The Cambridge Encyclopedia of the Jesuits

General editor
Thomas Worcester, SJ

Associate editors
Megan C. Armstrong, James Corkery, SJ
Alison Fleming, Andrés Ignacio Prieto

Assistant editor
Henry Shea, SJ

CAMBRIDGE
UNIVERSITY PRESS

CAMBRIDGE
UNIVERSITY PRESS

University Printing House, Cambridge CB2 8BS, United Kingdom

One Liberty Plaza, 20th Floor, New York, NY 10006, USA

477 Williamstown Road, Port Melbourne, VIC 3207, Australia

4843/24, 2nd Floor, Ansari Road, Daryaganj, Delhi – 110002, India

79 Anson Road, #06-04/06, Singapore 079906

Cambridge University Press is part of the University of Cambridge.

It furthers the University's mission by disseminating knowledge in the pursuit of
education, learning, and research at the highest international levels of excellence.

www.cambridge.org
Information on this title: www.cambridge.org/9780521769051
DOI: 10.1017/9781139032780

© Cambridge University Press 2017

First published 2017

Printed in the United States of America by Sheridan Books, Inc.

A catalogue record for this publication is available from the British Library.

Library of Congress Cataloging-in-Publication Data
Names: Worcester, Thomas, editor.
Title: The Cambridge encyclopedia of the Jesuits / general editor, Thomas Worcester, SJ;
associate editors, Megan C. Armstrong, James Corkery, SJ, Alison Fleming, Andrés Ignacio
Prieto; assistant editor, Henry Shea, SJ.
Description: New York: Cambridge University Press, 2017. |
Includes bibliographical references and index.
Identifiers: LCCN 2017022402 | ISBN 9780521769051 (hardback)
Subjects: LCSH: Jesuits – Encyclopedias. | BISAC: RELIGION /
Christian Church / History.
Classification: LCC BX3702.A1 C36 2017 | DDC 271/.53003–dc23
LC record available at https://lccn.loc.gov/2017022402

ISBN 978-0-521-76905-1 Hardback

Dedicated with joy and in gratitude to
POPE FRANCIS
Jesuit priest, Latin American, Voice for the Poor, Bishop of Rome

Contents

Figures

Contributors

Amoussou, Luc, SJ
Hekima University College
Nairobi, Kenya

Armstrong, Megan C.
McMaster University
Hamilton, Ontario, Canada

Barnes, Michael, SJ
Heythrop College
London, UK

Begheyn, Paul, SJ
Netherlands Institute of Jesuit Studies
Amsterdam, Netherlands

Bernauer, James SJ
Boston College
Chestnut Hill, MA, USA

Buckland, Stephen, SJ
Arrupe College
Harare, Zimbabwe

Burke, Kevin F., SJ
Associate Professor, Fundamental and Systematic Theology
Jesuit School of Theology of Santa Clara University
Berkeley, CA, USA

Carey, Patrick W.
Professor Emeritus, Theology Department
Marquette University
Milwaukee, WI, USA

Cassar, Carmel
Associate Professor
Institute for Tourism, Travel & Culture
University of Malta
Malta

Catta, Grégoire, SJ
Maître de conférences en théologie morale
Centre Sèvres – Facultés Jésuites de Paris
Paris, France

Chase, Martin, SJ
Professor, English and Medieval Studies, Fordham University
Bronx, New York, USA

Chen, Hui-Hung
Associate Professor, History, National Taiwan University
Taiwan

Clark, William A., SJ
Associate Professor, Religious Studies,
College of the Holy Cross
Worcester, MA, USA

Colombo, Emanuele
Associate Professor, Catholic Studies
De Paul University
Chicago, IL, USA

Consolmagno, Guy, SJ
Director, Specola Vaticana (Vatican Observatory),
Vatican City State

Corkery, James, SJ
Professor, Theology
Pontificia Università Gregoriana
Rome, Italy

Danieluk, Robert, SJ
Archivist, Jesuit Roman Archives,
Rome, Italy

Donohue, John, SJ
Writer, Campion Center,
Weston, MA, USA

Duffy, Kathleen, SSJ
Professor, Physics
Chestnut Hill College
Philadelphia, PA, USA

Eggemeier, Matthew T.
Associate Professor, Religious Studies
College of the Holy Cross
Worcester, MA, USA

Endean, Philip, SJ
Professor of Theology
Centre Sèvres – Facultés Jésuites de Paris
Paris, France

Fahey, Michael A., SJ
Scholar in Residence
Fairfield University
Fairfield, CT, USA

Fernández, Eduardo C., SJ
Professor, Pastoral Theology and Ministry
Jesuit School of Theology of Santa Clara University and the Graduate Theological
 Union
Berkeley, CA, USA

Fernández Arrillaga, Inmaculada
Professor of Modern History
Universidad de Alicante
Spain

Fernando, Leonard, SJ
Principal and Professor, Church History and Systematic Theology
Vidyajyoti College of Theology
Delhi, India

Fleming, Alison
Associate Professor
Department of Art and Visual Studies
Winston-Salem State University
Winston-Salem, NC, USA

Francisco, Jose Mario C., SJ
Professor, Theology
Ateneo de Manila University, Philippines
and Pontificia Università Gregoriana, Rome, Italy

Fritz, Peter Joseph
Edward Bennett Williams Fellow and Assistant Professor, Religious Studies
College of the Holy Cross
Worcester, MA, USA

Gallagher, Charles, SJ
Associate Professor, History
Boston College
Chestnut Hill, MA, USA

Gannett, Cinthia
Professor Emerita, English
Fairfield University
Fairfield, CT, USA

Garcia, José Ignacio, SJ
Director, Jesuit European Social Centre
Brussels, Belgium

Gavin, John, SJ
Associate Professor, Religious Studies
College of the Holy Cross
Worcester, MA, USA

Gay, Jean-Pascal
Professor, History of Christianity (Early Modern and Modern periods)
Université Catholique de Louvain
Louvain, Belgium

Genilo, Eric Marcelo O., SJ
Professor, Moral Theology
Loyola School of Theology
Quezon City, Philippines

Habsburg, Max von
Head of History, Oundle School
Oundle, Northamptonshire, UK

Hawkes-Teeples, Steven, SJ
Assistant Professor, Medieval Christianity
Saint Louis University
St. Louis, MO, USA

Hinsdale, Mary Ann
Associate Professor, Theology
Boston College
Chestnut Hill, MA, USA

Howell, Patrick J., SJ
Distinguished Professor, Catholic Thought and Culture
Seattle University
Seattle, WA, USA

Janowiak, Paul A., SJ
Associate Professor, Liturgical and Sacramental Theology, Jesuit School of Theology of
    Santa Clara University Berkeley, CA, USA

Jurgensmeier, Charles, SJ
Associate Professor, Fine and Performing Arts
Loyola University Chicago
Chicago, IL, USA

Kaslyn, Robert J., SJ
Dean, School of Canon Law
Catholic University of America
Washington, DC, USA

Keenan, Charles
Associate Director, Core Program
Boston College
Chestnut Hill, MA, USA

Keenan, James F., SJ
Canisius Professor
Boston College
Chestnut Hill, MA, USA

Kim, Yongsu Paschal, SJ
St. Aloysius House of Studies
Seoul, South Korea

Knaap, Anna C.
Adjunct Professor, Art History, Emmanuel College
Cambridge, MA, USA

Kozhamthadam, Job, SJ
Indian Institute of Science and Religion
Pune, India

Kuzniewski, Anthony, SJ, RIP (d. 2016)

Laffey, Alice L.
Professor Emerita, Old Testament
College of the Holy Cross
Worcester, MA, USA

Lapomarda, Vincent A., SJ
Associate Professor Emeritus, History Department
College of the Holy Cross
Worcester, MA, USA

Lazar, Lance Gabriel
Associate Professor, History
Assumption College
Worcester, MA, USA

Lewis, Mark A., SJ
Associate Professor, History and Cultural Heritage of the Church
Pontificia Università Gregoriana
Rome, Italy

Llanos, Christopher, SJ
Lecturer, St. Michael's Theological College
Kingston, Jamaica

Lucas, Thomas, SJ
University Professor, Art and Art History,
Seattle University
Seattle, WA, USA

Maczkiewicz, Keith, SJ
Graduate student, Jesuit School of Theology of Santa Clara University
Berkeley, CA, USA

Marcocci, Giuseppe
Associate Professor, Early Modern History
Università degli Studi della Tuscia
Viterbo, Italy

Mariani, Paul
University Professor, English
Boston College
Chestnut Hill, MA, USA

Maryks, Robert A.
Associate Professor, History
Boston College
Chestnut Hill, MA, USA

Massaro, Thomas, SJ
Professor, Moral Theology
Jesuit School of Theology of Santa Clara University
Berkeley, CA, USA

McCoog, Thomas, SJ
Curator, Avery Cardinal Dulles Archives, and Archivist, Maryland province of the
    Society of Jesus,
Fordham University
Bronx, New York, USA

McDermott, James, SJ
Screen and Magazine Writer, Loyola Marymount University
Los Angeles, CA, USA

McKevitt, Gerald, SJ, RIP (d. 2015)

Mendonça, Délio, SJ
Associate Professor, History and Cultural Heritage of the Church
Pontificia Università Gregoriana
Rome, Italy

Menkhaus, James
Assistant Professor, Theology
Gannon University
Erie, PA, USA

Mesa, José Alberto, SJ
Secretary, Secondary and Pre-Secondary Education for the Society of Jesus, and Visiting
    Professor, Cultural and Educational Policy Studies
Loyola University Chicago
Chicago, IL, USA

Mkenda, Festo, SJ
Director, Jesuit Historical Institute Africa, and Lecturer, Church History
Hekima University College
Nairobi, Kenya

Molina, J. Michelle
John and Rosemary Croghan Chair, and Associate Professor, Catholic Studies
Northwestern University
Evanston, IL, USA

Mondoni, Danilo, SJ
Professor, History of Christianity
Faculdade de São Bento/São Paulo, and Faculdade Jesuita de Filosofia e Teologia/Belo
    Horizonte
Brazil

Monet, Jacques, SJ
Historian, Archive of the Jesuits in Canada
Montreal, Québec, Canada

Mormando, Franco
Professor, Italian
Boston College
Chestnut Hill, MA, USA

Morrissey, Thomas J., SJ
Historian of the Irish province and Writer
Manresa Centre of Spirituality
Dublin, Ireland

Murphy, Edward P., SJ
Mucks Community
Harare, Zimbabwe

Murphy, Thomas, SJ
Associate Professor, History
Seattle University
Seattle, WA, USA

Oberholzer, Paul, SJ
Professor, History
Pontificia Università Gregoriana
Rome, Italy

O'Brien, William P., SJ
Assistant Professor, Theology
Saint Louis University
St. Louis, MO, USA

O'Collins, Gerald, SJ
Research fellow, University of Divinity
Melbourne, Australia

O'Hanlon, Gerard, SJ
Jesuit Centre for Faith and Justice
Dublin, Ireland

O'Leary, Brian, SJ
Associate Professor (retired), Spirituality
Milltown Institute of Philosophy and Theology
Dublin, Ireland

Orobator, Agbonkhianmeghe E., SJ
Professor, Theology
Hekima University College/Jesuit School of Theology & Institute of Peace Studies and
    International Relations
Nairobi, Kenya

Otto, Brent Howitt, SJ
Ph.D. student, History, University of California-Berkeley
Berkeley, CA, USA

Pabel, Hilmar M.
Professor, History
Simon Fraser University
Burnaby, BC, Canada

Padberg, John W., SJ
Former Director, The Institute of Jesuit Sources
St. Louis, MO, USA

Palmisano, Joseph, SJ, RIP (d. 2015)

Phạm, Hưng Trung, SJ
Assistant Professor, Ignatian Spirituality
Jesuit School of Theology of Santa Clara University
Berkeley, CA, USA

Picó, Fernando, SJ
Professor, History
Universidad de Puerto Rico
Rio Pedras, Puerto Rico

Pierce, Joanne M.
Professor, Religious Studies
College of the Holy Cross
Worcester, MA, USA

Poché, Justin
Associate Professor, History
College of the Holy Cross
Worcester, MA, USA

Prieto, Andrés Ignacio
Associate Professor, Spanish and Portuguese
University of Colorado Boulder
Boulder, CA, USA

Rafferty, Oliver P., SJ
Professor, Modern Irish and Ecclesiastical History
Boston College
Chestnut Hill, MA, USA

Redden, Andrew
Director, Latin American Studies
University of Liverpool
Liverpool, UK

Reiser, William, SJ
Professor, Religious Studies
College of the Holy Cross
Worcester, MA, USA

Robertson, Clare
Professor, History of Art
University of Reading
Reading, Berkshire, UK

Salcedo, Jorge, SJ
Director, Centro de Formación Teológica
Pontificia Universidad Javeriana
Bogotá, Colombia

Schineller, Peter, SJ
Pastoral Ministry, Jesuit Center and Sacred Heart Parish
Amman, Jordan

Scully, Robert E., SJ
Professor, History and Law
Le Moyne College
Syracuse, NY, USA

Shea, Henry, SJ
Graduate student, School of Theology and Ministry
Boston College
Boston, MA, USA

Shore, Paul
Adjunct Professor, Religious Studies
University of Regina
Regina, Saskatchewan, Canada

Simmonds, Gemma, CJ
Senior Lecturer, Pastoral and Social Studies and Theology
Heythrop College
London, UK

Standaert, Nicolas, SJ
Professor, Sinology
University of Leuven
Leuven, Belgium

Stott, Jonathan, SJ
Assistant Professor, Physics
Fairfield University
Fairfield, CT, USA

Strasser, Ulrike
Professor, History
University of California, San Diego
La Jolla, CA, USA

Strong, David, SJ
Arrupe House
Pymble, NSW, Australia

Tran, Anh Q., SJ
Assistant Professor, Historical and Systematic Theology
Jesuit School of Theology of Santa Clara University
Berkeley, CA, USA

Ucerler, M. Antoni J., SJ
Associate Professor, East Asian Studies, and Director, Ricci Institute for Chinese–
    Western Cultural History
University of San Francisco
San Francisco, CA, USA

Waddell, Mark A.
Associate Professor, History
Michigan State University
East Lansing, MI, USA

Ward, Haruko Nawata
Professor, Church History
Columbia Theological Seminary
Decatur, GA, USA

Wardaya, Baskara T., SJ
Lecturer, History
Sanata Dharma University
Yogyakarta, Indonesia

Wood, Susan K., SCL
Professor, Theology
Marquette University
Milwaukee, WI, USA

Worcester, Thomas, SJ
Professor, History
College of the Holy Cross
Worcester, MA, USA

Wright, Jonathan
Honorary Fellow, Department of Theology and Religious Studies
Durham University
Durham, UK

Zampelli, Michael A., SJ
Associate Professor, Theatre
Santa Clara University
Santa Clara, CA, USA

Acknowledgments

Pope Francis, the Jesuit pope, has provided enduring inspiration by the example of his zeal and love for his vocation, his mission, his work.

Work on this project was supported by funds donated to the College of the Holy Cross by Cornelius B. Prior to honor Rev. Maurice F. Reidy, SJ. I acknowledge with much gratitude this very generous support.

I also acknowledge assistance of various kinds provided by the following: Jeffrey Klaiber, SJ (1943–2014), was one of the encyclopedia's associate editors in its early, formative stages. His long years of work in Peru gave him valuable perspectives that were of much help in the conceptualization of the encyclopedia's priorities. His death was a major loss in many ways. Andrés Ignacio Prieto graciously agreed to replace him among the associate editors. Associate editor and art historian Alison Fleming did a masterful job of selecting and obtaining the encyclopedia's images. Associate editor James Corkery, SJ, contributed the nuanced judgments and skills of a systematic theologian. And associate editor Megan Armstrong, a specialist in Franciscan history, gave us a healthy comparative perspective that helped to prevent or at least minimize false assumptions of Jesuit uniqueness. Henry Shea, SJ, joined the project in 2015 as an assistant editor and played an exceptionally important role in editing content and style in many of the more complex entries. The Jesuit Community at the College of the Holy Cross hosted several editorial meetings. Elizabeth Begley proofread nearly all of the entries before they went to the Press. Holy Cross student Sean MacKenzie spent part of a summer organizing lists and files critical to the project's progress. Emily Conn, Holy Cross valedictorian in 2016, carefully and judiciously drafted the cross-references to other entries provided with every encyclopedia entry. Richard Lent, of the Holy Cross Educational Technology staff, facilitated the preparation and formatting of the manuscript as a single document. Finally, I thank my students, both at the College of the Holy Cross, where I have taught for over two decades, and at three institutions where I have served as a visiting professor: Marquette University, Loyola University Chicago, and Seattle University. Intriguing, surprising, probing, and sometimes difficult questions and comments from students have made this a better work than it might otherwise have been.

Thomas Worcester, SJ
General editor

Alphabetical List of Entries

A

Acosta, José de, SJ (1540–1600)
Acquaviva, Claudio, SJ (1543–1615)
Acquaviva, Rudolf, SJ (1550–1583) and His Companions
Action Populaire / CERAS
Ad Gradum Exam
Africa, East
Africa, Northwest
Africa, West
AJCU (USA)
Alcalá
Alumbrados
Alumni/ae
AMDG
America Magazine
Anchieta, José de, SJ, St. (1534–1597)
Angels
Anima Christi
Anti-Jesuit Polemic
Anti-Semitism
Antwerp
Apostleship of Prayer
Apostolate
Applied
Arauco
Arca
Architecture
Archives and Libraries
Archivum Romanum Societatis Iesu (ARSI)
Argentina
Arnauld, Antoine
Arrupe College
Arrupe, Pedro, SJ (1907–1991)

Introduction

In the history of print and publishing, encyclopedias are above all associated with the eighteenth century, also the period in which the Society of Jesus was expelled by several states and then suppressed by the pope. This was the age of the Enlightenment, an age in which certain publications played an exceptionally prominent role, and none more so than Denis Diderot's *Encyclopédie*. The Enlightenment era has even been called the Age of the Encyclopedia. Diderot's consisted of seventeen volumes, first published between 1751 and 1772, with some 24,000 entries, by many contributors. The subtitle of his encyclopedia indicated that the topic was sciences, arts, and the professions. In these volumes, reason was exalted and traditional religion marginalized; progress was imagined as requiring leaving a priestly past, including the Jesuit past, behind.

Diderot's massive encyclopedia helped to change the world, in no small ways, for good or for ill. And it was so influential that even now the very genre of an encyclopedia may bring his volumes to mind. An encyclopedia of the Jesuits would, I dare say, have horrified Diderot, unless it were but a relentless catalogue of Jesuit misdeeds.

A Jesuit encyclopedia proposed by, and published by, Cambridge University Press, a press that was founded in Elizabethan England – a time and place hardly friendly to the Jesuits, to say the least – helps to show just how much times have changed. All of the entries for this *Cambridge Encyclopedia of the Jesuits* were written during the pontificate of Pope Francis, the first Jesuit pope. I am and my associate and assistant editors are delighted to dedicate this encyclopedia to him.

Thus, what is in and what is not in this encyclopedia? What matters enough to be included? This one-volume reference work was commissioned as a publication of no more than 500,000 words, with some 600 entries, to appear in hardcover and electronic versions. It has required a great many decisions as to what's in and what's out, who's in and who's out, and so on. This process of selection required a lot of time; in Jesuit terms it required discernment. What I believe matters most about the Jesuits is in; no doubt some will contest some of these decisions. But in fact the decisions were made collaboratively with the other editors and in the light of the generous advice of a great many people, Jesuits and others, from across the world, ranging from graduate students to professors emeriti/ae. Of the 600 entries, approximately 230 are biographies of individual Jesuits and of other persons important for Jesuit history; approximately 370 entries treat concepts, terms, places, institutions, events that matter for Jesuits. Depending on the topic, some entries are as brief as 300 words, while some are as long as 3,000 words; many are about 800 words. Most entries include a bibliography. Entries are signed by their authors, of whom there are 110, a distinguished and international group of scholars, ranging from

Figure 1 Pope Francis mural in New York, September 2015. Photograph Theresa Racht

Church historians and cultural historians to theologians and art historians, from Jesuits and other Catholics, to persons of other faiths or of none. Opinions expressed in entries represent the views of the authors, not necessarily those of the volume's editors. Some seventy images/illustrations point to the visual dimension of Jesuit experience.

One way of approaching Jesuit history is to focus on ideals, and on their expression in the writings of the founder, and/or in official Jesuit documents. Thus, if this is the way to get at what matters most about the Jesuits, one will emphasize reading the autobiography of Ignatius, his *Spiritual Exercises*, perhaps some of his thousands of letters, and then the *Constitutions*, of which he is the principal author. And there have been important studies done recently on these topics. One could also turn to decrees of Jesuit General Congregations, up to the most recent, along with perhaps letters and other documents from superiors general, from Ignatius to superior general Adolfo Nicolás. Many of these topics are included in this encyclopedia.

Yet even though all of these writings, decrees, and so on are certainly very important, I am not convinced that they are always what matters most, or where one might glean what matters most, about the Society of Jesus. How ideals and the prescribed have actually been lived out (or not) is something much, much messier, and much more time-consuming to access and study. But I believe that how Jesuits have lived their lives and what they have actually done are essential topics if one is to be able to talk with any credibility about Jesuit history. I am not suggesting that there has always been a huge gap between ideal and reality, but I suspect that there has usually been at least some significant disparity, human nature being what it is. Jesuits are human beings, with strengths, weaknesses, inclinations and actions ranging from heroic sanctity to deep-seated evil. Most Jesuits are somewhere in-between, most of the time.

The sources for studying what Jesuits have done over the centuries are phenomenal; an amazing quantity of manuscripts, printed sources, and other primary sources – such as Jesuit architecture, painting, other visual arts – have survived, despite expulsions of the Society from various countries, despite the suppression of 1773–1814, despite the vicissitudes of time. Archives and libraries rich in Jesuit sources have helped to make this reference work possible.

Expulsions and suppression: These kinds of events recall the fact that the Society of Jesus has not always been appreciated or well received. The extremely varied reception of the Society of Jesus is surely one of its characteristics: Jesuits have been used as scapegoats for just about everything wrong with culture and society; some Jesuits have been killed for simply being Jesuits, while others have been revered as saints and heroes in their lifetimes, whether or not they are ever officially beatified or canonized. The Society itself, as an institution, has experienced just as broad a range of responses, from demonization to an embarrassing flood of unqualified praise. Enemies of the Jesuits, as well as their friends, must be given ample space in this encyclopedia.

The bicentennial of the "restoration" of the Society in 2014 was not a minor anniversary. The significance for Jesuits of the decision of Pope Pius VII, promulgated on August 7, 1814, can hardly be exaggerated. Without it, there would be no Society of Jesus today, there would be no Jesuit schools, no retreat houses, or anything else. In Jesuit history, Pope Pius VII matters a lot. He was also a witness for the Church's freedom in the age of Napoleon's imperialism.

Questions remain for historians to sort about the Society post-1814. This is a period of Jesuit history that has yet to gain the kind of intense attention currently being given to the pre-1773 Jesuits. Among the key questions: To what extent was post-1814 a restoration of what had existed before? Or was it really a new Society of Jesus, inspired by the old Society in many ways, to be sure, but really something new? This question of continuity and discontinuity pre-1773/post-1814 is a question that informs many of the entries that follow.

But many people approach Jesuit history as a matter of great individuals: both Ignatius and other first-generation Jesuits such as Francis Xavier or Peter Faber, and then as we move along chronologically, to consider superiors general and other Jesuit administrators. Or perhaps to focus on Saints, Blesseds, and martyrs, from Ignatius and Xavier, to Peter Canisius, to Robert Bellarmine or Aloysius Gonzaga, to Claude La Colombière, the North American martyrs or, in the twentieth century, Miguel Pro, Alberto Hurtado, and the Jesuit martyrs in El Salvador. Or Jesuit scholars, theologians, writers, artists and scientists, from Christopher Clavius to Athanasius Kircher, Daniel Seghers and Andrea Pozzo to Gerard Manley Hopkins, Pierre Teilhard de Chardin, John Courtney Murray, Karl Rahner, Walter Ong, Jean-Yves Calvez, Pedro Arrupe, Avery Dulles. Jesuits such as these have their own entry in this work.

Lists of names may shed light on the accomplishments of some great individuals, but these lists may also be a bit tedious and, worse, may also occlude a key dimension of Jesuit life. Most of the time, most Jesuits are not simply lone warriors, as it were, carrying out a mission given to them as individuals and that's that. Jesuits are formed in community, and most of them spend most of their lives in community. To put this another way, what matters most about the Society of Jesus may not be a list of great individuals, but a Jesuit collective identity, or corporate culture. Shared priorities, attitudes, values, experiences; a shared project, shared goals, shared commitments, shared resources. These change somewhat, or perhaps a great deal, over time. Each generation of Jesuits may have a specific identity.

The Jesuit vows of poverty, chastity, and obedience may reveal shared values, priorities, shared commitments, and thus at least some of what matters most about the Jesuits. The Jesuit vow of poverty, I would suggest, has been and is a promise to let go of rugged individualism and independence in favor of mutual support and interdependence. This goes against what capitalist culture tells Jesuits they ought to be. The Jesuit vow of poverty is profoundly counter-cultural; my students are invariably shocked, indeed astonished, if I mention that Jesuits sign their salaries over to their Jesuit community. Jesuit obedience, too, means putting choice of works and other major life choices in a much broader context than simply individual preferences. It means opting for a life in which personal preferences may give way to more significant considerations. Availability for works one would not, on one's own, be likely to choose, is a central part of Jesuit obedience and identity. An effort to serve others, to help to meet their needs, not solely one's own needs and preferences, is at the heart of the matter. Jesuit chastity is articulated in a similar way: availability for mission, for serving others, those most in need, anywhere in the world, perhaps on short notice.

And yet, as I say these things, I am also concerned to caution against ahistorical generalizations, and to insist on paying attention to the particularities of Jesuit practice in different times and places. The encyclopedia entries on schools or anything else Jesuit must take account not so much of a timeless meaning, but of change over time. History means change, and since the sixteenth century the Society of Jesus has been no more exempt from change than anyone else. There is no direct or short path from what John

O'Malley called the "first Jesuits" to Jesuits today. There is, rather, a complex path, winding and meandering at times, doubling back, and then perhaps moving forward in some way.

Is a close look at periods of growth for the Society the way to elicit what matters most about the Jesuits? My own field as a historian is the seventeenth century, the religious history of seventeenth-century France and Italy in particular. That era was in some ways the golden age for Jesuits in Europe, with rapid expansion in many other parts of the world as well. In 1640 the centennial of the Society was celebrated, and such celebration included publication in Antwerp of a self-congratulatory commemorative book, *Imago primi saeculi Societatis Iesu*. In France, there was strong royal support for Jesuits, and a growing and large number of Jesuit colleges, churches, publications, etc; a Jesuit was the king's confessor, and Jesuits ministered to all levels of society, from the court in Paris and Versailles to poor workers and peasants. And yet it was also a period of intense opposition to the Society of Jesus.

Another key question is who are/or have been the real leaders, the ones that actually matter, in a given era and venue of Jesuit life and work? Many Jesuits would say that Fr. Pedro Arrupe, superior general 1965–83, was a great leader, but if he was, was it as an administrator, or as a charismatic and prophetic figure? Did he perhaps lead by the example of a holy life rather than by his administrative decisions? If leaders are not necessarily administrators, are they perhaps spiritual directors and confessors? Preachers? Teachers? Writers? Scholars? Advocates for and agents of social justice? Chaplains in hospitals and prisons? No doubt for various times and places the answer may differ. Some would say that in recent decades the voices for social justice stand out. One may think, for example, of the Jesuit Refugee Service, founded in 1981. It may be that leaders in the Society are those that serve where the needs are greatest, and this can be a lot of different places.

One may also think of leaders as innovators. Is innovation what matters most? Though the word 'innovation' had very negative connotations in the time of Ignatius – more or less equivalent to heresy – today it has a rather positive resonance for most people. And I think that Jesuits tend to think of the Society of Jesus as innovative, from its very beginnings. For example, unlike monastic orders, and even unlike the friars such as Franciscans and Dominicans, Jesuits do not chant the divine office in choir. Jesuit spirituality is centered on the *Spiritual Exercises*, not on a liturgical calendar, especially not on the divine office in common. Jesuit spirituality is not tied to the seasons of the liturgical year, and yet the Eucharist has been at the heart of Jesuit spirituality. That no female branch of the Society developed was also a kind of innovation, but one Jesuits may find embarrassing today. But this lacuna is one of the things that distinguished Jesuits from monastic orders or from the mendicant orders: they had male and female branches. And yet, to be fair, religious life for women in the sixteenth century was almost always cloistered monastic life only. This began to change by the seventeenth century, and Jesuits did at times support efforts to create active women's communities similar to the Jesuits: for example, Fr. Jean-Pierre Médaille, SJ, played a central role in the establishment of the Sisters of St. Joseph, in seventeenth-century France.

As an active religious order, indeed some might say the active religious order par excellence, the Society of Jesus may tend to be identified by its works, by what its members do. Is then what matters most about the Jesuits *what* they do? In a similar vein, are Jesuits best understood as hyphenated priests? Priest-teachers, priest-scholars, and so on?

But perhaps *how* Jesuits do what they do is a better gauge of what matters most than what we do. Ignatius was very keen to prevent greed from taking hold of what would be the Jesuit way of doing things. Ministry was to be offered gratis, and this included not only pastoral or sacramental ministry but also education. Up to the Suppression, Jesuit schools did not charge tuition. As I tell my students, perhaps those really were the good old days! And yet those days are not completely gone. In recent times, in the United States, where high-priced tuition and fees are the norm in private schools, Nativity middle schools actually live out the older tradition and provide a free education. Generosity is at the heart of Ignatian ideals, and Jesuits today do at times manifest this in a variety of ways, not just in some schools.

One may also ask: Is what matters most *who* Jesuits are? Jesuits call themselves companions of Jesus and the company of Jesus: Is this companionship what matters most? Jesuits have often had a reputation as men of hope and optimism, as men who live in the world and see it as filled with the presence of God. Jesuits have often been seen as taking a very positive view of human nature, emphasizing human dignity and freedom and how human beings are created in the image of God. And Jesuits tend to be optimistic about where God may be found: everywhere, not just in church, not just among the pious, and the good people; not just among the respectable but also, and perhaps especially, among the outcasts, the outsiders, the despised, the excluded, the marginalized, in all corners of the earth, Christian or otherwise. Jesuits commit themselves to following and walking with the Jesus who favored the scorned people, the ones that were wrongly thought not to count or somehow to be inferior. Pope Francis is relentless in drawing attention to the marginalized and in insisting that priests, Jesuits among them, give priority to their needs.

Attention to the *Spiritual Exercises* of St. Ignatius reveals a spirituality that is grounded in dependence on God's abundant and utterly undeserved grace, but it is also a spirituality that emphasizes the freedom and the ability of the human being to make a choice to cooperate with that grace, to engage in a cooperation rooted in a love that manifests itself in deeds. There is a kind of balance of hard work and radical dependence on grace. Indeed the very notion of "exercises" suggests an important role for human effort, for human practice, not merely for some passive reception of, or submission to, something entirely external to oneself and one's actions. Thus Jesuits embrace not nature or grace, but both nature and grace. Jesuit spirituality is focused on Jesus, his life, his ministry, his death and resurrection. Jesuits are Christocentric, but at the same time Jesuits, following Ignatius, also find God in all sorts of places others might spurn as godless. God, for Jesuits, is revealed in Jesus Christ in a particular way, but God is also revealed in an amazing array of places, persons, and situations that many people would find unlikely to reveal the presence of God. "Both … and" may be a Jesuit way of thinking. The *Spiritual Exercises* are thoroughly Christocentric, and they are more than that too.

In relation to the *Exercises*, and in many other places, including daily life and how they talk about it, Jesuits often use a specialized vocabulary. Is this Jesuit language, is this Jesuit-speak, perhaps the key, the entrée, to what matters most? The encyclopedia entries that follow include many examples of Jesuit terminology. Jesuit terminology grounded in the *Spiritual Exercises* includes the principle and foundation, composition of place, the examen, discernment, and three degrees of humility. There is contemplation and the *Suscipe*. And Jesuit language goes well beyond the *Exercises*; Jesuits speak of novices, scholastics, regents, temporal and spiritual coadjutors, professed fathers, the provincial. Jesuits are called to be zealous for helping souls. There are Jesuit houses, regions, provinces, and assistancies; there is the *ratio studiorum*, the preferential option for the poor, men and women for others, the *magis*; there is AMDG and the faith that does justice. There is villa; there are *informationes*; there are *degentes*; there is much, much more.

Jesuits belong to particular local Jesuit communities and to Jesuit provinces. But they also belong very much to the entire, worldwide Society of Jesus. The international dimension of the Society goes back to its very origins. The first Jesuits, Ignatius included, were foreign students studying at the University of Paris. This fact points to two central characteristics of the Society of Jesus: its international membership and identity, and its focus on education. Ignatius understood himself as a pilgrim, on the road. And pilgrimage, in various ways, is a part of a Jesuit's formation. A Jesuit is formed to be available to be sent to the ends of the earth, wherever the needs are greatest. The great variety of places to which Jesuits have been sent must figure in this encyclopedia. Jesuits are called to transcend national, ethnic, cultural, and racial boundaries; a good Jesuit is an antidote to the fear fostered by xenophobia. For a Jesuit, the pope is the universal pastor, a pastor able to transcend national barriers. When Jesuits make a vow to God of obedience to the pope, they mean obedience to one concerned to provide for the needs of persons all around the globe.

Recent historical work has documented that many European Jesuits in the first two centuries of the Society's existence wrote letters to provincials and to Fr. General asking to be sent overseas to the missions; some of these volunteers were accepted and some were not. At the margins, yet in the center: Jesuits in China is a topic that seems to fascinate a very large numbers of scholars in recent years, a fascination that was further energized by the 400th anniversary, in 2010, of the death of Matteo Ricci. But in some ways, the Jesuits in China were not typical of what Jesuits did in the sixteenth to eighteenth centuries; for one thing, they founded no school in China. By most standards their work in China was not very successful. But then what criteria do we use to gauge Jesuit success? Are they somehow different from criteria used elsewhere?

To return to the theme of education, a few years ago I was asked at the College of the Holy Cross to write a brief summary of what Jesuit education is all about, and this summary was to help a college committee on strategic planning do its work. This is what I wrote:

> Optimistic in its assessment of human possibilities, the Society of Jesus views each person as an image of God. Jesuit education values the beauty and dignity of that image, and cherishes the diversity of ways in which human beings manifest the glory of God. Academic excellence is understood to play an indispensable role in making that glory evident.

> Interdisciplinary in its structure and rationale, Jesuit education privileges the links between the humanities, the sciences, and social sciences. Respecting and valuing the particular methodology of each discipline, Jesuit education also poses broad questions of ultimate meaning and purpose, questions that cut across the curriculum and shed light on its interconnections.

> Jesuit education spares no effort in developing as fully as possible the unique potential of each student for growth in knowledge and wisdom.

One may ask: Are Jesuit schools the premier example of Jesuit success? Though the Society of Jesus was not founded as a teaching order, that is, as a religious order devoted exclusively or almost exclusively to teaching, within the lifetime of Ignatius Jesuit schools were founded and began in various ways to take precedence over most other work. More and more Jesuits were missioned to work in the schools. Of the hundreds of Jesuit schools, from those for young children to research universities for graduate students, selected institutions have their own entries in this encyclopedia, institutions representative of the diverse countries and cultures where Jesuit schools have been founded.

It should be kept in mind that the Jesuit community attached to a school has very often included men working in other ministries such as itinerant preaching or hospital chaplaincy. But is education in fact what matters most about the Jesuits? Jesuits themselves are often highly educated, beyond the already long formation in philosophy and theology required for ordination. It is not uncommon to hear Jesuits in studies joke about being in the 20th grade or higher. And some Jesuits along with others would say that Jesuit schools are what matters most about the Society of Jesus.

Jesuit schools have often done a lot with the arts, with the visual arts, and with performing arts, theater in particular. Indeed, Jesuits tend to be very aware of the pedagogical power of images. The plain, bare style of some monastic traditions and of many Protestant churches is not a Jesuit style. Jesuits have known how to use images in teaching, and in propagating the faith. Jesuit spirituality is incarnational: There is emphasis on seeing and on other senses as a way to believing and to living out the faith. The visual imagination plays a major role in the *Spiritual Exercises*; Jesuit spirituality focuses on God as taking on flesh in Jesus, thus on a transcendent God who chose to be made as visible and tangible as any human being. Some seventy images are included in this encyclopedia, and not as mere "illustrations" somehow ancillary to the text but as integral parts of Jesuit history and identity, as central to what matters most about the Jesuits.

In their efforts to teach something about God to peoples in Asia, in the Americas, and elsewhere, Jesuits often relied on images, even as they worked hard to learn local languages. Jesuit missionaries, in some parts of the world, made the founding of schools a priority, for the benefit of both the children of European colonists and the native population. In North America, the first Jesuit school was founded in Quebec City, in 1639. From the sixteenth century on, as Jesuits went all over the world, they often gained a reputation, through their preaching and teaching, for accommodating local cultures. That is, rather than take a tabula rasa approach, as some other missionaries did, to the cultures they encountered in places such as Asia or the Americas, Jesuit missionaries tried to separate Christian faith from European cultures and to respect local cultures. And this kind of accommodation got the Jesuits into a lot of trouble in Europe, where some popes and other authorities saw the Jesuits as soft on paganism (e.g., Chinese Rites Controversy). In recent decades, most scholars working on this kind of topic tend to view favorably Jesuit efforts at accommodation, even if by post-colonial standards (post-1945 perspectives) Jesuits remained limited by, and at times gave way to, European arrogance, racism, condescension.

But it was not necessarily a good thing to always embrace accommodation. Is it a good thing for Jesuits to accept the caste system of India and to despise those considered of low caste or as untouchable? Or if a Jesuit were to find himself in Nazi Germany, would accommodation of Nazi culture be appropriate? Jesuits once owned slaves in the southern United States – a case of accommodation of local culture, but hardly a witness to the Gospel.

Collaboration with others is something Jesuits have never done without, certainly in a time and place of declining Jesuit numbers, as is the case in parts of the world at present, but it is also true that Jesuits have always needed co-workers, supporters, allies. This is part of the Jesuits' story, too. Benefactors have always been needed, and so too at least tacit tolerance of Church and State authorities for Jesuit schools and other works; lay collaborators were envisioned as playing a role from the beginning. In the early modern period, confraternities and Marian congregations had Jesuit chaplains but were largely run by and for persons other than Jesuits.

As for Jesuit schools, Ignatius insisted that Jesuits not administer corporal punishment, though they could have such punishment meted out by a corrector, a person other than a Jesuit. This may seem a rather odd, perhaps awkward, example of persons collaborating with Jesuits, but the point here is simply that, from the sixteenth century on, Jesuits did not engage in their works without collaborators. It is not merely a recent development, though General Congregation 34 of the Society of Jesus, meeting in 1995, issued a decree on cooperation with laity in mission as well a decree on women. Both decrees acknowledge the dependence of Jesuit works on contributions of persons other than Jesuits.

In 2008, at the 35th General Congregation, Pope Benedict XVI called on Jesuits to serve the universal Church, especially by going to the frontiers, not only geographic frontiers, but cultural and intellectual ones, in order to live out a faith that is harmonious with reason and with science, a faith that promotes justice for the poor and the excluded. And in a talk in Mexico City in 2010, Fr. General Nicolás pointed to a "world of globalized superficiality of thought" and called on Jesuits and their collaborators to "promote in creative new ways the depth of thought and imagination that are distinguished marks of the Ignatian tradition"("Depth, Universality, and Learned Ministry").

This encyclopedia considers not only the history of the Jesuits since their founding in 1540 but also the contemporary Society of Jesus.

Though it may seem self-evident to say that an encyclopedia is encyclopedic, in the sense of all-inclusive, in fact this one-volume reference work does not and cannot cover everything about the Jesuits. Even ten volumes or twenty volumes would not suffice for that. No doubt some readers will regret this or that silence or absence. In order to stay within the word limit of the project, tough choices have had to be made, but they have been made with a view to putting forward what matters about Jesuits, from a variety of perspectives, and including religion, culture, education, and the arts. The goal has been to include what sheds the most light on the significance of the Jesuits since their founding in the sixteenth century, and to do so in a reference work of manageable size, accessible and useful for a multiplicity of audiences: students of various levels, an educated public, scholars, Jesuits, and other clergy and religious. Many readers of this encyclopedia will already be aware of the *Diccionario histórico de la Compañia de Jésus*, published, after various delays, in Spanish only in 2001. Among the *Diccionario*'s obvious limitations is a complete lack of illustrations or images. Its entries are already somewhat dated, having been commissioned and written some two or three decades ago; yet it remains a useful reference work, especially for basic biographical information on a great many obscure Jesuits.

Entries for this *Cambridge Encyclopedia of the Jesuits* were commissioned in 2013 and later; an English-language project for Cambridge University Press, it is far more concise than the the *Diccionario* and includes as its authors both well-known experts and younger scholars charting new paths in Jesuit studies, a burgeoning, lively field for the twenty-first century, a field given fresh energy by a Jesuit pope full of surprises. This encyclopedia has sought to take into account Jesuits from the time of Ignatius to the first years of the papacy of Pope Francis. Some of the possible topics have been very much moving targets, as it were. Changing boundaries and names of Jesuit provinces offer a good example of such movement, and they are a topic on which whatever is said may be outdated very quickly. So that the ever-present prospect of one more update not delay publication, any Jesuit events or developments later than mid-2016 are not included in this encyclopedia.

Burke, Peter, *A Social History of Knowledge*. Vol. II: *From the Encyclopédie to Wikipedia.* Cambridge: Polity Press, 2012.

Diccionario histórico de la Compañia de Jésus: biográfico-temático. Ed. Charles O'Neill and Joaquín Ma. Domínguez. 4 vols. Rome: Institutum Historicum Societatis Iesu; Madrid: Universidad Pontificia Comillas, 2001.

Ivereigh , Austen, *The Great Reformer: Francis and the Making of a Radical Pope.* New York: Henry Holt, 2014.

Fabre, Pierre Antoine, and Catherine Maire, eds., *Les Antijésuites: discours, figures et lieux de l'antijésuitisme à l'époque moderne.* Rennes: Presses Universitaires de Rennes, 2010.

Molina , J. Michelle, *To Overcome Oneself: The Jesuit Ethic and the Spirit of Global Expansion, 1520– 1767.* Berkeley: University of California Press, 2013.

Nicolás, Adolfo, "Depth, Universality, and Learned Ministry: Challenges to Jesuit Education Today." Mexcio City, April 23, 2010.

O'Malley, John W., and Gauvin A. Bailey, eds., *The Jesuits and the Arts, 1540–1773.* Philadelphia, PA: St. Joseph's University Press, 2005.

Worcester, Thomas, ed., *The Cambridge Companion to the Jesuits.* Cambridge: Cambridge University Press, 2008.

Thomas Worcester, SJ
General Editor

Entries

Acosta, José de, SJ (1540–1600)

José de Acosta was born in Medina del Campo, Valladolid, Spain, in 1540. He joined the Society of Jesus in Salamanca in 1552. After taking his first vows, he taught humanities in Medina del Campo and then studied philosophy and theology at Alcalá. He was ordained in 1566.

In 1571 he was sent to Peru. In the city of Lima, he taught theology at the University of Saint Marcos and at the Jesuit College of Saint Paul, where he became rector. He was provincial superior between 1576 and 1581. Under his leadership, the Jesuits sought to evangelize the Indians through catechesis and popular missions in the colonial cities. He founded schools for offspring of native nobility. Acosta, along with his Jesuit companions, saw the urgency of composing catechisms and grammars in the two major languages of the Viceroyalty: Quechua and Aymara. Under Acosta's leadership, the Jesuits also took care of the *doctrina* (native parish) of Juli, in the shores of Lake Titicaca (present-day Bolivia). Juli was promoted as a pastoral experiment and eventually became the training ground for all Jesuit missionaries destined to work in Peru. Its influence is still felt in the missionary work carried out in present-day Peru, Bolivia, Chile, Ecuador, Argentina, Paraguay, and Brazil.

Acosta traveled with the Viceroy Francisco de Toledo to La Paz, Chuquisaca, and Potosí (in current Bolivia), and along the way set up Jesuit schools in these cities. From 1574 on, Acosta was consultor of the Inquisition.

Acosta also participated as a theologian in the Third Lima Council (1582–83). He drafted the minutes and the canons. He also wrote two catechisms in Spanish and played an important role in the drafting of the confessionals and sermons. In 1587 he returned to Spain, where he served as King Philip II's envoy to the Fifth Jesuit General Congregation (1592–94). He was also rector of the College of Salamanca. Acosta died unexpectedly on February 15, 1600.

José de Acosta was an important writer on the nature and history of the Americas and one of the most important missiologists of his time. During his stay in the Viceroyalty of Peru, he wrote the following works: 1. *De natura novi orbis* (published in Salamanca in 1588 and 1589); 2. *De procuranda indorum salute* (published in Salamanca in 1588); 3. *Historia natural y moral de las Indias* (published in Seville in 1590); 4. *De Christo Revelato* (published in Rome in 1590); 5. *De Christo Incarnato* (published in Rome in 1590); 5. *De temporibus novissimis* (published in Lyon in 1592), and three volumes of sermons published between 1596 and 1599.

In his work *Historia natural y moral de las Indias*, Acosta described the nature of the western hemisphere and focused on the history of the Aztecs and the Incas before the conquest. Acosta was a pioneer of the geophysical sciences with his studies of weather, volcanoes, earthquakes, minerals, plants, and animals. An ethnographer and sociologist of high esteem, he studied Incan and Aztec cultures and discussed their characteristics at a depth beyond other authors of his time. *Historia natural y moral de las Indias* features his theories about the origin of the Indians of America and their cultural evolution. Contrary to the prejudices of his time, he attempted to demonstrate to his fellow Europeans that the natives were members of the human family and that they needed to be integrated into the Christian flock.

De procuranda was the first book written by a Jesuit in America. It is a systematic reflection on the problems of the evangelization of the Indians as well as a resolution to oppose the old method of destroying idols and suppressing ancient rites. He advocates, alternatively, for preserving indigenous culture as much as possible while promoting integration into Christianity. The book is divided into six parts in which he proposes the conversion of Native Americans to the Catholic faith. Acosta is optimistic about the future outcomes of evangelization in the Americas. He denounces slavery, unjust taxes, the repression and exploitation of the natives, and criticizes the greed and abuses of the Conquistadors. In addition, he denounces corrupt members of the secular and regular clergy.

See also Bolivia; Catechisms; Peru

Vázquez, Isaac, "Pensadores Eclesiásticos americanos." In Pedro Borges Pedro, ed., *Historia de la Iglesia en Hispanoamérica y Filipinas*. Vol. I. Madrid: BAC, 1991.

Jorge Salcedo, SJ

Acquaviva, Claudio, SJ (1543–1615)

Claudio Acquaviva was the fifth superior general of the Society of Jesus, holding the office between 1581 and 1615. Born in 1543, son of the Duke of Atri, Acquaviva studied at Perugia before becoming chamberlain to Pope Pius IV. He entered the Society of Jesus in 1567 and rapidly advanced through its ranks. After being ordained in 1574 and teaching at the Roman College, he became rector of the Collegium Maximum in Naples in 1575, provincial of Naples in 1576, provincial of the Roman province in 1579, and finally, in 1581, he was elected superior general. Acquaviva enjoyed one of the longest terms as superior general in the Society's history, which lasted thirty-four years and spanned eight pontificates.

The Society's rapid growth continued during Acquaviva's term, numbering 13,000 members and over 350 colleges by the time of his death. As a result of such growth, Acquaviva's generalate revolved around the consolidation and regulation of the Society's activities. As superior general he oversaw the revision and promulgation of the *Ratio studiorum* (1599), the educational guidelines used by Jesuit schools and colleges throughout the world, and in 1591 he published the *Directorium exercitiorum spiritualium P. N. Ignatii*, a guide for the Society's directors giving the *Spiritual Exercises*. Acquaviva commissioned the first general history of the Society, published in 1614, and he also oversaw the compilation of the Society's annual letters (*litterae annuae*), which reported the actions of Jesuit houses around the world and were meant for public consumption.

Politically, Acquaviva had to navigate treacherous waters. For his part, Acquaviva interpreted the Society's *Constitutions* to mean that Jesuits were forbidden from participating in political affairs altogether, an admonition confirmed by the 5th General Congregation (1593–94). Acquaviva wrote his *Instructions for Confessors of Princes* (1602) to further underline this point, urging Jesuit confessors to avoid becoming entangled in political matters at court. However, Jesuits remained in the forefront of European politics, even as Acquaviva attempted in vain to control the writings and actions of Jesuits across Europe from Rome. The Jesuits were expelled from the kingdom of France in 1594 after being linked to an assassination attempt on Henry IV. Though the Society was eventually reintroduced to the kingdom in 1603, accusations that Jesuits advocated tyrannicide refused to go away. The publication of Juan de Mariana's *De rege et regis institutione* (1598) did not help matters, since Mariana allowed for the overthrow of temporal rulers – including by force – in the text. Acquaviva demanded that its sections on assassination be removed, and he forbade any other Jesuits from defending the work. The Society came under fire again in 1610 after the assassination of Henry IV. Once more the Superior General attempted to demonstrate the Society's loyalty to the French monarchy, with limited success. After the publication of Francisco Suárez's *Defensio fidei* in 1614, which permitted tyrannicide in certain cases, Acquaviva reiterated that he had banned any discussion of tyrannicide by Jesuits. Acquaviva's term also saw the Jesuits expelled from the Venetian republic following the interdict crisis there (1606–07), and although he had instituted Jesuit missions to England and Scotland (in 1580 and 1581, respectively), they met with limited success.

In addition, Acquaviva faced opposition from his own Society. During his generalate some Spanish Jesuits, led by José de Acosta and Cardinal Francisco de Toledo, advocated for decentralization of the Society, hoping for more independence at the provincial level for Spanish Jesuits like themselves. This led to the convocation of the 5th General Congregation in 1593, the first that did not meet to select a new superior general. Acquaviva successfully weathered the storm, however. As superior general Acquaviva also had to respond to papal attempts to intervene in the Society's governance. Sixtus V (r. 1585–90) intended to review the Society's *Constitutions* personally and suggested that the Holy Office review them as well, though Sixtus's death prevented any action being taken. In addition, due to Cardinal Toledo's influence, Clement VIII (r. 1592–1605) was suspicious of Acquaviva and attempted to name him archbishop of Naples so that he would be removed from Rome and governorship of the Society. Acquaviva and other Jesuits successfully protested this decision.

Acquaviva died in Rome in 1615.

See also Anti-Jesuit Polemic; Superior General; *Ratio Studiorum*

Broggio, Paolo, Francesca Cantù, Pierre-Antoine Fabre, and Antonella Romana, eds., *I gesuiti ai tempi di Claudio Acquaviva: strategie politiche, religiose e culturali tra Cinque e Seicento*. Brescia: Morcelliana, 2007.

Fois, Mario, "Il generale dei gesuiti Claudio Acquaviva (1581–1615): i sommi pontefici e la difesa dell'Istituto ignaziano." *Archivum Historiae Pontificiae* 40 (2002), 199–233.

de Guibert, Joseph, "Le généralat de Claude Acquaviva (1581–1615): sa place dans l'histoire de la spiritualité de la Compagnie de Jésus." *Archivum Historicum Societatis Iesu* 10 (1941), 59–93.

Mostaccio, Silvia, *Early Modern Jesuits between Obedience and Conscience during the Generalate of Claudio Acquaviva (1581–1615)*. Trans. Clare Copeland. Burlington, VT: Ashgate, 2014.

Charles Keenan

Acquaviva, Rudolf, SJ (1550–1583) and His Companions

Born in 1550, Rudolf Acquaviva was the nephew of Claudio Acquaviva, fifth superior general of the Society of Jesus. He entered the Jesuit novitiate in Rome in 1568 and in 1577 left for Lisbon, where he was ordained a priest. He departed for Goa the following year, and in 1579 he was named head of a Jesuit mission to Akbar, the Mughal emperor (r. 1556–1605), who had requested that priests be sent to his court. Acquaviva remained there for three years, learning Persian and speaking with Akbar about religious matters. Acquaviva and his fellow Jesuits made limited progress with the Emperor who, in the Jesuits' view, seemed easily distracted and quick to lose interest in their discussions. The Jesuits' denunciation of Muhammad and their refusal to give communion to Akbar, a Sunni Muslim, did not help matters.

After returning to Goa in early 1583, Acquaviva was named head of a mission to Salcete that included four other Jesuits: Francis Aranha, Peter Berno, Anthony Francis, and Alfonso Pacheco. The group intended to construct a church in the village of Cuncolim. However, on July 25, 1583, after only a week there, Acquaviva and the others were killed by natives. Also killed were fourteen native Christians and one Portuguese man, Gonçalo Rodrigues. The five Jesuits were recognized as martyrs and beatified by Pope Leo XIII in 1893.

See also Goa; India; Martyrs (Ideal and History)

Correia-Alfonso, John, ed., *Letters from the Mughal Court: The First Jesuit Mission to Akbar (1580–1583)*. St. Louis, MO: The Institute of Jesuit Sources, 1981.

Goldie, Francis, *The First Christian Mission to the Great Mogul: or, The Story of Blessed Rudolf Acquaviva, and of his Four Companions in Martyrdom of the Society of Jesus*. Dublin: M. H. Gill, 1897.

Charles Keenan

Action Populaire / CERAS

The Centre de Recherche et d'Action Sociales (CERAS, Center for Social Research and Action) – formerly Action Populaire (AP) – is an institute of the Society of Jesus in France dedicated to the promotion of justice and the support of those who work "at the service of the human person in society." Through its website, the publishing of a periodical (*Projet*), and various activities of formation, the center wishes to contribute to discerning the social challenges of the times by articulating grassroots experiences, social sciences, and the tradition of Catholic Social Teaching (CST).

AP was founded in 1903 by Fr. Henry-Joseph Leroy, SJ, then in exile in Belgium with the Jesuits in formation. His purpose was "to love the world" (implying the "modern" world), to bring the Church closer to the growing working class and to promote social engagement among Catholics. This happened in the aftermath of the publication of Leo XIII's *Rerum novarum* (1891), the first social encyclical and a powerful plea for the betterment of the condition of the workers, and also after the pope's call to French Catholics to accept the Republic (encyclical *Au milieu des sollicitudes*, 1892). Nonetheless, the tensions between the French State and the Church were at their peak with the expulsion of religious from their houses in 1901, and overall the Church was fighting fiercely any form of Modernism. In this context, to engage in a more positive dialogue with the culture while defending the Church was no little challenge.

Still a student of theology, Fr. Gustave Desbuquois, SJ, collaborated with Leroy. In 1905 he was named director, and AP settled in Reims. Until his replacement in 1946 by Fr. Jean Villain, SJ, he had been the great architect and charismatic leader of a work which has associated from the beginning Jesuits and laypeople. After World War I, AP relocated in Vanves, a southern suburb of Paris, and became an interprovincial institution. The name CERAS was added to AP in the 1960s and quickly replaced it. At this time, Fr. Jean-Yves Calvez, SJ, great specialist of Marxism and soon to become assistant of Fr. Arrupe, superior general, in Rome, was a pillar of the team. In the 1970s, because of fewer vocations and because of changes in the organization of the Jesuits in France, staff diminished. That led in 1984, to a move to rue d'Assas, central Paris, in order to be closer to the other three main Jesuit publications (*Etudes*, *Christus*, and *Croire Aujourd'hui*). In 2005 the CERAS settled in Saint-Denis, a northern suburb of Paris.

From the beginning, the central activity of AP/CERAS has been the publication of various leaflets, periodicals, and books in order to support those engaged in social change and to promote social concern among Catholics. The objectives are both documentary – to share experiences and practical, juridical, or technical resources – and formative – to improve social analysis and to diffuse the teaching of the Church on social issues. The AP started with the diffusion of the very popular *brochures jaunes* (yellow leaflets). At a pace of two or three per month, they dealt with topics such as unionization, just salary, value of work. Quickly, other more scholarly publications were added. In 1908 began *La revue de l'Action Populaire* which took various forms through the years until becoming *Projet* in 1966. It is now a bimonthly journal also accessible online. It takes a multidisciplinary approach on themes such as poverty, immigration, or environment and offers chronicles and book reviews as well.

Alongside publications, another major activity of the AP/CERAS is education and ongoing formation. Fr. Desbuquois started annual workshops for clergy and the members of AP, and he gave numerous talks to a variety of audiences. The CERAS still offers an annual one-week formation session attended by many laypeople working in Catholic charities or Church institutions as well as religious and priests. In 1923, AP helped to found the Institut d'Études Sociales (IES, Institute of Social Studies) at the Catholic Institute of Paris and provided a director and some professors for it until very recently. The AP/CERAS has been a regular partner of the French *Semaines Sociales* since their beginning in 1904.

Central to the mission of AP/CERAS is also the contribution to and the promotion and diffusion of CST in its magisterial form. Major encyclicals and documents have been published under its direction with documented introductions. They are gathered in a single volume regularly updated. The CERAS is now the editor of a reference website in French making available the documents of CST and a large collection of scholarly articles about them. AP/CERAS also directly collaborated in the composition of *Quadragesimo anno* (1931) and *Octogesima adveniens* (1971).

See also France; Justice

CERAS, *Le discours social de l'Eglise catholique: De Léon XIII à Benoît XVI.* 4th edn. Paris: Bayard, 2009.
Droulers, Paul, *Politique sociale et christianisme: Le Père Desbuquois et l'Action Populaire.* 2 vols. Paris: Éditions Ouvrières, 1968, 1981.

Grégoire Catta, SJ

Ad gradum exam

Colloquially known as the "ad grad," under revised norms this comprehensive exam before three examiners occurs at the end of four years of theological studies, to determine whether those who have not acquired a higher academic degree, at least a licentiate, have attained the level of learning in sacred sciences required for solemn profession of four vows (*Complementary Norms*, 93).

Traditionally, this exam was the ordinary way in which the academic part of the requirement for profession of four vows was determined. However, after General Congregation (GC) 31 (1965), perhaps motivated by the more egalitarian spirit of the age and to promote unity in the Society through "the avoidance of social distinction" (Decree 7, #6) and the division which different grades in the Society was felt to generate, the Society looked for ways to make profession of four vows – with concomitant rights to otherwise restricted roles of governance – more widely available. Both Pope Paul VI (at the time of GC 32) and John Paul II (GC 34) made it clear that any radical change – including the extension of the fourth vow to the Brothers (GC 31, Decree 5, #2) – was not to be permitted. While the Society obediently accepted this papal ruling, nonetheless it seems in practice to have engaged in more generous recourse to a provision in the *Constitutions* (519; *Complementary Norms*, 121, #3) which allows "some outstanding persons" to be admitted to profession of four vows without recourse to the "ad grad" exam. In this context – and in the context of the more pluralistic organization of scholastic studies – the *ad gradum* exam is no longer the conventional way for Jesuits in many parts of the world to fulfill the academic requirements for profession.

See also Formation; Scholastic

The Constitutions of the Society of Jesus and Their Complementary Norms. Ed. John W. Padberg. St. Louis, MO: The Institute of Jesuit Sources, 1996.
GC 31, *Decrees 5, 7, and 11*; GC 32, *Decrees 6 and 8.* In John W. Padberg, ed., *Jesuit Life and Mission Today: The Decrees and Accompanying Documents of the 31st–35th General Congregations of the Society of Jesus.* St. Louis, MO: The Institute of Jesuit Sources, 2009.

Gerard O'Hanlon, SJ

Africa, East

The Jesuit story in East Africa goes back to the sixteenth century. Francis Xavier (1506–52) briefly visited Malindi, Kenya, in 1542. Kenya is one of six countries that constitute today's Eastern Africa province of the Society of Jesus, the others being Ethiopia, South Sudan, Sudan, Tanzania, and Uganda. Other than Xavier's sojourn at Malindi, early Jesuit presence in this region was limited to Ethiopia. Only after the restoration of the

Society of Jesus in the nineteenth century did Jesuits explore the Sudan, and only in the decades of Africa's political independence did they move to other parts of the current province.

Desiring to bring the Ethiopian Orthodox Church to communion with Rome, Ignatius of Loyola (c. 1491–1556) created the province of Ethiopia in 1553 and assigned to it fifteen men. Two Jesuits entered the fabled Land of Prester John for the first time in 1555. In the end, only five Jesuits managed to enter and work in the country during this period, among them Bishop André de Oviedo (1518–77). A pious and resilient missionary, but probably a tactless diplomat, Oviedo supervised a mission that stood precariously in the face of Orthodox opposition and ended in 1593 with the death of its last member.

A second mission to Ethiopia was opened in 1603. First headed by Pedro Páez (1564–1622), it enjoyed relative success in its early years. A better diplomat than Oviedo, Páez found favor with the Ethiopian political class, especially the emperor, Sussenyos (r. 1607–32). Although the number of Jesuits, churches, and residences increased, and although Sussenyos himself embraced Catholicism, Páez's most important achievement was the avoidance of direct confrontation with the Orthodox hierarchy. Another important achievement was his 1622 *History of Ethiopia* in which he writes about the sources of the Blue Nile – the first known eyewitness account by a foreigner. Alphonso Mendez (1579–1656), who came in as patriarch, replaced Páez and pushed for mandatory conversions, completely disregarding venerable Ethiopian traditions. His intolerance was equalled by and opposed to that of Emperor Facilidas (r. 1632–67). Facilidas decreed the expulsion of Jesuits from Ethiopia in 1632. Eight Jesuits were martyred in the process, not counting hundreds – probably thousands – of Ethiopians.

After the expulsion from Ethiopia, several attempts were made in the eighteenth century to return there via Egypt, but most of them were unsuccessful. In the mid-nineteenth century, some Jesuits joined a mission of the Holy See to the Sudan. Maximilian Ryłło (1802–48) from Poland became the mission's pro-vicar apostolic in 1848. However, the Jesuits withdrew from this mission as quickly as they had joined it, and they were out of the region again for close to a century.

A more enduring presence started in 1945 when Emperor Haile Selassie I (1892–1975) invited Canadian Jesuits to Ethiopia and tasked them with modernizing the country's education system. They first ran a model secondary school in the capital and later on embarked on tertiary education, leading to the founding of what later became the University of Addis Ababa. Beyond Ethiopia, political independence opened the broader eastern Africa region to Jesuits from all over the world. Indian Jesuits went to Tanzania in 1961 to open an urban parish and begin the retreat ministry there. They were quickly absorbed into the country's school system and were in high demand as teachers in minor and major seminaries. Their success caught the attention of Maltese Jesuits, who joined them but focused more on parish ministry and seminary teaching in Uganda. In the early 1970s, the Tanzanian mission extended to Kenya where great emphasis was put on the retreat ministry.

Indian Jesuits also moved to the then undivided Sudan in a period of great crisis. All foreign missionaries had been expelled from the country in 1968. In 1972, the government allowed non-European missionaries to come in, at which point Jesuits from Ranchi took up the challenge. Their main task was to train local Sudanese clergy in minor and major seminaries.

The disparate missions in eastern Africa were amalgamated into an independent administrative region in 1976 and eventually became the full-fledged province of Eastern Africa in 1986. The province has experienced great progress, largely visible in the growth of local membership and institutional foundations. Slightly over 200 Jesuits belong to the province. About 60 percent of these are in training and the rest work in institutions that are spread throughout the region, including four parishes, eleven schools and colleges, a radio station, and a number of spirituality, youth, and social centers. The province invests heavily in the youth of eastern Africa, with educational ministries taking up to 82 percent of its financial resources.

See also Egypt; Hekima University College; Jesuit Historical Institute Africa; Kenya

Caraman, Philip, *The Lost Empire: The Story of the Jesuits in Ethiopia, 1555–1634*. London: Sidgwick & Jackson, 1985.

Belcher, Wendy Laura, and Michael Kleiner, eds. and trans., *The Life and Struggles of Our Mother Walatta Petros: A Seventeenth-Century African Biography of an Ethiopian Woman*. Princeton, NJ: Princeton University Press, 2015.

Mkenda, Festo, *Mission for Everyone: A Story of the Jesuits in Eastern Africa, 1555–2012*. Nairobi: Paulines Publications Africa, 2013.

Festo Mkenda, SJ

Africa, Northwest

There are mentions of Francis Xavier stopping somewhere along the West African coast, probably in today's Ghana, but these are historically unfounded. Neither is there evidence of a favorable response from St. Ignatius of Loyola to King John III's 1554 request for Jesuits to become chaplains at Elmina (also in Ghana). The territory that is today's Jesuit province of Northwest Africa (commonly referred to as Africa Northwest), comprising Nigeria, Ghana, Liberia, Sierra Leone, and Gambia, was the latest to receive Jesuits in Africa. Father Johannes Hofinger (1905–84) from Germany was probably the first Jesuit to spend time in this region. He visited Ghana in 1954 and conducted workshops in catechesis. Actual missionary presence happened in 1962 when Father Joseph Schuh (1914–96) from the New York province joined the faculty at the University of Lagos, Nigeria. He was joined in the following year by two other Jesuits from the same place. They all taught at the university and provided chaplaincy services in various institutions around the city. They also set in motion the history of what would later become a Jesuit province.

Some Jesuits visited Ghana for occasional retreat work between 1968 and 1974, often building upon the Lagos connection. A stable presence in this country started with Father Patrick Ryan, also from New York, who was sent to teach at the University of Ghana in 1974. Like those in Lagos, he assisted at the university chaplaincy and at its dependent stations in Legon, near Accra.

While Jesuit presence in Nigeria and Ghana has been tangible and effective since 1962, it remained somewhat tentative due to a small number of Jesuits and a lack of formal administrative structures on the ground. Moreover, the 1967–70 Biafran War in Nigeria significantly disrupted initial Jesuit ministry. In Ghana, a Jesuit community was officially established in Accra in 1986, and only then were its links with the Nigerian mission formalized. The Nigeria-Ghana mission, then dependent on the New York province, was established in 1987 and matured into the juridical status of a dependent region in 1992.

The region grew by leaps and bounds. In Ghana, Jesuits had already reached the city of Cape Coast by 1978, teaching in colleges and seminaries where they also served as spiritual directors. Cape Coast, known for its many colleges and schools, became particularly attractive as a place where younger members of the region could have their regency experience. With memories of the Biafran War still fresh, and with multiple military coups in Nigeria adding to a sense of insecurity, Cape Coast was developed not only for regents but also as an alternative center in case Nigeria closed down to expatriates. With a large donation from Mr. and Mrs. Richard Bennet of Madison, New Jersey, a huge residency was built in Cape Coast. The construction was supervised by Father Raymond Adams (1935–89), who was later murdered in the same place by a man he had been helping. Named Claver House, the building is still the focus of Jesuit presence in the area and serves as a retreat center, although it remains largely underutilized.

Despite initial fears, Nigeria never actually disappointed. By 1967, Jesuits had gone beyond Lagos to work in Nsukka, Kaduna, and Port Harcourt. In 1994 they were running two parishes and a school in Lagos. They were also involved in chaplaincy work in Lagos and in Benin City and were constructing Loyola Jesuit College in Abuja, which remains the province's most prestigious undertaking to date. Lagos still hosted the region's headquarters, but Benin City had gained prominence, with a retreat house, a novitiate, and a parish located there. At this point there were seventeen Jesuits assigned to Nigeria on a full-time basis, more than double the number that was in Ghana.

The most impressive progress of the region was seen in local vocations. Nigerian candidates first joined the Jesuits in 1969 and Ghanaian ones in 1971. In 1994 there were twenty-four African scholastics in various stages of formation. This continued growth in indigenous vocations saw the region turned into a full-fledged province in 2005, with 90 percent of its membership being indigenous. Ten years later the new province had 107 members, almost all of them indigenous.

For obvious historical reasons, the five-nation Northwest Africa province hinges on Nigeria, which is the most populous country in Africa. Only three out of its twelve community and apostolic centers are located outside this country: Claver House in Cape Coast and St. Anthony's Church in Accra, Ghana, and Holy Family Parish in Monrovia, Liberia. A new high school has been built in Port Harcourt in memory of sixty students of Loyola Jesuit College who died in a plane crash in 2005, and plans for a Jesuit university in Nigeria have been widely publicized. While Nigeria will most likely remain a crucial base, the province faces the challenge of transforming what currently looks like a heavy base into a springboard for new initiatives beyond the borders of Africa's population giant.

See also Africa, East; Africa, West Province

Anonymous, *From Generation to Generation: The Story of the Nigeria/Ghana Mission of the Society of Jesus.* [Lagos]: Something More Publications, 1994.

Ejembi, Gabriel Ujah, "Story of Success: The Golden Jubilee of the North-West Province of Africa (ANW)." *The Year Book of the Society of Jesus* 52 (2012), 25–28.

Festo Mkenda, SJ

Africa, West

In 1946 the first Jesuits arrived in the territory that would become the Jesuit province of West Africa. These Jesuit missionaries from France were asked to start a local church in Chad, and they soon founded two dioceses. In 1957 the Diocese of Douala in Cameroon asked the Jesuits to undertake the direction of Libermann High School, formerly under the leadership of the Holy Ghost Fathers. In 1962 the bishops of West Africa requested the help of the Jesuits in creating social institutions to assist the new independent nations of West Africa. This led to the founding of the African Institute of Economic and Social Development (INADES). The vice province of West Africa was established on July 31, 1973.

The Jesuit province of West Africa is one of the largest provinces of the Society of Jesus as far as the number of countries is concerned. The province covers the vast territory from Congo (Brazzaville) to Senegal and includes fourteen countries, namely: Benin, Burkina Faso, Cameroon, Central Africa, Chad, Congo, Ivory Coast, Gabon, Guinea, Mali, Mauritania, Niger, Togo, and Senegal. All these countries have French as common official language. This characteristic facilitates communication between the Jesuits of this province. The provincial house is located in Douala, Cameroon, but the provincial superior spends fewer than ninety days a year there and the rest of his time visiting the members of the province scattered around Africa and the world. It is a difficult charge that requires much strength, willpower, and generosity.

The Jesuits in the West Africa province are involved in various kinds of ministries, including intellectual, spiritual, and socio-pastoral assignments. At the core of their mission, wherever they find themselves, lies a strong commitment to social justice. The intellectual apostolate consists of colleges and higher education institutions. The province has two secondary schools, namely St. Charles Lwanga in Sarh, Chad, and College Libermann in Douala, Cameroon, and two universities, the Catholic University of Central Africa (UCAC) in Yaoundé, Cameroon, and the Center of Research and Action for Peace (CERAP) in Abidjan, Ivory Coast. It also has one preparatory school (IST-AC) for technological studies in Douala. CERAP is an important educational undertaking of the province because it will grow to become a full university. One of its missions is to foster peace by preparing students to build stable political institutions in Africa. The Center of Formation and Development (CEFOD) is an equivalent of CERAP in Chad and focuses on the formation of human development and administrative skills. There are other centers for research and publications in various other parts of the province as well, namely the Center for Research, Studies and Creativity (CREC) in Benin, the Center of Studies and Reflection for Students (CERCLE) in Burkina Faso, and the Loyola Cultural Center (CCL) in Togo. In addition, the Jesuit Institute of Theology (ITCJ), a work of the entire African Assistancy, is also in Abidjan.

The spiritual apostolate is done by every Jesuit through spiritual direction and four spiritual centers, namely "Les Rôniers" in Chad, the Spiritual Center of Bonamoussadi in Douala, Pam-Yôodo in Ouagadougou, and Vouela in Congo-Brazzaville. Spiritual assistance is also provided through chaplaincy work for the University of Yaoundé and the University of Bangui, Central Africa Republic.

The social apostolate consists of rigorous intellectual analysis of social and cultural changes and the use of such analysis to participate in the human and social development

Figure 2 *Schoolchildren at Centre Culturel Loyola, Lomé, Togo.* Photograph courtesy of Luc Amoussou, SJ

of the region. CEFOD in N'djamena, Chad, contributes to social and developmental studies that aim to sustain the political search for justice and prosperity in Chad. Foyer de l'Espérance in Lomé, Togo, focuses on the fight against the spread of HIV/AIDS.

Overall, the Jesuits of the West Africa province are committed to bringing cultural and political changes to the various countries of the province in keeping with the mission of the whole Society of Jesus, which is a faith that does justice. The promotion of faith and the work for justice are at the core of every undertaking in the province. The Jesuits of West Africa are all trying to seek and love God in everything they do and in every person they meet. The motto of the West Africa province is "To see the world as a place where God is at work." They want to labor with God in that part of Africa where many countries are facing sociopolitical disruption and unrest.

The West Africa province is still a very young province in its population. This is a blessing for the future but a challenge for today, since most members of the province are still in formation. The province is investing a lot in these men in formation, and this represents the greatest asset for the future. The province's goal is to participate as much as possible in the education and empowerment of the youth of today in order to create a better world for tomorrow.

See also Congo; HIV/AIDS; Peace and Reconciliation; Service of Faith and Promotion of Justice

Jésuites de la Province de l'Afrique Occidentale. www.jesuitespao.com/.

Luc Bonaventure A. Amoussou, SJ

AJCU (USA)

The Association of Jesuit Colleges and Universities (AJCU) has a full-time staff of five based in Washington, DC. A principal task is to seek Congressional support for private higher education. A board of trustees consists of the presidents of all twenty-eight Jesuit colleges and universities in the United States. The AJCU sprang in 1970 from the Jesuit Educational Association of 1936, an organization of both higher and secondary education. The older association communicated the decisions of the Roman Jesuit Curia and sought to protect the authenticity of Jesuit education from excessive Americanization.

Vatican Council II (1962–65) fostered grassroots links among the Jesuit institutes. As they exercised autonomous governance, greater academic freedom, and deeper research in the Council's aftermath, desire for collaboration grew. Conciliar decrees such as *The Pastoral Constitution on the Church in the Modern World* and *The Decree on the Lay Apostolate* influenced the new AJCU in a more dialogic attitude toward US culture. In 1975, General Congregation 32 of the Jesuits inspired the AJCU toward greater promotion of global social justice, especially in collaboration with Jesuit institutes in the developing world. The AJCU encourages foreign exchange programs and internationalization of home campuses.

The AJCU mediates between Catholic higher education and the Vatican, substantially influencing the drafting and application of the apostolic constitution *Ex corde Ecclesiae* of Pope John Paul II (2000). Its work increasingly involves encouraging communications among the specialized professional staffs of the member schools. There are currently over thirty-five conferences within the AJCU for this purpose.

As the number of actual Jesuits in higher education continues to diminish, the AJCU seems likely to become a principal nurturer of the lay collaborators who will increasingly carry the Jesuit educational tradition.

See also United States of America; Universities, 1773–Present

Association of Jesuit Colleges and Universities (AJCU). www.AJCUnet.edu.
Schroth, Raymond J., *The American Jesuits: A History.* New York: New York University Press, 2009.

Thomas Murphy, SJ

Alcalá

Alcalá de Henares is a university town only 31 kilometers away from Madrid, with a current population of about 200,000 people. UNESCO declared Alcalá a World Heritage City in 1998, and it is most famous for its University of Alcalá, officially founded in 1499 by Cardinal Ximénes de Cisneros, then regent of Spain. A variety of significant Jesuits have set foot in its classrooms: Ignatius Loyola was enrolled at the university between 1526 and 1527 while working at Antezana hospital and engaging in spiritual ministries. Juan de Mariana studied the arts and theology at the University of Alcalá, and St. Francis Borja did his novitiate here. Perhaps most notably, Francisco Suárez served as professor of this university between 1585 and 1592.

In 1620 construction began on the first college of the Society of Jesus in Alcalá, an impressive building that today houses the university's Faculty of Law. After the suppression of the Society in 1773, the school reopened in 1827 and would operate until the exile of the Jesuits seven years later, in 1835. In 1953 the Society returned to Alcalá to provide pastoral ministry and open a primary school. Two years later, in 1955, this would also lead to the establishment of a College of Philosophy for Jesuit scholastics. Today, the Jesuits have an urban complex in the city that includes a retreat house, Jesuit residence, and the Colegio San Ignacio de Loyola, an institution that provides a primary and secondary education as well as specific vocational training. This site is also home to the historic archives of the former Jesuit province of Toledo. It may be noted, finally, that Jorge Mario Bergoglio, now Pope Francis, completed his tertianship in this Jesuit residence in Alcalá between 1970 and 1971.

See also Loyola, Ignatius of, SJ, St.; Spain

Jurado, Juan José Zorrilla, *Alcalá de Henares, ciudad patrimonio de la humanidad.* Madrid: Ediciones Alfonso Martínez, 2005.
Pareja , Luis Miguel de Diego, *La expulsión de los jesuitas de Alcalá de Henares en 1767 y vicisitudes de sus propiedades hasta su regreso en 1827.* Alcalá: Fun. Colegio del Rey, 1997.

Inmaculada Fernández Arrillaga

Alumbrados

Alumbrados, meaning "illuminated" in English, was the name given to a spiritual movement that originated in the Spanish region of Castile in the early seventeenth century. Its practices were adopted by devout women and men who were not highly educated but sought a path of perfection based on pure love, away from worldly interests and distractions. As the movement attracted converts, elements of its theology received much criticism, culminating in a decree of condemnation entitled the "Edict against the Alumbrados of the Kingdom of Toledo" in 1525. It is no coincidence that this event took place in an area where Jews, Muslims, and Christians used to live side by side.

In 1526 Íñigo (Ignatius) de Loyola came to Alcalá, a small college town heavily guarded by the Inquisition where the kind of religiosity he advocated fell under suspicion. Additionally, he enjoyed the friendship of influential women who protected him because of his austere lifestyle and the kind of interiorized spirituality he promoted. All of this drew severe criticism toward him, and he was persecuted for sharing spiritual practices without possessing an ecclesiastical degree or office.

From 1540 onwards, many attacks against Ignatius and his followers in Rome focused on the practice of the Spiritual Exercises. Its promotion of interior prayer and the innovative concepts of Ignatian spirituality were viewed as suspiciously similar to the confusing concepts defended by *alumbrados*. In this respect, the Spanish roots of the initial group of Jesuits would also encourage these suspicions, as many of the companions of Ignatius had a Hispanic origin: Francis Xavier, Diego Laínez, Alfonso Salmerón, Juan Alfonso Polanco, Jerome Nadal, and Francis Borja.

See also Anti-Jesuit Polemic; Loyola, Ignatius of, SJ, St.; *Spiritual Exercises*

Fernández, Luis, "Íñigo de Loyola y los alumbrados." *Hispania Sacra* 35 (1983), 585–680.
Hamilton, Alastair, *Heresy and Mysticism in Sixteenth-Century Spain: The Alumbrados.* Cambridge: James Clarke & Company, 1992.

Inmaculada Fernández Arrillaga

Alumni/ae

A major source of the Society's historical influence has been the graduates of its various colleges and universities. In the seventeenth century, these ranged from Peter Paul Rubens to René Descartes and from Ferdinand II of Austria to Pope Innocent XI. In modern times, alumni have been heads of state, including Bill Clinton in the United States, Fidel and Raúl Castro in Cuba, Gloria Macapagal-Arroyo in the Philippines, Rafael Caldera in Venezuela, and King Abdullah II in Jordan. They have been as varied as James Joyce, Alfred Hitchcock, Sandra Cisneros, and Gabriel García Márquez. This diversity reflects both the global reach and the variety of the order's educational institutions.

Historically, there were three kinds of Jesuit colleges: the institution with exclusively Jesuit students, the mixed Jesuit and lay school, and the college with an entirely lay student body. Part of a worldwide network, these schools bestowed the Bachelor of Arts diploma after a seven-year course of studies. By 1710, in addition to 612 colleges and 176 seminaries, Jesuits taught at twenty-four universities that bestowed professional and doctoral degrees in theology, philosophy, law, and medicine.

The Jesuits' humanistic curriculum, uniquely adapted to sixteenth-century needs, sought to prepare students for advancement in the civil service, Church, and professions. To this end, it cultivated *eloquentia perfecta*, or rhetorical virtuosity, embodied by three alumni who became renowned court preachers in the golden age of the French pulpit in the seventeenth century: Jacques-Bénigne Bossuet, Louis Bourdaloue, and Claude La Colombière. Jesuit institutions were also incubators of theatrical talent, evidenced by dramatist alumni such as Pedro Calderón de la Barca and Lope de Vega in Spain and the Italians Tasso, Maffei, and Goldoni. Master playwrights of seventeenth- and eighteenth-century France were Jesuit-trained: Corneille, Molière, Dancourt, Racine, and Voltaire.

Many students pursued ecclesiastical careers. Founded in 1551, the Roman College (today's Gregorian University), was one of several seminaries that trained clergy. From its classrooms came future missionaries, priests, pastors, theologians, and bishops. Notable Jesuit graduates of the Roman College were Christoph Clavius, chief architect of the Gregorian calendar; Athanasius Kircher, Renaissance polymath; and Roger Boscovich, physicist and mathematician. Through the seventeen popes and countless cardinals and bishops who studied at the institution in the course of five centuries, the Society gained access to powerful patrons in the hierarchy.

Contrary to a stereotype asserting they educated only the rich, the colleges did not favor the privileged over others. Indeed, some schools catered especially to the poor so that, as St. Ignatius explained, they might "obtain gratis an education which they could hardly succeed in obtaining at great expense." His mandate that schools were "for everybody, poor and rich" alike, assured that alumni arose from all economic classes. Because of the attraction of free schooling, the majority of students in Jesuit institutions who commuted daily to class from home came from lower-class and middle-class backgrounds. When in the mid-seventeenth century the Society bowed to parental pressure to accept boarders – who paid for their room and board – caste and class crept upward and bourgeois enrollments increased. The Jesuits also turned their attention to educating the ruling classes in the residential colleges for nobles. The vast majority of schools, however, continued to offer opportunities for upward social mobility to middle-class and lower-class youths.

When the Society was suppressed in 1773, enrollment in its schools worldwide stood at 200,000. After its restoration in 1814, the Order slowly resumed educational work, but social unrest, war, and anticlerical persecution meant it never attained in Europe the prominence of previous centuries. Exiled from many European nations, Jesuit schoolmasters broke new ground in the nineteenth century in China, Japan, India, Egypt, and the Americas. By 1896 there were 209 colleges and universities serving 52,692 students around the globe. The United States, committed to religious toleration, proved an exceptionally fertile field.

Notable figures educated in Jesuit institutions in recent times include Pierre Trudeau and Justin Trudeau, father and son respectively, both Canadian prime ministers; Tony Abbott, Australian prime minister; Vicente Fox, president of Mexico; Alejandro Toledo, president of Peru; John Kerry, US secretary of state, and John Boehner, speaker of the US House of Representatives. In the arts and sciences, Jesuit alums include Georges Lemaitre, the Belgian physicist and priest who developed the Big Bang theory, actors such as Denzel Washington and Salma Hayek, and authors as diverse as Arthur Conan Doyle, Rubén Darío, Mary Higgins Clark, and Will Durant.

The most prominent alumni association is the World Union of Jesuit Alumni, which was founded in 1956 in Bilbao, Spain. Every four years the World Union hosts a global congress of Jesuit alumni in different locations around the world. The most recent of these congresses was held in Medellín, Colombia, in 2013, and drew over 700 representatives from more than forty different countries. Prominent regional affiliates of the World Union include the Federation of Jesuit Alumni Associations of India (JAAI), which seeks to unite alumni from the more than 200 Jesuit educational institutions on the Indian subcontinent, and the European Confederation of Jesuit Alumni/ae, which unites more than a dozen national Jesuit alumni associations throughout Europe. In other regions, such as the United States, alumni associations have been more directly affiliated with individual Jesuit schools and institutions.

See also Descartes, René; Rubens, Peter Paul; Universities, 1540–1773; Universities, 1773–Present; Voltaire, François-Marie Arouet de

Gerald McKevitt, SJ

AMDG

AMDG, the abbreviation for the Latin phrase *Ad majorem Dei gloriam*, meaning "for the greater glory of God," became a leitmotif of the Society of Jesus. There were a number of factors that propelled Ignatius of Loyola's own personal conversion as well as his founding of a new religious order. While no one phrase can capture the full breadth and depth of Ignatius's spiritual zeal, this one perhaps comes closest of all. In fact, these words or their equivalents appear well over 300 times in the Jesuit *Constitutions*, which Ignatius spent many years writing and rewriting, and which were for him as much a spiritual as a juridical guide for his nascent order. As a prime example, the preamble to the *Constitutions* states that, because "the consideration which comes first and has more weight in the order of our intention [as] regards the body of the Society as a whole, whose unity, good government, and preservation in well-being for the greater divine glory are primarily in view, ... it is from this consideration that we shall begin" (#56). The text of the *Constitutions* ends with the logo: "AMDG." On the part of Ignatius,

Figure 3 "AMDG" inscribed on a book held by St. Ignatius, stained glass window, Church of St. Ignatius Loyola, New York. Photograph Alison Fleming

this impetus regarding the greater glory and praise of God is clear from the time of his spiritual awakening onward. In his discussion about advising someone making a choice concerning his or her life, he says, "I will consider what I would say in order to bring such a one to act and elect for the greater glory of God our Lord and the greater perfection of his or her soul" (*Spiritual Exercises*, # 185). Owing to its concise and compelling rationale, in time the Jesuits unofficially adopted this phrase as their motto.

See also Constitutions; Loyola, Ignatius, SJ, St.; Mission; *Spiritual Exercises*

The Constitutions of the Society of Jesus and Their Complementary Norms. Ed. John W. Padberg. St. Louis, MO: The Institute of Jesuit Sources, 1996.
O'Malley, John W., *The First Jesuits*. Cambridge, MA: Harvard University Press, 1993.

Robert E. Scully, SJ

America Magazine

America, a Catholic journal of opinion on culture, politics, and religion, was founded in 1909 by John J. Wynne, SJ (1859–1948).

Throughout its history, *America* has been a strong advocate for human rights and Catholic social teaching. In the early years it heightened the plight of the Irish under British colonial rule, and it favored the Nationalists in the Spanish Civil War, which saw 7,000 priests murdered. It promoted racial and social justice and deplored anti-Semitism.

The elections of John XXIII as pope and of John F. Kennedy as the first Catholic president, followed by the Second Vatican Council, augured a new time in the American

Church. Thereafter, *America* gave much more attention to theological developments and to the multiple reforms occurring in the Church.

The magazine gave attention to the new prominence of Hispanics in the Catholic population; to separating heresy from dissent to Church teaching; to the expanding roles of women in parishes; to urging the abolition of the death penalty. It offered blunt assessments of the flawed leadership skills of bishops and the moral need to clean up the Vatican's financial mess. It deplored Rome's rigid approach to ecumenism and its ever more insistent demand for orthodoxy. *America*'s even-handedness gave the magazine a reputation for temperateness.

The sexual abuse scandal and cover-up of the abuses by bishops by shifting known offenders from parish to parish created a "Catholic Watergate," as one commentator called it.

Under the editorship of the entrepreneurial Matt Malone, SJ, *America* in 2013 established new "firsts": an exclusive interview with Pope Francis and a special issue by women on women's roles in the Church and civil society.

See also LaFarge, John, SJ; Revues/Journals; United States of America

Morris, Charles R., "The First 50 Years." *America*, April 13, 2009, and "A Catholic Moment." *America*, April 20, 2009.

Patrick J. Howell, SJ

Anchieta, José de, SJ, St. (1534–1597)

Born on March 19, 1534, in San Cristóbal de la Laguna (Canary Islands). In 1548 he was sent to study at the Royal College of Arts in Coimbra, where he excelled at Latin poetry. He entered the Society of Jesus on May 1, 1551. The letters from the Jesuits in the East awakened in him the desire to be a missionary. Anchieta was sent to Brazil and arrived at Bahia on July 13, 1553. From there, he proceeded to the captaincy of São Vicente. Together with Manuel da Nóbrega, he established the College of São Paulo on January 25, 1554. In Piratininga he worked as a confessor, a preacher, and a catechist. He taught Portuguese to native and Portuguese children, studied the native language, and composed the first grammar of the Tupi language – *Arte da língua mais usada na costa do Brasil* (Art of the Language Most Used on the Coast of Brazil, 1595).

Anchieta noticed the natives' interest in singing and music. He wrote a catechism, several plays, and hymns in Tupi, incorporating cultural elements from the Brazilian native peoples.

In 1560 he wrote *De gestis Mendi de Saa*, the first epic poem written in the Americas, portraying the struggle of the Portuguese led by the governor-general Mem de Sá to expel the French from the Guanabara Bay.

From May to September 1563, he accompanied Nóbrega to the peace talks between the Portuguese and the Tamoios, who were threatening the colony of São Vicente. To prove the sincerity of the Portuguese, he surrendered himself as a hostage to the natives, while Nóbrega and his companions negotiated with the Tamoio Confederation. At this time, he wrote his poem "The Blessed Virgin Mary" (*De beata Virgine Matre Maria*), consisting of more than 5,700 lines in Latin distichs. Also in 1563, a smallpox epidemic killed 30,000 Indians on the Brazilian coast. Anchieta tended to the sick, making use of his knowledge of native herbs; in the most serious cases he resorted to a bleeding.

In May 1565, he took part in the founding of São Sebastião do Rio de Janeiro.

Ordained a priest in 1566 in Salvador, in January 1567 he went with Nóbrega to Rio de Janeiro in order to establish the local college, which he directed from 1570 to 1573. From 1567 to 1577, he was responsible for the mission of São Vicente. In 1577 he was rector of the College of Salvador. From 1577 to 1588, he was the fifth provincial of the Society of Jesus in Brazil. In spite of his frail health, he traveled constantly along the coast from Cananeia as far as Recife. He visited the Jesuits twice a year, giving rise to new missionary initiatives and establishing schools and colleges.

At the request of the Tucumán bishop, Francisco da Vitória, he sent five priests to found the mission of the Guanarís or Carijós in Paraguay. The fathers took with them the *Grammar*, the *Dialogue of Faith*, and other writings by Anchieta.

From 1587 on, he was rector of the College of Vitoria and superior of the Jesuit houses of Espírito Santo. In May 1597, he had himself transported to Reritiba (now Anchieta), a town founded by him in 1569. He died there on June 9, 1597. His body was taken by the Indians to Vitória and buried in the Church of Saint James. At the funeral, Bartolomeu Simões Pereira, the prelate of Rio de Janeiro, proclaimed him Apostle of Brazil.

Educator, poet, dramatist, and historian, his fame resulted from the influence of his personality over natives and settlers, from his humanistic education, and from the composition of Latin poems, religious songs, and popular plays in Tupi, Portuguese, and Spanish. His oratory was characterized by a biblical flavor, and by its simplicity, clearness, and strength of conviction. Deeply interested in people, he devoted himself to the poor and suffering, the threatened native groups, and the enslaved Africans.

A fine observer of the natives' custom and usage, his letters are full of precious elements for the anthropological studies of the first inhabitants of Brazil. He also penned many notes describing the flora and fauna, the geography, and the climate of the Brazilian land.

Beatified on June 22, 1980, by Pope John Paul II, he was canonized on April 3, 2014, by Pope Francis.

See also Brazil; Catechisms; Nóbrega, Manuel da; Portugal

Cardoso, Armando,*Vida de São José de Anchieta: um carismático que fez história*. São Paulo: Edições Loyola, 2014.

Leite, Serafim, *História da Companhia de Jesus no Brasil*. Vols. I–II. Lisbon/Rio de Janeiro: Civilização Brasileira, 1938.

Viotti, Hélio Abranches, *Anchieta: O apóstolo do Brasil*. São Paulo: Edições Loyola, 1980.

Danilo Mondoni, SJ

Angels

Like many other Catholic religious orders in early modern Europe, Jesuits stressed devotion to the saints and the angels. Ignatius himself referred to the role of the "good angel(s)" and the "evil angel" in the *Spiritual Exercises* (##329, 331). Peter Faber (1506–46) noted in his *Memoriale* (1542) his resolution to invoke the "angelic Principalities, the Archangels, the guardian angels and patron saints" of each nation or region in which he would work. Other early Jesuit authors who wrote on the subject of angels include: Aloysius Gonzaga (1568–91); Francesco Albertini (?–1619); Juan Maldonado (1533–83); Pierre Coton (1564–1626); Francisco Suárez (1548–1617); and Jeremias Drexel (1581–1638).

In the contemporary period, Karl Rahner, SJ, has contributed the most to a theological and devotional understanding of the role of angels. In addition to at least one published sermon, Rahner contributed a lengthy entry, "Angel," to the encyclopedia *Sacramentum mundi* (1968). Here, he stresses the real existence of angels as part of both created reality and the "context" of divine revelation and human salvation in Christ. Even the veneration of "guardian angels" can be supported by tradition and theological reflection (if not too "anthropomorphic" or "childish").

See also Loyola, Ignatius of, SJ, St.; Rahner, Karl

Guibert, Joseph De, *The Jesuits, Their Spiritual Doctrine and Practice: A Historical Study*. St. Louis, MO: The Institute of Jesuit Sources, 1964.

Johnson, Trevor, "Guardian Angels and the Society of Jesus." In Peter Marshall and Alexandra Walsham, eds., *Angels in the Early Modern World*. Cambridge: Cambridge University Press, 2006, pp. 191–213.

Julia, Dominique, "Le culte des saints dans le Mémorial de Pierre Favre." In Jürgen Beyer, Albrecht Burkardt, and Fred van Lieburg, eds., *Confessional Sanctity (c. 1500 – c. 1800)*. Mainz: Verlag Philipp von Zabern, 2003, pp. 25–48.

Joanne M. Pierce

Anima Christi

An anonymous prayer, perhaps of fourteenth-century origins, it was known to Ignatius of Loyola; he mentioned it twice in the *Spiritual Exercises*, in connection with the meditation on Two Standards of Christ or Satan (#147), and with the Second Method of Prayer (#253). In each case Ignatius clearly presumed that it was a well-known prayer, for he recommended saying it along with the Hail Mary and other such prayers. He was not the author of the *Anima Christi*, though the fact that many editions of the *Spiritual Exercises* have printed this prayer as a kind of preface or foreword has led some to draw this erroneous conclusion.

The *Anima Christi*, directed to Jesus the crucified one, is a heartfelt, intimate petition for an extraordinarily close, personal, embodied relationship. Asking "Blood of Christ, inebriate me," and "Within your wounds, hide me," the one praying this prayer asks for salvation and sanctification through the passion of Jesus. The prayer reflects in a vivid, emotional way Eucharistic piety of the late Middle Ages, with its emphases on the real presence of the body of Christ in the Eucharist, and on the Eucharist as a privileged means of access to Jesus. Though frequent reception of the Eucharist had not yet become the norm for laity, seeing the consecrated host, at Mass, or outside Mass in processions for feasts such as Corpus Christi, was at the heart of the religious experience of a growing number of devout Catholics by the time of Ignatius. The *Anima Christi* also reflected the desire for a good "hour" of death, by asking Jesus to "call" one to himself at that most critical of moments.

See also Communion, Frequent; *Spiritual Exercises*

Homza, Lu Ann, "The Religious Milieu of the Young Ignatius." In Thomas Worcester, ed., *The Cambridge Companion to the Jesuits*. Cambridge: Cambridge University Press, 2008, pp. 13–31.

Rubin, Miri, *Corpus Christi: The Eucharist in Late Medieval Culture*. Cambridge: Cambridge University Press, 1991.

Viladesau, Richard, *The Triumph of the Cross: The Passion of Christ in Theology and the Arts, from the Renaissance to the Counter-Reformation*. Oxford: Oxford University Press, 2008.

Thomas Worcester, SJ

Anti-Jesuit Polemic

From their origins, Jesuits have been highly praised and highly valued as well as vilified, slandered, mocked, scapegoated, rejected, imprisoned, expelled, persecuted, and even killed. Anti-Jesuit polemic has very often been expressed in print: in books, articles, pamphlets, tracts, etc. There is an astounding abundance of such material extant, much of which is little studied. This entry offers a kind of overview of at least some of the major themes in anti-Jesuit discourses.

The history of anti-Jesuit polemics begins with opposition to the Jesuit founder Ignatius of Loyola (1491–1556). His *Spiritual Exercises* were repeatedly the subject of hostile examination by inquisitors and the like looking for links between Ignatius and what were considered heretics at the time. The focus in the *Exercises* (first published in 1548) on an individual's direct, personal experience of God did not please those seeking to uphold institutional authority and clerical control of religious experience. In a similar way, and since the time of Ignatius, Jesuits have been periodically accused of not being sufficiently obedient to church authority.

And yet Jesuits have often been challenged and excoriated because of what has been perceived as their too-close relationship with the papacy. In the sixteenth century, Spain was the world's superpower; perceived as a Spanish order, the Society of Jesus was vilified in France and elsewhere as Spanish and papist. In France, especially, Jesuits were accused of not being good subjects of the king, an accusation strengthened in the wake of the 1589 assassination of King Henri III, the 1594 attempt on the life of King Henri IV, and the 1610 assassination of Henri IV. Jesuits were repeatedly accused of advocating regicide and of helping to carry it out. Writings by the Spanish Jesuit Juan de Mariana (1536–1624) that dealt in a theoretical way with circumstances that might justify killing a tyrannical monarch were used to tarnish French Jesuits as disloyal, untrustworthy, murderous foreigners, and as anything but good Frenchmen. Such accusations and insinuations were used as the reason to expel Jesuits from certain parts of France in 1594, expulsions revoked by Henri IV in 1603. Jesuit writers produced a flood of publications declaring their loyalty to the French monarchy, flattering the king, and seeking to obtain a secure place for themselves and their schools and other works in the France of the Most Christian King (*Le Roi Très Chrétien*). Such a strategy worked with the king, but even in an increasingly absolute monarchy, as was the French monarchy of the 1600s, many other French voices and other French institutions did not revise or tone down their anti-Jesuit agenda and discourse.

Not too surprisingly, early modern Protestants had little or nothing good to say about the Jesuits, seeing them as a threat, theological and political. In England, some Jesuits, such as Edmund Campion (1540–81), suffered martyrdom, for the monarch was head of the Church as well as head of State, and thus disobedience to the royal will in religion could be hard to distinguish from political disloyalty. Catholic priests, especially Jesuit priests, were assumed to be guilty of treason and thus worthy of death. In various parts of Germany and central Europe, in the late sixteenth and seventeenth centuries, Jesuit preachers sought to bolster Catholicism and to bring people back to what they believed was the true faith. By the era of the Thirty Years War (1618–48), Jesuit confessors to the Habsburgs and the Wittelsbachs used their positions at court to promote Counter-Reformation in a military and political sense. Protestant polemicists, using broadsheets and other printed means, alleged that Jesuits concealed large quantities of weapons and money, that they were hypocritical in their vow of chastity, that they were disciples of Machiavelli, and that they were similar to Jews, witches, and Ottoman (Muslim) troops.

But Lutheran and Reformed leaders were not the only critics of the Jesuits. When Catholic armies "recovered" Catholic territory, including religious houses such as monasteries and their lands, Jesuits sought to obtain some of these for their various works. This elicited vigorous anti-Jesuit responses from the older religious orders, eager to limit the growth of such upstart newcomers as the Jesuits, and to protect and preserve the more traditional forms of religious life and their institutions and property.

A particularly virulent anti-Jesuit publication that had a very long life was the *Monita secreta*, first published in 1614, in Poland, by a former Jesuit, Jerome Zahorowski (1583–1634), disgruntled, at least in part, by his failure in a theology examination that had disqualified him from taking the fourth vow of Jesuits. The forged document read as if it were the secret instructions, now made public, that guided the Society of Jesus in a lust for wealth and power. Thus, the publication of the *Monita secreta* was intended to severely compromise the credibility of the Society of Jesus by showing its real purpose to be anything but spiritual. Despite the fraudulent nature of the *Monita secreta*, many editions, translated into various languages, including French, English, German, Dutch, Spanish, and Portuguese, were published from the seventeenth to the twentieth centuries.

By the 1640s Jansenists were honing their anti-Jesuit accusations and insinuations. With a rather dour, pessimistic appropriation of certain aspects of St. Augustine's theology, Jansenists in France relentlessly excoriated the Jesuits as soft on sin and as given over to worldly pursuits and ideals. Antoine Arnauld lambasted Jesuit sacramental practice as too quick to grant absolution in the sacrament of penance and as too ready to encourage frequent reception of communion, and communion without a period of rigorous penitential preparation. Frequent communion, Arnauld and other Jansenists argued, would promote an overly familiar approach to the Eucharist, and thus a diminishment of awe and respect. For the Jansenists, the genuinely devout received communion but rarely and only after confession and a period of penance that could be lengthy. While the Jesuits emphasized creation of the human being in the image and likeness of God, Jansenists stressed the devastating consequences of original sin and the small number of elect that would be saved through God's inscrutable will and commands. In hearing confessions, Jesuits often considered circumstances that could reduce the gravity of a sin; however, Jansenists denounced what they called Jesuit laxity and Jesuit failures to uphold a traditional, unchanging morality that, Jansenists argued, was articulated in the Bible and the Church Fathers, and not subject to revision. Blaise Pascal (1623–62) was the most eloquent and clever of Jansenist writers; his *Lettres provinciales*, still in print in French and various translations, remains an extraordinarily successful misrepresentation of Jesuit pastoral practices.

If Jesuit confessors in Europe attempted to bridge the gap between abstract moral principles and the particularities of human experience, Jesuits sent to Asia and elsewhere around the world sometimes sought not only to announce the Gospel but to do so while accommodating (preserving, honoring, valuing) local cultures and practices. This was especially so in China. Negative reactions to Jesuit accommodation of Chinese rites that honored ancestors were loud and insistent. When Jesuits permitted Chinese converts to Christianity to continue to perform such rites, rival Catholic missionaries in Asia, and their supporters in Europe, denounced the Jesuits as guilty of accepting and fostering paganism. Popes responded variously in the 1600s, but Clement XI (r. 1700–21) forbade missionaries from accepting the Chinese rites as compatible with Christianity. Anti-Jesuit agendas carried the day and the papacy with it, though Clement XI was anything but friendly to the Jansenists, arch-enemies of the Jesuits.

The eighteenth century represents the high-water mark of anti-Jesuit fury. Papal and royal efforts to limit if not eliminate Jansenism seemed only to strengthen an image of Jansenists as courageous martyrs and champions of conscience and local authority, and the purveyors of an alternative to the pretensions of centralizing and absolutist kings and popes. None of these dynamics was helpful to the Jesuits. The 1700s saw Jesuits mocked and slandered, from left and right, by deist *philosophes* and Jansenist sympathizers, by left-wing secularizers and right-wing religious zealots. Jesuits can be said to have tried to hold a middle ground, a ground that did not hold. Enlightenment discourse despised priests as enemies of human progress and reason, as obstacles to science and learning, as salesmen for superstition. Religious orders and communities were portrayed as dens of iniquity and sexual perversion, and as dungeons where young women were imprisoned by their families. Jesuits were viewed as using their missions in Latin America as gold and silver mines for their own enrichment, and as stirring up native populations against Spanish and Portuguese royal authorities.

A famous legal case in France was the 1731 trial of Jean-Baptiste Girard, SJ (1680–1733), accused of seduction, procurement of abortion, and witchcraft. The courts did not find him guilty, but in books and pamphlets, published in French and other languages, he continued to be not only tried but condemned. The Girard case offers an excellent case of how, in the decades leading up to the Suppression of the Society of Jesus, the reputation of Jesuits was dismantled by anti-Jesuit forces little concerned with facts or justice.

Meanwhile, Enlightenment-era Catholic monarchs sought to bring the Church in their realms under ever-tighter state control. Though such an agenda did not necessarily single out the Jesuits, they were especially vulnerable in view of their vow of obedience to the pope and their international structure and charism. Jesuits were perceived as incompatible with national churches under state control, in Portugal, in Spain, in France, and in their overseas territories. Anti-Jesuit polemics and accusations of various kinds paved and eased the way for national expulsions and dissolutions of the Society of Jesus, beginning in Portugal, in 1759. These would eventually be followed, in 1773, by Pope Clement XIV's universal Suppression of the Society, in response to pressure from heads of state and their ministers only too happy to propagate every manner of anti-Jesuit discourse.

Restoration of the Jesuits by Pope Pius VII (r. 1800–23) in 1814 did not mean that anti-Jesuit polemics had ceased. On the contrary, the nineteenth century saw some of the greatest hostility to the Society of Jesus, and expulsions of Jesuits from one or another country were at least as frequent as they had been pre-1773. In the new republic of the United States of America, political leaders such as John Adams and Thomas Jefferson deplored Pius VII's decision and described Jesuits as worthy of eternal hellfire, but they nevertheless allowed that Jesuits might enjoy the religious freedom afforded by the American Constitution. English-speaking countries and territories, though more-or-less Protestant in their heritage, often proved to be quite tolerant of the restored Society of Jesus, more so than many traditionally Catholic countries.

In France, the familiar catalogue of anti-Jesuit accusations proved very resilient, and as nineteenth-century France underwent frequent regime change, from empire to monarchies, to republic, to empire, to republic, Jesuits were at the mercy of politicians eager to praise or blame, reward or scapegoat and punish the Society of Jesus. Schools were a particularly sensitive issue, with anticlerical politicians keen to eliminate Jesuit and other Catholic influence over impressionable children and to guarantee that all schools taught a patriotic historical narrative in which clergy played little positive role. The nineteenth century was an age of especially fervent nationalism and, in Europe at least, this made Jesuits more vulnerable than ever to attack as papists insufficiently loyal to the nation-state. Anti-Jesuit paranoia meant that the Society of Jesus was imagined as conspiring against liberty and equality and progress and all that the French Revolution had accomplished. Jesuits were also depicted as parasites preying on wealthy women, especially widows, and seeking to use them to gain wealth and power. Anti-Jesuit polemics could pave the way for murder: during the Paris Commune of 1871, five French Jesuits were executed.

In the late 1800s – in the wake of Vatican I's definition of papal infallibility, and with the dissolution of the Papal States by the kingdom of Italy, in the wake of the creation of Bismarck's German Empire and the establishment of the French Third Republic – Jesuits were relentlessly portrayed as enemies of the nation and of the state, and as crafty and untrustworthy. Such polemics were expressed in image as well as in word. An example of the former is a cartoon published in Rome in 1872 showing Jesuits departing into exile in Austria, dressed in cassocks but with serpents' tails emerging beneath their religious habits. Bismarck's *Kulturkampf* was anti-Catholic in various ways, but it was especially anti-Jesuit. When in 1901 the French state forced nearly all religious orders and congregations into exile, the French Jesuits were already very familiar with such treatment.

Jesuit participation in World War I, on both sides, and as both soldiers and chaplains, helped to some extent to improve their patriotic credentials in various nations. But even an event as significant as the Great War did not fundamentally alter centuries of anti-Jesuit discourse. Still, in post-1918 France, Jesuits came to enjoy at least a kind of de facto tolerance, and Jesuit numbers in France rose dramatically between the two world wars. But in the1920s in Mexico, and in the 1930s in Spain, not only were Jesuits maligned by secularizing, anticlerical governments, but some were martyred, including Blessed Miguel Pro (1891–1926) in Mexico, and Blessed Tomás Sitjar (1866–1936) in Spain. Fascist governments, especially the Nazi regime, envisioned the state as controlling everything, religion included, and this model of the state did not always leave much breathing room for the Society of Jesus. German Jesuit Alfred Delp (1907–45) and French Jesuit Yves de Montcheuil (1900–44) are examples of Jesuits executed by the Nazis. Communist regimes of the twentieth century varied in their degree of persecution of Jesuits: Hungarian Jesuits formed a Jesuit province in exile, but Polish

Jesuits remained in Poland and were able to do a great deal of pastoral work, though Jesuit schools were seen as incompatible with the Communist state. Officially atheistic regimes could hardly be well disposed to an order of priests working for the greater glory of God.

And yet "communist" eventually became one of the main accusations against the Society of Jesus in the decades after Vatican II. As the Society of Jesus affirmed a preferential option for the poor, and as Jesuits played major roles in the development of liberation theology, defenders of wealth and its privileges disparaged the Society of Jesus and sought to portray it as at odds with authentic Catholicism. Anti-Jesuit polemic, from the religious and political right, frequently targeted Pedro Arrupe (1907–91), Jesuit superior general from 1965 to1981. The 1989 assassination of six Jesuits in El Salvador marked the most violent expression of hatred of the Society of Jesus in the post-Vatican II era.

Also in the decades after Vatican II, some of the most virulent criticism of Jesuits saw them as turning their backs on their own traditions. Former Jesuit and Irishman Malachi Martin (1921–99) was prominent among such critics. These critics saw nearly everything wrong with the Jesuits, and with the Catholic Church, as a kind of betrayal and abandonment of what they imagined as the glorious era of the 1950s and earlier. Accusations of betrayal and the like also dominated claims that the Jesuits had renounced their tradition of loyalty and seemingly set aside their vow of obedience to the pope, replacing it by dissent and disloyalty. The US author George Weigel often articulated this sort of polemic against the Jesuits.

The election of a Jesuit pope in 2013 surprised almost everyone, including and maybe even especially Jesuits. Though the election of Francis and his first years as pope saw enormous enthusiasm around the world, negative reactions were not lacking either. Not everyone was pleased with the beatification of Oscar Romero (1917–80), assassinated archbishop of San Salvador, long defamed by some as a communist but declared a martyr by Pope Francis in 2015. In the USA, dismissive and condescending reactions to the 2015 encyclical *Laudato Si'* suggested the persistence of North American and Anglo-Protestant bias against Latin America and against the Society of Jesus. Die-hard defenders of so-called "free" market capitalism refused to give a hearing to Pope Francis when he dared to question profit-driven environmental degradation. Though the election of Jorge Bergoglio, SJ, as bishop of Rome in some ways offered an unexpected vindication of the Society of Jesus, it also exposed it more than ever to being used as a scapegoat for anything perceived as wrong in the Catholic Church and beyond. No Jesuit has ever had such a high profile worldwide as Pope Francis, a profile carrying enormous risks and enormous opportunities.

See also Chinese Rites Controversy; Ex-Jesuits; France; Jansenism; *Monita Secreta*; Portugal; Scandal; Spain; Suppression; United Kingdom

Burke, Peter, "The Black Legend of the Jesuits: An Essay in the History of Social Stereotypes." In Simon Ditchfield, ed., *Christianity and Community in the West: Essays for John Bossy*. Aldershot: Ashgate, 2001, pp. 165–82.

Cubitt, Geoffrey, *The Jesuit Myth: Conspiracy Theory and Politics in Nineteenth-Century France*. Oxford: Clarendon Press, 1993.

Fabre, Pierre-Antoine, and Catherine Maire, eds., *Les Antijésuites: discours, figures et lieux de l'antijésuitisme à l'époque moderne*. Rennes: Presses Universitaires de Rennes, 2010.

Fumaroli, Marc, "Between the Rigorist Hammer and the Deist Anvil: The Fate of the Jesuits in Eighteenth-Century France." In John W. O'Malley, Gauvin A. Bailey, Steven J. Harris, and T. Frank

Kennedy, eds., *The Jesuits II: Cultures, Sciences, and the Arts, 1540–1773*. Toronto: University of Toronto Press, 2006, pp. 682–90.

Martin, Malachi, *The Jesuits: The Society of Jesus and the Betrayal of the Roman Catholic Church*. New York: Simon & Schuster, 1987.

Paintner, Ursula, '*Des Papsts neue Creatur*': *Antijesuitische Publizistik im Deutschsprachigen Raum (1555–1618)*. Amsterdam: Rodopi, 2011.

Pavone, Sabina, *The Wily Jesuits and the Monita Secreta: The Forged Secret Instructions of the Jesuits, Myth and Reality*. Trans. John P. Murphy. St. Louis, MO: Institute of Jesuit Sources, 2005.

Ross, Andrew, *A Vision Betrayed: The Jesuits in Japan and China, 1542–1742*. Maryknoll, NY: Orbis, 1994.

Weigel, George, "Questions for Father General," *Denver Catholic Register*, February 20, 2008. www. archden.org/dcr/news.

Whitfield, Teresa, *Paying the Price: Ignacio Ellacuría and the Murdered Jesuits of El Salvador*. Philadelphia, PA: Temple University Press, 1994.

Thomas Worcester, SJ

Anti-Semitism

Although Jesuits of Jewish ancestry were very numerous and very influential in the early Society, the Order explicitly banned members of "Hebrew or Saracen stock" in a decree of 1593. This prohibition, motivated by anti-Spanish nationalism, stayed in effect until 1946 when it was abrogated in the wake of the Holocaust. German anti-Semites had praised the Order's commitment to racial purity in its ban on Jewish members. Although it was an exaggeration, Hannah Arendt identified anti-Semitism as the special charism of the Society: "It was the Jesuits who had always best represented, both in the written and spoken word, the anti-Semitic school of the Catholic clergy" (*The Origins of Totalitarianism*, 102). Unfortunately, there has as yet been no systematic effort to trace the history of Jesuit hostility toward Jews and the very term "anti-Semitism" would be judged inaccurate as a Jesuit attitude if racism was taken as central to its meaning. Various terms have been utilized to chart Jesuit attitudes: ontological anti-Semitism, Judeophobia, Jew-hatred, anti-Jewish prejudice, and anti-Judaism among others. A widespread form was "asemitism" which advocated a separation between Jews and Christians while renouncing violent anti-Jewish activity. This hope for Jewish invisibility may very well be rooted in the particular historical circumstances of a Spanish religious order that would readily remember the 1492 expulsion of the Jews as well as in the prohibition against Jewish membership.

Jesuits have been accused of combining the religious rejection of Judaism with a secular denunciation of Jewish power, a very toxic mix. The single Jesuit institution that evokes the most criticism for its anti-Jewish polemic is the Italian journal *La Civiltà Cattolica* that followed the Vatican program of demonizing modernity and the forces that were believed to be behind it, among which the Jews were often targeted as prominent. The traditionally close relationship between the Jesuits and the papacy has given the Society a particular importance in the scrutiny of papal activity before and during the Holocaust. For example, Pope Pius XI commissioned a never promulgated encyclical on racism (*Humani generis unitas*, 1938) from a group of Jesuits, and the document exhibits at times the sorry state of attitudes toward Jews even when criticizing racial thinking: The Israelites have been "blinded by a vision of material domination and gain" and were doomed to "perpetually wander over the face of the earth." "Israel has incurred the wrath of God because it has rejected the Gospel." The Church is not "blind to the spiritual danger to which contact with Jews can expose souls," and she knows of the need to "safeguard her children against spiritual contagion."

There were more than a few Jesuits, however, who overcame the common prejudices and hostility toward Jews, and their contribution was especially significant during World War II. In France, Belgium, Poland, as well as in Germany, Jesuits spoke out against the Nazi persecution of the Jews. A sign of the heroism that was shown by some is the recognition of fourteen Jesuits by the State of Israel's program to recognize non-Jews who risked or lost their lives in efforts to save Jewish life ("Righteous Gentiles" project of Jerusalem's Yad Vashem institution). Among the fourteen was the Belgian Jean-Baptiste Janssens who was elected the leader of the Order in 1946. The witness of these Jesuit critics and their postwar writings influenced many Catholics to reconsider their attitudes toward Jews in the period leading up to the Second Vatican Council. The French Jesuit biblical scholar, Joseph Bonsirven, prepared the way for the positive religious apprecia-tion of Judaism even while criticizing Jesuit leadership for anti-Semitic attitudes. He was certainly one of the intellectual sources for the 1960 petition from the Jesuit Pontifical Biblical Institute in Rome that first called for a declaration from the Council on the Jews. In 1965 the Council adopted the document *Nostra aetate* and, thus, inaugurated the most positive relationship between Catholics and Jews that has ever existed in their long histories.

See also Jews and Jesuits

Bernauer, James, and Robert Maryks, eds., *"The Tragic Couple": Encounters between Jews and Jesuits.* Leiden/Boston: Brill, 2014.

Lapomarda, Vincent, *The Jesuits and the Third Reich.* Lewiston, NY: Edwin Mellen Press, 2005.

de Lubac, Henri, *Christian Resistance to Anti-Semitism: Memories from 1940–1944.* San Francisco: Ignatius Press, 1990.

Passelecq, George, and Bernard Suchecky, eds., *The Hidden Encyclical of Pius XI.* New York: Harcourt, Brace and Company, 1997.

James Bernauer, SJ

Antwerp

The city of Antwerp, located on the frontier with the Protestant Dutch provinces, was an important center for the Jesuits' evangelizing mission. Twelve years after settling in the city in 1562, the first Jesuits founded a modest college and church in the center of town. After being banned from the city in 1578 by Protestant rebels, the Belgian Jesuits were welcomed back in 1585 by the Spanish general Alessandro Farnese, who had brought the city back under Catholic governance. The years fol-lowing their return inaugurated a period of great expansion. In 1585 they founded their first Marian sodality, a lay congregation intended for young men of divergent social and economic backgrounds. In 1607, they relocated their college to a larger site on the outskirts of the city, and in 1612 they turned their main residence into the first professed house of the Flemish-Belgian province. By 1619 the Jesuits had grown into the largest order in Antwerp, with 157 members. This expansion led to the building (1615–21) of one of the most splendid Jesuit churches north of the Alps. Designed by the Jesuit architects Franciscus Aguilonius and Pieter Huyssens, the

Figure 4 Sebastian Vrancx: *Interior of the Jesuit Church in Antwerp*, 1630, oil on wood, Kunsthistorisches Museum, Vienna. Photograph © Erich Lessing / Art Resource, New York

church featured polychrome marble and a scheme of paintings by Peter Paul Rubens (partly destroyed in a fire in 1718), which showed the Order's commitment to using the visual arts in their program of reform. Other noteworthy accomplishments of the Antwerp Jesuits included the publication of Jerónimo Nadal's *Adnotationes et meditationes in Evangelia*, a series of devotions with images engraved by the Wierix brothers of Antwerp (1595); Heribert Rosweyde's edition of the lives of the saints (the *Acta Sanctorum*, started in 1607 and continued by Jean Bolland in 1629); and the *Imago primi saeculi* (1640), a history of the Order lavishly illustrated with emblems.

See also Imago Primi Saeculi; Rubens, Peter Paul; Wierix Brothers

Lombaerde, Piet, ed., *Innovation and Experience in the Early Baroque: The Case of the Jesuit Church in Antwerp*. Turnhout: Brepols Publishers, 2008.

Anna C. Knaap

Apostleship of Prayer

The Apostleship of Prayer (AOP) was born out of a profound missionary zeal. In 1844 a number of Jesuit scholastics studying theology in Vals, France, expressed their fervor to work in overseas missions. Responding to their plea, Fr. François-Xavier Gautrelet exhorted the students to devote themselves to prayer and a morning offering of self as a present apostolic endeavor. After Fr. Gautrelet introduced the practice, Fr. Henri

Ramière organized the scholastics' daily devotional practice into the AOP. He also added the devotion of the Sacred Heart of Jesus as part of its spiritual practice.

In 1861, under Fr. Ramière's direction, the first edition of the organization's periodical, *Messengers of the Sacred Heart of Jesus*, was published in Toulouse. In 1866 Pope Pius IX granted papal approval to the Apostleship's first statutes. Subsequently, devotion to Our Lady and prayers for the Pope's intentions were added to the Apostleship's set of devotional prayers and mission. The Apostleship's statutes of 1896 submitted its governing oversight to the Jesuit superior general or one of his delegates. In 1927 its headquarters was moved from Toulouse to the Jesuit Curia in Rome.

According to Decree 13 of General Congregation 34, "the Apostleship of Prayer seeks to form Christians shaped by the Eucharist, devoted to the Heart of Christ through the daily offering and prayer for the intentions of the Church, and committed to apostolic service. The Society supports and promotes this pastoral service entrusted to it by the Holy Father." In his letter "To the Whole Society," dated January 3, 2015, Father General Adolfo Nicolás insisted on the Society's commitment to the Apostleship of Prayer, particularly for prayer dedicated to the intentions of the pope. He subsequently introduced a new proposal entitled *Journeying with Jesus in Apostolic Availability*, which re-creates the Apostleship of Prayer by renewing its initial vision through new modalities that are more attractive and compelling.

See also Christian Life Communities; Confraternities; Sacred Heart

Kolvenbach, Peter-Hans, "El Apostolado de la Oración hoy." *Oración y Servicio* (1995), 3–104.
Nicolás, Adolfo, "To the Whole Society: On Re-creating the Apostleship of Prayer." Curia Generalizia della Compagnia di Gesù, Rome, January 3, 2015.

Hưng Trung Phạm, SJ

Apostolate

The word "apostolate" has its origin in *apostolos*, Greek for an apostle – one who is sent on mission. Over the centuries Jesuits have developed a multitude of apostolates. Some have been unique to a particular individual, such as a Jesuit who composes operas or one who researches embryonic biology. Others have been apostolates taken up by the Society itself, such as the founding of the first Jesuit college in Messina, Sicily, at the invitation of the local civic leaders.

During the Suppression, 1773–1814, the state took over almost all of the Society's apostolates and properties.

Over the last fifty years, dedicated laypeople have made possible the extension and success of many Jesuit apostolates. A prime example would be the founding of Copper Valley School in Alaska. At "Copper," the original Jesuit Volunteer Corps, founded by Jesuit scholastic Jack Morris, provided the lion's share of the instruction. Another example of lay leadership is the founding of Cristo Rey high schools and Nativity middle schools for at-risk students

A vital apostolate for Jesuits has always been work with indigenous peoples. Often Jesuits produced the first dictionaries of the native languages.

In the two decades after Vatican II, tensions often existed between the social apostolate and the educational apostolate. The former tended to draw entrepreneurial Jesuits who worked side by side with the poor or who directly confronted unjust social structures. The latter tended to be more steeped in tradition, slower to change, engrossed in scholarly research and teaching. In recent years, however, these two apostolates have often partnered to form a more dynamic institution for educating leaders for a more just and humane society.

See also Ministries; Mission

Padberg, John W., ed., *Jesuit Life and Mission Today: The Decrees and Accompanying Documents of the 31st–35th General Congregations of the Society of Jesus.* St. Louis, MO: The Institute of Jesuit Sources, 2009.

Patrick J. Howell, SJ

Applied

This is the process by which Jesuits are given permission to work or reside for a period of time in a province not officially their own. Although Jesuits belong to the province to which they were formally admitted, they may under certain circumstances wish or be asked to spend time residing and working elsewhere. According to the Complementary Norms of the Jesuit *Constitutions*, "By mutual consent of the provincials involved, members of one province can be sent to another province or applied to it temporarily" (389, #2). The criterion for individual Jesuits to be applied to another province is that their principal ministry centers on "a stable assignment directed primarily to the good of that province and not their own, whether for a definite or an indefinite time" (389, #3). This application can last until such time as other provisions are made. There are, however, some instances in which members of the Society may be living in another province but should not be applied to it (i.e., *degentes*), including "for reasons of studies, probations, health, or business that is not the responsibility of that province" (389, #4). This rationale also extends to "those who are assigned to a house or a work that is immediately dependent on the general" (389, #4), or that he has deemed to be a work common to the Society or to several provinces. In any event, a Jesuit who is applied to another province receives all of his financial support from there and gives his annual manifestation of conscience to that provincial. In these and other ways, the Society promotes a fuller union of minds and hearts among its members.

See also Province; Transcribe

The Constitutions of the Society of Jesus and Their Complementary Norms. Ed. John W. Padberg. St. Louis, MO: The Institute of Jesuit Sources, 1996.

Robert E. Scully, SJ

Arauco

In 1608 the Jesuits Martín de Aranda Valdivia and Horacio Vecchi were tasked with beginning a mission to the indigenous people known as the Araucanians (or Mapuche). This took place in a context of fierce conflict between the Mapuche and the Spanish. By the time of the mission, only the forts of Arauco and Paicaví remained south of the River Bío Bío, and a community of indigenous allies to the Spanish had grouped around them. As such, Arauco, while far from ideal, seemed like the best place to establish the first mission. In 1612 Luis de Valdivia returned from Spain with instructions to implement the strategy of *Defensive War*, and for this he enlisted the help of Aranda, Vecchi, and a Jesuit novice, Diego de Montalbán, who combined their peace-brokering with a mission to the indigenous people of Elicura. During the course of this mission, however, the three Jesuits were killed.

Despite this major setback, the mission to Arauco continued. Letters talk of the hardships suffered by missionaries, not just because of the rough terrain, lack of supplies, and the inclement weather but also because of the constant danger. The annual letter of 1629–30, for example, describes how one of the missionaries to Arauco found himself caught up in a battle between the Spanish and the Mapuche. Another major uprising in 1655 destroyed the mission of Arauco, and it was not reestablished until 1664. Nevertheless, the Jesuit missionaries on the frontier, and in particular those working in Arauco, were of fundamental importance to facilitating dialogue in what was known as "parliaments" between the Mapuche and the Spanish. This missionary work that emphasized the role of peacemaking at least helped bring about an uneasy truce and opened the way for the further expansion of the Society in the eighteenth century.

See also Chile; Spain; Valdiva, Luis de, SJ

Foerster, Rolf, *Jesuitas y mapuches, 1593–1767*. Santiago de Chile: Editorial Universitaria, 1996.
de Ovalle, Alonso, *Histórica relación del reino de Chile [1646]*. Santiago de Chile: Pehuén, 2003.

Andrew Redden

Arca

The dictates of poverty impose certain restrictions on the Society as a whole, and additional restrictions on provinces and regions, with regard to the possession of revenue-bearing capital and of fixed and stable revenues. Provinces as well as independent and dependent regions (or missions) can possess and make use of revenues or trust funds only for a restricted set of purposes. The first of these purposes is for the support of Jesuits in formation, including studies, which is known as the *Arca seminarii* (Seminary Fund). The second of these set-asides is for the care of the sick and aged, the *Arca praevisionis* (Retirement Fund). Thirdly, funds can be built up for the establishment or development of houses and foundations, as either needs or opportunities arise, constituting the *Arca fundationum* (Foundations Fund). A final category relates to the broadly apostolic nature of the Society itself. As expounded in the Complementary Norms of the *Constitutions*, certain funds can be used to support such works as "retreat houses especially for non-Jesuits, centers for the social apostolate or for the diffusion of Catholic teaching by means of the media of social communication, for charitable enterprises both in and outside the Society, and for other apostolates that otherwise would lack sufficient resources" (205, #4). This constitutes the *Arca operum apostolicorum* (Apostolic Works Fund).

See also Gratuity of Ministries; Poverty

The Constitutions of the Society of Jesus and Their Complementary Norms. Ed. John W. Padberg. St. Louis, MO: The Institute of Jesuit Sources, 1996.

Robert E. Scully, SJ

Architecture

Prior to the Suppression of the Society, Jesuit churches were often designed by Jesuit architects. Giuseppe Castiglione, Andrea Pozzo, Orazio Grassi, François d'Aguilon, Pieter Huyssens, Etienne Martellange, and Carlo Spinola are among the Jesuits of the sixteenth and seventeenth centuries who constructed spaces for use by the Society. Jesuit architects also worked for secular patrons, constructing diverse works including military fortifications. In the early modern period, the Jesuits were able to rely on their own, as so many of their number had received artistic and architectural training. While this is less frequent today, the Society of Jesus continues to hold high regard for architecture. Father Gilbert Sunghera, SJ, stands out as a contemporary Jesuit, trained as an architect, who maintains a consulting practice focused on developing liturgical space and connecting architecture with issues of social justice.

At the time of the restoration, the neo-Gothic movement in art and architecture was emerging, and an embrace of this style allowed the Society to associate themselves with a new visual image. This was true in Europe as well as the Americas and Asia. The Cathedral of St. Ignatius in Shanghai, built by the Jesuits in the mid-nineteenth century after their return to China, stands out as an exemplar.

In contrast to the "old" Society, in the nineteenth century fewer buildings were designed by Jesuits. There are some prominent exceptions, most notably Ignatius Scoles (1834–96). Scoles was the son of architect Joseph John Scoles, who worked extensively for the English Jesuits. His principal building is the Church of the Immaculate Conception, also known as Farm Street Church, in central London. Constructed for the Jesuits in 1844–49, it is considered an outstanding example of the Gothic Revival style in England. He named his son for St. Ignatius of Loyola and had him educated at Stonyhurst College. Like his father, Ignatius Scoles trained as an architect and designed churches in his native England. He entered the Society in 1860 and was ordained six years later. In 1868 he was sent to British Guyana and designed structures in Georgetown that include the city hall and the tower of St. Mary's chapel in Brickdam Cathedral, in neo-Gothic style. Three other examples of Jesuit architects who built structures in the context of the missions were Alphonse Taix (1835–62), a French Jesuit missionary in Madagascar, and designer of cathedrals in Tananarivo and Fianarantsoa, and Jesuit brothers Polydor Verbrugge (1870–1949) and Theofiel Roelandt (1872–1942), both Belgians who worked in Sri Lanka.

In the nineteenth and twentieth centuries, the Society of Jesus increasingly became known as significant patrons of architecture. The Gothic Revival style, so popular worldwide for most of the nineteenth century, became the style associated with Jesuit colleges and universities established in the United States, including Fordham University, Boston College, and Georgetown University.

As new architectural styles developed throughout the twentieth and into the twenty-first century, the Jesuits responded accordingly. Many contemporary buildings exemplify the Society's continued appreciation of well-designed spaces. The Chapel of St. Ignatius at Seattle University (Steven Holl) was built in 1997 with a focus on the light that enters the space. The Jesuit Residence and Spirituality Centre at St. Aloysius College, constructed in Glasgow in 2007 (Elder & Cannon) sought to bring modern buildings into an existing neighborhood and integrate them seamlessly. The Jesuit Community Center at Fairfield University, CT (Gray Organschi Architecture), built in 2010, has won numerous awards

Figure 5 Jesuit Church of the Immaculate Conception (Farm Street Church), Mayfair (London), 19th century. Photograph Thomas Worcester, SJ

for its ecological focus and strong design. Colombière Jesuit Community Residence and Chapel in Baltimore (Bohlin Cywinski Jackson), 2011, and the Jesuit High School Chapel of the North American Martyrs (Hodgetts + Fung) in Carmichael, CA, 2014, demonstrate that the Society of Jesus continues to embrace a strong architectural tradition. Seattle Preparatory School opened a new chapel on campus in September 2014. Named for a transformational event in the life of the young Ignatius of Loyola, Our Lady of Montserrat Chapel (Hennebery Eddy Architects in collaboration with Francis Nguyen, SJ) is positioned as a place for students to address their own spiritual formation. The chapel won an award for religious architecture. Finally, the 2015 announcement by the College of the Holy Cross that acclaimed architectural firm Diller Scofidio + Renfro would design a new performing arts center on the campus reinforces the notion that the Society of Jesus remains a significant patron of architecture.

See also Art Patronage; Arts, Visual; Baroque Art and Architecture; Castiglione, Giuseppe, SJ; Grassi, Orazio, SJ; Pozzo, Andrea, SJ

De Lucca, Denis, *Jesuits and Fortifications: The Contribution of the Jesuits to Military Architecture in the Baroque Era*. Leiden: Brill, 2012.
Guillen-Nunez, Cesar, "Rising from the Ashes: The Gothic Revival and the Architecture of the 'New' Society of Jesus in China and Macau." In Robert Maryks and Jonathan Wright, eds., *Jesuit Survival and Restoration: A Global History, 1773–1900*. Leiden: Brill, 2015, pp. 278–98.

Klaiber, Susan, "Architecture as a Form of Erudition: Early Modern Priest-Architects." *Sacred Architecture Journal* 24 (2013). www.sacredarchitecture.org/articles/architecture_as_a_form_of_erudition.

Primrose, Tracey, "Answering God's Call: Father Gilbert Sunghera, SJ." *Jesuits.org* (2013). http://jesuits.org/story?TN=PROJECT-20131122025541.

Alison Fleming

Archives and Libraries

The importance of archives for an efficient functioning of the Society of Jesus emerged early in its history. In addition, many of its members' activities (not only teaching, or polemics with various adversaries, but also preaching, hearing confessions, and other forms of pastoral work, as well as foreign missions) quickly necessitated the use of books and the establishing of libraries. Thus, both archives and libraries were organized, protected, and esteemed by the Jesuits. They gathered documents for administrative purposes but also preserved them for the future writing of the Society's history, in accordance with the norms of superiors general.

Jesuit archives reflect the structure of the Order's administration: each province, house, or institution had its own archives, and similarly the Roman archives (Archivum Romanum Societatis Iesu, ARSI) reflects the Society's central government. Many documents (such as the catalogues, and the formulas of final vows) were produced in several copies: those required in Rome were sent there, while one copy remained in the local archives. A special instruction called *Formula scribendi* was promulgated at the end of the sixteenth century which regulated during the following two centuries the entire Jesuit system of communication of which the archives are a mirror. Only in the nineteenth century were these rules reformulated under the title of *Practica quaedam*; this remains up to the present (although in an updated form) the main reference for the contemporary administration of the Society.

Many pre-Suppression Jesuit archives were lost after 1773 or are no longer the property of the Society, while those after its restoration in 1814 are generally owned by the Order. Jesuit libraries, too, were in their structure and content representative of the Society's character and apostolate. Each community had its own collection of books. Those of professed houses, universities, and bigger colleges could count several thousand titles, while residences had more modest collections. Usually each college had a main library in a room especially assigned for that purpose, and smaller collections corresponding to diverse special studies or research entrusted to the Jesuits living there. Individual Jesuits were allowed to have some volumes in their rooms if their work required these. A Jesuit was appointed librarian with the task of caring for the books according to special rules (*Regulae praefecti bibliothecae*). These rules concerned his role as well as the functioning of the library, including such practical aspects as cleanliness (one rule prescribed that the floor of the library was to be swept twice a week, and the books were to be dusted once a week).

Several Jesuit libraries from the sixteenth to the eighteenth centuries have survived up to the present as have some of their catalogues. As with the archives, the majority of the books that the Order owned before 1773 have been lost, dispersed, or changed owner because of the well-known vicissitudes experienced by the Society (for example, the majority of books belonging to the Roman College library before 1870 is to be found at present in the National Library in Rome, while the plans of Jesuit colleges are now in the National Library in Paris). Thus, after 1814 the restored Society had to reassemble entirely both its archives and its book collections. The older Jesuit libraries became the object of several studies, while the contemporary activities of the Society require, as in the past, a constant use of books. As in the case of archives, the Jesuits continue to take care of their libraries. As in the past, structure and content correspond to the specificity of the mission of each house. Besides the general collections of a school or a university, there are more specialized libraries, such as in ARSI (incorporating the Jesuit Historical Institute in Rome), dedicated to the Society's history, or the library of the Bollandists in Brussels focused on hagiography. As a result of internal prescriptions obliging each Jesuit author to send a copy of any of his publications to the library of the General Curia, the latter is provided with a rich collection of the writing endeavors of the Society's members, while the Order's bibliographies complete the inevitable lacunae arising from missing titles.

See also Annual Letters; Archivum Romanum Societatis Iesu (ARSI); Bibliographies; *Lettres édifiantes et curieuses*

Koch, Ludwig, "Archive." In *Jesuiten-Lexikon: Die Gesellschaft Jesu einst und jetzt*. 2nd edn. Löwen-Heverlee: Verlag der Bibliothek SJ, 1962, cols. 86–87.

"Bibliotheken." In *Jesuiten-Lexikon: Die Gesellschaft Jesu einst und jetzt*, cols. 207–08.

Julia, Dominique, "La constitution des bibliothèques des collèges: remarques de méthode." *Revue d'Histoire de l'Église de France* 83 (1997), 145–61.

McCoog, Thomas M., *A Guide to Jesuit Archives*. St. Louis, MO: The Institute of Jesuit Sources; Rome: Institutum Historicum Societatis Jesu, 2001.

"Practical Proposals Regarding Archives of Provinces, Houses and Apostolic Works." *Acta Romana Societatis Iesu* XXIII. fasc. 1 (2003), 378–92.

"*Scriptis tradere et fideliter conservare*": *Archives as "Places of Memory" within the Society of Jesus*. Rome: General Curia, 2003.

Robert Danieluk, SJ

Archivum Romanum Societatis Iesu (ARSI)

The Roman Archives of the Society of Jesus (usually abbreviated ARSI because of their official name in Latin) is the archives of the central government of the Jesuit order, situated in its headquarters in Rome. Their mission is to preserve documents related to the activity of the Society's superior general, to put them in order and to make them available for historical research. In 1995 a new building was opened to store the archives' holdings together with those of the library of the Jesuit Historical Institute and to provide improved facilities for the growing number of researchers (around 400 a year) from all over the world. The archives comprise circa 1,800 meters of shelves; they are organized according to the structure of the Society's government, and its history. Thus, three main sections should be distinguished: "Old" Society (the period 1540–1773), "New" Society (the period since 1814), and *Fondo Gesuitico* (Archives of the General Procurator of the Order, separated for historical reasons from the two previous sections, although chronologically corresponding mostly to the "Old" Society). A fourth section contains all materials which do not belong to the three main parts, such as the archives of the Jesuit churches in Rome, photographs, Chinese and Japanese books, medals and seals, etc. Each section of ARSI is provided with general inventories, while for some sections detailed inventories are also available. Some series have been digitized, and the process of digitization continues. General information about ARSI is available on the website www.sjweb.info/arsi/.

See also Archives and Libraries; Bibliographies

Danieluk, Robert, "Archivum Romanum Societatis Iesu: un luogo privilegiato per lo studio dell'attività evangelizzatrice dei gesuiti." *Archiva Ecclesiae* 53–55 (2010–12), 221–254.
Lamalle, Edmond, "L'archivio di un grande Ordine religioso: L'archivio Generale della Compagnia di Gesù." *Archiva Ecclesiae* 24–25 (1981–82), 89–120.

Robert Danieluk, SJ

Argentina

The present configuration of the Latin American provinces developed over several centuries. The first Jesuits reached Argentina in 1585 and immediately began missionary work among the numerous indigenous groups, but Argentina initially belonged to the province of Peru and then to Paraguay. Jesuits were expelled from Latin America in 1767; they returned to Argentina in 1836. The local governor forced them to leave Buenos Aires in 1842 and persuaded other governors to expel them from their territories, but the Jesuits were invited back in 1854. In 1918 Argentina became part of the Argentine-Chilean province, which lasted until Chile was named its own province in 1958. In 2010 Argentina joined with Uruguay and was named the Argentine-Uruguayan province. The gradual formation and realignment of the Society's Latin American provinces reflect the development and expansion of its work among the native peoples, the increase (and eventual decrease) of its membership, and the political and cultural forces of the nations and peoples that make up South America. Work among the indigenous people required linguistic proficiency, since there were many languages; it led to the writing of grammars and dictionaries, to ethnographic, historical, and cultural study, as well as to considerable exploration. But the early Jesuits also began several *colegios* and a university (1622, in Córdoba). Jesuits later founded a university in 1956 (Universidad del Salvador in Buenos Aires) and another in 1964 (Universidad Católica de Salta in the Andean northwest of the country); but they had to withdraw from these works in 1974 and 1975 because of a decrease in vocations and departures from the Society.

In the 1950s both the Church in Argentina and the Society were confronted with the open hostility of a Peronist government that had turned dictatorial, although initially the social idealism of President Perón matched important elements of Catholic social teaching. But it was the military dictatorships that ruled so many nations in Latin America during the last century, together with the grinding poverty of their peoples, the bringing to consciousness of 500 years of oppression since the arrival of the colonial powers, and heightened cultural awareness among indigenous peoples everywhere, which forced a turning point for the Church in Latin America. The poor had begun to find their voice and to mobilize. In 1973 Jorge Mario Bergoglio was named provincial, and shortly thereafter the 32nd General Congregation (1974–75), at which he was present, issued its celebrated Decree 4 on the service of faith and the promotion of justice. The evangelical principle of the "preferential option for the poor" of liberation theology (a phrase first used by Fr. Pedro Arrupe in a letter to the Jesuits of Latin America in 1968)

Figure 6 Coat-of-arms of Pope Francis, photographed at the Church of Sant'Andrea al Quirinale, Rome, 2016. Photograph Thomas Worcester, SJ

was spreading fast among Jesuit communities and throughout the Church, often creating fierce tension on how to implement it.

In 1976 the scandalous, traumatic "Dirty War" (Spanish: *Guerra Sucia*) broke out in Argentina, which last-ed until 1983. While the attitude and response of Argentina's hierarchy toward the military junta appear to have been ambivalent at best, remarkable witness came from the mothers of the Plaza de Mayo, whose weekly vigils in silent, courageous remembrance of the "disappeared" – *los desaparecidos* – gradually riveted the conscience of a nation and the attention of the world. The Jesuits thus found themselves once more navigating treacherous waters: standing alongside the poor and marginalized in the midst of state-sponsored terrorism was, in some ways, reminiscent of their eighteenth-century efforts to protect the indigenous of the *reducciones* or missions in the face of predatory *conquistadores*. Such was the religious, social, and historical context that schooled the province's best-known member. Fr. Bergoglio, becoming archbishop of Buenos Aires in 1998 and a cardinal in 2001, participated in the conclaves of 2005 and 2013. His election as pope surprised the world and marked the first time a Jesuit or a Latin American had been elected bishop of Rome.

Today the Argentine-Uruguayan province (Provincia Argentino-Uruguaya) sponsors three institutions of higher education (the Universidad Católica de Córdoba, the

Universidad Católica de Uruguay, and the Colegio Maximo de San José), a network of secondary schools (RAUCI, or Red Argentino Uruguaya de Colegios Ignacianos), and the Fe y Alegría network. In addition, the province's works include parishes, spirituality centers, and retreat houses.

See also Paraguay Missions ("Reductions"); Peru; Preferential Option for the Poor; Uruguay

Ivereigh, Austen, *The Great Reformer: Francis and the Making of a Radical Pope*. London: Picador, 2015.
Jesuits of Argentina and Uruguay. www.jesuitasaru.org.
Klaiber, Jeffrey, *The Jesuits in Latin America, 1549–2000*. St. Louis, MO: The Institute of Jesuit Sources, 2009.
Morello, Gustavo, *The Catholic Church and Argentina's Dirty War*. Oxford: Oxford University Press, 2015.
Nunca Más: The Report of the Argentine National Commission on the Disappeared. New York: Farrar, Straus and Giroux, 1986.

William Reiser, SJ

Arnauld, Antoine

Known as "le Grand Arnauld," Antoine Arnauld came from a political family famous for its opposition to the Jesuits and its support for the Jansenist movement. His sister Jacqueline (Mère Angélique) was abbess of the monastery of Port-Royal, which included in the community their mother, sisters, and niece, while their brother and nephews lived among the *Messieurs*. Under the influence of the radical Augustinianism of the Abbé de Saint-Cyran, spiritual director of Port-Royal and friend and collaborator of Cornelius Jansen, Arnauld shocked Paris by retiring from a brilliant legal career and becoming a doctor of Paris University's theological faculty in 1641.

Arnauld became the central polemicist of Port-Royal, much admired by Jansenist sympathizers but opposed by influential figures in church and at court. In 1643, two years after the Inquisition's condemnation of Jansen's *Augustinus*, he published *De la fréquente communion*, arguing against easy access to the sacraments of penance and Eucharist. He compared rigorous apostolic and patristic practice with the laxity of contemporary "Pelagian" Jesuits who allegedly permitted grave sinners to be admitted to communion without adequate repentance. His famous book placed him in direct conflict with the Jesuit pastoral strategy, which opposed Protestant limitation of sacraments and weak Catholic sacramental attendance through the Marian congregations which encouraged frequent reception.

In 1655 Arnauld was censured by the Sorbonne for his support of Jansen and stripped of his doctorate, an attack which provoked Blaise Pascal's bitterly anti-Jesuit *Lettres provinciales*. Arnauld's enduring hostility to the Jesuits lay in his opposition to increasing royal and papal absolutism, which he saw them as supporting, and in his dream of a pure, rigorous, primitive Church as the norm for all subsequent Christian communities. A lifelong polemicist, he died in exile in Brussels in 1694.

See also Anti-Jesuit Polemic; Jansenism; France; Paris

Antoine Arnauld, 1612–1694: philosophe, écrivain, théologien. Paris: Bibliothèque Mazarine 1995.
Lesaulnier, Jean, and Antony McKenna, eds., *Dictionnaire de Port-Royal*. Paris: Honoré Champion, 2004.

Gemma Simmonds, CJ

Arrupe College

The first house of studies for African Jesuits, the Institut S. Pierre Canisius, was opened in 1954 by the Central African province, admitting students from other provinces as space allowed. In 1968, new General Norms called for greater inculturation in Jesuit studies, a theme dear to Father General Pedro Arrupe. In 1984 Hekima College interprovincial theologate started in Nairobi, and planning began in 1991 for an interprovincial English-speaking philosophate, with Fr. Cecil McGarry, dean of Hekima and former general assistant for Formation, commissioned to direct the project's development.

Arrupe College Jesuit School of Philosophy and Humanities opened in Harare, Zimbabwe, in 1994, moving to the present Mount Pleasant site in 1996. The first rector was Fr. Valerian Shirima (East African province); six of the ten pioneering lecturers came from Jesuit provinces in the United States. In the spirit of Fr. Arrupe and General Congregations 31 and 32, the four-year undergraduate program situated philosophy in an African context through literature, history, African studies, and the human sciences, including the equivalent of one year's theology, and led either to the Pontifical Gregorian University's baccalaureate or to the University of Zimbabwe's BA Honours in Philosophy. A three-year diploma in philosophy and theology was added in 2000 and a master's in philosophy in 2007, both from the University of Zimbabwe.

The College Chapel of the Holy Name, decorated by Fr. Tony Berridge, opened in 2001. Books were gathered, largely from academic programs closing in the United States, from 1992, and the two-story library now has over 90,000 volumes. The college is governed by a board of Jesuit major superiors of Africa and Madagascar. In 2014, the Jesuit community of eighty-eight students and ten formators lived in eight nearby residences under a single rector. A small number of non-Jesuit students, mainly other religious, are admitted to academic programs.

See also Arrupe, Pedro, SJ; Zimbabwe

Stephen Buckland, SJ

Arrupe, Pedro, SJ (1907–1991)

Introduction

Fr. Pedro Arrupe, SJ, was born in the Basque region of Spain on November 14, 1907, and became the first Basque superior general since the Society's founder, St. Ignatius of Loyola. He served the Society of Jesus as the twenty-eighth superior general from 1965 to 1983. Considered by some Jesuits to be a "second founder" of the Society of Jesus, Arrupe left his mark on nearly every aspect of Jesuit identity, especially in education, as he attempted to update the Society of Jesus in light of the transformative event of the Second Vatican Council. Suffering a devastating stroke on August 7, 1981, Arrupe officially resigned his position as superior general at the 33rd General Congregation in 1983. Pedro Arrupe died on February 5, 1991.

Early Life

Pedro Arrupe was born in the Basque city of Bilbao, Spain, to Marcelino and Maria Dolores Gondra Arrupe. He was the youngest of five children, which included four sisters: Catalina, Maria, Margarita, and Isabel. Arrupe fondly remembered his childhood and his family's dedication to their Catholic faith. When he was 10 years old, his mother died unexpectedly. After completing high school, Arrupe began to study medicine at San Carlos University in Madrid, Spain. A strong student, Arrupe enjoyed reading science journals, and he received prizes for study in anatomical studies, physiology, and therapeutics. His professors saw great potential in him to become a skilled physician, and he was voted student of the year by the faculty.

One of Arrupe's early formative moments occurred when he was in medical school working with the St. Vincent de Paul Society, a lay group dedicated to helping the poor. One day, Arrupe approached a boy who was eating a roll on the side of the road. After conversing with him, Arrupe realized that the boy did not have a father and that the small roll he was eating was going to be his only meal for the day. Arrupe recalled that this was the first time he was exposed to the hunger of a child. The encounter and the face of the boy were experiences that Arrupe held close to his heart for the rest of his life.

In 1926 Arrupe's father passed away. Following his father's death, Arrupe decided to make a pilgrimage to Lourdes, France. Remaining there for three months, he visited the Office of Verification where he was given permission to examine claims of miraculous cures that were common in the city. He observed the Blessed Sacrament carried down the street, and before his eyes a series of experiences that he would later call miracles occurred. A nun who had been paralyzed stood up and praised the Sacrament, a woman with stomach cancer was cured, and a young man who had suffered from infantile paralysis stood up. In all three of these cases, Arrupe was able to examine the medical records of those who claimed to have been cured. In all three cases, he confessed that there was no natural explanation that he could find. He later reflected that it was here that his vocation was born. Arrupe entered the Jesuit novitiate at Loyola, Spain, on January 15, 1927, at the age of 19.

Having completed two years as a novice, undergoing the traditional experiments and instruction outlined in the *Constitutions of the Society of Jesus*, Arrupe took his first vows. During his annual retreat, Arrupe felt a strong inclination to be sent to Japan and wrote to his Jesuit superiors with this request. Although his request was initially denied, the reply left open the possibility of a future assignment in Japan. Arrupe's studies of philosophy and theology were altered by the political climate in Europe. Spain declared itself a socialist republic in 1931. All Jesuits were exiled from the country, and Arrupe was sent to Marneffe, Belgium, for his philosophy studies and later to Valkenburg in Holland to study theology and medical ethics. Arrupe was ordained a priest in Belgium on July 30, 1936. Soon after his ordination, he was sent to the United States to complete his theology studies at Saint Mary's College in Kansas. While in North America, Arrupe traveled to Texas and Mexico to work with orphans. He did his tertianship in Cleveland, Ohio, and again underwent the *Spiritual Exercises*. He also spent a few months working in New York City at a prison with primarily Spanish-speaking immigrants. In 1938 Arrupe received a message from the Father General advising him that he was being sent to Japan. The experiences of Arrupe's early life exposed him to multiple realities of suffering and poverty that would later influence his work in Japan and his policies as superior general.

Japan

On September 30, 1938, Arrupe left Seattle for Japan and arrived at the Bay of Tokyo on October 15. Despite his background in languages, Arrupe struggled to learn Japanese. He also suffered from culture shock as he attempted to learn Japanese customs. After eighteen months in Tokyo, he was sent to Ube to continue practicing Japanese. Later that year, he was appointed as the assistant parish priest in Yamaguchi at the same parish where Francis Xavier had begun his work. Arrupe slowly began to win the hearts of the people and would give concerts with his fellow Jesuits to help make Christ better known. He realized that the only way to gain converts was to focus on coming to know the heart of the Japanese people.

On December 8, 1941, following the Japanese attack on Pearl Harbor, Arrupe was detained for questioning by the *Kempetai* (the Japanese military police). Finding letters from Jesuits all over the world in his office, written in a variety of languages, the police felt they had enough evidence to take him away as a spy. He was accused of preaching peace in a time of war. Arrupe was placed at the end of the open truck so that people could see his disgrace as the truck carrying the prisoners drove through the busy market in town. He was put into a cell with an area of four square meters with nothing except a dirty straw mat and a metal receptacle in the corner.

Arrupe's time was spent either alone in the quiet of a cell or under interrogation from the *Kempetai*. At midnight on January 11, 1942, Arrupe began 37 hours of continuous interrogation, where he was questioned about politics, religion, and numerous other "inconsistencies" concerning his beliefs. Following the investigation, he was escorted to the prison governor's office and, to his surprise and delight, was told that he was being released. It was not his theological arguments that had saved his life but rather, he was told, "his internal completeness, his simplicity, his transparency of soul" that the Japanese believed revealed his inner character.

Arrupe thanked his guards upon hearing news of his release. To their astonishment, the same man who had been mistreated and isolated for over a month was thanking them for the experience. Arrupe explained that the experience had taught him to suffer. He had come to Japan to suffer for the Japanese people, and this experience allowed him to do that. The police fought back tears and told Arrupe he was free to preach his religion.

The superior, Father Lasalle, asked Arrupe if he would go to Nagatsuka on March 9, 1942, to become the novice master because the current novice master was very ill. Arrupe was apprehensive of accepting because he knew his knowledge of Japanese language and customs was still not strong enough to warrant that position. However, two days later, he said goodbye to his parishioners in Yamaguchi and traveled to Nagatsuka on the outskirts of Hiroshima.

The Jesuits had two houses in Hiroshima. One was a parish church in the city and the other the novitiate in the hills outside the city at Nagatsuka. Arrupe was charged with the care of thirty-five young Jesuits in the novitiate house. When the atomic bomb was dropped on August 6, 1945, at 8:15 a.m., a blinding flash of light filled the house and threw some of the men across the room. Making their way outside, they saw Hiroshima a few miles away engulfed in flames. Given that many of the structures in the city were built of wood, paper, and straw, and that the timing of the blast coincided with the time when ovens were lit for cooking morning meals, the city was consumed in a lake of fire. Clouds gathered in the sky above the city, and a black, heavy rain fell in the northern part of the city. Arrupe and his novices tried to enter the city but were prevented at first because of the wall of fire.

After 12 hours the Jesuits were able to enter the city but still could not get near the center. The men cleared as much room as they could in the chapel of the house where they were and made it into a hospital. They were able to care for 150 people. Arrupe's expertise from his early medical training gave him the ability to work with the sparse means at his disposal. Nearly every person treated in that chapel lived through the disaster. Using his medical skill, Arrupe poured acid into the unknown wounds that would later be identified as side effects of radiation, and kettles had to be used to catch the liquid that flowed from these wounds. Despite the many people who needed aid, Arrupe and his fellow Jesuits continued to celebrate Mass in the chapel with the sick and injured strewn across the floor. Arrupe recalled seeing people who did not know Christ and who were unaware of what he was doing. Despite the horrible circumstances and the suffering that surrounded him, Arrupe recalled that he had "never said mass with such devotion."

After the Japanese surrender and the end of the war, the number of those entering the novitiate increased, including sixteen former officers of the Imperial Japanese Army and Navy. Arrupe knew that pride would be an issue for these men and thus had them dress in their formal attire and do lowly tasks. This was not meant as a humiliation for their rank, but to make them realize that they, like he, must be humble before Christ. Arrupe knew what these men needed to learn most and again, knowing the Japanese soul as well as he did, he was able to bring them closer to Christ. These men became cornerstones for the future of the Japanese province.

Arrupe remained the novice master until March 22, 1954, when he was appointed vice provincial. On October 18, 1958, he was appointed first provincial of the newly formed province of Japan. The Japanese province expanded rapidly, and Arrupe routinely visited each Jesuit house and spent time with each Jesuit. He also traveled the world and spoke as a survivor of Hiroshima. He was constantly on the move, consoling Jesuits, inspiring people with his words, and offering his genuine warmth to people. His time in Japan would end surprisingly in 1965.

Superior General

On October 5, 1964, Superior General Jean-Baptiste Janssens, a Belgian who had been elected as superior general in 1946, died after suffering numerous medical complications during his final years as general. On May 7, 1965, the Jesuits gathered in Rome to begin the 31st General Congregation to elect a successor to Janssens. Meeting between the third and fourth sessions of Vatican II, the Jesuits voiced their desire to elect a successor who would lead them in the vision of reform voiced by the Second Vatican Council. Pope Paul VI opened the General Congregation and reminded the Jesuits of their duty to the vision of Ignatius and their fidelity to the Church. The over 200 delegates present at the General Congregation set out to elect a general who would be faithful to their past and yet pave the way to their future.

On May 22, 1965, Arrupe was elected superior general after the third vote and was now charged with the leadership of over 30,000 Jesuits around the world. His vision and temperament would affect the future of every Jesuit. As he walked forward to offer his first remarks, the newly elected general and speaker of seven languages quoted Jeremiah, "Ah! My Lord God, I do not know how to speak . . ." Causing laughter among the assembly, Arrupe continued the quote, "Be not afraid, for I am with you." The Spaniard, who had spent over twenty-five years in Japan, returned to Rome and became the 28th superior general of the Society of Jesus.

One of the hallmarks of Arrupe's time as superior general was his speech on the Feast of St. Ignatius, given on July 31, 1973, in Valencia, Spain. Many of those gathered were affluent, Jesuit-educated alumni from around Europe. Drawing upon the 1971 Synod of Bishops and their document "Justice in the World," Arrupe challenged and angered many in the audience. Explaining that a Jesuit education should form "men (and women) for others," Arrupe proclaimed that an education that fails to do this and that fails to "issue in justice for others is a farce." Challenging any notion that the faith does not call one to action, Arrupe established the mission of Jesuit education as forming people who will live for others. For Arrupe, life for others included a life dedicated to Christ and to God, not to self-gain and personal achievement.

The major official contribution Arrupe made to the Society of Jesus was the convening of the 32nd General Congregation from December 2, 1974 to March 7, 1975. The General Congregation (GC) was meant to either solidify Arrupe's "new" trajectory following his speech at Valencia or inform him that the Spirit was not leading the Jesuits in that direction. While GC 31 focused on implementing the challenges of Vatican II within the Society, GC 32 addressed the divisions that had occurred among the Jesuits about the most appropriate way to implement these changes.

The most controversial section in GC 32 is Decree 4, "Our Mission Today: The Service of Faith and the Promotion of Justice." The decree begins by addressing "the many requests received from all parts of the Society for clear decisions and definite guidelines concerning our mission today" and in no uncertain terms states, "The mission of the society is the service of faith, of which the promotion of justice is an absolute requirement." While the service of faith had always been central to the Jesuits, the importance of the promotion of justice was now linked with faith. The service of faith and the promotion of justice were now codified by the highest governing body of the Society, a General Congregation.

During Arrupe's time as superior general, the relationship between the Jesuits and the Vatican was sometimes strained by the actions of some Jesuits, especially those who applied liberation theology to their decision to side with the poor. Arrupe had warned that if the Jesuits embarked on implementing Decree 4 that some would be martyred. Six Jesuits, along with their housekeeper and her daughter, were killed in El Salvador on November 16, 1989: an instance of Arrupe's prophetic warning. Despite such atrocities, the Jesuits remained steadfast in their support of the poor and strongly influenced the development of liberation theology in Latin America. Arrupe pioneered the development of the Jesuit Refugee Service, refugees and migrants being a population that Arrupe specifically set out to help. As superior general, Arrupe continued his earlier commitments to devoting time to as many Jesuits as possible, spending time with them personally, and championing the cause of the poor and the powerless.

Final Years

On August 6, 1981, thirty-five years after Arrupe aided the survivors of the atomic bomb, he was flying back from visiting the Jesuits in the Philippines and refugee camps in Thailand. The next morning, August 7, the plane landed in Rome. While reaching down for his bag on the carousel, Arrupe froze. He could not close his hands around the bag. Those with him offered assistance and realized that something was wrong. They immediately rushed Arrupe to the hospital, where it was declared that he had suffered a severe stroke.

Despite Arrupe's wish that Fr. Vincent O'Keefe, one of his four general assistants, would take temporary charge of the Order, Pope John Paul II appointed Fr. Paolo Dezza as his delegate and interim head of the Society of Jesus. Some feared this intervention would cause a rift between the Jesuits and the Pope, but after two years there were no incidents, and the 33rd General Congregation was convened to elect Arrupe's successor. Fr. Peter-Hans Kolvenbach was elected to follow in the footsteps of Arrupe as the 29th successor to St. Ignatius.

In his closing address as superior general, read by Fr. Ignacio Iglesias, Arrupe mused over how he was "totally in the hands of God," something he had wanted since his youth. Those assembled gave Arrupe a standing ovation. Unable to move freely and communicate on his own, Arrupe offered his condition fully to God and reacted out of thankfulness for his life, rather than bitterness about his condition.

In his final homily as general of the Society the following day, read by Fr. Fernandez Castaneda, Arrupe recalled the faith of St. Ignatius at La Storta where Ignatius had a vision of God and was told He would place Ignatius with his Son and that He would be favorable to him in Rome. Arrupe reflected on how favorable God had been to him, even through his illness.

Arrupe lived for ten years following his stroke, during which time he continued to welcome visitors. Ironically, the man who had spoken seven languages was reduced to a form of broken Spanish. However, with the help of the Jesuits who cared for him, his messages could often be interpreted. On January 27, 1991, Pope John Paul II visited Arrupe for a second time, but Arrupe was unconscious. A few days later, on February 5, 1991, he died. On the anniversary of the martyrs of Nagasaki, and with his last known word being "amen," the man who had spoken on behalf of the suffering of millions, breathed his last.

See also Japan; John Paul II; Justice; "Men and Women for Others"; O'Keefe, Vincent, SJ; Preferential Option for the Poor; Superior General

Arrupe, Pedro, *One Jesuit's Spiritual Journey: Autobiographical Conversations with Claude Dietsch, SJ.* Trans. Ruth Bradley. St. Louis, MO: The Institute of Jesuit Sources, 1986.
  Pedro Arrupe: Essential Writings. Ed. Kevin Burke. New York: Orbis Books, 2004.
  Recollections and Reflections of Pedro Arrupe, SJ. Trans. Yolanda T. De Mola. Intro. Vincent O'Keefe. Wilmington, DE: Michael Glazier, 1986.
Bishop, George D., *Pedro Arrupe, SJ: Twenty-Eighth General of the Society of Jesus.* Anand, India: Gujarat Sahitya Prakash, 2000.
LaBella, Gianni, ed., *Pedro Arrupe, general de la Compañia de Jésus: nuevas aportiones a su biografía.* Bilbao: Edicones Mensajero; Santander: Sal Terrae, 2007.
Lewis, Hedwig, *Pedro Arrupe Treasury.* Anand, India: Gujarat Sahitya Prakash, 2007.
Modras, Ronald, *Ignatian Humanism: A Dynamic Spirituality for the 21st Century.* Chicago, IL: Loyola Press, 2004, pp. 243–83.

James Menkhaus

ARSI

See Archivum Romanum Societatis Iesu (ARSI)

Art Patronage

Following papal approval of the order in 1540, the Society of Jesus underwent a period of growth and expansion. In the course of the sixteenth and seventeenth centuries the Jesuits established residences in the great Catholic centers of Europe and sent missionaries to new territories in Asia, South America, and Africa. To accommodate their growing order, the Jesuits contributed significantly to the building of new complexes, which included churches, professed houses (residences for fully trained Jesuits), colleges, chapels for their lay congregations, and novitiates. They further enhanced their urban presence by organizing festivals and theatrical performances, and by publishing meditational treatises and devotional prints. As patrons of major church complexes, the Jesuits played a leading role in redefining sacred space in the early modern period. They conceived of the interiors of their churches as theatrical spaces that not only framed traditional liturgical rituals but also served to overwhelm, uplift, and persuade the viewer.

By far the most important commission undertaken by the Jesuits was the building of the mother church in Rome, the Gesù (1568–1575). Nanni di Baccio drew the earliest plans for the church in 1549–50 to replace the older, smaller Church of Madonna della Strada, but construction was delayed due to a lack of funds. Their ambitious building plan was realized only with the support of Cardinal Alessandro Farnese, the grandson of Pope Paul III, who had approved the Order in 1540. Farnese clearly put a stamp on the building by commissioning his own favorite architect Jacopo Vignola to draw up the plans and by stipulating that the church be built with a barrel vault rather than a flat wooden ceiling as the Jesuits had preferred.

The design of the church inaugurated a new conception for post-Tridentine church interiors. The church boasted a wide, aisleless nave, a domed crossing, a choir, and a series of side chapels on either side of the nave. Its nave was articulated by paired Corinthian pilasters crowned by a continuous entablature. This vast, clearly structured interior was designed to hold large crowds and to serve as an appropriate setting for preaching, an activity central to the Society's program of reform. The Jesuits also promoted the frequent reception of the Holy Sacrament. To this end, they created an impressive setting for the high altar and incorporated numerous side chapels where masses could be celebrated simultaneously. In the Gesù the uninterrupted entablature leads the eye to the choir, which originally housed an altarpiece by Girolamo Muziano, a painter favored by Farnese. Notably, the Jesuits did not sing the liturgical hours in common, so they did away with the choir screen, which separated the laity from the high altar in mendicant churches.

Giacomo della Porta, who succeeded Vignola as the main architect of the church in 1571, was responsible for the façade (completed in 1575). His design, which replaced the more densely decorated plan by Vignola, adopts the idea of a flat double-storied elevation connected by scrolls, as seen on the façade of Santa Maria Novella in Florence. Yet Della Porta gave the façade a more robust appearance by focusing on the interplay between the paired Corinthian pilasters and the niches and half-columns flanking the main entrance. Moreover, by reducing the number of niches to four and by eliminating some statues and ornamental decoration, he created a façade of great clarity, monumentality, and restraint.

Besides their main church, the Jesuits established a number of educational institutions throughout Rome in the second half of the sixteenth century. As in the case of the

Gesù, they employed both Jesuit and lay artists and attracted wealthy patrons to realize their ambitious building projects. Remarkably, at this early stage in the order's development, the Jesuits relied especially on the charity of female patrons, principally wealthy widows of noble families. For example, in 1560, Marchesa Vittoria della Tolfa offered financial resources and private land for the building the Collegio Romano in Rome. Likewise, Isabella della Rovere, wife of the Neapolitan nobleman Nicolò Bernardino di Sanseverino, supported the construction of the new Jesuit church in Naples (1585) and paid a staggering 90,000 *scudi* for the renovation of the novitiate Church of San Vitale (1596) on the Quirinal hill in Rome.

The late sixteenth and early seventeenth centuries saw a virtual building boom of Jesuit churches worldwide. Building programs from the Jesuit provinces had to be approved by the Roman general, and certain plans and designs circulated widely. The Roman church of the Gesù exerted an especially strong influence. Perhaps the closest example of a church built according to the Roman model is the Church of Saints Peter and Paul in Krakow (1597–1625). For this building, the Jesuits attracted several Italian architects, including Matteo Castello and Giovanni Trevano. The façade displays a two-story elevation with paired Corinthian pilasters and half-columns marking the bays, as seen in the Gesù. The Italian architects also adopted the niches with statues of saints as well as the IHS emblem above the entrance. The impetus for the emphasis on Italian architectural design may not have come directly from Rome, however, but rather from the patron, King Sigismund III Vasa of Poland. Sigismund favored Italian culture, as exemplified by his employment of Italian musicians and his collection of Italian art.

The Jesuits were especially active in centers on the frontier with Protestant territories, including Antwerp, Münster, Düsseldorf, Freiburg im Breisgau, and Krakow. Yet they also had a strong presence in Catholic strongholds such as Spain and Portugal. In Spain, Portugal, and later Latin America, we see a greater development toward sumptuous, multimedia church interiors that moved away from the starker Roman model. The Church of San Ildefonso in Toledo (also called the Iglesia de Los Jesuitas), begun in 1629 and consecrated in 1718, ranks as one of the earliest examples of Jesuit Baroque architecture in Spain. The church is attributed to Juan Bautista de Monegro. Pedro Sánchez and Francisco Bautista, both Jesuit architects, oversaw the construction. The façade rises to three stories and includes two large bell towers on the corners. It is further brought to life by wall planes set forward and by the application of ornaments visible in the consoles and sculptural reliefs. The whitewashed interior still follows the ground plan of the Gesù, but it distinguishes itself from the Roman model in its use of decoration. The interior features richly decorated consoles, carved reliefs, and niches, which were filled in the eighteenth century with polychrome statues of the apostles, attributed to Germán López. Color is introduced not only in the gilded altarpieces but also in the yellow stained glass window containing the IHS emblem of the Jesuit order, filling the interior with a glowing, golden light.

The most ornate early Jesuit church erected north of the Alps is in the city of Antwerp (1615–21). Franciscus Aguilonius and Pieter Huyssens, two local Jesuit architects, designed both the church and the surrounding professed house and sodality house, but it was Peter Paul Rubens who transformed the church into a visually stunning and splendid sacred space. Among the patrons of the church were the Spanish governors of the Southern Netherlands, the archdukes Albert and Isabella, King Philip IV of Spain, the city government, and the population of Antwerp. As in Rome, rich, unmarried women, who received spiritual guidance from Jesuit priests, played an important role as well. The daughters of Godfried Houtappel, Maria, Anna, and Christina, and their cousin Anna 's Grevens paid large sums of money for the building and decoration of a side chapel dedicated to the Virgin.

The first building in the world to be dedicated to Ignatius, the Jesuit church featured a three-story façade fronted by a piazza as seen in Rome. But unlike the austere exterior of the Gesù, the Antwerp façade teems with ornament and, like the Jesuit church in Toledo, displays two bell towers. In deviating from the advice of Rome to avoid "superfluous ornaments," the Antwerp Jesuits favored a type of architecture that fulfilled the same goals as ancient rhetoric, namely to teach, delight, and move the viewer.

The interior of the Antwerp church was partly destroyed by a fire in 1718 but was rebuilt in the early eighteenth century. Early descriptions and paintings provide a good idea of its original appearance. Like the Gesù, the Antwerp church had a barrel-vaulted nave, yet with significant new changes. Following the model of early Christian churches, the church shows a three-aisled basilica ground plan. Equally innovative was the profuse use of colored marble. Moreover, the church was the first Jesuit building to showcase a suite of ceiling paintings (destroyed in the 1718 fire), which were designed by Rubens. The light reflecting on the polished marble and the illusionistic ceiling paintings transformed the church interior in what early commentators described as a "heavenly court." At the same time, the integration of art, sculpture, architecture, and light created a new type of theatrical church environment that was directed at moving the minds of the congregation.

This predilection for ornate, theatrical church façades and interiors culminated in the missionary churches that sprang up all over the Americas and Asia. Perhaps the most characteristic of these is the novitiate church of San Francisco Javier in Tepotzotlán, north of Mexico City (1670–82, façade restored in 1760–62). The church (today the Museo de Arte Virreinal) is a prime example of the ultra-Baroque style. The three-tiered façade, which features one bell tower, dissolves in a wealth of elaborate ornament. Most prominent are the inverted pilasters and half-columns, called *estípite*, which are overlaid by densely decorated ornaments, ranging from garlands and vegetal motifs to shells, scrolls, masks, and figures. The bays, in turn, are heavily decorated with niches containing statues and cartouches featuring relief sculpture. Yet the highpoint of the church is the interior, an amalgamation of eleven imposing gilded *retablos* and dramatic indirect light sources, which envelop the spectator. Replicating the dense ornamentation of the façade, the *retablos* create an exuberant environment that evokes the earthly paradise.

Building churches fulfilled an immediate need for the Jesuits to foster religious communities in Europe and territories overseas. In addition to acting as patrons of architecture, the Jesuits also maintained a sustained interest in images. Not only did they invest in ambitious church decorations, but they also promoted the use of devotional prints, illustrated meditational treatises, and emblem books. Their interest in the visual arts was predicated on the idea that images could serve as tools to instruct the faithful in the articles of Christian faith. Jesuit missionaries, such as Francis Xavier, relied heavily on images as teaching and preaching tools to evangelize the local population of the countries they visited, including India, China, and Japan. Moreover, the Jesuits used images in engaging the viewer/reader in the practices of meditative prayer. Indeed, images were a natural extension of Ignatius of Loyola's *Spiritual Exercises*, a devotional text first published in 1548, which directed the devotee to vividly imagine the place, personages, and sounds of the Christian subjects suggested for meditation. The Jesuits also recognized the rhetorical power of images to persuade the viewer and move him or her to piety.

The late sixteenth- and seventeenth-century Jesuit church ensembles were conceived as unified iconographic programs that focused on the lives of Christ, the Virgin, and the saints. The decorative program of the Gesù (1580s and 1590s) progressed along a series of coordinated altars displayed in the paired side chapels of the nave. Decorated by Giuseppe Valeriano (a Jesuit artist), Federico Zuccaro, Scipione Pulzone, Caspare Celio, and others, the chapels were dedicated to the Apostles, the early martyrs, the Infancy of Christ, the Passion of Christ, the Trinity, and Angels. The transept altars, in turn, were dedicated to the Crucifixion and Resurrection while the high altar displayed Muziano's *Circumcision of Christ*. The Circumcision represents the moment not only of Christ's first blood shedding, but also of his naming. Since the Society was named after Jesus, the subject and feast day of the Circumcision fulfilled a particularly important role in Jesuit worship – and by extension within Jesuit church programs. Important examples include Federico Barcocci's high altarpiece for the Jesuit church in Pesaro (1590), Juan de Roelas's altarpiece for the professed house in Seville (1604), and Rubens's altarpiece for the high altar of Sant'Ambrogio in Genoa (1605).

Besides iconography focused on the life of Christ and the Virgin, the Jesuits also favored cycles dedicated to the early martyrs, as exemplified by the frescoes of Niccolò Circignani for Santo Stefano Rotondo (1581), the church of the Collegio Germanico in Rome. Circignani painted a series of thirty-nine frescoes of gruesome martyrdom scenes. The focus on the martyrs aligned with the Jesuits' aim to show their practices and beliefs as a direct continuation of those of the revered early Christian Church. Furthermore, the terrifying images of dying martyrs fulfilled the Society's goal of promoting rhetorical and vivid imagery that had the power to persuade the young novices to go as missionaries to non-Catholic lands.

Early Jesuit programs outside Italy typically followed the Christological and Marian focus of the Gesù. St. Michael's in Munich (1583–97), which was patronized by Duke Wilhelm V of Bavaria, featured side altarpieces dedicated to saints and martyrs, the life of Christ, the Trinity, and the Name of Jesus (both paintings executed by Antonio Maria Vianai), and a high altarpiece of *St. Michael and the Fall of the Rebel Angels* by Christoph Schwartz (1589). This Christological focus has led scholars to conclude that the iconography of the early Jesuit programs was firmly rooted in Ignatius's *Spiritual Exercises*. In Ignatius's instructions, the devotee is led through a four-week program, progressing from meditations on Hell, the Nativity, the Passion, and the Resurrection of Christ. Yet, although there are some parallels between the themes and structure of both the *Spiritual Exercises* and the images laid out in Jesuit churches, Ignatius's text should not be identified as the primary source for Jesuit programs. Rather, Jesuit art draws on a wide variety of texts, from sermons and exegetical writings to liturgical practices and early devotional books.

Following the canonization of Ignatius and Francis Xavier in 1622, ensembles glorifying the history of the Order and the lives of the first Jesuits gradually replaced programs centered on the Circumcision and the life of Christ. The Antwerp church was the first Jesuit edifice to display altarpieces of Ignatius and Francis Xavier on the high altar (1617–18). Rubens's altarpieces, which were completed a few years prior to their official canonization, showed the saints triumphantly standing among a group of onlookers. Francis Xavier preaches to a group of exotically clothed pagans as an Indian idol crashes to the ground. Ignatius, dressed in a glowing chasuble, stands in a church interior as he cures two figures possessed by demonic forces.

In the wake of their canonization, the transept altars in the Gesù were rededicated to Ignatius and Francis Xavier. However, Gian Paolo Oliva (father general, 1664–81) commissioned the more extravagant programs to honor the Jesuit saints and the order. Jesuit artist Andrea Pozzo, for example, transformed the barrel vault of the nave of Sant'Ignazio in Rome into an exuberant display of illusionistic foreshortening. Highlighting the *Triumph of the Missionary Efforts of the Jesuits* (1691–94), the ceiling fresco shows Ignatius in a heavenly light surrounded by personifications of the four continents.

In keeping with their recognition of images as aids to private meditation, the Jesuits established a leading role in the production of devotional books and prints. Popular and widely circulating devotional books, such as Jan David's *Veridicus Christianus* (Antwerp, 1601), Louis Richeome's *La peinture spirituelle* (Lyon, 1611), and Antonius Sucquet's *Via vitae aeternae* (Antwerp, 1620) all relied on suggestive relationships between words and images. Yet Jerónimo Nadal's *Adnotationes et meditations in Evangelia* (Antwerp, 1595) had the greatest influence worldwide. Designed at the recommendation of Ignatius himself, the book features a series of 153 elaborate engravings by the Wierix brothers of Antwerp, which depict Christ's life, death, and Resurrection. Nadal's book was instrumental in the Jesuit project of the cultural transmission of ideas, because missionaries in China and South America used it as a teaching and meditative tool. Moreover, artists in South America and China copied illustrations of the *Adnotationes* as evidenced by the illustrated life of Christ published by the Jesuit Giulio Aleni in 1637 in the Chinese city of Jinjiang.

Unlike the sixteenth and seventeenth centuries, which saw a period of remarkable growth for the Society, the eighteenth century inaugurated a period of decline. Spurred by the expulsions of Jesuits in Portugal and Spain, Pope Clement XIV issued a decree suppressing the Society of Jesus in 1773. The decree led not only to the dismissal of Jesuit priests but also to the confiscation and sale of Jesuit property. Many of the Jesuits' magnificent churches were repurposed as parish churches, as happened in Düsseldorf, Neuburg am Donau, Munich, and Antwerp.

Perhaps the greatest loss to the artistic heritage of the order was the dispersal, sale, and destruction of church property. Nowhere was the damage to the artistic patronage greater than in the Jesuit foundations in the Southern Netherlands, which housed some of the greatest treasures of seventeenth-century Baroque art. Between 1774 and 1776, the Austrian rulers of the Southern Netherlands, Maria Theresa and Joseph II, who had mandated the expulsion of the Jesuits in 1773, obtained thirty of the best paintings from the churches in Antwerp, Ghent, and Brussels and ordered the melting down of liturgical objects. Among the greatest losses to Antwerp were Rubens's altarpieces of the *Miracles of Ignatius of Loyola* and the *Miracles of Francis Xavier*, which were moved to Vienna in 1776. Joseph de Rosa, the director of the Imperial Gallery in Vienna, also selected masterworks by Anthony van Dyck, Jan Brueghel, and Daniel Seghers from Flemish residences. Moreover, in 1777 a large group of paintings by Flemish masters in Jesuit foundations in the Flemish-Belgian province were sold at public auction in Antwerp.

Figure 7 *Portrait of Alessandro Farnese (1520–89) and Odoardo Farnese (1573–1626), Italian Cardinals who Financed the Chiesa del Gesù in Rome* (unknown artist), 17th century, Church of Il Gesù, Rome. Photograph © Gianni Dagli Orti / The Art Archive at Art Resource, New York

Despite the dispersal of Jesuit property, scholars have been able to reconstruct the role of the Jesuits as patrons of major works of art, architecture, prints, and books. Taken together, the Jesuits not only transformed the post-Tridentine church interior into a densely decorated, theatrical space but also acted as agents of cultural transfer and transmission, creating networks between Europe, the Americas, and Asia and using art as a key instrument of communication and conversion.

Today, Jesuits continue to work as artists and to serve as patrons of the arts. Jesuit colleges and universities, such as in the United States, may be seen as prominent patrons, commissioning buildings and artworks in myriad forms. These projects are executed by lay artists and members of the Society, as has always been done. The Chapel of St. Ignatius at Seattle University (Steven Holl Architects, 1997) is an excellent example of contemporary Jesuit artistic patronage, as are numerous academic buildings on other campuses, including the College of the Holy Cross, Boston College, and Marquette University. These institutions continue the significant legacy of Jesuit artistic patronage in the restored Society.

See also Antwerp; Architecture; Arts, Visual; Baroque Art and Architecture; Gesù, Rome; Pozzo, Andrea, SJ; Rubens, Peter Paul; Wierix Brothers

Bailey, Gauvin A., *Art on the Jesuit Missions in Asia and Latin America, 1542–1773*. Toronto: University of Toronto Press, 1999.

Melion, Walter, *The Meditative Art: Studies in the Northern Devotional Print, 1550–1625*. Philadelphia, PA: St. Joseph's University Press, 2009.

O'Malley, John W., and Gauvin A. Bailey, eds., *The Jesuits and the Arts, 1540–1773*. Philadelphia, PA: St. Joseph's University Press, 2005.

Smith, Jeffrey Chipps, *Sensuous Worship: Jesuits and the Art of the Early Catholic Reformation in Germany*. Princeton, NJ: Princeton University Press, 2002.

Anna C. Knaap

Arts, Performing

The performing arts creatively express perspectives on the world and human experience. Unlike visual or cinematic arts, however, the performing arts communicate via the bodies of performers who are most often physically present to their audiences. Theater, music, and dance exist less as static artifacts and more as dynamic events. The "art" is not simply the play text or score or libretto but rather its embodied realization at a given time and place; hence, performance "struts and frets its hour" in the space between those exercising their craft and those apprehending it.

Prior to the Order's suppression in 1773, the Jesuit investment in the performing arts was considerable. Jesuits employed theater, music, and dance not only in global educational contexts but also in pastoral and missionary settings. In the latter half of the sixteenth century, dramatic production became a staple of academic life in Jesuit schools and colleges. Not only did the theater exercise the students' growing competence in *eloquentia perfecta Latina*, but it also deepened their understanding of human and Christian virtues by allowing them to experience the challenge of choosing well by embodying dramatic characters. Despite some initial reticence, the Society regularly employed music to texture dramatic productions and to enhance the transporting nature of worship in its schools and churches. At the same time music was also used to facilitate religious education, particularly in mission territories where the content of the catechism was set to melodies or the lives of the saints became the subject of music dramas. Dance, particularly in France, affirmed that eloquence was as much a matter of the body as of the tongue. The ballet, theorized by Jesuits like Claude-François Ménestrier, aimed to help students grow in the physical graces required for active participation in early modern society. Though the historical record of Jesuit-related performance since 1814 requires more sustained investigation, it is clear that the restored Society utilized a range of performance forms in its apostolic works. Schools and other ministries in the young United States, for example, employed dramatic and musical productions to assist with language acquisition, to develop a persuasive public presence in a democratic society, to integrate Catholic and emerging American identities, and to publicize the reputation of the apostolic work in the larger community. Even in the contemporary world, Jesuit investment in the performing arts is noteworthy, not simply in educational institutions but also in the work of Jesuits who engage the performing arts to serve faith and promote justice (e.g., Teatro la Fragua in Honduras, Magis Theatre Company in New York City, InterPlay in India).

The Society's cultivation of the performing arts has never been immune to either internal or external criticism; yet these embodied aesthetic forms have proven consistently useful in glorifying God and "helping souls." Early modern religious rigorists routinely condemned the performing arts because of their associations with carnal sin and social disruption. Though some of these critics were themselves Jesuits, the Society discovered that, when rightly ordered, the performing arts could effectively teach, move, *and* please. The somewhat risky ventures into theater, music, and dance reflected the Society's distinctive approach to engaging its mission by accommodating itself to broader cultural contexts. Further, the inherent relationality of performance made theater, music, and dance apt media for pursuing effective, meaningful, and sustained communication with individuals and communities, "a consummation devoutly to be wished" by all Jesuit ministries.

The affinity between Jesuits and the performing arts has been nourished by a spirituality that emphasizes imagination as a means of encountering and responding to God's grace made flesh in Christ. Fresh explorations of the Ignatian charism in the wake of the Second Vatican Council not only resulted in a renewed appreciation for the place of imagination (and affectivity) in Jesuit spiritual practice but also likely set the stage for a more adequate understanding of the performing arts within the Society's mission. In an important 1973 essay reevaluating the place of art in Jesuit life, Clement McNaspy, SJ, noted that "[w]hoever would love Jesus with a self-giving generosity must bring him into view – by an imagination which is historical; by an empathetic imagination to the point of tears, joy, chagrin, pity; by a recreative imagination that not only envisions the cross but also that final state of union with the three-personed God" ("Art in Jesuit Life," 103). This kind of imagination addresses *the whole person* and calls forth a response, certainly in prayer but also in the performing arts.

See also Arts, Visual; Dance; Music; Theater

Arrupe, Pedro, "Art and the Spirit of the Society of Jesus." *Studies in the Spirituality of Jesuits* 5 (1973), 83–92.
McNaspy, Clement J., "The Place of Art in Jesuit Life." *Studies in the Spirituality of Jesuits* 5, 3 (1973), 93–111.
O'Malley, John W., and Gauvin A. Bailey, eds., *The Jesuits and the Arts, 1540–1773*. Philadelphia, PA: St. Joseph's University Press, 2005.

Michael A. Zampelli, SJ

Arts, Visual

Ignatius Loyola bequeathed a sensibility, an appreciation for the revelatory power of the imagination that was a breakthrough in the western spiritual tradition. Inspired by his conversion-period readings of Ludolph's *Vita Christi* and Voragine's *Legenda aurea* and the currents of the *devotio moderna* he encountered at Montserrat and elsewhere, Ignatius in his *Spiritual Exercises* (*SpEx*) encouraged retreatants actively to use their imaginations as well as their intellects. While some of the exercises are analytical or content-driven, the most important are exercises of the imagination: "contemplations" of the life of Jesus wherein the retreatant enters into the scene with eyes, ears, and heart open. They begin with a visual composition "made by imagining the place," and each day ends with an application of the senses: "to see the persons with the imaginative sense of sight ... to hear what they say or could say, to smell and to taste ... to touch with the sense of touch ... always seeking to derive some profit from this" (*SpEx* ##122–26). Ignatius thus connects the spiritual realm to the concrete world of the retreatant's own sensory experience. No stranger himself to the uncharted and sometimes confusing places such practices can lead to, he moreover laid out a simple yet effective check-valve mechanism for the overactive imagination in his rules for discernment.

Figure 8 Interior view of Church of St. Francis Xavier, New York, 19th century. Photograph Alison Fleming

During his lifetime, Ignatius did not hesitate to lavish money on the building and decoration of Jesuit churches. Although he eliminated the requirement of choral office for Jesuits, he himself loved music. Even before Ignatius's death in 1556, full-scale plays and musicales were being performed with his blessing at Rome's flagship Roman College, and at Jesuit colleges at Ingolstadt and Messina.

The 1586 *Ratio studiorum* recognized the dual value of performance for the young as training in poise and memory: "Our students and their parents become wonderfully enthusiastic, and at the same time very attached to our Society when we train the boys to show the result of their study, their acting ability and their ready memory on the stage." From these beginnings, a rich and complex tradition of biannual plays grew up in Jesuit colleges. Across the world, the work of the colleges gave way to vast spectacles that filled the courtyards and theaters of the colleges. In France, important court composers like Marc-Antoine Charpentier and Jean-Baptiste Lully provided the scores, royal ballet masters like Pierre Beauchamps and Jesuit Father Joseph Jouvancy provided the choreography. Jesuit theorists and historians produced five of the most important early treatises on ballet at the Collège Louis-le-Grand. An estimated 150,000 plays were performed across the world over the first two centuries of Jesuit education, and countless more since the nineteenth-century restoration.

This theatrical and artistic tradition was about more than entertainment and diversion. The arts were not considered as ends in themselves but were always seen as useful educational tools that formed morally astute citizens and socially competent persons who could comport themselves in public in a convincing way. Although what are now called studio arts were not formally taught, applied arts were part of the program: Students learned to sketch, construct, and paint *trompe l'oeil* scenery and were given practical lessons in rudimentary engineering so that their confrères could fly safely above the stage on painted clouds.

From the very beginning, the Jesuits used the arts for persuasion. They built grand and beautiful churches and imposing college buildings, recruited artists to join the Order, and employed a stable of some of the best lay musicians, architects, and artists of the early modern and Baroque periods. Bernini was a friend of General Gian Paolo Oliva, and Carlo Fontana designed the basilica of St. Ignatius at Loyola in Spain. Rubens was a devout member of Jesuit sodalities. The arts were always seen as instrumental, never an end in themselves: concrete, visible, audible ways to come into contact with the invisible and inaudible realm of spirit.

The 1814 restoration after the trauma of the Suppression saw the Jesuits return as shell-shocked survivors. Old artistic styles were embraced anew. Novelty was eschewed at all costs, and a kind of benign philistinism came to rule in the Jesuits' approach to the arts. For all practical purposes, no great art was inspired by or came out of Jesuit institutions, with the exception of the brilliant, unpublished verse of English Jesuit Gerard Manley Hopkins. Summarizing the attitudes of the age he wrote sadly, "Brilliancy does not suit us."

In 1973, Pedro Arrupe's landmark essay "Art and the Spirit of the Society of Jesus" invited the Society to honor and reclaim its artistic heritage, and encouraged Jesuit artists to put their talents again at the service of the Church and society.

See also Architecture; Art Patronage; Arts, Performing; Images

Arrupe, Pedro, "Art and the Spirit of the Society of Jesus." *Studies in the Spirituality of Jesuits* 5, 3 (1973), 83–92.
O'Malley, John W., and Gauvin A. Bailey, eds., *The Jesuits and the Arts, 1540–1773*. Philadelphia, PA: St. Joseph's University Press, 2005.
O'Malley, John W., Gauvin A. Bailey, Steven J. Harris, and T. Frank Kennedy, eds., *The Jesuits: Cultures, Sciences, and the Arts, 1540–1773*. Toronto: University of Toronto Press, 1999 and 2006.

Thomas Lucas, SJ

Asceticism and Mysticism

The mid-twentieth century witnessed a shift from the understanding of Jesuit spirituality primarily as a form of asceticism toward a greater emphasis upon its place in the mystical tradition. Yet, though useful as conceptual distinctions, asceticism and mysticism must always be considered within the whole of Ignatian spirituality

The term "asceticism" comes from the Greek word *askesis*, or exercise. It designates those spiritual and physical disciplines applied to the liberation from vices, the growth in Christian virtue, and, above all, the pursuit of divine union.

One may highlight three important elements of the Society's asceticism. The first is Christological: Growth in virtue is sought through a more intimate knowledge and imitation of Jesus. The *Spiritual Exercises*, for example, inspire a series of encounters with the Jesus of the Scriptures that foster affective responses, ranging from love to sorrow. Such experiences, in turn, lead to a concrete application in the Jesuit's life through a separation from disordered desires and a greater zeal to serve under the banner of Christ. This *imitatio Christi* has become a hallmark of Jesuit devotional literature and practice.

Second, Jesuit spirituality emphasizes the mortifications of service and the *examen*. While traditional ascetical practices such as fasting and physical deprivation have had their place in Jesuit life, from the beginning Jesuits have leaned toward mortifications that provide apostolic formation. Experiments with the sick and the poor, the education of youth, "low and humble tasks" within the community – all of these experiences discipline a Jesuit for mission. Even the practice of averting the gaze from temptations, the so-called custody of the eyes, allows a Jesuit to avoid distractions and negative influences while working in the apostolate. Above all, the *examen* stands out as a daily spiritual practice that aids the Jesuit in the elimination of disordered attractions and the discernment of God's will.

Finally, the vows of poverty, chastity, and, above all, obedience, have given form to the Jesuit vocation. In assuming these vows, the first Companions inserted their enterprise into the disciplinary framework of Christian religious congregations; yet they lived these vows apart from some of the generally accepted structures (the office in choir, the fixed community, etc.) for the sake of mission. Obedience to the superior and to the pope in regard to missions both humbles the individual Jesuit and frees him to embrace the Society's apostolic initiatives.

Jesuit spirituality also has a place in the mystical tradition. Mysticism may generally be defined as a personal and transformative experience of God. It may embrace numerous divinely bestowed phenomena: infused prayer, visions, ecstasies, physical manifestations such as tears, a heightened awareness of God's presence. Ignatius himself described mystical experiences in his life ranging from visions (e.g., Manresa, La Storta) to floods of tears when celebrating the Mass, and one may find other examples in the accounts of Jesuit saints (e.g., Peter Faber, Claude la Colombière, Alberto Hurtado). Yet the Jesuits have always maintained a sober mistrust of the radical impulses in such experiences and have demanded a careful discernment of spiritual phenomena.

Jesuit mysticism emerges from a living experience of the God who encounters humanity personally and historically. Karl Rahner highlights that this God is Trinity, the wholly Other, who, at the same time, has definitively revealed himself in Jesus and continues to draw creation into personal union with himself. Jesuit spirituality therefore fosters a state of readiness to respond to the free and transformative presence of divine grace in the world.

Furthermore, the Society's mysticism involves an affective movement toward ecclesial service. As already noted, the *Exercises* foster an encounter with Jesus that both stirs deep affections and leads to an election. The authenticity of spiritual gifts may be tested, above all, by the fruit that they bear in the exercitant. In the Contemplation to Attain Love (*SpEx* #230), for instance, Ignatius stresses that love is expressed more fully in deeds than in words.

There is not, in the end, a radical bifurcation between the ascetical and the mystical in Jesuit spirituality, but rather they are unified in the Society's end: the Greater Glory of God. The simplicity, flexibility, and practicality of the Jesuit experience have made it one of the most accessible and influential spiritualities in the Christian tradition for both religious and laity.

See also Examen; Mission; *Spiritual Exercises*

Egan, Harvey D., *Ignatius Loyola the Mystic*. Collegeville, MN: The Liturgical Press, 1987.

de Guibert, Joseph, *The Jesuits: Their Spiritual Doctrine and Practice.* Trans. William J. Young. Chicago, IL: Loyola University Press, 1964.

Rahner, Karl, "The Ignatian Mysticism of Joy in the World." *Theological Investigations.* Vol. III: *The Theology of the Spiritual Life.* Trans. Karl-H. Kruger and Boniface Kruger. New York: Seabury Press, 1967, pp. 277–93.

John Gavin, SJ

Asia

The Jesuits arrived in Asia in the early days of the Society, when Ignatius Loyola sent Francis Xavier (1506–52) to the "East Indies." Xavier landed in Goa (1542) before heading eastward to Malacca (1545), the Moluccas (1546), and finally to Japan in 1549. On his second trip to the east from Goa, Xavier had hoped to reach China, but unfortunately he died on Shangchuan Island in 1552 without setting foot on the mainland.

The Society continued to send Jesuits to Asia, and eventually missionary headquarters were set up in Goa and Macau. The chief architect of the Jesuit missionary endeavor in Asia was Alessandro Valignano (1539–1606) who believed that the key to successful evangelization involved learning the local languages and adapting to the indigenous cultures, as long as there was no conflict with the Christian message. Valignano's approach, *il modo suave* (the smooth way), departed from the *tabula rasa* (blank slate) method employed by Jesuits in the Americas and was applied by most missionaries to Asia.

Many Jesuit missionaries became masters of language. Together with native lay assistants, they composed lexicons, grammars, prayer books, and catechisms in the local languages in order to spread the Christian message to the people. A few Jesuits, such as Matteo Ricci (1552–1610) in China or Roberto di Nobili (1577–1656) in India, learned the sacred texts of the people and befriended the religious and civil elites by introducing them to western sciences, arts, and ideas. Others, like Alexandre de Rhodes (1591–1660) in Vietnam, adapted to the civil customs and ordinary life to reach the mass population. Cultural accommodation is the Jesuit way to evangelize among people of all social strata. The Spanish Jesuits in the Philippines also made some adaptation based on their experience with the *reducciones* (planned settlements) in South America.

The Jesuits in Asia were cultural transmitters and contributed significantly to knowledge of Asia for Europeans. They translated Chinese and Indian classical texts, wrote travelogues, composed books on the culture and customs of the local people, as well as taxonomies of the local fauna and flora.

However, the Jesuit missionary enterprise was not without difficulties. It was Rome's decision to set up its own mission office, *Propaganda fide*, in 1622 to direct the evangelizing activities of the whole Church. Consequently, Jesuits were often caught in tension and conflict between loyalty to their royal patrons and obedience to the new bishops appointed by Rome for the missions in Asia.

Other obstacles abounded, from a lack of cooperation between Catholic religious orders and the fierce political and economic competition between the Portuguese, Spanish, and Dutch traders. In Japan, conflicts of commercial interest and fear of a European expansion resulted in a series of edicts against Christianity beginning in 1587. Furthermore, European prejudice and fear of syncretism also prevented an understanding of missionary needs at the frontiers, and the controversies on the Chinese Rites

(1645–1743) and Malabar Rites (c. 1600–1744) were disastrous for the missions in China and India.

Jesuits were also caught up in political controversies in Europe and, as a result, made enemies among the ruling classes. In 1762, the Portuguese authorities expelled all Jesuits from Macau and Goa, and in 1768 the Spanish Crown evicted Jesuits from the Philippines. Then came the worldwide suppression of the Society of Jesus in 1773 that effectively ended the Jesuit missionary activities in Asia.

After the restoration, the Jesuits slowly returned to Asia. They were in British India by 1834, China by 1841, Dutch Indonesia and Spanish Philippines by 1859, and Japan by 1908. The missions in Asia grew steadily during the nineteenth and twentieth centuries. Before World War II, the majority of Jesuit missions were concentrated in Java (Indonesia), the Philippines, and various parts of China. China's mission prospered until the Jesuits were expelled from the mainland in the 1950s. They came to Korea and Thailand in 1954, and returned to Vietnam in 1957. Since the 1990s, new missions were set up in Cambodia, Myanmar, Laos, and East Timor. During the twentieth century, the Jesuits focused on building up educational institutions and social centers, and thus helped to revitalize the Church and modernize many Asian countries.

Although only the Philippines and Timor-Leste are predominantly Christian, Asia is a fast-growing part of the Society. Today, the Jesuits in Asia are organized into two conferences. The Jesuit Conference of South Asia (JCSA) includes the many provinces in the Indian subcontinent and Sri Lanka, while the Jesuit Conference of Asia Pacific (JCAP) covers Jesuit life and service in most countries of East Asia and Southeast Asia as well as Oceania (Australia, New Zealand, and Micronesia). With a significant presence in Asia, about a third of the worldwide Society, these Jesuits have made major contributions to the Society's mission in education, youth ministry, communication, spiritual, interreligious, social, and pastoral works.

See also China; India; Japan; Philippines; Xavier, Francis, SJ, St.

de la Costa, H., *The Jesuits in the Philippines, 1581–1768*. Cambridge, MA: Harvard University Press, 1967.
Moffett, Samuel H., *A History of Christianity in Asia*. Vol. II. Maryknoll, NY: Orbis, 2005.
Neill, Stephen, *The Story of the Christian Church in India and Pakistan*. Grand Rapids, MI: Eerdmans, 1970.
Phan, Peter C., ed., *Christianities in Asia*. Hoboken, NJ: Wiley-Blackwell, 2011.
Ross, Andrew C., *A Vision Betrayed: The Jesuits in Japan and China 1542–1742*. Maryknoll, NY: Orbis, 1994.
Uhalley, Stephen, Jr., and Xiaoxin Wu, eds., *China and Christianity: Burden Past, Hopeful Future*. Armonk, NY: M. E. Sharpe, 2001.

Anh Q. Tran, SJ

Assistancy

The Society of Jesus is organized into provinces or geographic regions, each of which is headed by a provincial superior who is appointed by the Jesuit superior general. The individual provinces are grouped into assistancies, which generally correspond to nations or wider regions. As an example, the collective provinces of North America (Canada and the United States) form a single assistancy. As a point of clarification, the 12th General Congregation (1682) decreed that "the place of birth or origin of an individual does not determine whether or not he is to be considered to belong to a certain assistancy; rather, it depends upon the province to which he belongs. Thus, a man who is a member of a province belonging to a given assistancy belongs to this assistancy and is eligible to be elected its assistant" (Decree 5). With regard to the "Continuing Evaluation of Our Apostolic Work" at various levels of the Society, the 32nd General Congregation (1974–75) directed: "In each province or region, or at least at the Assistancy level, there should be a definite mechanism for the review of our ministries." The Congregation urged the Society "to examine critically how [various] arrangements are working and, if need be, to replace them by others which are more effective and allow for a wider participation in the process of communal discernment" (Decree 4, #126).

See also Province; Region

Padberg, John W., ed., *Jesuit Life & Mission Today: The Decrees of the 31st-35th General Congregations of the Society of Jesus*. St. Louis, MO: The Institute of Jesuit Sources, 2009.

Padberg, John W., Martin D. O'Keefe, and John L. McCarthy, eds., *For Matters of Greater Moment: The First Thirty Jesuit General Congregations: A Brief History and a Translation of the Decrees*. St. Louis, MO: The Institute of Jesuit Sources, 1994.

Robert E. Scully, SJ

Astronomy

Jesuit work in astronomy is in keeping with the incarnational nature of Jesuit spirituality: to "find God in all things." Indeed, in his *Autobiography*, St. Ignatius noted that "the greatest consolation that he received … was from gazing at the sky and stars, and this he often did and for quite a long time."

The modern science of astronomy began with Copernicus's *On the Revolutions of the Heavens* (1543). That work was used in the Gregorian reform of the calendar in 1582, in which the Jesuit mathematician Christopher Clavius (1538–1612) played an important role. Clavius also promoted the teaching of mathematics, including astronomy, in the *Ratio studiorum*.

Clavius was one of Galileo's early supporters among the Jesuits of the Roman College, who feted Galileo in 1611. However, disputes between Galileo and the Jesuits Christopher Scheiner (1573–1650) on the nature of sunspots, and Orazio Grassi (1583–1654) on the nature of comets, soured relations between him and the Jesuits. When Cardinal Robert Bellarmine (1542–1621), himself a Jesuit, delivered an injunction to Galileo in 1616 against teaching the Copernican system, Galileo faulted the Jesuits for not supporting him. Later, he blamed Jesuit hostility as a cause for his infamous trial in 1633.

Scientific evidence in favor of heliocentrism was not yet well established in the seventeenth century. In *The New Almagest* (1651), Jesuit astronomer Giovanni Battista Riccioli (1598–1671) noted that observations of the planets alone could not distinguish the Copernican system from the Tycho Brahe system, where the planets orbit the Sun but the Sun orbits the Earth. In that same book, Riccioli produced an accurate telescopic map of the Moon, devising the nomenclature system still used today. Lunar craters are named for prominent scientists; Riccioli named two dozen for Jesuits. (The current count of Jesuits on the Moon is 33.)

A number of Jesuits served as astronomers at the Roman College from the seventeenth to the nineteenth century. Christoph Grienberger (1564–1636) observed with Galileo's telescope and invented the equatorial mounting (with one axis parallel to the Earth's). Odo van Melcote (1572–1615) observed the nova of 1604; his observations placed the nova in the same location as seen by observers elsewhere in Europe, showing that it was not merely an effect in Earth's atmosphere but a phenomenon that occurred well beyond the Moon's orbit. Nicola Zucchi (1586–1670) invented the reflecting telescope. Athanasius Kircher, SJ (1601–80), made some of the first detailed telescopic drawings of Jupiter and Saturn.

Thanks in part to the efforts of the Jesuit astronomer Roger Boscovich (1711–87), the Vatican lifted its prohibition against teaching heliocentrism in 1757. Boscovich studied telescope optics and cometary orbits, and he promoted observations of the transits of Venus in 1761 and 1769. By measuring where Venus appeared to cross the Sun as observed from many different locations on Earth, one could calculate the distance from Earth to Sun as a function of the distance between the terrestrial observing locations. At that time, 25 percent of all observatories in Europe were run by Jesuits; notably, the director of the Vienna Observatory, Maximilian Hell (1720–92), observed the transit from Sweden by invitation of the Swedish king, at a time when Jesuits were otherwise banned from Sweden.

Jesuit missionaries worldwide contributed to such observations. Notable among them were Ferdinand Verbiest (1623–88) and other Jesuits at the Imperial Observatory in China; and missionaries in South Africa, Siam, and India, including the first discoverers of double stars, Jean de Fontanay (1643–1710) and Jean Richaud (1633–93).

Jesuit astronomy continued after the restoration of the Society. Etienne Dumouchel (1773–1840) and Francesco de Vico (1805–48) were the first to recover Comet Halley in 1835. The most notable nineteenth-century Jesuit astronomer was Angelo Secchi (1818–78), famous for his observations of Mars and his pioneering work on stellar spectra. He was the first to develop a classification scheme for stellar spectra, classifying more than 4,000 stars, including the first identification of carbon-rich stars. He also made spectral observations of the atmospheres of Mars, Jupiter, Saturn, Uranus, and Neptune, and found carbon lines in comets, meteors, and nebulae. By changing the work of astronomy from measuring stellar positions to measuring stellar composition, he is often credited as the "Father of Astrophysics."

Secchi's success at representing the Holy See in scientific congresses may have inspired the foundation of a permanent Vatican Observatory in 1891. The Jesuit astronomer Johann Hagen (1847–1930) was made director of the Observatory in 1904, and the staffing of the Observatory was entrusted to the Jesuit order in 1934, who continue to operate it today. Among its notable achievements are its contribution to the international *Carte du Ciel* photographic star atlas, under Fr. Hagen; the spectroscopic laboratory under Alois Gatterer (1886–1953), including the founding of the journal *Spectrochimica Acta*; and the work of William Stoeger (1943–2014) in philosophy, religion, and science.

See also Galileo; Moon; Science; Vatican Observatory

Graney , Christopher M., *Setting Aside All Authority: Giovanni Battista Riccioli and the Science against Copernicus in the Age of Galileo*. South Bend, IN: University of Notre Dame Press, 2015.

Maffeo, Sabino, *The Vatican Observatory: In the Service of Nine Popes*. South Bend, IN: University of Notre Dame Press, 2002.

Udías, Augustín, *Jesuit Contribution to Science: A History*. London: Springer, 2015.

Guy Consolmagno, SJ

Ateneo de Manila University

Ateneo de Manila University (ADMU) is the oldest of five Jesuit universities under the Philippine province. Its campuses in Metro Manila offer highly recognized tertiary and basic education programs in a broad range of disciplines. Situated in the fast-changing Southeast Asian context, it aims to integrate Jesuit traditional values of humanistic education and social engagement with its development as a modern university.

In 1859, colonial authorities asked the restored Society to run Manila's primary school for Spanish children. It soon became Ateneo Municipal de Manila, licensed to grant the bachelor's degree. Courses, taught in Spanish, followed the Jesuit *Ratio studiorum*. Catholic services and Jesuit organizations were routine for its all-male studentry, now including native and mestizo. Here studied leaders of native diocesan clergy and of the nationalist and revolutionary movements in the late nineteenth century. José Rizal, 1877 Bachelor of Arts graduate, became its most prominent alumnus for being executed for his nationalist views and recognized subsequently as a national hero.

With no subsidy from the American colonial government (1898–1946), ADMU became privatized. Maryland-New York province Jesuits, designated for being sent to British Bombay but deemed unacceptable for being ethnic Irish, came to the Philippines instead. Upon assuming administration from 1921 onward, they continued to emphasize the humanities, especially literature and drama, but also brought an educational ethos with colonial and modern nuances that sometimes offended Spanish sensibilities. English became the medium of instruction, much later than in other Catholic schools. More student organizations, military parades, and sports like boxing were introduced. In 1932, it relocated to Padre Faura St., Ermita, when many facilities including the famous Museum of Natural History and the country's best physics laboratory were burned. It suffered further destruction when World War II razed the exquisite 1869 San Ignacio Church, Intramuros.

As a Jesuit institution amid poverty, Ateneo became involved in wider issues through the work of the Jesuits Joseph A. Mulry before World War II, and Walter B. Hogan after. Inspired by Catholic social teaching, their work initiated the formation of labor and peasant organizations to combat growing communist influence. However these organizations conflicted with other Church leaders during the 1956 labor strike at the Dominican University of Santo Tomas.

Six years after the 1946 Philippine Independence, Rector William F. Masterson transferred all programs except postgraduate to then-undeveloped Loyola Heights, Quezon City. This move met opposition but increased the population and programs. The Ateneo expanded its programs in the humanities, science, and technology. In the following decades, American-trained Jesuit and lay teachers initiated social science programs to understand Philippine society better. In 1958, the Ateneo received its first Filipino rector; the following year, its university status.

Social unrest in the 1960s made "Filipinization" and social inequality crucial concerns. Courses used Filipino as medium of instruction, focused on local issues, and incorporated exposure to marginalized sectors. Scholarship programs and more social organizations were established. This aligned with Jesuit Superior General Pedro Arrupe's mandate to form men and women for others. Formation programs in faith and justice for students, lay faculty, now regarded as full partners in mission, and alumni proved invaluable during the Marcos authoritarian years (1972–86). Government forces raided

Ateneo social organizations and imprisoned or executed some of those in the opposition. Following assassinations of prominent alumni Benigno Aquino, Jr., in 1983 and Evelio Javier in 1986, many in the Ateneo network supported Church and civil society movements during the historic People Power Revolution and restoration of constitutional democracy.

ADMU began to change from a liberal arts college to a teaching and research university. Its humanistic and service orientation still informed all programs, including new initiatives in information technology and environmental sciences. In 1974, the college turned coeducational, and later restructured to facilitate student-centered learning and to accommodate higher enrollment. The School of Government and School of Medicine and Public Health pioneered new approaches to leadership and health education. Supporting structures were built: at the Loyola Heights campus, new academic facilities for various schools, the University Church of the Gesù, and student centers for sports, organizations, and a dormitory. Postgraduate law and business programs moved to Makati; first Salcedo Village, then Rockwell Center. Moreover, ADMU's international profile has grown through linkages with foreign institutions and study programs focused on other countries. Faculty and student exchanges have increased as has the number of international students at the Ateneo.

Well known for Ateneo-educated leaders in various fields, ADMU strives to excel as a truly modern institution without compromising its foundational Jesuit tradition. Its expansion into new degree and research programs, especially in science, technology, and business, has not diminished its stature as a center for the humanities and social concerns. It is not uncommon to find faculty and students from various academic disciplines working together to address the social and technical impact of endemic poverty and chronic natural calamities exacerbated by environmental factors.

See also Philippines; Universities, 1773–Present

Arcilla, Jose S., *150: The Ateneo Way*. Quezon City: Media Wise Communications, 2009.
De Castro, Antonio B., "Jesuit Linguistic Battles, ca. 1898–1932: Language, Power, and the Filipino Soul." *Philippine Studies* 58, 1/2 (2010), 111–46.
Schumacher, John N., *Growth and Decline: Essays on Philippine Church History*. Quezon City: Ateneo de Manila University Press, 2009.

Jose Mario C. Francisco, SJ

Australia

Two Austrian Jesuits, Fathers Aloysius Kranewitter and Maximilian Klinkowström, having been expelled from the Austro-Hungarian Empire during the 1848 revolutions, accompanied a group of Catholic Silesian families emigrating to the twelve-year-old colony of South Australia. When established in Sevenhill, the bishop of Adelaide gave the Jesuits pastoral responsibility for the north and west of the State, an area the size of France. By 1901, fifty-nine Austrian priests and brothers had served in parishes and mission stations in South Australia and the Northern Territory. A secondary school was opened in 1856 at Sevenhill, and in 1869 the parish of Norwood in Adelaide was accepted.

The second coming to Australia was to the colonies of Victoria and New South Wales by the Irish Jesuits at the request of the Irish Catholic community to start a secondary school. The first Irish Jesuits came to staff St. Patrick's College, Melbourne, in 1865. The bishop also asked the Jesuits to administer the parochial mission of Richmond, preach occasional sermons, give retreats, and assist in the seminary training of priests. Further demands for a boarding school resulted in Xavier College, Kew, opening in 1878.

It was a similar story in New South Wales, where Benedictine Roger Bede Vaughan, the archbishop of Sydney, invited the Jesuits to start St. Kilda House (later St. Aloysius' College, Milson's Point) and to run the parish of the North Shore in 1879. The following year, a boarding school, St Ignatius' College, was established. Joseph Dalton was the founding father of all these early works.

In 1886, the *Messenger of the Sacred Heart* was founded, and a second devotional magazine, *Madonna*, was published from 1897. *Messenger* circulation peaked at over 60,000. The contemporary province communications network sponsors the online *Eureka Street*, a journal of religious, political, and social comment.

In 1901 the two Jesuit missions to Australia were amalgamated under the control of the Irish province. Much growth subsequently occurred, especially in the field of tertiary education. In accepting Newman College in 1918, the Jesuits were given scope to foster both the academic life and the faith development of Catholic undergraduates attending Melbourne University by providing Catholic Action groups. The administration and pastoral ministry of other university colleges followed in Adelaide (1950), Brisbane and Perth (1954), and Hobart (1959). A few Jesuits took up teaching positions in the universities.

The Riverview Observatory, the only fully equipped seismological observatory in Australia, was established in 1909, and the first Jesuit foundation in Queensland, the parish of Toowong and Indooroopilly, began in 1916. A preparatory school to Xavier College, Burke Hall, was opened in Kew in 1921, and in 1922 the Society accepted the invitation to staff the regional diocesan seminary of Victoria, Corpus Christi College, Werribee. Staffing the Holy Name seminary in Christchurch, New Zealand, was accepted in 1946.

As the number of vocations increased, the Irish mission to Australia became an independent vice province in 1931. Houses of formation were built in Victoria in 1934, for novices and philosophers, and for theology in Sydney in 1939. New schools were founded in Brighton, Victoria, 1936; in Perth, in 1938; and in Norwood, South Australia, in 1951.

Australia became a full province in 1950, and the following year, the zealous new provincial, Austin Kelly, sent six Jesuits to the mission in Bihar, Northern India, which eventually became the Hazaribag province. Over fifty Jesuits were sent to this mission, engaging in education and working in tribal mission stations.

The flow of novices did not continue. In the aftermath of the Second Vatican Council, there was an initial growth in vocations, and then a relatively rapid decline. Province numbers reached a maximum of 365 in 1966, and then decreased to 128 in 2014. From 1969 until 2014, scholastics studied theology as part of an ecumenical consortium at the United Faculty of Theology in Melbourne.

Considering the geographical situation of the Australian province, and that Australian Jesuits were already working in Asia, it was transferred, in1968, from the English Assistancy to the East Asian Assistancy.

With renewed focus on Asia, and issues facing the poor and disadvantaged, the *Asian Bureau Australia* was established in 1971, and Jesuits were sent to work among the Aboriginals in the Kimberly region of Western Australia, and in Queensland. Managing a home for homeless alcoholics at Greenvale, Melbourne, began in 1976. The Jesuit Refugee Service was established in 1983, and a social justice research center, Uniya, opened in Sydney in 1989. In 1995 Jesuit Social Services was established.

Centers of spirituality were set up in Brisbane, Sydney, Melbourne, Sevenhill, and Adelaide from 1976, giving retreats, spiritual direction, and courses on Ignatian spirituality to the laity. With the declining number of Jesuits, the challenge for the future of the province institutions is the education of lay collaborators in the Ignatian ethos.

See also Asia; German-Speaking Lands; Ireland

Eddy, J. J., "The Society of Jesus (Jesuits) in Australia." In James Jupp, ed., *The Encyclopedia of Religion in Australia*. Cambridge: Cambridge University Press, 2009, pp. 245–53.
Strong, David, *Jesuits in Australia: An Ethnographic History of the Society of Jesus in Australia*. Richmond, Victoria: Aurora Books, 1995.

David Strong, SJ

Autobiography of St. Ignatius

The autobiography of Ignatius, often called *Acta*, spans eighteen years of the saint's life, from his wounding at Pamplona in 1521 through his conversion at Manresa, the trip to Jerusalem, his university studies in Spain and Paris, and his journey to Rome in 1538 when he placed himself and his companions at the disposal of the pope. These critical years reveal the incredible transformation and spiritual growth of Ignatius and the events that helped to bring about this change.

Thus the *Acta* do not cover the entire life of Ignatius, and strictly speaking, neither were they written by him, nor is it strictly speaking an autobiography. The text is clearly inspired by the Acts of the Apostles wherein Ignatius could see God's spirit acting on the hearts of the apostles. In the early years Ignatius and his first companions had to face many difficulties quite similar to those described in the Acts of the Apostles. Ignatius experienced great opposition from some Church quarters and was unfairly persecuted by overzealous inquisitors and clergy who could not understand his ideals. On a few occasions his views even landed him in prison. Through Acts, Ignatius came to understand that one need not withdraw from the world in order to become holy. Rather, like the apostles, one can become holy through charitable work. Luke's Gospel and Acts of the Apostles provided a solid theological base for the *Acta*. Luke's spirituality thus served to enrich and renew Ignatius, and in this sense Luke's writings are most relevant to Ignatian spirituality.

Ignatius struggled against vainglory, which he considered to be his principal vice; as a result he was reluctant to give an account of his life and only agreed to do so after much insistence from his companions. Ignatius narrated his struggles to Luis Gonçalves da Câmara, whom he considered to be equally vainglorious, but there were many pauses and it took a long time for the text to evolve as the *Acta* that we know. Gonçalves da Câmara jotted down notes based on his memory of the verbal account delivered by Ignatius. These were then dictated to secretaries and came to form a completed narrative written predominantly in Spanish, while its final segment was transcribed in Italian.

The *Acta* illustrate the difficulties experienced by Ignatius and helped to show that vainglory was a major fault of the human character. Though not an autobiography, the

Acta expose the manner by which Ignatius made the examination of conscience and review the actions of God during this most crucial phase in his life.

The *Acta* were consciously intended as a narrative of God's activity in the life of Ignatius and primarily intended to assist his companions in their apostolate and in changing their interior disposition. Ignatius chose which events to include and which to leave out, in such a way that one can see his perception of things, and how events included reflect conscious decisions taken by Ignatius. The *Acta* show what it means to be a Jesuit, and Ignatius emerges as the sole founder of the Society of Jesus. Finally the *Acta* present Ignatius as a Renaissance man who might not always conform to the teachings of the Counter-Reformation Church. This made the early Jesuits rather uncomfortable with the *Acta* which were later suppressed in favor of official biographies by Jesuits who wrote in line with the teachings of Trent.

Thus fifteen years after its completion, all copies of the *Acta* were removed from circulation in favor of a new biography by Pedro de Ribadeneira. The *Acta*, as dictated by Ignatius, were said to leave out important details on the life of Ignatius. Ribadeneira even claimed that the *Acta* were written when Ignatius was past 60, and they reflected the weakness of his memory. Ribadeneira's biography was published in Latin in 1572 and a Spanish translation came out in 1583.

In Ribadeneira's biography, Ignatius is presented as the former soldier who endowed the Society of Jesus with a quasi-military discipline. This was in sharp contrast with the *Acta*, wherein Ignatius expressed his distaste for misguided military heroics and crusading fervors. Ribadeneira presented an Ignatius firmly entrenched in the camp of the Counter-Reformation Church. He is depicted as the antithesis of the heretical Martin Luther and is even portrayed as an opponent of Erasmus from the start of his education, which is far from the truth.

It was not until the mid-eighteenth century that the Bollandists first published a Latin translation of the *Acta* and presented it as the seventh volume of the *Acta Sanctorum*. It was only in 1904 that it was edited and published in the vernacular. By 1943 the vernacular original and the Latin translation were published side by side.

See also Gonçalves da Câmara, Luis, SJ; Loyola, Ignatius of, SJ, St.; Ribadeneira, Pedro de, SJ

Boyle , Marjorie O'Rourke, *Loyola's Acts: The Rhetoric of the Self.* Berkeley: University of California Press, 1997.

McManamon, John M., ed., *The Text and Contexts of Ignatius Loyola's "Autobiography."* New York: Fordham University Press, 2013.

Olin, John C., ed., *The Autobiography of St. Ignatius of Loyola, with Related Documents.* Trans. Joseph F. O'Callaghan. New York: Harper & Row, 1974.

Tylenda, Joseph N., trans., *A Pilgrim's Journey: The Autobiography of St. Ignatius of Loyola.* Wilmington, DE: Michael Glazier, 1985.

Carmel Cassar

Azevedo, Ignatius, SJ, Bl. (1527–1570)

Born in 1527 in Oporto, Azevedo was brought up at the court of John III of Portugal. When he was 18 years old, Azevedo became the administrator of his family estates, but after listening to the homilies of the Jesuit Francis Estrada he decided to renounce them.

On December 28, 1548, he joined the Society of Jesus. Before completing his theology studies, he was appointed rector of the College of Saint Anthony in Lisbon, and he was sent to Braga in order to establish the college of Saint Paul. He was vice provincial of Portugal.

Troubled by the full awareness of his origins (his father was a clergyman and his mother a nun) and inclined to be a missionary, he asked to leave Portugal. He was the procurator of India and Brazil at the 2nd General Congregation (1565). On February 24, 1566, he was appointed visitor (inspector) of Brazil. In May 1569 he went back to Rome. Before returning to Brazil, he recruited seventy young men from Portugal and Spain. After five months training for their missionary labors at the Quinta de Val de Rosal (near Lisbon), on June 5, 1570, forty missionaries left for Brazil on board a merchant ship, while thirty others followed on a warship.

They were attacked by a French ship commanded by the Huguenot Jacques Sourie near the island of Palma on July 15, 1570. The forty missionaries (except João Adauto, spared because he was a cook) were beheaded and thrown into the sea. News of Azevedo's martyrdom soon reached Madeira. He and his companions were beatified on May 11, 1854.

See also Brazil; Martyrs, Ideal and History

Leite, Serafim, *História da Companhia de Jesus no Brasil*. Vols. I–II. Lisbon/Rio de Janeiro: Civilização Brasileira, 1938.
    Monumenta Brasiliae. Vol. IV. Rome: Monumenta Historica Societatis Iesu, 1960.

Danilo Mondoni, SJ

Azpeitia

The town of Azpeitia is situated in the province of Guipúzcoa, on the banks of the River Urola, surrounded by green limestone hills. Azpeitia's surroundings include a small urban center and a series of rural neighborhoods; the most notable is Loyola because Ignatius Loyola was born there and because there is a monumental religious complex in the baroque style. Its population is around 15,000 people, and it celebrates the festivities on July 31, in honor of San Ignacio. The word *Azpeitia* comes from the Basque language (Euskera), and it means "rock" or "mount up," while the neighboring town of Azkoitia means "mount below," as Father Larramendi explained in his work *Corografía*, published in 1759.

Besides the aforementioned Sanctuary of Loyola, the town has other important monuments, such as the parish of San Sebastian de Soreasu; associated with the Templars and with a neoclassical front of Ventura Rodríguez, it is the place where San Ignacio was baptized. In the nearby village of Azkoitia, there is also another significant monument, popularly known as *Etxe Beltza* (black house), because of its dark façade. It was the tower house of the dukes of Granada.

See also Loyola (Place)

Instituto Geográfico Vasco. www.ingeba.org/klasikoa/geografi/mug302/g813821.htm.
de Larramendi, Manuel, *Corografía o descripción general de la muy noble y muy leal provincia de Guipúzcoa*. Valladolid: Maxtor, 2010.

Inmaculada Fernández Arrillaga

Baghdad

In 1932, the year Iraq gained its independence following World War I, the Chaldean Patriarch of Babylon, Mar Emmanuel II, arranged for American Jesuits to come to Baghdad and open a secondary school for boys. Christians in Iraq were a small minority, less than 5 percent. Minorities had long functioned as semi-autonomous communities under the Ottoman system and following World War I all communities were focusing on education with help from outside. Iraq was put under English mandate by the San Remo Conference in 1920, so aid for educational development was sought from English-speaking sources. Fr. Edmund Walsh of Georgetown made first contact and helped recruit the four Jesuits who would establish the school. Incidentally, the Patriarch had studied at the Jesuit University of St. Joseph in Beirut.

Much earlier, in the late sixteenth and early seventeenth centuries, Jesuits had passed through Baghdad on their way east to Persia and China. The *Monumenta Historica Societatus Jesu* also records the death of two Jesuit brothers there in 1661 and 1664. The famous Jesuit missionary of Vietnam and Indonesia, Alexander de Rhodes, had also been in Baghdad briefly. He was buried next door in Persia in 1660.

The four Jesuits who arrived in 1932 inaugurated the school in downtown Baghdad but shortly thereafter purchased 25 acres of land in Sulaikh, on the northern outskirts of the city. There they gradually built a complex containing a residence, a class room and laboratory buildings, a boarding house, and a chapel. The Society of Jesus was not recognized as a moral person in Iraq, so these Jesuits were sponsored by the Iraqi-American Educational Association formed by the presidents of several American Jesuit institutions (Boston College, the University of Detroit, Georgetown University, Loyola University Chicago, Loyola University New Orleans, St. Louis University, and the University of San Francisco). The first Jesuits sent were from the California, Chicago, New York, and New England provinces, but the school was soon assigned to New England.

The school began with 107 students and nine faculty (four Jesuits and five Iraqi laymen). Growth was slow until the outbreak of World War II, and when travel restrictions prevented well-to-do families from sending their sons abroad to English-speaking schools, they opted for the new Jesuit school. This upgraded the reputation of the school sufficiently to assure capacity enrollment for the years to come. The student body included Christians and Muslims in equal numbers.

The Jesuits followed the Iraqi curriculum set up under English supervision for the five years of secondary education. Primary education was spread over seven years. Secondary education offered a choice of a scientific or a literary track. The Jesuits offered only the scientific. Certain subjects (civics, history, and Arabic literature) had to be taught in Arabic. Other subjects could be taught in English. However, the obligatory government exams to pass from third high to fourth and to finally obtain the secondary diploma were in Arabic only. The Jesuits arranged for the students to have preparatory sessions in Arabic for the subjects taught in English. The formula worked well. Exam results were excellent, and the graduates were well prepared for university studies in Baghdad, which were taught in English. Thus, the Jesuits shaped their own contribution within the parameters set by the government. Extracurricular activities included drama, sports, and debating.

Proselytizing was forbidden. Classes in religion were offered to Christian students. There was limited opportunity for directly apostolic work with the Christian community. Scholastics and a few fathers were regularly set aside to study Arabic.

Figure 9 Photograph of Jesuits ("Four Founders") living in Baghdad, *c.* 1933. Photograph ©
Archives of the New England Province, Society of Jesus

Early projections for enrollment were set at 200 students. By 1945 the actual enrollment was double that. Facilities for boarding students enabled families from Basra and
Mosul to send their sons to Baghdad. Numbers, however, were not allowed to increase
with demand. The peak was sixty-two boarding students.

Following World War II, enrollment at Baghdad peaked at 980 students in the late
1960s. In 1955 the government considered that the Jesuits' contribution to education
should be rewarded. They had brought innovation to secondary education and the
authorities hoped the Jesuits could offer constructive competition at the university level.
The prime minister donated a tract of land (168 acres) south of the city in Za'franiyya to
the Jesuits to open a university. In 1956, al-Hikma (Wisdom) University was opened for
studies in civil engineering and business administration.

The Six Day War of 1967, in which Israel crushed Arab armies and occupied more
territory, provoked reactions which brought an end to the work of the Jesuits in 1968 and
1969. Minor problems centering around a few Jewish students at al-Hikma University
were magnified by a faction of the ruling Baath Party that had been sidelined. This
led the minister of the interior to expel the Jesuits, from al-Hikma in 1968 and from
Baghdad College in 1969.

See also Middle East

MacDonnell, Joseph F., *Jesuits by the Tigris: Men for Others in Baghdad*. Boston, MA: Jesuit Mission Press, 1994.

John Donohue, SJ

Baja California (Antigua California, California)

California was named by explorers in the 1530s, yet efforts to found a Spanish-styled civilization in the harsh environs of Baja California foiled no less than Hernán Cortés, and future attempts remained unsuccessful until Jesuit Fathers Eusebio Kino and Juan María Salvatierra joined forces in the 1690s. These Italian-born Jesuits combined a wealth of experience, knowledge, patronage networks, and persuasive ability to convince a reticent Spanish Crown and an equally reticent Society of Jesus to make yet one more attempt. Kino and Salvatierra shared the view that evangelization efforts had been compromised by the presence of other settlers, namely, miners, soldiers, and ranchers. Crown support derived from the desire to establish a northern port of call for the returning Manila Galleon. The California mission was unique in that its foundation was funded by private donors.

The first mission, Loreto, was founded in 1697. The nomadic indigenous peoples of California used lightweight agave fiber to support a way of life that found them on the move in search of sustenance and fresh water sources. Yet when Francisco Piccolo returned from California to serve as *procurador*, his infamous *Informe de 1702* "described the economic potential of peninsular California in terms that would make a modern real estate swindler blush" (Crosby, *Antigua California*, 46). The reality was that scarcity of water made it difficult to grow the food and feed the livestock needed to attract and support mission Indians, compelling the California missions to depend for supplies upon the wealthier Sonora missions across the Sea of Cortez. The mission was not self-sustaining, compelling Salvatierra to make a formal request for Crown funds in 1700, which opened the Jesuit monopoly in California to criticism and countermeasures. The new Bourbon Crown frowned upon the fact that Jesuit missionaries had been granted oversight of the *presidio*; soldiers, who typically expected opportunity for personal gain through access to land and Indian labor, complained that Jesuits stifled their extra-economic activities. When the Jesuits were eventually expelled in 1767, the Bourbon authorities, still operating under the illusion of potential riches promoted by Piccolo's *Informe*, were disappointed to find no hidden Jesuit treasures of pearls and silver. The missions were turned over to the Franciscan order under the leadership of Junípero Serra.

See also Kino, Eusebio, SJ; Mexico (Viceroyalty of New Spain)

Crosby, Harry W., *Antigua California*. Albuquerque: University of New Mexico Press, 1994.

J. Michelle Molina

Balthasar, Hans Urs von

Hans Urs von Balthasar was born on August 12, 1905, in Lucerne, Switzerland, the oldest of three children. He began his education in a Benedictine high school but

transferred to the Jesuit-run Stella Matutina. He left the school a year before his graduation in order to study German language and culture at the university level, spending
semesters in Zurich, Vienna, and Berlin. He completed his doctorate at the University
of Zurich in 1928 with his thesis, "History of the Eschatological Problem in Modern
German Literature."

Balthasar received his call to a complete availability before God during a thirty-day
retreat with Fr. Friedrich Kronseder, SJ, in 1927. This openness to the divine will led him
first to the Society of Jesus. After completing the novitiate in 1931, he went on to philosophy studies in Pulach and theology studies in Fourvière. Forced to abandon his love for
music and literature during these years, Balthasar found his studies in the Society, with
its "sawdust Thomism," a trial. Yet he did find two Jesuit mentors – neither of whom were
ever his professors – who ignited new intellectual and spiritual passions. Eric Przywara
(1889–1972), SJ, provided him with creative bridges between scholastic philosophy and
contemporary thinkers. At Fourvière he came to know Henri de Lubac, SJ, who showed
him the rich harvest that could be drawn from the Church Fathers. During his time in
Fourvière, he also discovered such French authors as Charles Péguy, Paul Claudel, and
Georges Bernanos, figures whose works he would later translate and comment on.

After ordination on July 26, 1936, he began work at the journal *Stimmen der Zeit*
in Munich, but the tensions of the war forced his return to Zurich to be a university
chaplain. He worked tirelessly as a lecturer, retreat director, spiritual guide, and editor
for the "European Series" of the Klosterberg Collection. It was during this time that he
also formed two relationships that would shape his future works. The first was with the
Protestant theologian Karl Barth (1886–1968), whose theology Balthasar treated in both
a lecture series and a book. More importantly, however, he encountered the married
medical doctor and mystic, Adrienne von Speyr (1902–67).

Balthasar would become Speyr's spiritual guide during her conversion to Catholicism.
Eventually, they discerned a common call to found a secular institute, the Community
of St. John (*Johannesgemeinschaft*), that would "unite the evangelical counsels of Jesus
to an existence in the midst of the world." His involvement with the community would
lead to tensions within the Society and conversations with the Fr. General, Jan Baptiste
Janssens. Confronted with the choice between "obedience to the Society and obedience
to God," Balthasar chose to leave the Jesuits in 1950 in order to dedicate himself to the
Community and the appropriation of the fruits of Adrienne von Speyr's mystical experiences. He would, however, always see a continuity between his vocation as a Jesuit and
the fundamentally Ignatian form of his project with Adrienne.

For some years Balthasar made his living through lectures and publishing through
the Community's Johannesverlag. He moved in with the Kaegis and eventually received
incardination in the Diocese of Chur in 1956. These years of intense activity included
the publication of his major theological works, the foundation of the international journal *Communio* (1973), membership in the Pontifical Theological Commission, and
the reception of numerous honors and prizes. Toward the end of his life, he entered
into discussions with Fr. General Kolvenbach regarding his return to the Society, but
the Jesuits' refusal to assume responsibility for the Community of St. John remained an
obstacle. In 1988, John Paul II named him a cardinal, but he would not live to receive
the honor. He died on June 26, 1988.

Balthasar's prolific writings on numerous topics have grown in influence since his
death. His major trilogy – *The Glory of the Lord*, *The Theodrama*, and *The Theologic* – treats

revelation from the standpoints of the Beautiful, the Good, and the True. His writings on the Fathers offer critical appropriations of early Christianity's vision. Other writings on theology, literature, drama, music, and spirituality present a staggering wealth of knowledge and profound reflection. Yet, despite the celebrated impact of his scholarship, Balthasar always understood his primary mission to be his common project with Adrienne von Speyr – a project that embraced the Ignatian call to be a transforming Christian presence in the heart of the world.

See also Ex-Jesuits; John Paul II

Henrici, Peter, "Hans Urs von Balthasar: A Sketch of his Life." *Communio* 16 (Fall 1989), 306–50.
Oakes, Edward T., *Pattern of Redemption: The Theology of Hans Urs von Balthasar*. New York: Continuum, 1997.
Servais, Jacques, *Théologie des exercices spirituels: H. U. von Balthasar interprète saint Ignace*. Brussels: Culture et Vérité, 1996.

John Gavin, SJ

Barat, Sophie, St.

Madeleine Sophie Barat (1779–1865) was born in Joigny, Burgundy, shortly before the French Revolution and became founder of the Society of the Sacred Heart, a religious congregation of women of Ignatian inspiration. Her family region was strongly marked by the religious rigorism and Gallican ecclesiology associated with Jansenism. As a child Sophie witnessed the fall of the *Ancien Régime* and the Reign of Terror, with further revolutions continuing throughout her life. While a period of extreme social, religious, and political upheaval, the post-revolutionary period also saw an extraordinary flourishing of new religious communities of women throughout France, mostly undertaking works of education and health care.

Sophie was highly educated by her severe young brother and godfather Louis, a seminarian who suffered persecution during the Terror and whose brutal dominance was to cast a long shadow on her life. Through Louis, Sophie met Joseph Varin, a member of the priestly Society of the Sacred Heart working actively for the restoration of the Jesuits in France. The Society of Jesus had been expelled from France in 1764 and suppressed altogether by Clement XIV in 1773 until its restoration by Pius VII in 1814. A similar Italian group, the Fathers of the Faith, had hopes of a women's association, inspired by the Jesuit rule, which was to live a contemplative life while undertaking educational and spiritual apostolates. Both groups came together under Nicholas Paccanari's leadership and a small group of women emerged called Diletti di Gesù (Beloved of Jesus). Sophie joined the Diletti, beginning teaching in a school in Amiens. Poor leadership within the community and Paccanari's imprisonment for sodomy led the French Fathers of the Faith to break with him, but they themselves were suspected by Napoleon's regime of being secret Jesuits.

In 1802 Sophie was appointed leader of the women. She traveled to Grenoble to meet Rose Philippine Duchesne, a former Visitandine nun struggling to restore the order there, with a view to merging the two groups. Philippine would later initiate a mission in America and was canonized in 1988. There followed a long period of power struggles and confusion between Varin, Sophie (now elected superior general of the newly named Association des Dames de l'Instruction Chrétienne), and Fr. Saint-Estève, the meddling chaplain to the Amiens community, as a clear way was sought between various conflicting models of religious life. Further struggles involved bishops seeking authority over such groups of women religious and averse to the independence and mobility Sophie adopted. In 1807 the Fathers of the Faith were suppressed, many later joining the restored Society of Jesus. Meanwhile the Association sought and received recognition from Napoleon's government for its activities in France and beyond. Sophie's insistence on the Jesuit model of religious life, with the lifelong office of superior general and the spirituality of the Sacred Heart, caused increasing opposition. Saint-Estève attempted to manipulate matters in Rome, where memories of the prohibition on a female Jesuit branch survived, accusing Sophie's group of wanting to be "Jesuitesses."

In 1815 new constitutions, based on those of the Jesuits and other French religious orders and traditions, were approved for the Society of the Sacred Heart of Jesus, Sophie being confirmed as superior general for life and its seat moving to Paris. Struggles to confirm the identity and nature of the Society continued as powerful clerics sought control over the Order and political upheavals made association with the Sacred Heart difficult, the Sacred Heart emblem being associated with counter-revolutionary political causes. Communities and schools expanded and flourished despite conflicts over styles of education and of religious life, the question of cloister, solemn vows, and the role of the local bishop over communities being most contentious. The Society was approved in 1825, and Sophie petitioned the Jesuit Superior General Luigi Fortis, for a form of spiritual affiliation with his Society. Both Societies were associated in many minds, but further political upheavals in France threatened another expulsion of the Jesuits, preventing Sophie from pressing for closer structural links. In time a new generation of Jesuits proved reluctant to maintain previous associations, again for fear of encouraging women's aspirations to be "Jesuitesses."

Sophie endured years of bitter opposition and attempts to undermine her leadership from former close friends within the Society and numerous bishops and prelates opposed to her attempts to bring it closer to the universal mission and governance structures of the Jesuits. This was further exacerbated by tensions between Gallican and ultramontanist factions within the Church. Despite Sophie's chronic ill health, this almost constant internal warfare, and struggles to maintain her authority as superior general, the Society continued to expand schools and communities across Europe and the Americas, counting over 3,500 members at her death. Madeleine Sophie Barat died in 1865 and was canonized in 1925.

See also France; Sacred Heart; Women, as Co-Workers with Jesuits

Kilroy, Phil, *Madeleine Sophie Barat 1779–1865: A Life*. Cork: Cork University Press, 2000.
Luirard, Monique, *Madeleine-Sophie Barat: une éducatrice au cœur du monde, au cœur du Christ*. Paris: Nouvelle Cité, 1999.

Gemma Simmonds, CJ

Baroque Art and Architecture

Many early western historians characterized Baroque art and architecture as extravagant, highly emotional, and resolutely propagandistic successors to the classical restraint of the Renaissance. First appearing in Italy in the aftermath of the Council of Trent, Baroque art and architecture were often described as anti-democratic, manipulative, and low-brow, calculating attempts to overwhelm the viewer through sheer bravado and dazzling effects. In the mid-nineteenth century, at the very beginnings of modern academic western art historiography, the Jesuits were credited or blamed for its invention and diffusion. Indeed, the term "Jesuit style" preceded the common use of the word "baroque" by almost half a century. The story is much more complex.

Most contemporary art historians would maintain that such theorists were prejudiced by their own cultural contexts: the German Protestant tradition that sought to revalue the "native" Gothic art of northern Europe, and the emphatically anticlerical and anti-Jesuit culture of France in the nineteenth century. Moreover, these German and French commentators, influenced by the late Enlightenment's neoclassical revival, respected and defended the classicism of the Renaissance while railing against the opulence and what they interpreted as almost Asiatic vulgarity in the art that followed it. The art of the Mediterranean was considered the vanguard of counter-revolutionary, anti-humanistic, and manipulative Catholic culture, in direct opposition to northern Europe's pretended sobriety and rationality. Ironically, this interpretation blossomed, as Romanticism was in full flower in northern Europe. In this worldview, however, the crafty Jesuits were entirely to blame.

Anti-Jesuit sentiments and literature were hardly new phenomena. To twenty-first-century sensibilities, they betray a deep-seated anxiety about alterity, fear of the emotional and non-linear, and suspicion of the international. The Jesuit straw man, ultramontane and anti-nationalistic yet externally flexible and accommodating, was raised and knocked down again and again during the nineteenth century, even as Jesuits were repeatedly expelled, readmitted, and expelled again from countries across Europe and Latin America. Pascal's famous *Provincial Letters* (1657–58) were a devastating and direct attack on the casuistry of the Society, and a vigorous defense of Jansenism, itself an emphatically anti-aesthetic theological stance. Voltaire, an alumnus of the Collège Louis-le-Grand in Paris, satirized the alleged opulence and extravagance of the Jesuits at the Paraguayan Reductions in his *Candide* (1759). The topos of the conniving, degenerate, and manipulative Jesuit reappeared with renewed vigor with the restoration of the Society in 1814. Eugène Sue's wildly popular serial novel *The Wandering Jew* (1844) portrayed an international Jesuit conspiracy aimed at world domination and appeared at about the same time that art historians first began using "Jesuit style" as a pejorative term.

The "Jesuit style" argument began to break down at the end of the nineteenth century. Heinrich Wölfflin's classic *Renaissance and Baroque* (1888) pointed to the fact that the Jesuits were not in fact the instigators or inventors of a new style, although he remained suspicious of the manipulative qualities of the art of Jesuit churches. Early in the twentieth century, historians Joseph Braun and Louis Serbat produced detailed typologies of Jesuit buildings across Europe and effectively disproved the notion of a single, monolithically imposed and premeditated Jesuit style. They definitively showed that Jesuit construction design up to the Suppression incorporated a wide variety of local materials and architectural idioms (including the paleo-Christian, Romanesque, and Gothic), and used lay as well as Jesuit architects. Gauvin Alexander Bailey and Evonne Levy's recent scholarship has effectively summarized the *status questionis* of the "Jesuit style" as it stands today.

Nevertheless, important questions remain. In a provocative study, Levy explores the relationship between the contemporary understanding of propaganda and the Jesuit rhetorical tradition grounded in Cicero's hallowed triad of *docere, movere, et delectare*, "to teach, move, and delight." Levy and Bailey have also helped to unpack a dense phrase from Jesuit documents that has caused much confusion: *noster modus procedendi*, "our way of proceeding." They have demonstrated that the Jesuit way of proceeding was not a cold-blooded imposition of a single artistic or architectural style or form. Rather, the "way of proceeding" is analogous to a whole constellation of activities described in Jesuit foundational documents, including passages in the Jesuit *Constitutions* and documents of the early General Congregations, which specify process rather than product. In the case of the visual arts and architecture, the way of proceeding includes a series of practical, economic, and political guidelines that regulated *how* commissioning, design, and construction should take place, not what the product should look like. Such a "way" was certainly required, given the vast construction boom that accompanied the development of Jesuit colleges and their attendant churches. From the 1580s to 1650, some 24 churches were built in Germany alone, and by the time of the Suppression, the Society had built 160 churches in Italy and 1,200 worldwide.

Major elements that evolved in this "way" included careful project management and limiting change orders to control costs and to speed up construction; use of the best available artists and architects within the limits of budget; and a strong focus on the pastoral and practical needs that a building or art work would satisfy. To this end, the superiors general required that plans and elevations of proposed constructions be sent to the Roman headquarters for review by their own in-house architectural consultant (the *consiliarius aedificiorum*), who was usually a Jesuit architect or mathematician from the Roman College. While some discussions about the regularization of church design occurred in the late sixteenth century, attempts to promulgate a "view book" of approved and suggested plans were never realized.

The 1st General Congregation (1558) established what might be considered the Society's Uniform Building Code. Jesuit residential and college buildings were to be *sana*, *utilia*, and *fortia*, "healthful, practical, and sturdy, neither sumptuous nor novel," but churches were specifically exempted from this regulation. Ignatius himself insisted on the need to beautify places of worship, beginning with the Jesuits' first chapel of the Madonna della Strada in downtown Rome.

The Roman Chiesa del Gesù's floor plan, though often copied or adapted throughout the world, was a simple variant of the medieval hall churches of the mendicants and early Renaissance plans already in use in Rome and central Italy. There is evidence that Michelangelo drew up sketches for a large single-nave Jesuit mother church during Ignatius's lifetime, but construction did not begin until Francis Borja became superior general and Cardinal Alessandro Farnese, grandson of Paul III Farnese who had approved the Society in 1540, endowed the project. Construction began in 1568.

Its broad, single nave with small, lateral chapels served the Jesuits' practical goals of providing clear sight lines for liturgical celebrations, a large space for extra-liturgical preaching, catechesis, and hearing confessions, and more intimate devotional spaces, whose frescoes, in the case of the Gesù, followed a thematic rhythm that perhaps echoed the weeks of the *Spiritual Exercises*. A similar program of imagery was adopted at the Michaelskirche in Munich, painted at the same time as the Gesù. While the Gesù is often cited as the prototypical Baroque church, it is important to recall that its lavish ceiling, dome, and tribune decorations were added almost a century after its construction. Until General Gian Paolo Oliva and Giovanni Battisa Gaulli (known as "Il Baciccio") began a ten-year campaign of decoration (1676–85), its interior was a largely unadorned shell that stylistically lagged far behind the more elegantly decorated Roman churches of the Theatines (Sant'Andrea della Valle) and the Oratorians (Chiesa Nuova).

The late Renaissance and Baroque periods were eras of tremendous artistic patronage. The complicated relationship between a centralized and financially strapped Jesuit leadership and the emphatic will of major benefactors goes back to the Society's earliest days. Cardinal Farnese and Jesuit General Borja disagreed about the choice of architect and the form of the Society's mother church, the Chiesa del Gesù. Borja proposed his *consiliarius*, Jesuit brother Giovanni Tristano, as architect, and preferred a flat ceiling to enhance acoustics for preaching and catechesis. Farnese imposed his house architect Giacomo Barozzi da Vignola on the project and insisted on a more elegant barrel vault in the nave. Analogous difficulties arose with Cardinal Negroni's commissioning of the Pietro da Cortona/Carlo Maratta Chapel of St. Francis Xavier in the Gesù (1660s), and Emperor Leopold II's insistence on the transfer of Brother Andrea Pozzo, the Society's most famous Baroque artist, to Vienna in 1702. Similarly, Jesuit leadership was often required to negotiate with important local artists and architects when competitions for important commissions were pending. Gian Lorenzo Bernini convinced General Oliva to employ an untried 22-year-old, Giovanni Battista Gaulli, in place of a more seasoned Jesuit artist, Jacques Courtois, for the decoration of the Gesù. In the interest of maintaining credibility and good will, superiors sometimes brought in outside counsel to advise Jesuit architects and artists on important projects like Father Orazio Grassi's design for the Church of Sant'Ignazio (Domenichino, Borromini, and Carlo Maderno) and Andrea Pozzo's tomb of St. Ignatius in Il Gesù (Carlo Fontana).

Papal patronage dominated the Roman art scene until well into the seventeenth century and absorbed the efforts of many of Italy's most talented artists. In addition, the frantic pace of Jesuit building in the Society's first century (1540–1640) and very limited financial resources made the commissioning of art a secondary consideration for the Society. When commissions were made, they frequently went to second-tier artists who were available and less expensive. The first campaign of decoration of the Gesù's side chapels was undertaken by a "B-list" of late Renaissance and Mannerist artists including Jesuit painter Giuseppe Valeriano, who also designed the immense palazzo of the Collegio Romano and the Gesù Nuovo in Naples.

The Jesuits' determination to use the arts for educational and devotional purposes was underscored in a project of Jerónimo Nadal, approved by Ignatius himself: the production of *Evangelicae historiae imagines*, an impressive volume of fine Flemish engravings illustrating the gospel readings for all the Sundays and major feasts of the year. The project was long in gestation and was finally published in 1593 with 153 engravings by the Wierix brothers. Early on, the use of printed media became a characteristic Jesuit tactic for diffusing images and promoting the canonization of its members. Borja commissioned both painted and engraved copies of the icon at Santa Maria Maggiore, the *Salus Populi Romani*, and sent printed copies by the thousands to Jesuit missions around the world. Peter Paul Rubens collaborated with the Flemish studio of Cornelius Galle and engraver Jean-Baptiste Barbé on the production of a volume of seventy-nine biographical engravings of the life of Ignatius published in 1609 (*Vita beati P. Ignatii Loiolae fundatoris Societatis Iesu*) shortly after Ignatius's beatification. These engravings, the first diffused cycle of Ignatian images, were widely copied around the world. Ignatius and Francis Xavier's canonization in 1622 led to further publications. The German

Assistancy used the engravings of Boethius à Bolswert and other artists to great advantage, illustrating the dynamics and meditations of the *Spiritual Exercises* as well as the Society's own narrative hagiography.

In Rome, the first important Jesuit fresco cycles besides those in the Gesù were found in the seminary chapels of Santo Stefano Rotondo, the Venerable English College, Sant'Apollinare, and the Jesuit novitiate Church of San Vitale. In the context of a brief paleo-Christian revival in late-Renaissance Rome, the goal of these gruesome martyrdom frescoes was to encourage – literally, to give courage to – recruits who could and would face a similar fate in the lands of the Reformation. Niccolò Circignani's brutal cycle at Santo Stefano Rotondo – some thirty large panels – graphically, yet in a strangely detached way, depicts the martyrdom of early Christian saints set against classical backdrops. The San Vitale cycle places similar scenes in bucolic landscapes: scenes of horror set in serene gardens. The English College's frescoes included images of Edmund Campion (1540–81) and other very recent English martyrs.

Educated by the Jesuits in Cologne, Peter Paul Rubens was and remained a sodalist for the rest of his life. He had visited Italy as a young man, where he painted for the Jesuit churches in Genoa and Mantua. On his return to Antwerp, he received a major commission for the Church of St. Ignatius. There he created a cycle of thirty-nine large ceiling paintings (now lost) and two heroic portraits of Ignatius and Francis Xavier. The three-year commission coincided with the canonization of the two Jesuit founders. Rubens was but one of several prominent Flemish painters including Antony Van Dyck, Jacob Jordaens, and Jesuit brother Daniel Seghers who decorated Jesuit churches and colleges in the early Baroque idiom. Given the political and artistic connections between the Low Countries and Spain, and the deep Iberian roots and diffusion of the Society in Spain, it is not surprising that the Jesuits were affiliated with some of the most important artists of the Spanish Golden Age, including Francisco de Zurburán, Alonso Cano, Bartolomé Murillo, Francisco Pacheco, and Diego Velázquez, all of whom produced devotional works for the Society.

The election of Genovese Gian Paolo Oliva as general of the Society (term 1664–81) was a watershed moment for Jesuit involvement in the visual arts. A highly respected and sought-after preacher, Oliva was a resolute leader and a man of very high culture. He communicated with and commissioned some of the foremost artists and architects of his day. He was a personal friend and counselor to Gian Lorenzo Bernini, who illustrated Oliva's sermons and who was acquainted with the concepts if not the actual practice of the Spiritual Exercises. In 1664 Bernini designed a new chapel for the Roman novitiate *gratis*, and his jewel-like Sant'Andrea al Quirinale became his only work that ultimately satisfied his exacting standards.

Oliva had resources enough in hand to propose the interior decoration and modernization of the Gesù in Rome and, through Bernini's influence, commissioned Gaulli to undertake the breathtaking and backbreaking work of turning the dowdy late Renaissance interior into a masterpiece of *quadratura* or illusionistic painting. Gaulli literally blew the roof off the center of the nave and created a luminous vision of the "Triumph of the Name of Jesus" in which light from the name of Jesus pours through an apparent window in the roof of the building, while the Magi, members of the Farnese family, and saints and angels ascend into light while heretics are cast into nether darkness. Oliva was certainly involved in developing the complex iconography of the ceiling and its attendant gilded stucco work done by Antonio Raggi.

Oliva's great act of artistic prescience was summoning Andrea Pozzo to Rome shortly before Oliva's death in 1681. Pozzo, an alumnus of the Jesuit college at Trent, had entered the Society at 23 years of age after artistic apprenticeship across northern Italy. He became known as a designer of extravagant ephemeral installations for canonizations and Forty Hours Devotions and also painted Jesuit church interiors in Modena, Arezzo, Turin, Mondovì, and (after his Roman years) Vienna.

At Rome, Pozzo's first major work was the decoration of a narrow corridor outside the rooms of St. Ignatius in the Casa Professa at the Gesù. Pushing the anamorphic tradition of Carracci and Pietro da Cortona to breaking point, he created a gallery of the founder's miracle scenes set into a dramatic yet entirely nonexistent architectural framework. Pozzo's other work at the Gesù, his pharaonic design for the tomb of St. Ignatius (1695–99), was a dazzling display of rich materiality and operatic scenography.

Pozzo is best known for his work at the Roman College's Church of Sant'Ignazio. The college's original chapel of the Annunziata, designed by Giovanni Tristano in 1567, was subsumed into the much larger fabric of the Church of Sant'Ignazio designed (at least in part) by Orazio Grassi and funded by the Ludovisi family after the canonization of Ignatius (1622) and the death of the Ludovisi Pope Gregory XV a year later. The design and construction history is long, complex, and still not entirely clear. One result of many changes – in this case due both to neighborhood opposition and to financial constraints – was the elimination of the church's tall dome. In 1684–85, Pozzo painted a canvas 17 meters in diameter that creates a convincing illusion of the interior of a (nonexistent) dome to cover the blank ceiling at the crossing where the intended dome had never been built. This work, detailed in Pozzo's two-volume "how-to" manual, *Perspectiva pictorum et architectorum* (1693 and 1700), was widely imitated throughout Poland and Central Europe after 1702, when Pozzo brought the concept to the decoration of Vienna's Universitätskirche. The treatise was quickly translated into eight languages, including Chinese.

Pozzo's nave fresco in Sant'Ignazio, the "Allegory of the Missionary Work of the Society of Jesus," sometimes referred to as "The Apotheosis of St. Ignatius," serves as a kind of compendium of Jesuit art. Deeply devotional, engaging, and certainly dynamic, it shows the interplay of this world and the next in a most dramatic and even triumphalistic fashion. Pozzo's illusion removes the ceiling of the nave entirely, and at its very apogee, a beam of light shoots from the wounded side of Christ to the heart of the ascending Ignatius, from whose heart the beam is refracted to various Jesuit saints, a mirrored shield showing the IHS monogram of the Society, and four gigantic allegorical figures representing the four known continents of Europe, Asia, Africa, and the Americas where the Jesuits served as missionaries.

The use and development of art in the Jesuit missions is an impossibly vast subject. Bailey has provided a lapidary introduction in his 1999 omnibus volume *Art on the Jesuit Missions in Asia and Latin America, 1542–1773*. In general, the principles laid out above concerning the Jesuit use of art in Europe applied equally to the missions. Art was seen and appreciated as a useful and even necessary tool for capturing the indigenous imagination, for persuasion, and for the propagation of the faith. The logic of rhetoric (*docere, delectare, movere*) and need for visual and narrative tools and propaganda caused missionaries from the time of Francis Xavier to request and even demand that first-quality art, illustrated books, and liturgical objects be sent from Europe to worldwide missions. Architectural tomes of Vitruvius, Serlio, Palladio and Pozzo, the gospel engravings commissioned by Nadal and the illustrated lives of Ignatius as well as theology books went across the globe in the saddlebags of missionaries.

An important nuance in the missionary sphere was the frequent Jesuit impulse to incorporate local vernaculars into their art and architecture. Where possible, they used local talent, most notably in Mexico where Miguel Cabrera, Cristóbal de Villalpando, and Juan Correa were frequent contributors to the Jesuit inventory of paintings. The Jesuits established ateliers from Japan to Paraguay for the training of local talent and the production of acculturated works of art. Carlo Spinola, martyred in Japan in 1622, and Giovanni Niccolò, who founded the Seminary of Painters in Japan around 1583, designed the great college Church of the Mother of God in Macau, and its craftsmen, exiled Japanese Catholics, incorporated local flora, fauna, dragons, and Buddhist clouds into its Baroque façade. The Baroque *retablo* of the Church of the Candelaria in Silang not far from Manila shows Christ, the Holy Family, and Jesuit saints with distinctly Asian features. At Arequipa, Peru, the chapel of San Ignacio is a mini-Pantheon in form, but its interior vault is overpainted with lush tropical vines and adorned by Jesuit Bernardo Bitti's haunting late-Mannerist Risen Christ. The Reductions of Paraguay and its neighboring countries produced thousands of hybrid sculptures that combined the flamboyant techniques of its German Jesuit wood carvers with the serene and even severe local idioms of the Guaraní and other tribes. Giuseppe Castiglione (†1766), a late Baroque painter, "went native" in China and learned and adapted Chinese art and techniques at the court of the Qianlong emperor, even as he created what Bailey calls "an Occidentalist theme park" (*The Jesuits and the Arts*, 344) as part of the imperial Yuanming Yuan summer palace outside Beijing.

To summarize, the Jesuits were not inventors of the Baroque but were certainly among its most fervent adopters and patrons, especially after the 1650s. Baroque sensibilities of high drama, emotional engagement, and appeal to the imagination were certainly in line with the imaginative pedagogy of the *Spiritual Exercises*, and with Jesuit rhetorical and propagandistic aims. An understanding of art as instrumental and a profound desire to edify (literally, to build up) informed the Society's aesthetic choices. Art was never seen as an aesthetic end in itself but was put in service of meta-narrative, both scriptural and hagiographic, attempting to connect both believer and non-believer with the possibility of union with God in this world and the next.

See also Architecture; Art Patronage; Arts, Visual; Bernini, Gian Lorenzo; Gaulli, Giovanni Battista; Gesù, Rome; Pozzo, Andrea, SJ

Bailey, Gauvin A., *Art on the Jesuit Missions in Asia and Latin America, 1542–1773*. Toronto: University of Toronto Press, 1999.
    Between Renaissance and Baroque: Jesuit Art in Rome, 1565–1610. Toronto: University of Toronto Press, 1992.
Haskell, Francis, *Patrons and Painters: A Study in the Relations between Italian Art and Society in the Age of the Baroque*. New Haven, CT: Yale University Press, 1980.
Levy, Evonne, *Propaganda and the Jesuit Baroque*. Berkeley: University of California Press, 2004.
O'Malley, John W., and Gauvin A. Alexander, eds., *The Jesuits and the Arts, 1540–1773*. Philadelphia, PA: St. Joseph's University Press, 2003.
O'Malley, John W., Gauvin A. Bailey, Steven J. Harris, and T. Frank Kennedy, eds., *The Jesuits: Cultures, Sciences, and the Arts, 1540–1773*. Toronto: University of Toronto Press, 1999 and 2006.

Figure 10 Andrea Pozzo: Sant'Ignazio ceiling frescoes, 1693, engraving. Photograph Thomas Lucas, SJ

Pozzo, Andrea, *Perspective in Architecture and Painting: An Unabridged Reprint of the English-and-Latin Edition of the 1693 "Perspectiva Pictorum Et Architectorum."* Mineola, NY: Dover Publications, 1989.

Smith, Jeffrey Chipps, *Sensuous Worship: Jesuits and the Art of the Early Catholic Reformation in Germany.* Princeton, NJ: Princeton University Press, 2002.

Wittkower, Rudolph, and Irma Jaffe, eds., *Baroque Art: The Jesuit Contribution.* New York: Fordham University Press, 1972.

Thomas Lucas, SJ

Bea, Augustin, Cardinal, SJ (1881–1968)

Augustin Bea, biblical scholar, ecumenist, and confessor to three popes, was born on May 28, 1881, in Riedböhringen (Baden), Germany. Although his father was a master-builder and carpenter, his parents were quite poor and could not afford Augustin's school fees. Fortunately, their son's intellectual talents merited him scholarships that funded his education.

Augustin expressed a desire early on to become a priest. During a retreat with the Austrian Jesuits in his last semester of high school, he decided to become a Jesuit. Since the Society had been expelled by Bismarck during the *Kulturkampf*, this would have meant leaving Germany. His father was reluctant to grant permission, hoping his only son would succeed him in carpentry and provide his parents with financial support in their old age. As a compromise, he persuaded Augustin to enter the diocesan seminary instead and to begin studies with other diocesan seminarians at the University of Freiburg.

In 1902 Bea received his parents' permission to enter the Jesuits. After novitiate in Holland, he studied philosophy and ethnology in Valkenburg and taught classical languages to high school students. Bea thereafter returned to Holland for theological studies, where his considerable talents became ever more apparent. Following his ordination (1912), he was sent to Berlin to pursue ancient oriental history and languages with the intention of becoming a biblical scholar.

The outbreak of World War I interrupted Bea's studies, and he was made superior of the Jesuit house in Aachen. In 1921, at age 40, he was appointed provincial of the newly established Jesuit province of Southern Germany. As provincial, Bea sent young Jesuits to German universities rather than to Rome, believing the German programs to be far superior. Three years later he was called to Rome to direct an international Jesuit house of studies and teach New Testament at the Pontifical Gregorian University (1924–28). In 1928 he was relieved of his administrative responsibilities to lecture full time at the Pontifical Biblical Institute (Biblicum), a post he would occupy for thirty-four years.

Bea was appointed rector of the Biblicum in 1930. During his tenure he served as editor of the journal *Biblica*, visited the Institute's branch in Jerusalem several times, engaged in an archaeological dig in the Jordan Valley and established the Oriental Institute. Bea's talents also led to his appointment as consultor to several bodies of the Roman Curia. His 1931 draft of Pius XI's apostolic constitution *Deus scientiarum Dominus*, which reformed ecclesiastical studies, facilitated his obtaining permission to attend the first international meeting of biblical scholars in Göttingen, which included Protestant and Jewish exegetes as well as secular scholars – a significant achievement that presaged Bea's future ecumenical involvement.

He was appointed to the Pontifical Biblical Commission in 1931 and in that capacity contributed significantly to Pope Pius XII's encyclical *Divino afflante Spiritu* (1943), which enabled Catholic scholars to utilize modern biblical criticism. Bea was appointed a consultor to the Holy Office in 1949 and became heavily involved in the preparation of Pius XII's dogmatic definition of the bodily Assumption of Mary (1950). When the Pope's confessor became ill, Bea was asked to assume this duty, a role he filled for more than thirteen years until Pius XII's death.

Bea's work also put him in contact with pre-Vatican II renewal movements in Germany, several of which promoted Jewish–Christian relations and ecumenism. By the 1950s Bea's work for the Holy See had become so demanding that he asked to be relieved of his position as rector of the Biblicum. In gratitude, Pius XII wanted to name him a cardinal, but the Jesuit General, Jean-Baptiste Janssens, opposed the idea, saying it was contrary to Jesuit vows and would provoke hostility among the curia. But when Pope John XXIII was elected in 1958, he made Bea a cardinal deacon and appointed him to the most significant role of Bea's life: president of the new Secretariat for the Promotion of Christian Unity (1960–68).

Bea played an influential role at defining moments of the Second Vatican Council, such as the dramatic rejection of the curial schema on revelation, *De fontibus*, and the eventual acceptance of the Council's controversial document on religious free-dom. Under Bea's prudent but open leadership, several other conciliar documents were brought to fruition, including those on divine revelation, ecumenism, and the relation-ship of the Church to non-Christian religions.

Bea died on November 16, 1968, in Rome.

See also Cardinals, Jesuit; Ecumenism; Papacy; Vatican II

Augustin Cardinal Bea: Spiritual Profile. Ed. Stjepan Schmidt, trans. E. M. Stewart. London: Geoffrey Chapman, 1971.

Jung-Inglessis, E. M., *Kardinal Bea: Sein Leben und Werk*. St. Ottilien: EOS Verlag, 1994.

Schmidt, Stjepan, *Augustin Bea: The Cardinal of Unity*. Trans. Leslie Wearne. New Rochelle, NY: New City Press, 1992.

Vereb , Jerome-Michael, *"Because He Was a German!" Cardinal Bea and the Origins of Roman Catholic Engagement in the Ecumenical Movement*. Grand Rapids, MI: Eerdmans, 2006.

Wicks, Jared, "Augustin Cardinal Bea, SJ: Biblical and Ecumenical Conscience of Vatican II." In Massimo Faggioli and Andrea Vicini, eds., *The Legacy of Vatican II*. New York: Paulist Press, 2015, pp. 185–202.

Mary Ann Hinsdale, IHM

Beek, Joop, SJ (1917–1983)

From an Amsterdam family with Indonesian connections, Joop Beek became a Jesuit in 1935 and was sent to the Dutch Indies in 1938 to teach in a college in Yogyakarta. During World War II the Japanese occupying forces put him in an internment camp until 1945, followed by seven months of imprisonment by the Indonesians. In 1946 he returned to the Netherlands for his theology study in Maastricht, where he was ordained a priest in 1948.

Back in Indonesia, Joop Beek worked again in Yogyakarta and started organizations of Catholic students, which became very influential. Sent to Jakarta in 1960, he set up a leadership training for Catholic students (KASBUL, Kaderisasi Sebulan) as a defense system against communists and Muslims. During a failed coup in 1965, six pro-western generals were assassinated. General Suharto was able to oust President Sukarno and to eliminate half a million communists, while huge numbers of people were taken pris-oner. Followers of Beek became influential in the army, government, and economics. At his request Suharto founded Golkar, a political party for non-Islamic middle classes and Catholics that could keep the Muslims under control and stop the spreading of Islamic fundamentalism. The presidency of Suharto (1967–98) led to great corruption and nep-otism, and at the same time economic growth could be seen. Only twenty years after the death of Joop Beek has his role become clearer.

In 2007 the Dutch scholar Saskia Wieringa wrote the political thriller *Het krokodil-lengat* (The Crocodile Hole), in which she describes the role of "Father Bron" (Beek) in the coup of 1965.

See also Indonesia

Hunter, Helen-Louise, *Sukarno and the Indonesian Coup: The Untold Story*. Westport, CT: Praeger Security International, 2007.

Soedarmanta, J. B., *Pater Beek, SJ: Larut tetapi tidak hanyut. Biografi (1917–1983)*. Jakarta: Obor, 2008.

Paul Begheyn, SJ

Belgium

In the sixteenth century, the Low Countries were ruled by Spain. This helps to explain how it was that, while a student in Paris, Ignatius of Loyola (1491–1556) made more than one trip to urban centers such as Bruges and Antwerp to seek financial support from Spanish merchants. In 1566 a long period of war for independence from Spain engulfed these territories and led ultimately to the division between a mostly Protestant north (a Dutch Republic independent from Spain) and a Catholic south (Belgium) that remained loyal to the Spanish Crown.

A Belgian Jesuit province had first been created in 1564, by Jesuit Superior General Diego Laínez. By then, Belgian Jesuits were also being sent to study and to work elsewhere. For example, in Rome, in 1563, the Belgian Jesuit Jan Leunis (1532–84) had founded the first Marian congregation of the Society of Jesus. By 1600 Jesuits and Jesuit activities were proliferating in Belgian cities such as Antwerp, Brussels, and Leuven. In 1612 Superior General Claudio Acquaviva divided the Belgian province into a northern Flemish province and a southern Francophone province. Up to the Suppression of the Society in the late eighteenth century, these provinces were important centers of Jesuit intellectual work, including education at various levels, and the publication of books, many illustrated, both scholarly books and some aimed at broader audiences. The Italian Jesuit theologian, prolific author, and future cardinal Robert Bellarmine (1542–1621) taught for a time at Leuven. The Flemish Jesuit Cornelius a Lapide (1567–1637) published detailed commentaries on Scripture. In 1640, the *Imago primi saeculi* was published in Antwerp: it celebrated the first century of Jesuit life and work. In the mid-seventeenth century, Jean Bolland, SJ (1596–1665), promoted the historical-critical research and publication on the lives of the saints that continues to be a ministry of Jesuits in Belgium to this day. Large, pre-Suppression Jesuit churches, in which preaching and sacramental ministry were the focus, can still be seen in many Belgian towns and cities. Some Belgian Jesuits also went to the ends of the earth, among them Ferdinand Verbiest (1623–88), to China.

In the early eighteenth century, the southern Low Countries passed from Spanish to Austrian rule, and this would continue to the French Revolution. After a period of French rule, and after the Congress of Vienna that redrew the map of Europe in the wake of Napoleon's defeat, Belgium was for a time reunited with Dutch territories. Since 1830 Belgium has been an independent kingdom.

The Society of Jesus had been restored in 1814 by Pope Pius VII; in 1832 Jesuit Superior General Jan Roothaan created a Belgian province that included all of Belgium and Holland. In 1849, he made his native Holland an independent province. In the nineteenth and early twentieth centuries, Belgian Jesuits resumed much of the work they had pursued prior to the Suppression, but they also adapted to changing times. As the Congo became an important Belgian colony, Jesuit missionaries followed. Belgian Jesuits also went to places as diverse as India and the Midwest of the USA. Peter John De Smet, SJ (1801–73), is the best known of the Belgians active in nineteenth-century America. Meanwhile, educational and intellectual work continued to be a focus in Belgium itself; for example, Augustin de Backer, SJ (1809–73), spent many years compiling bibliographies (still used today) of Jesuit works. After 1901, when religious orders were expelled from France, Belgium became a place of refuge including for French Jesuits.

For the past hundred years or so, several things merit inclusion here. In 1935 Superior General Włodomir Ledóchowski divided the Belgian province in two as Acquaviva had done: into a northern Flemish province and a southern Francophone province. The Jesuit superior general 1946–64 was the Belgian Jean-Baptiste Janssens. Outstanding Belgian Jesuits in the post-Vatican II era include Jacques Dupuis (1923–2004) whose work in India on interreligious relations brought both much praise from many quarters and investigation by the Vatican Congregation for the Doctrine of the Faith. At the writing of this entry, the southern Belgian Jesuit province is poised to join France in creating a European Francophone province, and the northern Belgian Jesuit province was working ever more closely with the Dutch, British, and Irish provinces. Moreover, in recent decades, Brussels, in view of its role as a center of the European Union, has become a home base for pan-European Jesuit works and offices, among them the Conference of European Provincials, and a regional office for the worldwide Jesuit Refugee Service.

See also Antwerp; Berchmans, Jan; Bollandists; Congo; De Smet, Peter John; Dupuis, Jacques; *Imago Primi Saeculi*; Lessius, Leonard; Lievens, Constant; Mercurian, Everard; Netherlands; Scribani, Carlo; Verbiest, Ferdinand.

Begheyn, Paul, Viviane Deprez, R. Faesen, and L. Kenis, eds., *Jesuit Books in the Low Countries, 1540–1773*. Leuven: Peeters, 2009.

Deneef, Alain, Xavier Dusautoit, Christophe Evers, Maurice Pilette, and Xavier Rousseaux, eds., *Les Jésuites belges, 1542–1992: 450 ans de Compagnie de Jésus dans les Provinces belgiques*. Brussels: AESM éditions, 1992.

Deneef, Alain, and Xavier Rousseaux, *Quatre siècles de présence jésuite à Bruxelles*. Brussels: Editions Prosopon; Leuven: Kadoc-KU, 2012.

Dusausoit, Xavier, *Les Jésuites dans la ville: les collèges jésuites et la société belge du XIXe siècle (1831–1914)*. Brussels: Le Cri, 2011.

Volper, Julian, *Giant Masks from the Congo: A Belgian Jesuit Ethnographic Heritage*. Tervuren: Royal Museum for Central Africa, 2015.

Thomas Worcester, SJ

Bellarmine, Robert, SJ, St. (1542–1621)

Born in Montepulciano in 1542, Robert Bellarmine joined the Society of Jesus in 1560 and studied at the Roman College. After teaching in Florence and Mondovì, he began to teach theology in Padua. However, in 1569 Superior General Francis Borja sent Bellarmine to Louvain, where he was ordained a priest the following year. In 1576 Bellarmine was reassigned to the Roman College, where he held a newly created chair in controversial theology. It was out of his lectures during this period that he wrote his famous *Disputationes de controversiis Christianae fidei adversus huius temporis haereticos* (Vol. I published in 1586, Vol. II in 1588). Bellarmine also traveled to Paris in 1589 as a theologian in the entourage of Cardinal Enrico Caetani, who had been sent there as a legate following the assassination of Henry III.

In 1590 Bellarmine returned to Rome, beginning the most famous and productive period of his life. Given his position and influence, Bellarmine became a central figure in the Counter-Reformation Church. Rector of the Roman College from 1592, Bellarmine served on the committee that revised the *Ratio studiorum*, as well as the committee that produced the Clementine edition of the Vulgate (1592). In 1597 he became a consultant to the Holy Office of the Inquisition. Then, after being created cardinal in 1599, Bellarmine's curial role expanded even further when he became a member of the congregations of the Holy Office, Rites, the Index, and the Reform of the Breviary. After the death of Cardinal Francisco de Toledo in 1596, Bellarmine became a key adviser to Clement VIII (r. 1592–1605) and, later, to Paul V (r. 1605–21). Though he had already been created a cardinal-priest, it was only in 1602 that he was consecrated as archbishop of Capua.

In his teaching and writing, Bellarmine championed the power of the papacy. He is perhaps most famous for his development of the theory of the indirect power of the pope (*potestas indirecta*). Bellarmine declared that the pope did not hold any direct authority in temporal matters, only in spiritual ones. Nevertheless, by virtue of his spiritual authority, the pope did enjoy an indirect authority to intervene in temporal matters. While Bellarmine conceded that temporal and spiritual authorities were separate, he insisted that temporal rulers were subject to the spiritual ruler – here, the pope. The pope could act for a spiritual good (*in ordine ad bonum spirituale*) that Bellarmine regarded as superior to any temporal good.

These issues came under intense scrutiny at the beginning of the seventeenth century because of two separate, but nearly simultaneous, incidents. The first erupted in 1605 when the Venetian republic decided to try two clerics in civil, rather than ecclesiastical, court. Paul V responded by placing an interdict on the republic. This crisis lasted into 1607, when France mediated a resolution between Rome and Venice. Bellarmine was heavily involved in the pamphlet war that took place during the conflict, composing numerous treatises against Venice and its supporters, and especially against the Servite friar Paolo Sarpi, who served as a theologian and adviser to the Venetian senate. The second issue was James I of England's promulgation of the Oath of Allegiance (1606), which required his subjects to swear loyalty to him and to deny the proposition that subjects of an excommunicated monarch could rightfully overthrow him or her. Paul V condemned the oath twice, and Bellarmine also wrote a letter addressed to Catholics in the kingdom. When James personally took up his pen in response to these three documents (*Triplici nodo triplex cuneus*, 1608), Bellarmine offered a *Responsio* of his own under the pseudonym Matthaeus Tortus (1608), defending the pope's universal spiritual authority. Then, in response to the writings of William Barclay, the Jesuit produced a treatise entitled *De potestate summi Pontificis in rebus temporalibus adversus Gulielmum Barclaium* (1610) to defend the pope's spiritual and temporal authority. Bellarmine was not the only Catholic author to enter these debates, but his writings do point to his dual role as theologian and polemicist.

Bellarmine remained active in curial affairs for the rest of his life, famously taking part in the trials of Galileo Galilei, Giordano Bruno, and Tommaso Campanella. Bellarmine died in 1621. Pope Pius XI beatified him in 1923, canonized him in 1930, and in 1931 declared him a Doctor of the Church.

See also Cardinals, Jesuit; Papacy; Theology; Ultramontanism

Maio, Romeo De, ed., *Bellarmino e la Controriforma: atti del simposio internazionale di studi Sora 15–18 ottobre 1986.* Sora: Centro di Studi Sorani "Vicenzo Patriarca," 1990.

Godman, Peter, *The Saint as Censor: Robert Bellarmine between Inquisition and Index.* Leiden: Brill, 2000.

Motta, Franco, *Bellarmino: una teologia politica della Controriforma.* Brescia: Morcelliana, 2005.

Tutino, Stefania, *Empire of Souls: Robert Bellarmine and the Christian Commonwealth*. Oxford: Oxford University Press, 2010.

Charles Keenan

Berchmans, Jan, SJ, St. (1599–1621)

Oldest of five children of a shoemaker, Jan Berchmans studied at the gymnasium of his home town and became one of the first students to enroll in the new college opened by the Jesuits in 1615 at Mechelen. Inspired by the example of Aloysius Gonzaga (1568–91) and the Jesuit English martyrs, he entered the Jesuit novitiate in 1616, hoping to become an army chaplain and then be martyred on the battlefield. After his first vows in 1618, he began his study of philosophy, first in Antwerp and then in Rome. In August 1621 he was selected to participate in a discussion of philosophy at the Greek College, then under the charge of the Dominicans. Shortly afterwards he was infected with fever and died of dysentery on August 13, 1621. He was buried in Sant'Ignazio, apart from his heart that was returned to the Onze-Lieve-Vrouw van Leliëndaal church at Mechelen. After his death the Duke of Aarschot asked Pope Gregory XV for the beatification of the young Flemish scholastic, which eventually took place in 1865. He was canonized in 1888.

Jan Berchmans was known for his humility and friendliness ("Frater Hilaris"), his Flemish mystical piety, and attachment to the Society of Jesus. He is often depicted smiling, with hands clasped, holding his crucifix, his book of Jesuit rules, and his rosary. His motto was: "Doing the ordinary in an extraordinary way."

All over the world churches, schools, and institutions have been named after him, like Berchmanskolleg (Munich, Germany) and Berchmanianum (Nijmegen, The Netherlands). In 1965 the Belgian mail issued a Berchmans stamp.

See also Gonzaga, Aloysius, SJ, St.

Schoeters, Karel, *St. John Berchmans, the Shoemaker's Son*. Brandra: St Paul, 1965.

Paul Begheyn, SJ

Bernini, Gian Lorenzo (Giovanni Lorenzo)

One of the founding fathers and preeminent exponents of the Roman Baroque style of art and architecture, Bernini (1598–1680) was in large part responsible for creating the enduring visual representation of the Counter-Reformation papacy and Roman Catholicism. The Society of Jesus likewise adopted, and was long identified with, the same Bernini-inspired Baroque style in the art and architecture of many of its houses of worship and in its rituals (e.g., the Forty Hours), though that choice was never a matter of universal, institutional mandate and though Bernini himself received few actual commissions from the Order. Since the whole of Bernini's career is beyond the scope of this article, what follows will focus on three aspects of his life and production: those works produced by Bernini specifically for the Jesuits; the influence of Jesuit spirituality on the artist's own faith; and his personal rapport with individual Jesuits.

Though often described as "Jesuit artist par excellence," Bernini's significant interactions with the Society, in reality, all date to the relatively short pontificate of Alexander

VII (1655–67) in which period he produced (completely *gratis*) his most substantial work for the Jesuits, the Church of Sant'Andrea al Quirinale. Before then Bernini had done no architectural work for the order, nor, for that matter, any large-scale artistic work of any kind. Before 1658 his Jesuit-related work amounted to just three items: the funerary bust of Robert Bellarmine (the Gesù, Rome, 1621–24), a frontispiece for the Jesuit-sponsored 1631 edition of Pope Urban VIII's poetry, and some unidentified ephemeral decorations for the Order's 1640 centenary celebrations at the Collegio Romano. Though the sources record no relationship between the artist and specific Jesuits in these earlier years, Bernini did have other, non-professional contacts with the Society, through his participation in the "Good Death" (*Bona Mors*) devotions and weekly Mass attendance and Eucharistic adoration at the Gesù. But the choice of the Gesù may have been in part due to its convenient "downtown" location: Bernini's own parish was Sant'Andrea delle Fratte, located next to his home on the outlying Via della Mercede and presided over by the Order of the Minims with whom he presumably also interacted on a regular basis. Bernini also had close, personal relations with various members of the Congregation of the Oratory (the Oratorians). Significantly, during his five-month stay in Paris, Bernini worshipped almost exclusively at the Benedictine church of the Feuillants, rarely even visiting a Jesuit church. Moreover, despite repeated claims by especially Jesuit historians, there is no evidence at all that Bernini ever did the *Spiritual Exercises* of St. Ignatius in any form: no contemporary source even alludes to this, including son Domenico Bernini's hagiographic account of his father's life and piety. (That legend may have its origins in the fact that Bernini's name appears in the records of Sant'Andrea al Quirinale in July 1673 as having done a three-day retreat there, but note that he was there to mourn the recent death of his wife and not to do the *Exercises*.) Furthermore, there is nothing in Domenico's detailed description of his father's piety and spiritual practices that is particularly Jesuit in nature, except his aforementioned participation in the *Bona Mors* devotions. Finally, in none of the voluminous Bernini primary sources is there even mention of St. Ignatius or the *Spiritual Exercises* in any context.

The fact that the major period of Bernini's interaction with the Jesuits coincided with the reign of Alexander VII was due to that pontiff's predilection for two prominent Jesuits, Father General Gian Paolo Oliva, who also served as preacher to the papal court, and scholar-historian Sforza Pallavicino. As official papal architect, Bernini was in the papal inner sanctum that included Oliva and Pallavicino, and a friendship developed between them, both Jesuits serving as trusted counselors to and protectors of Bernini and his family interests. Most significantly, it is Oliva whom Bernini credited with overcoming his resistance to traveling to Paris to enter into the service of King Louis XIV in 1665, a major event in the annals of early modern art history. Yet, except for Sant'Andrea al Quirinale, Bernini's Jesuit works in this period took the form of only drawings: a chalk portrait for Pallavicino and two frontispieces for Oliva's published sermons (Bernini also supplied a frontispiece for another Jesuit friend, Niccolò Zucchi). Bernini did, however, play a crucial role in the creation of one of the order's most famous icons, the *trompe l'oeil* ceiling of the Gesù: it was thanks to Bernini's intervention that Father General Oliva gave that commission to Bernini's young protégé Giovanni Battista Gaulli, who received crucial assistance in its design and execution from Bernini himself. Finally, it should be noted, Bernini's son and future biographer, Domenico, entered the Jesuit novitiate in Rome in 1671 but left before vows in 1673.

See also Baroque Art and Architecture; Gesù, Rome

Figure 11 Interior view of Church of Sant'Andrea al Quirinale, Rome, 17th century.
Photograph Franco Mormando

Bernini, Domenico, *The Life of Gian Lorenzo Bernini*. Ed. Franco Mormando. University
    Park: Pennsylvania State University Press, 2011.
de Chantelou, Paul Fréart, *Diary of the Cavaliere Bernini's Visit to France*. Ed. Anthony Blunt; anno-
    tated by George C. Bauer; trans. Margery Corbett. Princeton, NJ: Princeton University Press, 1985.
Mormando, Franco, *Bernini: His Life and His Rome*. Chicago, IL: University of Chicago Press, 2011.

Franco Mormando

Beschi, Constanzo Giuseppe, SJ (1680–1747)

Constanzo Beschi was an Italian Jesuit born in 1680 in Castiglione, Italy, also the hometown of St. Aloysius Gonzaga (1568–91). He joined the Jesuits at the age of 18 and
began his formation. Shortly after being ordained a priest, he followed in the footsteps of
Robert de Nobili and John de Brito by joining the Madurai mission in 1710. Beschi had
a profound ability to adapt to new circumstances. His quick ability to become fluent in
Tamil and master the local cultural idioms of dress, food, and social etiquette won him
a warm reception from many. He spent most of his first decade in India as a traveling
preacher, fashioning himself as an Indian *sannyasi* (a wandering ascetic). Beschi composed works of apologetics in Tamil, explaining Christian doctrine and also defending
Catholicism against the teachings of the Dutch Lutherans who had started their own
mission in nearby Tranquebar. His Tamil became so exceptional that he composed fine
poetry including the epic poem *Thembavani*. Beschi was responsible for the catechesis
and baptism of thousands of new Christians in the region as well as the construction
of several churches for new Christian communities. Beschi was, however, impeded by
disapproving kings from ministering to some extant Christian communities. While his

charisma generally helped to protect the Christian communities with which he was associated, this did not entirely prevent persecution. He was arrested and condemned to death in the winter of 1714–15 but, owing to the help of Hindu friends, he was ultimately released and continued to minister in the Madurai mission until his death in 1747.

See also Brito, John de, SJ, St.; India; Nobili, Roberto de, SJ

Echaniz, Ignacio, *Passion and Glory: A Flesh-and-Blood History of the Society of Jesus.* Vol. III: *1687–1773–1814.* Anand, India: Gujarat Sahitya Prakash, 2000, pp. 49–54.
Pillai, A. Muttusami, *Brief Sketch of the Life and Writings of Father CJ Beschi, or, Vira-mamuni, tr. from the original Tamil.* Madras: J. B. Pharoah, 1840.

Brent Howitt Otto, SJ

Biblical Studies

Situating the Jesuits within the world of biblical studies requires a careful examination of premodern, modern, and postmodern assumptions and methods of biblical interpretation. By the time Ignatius of Loyola founded the Jesuits in 1540, Gutenberg had already invented the printing press (*c.* 1450), and Martin Luther had already posted his Ninety-Five Theses on the doors of the Castle Cathedral at Wittenberg, Germany (1517). These events, to which can be added the Renaissance, the Council of Trent, and the spread of Jesuit education, provide an important historical context for understanding the Jesuits' contribution to biblical studies.

The Church's long tradition of Scripture study, which can be traced through the theology of Origen (185–254), Augustine (354–430), Jerome (*c.* 347–420), the Antiochene school (*c.* 350–450), Thomas Aquinas (1224–74), and many others, welcomed Jesuit commentators. Early Jesuits rarely deviated from traditional assumptions and methods of interpretation held and practiced by the Fathers of the Church, medieval commentators, and biblical homilists such as Bede (*c.* 672–735) and Bernard of Clairvaux (1090–1153). As Augustine summarizes this approach at the beginning of his commentary on Genesis, "In all the sacred books, we should consider the eternal truths that are taught, the facts that are narrated, the future events that are predicted, and the precepts and counsels that are given."

Since Jesus was assumed to be the center of history, the Old Testament was primarily studied for its foreshadowing of the New Testament. While different commentators might have their own emphases, methods of interpretation generally included considerations of the literal sense, the allegorical or figurative sense, the tropological or moral sense, and the anagogical or mystical/heavenly sense of the sacred texts.

Jesuits joined this traditional enterprise, sharing the traditional assumptions and using the traditional methods. Their training in classical languages as taught in their schools made many of them competent translators and exegetes. In addition to preaching on the liturgical readings from Scripture, almost all of the early Jesuits commonly gave lectures on the biblical books. For example, Francis Borgia lectured on the book of Lamentations; Nicolas Bobadilla, on the book of Jonah and Paul's letter to the Romans; Claude Jay and Diego Laínez, on the epistle to the Galatians and Laínez on the letter to the Romans; André de Freux, on one of the letters to the Corinthians and the letter to the Romans; Paolo d'Achille and Jerome Nadal both lectured on Romans.

The sixteenth century produced a surprising number of Jesuit biblical scholars who came from all parts of Europe – Spain and Italy and France, of course, but also Belgium and Portugal. A listing of sixteenth- and early seventeenth-century Jesuit biblical scholars who wrote commentaries on books of the Bible appears in the 1908 *Catholic Encyclopedia*. The work of a couple of those Jesuit biblical scholars is available for purchase even today.

Alfonso Salmerón (1515–85) was a Spanish Jesuit who is believed to have written sixteen volumes of scriptural commentaries, eleven on the Gospels, one on the Acts of the Apostles, and four on Pauline Epistles; Manuel de Sa (1530–96) was a Portuguese Jesuit who produced notes on the four gospels and provided annotations on the entire Bible. Born two years later than de Sa in Córdoba, Spain, Francisco de Toledo, the first Jesuit cardinal, wrote commentaries on the Gospels of Luke and John and on Paul's Epistle to the Romans; he died in 1596. Juan Maldonado/Maldonatus (1533–83), another Spanish Jesuit, produced commentaries on Isaiah, Ezekiel, Psalms, Proverbs, the Song of Solomon, Ecclesiastes, Daniel, and Baruch, as well as a commentary on the four gospels. Benedict Pereia (1536–1610), a Jesuit born in Valencia, Spain, produced a commentary on Genesis as well as work on Exodus, Daniel, the Gospel of John, Paul's letter to the Romans, and the Apocalypse.

Better known than those aforementioned, Robert Bellarmine (1542–1621), an Italian Jesuit, served as a papal theologian during the Council of Trent and produced, in addition to many theological writings, a commentary on the Psalms. Sebastiao Barradas (1543–1615), a Portuguese Jesuit, wrote at least two commentaries, one on the book of Exodus and the other on the Gospels. Gaspar Sánchez (1553–1628), a Jesuit born in Alcalá, Spain, published in folio form various commentaries on the Scriptures. These were later used by Matthew Poole (1624–79) in his three-volume commentary on the Bible. Luis del Alcazar (1554–1613), a Jesuit born in Seville, Spain, produced a commentary on the book of Revelation and another volume that contained Old Testament texts that he thought to be related to the book of Revelation. John de Pineda (1558–1637), another Jesuit from Seville, wrote commentaries on the books of Job, Ecclesiastes, the Song of Solomon, and the Wisdom of Solomon.

Uncontested, the most outstanding and prolific Scripture scholar of this period was Cornelius a Lapide (1567–1637), a Flemish Jesuit. He wrote commentaries on all the canonical and deutero-canonical books of the Bible, with the exception of the books of Job and the Psalms. In 1681 a major commentary appeared, published in Antwerp, which contained commentary on all of the books of the entire Bible. It comprised his work – including some of his commentaries that were edited after his death – and commentaries on Job and Psalms written by others. This achievement went through many editions and was republished in Italy, Germany, and France; it can still be purchased today.

Jacques Bonfrère (1573–1642), a Belgian Jesuit born in Dinant, was a leading commentator on the Old Testament; he wrote a commentary on the Pentateuch, one on the books of Joshua, Judges, and Ruth, and one on the books of Kings and Chronicles. Unfortunately, this latter commentary was burned in a fire at the publishing house where it had been sent to be printed. Bonfrère may even have written commentaries on other books of the Old Testament. Giovanni Stefano Menochio (1575–1655), an Italian Jesuit born in Pavia, besides writing a volume on the literal sense of Sacred Scripture, produced a volume on politics in Sacred Scripture, and another volume on economics in Sacred Scripture. Finally, Jacob Tirinus (1580–1636), another Belgian Jesuit, wrote a two-volume commentary on the Old and New Testaments that is still available. Three other Jesuits are known to have published commentaries on Scripture but, beyond their names and the approximate time in which they lived, not much is known of them: Francis Ribera of Castile (1514–?); Nicolaus Serarius of Lorraine (1555–1609), and Lorinus of Avignon (1559–1634).

And then there was silence. Because of the controversies surrounding the interpretation of Scripture during the Reformation, the Council of Trent at its first session (1545–47) declared that the Catholic Church (its Magisterium) was to have the sole right in interpreting the Bible. Consequently, little Roman Catholic biblical interpretation took place after the Council until the end of the nineteenth century. What developed in the field of biblical studies in the approximately 250 years between the mid-seventeenth century and the end of the nineteenth century took place in Protestant circles.

The Enlightenment brought its own challenges to Protestants. They who had rejected the teaching authority of the Church at Rome and clung to Scripture's authority (*sola scriptura*) were challenged by the deists and atheists of the Enlightenment and the Scientific Revolution. In an effort to respond to the challenges to a Scripture-based faith, faith-filled Protestant ministers developed scientific methods based on reason and applied them to the study of the Bible. Certain of the Bible's ultimate divine authority, they set out to 'prove' the truth of the Bible. They would find the historical route of the Exodus, discover the archaeological remains of the city of Jericho, and find rational explanations for the Bible's many repetitions and contradictions and even for its miracles. But their efforts yielded more than they could have expected. They discovered at least four possible routes of the Exodus; their archaeological pursuits showed that no such city as Jericho was destroyed at the time their biblical calculations suggested; they concluded that there were likely multiple sources that accounted for the discrepancies in the Pentateuch, which 'proved' that all five books could not have been written by Moses; they determined that the New Testament contains interpolations and that it was likely redacted before it arrived at its final form. In light of Darwin's theory of evolution (1859), it was unlikely if not impossible that creation took place within seven days. But if the Bible was 'word of man' as much as it was 'word of God,' if it contained factual inaccuracies, how could it be inspired and the deposit of revelation? By the end of the nineteenth century, the assumption that the Bible was the inerrant word of God was strongly questioned if not out-and-out rejected. And the irony was that conscientious and pious Protestant ministers had been at least partially responsible for this dilemma in their congregants. But there was no way back. People could no longer believe what they did not reasonably understand. Whatever the cause or source, modernity's reason had become an integral part of biblical study.

While Protestant ministers had been seeking to address their communities, now heavily influenced by rationalist and scientific thinking, Catholics had been attentive, for the most part, to the Church's magisterium. Still, they had not been immune to the cultural shifts affecting modern Europe, nor were they totally ignorant of the developments of modern methods of biblical study. Though Catholics did not themselves overtly practice them, the Church felt mounting pressure to respond. Several events occurred in quick succession, within twenty years, with respect to Catholics and biblical study. In 1890, Marie-Joseph LeGrange, OP, established the École Biblique in Jerusalem. Three years later, in 1893, Pope Leo XIII issued an encyclical "On the Study of Holy Scripture," *Providentissimus Deus*. Within a decade (1902), Pius X established the Pontifical Biblical Commission. Five years after that Modernism was declared a heresy. Then, in 1909, Pius X established the Pontifical Biblical Institute and entrusted it to the Jesuits. This intellectual endeavor was created to ensure that the clergy, those who would be ordained, and ultimately the faithful, would not be corrupted by rationalist approaches to the Bible. Finally, in 1910, the Oath against Modernism was promulgated. Among other things it required that those who would teach Scripture conform, obediently, to the Church's teachings and authority. It was only in 1967 that Paul VI abolished the Oath.

The scurry of activity within Catholicism was collectively an effort to stave off rationalist and scientific thinking with respect to the Church in general, but especially with respect to its biblical foundations. No one could study the Bible at the École Biblique and then proceed to teach Scripture to seminarians or priests without first passing under the scrutiny of the Pontifical Biblical Commission. Those papal representatives sought to ensure that the traditional teaching, particularly regarding Genesis 1–3, was upheld. When the Pontifical Biblical Institute was founded, its purpose was to ensure that those who studied there learned and embraced the traditional rather than the modern approaches to Scripture. Only those who had either passed the Pontifical Biblical Commission's test or, after 1928, were graduates of the Pontifical Biblical Institute were permitted to teach Scripture to clergy, aspiring clergy, and other Catholics. Moreover, almost since the Biblical Institute's founding, all its students were required to take the Oath against Modernism that required, among other things, that one "reject that method of judging and interpreting Sacred Scripture which, departing from the tradition of the Church, the analogy of faith, and the norms of the Apostolic See, embraces the misrepresentations of the rationalists and with no prudence or restraint adopts textual criticism as the one and supreme norm." No one was allowed to teach Scripture who interpreted "the writings of each of the Fathers solely by scientific principles, excluding all sacred authority, and with the same liberty of judgment that is common in the investigation of all ordinary historical documents." Such were the constraints conferred upon the Jesuits in the execution of their educational mission to teach Scripture at the time of the founding of the Pontifical Biblical Institute in 1909.

Though there is some record of the tension that existed at the Institute during its early years (Gilbert, *Pontifical Biblical Institute*), one can easily imagine the struggle of the Jesuit faculty to be both faithful to the Church and faithful as educators to the pursuit and dissemination of truth.

There is also another complication that led to tension and turmoil. The Pontifical Biblical Institute established a branch in Jerusalem. While it made sense to study the Scriptures in the land of the Bible and while the means were available to make the endeavor possible, at first it did not have papal approval, but especially, it did not have the approval of the Dominicans at the École Biblique. After all, they had been twenty years ahead of the Jesuits doing biblical study in Jerusalem. So the Jesuits were hemmed in from all sides: objections to assumptions and methods of biblical interpretation from without (the spirit of the age) and from within (from those in the Church who wanted to limit their influence). Despite objections and conflict, in 1927 a branch of the Pontifical Biblical Institute was opened in Jerusalem. It was not then, nor is it still, nor was it ever meant to be an independent institution in its own right, with its own proper academic program. Rather, it is a house at the service of the professors and students of the school in Rome as a base of operations for their studies elsewhere in the Holy Land. Toward this end it does have both a library and a museum, and students who are enrolled at the Pontifical Biblical Institute toward the attainment of a licentiate can study, as an integral part of their curriculum, at the Hebrew University, the École Biblique, or the Studium Biblicum Franciscanum.

For multiple reasons, including those cited above, the years prior to the promulgation of the encyclical *Divino afflante Spiritu* (1943) were filled with great turmoil. Pius XII issued the encyclical on the occasion of the fiftieth anniversary of *Providentissimus Deus*; it was the first official papal indication of increasing openness to modern methods of biblical study. For the thirty-five years preceding the encyclical, most official biblical study was done in Rome at the Pontifical Biblical Institute or at the École Biblique in Jerusalem, and most was highly philological. Most teachers of Scripture were Jesuits, though some were Dominicans. Then, between 1943 and the opening of Vatican Council II in 1962, a gradual shift in emphasis could be perceived. More Jesuits began to study and teach the 'modern methods' of biblical study, that is, textual and historical criticism, although the Institute's faculty for many years shied away from teaching Genesis 1–3. Ignace de la Potterie continued to cling to the premodern methods of interpreting Scripture developed by the Church Fathers. Several other Jesuit faculty at the Biblical Institute, more in line with modern French methods of biblical interpretation, promoted literary methodologies and the insights of Paul Ricoeur (e.g., Luis Alonso-Schoekel, Dionisio Minguez, Pietro Bovati, Jean-Noël Aletti).

The "Biblicum," as the Institute is popularly known, with a predominantly Jesuit faculty who are themselves mostly alumni of the Institute (e.g., Stanislaus Lyonnet, Fritzleo Lentzen-Deis, Édouard Barbou des Places, Pietro Boccaccio), remained the primary school for educating clergy in the field of Scripture. Most Jesuit and non-Jesuit graduates of the Biblicum return to their native countries and seminaries to teach Scripture. Roderick MacKenzie, Carlo Martini, Maurice Gilbert, Albert Vanhoye, Klemens Stock, Robert O'Toole, Stephen Pisano, José María Abrego de Lacy, all Jesuit graduates of the Biblicum (and two of whom were named Cardinals), have served as rectors of the Institute.

The illustrious Jesuit biblical scholars named above represent Italy, the United States, Canada, France, Belgium, Germany, and Spain. William Dalton, an Australian Jesuit, taught at the Institute while serving as the Community's superior. H. Simian Yofre, an Argentinian Jesuit who did his doctorate at the University of Würzburg, taught the prophets; Joseph Nguyen Cong Doan, a Vietnamese Jesuit, studied at the Biblicum and served from 2008 to 2014 as the director of the Institute's house in Jerusalem. Some Jesuits became experts in biblical or comparative languages rather than exegesis.

Vatican II really opened the windows to biblical study. Jesuits began to study Scripture outside Rome. An ecumenical spirit made possible the education of Jesuits at Harvard University (e.g., Daniel Harrington, Richard Clifford), Vanderbilt University (e.g., John Endres), or at any of the many Jesuit or other universities throughout the world that taught the Bible and awarded advanced degrees. While the Biblicum's enrollment from Europe and the United States has decreased, enrollment from the developing world has increased.

After the Council, in light of its document *Dei Verbum*, on Divine Revelation, Catholics were encouraged to return to the sources and begin serious Scripture study. While some turned to Catholic Scripture scholars, many, in light of Vatican II's openness to Protestants, took advantage of their history of uninterrupted biblical study. The laity became increasingly familiar with historical criticism. Meanwhile, in Jesuit circles, while a strong philological emphasis persisted, most scholarship was done using the modern methods of historical criticism originally developed in Germany.

Today the Jesuits can claim outstanding biblical scholars among their numbers throughout the world, and while many have had some part of their education at the Biblicum, that education is no longer a requirement for teaching Scripture. The Biblicum now possesses a curriculum very similar to that of most other graduate schools of biblical study throughout the world.

Finally, while most Jesuits continue to teach Scripture using the modern methods of historical criticism, a word needs to be included regarding biblical interpretation by Jesuits in the postmodern period. Rejecting the assumption that total objectivity is possible, postmodern biblical interpretation privileges the social location of the interpreter/ interpreting community in the act of interpretation. Contemporary Jesuits, steeped in their Ignatian roots (preaching, lecturing, the *Spiritual Exercises*, etc.) and sensitive to "the signs of the times" (Vatican II's *Gaudium et spes*, 4), have used and encouraged their lay communities to use their own social location as the starting point of biblical interpretation. In this way Jesuits interpreting Scripture with the Church in a postmodern world have developed theologies of liberation for particular communities.

See also Bea, Augustin, SJ; Lapide, Cornelius a, SJ; Martini, Carlo Maria, SJ; Pontifical Biblical Institute

Augustine, *The Literal Meaning of Genesis*. 2 vols. New York: Paulist Press, 1982.
Gilbert, Maurice, *The Pontifical Biblical Institute: A Century of History (1909–2009)*. Rome: Pontifical Biblical Institute, 2009.
O'Malley, John W., *The First Jesuits*. Cambridge, MA: Harvard University Press, 1993.

Alice L. Laffey

Bibliographies

The Jesuits wrote and printed books from the beginning of the Society's history; thus from an early date lists of their publications appeared. The first such bibliography was Pedro de Ribadeneira's *Illustrium scriptorum religionis Societatis Iesu catalogus* (Antwerp, 1608), but the most complete repertory of both Jesuit authors and the history of the Order for the period 1540–1900 is Carlos Sommervogel, *Bibliothèque de la Compagnie de Jésus* (12 vols. Bruxelles/Paris/Toulouse, 1890–1932). This work has been continued, but with unequal success.

Its first part – the bibliography of Jesuit authors – exists for the years 1888–1914 and 1937–77 thanks to *Moniteur bibliographique de la Compagnie de Jésus* (43 fascicles published 1889–1921 as a supplement to the periodical *Études*) and *Index bibliographicus Societatis Iesu* (20 vols. published by the General Curia in Rome, 1938–79). However, there are gaps for the years 1915–36 and since 1978 when the idea to continue the *Index bibliographicus* with a card catalogue (preserved in ARSI) was eventually abandoned. The bibliography of the Society's history (the second part of Sommervogel's project) covers the entire period of the Order's existence. László Polgár's *Bibliographie sur l'histoire de la Compagnie de Jésus, 1901–1980* (6 vols., Rome, 1981–90) and its supplements for the years after 1981 published by *Archivum Historicum Societatis Iesu* (since 2006 the supplements have been edited by Paul Begheyn, SJ) list titles published during the last and the beginning of the present century. Also the *Journal of Jesuit Studies* (founded 2014) published by Brill will include a bibliography on Jesuit history.

See also Archives and Libraries; Archivum Romanum Societatis Iesu (ARSI); Ribadeneira, Pedro de, SJ; Sommervogel, Carlos, SJ

"Breve historia de la Biblioteca de Escritores de la Compañía de Jesús." In José Eugenio de Uriarte and Mariano Lecina, *Biblioteca de escritores de la Compañía de Jesús pertenecientes a la antigua Asistencia de España desde sus orígenes hasta el año de 1773*, part 1. Madrid: Imprenta de la Viuda de López del Horno, 1925, pp. XI–LXXXVI.

Danieluk, Robert, *La "Bibliothèque" de Carlos Sommervogel: le sommet de l'oeuvre bibliographique de la Compagnie de Jésus (1890–1932)*. Rome: Institutum Historicum Societatis Iesu, 2006.

Robert Danieluk, SJ

Bishops, Jesuit

Since the beginning of the Society of Jesus in 1540, there have been over 350 Jesuit bishops. A complete list up to the year 2000 is found in the appendix of the *Diccionario histórico de la Compañía de Jesús* (Madrid, 2001). The list begins with João Nunes Barreto, patriarch and bishop of Ethiopia, and ends with No. 338, Iuliura Kema Sunarka, ordained a bishop in the year 2000. Since that listing, a number of Jesuits have been ordained bishops, including a small number during the papacy of Pope Francis (2013–). First among these was Michael Charles Barber, appointed in 2013 as bishop of Oakland, California. Among other Jesuit appointees of Francis are Alojzij Cvikl, as archbishop of Maribor in Slovenia, Donat Bafudinsoni, as auxiliary bishop of Kinshasa in Congo, and Bishop Lionginas Virbalas, SJ, as archbishop of Kaunas, Lithuania. At the time of writing, Pope Francis continues to appoint Jesuits as bishops occasionally.

Yet for Jesuits to serve as bishops was strongly opposed by St. Ignatius. When he heard that Ferdinand of Austria wanted an early Jesuit to be appointed bishop, he wrote: "We are convinced in conscience that for us to accept the prelacy would be to demolish the Society. Indeed, if I wanted to think up or imagine a variety of methods for overthrowing and wrecking this Society, one of the most effective, indeed the most effective of all, would be to accept a bishopric."

Ignatius, however, did agree to the episcopal ordination of three early Jesuits, João Nunes Barreto, Andres de Oviedo, and Melchor Carneiro for the mission to Ethiopia. This mission promised hardship without honor and benefice, and so Ignatius did not consider it a violation of the Jesuit injunction against ambition. In fact, only Oviedo reached Ethiopia, and the mission was a total failure.

Throughout Jesuit history, the main reason why Jesuits accepted to serve as bishops was in view of the need for leadership in mission lands, such as India, other parts of Asia, Alaska, and countries of Africa. Yet at the First Vatican Council (1869–70) seven Jesuit bishops (vicars apostolic) were in attendance. At the Second Vatican Council, fifty-four Jesuit bishops were invited to attend.

Highlighting several of the more interesting Jesuit bishops shows the variety of contexts where these bishops served. John Carroll, archbishop of Baltimore (#51) was the first Catholic bishop in the United States. He founded what would become Georgetown University. Leonard Neale (#63) was his successor as the second archbishop of Baltimore and also served as the president of Georgetown. Bishop Benedict Fenwick (#80) was appointed the second bishop of Boston. He founded, in 1843, the College of the Holy Cross in Worcester, Massachusetts.

Moving to the Midwest, James Oliver Van de Velde (#83) was the second bishop of Chicago from 1849 to 1853, after which he became bishop of the Diocese of Natchez, Mississippi. John Baptiste Miege (#84) was the first bishop of the Kansas Territory, which eventually became the Archdiocese of Kansas City.

Outside the United States, Alban Goodier (#138), an author of many books on saints, Christ, and spirituality, was made bishop of Bombay in 1919. Archbishop Thomas Roberts (#179) was also appointed archbishop of Bombay in 1937. He resigned in 1950 so that a native Indian could govern his diocese. Roberts dedicated himself to lecturing and writing. At the Second Vatican Council, he promoted the recognition of conscientious objection to war and greater participation of the laity in the Church. Francisco Claver (#245) completed his doctorate in anthropology at the University of Colorado and was appointed bishop of the Malaybalay Diocese in the Philippines. He resigned in 1984 but was appointed vicar apostolic of the new Vicariate Apostolic of Bontac-Lagawe, Philippines. He took a strong stand on human rights and was a foe of martial law. Alfred James Jolson (#301) was originally from Pittsburgh, Pennsylvania. After several years of teaching in the United States, Italy, and Iraq, he was appointed to the Diocese of Reykjavik, Iceland, in 1987. Also on the list of bishops, Jorge Mario Bergoglio (#316) became a bishop in 1992, and a cardinal in 2001. In 2013 he was chosen to be bishop of Rome, taking the name Pope Francis.

If a Jesuit becomes a bishop, he continues to be a Jesuit, but he is no longer under obedience to a Jesuit superior. Yet he has promised that if "I should happen to be ordained a bishop, I shall not refuse to listen to the General of the Society if he … will do me the favor of giving me some counsel."

Jesuit bishops are a rare species, in positions that contrast with the normal Jesuit way of serving the Church. Yet, especially in mission lands, Jesuit bishops have made major contributions to the foundation, growth, and stability of the Church.

See also Cardinals, Jesuit; Papacy

Aixala, Jerome, *Black and Red SJ*. Bombay: Messenger Office – St. Xavier's High School, 1968.
Schineller, Peter, "Jesuits in the Hierarchy." *America*. May 3, 2013.

Peter Schineller, SJ

Bitti, Bernardo, SJ (1548–1610)

Democrito Bernardino Bitti, a Jesuit brother, was the first artist to travel on the missions to South America. From the Italian Marche, he studied painting in Rome for five years before entering the Society. He may have painted works while at the

Roman novitiate of Sant'Andrea al Quirinale (1568–73), but none survive. Bitti was artistically trained in Late Renaissance Italy; however, his only known paintings were executed in Peru.

Bitti arrived in Peru in 1574 and worked there until his death in 1610. He spent the first eight years working in Lima. After that, he traveled extensively throughout the region, painting in Cuzco, Arequipa, Juli, Acora, La Paz, Sucre, and Chucuito. He executed individual commissions and worked with other artists. One notable collaborator/student was the Andalusian Jesuit sculptor Pedro de Vargas, who described, in a 1585 letter, working with Bitti on an altarpiece for the Church of San Pedro in Lima. Most of Bitti's paintings illustrate Christ, the Virgin, or episodes from their lives. Numerous representations of the Immaculate Conception, a subject popular in this region, survive.

Bitti's style is typical of Italian Mannerism, with elegant figures and saturated colors. These characteristics created a painting style new in Peru, and thus Bitti's talents were avidly sought. Other Italian artists made their way to South America, but few exerted his influence. Bitti is regarded as the founder of the Cuzco School of Painting.

See also Peru

Bailey, Gauvin A., "Creating a Global Artistic Language in Late Renaissance Rome: Artists in the Service of the Overseas Missions, 1542–1621." In Pamela M. Jones and Thomas Worcester, eds., *From Rome to Eternity: Catholicism and the Arts in Italy ca. 1550–1650.* Leiden: Brill, 2002, pp. 225–51.

de Mesa, José, and Teresa Gisbert, *Bernardo Bitti.* La Paz: Dirección Nacional de Informaciones de la Presidencia de la República, 1961.

Alison Fleming

Black Pope

The term "Black Pope" generally refers to the superior general of the Society of Jesus whose religious dress is black while that of the Roman Pontiff is white. The first recorded use of the term, however, was in fact not made in reference to any Jesuit but to the Abbé Dominic Sala, who played a key role in ecclesiastical affairs throughout the tumultuous events of the Napoleonic era and particularly in Rome during the imprisonment of Pope Pius VI in 1798 and 1799. Decades later, as the restored Society of Jesus rose to greater prominence during the pontificate of Pope Pius IX (1846–78), the term would be applied to the Jesuit general. The first written instance of this is found in a novel of Jean Hippolyte Michon, a French priest who anonymously published works of fiction written from a liberal perspective. In Michon's *Le jésuite* (1865), the Jesuit Superior General John Roothan returns to Rome in 1850 amid crowds that exclaim, "Long live the Black Pope!"

By the end of the nineteenth century, "Black Pope" had become a well-known appellation for the Jesuit general across the European continent. The term usually possessed a negative connotation, and it has often been used in connection with conspiracy theories involving the Society of Jesus. As early as 1892, the term would be used in the United States by the Rev. Oliver Murray, a Methodist pastor who published a 255-page work entitled *The Black Pope: Or, the Jesuits' Conspiracy against American Institutions.*

When Jesuit Superior General Adolfo Nicolás visited Los Angeles (November 24, 2009), a reporter asked him about the term and he replied: "I'm not pope, and I have no power."

See also Papacy; Superior General

Cusack, Mary F., *The Black Pope*. Seattle: CreateSpace, 2014.
Hales, E. E. Y., *Pio Nono*. London: Eyre & Spottswoode, 1954.
"Journals of the 62nd Congress, 3rd Session, of the United States Congressional Record." House Calendar No. 397, Report No. 1523, February 15, 1913, pp. 3215–16.

Vincent A. Lapomarda, SJ, written in collaboration with Henry Shea, SJ

Blesseds

The Jesuit blesseds, a larger group than the canonized Jesuit Saints, consist of 146 priests, brothers, scholastics, and novices from all continents. Almost all of them were martyrs.

Starting with Africa, there was Jan Beyzym (1850–1912), a priest from the Ukraine who cared for the lepers at Fianarantsoa in Madagascar.

In America, the blessed were mainly from South America. In Brazil, they include the forty Jesuits missionaries who were martyred when their ship was intercepted by Huguenot pirates near the Canary Islands. Among them were the priests Ignatius de Azevedo (1526–70) and Diogo de Andrade (*c.* 1531–70); the scholastics Bento de Castro (*c.* 1543–70), Luis Correia (d. 1570), Manuel Fernandes (d. 1570), João Fernandes I (*c.* 1547–70), André Gonçalves (d. 1570), Simão Lopes (d. 1570), Francisco de Magalhães (*c.* 1549–70), Álvaro Borralho Mendes (d. 1570), Pedro Nunes (d. 1570), Luís Rodrigues (*c.* 1554–70), Manuel Rodrigues (d. 1570), Juan de San Martín (d. 1570), and António Soares (d. 1570); among the brothers were Francisco Alvares (*c.* 1539–70), Gaspar Alvarez (d. 1570), Manuel Alvarez (*c.* 1536–70), Alfonso de Baena (*c.* 1539–70), Simão de Costa (d. 1570), Gregorio Escrivano (d. 1570), António Fernandes (*c.* 1552–70), Domingos Fernandes (*c.* 1551–70), João Fernandes II (*c.* 1551–70), Pedro de Fontoura (d. 1570), Juan de Mayorga (d. 1570), Brás Ribeiro (*c.* 1546–70), Amaro Vaz (*c.* 1553–70), Juan de Zafra (d. 1570), Esteban Zuraire (d. 1570); regarding the novices, they were Marcos Caldeira (*c.* 1547–70), Antonio Correia (*c.* 1553–70), Aleico Delgado (*c.* 1555–70), Nicolau Dinis (*c.* 1553–70), Fernando Sánchez (d. 1570), Manuel Pacheco (d. 1570), Francisco Pérez Godoy (*c.* 1540–70), and Diogo Pires Mimoso (d. 1570); and to these can be added a candidate, João "Adauctus" (d. 1570). In Mexico, there was the popular priest and martyr, José Ramón Miguel Pro (1891–1927).

Turning to Asia, there were Jesuits who spread the Catholic faith in Guam, India, and Japan. In Guam, there was Diego Aloysius de San Vitores (1627–72), a priest and martyr. In India, there were priests such as Rodolfo Acquaviva (1550–83), Pietro Berno (1552–83), Antonio Francisco (1550–83), and Alfonso Pacheco (1549–83) as well as one brother, Francisco Aranha (1551–83), all of whom were martyrs. In Japan, there were martyrs among the priests, scholastics, and brothers who came not only from Japan but also from Italy, Korea, Portugal, and Spain. Among the priests were Diogo Carvalho (1578–1624), Miguel Carvalho (1579–1624), Camillo Costanzo (1571–1622), Girolamo DeAngelis (1567–1623), Kyūtaku Antonius Ishida (1570–1632), Peter Kibe Kasui (1587–1639), Sebastian Kimura (1565–1622), João Baptista Machado de Távora (1581–1617), Pietro Paolo Navarro (1560–1622), Francisco

Pacheco (1566–1626), Carlo Spinola (1564–1622), Baltasar de Torres (1563–1626), Thomas Tsuji (1570–1627), and Giambattista Zola (1575–1626); among the scholastics were Thomas Akahoshi (*c.* 1565–1622), John Chūgoku (*c.* 1573–1622), Nicholas Keian Fukunaga (1569–1633), Gonzalo Fusai (*c.* 1580–1622), Gaius (1572–1624), the first Korean Jesuit, Luis Kawara (1583–1622), Anthony Kyuni (*c.* 1572–1622), Julian Nakaura (*c.* 1567–1633), Peter Sampo (*c.* 1580–1622), and Michael Shumpo (1589–1622); and the brothers were Leonard Kimura (1575–1619), Ambrósio Fernandes (1551–1620), Dionysius Fujishima (1584–1622), John Kisaku (*c.* 1605–26), Michael Nakashima (1583–1628), Augustine Ota (1572–1622), Peter Rinsei (*c.* 1588–1626), Didacus Yuld Ryoseetsu (*c.* 1574–1630), Gaspar Sadamatsu (*c.* 1565–1626), Peter Onizzuca Sandaju (1604–22), Michael Tozo (*c.* 1588–1626), Paul Xinsuki (*c.* 1581–1626), and Simon Yempo (1580–1623).

   In Europe, the Jesuit blesseds were martyrs, mainly from England and France. From England, the blesseds who were priests include William Barrow [William Harcourt] (1609–79), Ralph Corby (1598–1644), John Cornelius (1557–94), Thomas Cottam (1549–82), John Fenwick (1628–79), Roger Filcock (1570–1601), John Gavan (1640–79), Thomas Holland (1600–42), William Ireland (1636–79), Robert Middleton (1571–1601), John Nelson (*c.* 1535–78), Edward Olcorne (1561–1606), Francis Page (d. 1602), Anthony Turner (1628–79), Thomas Whitbread (1618–79), Thomas Woodhouse (1535–73), and Peter Wright (1603–51); and a brother, Ralph Ashley (d. 1606). In France, there were the martyrs of Aubenas, namely, Jacques de Salès (1556–93), a priest, and Guillaume Saultemouche (1557–93), a brother. There were the priest martyrs of the French Revolution: Jacques-Jules Bonnaud (1740–92), Alexander-Charles Marie Lanfant (1726–92), and twenty-one companions: François Balmain (1733–92), Charles-Jérémie Bérauld du Pérou (1737–92), Claude Cayx-Dumas (1724–92), Jean Charton de Millou (1736–92), Guillaume Delfaud (1733–1792), Jacques Friteyre-Durvé (1726–92), Claude-François Gagnières des Granges (1722–92), Claude-Antoine Raoul Laporte (1734–92), Mathurin de La Villecrohain (1731–92), Charles-François Le Gué (1724–92), Vincent Joseph Le Rousseau de Rosencoat (1726–92), Louis Thomas-Bonnotte (1719–92), François Vareilhe-Dueteil (1734–92), René-Marie Andrieux (1742–92), Jean-François-M. Benoit-Vourlat (1731–92), Pierre Guérin du Rocher (1731–92), Robert François Guérin du Rocher (1736–92), Eloi Herque du Roule (1741–92), Jean-Antoine Seconds (1734–92), Nicolas-Marie Verron (1740–92), and François-Hyacinthe Le Livec (1726–1792). There were the priest martyrs of the Reign of Terror: Jean-Nicolas Cordier (1710–94) and Joseph Imbert (1720–94). Finally, among the French blesseds was Julian Maunoir (1606–83), "The Apostle of Brittany," a priest. In Germany, there was Rupert Mayer (1876–1945), "The Apostle of Munich." In Ireland, there was Dominic Collins (1566–1602), a brother. In Italy, there was Antonio Baldinucci (1665–1717), a priest. And, in Spain, there was Bernando de Hoyos Seña (1711–35), a priest who was known as "The Apostle of the Sacred Heart," and Francis Gárate (1857–1929), a brother who was the doorkeeper at the college in Bilbao. There were also the martyrs of the Spanish Civil War: Tomás Sitjar Fortiá (1866–1936), a priest, and ten Jesuit companions: Narciso Basté Basté (1866–1936), Pablo Bori Puig (1864–1936), Constantino Carabonell Sempre (1866–1936), Juan Bautista Ferrerres Boluda (1861–1936), Darilo Hernández Morató (1880–1936), and Alfredo Simón Colomina (1877–1936), who were all priests, and these brothers: Pedro Gelabert

Amer (1887–1936), Ramón Grimaltos Monllor (1861–1936), Vicente Sales Genovés (1881–1936), and José Tarrats Comaposada (1878–1936).

See also Martyrs, Ideal and History; Saints

Jdel Rio, Jorge Delpiano, and Victor Gana Edwards, *Testigos de Santidad en la Compañía de Jésus*. Santiago, Chile: Manuel Sales, 2008.

Rochford, Tom, ed., *The Complete List of Jesuit Saints and Blesseds*. Rome: The Jesuit Curia, 2016.

Tylenda, Joseph N., *Jesuit Saints and Martyrs*. 2nd edn. Chicago, IL: Loyola Press, 1998.

Vincent A. Lapomarda, SJ

Bobadilla, Nicolás, SJ (1509–1590)

Born in 1509 to a poor family in Spain, Nicolás Bobadilla studied at the University of Alcalá, taking a degree in 1529, before teaching logic at Valladolid for several years. Bobadilla then traveled to Paris, where he met Ignatius of Loyola and the other companions, taking vows of poverty and chastity with them at Montmartre in 1534. After the group arrived in Venice, hoping (in vain) to go to the Holy Land, Bobadilla was ordained a priest in 1537 and engaged in the company's early ministry, preaching in Bologna, Ferrara, Verona, and Vicenza between 1537 and 1539. Although selected to go to India in 1540, Bobadilla was too ill to make the journey and instead worked in southern Italy from 1540 to 1542.

In 1542 Bobadilla was sent to Germany and Austria, where he attended seven imperial diets. Bobadilla protested the *Interim* of 1548, which granted concessions to Lutherans, so forcefully that Charles V ordered him to leave the Empire. Ignatius was embarrassed by Bobadilla's conduct, and the relationship between the two men became fraught, with Bobadilla eventually referring to Ignatius as a "tyrant." Bobadilla's issues with the governance of the Society – particularly his distaste for the manifold rules being put in place to govern it – continued after Ignatius's death in 1556, when Bobadilla protested the decisions being made by Laínez, Polanco, Nadal, and others, and he briefly managed to gain the support of Pope Paul IV for his protests. Finding himself isolated, however, Bobadilla sought and received reconciliation from Laínez. Nevertheless, Bobadilla was respected as the last surviving companion, and he continued his itinerant ministries, such as preaching and hearing confessions, in Italy until his death in 1590.

See also Loyola, Ignatius of, SJ, St.

Parente, Ulderico, "Nicolás Bobadilla (1509–1590)." *Archivum Historicum Societatis Iesu* 59 (1990), 323–44.

Charles Keenan

Bobola, Andrew, SJ, St. (1591–1657)

A missionary from Poland to the people of Lithuania, Andrew Bobola died a martyr's death at the hands of czarist Cossacks. Because of his exceptional work preaching the Gospel and sustaining whole villages in the Catholic faith in the face of pressure from fanatics representing the Orthodox Church, Bobola was nicknamed "soul-hunter."

Bobola was born in southern Poland on November 30, 1591, to parents devout in their practice of Catholicism. The future saint studied at the Jesuit school in Braniewo in northern Poland and entered the Jesuit novitiate five years later. Following the standard course of Jesuit formation in philosophical and theological study, Bobola was ordained to the priesthood in 1622.

Father Bobola spent most of his life as a pastor and itinerant preacher, traveling to communities in eastern Poland that had once been Catholic but had abandoned the faith because of an insufficient number of priests and churches. He built churches and worked among the sodalities of Our Lady; his ministry to the imprisoned and those dying of plague brought many people back to the Catholic faith. His success and charisma brought the attention and the hatred of the Cossacks, who captured him on May 16, 1657.

Refusing to submit, Bobola was mercilessly tortured to death, skin torn from his body. He was mocked with a crown of twigs, and holes were cut into his palms, both of which Bobola no doubt welcomed as a grace: to suffer as Christ suffered. Canonized on April 17, 1938, St. Andrew Bobola's body is venerated in the Jesuit church in Warsaw.

See also Lithuania; Martyrs, Ideal and History; Poland

Gallagher, Louis, and Paul Donovan, *The Life of Saint Andrew Bobola of the Society of Jesus, Martyr.* Boston, MA: B. Humphries, 1939.
Tylenda, Joseph N., *Jesuit Saints and Martyrs.* Chicago, IL: Loyola University Press, 1984.

Keith Maczkiewicz, SJ

Boka, Simon-Pierre, SJ (1929–2006)

Simon-Pierre Boka of Mpasi Londi was born on September 20, 1929, in Inkisi in Lower Congo and died on September 7, 2006, in Abidjan, Côte d'Ivoire. He was a composer, writer, professor, and skilled theologian. He entered the Society of Jesus in 1951 and was ordained a Jesuit priest in 1962. His doctoral thesis at the Gregorian University in Rome was written on the mediating role of the Holy Spirit in the revelation of Christ in the writings of Saint Augustine. He is the founder of *Telema* (*Get up!*), a theological and pastoral review that remains highly regarded in Africa. During his long tenure as director of the review from its creation in 1975 to 1998, Boka strove to incorporate the contributions of many African thinkers and theologians within the review and thereby make it helpful and insightful for the Church in Africa.

He was professor in various institutions: Lumen Vitae in Brussels (1974–91), the Gregorian University in Rome (1983–99), Hekima College in Nairobi (1984–93), Regina Mundi in Rome (1991–99). He also taught at St. Peter Canisius, the Jesuit school of philosophy in Kimwenza, Democratic Republic of the Congo, where he lived for most of his life.

A talented musician, he composed the two national anthems of his country: *Debout Congolais* in 1960 and *La Zaïroise* in 1971. It was primarily for this reason that an avenue was named after him in Kinshasa, the capital city of Congo. He was also a spiritual father to many and a great adviser to many African bishops. Among his many important publications are *Rôle médiateur du Saint Esprit dans la révélation du Christ chez Saint Augustin* (Rome, 1986); *Verso una cattolicità arcobaleno: avanti, Chiese della 11a. ora (Mt 20, 1–16)* (Rome, 1998–99; *Théologie africaine: inculturation de la Théologie: bien-fondé, enjeux, évolution et réalisation* (Abidjan,

2000); *Théologie africaine II: Jesus-Christ Sauveur, pourquoi faire en Afrique?* (Abidjan, 2003).

See also Congo; Hekima College; Lumen Vitae; Music

Luc Bonaventure A. Amoussou, SJ

Bolivia

Although Jesuits first came to Bolivia in 1572, the country did not become an independent province of the Society until 1983. The work of the province currently consists of four secondary schools or *colegios* (the most notable of which is San Calixto in La Paz), parishes, retreat houses, literacy programs and education through radio broadcasting (e.g., Radio Fides, Radio Santa Cruz), and centers for technological and vocational training. Jesuits are involved with the Fe y Alegría network of primary and secondary schools which reaches largely rural and under-served populations, as well as with grassroots organizations aimed at developing social, cultural, and economic life among neglected sectors (e.g., Centro de Investigación y Promoción del Campesinado [CIPCA], Acción Cultural Loyola [ACLO]).

At the time of their expulsion by Charles III in 1767, Jesuits numbered 152, the majority of whom were working among and protecting the indigenous peoples in the eastern part of the country (the Mojos and Chiquitos), a venture that began with the founding of the first of the "reductions" (*reducciones*) on March 25, 1682, *Nuestra Señora de Loreto*. In the level of economic and social organization, together with the artistic and architectural accomplishments of those communities, so centered around liturgical life, they were remarkable achievements, which is evident today in the Baroque musical tradition they both owned and preserved, as well as in the churches that have been restored. One must be cautious about judging the utopian idealism behind that missionary work in light of postcolonial theory. Life in the reductions was highly regimented and paternalistic; nevertheless, the extraordinary cultural achievements of the indigenous people reflect both a patient pedagogy on the part of the Jesuits and a great aptitude for the arts on the part of the Mojos and Chiquitos. The expulsion of the Jesuits proved tragic for the indigenous people, who fell into the hands of the *conquistadores*.

The Society returned to Bolivia in 1881 and resumed its connection with the descendants of the reductions. Historically, Jesuits have been heavily engaged in anthropological, ethnographic, and linguistic studies in a country that describes itself today as *plurinational* (the Bolivia Constitution recognizes over thirty languages, one of which is mojeño-ignaciano, a language created by the early Jesuits to serve as a common language among the indigenous peoples). Committed to social and economic development, many Jesuits were considered Marxists in the time of the dictatorships (1971–82); some were forced into hiding. Luis Espinal – film critic and producer, journalist, poet, and outspoken defender of the people – was killed by paramilitaries in La Paz on March 22, 1980, two days before Oscar Romero was murdered in El Salvador. Espinal's story is told in the film *Lucho San Pueblo* (2010). The province also publishes the review *Cuarto Intermedio*.

Although the town of Juli is located in Peru, the historic Jesuit mission in this Aymara-speaking region on the shores of Lake Titicaca in the Andes, very close to Bolivia, should be mentioned. The Spanish viceroy entrusted Juli to the Jesuits in 1576 (it had formerly been overseen by the Dominicans). But whereas the viceroy had in mind that they would take charge of many parishes in the region, the Jesuits agreed to assume responsibility for only a few. They feared that taking charge of too many would lead to religious isolation and loss of corporate vision, and they believed that parish work, as traditionally conceived, would compromise their availability for mission. So they agreed to accept the Juli *doctrina* (or parish) on the condition that it would be used to create an experimental community, much like the future reductions. Juli soon became a training ground for missioners; in Juli they learned the language and culture of the Aymara, and they witnessed effective community organization and economic development. Juli became a center of inculturation. Furthermore, in order to protect the indigenous population, with the exception of Jesuits themselves, Spaniards were not allowed there.

See also Acosta, José de, SJ; Fe y Alegría; Paraguay Missions ("Reductions"); Spain

Eder, Francisco J., *Breve Descripción de las reducciones de Mojos*. Trans. Josep M. Barnadas. Cochabamba: Historia Boliviana, 1985.

Menacho, Antonio, *"Jesuitas en Bolivia: 1572–1767, 1881–1981. Centenario de la segunda llegada de los Jesuitas a Bolivia."* Privately circulated.

"La Compañía de Jesús y la educación en Bolivia." Anuario de la Academia Boliviana de Historia Eclesiástica 13 (2007), 43–52.

Morales, Javier Baptista, "La Compañia de Jesús en Bolivia." *Blog de Historia de la Compañía de Jesús en América Latina.* February 21, 2008.

Pedrajas, Alfonso, *¡Lucho vive!* La Paz: Editorial Verbo Divino, 1999.

Querejazu, Pedro, ed., *Las misiones jesuíticas de Chiquitos.* La Paz: Fundación BHN, 1995.

de la Rosa, Alexandre Coello, "La doctrina de Juli a debate (1575–1585)." *Revista de Estudios Extremeños* 63 (2007), 951–90.

Torrico, Percy Brun, and Eduardo Pérez Iribarne, *Fides: combate permanente.* La Paz: Radio Fides, 2014.

William Reiser, SJ

Bollandists

Known formally as the Society of Bollandists, the Bollandists describe themselves as "a Jesuit research institute dedicated to the critical study of Greek, Latin, Oriental and vernacular hagiographic literature as well as to the history of the saints and their cults." The four-member team, headquartered in Brussels, collaborates with a scientific committee from western Europe and North America.

The Society developed in the first part of the seventeenth century following the publication by Dutch Jesuit Heribert Rosweyde (1569–1629) of the *Fasti sanctorum* (Antwerp, 1607), in which he announced an eighteen-volume collection of the lives of some 1,300 saints based on accurate reproductions of Latin ancient and medieval manuscripts. Although the project did not materialize, Rosweyde published a collection of the lives and writings of the Desert Fathers entitled *Vitae Patrum* (Antwerp, 1615). In 1630, Jean Bolland (1596–1665), a Jesuit from Julémont (Liège), went to Antwerp to develop Rosweyde's project, expanding it to include all saints named in the ecclesiastical calendars, martyrologies, and other sources.

In preparing the first installment of the monumental *Acta Sanctorum* (2,400 pp., 2 vols., in-folio, 1643), which included the January saints, the Bollandists used the historical and philological methods suggested by compatriot and fellow Jesuit Godfried Henskens (1601–81). They followed this publication with three-volume installments each for February (1658), March (1668), and April (1675), the last of which featured the first illustrations. The publication for the May saints (7 vols., 1680–88), to which they added a volume dedicated to the chronology of the popes, incorporated material that Henskens and new collaborator Daniel Van Papenbroek collected on a trip through western Europe (July 1660–December 1662). Correspondence in search of specific documents would supplement such "literary travels" in the preparation of subsequent volumes of the *Acta*. At times their research ended in censure, as when Van Papenbroek challenged both Carmelite tradition, resulting in condemnation by the Spanish Inquisition (1695, lifted in 1715), and the authenticity of Merovingian charters, earning criticism from French Maurist Jean Mabillon (1632–1707). Mabillon's *De re diplomatica* (1681; supplement 1704), which responded to Van Papenbroek's claims, established foundational principles for the scholarly fields of paleography and diplomatics.

With the Suppression of the Society of Jesus in 1773, the Bollandists moved from Antwerp to the Coudenberg Abbey (Brussels, 1778), where they stayed until its closing (1786). They then transferred operations to Tongerlo Abbey (Westerlo), where they printed Volume 6 for the October saints and stayed until the occupying French forces confiscated and sold the property, dispersing the library. Years later, after the restoration of the Society of Jesus (1814) and the recreation of the Belgian province (1832), four Jesuits were sent to Brussels (1837) in order to complete the *Acta Sanctorum*. Under the leadership of polymath Victor De Buck (1817–76) and with the collaboration of Russian Jesuit Ivan Martinov, the *Acta* began to include saints of the Slavonic countries. Charles De Smedt (1833–1911) brought further renewal with his knowledge of German and French historical criticism, compiling three *Bibliothecae hagiographicae* that provided an exhaustive catalogue of pre-1500 Latin, Greek, and Oriental literature dealing with saints. Then, in 1882, the first issue of *Analecta Bollandia* appeared, followed by the complementary series *Subsidia hagiographica* and the transfer of the Bollandist library to a new wing of the Collège Saint-Michel (Etterbeek, 1905).

In the twentieth century, Hippolyte Delehaye (1859–1941) produced critical editions including commentaries on the Synaxarium of Constantinople, the Hieronymian Martyrology, and the Roman Martyrology as well as books on hagiographical method (*Les légendes hagiographiques*, 1905), historical syntheses (*Les origines du culte des martyrs*, 1912; *Sanctus: essai sur le culte des saints dans l'Antiquité*, 1927), and monographs about the passions of the martyrs and their cults, while Jesuit linguist Paul Peeters (1870–1950) pioneered study of Oriental hagiography. With the further development of critical standards, however, the Bollandists ceased publication of the *Acta Sanctorum* after 1940, which freed them from conforming their research agendas to the progression of the calendar. In the second half of the twentieth century, Bollandists Paul Grosjean (Celtic hagiography), Baudouin de Gaiffier (Spanish hagiography), and François Halkin (editions of Greek texts) helped make the Society of Bollandists the international center of hagiographic studies that it is today. Recent projects include the online database *Bibliotheca hagiographica Latina manuscripta*, a series Tabularium hagiographicum for publishing Bollandist and related archives, and an online version of the *Acta Sanctorum*, which the Bollandists developed with ProQuest.

See also Encyclopedias; Saints

Godding, Robert, Bernard Joassart, Xavier Lequeux, and François De Vriendt, eds., *De Rosweyde aux Acta Sanctorum: la recherche hagiographique des Bollandistes à travers quatre siècles: actes du colloque international (Bruxelles, 5 octobre 2007)*. Brussels: Society of Bollandists, 2009.

Godding, Robert, Bernard Joassart, Xavier Lequeux, François De Vriendt, and J. van der Straeten, *Bollandistes, saints et légendes: quatre siècles de recherche*. Brussels: Society of Bollandists, 2007.

Société des Bollandistes. www.bollandistes.org. Accessed on October 10, 2014.

William P. O'Brien, SJ

Borja (Borgia), Francis, SJ, St. (1510–1572)

St. Francis Borja (Borgia) was born in the Valencian town of Gandía on October 28, 1510. His family belonged to the Spanish high nobility: His father was the Duke of Gandía and his mother was the granddaughter of King Ferdinand of Aragon. When he was 18 years old, he began to serve in the court of Charles V, emperor of the Holy Roman Empire and king of Spain. The Emperor's wife, the Empress Isabel de Avís, princess of Portugal, proposed her maid of honor, Leonor de Castro, as a bride for Borja. They married in 1529. As a wedding gift, the Emperor made Borja the marquis of Lombay, and the Empress appointed him honorary equerry. The Empress also made Leonor her chief lady-in-waiting, indicating the close relationship between the two couples. In 1538 the Empress died, and this event affected them very much. Borja was part of the procession that brought the remains of Empress Isabel to Granada, and it is said that when the coffin was uncovered and he saw the degree of putrefaction of the queen's corpse, he declared famously: "Never again will I serve a master who may die on me."

He was appointed viceroy of Catalonia in 1539, the highest office within the Principality of Catalonia and the counties of Roussillon and Cerdanya. It was during his viceroyaltyship that he came into contact with the first Jesuits to visit Spain: Peter Faber and Antonio de Araoz. In 1543 Borja finished this important commission and returned to his hometown, Gandía, where he took care of his properties. A devout man, he also began to write his first spiritual treatises. They were published in Valencia under the title *Six Very Devoted and Useful Treatises for Any Member of the Christian Faithful.*

Leonor died in March 1546, and it is then, when already a widower, that Borja decided to enter the Society of Jesus due to the good epistolary relationship he had with the Jesuits named above and with Ignatius himself. It seems that this decisive step was taken after he made the Spiritual Exercises under the direction of Andrés de Oviedo. Ignatius admitted Borja to first vows in June 1546, but Ignatius recommended that his entry in the Society be kept secret "because this world does not have ears to hear such an explosion."

Francis Borja met Ignatius in 1550 when he traveled to Rome to attend the presentation of the "Constitutions," and before leaving the Holy City, Borja helped to finance the founding of the Roman College. He was ordained a priest in 1551 and celebrated his first Mass privately in the Chapel at the House of Loyola on July 31. Ignatius had thought that for Borja's first public Mass it would be suitable to obtain a special indulgence from the pope for the participants. Finally, the Mass was held in Vergara on November 15, 1551, and was attended by over 10,000 people. In 1554, he was appointed commissioner of the three new Spanish provinces: Aragon, Andalusia, and Castile in addition to Portugal and its overseas territories. He combined the many trips required to these destinations with spiritual counseling, and among those who came to apply for his advice we find St. Teresa of Avila, the Infanta Juana, daughter of Charles V, and the Emperor himself, who called Borja to come to his voluntary retreat at Yuste where he used to go. In 1557 he was asked to conduct diplomatic negotiations with Portugal and was appointed the Emperor's executor.

Nevertheless, Borja did not escape from the long arm of the Inquisition. During the summer of 1559, the works written by the Duke of Gandía were included in the Index of Prohibited Books because members of the Holy Office evidently intuited in his writings reminiscences of Lutheranism when the author spoke about the redemption made by Christ. In November of that same year, Borja traveled to Portugal at the invitation of the Cardinal Infante Henrique. At the end of 1561, Borja went to Rome in response to the call of then-Superior General Diego Laínez, who had nominated him general assistant of the Society. Laínez died four years later, and on July 2, 1565, the 2nd General Congregation would elect Francis Borja the third superior general of the Order. He was 54 years old.

During his generalship the formation of novices was greatly encouraged and the opening of new colleges increased greatly, reaching the number of 163 in 1574, whereas in 1556, the date Ignatius died, there were only 50. He also enacted the first *Ratio studiorum* for the lower grades and maintained a close and protective relationship with Pius V, who gave positions of responsibility to Jesuits during his papacy. The Society of Jesus increased significantly in number, and in Rome alone, between forty to fifty individuals were admitted each year. In 1568 the foundation stone was laid for the construction of the Gesù, the iconic main house of the Order. It was also the beginning of the important and controversial Jesuit missions and reductions in Hispanic America, a territory previously reserved only for Augustinians, Dominicans, Franciscans, and the Order of Mercy. The Society of Jesus entered Brazil with force, thanks to the work of Father Azevedo. The number of Jesuits in the East Indies also increased, reaching nearly 200 men in 1570. St. Francis Borja died on September 30, 1572, after returning to Rome from a long and painful journey commissioned by Pius V.

See also Faber, Peter, SJ, St.; Loyola, Ignatius of, SJ, St.; Superior General

de Dalmases, Candido, *Francis Borgia, Grandee of Spain*. St. Louis, MO: The Institute of Jesuit Sources, 1991.

Hernán, Enrique García, *Francisco de Borja y su tiempo: política, religión y cultura en la Edad Moderna*. Valencia: Albatros, 2012.

Iparraguirre, Ignacio, "Francisco de Borja visto a través de sus biógrafos." *Manresa* 44 (1972), 195–206.

Inmaculada Fernández Arrillaga

Boscovic (Boscovich), Rogerius Joseph (Ruđer Josip Bošković), SJ (1711–1787)

Scientist and polymath, born in Dubrovnik (Ragusa) to Croatian and Italian parents (although he is also claimed by Serbs since his grandfather came from a historically Serbian district of Bosnia), Boscovic was educated in Jesuit schools in Croatia and Rome, where he received training in mathematics and physics. Made a professor of mathematics at the Collegium Romanum before he was 30, Boscovic had already embarked upon a wide-ranging program of investigations of natural phenomena that included the aurora borealis and gravitation. Jesuits of Boscovic's day could not openly embrace Newtonian physics without modification, so one of the major undertakings of the young scientist was to attempt to construct a gravitational model midway between Newton's and Leibniz's. The resulting *De viribus vivis* (1745) is an ingenious exposition of "impenetrability" which described Cartesian atoms as being without matter.

Of more lasting importance were Boscovic's researches on the orbits of Saturn and Jupiter, which earned the admiration of the Académie Française, and his essay on sunspots, the first in the history of astronomy to give a geometrical solution to an astronomical problem. Yet Boscovic never formally and absolutely repudiated the possibility that the earth was stationary, or at least stationary in an "absolute space" unlike the "relative space" posited by Newton. He persuaded the relatively liberal Benedict XIV to remove the *De revolutionibus* of Coperincus from the *Index librorum prohibitorum* and advised his successor, Clement XIII, on the draining of the Pontine Marshes. Other practical projects undertaken by Boscovic include surveying the meridian of the Papal States and recommending repair work for the Milan Duomo and iron rings to support the dome of St. Peter's in Rome.

Boscovic's most ambitious undertaking was his *Theoria philosophiae naturalis* (1758) which outlines his atomic theory and also placed great emphasis on the relations between these "directionless points" whose mutual attraction was a general function of the distance between them, represented by an oscillatory curve. In this work Boscovic distanced himself both from the Lucretian concept of atoms as solid and elastic, and also from Newtonian ideas of absolute space and time (although elsewhere he accepted Newton's gravitational theories).

Boscovic traveled in 1759 to France, in part to avoid the tensions he was encountering in Rome, where his theories were regarded with suspicion by some. Elected as a foreign Fellow to England's Royal Society during a triumphal tour of that country in 1760–61, and later made a French subject by Louis XV, Boscovic was in a position to negotiate the Suppression with less difficulty than many of his brethren. But the collapse of the Society caused him great pain, and disputes and controversies dogged him; late in life Laplace would challenge Boscovic's measurement of cometic orbits. Deprived of his post as astronomer in Brera near Milan, Boscovic became director of Naval Optics in France where he remained for nine years, producing works of applied astronomy. Knowledge derived from strictly human sources for Boscovic remained a limited and relative thing; although in contact with many of the *philosophes*, the Jesuit had only disdain from Rousseau and rejected the human-centered views of many other Enlightenment intellectuals. The feeling was often mutual: D'Alembert made considerable efforts to impede the spread of Boscovic's ideas in France. The desire of many *philosophes* to defeat all things Jesuit also added to Boscovic's troubles.

Boscovic's later years were darkened by depression and failing health, which found the climate of France inimical. His reputation waning, he returned to Italy and, lapsing eventually into a fearful and even suicidal state, died there three years later. His funeral was sparsely attended and today his grave is unknown.

In addition to his scientific writings, Boscovic published an account of his travels in eastern Europe and the Balkans, undertaken in 1762–63. He was one of the last major Jesuit scientist-poets writing in Latin, devoting decades to the completion of *De solis ac lunae defectibus*, a treatise on eclipses, and, like many of his Jesuit contemporaries, produced devotional poetry. His correspondence with figures such as Euler survives but remains unpublished, and thus his precise role in the intellectual life of late eighteenth-century Europe has yet to be ascertained. The lunar crater Boscovich is named after him.

See also Astronomy; Science

Gill, Henry Vincent, *Roger Boscovich, SJ (1711–1787): Forerunner of Modern Physical Theories*. Dublin: M. H. Gill and Son, 1941.

Hill, Elizabeth, "Biographical Essay." In Lancelot Law Whyte, ed., *Roger Joseph Boscovich, SJ*. New York: Fordham University Press, 1961, pp. 17–101.

Mlikotin, Anthony M., "Roger Boskovich's *Theoria Philosophiae Naturalis* and the Rise of Modern Philosophy." *Journal of Croatian Studies* 28/29 (1987–88), 54–64.

Wolff, Larry, "Boscovich in the Balkans: A Jesuit Perspective on Orthodox Christianity in the Age of Enlightenment." In John O'Malley, Gauvin A. Bailey, Steven J. Harris, and T. Frank Kennedy, eds., *The Jesuits II: Cultures, Sciences, and the Arts, 1540–1773*. Toronto: University of Toronto Press, 2006, pp. 738–57.

Paul Shore

Boston College

Founded in 1863, Boston College (BC) is one of the twenty-eight Jesuit colleges and universities in the USA. Though not the oldest (it ranks eleventh by order of founding), it is one of the largest, wealthiest, and, by any reckoning, most prestigious among them, and indeed among all American Catholic institutions of higher education. Yet, its origins were humble, and its academic and financial status relatively undistinguished and at times precarious until the late twentieth century. Together with its affiliated preparatory school (BC High School, separately incorporated in 1927), BC had its beginnings in the Irish Catholic working-class neighborhood of the South End as a small, non-residential college. The idea of founding such a college had been born in the 1840s and, after fits and starts lasting some twenty years due to obstacles posed by financing and an anti-Catholic legislature, it finally obtained a charter from the Commonwealth of Massachusetts in 1863, enrolling an inaugural class of twenty-two boys. By 1900 that number had reached 500. Then and until the late twentieth century (when the college became coeducational [1970] and began attracting a more diverse applicant pool), its student population was composed predominantly of the sons and grandsons of local Irish Catholic immigrants.

By 1908 the school had grown sufficiently in size, status, and ambition to warrant a move from its cramped South End location, and in that year its president, Thomas Gasson, SJ, purchased the Amos Adams Lawrence farm in what is now the wealthy, attractive suburb of Chestnut Hill, 6 miles west of city center. Gasson also commissioned a campus master plan in elegant English Gothic style from architect Charles Donagh Maginnis. Though finances made it possible to construct only a few of the twenty planned buildings, this core collection of Maginnis architectural masterpieces continues to set an impressive tone for the entire campus. By the early 1920s the newly expanded campus and academic reputation enabled the school to expand its institutional structure as well: to the undergraduate liberal arts college were added in this decade the Graduate School of Arts and Sciences, the Law School, and what is now known as the Woods College of Advancing Studies; soon after came the Graduate School of Social

Work, the Carroll School of Management, the Connell School of Nursing, and the Lynch School of Education. In 2008 the university added a further graduate faculty by absorbing the former national Jesuit theologate, the Weston Jesuit School of Theology, renamed the School of Theology and Ministry. The expansion of its academic and non-academic divisions necessitated a further expansion of its campus, which in 1974 was notably increased by the purchase of the 40-acre property of the former Newton College of the Sacred Heart, 1.5 miles west of the main campus. In 2004 came the purchase of 65 acres formerly occupied by the Archdiocese of Boston, just opposite the main campus in the adjacent Brighton neighborhood of Boston. Currently, the various campus properties comprise a total of some 335 acres.

Unfortunately, for most of its history until the early 1980s, BC's academic ambitions and development, though guided by hard-working, devoted Jesuits, were never matched by a sufficiently robust financial growth nor sufficiently professional executive leadership. The school's ever precarious institutional status reached a crisis point in the early 1970s when the school found itself on the verge of bankruptcy, with $30 million in debt and an endowment of less than $6 million. Fortunately in 1972 J. Donald Monan, SJ, the most capable financial and academic administrator in the school's history, assumed the university presidency and through a series of bold, astute measures (which included legal separation from the Society of Jesus) rescued the school from its dire straits slowly but surely over the course of his twenty-four-year tenure, aided by a new generation of generous trustees and the university's newly galvanized, loyal alumni. The new foundation of financial stability achieved during the Monan years and strengthened during the tenure of his successor, William P. Leahy, SJ (assumed office in 1996), paved the way for the university's remarkable rise in academic quality and national prestige. This rise was also helped to no small degree by the dramatic new success of the school's football and other athletic programs, as well as by its highly desirable location in the culturally rich Boston metropolitan area. According to the national polls, for the past decade the university has consistently ranked among the top forty US universities (usually placed in the low thirties by the *US News and World Report*). Its endowment (as of May 2014) stood at $2.1 billion while its now internationalized student population has reached 14,400 (9,100 of whom are undergraduates). The ratio of number of applicants to available undergraduate seats now classifies BC in the same highly competitive category as the Ivy League universities.

See also AJCU; College of the Holy Cross; United States of America; Universities, 1773–Present

Donovan, Charles, *History of Boston College: From the Beginnings to 1990*. Boston, MA: University Press of Boston College, 1990.
O'Connor, Thomas H., *Ascending the Heights: A Brief History of Boston College from Its Founding to 2008*. Boston, MA: Linden Lane Press at Boston College, 2008.

Franco Mormando

Bouyges, Maurice, SJ (1878–1951)

Born in Aurillac, France, Bouyges entered the Jesuit order in 1897 and was sent to Beirut for his first eleven years of training. There he acquired a mastery of Arabic as well as a good grasp of Syriac and Hebrew along with some Geez and Akkadien. He did his studies of philosophy and theology in Jersey and France, and during that time his provincial asked him to undertake a critical edition of the Arab philosophers who had been translated into Latin in the medieval period. After serving as librarian in Beirut, he began in 1926 with a visit to the libraries of Europe to collect the manuscripts and publications required for his critical work. To make critical editions of the Arabic texts, their medieval Latin translations, and to offer a French translation of these works was a project for a committee, but Bouyges was not of a cooperative temperament and consequently achieved only part of his project. He did edit several works of al-Ghazzali, al-Farabi, and Ibn Sina (Avicenna) in the series *Bibliotheca Arabica Scholasticorum* published by the Jesuits at Beirut (l'Imprimerie catholique now *Dar el-Machreq*).

See also Lebanon; Middle East

Jalabert, Henri, *Jésuites au Proche Orient*. Beirut: Dar el-Machreq, 1987.

John Donohue, SJ

Brazil

The landing of six Jesuits led by Fr. Manuel da Nóbrega at the Bahia de Todos os Santos on March 29, 1549, together with the first governor-general of Brazil, Tomé de Souza, marked the first attempt at systematic evangelization in Brazil.

Semi-nomadic groups that practiced a rudimentary agriculture and depended on hunting and fishing occupied the jungle-covered territory. Portuguese settlers were already exploiting the riches of the land, living in tiny villages along the coast. The Brazilian mission belonged to the province of Portugal until 1553, when it was designated as an independent province.

The Jesuits developed their apostolic activity with the approval and under the protection of the colonizing power. They accepted slavery as an inevitable aspect of the Portuguese colonial project. The missionaries resorted to the colonial authorities both to gather the natives into villages under the fathers' guidance and to defend them from slave hunters. Because of the nomadism of the native groups, the settlements – known as reductions – seemed an indispensable requirement for their conversion to the Christian faith. Christianizing the natives implied imposing on them European customs and morals.

The Jesuits opposed ritual anthropophagy and polygamy. In the missionaries' view, the natives' conversion justified both the immense sacrifices made by the Jesuit missionaries and the use of force whenever persuasion was not enough.

In 1556, and under the influence of the newly published *Constitutions*, the Jesuits began opening schools for the reduction children. At the end of the seventeenth century, Fr. Alexandre Gusmão began opening boarding schools. Funded by the Crown, the colleges taught free of charge. Besides elementary education, they gave systematic courses of humanities, sciences, philosophy, and, in the case of Bahia, Rio de Janeiro, and Maranhão, also theology. The Portuguese Crown, however, denied Jesuit colleges the permission to grant university degrees or to print books.

Since 1575, the provincial had a boat. A little afterwards it was fitting for the Jesuits to have their own means of transportation. The building of small boats, which had begun in Bahia in the sixteenth century, spread to the farms to offer greater ease to transport

Figure 12 Igreja de Jesus, Salvador (Bahia), Brazil, on the occasion of World Youth Day, 2013. Photograph Gregory Lynch, SJ

timber. At the beginning of the eighteenth century, the Society had at their disposal a fleet of seven ships.

Besides ship building, the timber industry was also necessary to build churches and colleges. The carpenters' workshops, joinery, and sculpture-making reached their peak between the second half of the seventeenth century and the first quarter of the eighteenth century, the period of the greatest Jesuit constructions in Brazil. The building of monumental churches led to the establishment of fine art workshops in the colleges of Bahia, Pará, and Maranhão.

The productive farms transformed cassava into flour, cotton into cloth, cane into sugar and brandy, cattle into food staples and into the tanning industry. Quinta do Tanque, in the town of Bahia, was an experimental agricultural station where plants from four continents (America, Europe, Africa, and Asia) were grown.

The study of native languages, mainly Tupi, was always highly regarded by the priests in Brazil, and they insisted on their learning as an evangelization tool, authoring several dictionaries and grammars: José de Anchieta, *Arte de gramatica da língua mais usada na costa do Brasil* (1595); Leonardo do Vale, *Vocabulário na língua brasílica* (1591). Besides Tupi, the language of Brazil, Vieira also encouraged the study of the language of Angola – Pedro Dias, *A arte da língua de Angola* (1697) – and of languages specific to the Amazon region – José Vidigal, *Caderno da doutrina pela língua dos Manaos* (1740).

The Jesuit Brazilian mission came to an end as a result of King Joseph I's law of September 3, 1759, which banned the Society from Portugal and its dominions, confiscating its houses and assets. The Society returned to Brazil in 1843, by means of Spanish

Jesuits expelled from Argentina. From 1858 onwards, there arrived German and Italian Jesuits. From 1911, the expelled Portuguese Jesuits assumed responsibility for a mission in the north and northeast of Brazil.

The Jesuits devoted themselves to the educational apostolate, the instruction of the clergy, to retreats, to associations of Ignatian character, to the intellectual apostolate, to the evangelization of the natives, and to initiatives on behalf of Japanese immigrants.

The creation of the Conference of Provincials of Brazil in 1973 encouraged interprovincial cooperation.

See also Anchieta, José de, SJ, St.; Nóbrega, Manuel da, SJ; Portugal

Leite, Serafim, *Artes e ofícios dos jesuítas no Brasil (1549–1760)*. Lisbon/Rio de Janeiro: Edições Brotéria, 1953.
    Breve história da Companhia de Jesus no Brasil (1549–1760). Braga: Edições Brotéria, 1965.
    História da Companhia de Jesus no Brasil. 10 vols. Lisbon/Rio de Janeiro: Civilização Brasileira, 1938–1950.
Mondoni, Danilo, *Os expulsos voltaram: os jesuítas novamente no Brasil (1842–1874)*. São Paulo: Edições Loyola, 2014.

Danilo Mondoni, SJ

Brébeuf, Jean de (1593–1649)

See Canadian/North American Martyrs

Brito, John de, SJ, St. (1647–1693)

John de Brito was a Portuguese Jesuit of high birth and a former courtier of King John IV. He desired to be a missionary to India and entered the Society of Jesus in 1662. He sailed for India in 1673 with seventeen companions, thirteen of whom died during the voyage. Unlike some of his Portuguese forebears, Brito distinguished himself, much as the Italian Jesuits had done in India, by carefully attempting to inculturate Christianity to the context.

Upon arrival in Goa, he completed his theological training before setting out the following year for the Madurai mission. Like Robert de Nobili before him, Brito fashioned himself in the practices and attire of a Hindu *sannyasi* and became fluent in Tamil. Unlike Nobili, who was a guru to whom people flocked, Brito was a roving missionary who preached throughout the five ancient kingdoms of Vellore, Jingi, Tanjore, Madura, and Marava. He was responsible for many conversions to Christianity, including people of high birth. The future of the Madurai mission came into question due to limited manpower and opposition by some potentates.

While the mission and Brito himself were successfully defended in front of the provincial, a period of persecution commenced. In 1686 Brito was expelled from the kingdom of Marava and sent back to Europe as procurator for the mission. Having vowed to die in India, he returned in 1690. Brito was ultimately martyred after baptizing Thadya Thevar, a man of noble standing. One of the wives he had dismissed after converting complained to her relative, King Ranganatha Thevar, who had Brito beheaded on February 4, 1693. Pope Pius XII canonized Brito in 1947.

See also Beschi, Constanzo Giuseppe, SJ; India; Martyrs, Ideal and History; Nobili, Roberto de, SJ

Nevett, Albert, *John de Britto and his Times*. Anand, India: Gujarat Sahitya Prakash, 1980.
Echaniz, Ignacio, *Passion and Glory: A Flesh-and-Blood History of the Society of Jesus*. Vol. II: *1581–1687*. Anand, India: Gujarat Sahitya Prakash, 2000, pp. 201–14.

Brent Howitt Otto, SJ

Broët, Paschase, SJ (*c.* 1500–1562)

Along with Jean Codure and Claude Jay, Paschase Broët is what John Padberg has deemed one of three "forgotten founders" of the Society of Jesus. After joining the small group of companions in 1536, Broët would hold many important roles in the Society, and his magnanimity and availability for mission made him an early exemplar of the Jesuit charism.

Born in or around 1500 in the Picardy region of France, Broët, like Codure, encountered Ignatius and his companions at the University of Paris where Peter Faber served as his spiritual director. In 1536 he, along with Codure, bound themselves by the same vows as the others. With this act, the group of ten original companions was complete.

The group had vowed to place themselves at the service of the Pope, and Broët was the first to receive a direct mission. In 1539 Paul III sent him to Siena to settle a controversy among Benedictine nuns. Afterwards, Broët was sent as nuncio to Ireland, but the mission to bring back the faithful proved impossible, and Broët returned to Rome only a month after arriving.

Ignatius was impressed by Broët and appointed him first provincial of Italy in 1551 until his appointment as provincial of France in 1552. His ten years in France proved difficult and long as he spent much time convincing suspicious members of the Parlement to grant legal recognition to the Society of Jesus there. The Parlement relented in 1562, the year of Broët's death, but not before Broët had laid the foundation for apostolates that would flourish until the Suppression.

See also Codure, Jean, SJ; France; Italy; Jay, Claude, SJ

O'Malley, John W., *The First Jesuits*. Cambridge, MA: Harvard University Press, 1993.
Padberg, John W., "The Three Forgotten Founders of the Society of Jesus." *Studies in the Spirituality of Jesuits* 29, 2 (March 1997), 1–45.

Keith Maczkiewicz, SJ

Brothers

Brothers, also known as temporal coadjutors, are Jesuits who participate in the mission of the Society of Jesus. What makes brothers unique in the Society of Jesus is that they serve without seeking priestly ordination. Like spiritual coadjutors, brothers do not profess a solemn fourth vow of obedience with regard to mission. Historically, brothers made up roughly one-third of the membership of the Society of Jesus, although in recent years their numbers have fallen below 10 percent.

The first official mention of brothers in the Society of Jesus occurs in the revised *Formula of the Institute* of 1550. In the early years, brothers were laymen, often skilled in a trade, who sought admission to the Society of Jesus. Within the Society, their role was "to exercise themselves in all the low and humble services which are enjoined upon them, although they may be employed in more important matters in accordance with the talent God may have given them." While many brothers served the ordinary day-to-day needs of Jesuit houses, brothers also played an essential role in establishing the early institutions of the Society. For example, a number of the early Jesuit churches and houses were designed and built by brothers who had been architects and artists before becoming Jesuits. Perhaps the best-known examples are the frescoes on the ceilings of the Church of St. Ignatius in Rome and on the corridor outside Ignatius's rooms, both of which were designed and painted by the Jesuit brother Andrea Pozzo.

With time, however, the status of brothers within the Society shifted. In the *Constitutions*, for example, brothers are enjoined not "to seek more learning than [they] had when [they] first entered [the Jesuits]." Fifty years later, however, the Society's attitude had shifted and in 1616 a harsher rule came into force: "Let no one of those who are admitted for domestic service learn either to read or write, or if he has any knowledge of letters, acquire more; and let no one teach him without leave of the General." This distinction between priests and brothers became even more pronounced after the restoration of the Society of Jesus in 1814. In the restored Society, the brothers were the domestic servants of the Jesuit community who labored out of sight. Thus, while recognized for their holiness, the brothers were not the social equals of priests.

This social distinction ("grades") was also reflected in both the selection and the formation of Jesuits. Up through the 1960s, theological studies and ordination to the priesthood required a working knowledge of the Latin language. Men applying to the Society of Jesus who had already learned some Latin would be directed to become priests; those with less education were either turned away or told to become brothers. Once accepted, the brother novices would begin to learn how to become tailors, cooks, and the like, while the scholastic novices, destined to become priests, would spend their time on spiritual reading and improving their Latin. Thus, there was not only a social distinction but also a very real difference in education between the brothers and the priests. After formation, the practice of grades continued into the Jesuit communities themselves where brothers and priests lived almost parallel lives, with separate areas for socializing and often separate tables for meals.

By the mid-twentieth century, however, the life of the brother began to change for the better. First, the 27th and 30th General Congregations loosened and then removed the prohibition on the brothers' receiving additional education. Then, in 1966, the 31st General Congregation promulgated a revolutionary decree on Jesuit brothers. Recognizing the historical injustices that had been imposed on them, this decree ordered three important changes to the brothers' lives. First, it explicitly defined the life of the brother to have a full share in the apostolic life of the Society of Jesus. Second, it encouraged superiors to assign brothers tasks for which they showed a natural talent, even if they were not jobs typically held by brothers. Finally, it required that brothers should receive at least some spiritual and theological education. These changes were then confirmed and extended by subsequent General Congregations, which declared brothers to be full co-workers in the mission of the Society of Jesus.

Today, as in the time of St. Ignatius, brothers are once again integrated into the life of the Society of Jesus and are free to receive any mission the Society asks of them except for those that require priestly ordination. Jesuit brothers, for example, now serve as university professors, spiritual directors, business and property managers, astronomers, directors of vocations, and school presidents, as well as in the more traditional tasks of running Jesuit communities. In this way the brothers continue to live out Ignatius's vision of men whose lives are dedicated to the service of the Society of Jesus and its mission.

See also Coadjutor, Temporal and Spiritual; Grades; Pozzo, Andrea, SJ; Priesthood

The Constitutions of The Society of Jesus and Their Complementary Norms. Ed. John W. Padberg. St. Louis, MO: The Institute of Jesuit Sources, 1996.

Padberg, John W., Martin D. O'Keefe, and John L. McCarthy, eds., *For Matters of Greater Moment: The First Thirty Jesuit General Congregations.* St. Louis, MO: The Institute of Jesuit Sources, 1994.

Rehg, William, "The Value and Viability of the Jesuit Brother's Vocation: An American Perspective." *Studies in the Spirituality of Jesuits* 40, 4 (2008), 1–38.

Jonathan Stott, SJ

Browne, Francis, SJ (1880–1960)

Frank Browne was an Irish Jesuit who took over 42,000 photographs over a sixty-year period, in twenty-eight countries. While the vast majority of his photographs were not printed in his lifetime, those that were – largely the last photographs of the Titanic – were seen by a wide audience. In addition to his role in the tradition of Jesuit artists, he was also a highly decorated military chaplain in the Irish Guards during World War I.

Browne's life as a photographer began at his high school graduation, when his uncle, Robert Browne, bishop of Cloyne, gave him a camera. Browne set off for Europe and captured images of France, Italy, and Switzerland. Upon his return to Ireland, he entered the Jesuit novitiate at Tullabeg and took his first vows in September 1899. In 1902 he completed his education at the Royal University of Dublin and returned to Italy to study philosophy at Chieri (near Turin). While he had been required to give up his camera upon entering the novitiate and no photographs exist from those years, he began taking photographs again in Italy. On summer holidays, he traveled around examining art in northern Italy, notably Florence and Venice, and studying aspects of artistic composition to improve his own work.

Many of Browne's significant photographs were the result of being in the right place at the right time; he had unusual opportunities to capture moments in history through his photography. In 1909 Browne's uncle Robert took him on a summer trip to Rome, where his sister Mary, a nun, worked in the papal household. She was able to arrange a visit with Pope Pius X, who allowed Browne to take his photograph. Three years later his uncle arranged for his passage on the maiden voyage of the Titanic, from Southampton to Cobh (Queenstown). Browne took many photographs of his voyage, from recording passengers on the platform of Waterloo station on the morning of April 10, 1912, to the ship pulling away from the harbor in Queenstown on the afternoon of April 11, after Browne had disembarked. He captured many people and spaces on board, including the only known photograph of the Marconi room

Figure 13 Francis Browne, SJ: Last photograph of the *Titanic*, as the ship sailed away from Queenstown, April 11, 1912. Photograph © Davison & Associates

on the ship. Browne met an American couple who offered to pay his fare to travel on the ship to New York with them, and his fare to return home, in order to enjoy his company. Browne wired his provincial in Dublin to ask permission to stay aboard and received a response that said simply "GET OFF THAT SHIP – PROVINCIAL." E. E. O'Donnell, in his book on Browne's Titanic voyage, noted, "In later years, Frank Browne used to say that it was the only time that Holy Obedience had saved a man's life!" (40). After the sinking of the Titanic, Browne's photographs appeared on the front pages of newspapers all over the world, and his shot of the ship departing for the Atlantic is one of the last images of it ever captured.

Having survived the Titanic disaster, Browne returned to his studies in Dublin and was ordained in 1915. He joined the First Battalion of the Irish Guards as a military chaplain in 1916 and served on the front lines, being wounded five times. His bravery was heralded and he won numerous awards, including the *Croix de Guerre*. He continued to take photographs during the war and purchased a new camera in Germany in 1919. After the war he completed his tertianship and took his final vows in 1921. Browne suffered numerous problems with his health due to his war injuries: his lungs especially troubled him as a result of gassing. In 1924 his doctors recommended that he move to a drier and warmer climate, and he departed for Australia. He took thousands of photographs in Australia, and on the voyage there and back, in Asia, the Middle East, and Africa. After his return to Dublin, he spent years photographing Ireland. He became a member of the Photographic Society of Ireland, the Dublin Camera Club, and the vice president of the Irish Salon of Photography. He also photographed extensively in

England, being commissioned by the Church of England to photograph numerous churches prior to World War II.

Prior to his death in 1960, Browne completed a meticulous cataloging of his photographs, including lists of the different places, people, and types of photos he had taken. Despite his famed photographs of the Titanic, his later photographs were not printed or published. A trunk filled with his carefully labeled negatives was put in storage after his death, and forgotten about for decades. The trunk was rediscovered by Father O'Donnell in 1986, who has since published great numbers of the photographs and revived interest in Browne's work. As a result, all of the negatives were conserved before they deteriorated and have therefore been preserved.

See also Photography

Davison, David, and Edwin Davison, *Frank Browne: A Life through the Lens*. New Haven, CT: Yale University Press, 2014.

O'Donnell, E. E., *Father Browne's First World War*. Dublin: Messenger Publications, 2014.
    Father Browne's Titanic Album: A Passenger's Photographs and Personal Memoir. Dublin: Messenger Publications, 2011.

Alison Fleming

Brzozowski, Tadeusz, SJ (1749–1820)

Born to Polish parents in Koenigsberg, East Prussia, on October 21, 1749, Thaddeus Brzozowski entered the novitiate in 1765. After the Suppression, he completed studies in Vilnius, was ordained in 1775, and taught at Minsk and Polotzk. A well-known preacher, he also translated several works into Polish, including the *Dictionnaire philosophique de la religion*, by Claude-Adrien Nonnotte. In 1797, he was named Secretary of the Society and served in this capacity for three superiors of the Society in Russia: Gabriel Lenkiewicz, Franciszek Kareu, and Gabriel Gruber; the last two, at the direction of Pius VII, had been designated as generals. At the regional council at Polotzk in 1805, Brzozowski was elected to succeed Gruber and held office in the partially restored Society until 1814; thereafter, he served as the nineteenth general of the Society until his death on February 5, 1820.

Under complicated circumstances before 1814, Brzozowski faced difficult challenges. He had to cultivate the support of the Russian court for the Society's educational and pastoral projects in an Orthodox country where Jesuits' presence as educators was welcome but their identity as Roman Catholics rendered them somewhat suspect. He had to attend to pleas from religious and secular rulers around the world to take advantage of new opportunities being opened to the Society by Pius VII, and to harmonize an increasingly diverse group of Jesuits in Russia. After universal restoration in 1814, the challenge was to direct the Society from within Russia, since Czar Alexander I withheld permission to move the headquarters to Rome.

As general during the final years of partial restoration, Brzozowski supported the revival of the Society, gradually broadening and extending its work in Europe and across the Atlantic. To the United States, he sent Anthony Kohlmann and Giovanni Grassi, among others, to provide internal leadership and invigorate the educational apostolate at Georgetown. Within Russia, Jesuits expanded their work as far as Siberia and worked with German immigrants at Saratov on the Volga. From a distance, Brzozowski also supervised the work of Jesuits in Italy and England. His leadership followed a fixed formula: "Everything should be fitting, as reason, the Institute, good order, and the glory of God requires." Responding to Pius VII on behalf of the Society after issuance of *Sollicitudo omnium ecclesiarum*, Brzozowski offered a thank-you gift of 2,000 Masses for the Pope's intentions and prompted Jesuits' observance of August 7 thereafter as a day of remembrance and gratitude.

Until 1815 he worked in St. Petersburg, where the czar had allowed Jesuits to open an academy in 1800. There he used his linguistic talents and engaging personality to foster the affairs of the Society, whose schools were popular with the nobility. In 1811 the Jesuit college at Polotzk was raised to the rank of a university. The following year, Jesuits rendered material and pastoral aid to wounded soldiers during the Napoleonic invasion. However, the Society's prestige in Russia declined after 1814. Brzozowski clashed with his one-time friend, Prince Aleksandr Golitzyn, head of the Ministry of Spiritual Affairs and Public Education, who was disturbed that his nephew, a student at the Jesuit school, intended to convert to Catholicism, even after Brzozowski's directive against proselytization of Orthodox students and his controversial decision to allow them the use of their own catechism. Golitzyn was also head of a Bible society committed to the spread of a sort of creedless Christianity that Brzozowski was unable to support. A final neuralgic point was rising xenophobia among influential Russian conservatives who were reacting against the Enlightenment in the aftermath of the Napoleonic invasion.

In 1815 Jesuits were expelled from St. Petersburg, and the Society's headquarters were relocated to Polotzk. Despite Brzozowski's pleas, the Russian government refused permission to relocate to Rome, seeking to preserve its hegemony over the Society and to counter western European influence after the restoration. To facilitate governance, Brzozowski appointed Mariano Petrucci in Rome to be vicar general with broad powers. A hard worker, he did what he could to promote restoration of the Society's work in Italy: the opening of a second novitiate in 1816 and work at a dozen colleges. He also presided over the revival of the Society's work in Spain, England, Ireland, Belgium, France, and America. And he welcomed the reaffiliation with the Society of elderly former Jesuits who were eager to restore a fraternal connection that had been severed in 1773.

Five weeks after Brozozowski's death, the Jesuits, numbering 358, were expelled from Russia; normal governance resumed with the 20th General Congregation later in 1820. By the time of his death, there were 436 Jesuits in twenty-one houses of the Society.

See also Russia; Suppression

Bangert, William V., *A History of the Society of Jesus.* 2nd edn. St. Louis, MO: The Institute of Jesuit Sources, 1986, pp. 413–35.

Anthony Kuzniewski, SJ

Burghardt, Walter J., SJ (1914–2008)

Walter Burghardt, noted theologian, was once cited as one of the twelve most brilliant preachers in the United States. He was known for his wide learning, his cultured manner, and incisive writing style.

In 1931 at age 17, Walter entered the Jesuit novitiate at St. Andrew's on Hudson. He was ordained in 1944 and then taught at Woodstock College seminary from 1946 until it closed in 1974.

From 1946 to 1990, he set a high standard as managing editor and then editor of the influential journal *Theological Studies*. He often criticized the restrained preaching style of his fellow priests: "imagination seems to be a vestigial organ that many a Catholic priest was trained to leave in the seminary."

In 1957 he completed a doctorate on Cyril of Alexandria at the Catholic University of America under Johannes Quasten. He credited the German exile Quasten for a "sense of history, an awareness of cultural contexts, and a realization that Christianity is inescapably involved in the ebb and flow of time."

In 1991 at age 77, he set out on a global project called "Preaching the Just Word." He led more than 125 intensive, five-day retreats for priests and deacons in order to instill both moral fervor and a "fire in the belly" for preaching. In 1992 he founded the ecumenical quarterly *The Living Pulpit*.

He published twenty-five books and more than 300 articles primarily on the art of preaching and Church history. Highly acclaimed and widely loved, he received twenty-three honorary doctorates.

See also Preaching; United States of America

Burghardt, Walter J., *Preaching the Just Word* (expanded version of the LymanBeecher lectures). New Haven, CT: Yale University Press, 1996.
O'Donovan, Leo J., "Ambassador of Christ: In Memory of Walter J. Burghardt, SJ." *Theological Studies* 69 (September 2008), 492–508.

Patrick J. Howell, SJ

Cabral, Francisco, SJ (1533–1609)

Born in the Saõ Miguel Islands, in the Portuguese archipelago of the Azores, Cabral studied in Lisbon and traveled to India as a soldier. He joined the Society of Jesus in Goa (1554) and held the office of rector in Bassein (1566) and Cochin (1567–70). For eleven years (1570–81), he was the superior of the Jesuit mission in Japan. Subsequently, he was the rector of the Jesuit residence in Macau (1583) and responsible for the mission in China. Later, he returned to Goa, and during the years 1593–96 he was the provincial of India.

When Cabral arrived in Japan in 1570, he enacted several reforms which aimed at reshaping the Jesuit missionary approach. He attempted to restore the austerity that in his view had been lost among Jesuits and was persuaded that certain strategies of accommodation – such as luxurious clothing – and excessive involvement in the silk trade had changed the nature of the Jesuit presence in Japan. Highlighting the differences between the Jesuits and the Japanese, and not adapting to Japanese habits, was in Cabral's mind the most powerful method of evangelization; the Jesuits' strategy should be based on showing their own originality.

Cabral studied the Japanese culture and acknowledged the importance of a Japanese clergy, but he also underlined its status of subordination and need to act in service to European clergy.

In 1579 Alessandro Valignano (1539–1606) arrived in Japan as a visitor to the mission and strongly opposed Cabral's approach. The two Jesuits' debates on missionary methods continued during the following years, when Cabral left Japan, and may be seen in several letters they sent to General Claudio Acquaviva.

See also China; India; Japan; Portugal; Valignano, Alessandro, SJ

Correia, Pedro Lage Reis, "Francisco Cabral and Lourenço Mexia in Macau (1582–1584): Two Different Perspectives of Evangelisation in Japan." *Bulletin of Portuguese–Japanese Studies* 15 (2007), 47–77.

Ucerler, M. Antoni J., "The Jesuit Enterprise in Japan (1573–1580)." In Thomas McCoog, ed., *The Mercurian Project: Forming Jesuit Culture, 1573–1580*. Rome: Institutum Historicum Societatis Iesu, 2004, pp. 831–76.

Emanuele Colombo

Calvez, Jean-Yves, SJ (1927–2010)

Jean-Yves Calvez (1927–2010), French Jesuit, was a major scholarly voice in the promotion and development of Catholic social thought in the twentieth century and into the twenty-first. Perhaps best known to Jesuits because he served as a general assistant to Pedro Arrupe from 1975 to 1983, he played a key role in the development of Decree 4 of the 32nd General Congregation (GC 32) which dealt with the service of faith and the promotion of justice. During his time in Rome as general assistant, he visited nearly every Jesuit community in the world. But what gave Fr. Calvez such extraordinary credibility both within and outside the Society was not only his passionate concern for social justice and his love of the Church but also his scholarly credentials. In 1956 he published his doctoral research *La pensée de Karl Marx*, a non-polemical, constructive study of Marx's work that established Calvez as a major social thinker and theorist. This background later proved extremely valuable in helping Jesuits to understand and implement Decree 4, especially its call for the transformation of social structures.

Paul VI had misgivings about the particular direction in which he saw the Society moving with GC 32's focus on the promotion of justice, especially if such work were to compromise the Society's priestly character. Fr. Calvez realized that while a naive recourse to Marxist social analysis was not helpful, any practical involvement in promoting justice and transforming social structures was going to be, of necessity, political; however, it need not be ideological, and it need not compromise one's vocation as a priest. And, to be fair, the sentiment behind Decree 4 was in keeping with the spirit of the Pastoral Constitution on the Church in the Modern World (*Gaudium et spes*) of Vatican II, which Fr. Calvez attended as a *peritus*. A prolific writer and frequent contributor to *Études*, he served as the journal's editor from 1985 to 1995.

See also Arrupe, Pedro, SJ; Service of Faith and Promotion of Justice

Calvez, Jean-Yves, *Faith and Justice: The Social Dimension of Evangelization*. St. Louis, MO: The Institute of Jesuit Sources, 1991.

Calvez, Jean-Yves, and Jacques Perrin, *The Church and Social Justice: The Social Teaching of the Popes from Leo XIII to Pius XII*. Chicago, IL: Henry Regnery, 1961.

Politics and Society in the Third World. Trans. M. J. O'Connell. Maryknoll, NY: Orbis Books, 1973.

de Charentenay, Pierre, "Jean-Yves Calvez: A Servant of the Gospel and of the Church." *Promotio Iustitiae* 104, 1 (2010), 145–47.

William Reiser, SJ

Campion, Edmund, SJ, St. (1540–1581)

Popular and influential at Oxford University, Campion abandoned a very promising career for religious reasons. Reconciled to the Roman Church in 1571 at Douai, he studied for two years at the English College before departing for Rome in 1573 to enter the Society of Jesus. He was sent to the novitiate in Prague. For nearly eight years Bohemia was a "pleasant and blessed shore." Unlike Robert Persons, Campion had no desire to return to England. Everard Mercurian's summons to Rome in January, 1580, for the English mission aroused Campion's anxiety. With considerable reluctance and after more than a few delays, he arrived in Rome in April, 1580, to depart shortly thereafter with Persons and a Jesuit brother Ralph Emerson. Impersonating an Irish jewel merchant, Campion crossed the English Channel in June.

Fearing eventual capture and the possible dissemination of misinformation, Campion and Persons drafted *apologiae* explaining the nature and purpose of their mission to be released in the event of their apprehension. Campion's statement, known as his "Brag," was released prematurely, but probably intentionally. He challenged government, judiciary, and universities to debate the religious settlement. Cowed and persecuted Catholics proclaimed him a "champion"; a provoked establishment declared him a hunted man. In the winter and spring of 1580–81, as he traveled throughout northern England, he wrote a detailed follow-up: *Rationes decem* – the intended title was *De haeresi desperata* – distributed surreptitiously in Oxford in June. Campion was captured at Lyford Grange (Berkshire) on July 17, 1581. Because of Campion's challenge, the government staged disputations between Campion and leading Protestant controversialists, debates that did not proceed according to the government's plan. Tried on November 20 on a trumped-up charge of high treason, Campion was found guilty, sentenced to death, and hanged, drawn, and quartered at Tyburn on December 1, 1581.

See also Persons, Robert, SJ; United Kingdom

Kilroy, Gerard, *Edmund Campion: A Scholarly Life*. Farnham: Ashgate, 2015.
McCoog, Thomas M., *The Reckoned Expense: Edmund Campion and the Early English Jesuits*. 2nd edn. Rome: Institutum Historicum Societatis Iesu, 2007.
Simpson, Richard, *Edmund Campion*. 2nd edn. London, 1896.

Thomas McCoog, SJ

Canada

The Society of Jesus was never suppressed in Canada. During the early 1760s, while the ceding of Canada to the British Empire in the Treaty of Paris (1763) was being negotiated, the various French *parlements* were systematically expelling Jesuits from their territories. Then, in November 1764, King Louis XV proscribed the Society from his entire Kingdom. By then the Jesuits in Canada were safely outside his jurisdiction. Later, when the papal brief of suppression arrived in Quebec in 1773, Bishop Jean-Olivier Briand made arrangements with Lt. Governor Hector Cramahé to forbid its publication. And so the Jesuits were never suppressed.

They did, however, die out by attrition. In 1763 there were 17 Jesuits in Canada: some in the *collège* at Quebec and others among the Native people; in 1773 there were 15; in 1781 there were 11; in 1791 there were 3. Fr. Jean-Jacques Casot, who died in 1800, was the last to survive, and to his dying days he kept oversight of the "Jesuit Estates" that, at one time, were estimated to be equivalent to one-fifth of the settled lands in the Canadian colony. At his death they passed in trust to the Crown.

Decades later, at the pressing invitation of Bishop Ignace Bourget of Montreal, Fr. Clément Boulanger, then provincial of France, agreed that French Jesuits should return to Canada. Since a group of nine Jesuits was to leave for the French mission in Madagascar, Boulanger had them immediately rerouted. In 1842 the group arrived at Laprairie in eastern Canada led by Pierre Chazelle (1789–1845). Among their number was Félix Martin (1804–86), who would publish the first full set of the Jesuit *Relations* and build the Collège Sainte-Marie in Montreal. Also among them was Joseph-Urbain Hanipaux, who in 1844 would join Jean-Pierre Choné in bringing the Jesuits to the Wikwemikong Unceded Indian Reserve, where Jesuits have been serving ever since.

Before the death of the last of these men in 1900, the number of Jesuits in Canada had reached 273. The Canadian Jesuits became an independent mission in 1887, ushering in years of development and expansion until a new province of Canada was established in 1907 with 145 priests, 88 brothers, and 96 scholastics. By 1924 there were colleges in Sudbury, Edmonton, and Regina. The Native Industrial School operating at Wikwemikong moved in 1913 to Spanish, Ontario, as a new Industrial Residential School.

These developments were unfortunately accompanied by growing nationalist tensions between the English-speaking and French-Canadian Jesuits. By 1917 the crisis had become such that Fr. William Power, an official visitor sent from Rome, strongly recommended that the province be divided in two. The division became effective on June 27, 1924, when a French-speaking Lower Canadian province was created with 468 members and a Curia in Montreal, and an Anglophone vice province of Upper Canada was established with headquarters in Toronto and 130 members. In 1939 the latter became a province numbering 300 Jesuits.

The Lower Canadian province focused on the *collège classique*. By 1942 it administered eight of them, three of which were in Montreal. It was also responsible for large parishes in Montreal, Quebec, and Sudbury, as well as a half-dozen retreat houses. Under the leadership of Fr. Joseph-Papin Archambault (1880–1966), l'École Sociale Populaire and the periodical *Relations* promoted the social doctrine of the Church.

By 1960 the number of French Canadian Jesuits reached an unmanageable 770, and the decision was made to divide the province of Lower Canada into two provinces: Montreal and Quebec. Within five years, however, the Second Vatican Council and Quebec's "Quiet Revolution" combined to provoke a sudden drop in the number of men entering religious life or persevering in it. As a result the new Montreal and Quebec provinces were reunited in 1968 as the province of French Canada. In neither the French- nor the English-speaking province has there been a significant increase in vocations since this time.

The "winds of change" blowing through western society and the "Spirit of Vatican II" all transformed the ministries of the Canadian Jesuit provinces. In Quebec the educational institutions, often with the strong encouragement of the Society, passed from religious to lay control. So did most of the social services. In English-speaking Canada, as government policies increased funding for universities and denominational schools, the need declined for the contributed services of religious administrators, professors, and teachers. Accordingly, in both provinces the Society increasingly entrusted its responsibilities to lay professionals.

Simultaneously, increasing emphasis was placed on issues of social justice and the development of spiritual centers. Spiritual centers in Guelph and Quebec pioneered new insights into the *Spiritual Exercises*. The Jesuit Centre for Social Faith and Justice was founded in Toronto in 1979. In French Canada *le Centre Justice et Foi* focused on the publication of the periodical *Relations*. At Espanola the new Anishinabe Spiritual Centre developed the Aboriginal Native Lay Deacons Programme.

In the last dozen years, the two Canadian provinces have been drawing closer. The two provinces now share a common novitiate in Montreal, and the father general has given them permission to found a new single province of Canada.

See also Canadian/North American Martyrs; Marquette, Jacques, SJ; Québec

Curran, Francis,*The Return of the Jesuits: Chapters in the History of the Society of Jesus in Nineteenth-Century America*. Chicago, IL: Loyola University Press, 1966.
Dictionary of Jesuit Biography: Ministry to English Canada, 1842–1987. Toronto: Canadian Institute of Jesuit Studies, 1991.

Jacques Monet, SJ

Canadian/North American Martyrs

In the United States of America, Saints Jean de Brébeuf, Isaac Jogues, and their six companions are generally referred to as the North American Martyrs. However, devotion to the memory of their extraordinary lives and heroic deaths took deep root in Canada as it did in the missionaries' own French homeland, thanks to the widespread diffusion of the Jesuit *Relations*.

The *Relations*, which are almost the only source of information we possess on the lives of Jean de Brébeuf and his companions, are a set of some forty volumes of notes, letters, and reports sent annually between 1632 and 1672 by the Canadian missionaries to their superiors in France and published by the latter. They provide a powerful insight into Ignatian spirituality and a detailed record of the earliest Jesuit exploration into the vast regions of the northeastern region of the "New World." They also marginally record the courage and perseverance of the earliest French-Canadian settlers in learning how to tame and be tamed by the strongest expressions of the forces of nature.

Six of the martyrs – Jean de Brébeuf (1593–1649), Charles Garnier (1606–49), Antoine Daniel (1601–48), Isaac Jogues (1607–46), Gabriel Lalemant (1610–49), Noël Chabanel (1613–49) – were Jesuit missionary priests; one, René Goupil (1608–42), was a surgeon who pronounced vows as a Jesuit just before his assassination, and the last, Jean de Lalande (c. 1630–46), was a *donné*, that is, a lay collaborator with a defined commitment, who had volunteered to travel with Fr. Jogues.

All of the Jesuit missionaries were Frenchmen who had undertaken to work in New France. Some, in their own lifetime, were considered to be living the lives of saints: Isaac

Jogues, for instance, was declared a "Martyr of Christ" by Pope Innocent X two years before his death. And, likewise, Christophe Regnaut (1613–97), the infirmarian who prepared Brébeuf's body for burial, wrote convincingly of the sacred quality of its relics. For over two centuries, Jean de Brébeuf's enshrined skull has been venerated without interruption at the Convent of the Hospital Sisters of Saint Joseph in Quebec. Later, noted Jesuit archivists such as Félix Martin (1804–86) gathered rare documents about them, while such dedicated archaeologists as Arthur Edward Jones (1838–1918) discovered and produced relevant artifacts and ancient maps.

By the 1880s devotion to the Martyrs was growing among Catholics in the United States as well. In 1884, at the Third Council of Baltimore, the American bishops proposed advancing the cause of the three who had been put to death in what has now become Auriesville, New York. Rome agreed in 1885, and the American Jesuits immediately organized a massive pilgrimage that attracted 3,000 people to the site that would eventually be called the National Shrine of the North American Martyrs.

The Canadian bishops acted quickly. From their Provincial Council at Quebec, they wrote to Rome in 1886 asking that the names of Brébeuf, Daniel, Garnier, and Lalemant be added to those proposed by the Americans. They also dedicated a parish church in Penetang, Ontario, to the memory of Brébeuf and Lalemant, whose deaths they then thought had taken place very close by. Later, in 1906, another site at Waubashene was decided to be the more authentic one. This site, however, was also to be abandoned in 1947 when Wilfrid Jury, the director of the archaeological digs in Huronia, provided the since-uncontested archaeological proof for the true location of Brébeuf's and Lalemant's martyrdom.

The canonical process for the Martyrs' beatification began in Quebec City in 1904, though it was mostly carried forward after 1919, the most intensive work being done in 1922. It was then that Fr. Edward J. Devine testified for eighteen and a half hours as the expert witness, never once faltering in his detailed knowledge of the Martyrs' lives and deaths.

The vice-postulator of the cause in the Archdiocese of Quebec, Fr. Théophile Hudon, SJ, as well as Fathers Jacques Dugas and John J. Wynne, the promoters in Canada and the United States, hoped to have the beatification decreed on the exact 300th anniversary of Brébeuf's landing at Quebec, June 21, 1625. So it was, in St. Peter's Basilica on June 21, 1925.

For the canonization, the required miracles followed fairly quickly. Georgina Robichaud, an Acadian Sister Hospitaler of St. Joseph, was cured of tubercular peritonitis on July 9, 1926, and a French-Canadian Sister of the Presentation, Alexandrine Ruel, was cured of the same illness on December 30, 1927. Both cures were officially recognized on May 11, 1930. The canonization by Pope Pius XI took place on the patronal feast of Rome, June 29, 1930.

In 1932 the Canadian Martyrs were assigned as the patron saints of the vice province of Upper Canada. In 1940 they were declared by Pope Pius XII to be the secondary patrons of Canada, the first, Saint Joseph, having been chosen by the Récollet missionaries in the 1620s.

See also Canada; Martyrs, Ideal and History

Anderson, Emma, *The Death and Afterlife of the North American Martyrs*. Cambridge, MA: Harvard University Press, 2013.

Latourelle, René, *Étude sur les écrits de Saint Jean de Brébeuf*. 2 vols. Montreal: Les Éditions de l'Immaculée Conception, 1952–53.

Jacques Monet, SJ

Canillac, François de Montboissier de, SJ (1574–1628)

Superiors received him into the Society in Rome in 1593, once his mother, widow of the Marqués de Canillac, passed away, thus removing objections. Following ordination in 1602, he served as master of novices in Lyon before being chosen to lead a new mission to Istanbul in 1609. An earlier attempt (1583) to establish a mission to serve the Latin Catholics in the city was terminated when the five Jesuits there fell victims to the plague. Once established in the old monastery of St. Benedict in Galata, Canillac refurbished the chapel, established a school, and inaugurated cordial relations with the Ecumenical Patriarch, Theophilos. His vision for Jesuit work in the region went far beyond Istanbul to the Christians in the area, living under Ottoman rule. In 1613 he returned to Paris and laid his projected plans before the French king. He sent copies to the superior general of the Jesuits and to the Vatican Congregation, *Propaganda fide*. He returned to Istanbul with permission to make a pilgrimage to Jerusalem and study possibilities for a Jesuit mission there. Rebuffed by the Franciscans in Jerusalem, he returned to Istanbul by way of Lebanon and Syria. He counseled a mission to Aleppo. His advice was heeded by the new Jesuit General, Fr. Vitelleschi, elected in 1615. The first Jesuit missionaries arrived in Aleppo in 1625. Meanwhile Fr. de Canillac retired from Istanbul and, after aiding the bishop of Smyrna for a few years before poor health forced a return to France, he spent his final years encouraging vocations for the Levant.

See also Lebanon; Middle East; Syria

John Donohue, SJ

Canisius, Peter, SJ, St. (1521–1597)

Canisius was one of the most dynamic and prolific of the early Jesuits. A champion of internal Church reform and a vital force of the Counter-Reformation, he is credited with reinvigorating Catholicism within a largely Protestant Holy Roman Empire. Born into an influential patrician family in Nijmegen on May 8, 1521, he became the first Dutch Jesuit. He moved to Cologne in 1536 to study at the university, taking a BA (1536), MA (1540), and a bachelor's degree in theology (1546). A brief stint in 1539 at the University of Leuven introduced him to canon law. In April 1543, he traveled to Mainz to meet Peter Faber, the first Jesuit to arrive in Germany. After Faber directed him in the Spiritual Exercises, Canisius promptly entered the Society of Jesus in Mainz on May 8, 1543. He returned to Cologne, where he was ordained a deacon (1543) and a priest (1546) and led the fledgling Jesuit community, supporting the local Catholic clergy against their archbishop (Hermann von Wied), who had become a Protestant. Ignatius of Loyola summoned Canisius to Rome in 1547 to ground him more deeply in the spirituality and ministries of the Society of Jesus. In 1548, Canisius joined the first formal Jesuit educational mission at the college of Messina in Sicily, where he taught rhetoric. In 1549, he journeyed northwards to profess his solemn vows before Ignatius in Rome, take his doctorate in theology from the University of Bologna along with his confrères Alfonoso Salmerón and Claude Jay, and arrive at the University of Ingolstadt, where he began teaching theology with them. Canisius served as rector of the university in 1550. In 1552, Ignatius sent him to Vienna, where he taught theology at the university and preached at the court of Archduke Ferdinand. Canisius governed the Diocese of Vienna as administrator (1554–55) after the death of Bishop Christoph Wertwein. In June 1556, Ignatius named Canisius the first head of the Society's Upper German province. His provincialate (1556–69) represented the busiest period of his life, in which he founded several Jesuit colleges, held the post of cathedral preacher in Augsburg (1559–66), and preached wherever his many travels took him. In 1557 he participated in the Colloquy of Worms, a fraught effort to find common ground between Catholics and Protestants. Canisius contributed to the breakdown of the discussions by emphasizing the doctrinal divisions among his Protestant opponents. In 1562 he briefly attended the Council of Trent, where at a theologians' congregation he spoke in favor of a limited concession of the lay chalice to keep Catholics living among Protestants faithful to the Church. In 1565 Pope Pius IV commissioned Canisius to deliver the decrees of the Council of Trent to the Catholic princes and bishops of Germany. In the 1570s, tensions emerged between Canisius and his successor as provincial, Paul Hoffaeus. After an unsuccessful attempt to transfer Canisius to the Rhenish province, Hoffaeus sent him in 1580 to found a Jesuit college in Swiss Fribourg, an outpost in the Upper German province. Until his death in Fribourg on December 21, 1597, Canisius devoted himself to pastoral ministry and to writing.

Canisius's first publications were editions of the fourteenth-century mystic Johannes Tauler (1543) and of the Church Fathers Cyril of Alexandria and Leo the Great (1546). His edition of an anthology of the letters of St. Jerome (1562), intended for use in schools, remained in print until the nineteenth century. His familiarity with the Church Fathers signaled his preference for positive over scholastic theology.

Canisius's knowledge of Greek, capacity for elegant Latin, and biblical and patristic proficiency indicate a humanist style, but his humanism was confessionalized, dedicated to the triumph of Catholic truth over Protestant heresy. His letters and publications often gave voice to hostility toward Protestants, whom he attacked for corrupting Scripture and rejecting long-established Church traditions. In the 1570s, Canisius published two voluminous polemics against the Lutheran Magdeburg Centuriators.

Canisius is best known as a catechist. He wrote for audiences of varying sophistication. The Large Catechism (*Summa doctrinae christianae*) first appeared anonymously in Vienna in 1555. The so-called Smallest and Small Catechisms followed in 1556 and 1558. The three catechisms were published many times in Latin, German, and other European languages. Canisius also published prayer books, saints' lives, and a series of meditations for priests on the Gospels for Sundays and saints' days.

In 1864 Pope Pius IX beatified Canisius. Pope Leo XIII proclaimed him the second apostle to Germany in an encyclical of 1897. Pope Pius XI canonized Canisius in 1925 and declared him a doctor of the Church.

See also Germany-Speaking Lands; Holy Roman Empire

Figure 14 Exterior view of Church of St. Peter Canisius, Berlin, 20th century. Photograph Alison Fleming

Brodrick, James, *Saint Peter Canisius*. London: Sheed and Ward, 1935; repr. Chicago, IL: Loyola Press, 1998.
Pabel, Hilmar M., "Peter Canisius and the Protestants: A Model of Ecumenical Dialogue?" *Journal of Jesuit Studies* 1 (2014), 373–99.

Hilmar M. Pabel

Canon Law and the Society of Jesus

Ecclesiology provides the context for canon law; see Vatican II, *Lumen Gentium* 8: The Church is both the Mystical Body of Christ and a visible society. Law provides the structure necessary to foster the life of faith, grace, and charisms (Saint John Paul II, *Sacrae disciplinae leges*, *Acta Apostolicae Sedis* [AAS] 75.II [1983], xi). Therefore, no distinction can exist between, e.g., the Church of law and the Church of charity (Blessed Paul VI, *AAS* 57 [1965] 986).

Broadly understood, *ius canonicum* encompasses a variety of *ordinationes* — the various official acts that structure the Church's life: law as a binding norm deriving from a person or body with legislative power; decrees, instructions, and other documentation issued by those with executive power; statutes of juridic persons; proper law of institutes and societies of consecrated life; divine/natural law.

Three texts provide for the "canonical ordering of the whole Church" (Saint John Paul II, *Sacri Canones* [AAS 82 (1990), 1038–39]): the *Code of Canon Law* (1983; for the Latin Church); the *Code of Canons of the Eastern Churches* (1990; for the Eastern Churches *sui iuris*); and *Pastor Bonus* (1988) regulating the Roman Curia which is at the service of the Roman Pontiff "for the good and service of the whole Church and of the particular Churches." These constitute but not exclusively the "universal law" governing the Church. "Particular law" is for a specific territory, e.g., a diocese, an ecclesiastical province, the territory of a conference of bishops. "Proper law" applies to members of a religious or secular institute or apostolic society through profession of the evangelical counsels or other bonds. "Proper law" in reference to the Society of Jesus refers primarily to its foundational documents governing its life and mission.

General Congregation 33 (Decree 6, #2) mandated the revision of the Society's proper law from the perspective of Vatican II and the two codes cited above. This revision was approved by General Congregation 34 on March 18, 1995. The "proper law" of the Society of Jesus consists of a primary text – the original text of the *Constitutions* – and a collection of norms complementary to the *Constitutions*. As revised, "The *Constitutions* of Saint Ignatius, an explicitation of the *Formula of the Institute of the Society of Jesus* as approved by the supreme pontiffs Paul III (*Regimini militantis Ecclesiae*, 1540) and Julius III (*Exposcit debitum*,1550) […] should serve to inspire and govern our entire present-day lives" (Peter-Hans Kolvenbach, September 27, 1995).

The proper law of the Society – the *Constitutions* and their Complementary Norms – has been published in one volume introduced by the *Formulas of the Institute*. The *Constitutions* has not been changed but annotated by the authority of the General Congregation through the addition of notes reflecting modifications, abrogations, and clarifications necessitated by universal Church law or by the acts of General Congregations. Complementary Norms issued by the authority of various General Congregations were reformulated and arranged according to the order of the *Constitutions*, after obsolete or unnecessary elements were removed. These fundamental texts have the nature of pontifical law (*Complementary Norms*, 9).

Dependent on these texts are the *Statutes on Religious Poverty in the Society of Jesus* (first promulgated in 1967; updated and promulgated in 1976 and 2003) and *Instruction on the Administration of Goods* (promulgated 2005), published in one volume in 2005. Secondary legal texts – to fulfill the requirements of the *Formula of the Institute*, *Constitutions*, and *Complementary Norms* – include the *Formula of a General Congregation*, and procedures for *Congregation to Elect a Temporary Vicar*, *Congregation of Procurators*, *Province Congregation*, all of which have been established by a General Congregation or by its authority (*Complementary Norms*, 331).

The responsibility for "good government, preservation and growth of the whole body of the Society" (*Constitutions*, #719) is entrusted to the superior general (*praepositus generalis*). General Congregations are the sole subject of full legislative power (*Complementary Norms*, 333, #1) and have as their primary purpose the election of a new superior general (*Constitutions*, #677) and/or to address matters of more importance and urgency (*Constitutions*, #680). The Society of Jesus does not have capitular governance. The proper law of the Society is directed to mission: "The monarchical model of sharing of authority fosters an organization which streamlines sending and mission, a mission always meant to be at one with Christ and his Vicar on earth" (Geisinger, "Religious Authority," 987).

See also Constitutions

Aldama, Antonio De, *Constitutions of the Society of Jesus*. 5 vols. St. Louis, MO: The Institute of Jesuit Sources, 1989–99.

The Constitutions of the Society of Jesus and Their Complementary Norms. Ed. John W. Padberg.
    St. Louis, MO: The Institute of Jesuit Sources, 1996.
Geisinger, Robert, "Religious Authority in the Society of Jesus." *Angelicum* 83 (2008), 965–1023.
Padberg, John W., ed., *Jesuit Life and Mission Today: The Decrees and Accompanying Documents of
    the 31st–35th General Congregations of the Society of Jesus.* St. Louis, MO: The Institute of Jesuit
    Sources, 2009.

Robert J. Kaslyn, SJ

Caravaggio, *The Taking of Christ*

Known as the "Jesuit Caravaggio" for its rediscovery in a Jesuit house two hundred years
after its disappearance from Rome, *The Taking of Christ* is a large canvas (53 x 67 in.)
by Baroque master Michelangelo Merisi da Caravaggio (1571–1610), commissioned in
1602 by Marquis Ciriaco Mattei. It depicts the dramatic moment in which Jesus, having
just received Judas's kiss of betrayal, is seized by armed Roman guards. That Caravaggio
had painted the subject had long been known to scholars through the existence of several contemporary copies, but the location of the original and the circumstances under
which it left Rome were unknown. Though still the property of the Society of Jesus, the
painting is on indefinite loan to the National Gallery of Ireland. It has traveled extensively
in Europe but only once to North America, as the centerpiece of the 1999 exhibition

Figure 15 Caravaggio: *Taking of Christ*, 1602, oil on canvas. On loan to the National Gallery
of Ireland from the Jesuit Community, Leeson Street Dublin, who acknowledge the kind
generosity of the late Dr. Marie Lea-Wilson. Photograph © National Gallery of Ireland

Saints and Sinners: Caravaggio and the Baroque Image organized by the McMullen Museum of Art of Boston College, the city's Jesuit university. The exhibition catalogue contains a first-hand account of the painting's rediscovery by Noel Barber, SJ, superior of the Leeson Street Jesuit community, where the painting had resided for decades. The painting was a gift of Marie Lea Wilson (d. 1971) in the 1930s, who purchased the work (attributed to Dutch *caravaggista*, Gerard van Honthorst) in Edinburgh in the 1920s. The painting, already misattributed to Honthorst, had arrived in Scotland in 1802 when sold by the Mattei to William Hamilton Nisbet. In 1990 Fr. Barber arranged for the painting to undergo conservation work at the National Gallery. Fortunately the task was assumed by Italian conservator and baroque connoisseur, Sergio Benedetti, who soon suspected the painting's true identity and gathered an impressive array of evidence proving its now undisputed attribution to Caravaggio.

See also Arts, Visual; Baroque Art and Architecture

Benedetti, Sergio, "Caravaggio's 'Taking of Christ': A Masterpiece Rediscovered." *Burlington* 135, 1088 (1993), 731–46.
Saints and Sinners: Caravaggio and the Baroque Image. Ed. Franco Mormando. Boston, MA: McMullen Museum of Art, Boston College, 1999.

Franco Mormando

Cardinals, Jesuit

Pope Francis is the first Jesuit pope, but not the first Jesuit cardinal. The first was Francisco Toledo, created in 1593. Overall there have been forty-three Jesuit cardinals. Most famous would be Robert Bellarmine, created in 1599. He was the second Jesuit made a cardinal and the only one who is a saint and doctor of the Church. Cardinal Juan de Lugo (1643 – the year of creation is listed in parentheses) was famed for recommending quinine, so it became known as "De Lugo's Powder." Two Jesuit priests who later became cardinals, Camillo Mazzella (1886) and Avery Dulles (2001), taught at Woodstock College, the Jesuit theologate in Woodstock, Maryland. Cardinal Billot (1911) resigned the cardinalate in 1927 because of his involvement with *L'Action française*.

At the beginning of 2015 there were five living Jesuit cardinals: Jan Chryzostom Korec (1991); Julius Riyadi Darmaatmadja (1994); Roberto Tucci (2001); Albert Vanhoye (2006); and Karl Josef Becker (2012). This number is rare in the history of the Jesuits. Often there were none and rarely two.

Jesuit cardinals appointed since Vatican II, but now deceased, are: Augustin Bea (1959); Jean Daniélou (1969); Pablo Muñoz Vega (1969); Victor Razafimahatratra (1976); Lawrence Trevor Picachy (1976); Henri de Lubac (1983); Carlo Maria Martini (1983); Paolo Dezza (1991); Aloys Grillmeier (1994); Augusto Alzamora (1994); Adam Kozlowiecki (1998); Paul Shan Kuo-hsi (1998); Avery Dulles (2001); Roberto Tucci (2001); Tomas Spidlik (2003); Urbano Navarrete Cortés (2007); and Karl Josef Becker (2012).

A Jesuit can be created a cardinal at an advanced age because of his achievements, and most recent appointments have been honorary. Such cardinals serve as honorary advisers to the pope.

See also Bishops, Jesuit; Papacy

Aixala, Jerome, *Black and Red SJ*. Bombay: Messenger Office – St. Xavier's High School, 1968.
Schineller, Peter, "Jesuits in the Hierarchy." *America*. May 3, 2013.

Peter Schineller, SJ

Caribbean

The Caribbean islands, though sharing a common history of chattel slavery and European domination, are composed of diverse and distinct peoples. The history of the Society of Jesus in the islands partly reflects this diversity and separateness. Nevertheless, the Society's universal character can still be recognized in similar but independent efforts on separate islands, coordination across islands within single language groups, and occasional cross-language enterprises. This entry provides a few examples of this universal character.

Prior to 1773, there was coordination among French-speaking Jesuits centered out of Martinique. In the seventeenth century, the French-speaking Jesuit missions included several eastern Caribbean islands, including St. Kitts and St. Vincent. In the eighteenth century, what is now northern Haïti also became part of this wider activity. Jesuits quickly diversified their pastoral work to include work with slaves and the Carib peoples. It was not long before they also entered the field of formal education. Jesuit ministry to the Carib peoples on the island of St. Vincent would produce the first "Jesuit martyrs" in the eastern Caribbean.

In March 1653, Fr. Guillaume Aubergeon arrived in St. Vincent in response to the invitation of a Carib delegation. After two hurricanes did much damage in St. Vincent in 1653, Fr. François Gueymeu was sent to help. Two young French laymen accompanied them in their work. On January 24, 1654, all members of the Jesuit mission were killed as part of a Carib uprising against Europeans in the Lesser Antilles. It is likely that Jesuit cooperation with French authorities and companies served European attempts to gain control of the Carib peoples across the Lesser Antilles, even if Jesuits did not share this purpose. Despite the killing of the four missionaries, a Jesuit mission to St. Vincent was maintained from Martinique until at least 1679.

With the arrival of Fr. Jean Gerard in 1704, the Society's work in what is now northern Haïti began. The Jesuits dedicated energy and time to an apostolate among the slaves and established the institution known as "Cure des Nègres." By 1725 the pastoral work was touching the lives of about half of the slaves in the colony, but it eventually became a source of tension with local authorities. It should be noted that Jesuit work in Haïti was partly financed by Jesuit-owned enterprises, which employed large numbers of slaves. Following a royal decree in 1764 expelling the Jesuits from France, the Jesuits were expelled from Haïti as well. Their Spanish Jesuit confrères would be expelled from the Spanish Caribbean territories in 1767.

Jesuits first returned to the Caribbean islands with the arrival in Jamaica of Frs. William Cotham and James Dupeyron on December 2, 1837. The return to the rest of the Caribbean was gradual, with the Society not arriving in Haïti until 1953. After 1814, with the exception of Trinidad and Barbados, Jesuits did not reside in the eastern Caribbean islands.

The post-1814 Society in Jamaica, Cuba, and Puerto Rico has been renowned for its premier high schools: St. George's, Belén, and San Ignacio, respectively. In these schools some prominent leaders of the respective nations have been educated. In the Dominican Republic (DR), Jesuits have had a particular influence on technical education.

The work of Fr. John P. Sullivan with the Credit Union movement stands out as one of the cross-language and multi-island Jesuit endeavors that has had a widespread impact in the Caribbean. Fr. Sullivan visited the DR from Jamaica in 1946 as part of a program aimed at spreading the Credit Union movement. He returned again in 1947 for a conference in which he once again promoted the Credit Union movement. As a result, Credit Unions developed in the DR with the help of several priests, including Jesuit Fr. Gerardo Vásquez, who had attended the 1947 conference. The work of Fr. Sullivan and his collaborators was largely responsible for the birth of the Credit Union movement throughout the Caribbean.

In recent years, the Society has been trying to foment greater Jesuit collaboration across islands and languages. Impacts of these new efforts on the Church have been minimal, though they have had visible effects at the level of the Society's formation programs. The Novitiate in Santiago, DR, has served Cuba, Puerto Rico, Miami, Jamaica, and the DR. The First Studies program in Santo Domingo serves Haïti, the DR, and Cuba. Though a slow and sometimes painful process, collaboration in Jesuit formation may equip future Jesuit generations for a more coordinated mission in an often divided and insular Caribbean.

See also Cuba; Dominican Republic; Haïti; Jamaica; Puerto Rico

Chatrie, Emilie, "Pierre Pelleprat: A Missionary between the Lesser Antilles and the Continent." In C. L. Hofman and A. van Duijvenbode, eds., *Communities in Contact: Essays in Archaeology, Ethnohistory and Ethnography of the Amerindian circum-Caribbean.* Leiden: Sidestone Press, 2011, pp. 367–77.

Kawas, François, *Sources documentaires de l'histoire des jésuites en Haïti aux XVIII et XX siècles.* Paris: L'Harmattan, 2006.

González, Manuel Revuelta, *Once Calas en la historia de la Compañía de Jesús.* Madrid: Universidad Pontificia Comillas, 2006.

Osborne, Francis J., *History of the Catholic Church in Jamaica.* Chicago, IL: Loyola University Press, 1988.

Christopher Llanos, SJ

Carroll, John, SJ (1735–1815)

By the eighteenth century, the Maryland Jesuit mission ministered largely to the Maryland planter elite into which John Carroll was born in 1735. His parents opted for his education in Europe. Carroll remained overseas for twenty-six years, mostly in French Flanders, where he enrolled in Jesuit schools prior to entering the Society at Watten in 1753. His associations with English Catholic recusants traveling and living on the Continent exposed Carroll to both the British monarchy's anti-Catholicism and the role of Catholic monarchies in fostering the Suppression. Carroll's letters and reports form valuable historical testimony to this period.

Returning to Maryland in 1774, Carroll quickly joined his well-to-do relatives in support for American independence. To their concerns about the British threat to colonial property-holders, Carroll added a conviction that it would be worthwhile to gamble that the Church might fare better under a republican form of government. Carroll joined

Benjamin Franklin in an unsuccessful diplomatic mission to attract Catholic Quebec to join the rebellion. He was more effective in securing Catholic support for the adoption and implementation of the Constitution so long as it respected religious liberty. Thus, Carroll began a process of dialogue between the Church and American constitutional law that would see fruition exactly 150 years after his death in Vatican II's teaching on religious liberty.

Carroll's other preoccupation was to preserve the Jesuit legacy in the United States throughout the Suppression. The lack of episcopal authority in North America and the neutrality of the new government in religious matters were advantages for this project. Carroll helped former Jesuits to maintain a sense of spirituality and community through the establishment of a clergy corporation under Maryland law. While the resulting security of the Jesuit estates ensured the survival of clerical slaveholding in the state for another half century, it was also true that the estates became refuges for Jesuit formation and ministry. Carroll also recognized that future vitality depended on an expansion of ministries and was instrumental in the formation of Georgetown Academy in 1789.

Carroll's spiritual leadership and practical organization made him a logical choice to become the first bishop in the United States in 1789, with Baltimore as his see. In 1808, he became a metropolitan archbishop. Carroll was greatly disturbed when the Napoleonic Wars impeded communications between the Holy See and the American Church for a generation. This phenomenon worsened amid two French incarcerations of the papacy and a British blockade of Europe and was particularly worrisome to a bishop convinced that one cause of the Suppression had been papal misinformation about the Society. Carroll worked hard to make sure that the same fate would not befall the American Church. At the same time he sought to reassure Americans that the Church was no threat to their liberty. For this reason, he corrected clerical refugees from Europe, including Georgetown faculty, who were inclined to interpret the American Revolution as a variant of the French one.

Historians have debated two issues concerning Carroll's legacy, beginning with his attitude toward the American Enlightenment. The consensus is that Carroll shared the movement's general enthusiasm for learning without ever allowing the primacy of reason to eclipse a thoroughly Catholic humanism. The realistic Carroll saw the emerging American system as the most beneficial option for the Church in an otherwise oppressive era. He was grateful to the Enlightenment for fostering this system but felt the Church had much to say to the system in return.

Historians have also debated the extent to which Carroll, once a bishop, truly desired the restoration of the Jesuits. Here the consensus is that he did indeed want a revival but was cautious to ensure that the reconstituted Society would be adaptable to American culture. Carroll also desired that the American Society would not antagonize the Holy See.

At Carroll's death in 1815, the Society was restored worldwide, the Church's Napoleonic ordeal was over, and American independence had been reconfirmed in the War of 1812. By preserving the American Church and the American Jesuits through these crises, Carroll prepared the way for the remarkable growth of each during the remainder of the nineteenth century.

See also Bishops, Jesuits; Maryland Mission; United States of America

Dolan, Jay P., *The American Catholic Experience: A History from Colonial Times to the Present.* New York: Doubleday, 1985.

Hanley, Thomas O'Brien, ed., *The John Carroll Papers.* 3 vols. Notre Dame, IN: University of Notre Dame Press, 1976.

Hoffman, Ronald, *Princes of Ireland, Planters of Maryland: A Carroll Saga, 1500–1782.* Chapel Hill: University of North Carolina Press, 1982.

Kupke, Raymond J., ed., *The American Catholic Preaching and Piety in the Time of John Carroll.* Lanham, MD: University Press of America, 1991.

Thomas Murphy, SJ

Cartography in China

Cartography encompasses geography, mathematics, and astronomy. In the Jesuit educational system, students were provided basic training in mathematics and astronomy as preparation for theological studies. Michele Ruggieri (1543–1607), one of the first Jesuits to arrive in China in the 1580s, expressed interests in Chinese geography and cartography and created a series of Chinese provincial maps. Ruggieri completed this work after returning to Italy around 1589, although his manuscript remained unknown until 1989. Ruggieri's compilation of twenty-eight maps for the whole of China, with Chinese place names and separate Latin descriptions, can be considered the first Jesuit cartographical work *on* China.

The world map designed by Jesuit Matteo Ricci (1552–1610) was the first European-style map presented to the Chinese. Ricci presented a European world map to the Chinese in 1583–84 in Zhaoqing (肇慶), the province of Guangdong (廣東省), several months after he arrived in Macau in 1582. Ricci probably brought maps for the Jesuits' own academic purposes; that is, for the same reason that he imported mathematical devices such as globes and clocks. Among several European books brought to China by the Jesuits in the early years of their mission, Abraham Ortelius's cartographical work, *Theatrum orbis terrarum* (Antwerp, 1570) was the only European publication mentioned in Ricci's list of items presented to the Chinese emperor. The first public appearance of the European-style world map elicited telling reactions from the local people: Chinese officials urged Ricci to annotate the map in Chinese and to print and distribute it throughout China. The first edition of Ricci's world map in Chinese was entitled *Shanhai yudi quantu* 山海輿地全圖 (*Universal Map of Mountain, Sea, and Geography*). This map was continuously revised and reprinted; for example, in Nanchang (*c.* 1596), Nanjing (1600), Beijing (1601–03), and later in Japan. The 1602 revision in Beijing was supervised by Chinese literati Christian Li Zhizao 李之藻 (*c.* 1564–1630), and a refined format with supplementary contents and commentaries was developed. This *mappamundi* was the exemplar most cited, and re-entitled *Kunyu wanguo quantu* 坤輿萬國全圖 (*Universal Map of the World and Countries*).

The universal mapping method of Ricci was based on Ptolemy's model, intentionally modifying China's position with respect to the other continents in the middle of the world. The reduction of China's size produced a culturally shocking visual experience for the Chinese. Cartography became a thriving field in which knowledge exchanged between the missionaries and the Chinese yielded a product showing the impact of the European worldview and technology on a non-Christian Asian culture.

After Ricci, the world map of Giulio Aleni (1582–1649), *Wanguo quantu* 萬國全圖 (*Universal Maps of Countries*), was made around 1620, based on the format and contents of Ricci's map. Other Jesuits in China, Diego de Pantoja (1571–1618) and Francesco Sambiaso (1582–1649) also continued to design world maps. The map of Ferdinand Verbiest (1623–88), *Kunyu quantu* 坤輿全圖 (*Universal Map of the World*, 1674), shows two hemispheres, and the two outer scrolls contain several types of information on geography and meteorology in cartouches. This mapping projection deriving from Gerard Mercator (1512–94) was a different mode from the Ptolemaic method. At least fourteen copies and editions of Verbiest's *Kunyu quantu* exist. The Jesuit efforts to introduce a western format of world map and share western knowledge of cartography would have two primary purposes. First, it ensured greater knowledge of the world and an enhanced Chinese understanding of the missionaries and European cultures. Second, embodying the Christian dimension in Jesuit cartography helped the Chinese to comprehend the greatness of Earth and Heaven, and thus the grace of God. Jesuit cartography directs the reader to the spiritual world through a visualized geographical configuration and helped propagate the concept of the Creator.

The Jesuit Martino Martini's (1614–61) atlas of China was published in Europe in 1655. It was the most complete cartographical work on China that had appeared in Europe up to then, as the similar works of the Jesuits Ruggieri and Michael Boym (1612–59) remained unpublished. This atlas's popularity exemplified the Jesuits' prominent position in the fields of cartography as well as the knowledge of China in seventeenth-century Europe. Moreover, during the golden reigns of Qing emperors Kangxi, Yongzheng, and Qianlong, the reliance of the rulers on the capability of science and the mapping skills of the French Jesuits for surveying the expanded territories of the country and creating imperial maps of China was apparent. By offering the first-hand sources of Chinese geography and cartography, Jesuit missionaries in China contributed to prosperous European publications on China in the eighteenth century.

See also China; Ricci, Matteo, SJ

Chen, Hui-Hung, "The Human Body as a Universe: Understanding Heaven by Visualization and Sensibility in Jesuit Cartography in China." *The Catholic Historical Review* 93, 3 (July 2007), 517–52.

Feng, Huang Xiu, and Gianfranco Cretti, eds., *La Cina nella cartografia da Tolomeo al XVII secolo* 中國地理學：從托勒密時期到十七世紀. Macerata: Fondazione Internazione Matteo Ricci; Brescia: Fondazione Civiltà Bresciana-Centro Giulio Aleni, 2011.

Hui-Hung Chen

Castiglione, Giuseppe, SJ (1688–1766)

Giuseppe Castiglione was a Jesuit brother, artist, and missionary, who served at the court of the Chinese emperors for over fifty years. Born in Milan, he trained as an artist and then entered the Society at age 19. He produced a few works in Italy and Coimbra, Portugal (where he completed the novitiate) prior to departing for China in 1714. After being tutored in the local language and customs in Macau, he was successfully presented at the Qing court in Beijing and adopted the name Lang Shining.

Figure 16 Giuseppe Castiglione, SJ: *Portrait of Qianlong (Chinese Emperor, r. 1736–96),* *c.* 1737, colors on paper. Musée des Arts Asiatiques-Guimet, Paris. Photograph © RMN-Grand Palais / Art Resource, New York

Castiglione's abilities in portraiture were sought-after and prized in the competitive environment at the court, where much was demanded of artists. In addition to portraits of the royal family (and their dogs and horses), he also painted military expeditions, hunts, and other court spectacles. His precise and detailed style is often described as combining eastern brushwork – especially seen in landscapes – and western naturalism and color. Castiglione also taught students, collaborated with visiting artists, and painted church interiors in Beijing, among them a faux cupola modeled on the one earlier produced by Andrea Pozzo in the Church of Sant'Ignazio in Rome.

The Chinese were intrigued by his technical skills in perspective, and he is considered the first western painter to be admired in China. He also assisted in the Chinese translation of Pozzo's treatise on perspective. However, even after fifty-one years, his western style seems to have not had a lasting impact on Chinese artists of the period.

Some of Castiglione's works remain in Beijing, but most are today in the National Palace Museum in Taipei.

See also Architecture; Arts, Visual; China

Beurdeley, Cécile, and Michel Beurdeley, *Giuseppe Castiglione: A Jesuit Painter at the Court of the Chinese Emperors.* Trans. Michael Bullock. Rutland, VT: Tuttle, 1971.

Musillo, Marco, "Reconciling Two Careers: The Jesuit Memoir of Giuseppe Castiglione Lay Brother and Qing Imperial Painter." *Eighteenth-Century Studies* (2008), 45–59.

Alison Fleming

Casuistry

Casuistry is the common method of moral reasoning by which one compares a settled and recognizably authoritative case with an unresolved one. Each case incorporates the particularity of a situation and its attendant circumstances within a short narrative depiction. Authoritative cases could be of three kinds. The Scottish logician John Mair (1467–1550) used commonsense cases when he developed the argument for legitimating the work of maritime insurance agents. Using the captain of a ship who guarantees that the cargo of a ship gets from one port to another, Mair argued that similarly the agent guarantees that the worth of the cargo gets from one port to another. Biblical cases were also frequently used. The most used case to entertain legitimate forms of dissemblance was Jesus's discourse with the disciples at Emmaus (Luke 24:13–35) where he asked them (v. 17) what they were discussing and when they asked him, "are you the only one in Jerusalem who does not know about these things?" Jesus answers, "what things?" (v. 19). Later, Jesus provides a non-verbal form of dissemblance as "he appears to be continuing on" (v. 28). Finally, civil and canonical legal cases gave precedence to other cases, such as the extensive casuistry that arose over the marriages of Henry VIII.

In continental Europe, casuistry enjoyed considerable popularity throughout the sixteenth century. Explorations of the New World and extensive trading with the East prompted new questions about property, financing, governance, and evangelization that long-standing principles never anticipated. Casuistry was introduced because of the inability of contemporary moral principles to address new, emerging, and urgent moral concerns.

At the same time, scholastic philosophy was influenced by fifteenth-century nominalism, a school of philosophy that insisted on the priority of the individual and on the radical singularity of each existent. At the start of the sixteenth century, John Mair is both the most influential nominalist at the University of Paris and arguably the first modern casuist. In determining standards for right ways of acting, he referred not to an existing rule or norm, but rather to an authoritative case of right acting (like the captain of a ship or Jesus at Emmaus) to serve as suitable standards against which new cases could be resolved by comparison and contrast. The authoritative case eventually replaced the inadequate principle or rule as the moral standard for the sixteenth century. Likewise the method of casuistry replaced the deductive moral logic of principle-based ethics with an inductive comparison of congruencies between the authoritative case and the unsolved analogous case with a different set of circumstances. Mair and others used their new method to answer new questions relating, for example, to maritime insurance but also to revisit old ones, such as marital pleasure and money-lending.

Members of the newly developing Society of Jesus, having studied at Paris with Mair, opened their own schools and appropriated the method. Their missionary companions would report to Rome first-hand cases of new moral complexity, e.g., could one baptize someone whose tribal chief forbade it? Could one take possession of lands if the lands had no deeds? Could one participate in native people's rituals even if they were religious? Entertaining these cases at the Roman university provided faculty and students with material that was rich in circumstances and imaginatively captivating.

The Jesuits used casuistry also for the pastoral praxis of hearing confessions. Sixteenth-century confessors had two major roles: judge (to determine a sin's gravity and its appropriate penance) and physician (to assign the proper remedy to cure the sinner from attraction to particular sins). But Jesuits were known as ministers of consolation, and the role of consoler influenced the other two roles that they assumed in the confessional. In training to be confessors, Jesuits introduced more and more circumstances into their cases in order to highlight the uniqueness of the subject's situation. The Jesuit confessor became as consoling as the Jesuit spiritual director, particularly in appreciation of/for the uniqueness of the particular penitent.

By the end of the sixteenth century, casuistry generated an enormous number of new moral insights that were articulated into rules, e.g., for war as in distinguishing soldiers from civilians or for abortion as in distinguishing an indirect abortion to save a mother's life. Methodological principles like double-effect, cooperation, and toleration were all also first formulated at the end of the sixteenth century. All these rules become the standards for the moral manuals of the next three centuries.

See also Confession, Confessor; Ethics; Probabilism

Jonsen, Albert, and Stephen Toulmin, eds., *The Abuse of Casuistry: A History of Moral Reasoning*. Berkeley: University of California Press, 1988.

Keenan, James F., and Thomas Shannon, eds., *The Context of Casuistry*. Washington, DC: Georgetown University Press, 1995.

Mahoney, John, *The Making of Moral Theology: A Study of the Roman Catholic Tradition*. New York: Oxford University Press, 1987.

James F. Keenan, SJ

Catechism

In the second half of the sixteenth century, both Protestants and Catholics published many catechisms, large and small, for adults or for children, for clergy or for laity, designed to delineate clearly what was (and what was not) the Christian faith, as their church understood and articulated it. Behind this proliferation of a certain kind of doctrinal manuals and textbooks lay a fear that ignorance of Christian doctrine abounded, and that this had to be corrected for the sake of the salvation of souls and the good of society. On the Catholic side of the confessional divide, Jesuits played a major part. Ignatius of Loyola insisted that the teaching of basic Christian doctrine to children and others in need of education be part of what Jesuits do, and that such work not be scorned as if it were beneath the dignity of Jesuit priests. The teaching of Christian doctrine to children was one of the priorities of Ignatius for the work that Jesuits were to do; in the very first paragraph of Pope Paul III's 1540 approval of the Society of Jesus, this priority is explicit.

After the Council of Trent (1545–63), and the publication by Pope Pius V (1566–72) of a catechism based on the Council's canons and decrees, Jesuits were prominent among those that propagated Trent's teachings, through preaching, teaching, and publications. The catechisms of Dutch Jesuit Peter Canisius (1521–97) appeared in various languages, while he focused on ministering to Catholics in Germany. By the early 1600s, catechisms of the Italian Jesuit and cardinal Robert Bellarmine (1542–1621) were available in several languages, English among them. Many other Jesuits in the early modern period produced catechisms, and even more taught catechism. As Jesuit missionaries went both into rural Europe and across the globe to many peoples and cultures, they often used images as well as (or instead of) words or texts to communicate. This was due not only to language barriers but also to the fact that images could be more powerful and more persuasive than words or words alone. Word and image went together and reinforced each other. For example, in Europe, Jesuits produced emblems and emblem books that paired an image with an inscription, a pairing that taught some moral message. Jesuit adaptation to a wide variety of circumstances included translating catechisms into local languages and cultures and making them accessible and comprehensible to peoples across the globe who had not been even remotely in or on the minds of the bishops at Trent. Among the challenges Jesuits faced was whether or not doctrines such as the Trinity, hard enough to explain even in Latin or in familiar western vernaculars, could be accurately expressed and convincingly taught in languages ranging from those spoken by Native Americans in the forests of Canada to those spoken by the intellectual and political elites of China or Japan. Still, Jesuits strived to overcome these challenges to some degree by training lay catechists among converts to Christianity, women as well as men.

In the last 200 years, the restored Society of Jesus has continued such traditions, both producing catechisms and teaching catechism, and adapting catechetical pedagogy to times and places and persons and circumstances. US Jesuits helped to propagate the Baltimore catechism, produced by order of a council of American bishops meeting at Baltimore in 1884. A catechism published in the 1920s by Jesuits Jerome O'Connor and William Hayden explicitly mentioned the Baltimore catechism in its subtitle. Thus did generations of Catholic children learn by heart the "correct" responses to questions such as who is God, what is perfect contrition, was anyone ever preserved from original sin, and what is heaven. Morality, especially sexual morality, could be featured prominently in some catechisms; a good example of this is a "catechism" published in the early 1930s by Flemish Jesuit Arthur Vermeersch (1858–1936) on the encyclical of Pope Pius XI, *Casti connubii*, treating marriage and birth control.

More recently, catechetical and other works published by Jesuits have helped to make Vatican II (1962–65) and its teachings accessible and well known on topics such as the liturgy, the laity, ecumenism, and the Church in the modern world. The growing centrality of Scripture in Catholic thought and life has also affected what Jesuits do in the field of catechetical literature. A good example is the Christological "catechism" of Joseph Fitzmyer, SJ. In the twenty-first century, Jesuit adaptation to circumstances will very likely integrate ever greater use of electronic media in the teaching of catechism.

See also Bellarmine, Robert, SJ; Canisius, Peter, SJ; Catechists, Women; Emblem Books; Theology

Filippi, Daniele, "A Sound Doctrine: Early Modern Jesuits and the Singing of the Catechism." *Early Music History* 34 (2015), 1–43.

Fitzmyer, Joseph A., *A Christological Catechism: New Testament Answers*. New York: Paulist Press, 1991.

Gagnon, François-Marc, *La conversion par l'image: Un aspect de la mission des jésuites auprès des indiens du Canada au XVIIe siècle*. Montreal: Bellarmin, 1975.

O'Connor, Jerome F., and William Hayden, *Chalk Talks: or, Teaching Catechism Graphically (Based on the Baltimore Catechism)*. St. Louis, MO: Queen's Work, 1928.

Vermeersch, Arthur, *What Is Marriage? A Catechism Arranged according to the Encyclical "Casti connubii" of Pope Pius XI*. Trans. T. Lincoln Bouscaren. New York: The America Press, 1932.

Thomas Worcester, SJ

Catechists, Women, and the Jesuits in Japan

Japanese catechists, both male and female, contributed greatly to the Jesuit mission in Japan between 1549 and 1650. Because of the shortage of priests, these catechists carried out many daily pastoral tasks.

Early on, the mission adopted the Zen acolyte ranks of *dōjuku* and *kambō* into their classes of coadjutors. These men often were former Buddhist monks. Most Jesuit *dōjuku* served as preachers in Japanese. Some taught Japanese language and literature at the seminaries and college. Others became interpreters for the missionaries, translators, and writers of the Kirishitanban literature, and debaters with Buddhist clergy. Still others were church artists, tea servers, and musicians. The mission sustained about 100 *dōjuku* in 1580 when Visitor Alessandro Valignano endorsed this system. There were about 300 *dōjuku* in 1609, assisting sixty-five *padres* (priests) and seventy-five *irmãos* (brothers). Well-known *dōjuku*, such as Yōhō Paulo (1508–95), a translator, and Ōta Augustino (1574–1631), the printer of the Jesuit Press, went on to become *irmãos*. Some eventually received ordination as priests.

Jesuit *kambō* maintained the local places of worship, led liturgy, and preached when *padres* and *irmãos* were not available. They regularly taught Christian Doctrine (catechism), visited the sick, heard confessions, and conducted baptisms, Christian funerals, and burials. In 1609 there were about 190 *cambō*, approximately one for every local congregation. *Kambō* became invaluable especially after the 1614 expulsion of the Jesuits. There were twenty-seven *kambō* between 1613 and 1630, of whom nineteen became martyrs, including Arakawa Adam (martyred 1614).

Many women also emulated the Jesuit active apostolate in their own ministries as catechists. Following their *Constitutions*, the Jesuits did not found a women's branch nor establish parallel coadjutor classes for women. Therefore, while the mission paid salaries and supplied expenses for the male catechists, similar women's activities remained without official sanction or support. Like their male counterparts, women catechists were evangelical preachers and pastors. Advantageously, women catechists had access to other women, who were not able to meet with the male clergy. In 1587, the Jesuits authorized Kiyohara Ito Maria to baptize Lady Hosokawa Tama Gracia (1563–1600), who was confined to her residence by her husband. Then, as the Jesuits went into hiding under Toyotomi Hideyoshi's *Edict of the Expulsion of Padres*, Ito Maria continued to minister to Tama Gracia as her "soul mother." In time she also baptized Tama Gracia's children. An unnamed lady-in-waiting heard Tama Gracia's confessions in later years.

The most prominent evangelist was Naitō Julia (*c.* 1566–1627), who before her conversion to Christianity had been a long-time Buddhist abbess of a Jōdo convent in Kyoto. In 1597, within a few months of her baptism in the Kyoto church, Bishop Luís

Cerqueira, SJ, confirmed her. She staged a religious disputation with Buddhist monks to prove her conversion. Around 1600, she formed a society of women catechists. She and her companions took the three monastic vows under the supervision of Gnechi-Soldo Organtino, SJ, and Pedro Morejón, SJ. The *Miyako no bikuni* (nuns of Miyako) set up their house next to the Jesuit house in Kyoto. For over a decade, these "nuns" preached, catechized, baptized, and if the need arose, heard confessions and engaged in interreligious debates. Because of her notoriety, the city magistrates ordered Julia's arrest several times between 1601 and 1605. Naitō Julia and the *Miyako no bikuni* worked together with another noteworthy catechist, Kyōgoku Maria (*c.* 1543–1618), and her women disciples and were said to have converted more than 60,000 women and men in the Osaka-Kyoto region by 1612.

When the Second Shogun Tokugawa Hidetada issued the definitive ban of Christianity in 1612, Kyōgoku Maria was forced to retire to the remote northern region. The authorities arrested and publicly tortured the *Miyako no bikuni*. In 1614 Naitō Julia and fourteen *bikuni* members were deported from Nagasaki to Manila, with P. Morjón and twenty-two Jesuits, and fourteen *dōjuku*. The *bikuni* became enclosed in a house next to the Jesuit house in San Miguel and devoted their time in visions and intercessory prayers. Julia died in 1623, and the last two members perished in 1656. The Jesuits celebrated their funeral Mass as if they were "their own." Other women catechists remained in Japan and became martyrs or went underground.

Even though the majority of these catechists were Japanese, notable Korean-born Christian converts, taken to Japan during Hideyoshi's invasion of Korea (1592–98), also became *dōjuku*, *kambō*, *bikuni*, and women catechists.

See also Japan; Women, as Co-Workers with Jesuits

Cieslik, Hubert, "Laienarbeit in der alten Japan-Mission." In Margret Dietrich and Arcadio Schwade, eds., *Publikationen über das Christentum in Japan: Veröffentlichungen in europäischen Sprachen*. Frankfurt am Main: Peter Lang, 2004, pp. 165–89.
López-Gay, Jesús, "Las organizaciones de laicos en el apostolado de la primitiva misión del Japón." *Archivum Historicum Societatis Iesu* 36 (1967), 3–31.
Schütte, Josef Franz, *Valignano's Mission Principles for Japan*. Trans. John J. Coyne. 2 vols. St. Louis, MO: The Institute of Jesuit Sources, 1980, 1985.
Ward, Haruko Nawata, *Women Religious Leaders in Japan's Christian Century, 1549–1650*. (Women and Gender in the Early Modern World). Farnham/Burlington, VT: Ashgate, 2009.

Haruko Nawata Ward

Catherine II ("the Great") of Russia

The daughter of the German prince of Anhalt-Zerbst, Catherine (1729–1796) married the heir to the Russian throne (the future Peter II) in 1745. Theirs was an unhappy marriage, marked by infidelity, and Catherine ascended to the throne upon the violent death of her husband (now czar) in 1762. On the one hand, Catherine II (r. 1762–1796) can be positioned as a monarch who embraced many of the intellectual trends of the eighteenth century, as witnessed by her affiliation with leading figures such as Diderot, d'Alembert, and Voltaire (though relations with such figures were not always cozy). On the other hand, portraying her as a typical Enlightenment figure determined to Europeanize her realm and usher in a brave new age of reason and liberty can be misleading. She certainly embraced western ideas in, for instance, her attempts at legal reform, but in many other spheres she preserved long-standing Russian policies and postures: during her reign the number of serfs in the empire increased, privileges were showered on the nobility, and her aggressive foreign policy did little to foster peaceful relations across the continent.

An ambivalent attitude toward western Europe can also be glimpsed in the history of the Society of Jesus in her dominions. As a result of the First Partition of the Polish-Lithuanian Commonwealth in 1772, the Russian Empire acquired White Russia and part of Livonia. This brought more than 200 Jesuits, responsible for four colleges, several missions, and residences, under the rule of Catherine II. A potentially disruptive event proved to be a blessing. When Clement XIV issued the papal brief *Dominus ac Redemptor* in 1773, suppressing the Society of Jesus, Catherine did not allow the document to be promulgated or enforced in her territories (a measure also taken, albeit temporarily, by the ruler of Prussia). The Jesuits were therefore able to sustain a corporate existence in the Russian Empire and foster moves toward formal restoration throughout the Suppression era. The irony that this was made possible in an Orthodox nation was not lost on contemporaries.

Catherine did not act primarily out of any great sympathy for the Jesuits, although she admired their educational achievements. Rather, her decisions stemmed from an attempt to resist papal interference in her realms. Tellingly, one of her first actions following the Partition was to remove Catholics in her new territories from the authority of bishops in the Commonwealth and to establish a new see at Mohilev. It is also reasonable to identify a note of infuriation with the Bourbon powers further west in Catherine's actions. She resented the assumption that she should fall into line with the agenda of the western Catholic powers. Nonetheless, the Society benefited greatly from the consequences of the Partition: a stroke of geopolitical good fortune. In short measure the surviving Jesuit community in White Russia, led by its former provincial, Stanisław Czerniewicz (1728–85), was able to begin ordaining candidates for the priesthood, open a novitiate, and resume courses in philosophy and theology. A General Congregation at Połock in 1782 elected Czerniewicz as "Vicar General for life," and he was granted all the powers of a father general "until a Father General is elected with the restoration of the Universal Society." A year later, papal confirmation of the "Russian" Society was given, although only orally at this stage, during an audience with Catherine's envoy Jan Benislawski.

It is important to note that Jesuits who had begun their careers within the Polish-Lithuanian Commonwealth worked hard during the post-Partition years to sustain the cultural legacy they had inherited but, beyond question, the survival of a newly minted "Russian" fragment of the Society was a source of great sustenance during the Suppression era. Ex-Jesuits around the globe would seek affiliation, those with ties to the "Russian" Society would play a starring role in revitalizing Jesuit activity from Parma to the USA, and the college at Połock would emerge as one of the most dynamic educational institutions in eastern Europe.

See also Russia; Suppression

Inglot, Marek, *La Compagnia di Gesù nell'impero Russo (1772–1820) e la sua parte nella restaurazione generale della Compagnia*. Rome: Gregorian University, 1997.

"The Society of Jesus in the Russian Empire (1772–1820) and the Restoration of the Order." In Robert Maryks and Jonathan Wright, eds., *Jesuit Survival and Restoration: A Global History, 1773–1900.* Leiden: Brill, 2014, pp. 67–82.

de Madariaga, Isabel, *Catherine the Great.* New Haven, CT: Yale University Press, 2002.

Pavone, Sabina, *Una strana alleanza: la Compagnia di Gesù in Russia dal 1772 al 1820.* Naples: Bibliopolis, 2008.

Jonathan Wright

Caussade, Jean-Pierre de, SJ (1675–1748)

Jean-Pierre de Caussade is a prominent figure of French spiritual literature who was active mostly in the second quarter of the eighteenth century. Born in the town of Cahors, in southwestern France, Caussade became a Jesuit in 1693 in Toulouse and completed his training in the final years of Louis XIV's reign. His missionary activity focused on the towns of his native province as well as on some others in France (in Lorraine or Picardy). In Nancy he built a strong relationship with the local Visitandines, a congregation of women founded in the early seventeenth century by Jeanne de Chantal with whom he shared a common esteem for François de Sales's spirituality.

Caussade confronted the crisis of mysticism in late seventeenth- and eighteenth-century France. The first part of his main work, the *Instructions spirituelles*, published anonymously by Paul-Gabriel Antoine, a major eighteenth-century Jesuit theologian, commented on Bossuet's *Instruction sur les états d'oraison*, a text that the late bishop of Meaux had written in 1694 to impugn Madame Guyon's *Moyen court de faire oraison*. He tried to defend the Salesian vocabulary of spiritual "indifference" and did so by painting it as a heroic faith in God's will.

While he played a significant role in spiritual circles in eighteenth-century France, he was reclaimed as a major figure of the history of the Society of Jesus only in the second half of the nineteenth century (his *Abandon à la Providence divine* remained unknown until its publication in 1861) along with others who, like him, had attempted to find common ground between quietist practice of spirituality and doctrinal orthodoxy.

See also France

Gagey, Jacques, "'Le Traité où l'on découvre la vraie science de la perfection du salut' et la tradition spirituelle caussadienne: histoire, critique et théologie." Doctoral thesis, Pontifical Gregorian University, Rome, 1994.

Olphe-Gaillard, Michel, *La théologie mystique en France au XVIIIe siècle: Le Père de Caussade.* Paris: Beauchesne, 1984.

Jean-Pascal Gay

Caussin, Nicolas, SJ (1583–1651)

Nicolas Caussin remains famous both as a spiritual writer and as confessor to King Louis XIII at the time of Richelieu's ministry. Caussin, born during the years of the Wars of Religion, became a Jesuit in 1607, shortly after Henry IV recalled the Order in the parts of France it had been banished from. After having taught the humanities, he became a preacher at the professed house in Paris, where he enjoyed tremendous popularity particularly among the aristocracy. His apostolate to the upper classes inspired his most famous spiritual work, *La cour sainte*, in which he sketched a path for aristocratic devotion.

He succeeded Jacques Gordon as confessor to the King in1637. The appointment came in a dire political context as France stepped up its involvement in the Thirty Years War. French diplomacy, namely the Protestant alliances, was the object of strong criticism from *dévots* circles who portrayed it as detrimental to the global cause of Catholicism. Caussin, who had fostered reconciliation between Louis and his wife, came under suspicion from Richelieu for being in league with his political adversaries and for trying to use his influence as confessor to affect French policies. Muzio Vitelleschi had indeed encouraged him to remind the King of the sufferings that war brought upon Europe. Louis granted Richelieu Caussin's exile to Brittany with the approval of the Jesuit curia. The episode proved decisive in bringing about a distinction between the public and private persons of the sovereign that later confessors acknowledged as a given.

During her regency, Anna of Austria recalled him from his exile, and he took part in the controversies between the Society of Jesus and its adversaries in the early 1640s.

See also France

Bireley, Robert, *The Jesuits and the Thirty Years War: Kings, Courts and Confessors*. Cambridge: Cambridge University Press, 2003.

de Rochemonteix, Camille, *Nicolas Caussin, confesseur de Louis XIII et le Cardinal de Richelieu*. Paris: Picard, 1911.

Jean-Pascal Gay

Centre Sèvres – Facultés Jésuites de Paris

The Centre Sèvres – Facultés Jésuites de Paris is an institution of higher education of the Society of Jesus in Paris. It was founded in 1974 at the instigation of Jacques Sommet, SJ (the first president), Paul Valadier, SJ, and Pierre Vallin, SJ. It resulted from the fusion of two ecclesiastical faculties of philosophy and theology then located respectively in Chantilly and Lyon. At the core of its mission is the formation of Jesuit scholastics and brothers, but from the beginning it has welcomed male and female religious from other orders, as well as laypeople. A central intuition which led to the foundation was the desire for a fruitful dialogue between philosophy and theology both among faculties and during the process of formation. A first cycle of studies is thus offered which is called "integrated" because it combines philosophy and theology for five years instead of the traditional curriculum in Catholic seminaries (a cycle of philosophy followed by one of theology). Following the Ignatian tradition, the pedagogy stresses personal tutoring and in-depth integration of the various elements of the education, including personal life and apostolic experiences, thanks to regular re-reading of the intellectual journey accomplished by a student.

In 2014 the Centre Sèvres welcomed some 250 students pursuing ecclesiastical degrees in philosophy and/or theology (bachelor degrees, licentiates, doctorates) and some 2,000 auditors simply taking classes or attending talks. In addition to the two ecclesiastical faculties, the institution comprises six specialized departments: (1) aesthetics, (2) biomedical ethics, (3) public ethics and international relations, (4) patristic, (5) cultures and religions, (6) spirituality and religious life. It also hosts a center for Chinese studies, the Ricci Institute of Paris. There are forty permanent professors, half of them Jesuits. The library, which came from various older Jesuit formation centers, is renowned for its collection of Jesuit archives, *Jesuitica*. The Centre Sèvres publishes two scholarly journals: *Recherches de science religieuse* and *Archives de philosophie*.

See also Formation; France; Paris; Philosophy; Theology

Grégoire Catta, SJ

Certeau, Michel de, SJ (1925–1986)

A Savoyard born in Chambéry on May 17, 1925, Michel de Certeau came from a family of the *petite noblesse*. As a young man, de Certeau traversed the mountain paths of the Savoy as a messenger of the French Resistance. When the war drew to a close, he traveled throughout France in the style of a medieval *peregrinatio academica*, attending lectures and seeking out celebrated figures of the French Academy. During this time he studied formally at the universities of Grenoble, Paris, and Lyon, receiving degrees in classics and philosophy.

In 1950 de Certeau entered the Society of Jesus. His formation was expedited because of his previous study, and he was ordained at Lyon in 1956. Thereafter, he returned to the Sorbonne to complete a doctoral dissertation on the writings of Peter Faber, publishing a scholarly edition of Faber's *Memoriale* in a celebrated French translation and commentary (1960). With a continued interest in spirituality, he turned his attention to the seventeenth-century French Jesuit mystic Jean-Joseph Surin, publishing an edition of Surin's *Guide spirituel* in 1963 and his *Correspondance* in 1966.

In 1967 de Certeau was the victim of an automobile accident in which his mother died and he lost vision in one eye. A year later, the demonstrations of May 1968 in Paris and across the world exerted a profound effect upon him. Describing the events as a "foundational rupture," de Certeau emerged as a prominent intellectual interpreter of them for the French public. In interviews and articles, he argued that "the 'revolutionary' speech of May 1968" was "a symbolic action" that called "for a global revision of our cultural system." An essay of his in *Études* famously began: "Last May speech was taken just as in 1789 the Bastille was taken."

In 1970 de Certeau produced a study of the strange events at Loudun in seventeenth-century France in which Surin was called to perform exorcisms on a group of Ursuline nuns. Entitled *La possession de Loudun*, the work offered critical analysis that dissected power dynamics operative in the marginalization of the religious women and the validation of dominant religious and political structures. His work on Surin also led to an interest in psychoanalysis, and de Certeau is counted among the founding members of the École freudienne of Jacques Lacan in Paris.

In the years that followed, de Certeau became increasingly focused upon cultural analysis. Having published *La culture au pluriel* in 1974, he released a study in 1980 that became a classic in cultural theory, *L'Invention du quotidien*. The work analyzed the ways in which an anonymous majority develops daily practices of resistance to the socio-cultural productions imposed upon them by those in power. De Certeau proposed a signature distinction between "strategy" and "tactics." Whereas "strategies" are imposed from above by those in power, "tactics" are creative, everyday methods of resistance deployed by the subjugated and repressed.

Luce Giard, de Certeau's longtime collaborator in scholarship, notes that while he is "internationally known mainly as a cultural theorist, de Certeau invariably called himself a 'historian of spirituality.'" Philip Sheldrake has argued that, for de Certeau, the two were ultimately interconnected, for he understood "the 'privileged places' for the development of mystical practice" as paradoxically inhabited by "people of little or no power in the public realm."

De Certeau also continued to publish more explicitly historical works, such as *L'Écriture de l'histoire* in 1975 and *La fable mystique (XVIe–XVIIe siècle)* in 1982. Throughout his writings, emphasis is placed upon *altérité*, or the otherness of the past, and the way in which interpretation involves *braconnage*, or poaching. He famously remarked: "Lire: un bracconage" (Reading: a kind of poaching).

Having taught in a multitude of places and countries throughout his career, including the University of Paris (VII and VIII) and the University of California in San Diego, in 1984 de Certeau was offered the prestigious position of *directeur d'études* (research professor) at the École des Hautes Études in Paris. A year later, however, he was diagnosed with pancreatic cancer and died on January 9, 1986.

His funeral at the Jesuit Church of Saint-Ignace in Paris drew an immense crowd, with hundreds participating only by way of loudspeakers posted outside the church. There they heard selections specifically chosen by de Certeau: a reading from 1 Corinthians about how "God has chosen the foolish things of the world to confound the wise," a recording of Edith Piaf's "Non, je ne regrette rien" (No, I regret nothing), and an excerpt from Surin's *Spiritual Canticle* about a wandering soul on pilgrimage, shedding all but divine love.

See also France; Paris; Surin, Jean-Joseph, SJ

Ahearne, Jeremy, *Michel de Certeau: Interpretation and Its Other*. Cambridge: Polity Press, 1995.
Bocken, Inigo, ed., *Spiritual Spaces: History and Mysticism in Michel de Certeau*. Leuven: Peeters, 2013.
de Certeau, Michel, *The Practice of Everyday Life*. Trans. Steven Randall. Berkeley: University of California Press, 1984.
Giard, Luce, ed., *Michel de Certeau*. Paris: Centre Georges Pompidou, 1987.

Henry Shea, SJ

Charism

Understood as broadly as possible, a charism is a specific gift bestowed on a person, or persons, by the Spirit of God for the purpose of making God better known in the Church and in the world. Charisms feature prominently in the writings of St. Paul, who points to there being a "variety of gifts" in the Christian community, all bestowed by the same Spirit (1 Corinthians 12:4); and these are given for the building up of the entire Body of believers. The root meaning of the word "charism" is gift: a free gift, or grace, bestowed by God.

The distinctiveness of a religious order or congregation has to do with the particular gift (charism) given to its founder (or founders). The decree of the Second Vatican Council, *Perfectae caritatis* (PC, October 28, 1965), encouraged a renewal of religious orders and congregations based on a return both to the sources of the whole of the Christian life and to the original inspiration of their own founders, with suitable adaptation for contemporary conditions (PC, 2). Thus, the Society of Jesus sought to reengage not only with the spirit of St. Ignatius and the early Jesuits but also with the Order's founding texts such as the *Spiritual Exercises* and the *Constitutions*. Through research, study, and a rediscovery of the dynamic character of Jesuit and Ignatian spirituality, there was a renewal, in various parts of the world, of the charism, the distinctive gift, given to St. Ignatius and the first Jesuits.

A charism can be difficult to capture and define. It refers to the Jesuits' characteristic "way of proceeding," to their particular way of being disciples of Christ. Expressions such as "finding God in all things," being a "contemplative in action," doing all "for the greater glory of God" seek to capture the heart of the Jesuit charism. A decree of the 35th General Congregation (in 2008) sought to articulate the identity of Jesuits today and its subtitle was: "Rediscovering Our Charism." What Vatican II asked for – renewal based on returning to a founder's inspiration and adapting it for today's circumstances – remains ongoing.

See also Loyola, Ignatius of, SJ, St.; Mission; Vatican II; Way of Proceeding

Witwer, Toni, "The Grace of Vocation and Charisms in the Church." *The Way* 49, 2 (April 2010), 7–19.

James Corkery, SJ

Charles III of Spain

The Spanish branch of the Society came under serious attack in the wake of a series of riots during 1766. They were chiefly prompted by food shortages and popular opposition to the fiscal reforms enacted by Charles III (1716–1788; r. 1759–1788) following his accession in 1759. The riots were also welcomed by some members of the ruling classes who were discontented with Charles's reforms and harbored hostility toward leading members of his government.

Charles was greatly alarmed by the riots and charged a special *sala* of the council of Castile to conduct an inquiry into the possible causes. Despite an absence of evidence, a judgment of December 1766 charged the Society of Jesus with involvement, to the extent of accusing the Order's Superior General Lorenzo Ricci with fomenting an attempted *coup d'état*. The council of state approved this document on February 20, 1767, and a week later, Charles issued a royal decree ordering the Jesuits' expulsion from his territories.

Charles's actions should be seen in the context of his broader religious policies. He was determined to assert royal control in ecclesiastical matters and to limit papal interference: He had previously brought the collection of some ecclesiastical taxes into royal hands and had imposed conditions on the publication of any papal documents in his realms. He perceived the Society of Jesus as an obstacle to this regalist agenda. Following the Spanish expulsion, Charles's ambassadors in Rome would interfere dramatically in the conclave (1769) that elected Clement XIV and play the leading role in pressuring that pope into ordering the global suppression of the Society in 1773.

See also Spain; Suppression

Guasti, Niccolò, *Lotta politica e riforme all'inizio del regno di Carlo III: Campomanes e l'espulsione dei gesuiti dalla monarchia spagnola (1759–1768)*. Florence: Alinea, 2006.
Paquette, Gabriel, *Enlightenment, Governance, and Reform in Spain and Its Empire, 1759–1808*. Basingstoke: Palgrave Macmillan, 2008.

Jonathan Wright

Charpentier, Marc-Antoine

Marc-Antoine Charpentier (*c*. 1643–1704) was a French Baroque composer, born in or near Paris. The exact date and place of his birth has not been given historical documentation. His father was a master scribe and came from a family of notaries in Meaux. Little is known about Charpentier's early life and education, and according to some indirect sources he may have been educated by the Jesuits in Paris. He did travel to Italy during the mid-1660s to study music, supposedly with Carissimi, though there is no evidence that he studied under him (according to an article published in the French literary magazine, the *Mercure Galant*, March 1688, he did study under the composer). However, Charpentier did have abundant contact with the mid-seventeenth-century Italian musical style in Rome that he soon incorporated into his own compositions. Upon his return to Paris, he did have copies of Carissimi's oratorio *Jepthe* and motets and masses by other Roman composers, including Alessandro Stradella and Domenico Mazzocchi.

After his return to Paris, he came into contact with Marie de Lorraine, a rich noblewoman known as Mademoiselle de Guise. He lived in an apartment in her vast residence, the Hôtel de Guise, and she hired him to be her composer-in-residence and singer. He composed dramatic sacred motets, settings of the Psalms, as well as secular works – small operas as entertainments for her and her guests. Owing perhaps to his employment with the Guise family, he was able to make connections with other artists, most notably Molière and the Comédie Française. His chief musical rival was Lully, the court composer to Louis XIV, who made it virtually impossible for Charpentier to be given a royal appointment. However, Mlle. de Guise recommended him to the Society of Jesus for a much higher postition.

Charpentier did possess credentials that made him appealing to the Jesuits. People believed that he was a pupil of Carissimi and that bolstered his reputation. He had lived in Rome, the center of the Catholic Counter-Reformation. He worked with two former students of the French Jesuit colleges, Molière and Corneille, two of the best French playwrights of the seventeenth century. Lastly, his compositions impressed the Jesuits, so much so that they hired him to be the organist and music master of their church in the rue Saint-Antoine. He had earlier composed music for the sacred dramas of the Collège de Louis-Grand. *Celse Martyr* was written in 1687 and *David et Jonathas* in 1688. The libretto for the former has survived and the music for the latter survives from a full score copied in 1690. Earlier in his career, Charpentier composed music and worked for the Jesuits at the Collège de Clermont as the *maître de chapelle* in the mid-1670s. The college was renamed as the Collège de Louis-le-Grand in 1683. He was also the *maître de musique* for the principal Jesuit church in Paris, St. Louis. With these two appointments, he achieved much success. With the appointment as the *maître de musique* in the Jesuit church, St. Louis, Charpentier also had the best singers and musicians from the Opéra and the Académie Royale to perform his compositions.

One of the many compositions he composed during his appointments with the college and church is a *Miserere des Jésuites* (H. 193). Long thought to have been written for the order, it was originally written for the Guise family, as the *des Jésuites* was not in the autograph but later added. It is possible that the work was performed in the Jesuit church, but there is no proof for that claim. By the 1680s Charpentier appeared to be working exclusively for the Society. Compositions from this decade include a *Salve regina des Jésuites* (H. 27), the sacred dramas *Mors Saülis et Jonathae* (H. 403), a "Grand motet ou dialogue, pièce pour les Jésuites en tragédie," and *Josue* (H. 404). The *Mercure Galant* published accounts of three very important ceremonies for the Jesuits in which Charpentier's music received notice: the 1691 April Tenebrae services (H. 126–34), the 1692 motet for the feast of St. Louis (August 25), *In honorem Sancti Ludovici Regis Galliae* (H. 418), and for the funeral of the Maréchal Duc de Luxembourg (April 21, 1695), the *Messe des morts à 4 voix et symphonie* (H. 10). For the feast day of Francis Xavier on December 3, he composed the motet *In honorem Sancti Xaverii Canticum* (H. 355) and the *Canticum de Sancto Xaverio reformatum* (H. 355a); these were most likely to have been performed in either 1691 or 1692. Along with the motets honoring Xavier, his *Motet pour Francis de Borgia* (H. 354) honors that saint. His music served as a means of contemplation and asked the listener to respond, in accordance with Jesuit spirituality.

See also Art Patronage; Music; Paris

Cessac, Catherine, *Marc-Antoine Charpentier*. Trans. E. Thomas Glasow. Portland, OR: Amadeus Press, 1995.

Hitchcock, Hugh Wiley, *Marc-Antoine Charpentier*. Oxford: Oxford University Press, 1990.

"The Latin Oratorios of Marc-Antoine Charpentier." *The Musical Quarterly* 41 (1955), 41–65.

Gosine, Jane, and Erik Oland, *Docere, Delectare, Movere: Marc-Antoine Charpentier and Jesuit Spirituality*. Oxford: Early Music, 2004.

Charles Jurgensmeier, SJ

Chastity

It should be noted straightaway that there is nothing distinctly "Jesuit" about the vow of chastity that Jesuits live. In writing the *Constitutions*, Ignatius seemed intent that this new religious congregation be known chiefly by the members' unique observance of the vow of obedience (practiced in large part through the annual account of conscience), while also laying out stringent guidelines for the observance of poverty regarding the use of material possessions and alms, especially for the professed.

On chastity, however, Ignatius said precious little, writing only that "What pertains to the vow of chastity requires no interpretation, since it is evident how perfectly it should be preserved, by endeavoring to imitate therein the purity of the angels in cleanness of body and mind" (*Constitutions*, #547). However, Ignatius's simple and pious brevity (which we can rightly assume is a product of his time) has been expanded greatly in the succeeding years, most especially in the documents produced by the 31st to 35th General Congregations in response to developments in the understanding of psychosexuality, changing sexual mores, and the scandal of child sex abuse.

Like the vows of poverty and obedience, the Jesuit's vow of chastity is understood first and foremost as apostolic in nature, or at the service of his work as an apostle of Christ. Never intended solely for personal sanctification, chastity is best lived by the Jesuit who has his eyes set on the Kingdom, working to bring about the Reign of God, intent on "saving souls." To that end, a Jesuit forgoes married life and the possibility of children so as to remain apostolically available and geographically mobile – to be sent on mission. However, since "no one lives without love" it is important to note that a chaste life is not a loveless life. Instead, the chastity lived by any Jesuit is a means to greater love, freely given in service to all, and not reserved for an exclusive partner or family.

While a Jesuit forgoes the possibility of raising children of his own, it does not mean that he is not actively generative, for the Kingdom is always in need of rebirth. Indeed, the vow of chastity is not a denial of generativity, only of genital activity. This distinction is important: Chastity is not meant to be emasculating, depressive, or suppressive, but rather a unique way in which a Jesuit is called to live his affective life with apostolic purpose and witness. And while regular periods of solitude should be a natural and healthy part of a Jesuit's life, loneliness – though at times inevitable and difficult – is never prescribed.

To live a life of perpetual chastity well, a Jesuit's affective needs must be known, nurtured, and well integrated. A Jesuit who lacks affective integration may bring ruin and pain to the lives of others or might live the life of a religious-bachelor: cold, aloof, unloving, and unaware. The documents of the most recent General Congregations (GCs) make it abundantly clear that neither example is acceptable, for chastity is not a pious or simplistic ideal, but a complex way of life that needs to be actively nurtured, persistently discerned, and continually integrated. Frequent references to boundaries for the Jesuit are meant to encourage him to live his chastity as a love that can be trusted.

To this end, the Society in its wisdom offers suggestions and helps for Jesuits to consider in their growth in the vow of chastity: openness to one's superiors, cultivating rich cultural interests, true charity, union with Christ in prayer and in the Eucharist, a special devotion to Our Lady, recourse to spiritual direction and the Sacrament of Reconciliation, and active participation in one's local community.

Though the value of chastity has been questioned, especially in light of the sexual abuse crisis, delegates to GC 32 wrote in Decree 11, #26 about the enduring place of chastity in the modern world:

> Celibacy for the sake of the Kingdom has a special apostolic value in our time, when men tend to put whole classes of their fellow human beings beyond the margins of their concern, while at the same time identifying love with eroticism. In such a time, the self-denying love which is warmly human, yet freely given in service to all, can be a powerful sign leading men to Christ who came to show us what love really is: that God is love.

See also Obedience; Poverty

The Constitutions of the Society of Jesus and Their Complementary Norms. Ed. John W. Padberg. St. Louis, MO: The Institute of Jesuit Sources, 1996.

Sonny Manuel, Gerdenio, "Living Chastity: Psychosexual Well-Being in Jesuit Life." *Studies in the Spirituality of Jesuits* 41, 2 (Summer 2009), 1–36.

Padberg, John W., ed., *Jesuit Life & Mission Today: The Decrees of the 31st–35th General Congregations of the Society of Jesus.* St. Louis, MO: The Institute of Jesuit Sources, 2009.

Keith Maczkiewicz, SJ

Chile

On February 9, 1593, eight Jesuits left Peru for Chile. They reached Santiago on April 11. There they founded a residence and a school and also began to carry out missions among the indigenous Mapuche. The Society had not long established itself before a major indigenous uprising (December 1598) destroyed all the Spanish settlements between the archipelago of Chiloe and the River Bío Bío. After initial uncertainty, by 1604 the Jesuits were convinced that the reasons for the uprising were due to the injustice of forced indigenous labor.

In 1607, the administration of the Chilean missions was transferred to the newly created Province of Paraguay. The Jesuits, meanwhile, were deeply committed to ending the war which was causing so much suffering and proving a significant obstacle to evangelization. Thus, in consultation with Viceroy Juan de Mendoza y Luna, Luis de Valdivia designed what became known as the Defensive War in which the Spanish were to withdraw to a line of forts along the Bío Bío. Philip III approved the plan on December 8, 1610. In 1611 Valdivia was appointed superior of the missions to be founded south of Concepción, and he returned to Chile in 1612 with another ten Jesuits to implement the strategic Defensive War on behalf of the Crown.

The strategy began badly. It was ill-received by the Spanish colonists and almost collapsed after a serious misunderstanding with a powerful Mapuche war leader named Anganamon resulted in the massacre of three Jesuits and the indigenous people of Elicura who had accepted the peace treaty. Word spread among the Mapuche of the treachery of both Spaniards and Jesuits, and Valdivia's plan began to unravel.

Despite the Society's best efforts, Philip IV suspended the Defensive War in 1625. That same year Chile was officially designated a vice province and was returned to the administrative jurisdiction of Peru. Notwithstanding regular polemics due to the Society's opposition to ongoing warfare and the enslavement of the Mapuche, throughout the seventeenth century they opened four colleges and two residences, and they also founded a significant number of missions.

In 1683 Chile became a province in its own right, and the Jesuits established a school for the sons of indigenous leaders in Chillán; they also continued to found residences and colleges, and took on the seminary in Concepción. During the eighteenth century, the missions grew further despite ongoing conflict. A general uprising in 1723 meant that all but five missions closed, but when hostilities died down, missionary work began again. This work was given new vibrancy between 1712 and 1754 by the arrival of expert Jesuit artisans and architects from Germany.

With the expulsion of the Society from all Spanish territories, on August 26, 1767, the Chilean Jesuits were exiled to the Papal States (Imola, Rome, and Bologna). It was not until the 1840s that the reestablished Society was finally invited to return.

In 1848 a number of Jesuits from Argentina founded a residence in Santiago and then Valparaíso (1850). German Jesuits were also sent to minister to German immigrant communities in Puerto Montt, in the south. By the late 1860s, the joint Chilean-Argentine mission had begun to regain a firm footing, and by the end of the century, Jesuits were teaching in Chilean seminaries and leading catechesis and popular missions, and their schools were full. In 1918 the Argentine-Chilean province was founded, and given the Society's continued expansion, the independent vice province of Chile was created in 1937. This, in turn, became a province in 1958.

The twentieth century saw active engagement with the social doctrine of the Church. In 1944 the parish of Jesus the Worker in a working-class district of Santiago was founded, while Jesuit ministry during the 1950s, exemplified by that of Alberto Hurtado (canonized October 23, 2005), created a significant intellectual, social, and cultural legacy. Centers for social research and development were set up: for example, the Center of Investigation and Social Action (CIAS) in 1957; the Center for Investigation and Educational Development (CIDE) in 1965; and the Latin American Institute for Social Studies (ILADES) in 1966. In 1973 the brutality of the military coup precipitated a shift in the Society's focus toward justice and the protection of Chileans from state persecution. This new emphasis formed a key part of the rationale for the foundation of the University of Alberto Hurtado in 1997. The Society's historical legacy of peacemaking and social justice continues to the present with Jesuit mediation in the ongoing conflict between the Mapuche and the Chilean state.

See also Arauco; Chiloé Mission; Paraguay Missions ("Reductions"); Valdivia, Luis de, SJ

Espindola, Walter Hanisch, *Historia de la Compañía de Jesus en Chile*. Buenos Aires/Santiago: Editorial Francisco de Aguirre, 1974.
Foerster, Rolf, *Jesuitas y mapuches 1593–1767*. Santiago: Editorial Universitaria, 1996.
Korth, Eugene, *Spanish Policy in Colonial Chile: The Struggle for Social Justice, 1535–1700*. Stanford, CA: Stanford University Press, 1968.

Andrew Redden

Chiloé, Mission

The first permanent Jesuit mission to the archipelago of Chiloé was founded in the year 1608 in the Spanish settlement of Castro. From the beginning, missionaries faced considerable hardship. The southern latitude of the archipelago meant that the weather conditions could be extremely unpleasant; frequent storms and difficult sea currents meant that those on the island were cut off from the Spanish mainland for half a year. Missionaries had to rely on what could be delivered to the island during summer or on what was produced on the island itself. While missionaries would be posted to Chiloé from Chile, the mission (which later expanded with the foundation of other permanent missions in Achao, Chonchi, and Cailín) was sustained by direct links with Lima. Timber was shipped to Lima where it would then be sold by the Jesuit procurator to pay for goods to be shipped back.

In order to evangelize the dispersed indigenous populations of the archipelago, the Jesuits pioneered the "itinerant missions" system, in which the missionaries would travel by canoe from community to community between the months of September and May. Each community would have its own chapel and a native catechist (*fiscal*) or sacristan, who would look after the chapel and the faith of the community in the missionary's absence. During the eighteenth century, Jesuit mission culture on the islands flourished with the arrival of German Jesuits. With the expulsion of the Society in 1767, the missions in Chiloé passed to the Franciscan order.

See also Arauco; Chile

Bailey, Gauvin A., "Cultural Convergence at the Ends of the Earth: The Unique Art and Architecture of the Jesuit Missions to the Chiloé Archipelago (1608–1767)." In John W. O'Malley, Gauvin A.

Bailey, Steven J. Harris, and T. Frank Kennedy, eds., *The Jesuits II: Cultures, Sciences and the Arts 1540–1773*. Toronto: University of Toronto Press, 2010, pp. 211–39.
Jería, Rodrigo Moreno, *Misiones en Chile austral: los jesuitas en Chiloé 1608–1768*. Seville: CISC/ Universidad de Sevilla, 2007.

Andrew Redden

China

General Characteristics

The Jesuit mission in China in the seventeenth and eighteenth centuries can be described in four characteristics. First, the policy of accommodation or adaptation to Chinese culture. While the first Jesuits dressed like Buddhist monks, they soon adapted themselves to the lifestyle and etiquette of the Confucian elite of literati and officials. This policy remained unchanged throughout the two centuries, and for most Jesuit missionaries, Matteo Ricci (1552–1610) became the reference with regard to this policy. Accommodation was facilitated by the significant similarity between China and Europe regarding the means of cultural transmission, i.e. the a widespread printing practice and a well-developed education system. As a result, the Jesuits actively promoted an "apostolate through books" destined for the educated elite. An impressive number of texts was produced in Chinese by missionaries and Chinese Christians. For the seventeenth century, in addition to some 120 texts dealing with the West and its sciences, there were some 470 texts mainly related to religious and moral issues, of which some 330 were written by missionaries, most of them by Jesuits.

Second, the evangelization "from the top down." Jesuits addressed themselves to the elite of literati. The underlying idea was that if this elite, preferably the emperor and his court, were converted, the whole country would be won for Christianity. The elite consisted mainly of literati who had spent many years of their life preparing for the examinations so as to enter officialdom. In the early period of the mission, several of them converted to Christianity. Since the 1630s, however, the contacts with the literati elite weakened and became mainly focused on the court and court officials in Beijing. Yet the predominant image of the Jesuit mission as primarily elite is cast in a different light if one looks at the statistics of the Christian population. In general, the elite represented merely 1 to 2 percent of the total Catholic population. By far the largest group of Christians being illiterate commoners.

Third, the indirect propagation by using European science and technology. Jesuits offered a European clock to the emperor, they introduced paintings which surprised the Chinese by their use of perspective, translated mathematical writings of Euclid, translated books on calendar, agriculture, and technology, and printed an enormous global map which integrated the results of the latest world explorations. These translations introduced a new worldview and were used to prove the solidity of their arguments that went hand in hand with their faith.

Fourth, the openness to and tolerance of Chinese values. In China, Jesuits encountered a society with high moral values expressed in a rich culture of book learning. They were of the opinion that the social doctrine of Confucianism should be complemented with the metaphysical ideas of Christianity. However, following Ricci, most Jesuits rejected Buddhism and Neo-Confucianism, which, in their eyes, was corrupted by Buddhism. Their use of traditional names for God and tolerant attitude toward certain Confucian rites led to the "Rites Controversy" and their condemnation in the early eighteenth century.

The Jesuit corporate culture in China, however, was not only the result of a conscious and well-defined policy conceived by the Jesuits themselves but also, to a large extent, the result of their reaction to what China was and who the Chinese were. In other words, their corporate identity was shaped by the Chinese other as well. If the Jesuits in China became who they became, it was also because the other encouraged them actively or passively to become like that. The many examples of how Jesuits' activities were shaped by the Chinese can be summarized under the label "cultural imperative," a characteristic belonging to the structure of Chinese religious life in late imperial China. No marginal religion penetrating from the outside could expect to take root in China unless it conformed itself to the Confucian orthodoxy and orthopraxy in a religious, ritual, social, and political sense. In order not to be branded as heterodox or heteroprax, a marginal religion had to prove that it was on the side of the Confucian tradition. In other words, the adaptation was not only a choice but also, to a large extent, constantly imposed on the Jesuits. In this process, it was the Chinese that occupied the dominant position, since they effectively hosted the foreigners on their own territory, obliging them to adapt to the native culture. The clearest example of this was the predominance of the Chinese or Manchu language throughout the exchange. With the exception of a very small number of Chinese educated for the priesthood, no Chinese involved in the interaction learned a foreign language.

Historical Overview

Based on developments proper to the mission as well as external to it, the Jesuit presence in China during the 200 years before the Suppression can roughly be divided into five periods, each covering approximately thirty to forty years. While in total over 400 Jesuits were active in China during this whole period of 1583–1775, the number of Jesuits who served at any one time was rather small. During this whole period, their number never reached one hundred.

The first period from 1583 to 1616 was the time of the pioneers. It was characterized by the person of Matteo Ricci, who was born the year that Francis Xavier died on an island before the Chinese coast. Under the encouragement of the Visitor of Asia, Alessandro Valignano (1539–1606), he developed a missionary attitude that laid the ground for the next 200 hundred years. Ricci was responsible for the geographical move from the south to the north and from the periphery to the capital in Beijing. His network-building was established through personal relationships and he proceeded from one city to another. Besides the translation of mathematical and astronomical texts, one of his most important texts was a treatise on "Friendship" (*Jiaoyou lun*, 1595). His catechism, entitled the "Solid Meaning of the Lord of Heaven" (*Tianzhu shiyi*, 1603), considered the ancient Chinese classics as a source of natural theology. Nicolas Trigault (1577–1628), who arrived in China the year that Matteo Ricci died, returned to Europe a few years later. There he published *De Christiana expeditione apud Sinas svscepta ab Societate Iesv* through which Ricci's work became well known in Europe. In 1610, at the moment of his death, there were sixteen Jesuits in China, eight Chinese and eight foreigners, with c. 2,500 Christians. A few years later, in 1616–17, an anti-Christian movement forced the Jesuits to withdraw to the middle region of the country.

Around 1620, when the threat of persecution calmed down, a new group of missionaries initiated a second period, which comprised large-scale translation activities, based on the books that had arrived in China at the return of Trigault. The group included several Jesuits versed in mathematics or Aristotelian philosophy, among them Johann Adam Schall von Bell (1592–1666). An initiative stimulating the translation of a large number of astronomical or mathematical works into Chinese was the calendar reform project of 1629–35. In addition, the efforts by Francisco Furtado (1589–1653) and Alfonso Vagnone (1568/69–1640) to introduce Aristotelian philosophy resulted in several translations, including selections of the well-known Coimbra commentaries (*Commentarii Collegii Conimbricensis SJ*, 1592–1606). In this period there was a territorial expansion: First in the middle region of the country, next to the provinces of the southeast and the central-west. In the 1630s, in addition to the arrival of the mendicant orders, there was also a change in the Jesuit missionary policy. Jesuits made a double shift: In Beijing they mainly sought imperial protection and contacts with court officials who became more important than the literati, while at the local level they moved their attention to the lower levels of the literati and to commoners. An example of this move can be found in *Kouduo richao* (Diary of Daily Admonitions), an extensive selection of missionaries' sermons from the Fujian province over a period of ten years. More than twenty-five Christians, participated in the recording and editing of this work. It includes a lively description of the daily life of the mission, centered around the figure of Giulio Aleni (1582–1649).

The change of regime in 1644 led to a third period: the Ming court fell and was superseded by the Manchu leaders of the Qing. Johann Adam Schall von Bell secured the transition and was almost immediately appointed to the post of director of the Astronomical Bureau. From that time onward until the 1770s, Jesuits assumed leading positions in the Bureau. In the early years of the Qing dynasty, despite the numerous internal disturbances in China, Christian communities expanded due to the organization of confraternities. A conflict about the calendar in the years 1664–65 resulted in the expulsion of all Jesuits, except four, to Canton. This period of exile was important because they discussed with other religious orders the policy concerning the Chinese rites. In 1671 they were allowed to return to their former mission areas. In the subsequent years, Jesuits consolidated the efforts they had undertaken before the exile. While Ferdinand Verbiest (1623–88) was actively involved at the court, where he taught among others mathematics to the Kangxi emperor (reign 1662–1722), many others actively promoted the expansion of Christian communities in the provinces. These gradually came to function on their own. An itinerant priest would visit them once or twice a year. Most Jesuits were most of their time involved in fostering these communities through pastoral care. During this period, two Jesuits returning to Europe contributed to the spread of knowledge about China: Martino Martini (1614–61) published a book with maps of China, *Novus Atlas Sinensis* (Amsterdam, 1654), as well as a book on the early Chinese history, and a treatise on the Manchu War (of the 1640s). Philippe Couplet (1622–93) edited the *Confucius Sinarum philosophus* (1687), containing an extensive introduction on Chinese philosophy as well as the translations of three of the major Confucian classics.

In 1688, the year in which Verbiest died, the first three Chinese Jesuits were ordained in the mainland. The year 1688 was also characterized by the arrival of the French Jesuits who represented a new type of European Jesuit and thus introduced a fourth period. Known as "Mathématiciens du Roy," they did not fall under the Portuguese Patroado but were supplied with pensions from King Louis XIV of France while being corresponding members of the newly founded Académie Royale des Sciences. Though a considerable part of their efforts was dedicated to the Rites Controversy, the French Jesuits became known for their preoccupation with scientific matters, such as the major project of mapping the whole of China. Their writings about China were sent to Europe where they exerted significant influence on the Enlightenment thinkers, such as Gottfried Wilhelm Leibniz (1646–1716), Charles de Montesquieu (1689–1755), François-Marie Voltaire (1694–1778), and Jean-Jacques Rousseau (1712–72). They used the missionaries' portrait of China as a test for their own theories. In the early eighteenth century, a major source of information were the Jesuit letters *Lettres édifiantes et curieuses*, published in different editions since 1702. Jean-Baptiste Du Halde's *Description géographique, historique, chronologique, politique et physique de l'Empire de la Chine et de la Tartarie chinoise* (4 vols., Paris, 1735; 1736) introduced various aspects of Chinese culture on the basis of translations of Chinese sources. A particular group among the French Jesuits were the "Figurists," with as representatives Joachim Bouvet (1656–1730), Jean-François Foucquet (1665–1741) and Joseph de Prémare (1660–1736). In line with the ideas of prisca theologia, they were of the opinion that the ancient Chinese texts contained "vestiges" of the pure ancient religion of mankind as well as "figures" or "symbols" of the Old Testament and the Messiah. During this period, the number of Jesuits reached its zenith, when in the years 1701–03 more than ninety Jesuits operated in China.

During the reign of the relatively tolerant Kangxi emperor, the Jesuits succeeded in preventing several times the expulsion of the missionaries. After his death, however, Christianity became proscribed. In 1724, many missionaries in the provinces, including eighteen Jesuits, were deported to Canton and then expelled to Macau in 1732. This fifth and final period brought about a more articulated division between those Jesuits legally in the service of the emperor at the capital, and those who now illegally and secretly did pastoral work in the provinces outside Beijing. At the court, besides being astronomical and medical advisers, Jesuits were as technicians involved in artistic activities such as painting, architecture, and construction of artifacts (clocks, glass, and enamelware). The most well-known Jesuit in this regard is the painter Giuseppe Castiglione (1688–1766). Often there was a subtle interplay between the missionaries and the emperor, in which both sides took advantage of the other for their own purposes. The missionaries tried to please the emperor as much as possible, while the emperor, from his side, amply availed himself of their services and led them even to make ambivalent choices. In order to sustain the local communities in the rest of the country, the Society of Jesus accepted more Chinese into its ranks. In this period, there were for most of the time between fifty and seventy Jesuits in the country, with Chinese Jesuits constituting one-third of the Jesuits in China since 1748 and thus the largest nationality group. Some of them spent part of their formation in Europe. In 1773, the Society of Jesus was dissolved, which was promulgated in China in 1775. The former Jesuits remained in China working there as secular priests, subject to bishops or apostolic vicars. In this final period, some important publications about China saw the light: *Histoire générale de la Chine* (13 vols., Paris: 1777–85) by Joseph Marie Anne de Moyriac de Mailla (1669–1748) and *Mémoires concernant l'histoire, les sciences, les arts, les moeurs, les usages des Chinois* (16 vols., Paris, 1776–1814) with contributions from authors such as Jean-Joseph-Marie Amiot (1718–93), Antoine Gaubil (1689–1759), and Pierre-Martial Cibot (1727–80). They discuss subjects as diverse as Chinese history, music, philosophy, literature, sciences, etc. in most cases based on Chinese and Manchu primary sources.

The history of the Jesuits in China in the seventeenth and eighteenth centuries was not simply a successful transmission of knowledge by a "generation of giants." The interaction and communication that took place between them and their Chinese partners was such that very often they were not the originators of a dialogue but joined a dialogue that was already in progress.

After the Restoration

It took some time after the restoration of the Society in 1814 before new Jesuits were sent to China. After multiple requests by Chinese Christians, the first three French Jesuits, led by Claude Gotteland (1803–56), finally arrived in China in 1842. The history of the Jesuit presence during the century 1842–1949 is so rich and complex that it is impossible to treat it in one paragraph. As a result of the territorial division of the Catholic Church in apostolic vicariates or prefectures in the nineteenth century, Jesuits ultimately served in nine different areas, each area grouping Chinese Jesuits together with foreign Jesuits of the same country of province: Shanghai: French Jesuits of the Paris province (first Jesuits arrived in 1842); Xianxian: French Jesuits of the province of Champagne (1857); Wuhu: Spanish Jesuits of the province of Castile (1913); Anqing: Spanish Jesuits of the province of Leon (1913); Bengbu: Italian Jesuits of the province of Turin (1929); Xuzhou: French Canadian Jesuits of the province of Lower Canada (1931); Daming: Jesuits of the province of Hungary (1935); Jingxian: Jesuits of the province of Austria (1939); Yangzhou: American Jesuits from the California province (1928). During the very turbulent years of that century (including the Taiping Revolution, Boxer Rebellion, Japanese War and Civil War), Jesuits were involved in pastoral activities among the growing Catholic communities and also established small schools in various places. One of the major Jesuit centers was Xujiahui (Zikawei) in Shanghai, which included a secondary school (1850), the Aurore university (1903), the T'ou Se We art atelier and printing press, and a sinological study center.

In 1949 there were more than 900 Jesuits (of whom 250 Chinese) in China. After 1949 foreign Jesuits were expulsed or left on their own, while more than 150 Chinese Jesuits remained on the continent. A significant number of them were imprisoned and some of them died during incarceration. Those who had left the continent installed a new mission in Taiwan in 1951. With the opening up of mainland China in 1978, contacts with the Jesuits in China were gradually reestablished.

See also Asia; Castiglione, Giuseppe, SJ; Chinese Rites Controversy; Ricci, Matteo, SJ; Schall von Bell, Johann Adam, SJ; Valignano, Alessandro, SJ

For a very extensive bibliography to primary and secondary sources, see Ad Dudink and Nicolas Standaert, Chinese Christian Texts Database (CCT-Database). www.arts.kuleuven.be/sinologie/sinologie/english/cct.

Brockey, Liam Matthew, *Journey to the East: The Jesuit Mission to China, 1579–1724*. Cambridge, MA: Harvard University Press, 2007.

Dehergne, Joseph, *Répertoire des jésuites de Chine de 1552 à 1800*. Rome: Institutum Historicum Societatis Iesu, 1973.

Gernet, Jacques, *Chine et christianisme: action et réaction*, Paris: Gallimard, 1982; 1990; *China and the Christian Impact*. Trans. J. Lloyd. Cambridge: Cambridge University Press, 1985.

Golvers, Noël, *Libraries of Western Learning for China: Circulation of Western Books between Europe and China in Jesuit Mission (ca. 1650–ca. 1750)*. 3 vols. Leuven: Ferdinand Verbiest Institute, 2012–15.

Handbook of Christianity in China: Volume One (635–1800). Ed. N. Standaert. Leiden: Brill, 2000.

Malatesta, Edward J., *The Society of Jesus and China: A Historical-Theological Essay*. St. Louis, MO: The Institute of Jesuit Sources, 1997.

Pfister, Louis, *Notices biographiques et bibliographiques sur les jésuites de l'ancienne mission de Chine (1552–1773)*. Shanghai: Imprimerie de la Mission Catholique, 1932.

Rule, Paul A., *K'ung-tzu or Confucius? The Jesuit Interpretation of Confucianism*. Sydney: Allen & Unwin Australia, 1986.

Standaert, Nicolas, "Jesuit Corporate Culture as Shaped by the Chinese." In J. W. O'Malley, G. A. Bailey, S. Harris, and T. F. Kennedy (eds.), *The Jesuits: Cultures, Sciences, and the Arts, 1540–1773*. Toronto: University of Toronto Press, 1999, pp. 352–63.

Standaert, Nicolas, "Jesuits in China." In Thomas Worcester, ed., *The Cambridge Companion to the Jesuits*. Cambridge: Cambridge University Press, 2008, pp. 169–85.

Vermander, Benoît, *Les jésuites et la Chine: De Matteo Ricci à nos jours*. Brussels: Lessius 2012.

Zürcher, Erik, "Jesuit Accommodation and the Chinese Cultural Imperative." In David E. Mungello (ed.), *The Chinese Rites Controversy: Its History and Meaning*. Nettetal: Steyler Verlag, 1994, pp. 31–64.

Nicolas Standaert, SJ

Chinese Rites Controversy

The controversy about the Chinese rites concerned the name of God and the rituals in honor of Confucius and the ancestors. Regarding the name of God, the major question was whether terms like *tian* (heaven) and *shangdi* (high lord) taken from the Chinese classics could convey the Christian concept of God (this is also called the "term question"). The second point of dispute was the ceremonies in honor of Confucius, performed by the literati class in temples dedicated to him, and the cult of ancestors, which was embedded in the social structures on all levels and manifested by such forms of piety as prostrations, incense burning, offering of food, etc., in front of a corpse, grave, or commemorative tablet. In this issue the question was whether Christians should be forbidden to participate in these acts considered "superstitious," or should these be regarded as "civil," or at least not contrary to Christian belief, and therefore be tolerated?

Various phases in the controversy can be distinguished. The first phase (corresponding to the first fifty years of the mission) primarily concerned the term question and was debated within the Society of Jesus. Two opposite visions coexisted: Matteo Ricci (1552–1610) interpreted the ancient classics in such a way that *tian* and *shangdi* were identified with the Christian God, thus rejecting later Neo-Confucian interpretations. Niccolò Longobardo (1565–1655) argued that one should not interpret these ancient texts without the later ("materialistic") commentaries, thus rejecting some Chinese terms that were used for Christian concepts. The controversy was temporarily settled around 1633 in favor of the first view. The second phase coincided with the arrival of the Dominican and Franciscan friars in 1633. The friars were astonished by certain practices allowed or tolerated in the Christian communities established by the Jesuits. After having returned to Rome in 1643, Juan Bautista de Morales, OP (1597–1664), presented "Seventeen Questions" that basically attacked the Jesuit approach to the Chinese rites. A first decree approved by the pope (September 12, 1645) prohibited the practices described by Morales. In reaction, the Jesuits dispatched Martino Martini (1614–61) to Rome in 1651 to show that de Morales had not described their missionary practices accurately. A favorable decree followed on March 23, 1656, giving sanction to the practices as described in a statement by Martini. After the "Canton Conference" that was held among representatives of the Jesuits, Dominicans, and Franciscans around January 1668, Chinese Christians became more and more involved, and some Christian literati wrote important essays explaining the issues from a Chinese perspective. The conflict between the visions intensified at the end of the century when Charles Maigrot, MEP (1652–1730), vicar apostolic of Fujian, launched an indictment of the rites in his mandate of March 26, 1693. From that time the Holy See became involved in a juridical process of extraordinary complexity, while Jesuits' books about China became the subject of stormy debates and condemnations at the Sorbonne in Paris. The deliberations of a commission of cardinals in Rome resulted in the decree *Cum Deus optimus* of November 20, 1704, forbidding the use of *tian* and *shangdi*; prohibiting Christians to take part in sacrifices to Confucius or to ancestors; proscribing ancestral tablets inscribed with characters calling them the "throne" or "seat of the spirit" of the deceased. The text was reiterated by the apostolic constitution *Ex illa die* (March 19, 1715). The apostolic constitution *Ex quo Singulari* (July 11, 1742) closed the controversy. On December 8, 1939, the Sacred Congregation of the Propagation of the Faith issued the decree *Instructio circa quasdam cæremonias super ritubus sinensibus*, which nullified many of the prohibitions and abolished the anti-rite oath imposed upon the missionaries by the bull of 1742.

The Rites Controversy could be considered from the perspective of how various groups dealt with ambiguity. The whole attempt by the Jesuit missionaries consisted in taking away the inherent ambiguity, by insisting that these rituals are merely "as if" ancestors' souls were present, but not really present. Opponents of the rites, on the other hand, took away the ambiguity, by exposing the "real" intention of the rituals of offering food to the ancestors' souls who were considered to be "really" present and to consume the offerings.

See also China; Interreligious Dialogue; Ricci, Matteo SJ

Minamiki, George, *The Chinese Rites Controversy: From Its Beginning to Modern Times*. Chicago, IL: Loyola University Press, 1985.
Mungello, David E., ed., *The Chinese Rites Controversy: Its History and Meaning*. Nettetal: Steyler Verlag, 1994.
100 Roman Documents Concerning the Chinese Rites Controversy (1645–1941). Trans. Donald F. St. Sure; ed. Ray R. Noll. San Francisco: Ricci Institute, 1992.
Rosso, Antonio Sisto, *Apostolic Legations to China in the Eighteenth Century*. South Pasadena, CA: Perkins, 1948.
Rouleau, Francis A., "Chinese Rites Controversy." In *New Catholic Encyclopedia*. Vol. III. New York: MacGraw-Hill, 1967, cols. 610–17.
Standaert, Nicholas, *Chinese Voices in the Rites Controversy: Travelling Books, Community Networks, Intercultural Arguments*. Rome: Institutum Historicum Societatis Iesu, 2011.

Nicolas Standaert, SJ

Christian Life Communities

Christian Life Communities (CLCs) represent the modern descendants and a continuation on a global scale of the original Jesuit Marian congregations. At the sixteenth World

Assembly, held in Lebanon in 2013, the World Christian Life Community celebrated a 450th anniversary, commemorating the original "Annunziata" Congregation founded by Jan Leunis at the Roman College in 1563. Within this global organization, there are currently sixty-three participating national communities comprising thousands of individual groups, organized in six regional teams: Africa, North America, Latin America, Asia Pacific, Europe, and the Middle East. The World Christian Life Community is governed through General Assemblies, which are held every five years and are responsible for determining norms and policies. Its ordinary activities are coordinated by a World Executive Committee and a World Secretariat located at the Jesuit Curia in Rome and composed of laypersons, with a papally appointed "ecclesiastical assistant," such as the Jesuit General, Fr. Adolfo Nicolás, SJ. Individual CLC groups are led by an elected coordinator along with a guide (who is frequently a Jesuit priest or an individual "well formed in the Ignatian process of growth," according to the General Principles) and are typically composed of twelve or fewer members that meet either once a week or every fifteen days. After two to eight years of membership and a period of discernment, usually involving the *Spiritual Exercises*, members move from a temporary commitment to a permanent commitment. As of 2013, the total membership was estimated at roughly 25,000 (although this does not include students too young for commitment).

From the beginning, Ignatius and his companions actively supported confraternities, whether by encouraging or reforming existing institutions, or by founding their own. Ignatius promoted confraternities responsible for traditional charities like assisting orphans, prisoners, and the sick, as well as innovative charities for reformed prostitutes, daughters of prostitutes, and converted Jews and Muslims. But it was the Marian congregations, typically associated with Jesuit schools and their professed houses, that became the central model for Jesuit lay associations and that provide the foundation for CLCs today.

The first great spur to growth for the Marian congregations was the elevation of the original congregation founded by Leunis to an archconfraternity: after standardizing common rules for the Marian congregations in 1578, the Jesuit General Claudio Acquaviva obtained from Pope Gregory XIII in 1584 the bull *Omnipotentis Dei*, which conferred the power to affiliate similar institutions. After obtaining further bulls and privileges, Acquaviva added the Sodality rules to the *Ratio studiorum* in 1599, linking sodalities to every Jesuit college, and soon also Jesuit residences. By the time of the Suppression of the Jesuit order in 1773, there were roughly 2,500 affiliated Marian congregations throughout the world, in every Jesuit province, and their members included even the highest social circles.

During the Suppression of the Society, guidance of the sodalities transferred out of the hands of the general, and so various bulls clarified the affiliation of sodalities unassociated with the Jesuits. During the nineteenth century, new sodalities continued to form in Jesuit colleges as well as outside Jesuit circles. Given the ever-expanding diffusion of the congregations, the Common Rules were revised repeatedly, notably in 1855 and again in 1910, nevertheless maintaining the Ignatian emphasis on combining mental prayer and reflection with outward charitable activities. The apostolic constitution of Pius XII in 1948, *Bis saeculari*, reaffirmed the authority of the Jesuit general over new affiliations and invited a reform and assessment. By 1953, a new body and statutes for the World Federation of Sodalities of Our Lady gained papal approval. During the fourth assembly of the World Federation in 1967, following the conclusion of the Second

Vatican Council, the sodalities renamed themselves Christian Life Communities and called for another revision of the Common Rules, completed in 1971. The most recent "General Principles and General Norms" date from 1990, with minor amendments made in the General Assemblies of 1998, 2003, 2008, and 2013.

Since 1968 the World Christian Life Community has published a journal, *Progressio*, along with numerous supplemental publications and project pamphlets relating to global and regional charitable initiatives. The General Principles continue to reflect the Ignatian inspiration at the core of their charism: "The spirituality of our community is centered on Christ and on participation in the Paschal Mystery ... [W]e hold the *Spiritual Exercises* of St. Ignatius as the specific source and the characteristic instrument of our spirituality."

See also Confraternities; Marian Congregations

Christian Life Community Home Page with documents and organizational details. www.cvx-clc.net.
Frank, Daniela, "The Christian Life Community (CLC): Looking Back to 40 Years of Deepening Its Specific Identity." *Review of Ignatian Spirituality* 38.1, 114 (2007), 63–77.
Pope Pius XII, *Bis saeculari: Apostolic Constitution Sodalities of Our Lady.* St. Louis, MO: The Queen's Work, 1957.
The Relationship between the Christian Life Community and the Society of Jesus in the Church. Rome: Christian Life Community, 2010.

Lance Gabriel Lazar

Christina of Sweden

Christina (1629–1686), one time queen of Sweden, is perhaps better known as an important patron of art and learning in Counter-Reformation Rome. Contemporary accounts depict Christina as a larger-than-life figure. The only child of King Gustavus Adolphus of Sweden, Christina was raised from early on to rule. Adolphus was known to take Christina out to review the troops, traveling by his side throughout Sweden. Following the death of Adolphus during battle in 1632, Christina was entrusted to the tutelage of the High Chancellor of the kingdom, Axel Oxenstierna, who gave her a humanist education similar to that of the male rulers of Europe. By all accounts she was an excellent student, mastering several languages, including French and Latin, and claimed a good working knowledge of Greek, Hebrew, and Arabic. As early as 1644, Christina began turning her court into an illustrious center of arts and learning. Christina amassed an enormous library of over 8,000 manuscripts and attracted some of the most illustrious scholars in Europe to her court including Isaac Vossius, Gabriel Naudé, and René Descartes.

In 1655 Christina renounced her throne after converting to Catholicism. Two Jesuit fathers, Paolo Casati and Francesco Malines, played an important role in her conversion, providing her with spiritual guidance as early as 1652. Christina moved her court to the Palazzo Riario (now the Corsini) in Rome, quickly developing a reputation as an active patron of the artistic and literary life of the city. She is associated, for example, with the sculptor Bernini and the composer Alessandro Scarlatti. However, she was also a prominent patron of the Jesuit order. She chose Jesuits as personal confessors and supported a number of Jesuit artists including Andrea Pozzo.

See also Bernini, Gian Lorenzo; Pozzo, Andrea, SJ; Scandinavia; Women, as Co-Workers with Jesuits

Garstein, Oskar, *Rome and the Counter-Reformation in Scandinavia: The Age of Gustavus Adolphus and Christina of Sweden.* 2 vols. Leiden: Brill, 1991.
Zirpolo, Lilian H., "Christina of Sweden's Patronage of Bernini: The Mirror of Truth Revealed by Time." *Woman's Art Journal* 26 (2005), 38–43.

Megan C. Armstrong

Ciszek, Walter, SJ (1904–1984)

When Walter Ciszek stepped onto the tarmac at Idlewild Airport in New York on October 12, 1963, it was a resurrection of sorts. Ciszek's family and Jesuit superiors had long thought him dead and had even given up hope of finding his body and burying him. But in a moment, Ciszek's long ordeal behind the Iron Curtain – where he had spent over twenty years – was suddenly and surprisingly brought to an end.

Walter Ciszek was born on November 4, 1904, the son of immigrants who lived in a vibrant Polish enclave in Shenandoah, Pennsylvania. Ciszek expressed an early desire to be a priest, and his family sent him to a Polish minor seminary in Michigan. During his college studies, he read a biography of St. Stanislaus Kostka and, impressed by the story of the saint's determination, decided to become a Jesuit. Without consulting his parents, Ciszek entered the novitiate at Poughkeepsie, New York, in September 1928.

Early in his novitiate, Ciszek learned of Pius XI's call for missionaries to Russia, which he found immensely appealing. Soon after taking his first vows, Ciszek wrote to the superior general to volunteer for the missions; he was instructed to continue his studies. Eventually his studies brought him to Rome, where he studied at the Gregorian University and the Russicum Pontifical College, a Jesuit-run institution dedicated to the study of the culture and spirituality of Russia. After ordination in 1937, Ciszek was missioned to work among Russian Catholics in eastern Poland.

While ministering to the people there, Poland was invaded from both sides: the German army from the west, the Russians from the east. Since the village he was living in was suddenly part of Russia, Ciszek decided to move further into the country to work with Russian Catholics. However, traveling into Communist Russia was a dangerous proposition for a Catholic priest, so Ciszek decided to conceal his identity, becoming Vladjmir Lypinski, a widower. As Lypinski, he worked for a year as a common laborer in a lumber camp, hauling wood and driving trucks. He earned a meager wage and, like the people with whom he worked, lived in a perpetual state of hunger and hiding: He celebrated Mass in the woods for fear of being caught.

When the German army invaded Russia in June 1941, Ciszek, whose identity was known from the moment he entered the country, was arrested as a spy and sent to the infamous Lubianka prison. While incarcerated, Ciszek was subjected to brutal and frequent interrogations. Still, Ciszek managed to establish a daily order for himself, one that he based on his experience of early life in the Society with periods of prayer, meditation, the rosary, and recitation of the texts from the liturgy, which he had memorized. Unable to persuade his jailers that his motives were spiritual, not political, Ciszek was convicted as a spy and sentenced to fifteen years of hard labor at Dudinka, within the

Arctic Circle. While there, Ciszek began to minister to his fellow prisoners, hearing their confessions and distributing Holy Communion and providing a valuable and sustaining witness for his fellow prisoners.

A series of prison transfers followed, never explained. In each place, Ciszek's labor varied, from construction sites to coal mining. Most important to Ciszek, of course, was his priestly work, which he was able to complete inconspicuously, most days meeting one on one with men as they prepared to leave for work, offering them meditations from the *Spiritual Exercises*, which he had memorized, or hearing confessions while playing dominoes, to conceal his ministry.

Eventually, in 1955, Ciszek was released from the labor camps but was still under constant surveillance by Soviet authorities. Several times after his release, he was approached by the police and given instructions to move to another city, but in each place he found Catholics in need and would minister in private homes. During his final years in Russia, even as he ministered in secret, he worked as an auto mechanic, even though his hands were gnarled by the decades of forced labor and interrogations.

Without warning in early October 1963, Ciszek was sent by the Secret Police to Moscow where he was put on a plane bound for the United States as part of a deal that would free two Soviet spies. Back in the United States, Ciszek penned two books about his experience and devoted much of his time to retreat work, for which he was highly sought. He died on December 8, 1984, in New York. His cause for beatification is under consideration.

See also Russia; United States of America

Anderson, George, *With Christ in Prison: Jesuits in Jail from St. Ignatius to the Present*. New York: Fordham University Press, 2000.
Ciszek, Walter, *With God in Russia*. New York: McGraw-Hill, 1964.
    He Leadeth Me. Garden City, NY: Doubleday, 1973.

Keith Maczkiewicz, SJ

Civil Rights Movement (United States)

The formal African American Civil Rights movement began in the 1950s when efforts to end segregation in public transportation, schools, and other facilities prefigured a broader grassroots struggle for voting rights and economic justice in the 1960s. The movement nonetheless had deep roots in labor and political struggles before and during World War II. From its earliest stirrings, members of the Society of Jesus engaged African American demands for political and social equality in a number of ways. As leaders of prominent churches, colleges, and universities, Jesuit efforts to open institutional doors to all races set an important precedent for civic and religious leaders throughout the country. As community activists, social scientists, theologians, and pastoral leaders, many sought to bring the Civil Rights movement's moral lessons to bear on Catholic life and practice in the second half of the twentieth century. At all levels, Jesuits saw the most significant social movement of twentieth-century America as a critical proving ground for Catholic social and moral perspectives on interracialism, social justice, and the broader meaning of democracy and freedom in the nation's emerging global age.

Before World War II, a cadre of Jesuits throughout the country articulated important connections between the black struggle and Catholic social teaching. The latter's emphasis on economic inequality and labor rights generally overlooked the issue of racial oppression. Yet the country's struggle against a racist regime in Nazi Germany and the rise of a Soviet regime bent on exploiting American racism both brought the black struggle to the forefront of liberal thought in the 1940s. It also vindicated the efforts of Jesuit John LaFarge, who had sounded warnings since the 1920s about the effects of American racial violence in promoting communism. Leader of the Catholic Interracial Council in New York, LaFarge joined Missouri Jesuit William Markoe, who criticized Catholic institutional segregation and established a Catholic community for African Americans near St. Louis University.

The earliest Catholic interracial movements in the South remained closely tied with Jesuit institutions. A 1944 sermon by Claude Heithaus, SJ, an archaeology professor, inspired efforts to end segregation at St. Louis University, which became the first white institution in a former slave state to open its doors to all races in 1944. Heithaus joined Markoe and George H. Dunne, SJ, as the most aggressive voices for social change when they condemned Catholic leaders' prudence in the face of a social system that defied Catholic moral teaching. Following successful National Association for the Advancement of Colored People (NAACP) campaigns to target graduate programs in public higher education, Loyola University of the South in New Orleans desegregated its law school in 1952 and its undergraduate programs a decade later. The move inspired campus student and lay organizations that sought to confront white prejudice through church programs, lectures, and collaborations with the National Urban League and NAACP. Spring Hill College desegregated its undergraduate programs in 1954. There, sociologist Albert Foley, SJ, drew hostility from the Ku Klux Klan in 1957 when his open criticism of the organization and its collusion with police provoked a cross burning on the campus and led to confrontations between students and the Klan.

To be sure, all of these Jesuits confronted opposition at the dining table and among college administrators. Heithaus faced charges of insubordination for criticizing the president's limited integration of only classroom spaces. Dunne met a similar fate, returning to his home province of California where his pro-labor activism drew widespread attention. In New Orleans, Jesuit labor activist Louis J. Twomey, sociologist Joseph Fichter, SJ, and university chaplain Harold L. Cooper all voiced unpopular demands that Loyola University, and the southern province generally, take a more deliberate stance against discrimination.

Particularly as the so-called "race question" moved out of the south to confront the extent of racial injustice in the Catholic-heavy urban north, Jesuit-sponsored interracial programs highlighted Catholic complacency in the pews. The Second Vatican Council of the 1960s began to promote lay leadership in the Church's social apostolate and more active participation in liturgy. Both became arenas for the influence of Jesuit voices, such as that of LaFarge, who had long highlighted the parish as the central proving ground of interracial justice. Harlem Jesuit Joseph Roccasalvo echoed LaFarge's demand for a liturgy whose more active inclusion of laity would invariably transform its members' social attitudes.

While the antiwar activism of Daniel Berrigan, SJ, would overshadow Society participation in the later-1960s civil rights, by the end of the decade Jesuits at all stages of educational and pastoral apostolates understood the important ways in which the promises of Vatican II and the Civil Rights movement must be implemented in the day-to-day tasks of an inclusive and dynamic ministry that had long defined Jesuit life.

See also LaFarge, John, SJ; United States of America

Anderson, R. Bentley, *Black, White and Catholic: New Orleans Interracialism*. Nashville, TN: Vanderbilt University Press, 2005.

McGreevy, John T., *Parish Boundaries: The Catholic Encounter with Race in the Twentieth Century Urban North*. Chicago, IL: University of Chicago Press, 1996.

Southern, David, *John LaFarge and the Limits of Catholic Interracialism, 1911–1963*. Baton Rouge: Louisiana State University Press, 1996.

Justin Poché

Civiltà Cattolica

The first issue of the Italian journal *Civiltà Cattolica* appeared on April 6, 1850, and has remained in continuous publication until this day. Carlo Curci, SJ (1826–91), the founding editor, received the support of Pope Pius IX to publish a journal addressing the hostile liberal ideologies that had emerged after the 1848 revolutions and the collapse of the papal monarchy. With the contributions of such Jesuits as Luigi Taparelli d'Azegli (1793–1862), the renowned theologian at the Roman College, and Matteo Liberatore (1810–92), a significant contributor to Pope Leo XIII's social encyclicals, *Civiltà Cattolica* (CC) soon established itself as a major polemical and intellectual voice in defense of the papacy and tradition. In 1866 Pius IX promulgated the bull *Gravissimum supremi* that created a Jesuit College of Writers associated with the CC. Early issues included a mix of genres – philosophical and theological essays, polemic, and even a regular serial novel – aimed at a generally educated audience, including seminarians, religious, and lay Catholic activists. Its ideological targets would change with the decades – radical anarchists, masons, Modernists, and communists – but the writers also sought to promote a family-centered society, workers' rights, a renewed Thomism, and devotions such as the Sacred Heart. The journal was regretfully tarnished by elements of anti-Semitism and fascist leanings before and during World War II, causing some friction with the Vatican. Today CC has distanced itself from its more polemical past in order to promote a dialogue between faith and culture. In keeping with this new mission, it has embraced a more international outlook and has established a presence in the new media.

See also Italy; Revues/Journals; Ultramontanism

Logan, Oliver, "A Journal: *La Civiltà Cattolica* From Pius IX to Pius XII (1850–1958)". In R. N. Swanson, ed., *The Church and the Book*. Rochester, NY: Boydell and Brewer, 2004, pp. 375–85.

John Gavin, SJ

Claver, Peter, SJ, St. (1580–1654)

He was born on June 26, 1580, in Verdú, Spain, and died on September 8, 1654, in Cartagena, Colombia. Before joining the Society of Jesus, Claver completed four years of grammar and rhetoric in the General Study of Barcelona between 1596 and 1602. He joined the Society of Jesus in August 1602 in Tarragona, Spain. He studied philosophy between 1605 and 1608 in the College of Montesión at Palma de Mallorca. There, he met Alonso Rodríguez, the keeper of the College, who had a profound influence on his missionary vocation. Claver kept for the rest of his life a memento of Rodriguez, his spiritual notebook, which he later bequeathed to the novitiate of Tunja, on October 28, 1651. During his second year of theology, he was sent to the vice province of the new Kingdom of Granada (which encompassed today's Colombia and Ecuador), as he had requested two years earlier. Claver sailed from Seville on April 15, 1610. After working more than one year in Santafe de Bogotá, he finished his theology between 1612 and 1613. Later he made his tertianship in Tunja. Peter Claver was ordained on March 19, 1616, in Cartagena; he took his fourth vow on April 3, 1622.

In 1614 Claver began assisting Alonso de Sandoval in Cartagena with the evangelization of the newly arrived African slaves, an apostolate to which he would dedicate several years. Sandoval was his mentor and guide, and during Sandoval's absence from Cartagena between 1617 and 1620, Claver assumed the responsibilities of his waylaid master. Claver deeply loved the African slaves in their suffering and their poverty, and this love is reflected in the formula of their final vows, which he signed, "Petrus Claver, semper servus aethiopum."

To catechize the linguistically diverse population of African slaves, he gathered a group of black collaborators who acted as translators and did whatever else they could to care for new arrivals from Africa. According to one account, as a slave ship arrived at the port of Cartagena, he surprised the interpreters by boarding the ship to offer gifts to the frightened captives. He went down to the hold and consoled and encouraged the slaves in their nauseating conditions. He baptized the dying and tended the sick. Frequently, the slaves arrived suffering from smallpox or other diseases, and observers were amazed by Claver's charity and selflessness. Upon landing, he devoted long hours to catechize them, and after several days of instruction he baptized them by giving them a Christian name and hanging a medal around their necks in recognition of their human dignity. According to the 1696 beatification process initiated by brother Nicolás González, sacristan of the College and Claver's apostolate for twenty-two years, Claver baptized about 300,000 slaves.

Those slaves who stayed in Cartagena remained under the spiritual care of Claver, who was their friend and protector. He assisted them in their needs and defended them from the violence of their owners. He frequently visited the sick and performed remarkable acts of charity, overcoming the disgust he felt at the sight of certain diseases. Two hospitals in Cartagena, Saint Sebastian and the Leprosarium of Saint Lazarus, were the places where he unfurled his charity and zeal, and also where he attained several conversions of Muslims and Protestants.

In 1650 he fell ill and was immobilized. The illness coincided with the plague that ravaged Cartagena in 1651. His last years of life were an ordeal that he welcomed with generosity without limits. He became paralytic and was unable to undertake his pastoral work in the midst of the slaves of the city, and yet he maintained his spirit of kindness and generosity. Peter Claver has gone down in history as the great defender of African slaves. He has the merit of having done so before the Catholic Church took a position on that matter. The death of the "Apostle of Blacks" (as he came to be known) took place on September 8, 1654. There was a feeling of great loss in the city, among all social classes, as well as a sense of gratitude for the forty years of holy service they had been privileged to witness. From Cartagena, the Spanish Court in 1669 and the Holy See in 1670 were petitioned to ensure that the beatification process would be started. Claver was beatified by Pope Pius IX on September 21, 1851, and canonized by Leo XIII on January 15, 1888.

See also Colombia; Rodriguez, Alphonsus, SJ, St.; Slavery

Giraldo, Tulio Aristizabal, *Retazos de historia. Los jesuitas en Cartagena de Indias*. Bogotá: Ediciones Antropos, 1995.
Valtierra, Ángel, *El Santo que libertó una raza*. Bogotá: Editorial Pax, 1963.

Jorge Salcedo, SJ

Clavius, Christopher, SJ (1538–1612)

Christopher Clavius, SJ, was born in 1538 in Bamberg, Germany. We know virtually nothing, however, about his family or early life. In February 1555, Ignatius of Loyola personally received Clavius into the Society of Jesus. Clavius made his novitiate in Rome after which, in 1556, he was sent to study at the new Jesuit university in Coimbra, Portugal. He returned to Rome in 1560 to study theology at the Roman College. While still studying theology, Clavius started teaching mathematics at the Roman College. Clavius was ordained in 1564 and remained at the Roman College as a professor of mathematics until his death on February 6, 1612. On the Moon, Clavius crater is named after him.

Today, Clavius is best known for his work on the papal commission established by Pope Gregory XIII for the reform of the calendar. Despite the claims of some, Clavius was not the leader of the group and served as one of its scientific advisers. After the reform was promulgated in the bull *Inter gravissimas*, Clavius rose to prominence by writing *Novi calendarii*, the first of a series of books by Clavius which explained the mathematics and the science behind the new calendar and, more importantly, set forth the algorithm for calculating the correct date of Easter in the new Gregorian calendar.

Clavius's most important contribution to mathematics, however, was his work as a teacher of mathematics. Prior to the 1600s, and especially in Italy, the study of mathematics had very little prestige or importance and had virtually disappeared from the standard university curriculum. Clavius vehemently disagreed with this neglect of mathematics and as an adviser on the *Ratio studiorum*, he transformed mathematics into an integral part of the Jesuit educational project. To support the new Jesuit mathematics curriculum, Clavius wrote a number of mathematical textbooks on arithmetic, algebra, plane geometry, trigonometry, astronomy and astrology, calendars and sundials, and optics (perspective), all of which were considered to be branches of mathematics at the time. To give further support to mathematical education, Clavius created an academy for advanced mathematical studies at the Roman College. At the time of its foundation, this academy was the only university-level mathematical center in Europe and its students included many of the most important mathematics teachers of their day.

In particular, two of Clavius's textbooks for the Jesuit schools, his *Euclidis elementorum* (Rome, 1589) and his *Geometrica practica* (Rome, 1604) would go on to become the standard geometry texts used throughout Europe, in both Catholic and Protestant countries, during the seventeenth century. Both René Descartes and Marin Marsenne used them as students, and the books were even translated by Matteo Ricci and Adam

Schall into Chinese, where they were the first texts to introduce western mathematical techniques to China.

The *Geometrica practica* was a work in what we would now call applied mathematics: it showed how to use mathematics to solve a number of practical and every-day problems in geometry and astronomy. The *Euclidus elementorum* was a critical edition of Euclid's *Geometry*, containing the original text (in translation) with a wide range of commentaries, supplemented by Clavius's own additional proofs and axioms. These two texts used a number of Clavius's own notational innovations, including the radical sign for square roots, parentheses, positive and negative signs, and the decimal point. Clavius also helped to disseminate and popularize a number of other contemporary mathematical innovations, including the recently developed symbolic algebra of François Viète.

Clavius also regularly corresponded with all the leading mathematicians and astronomers of his day, including Johannes Kepler and Tycho Brahe. Another close friend of Clavius was Galileo Galilei, who was in turn well acquainted with Clavius's writings. Through his connections at the Roman College, Clavius and the Jesuits there were able to verify several of Galileo's astronomical discoveries, including sunspots, the rings of Saturn, and the phases of Venus.

In 1963, inspired by the example of Clavius, Andrew Whitman, SJ, and Lawrence Conlon founded the Clavius Mathematical Research Group. The Clavius Group is an international association of Jesuit and lay mathematicians who spend three weeks together every summer, sharing in mathematical research, prayer, and recreation.

See also Astronomy; Galileo; Science

Baldini, Ugo, "Christoph Clavius and the Scientific Scene in Rome." In George V. Coyne, Michael A. Hoskin, and Olaf Pederson, eds., *Gregorian Reform of the Calendar*. Vatican City: Specola Vaticana, 1983, pp. 137–70.

Lattis, James M., *Between Copernicus and Galileo: Christopher Clavius and the Collapse of Ptolemaic Cosmology*. Chicago, IL: Chicago University Press, 1994.

Smolarski, Dennis C., "The Jesuit *Ratio studiorum*, Christopher Clavius, and the Study of Mathematical Sciences in Universities." *Science in Context* 15 (2002), 447–57.

Jonathan Stott, SJ

Clement XIV

The conclave to elect Clement XIII's successor was dominated by the question of the Jesuits' future. The ambassadors of the Bourbon powers intervened in proceedings, and they appear to have been satisfied with the election, in May 1769, of the Franciscan Lorenzo Ganganelli (1705–1774) as Clement XIV (r. 1769–1774), though there remains debate about precisely what the new pope had or had not promised in regard to the possible global suppression of the Society. Ganganelli's feelings toward the Jesuits were not straightforward. Earlier in his clerical career, he had exhibited some sympathy toward the Society, even dedicating one of his books to Ignatius of Loyola. His attitudes appear to have shifted after he became a cardinal in 1759, and he voiced no overt opposition to the national attacks on the Society.

In the years following his election, Clement was bombarded with pressure to carry through the Suppression from the agents of the French and Spanish kings: There were both threats and promises – the prospect, for instance, of Avignon and Benevento being returned to papal hands should Clement prove pliable. Clement did take action against the Society, removing Jesuits from positions of influence in both Rome and the Papal States, but he was clearly reluctant to carry through global suppression. The arrival of the Spanish Ambassador José Moñino in July 1772 was a crucial turning point: He effectively bullied Clement into striking against the Society. The result was the papal brief of suppression, *Dominus ac Redemptor*, officially dated July 21, 1773.

See also Dominus ac Redemptor; Papacy; Suppression

Danieluk, Robert, "Some Remarks on Jesuit Historiography 1773–1814." In Robert Maryks and Jonathan Wright, eds., *Jesuit Survival and Restoration. A Global History, 1773–1900*. Leiden: Brill, 2014, pp. 34–48.

Gatti, Isidoro Liberale, *Clemente XIV Ganganelli (1705–1774): profilo di un francescano e di un papa*. Vol. I. Padua: Centro Studi Antoniani, 2012.

Jonathan Wright

Clorivière, Pierre-Joseph de, SJ (1735–1820)

A native of Brittany, Clorivière did not turn immediately to a religious vocation. Following his education from the Benedictines at Douai, he embarked upon a short-lived career as a sailor and contemplated a future in the legal profession. In Paris in 1756, however, he determined to enter the Society of Jesus. He embarked upon his novitiate in that year and made his vows in August 1758. He was ordained in 1763. He held various positions in Belgium, including a spell as spiritual director of the English Benedictine nuns at Brussels. He remained in that city immediately following the 1773 global suppression of the Order and then returned to France. He spent time at the monastery of Jarcy, close to Paris, and served as a pastor in Brittany.

The turmoil of the French Revolution inspired Clorivière to found congregations that attempted to sustain the Ignatian spirit: the Society of Daughters of the Heart of Mary (1790) and the Society of the Heart of Jesus (1791). Clorivière thus played a leading role in the survival of Jesuit ideals in France during the Suppression era and was keen to establish links with the outpost of corporate Jesuit existence in the Russian Empire. His efforts were rudely interrupted in 1804 when he was arrested on charges of involvement with the Cadoudal conspiracy against Napoleon's life. These charges were entirely false and stemmed from confusion between Clorivière and his nephew. Nonetheless, he remained incarcerated until April 1809. At the restoration of the Society in 1814, Clorivière took up the position of provincial, and, within three years, there was a novitiate with 144 members and five Jesuit colleges had been established. No figure provides a more notable example of continuity between the pre-Suppression and post-restoration Society.

See also France; Suppression

Reynier, Chantal, *Pierre-Joseph de Clorivière 1735–1820*. Namur: Lessius, 2014.

    ed., "La correspondence de P.-J. Clorivière avec T. Brzozowski 1814 à 1818." *Archivum Historicum Societatis Iesu* 64 (1995), 83–167.

Jonathan Wright

Coadjutor, Temporal and Spiritual

A coadjutor, either temporal or spiritual, is a Jesuit who participates in the mission of the Society of Jesus but does not profess a solemn fourth vow of obedience regarding mission.

The grade of coadjutor is first mentioned in the revised *Formula of the Institute* of 1550. There, coadjutors are understood as Jesuits who would assist the Society of Jesus by attending to routine matters and freeing up professed fathers to take on missions of greater urgency. Spiritual coadjutors would have been priests who wished to join the Society and were expected to "aid the Society by hearing confessions, giving exhortations, and teaching Christian doctrine or other branches of study." Temporal coadjutors (or brothers), on the other hand, were laymen whose role was "to exercise themselves in all the low and humble services which are enjoined upon them, although they may be employed in more important matters in accordance with the talent God may have given them."

Over time, however, the Society's understanding of coadjutors shifted. Where the original distinction between the spiritual coadjutors and the fully professed was based on one's availability to be sent on mission, the distinction was soon reduced to one of education. Temporal coadjutors, too, instead of being seen as men called to aid the Society of Jesus, would soon find their role reduced to that of cooks, tailors, porters, nurses, and general handymen. Since the Second Vatican Council, however, there has been great progress made in restoring the coadjutors, both temporal and spiritual, to their original role of co-workers within the Society of Jesus.

See also Brothers; Grades; Priesthood

The Constitutions of The Society of Jesus and Their Complementary Norms. Ed. John W. Padberg. St. Louis, MO: The Institute of Jesuit Sources, 1996.

Jonathan Stott, SJ

Codure, Jean, SJ (1508–1541)

Along with Paschase Broët and Claude Jay, Jean Codure is what John Padberg has deemed one of three "forgotten founders" of the Society of Jesus. One of the final additions to the original small group of "friends in the Lord," Codure's brief time in the Jesuits was spent almost exclusively in the founding events of the new Society of Jesus in Rome and in pastoral pursuits in the surrounding areas.

Born June 24, 1508, in Seyne, a town in the French Alps, Codure's first interactions with the men whose company he would join were at the University of Paris in 1534. There, Peter Faber acting as his spiritual director, gave him the *Spiritual Exercises*. In August 1536, two years after the original group of companions had pronounced their vows of poverty and chastity and one year after Claude Jay had, Codure took these same vows alongside Paschase Broët at Montmartre. Afterwards, this group would serve in Venice for the winter of 1537.

Though he served short stints in Padua, Velletri, and Tivoli, Codure's contributions to the canonical founding of the Society should be noted here. A participant in the three-month "deliberation of the first fathers" in 1539, Codure remained in Rome and, acting as a secretary for the nascent group, helped to draw up the first draft of the *Constitutions* of the Society of Jesus (completed in April 1541), and documents regarding the establishment of colleges and observance of poverty for the professed, both of which influenced Ignatius. Codure died after a brief illness on August 29, 1541, the first of the original companions to die.

See also Constitutions; Friends in the Lord

O'Malley, John W., *The First Jesuits*. Cambridge, MA: Harvard University Press, 1993.
Padberg, John, W., "The Three Forgotten Founders of the Society of Jesus." *Studies in the Spirituality of Jesuits* 29, 2 (March 1997), 1–45.

Keith Maczkiewicz, SJ

Coimbra

In 1537 the historic University of Coimbra was transferred back to Coimbra after sojourning in Lisbon for over a century and a half. Five years later, in 1542, Coimbra saw the foundation of the first Portuguese college of the Society of Jesus, though the construction of the Jesuit College of Jesus did not begin until 1547. After some initial difficulties, the Jesuits set down deep roots in the city. In 1555 they were also entrusted with running the Royal College of Arts, which had been overwhelmed by inquisitorial trials. Jesuits did figure among the denouncers, though they did not inspire the campaign of repression. The College's degree became obligatory for enrolling in university courses of Canons and Laws in Coimbra. But, unlike in Évora, the Jesuits never took over the running of the local university. This did not prevent a symbiosis between it and the Jesuit colleges, which sometimes supplied celebrated professors such as the theologian Francisco Suárez, and provided courses by prestigious teachers such as the philosopher Pedro da Fonseca and the theologian Luis de Molina. The most famous outcome of the Jesuits' intellectual activity in Coimbra was the eight-volume annotated edition of Aristotle's works (1591–1606). The College of Jesus also prepared Jesuits who were leaving for missions overseas. The prestige of the Jesuits' teaching in Coimbra was such that, significantly, harsh accusations were made against them in the new climate of the Enlightenment, which led to the expulsion of the Society of Jesus from the territories of the Portuguese Crown in 1759. After the Society was reestablished in 1814, the College of Arts was once again entrusted to the Jesuits between 1832 and 1834.

See also Portugal; Universities, 1540–1773

Alden, Dauril, *The Making of an Enterprise: The Society of Jesus in Portugal, Its Empire, and Beyond, 1540–1750*. Stanford, CA: Stanford University Press, 1996.
Rodrigues, Francisco, *História da Companhia de Jesus na Assistência de Portugal*. 4 vols. Porto: Apostolado da Imprensa, 1931–50.

Giuseppe Marcocci

Collaboration

Early on St. Ignatius sought out wealthy patrons to endow the colleges and provide funds for educating young Jesuits. In the case of the House of St. Martha, founded in Rome for the shelter of prostitutes leaving the profession, he enlisted women as collaborators. In the missions Jesuits relied on native catechists to give instruction to the people.

But the big shift in collaboration did not occur until the Second Vatican Council, which recovered the Pauline insight of each person endowed by baptism for building up the Body of Christ. Laypeople, of course, had assisted in Jesuit universities and high schools for centuries, but often in secondary roles such as male coaches or women secretaries. A mutuality in ministry at times had occurred among Jesuits and women religious – with Jesuits teaching boys in the high school and the sisters teaching in the corresponding grade school.

In the late 1960s the dire finances of some Jesuit institutions in the United States led to the rapid transfer of ownership to lay boards of trustees who had the resources and expertise to lay solid financial foundations. "Father, we'll handle the finances, and you do everything else" became an early mantra. Simultaneously high schools and universities enjoyed expanding enrollments, and more and more faculty were laypeople. Then in General Congregation 34, the Jesuits embraced a whole new way of collaboration. They identified their role as supporting laypeople in *their* ministry, rather than "inviting lay people into the ministry of the Jesuits." This new time matched the emerging trend in the Church for greater initiative by all the People of God.

See also Separate Incorporation; Universities, 1773–Present; Women, as Co-Workers with Jesuits

"Cooperation with the Laity in Mission," Decree 13, General Congregation 34 (1975).
"Jesuits and the Situation of Women in Church and Society," Decree 14, General Congregation 34 (1975).

Patrick J. Howell, SJ

Collins, Dominic, SJ, Bl. (1566–1602)

Born into a prominent family in Youghal, County Cork, in 1566, Dominic Collins was put to death in the same town on Sunday, October 31, 1602. Martyred at the hands of the English for his Catholic faith, his death was, nevertheless, mired in the politics of the period. Collins may have attended a Jesuit school which was opened at Youghal around 1576. Following the end of the Desmond rebellion in 1586, Collins went to France where he found employment as an innkeeper at Nantes. In three years he earned enough money to buy a commission in the army of the Duke of Mercoeur which, as part of the Catholic League, was fighting against the Huguenots. After nine years, and when the League was falling apart, Capitaine de la Branche, as he was known, left for Spain to join the armies of Philip III with a recommendation from the Spanish General Juan Del Agulia. He now met and came under the influence of an Irish Jesuit, Thomas White, who would publish, at Rome in 1604, the first account of Collins's life. Collins was received into the Society at Compostela in December 1598. A hardened soldier who was both obstinate and hot-tempered, Collins was accepted with reluctance as a temporal coadjutor. He was sent back to Ireland as *socius* to Fr. James Archer, SJ, who was chaplain to the forces of the Spanish king dispatched to aid O'Neill and O'Donnell in their rebellion against Queen Elizabeth I. This phase of the rebellion culminated in a rousing defeat at the Battle of Kinsale, 1601. Taken prisoner with two others following the siege of Dunboy Castle, seventy-six soldiers were summarily executed. Collins alone, given that he was a Jesuit, was to stand trial, and he was personally interrogated and tortured by the president of Munster, Lord Carew. From the scaffold he declared his loyalty to the Queen and told the onlookers that he had come to Ireland to defend and preach the Catholic faith. He was beatified by Pope John Paul II in September 1992.

See also Ireland; Martyrs, Ideal and History

Forristal, Desmond, *Dominic Collins: Irish Martyr, Jesuit Brother, 1566–1602*. Dublin: Messenger Publications, 1992.

O'Reilly, Myles, *Lives of the Irish Martyrs and Confessors*. New York: Sheehy, 1880, pp. 178–83.

Proinsius Ó Fionnagáin, "Dominic Collins SJ." In Patrick J. Corish and Benignus Millet, eds., *The Irish Martyrs*. Dublin: Four Courts Press, 2005, pp. 95–106.

Oliver P. Rafferty, SJ

Colloquy

It should be obvious that no relationship can be sustained without the benefit of regular communication and frequent contact. Friends can drift away from one another and rifts can develop between partners when opportunities for honest, thoughtful dialogue are neglected. If one understands prayer as relationship with God, then, one can see that a deep and lasting relationship will develop only if one takes advantage of these opportunities for intimate and open conversation.

In his *Spiritual Exercises* (*SpEx*), St. Ignatius insists on this point, including a conversation, or colloquy, as an essential element of almost every contemplation or meditation. Although the colloquy is prescribed for each meditation, it is worth noting that it is never detailed. Knowing that the "Creator will deal directly with the creature" (*SpEx* #15), Ignatius simply sets the stage for honest conversation, instructing the exercitant that "the colloquy is made by speaking (*hablando*) as one friend speaks to another" (#54).

In this way, the colloquy (whether with the Father, the Son, Mary, or all three in the so-called Triple Colloquy) is the proper end for any period of prayer, for it is the point of greatest intimacy within a relationship of trust where there is nothing to hide or fear. The colloquy ought not to be seen simply as the last and final part of a prayer period, like some sort of divine wrap-up, but rather as the point to which every exercise is leading: to open conversation with the One who has spoken first, with the One from whom the exercitant begs grace. In colloquy the exercitant has the space and trust to ask for more.

See also Spiritual Exercises

Aschenbrenner, George, "Becoming Whom We Contemplate." *The Way: Supplement* 52 (1985), 30–42.

Demoustier, Adrien, "Ignatian Contemplation and the Contemplative Way." *The Way: Supplement* 103 (2002), 16–24.

Keith Maczkiewicz, SJ

Colombia

We can divide the history of the Society of Jesus in Colombia into four periods:

1. *From 1599, the year the first Jesuits arrived in the present territory of Colombia, until their expulsion in 1767.* During this first stage, the Society of Jesus offered an invaluable contribution to the cultural, artistic, educational, scientific, religious, and social

life of what is now Colombia. Jesuit schools educated more than 6,000 students, an extraordinary number for the population at that time. They founded the Javeriana University with faculties of theology, philosophy, civil and Canon law in 1622. It was here that medicine was taught for the first time in the territory. The Jesuits introduced the first printing press in Colombia in 1737 and established the first pharmacy in Bogotá, attended by the Brother Diego Molina. The priest José Gumilla, a missionary to the Orinoco, introduced coffee as an important market commodity. Father José Dadey built the first harmonium in New Granada and was a consummate teacher of the Chibcha language.

At the time of their expulsion in 1767, the Jesuits left behind the prosperous missions among the native populations in the Llanos de Casanare and Meta, where 10,367 native people had been organized into communities called "reductions," for their religious, cultural, economic, and social development. The number of Jesuits expelled from the new kingdom was a total of 237, including 19 novices. After the independence of Colombia, the libraries of the colleges became an integral part of the current National Library.

2. *The Society of Jesus returned to Colombia in 1844, thirty years after the restoration of the Order by Pope Pius VII*. This second period lasted until 1850, when Colombian President José Hilario López expelled them again. The return of the Jesuits to Colombia took place through the initiative of a group of conservative politicians who, under President Pedro Alcántara Herrán (1841–45), passed new laws for the evangelization of native communities in Casanare, San Martín, Andaquí, Mocoa, Goajira, and Veraguas. The Jesuits who returned to New Granada in that year were all Spaniards. When the superior general summoned them to accept the invitation from the government of New Granada, they were living in exile in France, Italy, and Belgium, having been expelled from Spain in 1835.

Both the return and the presence of the Jesuits between 1844 and 1850 coincided with the rise of the new Liberal party, which elected José Hilario López to the presidency on March 7, 1849. López promoted a number of reforms geared toward developing a modern state. One of the measures concerning the Church was the expulsion of the Jesuits in 1850, without any legal process or defense on the part of those expelled. The ironic aspect of this expulsion was that, according to the President, the 1767 Expulsion Edict signed by Carlos III of Spain was still in force and, therefore, the presence of the Jesuits in the Republic was illegal.

3. *From 1858 to 1861*. In 1858, President Mariano Ospina Rodríguez (1857–61) invited the Jesuits to return to Colombia. However, after the Conservative defeat in the civil war of 1860, Ospina Rodríguez's successor, Cipriano de Mosquera (1861–64) expelled the pope's delegate in Colombia, Miecislao Ledóchowski, as well as Archbishop Antonio Herrán and some of his colleagues, and once again, the Jesuits. He dissolved all religious communities and expropriated Church property in defiance of Pope Pius IX. The two expulsions of the Jesuits coincide with these profound confrontations between Church and State.

4. *From the return of the Jesuits to Colombia in 1884 to the present*. The Jesuits opened a school in the city of Pasto, and two more in Bogotá and Medellín. In 1894, religious vocations in Colombia numbered 137, and as this number grew, it transformed the

Jesuit mission in Colombia into the independent province of Colombia (December 8, 1924). From that date until the present time, the Jesuits restored the Javeriana University in Bogotá in 1931 and in the 1970s established a university campus in Cali. In addition to these major works, the Jesuits founded colleges in Cali, Bucaramanga, and Manizales. Today, the Jesuits carry out important social work through the Center of Research and Popular Education (CINEP), the project Development and Peace of the Madgalena Medio, the Jesuit Service for Refugees (SJR), and several Fe y Alegría schools.

See also Claver, Peter SJ, St.; Fe y Alegría; Spain

Martínez, Jorge Enrique Salcedo, ed., *Los Jesuitas expulsados, extinguidos y restaurados. Memorias del Primer Encuentro Internacional sobre la historia de la Compañía de Jesús.* Bogotá: Pontificia Universidad Javeriana, 2014.
Las vicisitudes de los Jesuitas en Colombia en el siglo XIX. Una Historia de la Compañía de Jesús, 1844–1861. Bogotá: Editorial Pontificia Universidad Javeriana, 2014.
Pacheco, Juan Manual, *Los Jesuitas en Colombia.* 3 vols. Bogotá: Pontificia Universidad Javeriana, 1989.

Jorge Salcedo, SJ

Comillas, Universidad Pontificia (Madrid)

In 1978 Jesuit leaders integrated two long-standing educational institutions of the Society of Jesus in Spain – the Universidad Pontificia Comillas and the ICAI-ICADE institute in Madrid – under the common umbrella of the Universidad Pontificia Comillas of Madrid.

The Universidad Pontificia Comillas was originally founded in Comillas, Cantabria, in 1892 as a "seminary for the poor," providing tuition-free education to students from Spain and other Spanish-speaking countries who aspired to be priests. Its founding was the result of collaborative efforts among various agents: Tómas Gómez, SJ, its original source of inspiration; the Marquis of Comillas, its benefactor; and Pope Leo XIII, its original patron. Modeled as a seminary, the university was built in a quiet rural area on the Bay of Biscay, where it was isolated from much of the world. There, students immersed themselves in classical languages, philosophy, and scholastic theology. In 1904 the institution was granted the status of a pontifical university by Pope Pius X.

In contrast, the birth of the ICAI-ICADE institute took place in the busy urban setting of Madrid. In 1908, with funding from the Marquess of Vallejo, the Jesuits founded the ICAI (Instituto Católico de Artes e Industrias) to offer tuition-free technical training for factory workers. Decades later, as Spain underwent major development, the ICADE (Instituto Católico de Administración y Dirección de Empresas) was established in 1956 to provide programs in business management. In 1960 the ICADE was merged with the ICAI into one common institution, thus the ICAI-ICADE.

Beginning in 1969, the original Universidad Pontificia Comillas was gradually moved from Comillas to Madrid, where it could serve lay students as well as seminarians. With all these Jesuit-sponsored institutions now in Madrid, it was decided that their merger would enhance both institutions and enable the university to diversify and enrich its educational offerings. Having integrated faculties in the humanities and theology with those of business, law, and economics, the Universidad Pontificia Comillas serves as an example of Jesuit creative fidelity – adapting to the signs of the time while maintaining each of the institutions' original inspiration.

See also Spain; Universities, 1773–Present

González, M. Revuelta, "La Universidad Pontificia Comillas: un modelo de adaptación." *Once calas en la historia de la Compañía de Jesús: "Servir a todos en el Señor."* Madrid: Universidad P. Comillas, 2006, pp. 293–322.

Hưng Trung Phạm, SJ

Communion, Frequent

In the seventeenth century, an important theological dispute arose in France on the nature and relationship between grace and free will. Moral rigorists, who insisted on the importance of a strict moral code of behavior bolstered by disciplined penitential practice, became known as Jansenists (after the Dutch theologian Cornelius Jansen). Strongly opposed to Jansenist moral theology were many Jesuits, who stressed the freedom of the human will in moral decision making.

One Jansenist, Antoine Arnauld, applied Jansenist principles to the sacramental life of Catholics in *De la fréquente communion* (1643), discouraging the reception of communion by the laity without strict moral preparation. Jesuits, on the other hand, recommended the frequent reception of communion by laypersons, even those who had not engaged in penitential purification beforehand, since the grace received in the reception of communion was understood to strengthen the weak.

Jansenism, including its impact on sacramental participation, was condemned by several popes. In the early twentieth century, following Pope Leo XIII's 1902 encyclical *Mirare caritatis*, Pope St. Pius X rejected lingering local or regional practices involving delay in or reluctance to admit children to Communion, condemning:

> the injury caused by those who insist on extraordinary preparations for First Communion, beyond what is reasonable … such precautions proceed from the errors of the Jansenists who contended that the Most Holy Eucharist is a reward rather than a remedy for human frailty.

This decree established that children who have reached the age of reason (about the age of 7) should be admitted to both Confession and Holy Communion, and they need only to understand the meaning of the Eucharist (and act reverently) in a way appropriate to their age.

See also Jansenism; Liturgy

Dougherty, Joseph, *From Altar-Throne to Table: The Campaign for Frequent Holy Communion in the Catholic Church.* Lanham, MD: Scarecrow, 2010.
Pope St. Pius X (Sacred Congregation of the Discipline of the Sacraments), *Quam singulari* (1910; in English). www.papalencyclicals.net/Pius10/p10quam.htm.

Joanne M. Pierce

Community

The first Jesuit companions found it remarkable how they had all come together from so many diverse parts and nationalities and become "friends in the Lord." By making vows together at St. Denis chapel at Montmartre on the outskirts of Paris (1534), the seven companions cemented their relationship among themselves, even as they focused on the future of their mission together – ideally to go to Jerusalem to "convert the infidels" or, barring that, to journey to Rome to place themselves under the direction of the pope himself.

Once Pope Paul III began to mission them, they realized that they needed to form a more perfect union so that they could be united as companions, even as they were dispersed to distant places. So in 1539 the companions gathered for several weeks of prayer and communal discernment. They saw that their friendship and serving under the banner of Christ was their unique call, their charism: "to choose to be with Christ as servants of his mission, to be with people where they dwell and work and struggle, to bring the Gospel into their lives and labors" (General Congregation [GC] 34, Decree 1, #7, citing the *Deliberatio* of 1539). Community was vital – even if they were dispersed. And the superior was both to be a sign of their unity and to foster apostolic zeal and the bonds of affection.

Jerome Nadal, commissioned by Ignatius to explain the Jesuit *Constitutions*, described four types of Jesuit dwellings: "the house of probation, the college, the professed house, and the journey – and by this last the whole world becomes our house." For Nadal, "the journey," "pilgrimage," and "mission" were all equivalent.

Even at a distance Jesuit friendship flourished. The remarkable friendship between Ignatius and Francis Xavier was nourished by their letters. Francis Xavier wrote from Asia in 1549: "Among many other holy words and consolations of your letter, I read the concluding ones, 'Entirely yours, without power or possibility of ever forgetting you, Ignatio.' I read them with tears, and with tears now write them, remembering the past and the great love which you always bore towards me and still bear." Even at these monumental distances, they cherished their "friendship in the Lord." This welcomed tension between mission and community has always characterized Jesuits.

In response to the mandate of the Second Vatican Council to recover the charism of its founder and respond to the signs of the times, the Jesuits in GC 31 (1965–66) quickly realized that an accumulation of rules and arcane practices were obscuring their religious life and apostolic mission. After abrogating a multitude of rules, they called for a deeper appreciation of prayer, discernment, the *Spiritual Exercises*, and life in common, that is, their "friendship in the Lord." Obedience to the local superior shifted so that a greater responsibility was laid on each individual to build up the common good of all.

The separation of scholastics, brothers, and priests by grades, for instance – with separate recreation rooms for each group in the larger communities – was deemed no longer conducive to their common life in Christ.

Soon the restoration of the original method of Ignatius for retreats, given one-on-one with attention to each Jesuit's relationship with God, led naturally to a deeper appreciation and respect for the unique gifts of each individual. At the same time the dismantling of time-honored customs, such as the wearing of cassocks, reciting the Litany in common, reading at table, and so forth, led to some disorientation.

Nine years later in Decree 11 "Union of Minds and Hearts" (GC 32, 1975) addressed the void created earlier and laid a solid foundation for a more vibrant community life. As the title suggests, it sought to foster the bonds of fraternal love in Christ and a habit of prayer and discernment attuned to the Jesuit apostolic mission today.

GC 35 (2008) further refined the balance between apostolic work and community life. It declared, "Our mission is not limited to our works. Our personal and community relationship with the Lord, our relationship to another as friends in the Lord, our solidarity with the poor and marginalized and a lifestyle responsible to creation are all important aspects of our lives as Jesuits. They authenticate what we proclaim and what we do in fulfilling our mission … Thus, Jesuit community is not just for mission: it is itself mission" (GC 35, Decree 3, #85).

See also Friends in the Lord; Minister; Province; Region; Superior, Local

"Challenges to Our Mission Today." GC 35, Decree 3. In John W. Padberg, ed., *Jesuit Life and Mission Today: The Decrees and Accompanying Documents of the 31st–35th General Congregations of the Society of Jesus.* St. Louis, MO: The Institute of Jesuit Sources, 2009.

O'Malley, John W., "To Travel to Any Part of the World: Jerónimo Nadal and the Jesuit Vocation." *Studies in Jesuit Spirituality* 16, 2 (March, 1984), 1–28.

Patrick J. Howell, SJ

Company

The term "Company" (*Compañía* in Spanish, *Compagnía* in Italian) was used in the sixteenth century to identify groups of laymen or laywomen who came together to engage in a common apostolic activity. While modeled on the medieval confraternity (a pious association of persons who prayed and cared for one another), the company focused outwardly. One example, the Company of St. Ursula founded by Angela Merici in 1535, gathered a group of women of all ages to teach catechism to young girls. Merici hoped that by educating well-prepared young women to become devout mothers, the Christian family would be strengthened and the Church reformed. Their Primitive Rule states: "Let each member be concerned with the works of charity, particularly with Christian education … but also right conduct," so as to "give their students a living model [of Christian life]." Concern for teaching catechism and presenting a model of Christian life became fundamental components of a company.

When a branch of the Oratory of Divine Love was established in Rome in 1514, it attracted clergy as well as laity. Known as the Company of Divine Love, it centered its work at a hospital near Santa Dorothea in Trastevere. Founders of later reform orders, Gaetano of Thiene, Gian Pietro Carafa of the Theatines, and Giroloamo Emiliani of the Somaschans, belonged to this Company. The Somaschans, founded in 1528, were originally the Company of Servants of the Poor. They, too, emphasized apostolic activity through their orphanages and hospitals.

Ignatius of Loyola and his companions encountered these companies during their sojourn in Venice in 1537–38. Some of them lived with the Theatines; Ignatius lived at the Priory of the Trinity where Emiliani had lodged only a few months earlier. Thus, the Jesuits' decision to refer to themselves as the *Compagnía di Gesù* made use of a term that had already been well established.

See also Christian Life Communities; Confraternities; Friends in the Lord; Loyola, Ignatius of, SJ, St.

Iparraguire, Ignacio, *Historia de la espiritualidad.* Barcelona: Juan Flors, 1969.

Martin, Marie, *L'Éducation des Ursulines.* Rome: Aurora, 1947.

Mark A. Lewis, SJ

Composition of Place

An essential component of the imaginative meditations of the *Spiritual Exercises* (*SpEx*), the "composition of place" refers to the initial step, or "prelude," of a meditation in which the person praying considers the material to be contemplated and thereby composes a scene in his or her imagination. Ignatius bids the person praying to reconstitute the material setting of the scene, which often involves a passage from the Gospels, with "the vision of the imagination (*la vista de la imaginación*)" in all its concrete and vivid detail (*SpEx* #47).

In the contemplation on the Nativity, for instance, Ignatius invites the retreatant to imagine the cave in which Jesus was born, considering "how large, how small, how low, how high" the cave is, and "how it is arranged" (*SpEx* #112). In a similar fashion, when contemplating the Last Supper, the retreatant is instructed to consider the place, "whether great or small, whether of this or that appearance" (*SpEx* #192). Ignatius was not so concerned with the historicity of these imagined details as with the way in which this method enables retreatants to let the gospel scene become their own, facilitating an encounter with Christ within the context of personal experience, an experience that supplies the material by which the imagination creatively works.

This is merely a prelude, however, for the actual contemplation that follows, and the composition of place is like a *mise-en-scène* for the dramatic acts that form the main body of the contemplation, into which even the retreatant may personally enter. As this entire dynamic takes place within the context of faith, Ignatian spirituality trusts that these acts of the imagination, moreover, are not merely of our own making but also guided and shaped by the Holy Spirit who accompanies the retreatant in prayer.

See also Images; Imagination; *Spiritual Exercises*

Standaert, Nicolas, "The Composition of Place: Creating Space for an Encounter." *The Way* 46, 1 (2007), 7–20.

Henry Shea, SJ

Conference, Jesuit

There are at present six Jesuit Conferences of Major Superiors – Africa and Madagascar, Asia Pacific, Europe, Latin America, South Asia, and Canada and USA.

These conferences represent a "significant initiative in the governance structure of the Society" (General Congregation [GC] 35, Decree 5, #17). They derive from a growing sense – already articulated in 1965 in GC 31 (Decree 48), which referred to the need for "interprovincial cooperation" and authorized experiments in new structures to bring this about, in particular to meetings of "boards of Provincials," albeit without any juridical authority – of the need to create more adequate governmental and administrative structures to ensure that the universality of the Ignatian vision of mission could correspond to the new exigencies of our globalized world (see also GC 34, Decree 21).

By the time of GC 35 (2008), the experiments advocated in 1965 had developed to the point of the six conferences mentioned, each with its own moderator or president, and with its own set of statutes, taking into account regional differences, and approved by father general. The moderator by now has himself the faculties of a major superior (GC 35, Decree 5, #19), with the authority (specified by the statutes) to request and to assign persons from the provinces or regions needed for the activities and works dependent on the conference. It is also stated, however, that "Conferences do not constitute a new level of government between the General and the Provincials" and stress is laid on the "moral authority" of the moderator (GC 35, Decree 5, #18 b and #20 b, b2).

It is clear that Jesuit conferences are still somewhat experimental in nature, "in formation." But it is also clear that they represent an important Jesuit response to the challenges of our increasingly globalized world.

See also Curia, Jesuit; Province; Region

Padberg, John W., ed., *Jesuit Life and Mission Today: The Decrees and Accompanying Documents of the 31st–35th General Congregations of the Society of Jesus.* St. Louis, MO: The Institute of Jesuit Sources, 2009.

Gerard O'Hanlon, SJ

Confession, Confessor

Confession and confessors are of major significance in the history of the Jesuits, and in several distinct ways: confession of sins as a part of the *Spiritual Exercises* of Saint Ignatius; Jesuit priests as confessors hearing confessions; canonized Jesuit saints as confessors in the sense of confessing the faith; Jesuits as confessors to kings and powerful persons, both by hearing their confessions in the sacrament of penance and by functioning as confidential advisers on the morality of private matters (if a head of state may be said to have any) as well as of matters of state, such as foreign policy and war.

In the first "Week" of his *Spiritual Exercises* (##42–44), Ignatius of Loyola invites persons doing these "exercises" to make a general examen (or examination) of conscience, a kind of patient review of their history of receiving and responding to God's love and grace. Gratitude for grace leads the "exercitants" to ask for the grace of knowledge of their sins and for the grace to reject them. Ignatius then encourages those who wish to do so to make a general confession of their sins, since with better knowledge of their sins they may make a better confession and may be well disposed to receive the Blessed Sacrament.

Pope Julius III, in his 1550 approbation of the Society, specifically mentioned the work of hearing confessions among the ministries of Jesuits. Already in its first years, and throughout its history, the Society of Jesus has been known for its supply of sought-after confessors; its urban churches and chapels, in particular, have often featured an abundance of priests available to hear confessions many hours each week. Like some other religious order priests, Jesuits have at times been chosen as confessors by diocesan clergy eager to avoid confessing to one of their own. Some Jesuits have been chosen to hear the confessions of bishops, cardinals, and even popes.

Jesuit confessors have frequently been considered more merciful than some other confessors, and this has at times been a source not of praise but of condemnation of Jesuit sacramental practices. In the early modern period, Jansenists, such as Blaise Pascal, were relentless in mocking what they considered to be Jesuit laxness and softness on sin. Jesuits were known to emphasize the role of the circumstances of an action in determining its sinfulness or lack of it, while some other confessors emphasized absolute, exception-less norms for which circumstances made no difference. Jesuits were said to work with the principle of where there is doubt there is freedom, and Jesuits often found the sinfulness of various actions doubtful. In the restored Society, post-1814, and at least up to Vatican II, Jesuit confessors once again became sought after. An example is Felix Cappello (1879–1962), an Italian diocesan priest who found his call to become a Jesuit during a visit to Lourdes. As a Jesuit he taught canon law and moral theology at the Gregorian University and spent countless hours hearing confessions at the Church of Sant'Ignazio in Rome. He is buried in Sant'Ignazio near the spot where his confessional stood, and the cause for his beatification is in process.

Another Jesuit buried in Sant'Ignazio is Robert Bellarmine (1542–1621), also a professor at the Gregorian University, and the author of a catechism, works of "controversial" theology, that is, theology written as a refutation of Protestant teachings, and several devotional works, including one on a happy death. Canonized in 1930, Saint Robert Bellarmine is referred to as a bishop, doctor, and confessor. Confessor is a title that has been given to male saints who are not martyrs but are considered to have been articulate "confessors" of the faith, that is, they effectively preached, taught, and defended the Catholic faith. Bellarmine may be the best known of Jesuit confessor-saints.

As confessors to nobles and members of royal and imperial families, and to other persons of the highest rank, Jesuits gained access to the consciences of many of the most powerful people in early modern Europe, including kings of France and emperors of the Holy Roman Empire. As what was said in the sacrament of penance was held by confessors in the strictest confidentiality, historians have little access to what would be a fascinating source on this type of Jesuit confessor. Yet historians have shown how French Jesuit confessors also advised the king on who should be named a bishop in France, and how Jesuit confessors played significant roles in Germany in determining political and military priorities in the Thirty Years War.

See also Spiritual Direction

Bireley, Robert, *The Jesuits and the Thirty Years War: Kings, Courts, and Confessors*. Cambridge: Cambridge University Press, 2003.

Delumeau, Jean, *L'aveu et le pardon: les difficultés de la confession XIIIe–XVIIIe siècle*. Paris: Fayard, 1990.

Keenan, James, *A History of Catholic Moral Theology in the Twentieth Century: From Confessing Sins to Liberating Consciences*. New York: Continuum, 2010.

Minois, Georges, *Le confessor du roi: les directeurs de conscience sous la monarchie française*. Paris: Fayard, 1988.

Thomas Worcester, SJ

Confraternities

For millennia, confraternities, sodalities, and other voluntary pious affiliations have been an integral part of Christian devotional life, appearing in myriad forms and reflecting the societies in which they developed. In the sixteenth-century Mediterranean world in which Ignatius established the Society of Jesus, confraternities were intrinsic to communities, from the smallest villages to the largest cities, enriching their festive life and charitable initiatives.

Not surprisingly then, after making vows with the first companions at Montmartre in 1534, Ignatius became actively engaged in confraternal life during his brief return to his native Azpeitia and then from the first weeks of arriving in Rome in 1537. Besides promoting numerous traditional confraternal charities, such as for orphans, prisoners, and the sick, Ignatius was directly responsible for founding three innovative institutions in Rome that reflected the more active type of charitable intervention characteristic of both the Catholic and the Protestant Reformation. The first Ignatian confraternities directed these innovative works, namely, the Casa di Santa Marta – a halfway house for repentant prostitutes and battered women, the Conservatorio di Santa Caterina – a boarding school for daughters of prostitutes – and the Casa dei Catecumeni – a boarding school for newly converted Jews, Muslims, and other non-Catholics. These three Roman models were emulated with dozens of similar institutions throughout the world, wherever the Jesuits had a presence. Because prostitutes, Jews, and Muslims represented public figures outside the Christian community, they became a primary focus of charitable attention, and Ignatius frequently recruited prominent members of the community to provide financial support and leadership for these endeavors.

However, because of the independent, lay character of these confraternities, such institutions often lost their Jesuit association after a few decades. In contrast, the confraternal institutions that became most closely associated with the Jesuits and benefited from their ongoing spiritual direction and support were the Marian congregations, beginning with the Prima Primaria Sodality for students of the Roman College, founded by Belgian Jesuit Jan Leunis in 1563. After Gregory XIII raised the Prima Primaria Sodality to an archconfraternity in 1584, it became the primary model for Jesuit lay initiatives. Jesuit colleges would typically have multiple student Marian congregations, and other Jesuit houses could have as many as six or more affiliated congregations for adults, organized around social groups, such as nobles, merchants, artisans, servants, or priests. By the time of the Suppression of the Society in 1773, there were roughly 2,500 affiliated Marian congregations, and emperors, popes, kings, and cardinals could be counted among their membership.

Thus, the Marian congregations functioned for the Jesuits like the earlier Rosary confraternities for the Dominicans or the Third Order for the Franciscans as the primary lay associations supported by the Society of Jesus. However, Jesuits always promoted a broad variety of other confraternal institutions as well, particularly as part of their missionary activity, whether in the hinterlands of Sicily, New France, Paraguay, or in China. Within Europe itself, itinerant Jesuits such as Peter Faber or Jerónimo Nadal used week-long missions to generate fervor in a community with the intent of leaving behind new or revitalized confraternities, a practice codified by the 5th General Congregation in 1594. Jesuit spiritual writers and preachers like Franz Coster, Gaspar Loarte, and Luca Pinelli were prolific promoters of confraternities such as Name of God, Christian Doctrine, Most Holy Sacrament, and Body of Christ as well as confraternities affiliated with other orders like the Scapular, Cordelier, or Rosary.

Just as Jesuit missionary preaching often utilized spiritual meditation and the active engagement of the imagination in prayer, as found in Ignatius's *Spiritual Exercises*, so such activities appear frequently in the rulebooks and devotional practices of Jesuit-inspired confraternities. In addition to prayer and contemplation, Jesuits enjoined active engagement in charitable initiatives among confraternal members, though the objectives of these initiatives varied enormously depending on the resources of the individual confraternity.

The confraternities and numerous Marian congregations played a vital role during the period of the Suppression of the Society from 1773 to 1814, sometimes shepherding properties, chapels, and resources that were returned to the Order when it was revived. The confraternities and congregations also had a history of producing Jesuit vocations, another feature of the symbiotic relationship between the Order and its lay associations. Following the apostolic constitution *Bis saeculari* of 1948, Pope Pius XII approved the World Federation of Sodalities of Our Lady, which numbered some 80,000 individual sodalities at the time. Since the Fourth General Assembly in 1967, these affiliated organizations throughout the world have called themselves Christian Life Communities and represent the rich inheritance of the Jesuit confraternal tradition.

See also Christian Life Communities; Marian Congregations

Black, Christopher F., and Pamela Gravestock, eds., *Early Modern Confraternities in Europe and the Americas: International and Interdisciplinary Perspectives.* Aldershot: Ashgate, 2006.
Clossey, Luke, *Salvation and Globalization in the Early Jesuit Missions.* Cambridge: Cambridge University Press, 2008.
Donnelly, John Patrick, and Michael Maher, eds., *Confraternities and Catholic Reform in Italy, France, and Spain.* (Sixteenth Century Essays and Studies, vol. 44). Kirksville, MO: Thomas Jefferson University Press, 1999.
Lazar, Lance Gabriel, *Working in the Vineyard of the Lord: Jesuit Confraternities in Early Modern Italy.* Toronto: University of Toronto Press, 2005.

Lance Gabriel Lazar

Congo, the Central Africa Province

The Central Africa Jesuit province was established on December 8, 1961, under the leadership of Fr. Victor Mertens. It was composed of three countries: Congo-Zaire, Rwanda, and Burundi, all of which were former Belgian colonies. Political instability and difficult relationships between Rwanda and Congo after the Rwandan genocide in 1994 contributed to the creation of the separate but dependent region of Rwanda-Burundi in 1995. In 1999, Fr. General Peter-Hans Kolvenbach established Rwanda and Burundi as an independent region (RWB), marking the end of what had been a common venture between the three countries for thirty-eight years. On August 2, 2010, the province of Central Africa (ACE), which had been reduced primarily to the Congo, incorporated the territory of Angola, which had been attached to the province of Portugal.

The Jesuits of Central Africa have been involved in a variety of apostolates and contributed to the formation of the intelligentsia in Rwanda, Burundi, and Angola. They prepared the elite who led those countries after the movements for political independence in the 1960s. They were involved in the formation of youth, the proclamation of faith, and the promotion of social justice through their various social centers and parishes. This same work continues today through a host of different ministries and apostolates, including schools, publications, a radio station, parishes, and spiritual centers in both Congo and Angola. For the formation of youth, the province has seven high schools: Kubama (1926), Boboto in Kinshasa (1980), Alfajiri in Bukavu (1941), Technical and Professional Institute in Kikwit (1953), Sadisana in Kikwit (1957), N'Tememo in Kasongo-Lunda (1960), and Bosomi in Kinshasa (1967).

The promotion of social justice is part and parcel of every activity, but there are visible centers in the province to foster this dimension of the mission of the Jesuits of Central Africa. Legal and juridical analysis is done through the Center of Studies for

Social Action (CEPAS). The formation of social leadership is done with the help of CADICEC, a Christian center for leaders and entrepreneurs. Compassionate care is given through the CHECHE in Bukavu and the Centre MGR Munzihirwa for street children in Kinshasa. The Hospital of Djuma serves to alleviate the suffering of many in Congo. Special attention is given to refugees and internally displaced peoples in the cities of Kinsagani, Goma, and Luanda in Angola through JRC Congo, one of the most active branches of the Jesuit Refugee Service on the continent.

The province of Central Africa has invested substantial resources in the printing apostolate. It has the presses of Loyola Editions in Kinshasa and Maisha's Collections in Kikwit. It has a recording studio called Losambo. *Congo-Afrique*, *Renaître*, and *Documentation et Information Africaine* (DIA) are well-known reviews that offer social, cultural, and theological analysis for the average reader. *Telema*, *Raison Ardente*, *Afrique d'Espérance*, and *Revue Philosophique de Kiwenza* are academic reviews through which African thinkers from all over the continent publish theological and philosophical scholarship. Under the dedication of Fr. Peter-Simon Boka, the theological review *Telema* became a major component of the intellectual apostolate of the province. The late Fr. Boka worked tirelessly to obtain contributions to the review from various theologians and thinkers to ensure that it remained ever relevant to the challenges of the Church in Africa.

The Jesuits of the Central Africa province are deeply involved in pastoral work in parishes. They are responsible for fourteen parishes in total: thirteen in Congo and one in Angola. The *Spiritual Exercises* of St. Ignatius also constitute an important part of the province's ministry and represent one the most fruitful contributions of the Jesuits to both the clergy and the laity of Congo and Angola. Five retreat houses were built to offer the experience of the *Spiritual Exercises*, four in Congo and one in Angola: Manresa in Kimwenza (1958), Amani in Bukavu (1968), Kipula in Kikwit (1969), La Storta in Pelende (1994), and Sao Jao de Brito in Luanda (2009).

The Central Africa province is credited with the founding of Lovanium University, the first public university of Congo. This institution contributed much to the formation of Congolese leaders and administrators. In 1971, this university was merged with other institutions into the National University of Zaire. Between 1980 and 1991, this university was made separate again into three different universities in distinct locations throughout the Democratic Republic of the Congo. One of these, the University of Kinshasa, is near the Jesuit philosophate in Kimwenza, and today its students still take advantage of the well-equipped library of the Jesuit philosophate.

Through their diverse ministries and apostolates, the Jesuits of Central Africa endeavor to seek and find God and foster the construction of a democratic Congo where justice and the rule of law prevail.

See also Africa, West; Boka, Simon-Pierre, SJ; Munzihirwa, Christophe, SJ

JESAM: Jesuit Superiors of Africa and Madagascar. www.jesam.info.

Luc Bonaventure A. Amoussou, SJ

Congregations

While other religious orders usually speak of "chapters" to refer to formal meetings where elected members gather to do official business or to elect a person to office, Jesuits speak of "congregations," of which there are four kinds: a General Congregation, a Provincial Congregation, a Procurators' Congregation and a Congregation for the Election of a Temporary Vicar. The most important is a General Congregation, which meets either to elect a superior general or to treat of important or difficult matters affecting the life and work of the Society of Jesus as a whole (or both). A General Congregation, when convened, is the supreme governing body of the Society and makes decisions that are binding on Jesuits everywhere. It is composed of elected and of *ex-officio* members drawn from every province in the world, the former exceeding the latter in number.

In a Provincial Congregation, members of a particular province, e.g., Spain or East Africa, meet to discuss questions concerning the state of the province, in particular those proposed by the provincial. When a General or a Procurators' Congregation is forthcoming, they elect whoever will attend it (not *ex-officio*). Jesuits in a particular province elect members of that province to the Provincial Congregation in accordance with a formula ensuring that Jesuits of every grade are at least minimally included; for example, there must be at least one formed Brother and two approved scholastics, one of whom is not ordained.

Procurators' Congregations occur every four years from the end of the previous General Congregation, with each province or region choosing one of its own members (not the provincial or the regional superior) to attend. These Congregations ensure that rank-and-file members of the Society have a voice in the Society at large (see Decree 5, on Governance, General Congregation 35, #6). The last Procurators' Congregation was held in Nairobi in July 2012. The superior general and his advisers are always present and the Congregation discusses the overall state and affairs of the Society, with the general proposing to the members points that he wishes them to consider also. At a Procurators' Congregation, a vote is taken on whether or not to call a General Congregation.

A Congregation for the Election of a Temporary Vicar General is convened when the superior general, usually for reasons of health, is no longer competent to discharge his duties and has not previously indicated who his vicar should be.

See also Constitutions; Curia, Jesuit; Province; Superior General

The Constitutions of the Society of Jesus and their Complementary Norms. Ed. John W. Padberg. St Louis, MO: The Institute of Jesuit Sources, 1996.

James Corkery, SJ

Conscience, account of

When Ignatius introduces the account of conscience in the *General Examen*, one of the founding documents of the Society of Jesus, he does so with more than usual solemnity. "After pondering the matter in our Lord, we consider it to be of great and even extraordinary importance in his Divine Majesty that the superiors should have a complete understanding of the subjects" (*Constitutions*, #91). Openness to one's *abba* or *amma* was part of the wisdom of the desert and merged with a subtle teaching on the discernment of spirits. The practice provided support, encouragement, and an assurance that one was following the right path on one's journey to God. (As with the examen, "consciousness" may be a more helpful term than "conscience," indicating the comprehensiveness of the self-revelation involved.)

Ignatius had called on this tradition in describing the relationship between the one giving and the one making the *Spiritual Exercises*. He later incorporated it into his *Constitutions*. But here some differences emerge. The self-revelation is now made to a superior rather than to a spiritual father or retreat director. Besides, it is made at fixed times, not just when problems arise. (While the account of conscience/consciousness can be made to any superior, the term usually refers to the Jesuit's meeting with his provincial at the time of the annual visitation.)

However, not only was Ignatius interested in the *cura personalis* of the individual Jesuit. He also wanted this ancient tradition to serve the body of the Society and its end. So he developed it as an aid to missioning and governance at the same time as it offered *cura personalis*. Hence, there are three inter-locking dimensions to this practice. These are the personal care of the one making this self-revelation, his appropriate and most effective missioning, and the governance and well-being of the body of the Society. All three require discernment.

See also Cura Personalis; Examen; *Spiritual Exercises*

Kolvenbach, Peter-Hans, "Le compte de conscience." *Acta Romana Societatis Iesu* 23, 3 (2006), 554–61.
O'Leary, Brian, *Sent into the Lord's Vineyard: Explorations in the Jesuit Constitutions.* Oxford: Way Books, 2012, pp. 130–36.

Brian O'Leary, SJ

Consolation

Although consolation is a familiar term in spiritual writings, its meaning can take on particular nuances when used by different authors. For Ignatius it is essentially a sensible sign of the presence of God communicating himself. This allows for a wide range of possible manifestations of the divine presence. But, in whatever form, it is always recognizable as coming *de fuera*, from outside oneself, not initiated by or under the control of the person receiving it. Unfortunately, it can sometimes be simulated by an evil spirit.

Ignatius's Rules for the Discernment of Spirits include the clearest description of what he understands by consolation (*SpEx* #316). He begins with an experience of marked intensity, of being caught up totally in the love of God. "As a result it (the soul) can love no created thing on the face of the earth in itself, but only in the Creator of them all." He then speaks of tears that can accompany a consideration of one's sins, or of Christ's passion, and so forth. Lastly he turns to more "ordinary" experiences such as any felt increase in faith, hope, or charity, or any attraction to the things of God. All these leave a person in tranquility and peace.

This depiction of the various modes of consolation is not meant to be exhaustive but suggestive. More important for Ignatius is that consolation is an inner movement whose dynamic draws a person toward God. This explains why consolation plays a key role in the discernment of spirits and in decision-making. Consolation becomes the criterion or touchstone by which a person recognizes whether a certain option (election) is in harmony with God's will or not. Genuine spiritual consolation is a sign of God's approval. However, it is not to be identified with God and so not to be sought for its own sake.

See also Desolation; Discernment; *Spiritual Exercises*

Gallagher, Timothy, *Spiritual Consolation: An Ignatian Guide for the Greater Discernment of Spirits.* New York: Crossroad, 2007.

Brian O'Leary, SJ

Constitutions

The term "Constitutions" (of the Society of Jesus) is most commonly employed to designate two documents: the *General Examen* and the *Constitutions* proper. Although distinct, they cannot be separated and are always published together. The former is used during the assessment of applicants who wish to join the Society. The title *General Examen* is actually a misnomer due to a copyist's error. The correct title for the whole document, now rarely used, is simply *Examen*. This is then subdivided into the General Examen, which constitutes the first four chapters, and the Particularized Examens, which constitute the remaining four. The first group of chapters is addressed to all applicants, while the last four are addressed to different types of applicants: priests and those destined for ordination (Chapter 5), those to be admitted as spiritual or temporal coadjutors (Chapter 6), scholastics before and after their studies (Chapter 7), and finally those who enter with an openness to accept the grade for which they will show themselves most suitable (Chapter 8). The purpose of the *General Examen* is to allow the applicant to get to know the Society and the Society, through its representatives, to get to know the applicant. When both sides are satisfied, the applicant may enter the novitiate. The nature of the Constitutions themselves will be treated below.

Three events occurring in Rome in successive years form the background to the composition of both these documents. In 1538 Ignatius and his first companions, a group of ten recently ordained priests, offered themselves to Pope Paul III for apostolic service anywhere in the world. The following year, 1539, during what became known as the Deliberation of the First Fathers, they decided to give greater substance and precision to this offering by becoming a religious order. Finally, in 1540, the Pope gave his approval to the *Formula of the Institute*, a text drawn up by the companions that summarizes their aims and their way of life. This *Formula* (a revised version was promulgated by Pope Julius III in 1550) corresponds to the Rule in the older religious orders.

The *Formula* gave the superior general of the new order authority to draw up Constitutions in consultation with the other companions. In 1541 six of these companions gathered in Rome for the purpose of electing a first superior general, and unsurprisingly, they chose Ignatius. While they were together, they also worked on certain issues that remained unresolved from their 1539 Deliberation. Their decisions became known as the "Constitutions of 1541" (although these were limited in scope and understood to be provisional). It soon became clear that it would be impossible for all the companions, now more and more widely dispersed, to collaborate on writing fuller Constitutions. Hence, this task became the responsibility of Ignatius alone.

The composition of the *Constitutions* was in progress up to the death of Ignatius in 1556, although they were substantially finished by 1550. However, for a variety of reasons the work had begun slowly in the early 1540s and only picked up real momentum with the appointment of Juan de Polanco as secretary to the Society in 1547. In addition to possessing remarkable skills in research, organization, and composition, Polanco also had the time (which Ignatius did not) to devote to the Constitutions. The nature of the collaboration between Ignatius and Polanco has been the subject of considerable debate. It is obvious that Polanco was much more than a secretary and that his influence on the Constitutions was significant. However, it would be an exaggeration to claim him as their author. On this complex question perhaps all that can be said with confidence is that the *thought* throughout the *Constitutions* is always that of Ignatius while the *expression* is often that of Polanco.

Ignatius's way of thinking was inductive rather than deductive. He was more interested in praxis than in theory and, above all, he learned from experience. The *Spiritual Exercises* came into being because he had reflected on his own experience of God and on his experience of helping others in their search for God. When he wrote the *Constitutions*, the dynamic was similar. While the *Constitutions* were to become normative for Jesuits, in their origins they echoed to a large extent what was already happening in the life of the first generation. This is not to question the creative genius of Ignatius but simply to state that he sought to insert into the *Constitutions* the "best practices" that the first Jesuits had discovered – often through trial and error. This explains why Ignatius was always hesitant about bringing the *Constitutions* to a conclusion and died leaving them open-ended. He had sent his trusted colleague Jerome Nadal to different provinces in Europe from 1553 to 1555, primarily to explain the *Constitutions* to the scattered communities but also to check that what he had written reflected what was happening on the ground. He was at all times willing to listen to new evidence.

Central to any understanding of the *Constitutions* is the recognition that Ignatius and the early companions expressly wished to pass on to later generations of Jesuits the particular *experience* they had shared with one another. Indeed, the two main decisions that emanated from the Deliberation of the First Fathers in 1539 (to form themselves into a body and to become a religious order) could be described as a commitment to continuity and permanence. The First Fathers regarded their experience over the years since they had come to know Ignatius as their formation, just as Ignatius was understood to have made his novitiate at Manresa. Formation takes place in the Society of Jesus through a pattern of experience closely similar to that of the early companions, and in continuity with that experience, just as their formation was an experience closely similar to, and in continuity with, that of Ignatius. Permanence depends on continuity of experience. Continuity of experience is another term for formation.

Some statements from the *General Examen* offer concrete illustrations of how this approach is envisaged:

> The intention of the first men who bound themselves together in this Society should be explained to the candidates (C53).
>
> For where the Society's first members have passed through these necessities and greater bodily wants, the others who come to it should endeavor, as far as they can, to reach the same point as the earlier ones, or to go farther in our Lord (C81).
>
> [They] should beg from door to door ... thus imitating those earliest members (C82).

It is also understood that whatever unites present-day Jesuits with Ignatius and the first companions (through their having similar goals and experiences) will necessarily unite them to one another. In summary, the *Constitutions* paint the continuity with the first companions as threefold:

1. In the externals of their way of life, and particularly through their experience of real poverty.
2. In their intention, i.e., their inner motivation and purpose: *aiudar las almas*, to help souls.
3. In the bond of love which continues to exist within the body and which is always *de arriba*, from above. This means that it is pure gift and a sharing in the love of the Triune God.

We notice how the thought of Ignatius moves from the externals (especially actual poverty) to the human intention, and ultimately to the love poured into our hearts by God. The interconnectedness shown here is rooted in his mystical experiences, especially his "great enlightenment" at the River Cardoner in Manresa.

When Ignatius turned his mind to working in a more focused manner on the *Constitutions* (pre-Polanco), he first addressed the topic of "the missions." There is a reference to this in his *Spiritual Diary*. On March 12, 1544, he ended his discernment on the kind of poverty that he wanted for the Society of Jesus. Then he wrote, "I took these four days to avoid considering any points in the *Constitutions*." There follow his notes on his inner experiences on March 13–16 before he inserts another heading that reads, "Here I began my preparation and first consideration concerning the missions." This leads eventually to the *Constitutiones circa missiones* and the accompanying *Declarationes circa missiones* (constitutions concerning the missions, supplemented by certain clarifications), completed sometime during 1544–45. From these primitive documents grew the quasi-definitive text of the entire *Constitutions* (1550) and the definitive text approved by the 1st General Congregation (1558). In these fuller texts Ignatius maintained his practice of adding declarations or clarifications, most likely to help superiors in applying the *Constitutions* in concrete circumstances. It is important to note that the decision made by Ignatius to begin with *missiones* is of interest not just in studying the genesis of the text but because it is strongly indicative of his spirituality and his vision of the Society of Jesus. Mission is at its core.

So it is that the ten-part dynamic structure of the *Constitutions* revolves around Part VII which deals with the dispersal of the incorporated members and their missioning into the vineyard of the Lord. Part VII is the axis, the fulcrum of the entire work. It describes how the long-awaited and carefully prepared-for sending of the professed Jesuit is to happen. Everything that comes before this in the sequence of Parts leads up to and prepares for this missioning: entry (Part I), possible dismissal (Part II), novitiate (Part III), intellectual and professional formation (Part IV), incorporation (Part V), and the life of the professed (Part VI). Everything that follows – union of minds and hearts (Part VIII), spiritual governance (Part IX), preservation and increase (Part X) – constitutes corporate supports for that same missioning. To change the metaphor, omitting Part VII would be like removing the cornerstone of a building.

It is helpful to note that the primary significance of the word "mission" in Ignatian usage is as a verb rather than as a noun. "Mission" has the active meaning of 'to send' (to mission) or the passive meaning of 'to be sent' (to be missioned). It is only secondarily that it is used as a noun, signifying some concrete task ("the mission I was sent to carry out"). Hence Part VII contains four chapters which deal with the four ways in which Jesuits can *be sent* (missioned) into the world. This is summarized in the opening paragraph:

- Whether they have been sent to some places or others by either the supreme vicar of Christ our Lord;
- Or the superiors of the Society, who for them are similarly in the place of his Divine Majesty;
- Or whether they themselves choose where and in what work they will labor, having been commissioned to travel to any place where they judge that greater service of God and the good of souls will follow;
- Or whether they carry on their labor not by traveling but by residing steadily and continually in certain places where much fruit of glory and service to God is expected (C603).

This sequence of four ways of being sent follows the changing pattern of the modes of distribution of the companions from 1539 to 1550. Its origins, therefore, are historical. For example, concerning the fourth way of being sent, the *Constitutiones circa missiones* (1544–45) make no mention of any established domicile for Jesuits. The members are presumed to be in almost continual movement. But by 1550 the existence of stable residences is taken for granted. The order of the chapters does not claim to prioritize the ways of being sent. Rather, the structure of Part VII underscores the variety of possible insertions into the common Jesuit experience of mission.

The *Formula of the Institute* had indicated in a general way the ministries in which Jesuits should be involved. Part VII does not deal with this issue as such but with the process of sending. Ignatius was conscious that the Society's superiors would need guidance in this crucial area of discernment. In Chapter 2 he offers multiple and detailed criteria for superiors to consider. The purpose of all this detail is succinctly expressed as follows:

> Hence, the superior general, or whoever holds this authority from him, ought to bestow much careful thought on missions of this kind, so that, in sending subjects to one region rather than another, or for one purpose rather than for another, or one particular person rather than another or several of them, in this manner or in that, or for a longer or shorter time, that may always be done which is conducive to the greater service of God and the universal good (C618).

Ignatius is asking that a process of discernment precede every sending of a Jesuit. Such is "our way of proceeding" that must always be in place as a necessary component of spiritual governance. It is a process built on "indifference" or that "thoroughly right and pure intention in the presence of God our Lord" (C618). It presupposes a common apostolic vision and desire shared by the superior (the one sending) and the individual Jesuit (the one being sent). Each has his contribution to make, through prayer and dialogue, in order that the discernment may lead to a good decision.

As indicated earlier, this "being sent" is the point which a Jesuit has always aspired to reach. Both before and after this turning point, he is on a journey. The Formula had referred to the Institute as "a pathway to God." The Jesuit, like the Ignatius of the *Autobiography*, is always a pilgrim in motion. The *Constitutions* are a vademecum or a compass for the journey. They do not claim to describe all the twists and turns of the many roads he will traverse. However, they throw light on the terrain and suggest tools and strategies by which to find a way through difficulties. In other words they help the

Jesuit to discern. Discernment is needed on a journey of many crossroads and numerous perils.

Consequently the theme of movement (both interior and exterior) pervades the *Constitutions*. A cluster of words and images convey this forward dynamic as in the following quotations:

- We think it necessary that *Constitutions* should be written to aid us to proceed better … along the path of divine service on which we have entered (C134).
- … by endeavouring always to go forward in the path of the divine service (C260).
- Just as it is necessary to restrain those who are running too rapidly, so it is proper to stimulate, urge on, and encourage those for whom this is necessary (C386).
- … it is presupposed that the professed will be men who are spiritual and sufficiently advanced to run in the path of Christ our Lord (C582).

At other times there is a change from the metaphorical to the literal or physical meaning of movement. The context is the special vow of obedience to the pope *circa missiones*.

- (They took the fourth vow) in conformity with their intention to travel throughout the world, and, when they could not find the desired spiritual fruit in one region, to pass on to another and another, ever intent on seeking the greater glory of God our Lord and the greater aid of souls (C605).

In the *General Examen* we meet the applicant who begins with the desire to set out along this "pathway," this *via*. Learning to be a pilgrim, a traveler, both in an interior and an exterior sense, he discovers that all else is uncertain. His only security is God. With this awareness and determination, he freely chooses to be incorporated into a body of men already traveling along the road. This body has mission as its *raison d'être*, and it now accepts him into apostolic companionship. Their movement in partnership is developmental, always forward in orientation, leading the person:

1. into the body of the Society through formation and gradual incorporation;
2. into the vineyard of the Lord through being missioned by superiors;
3. into the life of the Triune God through grace alone.

All of this movement, with the interplay of its divine and human dimensions, is carefully delineated in the *Constitutions*.

Until the appearance of vernacular translations, which only began to appear in the late 1960s, the *Constitutions* were never well known throughout the Society. In large part this was due to the dominance of a shorter document called the *Summary of the Constitutions*, promulgated by Mercurian in 1580 as superior general. This *Summary* was the final stage in a developing series begun by Nadal in 1553. (Strictly speaking they are not really summaries but selected excerpts from the *Constitutions*.) The earlier versions had in view the spiritual formation of young Jesuits, then rapidly increasing in numbers. Hence, the passages selected came mainly from the *General Examen* (aiding the assessment of candidates) and Part III (which treats of the novitiate). Unlike the *Constitutions*, the summaries were soon translated into the vernacular languages, leading to their greater accessibility and more widespread use. They soon lost their originally specific link with formation and, especially after Mercurian's initiative, were understood to be normative for all Jesuits. This development led to the neglect of the full *Constitutions* and brought about the de facto squandering of a major resource within the Society.

Over the years commentaries on the *Constitutions* have changed in their purpose and style. They began as expository works, answering difficulties that were experienced by Jesuits in understanding the text. But soon they became more like *apologias* for the new style of religious life represented by the Society. These oeuvres first set out to meet objections from within the Church, but later (especially from the time of the Enlightenment) they were also responding to criticism from secular and political sources. However, since the mid-twentieth century, and especially after Vatican II, almost all commentaries and other writings on the *Constitutions* have concentrated on revealing their underlying *spirituality*. The text is treated as wisdom literature, even as a spiritual classic, while at the same time acknowledging that it is also a managerial masterpiece. Connections are made with the other Ignatian writings, in the process illuminating both. In a word, the *Constitutions* are approached more as a book of life than a book of norms.

See also Apostolate; Formation; *Formula of the Institute*; Mission; Loyola, Ignatius of, SJ, St.; Polanco, Juan de, SJ; Way of Proceeding

Bertrand, Dominique, *Un corps pour l'esprit: essai sur l'expérience communautaire d'après les Constitutions de la Compagnie de Jésus*. Paris: Desclée de Brouwer, 1974.
Clancy, Thomas H., *An Introduction to Jesuit Life: The Constitutions and History through 435 Years*. St. Louis, MO: The Institute of Jesuit Sources, 1976.
Coupeau, J. Carlos, *From Inspiration to Invention: Rhetoric in the Constitutions of the Society of Jesus*. St. Louis, MO: The Institute of Jesuit Sources, 2010.
The Constitutions of the Society of Jesus. Trans. George E. Ganss. St. Louis, MO: The Institute of Jesuit Sources, 1970.
de Jaer, André, *Together for Mission: A Spiritual Commentary on the Constitutions of the Society of Jesus*. St. Louis, MO: The Institute of Jesuit Sources, 2001.
O'Leary, Brian, *Sent into the Lord's Vineyard: Explorations in the Jesuit Constitutions*. Oxford: Way Books, 2012.

Brian O'Leary, SJ

Contarini, Gasparo

Born in 1483 to a patrician family in Venice, Gasparo Contarini studied at Padua before holding several offices in the Venetian republic, serving as an ambassador on diplomatic missions to Charles V and to Rome during the reign of Clement VII. Contarini also composed numerous treatises, including *De officio episcopi* (1516), a guidebook on how to be an ideal bishop. Paul III elevated Contarini to the cardinalate in 1535 along with other reform-minded men. He was among the nine clerics Paul III charged with drafting a report on how to reform abuses within the Roman Church, though the resulting document, the *Consilium de emendanda ecclesia* (1537), was never put into effect. Contarini was later sent to the Colloquy of Regensburg (1541), aimed at resolving theological disagreements between Catholics and Protestants. Though the colloquy was unsuccessful, Contarini played a major role in its proceedings, helping to draft a joint treatise on justification.

It was as a cardinal that Contarini encountered Ignatius of Loyola and his early companions. The cardinal made the Spiritual Exercises under Ignatius's direction in 1538, and Contarini soon became an ally to the group in the papal curia. After the companions drafted the *Formula of the Institute*, Ignatius asked Contarini to hand the text over to the pope. When some opposition was raised regarding the unusual nature of the *Formula's* chapters – that the new group would not recite the liturgy of the hours together, for instance – Contarini defended them and urged that they remain unrevised. His role in securing Paul III's approval of the Society is unquestionable. Contarini died in 1542.

See also Loyola, Ignatius of, SJ, St.; Paul III

Fragnito, Gigliola, *Gasparo Contarini: un magistrato veneziano al servizio della cristianità*. Firenze: L. S. Olschki, 1988.
Gleason, Elisabeth G., *Gasparo Contarini: Venice, Rome and Reform*. Berkeley: University of California Press, 1993.

Charles Keenan

Contemplation

In *Spiritual Exercises*, Ignatius uses the terms "meditation" and "contemplation" in a distinctive way. Other Christian writers use the distinction in connection with the mental state of the person praying. The committed cerebral engagement of meditation gives way to contemplation: a more elusive, passive, or affective experience, said to be more intensely or directly the work of God. In *Spiritual Exercises*, the distinction serves a different function: "contemplation" involves an engagement with the work of God in history, while "meditation" denotes prayer round ideas and images, notably those concerned with sin. The history in question is both that of Jesus in the Gospels, in the "contemplations" of the Second, Third, and Fourth weeks of the Exercises, and a more diffused presence of God throughout the creation, as in the Contemplation to Attain Love. Indeed, one passage in *Spiritual Exercises* may be specifying *contemplación* as *meditación visible* (#47). In literature by and about Jesuits, both the conventional and the properly Ignatian sense may be in play.

A typical "Ignatian contemplation" begins with a preparatory prayer that all be for God's glory, and then three preambles (or "preludes"): a recall of the gospel story; an invitation to place oneself within the scene (in the traditional jargon "composition of place"); and a prayer of petition for a grace. Ignatius then gives us three "points." In the example texts at the beginning of the second, third, and fourth weeks, these points include an invitation to consider first the persons, then what they are saying, then what they are doing (there are extra points particular to the Third and Fourth Weeks). By contrast, the "Meditations on the Life of Christ" appearing as a kind of appendix to *Spiritual Exercises* typically contain three elements in the gospel story. Crucially, each "point" throughout the Ignatian day, even in the prayer of the senses (Application of the Senses) at the end, includes an invitation to "reflect and draw profit." The aim is the discernment of how best to follow the Lord. The intensity may increase as the process continues, but it is an intensity rather different from that evoked in the conventional discourse of "contemplation."

Though the Ignatian way of distinguishing meditation and contemplation is carried through with notable precision in the earliest texts of *Spiritual Exercises*, other Jesuits do not seem seriously to have perceived Ignatius's usage until the twentieth century. What is probably Jean Codure's expanded version of Ignatius's text, written as early as 1541, may use the word "contemplation" to name individual exercises, but it nevertheless inserts into the opening Annotations a long and obscure paragraph reaffirming two possible versions of the traditional distinction, seemingly without recognizing that Ignatius's text had subverted it. A similar absence is striking in the arguments about Jesuit spirituality during the institutionally formative decades after Ignatius's death, whether in the various preparatory texts culminating in the 1599 *Directory*, or in the anxious controversies regarding the compatibility of contemplation with Jesuit ministry and Jesuit obedience, to some extent resolved by an important letter of Claudio Acquaviva in 1590. The debates were about whether a more passive, intuitive, and affective "contemplation" could be seen as a legitimate extension of cerebral meditation. No one recognized that Ignatius had seen concentration on the mysteries of Christ's life, and the discernment of how best to know, love, and follow the Lord, as itself in some sense contemplation.

The persistence of the more general understanding of contemplation in Jesuit discourse can perhaps be explained by two factors. First, theological accounts of contemplation – like Christian doctrines in general – as such marginalize the historical and the particular. In *Spiritual Exercises*, Ignatius's vision of a God found through, rather than despite, this-worldly activity is presented precisely not as a theory but rather as a gradual discovery, through processes of prayer and reflection deeply connected to ongoing practice. The abstract noun "contemplation" may serve useful functions in holding open a challenge and a possibility – but it leaves unexpressed the subversive, transformational character of the experience. Jerónimo Nadal's throwaway line about Ignatius as a contemplative in action has become a Jesuit slogan, not because the theoretical contradiction has been solved but because modern theology has recognized that its speculative discourses are secondary, depending intrinsically on history, narrative, and testimony. Because that connection is inevitably insecure, "contemplation" – and indeed other doctrinal terms – is always liable to lose its properly Christian force.

Second, the standard idiom of "contemplation" addresses an important spiritual question not envisaged directly in *Spiritual Exercises*: how people grow spiritually over a lifetime. *Spiritual Exercises* presents us simply with a program for one retreat; the text does not treat of the kind of development typically fostered by regular practice. For that purpose, the powerful and influential accounts of contemplation offered shortly after Ignatius by Teresa of Avila and John of the Cross became the standard resource. Here, "contemplation" marks a transition, often painful, that typically occurs in any serious spiritual life, from a focus of regular disciplined practice to something different, conventionally designated through apophatic idioms and through metaphors of depth and passivity. Though opinions may differ on whether Ignatian and Carmelite accounts of contemplation are conflicting or complementary, followers of Ignatius over a lifetime inevitably face the developmental realities addressed classically by Teresa and John. It is not surprising, therefore, that many Jesuit spiritual writers, including distinguished ones, have worked with a discourse of "contemplation" rather different from Ignatius's.

See also Composition of Place; Contemplation to Attain Love; Imagination; *Spiritual Exercises*

Philip Endean, SJ

Contemplation to Attain Love

A major set piece placed during the Fourth Week of *Spiritual Exercises*. It begins with two "notes" about the nature of love: Love is expressed more in deeds than in words and consists in mutual exchange between the two parties. We are then invited first to imagine ourselves in God's presence, with the angels and saints interceding for us, and second to ask for the kind of awareness of the benefits we have received that will enable us "in everything to love and serve His Divine Majesty." The exercise proper contains four points evoking God's activity. The first invites us to remember benefits received: creation, redemption, more particular gifts. The other three center on images: God *dwelling within* the creation; God *working through* the creation; the creation *descending from* God. All four considerations are meant to provoke the same response: a reflection on how we might respond in kind, offering back to God with much feeling "everything that is mine, and myself with all that." Ignatius then gives a formula – sometimes called the *Suscipe* after its opening word in the official Latin text – that often appears in public Jesuit settings: "Take, Lord, and receive all my liberty, my memory, my understanding, and all my will, all that I have and possess. You gave it to me: to you, Lord, I return it; it is all yours; make disposition entirely to your will; give me your love (or, following the official Latin Vulgate, 'love of you') and grace – that is enough for me."

The intensity of the writing in this text, and its place near the end, suggests that it marks a climax, expressing values central to the Exercises. The text may be linked with Ignatius's experience near the Cardoner. However, there is no evidence outside *Spiritual Exercises* of how Ignatius himself intended it, while the Official Directory and its preparatory documents suggest that his immediate followers did not assign it major importance. It is only recent interpreters who have assigned it a pivotal role in what they have identified as "Ignatian spirituality."

See also Contemplation; *Spiritual Exercises*; *Suscipe*

Philip Endean, SJ

Contzen, Adam, SJ (1571–1635)

Born in western Germany in 1571, Adam Contzen studied at the Jesuit college in Cologne before entering the Society of Jesus in 1591. After assignments in Cologne and Würzburg, Contzen became a professor at the Jesuit academy in Mainz in 1609, first of biblical studies and then of controversial theology. A prolific author, Contzen published numerous works in the early seventeenth century. Most famous was his *Politicorum libri decem* (1621). In it, Contzen took a strong anti-Machiavellian position, arguing for the centrality of religion and piety in political life and describing a program for a successful Catholic state, in which ecclesiastical and political leaders would cooperate to inculcate piety and virtue in the people. The work was highly influential for early modern political thought.

In 1624 Contzen was summoned by Duke Maximilian of Bavaria to be an adviser on political issues at court (though Contzen never held the title of councilor). Contzen was a militant during the Thirty Years War, favoring the use of force against Protestants and the restitution of Catholic ecclesiastical property that had been seized. He was a firm supporter of the Edict of Restitution (1629), which required the return of all Catholic lands and properties seized by Protestants since 1555. The Jesuit maintained this position at the Convention of Regensburg in 1630, when there was disagreement on whether to alter or mitigate the edict's terms. For Contzen, God was on the Catholic side, and any concessions to Protestants were unthinkable. Contzen died in June 1635, soon after the Peace of Prague (1635) that saw Ferdinand II and Maximilian abandon the militant program advocated by Contzen and others.

See also German-Speaking Lands; Holy Roman Empire

Bireley, Robert, *The Counter-Reformation Prince: Anti-Machiavellianism or Catholic Statecraft in Early Modern Europe*. Chapel Hill: University of North Carolina Press, 1990.

Charles Keenan

Copleston, Frederick, SJ (1907–1994)

Born on April 10, 1907, in Somerset, England, Copleston was the son of a British officer in the Indian Civil Service and the nephew of two Anglican bishops. He attended Marlborough College from 1920 to 1925. Shortly after his eighteenth birthday, he converted to Catholicism and was received into the Catholic Church. In spite of his family's disapproval, Copleston's father still helped him continue his education at St. John's College, Oxford, where he studied classics from 1925 to 1929. After obtaining the M.A., Oxon., Copleston entered the diocesan seminary, only to depart the following year to enter the Society of Jesus in 1930.

Upon the completion of his philosophy and theology studies at Heythrop College in Oxfordshire, Copleston was ordained a priest in 1937. In 1939, he completed his tertianship in Münster, Germany, departing for England only shortly before the outbreak of World War II. Copleston thereafter returned to Heythrop College as a professor of the history of philosophy, a post he occupied for the next thirty years. Dissatisfied with the seminary textbooks available to him, Copleston began to write his own philosophical history. The eventual result was the monumental nine-volume *A History of Philosophy*, published between 1946 and 1975, for which he would receive widespread acclaim. Described by *The Times* of London as "the best all-round history of philosophical thinking from the pre-Socratics to Sartre" (April 2, 1994), Copleston's history became renowned for the erudition of its scholarship, the comprehensive scope of its content, and the relatively objective position from which it was written.

At the same time, Copleston published single volumes on Nietzsche (1942), Schopenhauer (1946), and Aquinas (1955). In 1948 the Jesuit professor famously debated the existence of God with Bertrand Russell on the *Third Programme* of the BBC. The following year he disputed the validity of logical positivism on the same program with A. J. Ayer.

Between 1952 and 1968, Copleston also served as a visiting professor for the first semester of the academic year at the Pontifical Gregorian University in Rome. When Copleston was appointed dean of the Faculty of Philosophy at Heythrop College in 1965, however, his dual teaching obligations in Rome gradually ceased. In 1970, Heythrop College closed its doors in Oxfordshire and was moved to London, where it received a new charter as a College of the University of London. Copleston was appointed its first principal, a position in which he served from 1970 to 1974.

In 1974, having reached the usual retirement age of 67, Copleston entered official retirement and was made Professor Emeritus by the University of London. His copious productivity, however, continued. In 1978 he delivered the D'Arcy Lectures at Oxford, which were subsequently published under the title *Philosophies and Cultures* (1980), and between 1979 and 1980, he delivered the Gifford Lectures at the University of Aberdeen, which were published as *Religion and the One* (1982).

Copleston continued to teach as well as lecture. On a reduced basis, he taught as a visiting professor at Santa Clara University between 1974–75 and 1977–82. Throughout his life and especially in retirement, he went on numerous lecture tours, primarily in Europe and the United States, but also in India, Japan, and Australia. He was awarded myriad academic honors, being made a Fellow of the British Academy (1970), an Honorary Fellow of his alma mater, St. John's College, Oxford (1975), and Commander of the Order of the British Empire (CBE) by the Queen (1993). In like measure, Copleston was awarded a host of honorary doctorates.

Famous for his reluctance to proffer his own philosophical positions, in various instances Copleston expressed attraction to thinkers as diverse as Aquinas, Hegel, and Jaspers. In the introduction to *A History of Philosophy*, Copleston openly identified with "Thomism in a wide sense," which he termed the *philosophia perennis*. Later, in his memoirs, Copleston described himself as "increasingly influenced by the idea of philosophy's movement of self-criticism and self-limitation" and "less optimistic" about the capacity of any single, historically conditioned "metaphysical vision of reality" to "deliver the goods." His "dialogue with positivism in various forms," he continued, however, only encouraged his understanding of the ultimate centrality of "the movement of the human spirit towards increasing union with … a transcendent One through an increasing union of active love with one's fellows." To many of his contemporaries, Copleston had made this ethos a way of life. James Felt, a Jesuit colleague of Copleston at Santa Clara University, observed that "for those who had the privilege of living with him, he was a man of droll humor, keen insight, and great charity: a true humanist who is much missed."

He died in London on February 3, 1994.

See also Heythrop College; Philosophy; United Kingdom

Copleston, Frederick, *A History of Philosophy*. 9 vols. New York: Image Books, 1993–94.
　On the History of Philosophy and Other Essays. London: Search Press, 1979.
　Memoirs of a Philosopher. Kansas City: Sheed & Ward, 1993.
Felt, James, "In Memoriam: Frederick C. Copleston, SJ." *The Review of Metaphysics* 48, 1 (1994), 237–38.

Henry Shea, SJ

Corbishley, Thomas, SJ (1903–1976)

Educated at the Jesuit-run Preston Catholic College, Lancashire, England, Corbishley entered the Society, aged 16, in 1919. Having completed the novitiate and juniorate at Roehampton, London, he went to St. Mary's Hall, Stonyhurst, where he studied philosophy. In 1926 he proceeded to Campion Hall, Oxford, and read classics, obtaining the coveted double first in classical moderations (1928) and Greats (1930). It was a brilliant achievement given that he had not studied Greek before joining the Jesuits. As a scholastic he published several articles: in the *Journal of Roman Studies* (1934), on the Syrian governorship of Titius, and the chorology of Herod the Great; he completed his thoughts on these matters with an article in the *Journal of Theological Studies* (1935). His final venture into strictly scholarly fields was a piece on the census of Quirinius, which appeared in *Clio* in 1936.

Corbishley's first major job as a priest was as prefect of juniors in 1938. By 1945 he was appointed master of Campion Hall, Oxford, in succession to Martin D'Arcy. Not an easy task, given D'Arcy's reputation, but Corbishley made a deep impression on many at Oxford and formed lasting friendships with, among others, the young dons Hugh Trevor-Roper (subsequently Lord Dacre) and Alan Bullock (Lord Bullock), who became master of St. Catherine's and vice-chancellor of Oxford. After thirteen years as master he was assigned to Farm Street, London, where he remained for the rest of his life. A ready ecumenist, he was the first priest to preach at St. Paul's Cathedral, and the first since the Reformation to preach at Westminster Abbey. He was a deeply committed European and served with distinction on numerous committees, including the Council of Christians and Jews. His many publications include *Religion Is Reasonable* (1960) and *The Spirituality of Teilhard de Chardin* (1970).

See also D'Arcy, Martin, SJ; United Kingdom

Oliver P. Rafferty, SJ

Corridan, John M., SJ (1911–1994)

Born in New York in 1911, Father Corridan held a number of assignments in Jesuit educational and pastoral ministries. But he was best known for his work during the decade immediately after World War II as the associate director (under Director Phil Carey, SJ, another notable labor priest) of the Xavier Institute of Industrial Relations in New York City. Corridan's activism among dockworkers became the subject of the book and movie *On the Waterfront.* The role of the tough and passionate film character Father Barry (played by the actor Karl Malden) was clearly inspired by Corridan, who served as a consultant to screenwriter Budd Schulberg.

Known to his friends as "Pete," Corridan exhibited a style of support and advocacy for manual laborers (and dockworkers in particular) that had been pioneered by Cardinal Henry Edward Manning of Westminster (England) in the late nineteenth century. His eager participation in an institutionalized response to workplace injustice, namely the system of Jesuit-sponsored labor schools which were intended to raise the skill levels and enhance opportunities for blue-collar workers, is emblematic of a distinctively Jesuit approach to socioeconomic concerns. His program to uplift these workers also included fighting organized crime and exposing the corrupt practices that characterized such influential institutions as the International Longshoremen's Association, the major union on the waterfront at that time.

Obituaries that appeared at the time of Corridan's death in 1984 credited him with contributing to major reforms in hiring practices and anti-graft measures in the New York area docklands. By raising his voice against corruption, Corridan created momentum for the 1953 appointment of the Waterfront Commission, a watchdog agency set up by the state legislatures of New York and New Jersey.

See also Film and Television: Themes and Characters; Labor Schools; United States of America

Raymond, Allen, *Waterfront Priest*. New York: Henry Holt and Company, 1955.

Thomas Massaro, SJ

Coton, Pierre, SJ (1564–1626)

Born in Néronde (Loire), on March 7, 1564, Coton entered the Society of Jesus in Arona (Novara) on September 30, 1583. He continued his studies in Milan and in Rome, where Robert Bellarmine served as his spiritual director, and finished his theology course in Lyon. Coton's gift for pulpit oratory won him the post as ordinary preacher to Henry IV (1603–10), for whom he also functioned as confessor and counselor. From the time of his arrival in Paris, Coton enjoyed a mutual friendship with Pierre de Bérulle (1575–1629), founder of the Oratory, whom he both encouraged and defended from criticism. Coton continued as preacher and confessor for Louis XIII until 1617, when accusations and court intrigue forced his departure. He was subsequently made provincial of the province of Aquitaine in 1622 and of the province of Paris in 1624. Coton died on March 19, 1626, leaving behind a large body of apologetic material addressing the Protestants and defending the Jesuits, and writings dealing with a wide range of spiritual matters. His masterpiece, the *Interieure occupation d'une ame devote* (1608), which contains prayers and meditations to help those in the world to stay in the presence of God, went through several editions and translations during the author's life and influenced a number of devotional works in that style. His theocentric spirituality incorporates elements of the devout humanism in which he was trained while drawing on devotional themes of the day, including resignation to and service of God, and the doctrines of pure love and the mystical body of Christ.

See also Confession, Confessor; France; Paris

d'Orléans, Pierre Joseph, *La vie du père Pierre Coton, de la Compagnie de Jesus, confesseur des roys Henry IV et Louis XIII*. Paris: Estienne Michallet, 1688.
Pitts, Vincent J., *Henri IV of France: His Reign and Age*. Baltimore, MD: Johns Hopkins University Press, 2009.
Prat, Jean Marie, *Recherches historiques et critiques sur la Compagnie de Jésus en France du temps du P. Coton (1564–1626)*. 4 vols. Lyon: Briday, 1876.

William P. O'Brien, SJ

Course of Studies

"Course of Studies" refers to the lengthy program by which Jesuits are prepared spiritually, academically, and practically for the ministries in which they will be called to serve. The purpose of studies is apostolic – helping Jesuits grow in their capacity to fulfill the mission of the Society of Jesus today.

Jesuits should be prepared and available for a variety of assignments at the request of the pope or the Jesuit superior. For this a broad background is needed. The Jesuit course of studies must fulfill the requirements of the Catholic Church and canon law. The Society of Jesus has its own General Norms of Studies promulgated by the superior general that are adapted in what is called the *Regional Order of Studies*.

Since the time of the Second Vatican Council, several major shifts have occurred in the Jesuit course of studies. The language of studies for philosophy and theology is no longer Latin, but the local languages. The setting for formation has shifted from the secluded, remote seminary to the town or city. Classes with a mix of Jesuit and lay students are often taken in an ecumenical institution. Finally, whereas for higher studies

Jesuits often traveled to Rome or Europe, now such studies can also be completed in Nairobi, Delhi, or Boston – that is, in a variety of centers around the globe.

The ordinary course of formation takes ten to eleven years for scholastics who will be ordained to the priesthood, and five to eight years for most Jesuit coadjutor brothers.

During the two-year novitiate program, a novice lives the life of the vows in community and learns the traditions and charism of the Society of Jesus. He makes the Spiritual Exercises in a thirty-day retreat and engages in a variety of "experiments," some of which involve service to the poor. The novice grows in a more intimate relationship with God and an increasing love for the Society. At the end of the novitiate, he pronounces perpetual vows of poverty, chastity, and obedience.

He then moves on to a two- to four-year period of studies in philosophy and theology, depending upon his background. If he enters without a bachelor's degree, he will complete his BA degree during this time. Courses in "social analysis" help to integrate study, reflection, and action. The ordinary coursework includes 36 graduate hours of philosophy, 24 graduate hours of theology, and 12 graduate hours of electives. Many Jesuits in first studies earn a master's degree in philosophy; some will earn a master's degree in an area such as English or history. The focus of studies here is on the context of mission.

Regency is the next stage, where the scholastic lives and works in a typical Jesuit apostolic community. He is engaged full-time in ministry, which often means teaching in a secondary school, but it may also be any ministry Jesuits are engaged in. Regency lasts for two to three years. The emphasis here is on the development of ministerial competencies.

Theology is the stage for Jesuits immediately preceding ordination. By canon law, every candidate for priestly ordination must complete four years in the study of theology. Thus, the scholastic who has completed a year of theology during First Studies will engage in a three-year period of theology studies leading to the Master of Divinity degree or, if an additional year is undertaken, bringing the total to five, a Licentiate in Theology. The focus of these studies is on the content of faith.

At the end of theology studies, candidates for the Catholic priesthood are ordained to the diaconate and serve as deacons for six months to a year. Ordination to the priesthood occurs after the fourth year of theological study.

Tertianship is so named because it is like a third year of novitiate. Lasting seven to nine months, it can begin after the completion of theology studies and three to five years of full-time ministry. Tertians study the foundational documents of the Society of Jesus, make the thirty-day retreat, and participate in apostolic experiments. After tertianship, the Jesuit may be called to final vows in the Society of Jesus.

One further possibility would be special studies, for example at the doctoral level. Again, this is apostolic, always in accord with the talents of the Jesuit and the needs of the Society of Jesus and its institutions.

The formation of the Jesuit brother has a much less structured form. He may pursue a highly academic formation or more practical training in areas such as pastoral counseling or spiritual direction, or he may be active in the more "supporting" roles traditionally occupied by Jesuit brothers.

Language studies: Today, all Jesuits are expected to learn English, and those who speak English as a first language are expected to learn Spanish.

See also Formation; Novitiate, Novice; Regency; Scholastic; Tertianship, Tertians

The Formation of Jesuits. A Collection of the Letters on Formation of Fr. Peter-Hans Kolvenbach, SJ. 1986–2003. Rome: General Curia of the Society of Jesus, 2003.

Peter Schineller, SJ

Coventry, John, SJ (1915–1998)

Coventry joined the Jesuits in October 1932 and followed the normal pattern of training in the then English province of the Society. He read Latin and Greek at Oxford from1938–42, and among his near contemporaries was Iris Murdoch, with whom he remained on friendly terms throughout his life. His double first might have ensured a scholarly career, but as a theology student at Heythrop College he wrote several books, one of which, *Faith Seeks Understanding*, dedicated to Alexander Durand, the well-known French Jesuit theologian, fell foul of the authorities in Rome. The book had to be withdrawn from circulation, and the province was forced to compensate the publisher, Sheed and Ward.

After tertianship Coventry was sent to the Jesuit public school Beaumont College as prefect of studies and was subsequently appointed Rector. From 1958 to 1964 he was provincial. Toward the end of his tenure, Rome ordered a visitation of the province, and as a result a number of important changes were made, including the closure of Beaumont College. With the transformation of the theological climate following Vatican II, Coventry was now, belatedly, permitted to teach theology at Heythrop College, which he did from 1966 to 1976. He was then made master of St. Edmund's College, Cambridge, a post he retained for a decade, and was the last priest to occupy that position.

Prone to depression in his later years, he continued to make a contribution in the field of ecumenism, especially with the Association of Interchurch Families. Despite his status as a well-known ecclesiastical figure on the English scene, he was content with even the lowliest positions, serving for several years as the minister at the novitiate. Although fairly productive as a writer – his last and longest book, *Our God Reigns*, was published in 1995 – the early interruption of his academic career meant that he did not achieve prominence as a theologian. Coventry looked upon this contingency with some indifference.

See also Ecumenism; Theology; United Kingdom

Oliver P. Rafferty, SJ

Cristo Rey (Model of Schools)

The first Jesuit Cristo Rey High School opened in Chicago, Illinois, in 1996 in the Pilsen area thanks to the leadership of the Chicago Jesuits and the enthusiastic support of Cardinal Bernardin, then archbishop of Chicago. Fr. John Foley, SJ, a Jesuit who had spent decades educating impoverished students in Tacna, Peru, was called back to Chicago to open the first college preparatory high school in a working-class Hispanic neighborhood starving for quality Catholic education for their children.

In 2014 the Cristo Rey Network included twenty-eight Catholic, college preparatory high schools across the United States, and it still continues to grow, with more schools to be opened in the next few years. The Cristo Rey model is grounded on the vision of offering a quality Catholic, college preparatory education for urban low-income families who cannot afford private education on their own.

One important element that makes the Cristo Rey model distinctive is the Corporate Work Study Program (CWSP). This program allows every student to work five days a month in entry-level jobs in the corporate/business world with a group of five students sharing one full-time job. Payment for their work is given directly to the school and is used to help the students offset the cost of their education. Equally important, this program also enables students to build the kind of self-confidence needed to succeed in their education and life – a key factor that can make a decisive difference. Moreover, this experiential learning program helps students acquire valuable social and professional skills for their future careers. The Cristo Rey model has created an innovative way to fund private education beyond the traditional heavy dependence on fund-raising. Primarily on account of this work-study program, Cristo Rey schools have become known as "the schools that work," a phrase that not only makes for an appealing marketing slogan but also captures the innovative link between school and workplace implemented in the Cristo Rey model.

The CWSP is combined with three other important elements that distinguish a Cristo Rey education: (1) a strong pedagogical component that combines the traditional Jesuit *cura personalis*, which emphasizes respect and care for the individual student, with current developments in effective teaching and learning; (2) an emphasis on the spiritual and moral development of students to provide a real education of the whole person; and (3) an accountability model that measures and evaluates all aspects of the school.

The model has also proved successful in the enrollment of its graduates in colleges and universities. Cristo Rey schools currently have a 90 percent college enrollment rate, which is far higher than an average school for similarly positioned low-income students (National Student Clearinghouse Student Tracker, April, 2013).

The rapidly growing number of schools following the model is even more amazing when considering the economic difficulties of many Catholic schools in the United States, especially the many inner-city schools that have been forced to close. This growth has also required the formation of the Cristo Rey Network with a central office in Chicago and the mission to support and guarantee the quality of the model. The network has adhered to ten Mission Effectiveness Standards that include the explicit Catholic identity of the school (while remaining open, however, to students from all religious backgrounds), service to economically disadvantaged students, financially sound schools, academic rigor, and local involvement. The network, which comprises not only the Jesuits but also several sponsoring dioceses and other religious orders, has a slogan of "Transforming Urban America, One Student at a Time."

Cristo Rey schools are also increasingly partnering with numerous universities, both Catholic and non-Catholic, to ensure that their students and others with similar backgrounds continue to succeed in higher education as well. In this sense, the Cristo Rey model is impacting ever more the wider society and inspiring school reform with a model that has proven to work in places where other models have failed. "The schools in the Cristo Rey Network are proving, through their outcome data, that the most vulnerable and at risk youth in America can and will succeed in college when given a high quality, college preparatory high school educational experience."

See also Education, Secondary and Pre-Secondary; Nativity School Model; United States of America

Cristo Rey Network: Impact. www.cristoreynetwork.org. Accessed on December 18, 2014.
Kearny, G. R., *The Cristo Rey Story: More than a Dream.* Chicago, IL: Loyola Press, 2008.
Parkes, Joseph, The Cristo Rey Model. *Promotio Iustitiae* 114, 1 (2014), 40–43.
Sweas, Megan, *Putting Education to Work: How Cristo Rey High Schools Are Transforming Urban Education.* New York: HarperCollins Publishers, 2014.

José Alberto Mesa, SJ

Cuba

The first attempt of the Jesuits to establish themselves in Cuba dates back to the year 1566. In that year three Jesuits arrived in Havana with the goal of later opening a mission in Florida, but in time they realized Havana was no longer a staging point. The problems they faced in the missionary field there kept them bound in service and unable to advance to Florida. Pedro Martínez was one of the missionaries who perished there and two others, Juan Rogel and Francisco Villareal, survived and settled in Havana after finding themselves committed to apostolic work there. Between 1566 and 1574, the Jesuits unsuccessfully tried to open a school in Havana. Their superiors in Spain and Rome were unwilling to grant authorization to a lack of resources that they believed would be necessary in founding the college. In 1574 the Jesuits who did pastoral work in Havana moved to Mexico, putting an end to the Jesuit presence in Cuba.

The Jesuits tried to open a school in Havana throughout the seventeenth century. They were unable to do so because of a consistent lack of funding. In spite of their difficulties, for a significant period during the seventeenth century there was a Jesuit presence on the island. On many occasions, Jesuit priests passed through Havana hoping to obtain the resources needed to found the school, while preaching the *Spiritual Exercises* to the Cuban people.

Thanks to the insistence and support of two bishops of Havana, Diego Evelino Hurtado y Vélez (1685–1704) and Jerónimo Nosti y Valdés (1705–29), General Michelangelo Tamburini sent Fathers José Arjó and Fernando Reinoso, who arrived on the island in 1713. However, it was not until December 19, 1721, that a royal decree was issued authorizing a Jesuit college in Havana. This time around, the school had sufficient resources and, as the Jesuits offered free education to young people in all the colleges in Latin America during the colonial times, the formation they provided was highly prized. By the year 1752, the college and the church had already been built, but a tremendous blow was dealt to the intellectual and pastoral life of Cuba when, in 1767, King Carlos III of Spain expelled the Jesuits from his dominions. The school in Havana as well as a residence in Camagüey were both closed. The expulsion of the Jesuits of the College of San José and their church in Havana in 1767 limited the influence the Society of Jesus might have had on the different levels and sectors of what was a highly insular society in Cuba.

A royal decree signed November 26, 1852, authorized the Jesuits to return to Cuba. Fathers Bartolomé Munar and Cipriano Sevillano, along with Brother Manuel Rubia, arrived on the island on April 29, 1853, and stayed in what had been their former school. However, on January 16, 1854, the governor and captain general of the island gave them the convent of Belén, which later was turned into Belén College. The Jesuits opened a meteorological observatory in the college in 1857, which became the main source of information on tropical cyclones.

In the 1920s the Jesuits transferred Belén College to a larger location. Adjacent to Belén College, the Jesuits ran the Free School of the Poor Child of Bethlehem. Later, they founded the Obrera de Belén University, which educated the marginalized youth of Cuba. Thousands of well-known Cubans have studied at Belén College, including Fidel Castro, who after the Cuban Revolution expropriated Belén College and, on May 3, 1961, expelled twenty-six Jesuits from the island.

Today, Cuba belongs to the Antilles province of the Society of Jesus, which was created on June 31, 1968. The Antilles province is currently made up of three parts: one of which corresponds to the Republic of Cuba. There, the Jesuits are currently working in the fields of spirituality, parish life, and education. The second part of the Antilles province is Miami, Florida, where Belén College was relocated after 1961, and where many daughters and sons of Cuban exiles pursue their education. In addition to Belén College, the Jesuits in Miami undertake pastoral work and support vulnerable populations. The third part of the Antilles province corresponds to the territory of the Dominican Republic. In this country the pastoral work focuses on communication, the defense of human rights, spirituality, and education. Pope Francis, the Jesuit pope, visited Cuba in September 2015.

See also Alumni; Dominican Republic; Haïti; Jamaica

Cuevas, Eduardo Torres, and Edelberto Leiva Lajara, "Presencia y ausencia de la Compañía de Jesús en Cuba." In José Andrés Gallegos (ed.), *Tres grandes cuestiones de la historia de Iberoamérica.* Madrid: Fundación Ignacio Larramenti, 2005.
Santos, Ángel, *Los jesuitas en América*. Madrid: Editorial Mapfre, 1992.

Jorge Salcedo, SJ

Cuevas García, Mariano, SJ (1879–1949)

Mariano Cuevas García was a Mexican Jesuit, historian, and writer. Born in 1879 in Mexico City, he entered the Society of Jesus in 1893 and made his novitiate in Loyola, Spain. After studying philosophy in Burgos, he returned to Mexico to make his regency in Saltillo and Puebla. He was ordained a priest in 1909 in St. Louis, Missouri, where he had also completed his theological studies. He later went back to Europe for further studies in history in Rome, Louvain, and Valkenburg, along with some additional archival investigations in Spain. While also known as a talented orator and pastoral minister, Cuevas García became famous for being an excellent archivist of historical documents and books, and to this day, the Cuevas Collection maintained by the Mexican province of the Jesuits remains highly valued.

During the Mexican Church–State conflict under the Calles presidency, he was exiled in the United States and made use of this time by studying further sources in archives. In 1928, he brought out the fifth and last volume of what would become a classic work on Church history entitled *Historia de la Iglesia en México*, published in El Paso, Texas. In total, his entire written corpus covers over thirty-eight published works, including a history of Mexico. While his career as a historical author and archivist was distinguished, he nonetheless fell victim to many of the Church–State polemics of his time. Cacho and Gomez describe him as being less of a historian and more of an apologist and polemicist. Nevertheless, he will be remembered for his impassioned defense of a version of history inspired by Catholic faith that was markedly different from the secularist version put forth by the Mexican government of his time as well as for his meticulous collection of sources for future historical research. He died in Mexico City in 1949 at the age of 70.

See also Mexico, Nineteenth Century to Present

Burrus, Ernest E. J.,"Obituary of Father Mariano Cuevas." *The Woodstock Letters* 79 (1950), 79–85.
Cacho, Xavier, and Jesús Gómez Fregoso, "Cuevas García, Mariano." In Charles E. O'Neill and Joaquín Ma. Domínquez, eds., *Diccionario histórico de la Compañía de Jesús*, Vol. II. Rome and Madrid: Institutum Historicum, SJ. and Universidad Pontificia Comillas, 2001, p. 1022.

Eduardo C. Fernández, SJ

Cultures

The word "culture" is difficult to define because it includes so much. It points to how we have "cultivated" or creatively modified nature, how our environment is changed and shaped by humans.

A descriptive definition would be: a set of symbols, stories, and norms for conduct that orient a society or group cognitively, affectively, and behaviorally to the world in which it lives. It includes the ways of living developed by a group of human beings, handed on from generation to generation – language, arts, technology, law; political, religious, and social organization and practices.

The study of culture and the relation between the Gospel and culture has been a central concern and interest of the Society of Jesus since its origins. Jesuits are on mission to carry the Good News of the Gospel to the ends of the earth, to cultures that are traditional, modern, and postmodern. Jesuits carry this out with the conviction that the Spirit and grace of God has touched all cultures, and that God can be found in all things and all cultures.

Jesuit missionaries, therefore, have often been pioneers in learning new languages and cultures around the globe. In a manner that has been repeated over the centuries, the local language was studied; grammars and dictionaries were composed. Frequently, the first two books to be translated into the local language were a Catholic catechism and the Bible.

At the same time, Jesuit missionaries were obliged to send back to the Jesuit headquarters in Rome reports on the missions. These reports not only provided church statistics but more broadly described the fauna and flora, the weather, diet, foods, and customs of the local communities. One example of this are the reports gathered into seventy volumes, *The Jesuit Relations and Allied Documents*. This is a treasure for anthropologists and historians of the cultures of the Americas. Two significant examples of the Jesuit encounter with culture would be the creation of the Paraguayan Reductions in South America and the encounter of Matteo Ricci with the cultures of the Far East.

In the last century, the Second Vatican Council signaled the openness of the Catholic Church to the modern world and modern culture. The title of the key document indicating this direction is "The Church in the Modern World." This thrust entered into the vocabulary of Christianity under the rubric of "inculturation." Fr. Pedro Arrupe, the superior general of the Jesuits, himself a missionary to Japan, described this as follows:

> inculturation is the incarnation of Christian life and of the Christian message in a particular cultural context, in such a way that this experience not only finds expression through elements proper to the culture in question, but becomes a principle that animates, directs and unifies the culture, transforming it and remaking it so as to bring about a "new creation."

More recently, Pope Paul VI and subsequent popes have pointed to the difficulties and challenges that inculturation faces. They point to "the split between the Gospel and culture which is without doubt the tragedy of our time." The struggle to evangelize or bring the Gospel to bear upon cultures can be seen in several key challenges. There is the complexity and diversity of cultures and sub-cultures. Jesuits encounter premodern, traditional, modern, and postmodern cultures. Cultures are not static but rapidly changing. There can be no fixed relationship of Gospel and culture. There is resistance to the Gospel, with the spread of atheism and agnosticism. The Church and the Society of Jesus must link together key aspects affecting culture today. Thus faith, justice, concern for culture, and interreligious dialogue are inextricably joined, as was outlined in the Decree "Servants of Christ's Mission" (##14–21) of the 34th General Congregation of the Society in 1995. Finally, as Pope John Paul II has explained, there is the powerful culture of death embodied in violence and terrorism.

In this confrontation of Gospel and culture, there is need for careful and critical discernment. The lights and shadows in the cultures and sub-cultures must be understood, the lights accepted and learned from, and the shadows confronted. Pope Francis sees this as a special contribution of the Jesuits. He explains that a particular treasure of the Jesuits is spiritual discernment, which seeks to recognize the presence of God's spirit in human and cultural experiences. Indeed, Ignatian spirituality, with optimism and openness to the new, will play a crucial role in this ongoing dialogue between faith and culture.

See also Asia; China; Japan; Paraguay Missions ("Reductions"); Ricci, Matteo, SJ; Valignano, Alessandro, SJ; Vatican II

Arrupe, Pedro, "On Inculturation." Letter to the Whole Society of Jesus, May 14, 1978. English version. *Acta Romana Societatis Iesu* 17 (1977–79), 256–81.

Modras, Ronald, *Ignatian Humanism: A Dynamic Spirituality for the 21st Century.* Chicago, IL: Loyola Press, 2004.

O'Malley, John W., and Gauvin A. Bailey, eds., *The Jesuits and the Arts, 1540–1773.* Philadelphia, PA: Saint Joseph's University Press, 2005.

Wright, Jonathan, *God's Soldiers: Adventure, Politics, Intrigue and Power – A History of the Jesuits.* New York: Doubleday, 2004.

Peter Schineller, SJ

Cura Personalis

The Jesuit characteristic of *cura personalis*, "care for the whole person," underscores the respect that every individual deserves.

Though the term itself was apparently not in use until the twentieth century (Włodimir Ledóchowski, general of the Society, 1915–42, may have been the first to use the term *cura personalis*), it is a hallmark of Ignatian spirituality wherein the spiritual director adapts the *Spiritual Exercises* to the unique relationship with God and the talents that each individual enjoys. Eventually, it is applied to describing the responsibility of the Jesuit superior to care for each man in the community with his unique gifts, challenges, needs, and possibilities. And now it applies more broadly to include the relationships among educators, students, and professional staff who work in an academic setting – generally either a university or a high school. It can be seen as a condition for the other Jesuit motto of the *magis*, that is, giving greater glory to God. And together these mottos echo Irenaeus's affirmation: "the glory of God is the human person fully alive."

As an example of *cura personalis*, St. Ignatius once wrote to Jesuit Father Antonio Araoz ordering him to take better care of his health after learning that he was not eating properly. Ignatius wrote, "For the next three months, from now until September, you are to do no preaching, but are to look after your health." And he ordered him under obedience to follow his doctor's directives.

The term *cura personalis* indicates that the Christian faith involves not just the head but the heart, not just the soul but the body. Physical exercises are as important as spiritual exercises. Learning is as important as a good diet. Students pray, learn, and eat healthily as ways to glorify God and care for their entire selves. All are gifts from God.

See also Spiritual Direction; Magis

Kolvenbach, Peter-Hans, "Cura Personalis." *Review for Religious* 28, 1 (2007), 9–17.

Patrick J. Howell, SJ

Curia, Jesuit

The seat of the superior general and his closest collaborators in Rome is traditionally called the General Curia. Its structure and organization correspond to the exigencies of the Society's centralized government. The superior general is helped in the exercise of his mandate by some major officials (*officiales maiores*), such as the secretary of the Society (the Curia remains under his direct authority), the procurator general (in charge of legal matters), the postulator general (responsible for the Society's causes of beatification and canonization), and the treasurer general (who oversees the Order's finances). Distinct geographical areas of the world where the Jesuits are operating are represented by nine general assistants. In addition, several apostolic sectors (Education, Apostolate of Prayer, Social Apostolate, etc.) are supervised by secretaries. Some of these reside elsewhere, while the Curia is also a Jesuit community of over fifty members reflecting the international character of the Order. All the offices mentioned, as well as others (archives, library, communications-public relations, etc.), work with several dozen lay employees. Until 1873 the headquarters of the Society were at the Professed House of the *Gesù* in Rome. When the Jesuits were expelled, Fr. General Beckx organized his Curia in Fiesole near Florence, where it remained until 1895. It then returned to Rome, and it was located in the German College until 1927 when it moved to the new building prepared by Fr. General Ledóchowski at Borgo Santo Spirito, which remains i-ts present address. The web page of the General Curia is available at www.sjweb.info/.

See also Rome; Superior General

Miccinelli, Carlo, *Excerpta selecta ex historia novae domus Curiae*. Rome: Pontifical Gregorian University, 1966.

Robert Danieluk, SJ

Dalits and Dalit Theology

The dominant religious worldview in the Indian subcontinent is a Hindu one, which divides society into a hierarchy of castes (or *varnas*) of which there are four. These in turn are further divided into numerous *jathis*, or subcastes. These divisions are largely occupational in nature but also vary by geographic location and local culture. One is born into a caste, is traditionally expected to marry within that caste, and cannot change castes. Yet many Indians remain outside this caste hierarchy, including all non-Hindus: such as Muslims, Buddhists, and Christians, and also the entire indigenous *adivasi* (tribal) population. The term *dalit* means "broken," "trampled," or "oppressed" and refers to all persons without caste, outside the body of the cosmic being and thus doomed to pariah status. *Dalits* are often called "untouchables," because they are seen by caste Hindus as polluting, and thus they have traditionally suffered physical and social ostracism, particularly in rural settings.

The majority of Christians in India are Dalit, non-caste persons; that is, they did not convert to Christianity from an original Hindu caste identity but were formerly of *adivasi*, or other non-Hindu backgrounds. On account of the exploitative practices of the upper castes, the social condition of Dalits has been of great concern to Christians. This has been especially the case after the creation of India's secular constitution in 1950, shortly after Independence from British rule (1947), which made provisions to ensure the fair treatment of historically oppressed castes, classes, and tribes through guaranteed political representation, education, and employment opportunities. This was in part the work of Dr. B. D. Ambedkar, one of the principal writers of the Constitution who was a Dalit himself. In recent decades, concern for Dalits has been in tension with inculturation of Christianity to the Indian context, because that cultural context is dominated by brahminical Hinduism.

Dalit theology was partly inspired by liberation theology, a movement that began in Latin America as a theological approach to understand and remedy the brutally oppressive social conditions of the poor. Dalit theology attempts to do the same for Dalits in the Indian context and employs similar methodological tools such as Marxist analysis. Dalit theology is distinct from another strand of Indian liberation theology whose approach is Gandhian.

Most importantly, Dalit theology takes the life, experience, and social context of Dalits as the locus and focus of theologizing. The goal is to interpret the Scriptures, sacraments, and Christian tradition from a Dalit perspective and express the faith in the sign and symbol, the way of life and particular culture, of Dalits. By encouraging what amounts to a retrieval of Dalit subjectivity – that is, of agency and voice – it becomes possible for Dalits to experience their inherent human dignity as made in the image and likeness of God, and to hope and work for social change that would reverse their oppression.

For Dalit theology, the suffering of Jesus Christ on the Cross is a poignant act of solidarity with Dalits in their own suffering, for he was tortured and executed as an outcast by the religious and political leadership of his own society. For the way Jesus lived his life challenged the dominant powers who exploited the poor and ostracized some of the sick and suffering on the basis of ritual impurity. Thus Jesus Christ, in his words and deeds, is also understood as a subversive initiator of social change. Dalit theology is, therefore, a prophetic project, a calling of the poor to evangelize the non-poor.

Jesuits in India have long been involved in Dalit theology. One of the first Jesuit expressions of concern for Dalits was the establishment in 1951 of the Indian Social Institute, to support research, reflection, and action on social problems. Jesuit theologians have approached Dalit theology from various disciplinary perspectives and worked in dialogue with Protestant theologians as well. Some prominent Jesuits voices in Dalit theology are Xavier Irudayaraj, SJ, Maria Arul Raja, SJ, and Dionysius Rasquinha, SJ. Various Jesuits who work on Asian Theologies of Liberation, such as Michael Amaladoss, SJ, Samuel Rayan, SJ, and George Soares-Prabhu, SJ, have also addressed Dalit theology in some of their works. In addition to monographs and collected works, Jesuit theologians have published frequently on Dalit theology in the *Vidyajyoti Journal of Theological Reflection*.

See also India; Interreligious Dialogue; Liberation Theology; Soares-Prabhu, George, SJ

Clarke, Sathianathan, Deenabandhu Manchala, and Philip V. Peacock, eds., *Dalit Theology in the Twenty-First Century: Discordant Voices, Discerning Pathways*. New Delhi: Oxford University Press, 2010.

Devasahayam, V., ed., *Frontiers of Dalit Theology*. New Delhi: Published for Gurukul Lutheran Theological College & Research Institute, Madras, by Indian Society for Promoting Christian Knowledge, 1997.

Irudayaraj, Xavier, ed., *Emerging Dalit Theology*. Madras: Jesuit Theological Secretariat; Madurai: Tamil Nadu Theological Seminary, 1990.

Rasquinha, Dionysius, *Towards Wholeness from Brokenness: The Dalit Quest: a Historical Analysis and Theological Response*. Delhi: Indian Society for Promoting Christian Knowledge, 2013.

Brent Howitt Otto, SJ

Dance

Of all the investments that the Society of Jesus made in early modern culture, none seems more startling than the Jesuit transaction with dance. The received wisdom that Christianity has always and everywhere been hostile to dance bears some responsibility for this surprise. In truth, religious attitudes toward the dance have never been monolithic, and though dance was often decried because of its potential lasciviousness and/or its connections with pagan worship, not a few premodern ecclesiastical authorities considered dancing to be a morally neutral activity best judged by the effects it wrought in people's lives. The Jesuit use of dance likely emerged from the Renaissance view that dance not only entertained but also performed a social function, teaching courtiers to comport themselves gracefully and appropriately on an increasingly choreographed public stage. Jesuit dance – like theater, fencing, equestrianism, and other physical activities – aimed to cultivate in students expressive and disciplined bodies. In keeping with the Society's incarnational spirituality, dance facilitated an integrated education that addressed all the faculties of a human being.

As early as the sixteenth century, Jesuit theatrical productions in Europe began incorporating dance and music between the acts of mostly Latin dramas. These interludes provided audiences with sensual alternatives for engaging a play's central dramatic themes. Theatrical dance achieved a particular prominence in France, mirroring the cultural importance of the *ballets de cour* during the reign of Louis XIV. French Jesuits succeeded in employing dance to educate their students in the physical eloquence necessary for becoming effective contributors to early modern society. Simultaneously, Jesuit ballets performed the political, social, and religious values of "the splendid century," publicizing the distinguished reputation of these culturally imbedded institutions. Despite the repeated condemnations of dance by Jansenists and other religious rigorists, the Collège Louis-le-Grand (formerly the Collège de Clermont) became a hub of choreographic activity in seventeenth-century Paris. To choreograph their spectacular ballets, the Jesuits engaged dancing masters like the renowned Pierre Beauchamps, personal dancing instructor to the king and director of the Académie Royale de Danse. They even hired dancers employed by the Paris Opéra to perform alongside the students in the hope that a professional presence would improve the quality of student work. Jesuits also made significant intellectual contributions to the history and theory of dance. Claude François-Menestrier (1631–1705), for example, is widely regarded as the first historian of the ballet. As Judith Rock notes, "of the ten books on the history and theory of dancing" written between 1658 and 1760 "five … were by Jesuits from Louis-le-Grand" (*Terpsichore*, 17–18).

Dance also proved an effective tool in early modern Jesuit missionary endeavors attracting native peoples to Christian faith and worship. The use of dance in the context of evangelization, however, required that it be distanced from its pre-Christian past and modified to avoid any lasciviousness that could contravene Christian morality. For the most part, Jesuits were predictably accommodating in their approach, often reinterpreting indigenous dance within a Christian frame; however, there were instances in which the Jesuits saw indigenous sacred dance as a hindrance to conversion efforts. Like music, dance was an important cultural component of the Paraguayan reductions. The formal courtly and processional dance styles prevalent in France and Spain mingled with native forms to enliven religious celebrations and texture theatrical presentations.

Jesuit involvement with dance has continued into the present with several Jesuits making vocational commitments to the art of dance and theatrical movement. Robert VerEecke, SJ, founder and artistic director of the Boston Liturgical Dance Ensemble, has used dance to facilitate and deepen liturgical and spiritual experience in both pastoral and theatrical settings. Saju George, SJ, of Kolkata's Kalahridya Dance and Arts Institution practices the ancient Indian *Bharatanatyam* to preach the Good News and engage in interreligious dialogue. George Drance, SJ, artistic director of Magis Theatre Company, works with colleagues to provide affordable performance training that integrates body, voice, and imagination in exploring the human condition. Prakesh Olalekar, SJ, employs the techniques of InterPlay (an improvisational performance form involving storytelling, music, and dance) to build peace and advance the work of social justice in India. Though the programmatic integration of body and spirit have largely migrated to physical education departments and sports programs within Jesuit educational

Figure 17 Avinash Pasricha: Father Saju George, SJ, dancing. Photograph © Avinash Pasricha

institutions, dance and the other performing arts continue to assert the importance of the human body in cultivating personal and civic virtue.

See also Arts, Performing; Theater

Arcangelo, Alessandro, "Dance under Trial: The Moral Debate 1200–1600." *Dance Research: The Journal of the Society for Dance Research* 12, 2 (1994), 127–55.
Casalini, Cristiano, "Active Leisure: The Body in Sixteenth-Century Jesuit Culture." *Journal of Jesuit Studies* 1 (2014), 400–18.
Rock, Judith, *Terpsichore at Louis-le-Grand: Baroque Dance on the Jesuit Stage in Paris.* St. Louis, MO: The Institute of Jesuit Sources, 1996.
Herczog, Johann, *Orfeo nelle Indie: I gesuiti e la musica in Paraguay (1609–1767).* Lecce: Mario Congedo, 2001, pp. 221–43.

Michael A. Zampelli, SJ

Daniélou, Jean, Cardinal, SJ (1905–1974)

Jean Daniélou was born on May 14, 1905, in Neuilly-sur-Seine and died on May 20, 1974 in Paris. He received a degree in letters from the Sorbonne in 1927, studied philosophy in Jersey, the Channel Islands, from 1931 to 1934, and theology in Lyon-Fourvière, from 1934 to 1938. He was awarded a Ph.D. at the Sorbonne in 1943 and a Ph.D. at the Institut Catholique, Paris, in 1944. Daniélou entered the Society of Jesus in 1929 and was ordained priest in 1938. He occupied the Chair of Christian Origins at the Institut Catholique from 1944 to 1969. He became a member of the editorial board of *Études* in 1943 and co-editor, with Henri de Lubac, of *Sources Chrétiennes* in 1944. He was a *peritus* at the Second Vatican Council (1962–65). He was ordained bishop in 1969, named cardinal the same year, and elected to the Académie Française in 1972.

Daniélou earned a reputation as an intellectual, theologian, preacher, spiritual director, and polemicist. Henri de Lubac and Hans Urs von Balthasar, confrères at Fourvière, oriented him toward patristics, his primary area of expertise, and toward the movement known as the "New Theology" (*nouvelle théologie*). He launched his scholarly reputation with his study of the mysticism of Gregory of Nyssa. His translation of Gregory's *Life of Moses* was the first volume of the series *Sources Chrétiennes*. He also wrote on

Philo of Alexandria, Origen, Judeo-Christian theology, and the Pre-Nicene Fathers. He considered *Le signe du temple* (*The Presence of God*, 1958) to be programmatic for his entire career. His typological and allegorical interpretation of Scripture appeared in works such as *Sacramentum futuri: études sur les origines de la typologie biblique* (1950) and *Bible et liturgie* (1958). Other writings explored the relationship between God and us, the non-Christian world, and the dialogue between faith and culture.

In his later years, Daniélou was critical of what he saw as the intellectual poverty of the post-Vatican II progressives. He protested against what he perceived to be the secularism of the Church after the Council. Produced while he engaged in more polemical activities, his mature work of this period includes the three-volume study *A History of Early Christian Doctrine before the Council of Nicea* (1973) and the spiritual works, *God's Life in Us* (1963) and *La Résurrection* (1969).

See also Études; Nouvelle Théologie; Sources Chrétiennes

Susan K. Wood

D'Arcy, Martin Cyril, SJ (1888–1976)

Born in Bath, of Irish extraction, the youngest of four children, two of whom died in infancy, D'Arcy followed his brother Conyers to Stonyhurst College, and then to the Jesuit novitiate. He entered the Society in 1906 and, having completed the early stages of formation, he studied philosophy at St. Mary's Hall, Stonyhurst. In 1912 he went to the Jesuit house of studies at Oxford, Pope's Hall, subsequently Campion Hall, to read classics. He took a second in classical moderations in 1914, and this relative failure spurred him to work for a first in Greats, which he obtained in 1916. Between 1915 and 1923 he obtained three Oxford prizes.

D'Arcy began his theology at Hastings but completed it at St. Beuno's College, Wales, and was ordained in 1921. Prior to this he spent a year at Stonyhurst, where he had done regency in order to teach, according to the provincial, three exceptional boys, one of whom was Henry John, the son of the well-known painter Augustus John. D'Arcy formed an obsessive and unhealthy dependence on the young John, and when D'Arcy was sent to Rome for the biennium in philosophy in 1925 John also applied and was admitted to the Gregorian University. D'Arcy disliked the atmosphere in Rome in those years shortly after the Modernist crisis and, unusually, was allowed to spend his second year in Farm Street, London, to complete his doctorate. He was then assigned to Campion Hall, eventually becoming master in 1933. These were the years when D'Arcy began to be prominent in English public life, partly because of a number of high-profile converts whom he instructed in Catholicism such as Evelyn Waugh and Frank Pakenham, the future earl of Longford. His dazzling conversation, arresting looks, and wide reading, matched with a sympathetic and winning personality, gave D'Arcy an *entrée* into a world well beyond that of many twentieth-century English Jesuits.

He began to lecture and tutor in medieval philosophy, and his classes attracted a wide range of students including the young and rambunctious A. J. Ayer, whom, in time, D'Arcy would come to regard as the most dangerous man in Oxford because of his atheism matched to a lively intelligence. Given his interests in Thomism in a faculty increasingly out of sympathy with ideas about God, D'Arcy was never highly regarded as a philosopher at Oxford, and his lectures, even on Aristotle, were thought to be at best competent. It was D'Arcy who persuaded Sir Edwin Lutyens, the most renowned architect of his generation, to accept the commission to build the new Campion Hall, at Oxford, a decision that occasioned an investigation by the British Architectural Association, since the commission had already been given by the previous master to Edward Berks Norris. Eventually Norris was paid a fee of £1,200 to prevent a public row.

D'Arcy's early years in Oxford were overshadowed by deterioration in his relationship with Henry John, who had joined the Order in 1927, but who left the Society as a scholastic in 1934 and died in an accident the following year. D'Arcy was devastated, as was Augustus John who came to terms with the death of his son partly as a result of painting D'Arcy's portrait. The need to obtain funding to build Campion Hall in Brewer Street led D'Arcy to make his first visit to the United States in 1935, a country that thereafter he visited frequently. In 1945 he was appointed English provincial and in the course of his tenure he purchased three English country houses, for what precise purpose remains unclear. His administration was not successful, and although humane and caring, he was removed from office in 1950 after four and a half years of a six-year term. D'Arcy never fully recovered from what he took to be this humiliation. The rest of his life was divided between Farm Street and the United States, where he lectured at several Jesuit universities and was a visiting scholar at the Institute for Advanced Study, Princeton University.

Regarded by many as a snob, D'Arcy was undoubtedly immensely elitist in his approach to people, and although gifted and clever he never attained to the highest ranks of scholarship. His early books such as *St. Thomas Aquinas* (1930) and *The Nature of Belief* (1931) are now virtually unreadable, and his most enduring work is certainly *The Mind and Heart of Love* (1945). Even this is rather stilted in style, and in general his writings never matched the verve and panache of his conversation. He retained the affection and friendship of many in high society on both sides of the Atlantic, inducing Edward Heath, British prime minster from 1970 to 1974, and his eightieth birthday party at Club 21 in New York was attended by, among others, Senator Mike Mansfield and the Duke of Windsor, the former King Edward VIII.

See also United Kingdom

Abell, William S., ed., *Laughter and the Love of Friends: Reminiscences of the Distinguished English Priest and Philosopher Martin Cyril D'Arcy*. Westminster, MD: Christian Classics, 1991.
Sire, H. J. A., *Father Martin D'Arcy: Philosopher of Christian Love*. Leominster: Gracewing, 1997.

Oliver P. Rafferty, SJ

Davis, Thurston N., SJ (1913–1986)

Thurston Davis established the strong journalistic position that *America* magazine continues to enjoy today. He was editor-in-chief from 1955 to 1968 during the transition from the severe Pius XII to the ebullient John XXIII. During his tenure, the election of the first US Catholic president, the Second Vatican Council, the turmoil of the Vietnam War, and the success of the Civil Rights movement all occurred.

He described *America*'s role as "a weekly raid on the City of God in order to publish, in the City of Man, a journal that talks common Christian sense about the world of human events."

Through prodigious fund-raising, he purchased the old Montclair Hotel at 106 W. 56th St. in Manhattan as the new headquarters for *America*. He also founded the popular Catholic Book Club and made valiant efforts to expand circulation.

As a teenager, Davis made the long commute from Bloomfield, NJ, to the Jesuits' Xavier High School in Lower Manhattan. He quickly rose to eminence and played Hamlet in the school play and was second in command of the high school Reserve Officers' Training Corps. He entered the Jesuits in 1931 and was ordained eleven years later at Woodstock College, Maryland.

From 1944 to 1947, he earned a doctorate at Harvard in the history of philosophy. Soon after, as a faculty member and as a dean at Fordham University, he urged, against some opposition, a much stronger curriculum and academic expectations for the students.

After his years as editor, he served with the US Conference of Catholic Bishops and eventually as director of the John LaFarge Institute and the John Courtney Murray lectureship. He died at *America* house of a heart attack in 1986.

See also America Magazine; United States of America

"Editorial: Thurston N. Davis, SJ, 1913–1986." *America*. October 4, 1986, pp. 157–58.

Patrick J. Howell, SJ

Degentes

A Latin word meaning "living" or "residing," the term *degentes* is used to describe Jesuits who are living outside of the province, mission, or house to which they belong. Historically, for instance, the term could be used to describe (1) Jesuits who are members of a given province but are living in another province, *degentes extra provinciam*, (2) Jesuits from other provinces who are living in a given province, *ex aliis provinciis in nostra degentes*, (3) Jesuits who are assigned to a given mission territory but are living outside it, *degentes extra missionem*, (4) Jesuits who are members of another province but are living in a given province's mission territory, *socii provinciae in missionibus degentes*, and finally (5) Jesuits who are attached to a given Jesuit house but are living outside it, *degentes extra domum*. An important distinction is that a Jesuit is "applied" to another province if he is working for an institution of that province, whereas he is deemed to be *degens* in that province if he is not connected with one of that province's institutions. However, those who are *degentes* in another province, even for a brief period of time, have the fundamental rights and responsibilities of all members of the Society. Therefore, according to the Complementary Norms of the Jesuit *Constitutions*, they are still "dependent upon the superiors of [that] province, particularly as regards religious discipline and the exercise of the ministry; [in turn,] these superiors are to look after them with no less paternal solicitude than they have for their own subjects" (390 #1). This mutuality is clearly designed to promote the Society's desire for a fuller union of minds and hearts among all of its members.

See also Applied; Province; Transcribe

The Constitutions of the Society of Jesus and Their Complementary Norms. Ed. John W. Padberg. St. Louis, MO: The Institute of Jesuit Sources, 1996.

Robert E. Scully, SJ

Deliberatio

The term *deliberatio* (deliberation) refers to a discernment whereby a community prayerfully seeks to find the will of God in a particular matter. The elements of a deliberation include the matter to be decided, the process to be followed, and the members to be involved. With the exception of the Deliberation of the First Fathers (1539), this form of discernment is only consultative in Jesuit governance, aiding the superior who makes the final decision.

For Ignatius and his companions at Rome in 1539, the matter to be decided was first whether they would remain together or go their separate ways. Once having decided to remain together, they then needed to deliberate the nature of their union. They had made vows of poverty and chastity in Paris in 1537, but now they asked whether they should make a vow of obedience to a superior. This would lead to the establishment of a new religious community. Since these questions did not present as immediate an answer as the first, they decided to take the time between the end of Lent until the feast of St. John the Baptist (June 24) in more concentrated prayer and discussion. They opted to stay in Rome and continue their ministries throughout the process. All of them would participate in the deliberation, taking one side or the other of each question. In this way they unanimously decided in favor of the vow of obedience. This decision was taken so as to better fulfill their missions at the service of the papacy. In all of this they sought confirmation from the Pope, Paul III.

Following Vatican II, Father General Pedro Arrupe reemphasized the role of communal discernment as an aid to the decision-making of the superior. The provincial is now required to have a commission for the choice of ministries to help carry out this type of discernment.

See also Discernment; Friends in the Lord

Arrupe, Pedro, "On Discernment as a Preparation for GC XXXII." *Acta Romana*. Rome, 1971.
Essays on Discernment. (Dossier "Deliberatio" C). 2nd edn. Rome: Centrum Ignatianum Spiritualitatis, 1981.

Mark A. Lewis, SJ

Delp, Alfred, SJ (1907–1945)

Alfred Delp was born in Mannheim, Germany, on September 15, 1907, the second of six children to Johann Adam Friedrich Delp and Maria Bernauer. Though baptized a Catholic, he was raised in his early years as a Lutheran, the religion of his father, and returned to the Catholic religion of his mother at age 14. He would later become one of the most significant figures in the Catholic resistance to Nazism.

Upon his completion of secondary education, Delp entered the Jesuit novitiate in Feldkirch, Austria, in 1926. After taking his first vows, he applied himself to the study of philosophy, publishing a critical study of the German philosopher Martin Heidegger. His Jesuit formation followed the standard course, and he was ordained to the priesthood on June 24, 1937, the 400th anniversary of the ordination of Ignatius of Loyola.

Noting his academic prowess, Delp's Jesuit superiors had intended that he begin studying for a doctorate in social philosophy, but he was denied admission to the University of Munich by the Nazi administrator there. For Delp, this would be the first realization that simply being a Jesuit was a priori an enemy and an opponent of the Reich.

Instead, Delp was missioned to join the staff of the Jesuits' opinion journal, *Stimmen der Zeit*, which had published *Mit brennender Sorge*, Pope Pius XI's 1937 encyclical against National Socialism. Delp worked at *Stimmen der Zeit* for two years as the editor for social and political pieces, which sometimes directly challenged the National Socialist policies of Hitler's government. Of particular note during this period was Delp's publication "The Christian at the Present Moment" (1939), in which he wrote about the obligations of the Christian in the modern world. The Gestapo, the political police of Nazi Germany, shut down the publication of *Stimmen der Zeit* on April 18, 1941, and Delp once again recognized himself as one labeled an enemy of the State. Within weeks he was named pastor of St. Georg's Church in Munich-Bogenhausen, the post from which he would be become an instrumental member of the Catholic resistance group that met in Kreisau in Silesia. (This group would be designated the "Kreisau Circle" by the Gestapo in 1944.) During his tenure as pastor in Munich, Delp would also assist Jews escaping to Switzerland.

Founded by Helmuth James Graf von Moltke, the German jurist, the group gathered to prepare for what they saw was inevitable: the day that National Socialism would fall apart, torn asunder by its own devastating policies and ideology. Composed of both Catholics and non-Catholics alike (including Delp's provincial superior, Augustin Rösch and another Jesuit, Lothar König), the resistance figures that gathered at Kreisau would be ready to reconstruct a just society in its place when the Reich would eventually fall. As leader of the group, Von Moltke approached Rösch to see if he could supply the services of a Jesuit social scientist to advise them on issues that would affect German workers in a post-Nazi era. Because of his background and work at *Stimmen der Zeit*, Delp was made available and contributed to the group's discussions by drawing heavily upon Catholic social teaching, particularly Pius XI's encyclical *Quadragesimo anno*, which had been issued in 1931. However, the resistance group that met at Kreisau was under constant surveillance by the Gestapo and on July 28, 1944, after celebrating Mass in St. Georg's Church, Delp was arrested.

In prison, Delp's suspicions about his a priori enemy status were confirmed: the Gestapo suggested he could go free if he abandoned the Society of Jesus. Instead, Delp committed himself to a daily order of prayer, celebrating Mass with his hands bound, devoting many hours to prayer and composing letters and a series of meditations for Advent, which were smuggled out of prison. As the months dragged on, Delp came to understand more fully his loving God and the frailty of the human condition he had written about earlier in life.

His trial, held January 9–11, 1945, was one of high theater. Delp was sentenced to death, and on February 2, he was hanged in Plötzensee Prison in Berlin.

Delp noted with resignation the reason for his execution in farewell letters: "The actual basis for the judgment is that I am a Jesuit and I have remained one … The whole thing was, on the one hand, a farce and, on the other, it became the defining motif of my life" (Delp, *Prison Writings*, xvi–xvii).

See also German-Speaking Lands; Martyrs, Ideal and History; Revues/Journals

Coady, Mary,*With Bound Hands: A Jesuit in Nazi Germany*. Chicago, IL: Loyola Press, 2003.

Delp, Alfred, *Advent of the Heart: Seasonal Sermons and Prison Writings 1941–1944*. San Francisco, CA: Ignatius Press, 2006.

Prison Writings. Maryknoll, NY: Orbis Books, 2004.

Keith Maczkiewicz, SJ

DeMello, Anthony, SJ (1931–1987)

Anthony ("Tony") deMello was born in Bombay on September 4, 1931, the first of five children, one of whom died as an infant. He grew up in the suburban Catholic stronghold of Bandra in a devout middle-class Catholic family and was educated in a Jesuit school. Having imbibed the strong Catholic ethos and the discipline of his Jesuit education, Tony expressed at a young age his desire to be a Jesuit priest. This desire persisted and upon completion of school at 16 years of age, Tony received his parents' blessing to join the Jesuits.

On July 1, 1947, he entered the Jesuit novitiate of the Bombay province in Andheri. DeMello would remain there through his first vows in 1949 and undergraduate studies, known as "Juniorate." From childhood through these first few years of Jesuit life, he was remembered by his family and Jesuit brothers as being pious, devout, and uncompromisingly self-disciplined. DeMello could at times appear overly serious and rigid, but nevertheless showed great balance, good judgment, and fairness.

In 1952 he was sent abroad to study philosophy for three years in Barcelona, Spain. He thrived in the new environment and established great friendships. Superiors even asked deMello to teach English to the Spanish Jesuits. Then he began to gain a reputation as a very skilled and encouraging teacher, and also as an engaging storyteller, which would become a hallmark of his personality and key to his later ministries.

Returning to India in 1955, deMello began the "regency" period of his formation, first at St. Mary's High School, a boarding school in Mazagaon, and later as an English teacher at the Juniorate in Andheri. From 1958 to 1962 he studied theology at the Papal Athenaeum in Pune and lived at the Jesuit De Nobili College. By this stage of deMello's formation as a Jesuit, some of his close family and friends noted that his piety and discipline, which in the past may sometimes have appeared rigid or harsh, had matured to manifest deep sensitivity and compassion for others. On March 24, 1961, he was ordained a priest and remained at Pune to complete his fourth year of theology studies, followed by tertianship (the final stage of Jesuit formation) in Hazaribagh.

In 1963 deMello was sent to the United States to study for a master's degree in pastoral counseling at Loyola University in Chicago. There he would begin to hone his skills as a spiritual guide, enriching his formation in the Ignatian tradition of the *Spiritual Exercises* with new learning in human psychology and best practices of counseling. This was followed by further studies in spiritual theology from the Gregorian University in Rome, where he also pronounced his final vows.

Returning to India in 1965, deMello began a career of both spiritual ministries and leadership of several Jesuit formation houses. Most notable is his founding of the Sadhana Institute in 1973 in Pune. The word *Sadhana* comes from Sanskrit and means a quest, a life journey, or an inner way. The institute began as a center to train retreat directors and spiritual guides and later expanded to become a center for integrating spirituality and psychology, as well as facilitating dialogue between Christian spirituality and other Indian spiritual traditions. The appeal of deMello's work lay in how he blended Christian mysticism with Indian and other Asian spiritualities. Drawing on yoga and similar spiritual practices, he promoted the embodied quality of contemplation that it is not primarily an exercise of the mind but of the whole being. This was conveyed both in writing and in person through his warm personality and skill as a storyteller. In 1979 Sadhana moved to Lonavala, a more bucolic mountainous environment in the rural Western Ghats. Until the end of his life, Sadhana was deMello's home base, though he made many trips all over India and the world giving retreats and workshops. On one such international trip to the United States, he unexpectedly suffered a heart attack and died at Fordham University in New York City. His body was returned to India for burial.

Beyond the six books he wrote before his death, to date a dozen more have been published posthumously as compilations of his various writings or transcriptions of the recordings of his retreats and workshops. Tony deMello remains arguably the most famous Christian spiritual writer from Asia, with a strong international following. In 1998 the Congregation for the Doctrine of the Faith, under the leadership of Cardinal Joseph Ratzinger (later Pope Benedict XVI), investigated the theological and doctrinal soundness of deMello's writings and expressed concern that some elements may be incompatible with the Catholic faith, while finding no fault with most of his works. This has not seemed to diminish the popularity of deMello's work.

See also India

deMello, Anthony, *Sadhana: A Way to God – Christian Exercises in Eastern Form.* Anand, India: Gujarat Sahitya Prakash, 1978.
deMello, Bill, *Anthony deMello: The Happy Wanderer.* Maryknoll, NY: Orbis, 2013.
Valles, Carlos G., *Unencumbered by Baggage: Fr. Anthony DeMello: A Prophet for Our Times.* Anand, India: Gujarat Sahitya Prakash, 1987.

Brent Howitt Otto, SJ

Descartes, René

French mathematician and philosopher René Descartes, born March 31, 1596, in La Haye (Touraine), received his primary intellectual formation (c. Easter 1606 to mid-1614) at the royal college of La Flèche (Sarthe). The Bourbon King Henry IV had founded the college in 1603 and entrusted it to the Jesuits, whom he had permitted, following his conversion to Catholicism, to return to France from exile. A ceremony in which Descartes was chosen to participate, the interment of Henry's heart (June 4, 1610), would have marked significantly his time at La Flèche. His course of studies followed the first two cycles outlined in the *Ratio studiorum* (1599). Exposure to Quintilian at the end of the first cycle would have raised the concerns for clarity and distinctness and epistemic certainty that predominate in his thought, although he later criticized both the use of logic and the general perspective of Aristotelian physics as taught in the Jesuit colleges. Descartes studied alongside the Jesuit scholastic Étienne Noël (1581–1659), who served as his part-time tutor and later correspondent, and learned rhetoric from Denis Pétau (1583–1652), a Jesuit who would gain renown teaching theology in

Paris. Traces of Ignatian spirituality appear in the *Meditationes* (1641, rev. 1642), and Descartes later wrote to distant relative Étienne Charlet (1570–1652), rector of the college from 1607 to 1616, characterizing him "as a father" (Clarke, *Descartes*, 25). His reflections (1637) on his schooling indicate above all a desire for more secure epistemic foundations than those which his studies had afforded him. Finally, his later efforts to win Jesuit support for his philosophical project, e.g., to adopt the *Météors* as a text in the colleges (1637), met with frustration.

See also Alumni/ae

Clarke, Desmond M., *Descartes: A Biography*. Cambridge: Cambridge University Press, 2006.
Gaukroger, Stephen, *Descartes: An Intellectual Biography*. Oxford: Clarendon Press, 1995.

William P. O'Brien, SJ

Desideri, Ippolito, SJ (1684–1733)

Ippolito Desideri was born in Pistoia, Italy, and entered the Jesuit novitiate in 1700 in Rome. Influenced by missionary accounts of the earlier but failed Jesuit and Capuchin missions in Tibet, Desideri desired to follow in their footsteps. Upon completing theology studies, his desire was fulfilled. Desideri sailed for Goa, the Jesuit province responsible for the defunct Tibet mission. From Goa he traveled north, met his mission companion, Fr. Manuel Freyre, in Surat, and then they entered Tibet in 1715. In Lhasa, Desideri befriended the king and took up residence. Soon after arriving, Freyre returned to India.

Besides Desideri, the only other missionaries in Tibet at the time were a group of Capuchins in Lhasa, engaged mainly in medical work. Desideri enjoyed privileged access to the libraries and scholars of Lhasa, became proficient in the Tibetan language, and studied Buddhist texts. In six years he wrote four major theological and catechetical texts that engaged the Tibetan Buddhist context, as well as rich accounts of the people and culture. Desideri is sometimes considered the founder of Tibetan studies in the west.

Ecclesiastical tensions arose over the Tibet mission between the Congregation for the Propagation of the Faith, the Vatican authority on missions, and the *Padroado*, the authority of the Portuguese Crown over Church activities within its territories. The conflict was resolved when Rome gave the Capuchins exclusive responsibility for Tibet and asked the Jesuits, who operated there under the *Padroado*, to leave. Upon learning of this decision, Desideri departed Tibet in 1721. He eventually returned to Rome and died in 1733. His writings were then lost until they were rediscovered in 1904.

See also Goa; *Patronato* and *Padroado*; Portugal

Pomplun, Trent, *Jesuits on the Roof of the World: Ippolito Desideri's Mission to Eighteenth-Century Tibet*. London: Oxford University Press, 2010.
Sweet, Michael J., trans., and Leonard Zwilling, ed., *Mission to Tibet: The Extraordinary Eighteenth-Century Account of Fr. Ippolito Desideri, SJ*. Boston: Wisdom Publications, 2010.

Brent Howitt Otto, SJ

De Smet, Peter John, SJ (1801–1873)

The Belgian-born Peter John De Smet spent the majority of his life in the western territories of the United States, where he became the preeminent Jesuit missionary to the region's Native American nations. As a superior of the Rocky Mountain mission, go-between for US government officials, and priest, he traveled several thousand miles from St. Louis into Oregon Territory and Canada, garnering a reputation among many communities as "the only white man who doesn't talk with twisted tongue" (Gaier, "Doom of the American Indian," 10). In 1868 he met the emerging Sioux leader Sitting Bull in efforts to broker a peace treaty signed at Fort Rice. De Smet's career in the American West reveals the complexity of Euro-American encounters with Native Americans at a time when federal policy began to expedite westward expansion through more aggressive Indian policies.

Born to a wealthy family, De Smet left Belgium in 1821 to enter the novitiate at White Marsh in Maryland before being missioned to Florissant, Missouri. After his ordination in 1827, he joined the main Jesuit mission in St. Louis in 1829 to teach English. His first major assignment came in 1838 as a missionary among the Potawatomi in Council Bluffs, Nebraska. During his stay he brokered temporary peace between the Potawatomi and a faction of the Sioux. However, he grew frustrated by the influence of Euro-American trade, particularly in alcohol, on his work among the community.

Within two years he headed into Oregon Territory on his most significant assignment as "Apostle of the Rocky Mountains." He rose to prominence among the Flatheads, Coeur d'Alene, Kalespels, and Pend d'Oreilles communities. The Belgian organized St. Mary of the Flatheads (modern-day Idaho) in 1841 as a "reduction." Like similar missions in South America, it aimed to protect the community from outside forces while teaching Euro-American language, culture, and custom as part of their larger religious conversion. These techniques informed his policy recommendations to government officials who increasingly sought his expertise in bringing "civilization" to Indian nations. In addition to providing invaluable information on custom and language, De Smet's journals remarked on the struggles facing his Native American charges at the hands of whites who, "nine times out of ten," provoked the ongoing conflicts. "In my quality of Black-robe I did my best to give them salutary counsels, as well as to console them," De Smet wrote in 1866. He denounced white influence as "the scum of civilization, who bring to them the lowest and grossest vices, and not of the virtues, of civilized men" (Chittenden and Richardson, *Life, Letters and Travels*, 856).

Despite De Smet's insistence on their efficacy, the reductions struggled amid outside pressure and lack of governmental support in comparison with their Spanish predecessor. Six missions that he left in Oregon Territory in 1846 declined as a newer generation of Indians became indifferent at best to Jesuit presence. De Smet's writings made him a celebrity in Europe, where audiences gathered to hear his accounts of North American Indians and raise financial and moral support for the St. Louis territories. Indeed, throughout his travels he embraced the Ignatian task of letter-writing as a means of both unifying this community and spreading Jesuit teaching from the local mission to the larger world. With his colleagues he was one of the first to map unexplored regions along the Columbia, Athabasca, and Missouri rivers. Along with reports of native communities, he brought a scientific eye to the region's geological and biological features while visiting over thirty tribes.

De Smet also brought a forceful and inflexible attitude to his work, particularly as Jesuits began to compete with Protestant influence. While he had previously lent a sympathetic ear to Brigham Young, the leader of the Church of Latter-day Saints, while in Missouri he served as chaplain of an 1858 military expedition against Utah Mormons.

The marginalization of Jesuit missions by the government especially drew his ire. De Smet derided Protestant – particularly Methodist – efforts to win federal support from Ulysses Grant as part of his "Peace Policy" that redistributed support away from Jesuits, who had long maintained an influential presence in the region.

The son of a businessman, De Smet nonetheless raised funds, managed finances, and is generally credited with maintaining the Society's activity west of St. Louis. His writings provide an invaluable resource to modern audiences. Collectively, they offer rich and detailed accounts of the land and nations that inhabited them. They also lend a foreboding tone as unrelenting westward movement effected the tragedy of the American Indian by the end of his life.

See also Native Americans

Carriker, Robert C., *Father Peter John De Smet: Jesuit in the West.* Norman: University of Oklahoma Press, 1995.

Chittenden, Hiram Martin, and Alfred Talbot Richardson, eds., *Life, Letters and Travels of Father Pierre-Jean De Smet, SJ, 1801–1878.* New York: Francis P. Harper, 1905.

De Smet, John, *Letters and Sketches: With a Narrative of a Year's Residence among the Indian Tribes of the Rocky Mountains.* Philadelphia, PA: M. Fithian, 1843.

Origin, Progress, and Prospects of the Catholic Mission to the Rocky Mountains. Fairfield, WA: Ye Galleon Press, 1985.

Flagg, Edmund, *Flagg's The Far West, 1836–1837: De Smet's Letters and Sketches, 1841–1842.* Cleveland: Arthur H. Clark, Co., 1906.

Gaier, Claude, "The Doom of the American Indian: A Belgian View of 1878." *Journal of the West* 30, 4 (October, 1991), 9–15.

Killoren, John J., *"Come Blackrobe": De Smet and the Indian Tragedy.* Norman: University of Oklahoma Press, 1994.

Justin Poché

Desolation

In treating (spiritual) desolation in his Rules for the Discernment of Spirits, Ignatius begins by stating that it is the opposite of (spiritual) consolation (*SpEx* #317). This emphasizes that desolation is an inner movement which, if not opposed, leads a person away from God. He then offers some examples, such as "an impulsive motion toward low and earthly things," being "listless, tepid, and unhappy," and feeling "separated from our Creator and Lord." Like consolation these feelings are *de fuera*, from outside oneself and so not under one's control. Therefore, they imply no moral judgment and are simply part of the spiritual warfare in which a Christian is called to engage. In fact, a person can be very close to God in a time of desolation (although feeling the opposite).

Most of the Rules that are offered as more suitable for the First Week of the *Spiritual Exercises* deal with desolation and how to react to it. Desolation distorts our vision, our way of viewing ourselves and our world. For this reason prior decisions should be adhered to and not changed until the desolation is lifted. It is a time to pray more rather than less, and to find "some suitable way of doing penance." The aim is not to allow desolation to overwhelm us but to turn it into an opportunity for increased self-knowledge and growth in inner freedom.

Consequently, struggling with desolation is by no means just damage-limitation. Once a person in desolation recognizes their situation and refuses to succumb, the whole meaning of the desolation changes. It now becomes, paradoxically, a way forward, offering its own wisdom. If consolation is a time for vision and bold decision-making, desolation purifies our commitment and strengthens it through endurance. While consolation facilitates our serving the Lord joyfully and with élan, desolation teaches us to serve him selflessly.

See also Consolation; Discernment; *Spiritual Exercises*

Gallagher, Timothy, *The Discernment of Spirits: An Ignatian Guide for Everyday Living.* New York: Crossroad, 2005.

Brian O'Leary, SJ

Dezza, Paolo, Cardinal, SJ (1901–1999)

Paolo Dezza entered the Jesuits in the province of Venice. His studies took him to Barcelona, Innsbruck, and Naples. He was ordained to the priesthood in 1928, and not long after, his provincial appointed him to the new philosophate at Gallarte (Milan) where he was also rector for two years. In 1941 he became rector of the Gregorian University, where he taught metaphysics in the Thomistic tradition. Among his students was the future Pope Karol Wojtyla, although the Polish seminarian was actually enrolled at the Angelicum.

During the difficult years of World War II, Father Dezza was known as an excellent superior within a multinational community. He listened well, but also had a strong capacity to make decisions easily and quickly. He was astute in dealing with any discord that arose within the Jesuit community at the Gregorian University. In the last years of the war, he managed to provide safe places for Jews and for other Italians sought out by the Germans. At the end of the war, he baptized the Chief Rabbi in Rome Israel Zoller (1881–1956), who took the name Eugenio (after Eugenio Pacelli who was Pope Pius XII).

During these years he was in intimate contact with Pope Pius XII and other cardinals in the Curia. He was one of the founders of the Pontifical Institute Regina Mundi and was its president (1954–62). In 1964 he was appointed delegate (equivalent to provincial) for the international houses in Rome.

At General Congregation 31 (1965–66), notwithstanding concerns about his health and especially his eyesight, he was considered as a possibility for general; instead, he was elected as one of four general assistants. During the Arrupe years, Father Dezza played a wise counselor among his colleagues. He was known for his solid spirituality, priestly presence, and capacity for dialogue within an international setting. He had an exceptional memory.

Much appreciated in ecclesiastical circles, he was the confessor for Pope Paul VI and for Pope John Paul I, as well as a consultor on several Roman congregations (dicasteries).

The years after Vatican II were characterized by extremely rapid change in society and in the Church itself. A large number of Jesuits left the Society, which rapidly declined from a peak of 36,038 in 1965 to approximately 25,000 by 1981. In addition, the papacy and Vatican officials were increasingly concerned by the apparent political involvement of Jesuits in Latin America. They viewed liberation theology as overly Marxist, and after

John Paul II, who had battled communism all his life, was elected pope in 1978, these concerns heightened. Vatican officials decided that something "needed to be done" about the misdirection in which they perceived the Society was headed under Pedro Arrupe.

Don Pedro, as he was affectionately known, asked the Pope for permission to resign in early 1981, but the Pope was not ready and then in May the Pope himself was almost killed by an assassin in St. Peter's Square. But when Father Arrupe suffered a stroke in August 1981 and Father Vincent O'Keefe was appointed vicar general, the Pope moved in to cut this off. He appointed Father Dezza as the papal delegate along with a younger Jesuit Fr. Giuseppe Pittau to assist him in governing the Society of Jesus.

This unprecedented papal intervention shocked Jesuits throughout the world. Suspicions were voiced about the role of Father Dezza, but these quickly dissipated as Jesuits saw how astutely Father Dezza set about mending the break in relationships between the Vatican and the Society. Rather quickly, Father Dezza persuaded the Pope to agree to the convening of a General Congregation (GC) to elect a new general, which, in fact, happened in October 1983, at which time the highly able and remarkably diplomatic Father Peter-Hans Kolvenbach was elected.

By 1995 when the next congregation (GC 34) met, Father Dezza had been made a cardinal by John Paul II and was retired, living in the Jesuit Curia. Father Kolvenbach invited Cardinal Dezza, who was not a delegate himself, to address the Congregation, which he did in grand style. He took as his theme the six previous congregations he had attended (since GC 28 in 1938) and his personal relationships with each of the popes during that time, especially with Paul VI, with whom it was clear he had had a very special relationship.

Paolo Cardinal Dezza died in 1999 and, in a sign of special affection and honor, John Paul II presided at his funeral and gave the homily.

See also Cardinals, Jesuit; John Paul II; Papacy

John Paul II, "Funeral Homily." *L'Osservatore Romano*, December 21, 1999, 171–74.

Patrick J. Howell, SJ

Dictionaries

As the Society of Jesus widened its scope of influence in the centuries after its formation, the humble dictionary became a critical tool of rapprochement with the diverse cultures that the Jesuits encountered. It was difficult, if not impossible, to secure the goodwill – and, ultimately, the souls – of foreign populations without the benefit of a common language, and this is why the Jesuits pioneered some of the earliest and most widespread dictionaries used beyond Europe's borders. By the end of the sixteenth century, the Jesuits were among the most proficient linguists operating in the West, and it was due in no small part to their efforts that Europe was introduced to languages and cultures far from its shores.

Some of the earliest Jesuit dictionaries were created to aid in the Society's missions to the Far East. One of the best known is the *Nippo jisho* (日葡辞書, literally "the

Japanese–Portuguese Dictionary") or, in Portuguese, *Vocabulario da Lingoa de Iapam*, which was first published in Nagasaki in 1603. It is unclear how many Jesuits were involved in its production, though some historians believe that the famous Jesuit linguist and translator João Rodrigues (1558?–1633) played some role in organizing it. Containing more than 32,000 Japanese words rendered into Portuguese, the *Nippo jisho* was intended primarily to teach Europeans how to speak Japanese, meaning that it had to account for such complexities as regional dialects, the different vocabularies employed by the stratified classes and populations in early modern Japan, and words that applied specifically to religions such as Buddhism. Other contemporary dictionaries included the *Dictionarium Latino Lusitanicum, ac Iaponicum*, which appeared in 1595 and combined Latin, Portuguese, and Japanese, and the Portuguese–Japanese *Arte da Lingoa de Iapam* (1604–08). The latter was compiled by João Rodrigues and focused more specifically on Japanese grammar; it remains the oldest extant example of a complete work dedicated to translating the Japanese language.

Later in the seventeenth century, one of the earliest printed Chinese dictionaries to appear in Europe did so as part of the 1670 French edition of Athanasius Kircher's magisterial *China illustrata*. This was probably a descendant of the much earlier manuscript dictionary, which was Portuguese–Chinese, compiled by Matteo Ricci (1552–1610); with a little more than 2,000 entries, it was considerably smaller than the *Nippo jisho*, but it appears to have been the only printed French–Chinese dictionary to appear in Europe for more than a century.

Dictionaries were also a critical part of Jesuit missionary activities among the indigenous peoples of North America. Many of those who first arrived in that part of the world quickly began to fashion simple dictionaries for their own use, and these expanded over time as more individuals became involved in their production. The French Jesuit Pierre-François Pinet (1660–1702) helped to create a dictionary that bridged the French and Miami-Illinois languages around the turn of the eighteenth century. Around the same time, the missionary-linguist Jacques Gravier (1651–1708) compiled what became known as the "Gravier dictionary," a manuscript dictionary of the Algonquin – specifically, Kaskaskia – and French languages. He was aided in this endeavor by several fellow Jesuits, including the French trader and, later, Jesuit brother Jacques Largillier (1644–1714). It is important to note that dictionaries focused on indigenous North American languages were still being produced by Jesuits almost 200 years after the first appearance of the Gravier dictionary. For example, the extensive *Dictionary of the Kalispel or Flathead Indian Language* was printed in Montana between 1877 and 1879, and was produced by a collaboration of missionaries that included the Jesuit fathers Gregory Mengarini (1811–86) and Joseph Giorda (d. 1882).

Dictionaries are not always devoted to translations of words from one language to another. In the restored Society of Jesus, 1814 to the present, many Jesuits have contributed entries to or edited reference works known as dictionaries but more similar in style and structure to encyclopedias. Jesuits have also been the subject of such dictionaries, among them the *Diccionario histórico de la Compañia de Jésus* (4 vols., 2001).

See also Canada; China; Cultures; Encyclopedias; Japan; Native Americans

Kishimoto, Emi, "The Process of Translation in *Dictionarium Latino Lusitanicum, ac Iaponicum.*" *Journal of Asian and African Studies* 72 (2006), 17–26.

McCafferty, Michael, "Jacques Largillier: French Trader, Jesuit Brother, and Jesuit Scribe 'Par Excellence.'" *Journal of the Illinois State Historical Society* 104, 3 (2011), 188–98.

Masini, Federico, "Notes on the First Chinese Dictionary Published in Europe (1670)." *Monumenta Serica* 51 (2003), 283–308.

Moran, J. F., *The Japanese and the Jesuits: Alessandro Valignano in Sixteenth-Century Japan.* London: Routledge, 1993.

Thomason, Sarah, Dorothy Berney, Gail Coelho, Jeffrey Micher, and Daniel Everett, "Montana Salish Root Classes: Evidence from the 19th-Century Jesuit Dictionary." *International Conference on Salish and Neighboring Languages* 29 (1994), 288–312.

Mark A. Waddell

Dictionnaire de Spiritualité (Dictionary of Spirituality)

The *Dictionnaire de spiritualité ascétique et mystique: doctrine et histoire* (DS) was initiated in 1928 by the publisher Gabriel Beauchesne with three Jesuit scholars from Toulouse, France: Joseph de Guibert, SJ, Marcel Viller, SJ, and Ferdinand Cavallera, SJ. It took more than sixty years from the publication of the first volume in 1932 until the dictionary was completed in 1995. Today DS comprises 9,000 entries, 15,100 pages, and seventeen volumes. The dictionary had 1,634 contributors under the direction of Marcel Viller, SJ, the first director, and then of his successors, André Rayez, SJ, André Derville, SJ, Paul Lamarche, SJ, and Aimé Solignac, SJ.

The full title reveals the initial goal and the methodology of the work. In the 1930s it seemed to be merely a review of techniques of prayers and a description of mystical states with the various phenomena which sometimes accompany them. The first volumes were composed of short articles with no real sense of historical development. Those articles have since been reviewed and expanded. However, very soon, the endeavor took on a greater dimension. The intuition was that Christian thinking enclosed in the rather rigid and deductive dogmatic theology of the times needed a new breath. Spirituality, which is founded on both human experience and human freedom at work in the variety of human ways to encounter God, was to provide a renewal for all theological questions. The methodology was then to retrieve rigorously the history of the burgeoning and development of multiple spiritual movements. In doing so, DS prepared for the blossoming of the Second Vatican Council and then incarnated its dynamism. It is an invaluable resource, today available online, for historians of religion and theologians alike.

See also Asceticism and Mysticism; Encyclopedias; Theology

Dictionnaire de spiritualité. Paris: Beauchesne, 1932–1995. www.dictionnairedespiritualite.com.

Grégoire Catta, SJ

Direction, Spiritual

In a Jesuit context spiritual direction refers either to the direction of one or more persons in a retreat based on the *Spiritual Exercises* of Ignatius of Loyola, or to ongoing direction of one or more persons in living a life in response to God's grace. Since the first generation of Jesuits, spiritual direction has been a principal or privileged ministry of the Society of Jesus, though its practice has varied somewhat over time and in different places. In annotation #15 to the *Spiritual Exercises*, Ignatius cautioned the director against interfering in the direct relationship between God and the one doing the *Exercises*. The director is to help the directee stay focused on and in that relationship, and to help him or her sort out which desires come from God and which do not. In annotation #18 the director is instructed to adapt the Exercises to the age and other circumstances of the directee. For Ignatius, the director needed to be an excellent listener, paying careful attention to what the directee says and to how God may be present to and active in that person.

By the late 1500s, with rapid growth in Jesuit numbers and in Jesuit schools and other works, a move toward greater centralization and uniformity in various matters, including how Jesuits taught in schools and how they gave the *Spiritual Exercises*, was underway. Claudio Acquaviva (1543–1615) was Jesuit superior general between 1581 and 1615, a period that included publication of an official "directory" of how to give the *Exercises*. Over time, it became common for the *Exercises* to be preached to large groups, such as novices entering the Society, or to members of Jesuit-sponsored confraternities, rather than individually directed. The *Exercises* were also given to other priests and members of religious orders, the latter including women's communities. Yet individual spiritual direction did not disappear; indeed, it was sometimes even conducted by means of letters between a director and a directee, perhaps over considerable geographic distances. By the seventeenth century, alumni of Jesuit schools included many prominent laymen as well as influential bishops and other clergy. St. Francis de Sales (1567–1622) is a particularly good example of such a person; a graduate of the Jesuit college in Paris, eventually bishop of Geneva, a best-selling author and popular preacher, he was also a spiritual director for individuals, especially elite women.

Both before the Suppression of the Society in 1773 and since its restoration in 1814, large numbers of Jesuits have been known for their work as confessors, that is, as priests hearing confessions in the sacrament of penance. There could at times be considerable overlap between the work of a confessor and the work of a spiritual director, though the two roles are also separable, and one need not be a priest to be a spiritual director. The sacrament of penance has a specific focus on sin and on forgiveness of sin, while the focus in spiritual direction is potentially much broader, that is, on however God may be acting in a person's life and how that person may or may not be responding to God's initiatives. In recent decades, some persons have suggested similarities between spiritual direction and psychotherapy, though the latter usually lacks a reference to a personal relationship with God, the matter, or heart and soul, of spiritual direction.

With Vatican II and the 1960s came a renewed emphasis on the central role of the Bible in Catholic intellectual, liturgical, and spiritual life. From this perspective, the *Spiritual Exercises* were reappropriated as a particular of praying with Scripture, in order to grow in self-knowledge and especially in intimate knowledge of God. A spiritual director could be expected to suggest Scripture passages for a directee not only to read but to savor slowly and repeatedly, and to enter into, through composition of place, an imaginative placing of oneself in the space and place of biblical narratives, and to engage in a personal dialogue or colloquy with Jesus, his mother, and other saints. Vatican II also promoted ecumenical and interreligious dialogue, and with improving relations between Catholics and those of other religious traditions came availability of spiritual direction in the Ignatian/Jesuit tradition to ever-wider contexts beyond that of the Catholic Church.

See also Spiritual Exercises

Barry, William, and William Connolly, *The Practice of Spiritual Direction*. San Francisco, CA: Harper & Row, 1982.

Cusson, Gilles, *Biblical Theology and the Spiritual Exercises*. Trans. Mary Angela Roduit and George Ganss. St. Louis, MO: The Institute of Jesuit Sources, 1988.

Hart, Thomas, *The Art of Christian Listening*. New York: Paulist Press, 1980.

Molina, J. Michelle, "Technologies of the Self: The Letters of Eighteenth-Century Mexican Jesuit Spiritual Daughters." *History of Religions* 47 (2008). 282–303.

Mostaccio, Silvia, *Early Modern Jesuits between Obedience and Conscience during the Generalate of Claudio Acquaviva (1581–1615)*. Trans. Clare Copeland. Farnham: Ashgate, 2014.

Silf, Margaret, *Companions of Christ: Ignatian Spirituality for Everyday Life*. Grand Rapids, MI: Eerdmans, 2005.

Thomas Worcester, SJ

Discernment

Discernment is the exercise of spiritual wisdom to identify what is and is not of God. The practice of Ignatian spirituality involves two overlapping yet distinct kinds of discernment. The first is the discernment of spirits, in which good interior movements are distinguished from those that are not. To guide this practice, Ignatius attached two appendices of "rules" to the end of the *Spiritual Exercises*. The second is the discernment of the will of God in a particular matter, which in the *Exercises* is done through an "election."

In the New Testament, Paul identifies "the discernment of spirits" (*diakrisis pneumatōn*) as among the gifts of the Holy Spirit (1 Corinthians 12:10), and the First Epistle of John instructs its recipients to "test the spirits to see whether they belong to God" (4:1). Hugo Rahner has shown that the practice of discerning spirits can also be traced through the spiritual writings of various patristic and medieval authors, whose insights correspond in many ways with those of Ignatius. Even though the discernment of spirits was not original to Ignatius, his counsels do represent an original synthesis, composed primarily on the basis of his own spiritual experience.

The rules for discernment presume a theological backdrop. Ignatius envisioned both the world and the interior life as places of struggle and conflict, in which both good and evil forces are at play. In keeping with Christian revelation, the *Exercises* present a God who, in infinite wisdom and love, desires to save the human race and to share the fullness of divine life with all humanity. More distinctively, as Karl Rahner illustrated, the *Exercises* also presume that God has a particular, discernible will for each person's life. The aim of discernment is to recognize and cooperate with the Spirit of God as opposed to the evil one, thereby enabling the loving intention of God, for the whole world as for each person, to be realized more and more completely.

In the first set of rules for discerning spirits, Ignatius distinguishes between two kinds of people, those mired in serious sinfulness and those sincerely striving to advance "in the service of God." With the former, he says, the "good spirit" stings the conscience to compel a change of ways, whereas the "evil spirit" goads onward. By contrast, with those advancing spiritually, the good spirit gives encouragement, consolations, and peace, whereas the evil spirit afflicts with discouragement, anxiety, and sadness. As a result, Ignatius insists that one should never make a change in a time of desolation but rather persevere, intensifying one's spiritual efforts. Ignatius also stresses the importance of bringing one's interior life into the light by manifesting it to a director; for the evil spirit, he memorably observes, acts as a "false lover" who requires that an illicit relationship be kept secret.

Discernment, for Ignatius, presupposes faith and prayer. The first set of rules corresponds with the interior movements of the First Week of the *Exercises*, the meditations of which focus upon receiving the mercy of God and advancing toward greater conversion and freedom. The second set of rules is for the Second Week, in which the contemplation of gospel scenes is meant to facilitate an encounter with Jesus and a "Christification" of one's disposition and vision. The rules of the second set are more subtle, cautioning how the evil spirit can "masquerade as an angel of light" and twist what is ostensibly good toward a corrupt end.

One of the principal purposes of the *Spiritual Exercises* is to make an election concerning the will of God for one's life. At the outset, Ignatius explains that such an election is made only between things that are "good or indifferent" in themselves, such as the choice between marriage or religious life. There are three different occasions in which this may be done, listed in descending order of preference. The first entails an especially powerful grace in which God "so moves and attracts the will" that the person is able to elect what has been manifested without even "the possibility of hesitation." In the second, a person traces the course of their affective consolations and desolations to discern where the Spirit is leading. Finally, in the third, a time of calmness and "tranquility," one engages in a more rational deliberation before God, weighing the various aspects of a decision and considering it from diverse perspectives.

See also Election; *Spiritual Exercises*

Barry, William A., "Toward a Theology of Discernment." *The Way Supplement* 64 (1989), 129–40.
Gallagher, Timothy V., *The Discernment of Spirits: An Ignatian Guide for Everyday Living.* New York: Crossroad, 2005.
    Spiritual Consolation: An Ignatian Guide for the Greater Discernment of Spirits. New York: Crossroad, 2007.
Ivens, Michael, *Understanding the Spiritual Exercises.* Leominster: Gracewing, 1998.
Rahner, Hugo, "The Discernment of Spirits." In *Ignatius the Theologian.* Trans. Michael Barry. San Francisco: Ignatius, 1990, pp. 136–80.
Rahner, Karl, "The Logic of Concrete Individual Knowledge in Ignatius Loyola." In *The Dynamic Element in the Church.* Trans. W. J. O'Hara. New York: Herder, 1964, pp. 84–170.
Toner, Jules J., A *Commentary on Saint Ignatius' Rules for the Discernment of Spirits.* St. Louis, MO: The Institute of Jesuit Sources, 1982.

Henry Shea, SJ

Dismissal

Dismissal refers to the separation of a person from membership in the Society of Jesus. Dismissal is effected in different ways according to the grade of membership a person has attained. A novice is usually dismissed by the director of novices. (While the provincial generally receives the faculty to dismiss a novice from the general, it is customary to delegate it to the novice master.) Scholastics who have not been ordained and brothers after first vows but before final vows may be dismissed by the provincial after receiving permission from father general. After final vows and ordination, the process requires more involvement from Rome.

A dismissal may be voluntary (*petens*) when a Jesuit writes a letter seeking to separate from the Society for personal reasons. It may also be initiated by the Order (*non petens*) for failure of a member to live out his vows, for certain serious offenses, or in the case of those not yet ordained or in final vows, if it is judged that an individual will not progress satisfactorily to the goal of becoming a competent and learned Jesuit. After final vows a *"non petens"* dismissal must go through an administrative process in Rome that verifies the grounds for dismissal. For those ordained to the priesthood, this also involves a canonical process to remove him from the clerical state. This would not be done for a *"petens"* dismissal, however, if the priest was to be incardinated into a diocese or other religious institute.

See also Ex-Jesuits; Formation

Manual for Juridical Practice of the Society of Jesus. Rome: Curia of the Society of Jesus, 1997.
Practica quaedam. Rome: Curia of the Society of Jesus, 1997.

Mark A. Lewis, SJ

Dispensations and Privileges

Dispensations and privileges are singular administrative acts requiring executive power of governance; privileges are reserved to those with legislative power; the latter may authorize executive authorities to grant privileges.

In universal law a dispensation is a relaxation of a merely ecclesiastical law (i.e., enacted by an ecclesiastical human legislator in distinction to divine and/or natural law) in a particular case. Dispensations may not be granted from: divine/natural law; procedural and penal law (to protect rights of individuals); constitutive law (that which is necessary for a particular entity to exist, e.g., residence for domicile or consent for marriage); laws whose dispensations are reserved to a specific and/or higher authority (e.g., dispensation from clerical celibacy). Provincials and regional superiors as major superiors may dispense from universal law provided: recourse to the Holy See is difficult; danger of grave harm exists in delay; and the dispensation is one the Holy See usually grants (does not pertain to clerical celibacy).

In Jesuit proper law, the superior general (*praepositus generalis*) may dispense from the *Constitutions* and *Complementary Norms* for individuals, houses, or provinces provided such is according to the mind of the legislator (for liceity; *Complementary Norms*, 19; *Constitutions*, 746–47). For admission, permission of the superior general is necessary for those who: withdrew from the Catholic Church after age of 16; committed voluntary homicide or effectively caused abortion and cooperators in either; lost good reputation; made first profession/incorporation in another institute (religious or secular) or society of apostolic life or as a hermit; converted within three years of intended entrance; reached 50 years of age (for liceity; see *Complementary Norms*, 28, ##1–2; *Constitutions*, 166, 176, 178). These do not bind in doubt of law; in doubt of fact, provincials may dispense from all except voluntary homicide. The superior general has limited dispensing power in reference to the two-year novitiate and third probation. The superior general may grant a dispensation allowing Jesuits to administer temporal goods of non-Jesuits, including relatives (*Complementary Norms*, 166).

Provincials and local superiors, by means of a habitual faculty from the superior general, may dispense individual Jesuits "in minor matters from Rules, Ordinances, Decrees, and even but with greater difficulty from the Constitutions themselves" (*Manuale practicum*, #10 2⁰).

A dispensation is granted for a particular case; once used, it ceases. A privilege is a favor given through a particular act to physical or juridic persons and is presumed perpetual. Appendix IV of *Manuale practicum* is titled *Compendium privilegiorum Societatis Iesu*. These privileges, faculties, and indulgences have been revised in light of the 1983 Code of Canon Law and the 1990 Code of Canons of the Eastern Churches. Footnote 1 explains that the *Compendium*, authorized by the Society's legislative body (the General Congregation), contains privileges which "are useful either for protecting the proper nature of the Society or for making its life and governance more fruitful for the service of the Church, for the good of its members, and the help of souls." The note explains that many previous privileges are now found in universal law or their purpose has been achieved by other means or are no longer appropriate and therefore are no longer in force.

Appendix IV is divided into three sections: A. "Compendium of Privileges of the Society of Jesus"; B. "Faculties for the Help of Souls, Derived from the Privileges of the Society Which Have Been Communicated to It," and C. "Indulgences Granted to the Society of Jesus."

A. "Compendium of Privileges" is subdivided into I. Generic privileges concerning general governance and II. Particular privileges. Particular privileges concern governance and life of the Society and aim to assist either Jesuits or the Christian faithful. The majority of privileges in *Compendium* reflect the Jesuit way of proceeding in governance and its life (e.g., account of conscience or duration of terms of superiors) and are reserved to the superior general, major superiors, and superiors to use.

B. "Faculties for the Help of Souls" are in favor either of Jesuits or of the faithful. These faculties are given to major superiors and/or superiors who in turn may grant these to individual Jesuits who already possess the faculty of hearing confessions from the local ordinary. Grant of a faculty by a major superior ceases on the expiration of his term unless renewed by his successor.

C. "Indulgences" derive from rescripts of the Apostolic Penitentiary which grants a plenary indulgence, all conditions being fulfilled, to the Society as a whole, individual Jesuits, and houses; members of the Apostleship of Prayer; and Jesuit members of the "Congregation for a Good Death."

See also Canon Law; *Constitutions*

The Constitutions of the Society of Jesus and Their Complementary Norms. Ed. John W. Padberg. St. Louis, MO: The Institute of Jesuit Sources, 1996.
Manuale practicum Iuris Societatis Iesu. Rome: Curia Praepositi Generalis, 1997.

Robert J. Kaslyn, SJ

Dominic, St., and Dominicans

In his autobiography, Ignatius of Loyola attributes his own decision to pursue the path of reform to reading the lives of St. Dominic as well as St. Francis. Dominic de Guzman (d. 1221) was a thirteenth-century Spanish reformer and founder of the Dominicans, formally known as the Order of Preachers (OP). That Dominic would go on to form a religious tradition that was similar in many respects to the Franciscan is perhaps somewhat surprising given the very different characters and backgrounds of the two founders. Dominic was a member of the noble Spanish Guzman family, destined for a career in the Church. His biographers describe him as relatively serious, learned, and known for leading a rigorously austere life. He joined the canons regular in 1194, an experience that also informed his later construction of a new model of monastic life.

Dominic was influenced as well by the currents of religious reform then sweeping through the Church from the end of the twelfth century. Population growth, urbanization, and the consolidation of European kingdoms challenged the ability of the existing parochial structure to tend to the pastoral needs of many Catholics, especially in the smaller communities. Catharism was one of a number of heretical traditions that flourished at this time, located in the difficult mountainous regions of southern France.

In 1216 Dominic received permission to start a new order. He had already established himself along with a few companions in the city of Toulouse, the Cathars the focus of their first mission. His new spiritual ideal mingled a traditional notion of monastic *communitas*, one predicated upon the communal fostering of spiritual perfection, with an active pastoral agenda defined by a wandering preaching ministry and a life of poverty.

Similar to Ignatius, Dominic considered education essential for ensuring orthodoxy. The Dominican order produced many important theologians including the most celebrated of all, Thomas Aquinas (d. 1274). The reputation of the Dominicans for learning in canon law as well as theology may well explain why they were a popular resort on the part of the papacy as papal inquisitors throughout the late medieval and early modern periods. Jacob Sprenger and Heinrich Kramer, the authors of the well-known fifteenth-century inquisitorial handbook known as the *Hammer of the Witches*, were both experienced inquisitors and members of the order.

Though canonized a saint in 1234, Dominic never developed the same popular appeal as his contemporary, Francis of Assisi. However, his order proved to be just as durable an institution over time. Within a few years of his death in 1221, the order had established communities across Europe and as far afield as Constantinople and Jerusalem. During the sixteenth century, the Dominicans ventured across the Atlantic with the support of the Spanish and Portuguese regimes.

Ignatius's admiration for Dominic led him to seek guidance from members of the order during his early years as a reformer, though he eventually found his own vision of reform set him at odds with the spirituality of the order. Indeed, the Dominicans appear early on in the history of the Jesuit order as missionary rivals as well as frequent opponents in theological controversy. The debate over grace and free will during the sixteenth century was a particularly bitter and long-running one, pitting the two orders against one another for several decades beginning in the 1580s. The Jesuit theologian Luis de Molina was at the center of this controversy, accused by the Dominicans of espousing an understanding of the operations of grace and free will that contradicted Augustinian thought. Thomistic thought was influenced significantly by Augustinianism. The Dominicans accused the Jesuits in particular of denying the efficacy of grace. The conflict grew sufficiently intense by 1597 to demand the intervention of the papacy. The papacy formed a special commission to investigate. Following successive investigations into the matter and many public theological debates, the papacy in 1607 ordered an end to the disputes and allowed each order to adhere to its own interpretation.

The Chinese Rites Controversy of the seventeenth and eighteenth centuries brought the two orders into conflict with one another once again, this time regarding the observance of Chinese ancestral rites. The Jesuits regarded these as secular and thus compatible with Catholic spirituality, while the Dominicans disagreed. This debate as well carried on for decades, long after the Dominicans came to agree with the Jesuits.

See also Chinese Rites Controversy; Francis of Assisi, St., and the Franciscans; Loyola, Ignatius of, SJ, St.; Theology

Ames, Christine Caldwell, *Righteous Persecutions: Inquisition, Dominicans and Christianity in the Middle Ages*. Philadelphia: University of Pennsylvania Press, 2009.
Cummins, J. S., *A Question of Rites: Friar Domingo Navarrete and the Jesuits in China*. Leicester: Scolar Press, 1993.
Hinnebusch, William, *The History of the Dominican Order*. 2 vols. New York: Alba House, 1973.

Megan C. Armstrong

Dominican Republic

In the Dominican Republic, the pre-Suppression Society of Jesus is probably best remembered for their contribution to lay and priestly education. Their presence began in 1650, primarily with pastoral work, but was transformed in 1701 by a royal decree of Philip V of Spain, the Bourbon king, authorizing them to begin a college in Santo Domingo. This venture led them into the education of laypersons and to the helm of seminary education. They continued this until their expulsion from Santo Domingo in 1767. Their post-Suppression presence has been more widespread and diverse.

In the early twentieth century, Jesuits were occasionally present, often as ministers of the *Spiritual Exercises,* a labor that continues to this day. However, on August 8, 1936, when Father Felipe Gallego took possession of the parish in Dajabón, a northern border town, a new, stable presence of the Society in the Dominican Republic began. Jesuits returned under a contract between the Church and government that linked their pastoral work to President Trujillo's Dominicanization and Hispanization program in border areas. Such cooperation between the Catholic Church and the state in predominantly Catholic countries was common at that time. Sadly, the contract juxtaposed the Society's work with Trujillo's plan, which flowed into the 1937 Parsley Massacre of Haïtians in which Dominican authorities slaughtered anywhere from 9,000 to 20,000 persons.

Despite the unhappy association with Trujillo's project, their work along the border and its extension into other predominantly rural areas was instrumental for integrating agricultural populations into the Catholic Church and Dominican society. Jesuit work in farming communities diversified beyond pastoral activities and spread into non-border areas such as La Vega. The work with farmers included social, organizational, and educational efforts in border areas, La Vega, and later Santiago. This work helped small farmers gain recognition as well as their own voice within Dominican society.

The Society would quickly expand into education. By 1940 the Jesuits began returning to seminary work. In 1946 they took the helm of the Major Seminary, Santo Tomás de Aquino, in Santo Domingo (handing it over to diocesan clergy in 1981). Around 1946 an institute for agricultural education, known today as ITESIL, was started in Dajabón by the government and directed by the Society. Two years later Jesuits joined the faculty of the University of Santo Domingo and soon began developing student organizations there. In 1952, with the help of funding from Trujillo, the Instituto Politécnico Loyola opened its doors and became an important contributor to the development of technical skills. In 1990, "Fe y Alegría" (Faith and Joy), a work that provides a holistic education for marginal populations, was introduced to the Dominican Republic. Although the Society does have a premier school serving primarily the middle and upper classes and has also made notable contributions at the university level, Jesuits have had a longer, stronger history in the education of working and poorer classes in both rural and urban areas of the Dominican Republic.

Over the last few decades, an integrated and sometimes controversial commitment to poor and marginalized populations has marked the Jesuit presence. In Santo Domingo, new approaches to parish work in marginal urban areas were combined with serious social research, social advocacy, and new ways of living inserted within these marginal populations. In 1972, Fathers Tomás Marrero, Benjamín González Buelta, and José Fernández Olmo began their work and life in Guachupita and La Ciénaga, later joined by Father Jorge Cela. The work in these marginal urban settings would inform the work of the Centro Bonó, a center for social research and advocacy. Some of the same Jesuits would both work and live in these neighborhoods as well as contribute to the Centro Bonó and its development.

This commitment to marginalized urban and rural populations has shaped the image of the Society in the Dominican Republic and influenced internal decisions. This is true even though many Jesuits have not participated in this commitment, as the Society maintains a surprising array of apostolic activities. Nonetheless, the selection of novice experiments reflects a preference to be with the poor. The placement of houses of formation in close proximity to marginalized urban areas and the choice of the Centro Bonó for their course of studies also express this commitment. Public advocacy for the rights of Haïtian migrants, through the Jesuit-run Solidaridad Fronteriza and the Centro Bonó, has arisen out of a lived commitment to different marginalized populations. This commitment has informed the recent life of the Society in the Dominican Republic and shaped its public image both inside and outside the country.

See also Caribbean; Fe y Alegría; Haïti

Klaiber, Jeffrey, *The Jesuits in Latin America, 1549–2000: 450 Years of Inculturation, Defense of Human Rights, and Prophetic Witness*. St. Louis, MO: The Institute of Jesuit Sources, 2009.
Sáez, José Luis, *Los Jesuítas en la República Dominicana*. 2 vols. Santo Domingo: Museo Nacional de Historia y Geografía Archivo Histórico de las Antillas. Vol. I: 1988, Vol. II: 1990.

Christopher Llanos, SJ

Dominus ac Redemptor

The papal brief of global Jesuit suppression, *Dominus ac Redemptor*, is dated July 21, 1773. From the moment of his election in 1769 Clement XIV came under enormous pressure from the agents of the Bourbon powers to suppress the Society of Jesus. Matters came to a head after the arrival of the Spanish Ambassador, José Moñino, in Rome in July 1772. Monino can be reasonably identified as the main mover behind *Dominus ac*

Redemptor. It argued that the destruction of the Society was an unfortunate necessity aimed at sustaining the bonds of peace and unity within the Roman Catholic Church. It highlighted previous examples of suppressing religious orders and contained a digest of the supposed dissensions and quarrels provoked by the Jesuits both within their own ranks and between the Society and other orders, the secular clergy, and a host of Catholic rulers. Tellingly, it placed the Suppression in the context of the national attacks on the Society in Portugal, France, and Spain over the previous fourteen years. It did not contain denunciations of supposed flaws in Jesuit morality and theology, much to the disappointment of Charles III of Spain. News of the brief reached the Jesuit Superior General Lorenzo Ricci on August 16, 1773, and in short measure Ricci found himself incarcerated. Catherine the Great of Russia did not allow the brief to be enforced or promulgated within her territories, allowing for an island of Jesuit corporate survival throughout the Suppression era.

See also Catherine II ("the Great") of Russia; Charlies III; Clement XIV; Suppression

Burson, Jeffrey, and Jonathan Wright, eds., *The Jesuit Suppression in Global Context: Causes, Events, and Consequences*. Cambridge: Cambridge University Press, 2015.

Jonathan Wright

Douai

This city in the Spanish Netherlands became a vital center of English Catholicism from the late sixteenth century onward with the establishment there of a college/seminary. After the Elizabethan Protestant religious settlement of 1559, pressure gradually increased on English Catholics to conform to the Church of England. An English priest (and later cardinal), William Allen, realized that if Catholicism was to survive in England, it needed the ministrations of priests. In 1568, therefore, Allen founded an English College at Douai for Catholic exiles, particularly for the training of priests, who, by 1574, began returning to minister to their coreligionists on the English mission. Allen served as president of the English College for its first seventeen years and increasingly shifted its focus from that of a general college to a seminary. In addition, as a friend and advocate of the Jesuits and their spirituality, he introduced the *Spiritual Exercises* as a basic part of the formation of all students. He also joined with the Jesuit Robert Persons in convincing Father General Everard Mercurian to launch the Jesuit mission to England in 1580 in order to reinforce and expand upon the mission of the seminary priests from Douai and elsewhere. Owing to various complications, the English College moved to Rheims in 1578, but it returned to Douai in 1593. Based upon its central role in the training of clergy, Douai became in many ways the seedbed of English Catholicism and leavened it with key insights of Jesuit spirituality. In all, over the course of about two centuries, this "seminary of martyrs" supplied more than a thousand priests for the English-Welsh Catholic mission.

See also United Kingdom

Scully, Robert E., *Into the Lion's Den: The Jesuit Mission in Elizabethan England and Wales, 1580–1603*. St. Louis, MO: The Institute of Jesuit Sources, 2011.

Robert E. Scully, SJ

Drinan, Robert F., SJ (1920–2007)

A New England province Jesuit who served (between 1955 and 1970) as professor and dean of Boston College School of Law, Father Drinan came to national prominence in 1970 when he was elected to the House of Representatives as a Democrat from Massachusetts.

Debates regarding the circumstances of his ascension to and his departure from this public office have generally eclipsed what Drinan actually accomplished while in Congress. Perhaps the most striking event during his decade in office was his July 31, 1973, speech before the House calling for impeachment proceedings against President Richard M. Nixon. The Watergate scandal was, of course, the development that eventually motivated the congressional action that prompted the 1974 resignation of the thirty-seventh president, but Drinan's primary motivation for introducing the first resolution to impeach Nixon was the President's duplicity regarding the illegal bombing raids on Cambodia during a pivotal juncture in the Vietnam War. Drinan's initial campaign to represent the Third District of Massachusetts had focused on the imperative of bringing morality and transparency to US foreign policy, particularly in Southeast Asia.

Although he was often embroiled in public policy debates on civil rights and foreign policy, no issue dogged Drinan more than his public stance on abortion. Although he never challenged Church teachings prohibiting Catholics from procuring elective abortions, he defended civil laws guaranteeing access to abortion. Drinan was not always consistent in explaining his support for abortion rights. His attempts to add nuance to his position often emphasized the drawing of necessary distinctions between what constitutes a sin (within the domain of religious morality) and what should rightly constitute a crime (within the domain of civil law fit for a pluralistic society). The 1973 Supreme Court decision in _Roe_ v. _Wade_ subjected Drinan to heightened scrutiny. The "immoral but not illegal" explanation he cited, like the later "personally opposed but obliged to carry out the law" position invoked by Governor Mario M. Cuomo of New York, has not settled these controversies to the satisfaction of all. Although accused by many Catholics of inconsistency or outright disobedience to Church authority, Father Drinan defended his acquiescence to civil laws permitting abortions as a consequence of the religion clauses of the First Amendment of the US Constitution, which mandate respect for the consciences of all and set implicit limits on the legislation of morality. Many prominent Catholics nevertheless vehemently opposed Father Drinan's positions on the application of prudence regarding the advisability of criminal sanctions against procured abortions. Long after Drinan's term in Congress, jurisprudence has not settled the difficult questions he addressed, such as the limits of religious tolerance and the relationship between civil law and tenets of religious morality.

John Paul II's 1978 ascension to the papacy lent momentum to existing pressure to force Father Drinan to end his tenure in Congress. The calls for Drinan to step down must be seen in the wider context of global Catholicism, which was grappling with neuralgic questions regarding the involvement of ordained priests in partisan politics during an especially turbulent era, when the boundaries of Church and State were being challenged and renegotiated in such places as Poland, Nicaragua, and El Salvador. The text of canon 285 of the 1983 Code of Canon Law (in prohibiting clerics from assuming public offices) may be seen as a legacy of these episodes, although the regulation has been enforced selectively. Eventually, Drinan's Jesuit superiors acquiesced to the wishes of the Holy See and forced Drinan to withdraw from the 1980 election rather than seek a sixth two-year term.

After vacating his seat in the House of Representatives, Drinan spent the remainder of his life as a popular professor at Georgetown University's School of Law.

In his later years, Father Drinan turned his attention to various legal and policy issues regarding the intersection of religious values and public life. In several scholarly volumes, in journalistic writings (particularly for *America* magazine and the *National Catholic Reporter*), in frequent speaking engagements and travels around the globe, Drinan advocated for peace, religious freedom, and social justice. He commented most frequently and eloquently on the struggle for human rights and religious liberty on the international scene, as well as for nuclear disarmament and justice for migrants. Despite the global nature of his advocacy, Drinan will always be remembered primarily for the distinctive role he played in domestic United States politics, as the first Catholic priest elected to Congress, as well as for the controversies into which he fearlessly waded during a turbulent decade in office.

See also Boston College; Georgetown University; John Paul II; United States of America

Drinan, Robert F., *Can God and Caesar Coexist? Balancing Religious Freedom and International Law.* New Haven, CT: Yale University Press, 2004.

Schroth, Raymond A., *Bob Drinan: The Controversial Life of the First Catholic Priest Elected to Congress.* New York: Fordham University Press, 2011.

Thomas Massaro, SJ

D'Souza, Jerome, SJ (1897–1977)

Jerome D'Souza was a Jesuit of the Madurai Jesuit province in South India. He had a distinguished career as a professor of English Literature, an administrator of Jesuit institutions, and a statesman who represented Indian Christians in various national and international arenas. His talent for public speaking won him a natural home in leadership of Loyola College in Madras, and Madras University from the mid-1930s through 1950. Recognized for balanced judgment, he was elected to the Indian Constituent Assembly as a representative of Christians in the years preceding Indian Independence (1947). Thereafter, D'Souza was part of the Indian delegation to the United Nations on four occasions and once to UNESCO. Having the confidence of India's first prime minister, Jawaharlal Nehru, he assisted with the negotiations of the transfer of Pondicherry from France to India in 1954. D'Souza also ably assisted with ecclesiastical negotiations, including Indian diplomatic relations with the Vatican and the Portuguese influence over ecclesiastical appointments within Goa and several smaller western Indian Portuguese territories, until the *Padroado's* final dismantling. From 1951 to 1957, D'Souza was asked to start an institute to study Indian social problems located in Pune. Subsequently, he was appointed rector of a Jesuit house of studies in Kodaikanal. In 1957 Jerome D'Souza was elected by the Madurai Jesuits as a delegate to the 30th General Congregation of the Society of Jesus. During the Congregation he was chosen to become the superior general's assistant for Asia, a position he held for eleven years while also serving as a member of various Vatican congregations and committees to advise on Asian affairs. After returning to India he attempted to write his memoirs, but this was impeded by his declining health. He died on August 12, 1977.

See also India

Sundaram, V. Lawrence, *A Great Indian Jesuit: Fr. Jerome D'Souza: Priest, Educationist and Statesman.* Anand, India: Gujarat Sahitya Prakash, 1986.

Brent Howitt Otto, SJ

Dulles, Avery, Cardinal, SJ (1918–2008)

Avery Dulles, one of the most distinguished and widely published theologians in the post-Vatican II era, entered the Society of Jesus in 1946, was ordained in 1956, received his doctorate in theology from the Gregorian University in 1960, and was created a cardinal in 2001.

Dulles was born into a prominent family of American Presbyterian pastors, theologians, lawyers, and politicians. His Wall Street lawyer father, John Foster Dulles, paternal uncle Allen, and aunt Eleanor became prominent members of the Dwight David Eisenhower administration in the 1950s, serving respectively as secretary of state, head of the Central Intelligence Agency, and member of the postwar Department of State.

Because of the family's moderate wealth, Dulles received an excellent early education in Europe and the United States. He attended Choate, a prestigious private school for wealthy and upwardly bound students, where John Fitzgerald Kennedy was one of his contemporaries. After Choate he matriculated at Harvard College, where he became interested in history, art, and philosophy. During his senior year (1939–40), he wrote a Phi Beta Kappa award-winning undergraduate thesis on the medieval philosopher and theologian Giovanni Pico della Mirandola (1463–94), which was published by Harvard University Press as *Princeps Concordiae* (1941).

In the fall of 1940, he entered Harvard Law School, intending to follow in his father's footsteps. His academic interests since his sophomore year at Harvard, though, were in history, philosophy, and religion. With respect to religion, he acknowledged that before his sophomore year he had little interest in things religious, declaring himself to be an agnostic or practical atheist. Once he came into contact with the classical Greek and medieval philosophical tradition, however, he began to seek out for himself a view of life that transcended his previous purely secular or materialistic concerns. He also began to visit churches in the Boston area and eventually became attracted to the Catholic Church because he found in it remnants of what he had been studying in his history and medieval philosophy classes and in his extracurricular reading of some contemporary neo-scholastics and theologians like Karl Adam.

During his 1940 fall term at Harvard, Dulles decided to become a Catholic, took instructions, and was conditionally baptized. He also began associating with other Catholic students in the Boston area and together with some of them helped to establish, in the fall of 1941, St. Benedict Center, a place where Catholic students in the area could come for conversation and for Catholic books, provided by the Center.

In 1941, as the rumblings of war were increasing and as the United States edged closer to war, Dulles signed up for the United States Naval Reserve. After Japan bombed Pearl Harbor in December 1941, he was called into the Navy, and became a naval intelligence officer, serving in the Atlantic, Caribbean, and Mediterranean campaigns until the spring of 1945. During those war years, he began to consider a religious vocation to the Jesuits and wrote an account of his conversion, which was published as *A Testimonial to Grace* (1946).

In October of 1945, as the war was coming to an end, Dulles contracted polio, was hospitalized for four months, and then returned to St. Benedict Center in Boston. He spent seven months in Boston and applied for admittance into the Jesuits. Admitted in August, he began his two-year novitiate, and then entered Woodstock College in Maryland for philosophy (1948–51), taught philosophy as a scholastic at Fordham University (1951–53), and returned to Woodstock for his theological education (1953–57). He spent his tertianship in Münster, Germany (1957–58), and thereafter was sent to the Gregorian University (1958–60) where he defended his doctoral dissertation, "The Protestant Churches and the Prophetic Office" (1960).

Dulles returned to the United States in 1960 and began a long and productive career as a theologian and theological consultant to the American bishops and to local and national ecumenical meetings. His foundational ministry, though, was in teaching and research, preparing Jesuit scholastics in theology at Woodstock College (1960–70 in Maryland; 1970–74 in New York City), and clerical and lay theologians at the Catholic University of America (1974–88). After retirement from the Catholic University, Dulles taught Jesuit scholastics as well as lay theologians at Fordham University (1988–2008). During these years he also became a visiting professor of theology at various universities: e.g., Boston College (1981–82), Notre Dame (1985), the Gregorian University (1990, 1993), North American College at Louvain (1992), Yale University (1996). He also lectured widely to priests, university students, and Catholic laity at various gatherings around the country, in Africa, and at various European institutions of higher learning.

Dulles's theological research and teaching led to multiple published works, many of which were influential not only in the United States but in other countries where they have been translated. By the time of his death, he had published over 800 articles, chapters, book reviews, and twenty-five books.

Dulles contributed to theology primarily in the areas of fundamental theology, ecclesiology, and ecumenism. Before and during the Second Vatican Council, he taught courses in fundamental theology and published on apologetics and the relationship between revelation and faith and doctrine. After the Council and the death of Woodstock's Gustave Weigel, SJ (1964), Dulles also taught courses on ecclesiology and began publishing in that area.

Dulles's early research on faith, revelation, and doctrine culminated in his *Survival of Dogma* (1971). He argued for the survival of a new or reformulated concept of dogma, one that was ecumenically sensitive and met contemporary needs in an increasingly secular world. The post-Tridentine, and especially neo-scholastic, manuals understood dogma in non-historical, juridical, absolutist, authoritarian, and intellectualist categories. That neo-scholastic approach, which had nearly identified dogma with revelation, presented a propositional view of truth that made dogma itself absolute, immutable, and irreformable and produced among some contemporary laity and theologians either a servile conformism or a defiant rebellion. Dulles's *Survival* reinterpreted Catholic notions of revelation and dogma in the developmental, interpersonal, and symbolic categories of theologians in the Transcendental and *nouvelle théologie* tradition at Vatican II. Although Dulles modified and reinterpreted older conceptions of dogma, he did not relativize dogmatic statements completely. They were indeed derivative and relative to revelation, but they provided a stable and permanent reflection of divine revelation that demanded fidelity. What was irreformable in them was their truth and meaning, while the conceptual terminology in which they were cast historically was subject to modification and reformulation. *Survival* reinforced Dulles's favorable reputation among the post-conciliar progressive theologians in the United States and drew criticisms from more traditionalist theologians who charged that he relativized notions of revelation and dogma.

Ecclesiology, the second area of his most significant theological contributions, had been one of Dulles's major interests since his conversion. He began to develop his approach to the theology of the Church once he started teaching courses on ecclesiology at Woodstock College. His several lectures and publications on the subject during the 1960s culminated in his most widely distributed and commercially successful theological monograph, *Models of the Church* (1974, expanded and revised editions 1987, 2002).

In *Models* he developed his typological approach to theology, which he used in several subsequent books and articles. *Models* intended to underline the mystery of the Church by showing the benefits and limits of five predominant twentieth-century Catholic and Protestant theological constructions of the Church (as institution, as mystical communion, as sacrament, as herald, and as servant). It was obvious in the text that Dulles preferred the sacramental model, but not without combining it with the benefits offered by the other four. Combined, those five models demonstrated something of the multifaceted nature and mission of the Church. No single model could capture the meaning of the mystery. Human language and theological constructs by their nature were limited, and therefore keeping the constructs in a kind of dialectic tension with one another would best serve theology and the mystery it tried to unveil.

Survival and *Models*, during the early period of Dulles's theological development, acknowledged and supported a theological pluralism that he hoped would heal and unify a Church and theological community in the United States divided over a host of ecclesiastical reforms and theological issues. The texts were well received in the United States and other English-speaking countries, and *Models* became a standard text for courses in ecclesiology. *Models* firmly established Dulles's reputation and prominence in the theological community, and shortly after its publication he was elected president (1975–76) of the Catholic Theological Society of America (CTSA) and president (1978–79) of the primarily Protestant American Theological Society.

For more than a decade after *Survival* and *Models*, Dulles continued to work on and publish his notions of faith and revelation, culminating in what is perhaps his most significant contribution to fundamental theology, *Models of Revelation* (1983). For him, the document on revelation at Vatican II was central to all that transpired at the Council, and understanding revelation was key to understanding what Vatican II had done. *Revelation* was a *tour de force* in analytical and constructive theology. After describing five models (i.e., the propositional, historical, mystical, dialectical, and new awareness) of revelation in twentieth-century Protestant and Catholic theologies (all of which he interpreted as symbolic forms of communication), Dulles constructed his own view of revelation as "symbolic mediation." He maintained that an understanding of revelation itself as symbolic mediation was the way to bring together into a symbolic whole the limited perspective of each of the five models. His models approach in this text, however, did not intend to justify a legitimate pluralism in theology (a position he had previously argued in ecclesiology) as much as it sought to transcend the polarities that existed in competing positions and bring them into a theological synthesis. That synthesis (symbolic mediation) was a constructive and coherent theology not identified with any one of the models he described. Dulles's understanding of revelation as symbolic mediation became foundational for various theological and pastoral proposals he periodically made: e.g., in evangelization, catechesis, apologetics, ecumenism, and social justice.

Dulles's research in fundamental theology continued for another decade after *Revelation*, coming to fruition in a treatise on the theology of Christian faith, *The Assurance of Things Hoped For* (1994), which provided US students of theology and professional theologians with the first major theology of faith to be published in English. Later he made his theology of faith available to a more general reading audience in *The New World of Faith* (2000). The inherent connection between revelation and faith had been one of Dulles's personal and research interests since the days of his own conversion to Catholicism. Revelation, mediated symbolically, evoked Christian faith. "Without a prior revelation on God's part," Dulles argued, "faith would be impossible, for it would have no basis and no object. And without faith, the whole edifice of Christian existence would collapse."

Assurance outlined the biblical and traditional notions of faith, compared and contrasted various models of faith, and offered Dulles's own constructive theology of faith in dialogue with the tradition and other contemporary theologies of faith. He presented the act of faith as assent, trust, and obedience and emphasized the harmony of the objective and subjective dimensions. Although he stressed the interior light of faith, as did many contemporary theologians, he did not see faith itself as a kind of subjective or transcendental revelation, as Dulles thought Karl Rahner and some of his followers tended to do.

Dulles's third most significant contribution to theology was in the area of ecumenism. He made his mark on ecumenism through his teaching, scholarship, and participation in ecumenical events. He taught classical and contemporary Protestant theology in his classes, served on diocesan ecumenical commissions, and attended and gave papers at various local, national, and international ecumenical meetings, but his most important and sustained contribution to ecumenism took place in the Lutheran–Catholic dialogue (1971–96). During those twenty-five years, he presented a number of theological position papers and collaborated with Lutheran and Catholic theologians and bishops in publishing five major consensus statements on various doctrinal issues that divided the churches: Papal Primacy and the Universal Church (1974); Teaching Authority and Infallibility (1978); Justification (1983); One Mediator, the Saints and Mary (1990); Scripture and Tradition (1992). These five statements indicated where Lutherans and Catholics were in agreement, where there were acceptable differences in theological expression that were not church-dividing, and where there continued to be unresolved differences. Overall these conversations aimed at convergence.

After the Lutheran–Catholic dialogues, Dulles participated in an informal dialogue with theologians and Church leaders in the American Evangelical Protestant tradition, hoping to create an atmosphere of trust that would eventually overcome long-lasting hostilities. The new adventure in ecumenism had a much narrower focus than had the Lutheran–Catholic convergence-style ecumenism. After 1996 he argued for what he called a mutual-witness or confessional approach to ecumenism. As an ecumenist throughout his theological career, Dulles was a pluralist with respect to accepting theological differences and doctrinal formulations, a gradualist with respect to moving churches toward the unity Christ desired, and a pragmatic realist with respect to what could be accomplished in the present, given the long separation and suspicions that had developed over time.

Dulles was a post-Vatican II theologian who saw himself as a theological representative of the Council's major objectives and trajectories. While theologians in the post-conciliar era might be able to agree on Vatican II principles, they were not in universal agreement on interpreting the Council. Dulles opposed what he considered a hermeneutic of discontinuity, one that interpreted the Council in terms of its innovations without considering the large continuities between Vatican II and previous councils. Before and after the 1985 International Synod of Bishops, Dulles stood on the side of Cardinal Ratzinger and others who articulated a hermeneutic of continuity.

In the late 1960s and early 1970s, Dulles's critics tagged him a liberal Catholic or a theological relativist because of his emphasis on the historically conditioned nature of all theological and doctrinal language and because of his support for theological rein-terpretation and reformulation of the Catholic tradition. In the late 1970s and early 1980s and beyond, different critics interpreted him as a conservative or even reaction-ary Catholic because of his criticisms of certain theological revisionists and dissenters and his support for the papacy and positions of Pope John Paul II and Cardinal Joseph Ratzinger. His theology, however, fits into neither of these caricatures of his position in the theological community.

Dulles, like his critics, used the categories of liberal (or progressive) and conservative to characterize different post-conciliar theological positions in the Church, categori-zations that had in fact emerged during the Council itself. In *The Resilient Church* (1977), Dulles differentiated his own theological stance from that of both conservatives and liberals in respect to the Church's and the theologian's adaptations to modernity. Unlike conservatives, who saw adaptation as a capitulation to the world, he believed that adaptation was necessary and made the Church and theology more effective in commu-nicating the message of the Gospel. Unlike liberals, he believed that the Church and theology should avoid adapting to the fashions of a non-believing world and have the courage to proclaim the gospel message when it differed from prevailing values in soci-ety. One needed to adapt in order to be effective, but one needed to resist in order to be true to the hard sayings of Christ and the Gospel. Dulles placed himself in between the two major post-conciliar traditions, neither of which he fully accepted.

The liberal-conservative categories are not very helpful in locating Dulles theolog-ically because they are so tied to political positions in American society and generally reflect the so-called "cultural wars" of the period. More appropriate for placing Dulles's theology is the category of postcritical or postmodern. Dulles was a postcritical theolo-gian in the sense that he accepted the benefits of the critical enterprise in theology since the Enlightenment (with respect to the application of criticism to the canonical sources of theology), but he asserted that the philosophical and epistemological presuppositions of the critical enterprise needed extensive critique. A postcritical theology, which he shared with other contemporary theologians such as the Lutheran George Lindbeck and Hans Urs von Balthasar, to name two, began with the presupposition of faith, not doubt (as the critical enterprise had done), a hermeneutic of trust in the sources, and ended with a systematic, constructive articulation of the Church's life of faith. Such a theolog-ical enterprise arose from the theologian's dwelling within the Church, appropriating its living faith, and articulating it in a way that was intelligible to modern thinkers and believers. In this view, the theologian was accountable to the sense of the faithful, the creeds, the tradition, the liturgy, the Scripture, and the magisterium.

In 2001, Pope John Paul II named Dulles a cardinal in recognition of his theological work and contributions to the Church. For the next seven years, he continued to publish theological works, particularly in the area of the new evangelization. Although at the time of his death his influence in the American Catholic theological community was waning, his reputation in the public press remained high. His lasting legacy, though, continued to be in the area of fundamental theology, where he published his most perceptive studies.

See also Cardinals, Jesuit; Ecclesiology; Fundamental Theology; Theology; United States of America

Carey, Patrick W., *Avery Cardinal Dulles, SJ: A Model Theologian.* Mahwah, NJ: Paulist Press, 2010.

Kirmse, Anne-Marie, and Michael M. Canaris, eds., *The Legacy of Avery Cardinal Dulles, SJ: His Words and His Witness.* New York: Fordham University Press, 2011.

McDermott, John M., and John Gavin, eds., *Pope John Paul II on the Body: Human, Eucharistic, Ecclesial: Festschrift Avery Cardinal Dulles, SJ.* Philadelphia, PA: Saint Joseph University Press, 2007.

Merrigan, Terrence, "Models in the Theology of Avery Dulles: A Critical Analysis." *Bijdragen, tijdschrift voor filosofie en theologie* 54 (1993), 141–61.

"The Theological Contribution of Avery Cardinal Dulles, SJ." *Chicago Studies* 47, 2 (Summer 2008), 129–254.

Patrick W. Carey

Dupuis, Jacques, SJ (1923–2004)

Jacques Dupuis published a trilogy in English, French, Italian, Spanish, and other languages, through which his theological contribution will endure: *Jesus Christ at The Encounter of World Religions* (1991), *Who Do You Say I Am? An Introduction to Christology* (1994), and *Toward a Christian Theology of Religious Pluralism* (1997). After the Congregation for the Doctrine of the Faith (CDF) investigated the third volume, Dupuis remains even better known and appreciated around the world.

The son of a Belgian engineer, Dupuis was born into a devoutly Catholic family. After German forces occupied Belgium, he continued his studies at a Jesuit High School in Charleroi and joined the Society of Jesus in 1941. He completed a licentiate in letters (Namur) and a licentiate in philosophy (Louvain) before being sent to India in 1948. He spent over thirty years in India, and until his death remained a member of the Calcutta Jesuit province. At his eightieth birthday, he recalled his time in India: "My exposure to the Indian reality has been the greatest grace I have received from God as far as my vocation as a theologian and a professor is concerned."

Before priestly ordination, Dupuis studied theology at St. Mary's College, Kurseong (near Darjeeling). He was sent for further studies in Rome and, under the direction of Antonio Orbe, secured his doctorate at the Gregorian University with a thesis on Origen. He returned to India to teach theology in Kurseong and then in New Delhi, when the theology faculty moved there in 1971.

Dupuis served as assistant editor of *The Clergy Monthly* (renamed *Vidyajyoti Journal of Theological Reflection* in 1974) from 1973 to 1977 and as editor from 1977 to 1984. He became an assiduous reviewer of theological works. From 1960 until his death in 2004, he published 562 reviews of books. Dupuis was a theological adviser to the Catholic Bishops' Conference of India (CBCI) and the Federation of Asian Bishops' Conferences (FABC). In 1973 Josef Neuner and Dupuis edited *The Christian Faith in the Doctrinal Documents of the Catholic Church*. From the first edition of 711 pages, it grew to 1,135 pages in the seventh edition of 2001.

In 1984 Dupuis was called to the Gregorian University, and a year later he became the editor of *Gregorianum*. He made the quarterly once again a means for implementing Vatican II. An effective director of doctoral dissertations, he also proved a first-rate teacher in the licentiate program. His classes on Christology and the theology of religions regularly drew over 200 students. He was a consultor for the Pontifical Council for Interreligious Dialogue and a major author of their 1991 document, jointly issued with the Congregation for the Evangelization of Peoples, *Dialogue and Proclamation*. As an interpreter he attended four bishops' synods in Rome (1974, 1983, 1985, and 1987). At the 1974 synod (on "The Evangelization of the Modern World"), Dupuis worked closely with one of the two secretaries of the synod and with Archbishop Angelo Fernandes (of Delhi), preparing what the Archbishop said at a challenging press conference.

Dupuis's *Toward a Christian Theology of Religious Pluralism* was evaluated in over a hundred reviews, as well as in book chapters and articles in major journals. The book brought many invitations to lecture in Europe, Asia, and North America. It addressed major questions: How can one profess faith in Jesus Christ as the Savior of all humankind and at the same time acknowledge the Holy Spirit to be present and active in religions and cultures everywhere? What role do the world's religions play as paths to salvation? A subsequent work, *Christianity and the Religions* (2001), clarified further some of Dupuis's positions (e.g., on the asymmetrical complementarity between Christianity and other religions) and introduced the expression "inclusive pluralism" to sum up his theology of religions.

In late 1998 the CDF sent Dupuis a nine-page document challenging his terminology (e.g., his use of "decisive" rather than "definitive" to describe the revelation and redemption effected by Christ) and accusing him of false views (e.g., by distinguishing between the eternal Word of God and Jesus of Nazareth). Yet the CDF could not quote passages in *Toward a Christian Theology of Religious Pluralism* that were incompatible with Christian faith. On February 27, 2001, the CDF published a "Notification" that simply said that the book contained "notable ambiguities and difficulties on important points, which could lead a reader to erroneous or harmful positions." But no specific pages were cited, and Dupuis was not even asked to change a single line in the book.

Dupuis found the whole affair wounding. His book remains a classic, post-Vatican II reappraisal of "other" religious traditions. He died of a cerebral haemorrhage in Rome on December 28, 2004, and was buried in the Jesuit mausoleum in the Campo Verrano.

See also India; Interreligious Dialogue; Theology

Burrows, William R., *Jacques Dupuis Faces the Inquisition*. Eugene, OR: Pickwick Publications, 2012.
Kendall, Daniel and Gerald O'Collins, eds., *In Many and Diverse Ways: In Honor of Jacques Dupuis*. Maryknoll, NY: Orbis, 2003.
O'Collins, Gerald, *Living Vatican II*. Mahwah, NJ: Paulist Press, 2006, pp. 173–201.
    On the Left Bank of the Tiber. Ballarat: Connor Court, 2013, pp. 213–51.

Gerald O'Collins, SJ

East Asian Pastoral Institute (EAPI)

The East Asian Pastoral Institute (EAPI), an international training institute of the Jesuit Conference of Asia Pacific located at Ateneo de Manila University, offers programs in continuing pastoral formation. From its inception in the early 1950s, it became the pioneer pastoral center in Asia where lay, religious, and ordained ministers expanded their theological horizons and grew in faith together. Its subsequent development provides an excellent view of the impact of the Second Vatican Council in Asia.

After World War II, Christian churches became increasingly aware of the fundamental changes in Asia and the concomitant need for the training of those missioned there. Among Jesuits expelled during the 1949 Chinese Revolution, Johannes Hofinger came to Manila and, in 1953, set up the Institute of Mission Apologetics that became the EAPI in 1961. With few resources and personnel, this institute conducted seminars based on Josef Andreas Jungmann's groundbreaking "kerygmatic theology" and published much-needed catechetical and liturgical materials. It became known for study weeks held in Eichstadt, Medellin, and elsewhere.

Jesuit superiors recognized its strategic influence and worked for its institutionalization. Through the negotiations of the Philippine provincial Horacio de la Costa and the Ateneo administration, EAPI was approved as an interprovincial ministry of the Jesuit East Asian Assistancy by Superior General Pedro Arrupe and given its site at the university. Alfonso Nebreda of the Japanese province was soon appointed director.

In September 1966, EAPI opened its seven-month renewal program. Though influenced by Lumen Vitae (Belgium) and Loyola University (Chicago), the defining spirit behind its studies program and community structure came from the then-ongoing Second Vatican Council's openness to modern culture and rediscovery of spiritual foundations. Courses and workshops focused on new pastoral themes of conciliar theology, among them inculturation and human development. The residential staff and visiting faculty of Jesuit, religious, and lay were drawn from institutions in many different countries. Participants with rich pastoral experience from Asia and beyond incorporated local symbols and rituals in community liturgies and deepened their faith through spiritual direction and counseling. This program of integrating faith and life helped prepare pastoral leaders for the Church's mission in modern Asia.

With the success of its programs, EAPI's reputation and ministry grew. Local churches not only sent their representatives for the renewal program but also requested special training for their pastoral teams, at times including bishops. EAPI staff and faculty conducted workshops throughout the region that often led to the establishment of local pastoral institutes. The *East Asian Pastoral Review* published seminal essays on theological issues faced by local churches by leading theologians such as Aloysius Pieris and Michael Amaladoss.

EAPI's character as an inclusive and intercultural faith community remains central to its pedagogy. Participants from different countries in Asia and the Pacific are divided into cross-cultural and regional/national groups which provide opportunities and structures for cross-cultural learning and community life. They engage each other in theological reflection and common worship in these groups.

From the late 1980s, further developments in Church and society called for corresponding changes in the program's content and organization. Since many participants come with some familiarity with Vatican II documents and theology, courses now included insights from the Federation of Asian Bishops' Conferences, especially their focus on the triple dialogue with cultures, religions, and the poor. Integrity of creation as well as issues concerning women and those marginalized by global forces have become central concerns. Moreover, because pastoral leaders need requisite skills in addition to theological renewal, shorter programs in leadership and management have been organized for those in the field especially the laity. Sabbaticals could be tailored to address individual needs for spiritual growth, theological updating, and personal research.

The institute's outreach program has been reinvigorated since the late 1990s. Participants from developing churches in Asia such as Vietnam, Myanmar, China, and Timor Leste have been given priority. Aside from the annual homecoming at the institute, EAPI maintains regular contact with alumni and elicits suggestions regarding emerging concerns. The staff and faculty offer consultancies and special workshops to various local churches.

EAPI continues to address the need for ongoing pastoral formation in the Asia Pacific. The continuing development of its programs and activities reflects the dynamic encounter between the post-Vatican II Church and the contemporary world. Its lasting legacy remains in the life and ministry of its countless alumni in diverse and challenging contexts.

See also Asia; Ateneo de Manila; Philippines

Calle, José María, "Remembering Some Highlights of the First Ten Years of EAPI." *East Asian Pastoral Review* 46, 2 (2009), 182–200.
King, Geoffrey, "EAPI at Twenty-Five: Evaluation, Mission Statement, Future Plans." *East Asian Pastoral Review* 28, 2 (1991), 175–88.
Leger, Arthur, "The East Asian Pastoral Institute: From Missionary Apologetics to Mission." *East Asian Pastoral Review* 50, 4 (2014), 324–36.
Nebreda, Alfonso, M., "The Beginnings of the EAPI: Reminiscing." *East Asian Pastoral Review* 24, 1 (1987), 4–20.

Jose Mario C. Francisco, SJ

Eastern Catholic Churches

The Eastern Catholic Churches are Eastern Churches that have retained their own non-Latin liturgy, theology, spirituality, calendar, hierarchy, and canon law but are in communion with the See of Rome and therefore are part of the Catholic Communion of Churches. Most of these Churches were part of the Orthodox Church, the Oriental Orthodox Church, and the Church of the East, whose communion with the See of Rome was broken between the Council of Ephesus (431) and the mutual excommunications of 1054. The two notable exceptions are the Maronite Church, whose communion with the Holy See was never formally broken, and the Italo-Greek Church of southern Italy.

One of the Society of Jesus's first projects among Eastern Christians was the attempt to unite the Ethiopian Orthodox Church to the Catholic Church in 1555. St. Ignatius of Loyola sent a group of Portuguese Jesuits to carry out this project, which did not succeed. The Jesuits were expelled from Ethopia in 1632.

Also in 1555, Maronite Patriach Mussa-el-Akkari sent a letter to Ignatius, asking the Jesuits to establish a seminary for the Maronites in Lebanon. The proposal was seriously studied but considered, in the words of J. Polanco, to be "beyond our capacities." The first Jesuits to go to Lebanon, Tommaso Raggio and Giovanni Eliano, arrived in 1578. Jesuits were involved in the Chaldean Catholic Church soon after its establishment in 1553. The Society was involved in the reception into the Catholic Church of the Antiochene Christians who formed the Syriac Catholic Church in the late seventeenth century. In a similar way, Jesuits were present in Syria and helped lay the groundwork for the reception of Melkites into the Church and the creation of the Melkite Greek Catholic Church in the eighteenth century.

In central Europe, Jesuits were deeply involved in the union of Eastern Christians, creating Eastern Catholic churches in Ukraine, Podkarpatska Rus' (the Ruthenian Church), and Romania.

Jesuits contributed to the preparations for the Union of Brest-Litovsk, which gave rise to the Ukrainian Greek Catholic Church in 1595. A. Possevino and P. Skarga argued forcefully in favor of the union in their writings, but they took no part in the actual negotiations of the union.

Jesuits from Hungary and other regions prepared for and helped effectuate the Union of Uzhhorod in 1655, which created the Ruthenian Catholic Church. The Society established new schools and seminaries and taught in them. Many among the Ruthenian clergy, including a number of its early bishops, were educated at the Jesuit seminary in Nagyszombat, Hungary (now Trnava, Slovakia). A printing press at the seminary produced some of the first catecheses for the Ruthenian Church. Another important institution was the college established in Uzhhorod. The Eastern monks of the various monasteries in the region joined to form the Basilian Fathers. From the late nineteenth century into the early twentieth, Jesuits assisted in the reform and formation of the Basilians in the Ruthenian Church.

Very early on, Jesuits were involved in the education of Eastern Catholics, first at residential colleges in Rome – the Greek College from 1567, the Illyrian and Germano-Hungarian colleges in 1580, and the Maronite and Armenian colleges in 1584. In the original countries of Eastern Catholics, Jesuits worked in many educational institutions, particularly in the Near East and central Europe. One of the premier Jesuit institutions for the education of Eastern Catholics has been St. Joseph University in Beirut (1875). In 1917 the Pontifical Oriental Institute was founded in Rome and placed under the direction of the Society of Jesus in 1922.

Jesuits' research and study of Eastern Christian theology contributed initially to the foundation of several Eastern Catholic churches from the late sixteenth into the eighteenth centuries. In addition, Jesuits were deeply involved in the controversies with non-Catholic Easterners (e.g., R. Bellarmine, A. Possevino, P. Skarga). Certainly from the twentieth century and into the twenty-first, most Jesuit theological writing on Eastern Catholicism has had a distinctly ecumenical tone (e.g., H. de Lubac, J. Daniélou). Jesuits largely began the development of the branch of theology considered Eastern Christian spirituality, particularly Irenée Hausherr and Tomáš Špidlík.

In the pre-Suppression Society, some studies on Eastern liturgies were polemical, attempting to demonstrate the superiority of the Latin liturgy. Others were genuine exploratory studies. Since the restoration, most of the Society's work on Eastern liturgical studies has had an overwhelmingly scholarly approach. The work of the Bollandists in Belgium, particularly on the Eastern calendars, has made a dramatic contribution. Far and away, the greatest Jesuit contribution to Eastern liturgiology has been the work of the professors of the Pontifical Oriental Institute in Rome, especially J. Mateos,

M. Arranz, and R. Taft. In addition, a number of Jesuits, either originally from Eastern Catholic churches or having become involved in them later, have served these churches by celebrating the Eastern liturgies in a pastoral setting, such as at the Russian Catholic Church of St. Anthony the Abbot on the Esquiline.

See also Eastern Europe; Ecumenism; Pontifical Oriental Institute; Tomáš Špidlík, SJ

Roberson, Ronald G., *The Eastern Christian Churches*. Piscataway, NJ: Gorgias Press, 2007.
Suttner, Ernst C., "Die Jesuiten und der christlichen Osten." *Stimmen der Zeit* 209 (1991), 461–76.

Steven Hawkes-Teeples, SJ

Eastern Europe

The earliest history of the Society in this region is connected with the activities of Peter Canisius, who in 1556 was present at a conference between Protestants and Catholics that witnessed a turning point in the struggle to reassert Catholic dominance of the kingdom of Bohemia. Other Jesuits soon began apostolic work in Bohemia, and a university (teaching only theology) was founded in Olomouc, Moravia, in 1573. Following his novitiate in Brno, Moravia, Edmund Campion spent six years in Prague, where he taught rhetoric and philosophy. The Jesuit presence in Prague grew to be a major factor in the direction of the university and became the single most important cultural force in Bohemia from 1620 on until the second half of the eighteenth century, an influence reaching from astronomy to music and producing some of the landmarks of Bohemian Baroque architecture. Jan Drachovský produced a Czech grammar as early as 1644 and the historian Bohuslav Balbín (1621–88) was a strong advocate for the use of "Slavic" in Communion (if perhaps not in the Mass itself). Natural scientists such as astronomer Joseph Stepling (1716–78) and historians such as Ignac Cornova (1740–1822) flourished during the eighteenth century, while the Society operated a huge complex of buildings in Prague, the Klementinum, a division of Prague University which housed educational and apostolic activities.

Connections between pre-Suppression Jesuit professors and leading lights of the late eighteenth- and early nineteenth-century Czech National Awakening were complex: many former Jesuits, such as Josef Dobrovský (1753–1829), mentored intellectuals whose influence extended well into the nineteenth century. However, the Society's reputation suffered among many nineteenth- and early twentieth-century Czech nationalists who came to see the Society as an ally of the Habsburgs and the fosterer of a "time of darkness" that descended over the kingdom after 1620. At the time of the Suppression, the Society operated numerous schools and was a major landowner in the territories of the Bohemian Crown, and although Jesuits did not regain these properties after 1814, they did establish schools in Prague and Šejnov-Bohosudov. Following World War I a Czechoslovak vice-province was established, which became a province in 1928 and survived until the establishment of a communist government. With the collapse of Communism, the Society resumed many of its activities, and Jesuits now have returned to several of the churches with which they were historically associated, including the Church of Saints Peter and Paul in Brno.

In Hungary, the first Jesuit, Juan Vitoria arrived in 1553 at the invitation of Nicholas Oláh, archbishop of Esztergom. The university founded in Trnava (now Slovakia) in 1635 became one of the leading cultural centers of central Europe and the forerunner of

Eötvös Loránd University in Budapest. During the Ottoman occupation Jesuit missionaries, sometimes incognito, served the Catholic population of the Danube Basin, and a permanent mission was established in Pécs in 1612. Along with the propagation of a "Danubian" version of Baroque architecture, the influence of Georgius Káldi's translation of the Bible (1626), the literary models of Peter Pázmány (1570–1637), and the development of modern Hungarian historiography, perhaps the Society's most important contribution to Hungarian culture was the thousands of school plays and other performances produced. In the nineteenth century the Hungarian Society produced a series of distinguished astronomers, while focusing its educational efforts on secondary schools. The twentieth century brought widely varying fortunes to the Society. The Hungarian province was separated from the Austrian in 1909, and Hungarian Jesuits served in Chinese missions until 1949. Post-1989 Hungary saw the return of Jesuit secondary schools and the reopening of the Jesuit church in Budapest.

In the territories now making up Romania, Jesuits were active by the middle of the seventeenth century, opening a school in Iaşi and tutoring the sons of boyars in Bucharest. In 1580 Stephen Báthory, Prince of Transylvania, had permitted Jesuits who had been present since 1571 to establish a *collegium*, although the Society was expelled in 1606, only to return in 1617 to establish a school in Alba Iulia. After 1690 Transylvania passed to Habsburg control, and Jesuits established a network of schools and became masters of extensive properties. The Society's church in Cluj-Napoca (1724), where a *collegium* was established, was the first Baroque building in the region. Paulus Beke worked among the Hungarian-speaking Csángos of Moldova in the 1640s and even penetrated Crimean Tatary. Following the Suppression and subsequent restoration of the Society, Polish Jesuits were active in the lands now constituting Romania, but a formalized Jesuit mission did not reappear until 1918. During the Communist and Ceauşescu years, Jesuits were persecuted, and the Uniate Church they had helped establish suffered: the Jesuit priest Cornel Chira died in captivity, and priests and brothers went into hiding. Today the Society manages several projects in Romania supporting refugees and providing service to youth, operating a university chaplaincy in Targu-Mures and a Spirituality Centre in Cluj.

The first Jesuit of probably Croatian origin was Tomo Zdelarić, who entered the Society in 1554. Nicholas Bobadilla, one of the First Companions, made an initial visit to Ragusa (Dubrovnik) in modern-day Croatia as early as 1560 but did not establish a permanent mission. In 1580 the Ragusan Jesuit missionary Bartol Sfondrato traveled to Turkish Hungary passing through Bosnia en route. Bartol Kašic (1575–1650) was working in the Ottoman-controlled hinterlands of Dalmatia, including Bosnia, and composing a Croatian dictionary as early as 1604, but a permanent Jesuit presence in the western Balkans appeared only with the creation of the *collegium Ragusinum* in 1658. Zagreb became an important center of Jesuit activity during the Habsburg era; a mission station was created in 1606, a gymnasium opened a year later, and a university, today the most important in the country, was founded in 1669. In the years immediately before and after the Suppression, one of the most famous Jesuits in the world was the Croatian Rogerius Boscovic. Jesuits currently operate a gymnasium in Osijek, a residence and novitiate in Split, and a Faculty of Philosophy functioning as an independent educational institution in Zagreb.

To the north, Jesuits arrived in Slovenia in 1597 and had founded a *collegium* in Ljubljana in 1601, which produced one of the most important Slovenian composers, the Jesuit priest Janez Krstnik Dolar (1620–73). The Ljubljana cathedral was designed by Jesuit brother Andrea Pozzo (1642–1709). Another Jesuit trained in Ljubljana was Ferdinand Augustin Hallerstein (1703–74), head of the Portuguese mission to China at the time of the Suppression, and a skilled astronomer. The former Jesuit Jurij Japelj (1744–1807) translated the Bible into Slovenian and produced a grammar of that language. The modern Society serves four parishes and maintains an apostolate for youth, as well as conducting missions in Africa.

Although the Society's missionary activities in Ottoman-dominated Bosnia-Herzegovina were limited, one of the most important early chroniclers of ecclesiastical history in Dalmatia and Bosnia was the Jesuit Daniele Farlati (1690–1773) who produced the eight-volume *Illyricum sacrum*. During and after the war of 1992, the Society operated a refugee service in Bosnia.

The Society maintained a mission in Belgrade intermittently from 1614 onwards, and the Jesuit Bartholomeus Sfondrati may have visited the city as early as 1580. After Belgrade passed under Austrian control in 1689, an entire "Jesuit quarter" with church, schools, and *residentia* was begun, and efforts to serve both the Catholics of the Imperial armies and to proselytize among Orthodox Serbs were undertaken. However, this was all lost in 1739 when the sultan's forces retook the city in a struggle in which several Jesuits were martyred. The Society was unable to reestablish a presence in Ottoman-dominated Serbia until the twentieth century. Belgrade is home today to a small Jesuit community which possesses an image of the Virgin that has been preserved in Serbia since the seventeenth century, and a parish church served by a Jesuit priest.

The Society's efforts in Poland, Ukraine, and Transylvania were closely connected with the creation of Uniate (Greek Catholic) Churches. The Unions of Brest (1595–96) and Uzhhorod (1646) and the Act of Union in Transylvania (1698) were in large part results of a Jesuit program to extend the influence of Rome, and Jesuits were key players in the training of Romanian and Rusyn Uniate clergy and intellectuals, many of whom played key roles in the nationalist cultural movements of the nineteenth century.

Jesuit activity in what is now Slovakia commenced as early as 1585 when a mission was established in Turiec. Jesuits played a key role in the development of literary Slovak and in Košice established a small university and the most important press in that part of Europe during the eighteenth century. *Cantus Catholici* (1655; Slovak edition 1700), collected by Benedikt Szőllősi, preserves folk melodies from what was then Upper Hungary, while school dramas and public performances featuring the Slovak language were taking place in the seventeenth century. Slovakia is one of the few regions in eastern Europe where pre-Suppression Jesuit priests were involved in the design of churches, and Jesuit libraries were focal points of literary culture. As in the Danube Basin, the Society's aggressive missionary efforts reestablished the Catholic Church in a region that had been strongly Calvinist and Lutheran. Also among those converted were Jews and a handful of Muslims and Roma scattered throughout the region. Adam František Kollár (1718–83), who after the Suppression became chief librarian of the Imperial-Royal Library in Vienna, is regarded as one of the first Slovak nationalist intellectuals. In Slovakia, then part of Hungary, the de facto end of the Suppression did not come until 1855. Following the disbanding of the Order in 1950, the Society had to wait until 1989 to reestablish its schools. Jesuits today teach in many Slovak schools, operate a mission to India, and publish four periodicals. In 2013 a Jesuit, Milan Lach, was made suffragan bishop of the Greek Catholic Prešov Eparchy.

In what is now Estonia, which in the seventeenth century was within the Polish-Lithuanian Commonwealth, Jesuits established a school and residence in Tartu (Dorpat) in 1583. Much printed material produced in Estonian by the Jesuit press has not survived, but records of the Society's missionary efforts in the countryside suggest that Jesuits were often well received there. This era ended, however, with the arrival of Swedish troops in 1625. As in many other parts of eastern Europe, the Society contributed to the flowering of a local variation of Baroque art and decoration in the seventeenth century. Of special note are the two-tower brick Jesuit churches of southern Latvia. There is currently no permanent Jesuit presence in Estonia, while the Society's undertakings in Latvia are directed from Lithuania.

In the seventeenth century, while part of the Ottoman Empire, Albania had been visited by Jesuits. In the mid-nineteenth century, the Society was suppressed but returned to conduct traveling pastoral missions that strove to overcome the violent feuds that dominated local life and founded Shkodër Jesuit College in 1877. The Society continued its work during the period of the Kingdom of Albania (1912–25; 1928–39), but the establishment of a Communist regime ended the Jesuit presence until 1990; today a Jesuit community exists in Tiranë. Jesuits arrived in Skopje, now Macedonia, in 1921. Currently the Society's refugee service operates in Lojane, Macedonia, and in neighboring Kosovo.

In Ukraine, by the mid-seventeenth century Jesuits established *collegia* in Jarosław, Lviv, Lutsk, Kamianets-Podilskyi, Bar, Brest, and Kyiv, among others. The Kyiv-Mohyla Academy (1632), while not staffed by Jesuits, modeled its organizational structure, teaching methods, and curriculum on those of Jesuit schools. Among the Jesuit monuments in what was formerly the Polish-Lithuanian Commonwealth but which today are in Ukraine is the Church of Saints Peter and Paul in Lviv, completed in 1630, where twenty-two years earlier the Society founded a university. Uzhhorod, now in Ukraine, was a center of the Society's work among the Rusyn; in 1698 the first book in the Rusyn or Ruthenian language was published by the Jesuit press in Trnava. In conflict with the Orthodox hierarchy, the Society was expelled during the reign of Peter the Great. In the nineteenth century, one of the Society's most important tasks in western Ukraine, then ruled by Austria, involved the reformation of the Basilian order, while they also established schools in Ternopil and Stanislaviv, where there had been a Jesuit school in the eighteenth century. Today there are Jesuits active in Ukraine of both the Byzantine and Latin Rites: their work includes operating two parishes, leading youth groups, publishing, and service as army chaplains. The Society took a stance strongly in favor of the "Maidan" protests in the spring of 2014 and has as one of its highest priorities reconciliation and healing between the Catholic and Orthodox Churches.

The Society has played a much smaller role in the cultural history of Bulgaria; Rogerius Boscovic passed through the region in 1762 and wrote an account of his encounters with local Orthodox clergy. In the twentieth century the Jesuit Augustin Cardinal Bea served as apostolic visitor to Bulgaria.

Eastern Europe has therefore functioned both as a frontier for Jesuit missionary activity – an "Indies" far closer to home – and as an extension of its well-established western European projects. Locally born eastern European Jesuits have often shared the stage with those from neighboring (and politically dominant) lands, and for most of the period that the Society has been present in the region, it has had to negotiate its continued existence with great powers that often ruled many of these territories. Among the most significant aspects of the Society's experience in the region has been the interface with Eastern Churches, an encounter that continues to be freighted with difficulties since the Society's promotion of Uniate Churches has often been seen as an attempt to undermine historic Eastern Orthodox Churches, and even as a threat to the cultural integrity and political autonomy of the region.

The great variation in the number of Catholics from region to region, ranging from solid majorities to tiny minorities, has shaped the Society's different approaches throughout eastern Europe. Another major influence on Jesuit activities has been difficulties in communications, especially in the Balkans. And while the Society survived the Suppression in large part through its refuges within the nearby Russian Empire, the nineteenth and early twentieth centuries saw far less Jesuit scientific or literary activity in eastern Europe than in the seventeenth or eighteenth. This was due in large part to the absence of any independent political power based securely within eastern Europe that might have supported these endeavors, but also because of the widening gap between the increasingly secular and scientific cultures of western Europe and sustained religious focus of many of the Society's schools in the east.

The interaction of local artistic and decorative styles with the transnational elements of the late Baroque is a salient characteristic of the Society's cultural contributions to these regions and is also an area meriting further investigation. Generally speaking, the post-Suppression Society has not developed distinctive styles in the visual arts as its predecessor had.

While eastern European Jesuits were consistently the target of Nazi persecution and widely involved in rescuing Jews, a few appeared to favor the policies of the far-right regimes that arose in the twentieth century. In the 1930s some young Hungarian Jesuits formed KALOT, a nationalist, anti-Semitic movement. The Jesuit provincial of Slovakia, Rudolf Mikus, was quoted in 1939 saying that Jews must be removed from the public life of the nation, although this process must be "just."

The collapse of the Soviet Union and the transfers of power in Warsaw Pact and neighboring countries after 1989 brought about the biggest changes for the Society's undertakings in this region since 1773 and ushered in a period of both great opportunity and immense challenges as Jesuits confronted societies that had lacked many aspects of organized religious life for decades. The division of linguistic and ethnic groups such as Ukrainians among several political entities during the previous three centuries should also be seen as a factor profoundly influencing the organization and effectiveness of Jesuit undertakings, as has been the spreading of confessional groups over wide geographical territories. Likewise the prominence of Austrian Jesuits in Hungary and Polish Jesuits in Lithuania suggests the tendency of Jesuits from neighboring regions to play major roles in apostolic work in many eastern European countries.

Eastern Europe makes up a major portion of the Society's Central and Eastern Europe Assistancy, which currently consists of the provinces of Austria, Bohemia, Croatia, Germany, Hungary, Lithuania, North Poland, South Poland, Romania, Russia Region, Switzerland, Ukraine District, Slovakia, and Slovenia. The inclusion within this Assistancy of regions not generally considered "eastern Europe" is suggestive of the way the Society has historically approached the abovementioned nations: not as a unit but in relation to their neighbors.

The reestablishment of a Jesuit presence in former socialist or communist nations since 1989 has progressed at different rates, depending on a variety of factors, including the historic reception of the Catholic Church among local populations, relations with current governments, and available manpower and material resources for educational and outreach work. The ongoing needs of refugees are a new regional challenge to which the Society has responded. Secondary schools, long a focus of Jesuit efforts, have reemerged here as a key component of the Society's apostolate, although the Jesuit presence in the many universities the Society had founded remains modest. The training of local diocesan clergy is another important task of Jesuit schools. Eastern Europe also continues to be a region generating many of the Society's vocations.

See also Boscovic, Rogerius Joseph, SJ; Eastern Catholic Churches; German-Speaking Lands; Poland

Butterwick, Richard, *The Polish Revolution and the Catholic Church 1788–1792*. Oxford: Oxford University Press, 2012.
Černejová, Ivana, *Tovaryšstvo Ježíšovo: jezuité v Čechách*. Prague: Hart, 2002.
Louthan, Howard, *Converting Bohemia: Force and Persuasion in the Catholic Reformation*. Cambridge: Cambridge University Press, 2009.
Murzaku, Ines A., *Catholicism, Culture, Conversion: The History of the Jesuits in Albania (1841–1946)*. Rome: Pontifical Oriental Institute, 2006.
Pelesz, J., *Geschichte der Union der ruthenischen Kirche mit Rom*. Würzburg–Vienna: Woerl, 1878–80.
Shore, Paul, *Jesuits and the Politics of Religious Pluralism in Eighteenth-Century Transylvania*. Aldershot: Ashgate, 2007.

Paul Shore

Ecclesiology

A history of the major developments in ecclesiology from the Catholic Reformation to the present time shows the consistent influence of Jesuit ecclesiologists.

Robert Bellarmine, SJ (1542–1621), identified the Church as a perfect society in the sense that the Church contains all the necessary elements to accomplish the end for which it was intended, the salvation of all humanity. He stressed its visible elements, defining the Church as "the community of men brought together by the profession of the same Christian faith and conjoined in the communion of the same sacraments, under the government of the legitimate pastors and especially the one vicar of Christ on earth, the Roman pontiff," concluding, "And it is as visible as the Kingdom of France or the Republic of Venice." His famous definition reinforced a notion of the Church as an institutional society (see *Disputationes de controversiis Christianae fidei adversus huius temporis haereticos*, 1586, 1588, 1593).

Ecclesiological developments in nineteenth-century ecclesiology included several Jesuits associated with the "Roman School" such as Giovanni Perrone, SJ, (1794–1876), Carlo Passaglia, SJ, (1812–87), Klemens Schrader, SJ (1820–75), and Giovanni Battista Franzelin, SJ, (1816–86).

Émile Marsch, SJ (1890–1940), spent much of his life working on a systematic study of the Church as the Mystical Body of Christ and influenced Pius XII's encyclical, *Mystici corporis* (1943). His works include *The Whole Christ: The Historical Development of the Doctrine of the Mystical Body in Scripture and Tradition* (1933, English translation [ET]

1938), *Le Christ, l'Homme et l'univers: Prolégomènes à la théologie du corps mystique* (1962), and *The Theology of the Mystical Body* (1944, ET 1951).

Sebastian Tromp, SJ (1889–1975), professor at the Pontifical Gregorian University from 1929 to 1967, appointed a consultor to the Holy Office in 1936, participated in the writing of Pius XII's encyclical, *Mystici corporis* (1943), which retrieved the biblical and patristic image of the body of Christ. He also greatly influenced the description of the Church as the body of Christ during Vatican II. His major ecclesiological works were *De nativitate ecclesiae ex corde Iesu in cruce* (1936) and *Corpus Christi quod est Ecclesia* (1946).

Henri de Lubac, SJ (1896–1991), contributed to a Eucharistic ecclesiology through his historical study, *Corpus mysticum: L'Eucharistie et L'Église au moyen âge* (1949, ET 2006), which traces the evolution of the term *Corpus Mysticum* from designating the Eucharistic body to its use, from the middle of the twelfth century, to designate the ecclesial body, the Church. He identifies the Church as a sacrament in *Catholicisme: les aspects sociaux du dogme* (1947, ET 1950). Other Jesuit theologians who also developed this idea prior to its use by the Second Vatican Council include Otto Semmelroth, SJ (1912–1979), in *Die Kirche als Ursakrament*, 1963, and Karl Rahner, SJ (1904–1984), in *Kirche und Sakrament* (1960, ET 1963), who also published numerous articles on the Church collected in the series *Theological Investigations*. *Lumen gentium* identifies the Church as a sacrament in three different articles, each with a slightly different nuance: sacrament or instrumental sign of intimate union with God and of the unity of all humanity (§ 1), the Church as the universal sacrament of salvation (§ 48), and the Church as the visible sacrament of saving unity (§ 9). Even though the concept of the Church as the sacrament of Christ is closely related to the image of the Church as the mystical body of Christ, it escapes a major weakness of this image by avoiding too close of an identification between Christ and the Church. The concept of sacrament expresses the unity between the sign and the referent of that sign while maintaining the distinction between them, because what is signified is not absolutely identical with the sign that makes it present.

After Vatican II, Avery Dulles, SJ (1918–2008), favored the model of Church as sacrament in his *Models of the Church* (1974). The most prominent American ecclesiologist of the twentieth century, Dulles authored twenty-two books including *A Church to Believe In: Discipleship and the Dynamics of Freedom* (1982), *The Catholicity of the Church* (1985), *The Reshaping of Catholicism: Current Challenges in the Theology of Church* (1988), and *Magisterium: Teacher and Guardian of the Faith* (2007).

Francis A. Sullivan, SJ (b. 1922), professor of ecclesiology at the Gregorian University 1956–1992, is especially noted for his work on the question of authority in the Church through such publications as *Magisterium: Teaching Authority in the Catholic Church* (1983), *Creative Fidelity: Weighing and Interpreting Documents of the Magisterium* (1996), and *From Apostles to Bishops: The Development of the Episcopacy in the Early Church* (2001).

Jon Sobrino, SJ (b. 1938), known mostly for his contributions to liberation theology, wrote a liberation ecclesiology, *The True Church and the Poor*, in 1984.

See also Bellarmine, Robert, SJ; Dulles, Avery, SJ, Cardinal; Lubac, Henri de, SJ; Theology

Susan K. Wood

Ecology

There is a long tradition of Jesuit scientists investigating natural phenomena. Not long after the founding of the Society, Jesuits were already involved in mathematics (Christopher Clavius), astronomy (Matteo Ricci), and natural sciences (José de Acosta, Cristóbal de Acuña). Jesuit schools very often had observatories, labs, and natural science collections in which the discoveries of curious missionaries were displayed.

Today new initiatives related to ecological issues and the environment continue this long Jesuit tradition. With a distinct focus upon ecological sensitivity, Jesuits and Jesuit institutions are engaged in agricultural training (INEA, Spain; Kasisi Agricultural Training Centre, Zambia), rural development (Xavier University, Philippines), the peasant movement (IMCA, Colombia), and the study of the interaction between the environment and society (ESSC, Philippines). There are large organizations like Taru Mitra, which promotes ecological sensitivity with more than 2 million young people in India, and there are individual efforts such as those of Fr. Al Fritsch, SJ, and his daily reflections on www.earthhealing.info. The main resource at the global level today is the newsletter *Ecojesuit* (www.ecojesuit.com), published jointly by the Jesuit Conference of Asia Pacific in the Philippines and the Jesuit European Social Center (JESC) in Belgium. There are academic initiatives such as the Research Group on Ecotheology (Universidad Javeriana, Colombia) or "Healing Earth" (http://healingearth.ijep.net/), the free online environmental science e-textbook from Loyola University Chicago.

In 1995 the 34th General Congregation of the Society of Jesus (GC 34) expressed, for the first time, concern on this issue in Decree 20, introducing it as a dilemma between development and ecology: "The contemporary debate between development and ecology frequently arises in terms which describe it as the opposition between the wishes of the First World and the needs of the Third World." The question of ecology versus development is described as causing tension in the relationship between ecology and justice. The Decree suggests that the Society can help "to overcome some elements of this dilemma." It requests that father general promote further discussion on this question and look for positive contributions from the Society through our spirituality, works, and Jesuit lifestyle.

Father General Kolvenbach instructed the Jesuit Secretariat for the Social Apostolate to produce a reflection on this topic that was entitled "We live in a Broken World": Reflections on Ecology" (1999). The document was the result of a consultation among more than fifty Jesuits worldwide. As Kolvenbach explained in the introduction, "the expression, 'our way of proceeding,' seems fairly clear when applied within Jesuit contexts. But when entering a multi-faceted, controversial new field like ecology; when seeking a clear, full, reliable and common picture; when reflecting, discerning, deciding upon policy and taking action: – how indeed should we proceed?" He offers Jesuit ecological objectives: a better scientific understanding of the complexity of the phenomena and their social impacts, policy engagement, and the transformation of our lifestyles.

As the ecological crisis continued to increase, in 2008 GC 35 took a much stronger position on ecology. In Decree 3, the document related to the mission of the Society today, the Congregation stated: "In this global world marked by such profound changes, we now want to deepen our understanding of the call to serve faith, promote justice, and dialogue with culture and other religions in the light of the apostolic mandate to establish right relationships with God, with one another, and with creation" (#12). In this sense reconciliation with creation appears central to the mission of the Society. Later in the document, the Congregation specifically establishes the cause of our response: "In heeding the call to restore right relationships with creation, we have been moved anew by the cry of those suffering the consequences of environmental destruction … This Congregation urges all Jesuits and all partners engaged in the same mission, particularly the universities and research centers, to promote studies and practices focusing on the causes of poverty and the question of the environment's improvement" (#34). The vision of GC 35 is mainly that of mediation: Jesuits should put their skills and resources at the service of those who suffer the impacts of environmental degradation and natural resources exploitation.

GC 35 gave official recognition to the new importance of ecological issues for the Society. To facilitate the implementation of its decrees, Father General Adolfo Nicolás asked for a new document from what was then renamed the Secretariat for Social Justice and Ecology. "Healing a Broken World" (2011) is the most comprehensive position on environmental issues by the Society of Jesus. This document provides a regional overview of the main environmental threats, and then it gives a theological and Ignatian spiritual foundation for ecological concern. Finally, it offers a series of recommendations to Jesuit provinces, communities, and works to encourage the adoption of more ecologically responsible lifestyles.

A new total perspective has emerged in the Catholic Church when we come to talk, and to act, on ecology. The encyclical *Laudato Si': On Care for Our Common Home* (LS) by Pope Francis, published in June 2015, has placed ecological and environmental questions at the heart of Catholic Social Teaching. The encyclical offers a strong challenge, saying: "to protect our common home includes a concern to bring the whole human family together to seek a sustainable and integral development, for we know that things can change" (LS 13). The encyclical wants to open "a new dialogue about how we are shaping the future of our planet. We need a conversation which includes everyone, since the environmental challenge we are undergoing, and its human roots, concern and affect us all" (LS 14). Pope Francis highlights the key elements for framing the Catholic understanding of ecological questions in our time: the human roots, which affect the whole of humanity and require open dialogue among all stakeholders, and, for Christians, he makes clear that "living our vocation to be protectors of God's handiwork is essential to a life of virtue; it is not an optional or a secondary aspect of our Christian experience" (LS 217).

See also Ecology and Justice; Science

Ecology and Jesuits in Communication: Ecojesuit. www.ecojesuit.com.
Social Apostolate Secretariat, "We Live in a Broken World: Reflections on Ecology" (theme of issue), *Promotio Iustitiae* 70 (1999).
Social Justice and Ecology Secretariat, "Healing a Broken World" (theme of issue), *Promotio Iustitiae* 106 (2011), 1–33.

José Ignacio Garcia, SJ

Ecology and Justice

Jesuit ecological consciousness, in general, is similar in the societies in which Jesuits live and in the Catholic Church. Historically, the Catholic Church has shown a limited interest in environmental issues up to the recent encyclical *Laudato Si': On Care for Our Common Home* by Pope Francis. The reasons for this skepticism are not obvious, but we can suggest three possible causes.

From a sociological point of view, though there are certainly exceptions, the Catholic Church has been skeptical of environmental protectionist groups. Protecting biodiversity has never been seen as a direct consequence of Catholic faith. Moreover, in some countries, environmental groups have formed "green" political parties with clear leftist positions, a phenomenon sometimes viewed with suspicion by the Church. In the case of climate change, it is well known that many conservative groups with a religious background – mainly Evangelical but also Catholic – support positions of denial.

Second, the most widely shared theology of creation has several limitations; for example, by insisting on the centrality of the human being, it reduces to a merely instrumental value the rest of creation. A positive development in recent theological reflection is to underline the human role of "guardians" of creation as found in Scripture. This eschews the utilitarian vision of creation by demanding a strong sense of responsibility and care toward the environment and biodiversity.

A third reason for the low engagement of the Catholic Church on environmental issues is the priority given, in recent years, to individual moral issues (gay marriage, abortion) instead of social moral questions such as the depletion of natural resources or climate change.

With regard to specifically Jesuit ecological concern, the direct relationship between the abuse of natural resources and justice has formed undoubtedly the strongest nexus in the response of the Society of Jesus. As the Jesuit 34th General Congregation (GC 34) declared: "Unscrupulous exploitation of natural resources and the environment degrades the quality of life; it destroys cultures and sinks the poor in misery" (Decree 3, #9). Such serious injustices may be understood in terms of human rights: "Respect for the dignity of the human person created in the image of God underlies the growing international consciousness of the full range of human rights, including rights such as development, peace and a healthy environment" (Decree 3, #6).

For some, conservationist positions have been understood as antagonistic to development. Today, however, there is a clearer awareness that environment and poverty are closely linked. Environmental degradation and economic poverty have to be faced jointly if we want to achieve paths for a sustainable future. A development that seeks only short-term solutions will jeopardize the sustainability of the planet and therefore the life of future generations.

The Society of Jesus, through its General Congregations, looks to adapt its mission to new circumstances and contexts. The mission of the Society of Jesus was defined by the 32nd General Congregation (GC 32) as the *service of the faith and the promotion of justice*, and it was amplified by GC 34 to include the *dialogue with cultures and with other religions*. Most recently, it was newly expanded by the 35th General Congregation (GC 35) by the addition of a ministry of reconciliation to *establish right relationships with creation*.

The call to establish right relationships with creation by GC 35 does not suggest the need to establish new organizations but asks those already existing – mainly universities and research centers – to put themselves at the service of these new challenges. We can identify three steps in this process.

The first step is to promote research, especially research aimed at understanding how the most vulnerable populations are impacted. This research should lead to concrete policy proposals to alleviate harmful impacts. The next step is to engage in advocacy to change sociopolitical conditions in favor of the most vulnerable. Advocacy covers a wide range of activities, from awareness raising to campaigning to lobbying. Advocacy should be always done in partnership with other Church and civil society organizations. The third element of this process refers to Jesuits' lifestyle. This step is much deeper than adapting Jesuit communities or schools to standards for energy saving, efficient water usage or waste sorting. Lifestyle concerns, primarily, the role given to the poor in our work and in our personal and community relationships.

The encyclical *Laudato Si'* (LS) offers a new, and challenging, horizon of understanding, for Catholics, of the relationship between environmental and social issues. As Pope Francis states: "We are faced not with two separate crises, one environmental and the other social, but rather with one complex crisis which is both social and environmental. Strategies for a solution demand an integrated approach to combating poverty, restoring dignity to the excluded, and at the same time protecting nature" (LS 139). Proposing an "integral ecology" (LS 137), Pope Francis is offering a challenging framework for understanding justice based on the common good, intergenerational justice, and the sustainability of life on the earth.

See also Ecology; Justice; Science; Service of Faith and Promotion of Justice

Ecology and Jesuits in Communication: Ecojesuit: www.ecojesuit.com.

Social Apostolate and Ecology Secretariat, "Healing a Broken World" (theme of issue) *Promotio Iustitiae* 106 (2011), 1–68.

Social Apostolate and Ecology Secretariat, "A Spirituality that Reconciles us with Creation" (theme of issue) *Promotio Iustitiae* 111 (2013), 1–34.

José Ignacio Garcia, SJ

Ecuador

Jesuits arrived in Lima in 1568, but they did not come to Ecuador (*la Audiencia de Quito*) until about four years later, giving missions, eventually opening a *colegio* in Quito (1586), and being entrusted with the running of the seminary San Luis Rey in 1594. Also in Quito they founded the Universidad de San Gregorio Magno in 1622, and *colegios* in the cities of Cuenca and Popayán. When the province of Quito was created in 1696, its works included the university, the seminary, five *colegios*, a novitiate, and several missions. At the moment of Charles III's decree for their arrest and expulsion (1767–68), the province consisted of over 260 Jesuits engaged in a wide variety of academic, pastoral, cultural, and spiritual works, including *reducciones* among the indigenous people of the Amazon. Juan de Velasco, one of the Jesuits expelled at the Supression and a native of Riobamba, left an invaluable legacy in a two-volume, unedited anthology of poetry (*El ocioso en Faenza*) but especially in his three-volume history (*Historia moderna del Reino de Quito y crónica de la Provincia de la Compañía de Jesús del mismo Reino*), which he managed to take with him to the Papal States.

Upon their return to Ecuador after the restoration, the political situation fluctuated between leaders who favored nineteenthth-century liberalism and those who longed for a Catholic theocracy. The Church was caught between those two extremes; the Jesuits were forced to leave the country a second time in 1852. With the restoration, Ecuador had become a mission of several Spanish provinces, eventually becoming a vice province of Andalucía (1930) and then its own province (1983). In addition to the Pontifical Catholic University in Quito and a number of other educational works, the province today sponsors the Center for the Working Child, two radio stations for educational outreach (IRFEYAL [Instituto Radiofónico Fe y Alegría] and La voz de Guamote), a number of parishes and churches, social projects, and centers of spiritual formation.

See also Peru; Spain; Suppression

Chamorro, H. David, "Resumen de la Historia de la Compañía de Jesús en la Real Audiencia de Quito." Available at https://issuu.com. Accessed December 3, 2016.
Lynch, John, *New Worlds: A Religious History of Latin America.* New Haven, CT: Yale University Press, 2012, 207–12.
Perez, S., "The Return of the Jesuits to Post-Colonial America: Science, Modernity and Catholicism in Nineteenth-Century Ecuador." Available at repositorio.educacionsuperior.gob.ec (2011).

William Reiser, SJ

Ecumenism, Jesuits and

Jesuits were not among the Roman Catholic pioneers in the ecumenical movement such as Yves Congar (1904–95), Lambert Beauduin (1873–1960), Paul Couturier (1881–1953), Max Metzger (1887–1954), and Paul Watson of Graymoor (1881–1940). One might ask why Jesuits had a difficult time adjusting to this ministry. The reasons are multiple and complex. For one thing, the Society of Jesus originated at the beginning of the Reformation, and its founder Ignatius of Loyola (1491–1556) strongly opposed Protestants. It is true that the Society was not founded primarily to address problems occasioned by the Reformation, yet its strong ties to the papacy especially in the sixteenth century explains in part its distrust of Protestantism. One has only to read Ignatius's *Rules for Thinking with the Church* to understand his negative attitude toward the Reformers. Many of the early Jesuits were prominent in shaping Counter-Reformation theology and piety. The Jesuits Claude Jay (1504–52), Diego Laínez (1512–65), Alfonso Salmerón (1515–85), Peter Canisius (1521–97), and Robert Bellarmine (1542–1621) were not the sort of churchmen who inspired ecumenical attitudes. Jesuits often gained a reputation as controversialists, as opponents of Protestantism, Jansenism, and Gallicanism. They were typically Ultramontanists, persons not sympathetic to dissenting views. Still, by certain logic, the Order that supported the Council of Trent showed consistency by later heeding the papal call for implementing Vatican II.

The unbending character of the Jesuit Counter-Reformation should not be exaggerated. Instructive is a letter of one of Ignatius's first companions, Peter Faber (1506–1546), to his Jesuit colleague Diego Laínez (Ep 138, *Monumenta Historica Societatis Iesu, Fabri Mon.* 399–402), about the attitude of Jesuits toward Protestants. Faber stressed the need for charity combined with self-discipline and personal conversion so as to remove from oneself whatever might create an obstacle in dealing effectively with the Reformers.

Other factors should be taken into account to explain the changes regarding non-Catholics that came about gradually in the Roman Catholic Church and among Jesuits in particular. One historical event was the Russian Revolution and the subsequent exodus of one million Russian Orthodox into western Europe. Another was the trauma of World War II and the redistribution of populations that held different confessional allegiances. The foundation during 1945 of the Unitas Center in Rome under the direction of Charles Boyer, Jesuit professor at the Gregorian University and editor of the journal *Unitas*, was a move toward Catholic ecumenism among conservative circles. A congress on Catholic attitudes toward ecumenism met at Grottaferrata, the Eastern Basilian monastery outside of Rome, September 19–22, 1950, with the official encouragement of Pope Pius XII and his sub-secretary Giovanni Montini, the future Paul VI. This meeting was prepared by Boyer and included among the chosen delegates several Jesuits: Santiago Morillo Treviño (1900–66), Emil Herman (1891–1963), Joseph Gill (1901–89), and from the USA, John Courtney Murray (1904–67). Other events included Pope John XXIII's convocation in 1959 of the Second Vatican Council and the establishment of the Secretariat for Promoting Christian Unity in 1960 whose first director was Jesuit Father Augustin Bea (1881–1968). Of the fifty-four Jesuit bishops who were entitled to attend Vatican II, forty-two did attend and some helped to formulate the Council's ecumenical vision.

The Catholic Church and the Society of Jesus in particular did not participate in the early days of the formation of the World Council of Churches (WCC) and its initial general assemblies. In fact, Jesuits such as Jean Gonsette (1915–2001) and Sebastiaan Tromp (1899–1975) were strongly opposed to Catholic participation in the First General Assembly (1948) in Amsterdam. However, the Vatican hesitation about official participation did not prevent some Catholics (including several Jesuits) from attending early assembly meetings as "journalists" or "bystanders." As time went on, several Jesuits collaborated in the WCC's goals, such as Edward J. Duff (1912–84), author of *The Social Thought of the World Council of Churches* (1956), who was later chosen by the Vatican to be one of the first official Catholic delegates to attend the General Assembly at New Delhi in 1961. At the Fourth General Assembly in Uppsala in 1968, the Jesuit Roberto Tucci (1921–2015) addressed the delegates and urged the possibility of eventual Catholic membership in the WCC, and even eucharistic hospitality among the churches. The Jesuit George Dunne (1905–98) became the first secretary of SODEPAX, the joint Roman Catholic and WCC commission to deal with issues of peace and justice. Later this position was held by another American Jesuit, John A. Lucal (1926–2007).

Prior to Vatican II, Jan Baptist Janssens (1889–1964), general of the Jesuits from 1946 to 1964, had addressed ecumenism briefly on several occasions. In a letter dated August 2, 1951, he laid down norms for Jesuits attending theological congresses that included non-Catholic participants (cf. *Acta Romana Societatis Iesu* [*ARSI*] 12 [1951], 105–06). This letter was an application to Jesuits of the instruction by the Holy Office published March 1, 1950, dated December 20, 1949 (cf. *Acta Apostolicae Sedis* 42 [1950], 142–47). One modest sign of the change in attitude came in the General's statement and letter dated June 5, 1959, which urged including Christian unity among the petitions of the Apostleship of Prayer (*ARSI* 13 [1959], 599–600 and 601–03). Another factor that led to a shift in Roman Catholic attitudes toward non-Catholics was international and interconfessional cooperation among biblical scholars who shared a common historical-critical method of exegesis. As early as 1959 the American Jesuit Walter J. Abbott (1923–2008) pleaded for greater cooperation across denominational divides for a new English-language translation of the Bible.

Pedro Arrupe, the Jesuit general from 1965 to 1983, frequently stated that ecumenism was not an extra option for a Jesuit but was at the core of the Jesuit's vocation. In April 1966, Arrupe spoke in New York City about interreligious and interconfessional cooperation to a group of Orthodox, Protestants, and Jews. He later delivered a homily on Church unity on January 23, 1970, in London's Jesuit Farm Street Church. The following year he attended the fourth International Congress of Jesuit Ecumenists in Dublin (Milltown Park) where he delivered an important statement on ecumenism. He later addressed ecumenists in Manila on September 20, 1971.

The 31st General Congregation of the Society (1965–66) devoted a special decree on ecumenism, Decree 26, ##1–14. At the 32nd General Congregation (1974–75), the delegates did not repeat what had been stated previously but did mention in Decree 4: "Our Mission Today: The Service of Faith and the Promotion of Justice" (#37) that "ecumenism will then become not just a particular ministry but an attribute of mind and a way of life."

The 31st Congregation had made reference to the "sin against unity" of which Jesuits were guilty in the past and present. But the reference is rather oblique. What sin might they have had in mind? Perhaps one element was the Romanizing tendencies of the Society in relationship to the Eastern Churches. There may be allusions to the polemic anti-Luther writings of the Jesuit Hartmann Grisar (1845–1932) or the anti-Anglican sentiments voiced by theologians such as Sydney Fenn Smith (1843–1922), Leslie Joseph "Ignatius" Walker (1877–1958), and Salvatore Maria Brandi (1852–1915). Also envisaged may have been the negative attitudes to Church unity movements in writers such as Peter Sinthern (1870–1952). It may also have had in mind the fact that Jesuits had actively participated as staff members of the Holy Office during the 1950s when negative restrictions were made concerning cooperation with non-Catholics.

Another factor that changed the character of Jesuit attitudes toward ecumenism was the involvement of many Jesuit theologians and biblical scholars in the various international and national bilateral consultations set up with the encouragement of the Secretariat for Promoting Christian Unity to promote dialogue with the Orthodox, Anglicans, and Protestants.

Mention should be made of several Jesuit ecumenical centers. In New York City, the Russian Center, originally set up on the Fordham University campus by several Jesuits who had served exiled Russian Christians in Shanghai, was founded in 1951, and later renamed the John XXIII Center. In Montreal, Irénée Beaubien (b. 1916) was instrumental in preparing for the Fourth World Conference of Faith and Order in Montreal in 1963, and the same year he opened a bilingual center for ecumenism. In 1967, he was joined by Stéphane Valiquette (1912–2004), and in 1975 the office became a national Canadian Centre for Ecumenism that still operates and publishes French and English editions of the journal *Oecuménisme/Ecumenism*. In Manila, the East Asian Pastoral Institute (1965) focused on ecumenical concerns. Also in Manila in 1968 the Cardinal Bea Institute for Ecumenical Studies was inaugurated under the directorship of Pedro de Achútegui (1915–98). In Frankfurt, an ecumenical center, Action 365, was founded in 1962 by Johannes Leppich (1915–92) to encourage and coordinate basic Christian communities under the leadership of Wolfgang Tarara (1931–2001) and others. Michael Hurley (1923–2011) founded the Irish School of Ecumenics (1970) in Dublin whose motto is appropriately *floreat ut pereat* (may it flourish so as to perish).

Beginning in the 1960s, a small group of European Jesuits held the first unofficial meeting of the Congress of Jesuit Ecumenists which subsequently met usually every two or three years, eventually in four different continents, to exchange information and methodologies, although not usually publishing the presentations. This congress met for the twenty-second time on July 15–21, 2013, in Tampa, Florida. More recently, biennial meetings have been held in Vienna and Rome.

The Jesuit Curia which once appointed one individual to oversee ecumenical and interreligious activities more recently replaced that office with a committee of eight Jesuits from around the word to meet with and advise the superior general every September. Jesuit Pope Francis has shown a personal commitment to Church unity as typified, for instance, in his meeting with Moscow Patriarch Kyrill in Cuba on February 12, 2016, and in his participation on October 31, 2016, in Lund, Sweden, at an ecumenical worship service leading up to the 500th anniversary of the Protestant Reformation.

Relations with the Orthodox. The interest of Jesuits in Eastern churches during the twentieth century especially in Russia was heightened by the fall of the Romanovs in 1917 and the October Revolution. Many Roman Catholics were convinced that the upheavals of the Revolution and the shifts of population at that time offered an opportune time to strengthen the Eastern Catholic Churches in Russia. Around the year 1920 some 1 million Russians emigrated to various intellectual centers especially in the Slavic capitals, and later to Berlin and Paris. This led to the founding of the Institut de Théologie Orthodoxe de Paris, popularly known as St. Serge (1926), which helped to serve as a bridge between Russian Orthodox theology and French Catholic theology.

In Rome, the Pontifical Oriental Institute (PIO), entrusted to the Society of Jesus by Pius XI, was at first somewhat triumphalistic in its dealings with Orthodoxy especially under the leadership of Michel d'Herbigny (1880–1957). But this Unionist stress softened as the Vatican's attitude changed and under the influence of Jesuits such as Wilhelm de Vries (1904–97), PIO professor, whose ecumenical vision was transformative. One of the first courses on ecumenism at the PIO was offered in 1955–56 by Mauricio Gordillo (1894–1961). After Vatican II, special courses on the importance of unity with the Orthodox were given by Belgian Georges Dejaifve (1913–82) in 1965, the English Jesuit Joseph Gill (1901–89), and later in 1967 by the Benedictine Emmanuel Lanne from Chevetogne.

In the United States as early as the late 1950s, there was contact with the Orthodox especially the Russian Orthodox at the Jesuit Russian Center, New York City. Among those who entered into informal, private dialogue with the Jesuits were Orthodox theologians Georges Florovsky, Alexander Schmemann, and John Meyendorff. When the Russian Center became the John XXIII Center, it established a journal, *Diakonia*, devoted to Eastern Christian studies. Its editor was the Jesuit George Maloney (1924–2005) noted for his studies of Palamite theology, the history of Orthodoxy especially since the fifteenth century, and various Eastern spiritual writers. An official dialogue has existed since 1965 between the Eastern Orthodox and Roman Catholics in the United States, in which several Jesuits have played an important role. Its first Catholic executive secretary was the Jesuit Edward J. Kilmartin (1923–94) followed by Michael A. Fahey (b. 1933). John Long (1925–2005) was also a member, as was Robert Taft (b. 1932). Brian Daley (b. 1940) continues to serve on that consultation. There is also an official dialogue in the USA between Catholics and the Ancient Oriental Orthodox Churches in which some of the same American Jesuits have played a part.

Relations with the Anglican Communion. Ecumenical contacts between Anglicans and Roman Catholics were difficult and painful in England until only recent times because of the persecutions at the time of the Reformation and later civil restrictions against Catholics. Anglicans perceived the Jesuits as representatives of a foreign power. Roman Catholics in England tended to see themselves in sharp contrast to the Anglicans. However, in the second half of the nineteenth century, a Belgian Bollandist Jesuit priest, Victor De Buck (1817–76), entered into private negotiations with Anglo-Catholics in England, including Professor Edward F. Pusey of Oxford University, in the hope of arranging corporate union. This unlikely ecumenist was later called by Pieter Beckx (1795–1887), superior general from 1853 to 1887, to be his personal theological adviser at Vatican I (1869–70).

Pope Leo XIII set up a committee to study the possibility of recognizing the validity of Anglican Orders. These consultations, which took place from 1895 to 1896, included two Jesuits, Cardinal Camillo Mazzella (1829–1900) and the theologian Emilio de Augustinis (1829–99). Both of these Italian Jesuits had taught at Woodstock College in Maryland but had differing views of the validity of Anglican priestly orders. De Augustinis, unlike Mazzella, argued that their validity should be recognized by the papacy, but his view was rejected by Leo XIII who ultimately judged in his apostolic constitution, *Apostolicae curae*, that these orders were in fact absolutely null and utterly void.

In the years that followed, two other Jesuits emerged as pre-Vatican II leaders in the ecumenical movement: Maurice Bévenot (1897–1980) and Bernard Leeming (1893–1971). Bévenot was ahead of his time when he attended the Faith and Order Conference held in Edinburgh in 1937 with ecclesiastical permission. It was hoped that he, like other Catholics, might be allowed to attend the First General Assembly of the World Council of Churches in 1948. When the Secretariat for Christian Unity was set up, Bévenot was invited as one of the official consultors. Leeming's book on ecumenism, based on lectures delivered in 1957, appeared in 1960 and was one of the major English works on Church unity before Vatican II. In the following years there were significant contributions of Jesuits to Anglican/Roman Catholic dialogue. John Coventry (1915–98) served as general secretary of the Ecumenical Committee of the Episcopal Conference of England and Wales. After the formation of the official Anglican/Roman Catholic International Commission (ARCIC), two Jesuits, Edward J. Yarnold (1926–2002) and Herbert J. Ryan (1931–2010), served as consultant theologians.

Relations with Protestants. Although many of the Jesuits already mentioned have had ecumenical dealings with Protestants as well as with the Orthodox and Anglicans, it is well to mention in this final section some of the specific initiatives with Protestants. For many ecumenists in Europe and North America, ecumenical contact came first and foremost through Protestants.

Here one of the first Jesuits to cite is Max Pribilla (1874–1956) who anticipated attitudes that were to become acceptable for Catholics decades later. Son of a Protestant parent, he was friendly with several Lutheran theologians including Nathan Söderblom. His two pioneering publications were *Um die Wiedervereinigung im Glauben* (1926) and *Um kirchliche Einheit: Stockholm, Lausanne, Rom: geschichtlich-theologische Darstellung der neueren Einigungsbestrebungen* (1929).

Augustin Bea, through his position as president of the Secretariat for Promoting Christian Unity (SPCU), was a major Jesuit presence in Church unity efforts. His own initiation into ecumenism came largely through his participation in international biblical congresses, and partly through contacts with Jan Willebrands and Lorenz Jäger who was associated in Germany with the Una Sancta Brotherhood and the Paderborn Ecumenical Institute. Bea's major ecumenical publication *L'unione dei Cristiani* (1962) appeared in a number of translations.

In France, a number of Jesuits assisted Paul Couturier by preaching and lecturing during the Week of Prayer for Christian Unity. Prior to Vatican II, French Catholic theologians were dialoguing with Protestants through the first Group of Les Dombes in which Henri de Lubac also took part. A new Group of Les Dombes was founded after the Council and continues to this day to produce important texts. Among the Catholic members have been Bernard Sesboüé (b. 1929), Robert Clément (1918–94), and Jean Roche (1900–88) who also has served on the Lyons Center, Unité Chrétienne. In Paris, the future Cardinal Jean Daniélou (1905–74) actively engaged in dialogue through his Cercle St. Jean Baptiste. His book *Unité des chrétiens et conversion du monde* (1962) records some of these initiatives.

The Dutch Jesuit theologian Jan Witte (1907–89) became a professor of ecumenical theology and trained generations of ecumenists at the Gregorian University. Several Jesuit specialists in Luther were members of the faculty, especially Belgian Jos Vercruysse (b. 1931), an active member of Europe's Societas Oecumenica, and the American Jared Wicks (b. 1929).

In Denmark, the Jesuit bishop Hans Martensen (1927–2012) had close ties with Lutherans especially through his work as co-chairman of the International Lutheran and Roman Catholic Consultation.

In Brazil, the Jesuit Paulo Olejak (1901–82) established a regular dialogue with Lutherans in Porto Alegre, Brazil, as early as 1957.

In the United States, one of the principal Jesuit leaders in ecumenical dialogue was Gustave Weigel (1906–64). During a trip to Europe in 1953, he met Luther scholar Joseph Lortz who urged Weigel to get more Americans involved in Church unity concerns. Although Weigel's lectures at Woodstock College (e.g., his *Summula ecclesiologica* in 1954) were somewhat negative toward Protestantism, he became involved personally with a number of American Protestants and published several works on ecumenism beginning with *An American Dialogue* (1960). His participation in the early sessions of Vatican II before his premature death further helped ecumenical understanding. Other American Jesuits participated in ecumenical dialogues, especially with Lutherans, among them Avery Dulles (1918–2008) and Joseph Fitzmyer (b. 1920). Walter Burghardt (1914–2008), especially through his editorship of *Theological Studies*, kept ecumenical issues in the forefront. Two Jesuits, Richard Rousseau (1924–2015) and David Bowman (1919–93), served for several years as staff members on the National Council of Churches in the USA. In the following decade, Thomas P. Rausch (b. 1941) has reached out to include the Pentecostal churches in fruitful exchanges,

India also saw remarkable ecumenical exchanges following Vatican II in which some Jesuits held a leading role. Edward R. Hambye (1916–90), a consultor for the Secretariat for Christian Unity in the early 1970s, published documentation about Indian ecumenism.

Conclusion. This summary overview of involvement of Jesuits in the search for Church unity does not mean to imply that they were the leading Catholic voices in ecumenical endeavors. Still, their contributions have not been negligible. While Jesuit ecumenism has not had the long history of institutional commitment such as Jesuit ministry of higher education, still a number of individual Jesuits, with official encouragement, have been involved in this ministry. Their future role in the twenty-first century will depend on decisions reached at the highest levels of leadership in the churches and in personal initiatives.

See also Bea, Augustin, SJ; East Asian Pastoral Institute (EAPI); Eastern Catholic Churches; Interreligious Dialogue; Pontifical Oriental Institute

de Achútegui, Pedro S., ed., *The Dublin Papers on Ecumenism: Fourth Congress of Jesuit Ecumenists.* Manila: Cardinal Bea Institute, 1972.

Borelli, John, and John Erickson, eds., *The Quest for Unity: Orthodox and Catholics in Dialogue.* Washington, DC: United States Catholic Conference; Crestwood: St. Vladimir Seminary Press, 1996.

Briggs, John, Mary Amba Oduyoye, and George Tsetsis, eds., A *History of the Ecumenical Movement.* Vol. III: *1968–2000.* Geneva: World Council of Churches, 2004.

Fahey, Michael A., "Ecumenismo." In *Diccionario histórico de la Compañia de Jesús: Biográfico-temático.* Vol. II. Ed. Charles O'Neill, SJ. Rome: Monumenta Historica Societatis Jesu; Madrid: Comillas University, 2001, pp. 1193–1201.

Hambye, Edward, and Harry C. Permulalil, *Christianity in India: A History in Ecumenical Perspective.* Alleppey: Church History Association of India, 1972.

"Jesuits and Ecumenism: History, Formation, Spirituality." *Centrum Ignatianum Spiritualitatis* 20 (1989), 1–101.

Michael A. Fahey, SJ

Education, Higher/Tertiary

See Universities, 1540–1773; Universities 1773–Present

Education, Secondary and Pre-secondary

From the earliest days – even during St. Ignatius's tenure as general of the Society – Jesuits became heavily involved in what we today call secondary education. Paradoxically, the first Jesuits founded the Society with the idea of a mobile group of men dedicated mainly to preaching and works of charity – an intention quite foreign to dedicating themselves to educational commitments that imply long-term residence and stability. Quite soon, however, St. Ignatius and other early Jesuits – Nadal, Polanco, Laínez, and Salmerón – discovered the value of education as a ministry to carry out their fundamental mission of "helping souls" and "serving God." They all embraced the vision of education expressed by the humanism of their time and that Fr. Bonifacio captured in a sentence that became a mantra for Jesuit education: "Puerilis Instituto est Renovatio Mundi" (Education of the young is transformation of the world). In 1548 the first school was founded in Messina (Sicily) under the name of Collegio di San Nicoló; many such schools would follow so that in 1556, at the time of St. Ignatius's death, more than thirty schools were already in place.

As the Jesuits found themselves increasingly committed to this new ministry, they felt a need for some common guidelines for the expanding network of schools. After several drafts and much discussion, Fr. General Claudio Acquaviva officially published the *Ratio studiorum* in 1599 as a document to guide Jesuit education worldwide. This document describes the offices, curriculum, and pedagogy to be used in the schools. It stresses the humanist tradition of forming good character (*pietas*) to be used in the service of the common good. It also enthusiastically reflects the belief that good character could be formed essentially through contact with classical literature. For these reasons, the schools of the Society adopted the basic curriculum of the humanists: grammar, humane letters (poetry, history, literature, oratory), and languages (Latin, Greek, and Hebrew). The *Ratio* further adopted the *modus parisiensis* as the pedagogy of choice, but it integrated all these elements within the framework of the religious experience inspired by the *Spiritual Exercises*. In addition, Jesuits incorporated into their schools practices that originated from their ministry, such as teaching Christian doctrine, the celebration of Mass, the practice of confession, the Marian congregations, and the importance of teamwork among teachers, creating an eclectic model of education that has inspired continual renewal.

The numbers of schools continued to grow during the seventeenth and eighteenth centuries. When the Jesuits were suppressed in the eighteenth century, they had created an international network of more than 700 schools, primarily in Europe, Ibero-America, and India. The restoration of the Society in 1814 provided a new beginning for Jesuit education and, by 1833, the Jesuits had reopened or founded around forty-five schools. Sadly, the tuition-free schools of the pre-Suppression Society were replaced by more and more paid schools due to a lack of donors and the new circumstances of the times. These new schools' need for tuition resulted in Jesuits serving mainly those families who could pay for their education, leading to the common perception that Jesuit schools catered only to the moneyed elite. That perception is still current today and has led to criticism of what some perceive as an elitist, ghetto-enclosed, and reactionary phenomenon.

On the other hand, at the beginning of the twenty-first century the number of Jesuit secondary and primary schools number more than 2,000, spread over the entire world. They serve all social groups but specialize in serving those whose life is on the "margins" of society. Fascinating contemporary developments in Jesuit education have happened in the education of the poor; networks such as Fe y Alegría in Latin America and Africa, models such as the Cristo Rey and Nativity Schools in the United States, and many schools serving the Dalits and Adivasis throughout India testify to this. Not all these models are exclusively Jesuit, but they have developed from our common vision of serving faith, promoting justice, and opting for the poor that the Church has encouraged since Vatican II and the Society of Jesus has firmly embraced since the generalate of Fr. Arrupe. He demanded that Jesuit education be a means of preparing *men and women for others* according to the new signs of the times named clearly at Vatican II. This process of renovation, as part of our living tradition, continues today and has produced two important documents: *The Characteristics of Jesuit Education* (1986) and *Ignatian Pedagogy: A Practical Approach* (1993). These documents have guided the process of renewal, the rediscovery of the spiritual experience of St. Ignatius in Jesuit education, and the central role of educating for social justice. This new understanding was captured by Fr. Kolvenbach in the "4Cs:" "our goal as educators [is] to form men and women of competence, conscience, and compassionate commitment."

See also Cristo Rey; Fe y Alegría; Nativity School Model; *Ratio Studiorum*

Duminuco, V. J., ed., *The Jesuit Ratio Studiorum: 400th Anniversary Perspectives*. New York: Fordham University Press, 2000.

Kolvenbach, Peter-Hans, Letter regarding the Ignatian Pedagogical Paradigm. 1993. www.sjweb.info/documents/education/PHK_pedagogy_en.pdf.

O'Malley, John W., *The First Jesuits*. Cambridge, MA: Harvard University Press, 1993.

Vasquez, Carlos, ed., *Propuesta educativa de la Compañía de Jesús: fundamentos y práctica*. Bogotá: ACODESI, 2006.

José Alberto Mesa, SJ

Egypt

The Jesuit presence in Egypt began as a renewed attempt to get into Ethiopia. Following the early contacts with the Coptic Patriarch in 1560 and 1582, it was not until 1697 that a residence was established in Cairo as a stepping-off point for Ethiopia. The first Jesuit to make the attempt, Fr. Charles de Brevedent, in 1698, died eight months later outside Gondar. A second mission in 1700 arrived at Gondar only to be expelled shortly afterwards. When a third mission under Fr. William Dubernat failed in 1703, he decided to focus on the Coptic community in Egypt. He opened a school and seminary, which would function until 1764, shortly before the Suppression of the Society of Jesus. Dubernat's studies of the Coptic hierarchy furnished the information for Fr. Jean-Baptiste Du Sollier's *History of the Coptic Patriarchate of Alexandria*.

Fr. Claude Sicard, sent to Cairo in 1712 as superior, would soon attract attention by his scientific descriptions of Egypt. Fluent in Arabic, he was able to traverse the country and satisfy his curiosity concerning its monuments and early history. But his main concern was the apostolate to the Copts. He founded the first Coptic Catholic community and ran foul of the Franciscans by failing to separate Catholics from Orthodox in his ministry. He died caring for those stricken by the pestilence in 1726.

When the Society of Jesus was restored, Egypt was not a primary concern. In the spring of 1847, Fr. Maximillien Ryllo arrived in Alexandria with a bishop, two diocesan priests, and a few Jesuits on his way to found a mission in Central Africa. They advanced no further than Khartoum where Ryllo died in February 1848. Fr. general recalled the others in 1852 and the mission was passed to the Comboni Missionaries.

In 1879, at the request of Pope Leo XIII, Fr. Remy Normand arrived in Cairo with three other Jesuits to establish a seminary for the Copt Catholic community. He also began the College of the Holy Family, which shared quarters with the seminary until 1899 when a new seminary was constructed at Tahta in Upper Egypt. Problems in the region would bring the seminary to Maadi, a suburb of Cairo, in 1953. For the most part, the Jesuits offered auxiliary services; they assumed direction for a brief period from 1953 to 1968.

Fr. Michel Jullien, in 1882, purchased land in Faggalah quarter, on the outskirts of Cairo, where the College of the Holy Family would develop, fed by a few primary schools run by sisters. Following the 1952 Revolution and unpalatable French diplomacy, the College risked extermination but finally survived as a "foreign language school." The government control of tuition posed serious financial problems, which were overcome by fund-raising. The school houses a valuable library including documents from the famous expedition of Napoleon. It has served as a center for Jesuits to branch out into many other social apostolates. The most notable, perhaps, is the foundation of the

Christian Association of Free Schools of Upper Egypt in 1939 by Fr. Henry Ayrout. The Association sustained a network of schools for the poor Christian peasants (*fellahs*) of the region. The direction later passed to laypeople. The Jesuits at the school in Garagous set up a workshop for pottery that is still flourishing today. From Upper Egypt, Jesuit activity has reached into Sudan

The Jesuits also founded a college at Alexandria in 1888. It functioned up to World War I. At present, the Society maintains a library and student center in the city.

See also Middle East; Sicard, Claude, SJ

Libois, Charles, *La Compagnie de Jésus au Levant: la province du Proche-Orient: notices historiques*. Beirut: Faculté des lettres et des sciences humaines, Université Saint-Joseph/Dar el-Machreq, 2009.

John Donohue, SJ

Election (in the *Spiritual Exercises*)

Ignatius uses this key concept to describe the making of significant choices or decisions in one's life. Within the framework of the *Spiritual Exercises*, the section on "The Election" or "Introduction to the Consideration of the States of Life" comes in the context and toward the end of the Second Week, after the exercitant has prayed through the reality of being a loved sinner (in the First Week), and while contemplating scenes from the life of Christ (in the Second Week). After "A Meditation on the Two Standards" (of Christ and Satan), "A Meditation on the Three Classes of Persons," and a contemplation on "Three Ways of Being Humble," one is prepared for the process of making an election. Of fundamental importance, "In every good election, insofar as it depends on us, the eye of our intention ought to be single. I ought to focus only on the purpose for which I am created, to praise God our Lord and to save my soul. Accordingly, anything whatsoever that I elect ought to be chosen as an aid toward that end" (#169). Central to the making of a good election is the Ignatian concept of "indifference," that is, awareness and avoidance of any disordered affections or inordinate attachments. Ignatius also distinguishes between what he calls "an unchangeable election," such as priesthood or marriage, and "a changeable election," like taking or rejecting temporal goods (#171). In many ways, the making of an election – especially with regard to life-changing decisions – is at the very heart of the *Spiritual Exercises*.

See also Discernment; Indifference; *Spiritual Exercises*

The Spiritual Exercises of Saint Ignatius. Trans. George E. Ganss. St. Louis, MO: The Institute of Jesuit Sources, 1992.

Robert E. Scully, SJ

Eliano, Jean-Baptiste, SJ (1530–1589)

Grandson of the renowned Jewish grammarian Elia Levita, Eliano was born in Rome, converted to Catholicism in 1551, following in the footsteps of his elder brother Vittorio, and later entered the Jesuit order in Venice. His brother joined the diocesan clergy. Jean-Baptiste met Ignatius in Rome and was assigned to the Roman College. His fluency in Hebrew, Arabic, and Turkish marked him for work in the Middle East. Eliano was sent with Cristobal Rodriguez to Alexandria, Egypt, in 1561–63, for discussions on unity. The talks came to nothing because of mutual misunderstanding, and he returned to Rome, having briefly met his mother while in Egypt. In Rome he taught Oriental languages at the Roman College. Later, between 1578 and 1582, Pope Gregory XIII sent him twice to Lebanon in response to the Maronite patriarch's request for relations with Rome. In Cannobin he organized a synod and on his return to Rome arranged the founding of a Maronite seminary and the printing of Maronite liturgical texts. He continued to teach in Rome and translated the profession of faith of Pius V into Arabic: *I'tiqād al-amāna*. Earlier he had written a piece depicting a discussion between two Muslims, a Sheikh and a savant, on their return from the pilgrimage. He died in Rome in 1589.

See also Egypt; Middle East; Roman College

Clines, Robert John, "Confessional Politics and Religious Identity in the Early Jesuit Missions to the Ottoman Empire." Ph.D. dissertation, Syracuse University, 2014.

John Donohue, SJ

Ellacuría, Ignacio, SJ (1930–1989), and Companions

The Salvadoran Jesuit priest, theologian, and martyr, Ignacio Ellacuría Beascoechea, one of more than 300 Jesuit martyrs of the twentieth century, lived and died during the tragic persecution of the post-Vatican II Catholic Church in El Salvador. Murdered in his intellectual prime at the age of 59, he nevertheless produced a profound body of philosophical, theological, social-political, spiritual, and university writings that place him among the foremost Catholic intellectuals of the twentieth century, joining such Jesuit luminaries as Pierre Teilhard de Chardin, Karl Rahner, Bernard Lonergan, Henri de Lubac, Jean Daniélou, John Courtney Murray, and William Lynch.

Ignacio Ellacuría was born in the Basque region of Spain on November 9, 1930. He entered the Jesuit novitiate in Loyola on September 14, 1947. The following year he moved to El Salvador to spend his second year as a novice in the Central American novitiate newly founded by Miguel Elizondo. After professing his first vows, he traveled to Quito, Ecuador, to begin five years of studies in the humanities and philosophy under the tutelage of an outstanding classicist, Aurelio Espinosa Pólit. He returned to San Salvador for three years to teach in the diocesan seminary which the Jesuits ran at that time and then began a theology degree in Innsbruck, where he studied with Karl Rahner in the years just before the Second Vatican Council.

Ellacuría was ordained a priest in 1961 and the following year he journeyed to Madrid to begin advanced studies under the direction of the eminent Basque philosopher, Xavier Zubiri. He completed a three-volume doctoral dissertation on Zubiri's thought and under his supervision received his degree from Complutense University in Madrid. He returned to Central America in 1967 to teach at the Universidad Centroamericana "José Simeón Cañas" (UCA) and serve in its administration. From 1970 until 1975, he split his energies between his position at the UCA and his work as the director of formation for the Central American Jesuits. After 1975 he worked full-time at the UCA and soon became both a major voice in Latin American liberation theology and philosophy and a leading commentator on the social, political, economic, and cultural realities of El Salvador.

Such commentary was desperately needed. El Salvador's colonial and postcolonial history had created a desperate and polarized society. Gross inequities in land distribution, education, health care, nutrition, and political access set the stage in the 1970s for the reemergence of revolutionary movements in opposition to the ruling elites who maintained their grip on the country by stealing elections, rigging the judicial system, eliminating the free press, and deploying vigilante gangs to terrorize the populace and murder anyone who dared to oppose them. The victims of this tragic situation included hundreds of Church catechists, four US missionary women, more than a dozen priests beginning with the Jesuit pastor, Rutilio Grande, and most infamously, the Archbishop of San Salvador, Oscar Arnulfo Romero, who was assassinated while celebrating Mass on March 24, 1980. During that same period, many civic and religious leaders were forced into exile or arbitrarily deported, including Ellacuría. He was one of seven priests denied readmission into the country on February 22, 1977, the same day Romero was installed as archbishop. He remained abroad until August, 1978.

Civil War engulfed El Salvador during the 1980s. The descent into that intractable conflict began shortly after the collapse of a moderate government that had briefly assumed power in October, 1979; it began to escalate wildly after the assassination of the Archbishop. More than 75,000 Salvadorans would die violently during the war, the vast majority as victims of human rights abuses perpetrated by the Salvadoran military and right-wing death squads. October 1979 also marked the beginning of Ellacuría's tenure as rector (president) of the UCA which ended with his assassination ten years later. He went into exile a second time (from November 1980 through May 1981) because of the mounting death threats he was receiving.

All during this time, whether he was leading the UCA from inside the country or working from abroad, Ellacuría found time to participate in civic life, teach and give public lectures, edit several journals and books, and write extensively, all while helping the new archbishop, Arturo Rivera y Damas, fill the leadership void in the Church caused by the murder of Romero. Moved by the terrible suffering of the Salvadoran poor and the futility of the Civil War, Ellacuría exerted all his influence to bring about a negotiated settlement to the conflict. In 1989, with a peace agreement seemingly within reach, yet another round of talks between government and revolutionary leaders broke down. The guerilla coalition launched a long-threatened offensive that enabled them to control large sectors of the capital city but without drawing closer to a military victory. In this embattled context, the military high command, in collusion with the government, ordered commandos from an elite Army battalion to infiltrate the UCA and silence those whom they falsely branded "the intellectual leaders" of the guerillas. Shortly after midnight on November 16, 1989, Ellacuría and four other Jesuit university professors, Ignacio Martín-Baró, Segundo Montes, Amando Lopez, and Juan Ramón Moreno, were executed outside their home. Finally, in order to leave no witnesses, a sixth Jesuit priest, Joaquín Lopez y Lopez, a seminary cook, Elba Ramos, and her 15-year-old daughter, Celina Ramos, were murdered inside the different parts of the compound where they were staying.

What made Ellacuría and his companions such a threat? What provoked this callous killing? Part of the answer lies with the history of violence and impunity in El Salvador's political culture. Part of it might be found in Ellacuría's intelligence and integrity, in his fearless and forceful personality, and in the real and symbolic power of the Jesuit order. But a key part of the answer can be traced to the role of the UCA in Salvadoran society and to Ellacuría's vision of university. At a time when nearly every opportunity for legitimate dissent, reasoned discourse, and impartial information had been crushed, the

UCA emerged as a place where freedom of conscience thrived. Through its institutes for human rights and public opinion polling, its journals, radio station, and other means of communication, and above all, its symbolic presence as a place for memory, imagination, and dialogue, the UCA championed an alternative future for El Salvador. As the UCA's president Ellacuría engaged academic, business, Church, government, military, and revolutionary leaders of all stripes in private meetings and occasionally in public events. He even successfully negotiated the release of the kidnapped daughter of the president of the nation in 1985. In the latter part of the 1980s, he played a leading role in advancing the peace process while urging the university to labor for peace precisely as a university.

Ellacuría never missed a chance to point out that the university was not a political party, labor union, extension of the government or the revolution, nor any other partisan entity within the social body. The university was a distinct social force, but one whose specific task was to study the national reality, to insert itself into that reality through a process he called "social projection," and to create space for public dialogue and problem-solving. His writings on a new vision for the Christian university insisted that the university's priorities went beyond the education of students and included the promotion of a more just society for all people. Under Ellacuría's leadership, the UCA *qua* university sought to make a preferential option for the poor. At a commencement address given in the United States in 1982, he famously clarified what this means.

> This does not mean that only the poor study at the university; it does not mean that the university should abdicate its mission of academic excellence – excellence needed in order to solve complex social problems. It does mean that the university should be present intellectually where it is needed: to provide science for those who have no science; to provide skills for the unskilled; to be a voice for those who have no voice; to give intellectual support for those who do not possess the academic qualifications to promote and legitimate their rights.

The real sufferings of the Salvadoran people provided the horizon contextualizing all of the UCA's activities, which in turn gave meaning to its option for the poor.

Along with his political diplomacy and administrative acumen, Ellacuría delivered countless talks, radio broadcasts, and television interviews, and he penned a large body of essays and editorials analyzing the underlying roots of El Salvador's polarized social and economic systems. Several years before the Civil War began, in a special edition that the UCA academic journal, *Estudios Centroamericanos*, dedicated to the vexing issue of land reform, Ellacuría submitted a nuanced hermeneutical-ethical analysis of the concept of private property. When the weak central government reneged on its modest commitment to land reform, he penned a scathing satire of the whole process entitled "¡A sus órdenes, mi Capitál!" Shortly thereafter a bomb tore through the central administration building of the UCA, the second of some fifteen state-sponsored terrorist attacks against the university between 1975 and the massacre of Ellacuría and his companions in 1989.

Ellacuría's political writings and reflections on the university were groundbreaking, but what lent special depth and ongoing significance to his academic contributions were the rigor and relevance of his philosophical vision, his way of integrating that vision with the *Spiritual Exercises* of Saint Ignatius Loyola to craft a dynamic, hermeneutical approach to theological method, and his original contributions to historical soteriology and a new vision of church.

All of Ellacuría's diverse writings find a unifying core in his insistence that "historical reality" is the object of philosophy. This represents his way of continuing the philosophical task after the so-called "end of metaphysics" announced by Martin Heidegger and his postmodern heirs. At once critical, historically conscious, and yet open to transcendence, Ellacuría's posthumously published *Filosofía de la realidad histórica* displays a rigorous grasp of the material, biological, temporal, and historical grounds of reality but never collapses history into a closed dialectical materialism. He understands the "historical" not as the succession of various events that occur over time, nor as a systematized account of those events, but above all as the ambit of reality and realization that gives an underlying structural unity to everything that occurs. This underlying structural unity is given in reality, by reality, through real things, and it is given to human sentient intelligence (Zubiri) which alone can apprehend reality *qua* reality. Hence, he refers to the human not as the "rational animal" but the "reality animal." Moreover, Ellacuría intensifies the political dimension of Zubiri's thought and explores its relevance to theology. In several important essays recently translated into English, he imagines anew the role of philosophy in the liberation process and sketches the philosophical foundations for a Latin American theological method.

Along with Zubiri's profound articulation of the way humans apprehend the realities that they encounter, Ellacuría's distinctive approach to the discipline of theology is inspired by the *Spiritual Exercises* of Saint Ignatius of Loyola which emphasizes the composition of place and unveils its mysticism in and through historically real events. Although Ellacuría's writings on Ignatian spirituality do not take up a large space in his oeuvre, his efforts to uncover the presuppositions and implications of the *Spiritual Exercises* for the life of faith today give evidence that, at root, theological method is not primarily an epistemology nor even an anthropology so much as a faith praxis, a spirituality. One way that Ellacuría sought to put the Ignatian spirituality of Christian discipleship at the service of the Latin American Church was by developing philosophical and theological categories that correspond to and clarify its demands. Thus, in a manner characteristic of all of his writings, Ellacuría interprets the relationship between contemplation and action in a mystical-political key, allowing him to speak of "contemplation in the action of justice."

In a further integration of Ignatian spirituality with philosophy and theology, Ellacuría speaks of the *Spiritual Exercises* of Saint Ignatius as a way to enter and engage historical reality, to critically assess it, and to take responsibility for it. This corresponds closely with his understanding of the role of theology. In an important ecclesiological essay written in 1977, he famously defined liberation theology as "a reflection from faith on the historical reality and action of the people of God, who follow the work of Jesus in announcing and fulfilling God's Reign." Such an approach to theology includes the task of interpreting the *meaning* of the tradition in new situations, and constructing internally consistent conceptual systems, but insists that this work must emerge with a profound *ethical* commitment and must be embodied in a *practical*, efficacious life of faith. Theology as ethical commitment and faith praxis are not subsequent or supplementary to theology as interpretation, but of its essence. As such, Ellacuría interweaves his philosophical-spiritual appropriation of historical reality as the place of theological encounter with his understanding of the Church as the followers of Jesus who cooperate with his Spirit by helping to realize the Reign of God in history.

This last point corresponds to the fundamental vantage point of all of Ellacuría's theological work: the relationship between Christian salvation and historical liberation.

His central soteriological thesis, *salvation history is a salvation in and of history*, shapes his approach to the theology of salvation which he calls "historical soteriology." In his development of this biblically grounded, historically conscious approach to salvation, Ellacuría underscores the central unity between theology and ecclesial spirituality, between the living out of faith and the reflective vocation of the theologian. Theology needs to *reflect on* salvation in such a way that it actually *contributes to* salvation in history. Its concepts do not by themselves establish the vital link between historical reality and the Reign of God. Something more is needed: the liberating praxis of the faith community. Hence, in a succession of concrete historical situations, theology helps the Church fulfill its role as the sign of eschatological salvation by relating that ultimate purpose to those ever-changing circumstances. Ellacuría thus underscores the role of theology as an ecclesial discipline, or in the words of an important essay from 1978, "the ideological moment of ecclesial praxis." Through its reflective discernment, the Christian community helps point history toward the Reign of God. By reading the signs of the times, it discovers and implements its primary responsibilities and commitments.

In 1980, shortly after Archbishop Romero's death, Ellacuría deepened this recognition of the centrality of discernment to the discipline of theology. He wrote: "Among so many signs always being given, some identified and others hardly perceptible, there is in every age one that is primary, in whose light we should discern and interpret all the rest. This perennial sign is the historically crucified people." To view the poor and the suffering victims of our world as *crucified peoples* requires of Christians an audacious and difficult act of faith, for this "title" links the passion of Jesus to our current and ongoing historical reality. Similarly, this title enables Ellacuría to infuse the familiar but often misunderstood phrase, "preferential option for the poor," with extraordinary Christological depth. Like the servant of Yahweh in Second Isaiah, and ultimately like Jesus himself, the crucified people appear not only as victim of the sin of the world but as savior and judge of the world. Finally, what is true of that people could also be said of Ellacuría himself. Jon Sobrino captures this poignantly in reflections addressed to his friend on the first anniversary of his death:

> you were a man of compassion and mercy, and what was deepest in you, your guts and your heart, was moved by the immense pain of this people. This never left you in peace. It drove your creativity and your service. And your life, then, was not only service. Rather, it was the specific service of "taking the crucified people down from the cross," very much your words, the kind of words that are invented not only with much intelligence, but with an intelligence moved by compassion.

The exercise of compassionate intelligence drew Ignacio Ellacuría into the sufferings and hopes of the crucified people precisely as a theologian, philosopher, public intellectual, university administrator, and Jesuit priest. Throughout his life he bridged the historical chasms isolating the powerful and educated from the poor and illiterate. In his reflections on faith, he indelibly linked the sacrament of liberation to the fullness of salvation. By his death he made the reality of the poor and the destiny of the poor Christ his own. Taken as a whole, Ignacio Ellacuría's theological life, faith witness, and passionate death give extraordinary density to the words of the Jesuit order's 32nd General Congregation (1975) inscribed on his tomb: "What does it mean to be a Jesuit today? It is to engage, under the standard of the cross, in the crucial struggle of our time: the struggle for faith and the struggle for justice which that same faith demands."

See also Liberation Theology; Martyrs, Ideal and History; Preferential Option for the Poor; Service of Faith and Promotion of Justice; Universidad Centroamericana (UCA)

Burke, Kevin F., *The Ground beneath the Cross: The Theology of Ignacio Ellacuría*. Washington, DC: Georgetown University Press, 2000.
Ellacuría, Ignacio, *Escritos teológicos*. 4 vols. San Salvador: UCA Editores, 2000, 2002.
    Filosofía de la realidad histórica. Ed. A. González. San Salvador: UCA Editores, 1990.
    Ignacio Ellacuría: Essays on History, Liberation, and Salvation. Ed. M. E. Lee, with commentary by K. Burke. Maryknoll, NY: Orbis Books, 2013.
    Veinte años de historia en El Salvador (1969–1989): escritos políticos. 3 vols. San Salvador: UCA Editores, 1991.
A *Grammar of Justice: The Legacy of Ignacio Ellacuría Today*. Ed. J. M. Ashley, K. Burke, and R. Cardenal. Maryknoll, NY: Orbis Books, 2014.
Whitfield, Teresa, *Paying the Price: Ignacio Ellacuría and the Murdered Jesuits of El Salvador*. Philadelphia: Temple University Press, 1994.

Kevin F. Burke, SJ

Emblem Books

The word "emblem" comes from the ancient Greek *en/bléma*, literally "struck in." The term "emblem" was first coined by the Italian lawyer and humanist Andrea Alciato (1492–1550), who published his *Emblematum liber* at Augsburg in 1531. It was translated and appeared in more than 150 editions. An emblem has three components: *motto* (title), *pictura* (picture), and *subscriptio* (verse). Emblem books, both secular and religious, became enormously popular throughout Europe at least until the end of the eighteenth century, especially in the Netherlands, Belgium, Germany, and France.

In the first of five volumes of the *Corpus Librorum Emblematum: The Jesuit Series*, published in 1997, and written by Peter Daly and G. Richard Dimler, SJ, then general of the Society of Jesus Peter-Hans Kolvenbach wrote a foreword, undoubtedly prompted by the two authors. This gives an excellent insight into the role of the Jesuits in the production of emblem books:

> Members of the Society of Jesus produced more books in this genre [emblem books] than did any other identifiable group of writers. Furthermore, they published in all major European languages as well as in Latin … Both as individuals and colleges, Jesuits published emblematic books on a wide variety of topics. Religious themes dominate with books devoted to Christ, the Virgin Mary, biblical figures, martyrs and saints. Spiritual and theological works deal with the sacraments, Church teaching, devotion and meditation. There are also books celebrating dignitaries of the Church, the founding of churches, the jubilee of a college, or of the Society itself. But there is also a substantial number of works devoted to secular rulers: books celebrating dynastic marriages, births, baptisms, and royal exequies; books giving advice to princes and rulers, recording triumphal entries and commemorating victories. Jesuits used the emblem form for a range of didactic purposes imparting information on topics ranging from symbology, poetry and rhetoric, through philosophy, ethics and mythology, to alchemy and medicine.

The complete *Jesuit Series* comprises 1,525 entries: about 500 first editions, and a further 1,025 subsequent editions, issues, and translations. The following Jesuits are the most important authors of emblem books: Étienne Binet (1569–1639), Jan David (1546–1613), Jeremias Drexel (1581–1638), Henricus Engelgrave (1610–70), Guilielmus

Domine, ante te ômne d fiderium meum , &
gemitus meus à te non est abfconditus. Pfal. 37.

Heere

Figure 18 Christoffel van Sichem: Woodcut from Dutch translation of *Pia desideria* (Amsterdam, 1645). Photograph Paul Begheyn, SJ

Hesius (1601–90), Herman Hugo (1588–1629), Claude-François Ménestrier (1631–1705), Adriaen Poirters (1605–74), Louis Richeôme (1544–1625), Thomas Sailly (*c.* 1553–1623), Maximilianus Sandaeus (1578–1656), and Antoine Sucquet (1574–1627).

In the Netherlands the development of the love emblem, from 1600 onwards, can be seen as a manifestation of the successful literary relationship between the northern and southern part of the Low Countries. Religious love emblems were thereafter to a large extent influenced by Jacob Cats's *Sinne- en minnebeelden* (1618) and by Herman Hugo's *Pia desideria* (1624). Hugo's *Pia desideria* would become the most influential emblem book published after Alciato's *Emblematum liber*. It was reprinted forty-nine times, and ninety translations and adaptations were published all over Europe, as can be seen in the research of the *Emblem Project Utrecht*. The *Pia desideria* was used to help shape and form the Counter-Reformation in the Southern Netherlands.

Flemish historian Karel Porteman, retired professor of Dutch literature at the University of Louvain, who in 1996 published the emblematic exhibitions (*affixiones*) at the Jesuit College in Brussels (1630–85), wrote about the way Jesuits used emblem books:

The Jesuits more than anyone else integrated the emblem in education, and used it not just as a favourite exercise, but as a pedagogical crowning-piece to recommend their education system to the outside world. In the hand of the Jesuits the emblem was both an artistic-ingenious and a persuasive means of communication. It made the spiritual insistently tangible, visible and admirable for the complete human being, viz. for the eyes and the other senses, the intellectual capacities, the heart, the emotions and the affects. In this respect the emblem was part of the high technology of Jesuit *eloquentia*.

Emblems not only appeared in Jesuit books but were also used as interior and exterior decoration in buildings, as in the Jesuit colleges of Toruń in Poland and of Portuguese America, in the dormitory of the deanery of Bristol cathedral, and in St. Katharina, Katharinenheerd on the peninsula of Eiderstedt in Germany.

See also Catechisms; Images; Rhetoric(s)

Daly, Peter, and G. Richard Dimler, *Corpus Librorum Emblematum: The Jesuit Series*. 5 vols. Montreal: McGill-Queen's University Press; Toronto: University of Toronto Press, 1997–2007.
Emblemata Sacra: Emblem Books from the Maurits Sabbe Library, Katholieke Universiteit Leuven. Philadelphia, PA: Saint Joseph's University Press, 2006.
Manning John, and Marc van Vaeck, eds., *The Jesuits and the Emblem Tradition*. Turnhout: Brepols, 1999.
Porteman, Karel, *Emblematic Exhibitions (affixiones) at the Brussels Jesuit College (1630–1685)*. Brussels: Royal Library; Turnhout: Brepols, 1996.

Paul Begheyn, SJ

Encyclopedias

As an institution dedicated to knowledge, education, and the free exchange of ideas, it seems inevitable that the Society of Jesus should become involved in the production of encyclopedias. It is also true that the Society was created during the first heyday of the encyclopedia; the rapid spread of ideas brought about by the advent of mechanical printing, the discovery and exploration of the New World, and increasing contact with the Far East forced Europeans in the sixteenth and seventeenth centuries to devise ever more elaborate and practical ways to organize knowledge. Encyclopedias were a critical part of this process, and by the middle of the seventeenth century the Jesuits had established an important foothold in this genre.

The archetype of the Jesuit encyclopedia was not a text, but an individual: Athanasius Kircher (1602–80). Widely acknowledged in his own time as a polymath, Kircher exemplified a thoroughly baroque approach to knowledge, combining a respect for ancient and medieval authorities with the early modern commitment to innovation. This was obvious both in his own works and in the museum he administered in the Collegio Romano. Kircher's encyclopedic interests were extraordinary, even by the standards of his time. He produced encyclopedic treatments of Egyptian language and history (his *Oedipus Aegyptiacus*) and of Chinese culture (his *China illustrata*), and published more than thirty other works devoted to subjects such as light, sound, geology, and magnetism, all thanks at least in part to the resources of the Society – certainly he had access to artifacts and correspondents that virtually no one else did.

Kircher's encyclopedic legacy transcended his own corpus of works; he also inspired other Jesuits to produce widely circulated encyclopedias such as Gioseffo Petrucci's *Prodromo apologetico alli studi Chircheriani* (1677) and Caspar Knittel's *Via regia ad omnes scientias et artes* (1682). The same was true of works written by his disciples within the Society, such as Gaspar Schott's *Cursus mathematicus* (1661) – the "encyclopedia of all of the mathematical sciences" – and Francesco Lana de Terzi's *Prodromo, ouero, Saggio di alcune inuentioni nuoue premesso all'arte maestro* (1670). Of course, the tradition of Jesuit encyclopedias did not flow from Kircher alone; one finds numerous examples of encyclopedias authored by other Jesuits, such as Michael Pexenfelder's *Apparatus eruditionis tam rerum quam verborum per omnes artes et scientias* (1670). Together, these works were opportunities for the Society to showcase its erudition, its willingness to innovate, and the sheer breadth of the knowledge encompassed by its members.

It would be remiss to write an article on Jesuits and encyclopedias without mentioning perhaps the most well-known example of the genre: that vast expression of Enlightenment ideals, the *Encyclopédie* of Denis Diderot and Jean le Rond d'Alembert. The Jesuits were opposed to the *Encyclopédie* throughout its formation; many at the time believed that the Jesuits were behind the attempts to suppress its production. The contemporaneous *Dictionnaire de Trévoux*, which began its life as one of the earliest attempts to synthesize the learning of the eighteenth century, was both influenced by the Jesuits and sharply critical of the *Encyclopédie*. Given the anti-religious and materialist tone that pervaded many of the articles in the *Encyclopédie*, Jesuit opposition was not surprising; the hostility with which the *Encyclopédie* discussed the Society was itself unsurprising as well, for the Society represented to Diderot and other *philosophes* the very worst of religion in general and Catholicism in particular. The lengthy article on "Jésuite" in the *Encyclopédie*, authored by Louis de Jaucourt (with editorial emendations provided by Diderot himself), was scathing in its treatment of the Society, and Diderot was so taken with this piece that he had it published separately in London in 1766.

For better or worse, this treatment of the Society in the *Encyclopédie* was rooted in a widespread sentiment that existed in the years leading up to the papal suppression of the Society in 1773. Thus, the encyclopedia holds a double edge for the Jesuits: it has showcased their collective mastery and erudition, but has also provided a potent vehicle for criticism and dissent.

Since the restoration of the Society of Jesus in 1814, many Jesuits have devoted much time and energy to contributing entries to modern encyclopedias, such as the *Catholic Encyclopedia* (15 vols., 1907–12), and its later editions. Jesuits have also served as editors and co-editors of encyclopedias, with one notable example being Karl Rahner, who served as the lead editor of *Sacramentum Mundi: An Encyclopedia of Theology* (German edition in 4 vols., 1967–69; English edition in 6 vols., 1968–70).

See also Bibliographies; Dictionaries; Kircher, Athanasius, SJ

Diderot, Denis, *Article "Jésuite," tiré de l'Encyclopédie par main de maître*. London, 1766.
Knobloch, Eberhard, "Kaspar Schott's 'Encyclopedia of All Mathematical Sciences.'" *Poiesis & Praxis* 7, 4 (2011), 225–47.
Stolzenberg, Daniel, ed., *The Great Art of Knowing: The Baroque Encyclopedia of Athanasius Kircher*. Stanford, CA: Stanford University Libraries, 2001.

Mark A. Waddell

Enlightenment

Conceptualizations of the historical category of "Enlightenment" have undergone significant refinement in recent decades. It is now perceived by many scholars as a transnational, multifaceted, and organic phenomenon, and its relationship with the

Society of Jesus epitomizes this protean character. In earlier scholarship the Jesuits were frequently positioned as the natural enemies of an intellectually uncluttered, broadly anticlerical Enlightenment, and it remains true that some of the era's leading thinkers (such as Diderot and d'Alembert) had little sympathy for the Society. Likewise, members of the Society of Jesus led criticism of some of the landmark achievements of the Enlightenment, as traditionally construed: the *Encyclopedia*, for instance. However, it has become increasingly clear that numerous Jesuits had much in common with, and made vital contributions to, the broader trends of eighteenth-century intellectual life. Jesuit missionary endeavor was vital in stirring interest in far-distant cultures (China is perhaps the prime example) and a broadly positive assessment of human nature (often seen as a hallmark of the era's intellectual trajectory) was fundamental to mainstream Jesuit moral theology, in contradistinction to that of their Jansenist foes. Perhaps most striking is the Jesuit contribution to scientific inquiry during the period. Some sectors of eighteenth-century Jesuit intellectual life retained a conservative complexion. Curriculum reform was not always speedy and many within the Society clung to Aristotelian paradigms. However, it would be erroneous to suggest that members of the Society did not engage constructively with the era's most challenging thought.

It would, though, be appropriate to identify a tension in the Society's response to the era's intellectual currents: a reluctance to abandon tradition alongside a passion to embrace new ideas. A figure such as the Jesuit Roger Boscovich provides a useful example. Boscovich was, by any standard, one of the most adventurous thinkers of his time and was engaged in an impressive array of scientific disciplines. Some of his musings incurred the displeasure of his Jesuit superiors, but his talents were well recognized. Boscovich himself was torn between a desire to embrace provocative thought and a duty to place his researches in the context of an orthodox religious worldview: something he greatly respected.

This tightrope walk, so to speak, was a constant in the lives of many eighteenth-century Jesuits. A complicating factor is the newly minted concept of an idiosyncratic "Catholic Enlightenment." While many individual Jesuits contributed to this phenomenon, a case has been made that the Society of Jesus was increasingly perceived (not least by those of Jansenist and Gallican sympathies) as, at best, a complication and, at worst, an obstacle to the process of Catholic engagement with the era's intellectual adventure. This case can, however, be overstated, and future research will doubtless reveal how the processes of a Catholic Enlightenment varied from country to country, and from decade to decade. Indeed, the multivalency of the Enlightenment looks likely to command our attention for many years to come, and Jesuit involvement offers an unusually useful prism. Purveyors of the concept of a later "radical" Enlightenment accept the idea that, earlier in the century, there was much to be decided but stress the emergence of a subsequent movement that apparently signaled the arrival of "modernity." It seems more likely that the pluralities of the Enlightenment, however construed, remained regnant from beginning to end.

One certainty is that a monolithic approach to the value and potential of reason did not define the eighteenth century. There were many ways to construe the concept, including one rooted in devotion (reason as a God-given gift), and many Jesuits took the lead in utilizing the latest philosophical work in their religiously driven work. A case in point is the Bavarian Jesuit Benedict Stattler who engaged actively with the adventurous thought of Christian Wolff in his theological endeavors. Such was Stattler's reputation that even the Munich Academy of Sciences, a body know for its anti-Jesuitism, awarded him membership. Because of his later opposition to the theories of Kant, Stattler has sometimes been portrayed as an anti-Enlightenment figure. In fact, he demonstrated that it was entirely possible for the holder of a chair of dogmatic theology at Ingolstadt to be at the heart of the Enlightenment project. Much the same could be said of Jesuits who, across Europe, made vital contributions to disciplines as various as epistemology and experimental physics. It is certainly misleading to construe the attack on the Jesuits between the late 1750s and the 1773 Suppression as primarily a symptom of Enlightenment animus against the Society, even if leading *philosophes* attempted to take the credit. More important factors, ranging from Jansenist antipathy to local political happenstance, were at play.

See also Boscovic, Rogerius Joseph, SJ; Jansenism; Science: Suppression

Burson, Jeffrey, and Ulrich Lehner, eds., *Enlightenment and Catholicism in Europe: A Transnational History.* Notre Dame, IN: University of Notre Dame Press, 2014.

Lehner, Ulrich, and Michael O'Neil Printy, eds., *A Companion to Catholic Enlightenment in Europe.* Leiden: Brill, 2010.

Porter, R., and Mikuláš Teich, eds., *The Enlightenment in National Context.* Cambridge: Cambridge University Press, 1981.

Jonathan Wright

Epeikeia

Law is "a body of rules of action or conduct prescribed by controlling authority and having binding legal force" (*Black's Law Dictionary*, 795). Within the Church and from the ecclesiological perspective of Vatican II's *Lumen gentium* 8, law provides a means by which the Church fulfills its mission, the salvation of souls, which underlies epeikeia. "Ecclesiastical law," from a human legislator and distinct from divine and/or natural law, is an abstract norm directed to that which is common (rather than specific) and intends to protect the common good. At times, an ecclesiastical law could lead to consequences unintended by the legislator and could harm rather than support the common good and justice. In such cases, *aequitas* (equity, Greek *epeikeia*) could be utilized. For St. Thomas, equity/epeikeia is a virtue by which strict observance of the law is moderated to follow the dictates of justice and the common good (*Summa theologica*, II–II, 120:1–2). Equity/epeikeia is not a negative judgment on a law but rather the judgment that applying this law to such circumstances involving these persons could lead to injustice and harm the common good, i.e., results the legislator could not have foreseen. Epeikeia/equity requires that legitimate authority confronted with such circumstances take into consideration the *mens legislatoris* (the legislator's intention in enacting this law); the value which the law intends to protect; and the common good. Certain authors distinguish between equity (external forum, by one with authority) and epeikeia (internal forum alone, by private individuals). As an aspect of justice, epeikeia/equity assists in fulfilling the teleology of Church law, that is, law is not an end in and of itself but serves the mission of the Church and, in particular, Jesuit proper law is directed to this mission.

See also Canon Law

Black, Henry, *Black's Law Dictionary*. 5th edn. St. Paul: West Publishing, 1979.
Coughlin, John, "Canonical Equity." *Studia canonica* 30 (1996), 403–35.

Robert J. Kaslyn, SJ

Erasmus

Erasmus of Rotterdam was the most influential Renaissance humanist of the early sixteenth century. He promoted eloquence, the compatibility of the wisdom of ancient Greece and Rome with Christianity, and a learned piety. Most likely born in 1466, he was the illegitimate son of a priest. In 1492, Erasmus was ordained a priest. He left the monastery of the Augustinian canons at Steyn near Gouda in 1493, never to return to the discipline of monastic life. He obtained a doctorate in theology in short order from the University of Turin in 1506. Erasmus gradually fashioned his reputation in the Renaissance republic of letters through contacts with fellow humanists and through his publications, many of which had pedagogical import. The *Adages* was a growing collection of ancient proverbial wisdom elucidated by his own commentary. In the *Praise of Folly* and the *Colloquies*, Erasmus satirized the religious foibles of his day. His New Testament scholarship brought him renown and infamy. In 1516, he published the first printed Greek New Testament with the Vulgate translation and annotations that corrected the Vulgate text. Four revised editions appeared between 1519 and 1535. Erasmus's annotations and his *Paraphrases on the New Testament* (1517–24) courted considerable controversy, especially in the religiously divisive climate of what he called the Lutheran tragedy. Many Catholic theologians viewed him as paving the way for Luther and Protestantism. His *Diatribe on the Free Will* (1524) provoked the wrath of Luther, who dismissed Erasmus as a skeptic. Embattled, Erasmus continued to write until his death in 1536, publishing polemics, patristic editions, and spiritual and pastoral works, including the *Ecclesiastes* (1535), a voluminous manual on preaching. The taint of heterodoxy dogged his reputation after his death. The first papal Index of Prohibited Books (1559) condemned all his writings in their various genres, even publications that had nothing to do with religion. Subsequent Roman Indices curiously condemned all of his works in the category of heretics of the first class but also listed Erasmus among heretics of the second class, subject only to the proscription or purgation of specific works.

The first generations of Jesuits had to contend with Erasmus's legacy, especially in their educational ministries and their activity as controversialists. It is probably a myth that the *Enchiridion militis christiani*, Erasmus's early manual on piety, repelled Ignatius of Loyola. Ignatius did not prohibit Jesuits from reading Erasmus. After 1552, however, he forbade the use of his publications as textbooks in Jesuit schools, most likely because Erasmus remained a controversial author. The ban on Erasmus was uncompromising at the Collegio Romano, but in other contexts Ignatius was capable of flexibility toward Erasmus's influence on pedagogy. Refusing to condemn Erasmus as a heretic, Diego Laínez, as superior general, demonstrated greater tolerance than Ignatius. But Everard Mercurian in 1575 forbade Jesuits from reading Erasmus's books without permission. Some Jesuits, like Antonio Possevino, reviled Erasmus as Luther's inspiration. Others, like Alfonso Salmerón, studied his exegetical works without appreciative acknowledgment. As a consultor to the Congregation of the Index, Robert Bellarmine recommended removing Erasmus from the list of heretics of the first class, since he did not consider Erasmus a heretic, despite his errors.

Ambivalence characterized Peter Canisius's interpretation of Erasmus. He shared Erasmus's love of proverbial wisdom and his preference for the Church Fathers as theologians over the medieval scholastic doctors. In literary refinement, Erasmus had no rival; in theology, Canisius maintained, he was an insufferable and dangerous dabbler. Canisius managed to associate Erasmus with Protestantism while at the same time enlisting his authority for Catholic doctrine.

In the twentieth century, Jesuits contributed to the rehabilitation of Erasmus's reputation. In his magisterial *Exégèse médiévale* (1959–64), Henri de Lubac devoted a long, sympathetic section to Erasmus, admiring his theological predilection for the Church Fathers and maintaining that he was a precursor of Catholic Reform more than of the Protestant Reformation. Georges Chantraine asserted the theological credentials of Erasmus, who combined exegesis with an authentic spirituality and fidelity to Catholic tradition. In emphasizing the centrality of piety in Erasmus's thought and writing, John O'Malley has advanced the historical reevaluation of Erasmus more than any other Jesuit. He insists that Erasmus's piety was not only learned but also Christological and pastoral and evinced significant affinities with the early Jesuits. Erasmus's integration of rhetorical style and theological method, O'Malley contends, anticipated the Second Vatican Council.

See also Catholic Reformers; Humanism

Grendler, Paul F., "The Attitudes of the Jesuits toward Erasmus." In Konrad Eisenbichler, ed., *Collaboration, Conflict and Continuity in the Reformation: Essays in Honour of James M. Estes on His Eightieth Birthday*. Toronto: Centre for Reformation and Renaissance Studies, 2014, pp. 363–85.

Pabel, Hilmar M., "Praise and Blame: Peter Canisius' Ambivalent Assessment of Erasmus." In Karl A. E. Enenkel, ed., *The Reception of Erasmus in the Early Modern Period*. Leiden: Brill, 2013, pp. 129–59.

Hilmar M. Pabel

Espinosa Pólit, Aurelio, SJ (1894–1961)

Aurelio Espinosa Pólit, SJ, was one of the most prominent literary critics of twentieth-century Ecuador. Born on July 11, 1894, in Quito, Espinosa Pólit was educated almost completely in Europe, first in Belgium and Switzerland, and later on in England. In 1911, after finishing his secondary studies, he joined the Society of Jesus and completed his novitiate in Granada, Spain. In 1922, Espinosa Pólit was ordained in Sarlat, France, and began his ministry in Barcelona. In 1927 he enrolled at Cambridge University, to complete his studies in Greek and Latin. In 1928 he traveled back to Ecuador, where he directed the Jesuit novitiate in Cotocollao. That same year, he published the first of twenty-nine books, which included original poetry, translations of the Greco-Roman classics, textbooks, and studies on Ecuadorian literature. In 1930, he began a modest library of Ecuadorian writers in Cotocollao that, in time, would become the Biblioteca de Autores Nacionales, one of the main research centers in that country. In 1943 he helped found the Academia Cultural Ecuatoriana (Academy of Ecuadorian Culture, later known as the Casa de la Cultura Ecuatoriana). In 1946, along with Julio Tobar

Donoso and Archbishop Carlos María de la Torre, Espinosa Pólit founded the Pontifical Catholic University of Ecuador. He became its first rector, and taught Greek language and literature. In 1956, he assumed the editorial direction of the *Biblioteca Ecuatoriana Mínima*, probably one of the most ambitious publishing projects in Ecuador, aimed at re-editing what was considered the fundamental works of Ecuador's culture since the Colonial period. Father Aurelio Espinosa Pólit died in Quito on January 21, 1961.

See also Ecuador

Pimentel, Rodolfo Pérez, *Diccionario biográfico del Ecuador*. Guayaquil, Ecuador: Litografía e Imprenta de la Universidad de Guayaquil, 1987.

Andrés Ignacio Prieto

Ethics

Jesuits have been significantly involved in the development of moral methods and approaches as well as the advancement of theological ethics as a discipline.

Casuistry. In the sixteenth century Jesuits were associated with the development of high casuistry, a method of analyzing hard moral cases through comparison with resolved cases. Jesuits used this case method in their formation of future priests and in their ministry in the confessional. Case studies were published by Jesuit casuists for use as textbooks and guides for confessors. Among the noted Jesuit casuists during the sixteenth century were John Azor, Herman Busenbaum, and Antonio Escobar y Mendoza. Blaise Pascal's harsh criticism of casuistry led to the association of the method with laxity. Albert Jonsen, with his co-author Stephen Toulmin, helped revive interest in casuistry in the twentieth century through the publication of their book *The Abuse of Casuistry*.

Probabilism. First proposed by the Dominican Bartolomeo Medina in 1577, the doctrine of probabilism allowed one to follow a probable (or plausible) moral opinion even if the opposite opinion was more probable. An opinion is judged probable if "wise men propose it and confirm it with excellent arguments." The Jesuit moralist Gabriel Vasquez developed Medina's theory by identifying and separating the two components that make an opinion probable: reasonable arguments that provide "intrinsic probability" and reputable authorities who provide "extrinsic probability." Another Jesuit moralist, Francisco Suárez, introduced reflex principles to the theory of probabilism that allowed persons to judge whether, in a situation of doubt, a moral rule obliges or not. Jesuits were the leading proponents of probabilism, and it became an important component of their use of high casuistry. Probabilism was criticized by rigorists in the seventeenth century for contributing to laxity in morality. Despite this criticism and papal condemnation of both rigorist and laxist moral opinions, the doctrine of probabilism was never condemned and continues to be used by Catholic moralists today.

Manualism. After the Council of Trent until the twentieth century, moral theology was shaped by the moral manuals used in seminaries to form future confessors. Manualist moral theology was concerned with avoidance of sin and obedience to law. Jesuit manualists whose writings were authoritative and widely used during this period include Thomas Slater, Henry Davis, John Ford, and Gerard Kelly.

Renewal of Moral Theology. By the mid-twentieth century before Vatican II, a number of moral theologians viewed the minimalism of the moral manuals as inadequate for authentic Christian discipleship. These moralists sought to move moral theology away from an over-emphasis on sin and law and to greater integration with Scripture, spirituality, and dogmatic theology. Along with the Benedictine Odon Lottin and diocesan priest Fritz Tillman, the Jesuit Gerard Gilleman (1910–2002) was an early significant contributor to this movement of renewal. Gilleman's work, *The Primacy of Charity in Moral Theology* (1952), emphasized charity as the font and primary motivation of the Christian moral life. In the field of social ethics, the writings of John Courtney Murray (1904–67) helped shape the Church's view on religious freedom and the relationship between the Church and State in Vatican II.

Moral Theology after Vatican II. Joseph Fuchs, SJ (1912–2005), was one of the most significant influences on moral theology in the twentieth century. Originally trained in the classicist tradition that emphasized the teaching authority of the Church, Fuchs experienced an intellectual conversion while participating in the Pontifical Commission on Population, Family, and Birth Rate in the mid-1960s. Fuchs drafted the Majority Report of the Commission. After his conversion, Fuchs's writings emphasized the competence of the individual conscience, personal responsibility, and moral objectivity. He developed the theory of fundamental option. A Jesuit student of Fuchs, Bruno Schüller (1925–2007) contributed to the understanding of moral norms by making a distinction between the origin of a norm and its validity. Richard McCormick (1922–2000) helped influence the development of moral theology through his authorship of the "Notes on Moral Theology" in the Jesuit journal *Theological Studies* from 1965 to 1984. Through the Notes, McCormick regularly surveyed and evaluated the writings of ethicists from different countries. His writings also contributed to the discussions on proportionate reason and conscientious dissent. Peter Knauer introduced a rethinking of the traditional principle of double effect and distilled the principle's conditions to the consideration of proportionately grave reasons to allow evil effects of an action. Knauer's writings contributed to the development of the ethical theory of proportionalism. James Keenan has written extensively on virtue ethics, moral methodology, HIV/AIDS, and the history of moral theology. He has contributed to a more global and culturally sensitive perspective on contemporary theological ethics. He is the founder of an international network of Catholic ethicists (Catholic Theological Ethics in the World Church) that has fostered contextual reflection and multicultural dialogue on moral issues.

See also Casuistry; Ford, John C., SJ; Fuchs, Josef, SJ; Probabilism

Jonsen, Albert, and Stephen Toulmin, *The Abuse of Casuistry: A History of Moral Reasoning*. Oakland, CA: University of California Press, 1990.

Keenan, James F., *A History of Catholic Moral Theology in the Twentieth Century: From Confessing Sins to Liberating Consciences*. London: Continuum, 2010.

Eric Marcelo O. Genilo, SJ

Études

A French Jesuit journal on contemporary thought and culture, *Études* was originally founded in 1856 by Jesuits Charles Daniel and Jean Gagarine under the title *Études de théologie, de philosophie et d'histoire*. In the twentieth century, however, the scope of the journal was steadily broadened to include themes beyond philosophy and theology, and today it publishes on a wide range of topics, including international events, social questions, religion and spirituality, literature and the arts, films, entertainment, and other points of cultural interest.

Based in Paris, *Études* publishes eleven issues per year. The journal reports a print circulation of 11,000 subscribers in France and abroad, but in recent years its expansive internet presence has garnered a considerably larger readership. It has been issued continuously since its founding, with the exception of the period between 1880 and 1888, during which time the Jesuits were expelled from France, and between 1940 and 1944, the time of the German occupation. The editor has always been a Jesuit, but a large portion of its articles are now written by academic laymen and women chosen both for their expertise and for their affinity with "the spirit of the magazine."

Since 2000, *Études* has been under the umbrella of the Société d'Édition de Revues (SER), a joint venture of the Society of Jesus and the Bayard Presse Group. Known for its contemporary Jesuit humanism, the journal outlines on its website its aim to serve as a forum for dialogue and discernment on issues such as "the question of the human being in an environment marked by the rapid development of technology and a globalized economy," "the ecological challenge," the "fluidization of benchmarks in a postmodern context," and the "expression of the Christian faith in a secularized culture."

See also France; Revues/Journals

Études: revue de culture cotemporaine. www.revue-etudes.com.
Vallin, Pierre, "*Études*, histoire d'une revue: une aventure jésuite. Des origines au Concile Vatican II (1856 à 1965)." *Études.* special no. (2000), 5–81.

Henry Shea, SJ

Examen

The examen (a shorthand term) is the quintessential Ignatian prayer. It is found in two forms in the *Spiritual Exercises* (*SpEx*): the particular and the general examination of conscience (*SpEx* ##24–31 and 32–44). In this context it forms part of the First Week, the period when a retreatant discovers both the seriousness of their sin and the depth of God's mercy. Outside of retreat the examen can also be a daily (or twice-daily) prayer. In *Exercises* (#43) Ignatius suggests a method for making the examen, consisting of five points (thanksgiving, petition for enlightenment, examination of conscience, contrition, resolve for the future). This outline has been preserved over the centuries as a prayer (usually of about 15 minutes' duration) that allows a person to see whether they are advancing or regressing in their relationship with God.

Yet however helpful this way of making the examen proved to be, it ran the risk of rigidity and of a concentration on the negative in a person's life. To examine one's conscience meant to look for sin. This focus could lead to discouragement or (in extreme cases) self-loathing or despair. It also seemed to call for a degree of willpower that many people did not possess. In 1972 a seminal article by George Aschenbrenner brought about a radical rethinking of this prayer. Instead of an examination of "conscience," he proposed a "consciousness" examen. Here the stress is less on uncovering sins and more on becoming aware of the varied ways in which God was present during the period under review. Instead of concentrating solely on freely initiated thoughts, words, or actions, a person is invited to notice also the non-free movements or spontaneities they had experienced. So the emphasis moved from conscience (guilt) to consciousness (awareness), from the negative to the positive, from sin to grace.

See also Spiritual Exercises

Aschenbrenner, George, "Consciousness Examen." *Review for Religious* 31 (1972), 14–21.
Gallagher, Timothy, *The Examen Prayer: Ignatian Wisdom for Our Lives Today*. New York: Crossroad, 2006.

Brian O'Leary, SJ

Exhortation

The use of the exhortation, a style of oratory that makes direct appeal in ordinary language to an action or behavior supported by the *ethos* of a community, first appears in the fifth chapter of the *General Examen*. There, Ignatius suggests that students should deliver an exhortation "to give some proof of their progress in what they have studied." Acquiring the communication skills necessary for the spiritual aid of one's neighbor, then, requires young Jesuits in studies to preach within their community so that "they may encourage themselves and acquire a facility of voice." Part of that preaching would include exhortations to the virtues, especially "to union and fraternal charity."

Not surprisingly, Jesuit schools encouraged their students, both Jesuit and lay, to recite exhortations at public declamations. The Rules for the German College (1569) encouraged older students to exhort the younger ones to progress in the spiritual life. Jerónimo Nadal suggested that the Jesuit confessor should exhort the penitent with words of warning, advice, and comfort in a sort of private sermon (*privatas [ut ita dicam] conciones*).

The only required exhortations occur before the election of a new superior general. At the beginning of a General Congregation, the *Constitutions* call for the vicar general to exhort those gathered to make their decision "in a way conducive to the greater service to God and the good governance of the Society." The most recent Rules for a General Congregation has the vicar general "propose for the approval of the Congregation one of the Electors" to do so.

See also Rhetoric(s)

The Constitutions of the Society of Jesus and Their Complementary Norms. Ed. John W. Padberg. St. Louis, MO: The Institute of Jesuit Sources, 1996.
O'Malley, John W., *The First Jesuits*. Cambridge, MA: Harvard University Press, 1993.

Mark A. Lewis, SJ

Ex-Jesuits

Men who enter the Society of Jesus do not always remain; some leave for a variety of their own reasons, and some are expelled by the Society for certain reasons. In the late eighteenth century, the Society itself was suppressed, and thus "suppressed" Jesuits formed for a time a very large group of ex-Jesuits, among them John Carroll, first bishop in the United States.

Some ex-Jesuits are bitter about their Jesuit experiences, and they may devote much energy to exposing what they believe are the Society's faults and failures. An example is Malachi Martin, a former Irish Jesuit who spent decades denouncing not only the Jesuits but in many other ways the direction of the Catholic Church after Vatican II as well. A more recent critique comes from Stephen Casey, a Canadian who left the Jesuits after nearly four decades; his 2007 book *The Greater Glory* is a kind of indictment of the Jesuit formation and way of life he endured for a very long time.

But other ex-Jesuits have been and are more positive about their time as Jesuits. An example is F. E. Peters, a novice and a scholastic in the New York province, who went on to a very successful career in Islamic studies. Ex-Jesuits sometimes work in Jesuit educational institutions. Bernard Cooke, a prominent sacramental theologian, and for some years chair of the Religious Studies Department at the College of the Holy Cross, is an example. Ex-Jesuits are also found in a great variety of career paths. Jerry Brown, multi-term governor of California, spent some time as a young man as a Jesuit novice and scholastic.

See also Anti-Jesuit Polemic; Dismissal; Formation; Suppression

Casey, Stephen, *The Greater Glory: Thirty-Seven Years with the Jesuits.* Montreal: McGill-Queen's University Press, 2007.
Martin, Malachi, *The Jesuits: The Society of Jesus as Trojan Horse in the Global War against the Papacy.* New York: Simon & Schuster, 1987.
Peters, F. E., *Ours: The Making and Unmaking of a Jesuit.* New York: Penguin, 1982.

Thomas Worcester, SJ

Experiment

In the *General Examen*, an early Jesuit document focused upon the admission of candidates to the Society of Jesus, frequent references are made to various so-called "experiments" that each candidate would undertake. These experiments, peculiar to novices, were detailed by St. Ignatius and have remained standard since the approval of the Society in 1540, though they have been adapted and developed over time. In essence, the experiments are designed to test a candidate's fitness for life as a Jesuit.

Each of the six principal testing experiments might be paired with a question with which the novice director could evaluate a candidate: (1) to make the *Spiritual Exercises* for one month: *is he a man of prayer?* (2) to serve for another month in hospitals: *is he suitable for apostolic work?* (3) to spend another month making a pilgrimage without money: *can he rely on God and the Society?* (4) to serve in various low and humble offices: *does he understand no work to be beneath him?* (5) to explain the Christian faith to children or those who are unfamiliar with it: *is he able to hand on the faith?* and (6) to preach or hear confessions: *how does a more public witness deepen his life of faith?* (*General Examen*, ##64–70). (Of special note is the first experiment, the *Spiritual Exercises*, since it is so fundamental to the life and ministry of a Jesuit.)

At the heart of the experiments is a testing of character and attitude, and the novice director has great latitude to place a novice under specific circumstances to better understand the man and his fitness for life in the Society.

See also Formation; Novitiate, Novice

The Constitutions of the Society of Jesus and Their Complementary Norms. Ed. John W. Padberg. St. Louis, MO: The Institute of Jesuit Sources, 1996.

Keith Maczkiewicz, SJ

Extern

The word "extern" is used in the Jesuit *Constitutions* to describe people with whom Jesuits work. It is introduced in Part IV in the context of colleges wherein "not only our own scholastics may be helped in learning, but also those from outside (*externi*) in both learning and good habits of conduct" (#392). Thus, an initial reference to externs in the *Constitutions* refers to students at Jesuit schools. In early Jesuit documents Jesuits are identified using the possessive "Ours" in distinction from externs.

At a practical level, the *Constitutions* limited financial interactions with externs and the influence of externs upon the missioning of Jesuits. In this case extern referred to anyone outside of the Society of Jesus, though particularly those with whom Jesuits regularly come in contact. After the Second Vatican Council, the 32nd General Congregation articulated new relationships with those outside of the Society. That Congregation articulated its mission as the service of faith through helping others to "become more open toward God and more willing to live according to the demands of the Gospel." Following the lead of post-conciliar synods, they tied the service of faith to the promotion of justice. This led to greater international cooperation among Jesuits, as well as with others seeking similar ends. Increasingly the language of collaboration has replaced "extern" to better reflect this sense of sharing a common mission.

See also Collaboration; Women, as Co-Workers with Jesuits

The Constitutions of the Society of Jesus and Their Complementary Norms. Ed. John W. Padberg. St. Louis, MO: The Institute of Jesuit Sources, 1996.
Padberg, John W., ed., *Jesuit Life and Mission Today: The Decrees and Accompanying Documents of the 31st–35th General Congregations of the Society of Jesus*. St. Louis, MO: The Institute of Jesuit Sources, 2009.

Mark A. Lewis, SJ

Faber, Peter, SJ, St. (1506–1564)

Born on April 13, 1506, in Villaret (Savoy, now Rhône-Alpes), the eldest of a devout, middle-class family, Peter began studies (1516) at the Latin school recently founded by Swiss priest Pierre Veillard in La Roche. There he met classmate Claude Jay (*c.* 1504–52), with whom Peter later would profess vows at Montmartre. In 1525 Peter enrolled in the College of Montaigu at the University of Paris, transferring shortly thereafter to the College of Saint Barbara, where he shared a room with Francis Xavier. Ignatius of Loyola (1491–1556), who moved in with them in 1529, would later give Peter the First Week of the *Spiritual Exercises* as a remedy to deal with Peter's anxiety and scruples.

Having received the degree of bachelor of arts (1529) and the licentiate in philosophy (1530), Peter began his study of theology, making the complete *Exercises* under Ignatius in the beginning of 1534. He received priestly ordination in May and celebrated his first Mass on August 15 in the martyrium on Montmartre. There he professed, along with Ignatius and five other companions from the university, vows of poverty and to make pilgrimage to Jerusalem, with the clause that they would decide by majority once in Jerusalem whether to remain there or to return to Europe, where they would put themselves at the service of the pope. Faber gave the *Exercises* while continuing his studies of theology in Paris, receiving the degree of master of arts in October 1536 after which he and the other companions met up with Ignatius in Venice.

They left Ignatius in January 1537 for Rome, where they requested permission of the pope to work in northern Italy. Returning to Venice in October with Diego Laínez (1512–65), the three set out for Rome, en route to which Ignatius had his mystical experience at La Storta. During the following years, Peter engaged in a variety of apostolic works, including spiritual direction, sacramental ministry, instruction in theology and Scripture, and work among the Protestants in Germany and Spain. He developed a reputation for joy and warmth in friendship and of excellence in giving the *Exercises* to all classes of people. On this note, Ignatius himself famously considered Peter the companion most apt to direct others in the *Exercises*. Upon receiving the mission to serve as theologian at the Council of Trent, Peter left Spain in July 1564 for Rome, where he died on August 1, fatigued from years of work and travel. With the approval of Francis de Sales (1567–1622), the inquest into Peter's virtues began in 1596 and concluded with his beatification by Pius IX on September 5, 1872. On December 17, 2013, Pope Francis added Peter to the canon of saints for the universal Church following the process of extraordinary or equivalent canonization.

Although Peter left behind few writings, the autobiographical notes and prayer journal, composed between June 1542 and May 1545 and edited as the *Memorial*, provide an exceptional source for coming to know both the state of his own soul and, along with the *Spiritual Exercises* and *Constitutions* of Ignatius, the spiritual orientation of the early Society of Jesus. In addition, his extant communications and correspondence provide both valuable information about the regions where Peter ministered and insight into his spiritual doctrine and capacity for human friendship.

Charles Morel outlines the principal traits of Peter's spirituality as they emerge from the *Memorial*: living according to the Spirit, receiving the call to apostolic service, and fostering devotion. Peter reports having felt around the age of 7 that the Lord wanted to take possession of his soul, and about the age of 12 made a private vow of chastity. Years later he learned from Ignatius to distinguish such interior movements of the "good spirit" from the counter-movements of the "evil spirit." For Peter, the touch of the Holy Spirit brings about an increase in *devotio*, which in turn impels to action. From this perspective, the goodness of Jesus Christ who gives himself completely in the Mass inspired Peter to respond in kind by making of himself a gift both to Christ and, through him, to others. For Peter, devotion as the movement of the Spirit thus expresses itself in the apostolate as well as in particular acts of public and private religious piety such as he learned in his early years and, late, from the *Exercises*. These acts would include petitionary and intercessory prayer invoking the angels and saints, as well as meditation on the Eucharist and the mysteries of the life of Christ. Peter's life and writings thus reveal a thoroughly relational spirituality that integrates contemplation and action according to the Holy Spirit.

See also Friends in the Lord; Loyola, Ignatius of, SJ, St.; Montmarte; *Spiritual Exercises*

Morel, Charles, "Pierre Favre." In *Dictionnaire de Spiritualité, Ascétique et Mystique, Doctrine et Histoire*. Vol. XII, Pt. 2. Paris: Beauchesne, 1986, pp. 1573–82.

Murphy, Edmond C., Martin E. Palmer, and John W. Padberg, trans. and ed., *The Spiritual Writings of Pierre Favre: The Memoriale and Selected Letters and Instructions*. St. Louis, MO: The Institute of Jesuit Sources, 1996.

William P. O'Brien, SJ

Fe y Alegría

José María Vélaz, SJ (Chile, 1910–1985), founded the school system known as Fe y Alegría. From his early education, Vélaz studied with the Jesuits and was inspired by their work. After having completed several years of college, Vélaz entered the Jesuits as a novice. When he was 36, he was sent to Venezuela, where he witnessed extreme poverty and traumatic social differences. Profoundly moved by his experiences, Vélaz began a pioneering work to change the country's situation. Working in the Jesuit school in Mérida, Tachira, he experimented with educational strategies and eventually developed what was to become the urban and rural network of schools called Fe y Alegría, Faith and Joy, so named in 1960.

Vélaz fits the profile of a leader and savior of the marginalized, channeling their legitimate demands and hopes toward a better life. The shocking contrast between the poor and the wealthy increased his awareness of the needs of the marginalized thousands; he then started knocking on doors of the well-to-do asking for their support. Not a single Fe y Alegría school could have opened its doors to the poor without their financial assistance.

Vélaz and his friends roved the suburbs looking for a place to start the first Fe y Alegría school. Vélaz formed a group of university students ready to work together with the marginalized. The first years of Fe y Alegría brought together groups of people willing to offer themselves for a Christian service. "A true sign of the presence of God's Kingdom, now and among us."

By 1964, there were already 10,000 students in Venezuela; the successful experience was replicated in other countries. In a period of two years, Fe y Alegría spread to Ecuador in 1964, Panama in 1965, Peru and Bolivia in 1966, then El Salvador in 1968, Colombia in 1972, Nicaragua in 1974, Guatemala in 1976, Brazil in 1980, the Dominican Republic in 1991, Paraguay in 1992, and Argentina in 1995. As we write these lines, 1,253 schools of Fe y Alegría educate 1,156,300 students around the world. Several religious congregations and many laywomen and men supported this urban and rural movement for the marginalized.

The experience continued growing, thus multiplying the hopes of those living in the remotest and most deprived corners of the Americas: "*Fe y Alegría* starts where the pavement ends, where drinking water does not drip, where the city loses its name" (www. feyalegria.org).

The movement is a commitment to Integral Popular Education, providing the poorest students with high-quality education. Fe y Alegría does not want to be a small bandage on a giant wound, nor a simple repair to cover up a devastating reality. The movement provides those with the least opportunities and resources an education enabling them to become the main agents in transforming their reality.

Fe y Alegría is committed to human dignity and to setting up a new order based on equality and respect. This is a clear expression of Fe y Alegría's Christian roots and the commitment of the Latin American Church during those first years and today.

Since 1960, Fe y Alegría has been a model in alternative education. After the birth of the Fe y Alegría International Federation in 1987, the task to consolidate much more coordinated work started, setting and keeping a common line of action.

Fe y Alegría continues to grow worldwide, always loyal to its original idea. Thus in 1985, Fe y Alegría started in Spain, and Italy in 2001, and in 2007 it reached the African continent in Chad. Fe y Alegría schools operate in nineteen countries across three continents.

The reach of the project and the huge challenges to face during this new millennium are enormous. Presently 939 religious people share with the Jesuits the determination to push forward this pioneering mission. Almost half a century full of hope and commitment has made a deep transformation of communities around a school. Neighborhoods without sewage systems and millions of people living at the margins have become organized communities, producing urban infrastructure, better economic conditions, and most importantly, people with a dignity sign on their faces.

See also Cristo Rey (Model of Schools); Education, Secondary and Pre-secondary; Nativity School Model; Venezuela

Federación Internacional de Fe y Alegría. www.feyalegria.org/es/.

Jorge Salcedo, SJ

Feeney, Leonard

Leonard Feeney (1897–1978) entered the Society of Jesus in 1914 and was ordained on June 20, 1928. He came to national attention in the Boston Heresy Case during the late 1940s because of his unorthodox interpretation of *Extra ecclesiam nulla salus*.

After graduate studies at St. Bruno's College in Wales and at Oxford, Feeney returned to the United States and taught literature at Boston College (1931–36), became literary editor of *America* (1936–40), returned to Boston College in 1940, and was assigned in 1942 to the St. Benedict Center near Harvard University, where he drew large audiences of students, encouraged numerous religious vocations, and developed a loyal following. During and after World War II, he criticized the dropping of atomic bombs on Japan, and the liberal views of large segments of the Catholic community, including those of his bishop and religious superiors. He protested in particular against what he considered their liberal and heretical views of *extra ecclesiam*. He interpreted that theological dictum to assert that only faithful Catholics could be saved.

In 1949, the Holy Office's *Suprema Haec Sacra* (August 8) condemned Feeney's interpretation, Boston's Archbishop Richard Cushing removed Feeney's priestly faculties, his Jesuit superiors dismissed him from the Society of Jesus, and after refusing to obey a Vatican summons to Rome, he was publicly excommunicated on February 4, 1953. Feeney and the religious community he formed after his excommunication were eventually reconciled to the Church in 1972. He died at the age of 80 and the religious community he had moved to Still River, Massachusetts, eventually became St. Benedict Abbey. It continues into the twenty-first century.

See also Boston College; Ex-Jesuits; United States of America

Pepper, George B., *The Boston Heresy Case in View of the Secularization of Religion*. Lewiston, NY: Edwin Mellen Press, 1988.

Patrick W. Carey

Film and Television: Screenwriters, Consultants

The work of Jesuits in film and television in many ways mirrors the paths of Jesuit missionaries. Some have entered into these fields as modern-day Riccis, taking jobs in the industry with the hope of making an impact from within. So, for instance, US playwright Bill Cain created and ran the 1997–98 ABC drama *Nothing Sacred*, a thoughtful and often funny portrait of life in an inner city parish. Well-received by critics and many Catholics, the show also faced attacks from some conservative groups for its take on some moral issues. Cain has since written a number of movies for television, and an episode of Netflix's blockbuster series *House of Cards*. In 2013 Jim McDermott sold and developed a pilot with the AMC network and today works as a consultant on another television show for them.

In the field of production, Jeremy Zipple has worked as a producer for a number of US television networks, most especially creating documentaries on such things as the effects of prolonged stress (2008), rats in India (2009), and King Solomon's Mines (2010) for National Geographic. He also wrote, shot, and directed a documentary on Francis Xavier that appeared on PBS.

Many Jesuits have served as consultants on media projects. Scripture scholar Bill Fulco translated the entirety of the script for *The Passion of the Christ* into Aramaic, Latin, and Hebrew. William O'Malley not only served as an adviser on *The Exorcist* but had a minor role in the film. In Great Britain Tony Nye has served as an adviser on the BBC's popular *Father Brown*.

And while a Jesuit, Chris Donahue worked as director of development for Paulist Pictures, co-producing *Entertaining Angels: The Dorothy Day Story* (1996). Shortly before leaving the Society, Donahue also won an Academy Award for Live Action Short Film for his *Visas and Virtue*, a retelling of the story of Holocaust rescuer Chiune Sugihara.

More often, though, Jesuits working in media have tried to multiply their potential apostolic impact by creating institutions, production companies where they can tell the stories they wish to or that others are not telling. So Charles Chilinda founded Loyola Productions Zambia in 2005 with the goal of offering a local, Catholic voice in a television market saturated with evangelical and South African programs. Loyola's programs have included ongoing shows on health issues, religious-themed series during Advent–Christmas and Lent–Easter, a 26-part series on Zambia's journey to independence, and a film on mining and development to be screened at the UN General Assembly.

In Taiwan, the Jesuit-founded Kuangchi Program Service (KPS) is the nation's oldest production company. Over its fifty-plus-year history, KPS has produced a wide variety of programs for audiences in Taiwan, Hong Kong, Macau, and mainland China. Its longest-running and wildly popular series, *Uncle Jerry's English*, had the director Jesuit Jerry Martinson teaching English while promoting human values.

More recently KPS has produced the children's program *Mr. Amour and His Cats*, a show about "how everyday life becomes special if open to love and acceptance" (Asia News, August 16, 2013), and the first television series on foreign missionaries that China has ever allowed. The acclaimed multi-part documentaries on Jesuit missionaries Paul Xu Guangqi, Matteo Ricci, Adam Schall, and Giuseppe Castiglione have been broadcast repeatedly to large audiences on the mainland and abroad.

Programming from Jesuit production companies often focuses on religious themes. So Jesuit Communications in the Philippines produces television programs on Scripture and prayer and also runs a religious music business that has had a huge impact in both the Philippines and abroad. The company is also currently developing a feature film about St. Ignatius.

But Jesuit production companies in such places as Ecuador, Argentina, Indonesia, Kenya, and Germany are equally notable for the apostolic work they've done in promoting education and culture. In Timor Leste Jesuit-founded Casa de Produção Audiovisual has worked to help build a sense of national identity since 2002, producing such things as animated versions of popular legends and short films on local languages, political issues, and peace. Xavier College's Educational Multimedia Research Center (EMMRC) in Calcutta, India, has likewise been producing educational television programs on a wide range of subjects since 1986. In 1993 EMMRC created the eight-part documentary *The Tribals of Chotanagpur*, which received high praise from government and Church officials for its portrayal of tribal life in northern India. Producer George Ponodath also made a point of having tribal members help produce the film.

As the world of media has evolved to include ever-expanding online programming, so too has the work of Jesuits in media. Loyola Productions in Hollywood has produced many promotional videos for Jesuit institutions since its founding in the year 2000 and has had a number of projects in development with television networks. In 2012 Loyola founder Eddie Siebert also expanded its efforts to a YouTube channel, the Ignatian News Network (INN), which offers series on such things as cooking, the film industry, and the experience of gay Catholics.

The Conference of the European Provincials also sponsors the Iñigo Film Festival, an international celebration of films on topics of faith and spirituality that occurs in conjunction with each World Youth Day.

See also Film and Television: Themes and Characters

Anderson, John, "A Mission Field behind the Camera." *The New York Times*, April 2, 2010, AR7.
"Jesuit Film on North Indian Tribals Called Model of Content and Style." *UCAnews.com*, June 30, 1994.
"Kuangchi's Jesuit Documentary on Matteo Ricci and Paul Xu Guangqi on China TV and DVD." *Signis.net*, March 23, 2007.
"Raising Consciousness through Film: Casa de Produção Audiovisual." *SJAPC.net*, May 23, 2012.
Xin, Yage, "Taiwanese Catholics Launch First Children's TV Program on Mime." *AsiaNews.it*, August 16, 2013.

Jim McDermott, SJ

Film and Television: Themes and Characters

Relatively few films and television shows have been about the Society of Jesus. By far the most well-known and interesting is *The Mission*, the 1986 Roland Joffé film written by playwright Robert Bolt about an eighteenth-century Jesuit missionary to the Guaraní people of Paraguay, and the slave merchant there who becomes a Jesuit missionary himself. Written by playwright Robert Bolt from a story in C. J. McNaspy, SJ's 1982 book *The Lost Cities of Paraguay*, the film depicts the struggles the two men face when political and ecclesial pressures demand they abandon the mission to Spanish forces. *The Mission* won the 1986 Palme d'Or at the Cannes Film Festival and was nominated for eight Academy Awards, winning one for cinematography. Twenty years later its soundtrack by composer Ennio Morricone – particularly the song "Gabriel's Oboe" – remains a staple at Jesuit events, and its story continues to offer a potent doorway into Ignatian spirituality. Three other films examine the Society's seventeenth-century missionary activity. The Martin Scorsese film *Silence* (2016) is based on Shusako Endo's 1966 novel about the Portuguese Jesuits martyred in Japan. In 1971 a Japanese-produced version of the novel was released under the name *Chinmoku*. *Black Robe* (1991) tells the story of French Father LaForgue, a missionary in North American New France sent to check on a Catholic mission to the Huron people. Based upon the book of the same name by Canadian writer Brian Moore and directed by Bruce Beresford, the film is notable for the harshness and complexity of its portrayal of seventeenth-century North America. Over the course of his journey, LaForgue meets a variety of different tribes, each with their own belief system and complicated intertribal relationships. Beresford compared the courage involved in being a missionary at the time to that of people going into space today, and called the film "a wonderful study of obsession and love" (*Signis*, December 7, 1991).

A few other films have also involved the Society of Jesus in significant ways. The 1989 film *Romero* about Salvadoran Archbishop Óscar Romero includes a number of Jesuit characters, most especially Romero's friend and advocate for the poor, Father Rutilio Grande, SJ; Grande's murder, in fact, inspires Romero to take a stand against the government's repressive policies. In the 1998 Three Musketeers film *Man in the Iron Mask*, Jesuit assassins are attempting to kill French King Louis XIV, who is allowing his people to starve. The King engages former Musketeer and now Jesuit priest Aramis to find the superior general of the order and kill him. In fact Aramis is himself the superior general, and with the other musketeers he plots to replace Louis with the twin brother no one knows he has. A 2006 independent film *The Novice* (also called *Crossroads*) tells the story of two Jesuit novices sent to work in a soup kitchen in Mobile, Alabama; there they discover their true vocations.

In still other films and television shows, reference is made to significant characters being Jesuits without that fact being explored in any way. For instance, on the long-running television show *M*A*S*H* Father Francis Mulcahy mentions on a number of occasions that he is a Jesuit and often wears a hooded Loyola sweatshirt, but nothing further is ever made of it. In the 1954 film *On the Waterfront*, the Karl Malden character of Father Barry, who organizes action amongst the dockworkers, is based on Jesuit Father John M. Corridan, but again, that fact is not dwelled upon.

Priests in supernatural films are occasionally identified as Jesuits: the protagonist in *Stigmata* (1999) is a Jesuit, as is the Anthony Hopkins exorcist in *The Rite* (2011) and the exorcist in *Deliver us From Evil* (2014). But only in *The Exorcist* (1973) and *The Exorcist III* (1990) does that mean anything; Jesuit psychiatrist Father Alex Karras is clearly seen as a part of community of priests and brothers with whom he works and lives. (The real-life case on which *The Exorcist* is based also involved Jesuits.)

Unlike most religious orders, no major film has yet been made about the Society of Jesus's founder St. Ignatius, nor about major Jesuit figures like Francis Xavier or Pedro Arrupe. For many years Antonio Banderas was rumored to be attached to a project about Ignatius, but nothing materialized. Banderas was also long connected to attempts to make a film of the popular "Jesuit missionaries in outer space" book *The Sparrow*, which offers perhaps the most accurate fictional depiction of Jesuit life ever. In 2014 the AMC network came close to green lighting a TV version, but ultimately passed.

See also Corridan, John, SJ; Film and Television: Screenwriters, Consultants; Novels

Canby, Vincent, "Saving the Huron Indians: A Disaster for Both Sides." *The New York Times*, October 30, 1991.
    "'The Mission' with DeNiro and Irons." *The New York Times*, October 31, 1986.
"Crossroads (The Novice)," *Hometheaterinfo.com*, November 23, 2008. Accessed on October 8, 2015.
"Interview with Bruce Beresford," *Signis* 7, December 7, 1991.

Jim McDermott, SJ

Finding God in All Things

Jerome Nadal famously described Ignatius as a man to whom God had become so present that he was "contemplative likewise in action," "finding God in all things."

At the outset of the *Spiritual Exercises*, in the Principle and Foundation, Ignatius bids the exercitant to cultivate a radical "indifference" to all created things so as to order one's whole life exclusively toward the "praise, reverence and service of God" (*SpEx* #23). This indifference, however, is not meant to deny the value of these things but rather to reveal their true worth in the God who creates them. Ignatius envisions a "love of one's Creator and Lord" so freeing that one "loves all things not in themselves but in the Creator of them all" (*SpEx* #316).

In the Contemplation to Attain Love, placed at the end of the *Exercises*, the grace of "finding God in all things" occupies a central place. Ignatius invites one to reflect with gratitiude upon the presence of God in every creature, including oneself, to whom God is presently "giving being, life, sensation and understanding." One considers how God is "working and laboring for me in all created things on the face of the earth," bestowing countless "gifts and blessings" that perpetually "descend from above" as "rays from the sun" or as "waters from a fountain" (*SpEx* ##235–37).

The grace that Nadal described in Ignatius is an interior freedom so centered in the love of God that Ignatius was able not only to find God at all times but, as in the Contemplation, to experience all things as shot through with divinity, engendering what Karl Rahner described as a "mysticism of joy in the world."

See also Asceticism and Mysticism; Loyola, Ignatius of, SJ, St.; *Spiritual Exercises*

Dupré, Louis, "Ignatian Humanism and Its Mystical Origins." *Communio* 18 (1991), 164–82.
Nadal, Jerónimo, *Epistolae P. Hieronymi Nadal, Monumenta Natalis*. Madrid: Typis Augustini Avrial, 1905, Vol. IV: 651; Vol. V: 162.

Rahner, Karl, "Ignatian Mysticism of Joy in the World." In *Theological Investigations*. Vol. III. Trans. Karl-H. and Boniface Kruger. Baltimore, MD: Helicon Press, 1967, pp. 277–93.
Sachs, John R., "Ignatian Mysticism." *The Way Supplement* 82 (1995), 73–83.

Henry Shea, SJ

Ford, John Cuthbert, SJ (1902–1989)

John Ford was a moral theologian of the manualist tradition who was a prominent figure in moral and pastoral theology in the United States from the 1940s to the late 1960s. His moral method was characterized by an adept use of casuistry and moral principles. He emphasized the role of the magisterium as the authentic and definitive interpreter of the moral law. His pastoral approach took careful consideration of the subjective culpability of penitents. Ford's writings expressed special concern for vulnerable persons in society such as individuals affected by addictions, war, and the abuse of power.

He taught at various institutions including Weston College in Massachusetts, the Pontifical Gregorian University in Rome, and the Catholic University of America in Washington, DC. He co-founded the journal *Theological Studies* and wrote its "Notes on Moral Theology" for six years. He co-authored, with Gerald Kelly, SJ, a widely read two-volume work *Contemporary Moral Theology: Questions in Fundamental Moral Theology* (Vol. I) and *Marriage Question* (Vol. II).

During World War II, Ford was the only American moralist to criticize the Allied strategy of obliteration bombing which involved the systematic destruction of enemy cities through aerial bombardment. In a famous 1944 article, "The Morality of Obliteration Bombing," Ford denounced the use of this strategy on German cities as a grave violation of the right to non-combatant immunity of German civilians. His moral objection to the use of weapons of mass destruction continued to be reflected in his later writings against the use of the atomic and the hydrogen bomb. Ford emphasized the humanity of all persons threatened by the violence of war, whether combatants or non-combatants.

Ford was a member of the Papal Commission on Population, Family, and Birth Rate formed during the papacy of John XXIII and continued in the papacy of Paul VI. The commission was tasked with advising the Pope on matters related to the Church's teaching on birth regulation. While the majority of the commission members recommended reform of the teaching on contraception, Ford was among the minority who insisted that the teaching should not be changed. Ford authored the minority report of the commission submitted to the Pope. He argued that a reform of the teaching would result in a grave diminishment of the credibility and authority of the magisterium to teach on moral matters. It would result in an unacceptable admission of grave error on the part of the Catholic Church and a confirmation of the Protestant position on contraception. Ford's defense of the traditional teaching during the commission discussions and his private audiences with Paul VI were contributory influences to the Pope's decision not to change the teaching on contraception after the commission ended its work. In 1978 Ford co-authored, with Germain Grisez, an article "Contraception and the Infallibility of the Ordinary Magisterium," which argued that the teaching on contraception has been infallibly taught by the ordinary magisterium.

A pioneer in developing pastoral approaches for the care of persons suffering from alcoholism, Ford drew on his personal experience of recovery from alcoholism through Alcoholics' Anonymous (AA) in devoting much of his time and energy to promote the AA program in the Catholic Church. He is credited with introducing the early AA books to Catholic audiences in a manner that avoided any religious controversy. Ford argued that alcoholism was not a moral problem to be condemned in the confessional but rather a disease that should be treated. He advocated a compassionate consideration of the diminished subjective culpability of alcoholic persons with regard to their addiction. He made special efforts to encourage clergy with alcohol addiction to enter the AA program. His personal commitment to assisting persons affected by alcoholism is evidenced by his long-term work as a telephone counselor for an alcoholism counseling service, a ministry that he continued until the age of 86.

In 1969 Ford retired from teaching due to frail health, advanced age, and personal reasons. His retirement coincided with the transfer of Weston College, the Jesuit house of formation of the New England province of the Society of Jesus, from the town of Weston to Cambridge, Massachusetts, in 1968. The transfer would allow Jesuits in formation to take courses in non-Catholic institutions such as Harvard and the Episcopal Divinity School, a development that Ford found objectionable. He also acknowledged that his manualist training was no longer compatible with the renewal of moral theology taking place after Vatican II.

Ford was honored by the Catholic Theological Society of America in 1956 with the Cardinal Spellman Award for his contributions to theology. In 1988, a year before his death, Ford received the Cardinal O'Boyle Award for the Defense of the Faith from the Fellowship of Catholic Scholars.

See also Casuistry; Ethics; United States of America

Ford, John C., and Gerald Kelly, *Contemporary Moral Theology*. Vol. I: *Questions in Fundamental Moral Theology*. Westminster, MD: The Newman Press, 1960.
Genilo, Eric Marcelo O., *John Cuthbert Ford, SJ: Moral Theologian at the End of the Manualist Era*. Washington, DC: Georgetown University Press, 2007.

Eric Marcelo O. Genilo, SJ

Formation

Formation refers to the progressive training and integration of a Jesuit into the spiritual and apostolic life of the Society of Jesus. This objective is achieved through a well-defined and coordinated program unfolding in successive stages over several years. Prior to formal admission into the formation program, some provinces and regions invite interested, potential candidates to undergo a period of candidacy. This introductory, exploratory, and preparatory phase is non-committal and non-binding. Jesuit formation begins formally with a two-year period of prayer, study, testing, and experience of Jesuit life in the novitiate. A Jesuit in the novitiate is called a novice. The prescribed components of novitiate formation include the study of the founding, history, spirituality, and constitutions of the Jesuits, and the full spiritual exercises lasting thirty days. At different times a novice undertakes a form of field education known as apostolic or community experiments or immersions during which he is required to spend time working and serving in a variety of apostolic settings, such as hospitals, nursing homes, orphanages, deprived communities, or schools. A component of novitiate formation known as pilgrimage – which requires a novice to travel to an assigned destination relying solely on the generosity of people for his needs – appears to have fallen into desuetude in some parts of the world. At the end of novitiate formation, a novice takes his first perpetual vows of chastity, poverty, and obedience either as a scholastic or a brother, depending on the choice of status confirmed in the course of novitiate formation. A transition phase called juniorate that prepares the novice for a life of studies through an intensive program of humanities and languages is now practiced with less and less consistency. Where it still exists, it consists of a period of college studies or in-house studies. After the stage of novitiate, a Jesuit begins first studies, usually two to four years of philosophical and liberal studies at a tertiary-level institution. This stage is followed by regency, during which the young Jesuit receives his first assignment to an apostolic work, on average lasting between one and three years. The choice of placement varies, albeit high school teaching tends to be the preferred ministry. Depending on the aptitude, desire, and interest of the Jesuit and the needs of the province or region, he may be assigned to special studies in a secular subject area or missioned to begin studies in theology, in preparation for ordained ministry. A brother would follow a different path of formation, including the option of professional training. Prior to the end of theological studies and in anticipation of ordination, it is mandatory for a Jesuit to spend a few weeks reviewing his vocation options through a series of workshops and prayer experiences known as "Arrupe Month," named after Pedro Arrupe, who instituted the program. At the conclusion of theological studies, the Jesuit is ordained – first as a deacon, then a priest. Although a long period of either apostolic assignment or further studies may follow, ordination to the priesthood does not mark the end of formation in the Society. Any time after three years of ordination, a Jesuit is sent to tertianship, variously referred to in Jesuit parlance as the second novitiate or school of the heart. Although it repeats all of the formal components of novitiate training, including the full spiritual exercises, as a stage of formation, tertianship enables the Jesuit to consolidate and appropriate in depth the spirituality and ways of proceeding of the Society. The call to final vows upon completion of tertianship formally marks the end of formation in the Society. Jesuits understand formation as an ongoing process. Some provinces and regions have programs of ongoing formation targeting different cohorts or age brackets (young priests, brothers, middle-aged, and third age) or Jesuits working in particular sectors of apostolic ministry, such as pastoral, educational, and social. Other programs of renewal or retooling, such as sabbaticals, special courses, and spiritual retreats, are considered forms of ongoing formation. Owing to demographic changes, recent decades have seen a marked decline in the number of Jesuits in formation in North America, parts of Europe and Oceania. Conversely, the provinces and regions of Latin America, Africa, and Asia have recorded steady growth in the number of Jesuits in formation, although financial resources for formation are more readily available in the northern hemisphere than in the southern hemisphere. The provincial or regional superior is ultimately responsible for formation of Jesuits in his province or region. It is customary to delegate this duty to an assistant, coordinator, or delegate for formation. At the General Curia, the superior general is advised on matters of formation by an assistant and counselor for formation. The changing contexts and challenges of formation in the Society and the requisite adaptation of structures and programs are

Figure 19 Jesuits in Zimbabwe taking their final vows. Photograph courtesy of Stephen Buckland, SJ

subjects of decrees of recent General Congregations and apostolic letters of the superior generals.

See also Brothers; Novitiate, Novice; Priesthood; Regency, Regent; Scholastic

The Constitutions of the Society of Jesus and Their Complementary Norms. Ed. John W. Padberg. St. Louis, MO: The Institute of Jesuit Sources, 1996.

Kolvenbach, Peter-Hans, *The Formation of Jesuits.* Rome: General Curia of the Society of Jesus, 2003.

Agbonkhianmeghe Orobator, SJ

Formula of the Institute

The *Formula of the Institute*, the basic "rule" of the Society of Jesus, exhibits the fundamental structure of the Society. Because specifically papally approved, it can be changed only with papal approval. The word "Institute" designates both the style or way of living and acting of a religious and also the expression of that way of life in a body of written legislation.

In 1539, the ten "friends in the Lord" who, under the leadership of Ignatius of Loyola, were to become the founders of the Society of Jesus drew up a brief kind of sketch or statement of the evangelical way of life that they proposed to follow and for which they sought approval as a religious order from the Church. That "first draft" of the *Formula*, known as the "Five Chapters," was approved by Pope Paul III on September 3, 1539. But then several members of the papal curia designated to draw up the official text of the document for formal papal approval objected to some of its provisions. In addition, there was a fundamental objection, as expressed in the Fourth Lateran Council, to the foundation of any new religious orders. The objections were resolved satisfactorily, and the "Five Chapters," with a few changes or corrections, became the so-called "second draft" of the *Formula* that Paul III approved in *Regimini militantis ecclesiae* on September 27, 1540, the date of the founding of the Society of Jesus. The first Fathers of the Society who were at the time resident in Rome professed their vows in accord with *Regimini* on April 22, 1541.

With a decade of development and experience to draw upon, a revised or "third draft" of the *Formula* was approved by Pope Julius III on July 21, 1550, in *Exposcit debitum*.

That 1550 definitive text of the *Formula* contains the revised five chapters and a conclusion. The first chapter describes the Society as existing "to serve the Lord alone and the Church, his spouse, under the Roman Pontiff, the Vicar of Christ on earth." Its members take solemn vows of perpetual chastity, poverty, and obedience in a society "founded chiefly for this purpose: ... for the defense and propagation of the faith and for the progress of souls in Christian life and doctrine." It then sets forth the means especially apt to do so. Furthermore, it describes the office of a superior general who, together with a council, now called a General Congregation, "shall possess the authority to compose ... constitutions" and to deal with "other matters of more than ordinary importance." Those Constitutions of the Society of Jesus, composed by Ignatius and formally approved by the 1st General Congregation of the Society in 1557, further developed and explained the provisions of the *Formula*. The second chapter describes the special vow of obedience to the pope in regard to specific missions upon which he might send members of the Society. The third chapter deals with the vow of obedience to the superior of the Society, who possesses full authority to govern it. The fourth chapter treats of the vow of poverty, the reasons for such a vow, and the matter and object of the vow. The fundamental reason for it is a life free from all avarice and as like as possible to the poverty that Jesus and the apostles followed in their evangelical life. The chapter then gives details of how that vow applies to individuals, to houses of the Society, and to the colleges or "facilities for studies" to be established for the training of recruits to the Society. The fifth chapter deals with certain externals that distinguish the Society. There is no choir or common choral celebration of the Divine Office. In food, clothing, and other external things, members will follow the common and approved usage of reputable priests. Thus there is no mention of a common habit or way of dressing. As for penitential practices, they are not of obligation but in accord with one's needs or desires for spiritual progress.

The conclusion to the *Formula*, pointing out that this way of life is arduous, says that the members of the Society are to be proven by long and exacting tests. In its absence of an earlier limit on the number of Society members, it reflects Paul III's bull of 1544 *Injunctus vobis*. Most importantly, it notes the existence not only of the professed members, those with solemn vows, but also of another grade of members, approved by Paul III's brief of 1546, *Exponi nobis*, coadjutors, either for spiritual or temporal concerns, who take simple vows. The *Formula* then ends with a brief prayer to Christ "that he might favor these modest beginnings to the glory of God the Father."

See also Constitutions; Obedience; Paul III; Poverty

de Aldama, Antonio M., *The Formula of the Institute: Notes for a Commentary*. Trans. Ignacio Echániz. St. Louis, MO: The Institute of Jesuit Sources, 1990.

Conwell, Joseph F., *Impelling Spirit: Revisiting a Founding Experience: 1539*. Chicago, IL: Loyola Press, 1997.

Toner, Jules J., "The Deliberation That Started the Jesuits: A Commentary on the 'Deliberatio Primorum Patrum.'" *Studies in the Spirituality of Jesuits* 6 (1974), iii–ix, 179–212.

John W. Padberg, SJ

Forty Hours Devotion

The Forty Hours Devotion is a devotional rite dedicated to the glorification of the Eucharist that originated in sixteenth-century Milan and spread rapidly through Italy. By the following century, the Jesuits were among the orders orchestrating such devotions regularly. Originally, the consecrated host was placed in an architectural structure resembling a sepulcher, where the faithful kept watch in continuous prayer for forty hours. Charles Borromeo, archbishop of Milan, outlined the procedure, prayers, and ceremonies for this kind of Eucharistic adoration; the period of devotion corresponded roughly to the period of Christ's entombment. The encasement of the Eucharist in a tomb-like structure is referred to in contemporary documents as a *teatro* or *apparato*. The devotion is premised upon the Catholic understanding of the real presence of Christ in the Eucharist and celebrates the redemptive power of Christ's bodily sacrifice. The manner in which all the senses were captivated during the rite is strongly associated with the Jesuits.

The staging of the devotion grew more elaborate over time, with large structures outfitted with hidden lamps magnificently illuminating the host and filling the apse of churches. At Il Gesù in Rome, surviving records detail the spectacles, which have been described as "visual sermons" (Weil, "Devotion of the Forty Hours," 232). An engraving and description of the devotion held at Il Gesù in 1640, designed by Nicolò Menghini, celebrated the centenary of the Society. It was held on the last three days of Carnival, as was popular, although the devotion did not specifically correspond to any particular time of year. Menghini's stage set depicted Old and New Testament figures adoring the Host, glowing among clouds above. The Jesuit artist Andrea Pozzo created the *apparato* for the Forty Hours Devotion, depicting the Marriage at Cana, at Il Gesù in 1685. The positive reception of his design paved the way for future projects at Jesuit churches.

See also Confraternities; Liturgy

Weil, Mark, "The Devotion of the Forty Hours and Roman Baroque Illusions." *Journal of the Warburg and Courtauld Institutes* (1974), 218–48.

Alison Fleming

Foucquet, Jean-François

Jean-François Foucquet was born in Vézelay, France, on March 12, 1665, and entered the Society of Jesus in Paris in 1681. There he completed his studies for the priesthood and was ordained in 1693. He arrived in China in 1699. The first ten years he spent in the southern provinces Fujian and Jiangxi. In 1711, the emperor called him to Beijing in order to assist Joachim Bouvet (1656–1730) with his studies on the *Yijing* (Book of Changes). He was soon asked to explain principles of mathematics and astronomy, on which he compiled several Chinese texts, which included recent information from the French Académie Royale.

Foucquet was a so-called "Figurist," who believed that the Chinese classics were sacred literature, for they came from God's revelation and possessed a marvelous doctrine hidden under the Chinese characters. They were "figures" of the Old Testament, the Trinity, the Eucharist and the Messiah. His approach implied the denial of early Chinese chronology. Foucquet went beyond the interpretation of his fellow Jesuits by his interest in Taoism. After some twenty years in China, he was recalled to Europe because of his controversial ideas and his refusal to accept a confrère as his superior. In Rome, Foucquet left the Society of Jesus and was ordained titular bishop of Eleutheropolis (1725). He continued his investigations on the basis of a large number of Chinese books he had carried to Europe. He died in Rome on March 14, 1741.

See also China; Interreligious Dialogue

Golvers, Noël, "'Bibliotheca in Cubiculo': The 'Personal' Library of Western Books of Jean-François Foucquet, SJ in Peking (Beitang, 1720) and the Intertextual Situation of a Jesuit Scholar in China." *Monumenta Serica* 58 (2010), 249–80.
Witek, John W., *Controversial Ideas in China and in Europe: A Biography of Jean-François Foucquet, S.J. (1665–1741)*. Rome: Institutum Historicum Societatis Iesu, 1982.

Nicolas Standaert, SJ

France

France has played a central role in Jesuit history, from the time Ignatius of Loyola came north from Spain in order to study at the University of Paris (1528–35) to the reception and implementation of Vatican II (1960s to the present). Though France has often been home to many Jesuit schools, retreat houses, scholarly as well as more popular publications, and other Jesuit works, it has also been a country where hostility to the Society of Jesus has been amazingly resilient, across a broad range of eras and circumstances, religious, political, and other.

It was in France, in Paris, that the Society of Jesus was born, with the decision of Ignatius of Loyola and a small group of fellow students – all of them foreigners – to go to Jerusalem, or if that were not possible, to go to Rome and offer their services to the pope. In the eyes of many in France, the Jesuits would be permanently tainted by foreign origins and loyalties, especially Spanish and papal. From the sixteenth to eighteenth centuries, Jesuits worked hard to retain the support of French monarchs, for with such support they could withstand every kind of criticism, accusation, and slander; without such support they would have no legal standing in the kingdom of France and could not function there. In 1555 a Jesuit province was created in France; in 1564 a Jesuit college opened in Paris.

The University of Paris, many of the older religious orders, and many diocesan priests in France advanced a Gallican ideology in which the French Church enjoyed a great deal of autonomy in relation to Rome, an autonomy they saw as threatened by Jesuits,

Jesuits who also were resented as newcomers and upstarts, as unwanted outsiders, as defenders of regicide, the ultimate crime against God and the State. The 1589 assassination of Henri III helped to make every accusation of any kind of implication in regicide an explosive one. An attempt on the life of Henri IV in 1594 elicited expulsion of the Jesuits from at least most of France, an expulsion decreed by the royal law courts (*parlements*) and that lasted until Henri readmitted the Society of Jesus in 1603. Lack of evidence of Jesuit guilt never stopped anti-Jesuit polemicists, and they did their best in 1610, after an assassin succeeded in killing Henri, to assign blame to the Jesuits.

From 1598 to 1685, French Protestants – mainly Calvinists – enjoyed a significant degree of toleration in France. But legal toleration did not mean an end to Protestant and Catholic hostility and polemics, in print and in the pulpit. Jesuits played a major role in efforts to show the superiority and the truth of the Catholic faith and to contrast it with the inferiority and falsehood of the *Religion prétendue réformée* (the religion pretending to be reformed), with its misreading of Scripture and contempt for many centuries of tradition handed down from the early Christians, and its assault on images and statues of Christ and the saints, and on the Mass.

Though France came later than Spain and Portugal to the business of overseas exploration, colonization, and evangelization, it began to catch up, at least in some ways, in the 1600s. By the 1630s, French Jesuits in Canada were sending back to Paris reports of their experiences, and publication in France of these annual reports (*Relations*) was one of the ways in which Jesuits encouraged missionary vocations and financial support of such missions. These reports also served as a kind of apology for Jesuit ministries, an apology that might mute at least some of the hostility directed their way. But Jesuit approaches to the conversion of "pagans" outside Europe soon became another area where Jesuit opponents could not be won over, and in fact they intensified their criticism. By the end of the seventeenth century, and with the support of Louis XIV, French Jesuits were in China on a mission more scientific than explicitly Christianizing.

From the 1640s, French Jesuits had to contend with Jansenist opposition. Champions of an interpretation of St. Augustine that emphasized the sinfulness of human nature and the likely very small number of the saved, Jansenists scorned and lambasted Jesuits as at odds with the teachings of the Church Fathers. According to the disciples of Cornelius Jansen, the disciples of Ignatius of Loyola were soft on sin, all too ready to minimize the consequences of original sin, much too worldly, and eager to compromise with the world, the flesh, and the devil, precisely where unbending fidelity to a severe, rigorous, and demanding Christianity was needed. Through their writings, Antoine Arnauld and Blaise Pascal led the Jansenist assault on the Jesuits. Arnauld deplored Jesuit encouragement of frequent reception of communion, as an encouragement of too little respect for, and awe before, the Eucharist and God. Pascal mocked Jesuit pastoral practices in the sacrament of confession as excusing sin where what they should be doing is exhorting sinners to conversion and lives of penance. While the French Jansenists published many works in French, often in an eloquent French that won over readers, French Jesuits sometimes responded in Latin and thus failed to reach at least a part of the audience entranced by their opponents, an audience that included many laymen and women, as well as clergy and religious.

The Jesuits were not alone in opposing the Jansenists; the most important Jesuit allies in this regard were the French monarchs and most popes. In the 1600s and 1700s,

Jesuits served as confessors to the kings of France, and from this position Jesuits could work to keep the French state on their side, a strategy that worked until the 1760s. As authors, French Jesuits were prolific in publishing works flattering to the king, another strategy that worked for at least a century and a half. In the first half of the eighteenth century, Jesuits and their allies, including many French bishops, increased the pressure on Jansenists by demanding acceptance of *Unigenitus*, the 1713 constitution of Pope Clement XI that condemned a long list of Jansenist propositions. Affirming a conciliarist ecclesiology, the Jansenists appealed to a future council for a decision against that of the papal magisterium, while Jesuits insisted on obedience to pope and king.

The Enlightenment brought to the fore talented French writers opposed to Christian tradition and in favor of a kind of deism or natural religion, with little place for doctrine or clergy. Though hardly the only targets of Voltaire and other *philosophes*, the Jesuits were a favorite nemesis, a convenient scapegoat to blame for promotion of superstition, religious intolerance, and other ills, real and imagined. Yet if what we might call a sec-ular Left criticized and mocked the Jesuits, their more determined and more dangerous foes in the 1700s were on the Right, a religious Right relentless in seeking the destruc-tion of the Society of Jesus in France and, better yet, everywhere. Jansenists dominated the Paris Parlement, and on August 6, 1762, it declared the Society of Jesus inadmissible; other *parlements* in other regions of France did or did not follow suit. On November 26, 1764, royal support for the Jesuits came to an end with a decree from Louis XV eliminat-ing the Society of Jesus in all of France and its territories. At the time there were some 3,000 French Jesuits; the henceforth individual ex-Jesuits were permitted to remain in France, and many of the Jesuits who were priests continued to work as such, under the authority of bishops. A few even became bishops themselves. By 1789 and the beginning of the French Revolution, some 500 ex-Jesuits were still resident in France. Papal sup-port for the Society of Jesus, in France and everywhere else, had ended on July 21, 1773, with a decree of suppression signed by Clement XIV.

During the years of the Suppression (1773–1814), France underwent enormous upheavals with not only the decade of the French Revolution, 1789–99, but also the fifteen years or so of Napoleon that followed. This quarter century had seen the French Church nearly disappear under waves of persecution of varying intensity. Some forty ex-Jesuits were massacred or executed in France in the years 1792–94. Though in 1801 Napoleon agreed to a Concordat with Pius VII that provided for the legal status of dioceses and their clergy and institutions, nothing was agreed on religious orders. Meanwhile, some ex-Jesuits, led by Pierre de Clorivière, had created the Society of the Fathers of the Sacred Heart, while others created a Society of the Heart of Jesus, possible substitutes for the Society of Jesus and/or anticipations of its eventual restoration.

Restoration did eventually come. Held a prisoner of Napoleon in France for some years, Pius VII returned in triumph to Rome in the spring of 1814; on August 7, 1814, he issued *Sollicitudo omnium ecclesiarum*, a decree that authorized restoration of the Society of Jesus throughout the world. In France, such restoration proceeded slowly, with plenty of setbacks, and amid resurgences of anticlericalism, in general, and anti-Jesuit agendas in particular. Hostility to Jesuit education, imagined as a threat, espe-cially to the values of the Revolution, and liberty in particular, was strong. And the two Bourbon monarchs that succeeded Napoleon, Louis XVIII (1814–24) and Charles X (1824–30), were no help to the Jesuits, even though the Jesuits professed loyalty to these two younger brothers of the guillotined Louis XVI. An 1828 royal decree banned Jesuits from teaching. King Louis Philippe (1830–48) was certainly no ally of the Jesuits; but during his reign French Jesuits established a major missionary presence in French colonies and in other countries as well, such as India and China. Meanwhile, Jesuits in France focused largely on pastoral work, establishing retreat houses where they could give the Spiritual Exercises and promoting devotion to the Sacred Heart.

In 1850 the Falloux law was passed in France, a law that permitted religious orders to run educational institutions. In the years that followed, the French Jesuits opened many colleges, and these years also saw the number of Jesuits rise quickly. In the 1850s, Saint-Ignace, a new Jesuit church in Paris, rose on the rue de Sèvres. In 1856 the journal *Etudes* began publication, a Jesuit journal aimed not at specialists but at an educated public, a journal that continues today. Thus the years of Charles Louis Napoleon Bonaparte (Napoleon's nephew) as president of the Republic (1848–52) and as Emperor Napoleon III (1852–70) were relatively good ones for the Jesuits.

Those relatively good times did not last. When, in 1870, the first Vatican Council defined papal infallibility and affirmed the immediate jurisdiction of the pope throughout the Catholic Church, anticlerical zeal was stoked in France and elsewhere. The Franco-Prussian War of 1870–71 saw the capture of Napoleon III himself by Prussian forces and later his departure in to exile. In Paris, the short-lived Commune seemed for a time to revive the Terror of 1793–94 and its violent anticlericalism. In May 1871 the archbishop of Paris was executed as were five Jesuits. The establishment of the Third Republic, with its ideal of a muscular *laïcité*, would lead, in 1880, to a decree dissolving the Society of Jesus in France. Of the nearly 3,000 French Jesuits at the time, approximately a third were young Jesuits in formation. For them, houses of studies were established outside France, on the English island of Jersey, and in Belgium and Spain. In France, some of the Jesuit colleges continued to function with Jesuit staffing, but with ownership of property and governance of the institutions legally conferred on diocesan priests or laity.

From 1880 to 1914, most French Jesuits took a dim view of the French Republic and a pessimistic view of the modern world. Many longed for restoration of the French monarchy. But Pope Leo XIII (1878–1903) called for French Catholics to accept a republican form of civil government, a call that fell on largely deaf ears, Jesuit and others. In his 1891 encyclical *Rerum novarum*, Leo appealed for fair wages and humane working conditions for workers, for the natural right of workers to unionize to be respected, and for the state to intervene in the economy to protect workers from unfair treatment. Action Populaire, founded by Jesuits in 1903 in Reims, echoed Leo's response to the Industrial Revolution, but many French Jesuits sided with the wealthy elite, not with the poor and with workers. When the Jewish military officer Alfred Dreyfus was accused of treason, more than a few French Jesuits embraced a tirade of anti-Semitic polemics. The French 1901 law on associations made it very difficult for a religious order to function in France; the Society of Jesus became one of many French orders living and working in exile.

From the outbreak of World War I, the attitude of the Republic began to change, under the pressure of extreme circumstances and of appeals to a "sacred union" of the French of all political and religious views in the face of German aggression. Jesuits and other male religious young enough to fight were welcomed back, and nearly 900 Jesuits served in the French military in 1914–18, of whom more than 160 died or were presumed dead. After 1918, the French Republic wavered in its view of the Church and of religious orders but was generally somewhat more tolerant, at least in practice, than it had been in 1880–1914. Also, Pope Benedict XV's 1920 canonization of Joan of Arc had helped to restore a relationship between the Holy See and France.

In the interwar period, two tendencies appeared among Jesuits in France: a progressive, forward-looking view focused on social justice and the rights of workers, a view that accepted the democratic institutions of the Republic; a reactionary view, longing for restoration of monarchy and an alliance between throne and altar, a view that went hand-in-hand with fear of Soviet Communism and with sympathy for Fascism in Italy, Germany, and Spain. Even with such a wide divergence of attitudes and values, the French Jesuits continued to attract large numbers of vocations in these years, and many went to the missions in the Middle East, Africa, and Asia. By 1930 there were over 1,000 French Jesuits in these missions. Within France, Jesuit intellectual life prospered, with the reopening of the Faculty of Theology at Fourvière, with a team of Jesuits editing the massive *Dictionnaire de spiritualité*, and with the training of a generation of Jesuit theologians who would have enormous influence in the years leading to Vatican II.

The years of German Occupation, 1940–44, elicited at least three different responses from French Jesuits. Most kept their heads down, went about their business, and hoped for the best – like most of the population of France. But some Jesuits were vocal in supporting the Vichy government and even its collaboration with Nazi Germany, while others actively resisted, in some cases helping Allied soldiers or Jews escape capture. Of those Jesuits taking such risks, some were sent to concentration camps, and some paid with their lives. Yves de Montcheuil was shot for his work as a chaplain to the Resistance.

The postwar years saw no shortage of controversies. There were tensions between cutting-edge French Jesuit theologians, such as Henri de Lubac, and Roman authorities eager to squelch anything other than a dull, textbook version of Aquinas. The French Jesuits helped to promote a return to scriptural and patristic sources; for the latter, the *Sources chrétiennes*, since the 1940s, has published hundreds of critical editions. In the postwar years, some French Jesuits became "worker priests" by taking jobs in factories and in similar circumstances. This was designed to facilitate the presence of the Church among the working class, but it was controversial, and voices calling for Jesuit priests to focus on teaching and scholarly work, and on pastoral ministry, were many. In this same era, mid-1940s to early 1960s, France eventually pulled back from its colonial empire and allowed independence for many countries, but not without more than one war and much difficult debate in France itself. French Jesuits had to reimagine what they were doing in places such as Africa, and to reconsider whether they should be there at all, and if so, what were they to do. No longer could there be talk of a "civilizing mission" from Paris for which "natives" were expected to be grateful.

Vatican II and its aftermath brought rehabilitation to the *nouvelle théologie* that had flourished in France before the Council. Some would say, the rest of the Church caught up with the French Church. The Council had also affirmed a Church in the world, and a Church with, for, and among the poor. In recent decades this focus has been a central one for French Jesuits, one they have prioritized without setting aside intellectual life as equally important. Though the number of French Jesuits continues to fall, a remarkable energy imbues them as they look ahead to the twenty-first century.

See also Action Populaire; Anti-Jesuit Polemic; Canada; Centre Sèvres; Confessors; Jansenists; Paris; Sacred Heart

Burnichon, Joseph, *La Compagnie de Jésus en France: histoire d'un siècle, 1814–1914*. 5 vols. Paris: Beauchesne, 1914–25.

Cubitt, Geoffrey, *The Jesuit Myth: Conspiracy Theory and Politics in Nineteenth-Century France*. Oxford: Clarendon Press, 1993.

Delattre, Pierre, *Les Etablissements des Jésuites en France depuis quatre siècles*. 5 vols. Enghien: Institut supérieur de théologie, 1940–57.

Fouqueray, Henri, *Histoire de la Compagnie de Jésus en France des origines à la suppression (1528–1762)*. Paris: Picard, 1910–25.

Lacouture, Jean, *Jesuits: A Multibiography*. Trans. Jeremy Leggatt. Washington, DC: Counterpoint, 1995.

Lécrivain, Philippe, *Les Jésuites*. Paris: Éditions Eyrolles, 2014.

Martin, A. Lynn, *The Jesuit Mind: The Mentality of an Elite in Early Modern France*. Ithaca, NY: Cornell University Press, 1988.

Moledina, Sheza, "Books in Exile: The Case of the Jesuit Seminary Library in Jersey, 1880–1945." *Library & Information History* 26 (June 2010), 105–20.

Padberg, John W., *Colleges in Controversy: The Jesuit Schools in France from Revival to Suppression, 1815–1880*. Cambridge, MA: Harvard University Press, 1969.

Rocher, Philippe, *Le goût de l'excellence: quatre siècles d'éducation jésuite en France*. Paris: Beauchesne, 2011.

Worcester, Thomas, "Jesuit Dependence on the French Monarchy." In Thomas Worcester, ed., *The Cambridge Companion to the Jesuits*. Cambridge: Cambridge University Press, 2008, pp. 104–19.

Thomas Worcester, SJ

Francis of Assisi, St., and the Franciscans

The Order of Friars Minor (OFM) was the creation of Francis of Assisi, a layman. Most of what we know of his life and ministry comes from biographies produced by early followers. The traditional account emphasizes his birth into a wealthy mercantile family in Assisi, spiritual awakening after a rather debauched youth, and subsequent renunciation of all earthly possessions. Francis famously removed all of his own clothing to give it back to his father, who was enraged by his abandonment of the family business for a spiritual ministry.

In an age in which the pursuit of evangelical poverty spawned numerous new religious movements, Francis very quickly developed a reputation for austerity and humility. He traveled barefoot, wore a roughhewn habit made of burlap with a simple rope belt, and accepted shelter and food in return for labor. He was also considered a mystic, receiving the marks of the stigmata in 1224. Francis's reception of the stigmata became an iconic image of the saint from early on, most famously rendered in the fourteenth-century frescoes of Giotto. These images, along with Francis's adoption of an itinerant preaching ministry and life of poverty, cemented his reputation as *alter Christus*. But it was also his simple piety, including its emphasis upon love and joy as facets of the Christian experience, that explains his broad and enduring appeal. He was canonized within two years of his death in 1228. To this day Francis remains one of the most popular saints, his image a common presence in parish churches. In more recent times, Francis's veneration for all living creations including animals and birds has also made him a patron saint for environmentalists, including Pope Francis, the Jesuit pope.

More than a mystic and preacher, Francis is also historically important for founding one of the most influential missionary traditions in the Catholic Church. Established in 1210, the Franciscan order was the first of the five great mendicant orders (Dominican,

Augustinian, Carmelite, Servite) to receive papal recognition – the term mendicant (beggar) referring to their rejection of material goods. The first constitution (Rule) of the order forbade the ownership of property and office-holding, and required brothers to live off alms. For Church authorities, the friars were useful because of their itinerant ministry and reputations as excellent preachers. They supplemented a clerical pastoral structure that was struggling to reach a growing European population.

By the time of the establishment of the Jesuit order in the sixteenth century, the Franciscans had established communities throughout Europe and were widely celebrated as preachers. Art historians also consider Franciscan spirituality, in particular its Christocentric piety, an important influence upon late medieval and Renaissance artistic traditions. By the sixteenth century as well, the friars were playing an important role on missions in distant parts of the known world. They would develop important missions in the regions under Spanish rule in North and South America in particular, as well as Asia. The friars were also the official custodians of the Custody of the Holy Land, a role that the Order has played continuously since the formation of the Custody in 1342. Indeed, it was the Franciscans who expelled Ignatius of Loyola when he attempted to remain there in 1523.

The reputation of the friars as bitter missionary rivals of the Jesuits is not without merit when one considers the rapid global reach of the Jesuits and their success in competing with the mendicant orders for royal and noble patronage both in Europe and in foreign lands. In fact, it was a Franciscan Pope, Clement XIV, who issued the brief that suppressed the Order in 1773. The two religious orders represented fundamentally different spiritual ideals, and that may explain some of the tension. Apostolic poverty, the foundation of the Franciscan ideal, was somewhat less a focus of Jesuit spirituality, in which obedience in the sense of availability for mission was central. The humanist-inflected learning of the Jesuits and emphasis upon education as a critical mechanism of evangelization contrasted with the Scotist (scholastic) formation of the friars and the pronounced charismatic and mystical cast of their theology. In their modes of evangelization, however, the Jesuits and Franciscans clearly had a great deal in common. For example, both orders took preaching seriously and considered the visual arts, including performance, important modes of spiritual communication. They also embraced acculturation as a conversion strategy in many of their missionary endeavors, though the Jesuits also practiced inculturation, or adaptation to local cultures, to a degree that Franciscans did not.

Today the male order recognizes several branches including the Observant (O.F.M.), Conventual (O.F.M.Conv.), Capuchin (O.F.M.Cap.), and the Third Order Regular of Saint Francis (T.O.R.). The order also includes many female communities as well, the earliest formed that of the Poor Clares. In contrast, the Jesuits remain one order, male-only, unified under one superior general.

See also Clement XIV; Dominic, St. and Dominicans; Holy Land

Moorman, John, *A History of the Franciscan Order from Its Origins to 1517*. Oxford: Oxford University Press, 1968.

Pardo, Oswaldo, *The Origins of Mexican Catholicism: Nahua Rituals and Christian Sacraments in Sixteenth-Century Mexico*. Ann Arbor: University of Michigan Press, 2004.

Roest, Bert, *Franciscan Learning, Preaching and Mission, c. 1220–1650*. Leiden: Brill, 2015.

Megan C. Armstrong

Fransen, Piet, SJ (1913–1983)

Piet Fransen entered the Society of Jesus in 1930, was ordained in 1943, and obtained his doctorate of sacred theology (STD) at the Gregorian in Rome, with a dissertation on the indissoluble bonds of matrimony according to the Council of Trent (1951). He became professor of dogmatic theology at the Jesuit faculty in Louvain, and later at the theological faculties of Louvain and Innsbruck, where he was given an honorary doctorate (1970). As visiting professor he was invited to teach at Maastricht, Heythrop, Fordham, University of San Francisco, and Loyola University at Chicago.

In his research he paid special attention to the hermeneutics of the Councils and mystical theology, especially of his compatriot Jan van Ruusbroec. As a scholar he collaborated on the second edition of the *Lexikon für Theologie und Kirche* (1957–68), and on *Sacramentum mundi*, an encyclopedia of theology in six volumes (English edition 1968–70), in both cases under the leadership of Karl Rahner. His own books, translated into several languages, include *Grace and the Sacraments* (1958), *Divine Grace and Man* (1962), *The New Life of Grace* (1969), *Authority in the Church* (with others, 1983), and *Hermeneutics of the Councils and Other Studies* (posthumously, 1985).

After his death several dissertations were written on different aspects of his theology: Cutinha, ecumenical councils, Catholic University of America, 1988; Yeiser, theological method and theology of grace, Duquesne University, 1997; and Van den Bossche, sacramentology, Louvain, 1999.

His papers are kept in the archives of the Flemish Jesuits (ABSE), and in the Centre for the Study of the Second Vatican Council, both at Louvain.

See also Rahner, Karl; Theology

de Graeve, Frank, "Piet Fransen: A Biographical Sketch." *Louvain Studies* 10 (1984/85), 87–96.
Stagaman, David, "Piet Fransen's Research on Fides et Mores." *Theological Studies* 64 (2003), 69–77.

Paul Begheyn, SJ

Friends in the Lord

On July 24, 1537, Ignatius wrote a letter from Venice to Juan de Verdolay, a priest friend of his in Barcelona. He had been in Venice since 1535, but his companions at the University of Paris did not join him until 1537. He records: "In mid-January nine friends of mine in the Lord arrived here from Paris." He then goes on to give an account of their priestly ordination and other recent developments.

This is the only occasion in which Ignatius used the phrase "friends in the Lord." It was a simple, informal way of referring to the companions. Ignatius did not present it as pregnant with deep meaning. We note that he used it of those whom he had known, interrelated with, and influenced at the University of Paris and not of the Society of Jesus which had not yet come into being. The Jesuit appropriation of the term, almost as a way of summing up the Society's identity, did not occur until modern times. To be precise, this development was due to Pedro Arrupe who, as superior general (1965–83), resurrected the term and employed it frequently. It then entered the documents of the 32nd and 34th General Congregations (GCs) as well as the Complementary Norms and, indeed, common parlance within the Society.

Two key passages illustrate its usage: "Moreover, it is in companionship that the Jesuit fulfills his mission. He belongs to a community of friends in the Lord who, like him, have asked to be received under the standard of Christ the King" (GC 32). "Jesuits today join together because each of us has heard the call of Christ the King. From this union with Christ flows, of necessity, a love for one another. We are not merely fellow workers; we are friends in the Lord" (GC 34).

See also Faber, Peter, SJ, St.; Loyola, Ignatius of, SJ, St.; Xavier, Francis, SJ, St.

Osuna, Javier, *Amigos en el Señor: unidos para la dispersión*. Bilbao: Mensajero, 1997.
   Friends in the Lord. Part 1 of *Amigos en el Señor*. Trans. Nicholas King. London: Way Books, 1974.

Brian O'Leary, SJ

Fróis, Luís, SJ (1532–1597)

Luís Fróis was a Portuguese missionary and prolific historian in India and Japan. Little is known of him prior to joining the Society in Lisbon in 1548. Shortly afterward, he sailed to India. In 1561, he completed his theological studies at the College of Saint Paul in Goa and was ordained a priest. He accompanied M. Nunes Baretto to Malacca between 1554 and 1557. Leaving Goa in 1562, he arrived in Japan in 1563, where he remained until his death in 1597. He labored in Miyako between1565 and 1576, served as superior of Bungo between 1577 and 1581, and assistant to Vice Provincial Gaspar Coelho between 1582 and 1587. He took his fourth vow in 1591. He accompanied Visitor Alessandro Valignano to Macau between 1592 and 1595. He was fluent in Japanese and often was a Jesuit spokesperson to Oda Nobunaga and Toyotomi Hideyoshi.

Fróis authored more than 130 letters and edited numerous annual reports from India, Malacca, and Japan, providing thorough and keen observations. His last letter was on the Nagasaki twenty-six martyrs (1597). His *Tratado* (1585) offers witty cultural comparisons between Europe and Japan. His masterpiece, *Historia de Japam* (History of Japan), covers the years 1549 to 1593. First commissioned by General Everard Mercurian to be included in J. P. Maffei's *History of India*, but suppressed by Valignano, *Historia* was never published and the original was lost. In the 1920s scholars began to rediscover eighteenth-century copies. *Historia* provides intimate, vivid but critical primary information not only about the mission but also about sixteenth-century Japan in the rapidly shifting world.

See also India; Japan; Portugal

Fróis, Luís, *Historia de Japam*. Ed. José Wicki. 5 vols. Lisbon: Biblioteca Nacional de Lisboa, 1976–84.
López-Gay, Jesús, "Fróis, Luis [sic]." In Gerald H. Anderson, ed., *Biographical Dictionary of Christian Mission*. Grand Rapids, MI: William B. Eerdmans, 1998. p. 230.

Haruko Nawata Ward

Fuchs, Josef, SJ (1912–2005)

Ordained a diocesan priest in 1937, Fuchs entered the Jesuit novitiate the following year. In 1940 he began graduate studies in ecclesiology, writing on the foundations of a new ecclesiological trilogy, *Magisterium, Ministerium, Regimen: Vom Ursprung einer ekkle-siologischen Trilogie*. After finishing his degree in 1946, he was assigned to teach moral theology and went for roughly eighteen months to Tübingen to study with Theodor Steinbüchel (1888–1949). In 1947 he began teaching at Sankt Georgen in Frankfurt. There he published his first manuscript on the sexual ethics of Thomas Aquinas (*Die Sexualethik des Heiligen Thomas von Aquin*). In 1954 he went to the Gregorian University in Rome where he taught until 1982. His doctoral students include Sergio Bastianel, SJ, Klaus Demmer, MSC, Franz Furger, Karl Golser, Bernard Hoose, James F. Keenan, SJ, John Mahoney, SJ, Warren Reich, Philipp Schmitz, SJ, Bruno Schüller, SJ, and Helmut Weber.

From 1952 to 1956, Fuchs critiqued situational ethics as relativistic, because it held that the single insight of Christian ethics was to love in the situation immediately, that is, without the mediation of any moral tradition with its attendant principles and rules. Still, Fuchs found in its claims three interesting insights: first, it was fundamentally theo-logical, and Fuchs looked to the theological exclusively as the foundation of Christian ethics. Second, its injunction was biblical, and Fuchs was profoundly influenced by the biblical moralist, Fritz Tillman (1874–1953), Steinbüchel's dissertation director. Third, the introduction of the "situation" captured Fuchs's theological imagination for his entire life. In 1952 he published *Situation und Entscheidung: Grundfragen christlicher Situationsethik*, a book on moral decision-making, and over the next four years several articles as well. Later, the Holy Office censured Fuchs for not being sufficiently intoler-ant of the new morality and, for a year, he was not allowed to teach those preparing for ordination, though he continued to teach and direct licentiate and doctoral students.

In 1955 Fuchs wrote *Lex Naturae. Zur Theologie des Naturrechts* (English trans-lation, *Natural Law: A Theological Investigation*, New York, 1965). In its preface he announced: "A more decidedly theological cast is now being given to natural law teach-ing" (xi). Therein Fuchs presented chapters on "The Testimony of the Bible" and "The Situations of History." The conscience of the Christian, however, did little more than apply the moral norm.

In 1960 Fuchs authored *De castitate et ordine sexuali*. In 1963 Pope Paul VI, con-cerned that the birth control commission appointed by his predecessor, Pope John XXIII, was moving to recommend reform of Church teaching, expanded its member-ship by adding, among others, Fuchs. Though the Pope anticipated that Fuchs would oppose the commission's inclinations, he instead became the draftsman of its majority report, which the Pope rejected by promulgating *Humanae vitae* in 1968.

Listening to the married couples on the commission, Fuchs learned about the complexity of moral decisions regarding the responsible regulation of births and the right exercise of parenthood. He realized that the genuine application of moral norms required Christians to engage in conscience all teachings and all responsibilities that they faced. Here, Fuchs learned the competency of a mature moral conscience and later described his transformation, from his doubts in 1963 about the direct applicability of Church teachings to his decision to not allow the Gregorian University Press to repub-lish *De castitate*.

Fuchs's later writings often appeared as single essays, more than ninety of them, which were translated into English and other languages. In *Human Values and Christian Morality* (Dublin, 1970), he developed his positions on Vatican II, the fundamental option, human progress, and the theological foundations of moral theology. In *Personal*

Responsibility and Christian Morality (Georgetown, 1983), Fuchs returned to theological foundations, explored the distinctiveness of Christian morality and the "absoluteness" of moral norms, argued that the virtue of *epeikeia* (on interpreting the moral law) belongs not only to bishops and moralists but to all people of conscience, and started his defense of a Christian's conscience. In *Christian Ethics in a Secular Arena* (Georgetown, 1984), he discussed intrinsic evil, described natural law as right reason, and focused on the tension between moralists and bishops. In *Christian Morality: The Word Becomes Flesh* (Georgetown, 1987), he explored the goodness of a person striving to love and the rightness of a person's actions as two different competencies of a person acting in conscience. Finally, in *Moral Demands and Personal Obligations* (Georgetown, 1993), he reflected on sin, conscience, historicity, law, and grace.

See also Ethics; Paul VI; Theology

Graham, Mark, *Josef Fuchs on Natural Law*. Washington, DC: Georgetown University Press, 2002.
Keenan, James F., A *History of Moral Theology in the Twentieth Century*. New York: Continuum Press, 2010.
Sautermeister, Josef, "Josef Fuchs." In Konrad Hilpert, ed., *Christliche Ethik im Porträt*. Freiburg: Herder, 2012, pp. 759–90.

James F. Keenan, SJ

Fundamental Theology

Fundamental theology is that branch of theology which studies such foundational issues as the divine revelation in the history of Israel and in Jesus Christ, the conditions that open up human beings to this self-communication of God, the signs that make faith in Christ a credible option, the transmission (through the Church's tradition and the inspired Scriptures) of the experience of God's self-communication, and theological method. The pre-history of fundamental theology stretches back to the second- and third-century apologists who rebutted objections and offered educated outsiders a case for the Christian faith.

When the Society of Jesus was founded in the mid-sixteenth century, apologetic literature took shape around three questions: the existence of God, the divine identity of Christ, and his establishment of the Church. In his "controversial theology," St. Robert Bellarmine (1542–1621) debated with Anglican and Protestant counterparts questions concerning the Church founded by Christ. The Enlightenment, a movement that typically resisted authority and tradition and aimed at deciding issues through the use of reason alone, started in seventeenth-century Europe and spread to North America and elsewhere. In religious matters many who belonged to this movement rejected divine revelation, miracles, and Christ's resurrection, opposed central articles of the Christian creed, and in some cases doubted or denied the existence of a personal God. The expulsion of Jesuits from France, Portugal, and Spain led on to the papal suppression of the Society of Jesus in 1773 and caused Jesuits to be absent for many years from debates with leading figures in the Enlightenment.

After their restoration in 1814 and as the nineteenth century unfolded, Jesuits began contributing to fundamental theology. A notable work by Johann Baptist Franzelin (1816–86) concerned tradition and Scripture. Neo-scholastic Jesuits structured their fundamental theology around a triple "demonstration" (of God, of Christ as "God's legate," and of the Church as founded by Christ). George Tyrrell (1861–1909), who was to be expelled from the Society in 1906, turned away from the arid externalism of neo-scholastic arguments and developed an experiential apologetic for faith. His condemnation as a Modernist delayed the full development of fundamental theology, to which five Jesuits were to contribute massively.

The first was Henri de Lubac (1896–1991). He affected thinking on such basic questions as biblical interpretation, the founding of the Church, the relationship between philosophy and theology, and the nature of tradition. He also discussed atheism, non-Christian religions, and the dialogue between faith and science – all matters that belong to fundamental theology.

The crowning work of Karl Rahner (1904–84), *Foundations of Christian Faith* (German original, 1976), drew together his response to fundamental issues with which he had grappled for a lifetime: What is Christian faith? How can one justify it and live it with intellectual honesty? Does faith cohere with the basic dynamism of the human spirit? Rahner's classic volume forms a holistic *apologia* for God's answer to the universal questions of human beings. It uses contemporary human understanding to validate the divine self-communication in Christ and the Church founded by him.

Rightly dissatisfied with nineteenth-century fundamental theology, Bernard Lonergan (1904–84) developed what he called a "fifth functional speciality, foundations," which followed four other specialities (research, interpretation, history, and dialectic). Lonergan's foundations present the horizon within which the meaning of doctrines can be apprehended. His foundations promise to elucidate conflicts revealed in dialectic and provide a principle to guide the remaining specialties concerned, respectively, with doctrines, systematics, and communications (*Method in Theology*, 1972).

After his *Apologetics and the Biblical Christ* (1963), Avery Dulles (1918–2008) offered a credible account of divine self-revelation (*Models of Revelation*, 1983), the human response of faith (*The Assurance of Things Hoped For: A Theology of Christian Faith*, 1993), and the Church founded by Christ through his apostles (*Models of the Church*, 1978, and *A Church to Believe in: Discipleship and the Dynamics of Freedom*, 1982).

A towering figure in modern fundamental theology, René Latourelle (b. 1918) was driven by the desire to show the credibility of Christian claims. After his best-selling *The Theology of Revelation* (1966), he put the case for Jesus and the Church (*Christ and the Church: Signs of Salvation*, 1972), for knowing the historical Jesus (*Finding Jesus through the Gospels*, 1979), for the authenticity and meaning of the miracles (*The Miracles of Jesus and the Theology of Miracles*, 1988), and for the correlation between the human quest for meaning and the person and message of Jesus (*Man and His Problems in the Light of Christ*, 1981). Latourelle argued for the basics of Christian faith, integrated the apologetic task into the broader scope of fundamental theology, and, in order to establish the identity of that discipline, co-edited (with Gerald O'Collins) *Problems and Perspectives of Fundamental Theology* (1982) and (with Rino Fisichella) the *Dictionary of Fundamental Theology* (1994).

See also Dulles, Avery, SJ, Cardinal; Lonergan, Bernard, SJ; Lubac, Henri de, SJ; Rahner, Karl, SJ; Theology

O'Collins, Gerald, *Rethinking Fundamental Theology: Toward a New Fundamental Theology.* Oxford: Oxford University Press, 2011.

Gerald O'Collins, SJ

Furlong Cardiff, Guillermo, SJ (1889–1974)

One of the most prolific Jesuit historians, Guillermo Furlong Cardiff was born on June 21, 1889, to an Irish family near Rosario in northeastern Argentina. He entered the Jesuit Colegio de la Inmaculada Concepción in Santa Fe, where he decided to join the Society of Jesus. After finishing his novitiate in Córdoba, he was sent to Spain in 1905 and later to Washington, DC, where he earned his doctorate from Georgetown University in 1913. He returned to Argentina, where he taught Greek and Latin in the Pontifical Seminary of Buenos Aires. In 1916 Furlong Cardiff joined the faculty of the Jesuit Colegio del Salvador, where he taught history, English, and world literature. Between 1920 and 1925, he was back in Europe, visiting archives and libraries in Spain, France, Belgium, England, and Germany. In 1938 Furlong Cardiff was elected a member of the Argentine National Academy of History and in 1956 collaborated in the creation of the National Academy of Geography. In 1960, as part of the celebrations of the 150th anniversary of the Revolución de Mayo (Argentine Revolution of Independence), the Argentine Library of Congress published a catalogue titled, *Bibliografía de la Revolución de Mayo, 1810–1828* (Bibliography of the May Revolution, 1810–1828), compiled by Furlong Cardiff. This work earned him a monthly pension granted by Congress in order to help him defray future research expenses.

Furlong Cardiff's diligent and extensive archival research has made him an ineludible author for anyone seriously interested in the cultural history of the American Southern Cone between the sixteenth and the early nineteenth centuries. His bibliography counts close to a hundred books and innumerable papers and journal articles, some published under one of his forty-eight different pennames. His research covered initially different aspects of Jesuit activities and cultural life in Paraguay and the River Plate before the 1767 expulsion. In 1933 he published *Los jesuitas y la cultura rioplatense* (The Jesuits and the Culture of the River Plate, revised edition in 1946) and, in 1962, *Misiones y sus pueblos guaraníes* (The Province of Misiones and Its Guaraní Towns). He uncovered and published the work of many Jesuits who had been active in what today are Paraguay, Uruguay, Bolivia, Chile, and Argentina, drawing scholarly attention to their contributions, in many cases unknown until that moment. Important figures, such as José Sánchez Labrador, Thomas Falkner, Niccolò Mascardi, and José Manuel Peramás, to name just a few, were rediscovered by Furlong Cardiff's indefatigable archival research, which continued for decades almost until his very last day.

Jesuit historiography was only one aspect of Furlong Cardiff's interests. One of his main goals as a historian was to recover the cultural and scientific contributions that had come from the River Plate during the colonial period, which he felt had been ignored by modern historians. His monumental *Historia social y cultural del Río de la Plata, 1536–1810: el trasplante cultural* (Social and Cultural History of the River Plate, 1536–1810: The Cultural Transplant), published in 1969 and divided in three volumes, devoted to the arts, the sciences, and social processes, respectively, has become the standard work on the subject. The same could be said about his books on colonial philosophy, cartography, and printing, *Nacimiento y desarrollo de la filosofía en el Río de la Plata, 1536–1810* (Birth and Development of Philosophy in the River Plate, 1536–1810) (1952); *Cartografía jesuítica del Río de la Plata* (Jesuit Cartography of the River Plate Region) (1936), and *Historia y bibliografía de las primeras imprentas rioplatenses* (History and Bibliography of the First Printing Presses of the River Plate) (3 vols., 1953–58).

Father Furlong Cardiff died in Buenos Aires, on May 20, 1974.

See also Argentina; Paraguay Missions ("Reductions")

Mörner, Magnus, "Obituary: Guillermo Furlong Cardiff (1889–1974)." *Hispanic American Historical Review* 55, 1 (February, 1975), 92–94.
Tesler, Mario, *La obra oculta del padre Furlong*. Buenos Aires: Instituto de Investigaciones Históricas Juan Manuel de Rosas, 1994.

Andrés Ignacio Prieto

Galileo

Galileo Galilei was born in Pisa in 1564 and studied medicine and mathematics at the University of Pisa, leaving without a degree in 1585. After further informal studies in mathematics, music, art, and literature, in 1589 he began teaching mathematics in Pisa. In 1592 Galileo moved to the University of Padua, where he spent eighteen years and constructed his first astronomical telescope in 1609. During that time he was in regular correspondence with Jesuits at the Roman College, especially Christopher Clavius. Galileo's descriptions of craters on the Moon and satellites around Jupiter in his 1610 book *Sidereus nuncius* (*The Starry Messenger*) created a sensation. In 1611 Galileo visited Rome to exhibit his telescope and was feted by the Jesuits at the Roman College.

Galileo argued that his telescopic discoveries, such as the Jovian satellites, sunspots, and phases of Venus, supported the heliocentric model proposed by Copernicus. However, they were equally compatible with the Brahe system, in which the planets orbited the sun but the planets and the sun orbited around the Earth. The Brahe cosmology was less elegant, but it was consistent with prevailing Aristotelian physics and the interpretation of certain biblical passages that assumed the Sun moved while the Earth was stationary. The heliocentric model also lacked scientific support because the astronomy of the day could not provide any measurable evidence of the Earth's motion.

Galileo originally hoped to convince the Jesuits to support the Copernican system and teach it in their network of schools. However, a series of conflicts quickly soured relations between them. In 1612, Christoph Scheiner, SJ (1573–1650), had published a series of letters about sunspots. Galileo disputed Scheiner's priority in their discovery and his suggestion that they might be objects passing in front of the sun, arguing in *The Sunspot Letters* that they must be fixed to the sun's surface. The dispute grew more heated with time, as Scheiner proposed alternate explanations while Galileo insisted on his own interpretation.

Galileo also encountered resistance from some theologians within the Church. In 1616 a commission of cardinals appointed by the Holy Office judged the Copernican system as "absurd in philosophy ... [and] contrary to scripture." Jesuit Cardinal Bellarmine was directed to instruct Galileo to no longer hold or teach Copernicanism.

Then in 1618, Orazio Grassi, SJ (1583–1654), observed several comets, the first person to do so with a telescope. He determined that the comets showed no parallax and thus were located beyond the Moon, a conclusion difficult to reconcile with the Copernican system. Over the next four years, Galileo and Grassi engaged in a battle of booklets arguing the point, ending with Galileo's masterpiece in the philosophy of science, *The Assayer.* Its wit and sarcasm won Galileo fame, while it embarrassed Grassi (often unfairly), abused Scheiner for good measure, and infuriated their Jesuit brothers.

With the election of Maffeo Barbarini as Pope Urban VIII in 1623, a fellow Tuscan and friend of Galileo, it appeared that the injunction against the Copernican system might be relaxed. Galileo dedicated *The Assayer* to Pope Urban, published replies to his critics, and began work on a dialogue that would contrast the Aristotelian and Copernican systems. *The Dialogue on the Two World Systems* was approved – with corrections – by the Pope's censor in Rome. Among the required additions was a speech at the end of the dialogue representing the concerns of Pope Urban, emphasizing God's omnipotence and acknowledging that no model of the universe could ever be held as certain. After various delays, the book finally appeared in 1632. That summer, Pope Urban suddenly turned against the book and Galileo, halting its sale and demanding that Galileo be tried before the Roman Inquisition. The trial occurred in 1633, with the Pope himself presiding. Galileo's attempt at a plea bargain was rejected, and he was sentenced to house arrest after publicly abjuring the heresies in the Copernican system. (Oddly, those heresies were never specifically outlined.)

Historians still argue about the roots of Galileo's trial. Some attribute it to the Pope's anger that his arguments had been placed in the mouth of the most foolish participant in the dialogue; others note that the trial occurred during the height of the Thirty Years War, when the Pope was under intense pressure from Spain and may have wished to shore up support from more conservative elements in the Church. Galileo himself blamed the Jesuits, reading sinister intent in the comment of the Jesuit mathematician Grienberger that if Galileo had "maintained the affection of the Fathers of the [Roman] College, he would be famous, rather than disgraced, and he could have written freely on any topic, for instance about the Earth's movements."

See also Astronomy; Grassi, Orazio, SJ; Scheiner, Christoph, SJ

Fantoli, Annibale, *Galileo: For Copernicanism and for the Church.* South Bend, IN: University of Notre Dame Press, 2002.

Finocchiaro, Maurice, *The Galileo Affair: A Documentary History.* Berkeley: University of California Press, 1989.

Heilbron, J. L., *Galileo.* Oxford: Oxford University Press, 2010.

Miller, David Marshall, "The Thirty Years War and the Galileo Affair." *History of Science* 46 (2008), 49–74.

Guy Consolmagno, SJ

Gallicanism

Gallicanism is a political theory, or rather a set of theories, that became influential in French juristic and ecclesiastical circles by the sixteenth century. In broad terms, this theory emphasized the independent origins and distinctive character of French ecclesiastical institutions, and the role of the French monarchy as their protector. The origins of Gallicanism lay in the notoriously fraught relationship between the medieval papacy and the French monarchy over questions of jurisdiction. Gallicanism took its early modern form after 1510, during a dispute between King Louis XII of France and Pope Julius II. Louis XII threatened to call a council of ecclesiastics in this year to support his bid to declare a holy war on the Pope. Though the council was in the end a failure, it stimulated ongoing discussion in France over the existence of a distinctly "Gallican" church.

The defeat of papal troops at the battle of Marignano by French forces led to the formulation of the Concordat of Bologna (1516); this treaty enhanced royal authority over French religious institutions at the expense of the papacy. According to the Concordat, the French monarchy had the right to collect tithes, and restrict the right of appeal to Rome. The agreement also recognized royal appointment of high ecclesiastical offices, though papal authority could still reject an unworthy candidate.

Tension between France and the papacy over jurisdiction, however, continued throughout the sixteenth century. The so-called "Gallican crisis of 1551" stimulated some of the most important literature on this political theory, much of it coming from humanist-trained jurists such as Jean du Tillet, Pierre Pithou, and Charles Dumoulin. The Gallican crisis was triggered by renewed concerns on the part of the French monarchy about growing papal authority stemming from the meetings of the Council of Trent (1545–63). At certain points a schism between the Roman and French churches during the reign of Henry II (1547–59) seemed to be a genuine possibility. However, in the end, a shared concern about the growing threat of Protestantism managed to temper the rhetoric on both sides, and the Gallican council was never called. Gallican conceptions continued to percolate in governing circles well into the seventeenth century, producing a number of visible strands described variously as magisterial, episcopal, and royal Gallicanism.

From the standpoint of the Jesuit order, Gallicanism at times posed a serious challenge to its mission in France especially during its first century. Gallicanists found the fourth vow of the Jesuits disturbing, since it bound them to obedience to the pope. From the first establishment of the Jesuits in Paris in the 1540s, the Order found itself under attack in political polemics as well as in the civil courts as a potential source of disruption. During the height of the Wars of Religion in the 1580s and 1590s, the Jesuits were branded by many as anti-royalists for their support of the Catholic party known as the League. The League was a radical Catholic association formed in 1585 that became increasingly critical of the rule of Henry III. In truth, the French Jesuits were politically divided throughout these years, and some formed a visibly Gallicanist party. Among these men was the well-known royal confessor Edmond Auger. Auger was a close adviser of King Henry III until the latter's assassination in 1589. The taint of anti-royalism persisted even as the Wars drew to a close after 1593. The attempted assassination of King Henry IV in 1594 by an alumnus of a Jesuit school provoked the immediate expulsion of the Order from the French kingdom. The terms upon which the Order was reestablished a few years later reveal the influence of Gallicanist thought in monarchical circles, since the Jesuits were required now to take an oath of loyalty to the French Crown. The request was extremely controversial in the Jesuit order, provoking significant debate between the French Jesuits and authorities in Rome between 1599 and 1601. The French Jesuits, however, were anxious to reclaim their old missionary ground and were willing to take the oath. This decision in the end proved extremely important for the French mission, inaugurating a period of remarkable political, economic, and religious influence in France.

Once regarded as potential enemies of the state, the Jesuits after 1603 became a favored order under Henry IV and Louis XIII, one closely associated with the Bourbon regime and critical agents of its global expansion. And yet, Gallicanism remained a thorn in the side of the French Jesuits long after this time, despite their visible support of Louis XIV in his controversies over French Episcopal sees with Pope Innocent XI.

Indeed, in the years leading up to the French Revolution, and amid growing criticism of the arbitrary nature of the French state, the Jesuits found their loyalty to the monarchy heavily criticized by Gallicanist bishops and magistrates.

See also France; Henry IV; Louis XIV

Martin, A. Lynn, *Henry III and the Jesuits*. Geneva: Librarie Droz, 1973.

Nelson, Eric, *The Jesuits and the Monarchy: Catholic Reform and Political Authority in France (1590–1615)*. Aldershot: Ashgate Publishing, 2005.

Parsons, Jotham, *The Church in the Republic: Gallicanism and Political Ideology in Renaissance France*. Washington, DC: CUA Press, 2004.

Megan C. Armstrong

Gaubil, Antoine, SJ (1689–1759)

Antoine Gaubil, born in Gaillac, France, joined the Society of Jesus in 1704. During his Jesuit formation he studied mathematics and astronomy and was assigned to the China mission, where he arrived in 1722. He soon acquired remarkable fluency in Chinese, which enabled him to delve into Chinese history, geography, cartography, and astronomy while teaching Latin and acting as chief interpreter for the emperor at receptions of Russian and European visitors. He was also director of the college for young Manchus for a period. He is said to have been the best astronomer and historian among the French Jesuits in China during the eighteenth century.

Gaubil carried on an extensive correspondence with the savants of his day, and his writings earned him membership in the Royal Society of London, the French Académie Royale des Sciences and the St. Petersburg Academy of Sciences. His chronology of Chinese history from the beginning to the start of the Han Dynasty (206 BC), published posthumously in 1814, is considered an important contribution to the study of Chinese history (*Traité de la chronologie chinoise, divisé en trois parties*). His publication of *A Critical and Historical Treatise on Chinese Astronomy* and his translation of *Chou-King* were another major achievement, and his *History of Jengis Khan and All the Mongol Dynasty*, published in 1739, is a work that alone would have sufficed to gain him a formidable reputation as a writer. In addition to his scientific pursuits, he also devoted time to the instruction and formation of catechumens and abandoned infants during the difficult period of papal interference and Chinese restrictions that ended with the Suppression of the Jesuit order.

See also Astronomy; China

Tricentenaire d'Antoine Gaubil: bicentenaire de la Révolution française dans le Tarn. (Journeés d'histoire de Gaillac). Gaillac: Mairie de Gaillac, 1989.

John Donohue, SJ

Gaulli, Giovanni Battista (Baciccio)

Giovanni Battista Gaulli (1639 – after March 26, 1709), or Baciccio, is best known for his nave decorations of the *Triumph of the Name of Jesus* in the Gesù, Rome. Born in Genoa, Gaulli had ample opportunity from an early age to study the work of Titian,

Veronese, Rubens, and Van Dyck there, which contributed to his achievements as one of the great colorists of the High Baroque. He moved to Rome in 1657, a year in which his entire family was wiped out by plague. There he initially worked for Genoese art dealer, Pellegrino Peri, through whom he met Bernini. The sculptor would become a keen supporter. In 1662 he became a member of the Accademia di San Luca, rising to become its *Principe*. Among his first major commissions – on Bernini's recommendation – was one to paint the pendentives of Sant'Agnese in Piazza Navona (1666–72) with allegorical figures, for the Pamphilj family. He subsequently collaborated with Bernini on the Altieri Chapel in San Francesco a Ripa, painting the *Virgin and Child with St. Anne* as the backdrop to Bernini's *Blessed Ludovica Albertoni* around 1675.

His work at Santa Marta, opposite the Collegio Romano, aroused the interest of Giovanni Paolo Oliva, the father general of the Jesuits. Again with Bernini's encouragement, Baciccio was included in the competition to fresco the interior of the Gesù. In 1672 he signed the contract to paint the cupola and nave for 12,000 *scudi*. The dome was to be completed by Christmas Eve 1674, to mark the centenary of the church's formal opening. It shows a vision of Heaven with Old Testament figures and saints, including the Jesuit saints, Ignatius, Francis Xavier, and Francis Borgia. The illusionistic design looks back to the prototype of Correggio in the Parma Duomo, seen through the eyes of Pietro da Cortona in his dome at the Oratorian Church of Santa Maria in Vallicella, Rome. Baciccio immediately completed the pendentives, replacing the work of Giovanni de' Vecchi and Andrea Lilio (1583). Each pendentive was filled with complex groups of four figures: the Evangelists, Doctors of the Latin Church, Lawgivers and Leaders of Israel, and Prophets of Israel, which are striking for their illusionism.

The *Triumph of the Name of Jesus*, which covers the nave of the Gesù, is the culmination of illusionistic Baroque ceiling decoration, inspired by Giovanni and Cherubino Alberti in the Sala Clementina (Vatican) and Pietro da Cortona in the Salone of Palazzo Barberini, where the viewer has the impression that the ceiling has been removed and that they are witnessing a celestial vision. Here it is transposed into a religious context with great theatricality. Divine light radiates from the IHS symbol of Christ's name, which had been adopted as a Jesuit emblem, illuminating the blessed and angels amid a mass of clouds, which burst over the architectural mouldings in a brilliant mixture of fresco and stucco. At the part of the ceiling toward the crossing, the damned appear literally to fall out of the fresco, enveloped in dark clouds. The subject of worshipping Christ's name is based on St. Paul's epistle to the Philippians (2:10), while the expulsion of the damned is unexpected in this context. Enggass, the author of the principal monograph on Baciccio, has suggested that this might have been an addition to the program, enhancing the spirit of the Church Triumphant.

Baciccio decorated the apse of the Gesù between 1680 and 1683 with the *Adoration of the Lamb*, which is based on the vision of St. John in Revelation (5:6–14). As in the nave, divine light emanates from the Lamb, supported on a bed of clouds by exuberant angels. Below, the twenty-four Elders each raise a jar of incense in praise. Above, a group of angels add their praises. Baciccio also painted a group of angels above the high altar. They point out the name of Jesus, complementing Muziano's altarpiece of the *Circumcision*, the occasion of Christ's naming (1589). His final work at the church was the decoration of the left transept vault with *St. Ignatius in Glory*, unveiled in 1685.

While working at the Gesù, Baciccio painted an altarpiece for Bernini's Sant'Andrea al Quirinale, the Jesuit novitiate, of the death of St. Francis Xavier (1676). Toward the

Figure 20 Baciccio: *The Apotheosis of St. Ignatius*, detail of ceiling fresco, 1685, Church of Il Gesù, Rome. Photograph Alison Fleming

end of his career, in an austere climate, opportunities for patronage were fewer, though he worked again at Sant'Andrea, and also for the Altieri at Santa Maria in Campitelli. He was also a highly accomplished portraitist.

See also Baroque Art and Architecture; Bernini, Gian Lorenzo; Gesù, Rome

dell'Arco, Maurizio Fagiolo, Dieter Graf, and Francesco Petrucci, eds., *Giovanni Battista Gaulli, Il Baciccio, 1639–1709.* Milan: Skira, 1999.

Enggass, Robert, *The Painting of Baciccio, Giovanni Battista Gaulli, 1639–1709.* University Park, PA: Pennsylvania State University Press, 1964.

"Pozzo a Sant'Ignazio e Baciccio al Gesù: tracce della fortuna critica." In Alberta Battisti, ed., *Andrea Pozzo.* Milan: Luni Editrice, 1996, pp. 253–58.

Pascoli, Lione,*Vite de' pittori, scultori ed architetti moderni.* Rome: A. de' Rossi, 1730, pp. 194–209.

Clare Robertson

Gélineau, Joseph, SJ (1920–2008)

Joseph Gélineau was a French Jesuit composer and liturgist, born in Champ-sur-Layon, Maine et Loire, on October 31, 1920. As a youth, he studied music at the École César Franck in Paris. He entered the Society of Jesus in 1941 and was ordained in 1951. He was seriously interested in the changes in the liturgy, writing books and articles before and after the Second Vatican Council. He also composed numerous sacred works during this time. While stationed in Paris he was professor of liturgical and pastoral music at the Institut Catholique and associated with the Centre de Pastorale Liturgique. He was a founding member of the Universa Laus, the international liturgical music society.

In his research, particularly in *Chant et musique dans le culte chrétien* (1962), he argued for increasing the participation of the faithful in the liturgy. This was a time when there were essentially two musical camps, one seeking to keep traditional plainchant and sacred music and Gélineau's position. He reasoned that liturgical music be regarded as "functional art," its value judged in its capacity to assist with the prayers and liturgical actions. His aim was to restore the congregation's singing of the mass parts.

Given his knowledge of Hebrew, he wrote his own form of psalm responses in French, striving to attain the nuances of both languages. This new approach, with simple melodies for the cantor and the congregation, came to be known as "Gélineau psalmody." An English translation was published in London in 1963 as *The Psalms: A New Translation*. Using his settings as a model, many other settings of the responsorial psalms have emerged over the years. He composed and published several editions of psalms, including *Psaumes* (1953–55 from the Jerusalem Bible) and Masses such as the *Festival Mass* (1974).

See also Liturgy; Music

Gélineau, Joseph, *Chant et musique dans le culte chrétien*. Paris: Fleurus, 1962.
Jefferey, Peter, "Chant East and West: Toward a Renewal of the Tradition." In Mary Collins, David Power, and Melonee Burnim, eds., *Music and the Experience of God*. Edinburgh: T. & T. Clark, 1989, pp. 20–29.

Charles Jurgensmeier, SJ

Georgetown University

The flagship school of Jesuit and Catholic higher education in the United States, Georgetown was founded in 1789 and opened its doors in 1792, an enterprise of former Jesuits including the founder, Bishop John Carroll. In 1805, Carroll transferred the college to the Jesuits after several former members reaffiliated with the Society in Russia. Georgetown obtained a Congressional charter in 1815 and two years later awarded the first baccalaureate degrees, following the *Ratio studiorum*. Enrollment rose to over 300 by 1860, but the outbreak of the Civil War reduced the numbers dramatically; some of the buildings were commandeered as military hospitals.

After the war, Patrick Healy (president, 1873–82) facilitated the transition to a full university with graduate schools and programs. At the time he took office, Georgetown had a medical school dating from 1851 and a law school since 1870. Healy worked to professionalize these programs and to enhance the physical plant, including the construction of Georgetown's landmark building, now known as Healy Hall. Joseph Havens Richards (1888–98) continued the process, establishing graduate courses in the arts and sciences, building new facilities for the law and medical schools, and opening Dahlgren Chapel in 1893. By 1898, enrollment in all schools totaled 634, including 106 in the graduate divisions.

With the twentieth century came Schools of Dentistry (1901), Nursing (1903), and Foreign Service (1919). After 1915, a scientific course allowed students to graduate without Greek, as the classics gradually lost priority in the undergraduate program. The Graduate School opened formally in the 1930s, with programs in mathematics, natural sciences, economics, history, and government. During World War II, Georgetown hosted an Army Specialized Training Program, with military enrollment reaching 75 percent of students. During the war, women were admitted to the School of Foreign Service, and coeducation came to the undergraduate college in 1969. The School of Business Administration and the School of Continuing Studies both opened in the 1950s.

Surging enrollments after World War II led to a sharp expansion of the faculty; and the emerging context of the Cold War added to the School of Foreign Service and its Institute of Languages and Linguistics the mission of contributing to the ideological and geopolitical resources of the United States. Edward Bunn (1952–64) seized the possibilities of the age with a successful fund-raising drive that supported major expansion of the physical plant and professionalization of the faculty according to enhanced academic standards of research and publication. He also unified Georgetown's governance, making a true university from what had formerly been "a college with professional school satellites grouped unevenly around it." By 1968, the separate incorporation of the Jesuit community made possible the transfer of responsibility for Georgetown to a separate board of trustees who were increasingly laypersons.

Under the leadership of Timothy Healy (1976–89) and Leo O'Donovan (1989–2001), Georgetown grew from a regional school to become a major international research university with eight schools (College of Arts and Sciences, Graduate School, Medical, Law, Nursing and Health Studies, Foreign Service, Business Administration, Summer School and Continuing Education) and an affiliated hospital. Helped by its location near the seat of government and with gifted leadership, Georgetown joined the ranks of elite colleges and universities. In these years, the building program continued, and the faculty, now much diversified regarding race and gender, grew to about 1,300 full-time and 900 part-time, with greatly enhanced participation in governance. By 2013, the endowment had risen to about $1.3 billion.

Over 12,000 students, including 7,500 undergraduates, pursue studies at four local campuses and one in Qatar. Nearly 20 percent are international students, representing over 130 countries. Highly selective, Georgetown College admits about 17 percent of applicants. In athletics, Georgetown supports 23 varsity programs and has enjoyed particular prominence in men's basketball, winning the NCAA Tournament in 1984. In the same era, greater diversity among students and faculty became characteristic. In 2001, Georgetown elected the first lay president, John DeGioia. Under his direction in 2003, an office of Mission and Ministry was established, with the leadership of a vice-president whose responsibilities include coordinating the work of thirty-four campus ministers representing many international faith traditions.

Among prominent Georgetown alumni are heads of state, including Abdullah II (Jordan), William Clinton (USA), Felipe VI (Spain), and Gloria Macapagal-Arroyo (Philippines). Other alumni include twenty-two state governors, about fifty US cabinet officers, presidential appointees, and White House staff members, over a hundred ambassadors of various countries, twenty-one members of the US senate, about seventy members of the House of Representatives, and numerous other leaders in the Church, as well as in fields of law, medicine, business, entertainment, military service, and diplomacy.

See also Carroll, John; United States of America; Universities, 1773–Present

Curran, Robert Emmett, *A History of Georgetown University*. 3 vols. Washington, DC: Georgetown University Press, 2010.

Anthony Kuzniewski, SJ

German-Speaking Lands

The German Cultural Area during the First Five Generalates (1540–1615)

The German cultural area determined the trajectory of the Jesuits initially not as the location of their apostolate but as the nucleus of Reformation thought that was present in the student days of the first Jesuits at the Universities of Alcalá de Henares and Paris. The first companions, with the exception of Ignatius, gained direct impressions on their journey from Paris to Venice in the year 1536, where already in the southern part of Germany several cities had joined the Reformation. Their first engagements led the Jesuits into northern Italian cities to contain the advancing Protestantism, which they clearly perceived as "German." In 1540 Paul III asked Ignatius to send two Jesuits to Germany; in 1544 the first foundation was started in Cologne. Although Ignatius, shortly before his death in 1556, set up the two provinces of Germania Inferior and Superior, Germany was not a main focus during his generalate. Only in Vienna and Ingolstadt did he set up further foundations. Ignatius saw the beginning of Catholic Reform in Germany as lying in a solid priestly formation in Rome, for which the requirements were met through the founding of the Collegium Germanicum there in 1552.

To the Assistentia Germaniae that was set up in 1558 belonged, in addition to the German and Slavic language areas, also France and England, these last two being divided off in 1608 with the creation of the Assistentia Galliae. Laínez set new accents with his founding of six colleges and the province of Austria and with his visitation of numerous foundations in the summer of 1562, while he slowed down expansion overseas. Under Laínez, Germany developed into the most important apostolate. In 1564 he divided Germania Inferior into Rhenania and Belgica. The four *Instructiones* of Jéronimo Nadal for Germany in 1566 placed further emphasis on the setting of these new trends. Peter Canisius exercised great influence on the expansion of the Order and put his mark on Germany in a way that no Jesuit did for any other country. Jesuits were for a time called "Canisiani." The founding of further colleges was given a new lease of life during the generalate of Mercurian and was intensified by Acquaviva, under whom the most college foundations occurred and Catholic Reform really began to gain a foothold.

In 1623 Bohemia was separated from Austria and in 1626 Rhenania was divided into Rhenania inferior and Rhenania superior. The landscape of provinces changed again with the founding of the Silesian province in 1754 and the Bavarian in 1770. The boundaries of the Assistancy moved only in 1756 through the creation of the Assistentia Poloniae.

The activity of the Jesuits stood under the sign of the Reformation challenge. In the sixteenth century, they sometimes founded colleges in cities with a Reformation presence, e.g., in Augsburg, Prague, and Vienna. Since the boundaries had not yet been completely drawn, they temporarily taught pupils of parents of different denominations.

Although the German language was dominant, one cannot speak of a space that was homogenous linguistically. The southwest of Germania Superior with the colleges of Fribourg and Porrentruy in Switzerland stretched into French-speaking territory and in the south, with Trent, into Italian-speaking. Bohemia and Austria covered, in the main, regions in which Slavic languages and Hungarian were spoken.

The researching of Jesuits in the Holy Roman Empire of the German nation poses, as opposed to in other empires, a particular challenge because this did not represent a unified political space but was divided into many princedoms loosely bound together. The Order itself never developed a unified "foreign policy," but the headquarters delegated the formation of the politics on the ground each time to those who carried responsibility in the regions. Therefore the Order developed in different ways in different political units.

Although the Assistentia Germaniae measured about a third of the Order as a whole and was the greatest in terms of numbers, its presence was small in the general leadership. Among the eighteen generals, it had only two – the Westphalian Goswin Nickel and the Bohemian Franziskus Retz.

The Thirty Years War

In the Thirty Years War, when the Jesuits were court confessors in Paris, Madrid, Munich, Vienna, and other German princedoms, it is evident, on the one hand, that the Society had an effect on the Catholic Reform in central Europe more than in the rest of Europe because here the Reformation had inflicted greater damages on the ecclesiastical institutions and on the orders up to then. At the same time it is evident through the activity of the court confessors that the Jesuits remained faithful to their *Constitutions* in not taking on any tasks in political bodies, but that, in order to advance the life of faith, they did contribute an unofficial advisory activity to the political process. In Vienna and Munich the court confessors put in strongly for a militant Counter-Reform and stood up for the Edict of Restitution successfully. Through what they did, the Thirty Years War took on the clear characteristics of a religious war. Certainly, they did not succeed in moving Spain and France, through the mediation of the court confessors, to greater commitment in Germany. After the Peace of Prague in 1635, it was once again the court confessors who called for a more tolerant politics of religion. In the Thirty Years War, an inner change also becomes visible in Jesuits, who slipped back from their initial mission to strengthen the position of the papacy and showed greater loyalty to the princes, with whose support those things sought by the Catholic Reform could be realized better.

German-Speaking Jesuits in the Overseas Missions

It was after the Thirty Years War that the overseas missions opened out to a broader membership. The Peace of Westphalia fixed the boundaries of the confessions, and this made projects of re-Catholicization impossible in the Empire. These overseas missionaries grew in significance insofar as the Society was the only order in central Europe that participated in overseas missions with more than a hundred members.

From a total of 463 Jesuits documented in China, 27 were German-speaking. Of greater importance in the field of the natural sciences were Johannes Schreck and Adam Schall von Bell (both arrived there in 1619). In 1645 Schall von Bell became head of the imperial astronomical institute in Beijing, an office that the Jesuits continued to hold until 1774. The last four were of German origin: Caspar Kastner (1665–1709), Kilian Stumpf (1655–1720), Ignaz Kögler (1680–1746), and Augustin von Hallerstein (1703–74).

Portugal and Spain did not command sufficient resources in personnel to keep abreast of the overseas demands. After its secession from the Iberian Union of Crowns in 1640, Portugal opened its colonies to central European missionaries who, in addition to the usual apostolates in Brazil, offered their services as impartial cartographers in border disputes with Spain. The Spanish Crown was untrusting of foreign missionaries up until the end of the seventeenth century and restricted their numbers repeatedly; in 1760 they put an end to sending them. The share of missionaries working among the indigenous population was above average among central Europeans by comparison with Spaniards. Of significance were Eusebio Kino in Mexico, Martin Dobrizhoffer (1718–91), Florian Paucke (1719–79), and Anton Sepp (1655–1733) in Paraguay, as well as the architect and musician Martin Schmid (1694–1772) in Bolivia. The written testimonies of these missionaries had a key effect on the perception of cultures outside Europe in the German-speaking area, for example, Matteo Ricci's description of China, already printed in Augsburg in 1615, and also the missionary letters published later from 1726 to 1758 in the "Neue Welt-Bott." The numerous theater-pieces with themes from Japan and China that were produced on the stages of Jesuit colleges were based on such reports. Of importance also were the "Historia de Abiponibus" about the Abipon Indians in Paraguay that were published in Vienna in 1784 by Dobrizhoffer, also the description of the journey to and from Paraguay by Sepp as well as the notes of von Paucke, first published in 1829.

Scientific Achievements

The most significant central European natural scientists of the Society of Jesus had their effect in places outside their native country: for example, the already named missionaries to China, but also Christoph Clavius and Athanasius Kircher, who were active at the Collegium Romanum and in turn educated numerous Jesuits as natural scientists. Thus did Christoph Scheiner (1575–1650), who taught in Ingolstadt, carry out independent observations of the sunspots, which he was the first to publish and for which Galileo Galilei accused him, unjustly, of plagiarism. Jakob Pontanus (1542–1626), with his studies of Latin philology and pedagogy, as well as Jakob Gretser (1562–1625), with his Greek teaching methods, were taken on board also by Protestant schools; in the area of Latin poetry, Jacob Balde (1604–68) deserves mention.

Anti-Jesuit Polemic

As the eighteenth century came to a close, anti-Jesuit thought was disseminated through media from France of a late-Enlightenment Jansenist character. Although the colleges had fallen behind in comparison with Protestant and enlightened Catholic grammar schools, the power of the anti-Jesuit circle never amounted to what it was in Romance-language lands; in central Europe friends of the Jesuits were as strong as almost anywhere else. In 1773 the number of Jesuits there, Bohemia included, was 5,375.

Suppression and After-Effects

The implementation of the Suppression occurred in a humane way, on the whole. While the Jesuits in the Habsburg monarchy were driven out of school service, they were able, in most of the remaining dominions, to continue their work as diocesan priests; they remained constituted as communities and dissolved themselves slowly on account of the lack of new members. Most members soon took on the identity of a city grammar-school teacher. Lay brothers were set up with a pension. Only in 1776 was the papal suppression document read out in Augsburg, Rottweil, and Prussia, where for the Society the "Royal School-College" had been created; it lasted until 1801.

The first voices for a restoration of the Society stirred themselves in the 1790s. The literary figure Novalis, who had converted to Catholicism, called for the return of the Jesuits from Russia for the founding of a new age. The Salvator-College in Augsburg became, by means of a huge publishing activity, a bastion of Anti-Enlightenment. The Berne aristocrat Niklaus Joseph Albert von Diessbach, who converted to Catholicism and after a short marriage entered the Society in Turin in 1759, was an important figure preparing for the restoration. After 1773 he lived in Turin, Fribourg, Vienna, and Berne and founded groups of "Amicizie Cristiane," consisting of priests and laity, who educated themselves through good literature without succumbing to polemic. Giuseppe Sineo della Torre, who was important for the new beginning of the Society of Jesus, grew from this circle.

New Beginnings

After the Napoleonic wars, voices were raised in different places, even in Protestant camps, for the restoration. In 1805 the authorities of the French-ruled autonomous republic of Wallis in the southwest of Switzerland reorganized the grammar school in Sitten to meet the demands of a contemporary education. Paccanarists from Italy made themselves available as teachers, of whom eight arrived at the end of 1805. All had become Paccanarists with the intention of preparing for the restoration of the Society of Jesus. Also, they were called Jesuits by the population of Wallis. Following French occupation in 1810, the authorities confirmed the fathers as state teachers. Pope Pius VII wanted Sitten to be the outpost of the newly forming Society of Jesus in middle Europe. Thus in 1810 they began, linked with the Society in Russia, a Distance-Novitiate with vows in *foro interno*. On September 4, 1814, news came of the canonical convalidation of these vows, whereby the life of the Society of Jesus in the German-speaking area began with a Missio Helvetica consisting of 23 members. In 1821 it became the Viceprovincia Helvetica and embraced Switzerland, non-Austrian Germany, and the kingdom of the united Netherlands with 140 members. The Provincia Germaniae Superioris, created in 1826, numbered 176 Jesuits. A reduction followed in 1832 with the separating off of the Netherlands.

Ex-Jesuits in German-speaking lands revealed themselves to be astonishingly few (only nine) in the new beginning. On the other hand, Paccanarists carried out significant work in the rebuilding. Sineo della Torre, the first superior of the mission, became provincial in Italy in 1818, Nicolas Godinot, his successor, in 1824 in France. Johann Baptist Drach and Georg Staudinger were the first provincials of Germania Superior.

In the Habsburg monarchy the Society gained a foothold through being driven out of the czar's empire in 1820, at first in Galicia and in 1829 with a novitiate in Graz. In

1837 a foundation in Linz followed as a place of pastoral care and as a philosophate, and in 1839 a foundation in Innsbruck with a grammar school, the care of the old Jesuit church, and a theologate. In 1846, the province was divided into a Galician and an Austrian province. The new beginning was marked by tension between the Josephine State–Church line, which was negative to the Society, and the politics of Metternich, which the Jesuits estimated as an anti-revolutionary force. From 1848 to 1852 the Society was expelled.

In Germany, already in 1805, it was possible to make a beginning with a residence in Düsseldorf; however, in the first half of the century there remained just small foundations of short duration.

In Switzerland, the Society established five colleges with an international student body. In Freiburg in 1824 a theology faculty was set up. The driving out of Jesuits from Belgium, Russia, and France led to increases in personnel through the influx of qualified staff. Everyday life was similar to pre-1773.

Despite an ultramontane attitude, the spectrum of opinion was broader than in the half-century that followed. Literary production, especially in the academic theological sector, was, however, thin. Until being called to Lucerne in 1841, the Society of Jesus did not have a negative political impact. But the fact that they were to take over the teaching of theology and the grammar school in the liberal and significant city led to paramilitary outcries from liberal cantons and, as a reaction, to a union of conservative cantons (called *Sonderbund*). After the Sonderbund War in 1847 there was an expulsion and a prohibition in the constitution that was removed only in 1973 through a referendum. The Jesuits fled to the kingdom of Savoy-Sardinia and to Austria.

Expansion from 1850

In Germany the Order was able to gain a foothold from 1850 but remained confined to the Catholic cities in Westphalia and the Rhineland that were ruled by Prussia. Prussia did not recognize communities of religious orders as legal persons, so they could not own property and this had to be ascribed to individual fathers. From 1853 the province took the simple name of Provincia Germaniae.

In consequence of a progressive polarization between liberalism and the Catholic Church, but especially on account of Vatican I and of the *Syllabus of Errors* (1864), the Jesuit order, as the spearhead of Ultramontanism, was more strongly exposed to attacks. On June 19, 1872, the German parliament decided with a 66 percent majority to expel the Jesuits. The Swiss *Bundesrat* (upper house of parliament) enacted a corresponding law on July 4. Westphalian nobility left their palaces to the Jesuits in the Netherlands so that the life of the Order continued without interruption. In Germany and in Switzerland, there was a cautious pastoral presence from 1880 to 1900 and, up to 1917, a partly more open emergence of the Society with the maintaining of stations, gatherings of Jesuits living dispersed under one superior. The formation houses were in Holland and England where up to 45 percent of the members of the province lived. Nevertheless the German-speaking area had a strong influence on the entire Order, which was evident in the three generals that came from it: Anderledy, Wernz, and Ledóchowski. The anti-Jesuit law fell in Germany in 1917. In 1921 the Provincia Germaniae was divided into a South and North province, the latter, in 1931, into a West and East province, which was reunited in 1978. After the Hungarian province was taken out of Austria in 1909, there followed on account of the war the Croatian province in 1918 and the Czechoslovakian province in 1919. In 1947, Switzerland became an independent vice-province. From 2004 there was once again a German province with *missiones* in Denmark and Sweden. As of 2016, a further coming together with the Austrian, Hungarian, Lithuanian, and Swiss provinces was being prepared.

Numerical Development

From 1850 until the ban on Jesuits in 1872, the Order grew from 233 to 755, which was above average in strength by comparison with the Order as a whole. Also the time of exile proved favorable with a growth in numbers to 1,207 in 1917. After 1917 the number of Jesuits working on the foreign missions dropped in favor of the number remaining in Germany where, until 1936, a further increase to 1,795 members is to be noted. In the postwar period up to 1965, the composition remained stable with 1,279, and then dropped by 1983 to 789. In 2016, there were 537 Jesuits in Germany, Austria, and Switzerland.

Apostolates

Activity in Germany after 1850 was confined – besides the running of its own formation houses – almost entirely to popular missions and congregations (sodalities). It was no longer the population of the cities but that of the countryside that was in the foreground. In 1856 the Order took on as its only school the state grammar school in Feldkirch, where the tradition of the Swiss colleges was carried on until 1978.

At this time the founding of *Stimmen aus Maria Laach* occurred; at first it consisted of a series of writings (1864) and then a journal (1871) for defending the Syllabus of Errors published by Pope Pius IX; from 1914 until the present it has been published as *Stimmen der Zeit*. The anti-Jesuit law in Germany caused the accent to be placed on external missions, scientific work, and writing that embodied important achievements in the natural sciences, literature, and history. After 1917 the main focus was placed on youth work, on the sodalities, and on priestly formation. The Düsseldorfer Rednertürme (Preaching Group) achieved significance above all in the National Socialist period with a comprehensive program of lectures on world questions. *Stimmen der Zeit* represented a clearly pro-democratic position, one critical of nostalgia. Significant into the present time are the Faculties (*Hochschulen*) of Philosophy in Munich and Theology in Frankfurt, founded in 1925 and 1926 respectively. After the war, the emphasis was put on the formation of elite Catholic laity and on particular forms of pastoral care in the dioceses, though the big institutions were restored so that by the end of the century, while the colleges as a whole had diminished in significance, the area of media had grown. Jesuits have maintained their presence in research and academic activity.

Overseas Missions

In 1854 the Provincia Germaniae took on a part of, and then in 1858 the entire vicariate of Bombay, which at that time was laboring under the *Goa schism*, that is, the dispute between the Portuguese *Padroado* and the Vatican Congregation for the Propagation of the Faith. However, there was success in setting up elementary schools in every mission station, as well as two middle schools in Bombay and one each in Karachi and Puna. Between 1868 and 1907, the Buffalo-Mission (USA) and between 1869 and 1925 the missions of Rio Grande do Sul (Brazil) were taken over; both served the pastoral care of immigrant Germans. In 1873 Denmark followed as a mission of Germany (until 2016), in 1879 Sweden and Zimbabwe, as well as from 1913–48 Japan. In India there remained from 1929–56 only the Puna Mission.

The Challenge of Totalitarianism

Confrontation with the Third Reich can be divided into three epochs: (1) Confrontation and accommodation (1933–36), (2) Annihilation of the works (1936–40), (3) Sharpening of the fight (1941–45). There were always differences between Jesuits of the resistance and those who at first believed in an enduring *modus vivendi* and later drew back into silence. Ever present was the fear of expulsion. All in all, the anti-Jesuitism of the National-Socialist regime can be described as more unified and more consistent than the anti-National Socialism of the Jesuits. Only in the case of Augustinus Röch, provincial of Germania Superior, can a concept of resistance be established, which expressed itself in contacts with the Kreisau Circle and in a committee for influencing the Bishops' Conference. Exponents of the resistance were Alfred Delp and Rupert Mayer.

Important Theologians and Academics

Johann B. Franzelin, Josef Kleutgen, and Clemens Schrader were important representatives of the Roman School who, through the theological faculty in Innsbruck that had been taken over in 1857, contributed decisively to the establishment of neo-scholasticism in formation. Wilhelm Wilmers was a dogmatic and fundamental theologian and Theodor Meyer a social ethicist. At the First Vatican Council, Leo Meurin as apostolic vicar of Bombay and Wilmers as his theologian, as well as Joseph Roh as theologian of the bishop of Paderborn, participated, the last belonging to the moderate-infallibilist direction.

In the 1920s and 1930s, intellectual reflection and creativity were found in *Stimmen der Zeit* and not in the faculties. In addition to Erich Przywara in theology, Oswald von Nell-Breuning and Gustav Gundlach in their time exercised competencies in social doctrine that had effects on the whole of society. In the time after World War II, the German province produced not only significant theologians (Hugo and Karl Rahner, Andreas Jungmann, Hans Urs von Balthasar [he left the Society in 1950], Otto Semmelroth, and Aloys Grillmeier) who exercised influence on the Second Vatican Council, but also advisers to Pius XII (Bea, Leiber); other Jesuits (Hirschmann, Wallraff) contributed to the formation of the political and social order of the Federal Republic of Germany.

See also Anti-Jesuit Polemic; Delp, Alfred, SJ; Holy Roman Empire; Kircher, Athanasius, SJ; Rahner, Karl, SJ; Suppression; *Welt-Bott*

Bireley, Robert, *The Jesuits and the Thirty Years War: Kings, Courts, and Confessors*. Cambridge: Cambridge University Press, 2003.
Duhr, Bernhard, *Geschichte der Jesuiten in den Ländern deutscher Zunge*. 4 vols. Freiburg-Munich-Regensburg: Herder Verlag, 1907–28.
Hausberger, Bernd, *Jesuiten aus Mitteleuropa im kolonialen Mexiko: Eine Bio-Bibliographie*. Vienna/Munich: Böhlau, 1995.

Meier, Johannes, ed. *Jesuiten aus Zentraleuropa in Portugiesish- und Spanisch-Amerika: Ein bio-bibliographisches Handbuch mit einem Überblick über das aussereuropäische Wirken der Gesellschaft Jesu in der früheren Neuzeit.* Vols. I (Brazil), II (Chile), III (New Granada), V (Peru). Münster: Verlag Aschendorff, 2005–13.

Schatz, Klaus, *Geschichte der deutschen Jesuiten.* 5 vols. Münster: Verlag Aschendorff, 2013.

Strobel, Ferdinand, "Die Gesellschaft Jesu in der Schweiz 1814–1848." In *Helvetia Sacra*, Vol. VII, *Der Regularklerus.* Bern: Francke Verlag, 1976, pp. 473–512.

Vallina, Augustín Udías, *Jesuit Contribution to Science: A History.* Cham, Switzerland: Springer, 2015.

Paul Oberholzer, SJ

(entry translated by James Corkery, SJ)

Gesù, Rome

The mother church of the Jesuits was built on the site of their first, tiny church of Santa Maria della Strada. It was designed by Jacopo Barozzi (Vignola, 1507–73), at the behest of Cardinal Alessandro Farnese (1520–89), whose grandfather, Paul III, had approved the foundation of the Order in 1540. It is estimated that Farnese spent over 100,000 *scudi* on the building that would house his tomb. Vignola's design for the Gesù, with its wide nave to accommodate large numbers to hear sermons and its interconnecting side chapels, became a blueprint for subsequent Counter-Reformation churches, especially for Jesuit churches around the world. It was the largest Cinquecento church built in Rome up to that time, apart from St. Peter's, and occupies a central site close to the Campidoglio. Farnese first offered to pay for the church in 1561, but because of difficulties in acquiring the land, building did not begin until 1568. The patron also imposed his own views on architecture, including the need for a barrel vault over the nave, often against the Jesuits' wishes. Vignola's elegant design for a façade that included much sculpture was rejected in favor of a more austere design by Giacomo della Porta (*c.* 1540–1602).

Cardinal Alessandro took control of the decoration of the most significant parts of the interior decoration, though the Jesuits retained control of the overall iconography, with the chapels paired thematically across the nave. Farnese had the dome and pendentives painted by Giovanni de' Vecchi with the Fathers of the Church, and the drum by Andrea Lilio with the Evangelists (1583). These were destroyed almost a century later to make way for Giovanni Battista Gaulli's spectacular frescoes. Farnese commissioned Muziano to paint the high altarpiece of the *Circumcision*, a subject that was particularly important to the Jesuits. The other chapels were decorated in the late Cinquecento under the patronage of various Roman families, including a number of noblewomen, by such artists as Scipione Pulzone, Federico Zuccaro, and Agostino Ciampelli. Jesuit artists, too, contributed to the decoration of the chapels, including Giuseppe Valeriano and Giovanni Battista Fiammeri. The Order's theological concerns are again apparent in the choice of subject, notably in Federico Zuccaro's Cappella degli Angeli, which arguably reflects the writings on angels of Robert Bellarmine and Luigi Gonzaga.

The Farnese tradition of support was continued by Alessandro's great-nephew, Cardinal Odoardo, who commissioned the adjacent Casa Professa, which incorporated the rooms of St. Ignatius, and the Sacristy, as well as a private suite to which he could retreat. He also had built the tomb of Cardinal Robert Bellarmine, of which only Bernini's portrait bust remains (1621–24).

Figure 21 Exterior view of the Church of Il Gesù, Rome, 16th century. Photograph Alison Fleming

The interior of the church was transformed in the later seventeenth century, notably with Gaulli's exuberant frescoes covering the nave, dome, and tribune. The church also erected extravagant monuments to its founding saints, Ignatius and Francis Xavier. Ignatius's tomb occupies the left transept and was designed by Andrea Pozzo between 1697 and 1704. Numerous artists were involved in the project. It is notable for its use of extravagant materials: the columns flanking the silver effigy of the saint by Pierre Le Gros the Younger (1666–1719) are clad in lapis lazuli, as is the orb held by a cherub, between the group of the *Trinity*, by Lorenzo Ottoni and Bernardino Ludovisi, above the altarpiece. Le Gros also sculpted the marble group of the *Triumph of Religion over Heresy*. A corresponding group of the *Triumph of Faith over Paganism* is by Jean Baptiste Théodon (1645–1713). Further marble reliefs illustrate the saint's life. The decoration was completed by Gaulli's ceiling fresco of *St. Ignatius in Glory*.

The right transept was dedicated to St. Francis Xavier, and its architecture was probably designed by Luca Berrettini, after a design by his father, Pietro da Cortona, between 1673 and 1678. Despite the use of colored marbles, it is much more austere than that of the Ignatius chapel. The altarpiece by Carlo Maratti shows the death of the saint. Above the altar is a stucco group of Francis rising to Heaven by an unknown artist. The vault decoration, which Gaulli was originally intended to paint was instead decorated by another Genoese artist Andrea Carlone, with scenes from the saint's life, on the wishes of the patron, Giovanni Francesco Negroni.

See also Baroque Art and Architecture; Bernini, Gian Lorenzo; Gaulli, Giovanni Battista

Bailey, Gauvin A., *Between Renaissance and Baroque: Jesuit Art in Rome, 1565–1610*. Toronto: University of Toronto Press, 2003, pp. 186–260.

Bösel, Richard, *Jesuitenarchitektur in Italien, 1540–1773*. Vol. I. Vienna: Verlag der Österreichischen Akademie der Wissenschaften, 1985. pp. 160–73.

Levy, Evonne A., "The Institutional Memory of the Roman Gesù: Plans for Renovation in the 1670s by Carlo Fontana, Pietro da Cortona and Luca Berrettini." *Römisches Jahrbuch der Bibliotheca Hertziana* 33 (1999–2000), 373–426.

Pecchiai, Pio, *Il Gesù di Roma*. Rome: Società Grafica Romana, 1952.

Robertson, Clare, '*Il Gran Cardinale': Alessandro Farnese, Patron of the Arts*. New Haven, CT/London: Yale University Press, 1992, pp. 181–96.

Clare Robertson

Goa

Goa was the entry point of Jesuits into the Indian subcontinent and later the first Jesuit province to be established in Asia. Francis Xavier led the way in 1542 at the request of the Portuguese king, under whose patronage (the *Padroado*) the Holy See had entrusted the mission. While the desire of King John III was for the Jesuits to minister to the Portuguese soldiers, Jesuits also ministered to the native population in Goa

Figure 22 Tomb of St. Francis Xavier, Church of the Bom Jesus, Goa, 17th century. Photograph Alison Fleming

and its environs, quickly becoming a base for missions throughout India. In Goa they took charge of St. Paul's College, out of which a school, hospital, and the first printing press in Asia began. Jesuit evangelization efforts spread from Goa up to Bombay, down the Malabar coast to Cochin, up the Coromandel Coast, to interior places such as Madurai, as far away as Tibet and even, upon the request of the Mughal Emperor Akbar, to the royal court in Fatehpur and later Agra. The Jesuits funded their mission through a combination of direct patronage from Portuguese authorities and the revenue from lands granted to or purchased by the Society of Jesus. As the Portuguese capital, Goa was also the locus of tensions over ecclesiastical authority over Latin and Syro-Malabar Christians, their liturgical rites, and matters of accommodation to Indian culture, in which the Jesuits were implicated through their missions to Indians of various castes. On account of the growing entanglement of Jesuits in political and economic power, not just in Goa but throughout the Portuguese Empire, tensions led to their suppression and expulsion by the Crown in 1759. Although Jesuits returned to other parts of India shortly after 1815, they did not return to Goa until 1889, where they continue to this day with ministries in education, spirituality, and social uplift.

See also India; Portugal; Xavier, Francis, SJ, St.

Borges, Charles J., *The Economics of the Goa Jesuits 1542–1759*. New Delhi: Concept Publishing, 1994.

Brent Howitt Otto, SJ

de Goës, Bento, SJ (1562–1607)

Bento de Goës, Benedetto di Góis, or anglicized as Benedict Goes, was a Portuguese Jesuit, born in the Azores. He served in the Portuguese army in India. Once, on entering a chapel of the Virgin Mary in Travancor, on the Malabar coast of India, Goes received divine inspiration: he had a vision of Jesus Christ in tears, and thus then he prayed to the Virgin Mary for forgiveness for his early degenerate life. Soon afterward, he entered the Society of Jesus and served in the court of the Mughal King Akbar (r. 1556–1605). He humbly appreciated the great favor of God for pardoning his previous sins and refused to be elevated to the academic preparation for priesthood, but remained a brother.

Nicolas Pimenta (1562–1604), the visitor of the Society for India, investigated whether the empires of Cathay and China were identical. The reason for this investigation was that Cathay was said to have many Christians. Goes was selected for this mission because of compliments he received in the court of Akbar and his comprehensive knowledge of the Persian language. He also hoped to determine the existence of a shorter land route to China. The journey started from Agra in 1602. To avoid suspicion, Goes dressed himself in the Armenian style and assumed the name Abdullah Isai. He brought necessities and goods for use as gifts. Goes and his lifelong and loyal Armenian companion Issac traveled in several commercial caravans, passing through Lahore, Kabul, Samarkand, Yarkand, and Turfan on the northwestern frontier of China. Despite various perils, robbery, and attacks during their voyage, they finally passed around the western ending of the Great Wall and arrived in Suzhou in the Province of Kansu (甘肅肅州) in 1605. They sent letters to Matteo Ricci (1552–1610), the supervisor of the China mission in Beijing, and Ricci sent a Chinese Christian Zhong Mingli 鍾鳴禮 (Giovanni Fernandez, 1581–1620) to meet with these two brave companions. Unfortunately, Zhong eventually arrived there in the missionary's final moments – Goes died in April 1607. Goes's journey eliminated doubts about the separation of Cathay and

China, but the long distance and grueling travel showed that the mission on this route from the Mughal kingdom to China was nearly impossible. Ricci praised the spirit and ingenuity of Goes in his account of China. It was said that Zhong and Issac brought the scattered diaries of Goes to Ricci, who reported it to Rome in letters in 1608, the earliest release of Goes's adventure. Later, in Jesuit Giulio Aleni's (1582–1649) Chinese biography of Ricci, published in 1630, this extraordinary Jesuit and adventurer was included, and he was given a Chinese name, E Bendu 鄂本篤.

See also China; India; Portugal

Payne, C. H., trans., *Jahangir and the Jesuits: With an Account of the Travels of Benedict Goes and the Mission to Pegu.* New Delhi: Munshiram Manoharlal Publishers Pvt. Ltd., 1997.

Pfister, Louis, *Notices biographiques et bibliographiques sur les Jésuites de l'ancienne mission de Chine, 1552–1773.* Vol. I. Shanghai: Imprimerie de la Mission Catholique, 1932, pp. 95–102.

Hui-Hung Chen

Gonçalves da Câmara, Luís, SJ (1520–1575)

Born in 1520, Luís Gonçalves da Câmara is chiefly known for two roles in the Society. First, in 1553 the Portuguese king requested that Gonçalves da Câmara and Diego Miró become his confessors. Though both wished to decline, Ignatius ordered them to accept the position. Gonçalves da Câmara also tutored the heir to the throne, Sebastian I.

Gonçalves da Câmara's second, and more famous, role was in the preparation of Ignatius's *Autobiography*. Francis Borgia had requested information on Ignatius's life while the founder of the Society was still alive, and Jerome Nadal had sent Gonçalves da Câmara to see if Ignatius would give an account of his life, the eventual *Autobiography*. The *Autobiography*'s creation was a complex process for several reasons. First, it occurred over three separate periods between 1553 and 1555. Next was the issue of translation. During these sessions, Ignatius spoke in Spanish to Gonçalves da Câmara, who was Portuguese and did not transcribe anything while Ignatius was speaking. Only later did he write notes and dictate a narrative based on them to a Spanish scribe, who copied Gonçalves da Câmara's words verbatim. However, when Gonçalves da Câmara was dictating material from the third period with Ignatius, it was to an Italian scribe. As a result, two-thirds of the *Autobiography*'s first copy are in Spanish, with the last third in Italian. The text has thus been heavily mediated. In addition, we still lack the section that describes Ignatius's early life, which Gonçalves da Câmara seems to have never recorded.

Gonçalves da Câmara died in 1575.

See also Autobiography of St. Ignatius; Portugal

Eaglestone Alexander, and Joseph A. Munitiz, eds., *Remembering Iñigo: Glimpses of the Life of Saint Ignatius of Loyola – The Memoriale of Luís Gonçalves da Câmara.* St. Louis, MO: The Institute of Jesuit Sources, 2004.

Charles Keenan

Gonzaga, Aloysius, SJ, St. (1568–1591)

St. Aloysius (also "Luigi") Gonzaga was born in 1568, eldest son of Ferrante Gonzaga, marquis of Castiglione delle Stiviere. As such, Aloysius was raised in preparation for a life at court. From a young age, however, Aloysius found courtly life distasteful, and he

Figure 23 Andrea Pozzo: Portrait of St. Aloysius Gonzaga, 1682–86, Casa Professa, Rome. Photograph Alison Fleming

instead became very devout, fasting, meditating, and attending Mass daily. After traveling to Spain in 1581, Aloysius resolved to become a priest. His father would not grant permission and instead sent Aloysius to various courts in Italy, hoping this would dissuade the young man from his choice. When Gonzaga returned resolute in his decision, his father relented. Not yet 18 years old, Aloysius renounced his inheritance and entered the Jesuit novitiate of Sant'Andrea in Rome in November 1585. He enrolled at the Roman College soon after, studying philosophy and later theology.

After a brief sojourn in Castiglione (1589–90) Aloysius returned to Rome, where, like other young Jesuits, he worked at hospitals tending to the sick. The year 1591 saw widespread plague and famine in Italy, and in March of that year Aloysius fell ill. He died of plague on June 21, 1591, at the age of 23. Gonzaga was buried in the Church of the Annunciation in Rome, and his remains were later moved to the Church of Sant'Ignazio. He was beatified by Pope Paul V in 1605 and was canonized by Benedict XIII in 1726. He is the patron saint of young people, and his feast day is June 21.

See also Plague; Saints

Barker, Sheila C., "Plague Art in Early Modern Rome: Divine Directives and Temporal Remedies." In Gauvin A. Bailey, Pamela M. Jones, Franco Mormando, and Thomas W. Worcester, eds., *Hope and*

Healing: Painting in Italy in a Time of Plague, 1500–1800. Worcester, MA: Worcester Art Museum, pp. 45–64.

Martindale, C. C., *The Vocation of Aloysius Gonzaga*. New York: Sheed and Ward, 1945.

Charles Keenan

González, Roque, SJ, St. (1576–1628)

Roque González was born in the year 1576 in Asunción, Paraguay. He was ordained a priest in 1598, but it was not until 1609 that he entered the Society of Jesus. Given his command of the Guaraní language, he was commissioned to explore the territory beyond the River Paraguay in preparation for the establishment of Jesuit missions. This task began in earnest in 1611 with the foundation of San Ignacio Guazú; it was there that González helped pioneer the mission system that was to become so important throughout the region among the Guaraní, Abipones, Guaycurues, and other ethnic groups. González participated in numerous further foundations in the region during the next two decades. In 1619 he made his fourth and final vow and became superior of the River Uruguay missions in 1627.

In 1628, together with Alonso Rodríguez and Juan del Castillo, he began establishing new missions in the Caaró region. Jesuit priests often upset indigenous sociopolitical systems, by removing religious authority from indigenous leaders and imposing monogamous marriage. Thus Ñezú, a powerful indigenous leader, led an uprising against the missionaries. Roque González and Alonso Rodríguez were killed on November 15, 1628, at the Reduction of Todos los Santos del Caaró, and Juan del Castillo was killed two days later at Nuestra Señora de la Asunción. All three were beatified by Pius XII on January 28, 1934, and canonized by John Paul II on May 16, 1988.

See also Paraguay Missions ("Reductions"); Saints

Mathes, W. Michael, ed., *Primeras noticias de los protomártires de Paraquaria: la historia panegírica de Juan Eusebio Nieremberg. León Francia: 1631*. Santo Tomé, Baja California: Casa de la Cultura "Concepción Centeno de Navajas", Carem, 2004.

de Montoya, Antonio Ruiz, *The Spiritual Conquest Accomplished by the Religious of the Society of Jesus in the Provinces of Paraguay, Paraná, Uruguay, and Tape* [1639]. Intro. C. J. McNaspy, trans. C. J. McNaspy, John P. Leonard, and Martin E. Palmer. St. Louis, MO: The Institute of Jesuit Sources, 1993, pp. 149–56.

Andrew Redden

González de Santalla, Tirso, SJ (1624–1705)

Born in Arganza, Spain, González joined the Society of Jesus in 1643. He studied philosophy in Valladolid (1645–47) and theology at Salamanca (1647–51), where he also spent two additional years to fulfill the Society's required curriculum for teaching theology. A brilliant debater, González taught philosophy in Santiago (1653–55) and theology in Valladolid (1655–56) and Salamanca (1656–65).

In those years, he paired his academic activity with the preaching of popular and rural missions throughout Spain, inspired by the prominent Jesuit missionary Jerónimo López (1589–1658). In 1664 González asked to be relieved from his teaching duties to become a full-time missionary; his request was granted, and for more than ten years (1665–76) he crisscrossed the Iberian Peninsula, often with his companion Juan Gabriel Guillén (1627–75). Later, while he held the prestigious chair of theology at the University of Salamanca (1676–86), he continued preaching rural missions during Lent and in his free time.

During his missions, González devoted himself to the apostolate among Muslim slaves and servants he met in Spanish cities, and completed a handbook for the conversion of Muslims (*Manuductio ad conversionem Mahumetanorum*, Madrid 1687); it was published many times and became the reference book on the subject within the Society.

González was an ardent opponent of *probabilism*, a theological doctrine which maintained that in difficult matters of conscience one may safely follow a "probable opinion," that is, an opinion approved by theologians and supported by reasonable arguments. At that time, probabilism was widespread among Jesuits but was not the only official doctrine within the Society. In fact, a few marginal Jesuit theologians criticized it, advocating different forms of *probabiliorism*, a doctrine that required choosing the "more probable opinion." Debates concerning moral theology had become particularly harsh during the second half of the seventeenth century, and opponents of the Jesuits identified it as a source of moral relaxation. González developed a particular form of probabiliorism that emphasized the subjective estimation of the degree of probability, somehow undermining the value of external authorities. His view created turmoil and debates within the Society, and the Jesuit reviewers did not approve for publication his book *Fundamentum theologiae moralis*. A few years later, González received encouragement from Pope Innocent XI (r. 1676–89) – a strenuous opponent of moral laxism – to study and teach probabiliorism, and the Holy Office issued by the Pope's order a decree (1680) ordering the superiors of the Society to allow their subjects to defend probabiliorism.

In 1686 González was invited as a delegate to General Congregation 13 in Rome, after the death of Charles de Noyelle (1615–86). There, he was unexpectedly elected the thirteenth superior general of the Society (July 6, 1687). It is thought that the appointment was due to the support of Innocent XI, but the Pope's precise role in the appointment is not clear.

During his generalate, González attempted in various ways to confine the consequences of probabilism and to spread his own doctrine. In 1691 he had a new version of his book secretly printed in Dillingen without any approval; this fact caused bewilderment within the Society and revived the internal disputes. Tensions between González and the assistants grew to the point that King Charles II of Spain (r. 1665–1700) intervened in support of González, fearing that he might be replaced by a non-Spanish general. Only in 1694, and after heated debates, was González able to obtain official approval for publishing another version of his book. In the following years, and until his death, he continued his campaign against probabilism, trying unsuccessfully to publish other works.

During his generalate, González faced a serious crisis between the French court and the French Jesuits on the one side, and the Jesuit Roman Curia on the other. King Louis XIV of France, who was battling Innocent XI over the *Declaration of the Clergy of France* (1682), forbade the French Jesuits to communicate with the Jesuit Curia in Rome, considered the stronghold of the pope.

González developed the missions of the Society of Jesus both in Europe and overseas, in particular in the Ottoman Empire and in China, but he also had to address the first hints of the Chinese and Malabar Rites controversies.

González's reputation in the Society after his death was mixed, mirroring the internal debates that developed during his life. The tensions that began during his leadership provoked an internal fracture in the Society that lasted for decades.

See also Ethics; Spain; Superior General

Colombo, Emanuele, "Even among Turks: Tirso González de Santalla (1624–1705) and Islam." *Studies on Jesuit Spirituality* 44, 3 (2012), 1–41.
"In virtù dell'obbedienza: Tirso González de Santalla (1624–1705) missionario, teologo, generale." In Claudio Ferlan and Fernanda Alfieri, eds., *Avventure dell'obbedienza nella Compagnia di Gesù: Teorie e prassi fra XVI e XIX secolo*. Bologna: Il Mulino, 2012, pp. 97–137.
Gay, Jean-Pascal, *Jesuit Civil Wars: Theology, Politics, and Government under Tirso González (1687–1705)*. Farnham/Burlington, VT: Ashgate, 2012.
Knebel, Sven, K., ed., *Suarezismus: Erkenntnistheoretisches aus dem Nachlass des Jesuitengenerals Tirso González de Santalla (1624–1705). Abhandlung und Edition*. Amsterdam/Philadelphia: Grüner, 2011.

Emanuele Colombo

Grace

"Grace" is the word used by theologians to express God's gratuitous self-gift to humanity, with all the favors accompanying this: love, pardon, generosity, mercy, freedom, and new life. Topics associated with reflection on grace, such as its relationship to human freedom, sin, and salvation have been at the heart of Jesuit theological writing on grace since the Society of Jesus began. These topics were hotly debated in the sixteenth and seventeenth centuries, and again in the twentieth century, and Jesuits were to the fore in all of these discussions. At the Council of Trent (1545–63), Jesuits Diego Laínez (1512–65) and Alfonso Salmerón (1515–85), particularly the former, played an important role in the debates seeking to do justice both to the absolute need for grace at every stage of justification, as the Reformers insisted, and to the role, minimal though it might be, of created human freedom, as Catholicism traditionally maintained. A distinguishing characteristic of Jesuit theologizing about grace emerged here that underlined the contribution made by human freedom to good acts for which divine grace, of course, was always acknowledged to be also indispensable. This position led Jesuits then, and subsequently, into disputes with Dominicans, the most famous of these being the *De auxiliis* Controversy that went on for a considerable time in the late sixteenth and early seventeenth centuries. It was concerned with what "helps" were afforded by divine grace and what, if any, was the contribution made by human freedom in the performance of good acts. Domingo Bañez (1528–1604) was the chief Dominican and Luis de Molina (1535–1600) the main Jesuit involved in the discussion, which extended beyond their lives and was ended not by agreement, but by a papal decree in 1607, in which each side was chastised but neither was condemned. The Apostolic See promised a final pronouncement on the matter, but this is still awaited!

The great Iberian Scholastic theologian Francisco Suárez, SJ (1548–1617), followed, albeit with modifications, Molina's line and, since Jesuits in many parts of the world were trained in Suarezian Scholasticism, Molina's position persisted in Jesuit theology of grace. In any case, St. Ignatius had warned – "especially in times as dangerous as ours" – against over-emphasizing grace at the expense of free will (*Spiritual Exercises*, #369), for which he and the early Jesuits, with their humanist heritage, had a high regard (as Avery Dulles, SJ, noted, reflecting on the character of early Jesuit theology). This high regard for free will did not prevent Ignatius, however, from indicating in the famous *Suscipe* prayer of the *Spiritual Exercises* (#234) that nothing could surpass the love and grace of God. So there was utter confidence in God *and* optimism about humanity in Jesuit theology from the start. These may have helped Juan Martínez de Ripalda, SJ (1594–1648), to suggest that pagans could be saved, in an argument similar to that of Karl Rahner centuries later regarding the salvation of non-Christians. Arguments such as these, and the optimism that underpinned them, led to Jesuits incurring opposition from conservative Protestants, Jansenists, and others. By the time the suppressed Society of Jesus was restored in 1814, the treatises in which theology was, by that time, being organized were highly systematized and conceptual in form; and by the end of the century, following the triumph of Thomism in the encyclical of Leo XIII, *Aeterni Patris* (1879), in which Jesuits played no small role, grace was being taught in Jesuit schools of theology in a neo-scholastic mode. Jesuits, on the whole, showed little opposition to this – until the French Jesuit Henri de Lubac changed everything.

Henri de Lubac, SJ (1896 to 1991), circumvented the neo-scholastic writing on grace of his time by returning to the Fathers of the Church and the medieval theologians in order to retrieve their more seminal insights in relation to grace. His publication, in 1946, of *Surnaturel: études historiques* and, in 1965, of *The Mystery of the Supernatural* focused on how the extrinsicist approach to grace of neo-scholasticism, which postulated an almost discontinuous and non-necessary relationship between nature and grace, was out of kilter with St. Thomas's clear insistence that the desire for God was firmly situated in human nature itself and that there was never any such thing as "pure nature," a nature not oriented to the divine and not called to union with God. Furthermore, the hypothesis of pure nature put forward by many theologians in order to safeguard (as they saw it) God's freedom in the matter of bestowing grace – how could God be free if grace was "asked for" by created nature, they wondered – was one which, in de Lubac's view, was not needed, though not all agreed with him. There had never actually existed, he said, a human nature that lacked a divine finality. In fact, were one to postulate a change in human finality, the same de Lubac pointed out, one would be changing what the human being actually was simply by so doing.

Karl Rahner (1904–84), concerned like de Lubac to avoid extrinsicism in talk about nature and grace but also to avoid being caught in the dispute that de Lubac's approach had landed *him* in – with other theologians and also with Pius XII's teaching in *Humani generis* (1950) – developed an approach to grace using the Heideggerian language of "existentials," thus situating God's self-offer, which is what grace is, at the heart of the concretely existing human being but *not* in his/her nature, and so dispensing with the element of necessity, or obligation, on God's part. For Rahner, grace was God's self-communication; with this gift, God bestowed God's own self freely on human beings. The work of Karl Rahner became a reference point for all subsequent Catholic theological writing about grace. Through the theology of such Jesuits as de Lubac, Rahner, and Bernard Lonergan (1904–88; Canadian, but teaching in Rome), which drew brilliantly on what was best in Thomas Aquinas concerning grace, and followed by Jesuits such as Piet Fransen (1913–83) and Juan Alfaro (1914–93), the landscape of the theology of grace changed in the twentieth century. This continued through the works of a later generation of Jesuits, many of them North American, like Roger Haight (b. 1936) and

Jean-Marc Laporte (Canadian, b. 1940) and some also in Latin America, e.g. Juan-Luis Segundo (1925–1996) and Jon Sobrino (b. 1928).

See also Theology

Congar, Yves, *A History of Theology.* New York: Doubleday, 1968.
Dulles, Avery, "Jesuits and Theology: Yesterday and Today." *Theological Studies* 52 (1991), 524–38.
Mettepenningen, Jürgen. *Nouvelle Théologie – New Theology: Inheritor of Modernism, Precursor of Vatican II.* London/New York: T. & T. Clark, 2010.

James Corkery, SJ

Grades

The term "grades" refers to the different categories of membership and profession that developed in the Society, and which have raised some significant issues down to the present time. For Ignatius, as in the Jesuit *Constitutions*, the spiritual qualities of candidates to the Society were paramount; however, their intellectual qualities were also an important factor, at least for those who wished to be ordained and fully incorporated into the Society. A basic distinction in grades and ministries developed between those who would or would not seek ordination. According to the *Constitutions*, the latter become temporal coadjutors (or lay brothers). They take the three classic religious vows (poverty, chastity, and obedience) and traditionally have served the Society through their manual labor, though that has somewhat changed over time. Approved scholastics take first vows after their novitiate and go on for studies and further formation toward the priesthood. As the practice developed, those with supposedly inferior training or intellectual gifts, or other possible reasons, take final vows as formed spiritual coadjutors. The others who are called to final vows take four solemn vows as fully professed members of the Society (the fourth vow being one of fidelity to the pope with regard to missions). Over the centuries, the percentage of priests in the Society who became either spiritual coadjutors or fully professed members has varied widely. Some have argued that these distinctions were not meant to become permanent features and that they have become divisive and can appear to be elitist. André de Jaer, however, tries to portray grades in a more positive light, suggesting that "the inspiration behind the grades in the Society [is] to honor the diversity of God's gifts and to recognize this diversity itself as a grace" (*Together for Mission*, 78).

See also Brothers; Coadjutors, Temporal and Spiritual; Priesthood; Professed; Scholastics

The Constitutions of the Society of Jesus and Their Complementary Norms. Ed. John W. Padberg. St. Louis, MO: The Institute of Jesuit Sources, 1996.
de Jaer, André, *Together for Mission: A Spiritual Commentary on the Constitutions of the Society of Jesus.* Trans. Francis C. Brennan. St. Louis, MO: The Institute of Jesuit Sources, 2001.

Robert E. Scully, SJ

Grande, Rutilio, SJ (1928–1977)

The Salvadoran Jesuit priest Rutilio Grande García was brutally assassinated with two companions while on his way to celebrate Mass on March 12, 1977. Among the first

Jesuits killed in the years immediately following the Society's 32nd General Congregation (1974–75), his death powerfully affirmed the intrinsic link between the service of faith and the promotion of justice so clearly announced in the seminal documents issued by that Congregation. Very shortly after his death, the Archbishop of San Salvador, Oscar Romero, and the Superior General of the Society of Jesus, Pedro Arrupe, began to speak of Rutilio as a true martyr. In the case of Archbishop Romero, Rutilio's death was a watershed. He interpreted Rutilio's murder as an attack on the Church and publicly demanded accountability from the Salvadoran government and judicial system – demands that were largely ignored, but which earned him powerful enemies among the leaders of the oligarchy and military dictatorship. On Sunday March 20, eight days after the murders of Rutilio and his two companions, having cancelled all the local Masses in the archdiocese, Archbishop Romero concelebrated a single mass demonstrating the unity of the Church and its solidarity with all victims of injustice. Nearly all the priests of his diocese, including Jesuits and other religious, concelebrated the overflow mass that was attended by over 100,000 people – at the time the largest crowd ever assembled in El Salvador – with many more listening to the event on the Archdiocesan radio station. Three years later, on March 24, 1980, an assassin's bullet to the heart during the celebration of Eucharist brought Archbishop Romero's own ministry to a dramatic and sudden end.

See also Ellacuría, Ignacio, SJ and Companions; Martyrs, Ideal and History

Kelly, Thomas M., *When the Gospel Grows Feet: Rutilio Grande, SJ and the Church of El Salvador.* New York: Orbis, 2014.
Rutilio Grande, SJ: Homilies and Writings. Trans. and ed. T. M. Kelly. Collegeville, MN: Liturgical Press, 2015.

Kevin F. Burke, SJ

Grassi, Orazio, SJ (1583–1654)

Architect, mathematician, astronomer, controversialist, scenographer, and polymath, Orazio Grassi was born in Savona, Italy, in 1583, and entered the Society of Jesus at the Roman Novitiate of Sant'Andrea al Quirinale in 1600. He studied at the Roman College's "Mathematical Academy" under Christopher Clavius, Christoph Grienberger, and Odo van Maelcote. From 1616 to 1628 he served intermittently as professor of mathematics at the Roman College, architectural superintendent of the Order (*consiliarius aedificiorum*), and as rector of college in Siena. During this period he entered into a long and complex series of controversies with Galileo Galilei, ranging from disputes on the natures of comets, to geocentric versus heliocentric models, and Grassi's critique of Galileo's atomism as an implicit denial of Eucharistic transubstantiation. These controversies inspired one of Galileo's most famous and most satirical writings on the scientific method, *Il saggiatore* (Rome, 1623).

In the 1620s, Grassi won a competition sponsored by Cardinal Ludovico Ludovisi for a design for the Roman College's chapel, the Chiesa di Sant'Ignazio. Recent scholarship shows that while the quietly refined design was clearly Grassi's, he also incorporated elements from Borromini's and Domenichino's submissions. Work on Sant'Ignazio, both directing its construction and remedying construction design mistakes made during his absences from Rome, occupied Grassi for the rest of his life. Construction deficiencies,

Figure 24 Interior view of the Church of Sant'Ignazio, Rome, 17th century. Photograph Alison Fleming

cost overruns, and disputes with the Jesuits' Dominican neighbors at Santa Maria Sopra Minerva eliminated Grassi's intended dome from the project. The deficiency was corrected when Andrea Pozzo's dramatic anamorphic painting of a faux dome was erected in the crossing after 1685.

In 1631 Grassi was transferred to his native Savona, where he worked for a dozen years. He traveled throughout Italy working on Jesuit projects, and as rector of the college in Genoa, consulted with the government there on the design of defensive works and unsinkable ships. Returning to Rome in 1646, he worked at the Roman College until his death in 1654.

See also Architecture; Astronomy; Galileo; Science

Bösel, Richard, *Orazio Grassi, architetto e matematico gesuita*. Rome: Argos, 2004.

Thomas Lucas, SJ

Gratitude

See Contemplation to Attain Love; *Suscipe*

Gratuity of Ministries

The "gratuity of ministries" has long been a guiding principle of Jesuit apostolic life. *The Formula of the Institute*, the founding document of the Society of Jesus, stipulates that all works in which Jesuits engage should be carried out "altogether free of charge and without accepting any salary for the labor expended." In like measure, the *Constitutions* mandated that Jesuits accept no "stipend or alms as compensation" for their "Masses," "preaching," "lecturing," or "any other ministry" so that they may progress "in the divine service with greater liberty and greater edification of the neighbor." As Jesuits had received freely, they were to give freely and, in the words of the General Examen, receive recompense only from "God our Lord."

Additionally, Ignatius of Loyola was intent that Jesuit schools provide their instruction *gratis*. While these institutions depended upon gifts and endowments from benefactors, the schools of the pre-Suppression Society generally adhered to Ignatius's wish and provided Jesuit education without charge. But when the Society was restored in the early nineteenth century and endeavored to rebuild the Jesuit educational system, the changed socioeconomic context made previous financial models unfeasible. Papal dispensations from the *Constitutions* allowing the acceptance of tuition fees followed.

For over a century the Society also relied upon papal dispensations from the prohibition of accepting stipends. After the Second Vatican Council, a series of reforms by successive General Congregations regarding this issue were codified in *Complementary Norms* to the *Constitutions* (1995). While the gratuity of ministries abides as a guiding principle and Jesuits "may demand no stipend for their work in spiritual ministries," these recent norms state that stipends, income, and "remuneration for work done according to the Institute" are "a legitimate source of material goods … necessary for the life and apostolate of Jesuits."

See also Arca; Ministries; Poverty

de Aldama, Antonio, *The Constitutions of the Society of Jesus Part VI: Jesuit Religious Life*. Trans. Ignacio Echáinz. Saint Louis, MO: The Institute of Jesuit Sources, 1995, pp. 65–73.
Barry, William, and Robert Doherty, *Contemplatives in Action: The Jesuit Way*. New York: Paulist Press, 2002, pp. 61–68.

Henry Shea, SJ

Gregory XIII

Ugo Boncompagni was born in 1502. He developed an expertise in jurisprudence, studying and teaching law in Bologna before rising through the ranks of the Church. Pius IV created him a cardinal in 1565, and in 1572 he was elected Pope Gregory XIII.

Gregory XIII was a firm supporter of the Jesuits. In 1572 he secured a new location for the Society's Roman College and ensured it would receive 6,000 *scudi* per annum. It was later renamed the Gregorian University in honor of the Pope's support. Gregory also secured additional funds for the Society's German College, and he completed construction on the Church of the Gesù, the Society's main church in Rome. Gregory also supported the Jesuit missions overseas. The Pope's favor for the Jesuits was apparent in other ways as well. For example, he appointed Christopher Clavius, a Jesuit mathematician and astronomer, to the commission charged with reforming the Julian calendar. (The new "Gregorian" calendar was issued in 1582.)

Not all of Gregory's relations with the Society were positive, however. When the 3rd General Congregation met to elect Francis Borgia's successor, Gregory XIII noted that the Society's first three generals (Loyola, Laínez, and Borgia) had all been Spaniards. The Pope therefore commanded the Jesuits to elect a non-Spaniard as their next leader. The Jesuits protested, saying the Pope's intervention was highly unusual and that it contradicted the Society's *Constitutions*. Gregory eventually backed down, no longer requiring but merely recommending that the Society elect a non-Spaniard. Whether due to Gregory's actions or not, the Belgian Everard Mercurian was selected as the next superior general.

Gregory XIII died in 1585.

See also Gesù, Rome; Papacy; Roman College

McCoog, Thomas M., ed., *The Mercurian Project: Forming Jesuit Culture 1573–1580*. Rome/St. Louis, MO: The Institute of Jesuit Sources, 2004.

Charles Keenan

Gregory XV

Alessandro Ludovisi was born in 1554. He became the first pope to receive a Jesuit education, studying at the Roman College between 1569 and 1571. After taking a doctorate in law at Bologna, Ludovisi moved rapidly through the Church's ranks during the reign of Pope Paul V (r. 1605–21). He was named archbishop of Bologna in 1612 and created cardinal in 1616, having mediated a peace settlement between Savoy and Spain that same year.

In 1621 he was elected Pope Gregory XV. The two years of Gregory's short pontificate were dynamic, thanks in part to his cardinal-nephew, Ludovico Ludovisi. Gregory XV established the Congregation for the Propagation of the Faith in 1622, which oversaw the activities of Catholic missions throughout the world, and he reformed the rules governing conclaves. Gregory also actively supported Catholic leaders throughout Europe, even attempting, unsuccessfully, to arrange a marriage between the Spanish Infanta and the English prince Charles (later King Charles I).

In March 1622 Gregory XV canonized five individuals: two Jesuits, Ignatius of Loyola and Francis Xavier, as well as Philip Neri, Teresa of Avila, and Isidore "the Laborer." Loyola and Xavier thus became the first Jesuit saints. Gregory XV died in 1623. His remains were initially placed in the Chapel of the Annunciation, attached to the Roman College, but they were later transferred to the Church of Sant'Ignazio that replaced it.

See also Congregation for the Propagation of the Faith; Papacy; Saints

Jaitner, Klaus, ed., *Die Hauptinstruktionen Gregors XV: für die Nuntien und Gesandten an den europäischen Fürstenhöfen, 1621–1623*. Tübingen: Niemeyer, 1997.
"Kurie und Politik – der Pontifikat Gregors XV." In Alexander Koller, ed., *Kurie und Politik: Stand und Perspektiven der Nuntiaturberichtsforschung*. Tübingen: Niemeyer, 1998, pp. 1–15.

Charles Keenan

Grillmeier, Aloys, Cardinal, SJ (1910–1998)

Born in rural Bavaria, Aloys Grillmeier entered the Society of Jesus in 1929, was ordained a priest in 1937, and completed his doctorate at the University of Freiburg in 1942. After serving for two years as a medical orderly on the Eastern Front, he began a long career of teaching fundamental and dogmatic theology for the Sankt Georgen faculty (Frankfurt). As a consultant for Bishop Wilhelm Kempf of Limburg, Grillmeier attended Vatican II, where he became a Council expert (*peritus*) for the second session and also served on the Doctrinal Commission (1963–65). He had a hand in drafting the Dogmatic Constitution on the Church (*Lumen gentium*), the Dogmatic Constitution on Divine Revelation (*Dei verbum*), the Declaration on Religious Liberty (*Dignitatis humanae*), and the Pastoral Constitution on the Church in the Modern World (*Gaudium et spes*). At the Council he came to know Archbishop Karol Wojtyla of Krakow, working with him on the text of *Gaudium et spes*. As Pope John Paul II, he created Grillmeier a cardinal in 1994.

A prolific author, Grillmeier is best known for his study on the development of Christology, *Christ in the Christian Tradition* (Vol. I, 1965; Vol. II published in four parts, 1986–96). A dedicated ecumenist, he contributed his vast knowledge of ancient teaching and controversies over the person of Jesus Christ to the work of the Pro Oriente Institute (Vienna) and its dialogues with the Oriental Orthodox Churches, the Churches which rejected the Council of Chalcedon (451). This work bore fruit in official, joint confessions of faith in Christ between the Catholic Church and the Coptic Pope Shenouda of Egypt (1973), the Assyrian Church of the East (1994), and the Armenian Catholikos Karekin I (1996).

On September 13, 1998, Grillmeier died. He was buried in the Jesuit cemetery in Pullach (near Munich).

See also Cardinals, Jesuit; Fundamental Theology; Theology

Gerald O'Collins, SJ

Gruber, Gabriel, SJ (1740–1805)

A native of Slovenia, Gruber entered the Society in 1755 and went on to a successful teaching career, notably at Ljubljana. His interests varied widely, from mathematics to architecture and from agronomy to theater design. Following the global suppression of 1773, Gruber spent time at the court of Joseph II before traveling to White Russia in 1784. Here, the Society still enjoyed corporate existence because the brief of suppression had never been promulgated or enforced.

Gruber made a major contribution to the expansion of the Jesuits' Polock academy and, beyond his teaching duties, assisted in the creation of new facilities, including a museum, laboratories, and galleries. The Jesuits in Russia were eager to secure formal papal approval of their outpost of survival, and Gruber did as much as anyone to bring this goal to fruition. He was on friendly terms with Emperor Paul I and in August 1800 convinced him to send a formal letter to Rome requesting written approval of the "Russian" Society. This arrived in 1802 with Pius VII's brief *Catholicae fidei*. This positive development encouraged Jesuits in other parts of the world to seek "aggregation" with the "Russian" Society: a process that Gruber, elected father general in 1802, strongly encouraged.

Italy was the other main focus of pre-restoration recovery. Jesuits had established a formal presence in Parma as early as 1793, but the greatest triumph was the formal papal recognition of the Society in Naples and Sicily in 1804 through the papal brief *Per alias*.

See also Russia; Suppression

Inglot, Mark, "Pater Gabriel Gruber (1740–1805): Student der Tyrnauer Universitaet, der Generaloberer der Gesellschaft Jesu wurde." In Alzbeta Holosova and Istvan Bitskey, eds., *Die Tyrnauer Universitaet der Geschichte*. Krakow: Towarzystwo Slowakow w Polsce, 2012, pp. 256–77.
"The Society of Jesus in the Russian Empire (1772–1820) and the Restoration of the Order." In Robert Maryks and Jonathan Wright, eds., *Jesuit Survival and Restoration: A Global History, 1773–1900*. Leiden: Brill, 2014, pp. 67–82.

Jonathan Wright

Guadalupe, Our Lady of

Long before the emergence of devotion to Our Lady of Guadalupe in Mexico, based on the four sightings by Juan Diego at Tepeyac in 1531, there existed a strong devotion in Spain (Guadalupe of Estremadura), based on the legendary discovery of a Marian image hidden for over 600 years. The Spanish Guadalupe, with all her blackness, came to the Americas through the conquistadores; *Nuestra Señora de Guadalupe* is, for instance, the patroness of Sucre, the capital of Bolivia. The story of the Spanish Guadalupe gets woven into the history of the monastery at Montserrat and its image of the Virgin. The image of the Spanish Guadalupe found a place in the affections of the indigenous population of New Spain, thereby assisting evangelization (and colonization) efforts. The Mexican Guadalupe spoke to the indigenous Aztec population but above all to the criollos; yet rather than serving colonial interests, the Virgin gradually figured into the emergence of criollo nationalism and ultimately became associated with liberation. "The cult of Guadalupe was the spiritual aspect of the protest against the colonial regime" (Lafaye, *Quetzalcóatl and Guadalupe*, 299).

Jesuits played a role in the promotion of the Tepeyac Mary (e.g., the work of Francisco de Florencia, SJ, *La Estrella del Norte de México … Nuestra Señora de Guadalupe* [1688]) and in securing papal recognition of the cult of Guadalupe in 1754. In the seventeenth century several Jesuit preachers argued for the real presence of Mary in the icon. Another Jesuit, Francisco Javier Carranza, proposed that eventually the Church would leave Rome and be centered in Tepeyac (*The Transmigration of the Church to Guadalupe*, [1749])! Jesuit promotion of the Guadalupe cult was fused with a sense of Mexico as a privileged spiritual and political space as a result of the Virgin's appearance there as Latina. Today Guadalupe figures as an icon of divine solidarity with the poor and indigenous; the history of the devotion is more complex.

See also Marian Congregations; Mexico; Montserrat

Brading, D. A., *Mexican Phoenix: Our Lady of Guadalupe – Image and Tradition across Five Centuries*. Cambridge: Cambridge University Press, 2001.
Brosseder, Claudia, *The Power of Huacas: Change and Resistance in the Andean World of Colonial Peru*. Austin: University of Texas Press, 2014.
Lafaye, Jacques, *Quetzalcóatl and Guadalupe: The Formation of Mexican National Consciousness 1531–1813*. Chicago, IL: University of Chicago Press, 1976.
Peterson, Jeanette Favrot, *Visualizing Guadalupe: From Black Madonna to Queen of the Americas*. Austin: University of Texas Press, 2014.

Taylor, William B., "The Virgin of Guadalupe in New Spain: An Inquiry into the Social History of Marian Devotion." *American Ethnologist* 14, 1 (1987), 9–33.

William Reiser, SJ

Guatemala

Jesuits first arrived in Guatemala, now part of the Central American province, in 1582. Over the years they engaged in teaching and pastoral ministry (although the mission was not uninterrupted) until they were expelled from all Spanish lands in 1767. From the beginning of the mission to the expulsion, about 350 Jesuits worked in Guatemala, many of whom were born there.

In 1842 two Belgian Jesuits arrived in Guatemala to work as chaplains, and in 1851 a group of Jesuits forced to leave Colombia arrived. Educational ministry resumed; they also opened a house of formation. But in 1871 the Jesuits were again forced out because of political turbulence and anticlerical sentiment spreading from Mexico throughout Central America. They did not return until 1938, founding the Universidad Rafael Landívar (1961), as well as two *colegios*, a number of social/literacy projects, and a spirituality center.

If the early Jesuit history in Guatemala was a tortured one because of events in Europe that led to the Society's suppression, the later history proved difficult because of conflict in Guatemala itself. The civil war (1960–96) claimed over 200,000 lives. (Ricardo Falla, a Jesuit anthropologist, documented atrocities among the rural poor.) The story of the Society in Guatemala cannot be understood apart from the country's political, social, and economic history. Guatemalan Jesuit historian Ricardo Bendaña Perdomo analyzed the history of the Church in terms of *cristiandad* (Christendom), *iglesia y estado* (Church and State), and *pueblo de Dios* (people of God). The same three moments or contexts illumine the evolution of the Society's face in Guatemala: the sense of Christendom that informed the earliest missionary efforts, complex relations between the Church and successive governments over four centuries, and recovery of identity among the oppressed Mayan population alongside an ecclesiology "from below" (building upon Vatican II's idea of Church as the people of God).

See also Mexico

Diez, Francisco Javier Gómez, "Guatemala en el proyecto misionero de la Compañía de Jesús (1845–1871)." *Anales de la Academia de Geografía e Historia de Guatemala* 75 (2000), 95–138.

Falla, Ricardo, *Massacres in the Jungle: Ixcán, Guatemala, 1975–1982.* Boulder, CO: Westview Press, 1994.

   The Story of a Great Love: Life with the Guatemalan "Communities of Popular Resistance." Washington, DC: EPICA, 1998.

Klaiber, Jeffrey, "The Jesuits in Latin America: Legacy and Current Emphases."*International Bulletin of Missionary Research* 28, 2 (2004), 63–66.

Lynch, John, *New Worlds: A Religious History of Latin America.* New Haven, CT: Yale University Press, 2012.

Miller, Hubert, "The Expulsion of the Jesuits from Guatemala in 1871." *The Catholic Historical Review* 54, 4 (1969), 636–54.

Perdomo, Ricardo Bendaña, *Ella es lo que somos nosotros y mucho más.* Guatemala: Artemis Edinter, 2001.

Sariego, Jesús, *Tradición jesuita en Guatemala: una aproximación histórica*. Guatemala: Universidad Rafael Landívar, 2011.

William Reiser, SJ

Guillotin, Joseph-Ignace

Born in Saintes (France) on May 28, 1738, Guillotin was a student at the Jesuit Collège de La Madeleine in Bordeaux before entering the Society of Jesus on October 20, 1752. He would not profess vows until Christmas Day, 1755, while already a student of philosophy. After completing philosophy studies in 1756, Guillotin taught classical texts in Limoges for three years. In 1759 he left the Society.

He soon embarked upon what would be a celebrated medical career. In 1770 the Faculty of Paris made him a Regent-Doctor of Medicine. Esteemed a premier physician in Parisian society, his office on the rue Croix-des-Petits-Champs was frequented by people of every social class.

In 1789 he was elected as one of ten Paris deputies to the Estates-General at Versailles. There, in the newly formed National Assembly, Guillotin would deliver a speech proposing, among other things, that judicial sentences be delivered without regard to nobility or rank and that capital punishments be executed by a simple mechanism, which he fatefully referred to as "my machine."

In spite of the fact that the notorious *guillotine* of the revolution was neither invented nor designed nor built by Guillotin, the sobriquet stuck. In 1791 he withdrew from politics to return to medicine and was himself briefly imprisoned during the Terror. A man of broad humanitarian ideals, Guillotin later deplored the fact that his name had become unalterably attached to an instrument responsible for so much carnage.

He died in Paris on March 26, 1814.

See also Ex-Jesuits; France; Paris

Arasse, Daniel, *The Guillotine and the Terror*. Trans. Christopher Miller. London: Penguin, 1989.

Delattre, Pierre, "Saintes." *Les établissements des jésuites en France depuis quatre siècles*. Vol. IV. Enghien: Institut supérieur de théologie, 1956, pp. 646–47.

Duchet–Suchaux, Gaston, "Joseph-Ignace Guillotin." In M. Prevost, R. d'Amat, and H. Tribout de Morembert, eds., *Dictionnaire de biographie française*. Vol. 17. Paris: Letouzey et Ané, 1989, pp. 269–70.

Henry Shea, SJ

Gunpowder Plot

Also known as the Gunpowder Treason Plot, or the Jesuit Treason, the conspiracy led by Robert Catesby, Guy Fawkes, and others was to assassinate King James I, as a prelude to a revolution. When James became king in 1603, Catholics hoped that, because of his Catholic mother, the late Mary, Queen of Scots, he would be well disposed to the Catholic community. Catholic frustration at James's foot-dragging on the Catholic question led to the conspiracy to murder him at the state opening of parliament on November 5, 1605. The evening beforehand, Guy Fawkes was discovered guarding thirty-six barrels of gunpowder in the undercroft of the House of Lords. The conspirators were then arrested, with Catesby being shot dead in resisting arrest.

Fr. Henry Garnet, SJ, the superior of the Jesuits in England and Wales, was also arrested. Garnet knew of the plot from hearing the confession of another Jesuit, Fr. Oswald Tesimond. Tesimond also learned of it in the confessional from Catesby. Garnet wrote in late July 1605 to Fr. General Acquaviva, urging him to have the new pope, Paul V, declare that English Catholics should live in peace and not resort to violence. For a year before learning of the plot, he had already written several times to Rome in similar terms. Garnet was tried for treason and executed on May 3, 1606. In all fourteen were to die, with Fr. Tesimod and Fr. John Gerard, SJ, also implicated, managing to escape from England. In 1969 the English Jesuit Fr. Francis Edwards published a book alleging that the plot had been orchestrated by the King's chief minister, Robert Cecil. It is not a view that has gained much traction with historians. The plot helped to confirm at a popular level a deep animus in England against the Jesuit order.

See also United Kingdom

Caraman, Philip, *Henry Garnet 1555–1606, and the Gunpowder Plot.* New York: Farrar, Straus, 1964.
Edwards, Francis, *Guy Fawkes: The Real Story of the Gunpowder Plot?* London: Hart-Davis, 1969.

Oliver P. Rafferty, SJ

Habit

In general, a habit is a more or less stereotyped garment or manner of clothing that serves as a visual mark to identify members of a religious group or community within a wider society. Depending on its design, the habit can also become a focus for spiritual reflection by the individual community member, or for the community itself as a whole.

In Christianity, many elements of religious and liturgical vesture were derived from pieces of ancient Greek and Roman clothing. Both the cassock worn by diocesan clergy, and the tunic worn by male and female members of many religious orders, were thought to be related to the Greek *chiton* and the Roman *tunica*. Anchoritic and cenobitic monks of the fourth century adopted very plain, rough tunics based on the style of peasant dress as a visible sign of penitence for sins and renunciation of the world in poverty and ascetic lifestyle. However, in the early centuries, Christian priests did not adopt a style of dress different from the laymen of the locale, and in fact, were sometimes officially chided for doing so. By the sixth century, however, the ordinary dress of the layman in Europe had changed, and priests were increasingly required to retain traditional elements in their daily dress. For example, clergy were still required to wear a long tunic (the *vestis talaris*) that covered their lower legs instead of the Germanic-style short tunic with pants and leggings increasingly worn by men in both military and civilian life. In the early Middle Ages, local canonical legislation also forbade other forms of showy or ornamented dress; members of the clergy were urged to avoid wearing bright colors, exaggerated sleeves, or jeweled clasps for cloaks. Later in the medieval period, Roman and local canonical legislation became more rigorous. The Fourth Lateran Council (1215) mandated that the cleric's "outer garment" should be "closed" and of a moderate length; forbidden were the colors red and green, "long" sleeves, decorated shoes, and "gilded" accessories like bridles and spurs.

Figure 25 Photograph of Louis Gallagher, SJ, wearing cassock and biretta, at Woodstock College, 1917–22. Photograph © Archives of the New England Province, Society of Jesus

As St. Ignatius explicitly stated in the *Constitutions* (1553), Jesuits were not to have a particular religious habit. Instead, their clothing should have three characteristics: (1) to be "proper"; (2) to be "conformed to the country of usage" (at least, "not altogether different"); and (3) not to "contradict the poverty we profess," for example, in the use of expensive fabrics (*Constitutions*, #577). At first, Jesuits adopted the style of clerical cassock in common use in Rome, a style enforced on all clergy under pain of penalty by Pope Sixtus V (1589) and more narrowly standardized by Pope Urban VIII (1624).

As time passed, a specific "Jesuit" style of cassock developed, without the front buttons associated with diocesan priests, but closed at the top with an inner clasp and at the waist with a black sash. Other features included a full white collar worn over the neck of the cassock, and a set of rosary beads attached to the sash (made optional in the mid-twentieth century). Like diocesan clergy, Jesuits also wore the black clerical hat (the biretta). Depending on the time period and geographical region, the square cap of the biretta could have either four or three stiff fabric "horns," "blades" or "wings" radiating from the top center to each corner of the square frame. A biretta with only three blades, which came to be the style most associated with the Jesuits, was worn with the "empty" corner on the left side. The Jesuit biretta was not topped with the black tuft or "pom" used by diocesan clergy, but instead often had a simple black piece of fabric (a "tongue") at the top of the biretta.

Beginning in the late eighteenth century and lasting into the twentieth century, anti-clericalism in several countries in western Europe, the United States, and Mexico led to restrictions on the wearing of clerical dress in public places. For reasons like this, particular legislation was needed in a number of countries regarding clerical clothing. For example, in the United States, the Third Council of Baltimore (1884) reaffirmed that the cassock was the proper priestly dress at "home" and in church, but that when leaving these areas for other reasons, or when traveling, the priest might wear a black, knee-length "short" coat with the Roman collar. In accord with the *Code of Canon Law* (1983), canon 284, the US Conference of Catholic Bishops issued a contemporary interpretation (1999) of this national custom: "Outside liturgical functions, a black suit and Roman collar are the usual attire for priests." Members of religious communities were to follow their own rules about wearing their habits.

See also Constitutions

"Fourth Lateran Council: Constitutions." www.papalencyclicals.net/Councils/ecum12-2.htm.

Fucinaro, Thomas, "Clerical Attire: The Origin of the Obligation: Codicial and Recent Discipline, Governing Legislation from the Conference of Bishops in the United States of America, and Particular Legislation in the United States of America" (2009). www.clerus.org/clerus/dati/2009-07/29-13/Fucinaro_en.html.

"The Phillipi Headwear Collection." http://philippi-collection.blogspot.com/2013/09/jesuit-biretta.html.

"Religious Habit." In *New Catholic Encyclopedia*. 2nd edn. Vol. XII. Washington, DC: Thompson Gale, 2003, pp. 98–101.

United States Conference of Catholic Bishops. "Canon 284: Clerical Garb" (1999). www.usccb.org/beliefs-and-teachings/what-we-believe/canon-law/complementary-norms/canon-284-clerical-garb.cfm.

Joanne M. Pierce

Haciendas (and Jesuit Estates)

Haciendas were economic institutions established to support the Society's better-known foundations in the Americas, notably the colleges and the missions. While the term refers to a landed rural estate, the primary aim of Jesuit hacienda production was cash revenue. The Jesuits became involved in producing many important staples, including maize, barley, cattle, sheep, sugar, goats, hogs, horses, wool cloth, and "Jesuit tea" (*yerba mate*). Haciendas provided a range of occupations, from cowboys and sheep-herders to textile workers and tortilla-makers, employing both slave and free labor.

The institution predated Jesuit arrival in the Americas in 1572. The Mexican case provides a useful example. Upon arrival, the first Mexican Jesuits were dependent upon a gift-economy. A Spanish patron donated urban properties to help the Jesuits establish their presence in Mexico City and, shortly thereafter, in 1576, donated an existing hacienda, Santa Lucia, to support directly the newly established Jesuit college. There was some debate about whether managing an estate was consistent with the Society's understanding of missionary service, and there was even discussion of selling the lands in the 1580s. But the alternative investments were mining and merchant activities, so the hacienda was deemed least problematic. Moreover, it was quickly becoming lucrative. The Spanish development of the mining industry and the rapid growth of Mexico City meant there were ready markets for hacienda products. The Jesuits had some advantage among competing *hacendados* (hacienda owners) as they were not required to tithe. They reinvested in the hacienda, strategically purchasing lands for pasture, access to water, and roads. Only the first Mexican Jesuits had qualms about slaveholding; the continued purchase and sale of slaves went unnoted in the seventeenth and eighteenth centuries. The Jesuit haciendas differed from neighboring haciendas in that they had chapels, began the day with Mass (mandatory for slaves), and provided religious instruction for children of workers, both slave and free (in native languages as well as in Spanish).

See also Mexico; Slavery

Konrad, Herman, A *Jesuit Hacienda in Colonial Mexico: Santa Lucia, 1576–1767*. Stanford, CA: Stanford University Press, 1980.

J. Michelle Molina

Haïti

Jesuits first arrived in Haïti in 1704 at the urging of the Capuchins, who had been serving there since the 1630s. The Society was expelled in 1764 following a royal decree expelling the Jesuits from France and the French colonies.

In 1953 it was at the express wish of Pope Pius XII that Fr. Jean-Baptiste Janssens asked the province of Lower Canada to take responsibility for the interdiocesan Grand Séminaire at Port-au-Prince, Haïti. Accordingly, Fr. Arthème Tétreault (1891–1963), as superior of the mission, led five Jesuit priests to take over the administration of the Seminary. Between then and February 12, 1964, those five were joined by twenty-eight other French-Canadian Jesuits. The Grand Séminaire Notre-Dame was the main focus of Jesuit activity as the student body of seminarians grew to thirty-five.

In 1956 Fr. Maurice Champagne was asked to take over Saint-Louis de France Parish in Cap-Haïtien. He was followed there in 1957 by Fr. Bernard Bourassa, who was the longest to serve at Saint-Louis and saw attendance grow to 8,000 parishioners in 1964. It was also in 1956 that Fr. Antonio Poulin began to make plans for a retreat center, the Villa Manrèse, which was eventually inaugurated in October 1959, the first retreat house of its kind in Haïti. Before it was shut down in 1964, it would welcome some 12,000 retreatants.

It was from the Villa Manrèse that Brother François-Xavier Ross started the publication of a small devotional journal, *Haïti chérie*, and, most especially, that Fr. Origène Grenier opened Radio-Manrèse in 1961, a station exclusively dedicated to religious and educational programming.

It may well have been the popularity and strength of Radio-Manrèse that frightened the François Duvalier government. On January 31, 1964, its director, Fr. Paul Laramée, and his two assistants, Paul Hamel and François-Xavier Ross, were imprisoned in the notorious Fort-Dimanche prison, accused of plotting against the security of the state. No evidence of any such subversive activity was ever produced, but despite official protests from the Apostolic Nunciature and the Canadian chargé d'affaires, a decree of expulsion was issued on February 13. That evening the eighteen French-Canadian Jesuits working in Haïti landed in Montreal.

After the end of the first Duvalier regime in 1971, Jesuits returned to Haïti progressively. The first, Fr. Fritz Wolfe, returned to the Grand Séminaire in Port-au-Prince at the invitation of the bishop in 1973. He was followed in 1977 by Brother Mathurin

Charlot, whose degrees in forestry and rural agricultural planning made him welcome in many quarters. By 1981, at the urging of the bishop, several French-Canadian and native-born Haïtian Jesuits returned quietly to form a new community with Fr. Wolfe as superior. Before the end of the second Duvalier regime in 1986, the 1964 decree expelling the Jesuits was rescinded. In 2009 one of them, Gontran Décoste, was consecrated as bishop of the Diocese of Jérémie.

In recent years, Jesuit vocations and ministries have been thriving in Haïti. In addition to two French-Canadian Jesuits, there are now eighteen Haïtian Jesuits who work in a variety of ministries, including Fe y Alegría schools and refugee services. A new Jesuit novitiate was opened in 2015 in Dumay on the outskirts of Port-au-Prince, and there are presently thirty-five Haïtian Jesuits in formation studying philosophy and theology abroad.

See also Canada; Dominican Republic; Fe y Alegría; France

Les Jésuites en Haïti. www.jesuites.org/haiti.

Jacques Monet, SJ

Hebga, Meinrad, SJ (1928–2008)

Born on March 31, 1928, in Edea, Cameroon, Meinrad Hebga was a Jesuit priest. He was also an academic, philosopher, anthropologist, and charismatic preacher. His main contribution to African philosophy was to offer a scientific analysis of witchcraft and to study paranormal phenomena like bilocation, levitation, apparitions, encounter with spirits, and bewitching, which are commonly attested to in Africa. Hebga argued that such paranormal activities have their own rationality that cannot be measured only by a Cartesian perception of the world. For Hebga, paranormal activities are not merely a matter of primitive beliefs. He spent his life reflecting on paranormal phenomena and even used his priestly power as an exorcist to combat evil spirits and heal many people across the continent of Africa and elsewhere. In his doctoral thesis, completed at the Sorbonne in 1986 and entitled "Rationalité d'un discours africain sur les phénomènes paranormaux," Hebga argues that to deny any rationality to paranormal happenings on account of relativism is an oversimplistic answer to a very complex reality that is affecting many peoples in Africa and elsewhere.

As a Jesuit priest, Hebga was deeply involved with the charismatic movement. He founded a charismatic group of prayer and deliverance in Yaoundé, Cameroon. He traveled the world preaching and casting out demons. At the same time, he published many books and wrote more than a hundred articles in different reviews. He died on March 3, 2008, in Château-Thierry in France. Among his most important books are: *Personnalité africaine et catholicisme* (1963); *Les étapes des regroupements africains* (1968); *Émancipation d'Église sous tutelle: essai sur l'ère post-missionnaire* (1976); *Dépassements* (1978). *Sorcellerie, chimère dangereuse …?* (1979); *Sorcellerie et prière de délivrance: réflexion sur une expérience* (1982); *Afrique de la raison, Afrique de la foi* (1995); *La rationalité d'un discours africain sur les phénomènes paranormaux* (1998).

See also Africa, West

Luc Bonaventure A. Amoussou, SJ

Hekima University College

A theological school with an African character was first proposed by a group of young African and European Jesuits that met in Louvain, Belgium, in 1970. Their proposal fit well in the program of Pedro Arrupe (1907–91), then superior general, to establish structures for Jesuit administration and formation in Africa. For Arrupe, such a school would add a theological input to the ongoing pursuit of social and economic development in Africa, which tended to borrow too much from communist ideologies. It would also contribute toward critically needed inculturation of Christianity. Subsequent deliberations culminated in the opening of Hekima College in Nairobi, Kenya, in1984, with Henri de Decker (1927–95) as its first rector and principal.

From the outset, Hekima University College combined the teaching of the faith in the Vatican II tradition with pastoral experience and reflection. Although initially envisaged for the formation of Jesuits, the program quickly attracted students from other congregations of men. However, women religious and lay students remained very few. The College had other programs in spirituality and in the Christian faith, which served more people than its regular student body. An outreach initiative in community peace building eventually formed the basis for a full-fledged master's degree program offered by the Hekima Institute of Peace Studies and International Relations (HIPSIR) since 2005. The College has also been home to the Jesuit Historical Institute in Africa (JHIA) since 2012.

Hekima College has prepared many candidates for further studies elsewhere and has trained even more for pastoral practice. Its library is one of the best theological libraries in the eastern African region. Its biannual journal, *Hekima Review*, has been consistently produced since 1988. In 2015 the College acquired the status of a university college, though still as a constituent college of the Catholic University of Eastern Africa. The new status has raised optimism and generated activity toward becoming a full-fledged university.

See also Africa, East; Jesuit Historical Institute Africa; Universities, 1773–Present

de Decker, Henri, "Hekima College Nairobi, Kenya." *The Jesuits: Year Book of the Society of Jesus* (1986), 129–33.
McGarry, Cecil, "Hekima College: The First Twenty Years, 1984–2004." *Hekima Review* 32 (2004), 87–93.

Festo Mkenda, SJ

Hell, Maximillian, SJ (1720–1792)

A scientist and scholar, Hell was born of German-speaking parents in a mining community of Upper Hungary. Hell's theological training was completed in Vienna. After service in more remote locations, such as Cluj, Hell returned to Vienna to become the director of the Observatory there in 1756. In this post he published the yearly *Ephemerides astronomicae ad meridianum Vindobonensem*, which he continued to produce until his death. A committed Jesuit, he never openly rejected any of the cosmological positions held by the Church, even while carrying on correspondences with astronomers who had done so long before.

Highly regarded during his lifetime as an astronomer, Hell's reputation plummeted in the nineteenth century when he was wrongly accused by Carl Littrow of falsifying entries in his log, only to be rehabilitated by Simon Newcomb. In addition to his activities as an astronomer, Hell used a lodestone to devise an arrangement of magnetic plates for reducing pain associated with a number of diseases, including rheumatism, from which he himself suffered. Hell initially took an interest in, and then debunked, Franz Anton Mesmer's theory of "animal magnetism." Hell's best-known undertaking commences with an invitation from King Christian VII of Denmark and Norway to travel to the island of Vardø near Lapland to observe a transit of Venus in 1769. It was on this expedition that Hell's fellow Jesuit Joannes Sajnovics began to propound his theory (since proven correct) that Hungarian and Finnish were linguistically related. Plans to compile the findings from this expedition were thwarted by the Suppression. Following 1773 Hell continued to make astronomical observations and to make star charts. Hell's later writings reveal his persisting baroque piety and mistrust of Protestantism.

See also Astronomy; Science

Pärr, Nora, *Maximilian Hell und sein wissenschaftliches Umfeld im Wien des 18. Jahrhunderts*. Nordhausen: Verlag Traugott Bautz, 2013.

Paul Shore

Henry IV

King Henry IV's reign (1589–1610) is indeed decisive for the history of the Society in France. Not only did it expand considerably at that time, as well as face difficult vicissitudes, it also witnessed a considerable redefinition of its relationship to the monarchy and thus of its engagement with French society and culture.

After the assassination of Henry III by a *ligueur* Dominican friar, a high point in the French Wars of Religion, the Society had already made significant strides in France. There already were three provinces (Francia for the northern part of France, Lyon, and Aquitaine). By 1580 it already supervised fourteen colleges with a considerable number of students, even if some prominent colleges, founded by wealthy patrons, were not yet in the most important French towns (such as the colleges of Tournon or Eu). While Jesuits, such as Maldonado, had played a significant part in controversies with the Protestants, and while the *Ligue* certainly enjoyed large support in French society, an example of such being the Jesuit *ligueur* preacher Jacques Commolet, the Society cannot nonetheless be described as particularly committed to this cause. It did nonetheless become a scapegoat of the political process of pacification after the defeats of the *Ligue* in the early 1590s. The Parlement of Paris, with support from the Sorbonne whose doctors were threatened by the educational competition of the Jesuits, targeted the Society as a symbol of what the *Ligue* was or had been. In 1594, after the King's conversion was sanctioned by pontifical authority, the Parlement took the occasion of an attempted regicide perpetrated by a former pupil of the Jesuits, Jean Chastel, to act against the Society. The Jesuits were expelled from the *ressort* (extent of jurisdiction) of the Parlement and soon after from those of Rouen and Dijon. While this meant that the Jesuits had to abandon their colleges in what amounts to more than two-thirds of France, this decree cannot be properly pegged as expulsion since, partly because of royal protection, some other *parlements* did not emulate their Parisian counterpart, and the Jesuits could remain active and regroup in the rest of France.

This partial expulsion was short-lived, and in 1603 the King recalled the Jesuits in the entire country and restored the Order in its properties. As Eric Nelson has most convincingly shown, this was part of a greater struggle between the Parlement and the Crown. By recalling the Jesuits, the King asserted that he was the true judge of pacification and that the country was to be brought peace not by the affirmation of judicial power but rather by that of the gracious power of the would-be absolute monarch. This explains the public display of royal patronage over the Society during the rest of the reign. The King favored the opening of new colleges and sponsored the establishment of the most important college of the French province in La Flèche. In 1608, the 6th General Congregation approved the formation of a fourth province (that of Toulouse), and granted the King the creation of the Assistancy of France he asked for.

The emergence of this new level of government would later prove a first major step in the process of nationalization of the French Society of Jesus. Indeed, Henry IV initiated a process of transformation of the Society in a dynastic order that was continued by his successors. Henry also inaugurated the Bourbon tradition of having Jesuit confessors. This process of growing dependence on the dynasty protected the Jesuits, who managed, for example, to survive the renewal of the campaign for their expulsion when Henry was assassinated by Ravaillac in 1610. Yet the weight of royal patronage was also at times a liability for the Order. The question of the position of the Jesuits in France was therefore inevitably politically loaded and became recurrent in the relationship between the monarchy and other French political institutions, particularly the Parlement. Overdependence on royal patronage certainly still played a major part when the Jesuits came under attack in the second half of the eighteenth century. Attacking the Jesuits could also be a means of questioning some of the new claims of royal power. This particular connection between the Society and the monarch was indeed a political backdrop for the development of anti-Jesuitism, which was significantly on the rise in the early seventeenth century. Such texts as Pasquier's *Catéchisme des Jésuites* (1602) point to this connection between anti-Jesuitism and politics in France.

See also Anti-Jesuit Polemic; France

Fouqueray, Henri, *Histoire de la Compagnie de Jésus en France des origines à la suppression (1528–1762)*. Paris: Picard, 1910–25.

Nelson, Eric, *The Jesuits and the Monarchy: Catholic Reform and Political Authority in France (1590–1615)*. Aldershot and Burlington, VT: Ashgate, 2005.

Parsons, Jotham, *The Church in the Republic: Gallicanism and Political Ideology in Renaissance France*. Washington, DC: The Catholic University of America Press, 2005.

Wolfe, Michael, *The Conversion of Henri IV: Politics, Power and Religious Belief in Early Modern France*. Cambridge, MA: Harvard University Press, 1993.

Jean-Pascal Gay

Heythrop College

Heythrop College takes its name from a tiny village some 20 miles north of Oxford. Its origins, however, can be traced back to penal times when in 1614 a generous gift established the first version of "Heythrop" in Louvain. A very few years later, the College moved to Liège where, bolstered by an endowment from the dukes of Bavaria, it remained until the French Revolution forced the Jesuits to embark on a perilous journey to England where they moved into a largely derelict house at Stonyhurst in Lancashire. With the restoration of the Society in 1814 and the act of Catholic emancipation in 1829, the College became more firmly settled. In 1848 the theologians moved to St. Beuno's in North Wales, while the philosophy students remained at Stonyhurst. The two faculties were reunited in 1926 in a massive early eighteenth-century country house, Heythrop Hall, the sometime property of the earls of Shrewsbury. In the early 1960s moves were made to establish a Pontifical Athenaeum; a new library was built and preparations made to bring some fifteen religious orders together on the 400-acre site. In the wake of the Council, however, the move from rural retreats to city-based universities was in full swing. In 1970 Heythrop was formally accepted into the federal University of London, with premises first in the West End and, since 1993, in Kensington. There it has become one of the most esteemed centers of theological and philosophical reflection in the country. In 2015 – ironically less than a year after the College celebrated its 400th anniversary – financial problems led to the decision that the College would close "in its present form." The College has, however, long been used to an unstable, peripatetic existence. At the time of writing, plans were afoot to ensure that Heythrop's historic mission, to promote excellence in theological and philosophical learning, goes on in some way.

See also United Kingdom

Michael Barnes, SJ

HIV/AIDS

AIDS is new in human history, and AIDS ministry is extremely new for the Church. To this day, many pastoral agents are reluctant to touch AIDS, because they fear they will be stepping into a minefield littered with theological, pastoral, moral, and personal bombshells. In more than three decades since the first diagnosis of AIDS, the Church has sought to respond with compassion and wisdom. Scholars have formulated a theology that rejects notions of AIDS as divine retribution, an unequivocal basis from which to preach and practice an AIDS ministry that mirrors the justice and compassion of Jesus. The chosen direction of the Church is clear, and it is this path that the Jesuits walk.

When AIDS first exploded into the world, it was lone Jesuits who reached out. They did this everywhere and especially in sub-Saharan Africa, the continent hardest hit, with extraordinary compassion and courage. Leading pioneers among the Jesuits were Angelo D'Agostino (1926–2006), who set up the first hospice in Kenya for HIV-positive orphans who were abandoned to die; and Paul Besanceney (1924–2009), who started to visit families in slums around Khartoum in his seventies, prompted by "the realisation that people with HIV had so many problems tied with this one: the stigma, the ignorance, what it does to families." Given the huge damage caused by AIDS across sub-Saharan Africa, Jesuits who were involved felt that the Society of Jesus needed to do more. In 2000, nine Jesuits and one co-worker wrote a letter to father general and the Society that called for more intensive involvement in AIDS ministry by Jesuits in Africa. The participants made a heartfelt appeal, "recognising that the hopes and joys, the pains and sufferings of those infected or affected by HIV and AIDS are also the hopes and joys, the pains and sufferings of Christ in our world today." On June 21, 2002, the Jesuit Superiors of Africa and Madagascar (JESAM) established the African Jesuit AIDS Network (AJAN).

The very fact that the Jesuits have a network to deal with AIDS is quite unusual. AJAN encourages Jesuits to ask two questions: *What impact has HIV on my work? What impact does my work have on HIV?* AJAN educates Jesuits about the reality of AIDS today and how to deal with it in their daily ministry. AIDS remains shrouded in stigma and denial, and a popular misunderstanding persists that tackling AIDS requires a strictly medical, linear approach. AJAN approaches AIDS not just as a disease, but as one with profound social, personal, and economic ramifications. AJAN adopted the vision of Zambia-based Michael J. Kelly, whose writing and talks about AIDS have won much acclaim and who underscores that HIV and AIDS are powerful factors, permeating almost every facet of life, that undermine the universal right to personal dignity and integral human development. AIDS feeds off and in turn feeds endemic poverty and injustice. It is a crosscutting issue touching all sectors that Jesuits are engaged in, such as parishes, education, development, spiritual direction, and social justice. Jesuits implement the AJAN vision of *empowered individuals, families and communities working toward an AIDS-free society and fullness of life* in their daily work, responding to perceived needs. The services offered vary, but the approach is characterized by two elements: *comprehensiveness* and *person-centered action*. For example, the Service Yezu Mwiza, run by the Jesuit region of Rwanda-Burundi in Bujumbura, is officially recognized for voluntary counseling and testing, antiretroviral treatment (ART), and treatment of tuberculosis (TB). This medical care is offered as part of a comprehensive package that includes pastoral and psychosocial support, nutritional education, income-generating activities, material aid for those who need it, and help to pay the school fees of vulnerable children. Indeed, such are the services offered, to a greater or lesser extent, by most ministries that are run either by the Jesuits or by associations and organizations closely affiliated to AJAN. The AIDS ministry of Jesuits and of other organizations also focus on HIV prevention among youth. Some offer medical treatment; others facilitate access to it. This comprehensive approach restores human dignity and zest for life.

Thanks to rapid advances in medical treatment, AIDS is no longer a mandatory death sentence. There are 35 million people living with HIV worldwide, 71 percent in sub-Saharan Africa. By 2015, 15 million people had access to antiretroviral treatment (ART). However, stiff challenges remain, at the international level to sustain the progress and at the individual level to live positively with HIV. Staying well consumes time, effort, and money – things that many simply do not have. And stigma persists. Despite the hardships, AJAN continues to encourage and foster resilience, hope, and joy among people living with HIV and to boost their determined efforts to live positively.

See also Africa, East; Africa, Northwest; Africa, West; Zambia

Czerny, Michael, ed., *AIDS and the Church in Africa*. (African Jesuit AIDS Network). Nairobi: Paulines Publications Africa, 2008.

Kelly, Michael, *Education: For an Africa without AIDS*. Nairobi: Paulines Publications Africa, 2008.
    HIV and AIDS: A Social Justice Perspective. Nairobi: Paulines Publications Africa, 2010.

Mombé, Paterne A., Agbonkhianmeghe Orobator, and Danielle Vella, eds., *AIDS: 30 Years Down the Line*. Nairobi: Paulines Publications Africa, 2013.

Agbonkhianmeghe Orobator, SJ

Holy Cross, College of the

Founded in 1843 by Jesuit Benedict J. Fenwick, the second bishop of Boston, Holy Cross is the oldest Catholic educational institution in New England. Fenwick's priorities made the college an anomaly in Jesuit higher education: because of anti-Catholic nativism in Boston, he placed the school in Worcester, overriding the Jesuit preference for schools inculturated in large cities; and to foster vocations to the priesthood, he restricted admission to Roman Catholic students. Thomas Mulledy served as first president.

Initially, Holy Cross followed the model of the *Ratio studiorum*. After a disastrous fire in 1852, classes were suspended for fourteen months until the school reopened on a reduced scale. After the General Court of Massachusetts denied the College's first petition for a charter in 1849, Holy Cross awarded Georgetown degrees, since the academic programs were essentially similar. This situation lasted until 1865, when a charter was granted in the immediate aftermath of the American Civil War. Fenwick Hall, the original structure, was amplified after the war and complemented with O'Kane Hall in 1895, when the student body numbered about 350 students. By then, the Jesuit academic system was becoming less useful; compared with alumni of American colleges, Jesuit graduates were two years behind graduates of other colleges, insufficiently prepared for graduate and professional schools. After 1897, Presidents Joseph Hanselman and John Lehy revised the curriculum, separating the preparatory department from the College, where courses began to be organized by academic department: heavy requirements in classical languages, religion, and philosophy were maintained.

By 1910 Holy Cross was the largest Catholic college in the United States, and the preparatory division was dropped in 1914. After World War I, the campus gained three buildings expressing the architectural inspiration of Charles Maginnis: St. Joseph Memorial Chapel (1924), Dinand Library (1927), and Kimball Dining Hall (1935). Between the wars, academic departments grew; the student population grew to 1,200; and varsity teams achieved notoriety in baseball and football. After the United States entered World War II, the College contracted with the US Navy to host the V-12 Program, training naval officers. Between 1943 and 1946, the Holy Cross functioned as a branch of the Navy; Jesuit instructors and others worked as employees of the United States. During the war, non-Catholic students were assigned to the College, ending religious exclusivity. After the war, enrollment surged. New residence halls and classroom buildings were added; within twenty years, enrollment stood at 2,400. College football teams played in the Orange Bowl in 1946; while the basketball teams won the NCAA Tournament in 1947 and the National Invitational Tournament in 1954; and the baseball team won the College World Series in 1952. In those years, the academic enterprise was less successful, lagging behind many of the country's secular colleges in professionalization of the faculty, and in the requirement of a Ph.D. or equivalent for faculty.

Raymond J. Swords (Class of 1938), president from 1960 to 1970, addressed the issues with imaginative determination. He was one of the first American Jesuit presidents to introduce separate incorporation (1969); he also restructured governance to shift greater responsibility to the lay faculty. With his successor, John Brooks, SJ (Class of 1949, president 1970–94), he took measures to attract minority students to the campus, and to open the Department of Religious Studies, shifting the emphasis from catechetical to academic instruction, with the assistance of lay professors. During the Vietnam War, he defended the students' right to protest and endured strong criticism from some alumni.

Figure 26 Exterior view of Saint Joseph's Memorial Chapel, College of the Holy Cross, Worcester MA, 20th century. Photograph Thomas Worcester, SJ

He worked closely with the local bishop to implement the reforms of Vatican II, and, following a directive from Rome, eliminated the requirement of daily Mass. John Brooks continued the reshaping of Holy Cross by fostering the introduction of coeducation (1972) and maintaining vigorous building and fund-raising campaigns. By the end of his presidency, the endowment had risen from $6 million to $120 million.

Early in the twenty-first century, Michael McFarland (president 2000–12), reemphasized the school's Catholic and Jesuit identity through a number of programs that included an Ignatian pilgrimage for faculty and administrators to Spain and Rome. As enrollment grew to about 2,900, the College introduced Montserrat, a group-oriented academic program for first-year students that linked student life with rigorous academic seminars.

Despite many changes, Holy Cross has kept focused on undergraduate liberal arts education and is the highest rated Jesuit four-year college in the United States. Prominent graduates include David I. Walsh (1893), Massachusetts's first Catholic governor and US senator; Joseph Murray (1940), winner of the Nobel Prize in Medicine; Billy Collins (1963), Poet Laureate of the United States; and Clarence Thomas (1971), Associate Justice of the US Supreme Court.

See also Georgetown University; United States of America; Universities, 1773–Present

Kuzniewski, Anthony, *Thy Honored Name: A History of the College of the Holy Cross, 1843–1994*. Washington, DC: The Catholic University of America Press, 1999.

Anthony Kuzniewski, SJ

Holy Land

The only trip Ignatius of Loyola took outside Europe was to the Holy Land in September of 1523. He spent three weeks there and had his first contact with a Muslim, the guardian of the site of the Lord's Ascension. He considered staying there for the remainder of his life, but the Franciscans ordered him out. The Franciscans were Custodians of the Holy Land and could see no positive results coming from this mendicant pilgrim.

The desire to go to Jerusalem remained, and Ignatius and his first companions took a vow to travel to the Holy Land and seek "to spend their lives for the good of souls" (*Autobiography*, 85). If this were not possible, they would travel to Rome and put themselves at the disposal of the Holy Father. Ignatius's plan failed a second time when passage to the Holy Land proved impossible in 1537.

Later, in 1553, Pope Julius III issued a bull granting permission to the Society of Jesus to found colleges in Jerusalem, Cyprus, and Constantinople. Nothing came of this as far as Jerusalem was concerned.

Jesuits did pass through Jerusalem on pilgrimage, and a map of the Holy Land was drawn by the Jesuit, Jacobus Tirinus (1580–1636), a Belgian biblical scholar. He also published *Chorographia Terrae Sanctae*, a geographical description with a map of the region.

Since 1927 the Pontifical Biblical Institute, one of the institutions of the Holy See in Rome run by the Jesuits, has had a branch in the city of Jerusalem. This branch is not an independent entity, with its own proper academic program, but rather a house at the service of the professors and students of the school in Rome as a base of operations for their studies in the Holy Land. It houses a library and an archaeological museum with artifacts from the excavations at Teleilat Ghassul of the Chalcolithic Period.

There are also a few Jesuits working in the Holy Land today. David Mark Neuhaus is an Israeli Jesuit priest and serves as the patriarchal vicar for the Hebrew-speaking Catholic communities in Israel. He teaches Scripture at the Seminary of the Latin Patriarchate of Jerusalem and in the Religious Studies Department at Bethlehem University. Another Jesuit, Peter Du Brul, is head of the Religious Studies Department at the university.

See also Francis of Assisi and the Franciscans; Loyola, Ignatius of, SJ, St.; Middle East; Pontifical Biblical Institute

John Donohue, SJ

Holy Roman Empire

The Holy Roman Empire was an elective monarchy in central Europe of medieval origin that presided over a complex array of territories. Napoleon Bonaparte dissolved it in 1806. The emperors were members of the Catholic Austrian Habsburg dynasty for most of the period in which the Jesuits were active in the Empire. By the middle of the sixteenth century, the Protestant Reformation profoundly affected the political and social life of the Empire. Lutheranism predominated. Reformed Protestantism established itself in a clutch of territories. Catholicism survived principally in Bavaria and in the prince bishoprics.

The Jesuits, whose mission was to reinvigorate Catholicism, operated in an environment of confessional tensions. They were habitual targets of Protestant polemics. *Jesuwider* was a favorite Protestant pun to brand Jesuits as enemies of Jesus. During the Thirty Years War (1618–48), Jesuits were often the targets of Protestant troops, who banished them and plundered their schools. Some Jesuits, such as Lorenz Forer (1580–1659), were inveterate anti-Protestant controversialists.

A few pioneers began the work of the Society of Jesus. Peter Faber first entered the Empire in 1540. In 1543 in Mainz, he recruited the first Jesuit on German soil, Peter Canisius, and in the following year organized in Cologne the first Jesuit community in the Empire. During his travels in the Empire (1542–48), Nicolás Bobadilla argued against any imperial concessions to Protestants. In 1549 Claude Jay inaugurated Jesuit university teaching with Alfonso Salmerón and Canisius at the University of Ingolstadt. Jay moved to Vienna in 1551 to establish a Jesuit community and teach theology at the university.

The erection in 1556 of the Lower and Upper German provinces laid the institutional foundation of Jesuit ministries in the Empire. In 1564 the Lower German province was divided into a Belgian and a Rhenish province. The latter split into the Upper and Lower Rhenish provinces in 1626. In 1562 the Austrian province separated from Upper Germany. Out of Austria emerged the Polish province (1575) and the Bohemian province (1623). Protestant Prussia's conquest of Silesia in the War of the Austrian Succession (1740–48) led to the establishment in 1754 of the Silesian province, detached from Bohemia and Habsburg influence. The Bavarian province, carved out of Upper Germany in 1770, quickly came to an end with the Suppression of the Society of Jesus in 1773. At the time of the Suppression, the seven provinces in the Empire numbered 5,375 members, about 23 percent of Jesuits worldwide. With a membership of 1,819, the Austrian province was the most populous.

Education constituted the most conspicuous Jesuit ministry in the Empire. At their colleges and in Catholic universities, Jesuits adhered to humanist pedagogy, promoted Catholic piety, and contributed to scholarship in theology, philosophy, classics, and the sciences. The first four Jesuit colleges opened in Vienna (1553), Ingolstadt (1556), Prague (1556), and Cologne (1557). The sixteenth century witnessed a proliferation of more than twenty Jesuit colleges. Most of these were in Germany, such as in Munich, Würzburg, and Protestant Augsburg. Apart from Vienna, Austrian Jesuits operated colleges in Innsbruck and Graz. In Switzerland, which belonged to the Upper German province, they taught in Lucerne and Fribourg, in Silesia in Glatz, and in Moravia in Olomouc. In the seventeenth century, more colleges opened in Germany, Austria, and Switzerland, and the Jesuits began teaching in Hungary, Croatia, Friuli, and Istria. Jesuits held university professorships, controlled faculties of philosophy and theology, or administered entire universities on their own. The last foundation of a Jesuit university in the Empire took place in 1702 in Breslau.

Jesuits were active in several other ministries. Canisius began the ministry of court preacher. Jesuits also served as confessors at Catholic princely courts – in Vienna, Munich, Neuburg, and Dresden in the eighteenth century. At their colleges, Jesuits gave the Spiritual Exercises and established Marian congregations for the spiritual formation of their students and the promotion of charitable works. They also founded Marian congregations for urban men but refused to provide leadership for sodalities of women, especially in the Rhineland. Their rural missions emphasized preaching, catechesis, the hearing of confessions, and the visitation of the sick. Philipp Jeningen (1642–1704) was the most popular missionary in Upper Germany. In the second half of the seventeenth century, Jesuit missions in Austria often aimed at converting Protestants to Catholicism. In the Apostolic Vicariate of Nordic Missions, erected in 1667, Jesuits of the Lower Rhenish province provided pastoral care to Catholic minority communities in Protestant northern Germany, Denmark, and Sweden. Jesuits of the Bohemian province did the same in Protestant Saxony (Dresden, Leipzig). The German and Austrian provinces produced eager missionaries who ministered in Asia and Latin America in the seventeenth and eighteenth centuries.

See also Canisius, Peter, SJ, St.; German-Speaking Lands

Duhr, Bernhard, *Geschichte der Jesuiten in den Ländern deutscher Zunge.* 4 vols. Freiburg im
    Breisgau: Herder, 1907–13; Munich-Regensburg: Verlagsanstalt vorm. G. J. Manz, 1921–28.

Hilmar M. Pabel

Hong Kong

There had been many Jesuit missions to China prior to 1926 when two Irish Jesuits, Fr. George Byrne and Fr. John Neary, arrived there. Preceded centuries earlier in China by Italian Jesuit Fathers Michele Ruggieri and Matteo Ricci, who went there in the late sixteenth century, and followed by many others in the intervening years, the Irish Jesuits arrived in Hong Kong at a time when five provinces of the Society already had mission districts in China: Paris, Champagne, Castile, Leon, and Turin. When the Irish Jesuit province, encouraged by the foundation of the Maynooth (Ireland) mission to China in 1916, opened itself to the possibility of undertaking a mission in China, space was sought for it initially within the territory of the original – and extensive – Paris mission. And then, in 1926, a new apostolic vicar, Fr. Henry Valtorta, was appointed to the vicariate of Hong Kong. Italian priests had been working there but had had little success on the higher social and intellectual levels. So Bishop Valtorta wanted help, and his preference was for English-speaking priests. This prompted him to invite the Irish Jesuit province to send men to his diocese. And so it was that Jesuits from Ireland went to Hong Kong.

Within a decade, a small number of resourceful men, led by Fr. George Byrne, had more than fulfilled the Bishop's hopes. They established the basic framework for the future: providing lecturers in Hong Kong University; establishing a university hostel for Catholic students – Ricci Hall; managing and teaching in the Regional Seminary; editing the *Rock*, a quality magazine that had a circulation well beyond Hong Kong; running a successful school for Chinese pupils, Wah Yan College; and silencing the atheistic critics, who were a worry to the Bishop, by lectures, articles, and a challenge to public debate. In addition, a Chinese language school for newly arrived Jesuits had been set up in South China. Moreover, individual Jesuits visited China to give lectures and direct retreats for clergy and religious congregations. Their work in China and Hong Kong led the bishop of Canton to invite them to take over the running of primary and secondary schools in his diocese. After consideration, the offer was not accepted because of government restrictions on what was to be taught in the schools.

In 1941 the siege of Hong Kong resulted in the Japanese occupation. Most of the Irish Jesuits dispersed to Macau, Free China, and India. Some of the experiences of those remaining were indicated in *Jesuits under Fire*, by Fr. Tom Ryan, editor of the *Rock* and perhaps the most influential of the Irish Jesuits. He had worked with the Anglican bishop of Hong Kong by providing houses for workers (today a block of apartments is called after him – in his Chinese name). He influenced Fr. Joe Howatson in establishing his celebrated Shoeshine Boys Clubs. He was an inspiring teacher in Wah Yan College, gave public lectures on the local radio, and was music critic in a Hong Kong daily newspaper. During the war he worked in China on behalf of an international aid organization, and subsequently was appointed minister for forestry and agriculture in the Hong Kong Government. His appointment as superior of the mission came as no surprise. During his term he gave encouragement to younger men to undertake new ventures. Thus, Fr. Michael Morahan worked among the boat people, establishing the first school for their children and providing a football club and a playing pitch for them. Characteristically, he also became a welfare officer to the police and, with the approval of their superiors, drew up a code of practice for them.

Fr. Patrick McGovern was encouraged to study industrial relations. He became a leading figure in the field and was appointed to the Legislative Council of Hong Kong. Fr. Ryan expanded the workload of Wah Yan College by adding a special school for underprivileged children. In China, a school was established in Canton, links were made with university students, and a lectureship was obtained in Canton University. This Canton venture, however, had to be abandoned when Communist forces took over the region.

The next venture out of Hong Kong was in the 1960s, when foundations were made in Singapore and Malaysia. There, Irish Jesuits took part in Church work, in running a university hostel, acting as chaplains in third-level colleges, and participating in radio programs. In Hong Kong, a second Wah Yan College had been established across the harbor in Kowloon. A Residence for students was opened in the Chinese University. The Christian Life Community took on a new vitality. A Credit Union Movement was founded and other associations to meet social needs. Key principles of the *Spiritual Exercises* were applied to teaching in Jesuit schools, and later in other Catholic schools.

In time, the decline in religious vocations resulted in fewer and older Irish Jesuits. Meanwhile, however, there had been a modest growth in local vocations, and so, increasingly, the main burden of the apostolic activity passed to the Chinese colleagues of the aging Irish Jesuits and also to Catholic Chinese men and women. Native Hong Kong Jesuit Fr. William Lo served as regional superior for a time and other local Jesuits held important positions too. Jesuits today can take encouragement from the achievements of the Irish Jesuit mission to Hong Kong: the two Wah Yan Colleges, from which have emerged many committed Catholics and well-disposed non-Catholics, persons prominent in medicine, law, education, business, government and politics; the Regional Seminary, which has prepared priests to serve in China and beyond; a number of local vocations to the Society; the influence down the years of Ricci Hall; the effectiveness of the Christian Life Communities; the warm appreciation of Jesuits' work in Malaysia and Singapore; and the overall good will and respect that the Jesuits generated through their lives and work in Hong Kong.

See also China; Ireland

Morrissey, Thomas J., *Jesuits in Hong Kong, South China and Beyond: Irish Jesuit Mission – Its development 1926–2006*. Hong Kong: Xavier Publishing Association, 2009.

Thomas J. Morrissey, SJ

Hopkins, Gerard Manley, SJ (1844–1889)

One of the most original and influential voices on poetry of the twentieth and twenty-first century, the nineteenth-century Jesuit poet and priest Gerard Manley Hopkins went virtually unnoticed in his own short lifetime – he died of typhoid at the age of 44 – having published virtually nothing. The oldest of Manley and Kate (Smith) Hopkins's nine children, Hopkins was born on July 28, 1844, into a family of High Church Anglicans. His father was a London-based marine insurance adjuster who published a slim volume the year his oldest son was born. From the age of 10 until 19, the handsome, ascetic-looking Hopkins attended the renowned Highgate grammar school, winning a prize for his poem "The Escorial" and subsequently earning a scholarship to Balliol College, Oxford, which he attended between 1863 and 1867. And while the Pre-Raphaelites and Ruskin had an influence on the way in which Hopkins saw things, it was to poetry that he was most deeply drawn, his early poems especially influenced by Keats and Wordsworth, as well as by the religious sensibilities of two fellow Anglicans: George Herbert and Christina Rossetti.

At Oxford, he and other students came under the influence of the Tractarians, Anglican ministers who were searching for a way back to the original vision of the Catholic Church. In this way he sought out the writings of Blessed John Henry Newman, who had converted from Anglicanism to Roman Catholicism in 1845, and whose influence proved so strong that Hopkins asked to be received into the Catholic Church by Newman in 1866. Under the tutelage of the young Walter Pater and Benjamin Jowett, who called Hopkins "the star of Balliol," Hopkins graduated from Oxford a year later with First Class honours in Classics and "Greats," an exceptional feat in itself.

After teaching students at Newman's Birmingham Oratory and searching among the Benedictines and Franciscans, Hopkins joined the Society of Jesus and entered their novitiate in Roehampton in the fall of 1868. Believing that poetry was not something in which a Jesuit priest should indulge, he burned many of his early poems. But his Jesuit superiors, knowing Hopkins's poetic gifts, encouraged him in the writing of occasional pieces – in English, Latin, Greek, and Welsh, the last of which he learned in his three years studying theology at St. Beuno's in North Wales. The complex, playful, internal chiming evident in Welsh poetry, together with his understanding of early English poetry, and his reading of the medieval Franciscan philosopher Duns Scotus, with his emphasis on the *haecceitas* or the distinctive "thisness" of everything in creation, as well as his insights into the inscape and instress to be found in language, all came together when, in December 1875, he began writing his great ode, "The Wreck of the Deutschland," commemorating the sinking of a German passenger ship in which five Franciscan nuns, exiled by the German Second Reich and bound for the United States, perished off the coast of England. It was the final cry of one of the nuns in the midst of the havoc – "O Christ, come quickly" – which haunted the young Jesuit and which forced him to utter aloud his own deepest cry in the form of a profoundly brilliant poem which even his fellow Jesuits found too radical to publish, so that it would not see the light of publication until long after Hopkins's death.

In the months leading up to his ordination in September 1877, he wrote some of the world's most well-known sonnets, including "God's Grandeur" and "The Windhover." His overworked superiors tried finding him a position that would best fit his talents and strengths, serving as a preacher at Farm Street in London, then in the working-class section of Oxford, followed by three years working in the slums of Manchester, Liverpool, and Glasgow. In September 1881, the 37-year-old Jesuit spent ten months back at Roehampton completing his tertianship, after which he was assigned to Stonyhurst College in Lancashire to teach Latin and Greek. In February 1884, he was appointed

Professor of Greek and Latin at University College, Dublin, which – given the squalid conditions then prevalent in Ireland as a result of Britain's socioeconomic neglect and the subsequent rise of Irish nationalism – proved to be an extremely trying and depressing time for the lone English Jesuit in Ireland. Never robust, he found his work as an examiner and lecturer overwhelming. As a Fellow in Classics for the Royal University of Ireland, he was also responsible for grading thousands of exam papers each year.

It was here, then, that he spent his last five years, during which he underwent a particularly difficult dark night of the soul and also wrote his extraordinary "terrible" sonnets, terror-filled and awe-inspiring, reminding one of the poems of St. John of the Cross and influencing later generations of poets as diverse as Stevens, Auden, Hart Crane, Bishop, Lowell, Merton, Berryman, and Seamus Heaney, among so many others. In his last year – the depression lifted – he composed his extraordinary "That Nature is a Heraclitean Fire and in the Comfort of the Resurrection," his sonnet for his fellow Jesuit St. Alphonsus Rodriguez, and his final poem, in which he subtly explained to his closest friend, Robert Bridges, who could never understand why Hopkins had chosen to become a Jesuit – that if others saw his life as a wreck – he himself had come to see that the Holy Spirit had seen him through the refining fire. His last words, as he lay dying at 44 of typhoid fever on June 8, 1889, were, "I am so happy. I am so happy."

It was only in 1918, nearly thirty years after his death, that Bridges, then England's poet laureate, brought out a volume of his poems in an edition of 750 copies, which took ten years to sell. After that, however, Hopkins's poetic reputation spread – and still spreads – like some Pentecostal wildfire.

See also Poetry; United Kingdom

The Collected Works of Gerard Manley Hopkins. Ed. R. K. R. Thornton and Catherine Phillips. Oxford: Oxford University Press, 2006.
Mariani, Paul, *Gerard Manley Hopkins: A Life*. New York: Viking, 2008.
Phillips, Catherine, *Gerard Manley Hopkins and the Victorian Visual World*. Oxford: Oxford University Press, 2007.
Pomplun, Trent, "The Theology of Gerard Manley Hopkins: From John Duns Scotus to the Baroque." *Journal of Religion* 95, 1 (2015), 1–34.

Paul Mariani

Humanism, Renaissance

Sixteenth-century Jesuits, beginning with Ignatius and his companions at the University of Paris, received a philosophical and theological education that was rooted in medieval scholasticism, with its use of the Vulgate Bible and its emphases on logic, dialectic, and disputation. And yet they also were, in varying degrees, at least exposed to humanist ideals of a return to the classical languages and literature of ancient Greece and Rome, and in the humanist emphasis on oratory, rhetoric, eloquence, and on the "good" (moral) life. In addition to a rebirth of the Classics, "humanism" in the Renaissance has also been portrayed as an optimistic anthropology, a view of human beings and human nature that put more stress on the human being as in the image of God than as a fallen, depraved sinner and that celebrated human freedom to choose to imitate Christ and do the good, or to choose to do otherwise. It is fair to say that from the first generation of Jesuits onward, in Jesuit schools

Figure 27 Michael Flecky, SJ: Roman Amphitheater at Dougga, Tunisia, photograph, 1981. Photograph Michael Flecky, SJ

and in other Jesuit works, humanist perspectives such as these played a major role, even as scholasticism proved very resilient in Jesuit contexts.

Though first published in the nineteenth century, Jacob Burckhardt's *The Civilization of the Renaissance in Italy* continues to influence how historians talk about topics such as Renaissance humanism. Burckhardt emphasized an individualism that displaced a medieval focus on community and other groups that constituted one's identity. Burckhardt also posited a secularizing tendency in the Renaissance that few historians today would see as adequately describing that era. A kind of focus on the individual does play a key part in the *Spiritual Exercises* of Ignatius, and thus in Jesuit attitudes and values. Ignatius was convinced that God acts immediately in the life of an individual, and not exclusively through the mediation of the sacraments and the clergy. In this view, the individual is free to respond favorably or unfavorably to God's call and God's grace, to choose to follow Christ or Satan. Such a view of human freedom carried over into Jesuit pedagogy where students in Jesuit schools were challenged to use their freedom and develop their abilities in ways that served God and their neighbor.

And yet if "secular" is not a suitable adjective for Jesuit education, John O'Malley has emphasized that Jesuit schools served a cultural and civic mission at least as much as a pastoral or spiritual one. The curriculum in sixteenth- or seventeenth-century Jesuit colleges focused heavily on "pagan" authors such as Cicero and Vergil, and many Jesuits knew Cicero better than they did the Bible. Promotion of the common good was central to the purpose of Jesuit education, and this education was understood to include preparation of young men for a variety of careers such as law and civil service, where the ability to speak well and persuasively would be critical to success. The sixteenth century was an era when the printing press, invented in Germany *c.* 1450, spread rapidly not only in what became Protestant territories but in Catholic territories as well. From the sixteenth century onward, many Jesuits were prolific writers, in Latin but also in various vernaculars, and Jesuit houses and schools often amassed exceptionally large and diverse libraries that were the envy of many. Jesuit schools also promoted theater, using plays as a way to teach students how to perform well in public, and how to use language effectively. Study of ancient authors included study of poets, and some Jesuits themselves were poets. Jesuit pedagogy relied on images as well as words; Jesuits were important patrons of major and minor artists, and by the 1600s some Jesuits were themselves significant artists or architects.

The first hundred years or so (1540–c. 1640) of the Society corresponds to what many historians label as the late Renaissance, and a period when Renaissance ideas and ideals, such as humanism, spread far beyond Italy. As Jesuits traveled far beyond Italy and beyond Europe, humanism was a key part of the cultural goods they carried with them. And as Jesuits moved into later periods, in the seventeenth and eighteenth centuries, and then in the restored Society post-1814, they continued to carry with them humanist ideals and practices that both formed and informed them, and by which they formed and educated others. In the twenty-first century, while some Jesuit educational institutions have moved away from an education in the arts and sciences to a more narrow technical training, others continue to embody core ideals of Renaissance humanism.

See also Education, Secondary and Pre-Secondary; Erasmus; Formation; *Ratio Studiorum*; Rhetoric(s); Universities, 1540–1773

Burckhardt, Jacob, *The Civilization of the Renaissance in Italy*. Trans. S. G. C. Middlemore. London: Penguin, 1990.

Gannett, Cinthia, and John Brereton, eds., *Traditions of Eloquence: The Jesuits and Modern Rhetorical Studies*. New York: Fordham University Press, 2016.

Giard, Luce, "The Jesuit College: A Center for Knowledge, Art, and Faith 1548–1773." *Studies in the Spirituality of Jesuits* 40, 1 (Spring 2008), 1–31.

Haskell, Yasmin Annabel, *Loyola's Bees: Ideology and Industry in Jesuit Latin Didactic Poetry*. Oxford: Oxford University Press, 2003.

O'Malley, John W., "Five Missions of the Jesuit Charism: Content and Method." *Studies in the Spirituality of Jesuits* 38, 4 (Winter 2006), 1–33.

Thomas Worcester, SJ

Humility, Three Degrees of

When Ignatius wrote the *Spiritual Exercises* in the early sixteenth century, humility had long been key to monastic communal life and had become increasingly central to lay Christian devotional life in the late medieval era. Notably, the writings of the *devotio moderna*, a lay Christian movement oriented toward imitation of the humiliated and suffering Christ, were influential among early modern Catholics, the founder of the Jesuit order included.

Ignatius addressed the topic of humility in three degrees, or stages, in his *Spiritual Exercises*. To understand the importance of the three stages of spiritual advancement toward the third and highest degree of humility, one must appreciate Ignatius's conception of humility as a virtuous disposition to be cultivated. Here one worked, in stages, to abandon one's own will and, guided by love of Christ, to conform to God's will, this process being crucial to decision-making, especially arriving at and maintaining one's vocation. Accordingly, during the Second Week of the Spiritual Exercises, when the exercitant is to make an election concerning one's vocation, the three degrees of humility are not presented as a meditation, per se, but rather, as dispositional notes intended to guide the practitioner to hone the proper spiritual state of mind and, in an attitude of faith, to abandon oneself, in de Guibert's words, to "the lowliness and opprobrium of the Cross."

Of the three degrees or stages, the first confirms the desire to be bound to love Christ. The second commits one to leave behind or become detached from personal preferences. The third and highest stage is to abandon oneself so as to deliberately favor identification with Christ poor and humiliated.

See also Inordinate Attachments; *Spiritual Exercises*

de Guibert, Joseph, *The Jesuits: Their Spiritual Doctrine and Practice*. Trans. William Young. Chicago, IL: The Institute of Jesuit Sources, 1964.

J. Michelle Molina

Hurtado, Alberto, SJ, St. (1901–1952)

Luis Alberto Miguel Hurtado Cruchaga was born in Viña del Mar, Chile, on January 22, 1901. His father died when he was 4 years old, leaving him to be raised by his mother Ana. Though the family suffered from financial constraints over the years, Hurtado was able to attend the Jesuit Colegio San Ignacio in Santiago. After the completion of his schooling, he studied law at the Catholic University in Santiago, graduating in 1921. He entered the Jesuit novitiate in Chillán in 1923.

His formation in the Society then followed the normal course: novitiate (1923–25), juniorate in Córdoba, Argentina (1925–27), and further studies in the Colegio Maximo in Barcelona, Spain (1927–31). The declaration of the Second Spanish Republic in April 1931 and the rise of anti-Catholicism forced his transfer to Louvain for theology studies (1931–33), where his rector was Jean-Baptiste Janssens, the future father general. These years of study exposed him to important works that would shape his dedication to the social apostolate, including the encyclicals *Divini illius magistri* (1929) and *Quadragesimo anno* (1931), as well as the theology of the Mystical Body developed in the work of Émile Mersch, SJ (1890–1940).

He was ordained on August 24, 1933, in Louvain. He remained for two more years in order to complete his doctorate in education with a thesis on the American pragmatist John Dewey. While working on the dissertation, he received a commission from the Chilean government to study European educational institutions, allowing him to visit Italy, France, Germany, and England – a tour that enlightened him to the common problems of greed and radical individualism within the contemporary intellectual formation of youth.

He returned to Chile in 1935, ending an eight-year absence. From 1936 to 1941 he taught at the Catholic University and the Pontifical Seminary in Santiago. In 1941, however, he accepted a mission that proved to be the ideal field for his talents: the adviser to youth in the Catholic Action movement. Through retreats, congresses, and small group encounters, he sought to invest the youth with a solid spiritual and catechetical formation that demanded direct engagement with the reformation of social structures. His success in this work unfortunately led to accusations of partisan involvement in politics and a cult of personality. Hurtado's concern over the negative perceptions of both the hierarchy and some of his Jesuit brethren drove him to resign in 1944.

The liberation from these duties proved to be a blessing, since it allowed Hurtado to establish the apostolate that would remain his greatest legacy. An encounter with a homeless man in 1944 so moved Hurtado that he recounted the incident with tears during a homily at a women's retreat, where he likened the man to Christ and declared, "Christ has no home!" ("Cristo no tiene hogar!"). With the enthusiastic support of a group of women, he founded a network of services for the homeless and the poor known as El Hogar de Cristo. The organization came to include shelters – which Hurtado always sought to make genuine homes, and not impersonal institutions – and dormitories for the formation of abandoned youth. He also created an associated fraternity in 1950 for those collaborators who desired a genuine commitment to a simplicity of life and prayer within the Church.

Hurtado made other major contributions to the world of publishing and social action. He founded the journal *Mensaje* for the promotion of the Church's social apostolate and published his own writings on education and social reform, including *Es Chile un país Catolico?* (1941), *Humanismo social* (1947), and *Sindicalismo: historia, teoría, práctica* (1950). In 1947 he founded the Acción Sindical Chilena for the mobilization of leaders from the workers, intellectuals, government representatives, and members of the hierarchy in order to address the abuse of laborers and the need for a more just economic order.

In 1952 Hurtado's health began to deteriorate and doctors discovered that he had pancreatic cancer. In July he suffered two heart attacks and finally succumbed to his illness on August 18.

Though a controversial figure in his lifetime, even among his brother Jesuits, the importance of Hurtado's example and works became more and more evident in the Catholic Church after the Second Vatican Council. Initiatives such as El Hogar de Cristo and *Mensaje* continue to flourish and shape both the Church's and the Society's approach to social action. Pope Benedict XVI, who canonized Alberto Hurtado on October 23, 2005, declared that this humble member of the Society of Jesus was "a true contemplative in action."

See also Chile; Preferential Option for the Poor; Saints

Gavin, John, "'True Charity Begins Where Justice Ends': The Life and Teachings of St. Alberto Hurtado, SJ." *Studies in the Spirituality of Jesuits* 43, 4 (Winter 2011), 1–39.
Gilfeather, Katherine, *Alberto Hurtado: A Man after God's Own Heart*. Santiago: Fundacion Padre Alberto Hurtado, 2004.

John Gavin, SJ

Ignatian Spirituality Centers

Jesus's admonition to his tired apostles in Mark 6:31, "Come away by yourselves to a deserted place and rest a while," is at the heart of the mission of any modern-day Christian retreat center. But these centers, stand-alone facilities where one comes to spend time in intensive prayer, trace their roots back to the tradition of the Desert Fathers and the growth of Christian monasticism that flowed from their lives of prayer. And the explosive growth today in interest in all things "spiritual" means that spirituality centers have sprung up in many new places with many variations of form.

The birth of so-called traditional retreat houses traces its roots to the Desert Fathers, a collection of ascetics who lived in Egypt in the third century AD. These men moved into the desert in an attempt to flee the world, to embrace a solitude wherein they could focus solely on Christ's unique call to them. Over time, many others ventured into the desert to seek out these hermits, to discuss spiritual matters and obtain advice on how to order one's life. It could be said that this is the beginning of the ministry of spiritual direction, so important to the work of modern retreat centers: discussion of one's relationship with God with another.

Retreat centers often are tied to a specific spirituality, or way to God. Ignatian spirituality flows from the life of Ignatius, who was heavily influenced by the school of prayer he was exposed to at the Benedictine monastery in Montserrat. In his time there, Ignatius learned to contemplate and meditate; his experiences would form the basis for his *Spiritual Exercises* and the spirituality that would bear his name. Ignatian spirituality is based on an incarnational worldview, an understanding that God, having come into the world as Jesus Christ, both fully human and fully divine, has touched the world and imbued it with God's very self. It is this understanding that has led to the Ignatian aphorism that one might come to "find God in all things." Many have encountered God through this unique lens and indeed been transformed by being led through the *Spiritual Exercises* in which exercitants come to know this incarnate God in the figure of Jesus Christ.

Though the focus of Jesuit ministry has long been located in cities (as opposed to the life of the Desert Fathers and the monastic communities previously mentioned), many of today's Jesuit retreat houses offer places for a brief retreat from the city before returning to life and work in it. At these "traditional" Jesuit retreat houses, preached weekend retreats or directed retreats of five, eight, or thirty days are commonplace. In addition to these formats, many Jesuit retreat houses offer programs for those in recovery from substance abuse, partnering with twelve-step groups whose focus reframes the Ignatian ideals of interior freedom, detachment, indifference, and dependence on God.

Many of these same retreat houses also offer spiritually enriching sabbatical programs as well as programs to train spiritual directors. Still others offer opportunities for travel on pilgrimage, to walk in the footsteps of Ignatius in Paris, Spain, and Rome. Traditional retreat houses like these can be found in Jesuit provinces all over the world and include Loyola House in Guelph, Ontario, Canada; St. Beuno's Spirituality Centre in Wales, UK; the Centro Espiritualidad Loyola in Loyola, Spain; Notre Dame de la Route in Friboug, Switzerland; and Eastern Point Retreat House in Gloucester, Massachusetts, USA, among others.

Also of note is the recent addition of non-traditional centers for Ignatian spirituality that have become great resources in a variety of places. Many of these centers thrive in large metropolitan areas where the nineteenth annotation form of the *Exercises*, often called "the retreat in daily life," is popular and viable (see the Loyola Institute for Spirituality in Orange, California, USA, as an example). Centers for Ignatian spirituality can also be found among special populations or specific ethnic groups, like the Sioux Spiritual Center on the Native American reservation in South Dakota, USA.

Finally, other centers can be found on college and university campuses, serving as resources for faculty, staff, and students that bring the rich tradition of Ignatian spirituality into dialogue with other areas of academic life, especially in teaching pedagogy and the field of service learning. Centers like those located at Boston College, Fairfield University, Marquette University, Loyola Marymount University, and Creighton University, all in the United States, help to keep the incarnational worldview of Ignatius alive, by striving to help the various constituencies in the world of academia discover God's active presence in their various disciplines, extracurricular activities, scholarly work, indeed, "in all things."

See also Direction, Spiritual; *Spiritual Exercises*

Fleming, David, *What Is Ignatian Spirituality?* Chicago, IL: Loyola Press, 2008.
The Spiritual Exercises of St. Ignatius: Based on Studies in the Language of the Autograph. Trans. Louis J. Puhl. Chicago, IL: Loyola University Press, 1951.

Keith Maczkiewicz, SJ

IHS Monogram

The IHS monogram, an abbreviation of the Greek form of the name of Jesus, is arguably the most prominent visual icon of the Society of Jesus, marking in some fashion virtually all Jesuit establishments and important documents. It is also the central element in the official seal of the Society, as designed and used during St. Ignatius's generalate. Even before founding the Society, Ignatius had frequently inserted the monogram in his letters and other writings, this a manifestation of his intense devotion to the Holy Name of Jesus, after whom were eventually named his new religious order and its mother church in Rome. (Note that, contrary to what is often affirmed, the IHS does not represent the initials of the Latin phrase, *Iesus Hominum Salvator*.) Although today most associated with the Jesuits, the IHS monogram had been popularized by Observant Franciscan preacher Bernardino of Siena (d. 1444) as emblem of his new cult of the Holy Name of Jesus, which he succeeded in inserting into the mainstream of Catholic devotion. The Franciscan himself designed the icon's original form, a tablet featuring the IHS in Gothic minuscules surrounded by the rays of the sun. Lay people readily affixed the monogram to their homes and even their dress, encouraged by Bernardino's emphasis on its apotropaic power. As explained in Bernardino's sermons, the scriptural foundation for his new devotion was the Christological hymn of Philippians 2:3–10 (in the official Jesuit seal, therefore, the presence of the moon and the stars below the IHS refers to Philippians 2:10). After Bernardino's death, the exponential growth and phenomenal influence of the Franciscan Observant movement disseminated Bernardino's Holy Name devotion, along with its visual icon, throughout Europe, including the Basque country. Indeed, as historian Pacelli reports, it decorated the very crib of the infant Iñigo of Loyola.

See also Loyola, Ignatius of, SJ, St.

Pacelli, Vincenzo, "Il 'monogramma' bernardiniano: origine, diffusione e sviluppo." In Francesco D'Episcopo, ed., *S. Bernardino da Siena predicatore e Pellegrino*. Galatina: Congedo Editore, 1985, pp. 253–60.

Figure 28 IHS monogram on façade of the Church of Il Gesù, Rome, 16th century.
Photograph Alison Fleming

Pfeiffer, Heinrich, "IHS: The Monogram of the Society of Jesus." In *The Jesuits: Yearbook of the Society
of Jesus 2003*. Rome: General Curia of the Society of Jesus, 2003, pp. 12–15.

Franco Mormando

IHSI

See Institutum Historicum Societatis Iesu

Images

Imagery played a significant role in the spiritual development of Ignatius of Loyola,
from the time of his spiritual conversion through the last days of his life in Rome. After
his injury in battle at Pamplona in 1521, Ignatius cultivated mental images of the lives
of Christ, St. Francis, and St. Dominic, as a result of reading Jacopus de Voragine's
Golden Legend (thirteenth century) and Ludolph of Saxony's *Life of Jesus Christ* (fourteenth century) during his convalescence. These mental pictures of his new role models
would serve as his inspiration going forward when he found himself alone in seclu-
sion in Manresa and in traveling to the Holy Land. The concepts of envisioning and

imitating were thus firmly established early in the spiritual life of the Jesuit founder, which led rapidly to his development of this signature Jesuit practice in what became known as the *Spiritual Exercises*. During his period of retreat in Manresa, Ignatius cultivated this regimen of contemplation and prayer. The method begins with an effort to focus on *compositio loci*, or "composition of place." Ignatius believed that a visualization of the specific place where an event occurred, and an engagement of all of the senses, would aid in a better understanding of Christ. The goal is for participants to "place themselves" into the scene through a clear mental image, resulting in deeper prayer and meditation. From this point forward, Ignatius regularly led others through this process, and it evolved into an important aspect of what would eventually become the Society of Jesus. The *Spiritual Exercises* are still an important aspect of Jesuit formation. In this way, Jesuits have always cultivated the practice of visualization and imagination, and the practice has significantly influenced their creation of visual images.

After the formal establishment of the Order in 1540, Jesuit art proliferated, and a wide variety of images were created and commissioned by the Jesuits to aid in their pursuit of edification and devotion. Francis Borja, superior general of the Society (1565–72), specifically recommended the use of art to assist in meditation. The guided meditation of the *Spiritual Exercises* may be likened to the process through which the reader navigates and reflects upon the gospel images in Jerome Nadal's *Adnotationes et meditationes in Evangelia* (Antwerp, 1595). This illustrated gospel may be regarded as one of the very first artistic commissions of the Jesuits. Detailed engravings by the Wierix workshop allow viewers to "place themselves" in each scene through letters embedded in the images that guide the viewer through the scene visually and relate to accompanying text that elucidates the episode. These directed images were utilized extensively by Jesuits, not only in the teaching of novices but also in the missions to China, India, and South America. The frescoes by Niccolò Circignani in the Jesuit Church of Santo Stefano Rotondo in Rome depicting the martyrdoms of early Christian saints are similarly executed, with a direct relationship between text and image. In terms of the act of viewing and responding, both projects may be linked to the *Spiritual Exercises* in a general fashion. In recent decades, there has been much debate on Jesuit imagery in painted church decoration and how literally the *Spiritual Exercises* were employed by artists and patrons. While contemporary scholarship sees a less direct relationship, the keen interest the Jesuits developed in imagery, as a product of their meditational practices, cannot be ignored.

As is true with other religious orders, the Jesuits have employed images extensively in their missionary work. Visual representations had long served as the "books of the illiterate" in medieval Europe, and non-textual forms of communication were equally essential in dealing with native cultures, particularly when the language skills of the missionaries were not well developed. The Jesuits quickly learned and adopted alternate means of gaining notice, proselytizing, and imparting key concepts. In his letters to Ignatius and the Society in Europe, Francis Xavier described his attempts to connect with those with whom he did not share a common language. In addition to walking down streets ringing a bell to capture their attention and using music to teach prayers and lessons, images became indispensable aids in sharing information. These images were often in the form of prints, but also oil paintings, brought from Europe. In China in the 1580s, missionaries including Michele Ruggieri repeatedly wrote to Europe requesting images be sent to them; they primarily desired images of Christ and illustrations from the Bible. Matteo Ricci noted the necessity of images in general, and specifically praised the usefulness of Jerome Nadal's illustrated gospel in communicating concepts that simply could not be expressed adequately with words. Xavier himself brought two paintings of the Virgin Mary to be used in proselytizing when he entered Japan in August of 1549. But artistic images could also serve as currency, especially in the form of gifts to persuade, or pave the way: a thesis print by Anton Albert Schmerling (University of Vienna, 1690) depicts Francis Xavier presenting a printed image of the Virgin Mary to the daimyo of Bungo. To this end, other accounts complain that missionaries left Europe with hundreds of pictures but arrived at their destination having given them all away.

Soon, the Society recognized the overwhelming need for images in Asia, and the high cost of sending them there, not to mention the time required to wait for their arrival. Luís Froís reported from Japan in 1584 that more than 50,000 devotional images were needed to satisfy the present demand. This necessitated the export of a printing press to Japan in 1587. Earlier in the decade, a school to train local artists, the Seminary of Painters, was established at Arima, which also assisted in the production of devotional images. Finally, an incident recorded in Nagasaki, in 1633, reminds us of the powerful role of devotional imagery in the missionary context. A "foot-treading ceremony" was held, forcing Japanese citizens to renounce Christianity by walking on images (including paintings, prints, and sculptures), many of them created by the Seminary of Painters. From the very start of the missions, the Jesuits were keenly aware of the power of images – for devotion, for instruction, for communication – and they utilized a variety of means to send images to foreign lands, or create them on site, and sought to preserve and protect them.

Other images important to the Jesuits are hagiographic. With the canonization of the first Jesuit saints in 1622, the focus of image creation shifted from the imitation of Christ and early Christian martyrs to the illustration of the lives and miracles of Ignatius and Francis Xavier, both on the walls of churches and on the printed page. These images were used in devotional practice, as aids in prayer and meditation, and employed for didactic purposes, to communicate and teach. Images, especially in printed form, have long been used to spread ideas, concepts, and representations, and have even been attributed with miracles of healing. In the early seventeenth century, illustrated biographies of saints (or those being promoted for that status) began to appear with regularity. They were typically produced with detailed engravings outlining significant events and miraculous episodes in the figure's life, accompanied by captions, usually written in Latin. Depending on the subject, they ranged from modest books incorporating a dozen or so illustrations, to elaborate collections of as many as one hundred images, relating the biography in great detail. The first illustrated biography of this type connected to the Society of Jesus was the *Vita beati patris Ignatii Loiolae*, printed in Rome in 1609 to commemorate the beatification of Ignatius, but designed in the years preceding that event in order to promote his cause. This *vita* comprised seventy-nine engravings by Jean-Baptiste Barbé and was reprinted in 1622 with an additional image of the canonization of Ignatius. Widely distributed and still extant in many copies today, it is the most celebrated life of the Jesuit founder. This fame is in part due to the fact that many of the engravings were based on drawings made by Peter Paul Rubens. However, it was only the first of many *vitae* of this type. In the year after the beatification of Ignatius, the Galle workshop in Antwerp produced an elaborate, illustrated edition of Pedro Ribadeneira's biography, the *Vita beati patris Ignatii Loyolae religionis Societatis Iesu fundatoris*. This large-format work includes only sixteen plates (including the title page) but effectively utilizes the didactic format popularized by Circignani's frescoes of martyrdom and Nadal's illustrated gospels, with letters within the image tied to text below. In this case, parts of each image are connected to specific passages from Ribadeneira's textual biography. This allows each page to include myriad details that might occupy multiple engravings in other *vitae* and draw the viewer more deeply into the story.

The Wierix workshop, also in Antwerp, printed an illustrated biography of the blessed Ignatius in this period, and after his canonization numerous others were produced. These include the *Vita Sancti Ignatii* with thirty-one engravings by Petrus Firens (Paris, c. 1622–38), *S. Ignatii Loyolae Soc. Iesu Fundatoria quaedam Miracula* with twenty engravings by Valérien Regnard (Rome, c. 1622–30), and the *Vita Sancti Ignatii Loiola, Societatis Iesu Fundatoris* with one hundred engravings by Wolfgang Kilian (Augsburg, 1622). An analysis of the scenes represented (or omitted) in each *vita*, as well as the size, scale, and format of the books, reveals that each one was produced with a slightly different focus, ranging from descriptive or documentary to didactic, meditative, or devotional. The images of Firens and Regnard include captions written in vernacular languages in addition to Latin to broaden the audience beyond members of the Society and into the lay community. Regnard also produced an illustrated biography of Francis Xavier, canonized with Ignatius; both books are thought to reproduce the paintings hung on and around the Church of the Gesù at the time of their elevation to sainthood. Other *vitae* of the missionary appeared throughout the seventeenth and eighteenth centuries, as did those of later Jesuits saints, such as Aloysius Gonzaga. The diverse purposes and audiences of these *vitae* resulted in the broad transmission of persuasive, educational, and engaging images, frequently establishing key iconographical elements of the lives of Jesuit saints.

The Jesuits cultivated a keen interest in icons, especially the one known as the *Hodegetria* or *Salus populi romani*, preserved in the Church of Santa Maria Maggiore in Rome. A half-length portrait of the Virgin Mary holding the Christ Child reputed to have been painted by the hand of St. Luke, it is likely a medieval Byzantine icon. Long venerated in Rome, it also had an association with healing. In 590 an abatement of the plague resulted from Pope Gregory the Great carrying the icon in a procession around the city. Pedro Ribadeneira, in his 1592 biography of Francis Borja, reveals that the General had a copy of the icon produced in 1569, with permission of the Pope, to encourage the faithful. From this, more copies were made and distributed to the missions in South America and Asia as well as disseminated throughout Europe. By the end of the century, versions were being venerated across the world, in novitiates, professed houses, and schools. One copy was sent on the 1570 voyage of Ignatius Azevedo and his thirty-nine companions to Brazil. The ship was attacked en route by Huguenots, yet the sacred image miraculously survived. It made its way to Brazil, damaged by water and blood, according to the vision of the episode experienced by Teresa of Avila, which also helped solidify the cause of the missionaries for beatification as martyrs. According to a letter of 1596, another hung in the building that housed the Seminary of Painters in Japan. Still another copy was sent to the Jesuit College in Ingolstadt, in southern Germany. A significant Marian devotion sprang up around the image, which became known as the "Mater ter admirabilis," causing copies to be made of it that were disseminated through Bavaria. The visions, healings, and other miracles associated with these images are well documented by the Jesuits in letters, testimonials related to canonization processes, and other official accounts.

In 1583 Jesuit Visitor Alessandro Valignano ordered the creation of a portrait of Francis Xavier to be made from his extraordinarily well-preserved corpse in Goa in an effort to promote the missionary for beatification. Two images were created: one stayed in Goa and the other was sent to Rome. Neither original is extant, but numerous copies were made and circulated widely. These are the basis for the standard iconography of images of Xavier that proliferated in various forms (paintings, drawings, and prints) throughout the early modern period. Although these portraits are copies, they were regarded as imbuing the healing power of the saint himself. During the outbreak of bubonic plague in Naples in 1656, large numbers of people sought the healing power of a painted image of Xavier, a copy of the Goa portrait – and copies of the copy that circulated in printed form. The power of this particular image was due in part to its role in the 1634 recovery of Jesuit priest Marcello Mastrilli. He suffered a near-fatal head injury, and doctors were unable to stop the internal bleeding. Mastrilli asked for the image of Xavier to be placed next to his bed, and the saint spoke to him, ordering that a relic of the Holy Cross be placed on his wound, and even reaching out to direct the placement specifically. He asked Mastrilli if he would prefer to die, or to retrace the saint's missionary route through Asia. The wounded man eagerly accepted his fate as a martyr; he was killed in Nagasaki on October 14, 1537. On his way to Japan, he stopped in Goa to venerate the relics of Xavier in the Church of Bom Jesus. Determining that the silver casket was too plain, he commissioned a new covering, which allowed for thirty-two relief panels, which were completed in 1637, to illustrate the life and miracles of Xavier, including his posthumous healing of Mastrilli. The miracle-working portrait of Xavier remained in Naples, waiting to protect her citizens from the plague decades later, while a print voyaged to Asia with Mastrilli.

Visual images have played an extensive and powerful role in the Society of Jesus since its foundation. Today, the Society continues to embrace representations of Jesuit saints and Christological images, and contemporary artistic commissions reflect this tradition. For example, Seattle University's St. Ignatius Chapel (Steven Holl Architects, 1997), an airy and open space with extraordinary lighting effects, showcases traditional images of St. Ignatius in unexpected and modern ways. Icons in the narthex, painted by Bulgarian artist Dora Nikolova Bittau, highlight key moments in Ignatius's spiritual development, including *Wounded at Pamplona*, *Transformed at the River Cardoner*, and the *Confirmed in Mission at La Storta*. These works reinforce concepts deemed significant by the Society since the lifetime of its founder, in a modern style. A carpet below the icons, designed by the architect, portrays an abstracted waterway representing the River Cardoner and serves to both direct worshippers into the chapel and remind them of the transformational experience of Ignatius at that site.

Jesuit artists themselves offer both modern interpretations of these timeless subjects and new images that reflect various facets of Jesuit spirituality. Twentieth-century French Jesuit painter André Bouler communicated his spirituality through exuberant color. Mixed-media artist Sammy Chong creates installations that interpret contemporary spiritual concerns. Slovenian Jesuit Marko Rupnik works in the traditional medium of mosaic, continuing to re-envision religious subjects as his predecessors in the Society have long done. Seattle-based Trung Pham explores human relationships in painting. Images by these artists, and others, are found in Jesuit churches and chapels, schools and residences, and exhibited publicly in museums and galleries.

Magno apparatu à Rege Bungi excipitur
XAV: quem donatâ B: Virginis jcone ad
conversionem disponit.   2.ᵉ

Figure 29 Anton Albert Schmerling: *St. Francis Xavier Giving a Printed Image to the King of Bungo*, 1690, engraving. Jesuitica Collection, John J. Burns Library, Boston College. Photograph Alison Fleming

Jesuits since the nineteenth century have embraced photography for its documentary advantages as well as for artistic purposes. Images of Jesuits around the world have been captured and shared as a result of this transformative medium. Jesuits continue to maintain museums, such as the Martin d'Arcy Collection at the Loyola (Chicago) University Museum of Art, to preserve and celebrate these images. Ignatius and the early Jesuits lived in an age of abundant imagery: they were surrounded by visual representations in their residences and spaces of worship, and they recognized the ability of printed images to be disseminated widely throughout the world. They actively employed all sorts of images for learning, communicating, and as a fundamental component of their devotional practice, establishing practices that continue to the present day. Few other religious orders have cultivated and maintained such a profound relationship with images.

See also Arts, Visual; Baroque Art and Architecture; Composition of Place; Imagination; Nadal, Jeronimo, SJ; Photography; Wierix Brothers

Bailey, Gauvin A., *Art on the Jesuit Missions in Asia and Latin America, 1542–1773*. Toronto: University of Toronto Press, 1999.

de Boer, Wietse, Karl A. E. Enenkel, and Walter S. Melion, eds., *Jesuit Image Theory*. Leiden: Brill, 2016.

Dekoninck, Ralph, *Ad imaginem: statuts, fonctions et usages de l'image dans la littérature spirituelle jésuite du XVIIe siècle*. Geneva: Droz, 2005.

Fleming, Alison, "The 'Roles' of Illustrations of the Life of St. Ignatius of Loyola." In Erminia Ardissino and Elisabetta Selmi, eds., *Visibile teologia: il libro sacro figurato in Italia tra Cinquecento e Seicento*. Rome: Edizioni di Storia e Letteratura, 2012, pp. 115–25.

Levy, Evonne, "Early Modern Jesuit Arts and Jesuit Visual Culture." *Journal of Jesuit Studies* 1 (2014), 66–87.

Nadal, Jerome, *Annotations and Meditations on the Gospels*. Trans. Frederick A. Homann, intro. Walter Melion. 3 vols. Philadelphia, PA: St. Joseph's University Press, 2003–05.

O'Malley John W., and James P. M. Walsh, *Constructing a Saint through Images: The 1609 Illustrated Biography of Ignatius of Loyola*. Philadelphia, PA: St. Joseph's University Press, 2008.

Oy-Marra, Elisabeth, and Volker Remmert, eds., *Le monde est une peinture: Jesuitische Identität und die Rolle der Bilder*. Berlin: Akademie Verlag, 2011.

San Juan, Rose Marie, *Vertiginous Mirrors: The Animation of the Visual Image and Early Modern Travel*. Manchester: Manchester University Press, 2011.

Standaert, Nicolas, "The Composition of Place: Creating Space for an Encounter." *The Way* 46, 1 (2007), 7–20.

Alison Fleming

Imagination

"Imagination" plays at least three distinct roles in Jesuit parlance.

In his *Spiritual Exercises* Ignatius invites retreatants to a "composition of place" in which they imagine a story or scene in the Bible. They then place themselves in that scene and engage in dialogue with one or more persons, Jesus, Mary or one of the disciples, or others. Here imagination serves to bridge the chasm between present circumstances and what could otherwise seem a distant, hard-to-relate-to past, the gap between the time of the historical Jesus and later centuries.

From the first generation of Jesuits on, Jesuit churches and other institutions, such as schools, were patrons of the arts, commissioning at times the best artists of the day. Painting and other visual media were used to teach, to move, and to delight audiences. Against accusations of idolatry by some Protestant reformers, Jesuits reaffirmed a Catholic privileging of images of Jesus and the saints, images that were valued as teaching one what to believe and how to live one's life in such a way that one would reach heaven and there enjoy forever the beatific vision. In recent decades many Jesuit universities have placed a growing emphasis on the arts, as may be seen with the creation and expansion of art galleries and museums often devoted principally to the visual arts.

Jesuit "imagination" may also refer to a way of thinking optimistically and expansively, looking to go out to all the world and change it for the better. Such an imagination is rooted in a theological perspective that sees the goodness of creation as revealing God's love; it is a point of view that confidently looks to a future in which grace and reconciliation and healing and mercy overcome sin and suffering. Jesuit imagination looks for, works for, and celebrates the triumph of good over evil, love over hatred, generosity over greed, humility over arrogance.

See also Baroque Art and Architecture; Composition of Place; Emblem Books; Images

de Boer, Wietse, Karl A. E. Enenkel, and Walter S. Melion, eds., *Jesuit Image Theory*. Leiden: Brill, 2016.

Fabre, Pierre-Antoine, *Ignace de Loyola: le lieu de l'image*. Paris: Vrin, 1992.

Greeley, Andrew, *The Catholic Imagination*. Berkeley: University of California Press, 2000.

Melion, Walter S., and Lee Palmer Wandel, eds., *Image and Incarnation: The Early Modern Doctrine of the Pictorial Image*. Leiden: Brill, 2015.

Steeves, Nicolas, *Grâce à l'imagination: intégrer l'imagination en théologie fondamentale*. Paris: Éditions du Cerf, 2016.

Thomas Worcester, SJ

Imago Primi Saeculi

The emblematic Latin work *Imago primi saeculi* (952 pages) was composed by faculty and students at the Jesuit college of Antwerp to mark the centenary of the Jesuit order in 1640. In five chapters of prose and poetry, it describes the foundation of the Society of Jesus, its growth, acts, suffering, and honors. A sixth chapter presents the history of the Flemish-Belgian province, instituted in 1612. Each chapter is followed by a "poetic exercise" in Latin, Greek, or Hebrew. The Italian art critic Mario Praz (1896–1982) described the *Imago* as "the celebration of celebrations, the triumphal arch erected by the Jesuits in rich, luxuriant scrolls, in bizarre and pompous cartouches."

Provincial Jan de Tollenaere was editor, Jean Bolland chief historian, Sidronius de Hossche and Jacques van de Walle poets, all from the southern Netherlands. Philip Fruytiers, Abraham van Diepenbeek, Cornelis Galle, and Michael Natalis were responsible for the many engravings. Balthasar Moretus of the famous Officina Plantiniana in Antwerp was its printer.

A Dutch translation appeared in the same year, the prose written by Laurens Uwens, great-nephew of Peter Canisius, and the poetry by young poet Adriaen Poirters, both born in the northern Netherlands. Contemporary Jesuit author Daniel van Papenbroeck (Papebrochius) confessed that the poems by Poirters often surpassed the Latin original.

Pascal made a satirical remark on the *Imago* in his *Lettres provinciales*.

See also Antwerp; Netherlands; Poetry

Insolera, Lydia Salviucci, *L'"Imago primi saeculi" e il significato dell'immagine allegorica nella Compagnia di Gesù: genesi e fortuna del libro*. Rome: Editrice Pontificia Università Gregoriana, 2004.

O'Malley, John W., ed., *Art, Controversy, and the Jesuits: The Imago Primi Saeculi (1640)*. Philadelphia, PA: St. Joseph's University Press, 2015.

Roggen, Lien, "Celebration Time: The *Imago primi saeculi* Societatis Iesu and Its Dutch Translation as Part of the Festivities of 1640 Commemorating the Jesuit Order's Centenary." In S. McKeown, ed., *The International Emblem: From Incunabula to the Internet*. Newcastle: Cambridge Scholars, 2010, pp. 170–200.

Paul Begheyn, SJ

Imitation of Christ

A devotional work whose popularity was greatly enhanced by the Society of Jesus, the *Imitatio Christi* is generally attributed to Thomas à Kempis. Originally composed in Latin in the 1420s, by 1500 the *Imitatio* existed in over 800 manuscripts and 100 printed editions. As an accessible and effective guide to spiritual development, it remained a bestseller and became a core component of the Jesuit tradition. Carlos Sommervogel identified sixty Jesuit translators of the *Imitatio*, resulting in more than 450 editions between 1600 and 1900. In addition to providing numerous Latin editions, the Jesuits translated the *Imitatio* into over twenty languages (including Chinese, Hungarian, Japanese, Malagasy, Tagalog, and Turkish). There was some doubt about who wrote the *Imitatio*. The acquisition in 1595 of an autograph manuscript by the Antwerp Jesuit college stimulated Jesuit participation in the authorship debate. Heribert Rosweyde and Henri de Sommal responded to alternative claimants by reproducing copious editions of the *Imitatio* with Kempis as author.

Jesuit promotion of the *Imitatio* owes much to Ignatius of Loyola's enthusiasm for the work. Gonçalves da Câmara's *Memoriale* suggests that Ignatius first "discovered" it at Manresa, though he probably acquired a copy from his Benedictine confessor, Jean Chanon. The *Imitatio* was recognized as Ignatius's preferred choice of devotional reading: Juan Polanco noted how Ignatius was pleased by that "golden book"; Jerónimo Nadal affirmed Ignatius's attachment to the *Imitatio* the year that he joined the Society; for Olivier Mannaerts the *Imitatio* was a treasured book ("the partridge of spiritual books") and was one of the few texts permanently on Ignatius's desk. Ignatius's recommendation was also mentioned in Pedro de Ribadeneira's official biography. In response, Jesuits read, translated, and circulated it.

It is likely that Ignatius read the *Imitatio* at Manresa, thereby providing a stimulus for the *Spiritual Exercises*. In the original text of the *Exercises*, the *Imitatio* is recommended "for the second Week, as well as for the future." The Official Directory of 1599 described it as a "book calculated to nourish piety rather than busy the intellect with novelties." Many Jesuits first encountered the *Imitatio* while taking the *Exercises*. The *Imitatio* was frequently promoted within Jesuit houses and printed on college presses. It was read during meals and mentioned in the rules for the Master of Novices. Everard Mercurian's 1580 regulations were replicated as far afield as Japan, where the *Imitatio* was presented to the novices in Usuki. It was one of the few books that individual Jesuits owned: by 1559 almost every student in the Cologne college had a copy.

The *Imitatio* nurtured the piety of Jesuits and the laity within Jesuit houses, colleges, and beyond. The *Imitatio* was well suited to the task because of its parallels with Jesuit spirituality. G. Mercier's modern concordance of the *Imitatio* and the *Exercises* reveals their close relationship. The similarities in spiritual themes are extensive and include consolation and desolation, death, humility, contrition, suffering, and the centrality of Christ. The *Imitatio* was a useful text to prepare for the sacraments; Nicolás de Bobadilla recommended the *Imitatio* because it encouraged frequent communion. Book Four is devoted to the Mass, and parts of it are explicitly directed toward priests.

Jesuit documentation indicates that the *Imitatio* was widely circulated in educational circles, accommodating a range of academic abilities. Its non-technical language made it accessible to young boys and domestics. Juan de Vitoria informed Diego Laínez that a domestic helper used the *Imitatio* to learn how to read. The text was also well-received in scholarly circles. The *Imitatio*'s critique of learning reminded Jesuit theologians such as Robert Bellarmine (a strong advocate of the *Imitatio*) that they should not undertake intellectual pursuits at the expense of nurturing piety. The Jesuit Georg Mayr's parallel text edition in Greek and Latin suggests that the volume could be used for practicing Greek, thereby cultivating intellect as well as piety. An anti-intellectual rhetoric could complement the devotional life of a scholar.

Typical of the *devotio moderna*, the *Imitatio* has a spirituality suited both to the cloister and to the wider world. As such, it served well a form of consecrated life centered not on the cloister but on mission and on new forms of service. Ignatius confirmed the *Imitatio*'s suitability to monasticism by leaving copies to the Monte Cassino monks. But Ignatius and the early Jesuits did not regard the *Imitatio* as an exclusively monastic text. It is telling that the *Imitatio* was initially designated the "little Gerson" after Jean Charlier de Gerson, Chancellor of the University of Paris, who was not a monk. For the Jesuits, as for their lay followers, solitary contemplation and devotional reading were prerequisites for a purposeful ministry in the world.

See also Asceticism and Mysticism; Loyola, Ignatius, of, SJ, St.; *Spiritual Exercises*

von Habsburg, Maximilian, *Catholic and Protestant Translations of the Imitatio Christi, 1425–1650*. Farnham: Ashgate, 2011.
O'Malley, John W., *The First Jesuits*. Cambridge, MA: Harvard University Press, 1995.

Max von Habsburg

India

The Jesuit Indian mission lies at the very origin of the Society of Jesus. A more comprehensive history of the Jesuits in India is yet to be written, but what we can know is exclusively from European and Jesuit sources. This entry discusses select missions, activities, and the mentality of the Jesuits in India.

With the inauguration of the sea route to the East in 1498, India became a ground for missionary experiments to do what could not be done in Europe. The Society of Jesus had just come into being in 1540, when a year later King John III of Portugal asked it to leave behind outmoded European domestic preoccupations and instead shift its gaze to destinations overseas. Hearing the call of the King, the Society hastened to send Francis Xavier to join the Portuguese caravels bound for India. In 1542, India became the first Jesuit mission outside Europe in an endless succession of European Christian initiatives in the Orient.

First, the Portuguese seafarers brought along with them the Franciscans and diocesan clergy and settled them around their forts and factories just erected along the coast of India where they had commercial interests. The missionaries carried out conversion work with uncompromising zeal, giving rise to new Christian communities. John III sustained enthusiastically the missionary beginnings as well as the expansion of Christendom with revenue accruing from overseas gains.

The mission to convert millions of Indians necessitated massive human resources, but the constant requests for missionaries to greatly enlarge the boundaries of the Church remained throughout unanswered. The land was so vast that even "a hundred thousand priests would not be sufficient to Christianize everyone," Ignatius of Loyola was informed. The multiplication of mission houses and the ease with which some superiors dismissed allegedly unfit candidates and members aggravated the missionary lamentation. India appeared an almost impossible mission.

In the sixteenth century, evangelization in the East was carried out exclusively by Portugal despite its scant resources for the gigantic enterprise. Nevertheless, the Society was immensely favored and esteemed by the Portuguese Crown. But at the turn of the century, the power and prestige of Portuguese commerce and settlements in India waned, and mission work that depended on the *Padroado* missionaries and funds suffered equally. The Jesuits were the pillars of the *Padroado* – a system of rights, privileges, and duties granted to Portugal by the popes for evangelization of the East – that assisted them in building a network of missions across India. Portuguese politics coupled with their loss of monopoly in maritime commerce, prompted the Holy See to create the

Congregation for the Propagation of the Faith (*Propaganda fide*) in 1622, to answer the deficit in personnel and European political oscillations.

Jesuit missionary activity expanded rapidly with the creation of the extensive province of India in 1549 – with Francis Xavier as its first provincial and with headquarters in Goa, a colony of Portugal. For ten years (1542–52), Xavier laid the foundations of the Society in India. The province of Malabar in South India was established in 1611, facilitating further missionary progress.

The Jesuits could more easily convert peoples they lived with, around the Portuguese forts and storehouses as well as in some coastal towns where the Portuguese held sway, not from the large mainland. Missionary activity was more intense along the Malabar coast in the southwest and Coromandel or Fishery coast in the southeast, where a large number of fisherfolk converted.

The mission of the Society was the "conversion of the gentiles," "destruction of idolatry," "exaltation of the Christian faith," and "expansion of the empire of Christ," but the Jesuits did not display a uniform perception of the Indian cultural provinces, as the missions below show.

Goa Missions. Goa, the capital of the Portuguese Eastern Empire, became the cradle and bastion of the Society in India from 1542 until 1759, when the Jesuits were expelled from the Portuguese territories. The most spectacular Jesuit project was a Seminary of the Holy Faith for the formation of native diocesan clergy and Jesuits themselves. The story goes that the seminary was offered to the Jesuits soon after the arrival of Xavier. Since 1549, the Jesuits turned the seminary into a brilliant educational enterprise to prepare clergy from Africa and Asia, and the famed seminary housed the largest international community of students until 1759. The chief aim of the seminary, called also the College of St. Paul, was to extend the Society's presence throughout India and beyond. Although the College prepared priests and missionaries for the East, the need for personnel was a challenge the Society never met. No doubt, the Jesuits were responsible for the expansion of Catholic education.

The kings of Portugal, being zealous patrons of Christendom in the East and with the obligation to spread the faith, made generous donations to all the seminaries and colleges in India, since not many priests could come from Portugal. However, what reached us as historiography is the story of western missionary achievements, without the contribution of the indigenous clergy.

The Jesuits installed a fully functioning printing press in the College in 1556, the only one of its kind in India, which generated a vast body of printed material, including the first local-language (Konkani) grammar in 1640. Moreover, the Jesuits administered a "Royal Hospital" and other health-care units, pharmacies, and infirmaries. These works motivated the locals to convert in great numbers. The Jesuits were in charge of twenty-five parishes. They functioned as political and scientific advisers to the Portuguese governors, as their emissary envoys and as diplomatic intermediaries between rival parties, and as their confessors. They worked in foundries to manufacture cannons for the defense of their cities. In many cases the Jesuits served as administrators of storehouses and forts, and they had a hand in military and mercantile affairs of the Portuguese overseas state. The Society was also much involved in colonial civil-engineering works relating to the seventeenth-century infrastructure, such as maintenance of fortifications and city planning for the new capital city of Goa. By token of such broad scope of activity and all-pervading influence due to their institutions, the Jesuits naturally became a presence to reckon with, and a convenient target for both praise and blame from virtually every quarter.

If Jesuit proximity to political, financial, and ecclesiastical seats of Portuguese power in Goa caused their activity and property to expand by methods not always above doubts, it also caused serious conflict of interest. Despite constant warnings and recommendations from the Jesuit superiors in Rome not to participate in political affairs of the states, the Jesuits found it convenient and necessary to remain associated with the power structures so indispensable for the success of their various missions. The Jesuits had devised a complex network of material, political, and social activities in Goa, for which lavish financial capital and decision-making autonomy were required. Such complex networks were not always very transparent and free from suspicion and reprimands. The Jesuits enjoyed a reputation for being realists and practical, but they were not really cut out to be social and cultural revolutionaries. The Goa mission was successful and well established until the Portuguese government suppressed the Society in 1759; it granted them official entry only in 1933.

Mughal Mission. Remarkable experiments featuring the noted Mughal miniature paintings with Christian images in Indian style began at the Mughal court in Agra, North India, in the 1580s. Mughal emperors patronized those Qur'anic-Christian ecumenical artworks, but the Jesuits who brought along Christian art reprints assisted the Mughal artists to found a new school of Indian Christian art, whose paintings were eventually designated Mughal Christian miniatures.

The missionaries residing in the imperial court at the personal invitation of the Emperor Akbar served as his political ambassadors and theologians. There were three Jesuit missions to the Mughal court since 1580. The Jesuits expected Akbar to convert on seeing his great interest to learn about the other religions and cultures, particularly the Christian faith, but soon they understood that Akbar was not interested in conversion, nor his successors who were Muslim orthodox. However, the first three Mughal emperors were attracted to western and Christian art, and thus the court Jesuits did indirectly contribute toward an East–West cultural encounter. The three Jesuit missions to the Mughal court were not controversial, nor were they successful going by the number of conversions. We find also Jesuit artists and painters at the Vijayanagar Hindu court in South India; however, likewise those rulers were interested only in Christian art.

The Jesuits often played the role of cultural brokers and were responsible for the global expansion of Christian art. They brought religious images as objects of veneration and for catechetical purposes, but those images served as a portal for cultural exchanges with results beyond their expectations. The Jesuits would not have been able to imagine that the engravings and pictures they took along to the court would stir up a whole revolution and bring about a lasting influence on Mughal art, although the prints and paintings taken by the first Jesuit mission were not the first European Christian paintings to reach the court.

More than any other religious orders in India, the Jesuits were responsible for the global expansion of Catholic art and architecture. That artistic proliferation was the outcome of the Jesuit guidelines that urged them to use sacred imagery for the expansion of missionary activity. Mughal Christian art is a reminder that Indian Christian art originated in the initiative of the Muslim rulers and their openness to other faiths and cultures.

It was around art that the Jesuits drew the lines between the European and non-European, good and bad, morally pure and impure, civilized and uncivilized categories.

Generally, the Jesuits were not convinced of the ecumenical value of mixing cultural traditions. Mughal Christian art constitutes a momentous page in Jesuit history, as it forms part of the first experiments to erase those culturally created prejudices and barriers.

Madurai Mission. Traditional missionary strategies were ineffective among the high caste people who also prevented others from converting. Hindus regarded Christianity as a foreign religion meant for the low castes. Robert de Nobili, the remarkably talented Italian Jesuit (1577–1657), argued that the missionaries' refusal to adapt culturally had prevented the conversion of the high castes.

The Madurai mission, in which de Nobili occupied center stage, was the most spectacular as well as the most controversial. De Nobili's methods, writings, and lifestyle created a forceful debate known as the Malabar Rites, which intensified during the first half of the seventeenth century and lasted until the middle of the next century. The nucleus of that famous controversy was the Jesuit Madurai mission in Tamil Nadu in South India, a part of the Jesuit Malabar province. Soon it became an international clash of missionary methods and mentalities. Gonçalo Fernandes, of the same mission, was another protagonist of, and disputant in, the conflict opposing de Nobili.

De Nobili tried to impress on the Brahmans or high caste Hindus that Christianity was not a foreign religion meant for low caste people, and he did so not only by "going native" but also by cutting off social contacts with the lower castes. De Nobili's approach of privileging the Brahmans did not go down well with most Jesuits, nor did it please Dominicans, Franciscans, Carmelites, and Augustinians, who held that de Nobili was creating more divisions and discrimination. De Nobili's method did not endear the Society to other religious orders and to the secular clergy.

The project of de Nobili to convert the upper caste proved unsuccessful; nevertheless, it has been held as the first serious attempt in cultural adaptation of Latin Christianity in India. However, the Malabar Rites experiment is being recounted today as just a narrative of Christian cultural accommodation for the sake of converting the high caste. Yet there is more than meets the eye to these so-called very original Malabar Rites. De Nobili argued that European culture was not a privileged vehicle for the transmission of Christianity in India. Local social and cultural practices should be allowed to continue even after conversion, provided they were not contrary to Christianity, to permit a cogent presentation of the Christian message. De Nobili's approach did not end well, although Jesuits like Constanzo Beschi and John de Brito tried to follow it. In 1744 Rome ended the acrimonious Malabar Rites controversy by withdrawing concessions granted to the mission.

Exclusion of Indians. Until 1773, Jesuit personnel was European, and it is a moot question whether Jesuits were culturally equipped to deal with the Indian cultural provinces; nonetheless, the Society's success depended greatly on the disposition of the West toward it. European overseas commerce determined the expansion of Jesuit activities and human resources. Initially, the province of Portugal, never too large, sent Jesuits to India, but despite its best efforts, it could not dispatch enough recruits. It was imperative to increase vocations to meet the mission challenges without diluting the quality of personnel or public image, since support of the European elites, upon whom the Society so heavily depended, rested on that impression. To increase the number of candidates, the Society established the College of St. Paul and seminaries across India, but Indians were never admitted to the Society until after its restoration in 1814. Not even the daring and insightful Robert de Nobili advocated the admission of Indians to the Society. To resolve the shortage of missionaries and emancipate mission work from political vicissitudes, Rome established *Propaganda fide* in 1622. The missionaries of *Propaganda* clashed with those of the *Padroado*, and the Jesuits could be found on both sides of the divide.

Jesuit historiography reveals the existence of discontent and power struggles based on nationalities among the missionaries. India was not a level playing field for the missionaries. Portugal knew that political loyalty and nationality did not change after joining a religious order despite the pretension that the missionaries were "all dead to the world"; hence, Portugal reduced permits for missionaries of rival nations like Britain, Spain, and France and controlled their departure to India. Hostilities originating from nationalism among the Jesuits became so notorious that the superior generals of the Society recommended the scaling down of national rivalries and increase in fraternal union among them. Since the middle of the seventeenth century, the Jesuit leadership was exceedingly cautious and seemingly less concerned about the conversion of all mankind than about the defense of the Society's public image. On the other hand, the Jesuits, being multitalented and multinational, attained eminent positions of cultural influence and achieved respectability for themselves but not always for the Christian faith. The Jesuits could boast of so many resources, institutions, talents, and successes in their repertoire, but only until 1773 when the Society was universally suppressed. The Society that had expanded very quickly had also become a victim of its own vagaries. Where success abounds so do jealousy and arrogance.

Suppression–Restoration. Although all the plots and reasons that led to the Suppression of the Society in India even before 1773 were made in Europe, the Jesuits in India had also been accused of impious errors of amassing wealth, as in Goa, and of doctrinal laxity, as in the Madurai mission. Local rulers in Madurai, Calicut, and Travancore in South India rejected Portuguese requests for the extradition of Jesuits from their territories. French Jesuits continued to work in India even after they were expelled from France in 1767. The Portuguese government sent other religious orders, particularly Franciscans and diocesan priests, to vacant Jesuit mission stations in South India, and Capuchins and Augustinians took care of the missions in North India. Later the Jesuits themselves handed over their parishes to other missionary orders, and some of them joined other religious groups.

The return of the Society took place, slowly but steadily, in several phases spanning over a century, but the beginnings can be situated in Calcutta in 1834, first with British Jesuits. The British East India Company had extended its sway over India since 1758, and British imperialism was taking control of the resourceful India. For that enterprise the British needed missionaries to prepare personnel to service the Empire. The Jesuit educational system spread throughout India, and Francis Xavier's altruism and courage were projected as the model and inspiration for missionaries. Robert de Nobili's cultural experiments had been forgotten but were revived in the post-Vatican II period.

The mission field was divided and organized on the basis of European Jesuit provinces or nationalities. Indians were largely accepted into the Society after World War I, and native Jesuit leadership was perforce created as a post-colonial need. Since the 1960s, several Indian provinces began sending Jesuits to Africa.

The Indian mission produced a dramatic growth of educational institutions, as evidenced by the large number of schools, colleges, and seminaries established since the second half of the nineteenth century, initially all dependent on external manpower, material resources, and leadership until national independence. The Society developed intellectual and scientific works too. It sought to maintain a balance between educational and pastoral activities. The number of conversions increased as did mission stations and parishes. The effort by Constant Lievens (a Belgian Jesuit) in Chota Nagpur, Ranchi, North India, in 1884, to liberate the tribal population from the exploitation of the landlords and to empower them legally, led many tribal groups to convert.

Conclusion. The strategies the Jesuits employed varied from mission to mission. Some approaches appear remarkable. Jesuit methods of generating revenue to sustain their enterprise were equally daring and often not above suspicion. The conversion of rulers in India remained an illusion, and although xenophobia was absent in India, Christianity had no local patronage.

The old Society in India counted some excellent men of knowledge and of initiatives, men zealous and extremely hard-working, living in poverty and austerity. Monuments abound of geographical, lexicographical, and astronomical research and international exchange of knowledge. The circulation of, and contribution to, Indian knowledge by the Jesuits has been invaluable. The results, vision, tireless efforts, and heroic sacrifices of the Jesuits in India are inimitable monuments in need of further studies. Today the Jesuits in India form the largest segment in the Society of Jesus and some of them, like Jacques Dupuis, until his death in 2004, and Michael Amaladoss (b. 1936) have been engaged – not always uncontroversially – in interreligious dialogue in recent times.

See also Dalits; Goa; Nobili, Roberto de, SJ; Portugal; South Asia Jesuit Colleges and Universities; Xavier, Francis, SJ, St.

Alden, Dauril, *The Making of an Enterprise: The Society of Jesus in Portugal, Its Empire, and Beyond 1540–1750*. Stanford, CA: Stanford University Press, 1996.
Amaladass, Anand, ed., *Jesuit Presence in Indian History*. Anand, India: Gujarat Sahitya Prakash, 1988.
Correia-Afonso, John, *The Jesuits in India. 1542–1773*. Anand, India: Gujarat Sahitya Prakash, 1997.
Zupanov, Ines G., *Disputed Mission: Jesuit Experiments and Brahmanical Knowledge in Seventeenth-Century India*. Oxford: Oxford University Press, 1999.

Délio Mendonça, SJ

Indifference

The term "indifference" has a precise and distinct meaning in Ignatian spirituality. Its origins can be found in key meditations of the *Spiritual Exercises*, most notably the Principle and Foundation. There Ignatius explains that human persons are created to "praise, reverence, and serve God our Lord, and by this means to save [their] soul[s]." As a result, they ought to make themselves "indifferent to all created things," subordinating all desires and preferences to this transcendent objective. The logic of this derives from a Christian theological anthropology that understands the end and deepest desires of the human person as fulfilled in God alone. In light of this understanding, Ignatius reasons that all else should be made relative to this overriding concern and counsels that health should not be preferred to sickness, nor riches to poverty, nor a long life to a short one. For "our one desire and choice," he explains, "should be what is more conducive to the end for which we are created."

Characteristically, notes Joseph de Guibert, Ignatius's focus here is not only upon the end of union with God, as in other mystical traditions, but also upon whatever is "more" (Latin: *magis*) conducive to the praise and service of God, i.e., God's greater glory. Positively expressed, Ignatian indifference involves the realization of an interior freedom that enables one to habitually choose this *magis*. Through a liberating grace, the affect and will of a person are freed from what a long Jesuit tradition calls "inordinate attachments," or excessive attachments to created things that divert a person's focus away from the service of God. The resulting indifference is not apathy, but rather a harmonizing of the affect and will with the deepest desires of the person. Indifferent persons are thereby freed for a more complete love of God, and their interior life is integrated and ordered towards this love in such a way that they are also enabled to love all things in God.

See also Discernment; Inordinate Attachments; Magis; *Spiritual Exercises*

de Guibert, Joseph, *The Jesuits: Their Spiritual Doctrine and Practice*. Trans. William Young. Chicago, IL: The Institute of Jesuit Sources, 1964.

Henry Shea, SJ

Indonesia

The earliest presence of the Jesuits in Indonesia dates to 1546 when St. Francis Xavier (1506–52), one of the founding members of the Society of Jesus, came to the Spice Islands in the Moluccas. He came along with a Portuguese fleet in search of spices. While in the Moluccas, known today in Indonesia as Maluku, Xavier taught the Catholic faith to the locals, who comprised those of Portuguese descent and the natives of the islands. As a consequence of Spanish–Portuguese colonial rivalries, however, in the mid-1600s the Jesuit mission was terminated. When the Dutch colonial power came to the islands, many Catholics were forced to abandon their faith and converted to Protestantism.

It was only in the second half of the nineteenth century that the Jesuits returned to Indonesia, which was then a Dutch colony called the Dutch East Indies. In 1859 two Jesuits, Father Van den Elzen, SJ, and Father J. B. Palinckx, SJ, reopened a Jesuit mission in the colony. In 1893 Father W. J. Staal, SJ, was appointed as the apostolic vicar of Batavia, the colony's administrative headquarters. On December 14, 1904, Father Francis Van Lith, SJ, a Dutch missionary, baptized 171 Javanese in the village of Sendangsono, Central Java, following the earlier baptism of four Javanese on May 20 of the same year. The baptisms marked the beginning of a long period of Catholic missionization in Java, and later in other parts of Indonesia. In the town of Muntilan, Central Java, Van Lith also started a minor seminary, with the intention of training future native priests and lay leaders. This seminary produced the first native Indonesian Jesuits including Fathers F. X. Satiman, SJ, A. Djajasepoetra, SJ, and Albertus Soegijapranata, SJ. Later, on August 1, 1940, Soegijapranata (1896–1963) was appointed by Pope Pius XII as the bishop of the Archdiocese of Semarang, Central Java, making him the first native Indonesian bishop.

On August 15, 1970, Father Leo Soekoto, SJ (1920–95), a native Jesuit, was appointed as the archbishop of the Jakarta Archdiocese and served until his death on December 30, 1995. In 1983 another native Jesuit, Father Julius Darmaatmadja, SJ (b. 1934), was appointed as the archbishop of Semarang, when he had just started his term as the provincial superior of the Indonesian province of the Society of Jesus. Following the death of Archbishop Soekoto, in 1996 Darmaatmadja was appointed as the archbishop of the Jakarta Archdiocese. In 1994 he was made cardinal, making him the second native Indonesian cardinal.

Today Jesuits work in seven of the thirty-seven dioceses and archdioceses in Indonesia. A good number of Indonesian Jesuits also work outside the country, such as Japan, Thailand, Myanmar, Cambodia, Italy, and the Philippines. Following the invasion of East Timor (now Timor Leste) by the Indonesian military forces in 1975, the Indonesian province of the Society of Jesus was entrusted to care for the Timor Leste mission. The Jesuits worked in pastoral centers, educational institutions, and an agricultural center. Following Timor Leste's vote for independence in 1999, the presence of Indonesian Jesuits was reduced to a minimum.

Indonesian Jesuits work in different fields of ministries, such as parishes, educational institutions, social communication, pastoral services, and social works. In social communication Jesuits publish *Hidup*, a nationwide Catholic weekly magazine, and *Basis*, a bimonthly cultural-intellectual magazine. They also run Cipta Loka Caraka publishing house in Jakarta, Kanisius printing and publishing house in Yogyakarta, and two audiovisual production houses, namely Sanggar Prativi in Jakarta and Audiovisual Puskat in Yogyakarta. In the field of social work, Indonesian Jesuits serve in various ministries including the Jesuit Refugee Service-Indonesia.

In the area of education, Jesuits run high schools in Java and West Papua, such as Kanisius College in Jakarta and le Cocq d'Armandville College in Nabire, West Papua. They also run several vocational schools such as St. Michael College and St. Michael Industrial Machine Technical Academy, both in Surakarta, Central Java. In higher education they run Sanata Dharma University (student pop. 11,000), located in Yogyakarta, the only Jesuit university in Indonesia. Jesuits also provide spiritual direction and retreats, run centers for pastoral research and development, and manage institutes which deal with social and cultural issues.

The Indonesian province of the Society of Jesus has its own training centers, namely a novitiate, a philosophy training center, a theologate, and a tertianship center. By the end of 2014, the total number of Indonesian Jesuits was 315, including scholastics and brothers.

See also Muslims, Relations with; Sanata Dharma University; Timor Leste; Xavier, Francis, SJ, St.

Steenbrink, Karel, *Catholics in Indonesia 1808–1942: A Documented History*. Vol. I: *A Modest Recovery 1808–1903*. Leiden: KITLV Press, 2003.
    Catholics in Indonesia 1808–1942: A Documented History. Vol. II: *The Spectacular Growth of a Self-Confident Minority, 1903–1942*. Leiden: KITLV Press, 2007.
Susanto, A. Budi, ed., *Harta dan Surga: Peziarahan Jesuit dalam Gereja dan Bangsa Indonesia Modern*. Yogyakarta: Kanisius 1990.

Baskara T. Wardaya, SJ

Informationes

The *Constitutions of the Society of Jesus* (#63) instruct that a candidate should be asked "for the sake of greater progress in his spiritual life" whether "he will be willing to have all his errors and defects, and anything else which will be noticed or known about him, manifested to his superiors by anyone who knows them outside of confession; and further, whether he along with all the others will be willing to aid in correcting and being corrected, to manifesting one another with due love and charity." This willingness to be manifested and to manifest others is part of the Jesuit information gathering for the formation of Jesuit candidates.

The *Constitutions* (#92) also require as "not only highly but even supremely important" in missioning his members that the superior "have complete knowledge of the inclinations and motions of those who are in his charge." It adds that by having information regarding all the members, the superior will "be better able to organize and arrange what is expedient for the whole body of the Society."

For these three reasons (formation of candidates, specific appointments to mission, and responsible administration of all), superiors gather *informationes* from those members whom the superior deems knowledgeable of another. These *informationes* are standardized evaluation forms refereed and collected by the local superior but sent on with the superior's own assessment to the provincial. The information is gathered in secret and there are no provisions for the member being informed or to know anything of the procedure. All *informationes* have been archived since the Society's inception.

See also Formation; Superior, Local; Province, Provincial

Friedrich, Markus, "Government and Information-Management in Early Modern Europe. The Case of the Society of Jesus (1540–1773)." *Journal of Early Modern History* 12 (2009), 1–25.
Keenan, James F., "Are Informationes Ethical?" *Studies in the Spirituality of Jesuits* 29 (September 1997), 1–33.

James F. Keenan, SJ

Inordinate Attachment

When Ignatius of Loyola wrote his *Spiritual Exercises*, he explained in the First Annotation that prayer, meditation, and contemplation were "exercises" akin to physical activity but here geared toward disposing the exercitant's soul to be rid of "inordinate attachments."

Colloquially "inordinate" means excessive, but the use of the word in the *Exercises* carries an additional implication: human desires are not just abundant or excessive, but disordered and unregulated. In other words, one's choices and actions are driven by little understood and ill-directed desires. Accordingly, following the Annotations, Ignatius indicates that the purpose of the *Exercises* is to "overcome" or "conquer" oneself and to order one's life, without falling prey to these disordered tendencies. The *Exercises* instigate a process of self-evaluation that leads to understanding one's own inordinate attachments, allowing the exercitant to aim toward discovering what God wills for one's own life.

Key to regulating and thus overcoming one's own inordinate desires is to practice detachment. The particular meditations and exercises are geared toward self-knowledge that allows one to discern how he or she has stood in the way of understanding what God wills for his or her own life. Inordinate attachments are those tendencies that impede the vocation to which God has called each person individually.

See also Spiritual Exercises

Barry, William A., and Robert G. Doherty, *Contemplatives in Action: The Jesuit Way*. New York: Paulist Press, 2002.

Ganss, George E., ed., *Ignatius of Loyola: The Spiritual Exercises and Selected Works*. New York: Paulist Press, 1991.

de Guibert, Joseph, *The Jesuits: Their Spiritual Doctrine and Practice*. Trans. William Young. Chicago, IL: The Institute of Jesuit Sources, 1964.

Molina, J. Michelle, *To Overcome Oneself: The Jesuit Ethic and the Spirit of Global Expansion*. Berkeley: University of California Press, 2013.

J. Michelle Molina

Inserted Communities

Inserted (or insertion) communities are Jesuit communities located among the poorest of the poor, whether in inner cities or the rural countryside. Often they are found among immigrant communities in Europe and North America and among indigenous populations in Latin America, Africa, and Asia. Such communities proliferated in the wake of the 32nd General Congregation (GC 32), which reaffirmed ministry to the poor as a principal mission of the Society (see GC 32, Decree 4, ##47–50 and Decree 6, #10). *Complementary Norms* (#180) likewise asks provincials to "encourage those communities which … choose to practice a stricter poverty or to live among the poor, serving them and sharing some of their experience."

Jesuits in inserted communities work as they normally would during the day, but live side by side with the poor in decidedly modest housing, sometimes teaching the children of these communities or engaging in interfaith dialogue. Such a presence offers the Jesuits a unique perspective into the lives of the poor. In one's words, "We 'stoop' so as to be able to see things from below: from the gutter, from the anguish, from the tragedy" (Ferro, "Turning to the Poor," 20).

Inserted communities have become less common in recent years. In part, this is due to falling membership in the Society, which has led many provinces to close them to consolidate personnel. However, there has also been concern about the role of inserted communities. Some have seen such solidarity with the poor as dangerous, especially for connections (real or implied) with Marxist groups. For example, as provincial of Argentina Pope Francis (then Jorge Mario Bergoglio, SJ) closed all of the inserted communities there, not without dispute. Later, though, and especially as pope, he has shown support for clergy and religious living among the poor.

See also Community; Preferential Option for the Poor

Ferro, Alfredo, "Turning to the Poor out of Our Identity." *Promotio Iustitiae* 102 (2009/2), 17–21.

Riggio, Giuseppe, "Insertion Communities: A Brief Introduction." *Promotio Iustitiae* 100 (2008/3), 81–84.

Charles Keenan

Institute of Jesuit Sources/Institute for Advanced Jesuit Studies

Founded in St. Louis in 1961, the Institute of Jesuit Sources serves as a publishing house of texts and studies in Jesuit history, spirituality, and pedagogy. The Institute was originally founded by the Missouri province of the Society of Jesus under the direction of prominent Jesuit historian George Ganss, who served as its director and editor until 1986. He was succeeded by Jesuit historian John Padberg, the director and editor of the Institute until 2014. In that year the Institute of Jesuit Sources was transferred to Boston and subsumed under the newly founded Institute for Advanced Jesuit Studies at Boston College.

Over the past half-century, the Institute of Jesuit Sources has focused upon making Jesuit primary sources accessible in English translation, publishing foreign studies on Jesuits in English translation and providing resources for research on Jesuit topics. The Institute has published more than a hundred volumes related to the Society of Jesus, including multiple modern translations of the *Spiritual Exercises*, early directories on giving the Exercises, an English translation of *The Constitutions of the Society of Jesus and Their Complementary Norms*, and letters and writings of Ignatius of Loyola, Francis Xavier, and Peter Faber.

The Institute for Advanced Jesuit Studies at Boston College also sponsors the recently founded *Journal of Jesuit Studies* (2014), a peer-reviewed quarterly journal, and the Boston College Jesuit Bibliography, an online bibliographical library intended to serve as a "comprehensive open-access database" of all Jesuit-related publications. The Institute offers summer courses, workshops, and lectures focused upon Ignatian spirituality and Jesuit history, and it hosts an annual International Symposium on Jesuit Studies. Additionally, in-residence fellowships are awarded annually by the Institute to scholars engaged in research and publication related to the Society of Jesus.

See also Archives and Libraries; Bibliographies; Boston College

Henry Shea, SJ

Institutum Historicum Societatis Iesu

The Historical Institute of the Society of Jesus (Institutum Historicum Societatis Iesu, abbreviated as IHSI) started in Madrid when the first volume of *Monumenta Historica Societatis Iesu* appeared in 1894. At the same time, in Rome, Fr. General Martín organized a small group of Jesuit historians, giving them the task of preparing the history of their provinces. In 1930 Fr. General Ledóchowski merged these two initiatives and established a new community of historians in Rome (the name IHSI appeared only in 1935). They were responsible not only for the *Monumenta* series (a total of 166 volumes appeared up to 2014), but also for the twice-yearly periodical *Archivum Historicum Societatis Iesu* which started in 1932 (164 issues have appeared), the monograph series *Bibliotheca Instituti Historici Societatis Iesu* – BIHSI (75 volumes published since 1941), and a subsidiary series *Subsidia ad Historiam Societatis Iesu* – SAHSI (15 volumes published since 1957). As part of its mission of fostering and promoting the study of the Society's history, after over twenty years of preparation the Institute produced the four-volume dictionary, *Diccionario histórico de la Compañía de Jesús. Biográfico-temático*, co-published with the Pontifical University of Comillas in 2001. The work of the Institute has been facilitated by its library of up to 100,000 volumes which each year welcomes hundreds of researchers in a reading room shared since 2004 with the Jesuit Roman Archives (ARSI). Since 2010 the latter is responsible for carrying out all activities of the Institute.

See also Archives and Libraries; Archivum Romanum Societatis Iesu (ARSI)

Zapico, Dionisio Fernández, and Pedro de Leturia, "Cinquentenario de Monumenta Historica S.I. 1894–1944." *Archivum Historicum Societatis Iesu* 13 (1944), 1–61.

Robert Danieluk, SJ

Interreligious Dialogue

The 34th General Congregation of the Society (GC 34) in 1995 put the dialogue with religions firmly on the Jesuit map. "Our Mission and Interreligious Dialogue" makes reference to the now familiar post-Vatican II categories of the dialogues of theological exchange, religious experience, common life, and common action. Nothing like that existed in Ignatius's day. In the meditation on the Incarnation, Ignatius drew attention not to some romantic global village in which Hindus, Buddhists, and Muslims are next-door neighbours but to the "vast extent of the circuit of the earth, with its many and various races" (103). What today we call "the religions" was just one more phenomenon which the persons of the Trinity contemplated. Early Jesuits did not doubt the truth of Catholic Christianity as the source of the salvation of humankind. Nor did they have any hesitations about defending it robustly in the face of ignorance and error. They would, however, have appreciated the wider theological context of GC 34's renewal of the Society's mission. What is commended to a body of men keen to put themselves at the "service of faith" is a "culture of dialogue": not a new-fangled method of evangelizing appropriate to a postmodern world, but a certain capacity to make explicit in the world the signs of God's transforming grace.

That is the point of continuity between what John Paul II calls "a new experience for the Church" (*Redemptoris Missio*, 55) and that extraordinary outpouring of missionary dynamism that ran through the early period of the Society's history. In those decades Jesuits were schooled in rigorous Thomistic thinking and the richness of Renaissance humanism. It was this inner dialogue between a well-honed theological literacy and a fascination with the rich diversity of religious cultures that created the outer dialogue – not just a determination to bear witness to the truth revealed in Christ but a conviction that ultimately there can be no substantive distinction between what is known of God revealed in Christ and what is unknown but dimly perceived in other religious worlds. The challenge was to translate the Christian message so that it moved both head and heart. St. Francis Xavier, the greatest of all Jesuit missionaries, learned enough of the local language of south India to produce simple summaries which he repeated to people. More importantly, he taught them how to pray; in centering the words of faith round the life of Christ, they would come to understand the truth of the Gospel. His efforts became more "dialogical" when he encountered the intellectually sophisticated Buddhism of Japan. A powerful personality and a rudimentary competence in a new language were never going to be enough. It was a matter of entering deep into a very different world in order to appreciate its more subtle rhythms and ways of thinking. Alessandro Valignano (1539–1606), superior of the Eastern missions and the great architect of the Jesuit missionary efforts throughout the whole of Asia, insisted that his men become thoroughly imbued with local culture and customs. Without Valignano's influence, it is doubtful whether the genius of men like Matteo Ricci (1552–1610) or

Roberto de Nobili (1577–1656) would have made such an impact on the Confucian culture of China or the Brahmin-led world of India. They took their translation of the Gospel into a new religious world to the extreme of *translating themselves*, wearing the garb of local holy men, imitating their habits and customs, in order to become thoroughly familiar with their beliefs and practices.

Such moves were courageous and controversial, and they continue to raise critical questions today. But in 1659 the principle was established. *Propaganda fide* echoed de Nobili by stating unequivocally that European missionaries were to take with them not "France, Spain, or Italy or any part of Europe" but the Faith, "which does not reject or damage any people's rites and customs, provided these are not depraved." This is the basis of what has come to be known as inculturation, the process by which the Church grows into the culture of a people. For the first Jesuits it was less part of the missionary tool kit than an unstructured response to the needs of the situation. Two exact contemporaries, Jerome Xavier (1549–1617) and Thomas Stephens (1549–1619), stand for two different yet interrelated approaches. Both began as missionaries in Goa but soon moved into very different cultural and political worlds – the one, the great-nephew of St. Francis, at the court of the Mughal emperors Akbar and Jehangir, the other, the first English Jesuit in India, in the villages south of Goa. What they share is a reputation for resilience and an extraordinary capacity to improvise, not following some great missionary blueprint but knowing how to adapt and grasp the right moment. Xavier lived through a turbulent period of war and witnessed the martyrdom of the fifth Sikh guru, Arjun. His letter to Rome, the first recorded historical contact between Sikhs and Christians, manifests a sympathy for the Sikhs' "good pope" who sought to maintain spiritual integrity in a violent world. Stephens is today famous for the *Kristpurana*, an extraordinary retelling of the Old and New Testaments in classical Puranic style. But he was no more spared adversity than was Xavier. His painstaking work of translation of the Christian story into a popular form was forged out of disaster – the massacre of Christians at Cucolim in 1583. It fell to Stephens, as a young rector, to rebuild the community and to find a less antagonistic way to present the Gospel.

These men shared with Ricci and de Nobili a brilliance with languages, but it was as much their intellectual curiosity as their dedication to the needs of local people that inspired later generations. Alexandre de Rhodes (1590–1661) spent most of his life in Vietnam where he was responsible for resourcing later missionary efforts with a Portuguese–Latin–Vietnamese dictionary. Constanzo Beschi (1680–1747) mastered the Tamil language and became a renowned poet and teacher. Ippolito Desideri (1684–1733) learned Tibetan in order to debate the subtleties of Mahayana Buddhism at the royal court in Lhasa. Their texts vary in style and genre. What holds them together is the desire to *communicate* truth in a particular cultural medium – the sort of thing the early apologists attempted in their conviction that Greek philosophy could be seen as a *praeparatio evangelica* for the Gospel.

Whatever else may have changed between the era of missionary expansion and the contemporary multi-religious world in which "the other" has a far more powerful voice, this theme of communication remains constant. The structure of the later fourfold dialogue which melds affective qualities essential to building interpersonal relations with the careful reasoning proper to theological discernment is detectable in these and many less familiar examples of a great tradition. If there is such a thing as a "Jesuit instinct," it lies here, with the pastoral intent to root speech *about* God in what Ignatius in the

Exercises talks about as the inner "relish" of what God alone can reveal. The nineteenth-century restoration of the Society saw a much more European model of Church at work. From the critical but scholarly work on Islamic sources by Henri Lammens (1862–1937) in Beirut to the subtle Thomistic response to Advaita Vedanta pioneered in the 1920s by Pierre Johanns and Georges Dandoy in Calcutta, Jesuit interest in other religions had a distinctly Orientalist tinge. Nevertheless, in one regard Jesuits maintained a continuity with their own past. To make oneself understood it is always necessary first to understand. Study of the textual tradition remains essential to the properly critical practice of interreligious engagement.

With Vatican II, practice began to find a theory. Jesuits in India, Japan, and the Middle East responded to *Nostra aetate*'s invitation to move beyond textual study and engage in "conversations and collaboration" with persons from other faith traditions. The story of the tortured process which led to the promulgation of this brief – a mere thirty sentences in the Latin original – but enormously important text is well known and need not be repeated here. It did not lack for a very specific Jesuit influence, that of the elderly scripture scholar and rector of the Biblical Institute in Rome, Cardinal Augustin Bea. Without his dogged determination and capacity to learn from Jewish friends and colleagues such as Abraham Heschel, it is doubtful whether the declaration would ever have seen the light of day. The first drafts of *Nostra aetate* were designed to overcome supersessionist attitudes and "replacement" theologies which identified Judaism as little more than a relic of the Old Testament. A much richer theology began to emerge as the Council grappled not just with the Jewish origins of the Church but with questions arising from the experience of bishops, theologians, and missionaries dedicated to building better relations with their non-Christian neighbors in a rapidly changing postcolonial world. The eventual result, promulgated in October 1965, was a halting yet visionary account of the Church's place in a world of many religions, including specific reference to Islam and, more briefly, to Hinduism and Buddhism.

In the years since the Council, the opening up of the Church to the world in general, and other religions in particular, has gradually brought the lone efforts of a comparatively few Jesuit specialists into the mainstream of the Church's inner and outer life. They are inspired by *Nostra aetate*'s call to "acknowledge, preserve and encourage" the "spiritual and moral truths" to be found among other religions. Nothing is said in the text about what these are. And that may be the crucial element of *Nostra aetate*'s legacy, as far as Jesuits are concerned: the call for a critical discernment achieved in dialogue with the religious other.

Dialogue with Jews is carried on wherever the Church seeks to understand the original "parting of the ways" and to come to terms with its contemporary ramifications, particularly with regard to the Shoah. Jesuits such as David Neuhaus at the Biblical Institute in Jerusalem, James Bernauer at Boston College, and Christian Rutishauser in Munich and Rome walk in the footsteps of an earlier generation, scripture scholars alive to the baleful effects of the characterization of the rich and vibrant religious culture of Jesus's time as "late Judaism" and prophetic figures such as Stanislaw Musial at the Judaica Centrum in Cracow who did so much to overcome the effects of anti-semitic prejudice in postwar Poland.

Nostra aetate very quickly extended the dialogue with the Jews to Muslims, the third of the peoples of the Book. This providential opening up to the demands of a sometimes bitter three-way set of antagonisms has drawn in a number of Jesuits committed to this most demanding of all interreligious dialogues. Arij Roest Crollius began with studies in Cairo and Beirut, taught at the Gregorian University, and now teaches in Abidjan. After years of study in London, Christian Troll has taught in Delhi, Birmingham, Rome, Ankara and is now back in his native Germany. The Australian Paul Jackson has spent most of his life in Pakistan and India where he has specialized in Sufi mysticism. Thomas Michel joined the Society after becoming immersed in Muslim culture in Indonesia, spent some years in Rome at the Pontifical Council for Interreligious Dialogue, and now works in Ankara. Daniel Madigan teaches at Georgetown University, Felix Körner directs the Institute for the Study of Religions and Cultures at the Gregorian, while Damian Howard combines teaching of Muslim–Christian relations at Heythrop College with more face-to-face dialogue in the Bangladeshi-dominated streets of East London. Jesuits in dialogue with Islam are held together by a discerning spirituality that takes seriously the challenge made to Christian faith by a tradition which claims to be the final and definitive revelation of God's Word. No Jesuit, however, can be unaware of the risks run by close contact with the "civil war" that is tearing Islam apart in the contemporary Middle East. Paolo Dall'Oglio established a remarkable center of prayer and dialogue between Muslims and Christians at Dar Mar Musa, north of Damascus. He was kidnapped by ISIS militants in July 2013 and most likely executed.

A contrast between the politically and theologically sensitive dialogues with Judaism and Islam and the more "spiritual" dialogue with Hinduism and Buddhism is too easily drawn. Hinduism is, of course, more a loosely amalgamated set of ways of life than a "religion" based on overarching philosophical principles. But it also has its political edges, especially in today's India where ultra-nationalist perspectives have been carved out of ancient mythologies. The long-established dialogue with the Sanskritic traditions, evidenced most powerfully through Richard de Smet's influential reading of Aquinas through the lens of Śankara's version of classical Vedanta, needs to be held in tension with the focus on vernacular traditions, most importantly the mystical dialogue developed by Ignatius Hirudayam with Tamil traditions at his ashram, Aikiya Alayam, in south Chennai. Their work continues in India through the work of textual scholars like Noel Sheth in Pune and the philosopher Anand Amaladass in Chennai. At the same time emerging versions of Dalit theology, arising from the struggle of low-caste peoples, give much more attention to issues of justice and therefore to dialogues of common life and action. Some Indian Jesuit theologians, most importantly Michael Amaladoss in Chennai and Delhi, are engaged in a dialogue which takes both dimensions of Indian religious culture with utmost seriousness.

Of the non-Indian scholars of Hinduism, the best known is Francis Clooney, who has a specific expertise in the Vaishnava tradition. Now based at Harvard, Clooney is an exponent of one of the most important theological developments of Vatican II: comparative theology. This is a form of interreligious reading in which the religious imagination is stimulated by engaging with the symbols and thought-forms of another tradition. Clooney understands it, in the tradition of de Nobili, as a practice of "faith seeking understanding." It builds on a fairly common experience – that the more one learns about another tradition, the more one learns about one's own. That thesis is developed by another indologist-theologian, London-based Michael Barnes, who seeks to build a theology of dialogue, a reflection on the Christian experience of being in dialogue with the other. His version of comparative theology focuses not just on Hindu, Buddhist, and

Sikh textual traditions but on artifacts and architecture, whatever can be "read" as signs of God's Spirit.

The most celebrated figure in the dialogue with Buddhism is Aloysius Pieris in Śri Lanka. His center, Tulana, in a semi-rural setting on the fringes of Colombo, has become a place where Christians and Buddhists can talk and meditate in an atmosphere of mutual respect. Here the best of Śri Lankan culture is celebrated; the house and gardens are decorated with terra-cotta sculptures and friezes, bringing an evocative aesthetic dimension to the elusive interface between Buddhism and Christianity. At the more purely contemplative level, the extraordinary inner affinity between the *Spiritual Exercises* and Zen has inspired a number of dedicated teachers and spiritual directors, especially in Japan, such as William Johnston, Hugo Enomiya Lassalle, and Kakichi Kadowaki. A Jesuit tradition of contemplative Zen discernment has begun to build its own lineage. In the southern Indian state of Tamil Nadu, Arul Maria Arokiasamy (AMA Samy), who trained with Enomiya and Japanese Zen masters, has founded the Bodhi Centre, at Perumal high in the Kodai hills. In the USA Robert Kennedy leads Zen seishins in a dedicated zendo in the middle of the Jesuit university in Jersey City. Both are regular visitors to retreat centers in Europe. Their version of Zen is not treated as a convenient variation on some generic spiritual technology but, in the spirit of the *Exercises*, as pure gift to those who, both before and after the experience of the *Exercises*, seek the face of the Christ who is both present and absent, calling them to deeper intimacy yet always elusive to any purely human grasp.

Dialogue raises practical questions, about the proper exercise of spiritual discernment, and more fundamentally theological questions about the significance of other religions for a tradition defined by the language of God revealed in Christ. Karl Rahner's much-discussed thesis of the Anonymous Christian did not in the first place seek to address the traditional question of the salvation of the non-Christian; it was, more exactly, a corollary of his theological anthropology. It has, of course, been enormously influential beyond the confines of the Catholic Church and been integrated into the magisterial theology of religious pluralism espoused by Jacques Dupuis. Dupuis's major concern is the credibility of the Church. He is trying to show that the Paschal Mystery has a universal significance yet allows for a reciprocal relationship or mutuality, even though Christianity can never affirm the other as an equal. For Dupuis religious pluralism is not a "problem" to be solved by somehow being incorporated into the Christian economy but itself a manifestation of the superabundant richness and diversity of God's providential purposes. The tension between what is known through God's gracious act of self-revelation and what remains unknown and hidden in God runs through all forms of interreligious dialogue.

The theology of religions behind the Decree, "Our Mission and Interreligious Dialogue," of the 34th General Congregation, is not the product of a particular school of thought but a theological "style" that arises from the combination of the typically Jesuit tradition of a theologically principled accommodation to culture and *Nostra aetate*'s retrieval of the common heritage of divine revelation and human response that links Jews and Christians. The two are intimately linked.

For Jesuits dialogue is not a replacement for mission but an expression of the generous missiology that emerges from the Trinitarian vision behind the *Spiritual Exercises*. The Father sends the Son and the Spirit into the world – and the Church is caught up by and participates in this great movement of grace. For all that Ignatius can talk about people who are "all going down into Hell," the Jesuit sense of mission is inspired more by a vision of the world as the site of the compassionate action of God's grace than by an antagonism towards "the religions" as such. Jesuit spirituality is nothing if not apostolic, but that is only to say that companionship with Jesus Christ the King is itself a witness to what *God* is doing in the world. "Interior knowledge" of God's saving love is inseparable from an ever-growing sensitivity to the many ways in which the Spirit goes on laboring in human history and the world at large.

A dialogue that takes its rise from God's own dialogue with human beings opens up a vision of a world made new by what God reveals of Godself in the Paschal Mystery; that God is constant is the driving conviction behind Paul's passionate meditation on the fate of his own people in Romans 9–11. A Church touched by such a vision can never rest content with a grudging acknowledgement that the Covenant with Israel has never been revoked. It must follow the leading of the Holy Spirit – as depicted graphically in the historical genesis of the text of *Nostra aetate* itself – from one set of interreligious and interpersonal relations to another. *Nostra aetate* is more than an exhortation to address the "Jewish question," more even than an exercise in a sort of interreligious *ressourcement*. It sits alongside the other documents of the Council as intense reflections on the very experience of being a Church called once again to listen and learn, as Abraham was called. The Jesuit theological tradition has always consisted of an act of prayerful discernment that seeks to find new and imaginative ways of communicating the truth of the Gospel. In a religiously plural world, it seeks to provoke further variations on a richly complex story of faith, while inviting other persons from other communities together to make similar connections.

See also China; Chinese Rites Controversy; Cultures; Ecumenism; India; Japan; Jews and Jesuits; Middle East; Muslims, Relations with

Amaladoss, Michael, *The Asian Jesus*. Maryknoll, NY: Orbis, 2006.
Barnes, Michael, *Theology and the Dialogue of Religions*. Cambridge: Cambridge University Press, 2002.
Clooney, Francis X., *Comparative Theology: Deep Learning Across Religious Borders*. Chichester: Wiley-Blackwell, 2010.
Clooney, Francis X., and Anand Amaladass, eds., *Preaching Wisdom to the Wise: Three Treatises by Roberto de Nobili SJ*. St. Louis, MO: The Institute of Jesuit Sources, 2001.
Dupuis, Jacques, *Toward a Theology of Religious Pluralism*. Maryknoll, NY: Orbis, 1997.
Troll, Christian W., and C. T. R. Hewer, *Christian Lives Given to the Study of Islam*. New York: Fordham University Press, 2012.

Michael Barnes, SJ

Iparraguirre, Ignacio, SJ (1911–1973)

Ignacio Aldanondo Iparraguirre was born August 30, 1911, in Bilbao, Spain. He entered the Society of Jesus in 1926 and, after the novitiate and juniorate, went on to study in Belgium (1932–34), the Netherlands (1936–38), and Spain (1939–40). In 1945 he obtained his doctorate in Church history at the Gregorian University with his thesis "The Practice of the Exercises of St. Ignatius during the Life of the Author," which would become the first volume of his celebrated trilogy on the history of the *Spiritual Exercises*. He then assumed a position teaching the history and the theology of the

Exercises in the Spirituality Institute of the Gregorian University, which he held until his death on October 6, 1973.

His writings were numerous and remain influential. In addition to his trilogy, he collaborated in the publication of *The Complete Works of St. Ignatius* and a new edition of the *Directory of the Spiritual Exercises*. He wrote many articles on the history and practice of Ignatian spirituality. He was also one of the founders of the Centrum Ignatianum Spiritualitatis (CIS) in Rome.

Though an exceptional scholar, Iparraguirre was also known as a gifted spiritual director and teacher. In particular, he taught directors to know the text of the *Exercises* well and to adapt the movement of the retreat to the needs of the exercitant. His emphasis upon the personal assimilation of the *Exercises* would lead toward the greater popularity of the individually directed retreat and the formation of competent directors.

See also Loyola, Ignatius of, SJ, St.; *Spiritual Exercises*

Iparraguirre, Ignacio, *Historia de la práctica de los Ejercicios Espirituales de San Ignacio de Loyola.* Vols. I–III. Bilbao: El Mensajero del Corazón de Jesus, 1946–1973.
How to Give a Retreat: Practical Notes. Westminster, MD: Newman Press, 1961.

John Gavin, SJ

Ireland

With its long Christian tradition dating from at least the fifth century, Ireland by the sixteenth century was immersed in Henry VIII's break with Rome. Since the twelfth century, as a result of the papal bull *Laudabiliter* issued by the English Pope Adrian IV, Nicholas Breakspear, the English monarchs claimed "Lordship" over Ireland. Henry now had himself declared king and set about implementing the Reformation. Owing to confused reports as to what was happening in the country, two of the early companions of St. Ignatius, Paschase Broët and Alfonso Salmerón, at the request of Pope Paul III, were sent on a mission to Ireland to report on the state of religion. Spending about a month there in the early spring of 1542, Broët and Salmerón were convinced that Ireland was lost to Catholicism.

The Society was established in Ireland in 1561 with the arrival of Fr. David Wolfe, a native of Limerick and former rector of the Jesuit college at Modena. Given the circumstances of active persecution, the growth of the Order was slow, and by 1604 there were only six Jesuits in active ministry. Some, such as the English Jesuit Fr. James Archer, had immersed themselves in the Irish aspect of the political struggles of Counter-Reformation Europe, while others were content with applying themselves to the business of "saving souls." The war with England as represented by the Confederation of Kilkenny, 1642–49, gave scope for Fr. Robert Nugent, the mission superior, to embroil himself in political intrigue. Meanwhile the Society had established a college at Drogheda which attracted both Catholic and Protestant students. The organization and work of the Irish mission was a great concern to the Jesuit authorities in Rome, since Jesuit life in Ireland had little of the order and customs of Jesuit life in continental Europe. The notorious activities of Oliver Cromwell, especially the siege of Drogheda in 1649, claimed the lives of two Jesuits. Despite religious repression the mission made steady progress in terms of numbers, and by 1650 there were forty-seven Jesuits engaged in a variety of apostolates.

Figure 30 Michael Flecky, SJ: Clongowes Wood College, County Kildare, Ireland, 1993.
Photograph © Michael Flecky, SJ

A series of penal laws in the eighteenth century, aimed at extirpating Catholicism, made the work of the mission increasingly difficult. Most Jesuits labored in towns such as Dublin, Waterford, and Clonmel, and in addition to parishes a number of colleges were established, including a boarding school set up in Dublin in 1770 by Fr. John Austin and Fr. James Mulcaile. The Irish mission had long been supported by the work of Irish Jesuits in France and Spain, and with the expulsion of the Jesuits from those counties, the mission began to suffer. By the time of the general suppression of the Society in 1773, the Irish mission had shrunk to just nineteen members. Most of these remained working in parishes, with Fr. Thomas Betagh becoming vicar general of the Archdiocese of Dublin. Even before the general restoration of the order, Fr. Peter Kenney had set about reviving the Irish Jesuit mission. In time his activities would take him to the United States. He established Clongowes Wood College in March 1814. Clongowes would play a leading part in the education of Ireland's Catholic elite, including John Redmond, leader of the Irish Parliamentary Party. Clongowes was rivaled by St. Stanislaus College, Tullabeg, which, under its mid-century rector, Fr. William Delany, one of the greatest educationalists Ireland produced in the nineteenth century, had fair claims to be the best-performing school in the county. It would eventually be merged with Clongowes.

Irish Jesuits were also involved in university education, with the Royal University, and then, following the University Act of 1908, in University College Dublin. Jesuits also contributed to Irish cultural attainments with the *Irish Monthly*, under the brilliant editorship of Fr. Matthew Russell. The journal attracted a glittering array of talent to its pages, including W. B. Yeats. *Studies: An Irish Quarterly Review*, founded in

1912, became a vehicle for intelligent debate across an enormous intellectual range and for many decades was the most important Catholic review in the country. The province in the person of Fr. Francis Browne produced one of the most renowned photographers of the twentieth century. Irish Jesuits played little role in the emerging nationalist movement and indeed had a reputation for being pro-British. The official missions of the province were in Zambia and Hong Kong, but Irish Jesuits served with distinction in various other places including Japan, South America, and East Africa. Concern for issues of social justice led to the establishment in 1948 of the Catholic Workers' College, which by 1967 had evolved into the College of Industrial Relations. The province also contributed to philosophical and theological reflection through the Milltown Institute (1968–2015) and by the founding in 1970 of the Irish School of Ecumenics.

See also Browne, Francis, SJ; Hong Kong; Zambia

McRedmond, Louis, *To the Greater Glory of God: A History of the Irish Jesuits*. Dublin: Gill and Macmillan, 1991.
Morrissey, Thomas J., *As One Sent: Peter Kenney SJ (1779–1841) – His Mission in Ireland and North America*. Dublin: Four Courts Press, 1996.

Oliver P. Rafferty, SJ

Italy

The Italian province of the Society of Jesus was created by Ignatius in 1552. At that time, and until 1861, the Italian Peninsula was politically fragmented and under the control of different kingdoms and powers. Ignatius was the provincial de facto, while Diego Laínez (1512–65) was an official visitor to all the houses, with the exception of Rome and Sicily, the latter having become a separate province in 1553. In the years before the death of Ignatius (1556), twenty-four houses and about 400 Jesuits were active in the Italian Peninsula, and their number increased to 1,000 by the end of the sixteenth century. The growth of the Jesuit order was exceptional, and their geographic distribution depended on the support of local political and ecclesiastical authorities. In some cases, these authorities were extremely supportive of the Society, but in other cases – such as in the Diocese of Milan led by Archbishop Charles Borromeo (1538–84) – were more prudent and skeptical toward the growth of this new religious order.

By 1578 Jesuits in Italy were organized into five provinces: the Roman, Neapolitan, Lombardian, Sicilian, and Venetian – a structure that remained almost unchanged until the Suppression. Jesuits dedicated themselves to various types of ministries that became typical of their presence. First, they started missions in the towns and in the countryside where people who were already baptized were in need of education. Silvestro Landini (1503–54), who joined the Society under the guidance of Ignatius, became a famous missionary in various regions of Italy and – in the last part of his life – in Corsica. He began to call Corsica "my Indies," comparing his missions to the growing Jesuit missions overseas. The expression became common within the Society.

The Kingdom of Naples soon became the object of great interest to the Jesuits. Beginning in the 1550s, they undertook the task of civilizing the regions of Naples, creating confraternities, dedicating themselves to charitable work, and acting as itinerant preachers who sought the conversion of sinners and inculcated social virtues. For instance, during the Neapolitan Revolt of 1585, they went into the streets to bring an end to the violence and pacify the population.

At the beginning of the seventeenth century, Jesuits began the "urban missions" in the main cities of Italy, including preaching in the squares, processions, confessions, and the teaching of catechism. In Rome, the Oratorio del Caravita, an institution created in 1630 by Pietro Gravita (1587–1658), became the center of the urban mission.

Different methods of preaching were developed within the Society. During the seventeenth century, the prominent Jesuit Paolo Segneri senior (1624–94) traversed twenty-three dioceses with more than 500 missions in the Papal States and in northern Italy with his companion Giovanni Pietro Pinamonti (1632–1703). Segneri developed a theatrical missionary approach – including night processions and public penance – that became a model for generations of Jesuits, but he was also criticized and considered to be too emotional and ineffective in the long term.

From different provinces of Italy many Jesuits addressed to the general the *litterae indipetae*, letters requesting that they be allowed to leave for the Indies (*petebant Indias*). Borrowing the language from Ignatius's *Spiritual Exercises*, they considered the desire to leave for overseas missions as the first sign that God was calling, but always paired it with "indifference," that is, unconditional obedience to the decision of the superior.

Even if at the beginning education was not a ministry of the Society of Jesus, it quickly developed into one of the Jesuits' main activities. Italy saw the birth of the Jesuit involvement in education with the College of Messina (1548), the first of many others. At Ignatius's death, Jesuits were in charge of 18 colleges in Italy, which grew to 49 at the beginning of the seventeenth century and to over 100 at the beginning of the eighteenth century. The Roman College stood out as the greatest example of Jesuit educational enterprise. Opened in 1551, it enrolled almost 1,000 students in 1560, and it was later renamed the Gregorian University in honor of its greatest patron, Pope Gregory XIII (r. 1572–85).

Particularly important in the colleges was the presence of confraternities and sodalities promoted by laypeople – students, artisans, professionals, and also nobles – under the guidance of Jesuits. Members of the confraternities followed a rule of prayer, of meditation and examination of conscience, and were dedicated to charitable works such as visiting prisons, providing assistance in hospitals, and taking care of women who had suffered abuse and the mentally ill. Marian congregations were confraternities dedicated to the Virgin Mary; they were begun in 1563 at the Roman College and spread very quickly throughout Italy and Europe. The founding chapter (*Prima primaria*) received papal approval in 1584 with the bull *Omnipotentis Dei* by Gregory XIII and became the model for other congregations. Membership in the sodalities came from a broad range of society, including nobles, artisans, and women.

The Society of Jesus in Italy was often involved in political controversies; since the 1550s it had had a stormy relationship with the Republic of Venice. In 1606, following a diplomatic quarrel between Venice and Paul V (r. 1605–21), the Pope promulgated the Interdict that forbade the entire clergy from celebrating sacraments within the territory of the Republic. The Jesuits strongly supported the Pope and they were expelled from the Republic; even when the Interdict was lifted in 1607, resulting in a formal reconciliation with the Pope, Jesuits were not re-admitted into the Republic for fifty years, until 1656.

But it was the eighteenth century that was the most difficult period for the Society of Jesus in Italy. The growing aversion to the Society by the Bourbon dynasties was accompanied by the strengthening of anti-Jesuit and pro-Jansenist movements within the Church. The Jesuit expulsion from the Kingdoms of Portugal (1759) and Spain (1763) led to the expulsion from the Italian kingdoms which were most under Bourbon influence: the Kingdom of Naples (1767) and the Duchy of Parma (1768). The expelled Jesuits resided in the Papal States but, after the canonical suppression of the Society by Clement XIV (1773), they were able to relocate to towns and cities in central Italy where they progressively integrated into academic and cultural institutions.

Immediately after the Suppression, Italian ex-Jesuits shared hopes for an imminent restoration of the Society. Dispersed in different cities and often welcomed by Italian bishops in their dioceses – ten ex-Jesuits were later consecrated bishops – they maintained a network of letters, publications, and book exchanges, spreading prophecies and apocalyptic interpretations about the forthcoming death of Clement XIV and forecasts about the "resurrection" of the Society. The death of General Lorenzo Ricci (1775) in the prison of Castel Sant'Angelo showed that the restoration was not as imminent as they had hoped.

Prominent Italian ex-Jesuits such as Giovanni Vincenzo Bolgeni (1733–1811), Alfonso Muzzarelli (1749–1813), Luigi Mozzi de' Capitani (1746–1813), and Francesco Antonio Zaccaria (1714–95) dedicated themselves to scholarship in theology, literature, and the sciences; many of them published works against Jansenism, created confraternities and educational institutions, and preached popular missions. At the beginning of the nineteenth century, popular missions in the Italian cities and countryside were conducted by Jesuits according to the traditional method of Paolo Segneri. The appreciation and support of many bishops contributed to the reestablishment of the Society.

One of the most important figures of this period was the Spanish Jesuit José Pignatelli (1737–1811). After the expulsion of the Society of Jesus from Spain, he went to Corsica, Genoa, and Bologna. In 1799 he became the master of the novices for the novitiate of Colorno (Parma), the first one in Italian territory since the Suppression (but which was dependent on the province of White Russia, where the Society had never been suppressed). In the following years, Pope Pius VII (r. 1800–23), with the brief *Catholicae fidei* (March 7, 1801), approved the Society in Russia and with the brief *Per alias* (1804) extended the same approval to the Kingdom of Naples. Pignatelli became provincial of the province of the Kingdom of the Two Sicilies and in 1806 – after moving to Rome to escape the Napoleonic army – provincial of Italy. In this delicate phase of its history, the Society enjoyed the esteem of Pius VII, of many cardinals, and of Duke Ferdinand of Bourbon-Parma (r. 1765–1802), who became influential in reestablishing the Society in the Parma territories.

The renewed hope for the restoration of the Society introduced internal debates. One of the main issues of those years was the Paccanari affair. In 1797 Niccolò Paccanari (1786–1811) founded the Society of the Faith of Jesus whose rules were similar to those of Jesuits. This group was at first supported by prominent pro-Jesuit ecclesiastics, but its ambiguity in the relationship with the Society of Jesus immediately appeared. Accused of immoral conduct by many ex-Jesuits but also by former members of the Society of the Faith, in 1808 Paccanari was condemned by the Holy Office to eight years of imprisonment and died a few years later under mysterious circumstances.

In 1814, after over six years of confinement in Savona and Paris, Pius VII returned to Rome. He was determined to restore the Society and was supported by the enthusiastic endorsement of several bishops. The bull *Sollicitudo omnium ecclesiarum* (1814) was read in the Gesù Church in Rome in the presence of 150 Jesuits. The "New Society" was a small group of people – about 600 in total; some of them were old Jesuits who lived through the period of the Suppression, and others were young novices who did not have any knowledge of the Society as it was before 1773. Italian Jesuits were a significant group, and by the middle of the nineteenth century they represented about 40 percent of the entire order.

Pius VII nominated the former superior of the White Russia province, the Polish Jesuit Tadeusz Brzozowski (1749–1820), as general of the Society. The czar, who was upset with the restoration, did not allow Brzozowski to leave Russia. General Congregation 20 (1820) elected Luigi Fortis (1748–1829), the last Italian general of the Society up to the present. In Italy, Jesuits revived their traditional ministries: rural missions, especially in Sicily and in the Neapolitan province; urban missions, with the rebirth of the Oratorio del Caravita in Rome; education, thanks to restoration of control over their colleges (for example the Roman College in 1824) while new ones were founded; and extra-European missions, strongly encouraged by General Jan Philipp Roothaan (1785–1853) through a vibrant letter (*De missionum externarum desiderio excitando et fovendo*, 1833) that reminded the restored Society of the great examples of Jesuit missionaries of the past.

During the early nineteenth century, lively debates about the identity of the restored Society took place. While certain Jesuits highlighted the continuity with the past – supported by the fact that the Society had always survived in White Russia – others emphasized the need for a new religious order that should adapt to the current political and cultural environment. The Society followed both directions: on the one hand, several *litterae indipetae* written by Italian Jesuits at the beginning of the nineteenth century show the strong desire for a continuity with the past; on the other hand, Generals Fortis and Roothaan supported a reform of the *Ratio studiorum* (1832) in order to introduce new subjects to be taught (such as history and geography) and the use of modern languages in Jesuit teaching.

The difficult political situation in the Italian Peninsula during the nineteenth century caused many problems for the Jesuits, who became one of the favorite targets of the Italian Risorgimento through hostile campaigns, expulsions, and dispersions.

Following the First War of Independence (1848), Jesuits were expelled from the Papal States, the Kingdom of the Two Sicilies, the Kingdom of Lombardy-Venetia, and the Kingdom of Sardinia. When the Roman Republic was created (1849), the Pope escaped to Gaeta and Roothaan fled to Marseille, where he stayed until 1850. During this period, attacks against the Society also came from inside the Church. The abbot Vincenzo Gioberti (1801–52) accused the Society of anti-liberalism and strongly condemned Jesuit education methods. In his works *Prolegomeni al primato* (1845) and especially in *Il gesuita moderno* (1846–47), he launched a bitter attack against the Society that had a huge resonance on the Italian Peninsula; after initial prudence, Pius IX condemned the book in 1849. The Jesuits' response came quickly, resulting in numerous published works in opposition to Gioberti; among the defenders of the Society, the Neapolitan Jesuit Carlo Maria Curci (1810–91) was particularly active. The latter was the main founder of the biweekly journal *La Civiltà Cattolica* (Catholic civilization). The idea of a magazine of general culture, in Italian, for a well-educated lay public, whose aim was to defend the Jesuits and the Church, met with significant resistance within the Society (in particular from Roothaan) but was approved with enthusiasm by Pius IX and had unexpected success. Considered as the first Italian "national" journal, since its foundation it has had a special relationship with the Holy See.

Italian members of the Society also made important contributions to theological debates: many Jesuits at the Roman College advocated for defining the dogma of the Immaculate Conception (1854) and actively participated in the preparations of the First Vatican Council, while *La Civiltà Cattolica* was influential in readying the Church for the definition of papal infallibility.

The second half of the century saw another series of expulsions and dispersions of Jesuits. In 1859–60, they were expelled from the Kingdom of Sardinia and, after the creation of the Kingdom of Italy (1861), from the Venice province (1866) and from Rome (1873). General Pieter Beckx (1795–1887) had to flee to Fiesole, where he died. Beckx's successor, Anton Anderledy (1819–92), also died in Fiesole, while General Luis Martín (1846–1906), elected during General Congregation 24 that took place in Loyola, Spain (1892), was finally able to move the headquarters of the Society back to Rome from Fiesole (1895), owing to improved relations with the Kingdom of Italy.

Jesuits were engaged as military chaplains during World War I. During that war, some colleges of the Society were transformed into military hospitals; the Venice province in particular suffered badly from the destruction of the war. The postwar period was characterized by the Society's quick recovery, in terms of both numbers and its reengagement with internal and extra-European missions. New houses for spiritual exercises were built in numerous Italian cities, and every year they hosted thousands of people from every social status.

The Lateran Pacts (1929), an agreement between the Kingdom of Italy and the Holy See, opened a new season for Jesuit educational activities. Owing to the intermediation of the Jesuit Pietro Tacchi Venturi (1861–1956), a key character in the relationship between the Church and the Fascist regime, Jesuit schools and many other Catholic schools were approved by the state after verifying the programs and that professors had a university degree. During the Fascist period, *La Civiltà Cattolica* fluctuated between positions hostile to the regime – creating serious tensions – and positions that seemed to support some of the Fascist positions, as evidenced by the anti-Semitic views found in some articles.

Before World War II, Jesuit missions strengthened significantly, and new instruments to support them were created, such as the revival of the Marian congregations and the Lega missionaria studenti (Student Missionary League), a youth training organization begun in 1927 at Collegio Massimo in Rome that became a model for similar associations across Italy. The mission in Albania was particularly dear to Italian Jesuits: in 1946 Giovanni Fausti (1899–1946), a missionary in Albania and tireless promoter of dialogue with the Muslim world, was arrested by the Communist regime, accused of being a spy of the Vatican, and killed together with a companion; twenty other Jesuits were arrested. Italian Jesuits went back to Albania in 1991, at the request of John Paul II, and continue to be a significant presence in the country today.

In the postwar period, the number of Jesuit vocations began to decline, a phenomenon that, together with men leaving the Society, worsened dramatically after 1960. Jesuit teaching activity also underwent a crisis: the Constitution of the Italian Republic

(1948) allowed Jesuit schools some autonomy, but the drop in vocations and the need to hire lay teachers introduced the new problem of the cost of the schools. On the other hand, the university residences directed by Jesuits became a great success in the post-war years. Jesuits continued to be involved in the intellectual life of the country: some of them obtained prestigious chairs in Italian state universities and during the period from the 1940s to the 1960s, they promoted new cultural initiatives, such as the Centro di studi filosofici tra professori universitari in Gallarate (1945), later transformed into a foundation still active today, and the cultural center San Fedele in Milan (1954) which gave birth to *Aggiornamenti sociali* (1950), a still-active monthly journal analyzing polit-ical, social, and ecclesial life in Italy.

The end of the Second Vatican Council (1965) coincided with the election of General Pedro Arrupe (1907–91, generalate 1965–83) and the opening of a new era in the his-tory of the Society. Since the beginning of his generalate, but especially after General Congregation 35 (1975) – when a harsh debate between the Jesuits and Pope Paul VI (r. 1963–78) occurred – Arrupe led the Society toward a stronger emphasis on social jus-tice; in Italy this meant a weakening of the Jesuit intellectual and educational tradition. One of the most important figures in the Italian Jesuits after the Council was Cardinal Carlo Maria Martini (1927–2012), a renowned biblical scholar, the archbishop of Milan (1980–2002), and a prominent public figure.

Because of the progressive reduction in the number of members of the Society, the Italian provinces were gradually unified under the Arrupe generalate. In 1984 General Peter-Hans Kolvenbach (b. 1928) reorganized the provinces into three regions: Northern Italy, Central Italy (including Sardinia), and Southern Italy (including Sicily).

See also Messina; Papacy; Roman College; Rome; Suppression

Grendler, Paul F., *The Jesuits and Italian Universities 1548–1773*. Washington, DC: The Catholic University of America Press, 2016.

Guidetti, Armando, *Le missioni popolari: i grandi gesuiti italiani. Disegno storico-biografico delle mis-sioni popolari dei gesuiti d'Italia dalle origini al Concilio Vaticano II*. Milan: Rusconi, 1988.

Lazar, Lance G., *Working in the Vineyard of the Lord: Jesuit Confraternities in Early Modern Italy*. Toronto: University of Toronto Press, 2005.

Martina, Giacomo, *Storia della Compagnia di Gesù in Italia (1814–1983)*. Brescia: Morcelliana, 2003.

Murphy, Paul V., "Jesuit Rome and Italy." In Thomas Worcester, ed., *The Cambridge Companion to the Jesuits*. Cambridge: Cambridge University Press, 2008, pp. 71–87.

Rurale, Flavio, *I gesuiti a Milano: religione e politica nel secondo Cinquecento*. Rome: Bulzoni, 1992.

Scaduto, Mario, *Storia della Compagnia di Gesù in Italia*. Rome: La Civiltà Cattolica, 1930–64.

Zanardi, Mario, ed., *I gesuiti e Venezia: momenti e problemi di storia veneziana della Compagnia di Gesù: atti del convegno di studi, Venezia, 2–5 ottobre 1990*. Venice–Padua: Giunta Regionale del Veneto–Gregoriana Libreria editrice, 1994.

Emanuele Colombo

Jamaica

A Caribbean island of the Greater Antilles, 150 miles by 60 miles at its widest point, Jamaica was colonized by Spaniards in the sixteenth century but seized by English forces in 1655. Anglicanism dominated; no Catholic priest was permitted until 1792.

An apostolic vicariate was established in 1837; the first Jesuits, William Cotham (English) and James Dupeyron (French), with the Franciscan vicar apostolic and several secular priests, served a scattered flock of Spanish merchants, Haïtian refugees, and some Irish and English Catholics. Despite serious internal tensions, foundations were quickly laid for the mission's enduring framework: larger parishes, educational institutions, and other projects centered in Kingston, with a growing network of rural churches and mission chapels to the north and west. Fr. Dupeyron, the first priest to visit nearly every corner of the island, became vicar apostolic in 1855. For over a century after, Catholicism in Jamaica was fully dependent on Jesuit leadership and initiative.

With continued immigration, outreach to the poor, and increasing visibility and prestige, the Catholic population gradually increased (reaching something under 10 percent of island population by the mid-twentieth century). The variety of works grew correspondingly. In 1850, Spanish Jesuits exiled from Colombia began a school that, despite sporadic beginnings, eventually thrived as St. George's College, Jamaica's first secondary institution for classical education (continuing under Jesuit sponsorship as of 2017). With the involvement of the laity and, after 1857, communities of religious sisters, parochial elementary schools, orphanages, and other institutions were established. A newspaper, *Catholic Opinion*, was founded in 1896. The network of churches and chapels continued to spread across the island, requiring assistance from non-Jesuit missionary priests after 1901.

The first bishop was Charles Gordon, SJ, appointed vicar apostolic in 1889. In 1894 Jesuit administration passed from the English to the Maryland-New York province of the United States (and in 1929 to the New England province, newly formed in 1926.) The American Jesuits became embroiled in a dispute with Bishop Gordon over the relationship between the Jesuit mission and the vicariate as a whole, the overlapping roles of vicar and Jesuit superior, and ownership of various Church properties. The dispute was barely resolved when the great earthquake of 1907 struck Kingston, severely damaging or destroying most of the mission's churches and schools in the city. Recovery took years, but growth continued. Bishop Gordon was succeeded by a series of American Jesuit bishops, the last of whom, John McEleney, became bishop of the new Diocese of Kingston in 1956, archbishop in 1967, and was succeeded by native Jamaican Samuel Carter, SJ, in 1971.

The last half of the twentieth century brought great change. Jamaica was granted Home Rule in 1944 and independence from Britain in 1962. A democratic-socialist government won power in 1972 and held it until the election of 1980, which was marked by violent political unrest. Meanwhile, the Second Vatican Council (1962–65) and Jesuit General Congregations 31 (1965–66) and 32 (1974–75) published far-reaching decrees. Amid these events, Jesuits increasingly emphasized concepts such as "inculturation," "integral human development," and "the option for the poor." Internal debates about applying these ideals shaped new projects and experiments over the subsequent decades. A Social Action Center was opened in Kingston in 1958, continuing John Peter Sullivan, SJ's, pioneering work with credit unions, cooperatives, and labor organizations. While Campion College, established in 1960, developed a reputation as a school for the wealthier classes, St. George's became increasingly diverse socioeconomically and racially. Several Jamaicans studying for the Jesuit priesthood trained partially in Jamaica rather than abroad, some pursuing studies in sociology and anthropology. A few Jesuits became directly involved in increasingly turbulent Jamaican politics.

Disagreements over mission priorities and adaptation to social change continued as available personnel declined. In the late 1980s, Canadian Jesuits led by Fr. James Webb

Figure 31 Fred Foley, SJ: Jesuits celebrating Independence Day, St. George's College, Jamaica, August 6, 1962. Photograph © Archives of the New England Province, Society of Jesus

established an independent mission, eventually including both Kingston and north coast sites, providing a new model for integrating parish work, education, and social justice concerns. By 1997, this project had merged with the older mission, and Fr. Webb became the first of several Canadian mission superiors. This new era brought a small increase in Jamaicans entering the Jesuits, but also new dangers. In 2001, Canadian Jesuit Fr. Martin Royackers, engaged in a land redistribution project, was murdered outside his north coast rectory.

In the twenty-first century, the much-diminished mission (11 members in 2014, down from over 100 in the 1960s) has searched for appropriate organizational models. The creation of a united Caribbean province, encouraged by the superior general, faces serious cultural, political, and logistical hurdles, despite some cooperative efforts. Meanwhile, the mission, long classified as a "Dependent Region" of the New England province, was designated simply a community of the new USA Northeast province in 2014.

See also Caribbean; Royackers, Martin, SJ

Delany, Francis X., *A History of the Catholic Church in Jamaica, B.W.I.* New York: Jesuit Mission Press, 1930.

McLaughlin, Gerard L., *Jesuitana Jamaica: Historical Profiles, 1837–1996.* Kingston: Arawak Publications, 2000.

Osborne, Francis J., *History of the Catholic Church in Jamaica.* Chicago, IL: Loyola University Press, 1988.

William A. Clark, SJ

Jansenism

Jansenism is the name given to a supposed movement originating in the seventeenth century in circles attached to the monastery of Port-Royal, near Paris which, in religious terms, supported the radical Augustinianism of Cornelius Jansen, bishop of Ypres (1585–1638) and his friend and collaborator the Abbé de Saint-Cyran (1581–1643). Jansen had opposed the Jesuits and their advocacy of Luis de Molina's teaching on grace and free will in the University of Leuven. Many modern scholars have insisted that Jansenism never actually existed as a movement and was, instead, a phantom invented by its Jesuit-inspired enemies. The name was never used in Port-Royal, where they identified them-selves instead as "Friends of the Truth" or "Friends of Saint Augustine." The label stuck, however, to a shifting spectrum of religious or political views that continued into the nineteenth century and still has some roots within a group of minor religious sects. Opposition to papal and royal absolutism lies consistently at the heart of Jansenism's political aspect, while devotion to a rigorous interpretation of Saint Augustine's teaching and opposition to Jesuit casuistry and sacramental practice lies consistently (if not always coherently) at the heart of its religious side.

At its best the Jansenist movement was an attempt at Catholic reform in terms of con-ciliar governance, biblical, patristic, and liturgical scholarship, and the promotion of the role of the laity, which came to fruition only in the Second Vatican Council. Various earlier attempts at reform in liturgy or governance, such as those of the Synod of Pistoia, were condemned as "Jansenist" with little cause. Ironically the main thrust of reform, as well as various shifts in sacramental theology and ecclesiology which gained ascendance at Vatican II, were largely the fruit of the *nouvelle théologie*, itself largely a phantom movement invented by its opponents.

The quarrel between Jansenists and Jesuits has roots that reach far back in the history of the relationship between the Church, the Crown, and other sources of power within the state of early modern France. Jansenism not only embraces the traditional French resistance to excessive papal authority but an ecclesiology which valued the direct rela-tionship between Christ and the individual conscience over any structures of power. Jansen's *Augustinus* (1640) was condemned by Pope Innocent X's bull *Cum occasione* (1643) for containing five heretical propositions. All Jansenists were required to sign a formulary confessing their errors. The formulary controversy led Blaise Pascal to write his famous *Lettres provinciales* (1656–57) attacking Jesuit casuistry and moral laxity, while in return the Jesuits accused the Port-Royal party of crypto-Calvinism and of terri-fying the faithful away from the sacraments through their rigid teachings on grace.

Antoine Arnauld's claim that these propositions were not, in fact, contained in the *Augustinus* led to decades of theological and legal controversy at the heart of which lay a challenge to the extent of papal authority in matters of doctrine. Pascal and others more radically claimed that condemning Jansen was tantamount to condemning Augustine himself. They refused to sign the formulary and in 1661 the monastery of Port-Royal was closed and its lay community dissolved. By order of Louis XIV, the monastery was razed to the ground in 1710. Clement XI's bull *Unigenitus* (1713) condemned 101 propositions from Quesnel's *Réflexions morales* as heretical, and as identical with the earlier propositions condemned in Jansen's writings. Modern scholars, as well as many commentators of the time, view *Unigenitus* as a tragic error which rendered hundreds of innocent Catholics pseudo-heretics overnight. Many leading Jansenists fled to Holland where they founded what became the Jansenist Diocese of Utrecht, which became part of the Old Catholic Church after the First Vatican Council's formal declaration of papal infallibility.

The Jesuit-inspired Marian congregations fostered frequent sacramental access but were eventually suppressed as agencies of religiously inspired political unrest. Later Jesuit sources looked back on the suppression of the Congregations as a preliminary to the suppression of the Society of Jesus itself, fed by the triple hatred of the Jansenists, the University, and the Parlement. Jansenism also came to be equated with political subversion in the eighteenth century, where the *Nouvelles Ecclésiastiques* was a Jansenist-inspired clandestine journal which appealed directly to the public against the increasing despotism of crown and papacy. The "black legend" of Jansenism grew up chiefly among those who later blamed it for the destruction of the *Ancien Régime*.

In 1688 Cardinal d'Aguirre remarked to the Jesuit superior general: "There are three sorts of Jansenist. The first are those who uphold the Five Propositions and [are] extremely few … The second are those who are zealous for strict morality and rigorous discipline and, despite the laxity of our time, there is a reasonable number of these. The third are those who, in one way or another, are opposed to the Jesuits, and there is an infinite number of them."

See also Anti-Jesuit Polemic; Arnauld, Antoine; France; Paris; Pascal, Blaise; Suppression

Doyle, William, *Jansenism: Catholic Resistance to Authority from the Reformation to the French Revolution*. London: Macmillan Press, 2000.

Quantin, Jean-Louis, *Le Rigorisme Chrétien*. Paris: Cerf, 2001.

Simmonds, Gemma, "Jansenism: An Early *Ressourcement* Movement?" In Gabriel Flynn and Paul D. Murray, eds., *Ressourcement: A Movement for Renewal in Twentieth-Century Catholic Theology*. Oxford: Oxford University Press, 2012, pp. 23–35.

Van Kley, Dale K., *The Jansenists and the Expulsion of the Jesuits from France, 1757–1765*. New Haven, CT/London: Yale University Press, 1975.

Gemma Simmonds, CJ

Japan

The history of the Jesuit Japan mission can be divided into two separate phases. The first phase, often called the Christian Century, began with Francis Xavier's entry in 1549 and ended in the martyrdom of Mancio Konishi, SJ, in 1644. The second phase, of the restored Society, began in 1908.

The first phase of the mission experienced both phenomenal growth and a tragic outcome. Xavier and his successors under Portuguese patronage introduced Christianity for the first time in Japan's history. A papal bull of 1585 secured the Jesuit monopoly in mission. By 1599, the Society baptized about 40,000 Christians. Subsequent papal bulls in 1600 and 1608 allowed the Dominicans, Franciscans, and Augustinians under Spanish patronage to labor in Japan. The Jesuit presence remained dominant. The mission became a Jesuit vice province in 1582 and province in 1611. After the Diocese of Japan was established in 1588, the bishops of Japan were appointed from among the Jesuits.

Most field missionaries, such as Gnecchi Soldo-Organtino (1533–1609), pursued the principle of *omnia omnibus*. They adopted Japanese cultural and religious ideas and practices in their efforts to indigenize Christianity. One of the successful practices was the production of Kirishitanban (Christian literature). These translations and original works interwove transliterated Portuguese and Latin and Japanese Buddhist terms. Noting the importance of the literature mission, Visitor Alessandro Valignano brought a movable type press from Europe. The Jesuit Press in Japan published about sixty titles between 1591 and 1614. According to the detailed descriptions by Luís Fróis (1532–97), these books contributed to conversions of numerous Japanese and were effective in nurturing the new Christian community.

The recruitment of native leadership was another fruitful practice. In 1580, the mission founded a college and seminaries. In 1601 Bishop Luís Cerqueira, SJ (1542–1614), ordained two Japanese Jesuits, Sebastião Kimura (1565–1622) and Luís Niabara (1564–1618), as priests. Adopting Buddhist ranking, the mission created Japanese coadjutor-catechist classes of *dōjuku* (evangelical preachers) and *kambō* (local pastors). Many women catechists carried similar tasks to those of the *dōjuku*. Lay *confrarias*, again paralleling Buddhist tradition, became the base communities among the hidden Christians during the Suppression years.

A third pioneering practice was the attempt of interreligious dialogue. While their Thomist understanding of Japanese religions had limitations, the Jesuits studied texts of diverse religions, visited temples, and interacted with monks and nuns. Fabian Fucan's *Myōtei dialogue* (1605) suggests the content and format of such dialogues.

Increasing persecutions interrupted the mission. In 1587 Toyotomi Hideyoshi issued the *Edict of Expulsion of Padres* but still tacitly tolerated clandestine Jesuits because of his interest in Portuguese trade. In 1597, reacting to encroaching Spanish colonialism from Manila, Hideyoshi ordered the execution of twenty-six men, including Paul Miki (1563–97) and two other Jesuits in Nagasaki. In the ensuing years of Tokugawa Ieyasu's ascendancy to shogun between 1598 and 1603, the mission steadily grew. By 1612, the Christian population increased to above 600,000. The number of Jesuit priests was about 115. But in 1612 the second Shogun Hidetada took a decisively exclusivist foreign policy, except for the Dutch East India Company, and banned Christianity. In the Great Expulsion of 1614, most Jesuits were deported to Macau and others to Manila. Eighteen Jesuit padres and eight *irmãos* remained behind and several secretly reentered Japan. During the years of severe persecution, about 40,000 foreign-born missionaries, Japanese and Korean Jesuits, catechists, and laypersons became martyrs. After 1650 the "Hidden Christians" went totally underground until they resurfaced in 1865.

Following the Meiji government's lifting of the ban on Christianity in 1870, the Jesuit mission proceeded cautiously in 1908. It became a vice province in 1948 and province in 1958. Its energy has been centered in education. Its major foundation, Sophia University in Tokyo (founded 1913), recently celebrated its 100th anniversary. The mission founded other reputable schools including Elisabeth University of Music (1949) and Hiroshima Gakuin (1955). The Nagasaki Twenty-Six Martyrs Museum preserves the historical legacy of the first phase of the mission. In 1932, in the face of mounting military nationalism, several students at Sophia University refused to worship at the Yasukuni Shrine. The Jesuits went through delicate negotiations for their survival.

These crises from both of the two phases of the Jesuit Japan mission are reflected in the novel *The Silence*, by Shūsaku Endō (1923–96).

See also Arrupe, Pedro, SJ; Catechists, Women and the Jesuits in Japan; Froís, Luís, SJ; Miki, Paul, SJ, St.; Sophia University; Valignano, Alessandro, SJ; Xavier, Francis, SJ, St.

Farge, William J., *The Japanese Translations of the Jesuit Mission Press, 1590–1614: De imitatione Christi and Guía de pecadores*. Lewiston, NY: E. Mellen Press, 2003.

Schütte, Joseph Franz, ed. and annot., *Monumenta Historica Japoniae I: Textus Catalogorum Japoniae aliaeque de Personis Domibusque SJ in Japonia, Informationes et Relationes, 1549–1654*. (Monumenta Historica Societatis Jesu, Vol. 111). Rome: Institutum Historicum Societatis Iesu, 1975.

Ucerler, M. Antoni J., "Jesuit Enterprise in Sixteenth- and Seventeenth-Century Japan." In Thomas Worcester, ed., *The Cambridge Companion to the Jesuits*. Cambridge/New York: Cambridge University Press, 2008, pp. 153–68.

Ward, Haruko Nawata, "Japan and Europe: The Christian Century, 1549–1600." In Margaret King, ed., *Oxford Bibliographies in Renaissance and Reformation*. New York: Oxford University Press, 2015. Online.

Haruko Nawata Ward

Jay, Claude, SJ (1504–1552)

Claude Jay was born in Savoy in 1504. After early education there, he was ordained a priest in Geneva in 1528. At the University of Paris (1534–36), he received the licentiate and the degree of Master of Arts. In Paris, he had made the Spiritual Exercises under Peter Faber's guidance and joined the group of companions who, under the leadership of Ignatius of Loyola, were to become the founders of the Society of Jesus.

After the 1540 establishment of the Society of Jesus as a religious order, Jay was sent to Germany in 1541, where he spent most of the rest of his life. Up to 1545, he assisted at Diets at Speyer, Worms, and Augsburg. At Augsburg, Regensburg, and Ingolstadt, he engaged in the usual Jesuit ministries of preaching, spiritual direction, administering the sacraments, giving the Spiritual Exercises, and public lecturing, especially on Sacred Scripture. For his work, he was increasingly appreciated by Ferdinand I, William IV of Bavaria, and Emperor Charles V. That esteem brought strong pressure to accept a bishopric, which he and Ignatius successfully resisted. From 1545 to 1547, Jay represented Bishop Otto Truchsess at the first session of the Council of Trent.

Returning to Germany, Jay taught theology at Ingolstadt in 1549 and urged the establishment of a Jesuit college there. His letters to Ignatius of Loyola about the dire straits of the Church in Germany and the need for education helped move the Society to its growing involvement in that apostolate. In 1551 Jay went to Vienna to found a Jesuit college. He died in that city on August 6, 1552. Peter Canisius, himself later called the "Apostle of Germany," regarded Claude Jay as the true bearer of such a designation.

See also German-Speaking Lands

Bangert, William V., *Claude Jay and Alfonso Salmerón*. Chicago, IL: Loyola Press, 1985.

Padberg, John W., "Three Forgotten Founders of the Society of Jesus." *Studies in the Spirituality of Jesuits*, 29, 12 (1997), 1–45.

John W. Padberg, SJ

Jesuit Historical Institute in Africa (JHIA)

The Jesuit Historical Institute in Africa (JHIA) started in 2010 as an idea of the Jesuit General, Adolfo Nicolás, to promote the study of the Order's largely unexplored involvement in the evangelization of Africa. Further deliberations in Africa pointed to the need for such study to be carried out within a broader social, cultural, and religious context. The JHIA's vision was thus expanded to that of providing a cost-effective environment for groundbreaking research on the religious histories, cultures, and traditions of the people of Africa and Madagascar.

The JHIA pursues its vision by carrying out a fourfold mission. First, the Institute collects published and unpublished records on the religious traditions and cultures of Africa, including Islam. Second, it documents the evolution of Christianity on the African continent. In this process, it pays attention to the role of the Jesuits and other missionary societies in the spread of Christianity in Africa and also makes a deliberate effort to highlight the contribution of local agents of evangelization. The collected information is preserved in various formats at the Institute's premises in Nairobi, Kenya.

At the start of the Institute, a significant volume of Jesuit publications was transferred from the Jesuit headquarters in Rome to Nairobi. Subsequently, the JHIA undertook to solicit for documents and publications of interest from institutions and individuals, especially retiring Africanists with valuable collections that they were willing to donate gratuitously. Some of the most treasured books that are currently at the Institute came from Oxford's Bodleian Library of Commonwealth and African Studies and from the United Society for the Propagation of the Gospel. Several others were received from the late Dr. Margaret Mary Louise Pirouet (1928–2012), formerly senior lecturer in religious studies at Homerton College, Cambridge, and from the family of Kenneth Kirkwood (1919–97), who was professor of African history at the University of Oxford and the inaugural Rhodes Professor of Race Relations, among others. Furthermore, the JHIA's Africa Thesis Bank, which accepts masters and Ph.D. theses that touch on Africa, archives, advertises, and, depending on donors' instructions, makes accessible to readers research findings from universities all over the world. The work of collecting records and publications is ongoing and dominates the JHIA's operations in the early years of its existence.

Making the collected information accessible is the third aspect of the JHIA's mission. The Institute's collection serves a broad community of researchers in African studies. In some cases, missionary records and publications are the only written sources of past information about cultural, social, and political experiences of various communities in Africa. For instance, the works of the prominent historian George McCall Theal (1837–1919) indicate how indispensable Jesuit records are to any historical study of southern Africa from the sixteenth century that purports to be comprehensive. Thus, because of the nature of its collection, the JHIA serves all researchers that wish to treat African topics from a historical perspective.

The fourth aspect of the JHIA's mission is to promote targeted research. During its first three years, significant resources were directed to researching Jesuit history in Africa. However, other areas were explored and major resources are now directed to areas like the history of HIV and AIDS and the relations between Muslims and Christians in Africa over the centuries. By accumulating necessary sources, the JHIA aims at becoming a compelling research destination in these fields.

With an institution like the JHIA, researchers within Africa will be able to access easily some records that currently exist mainly in Europe and, in the process, avoid prohibitive visa regimes. In this way, the Jesuits intend to contribute directly to one of the most neglected aspects of scholarship in Africa: research. Currently, only 1 percent of internationally published articles on Africa comes from scholars based in Africa, which largely reflects an unequal access to documentary and financial resources. The JHIA is thus designed to circumvent this hurdle and stimulate a research revolution within Africa.

To a large extent, the JHIA remains a vision in the process of being fulfilled. A critical question is whether the Institute will attract sufficient funding for its operations and for more permanent structures, given that it currently operates from temporary premises. African governments and educational institutions have a lamentable record of funding research, and foreign donors rarely support projects that do not address emergency situations in Africa. Moreover, the JHIA is being established at a time when digital technology offers an unprecedented opportunity to make records easily accessible worldwide, and so it faces the challenge of having to operate at the very cutting edge of that technology. It will take many more years for the JHIA to navigate these challenges and become the compelling research environment that preserves memory and promotes historical knowledge in Africa.

See also Africa, East; Archives and Libraries; Hekima University College; HIV/AIDS; Interreligious Dialogue

Festo Mkenda, SJ

Jesuit Refugee Service (JRS)

In November 1980, moved by the plight of Vietnamese, Cambodian, and Laotian "boat-people" fleeing war-ravaged countries, as well as by refugees from Ethiopia struggling to live in Rome, Pedro Arrupe, superior general of the Society of Jesus, announced the establishment of the Jesuit Refugee Service (JRS) to coordinate worldwide efforts – both practical and spiritual – among provinces, institutions, and individuals who were already working with refugees. As general, Arrupe was well aware of the Society's universality and resources and thus reasoned that the Jesuits and their lay collaborators were uniquely positioned to offer a global response to a global problem. No doubt Arrupe's own experience as a refugee influenced him as well: Arrupe was a scholastic when the Jesuits were expelled from Spain in 1932 by the ruling anticlerical government.

So, too, was Arrupe influenced by the experience of Ignatius and his companions during the brutal Roman winter of 1538, when thousands of people were driven into the city from the surrounding towns, very few able to find shelter or adequate food. With many sleeping outside, the death toll was exceedingly high, and some estimate that in the course of a year, the first "companions in the Lord" cared for the temporal needs of over 3,000 refugees. Both Arrupe and his successor, Peter-Hans Kolvenbach, would cite this example in relation to the work and mission of JRS, highlighting the personal presence practiced by the early Jesuits as a model of accompaniment.

However, "refugee" is an inexact word. O'Brien's broad definition is used here:

> A refugee is one who crosses a national boundary because of (a) persecution based on race, religion, nationality, or membership in social or political groups, (b) armed conflict, (c) natural disaster, (d) violation of human rights, or (e) life-threatening economic

conditions. Displaced persons, on the other hand, are those forcibly uprooted from their homes for the same reasons mentioned above, but who do not cross a national border. Both groups of people live a provisional existence awaiting return to their home, resettlement to another country, or integration into their host country. ("Consolation in Action," 3)

The use of the terms "refugee" and "displaced persons" can be used interchangeably and help take into account distinctions – labeled artificial and punitive by Kolvenbach in 1990 – which various governments have taken to using in recent years to deny entry and vital services to refugees. According to Kolvenbach, regardless of name or cause, the effect is the same: human suffering caused by dislocation.

Since its inception, JRS has understood its mission in biblical terms: to welcome the widow, the orphan, and the stranger. This welcome is not to ensure survival alone, but to work toward the full development of persons, to ensure that the men, women, and children affected by dislocation are able to participate in all aspects of life: economic, social, ecclesial, educational, etc. To achieve this, JRS, while always cognizant of their founding mission, has adapted its own structures and guidelines throughout the years, shifting priorities and resources to areas and peoples of greatest need, deferring always to Ignatius's principle of the "greatest universal good," found in Part VII of the *Constitutions*.

In 1980, there were roughly 5 million refugees, but these numbers grew quickly and by the start of the twenty-first century, experts estimated over 45 million dislocated persons throughout the world. Though the early work of JRS was focused mainly on refugee camps in Asia (Thailand, Indonesia, Hong Kong, the Philippines, and Malaysia), JRS quickly began to respond to refugee situations in Africa (Ethiopia, Sudan, Kenya, Malawi, Mozambique, Angola, Liberia, Guinea and Ivory Coast, Burundi, Rwanda, Tanzania, and Zaire); Latin America (El Salvador, Guatemala, and Colombia); and Eastern Europe (Bosnia, Croatia, Albania, and the former Yugoslavia). The work of JRS in each of these places was and is as varied as the locales, and includes working for the reunification of families and offering legal assistance to asylum seekers in addition to education, language and vocational training, and the all-important ministry of personal accompaniment.

In the 1990s both Kolvenbach and the members of General Congregation 34, in the spirit of Arrupe's founding document, made clear that the service JRS offers to refugees is an apostolic commitment of the whole Society of Jesus, not the responsibility of a small group of specialists. This understanding, as well as the practice of personal presence and sense of accompaniment previously mentioned, are enshrined in the JRS Charter, promulgated in 2000.

See also Arrupe, Pedro, SJ; Preferential Option for the Poor; Service of Faith and Promotion of Justice

O'Brien, Kevin, "Consolation in Action: The Jesuit Refugee Service and the Ministry of Accompaniment." *Studies in the Spirituality of Jesuits* 37, 4 (Winter 2005), 1–45.
Jesuit Refugee Service, *Everybody's Challenge: Essential Documents of Jesuit Refugee Service, 1980–2000*. Rome: Jesuit Refugee Service, 2000.

Keith Maczkiewicz, SJ

"Jesuit Style"

See Baroque Art and Architecture

Jesuit Volunteer Corps (JVC)

"Ruined for Life." That's what Jack Morris, an Oregon province Jesuit, promises those who sign up to be members of the Jesuit Volunteer Corps (JVC). Each year about 300 young men and women, many recent graduates of Jesuit high schools, colleges, and universities, begin a one-year commitment as a Jesuit Volunteer (JV) in the United States or in placements abroad. These volunteers work full-time in various social service agencies and attempt to integrate the Christian faith into their work with marginalized members of society while also living in intentional communities centered around four main values: social justice, spirituality, community, and simplicity.

JVC began modestly in Alaska in the mid-1950s when a handful of young people were recruited to help the Jesuits, the Sisters of St. Ann, and the Ursuline sisters with their mission schools in Copper Valley, Alaska. These religious asked recent college graduates to join them and agreed to provide them with room, board, and the opportunity to teach. Eventually JVs were recruited for placements outside of the classroom and, by the early 1960s, Morris had given the group its title and a more formal structure, traveling the continental United States to actively recruit volunteers. Though his original promotional materials did not include the four values, Morris noted later these could readily be seen in the lives of the volunteers whose ranks had steadily grown over the years.

Morris's new project was in line with the liberalizing movements of the Second Vatican Council: never before had laypeople been invited to collaborate alongside priests and nuns in such numbers. From humble beginnings, JVC would grow into the largest young adult Catholic volunteer organization in the world. (Morris eventually convinced his superiors to support the rapidly expanding work until a total of five JVC regions were created, each an individual non-profit organization with a board of directors and fund-raising apparatus: Northwest, Midwest, South, Southwest, and East.)

The four main values of JVC – social justice, spirituality, community, and simplicity – are lived out in various ways. The daily work that JVs undertake, whether as advocates in domestic violence shelters, teachers in inner-city schools, or case managers for refugee resettlement projects, is designed to put them in contact with the poor and the systemic structures with which the poor have to contend. JVs are encouraged to develop a sustained spiritual life and, like Jesuits, to bring their spirituality to both the work they do and their continual examination of the causes of social injustice, to ask of God the hard questions that are born of gritty experience.

In addition to working full-time, JVs live in community with other JVs and share common prayer together and responsibilities for household chores like cooking and cleaning. Volunteers receive a small monthly stipend (around $80) from which food and other basic needs must be met. Though not bound by religious vows, the community life that JVs live is an intentional one, not wholly unlike community life in a religious order.

The influence of the structure of JVC and its four main values cannot be overstated. Each year the Catholic Network of Volunteer Services publishes their directory, listing hundreds of volunteer organizations based on the JVC model. The success of JVC over the years has provided a model that other religious orders have adopted, grafting their own spirituality onto new programs. Generally, the four main values are standard elements of these programs.

In 2006 JVC marked its fiftieth anniversary, claiming over 12,000 total former volunteers, whom they call FJVs. However, the numbers of volunteers has fluctuated each year, necessitating structural changes. In 2009, four of the JVC regions combined, streamlining fund-raising and recruitment operations and leaving only two separate non-profit organizations: JVC and JVC Northwest.

Also in 2006, JVC (in conjunction with Fairfield University) released its first major alumni survey, in which almost 2,000 respondents participated. The survey showed continuing strong identification with the four main values of the program and that FJVs were overrepresented in service-related careers, proportion of income given to charity, attendance at church services, and voting frequency when compared with their non-JV contemporaries. Though some have questioned the ability of JVC to properly form the young people in their charge – especially spiritually – the results of the study reveal "ruined lives" that have helped others.

See also Jesuit Volunteers International (JVI); "Men and Women for Others"; Preferential Option for the Poor; Service of Faith and Promotion of Justice; United States of America

Berggren, Kris, "50 Years of the Jesuit Volunteer Corps." *National Catholic Reporter* 42, 40, September 15, 2006.
Jesuit Volunteer Corps Northwest. http://jvcnorthwest.org/ and Jesuit Volunteer Corps. www.jesuitvolunteers.org/

Keith Maczkiewicz, SJ

Jesuit Volunteers International (JVI)

The history of Jesuit Volunteers International (JVI) is intimately connected to the Jesuit Volunteer Corps (JVC), the largest young adult Catholic volunteer organization in the world. Like their domestic counterparts, Jesuit Volunteers (JVs) living abroad work full-time in various social service agencies and attempt to integrate the Christian faith into their work with marginalized members of society while living in intentional communities with other volunteers. In the mid-1980s, JVC officials began placing small groups of JVs in a dozen developing nations across the globe, opening a new chapter in the history of JVC. As the international arm of JVC, JVI maintains the commitment to the four main values of the domestic program: social justice, spirituality, community, and simplicity.

In 1984, Jesuit Volunteers International was established as an individual non-profit organization with a separate board of directors, application process, and fund-raising apparatus (though it was later merged with four other JVC regions in 2009, streamlining operations and concentrating resources for common marketing and promotion).

Today, JVI stations volunteers in Belize, Nicaragua, Tanzania, the Federated States of Micronesia, Peru, and Chile where, like their domestic counterparts, volunteers serve in legal clinics, parishes, schools, health clinics, and social service agencies. JVs have served in the Federated States of Micronesia in Jesuit schools on the islands of Pohnpei and Chuuk; in Punta Gorda and Belize City, Belize, as members of the staff at the Jesuit parish and as social workers; and as teachers in the Jesuit school in Dar es Salaam, Tanzania. More recently, JVI has placed Spanish-speaking volunteers in Peru and Chile as parish assistants. Unlike their domestic counterparts, JVs who serve internationally make a two-year commitment.

See also Jesuit Volunteer Corps (JVC); "Men and Women for Others"; Preferential Option for the Poor; Service of Faith and Promotion of Justice

Jesuit Volunteer Corps, *Saving Stories: Former Jesuit Volunteers Remember*. Philadelphia: JVC East, 2000.
Jesuit Volunteer Corps. www.jesuitvolunteers.org/

Keith Maczkiewicz, SJ

Jesuits, Jesuitical

"Jesuit" is defined in the *Oxford English Dictionary* as "a member of the Society of Jesus." But the *Dictionary* continues to its second meaning by noting that "the stringent organization of the Order soon rendered it very powerful, and brought it into collision with the civil authority even in Roman Catholic countries." Secrecy, power, and casuistical principles render the term opprobrious both in English and French. The negative connotation is the univocal sense of the adjectival form, "jesuitical."

The notion of a Jesuit as deceitful, conniving, and dissembling through mental reservation arises from controversies involving the Society in the seventeenth and eighteenth centuries. By this point in their history, the Jesuits had established a reputation for teaching moral theology through the use of cases of conscience (casuistry) and had become renowned as confessors of the ruling elites. Because their moral reasoning in confessions often focused on the intention of the actor, they were caricatured as holding that "the ends justify the means." Since Juan de Mariana published his treatise *De rege et regis institutione* in 1599 with a chapter on tyrannicide, Jesuits have been impugned as the intellectual authors of assassinations by many conspiracy theorists. The trial and execution of Henry Garnet in 1606, following the Gunpowder Plot in England, combined the Jesuit reputation for secrecy, plotting, and violence into a compelling conspiracy theory. The outline of the charges against Garnet have been subsequently employed in assassination hypotheses. Father General Luis Martín established the Jesuit Historical Institute in 1893 to counter these accusations by providing material for accurate histories of the Jesuits using critical research methods.

See also Anti-Jesuit Polemic; Casuistry; Ethics; Mental Reservation

Cubitt, Geoffrey, *The Jesuit Myth: Conspiracy Theory in Nineteenth Century France*. New York: Oxford University Press, 1993.
The Oxford English Dictionary. Oxford: Oxford University Press, 1971.

Mark A. Lewis, SJ

Jews and Jesuits

The improved relationship between Jews and Christians, and particularly Jews and Jesuits, has been among the most significant and promising historical developments since World War II. The road toward that new situation has many markers, but it would be a very common perception to see the adoption of the declaration *Nostra aetate* during the Second Vatican Council (1962–65) as the most decisive early step toward reconciliation between these two faith communities. The Society of Jesus has been a leader in the Catholic Church's dialogue with the Jewish people, most clearly, but certainly not exclusively, in the role that the Jesuit cardinal Augustin Bea (1881–1968) exercised in formulating this groundbreaking document. The article explores the relationship between the Jesuit order and the Jews, and Jewish culture since the foundation of the Order. Because Jesuit racism and an opposition to it was the most significant defining conflict of their early relationship, this article pays special attention to the Jesuits' approaches to the concept of race in both early modern and modern periods, in which both Jews and Jesuits were important players.

Jesuits and Jews did form a distinctive couple, in part because they were both the most frequent victims for those who sought a total, diabolical explanation for how history operated, although it must be said that the suffering that was endured as a consequence cannot be compared. Both groups were characterized as evil or diabolic in infamous but popular fabrications: the *Monita secreta* (1614) for the Jesuits and the *Protocols of the Elders of Zion* (1903) for the Jews (the latter derived in part from the rhetoric of the former). Their alleged conniving character threatening the very fabric of societal order – and hence compared to the devil – was charted on the axes of space and time. Spatially, they operated outside of any specific territory and aspired for domination over the world; they lurked behind thrones at the same time that they were quite willing to overthrow those very rulers and nations. Jews and Jesuits were preeminently people of the city and, thus, were accused of being allied to wealth, loose morality, and a cunning, deracinated intelligence which was contemptuous of the traditions of the rural past. Temporally, they were at home in periods of decadence and collapse, and thus they were perceived as devotees of modernity: the same spectacles which detected the Jesuits as fathering the French Revolution saw the Jews as the creators of the Russian one.

The animosity directed toward the two groups did not just come from the outside, because the Jesuits had developed their own enmity toward the Jews. And this was unexpected to some extent. As far as the Jesuits were concerned, the opening moment in the Jewish–Jesuit encounter was both a stance of courage and a surrender to cowardice. The official name for the Jesuits is the Society of Jesus, and we know from his official biography by the *converso* Pedro de Ribadeneyra (1527–1611) that Ignatius of Loyola's desire for intimacy with his Savior even included an actual participation in the Jewish lineage ("secundum carnem") of Jesus and Mary. This account must be, however, contrasted with the fact that Loyola shared common prejudices of Christians against Jews, as proven, for example, in his support of Pope Paul IV's segregationist legislation against the Jews of Rome. Yet, Ignatius's devotion to the personal figure of Jesus saved him, and initially the Society, from a most common prejudice against Jewish converts to Christianity and their descendants, the so-called "new Christians" or "conversos" of Iberia, who were allegedly more Jewish than Christian, for they were of impure blood. Such "tainted" ancestry justified their exclusion from Church and civic posts and religious communities. Ignatius courageously resisted ecclesiastical and political pressures and refused to exclude Jewish converts or their descendants from the Society's ranks. Thus, some of the most distinguished early Jesuits were of Jewish heritage, including Ignatius's physician Baltasar de Torres (1518–61), his secretary, Juan Alfonso de Polanco (1517–76), his assistants Cristóbal de Madrid (1503–73) and Jerónimo Nadal (1507–80), and his successor, Diego Laínez (1512–65); the brothers Loarte, the brothers Acosta, the brothers Suárez, Juan de Mariana (1536–1624), Manuel de Sá (1530–96), Francisco de Toledo (1532–96), Alfonso de Pisa (1528–98), Andrés de Oviedo (1518–77), Alexandre de Rhodes (1591–1660), and not a few others.

Early Jesuits' approaches to Jews and *conversos* must be placed in a historical context in order to be better understood. The foundation of the Jesuits in 1540 – half a century after the expulsion of the Jews from Spain – coincided with the rise of a Spanish anti-*converso* hysteria that reached its peak in 1547, when the most authoritative expression of the purity-of-blood legislation in Iberia, *El Estatuto de limpieza* [*de sangre*], was promulgated by Juan Martínez Silíceo (1486–1557), joint archbishop of Toledo and Inquisitor General of Spain. The Society of Jesus could not avoid coping with the problem of *conversos*, because the Jesuits were founded by a group of so-called old and new Christians, most of whom were born in Iberia, as was their leader Ignatius of Loyola. In spite of the desired universal character of the Order envisioned by its founding fathers, the vexed purity-of-blood concern had produced from the very beginning a profound polarization in the Society of Jesus as it tried to implement its mission.

The death of Superior General Francis Borja in 1572 marked a turning point in the history of *converso* Jesuits, whose influence – after three decades of holding the highest posts of responsibility in the Jesuit administration – began to fade. After the deaths of Borja's two predecessors, Ignatius of Loyola and Diego Laínez in 1556 and 1565, respectively, the anti-*converso* Jesuits seized the momentum of political transition by campaigning against the *converso* presence in the Jesuit central administration. The campaign was successful – the anti-*converso* Italo-Portuguese lobby managed to block the election to the generalate of the *converso* Vicar General Juan Alfonso de Polanco. From the very start of his tenure, the newly elected superior general, Everard Mercurian (1514–80), began to "cleanse the house": he deprived almost all *converso* Jesuits of governmental posts in Rome, Italy, and possibly in other parts of Europe. Consequently, the period of the *converso* political sway ended, shifting the approach of the Jesuit administration in Rome away from both candidates and members of Jewish ancestry, a shift which under Mercurian's successor, Claudio Acquaviva (1543–1615), would eventually result in the important discriminatory legislation of 1593.

The discriminatory policy of Mercurian and the defeat of the *converso* lobby during the 3rd General Congregation triggered the anti-Roman separatist movement by Spanish Jesuits known as the *memorialistas*, or those who wrote reports called *memoriales*. The *converso* character of the *memorialistas* movement was denounced by the anti-*converso* lobby, which after the election of Acquaviva (1581) included high-ranking officials in the Jesuit curia, such as the German Paul Hoffaeus (*c.* 1530–1608), the Italian Lorenzo Maggio (1531–1605), and the Portuguese Manuel Rodrigues (1534–96).

Their Italian predecessor, Assistant General Benedetto Palmio (1523–98) had fueled their anti-*converso* bias in his memorial to Acquaviva. In it, he wrote that the first cause and origin of the evils in the Society of Jesus proceeded from the multitude and insolence of Spanish converts from Judaism. Other Jesuits shared Palmio's prejudice. Paul Hoffaeus claimed that one of the categories of people who compromised the Order's unity were so-called *confesos* (i.e. converts from Judaism) who were "either suspicious or hateful." Paraphrasing the Gospel of Luke, Lorenzo Maggio argued that "those from the circumcision subverted the entire house of the Society. As sons of this world who are shrewd in dealing with their own and avid of new things, they easily excite disorders and destroy the unity of souls and their bond with the government" (ARSI, *Instit.* 176, f. 154v).

Manuel Rodrigues's argument seemed more racist: "Jewish converts [and their descendants] are by *nature* contrary to the true and sincere spirit of religion and thus harmful … They promote genuine mortification and solid virtues very little and seem to be merchants, seeking first seats and being called rabbis; they are hardly eager to seek perfection … and readily admit others of the same blood who are very unworthy" (ARSI, *Instit.* 184/II, ff. 360–64). Rodrigues's description of Jewish converts and their descendants echoes the popular anti-*converso* work by Bishop Diego de Simancas, *Defensio statuti Toletani* (1573), in which he employed the concept of "hereditary vices," which were – according to Simancas – peculiar to Jewish converts and more frequent in them than in others. Simancas's predecessor, Inquisitor Silíceo, whose purity-of-blood statutes he defended, expressed this idea more eloquently: "[The Jewish converts] still hold on their lips the milk of their ancestors' recent perversity" (quoted in Sicroff, *Los Estatutos de Sangre*, 131). The difference between pure and impure Christians was, to Silíceo, similar to the one between bred and in-bred horses.

This enmeshing of anti-Judaic and anti-Semitic reasoning by the Jesuit leadership in the late sixteenth century was challenged by a group of Jesuit intellectuals, who were largely of Jewish ancestry. Most prominent among them was a prolific writer and diplomat from Mantua, Antonio Possevino (1533–1611). Following his engagement in the mission to Roman Jews after the 3rd General Congregation, he influenced Pope Gregory XIII's decision to create a college of neophytes aimed at training preachers to convert Jews in Italy and the Levant. He was one of the most prolific Jesuit writers, authoring close to forty books. The most famous of them was the *Bibliotheca selecta* (Cologne, 1603), part of which was dedicated to the topic of the conversion of Jews, who in his eyes were no more strangers and foreigners, but fellow citizens with the saints, and the domestics of God. Through this and other writings, Possevino became one of the fiercest opponents of purity-of-blood legislation in the Society, even though his description of Jews had often a taste of traditional Christian anti-Judaism. In his memorial to Acquaviva, Possevino argued that "either by procuring it or by consenting to it, both Jews and Gentiles dirtied their hands in shedding the innocent blood of Christ" (*Bibliotheca selecta*, 439).

In his argument another Jesuit opponent of purity-of-blood laws, García Girón de Alarcón (1534–97), evoked the authority of Cardinal Thomas Cajetan (1469–1534) who suggested that refusing candidates to religious orders only for the reason of their Jewish origin seemed irrational, for "our salvation comes from Jews, from whom Christ, the Apostles and many fathers of the faith were born according to the flesh" (ARSI, *Instit.* 184–I, ff. 302v–303r). A similar perspective was articulated by another Jesuit pioneer of the dialogue between Jews and Jesuits, António Vieira (1608–97), a Portuguese missionary to Brazil. Echoing Paul's letter to the Romans, he recalled the privileged role of the Jews in the history of Christianity, for even though they "are hated by God for their blindness … they are loved because of their faith and the merits of their ancestors." (Vieira, *Apologia das coisas profetizadas*, 71)

Unfortunately, however, the Society was to abandon its founder's brave policy on membership, and in 1593, under pressure from outside as well as from its own members, banned the admission of all with "Hebrew or Saracen stock" and dismissed those of that stock who had not yet made their final vows. Not even the superior general of the Order could dispense from this impediment of origin. The 5th General Congregation explained: "For even though the Society, for the sake of the common good, wishes to become all things to all men in order to gain for Christ all those it can, still it is not necessary that it recruit its workers from any and all human races." The decree was adopted

on December 23, 1593, "perhaps the most shameful day in Jesuit history" according
to one Jesuit historian. That shameful day would cast its shadow long into the future,
on many different activities of the Society, and those would shape a tragic profile to
that couple's history. The 1593 law was mitigated in 1608 by limiting the number of a
candidate's generations to be investigated to five. In the late 1800s and early 1900s, the
procedure of obtaining dispensation from the impediment of origin was made somewhat
easier.

This Jesuit racism regarding Jews as well as resistance to it from the earliest years
by Jesuits continued in the twentieth century. Among those who fought Nazi racial
anti-Semitism as well as among those who supported it, we find not a few influential
Jesuits. For instance, the Hungarian Bela Bangha (1880–1940) suspected baptized Jews
of being spiritually inferior or opportunistic. Georg Bichlmair (1890–1953), the future
superior provincial of Austria, argued that "Jews carried special defects in their genes
for the historic sin of rejecting Christ – defects so severe that baptism was powerless to
remove them." Bichlmair reflected the ideas of two prominent racist Jesuits: Wilhelm
Schmidt (1868–1954) of Vienna and the development biologist Hermann Muckermann
(1877–1962) who directed the section for eugenics at the Kaiser Wilhelm Institute for
Anthropology in Berlin. Muckermann wrote: "Let no one defend themselves on the
grounds of baptism making a Jew a Christian," for "baptism makes a person a child
of God, but never changes his basic hereditary structure." Muckermann's arguments
had found sympathetic ears in Germany and beyond: he advised Munich's Cardinal
Michael Faulhaber (1869–1952) and addressed a congress on racial hygiene sponsored
by Benito Mussolini (1883–1945), before being eventually censored by the Vatican in
1931. Similarly, a Viennese Jesuit Mario von Galli (1904–87) – under the pseudonym
of Andreas Amsee – published a book entitled *The Jewish Question*, in which he argued
that Jews had become a vermin-like destroyer of nations. This sort of anti-Semitism
was also widely reflected in the official periodical of the Jesuits in Rome, *La Civiltà
Cattolica*, and prepared the ground for racial laws in Europe on the eve of World War
II. Some Jesuits, such as Pietro Tacchi Venturi, were even directly involved in the introduction of the anti-Semitic legislation.

On the other side, there was Pierre Charles (1883–1954), a Belgian Jesuit who fiercely
criticized racism in his *Les Protocoles des sages de Sion* (Paris, 1938) with its revelation
of the work as a forgery, and the French Jesuit Pierre Lorson (1889–1954), the author
of *Christians before Racism* (1939) – the first book-length study of race from a Christian
perspective written in French. What characterized these and other Catholic anti-racists
was, according to John Connelly, that many of them were converts from Judaism (*From
Enemy to Brother*, 63). As Connelly put it, "without converts the Catholic Church would
not have found a new language to speak to the Jews after the Holocaust" (*From Enemy
to Brother*, 5). The Jesuit experience suggests that the potency of the converted is worth
being traced in earlier centuries because it is difficult not to notice certain parallelisms
between those interwar Jesuit border-crossers and the group of Jesuits, most of them of
Jewish origins, or *conversos*, who opposed purity-of-blood laws in the Society of Jesus in
the last quarter of the sixteenth century.

Their bold and tenacious fight against Jesuit racism was, however, voices crying in
the desert – their writings circulated mostly in manuscript and remained unpublished
until the twentieth century and thus had a limited impact on later generations of Jesuits.
The enemies of the *conversos* in the Jesuit administration prevailed and, despite the

absurdity of the anti-Judaic and anti-Semitic arguments they employed, they were able to orchestrate in 1593 the promulgation of the purity-of-blood law. This law was abrogated only in 1946, because Jesuits feared, in the shadow of the Holocaust, being accused of modern racism. Instrumental in this abrogation was a French Jesuit of Jewish ancestry, Auguste Valensin (1879–1953). The 1946 Jesuit abrogation was part of a more extensive postwar Catholic stream that would become the flood which brought down the barriers to *Nostra aetate*.

See also Anti-Semitism; Bea, Augustin, Cardinal, SJ; Interreligious Dialogue; Possevino, Antonio, SJ

Bernauer, James, and Robert A. Maryks, *"The Tragic Couple": Encounters between Jews and Jesuits*. Leiden: Brill, 2014.
Connelly, John, *From Enemy to Brother: The Revolution in Catholic Teaching on the Jews, 1933–1965*. Cambridge, MA: Harvard University Press, 2012.
Donnelly, John Patrick, "Antonio Possevino and Jesuits of Jewish Ancestry." *Archivum Historicum Societatis Iesu* 55 (1986), 8.
Maryks, Robert A., *The Jesuit Order as a Synagogue of Jews: Jesuits of Jewish Ancestry and Purity-of-Blood Laws in the Early Society of Jesus*. Leiden: Brill, 2010.
Reites, James, "St, Ignatius of Loyola and the Jews." *Studies in the Spirituality of the Jesuits* 13, 4 (September 1981).
Sicroff, Albert, *Los Estatutos de Sangre*. Madrid: Taurus, 1985.
Vieira, António, *Apologia das coisas profetizadas*. Ed. Adma Muhana. Lisbon: Edições Cotovia, 1994.

Robert A. Maryks, written in collaboration with James Bernauer, SJ

Jogues, Isaac, SJ (1607–1646)

See Canadian/North American Martyrs

John III, King of Portugal

Son of Manuel I and Maria of Aragon, John III of Aviz (Lisbon, June 6, 1502–Lisbon, June 11, 1557) came to the throne in December 1521, reigning until his death. He governed the kingdom during the delicate phase of the stabilization of the Portuguese Empire, which then had its main base in Asia. In a decade, the main lines of his cultural policy emerged, marked by the centrality of neo-scholastic theologians at court and the attempt to contain any breaches made by the Renaissance in the dictates of Catholic observance. This also led John III to relaunch decisively the missions beyond Europe. To this end he welcomed the recommendation that the theologian Diogo de Gouveia the Elder had made to him from Paris in 1538, suggesting that it would be "an inestimable good" to send to India men from the group that had coalesced around Ignatius of Loyola. These included Simão Rodrigues and Francis Xavier, who came to Portugal in 1540, making it the first kingdom to officially receive the Society of Jesus. John III's favor was never to abandon the Jesuits, who founded their first house in Lisbon and first college in Coimbra (1542), while Xavier went to Goa, inaugurating the Jesuit missions overseas. In the following years their influence at court increased: members of the royal family used Jesuit confessors, and increasing numbers of the nobility practiced the *Spiritual Exercises*. Thanks to the financial support of the King, they continued to set down roots in the kingdom and throughout the empire, reaching as far as Brazil (1549).

See also Coimbra; Portugal

Rodrigues, Francisco, *História da Companhia de Jesus na Assistência de Portugal*. 4 vols. Porto: Apostolado da Imprensa, 1931–50.
da Silva Dias, José Sebastião, *A Política Cultural da Época de D. João III*. Coimbra: Instituto de Estudos Filosóficos – Universidade de Coimbra, 1969.

Giuseppe Marcocci

John Paul II

Cardinal Karol Wojtyla (1920–2005) of Cracow, Poland, was elected pope, aged 58, on October 16, 1978 and, less than a year later, delivered an unforgettable address to the Superior General of the Society of Jesus, Fr. Pedro Arrupe, and his senior advisers. The day was September 21, 1979, and the Pope's address included the following words: "I am not unaware – drawing on not a few other sources of information – that the crisis which in recent times has troubled religious life and is still troubling it, has not spared your Society, causing confusion among Christian people and concern to the Church, to the Hierarchy and also personally to the Pope who is speaking with you."

Further light was shed on the Pope's concerns when, in the same address, he mentioned things that had been stressed also, he said, by his two immediate predecessors, Paul VI and John Paul I: "austerity in religious and community life to counter secularizing tendencies; sense of discipline at once interior and exterior; sound doctrine in complete fidelity to the supreme magisterium of the Church and the Roman Pontiff so fervently desired by Saint Ignatius, as everyone knows, and apostolic work appropriate to an Order of Priests." These statements, more general than specific, left the Jesuit superiors with the task of identifying concrete examples. Perhaps the Pope had in mind – he didn't say so – dissent by some Jesuits from Paul VI's encyclical, *Humanae vitae* (1968) on the regulation of birth, or involvement by Jesuits – in Central and Latin America particularly – with the poor in their struggle for liberation, an involvement inspired by the 32nd General Congregation's emphasis, in 1975, on a faith that does justice and informed, at least in some cases, by the emerging theologies of liberation in Latin America. Peter Hebblethwaite, writing in *America* magazine after the death of Fr. Arrupe in 1991, suggested that the real issue ran even deeper. While not denying papal concern about dissent from the magisterium or about Jesuit involvement in struggles for the liberation of the poor, "the real point of conflict" was that the papal analysis of the state of the Church at the time was at odds – thus Hebblethwaite – with the analysis of Fr. Arrupe and his collaborators. Thus it was inevitable, perhaps, that tensions arose between the Society and the papacy.

And then, on August 7, 1981, Fr. Arrupe suffered a debilitating stroke. More than a year earlier, he had asked the Pope for permission to resign, but this had been refused. Now, following a stroke that left him in a condition *requiring* the leadership of the Society to be handed over to a temporary (at least) vicar general, he designated one of his four assistants, Fr. Vincent O'Keefe, as this, and the Society worldwide was informed of Fr. O'Keefe's appointment on August 10, 1981. Shortly after that, Pope John Paul II made his dramatic intervention in the Society's life by appointing his personal delegate, the near-octogenarian Jesuit Fr. Paolo Dezza to take charge of the Society. Fr. Arrupe was informed of this on October 6, 1981, when Cardinal Casaroli, Vatican secretary of state, visited him at the infirmary of the Jesuit curia, carrying a letter from the Pope. Cardinal Casaroli "explained that the words in the Pope's letter 'in my name and by my appointment, superintend the government of the Society' should be understood in the sense that Fr. Arrupe remains Superior General of the Society, keeping the authority of his office, but because of his health, it is the Delegate who, in addition to the general superintendence, will also provide for the ordinary government which had been temporarily entrusted to Father O'Keefe as Vicar General." This – surprising – new arrangement was to begin on October 31.

Over the next two years, Fr. Dezza, working with Fr. Giuseppe Pittau (also appointed by the Pope) and (still) with Fr. Arrupe's four assistants, and drawing minimal attention to himself, ensured navigation of the ship of the Society into waters that made it ready for the restoration of normal government by means of a duly convened General Congregation that would elect a new superior general. This election occurred on September 13, 1983, when Fr. Peter-Hans Kolvenbach was chosen as general. On being told his name, the Pope asked who he was and was informed that he himself had appointed him rector of the Pontifical Oriental Institute two years previously. He is said to have replied: "it is good so." Sixteen years later, lauding (the then) Cardinal Dezza in his funeral homily, Pope John Paul recalled how "I myself created him a special Papal Delegate for the Society of Jesus in an important phase of its history." He did indeed.

Relations between the Society and John Paul II improved under the astute and diplomatic leadership of Peter-Hans Kolvenbach. The Pope admired certain Jesuits greatly and appointed some to important positions during his papacy. A Jesuit he admired and trusted all through his papacy was Fr. Carlo-Maria Martini whom he named archbishop of Milan on December 29, 1979.

See also Arrupe, Pedro, SJ; Dezza, Paolo, SJ; O'Keefe, Vincent, SJ; Papacy

Acta Romana Societatis Jesu. Vols. XVII and XVIII. Rome: Curia Praepositi Generalis, 1980, 1982.
"Bittere Pille." *Der Spiegel* 45. November 2, 1981, 161–64.
Hebblethwaite, Peter, "Don Pedro in History." *America* 146, 6, February 16, 1991, pp. 156–65.
"Mann aus dem Zylinder." *Der Spiegel* 39, September 29, 1983, p. 158.

James Corkery, SJ

Juana of Austria

Juana of Austria (1535–73) was the youngest daughter of Emperor Charles V and sister of Philip II of Spain. A deeply religious woman of high intelligence and considerable political acumen, she was the only female in history to have become a member of the Society of Jesus under permanent vows. Aged 17 she married her first cousin, Prince João of Portugal, who died two years later, shortly before the birth of their son, Sebastian. After being widowed, Juana returned to Spain and never remarried or saw her son again. When Philip traveled to England as the husband of Mary Tudor, Juana became regent of Spain. Under the spiritual guidance of Fray Luis de Granada and the Jesuit Francis Borgia, she lived in the palace of Valladolid as in a monastery, helping to carry out their religious reforms. Determining to become a Jesuit herself, she faced Saint Ignatius with a considerable dilemma. In 1554 the Society of Jesus had officially existed for only fourteen years and was still vulnerable to the Inquisition's suspicion and opposition. Ignatius could not afford scandal or to alienate Juana's father and brother by agreeing to a plan that would make further dynastic marriage impossible. Juana's support was essential for the Society's reforming plans, but a previous attempt by women to live as Jesuits had ended in disaster.

Ignatius and his early companions were involved in the Tridentine reform of female religious communities, several of whom became keen for incorporation into the Society of Jesus. Ignatius resisted tying his men down to this service, since it contradicted their identifying principle of universal mission and mobility, a freedom and flexibility which had already given rise to controversy. While Ignatius and his companions worked collaboratively with several women, enlisting their support in promoting the welfare and ministries of his nascent order, he was strongly averse to violating prevailing social and moral codes with a female branch. The outstanding personal piety and zeal of many early Jesuits inspired numerous women with a desire to imitate them without retiring behind monastic walls, but this dream could not have come at a less encouraging time in the history of the Church.

Strict enclosure had been imposed on all nuns in the Western Church from the time of Boniface VIII's (1294–1303) constitution *Periculoso*, which was confirmed at Trent. This rendered it impossible for female religious to undertake works of charity outside the monastic enclosure, with the limited exception of the education of girls. Women could live as tertiaries under simple vows, but Pius V's constitution *Circa pastoralis* (1566) confirmed Boniface and Trent and obliged even tertiaries to take solemn vows and observe pontifical enclosure. Full approbation was not given to women attempting to live an apostolic life under simple vows for nearly three centuries.

Ignatius's reluctance to involve himself with female aspirants to the Jesuit life stemmed in particular from an earlier episode involving Isabel Roser, a widowed early benefactress from Barcelona who in 1545 successfully petitioned the Pope to allow her and two companions to make profession in the Society of Jesus into Ignatius's hands. Difficulties arose almost immediately, culminating in Isabel and her nephews, who stood to inherit her fortune, accusing Ignatius of misappropriation of goods. Ignatius was vindicated in a court hearing and successfully appealed first to have the sisters' vows commuted to vows of obedience to the diocesan bishop and then to free the Jesuits in perpetuity from the spiritual direction of women living together in community and wishing to place themselves under obedience to his Society. This worked until he was faced with a petition from the daughter of the Emperor himself.

Ignatius appointed a committee to advise him in this fraught matter, enjoining such secrecy on the whole proceeding that surviving Jesuit correspondence does not use the Infanta's real name or title but uses the pseudonyms Mateo Sánchez or Montoya. The committee came to a compromise, recommending that Juana be received into the Society as a permanent scholastic. This would preclude the prohibition on a future marriage, since the vows of a Jesuit scholastic could lawfully be terminated, should she desire in the future to leave the Society. Juana pronounced her vows as a Jesuit, but in total secrecy, without any outward change to her manner of life, whose strict recollection anyway mirrored that of the *recogidos* (withdrawn ones) of the Catholic reform. She founded the Descalzas Reales monastery in Madrid, a religious haven for ladies of royal blood, and protected Catholic reformers as far as possible from the Inquisition. Juana educated her nieces and sisters-in-law, and had a profound influence on Infanta Clara Eugenia, later regent of Flanders, who protected Mary Ward and her "Jesuitesses." She remained a Jesuit until her death in 1573, the only female member of the Society in history.

See also Spain; Women, as Co-Workers with Jesuits

Baños, Antonio Villacorta, *La Jesuita: Juana de Austria.* Barcelona: Editorial Ariel, 2005.
Rodríguez-Salgado, M. J., *The Changing Face of Empire: Charles V, Philip II and Habsburg Authority 1551–1559.* Cambridge: Cambridge University Press, 1988.

Gemma Simmonds, CJ

Julius III

Giovanni Maria Ciocchi del Monte was born in Rome in 1487. After studying law, he became in turn archbishop of Siponto, governor of Rome, and legate to Bologna. Paul III (r. 1534–49) elevated him to the cardinalate in 1536 and sent him as legate to the Council of Trent when it opened in 1545. He was elected Pope Julius III in 1550.

As pope, Julius III reconvened the Council of Trent in 1551, though he was forced to dissolve its sessions because of war the next year. His reign also coincided with the brief return of Catholicism in England during the reign of Mary Tudor. However, Julius III grew frustrated by political life and spent more and more time at the Villa Giulia, the Renaissance palace he had built for himself just outside Rome. He also scandalized some by elevating a 15-year-old boy with whom he was infatuated to the cardinalate.

Like his predecessor, Julius III favored the Society of Jesus. The Society's *Formula of the Institute* was revised and reissued in a new bull, *Exposcit debitum*, that confirmed the Society and added "defense of the faith" as a primary goal of the Jesuits. It also removed the numerical limit of sixty members contained in Paul III's original bull, *Regimini militantis ecclesiae* (1540). Julius III's bull was promulgated on July 21, 1550. For the Jesuits the Pope also established the German College in Rome in 1552, which aimed at training German priests who would return to minister in northern Europe. In addition, Julius facilitated the Jesuits' pastoral and missionary work by granting the Society permission to absolve any person of heresy, sidestepping episcopal and inquisitional tribunals. Julius III died in 1555.

See also Papacy; Paul III; Trent, Council of

Brunelli, Giampiero, "Giulio III." In *Enciclopedia dei Papi.* Vol. III. Rome: Istituto della Enciclopedia Italiana, 2000, pp. 111–21.

Charles Keenan

Jungmann, Josef Andreas, SJ (1889–1975)

One of the most important figures in the twentieth-century liturgical renewal was the Austrian Jesuit Josef Andreas Jungmann. He was born in the South Tyrolean town of Sand in Taufers (November 16, 1889), then a part of the Austro-Hungarian Empire. As a young man, Jungmann attended the seminary at Brixen and served his first years after ordination (in 1913) as a diocesan priest. In 1917, he joined the Society of Jesus and spent the next few years in spiritual formation and academic studies. Jungmann earned two doctoral-level degrees in theology at the University of Innsbruck (his *Promotion* in 1923, and his *Habilitation* in 1925). He joined the theological faculty at Innsbruck in 1925 in catechetics and liturgical studies, and remained there for the rest of his academic career (retiring in 1956).

However, when the Innsbruck theological faculty were dismissed by the Nazis in 1938, Jungmann was forced to leave teaching temporarily and spent the war years (1939–45) first in Vienna, and then as chaplain to a community of Austrian nuns in Hainstetten (near Linz). After the war, Jungmann returned to his teaching position in Innsbruck for another decade. Liturgical scholars who studied under Jungmann included Hans Bernhard Meyer, SJ (d. 2002; succeeded Jungmann at Innsbruck), and Balthasar Fischer (d. 2001; priest of the Diocese of Trier and instrumental figure in the post-conciliar renewal of the rites of initiation). Even after his retirement, Jungmann remained an active and influential figure before, during, and after the Second Vatican Council (1962–65). He was a member of the preparatory commission for the Council, and then served as a *peritus* (expert) during the Council itself, where he was instrumental in drafting the first conciliar document, *Sacrosanctum concilium* (the Constitution on the Sacred Liturgy), promulgated December 4, 1963. Finally, Jungmann served on the post-conciliar Consilium as a member of *Coetus* X (working group 10), charged with shaping the reformed *ordo missae*.

Jungmann's list of publications is extensive. Exclusive of book reviews, he published articles and books from 1924 through 1974. It was during World War II that Jungmann started researching and writing what would become his monumental, two-volume history of the Mass, published in German as *Missarum Sollemnia: Eine genetische Erklärung der römischen Messe* (first edition, 1948). He would continue to update this study through five editions, the last published (in German only) in 1962. The second edition (1949) was translated into English and published as *The Mass of the Roman Rite: Its Origins and Development* (1951). This groundbreaking study of the history of the Mass paved the way for the liturgical reforms of Vatican II and is still essential reading for any serious student. Other key liturgical works included *Die Stellung Christi im liturgischen Gebete* (1925; English trans. *The Place of Christ in Liturgical Prayer*, 1965); *The Early Liturgy to the Time of Gregory the Great* (1959); *Liturgisches Erbe und pastorale Gegenwart* (1960; English trans. *Pastoral Liturgy*, 1962, 2014).

In addition to liturgical renewal, Jungmann also had an important impact on the parallel renewal of catechetics in the late 1950s and 1960s. In fact, one of his early publications was a catechetical work, based on a kerygmatic (rather than a simplified systematic) approach: *Die Frohbotschaft und unsere Glaubensverkündigung* (1936). However, this approach was considered so revolutionary at the time that the book was withdrawn from sale; an English edition was published in 1962 (*The Good News Yesterday and Today*), and a second German edition, in 1963 (*Glaubensverkündigung im Lichte der Frohbotschaft*). A later catechetical volume, *Katachetik: Aufgabe und Methode der religiösen Unterweisung* (1953), went through three German editions and by the late 1960s had been translated into several European languages (in English, as *Handing on the Faith: A Manual of Catechetics*, 1957, 1968). Another of his Innsbruck students, Johannes Hofinger, SJ (d. 1984), went on to himself become a major figure in twentieth-century religious education, with a special interest in global Catholicism and inculturation.

Josef Andreas Jungmann, SJ, is not to be confused with the nineteenth-century German Jesuit of the same name, Josef Jungmann (1830–85), who was also a professor at Innsbruck (from 1858), teaching and publishing in the areas of homiletics, catechetics, and aesthetics.

See also Liturgy; Vatican II

Fischer, Balthasar, and Hans B. Meyer, eds., *J. A. Jungmann: ein Leben für Liturgie und Kerygma.* Innsbruck: Tyrolia Verlag, 1975.

Jungmann, Josef A., *The Mass of the Roman Rite: Its Origins and Development.* Westminster, MD: Christian Classics, 1986. Repr. of F. A. Brunner's translation, Benziger, 1951–55.

Pacik, Rudolf, "Josef Andreas Jungmann. Liturgiegeschichtliche Forschung als Mittel religiöser Reform." *Liturgisches Jahrbuch* 431 (1993), 62–84.

Pierce, Joanne, and Michael Downey, eds., *Source and Summit: Commemorating Josef A. Jungmann, S. J.* Collegeville, MN: The Liturgical Press, 1999.

Joanne M. Pierce

Justice

Christian understanding of the virtue of justice is rooted in the incommensurate relationship between human beings and God. Jesuit interest in justice has been both theological (God's will for human salvation, and our free response), and practical (ensuring that human beings have the means for responding). St. Ignatius and his companions included service to the poor among the primary ways in which they sought to "help souls." Whether awaiting passage to the Holy Land or assisting at the Council of Trent, they attended the sick and poor. In Rome, Ignatius assisted women trying to escape prostitution and helped found or support orphanages, hospitals, and other works. The *Constitutions* ascribe first priority to situations exhibiting the greatest need "because of wretchedness and infirmity of the people and their danger of eternal damnation" (#622). The insistence on corporal works of mercy among the Society's ministries indicates a holistic understanding later summarized as "the service of faith and the promotion of justice" (General Congregation 32).

As the Society grew, works now popularly associated with Jesuits retained this view: lecturing and writing, engagement with those most influential in society, the establishment of schools, were works with a potentially long-term impact for the good of communities. In foreign missions, often continuing the strategy of influencing society "from the top down" (e.g., Matteo Ricci's work in China, 1582–1610), Jesuits also fought for recognition and defense of human dignity (e.g., St. Peter Claver in Colombia, 1610–54). Two frequent mission strategies were "model communities" (e.g., "Reductions" in South America) and, by contrast, individual Jesuits' insertion into the lifestyle of a community (later called a ministry of "inculturation" and "accompaniment"). Both approaches show an underlying desire to go beyond basic catechesis and piety to deep cultural influence. Theologically, the understanding of grace associated with Jesuits during protracted debates with both Dominicans and Jansenists maximized human agency against any suggestion undermining human cooperation with God's just action.

Pope Leo XIII's 1891 encyclical *Rerum novarum* dramatically altered the context for the Jesuit "social apostolate," introducing systemic social thought as a lens for viewing traditional charitable action. Jesuits quickly adopted the new perspective. General Congregation (GC) 24 (1892) urged the establishment of associations for workers and the poor. In France in 1903, Gustave Desbuquois founded Action Populaire, the first of many Jesuit social centers. In 1931, several Jesuits, notably Oswald von Nell-Breuning of Germany (drawing on work by Heinrich Pesch), contributed substantively to Pius XI's social encyclical, *Quadragesimo anno*. GC 28 (1938) declared the social apostolate among the most important of the Society's works. After World War II, centers were established in newly independent, postcolonial countries.

Development of the social apostolate introduced important new features into Jesuit work for justice. Consciousness-raising, organization, and education for the poor took their place alongside immediate physical and spiritual relief. Social centers published journals, contributed to internal Church discussions, and influenced legislation. Some Jesuits pursued graduate study in social sciences (called for by Superior General Jean-Baptiste Janssens in his 1949 letter "On the Social Apostolate"), signaling Jesuit desire to participate in vigorous public discussion regarding justice. This openness gradually raised new questions about practical cooperation, and theological understanding, beyond Church borders.

Fr. Pedro Arrupe's term as superior general (1965–81) marked the full maturing of these developments. In light of Vatican II's attention to the "signs of the times" and the place of "the Church in the modern world," GC 31 (1965–66) declared that the social apostolate aims beyond maintenance of particular Jesuit works and "strives directly by every endeavor to build a fuller expression of justice and charity into the structures of human life in common" (Decree 32, #1). Arrupe's assiduous promotion of this ideal, including the establishment of a Social Justice Secretariat, the Jesuit Refugee Service, and countless other endeavors, led to GC 32's (1974–75) placing of justice, in relation to faith, at the very heart of the Jesuit mission. This perspective was reaffirmed by GC 33 (1983), GC 34 (1995), and by a letter "On the Social Apostolate" written by Superior General Peter-Hans Kolvenbach to mark the fiftieth anniversary of Fr. Janssens's letter. GC 35 (2008) declared, "The service of faith and the promotion of justice, indissolubly united, remain at the heart of our mission. This option changed the face of the Society" (Decree 2, #15).

Despite demonstrable continuity, the evolution of Jesuit work for justice, particularly after Vatican II, provoked serious tensions and criticism. Jesuits themselves have continually debated the allocation of resources between traditional works and newer endeavors, and whether to emphasize research and education, activism and advocacy, or direct relief. Within the wider Church, the Society's commitment has occasioned objections like those raised against liberation theology: Is this justice "too human," not in fact "indissolubly united" to the "service of faith"? In the world at large, Jesuits have faced renewed objections to "meddling" in secular affairs; amid serious conflict in various places, scores have lost their lives to what Fr. Kolvenbach has called the "mysterious gift of martyrdom."

See also Action Populaire; Ethics; Liberation Theology; Mission; Preferential Option for the Poor; Service of Faith and Promotion of Justice

Arrupe, Pedro, *Justice with Faith Today: Selected Letters and Address*. Vol. II. St. Louis, MO: The Institute of Jesuit Sources, 1980.
Combs, Mary Beth, and Patricia Ruggiano Schmidt, eds., *Transforming Ourselves, Transforming the World: Justice in Jesuit Higher Education*. New York: Fordham University Press, 2013.
"The Social Apostolate In the Twentieth Century." *Promotio Iustitiae* 73 (2000), 1–33.

William A. Clark, SJ

Kateri Tekakwitha, St.

Kateri Tekakwitha, popularly known as the Lily of the Mohawks, is a saint associated with New France. Tekakwitha was born to a Mohawk father and Algonquin mother in the region of upstate New York sometime around 1656. She survived a smallpox epidemic that claimed her immediate family, but it left her pock-marked and vision-impaired. She was in the custody of her aunt and uncle when Jesuit missionaries arrived in her village in 1667. Their arrival followed the signing of a peace treaty between the Iroquois and the French in 1666, which allowed missionaries to operate in Iroquoian lands.

Most of what we know of her life comes from two Jesuits who were then a part of the mission: Pierre Cholenec who baptized Kateri (she took the name of Catherine), and Claude Chauchetière who was with her at her deathbed. Both men wrote biographies of her within sixteen years of her death. These accounts describe her as a determined young woman who defied her own family to join the Catholic faith. Kateri resisted familial pressure to marry, eager to protect her virginity and become a bride of Christ. By 1675 Kateri was studying the Catechism and was baptized at Easter that year. After a period of six months in the same village, Kateri was moved to another mission at Kanahwake (today Sault St. Louis). Kateri lived on this mission for only two years before dying in 1680.

By this time, however, her reputation as a holy woman was already in formation. This owed a great deal to her adoption of a rigorous model of Christian devotion. She was a member of a female group at the mission that engaged in rituals involving intense suffering. Flagellation, branding, exposure to extreme elements, fasting, sleeping on thorn-filled beds – these were some of the penitential rites reported by contemporaries. Kateri reportedly took a vow of chastity in 1679 and after this further intensified her mortifications. These practices may well have led to her death a year later. Since rituals of mortification were also important in Iroquoian culture, Kateri's attraction to similar practices in the Catholic faith could perhaps be considered evidence of cultural accommodation at work. These were practices, however, which were also admired by devout Catholics as manifestations of intense devotion.

Indeed, Kateri's modeling of chastity and rigorous asceticism was characteristic of female saints throughout the medieval and early modern periods, a fact which helps to explain the emergence of a cult around her following her death. Within two decades of her death, Kateri was the subject of two biographies, and as many as fifty would be produced by the eighteenth century. Seven miracles were attributed to her by the time of her beatification, though these were recognized as one. By the nineteenth century, Kateri was on the road to becoming the "savage saint," a popular model of New World Catholic holiness. It wasn't until the end of the nineteenth century, however, that the campaign for sainthood gained traction in papal circles. This was spurred by growing interest among American and Canadian Catholics interested in claiming a homegrown saint.

She was beatified in 1980 on the 300th anniversary of her death, and canonized in 2012. The establishment of her cult has not been without some controversy. Kateri is viewed in some circles as a betrayer of Native culture, and in others as a victim of European exploitation. Whether victim, betrayer, or saint, however, Kateri's emergence as a significant New World historical figure owes a great deal to her promotion

Figure 32 Léonard Bélanger, SJ: *Portrait of St. Kateri Tekakwitha*, 2012, oil on canvas. AJC-GLC, Art Collection 2013 005 1-2, artist Léonard Bélanger, SJ, Archives des Jésuites au Canada / The Archive of the Jesuits in Canada

by members of the Jesuit order. The Jesuit biographies of Cholonec and Chauchetière established the traditional narrative of her life, thus transforming her into a model of New World holiness that has proved enduring. This was a model, moreover, that was important for establishing the efficacy of the Jesuit mission in New France. As her biographers made quite clear, Kateri wished to see the work of the Jesuits prosper. She was dutiful and attentive to their spiritual direction while alive. After her death as well, she continued to demonstrate her support. Indeed, Chauchetière had several visions of Kateri, in which she urged him to publicize her life to ensure that the work of the Jesuits was not in vain.

See also Canada; Native Americans; Women, as Co-Workers with Jesuits

Greer, Allan, *Mohawk Saint: Catherine Tekakwitha and the Jesuits*. Oxford: Oxford University Press, 2005.

Hogue, Kellie Jean, "A Saint of Their Own: Native Petitions Supporting the Canonization of Kateri Tekakwitha, 1884–1885." *US Catholic Historian* 32 (2014), 25–44.

Koppedrayer, K. I.,"The Making of the First Iroquois Virgin: Early Jesuit Biographies of the Blessed Kateri Tekakwitha." *Ethnohistory* 40 (1993), 277–306.

Megan C. Armstrong

Kenya

With a population of over 46 million and the strongest economy in the region, Kenya is the social and economic hub of eastern Africa. Moreover, its central location on the continent endears it to regional and global businesses and organizations, giving its capital, Nairobi, an edge over cities like Lagos, Nigeria, and Johannesburg, South Africa. Nairobi is home to the regional headquarters of the United Nations, the World Bank, and the International Monetary Fund. The Jesuits, too, have the headquarters of the Eastern Africa province and the Conference of Major Superiors of Africa and Madagascar (JESAM) in Nairobi.

Kenya's attractiveness to outsiders goes far back in history. Its coastline has always been an opening to the world. As he rounded Africa on his way to the East, Vasco da Gama (d. 1524) erected a monument at the coastal town of Malindi, which still stands. Francis Xavier (1506–52) also stopped here in 1542, an event that is marked by an old Portuguese chapel that was dedicated to him. Fort Jesus is another historical monument at Mombasa, a coastal city that was also a doorway for explorers, traders, and missionaries.

As a single political entity, Kenya was first named British East Africa in 1895, following a gradual occupation of the territory by the British. After World War I (1914–18), it was renamed Colony and Protectorate of Kenya and remained under British rule until 1963. Colonial high-handedness and reckless land expropriation led to such extreme violence as was witnessed during the 1952–60 Mau Mau uprising. However, the British also established a strong economy, especially in plantation farming and industrial production. Under its first president, Jomo Kenyatta (c. 1896–1978), independent Kenya followed a capitalist model and maintained regional economic superiority in agriculture, tourism, and manufacturing. The country still enjoys this status, even as it fights endemic corruption, fractious ethnic politics, and frequent terrorist attacks.

See also Africa, East; Hekima University College; Jesuit Historical Institute Africa

Ogot, B. A., and W. R. Ochieng, *Decolonization and Independence in Kenya, 1940–93*. London: James Currey, 1995.

Wakhungu-Githuku, Susan, ed., *50 Years since Independence: Where Is Kenya?* Nairobi: Footprints Press, 2013.

Festo Mkenda, SJ

Kilsdonk, Jan van, SJ (1917–2008)

A Jesuit since 1934, Kilsdonk was ordained a priest in 1945. At a young age this miller's son "the divine dignity of the poor." This would show in his ministry came to understand among imprisoned Nazi sympathizers after World War II, surviving relatives of young men and women who had committed suicide, and numerous victims of AIDS. Apart from this he was a serious scholar of the early Christian communities.

With his striking language, baroque and imaginative, he presented old truths in a new, positive context and was able to put momentous questions into perspective. His objective was to present a liberating message regarding God in clear, understandable language. Thus he spoke and published about the virgin birth of Christ, homosexuality as an invention by the Creator, the role of women in the Church, and the exposure of the ecclesiastical hierarchy. It did not make him popular among bishops and other high-placed clergy.

He was a popular preacher, who attracted a large audience, and performed weddings and funerals for Catholics and non-Catholics alike. A selection of his sermons for men who died of AIDS was published in 2012. Even at an advanced age, he visited students in their homes and bars, until midnight. The morning after he wrote a reflective letter to those he had met.

From 1947, when he was appointed teacher of religion at the Jesuit college, until his death he lived and worked in Amsterdam, the city that gave him its Silver Medal in 1995, having already received the royal Order of Orange-Nassau in 1982.

See also The Netherlands

Begheyn, Paul, *Jan van Kilsdonk. Portret van een hartstochtelijk pastor.* Nijmegen: Valkhof Pers, 2008.
Verburg, Alex, *Pater van Kilsdonk. Raadsman in delicate zaken. Memoires.* Amsterdam/Antwerpen: Uitgeverij Atlas Contact, 2013.

Paul Begheyn, SJ

Kino, Eusebio, SJ (1645–1711)

Widely praised for his achievements as missionary and explorer in North America, Eusebius Franz Kühn was born in Segno in the Italian Tyrol on August 10, 1645. He attended the Jesuit *gymnasium* in Trent and the college of Hall, near Innsbruck, where he contracted a life-threatening illness. Attributing his recovery to the intercession of his patron, Francis Xavier, he entered the Upper German province of the Society of Jesus in 1665. After studies at Inglostadt and Innsbruck (including theology, but also mathematics, geography, and cartography), he was ordained in 1677. Desiring to be a missionary, he was sent to Spain, where he spent two years with Jesuits preparing for work in the Spanish Empire. There, he mastered Spanish, taught mathematics, and made scientific instruments for the missions. After he and a fellow Jesuit drew lots for the alternatives, Baja California in Mexico became his destination. Given his scientific skill, he was named both rector of the mission and Royal Cartographer of the Californias. Here in New Spain, he utilized his gifts of mind, spirit, and energy to leave a lasting mark as explorer, cartographer, astronomer, and founder of missions.

In 1681 he reached Vera Cruz, where he altered his name to Eusebio Kino and published a book of observations of the comet of 1680–81 that he had collected in Spain, *Exposicion astronomica*. In 1683, he worked as cosmographer and Jesuit superior on an expedition to Baja California where he endeavored to learn the language of the Guaicuro Indians and helped to establish a mission at San Bruno and a system of supply from the Mexican missions across the Gulf of California. When drought caused this mission to be abandoned, he worked in Pimería Alta, starting in 1687. From the existing chain of Jesuit missions in the Sierra Madre, he founded about two dozen missions in the San Miguel, Magdalena, Sonóita, Altar, Santa Cruz, and San Pedro Valleys. Kino and his contemporary missionaries faced a set of challenges in Mexico that differed significantly from those in areas further south where reductions were established. Here, the native population was grouped only loosely in tribal organizations, without a common language, and warfare was common. Eventually, the missionaries learned twenty-nine

Figure 33 Eusebio Kino, SJ: *Via Terrestris in California*, 1698, engraved map. Photograph ©
Rare Book and Special Collections Division, Library of Congress

different languages to further their work. Under the circumstances, one or two Jesuits resided in a central settlement, serving outlying groups on horseback.

Kino was an indefatigable traveler among the missions and was rarely out of the saddle. His base was the mission of Nuestra Señora de los Dolores in Sonora, which, by 1693, contained a sizable church: a water-powered mill; carpentry and blacksmith shops; cattle, oxen, and horses; a farm that included orchards, vineyards, and a winery. From here he made over fifty missionary journeys, often with Native American guides. Appreciative and protective of the Indians, he worked with sixteen different tribes, energizing the economy of that region by raising the standard of living, starting livestock ranches, and introducing European fruits, herbs, and cereals. Throughout his labors, opposition from public officials required him to plead the cause of those he served, including abolition of forced service in silver mines.

Laboring in Mexico until his death on March 15, 1711, he traveled over 20,000 miles and discovered an overland route to California. A superb cartographer, Kino made two expeditions down the Colorado River in 1701–02, gathering information that allowed him to draw the first maps representing Baja California as a peninsula and not an island; he was also the first to map about 50,000 square miles (80,500 km^2) of the Pimería Alta, an area now in the Mexican province of Sonora and southern Arizona in the United States. For over 200 years, these maps set the standard for precision and accuracy. He also kept a journal that vividly described his work and contained the first reliable description of the Casa Grande ruins in the Sonoran Desert, about 50 miles south of Phoenix, Arizona.

In 1711, at the mission of Santa Maria Magdalena (present-day Magdalena de Kino, Sonora, Mexico), he died of a fever. His skeletal remains were discovered in 1966 and may be viewed there in a crypt in a large plaza that bears his name.

In recognition of his contribution to history, the state of Arizona in 1965 placed Kino's statue in the Statuary Hall in the Capitol in Washington, DC. Equestrian statues stand near the cathedral in Hermosillo, Mexico, and in Phoenix and Tucson, Arizona. A movie, *Father Kino, Padre on Horseback*, was released in 1977 and is available in DVD format. The Mexican wine Padre Kino celebrates his introduction there of certain grapes.

See also Baja California; Mexico; United States of America

Kino's Historical Memoir of the Pimería Alta: A Contemporary Account of the Beginnings of California, Sonora, and Arizona, by Father Eusebio Francisco Kino, SJ, 1683–1711. Ed. and trans. Herbert Bolton. 2 vols. Cleveland: The Arthur H. Clark Co., 1919.

Polzer, Charles W., *Kino: A Legacy*. Tucson: Jesuit Fathers of Southern Arizona, 1998.

Anthony Kuzniewski, SJ

Kircher, Athanasius, SJ (1602–1680)

One of the most prominent Jesuits of the seventeenth century, Athanasius Kircher was a naturalist, collector, and polymath. He published almost forty works during his lifetime and also curated the famous museum in the Collegio Romano, which he turned into a spectacular illustration of his idiosyncratic worldview. He was both praised for his erudition and censured for his eccentricities by contemporaries, and while he remains one of the best-known Jesuits of the premodern era, historians have struggled to understand his contributions to the history of ideas, making him a contentious if fascinating figure in Jesuit history.

Kircher was born in Germany, close to the city of Fulda, and started his novitiate in the Society of Jesus in 1614. The turmoil of the Thirty Years War caught up with him more than once as he moved around Germany; he was ordained to the priesthood in 1628, but soon thereafter he was forced to flee to Avignon. There, in 1631, he attracted the attention of one of the foremost members of the Republic of Letters, the antiquarian Nicolas-Claude Fabri de Peiresc (1580–1637), who quickly became his patron and who helped to secure for him a teaching position at the Collegio Romano. Kircher arrived in Rome in 1633 and would remain there for the rest of his life, assembling the philosophical collection that would eventually blossom into his grand museum and producing a prodigious number of printed works.

Like many in Baroque Rome, Kircher was fascinated by the history of ancient Egypt. He claimed (erroneously) to have translated Egyptian hieroglyphs, and one of his greatest works, the *Oedipus Aegyptiacus* (1652–55), was devoted entirely to his intensive studies of Egyptian culture and language, as were a number of other, later works. He also developed a strong interest in China that culminated in his *China illustrata* (1667), one of the most comprehensive studies of the Far East to appear in Europe in this period. In fact, there was little to which Kircher did not turn his attention during his lifetime. He produced truly massive works devoted to such disparate subjects as cosmology (the *Itinerarium extaticum*), music and sound (both the *Musurgia universalis* and the *Phonurgia nova*), light (the *Ars magna lucis et umbrae*), geology (the *Mundus subterraneus*), and magnetism (most prominently, the *Magnes; sive, De arte magnetica*), in addition to books focused on biblical history, universal languages, and mechanics. Almost without exception, Kircher's works were a curious mix of rigorous erudition, imaginative speculation, and hearsay; his fierce love of learning led to an exuberant eclecticism that made his ideas difficult to understand even for contemporaries. He was intrepid in his quest for knowledge, however, once having himself lowered into the smoking crater of Vesuvius shortly before it erupted. He was also an innovator; he was one of the first to examine the blood of plague victims using the relatively novel technology of the microscope, recording in his *Scrutinium pestis* of 1658 the presence of what he called "animalcules" or small worms that he theorized might be responsible for the disease.

Kircher's many works were read widely by contemporaries, and he was one of the most visible members of the Society of Jesus in the seventeenth century. A great deal of this visibility was linked to the museum that he administered at the Collegio Romano almost from his arrival in Rome until his death. In its heyday, it was one of the greatest collections in Europe, filled with artifacts and specimens sent by Jesuits around the world. It was visited by cardinals, princes, and virtuosi from across Europe, and under Kircher's guidance it became one of the most spectacular manifestations of Jesuit power of its time.

Like many in the seventeenth century, Kircher balanced precariously between the bastions of traditional learning on one side and, on the other, the novel ideas emerging from the "new philosophies" of René Descartes, Johannes Kepler, Robert Boyle, and others. This explains why his own works at times hark back to the philosophy of Aristotle and then, only a few pages later, embrace the innovative theories of his contemporaries. First and foremost, however, Kircher was a Jesuit. He personified in himself the Society's commitment to erudition as well as its global character, but at the

Figure 34 Athanasius Kircher, SJ: Frontispiece engraving from *China Illustrata*, 1667.
Bibliothéque Nationale de France, Paris. Photograph © Art Resource, New York

same time his fascination with the universe, and with the invisible knots and chains that he saw as connecting so many disparate things, was rooted in a deep reverence for the Creator. He should be acknowledged as one of the most interesting and innovative thinkers of the so-called Scientific Revolution.

See also Encyclopedias; Museums; Rome

Findlen, Paula, ed., *Athanasius Kircher: The Last Man Who Knew Everything*. New York: Routledge, 2007.
Godwin, Joscelyn, *Athanasius Kircher's Theatre of the World: The Life and Work of the Last Man to Search for Universal Knowledge*. London: Thames & Hudson, 2009.
Sardo, Eugenio Lo, *Iconismi & mirabilia da Athanasius Kircher*. Rome: Edizioni dell'Elefante, 1999.
Stolzenberg, Daniel, ed., *The Great Art of Knowing: The Baroque Encyclopedia of Athanasius Kircher*. Stanford, CA: Stanford University Libraries, 2001.

Mark A. Waddell

Kleutgen, Joseph, SJ (1811–1883)

Kleutgen, born in Dortmund, Germany, was the most prominent and the most successful of the nineteenth-century Jesuit Neo-Thomists. He went to Rome in 1843, where he spent most of the rest of his life exercising various important roles: vice-secretary (1843–58), then secretary (1858–1862) of the Society of Jesus; professor of rhetoric at the German College (from 1848); and consultor of the Congregation of the Index (from 1851). He was a major influence on the two documents of the First Vatican Council (1869–70) and on the 1879 encyclical, *Aeterni Patris*, of Pope Leo XIII (1878–1903), following whose election in 1878 Kleutgen became prefect of studies at the Pontifical Gregorian University. One year later, in 1879, he suffered a debilitating stroke and he left Rome for South Tyrol where, following ever-declining health, he died in 1883.

Kleutgen's multi-volumed works, *Die Theologie der Vorzeit* (1853–70) and *Die Philosophie der Vorzeit* (1860–63), argued that only the philosophical and theological system of St. Thomas Aquinas could provide an adequate basis for articulating the relations between faith and reason and between nature and grace. His scholarship exhibited originality and breadth, but his work must also be seen as having had a Church-political dimension. It was a defense against other attempts by theologians to provide a philosophical-theological system that could do justice to the faith–reason problematic by drawing on more modern philosophical ideas. Kleutgen's successful efforts to restore the philosophy and theology of St. Thomas provided the papacy with the kind of support that it needed for an approach to the relations between faith and reason that enabled it to resist pressure on the Papal States and that offered it a theory to underpin the kind of independent Church–State relations that it wanted.

Kleutgen's personal and priestly life seems not at all to have been above reproach, as a recent book on his involvement with the nuns of the convent of Sant'Ambrogio reveals.

See also Philosophy; Scandals; Theology; Vatican I

McCool, Gerald A., *Catholic Theology in the Nineteenth Century: The Quest for a Unitary Method.* New York: The Seabury Press, 1977.
Wolf, Hubert, *The Nuns of Sant'Ambrogio: The True Story of a Convent Scandal.* New York: Albert A. Knopf, 2015.

James Corkery, SJ

Korea-Cambodia

Until now it has generally been held that Fr. Gregorio de Céspedes, SJ (1551–1611), a Portuguese Jesuit, was the first Westerner to come to Korea. He came in 1593 as a military chaplain when Japan invaded Korea in the years 1592–98. About 200 years later, the book *The Truth of the Lord of Heaven*, written in China by Matteo Ricci, SJ (1552–1610), deeply influenced Korean Confucian scholars. While these scholars studied this book on an academic level, they found the faith in it. Eventually, one of them, Lee Sung-hun (1756–1801), went to Beijing in 1783 and was baptized there by Fr. Jean Joseph Grammont, SJ (1736–c. 1812). Lee returned to Korea in 1784 and started baptizing his fellows. This is the origin of the Catholic faith community in Korea. In 1827, the Vatican Congregation *Propaganda fide* asked Fr. Luigi Fortis, SJ (1748–1829), twentieth superior general of the Society of Jesus, for Jesuit missionaries to Korea, but the Society, recently restored in 1814 after its suppression in 1773, had no personnel to send at that time.

The current Jesuit presence in Korea began in the twentieth century. It begins approximately with the establishment of Sogang University. The hierarchy of the Church asked Pope Pius XII (1939–58) to establish "a Catholic College for the spiritual and intellectual formation of Korean youth" in Korea. As a result, Fr. Thedore Geppert, SJ (1905–2002), a German missionary in Japan, was sent to Korea to prepare the Jesuit apostolate in 1954. This is the point of departure of the Jesuit presence in Korea (see Sogang University).

Fr. Jean-Baptiste Janssens, SJ (1889–1964), superior general of the Society, officially established the Korea mission on February 25, 1955, under the care of the Wisconsin Jesuit province. However, even before this time, four young Koreans had joined the Society abroad: three in Japan between 1939 and 1941 and one in China in 1948. All four transferred to the new Korean mission. Missionaries from the Wisconsin province also arrived in Korea to begin the Jesuit apostolate. In 1960, Sogang College was established. The Jesuits also administered Daegon College, the regional major seminary in Kwangju City, from 1961 to 1969. In 1985 Fr. Peter-Hans Kolvenbach, then Jesuit superior general, visited Korea and established Korea as an independent region. The first Korea Region Catalogue was published, listing fifty-eight members.

The Jesuits have tried to respond to the needs of Korean society. In the 1960s and 1970s, Korean society focused on economic development. The negative effects of this, such as growth of an urban poor and ignorance of the human rights of laborers, strongly emerged. In response Jesuits in Korea strengthened their social apostolate. In the 1980s, Jesuits could not expand their apostolate because of the shortage of personnel. Many of the Jesuits in Korea were in formation. As Korean society began to escape from poverty in the 1980s and to become stable economically as well as politically in the 1990s, Koreans showed a great interest in spirituality. The Jesuits responded to this phenomenon and strengthened their spiritual apostolate. As their number increased in the 2000s, Jesuits reached out to various new apostolic areas. These areas included an apostolate for migrant people, the Internet, and missions abroad.

In 2005 Fr. Kolvenbach established Korea as a province when he visited Korea on the occasion of the fiftieth anniversary of the Jesuit presence in Korea. The next year, he entrusted the Cambodia mission to the Korea province. From the historical point of view of the Cambodia mission, this marked the beginning of its third phase.

The first phase started in 1980 when Jesuit Refugee Service (JRS) members began to live at Site 2 Refugee Camp, on the border between Cambodia and Thailand, to which a number of Cambodians moved during the regime of Pol Pot. Then in 1990, as the domestic political situation of Cambodia was stabilizing and many refugees began returning from the camps to Cambodia, JRS accompanied them back to Cambodia. Thus, the second phase began with the establishment of the Jesuit Service for Cambodia (JS) in 1994. Reflecting on how to support Cambodians more effectively in the changed situation, the JS articulated a triple vision: to accompany, to serve, and to advocate for the poorest among the poor. In 2000, the Apostolic Prefecture of Battambang Diocese in Cambodia was established and entrusted to the Jesuits. Since then, the Jesuits have worked at two tasks: Battambang Diocese and Jesuit Service.

Currently, around 190 Jesuits, whose average age is 47 years old, serve in the Korea Jesuit province working in education, the spiritual apostolate, the social apostolate, mass communications, and mission abroad.

See also Asia; Sogang University

Acta Romana Societatis Iesu. Volumen XII: Fasciculus IV. Rome: General Curia, 1954.

Yongsu Paschal Kim, SJ

Košice Martyrs

Melchiar Grodziecki (Grodziecký), SJ, Marek Križín (Križevčanin), and Stefan (István, Stjepan) Pongrácz, SJ, were priests and martyrs who died on September 7 and 8, 1619, at Košice in the far eastern portion of Slovakia; were beatified in 1905; and canonized by Pope John Paul II, on July 2, 1995.

Grodziecký, a Silesian, and Pongrácz, a native of Transylvania, were sent by Peter Pázmány to Košice, a Calvinist stronghold with a significant Catholic minority in the extreme north-eastern corner of Hungary, then under Habsburg rule. Križín, a Croatian who had been trained by Jesuits although not himself a Jesuit, arrived a short time later. All had received extensive educations; Grodziecký was also trained as a musician. The city was multilingual, and the first two Jesuits concentrated on the different language groups: Pongrácz on the Hungarian speakers, Grodziecki the German and Polish speakers. The king's deputy had petitioned the Jesuits to send priests to tend to the minority population and gratefully housed the two respondents in his official residence outside the city. When the city fell to the Calvinist prince George I Rákóczi, the three priests were taken prisoner. After several days of starvation, they were tortured and beheaded on charges of treason.

The ascendancy of Habsburg-led Catholicism in the region after the middle of the seventeenth century led to the erection of a church that memorialized the martyrs and which served as an important adjunct to the Jesuit university established in Košice in 1657. Retrieved by the devout Catholic Countess Forgács, the bodies of the three martyrs were moved to Trnava in 1636, becoming the focus of devotion; their relics remain on display today. The Košice Martyrs were both an unusual instance of Jesuits killed by their opponents within the Kingdom of Hungary and a lesson in faith on which later Jesuits missionaries and teachers in the region capitalized.

See also Eastern Europe; Martyrs, Ideal and History

Tylenda, Joseph N., *Jesuit Saints and Martyrs*. Chicago, IL: Loyola Press, 1984.

Paul Shore

Kostka, Stanislaus, SJ, St. (1550–1568)

Along with Saints Aloysius Gonzaga and John Berchmans, Stanislaus Kostka is counted as one of the three "boy" saints of the Society of Jesus. Kostka's experience of entrance and novitiate in the Society was an arduous one; when he died at age 18, he had been a novice for less than a year.

Born to noble parents in Mazovia, Poland, Kostka was enrolled along with his brother in the recently opened Jesuit school in Vienna. While there, the future saint fell gravely ill and, unable to have Viaticum brought to him, prayed through the intercession of St. Barbara to receive communion. Kostka reported that the saint herself brought him communion and that just afterwards, the Blessed Virgin appeared to him, indicating that he should enter the Jesuits. His visions would continue throughout his brief life.

Figure 35 Pierre Legros: Portrait of St. Stanislaus Koska, 1702–03, polychrome marble, in novitiate of Sant'Andrea al Quirinale, Rome. Photograph Alison Fleming

Knowing that he would not be able to persuade his parents to consent to his entrance, Kostka, upon the advice of another Jesuit, undertook a journey to Augsburg, Germany, to request permission from German Provincial Peter Canisius, himself a future saint. Kostka walked 450 miles to Canisius and upon meeting him, requested permission to enter. Impressed with the young man's sincerity, Canisius agreed, sending him to Rome at Kostka's urging.

Upon arriving in Rome in October 1567, Kostka presented a letter of introduction from Canisius to Father General Francis Borja: "We expect great things of him," it read. Kostka entered the novitiate, where he would spend the next ten months devoted to prayer. But in August 1568, Kostka developed a fever and died on August 15. Beatified in 1605 (the first Jesuit ever to be beatified), he was canonized in 1726.

See also Poland; Saints

Gense, James, *The Spiritual Odyssey of Stanislaus Kostka (1550–1568)*. Bombay: St. Xavier's College, 1951.
Tylenda, Jospeh N., *Jesuit Saints and Martyrs*. Chicago, IL: Loyola University Press, 1984.

Keith Maczkiewicz, SJ

La Chaize, François d'Aix de, SJ (1624–1709)

François d'Aix de La Chaize was born August 25, 1624, at the family home in east-central France. Grandnephew of Pierre Coton (1564–1626), La Chaize began his studies at the Jesuit college in Roanne and entered the Society of Jesus in Avignon (1639). He completed his studies at Chambéry and at the College of the Trinity, Lyon, where he then taught poetry, philosophy, and theology to great acclaim, serving as rector from 1671 to 1674. The Jesuit general then appointed him provincial of Lyon, a post that he held only five months until, in February 1675, Louis XIV chose him as confessor. La Chaize retained that post for thirty-four years, during which he lived at the professed house in Paris (Saint-Antoine). With the dissolution of the *conseil de conscience* in the 1660s, the King adopted the habit of weekly, often private meetings with his confessor to consult on matters of ecclesiastical patronage. This put La Chaize at the center of Church–State relations, making him both a nexus of political information and a valuable intercessor for ambitious clergy and their promoters until his death in February 1709. Apart from his relationship with the King, La Chaize is perhaps best known as the namesake of the Père Lachaise [*sic*] Cemetery located in northeast Paris on the former grounds of Mont-Louis, the country house that he and others from the professed house would frequent.

See also Confession, Confessor; Louis XIV; France

Bergin, Joseph, *Crown, Church, and Episcopate under Louis XIV*. New Haven, CT: Yale University Press, 2004.

de Chantelauze, Régis, *Le Père de La Chaize, confesseur de Louis XIV: études d'histoire religieuse*. Paris: Durand, 1859.

Guitton, George, *Le Père de la Chaize: confesseur de Louis XIV*. 2 vols. Paris: Beauchesne, 1959.

William P. O'Brien, SJ

La Colombière, Claude, SJ, St. (1641–1682)

Claude La Colombière was born February 2, 1641, in Saint-Symphorien-d'Ozon. His paternal ancestry entitled him to use the particle *de*, although the particle does not appear in the extant autograph letters or the first editions of his writings. Claude began formal schooling with the Jesuits in Lyon, cutting his studies short to enter the Jesuit novitiate in Avignon (1658). After professing first vows, Claude entered the College of Avignon for a final year of study followed by a three-year teaching internship (regency) during which he gave his first public addresses. The Jesuit general then missioned Claude to study theology at the prestigious College of Clermont (Paris) where he made the acquaintance of Parisian literati (Bouhours, Patru, Rapin) before returning to Lyon to teach and to preach at the College of the Trinity. After tertianship, Claude's provincial superior sent him to Paray-le-Monial (1675), where he met Visitation nun Margaret Mary Alacoque (1647–90) and later authenticated her visions of the Sacred Heart of Jesus. Claude left for London in the fall of 1676 to serve as chaplain to Mary of Modena, duchess of York, at Saint James's Palace. Implicated in the Titus Oates affair, Claude was arrested, imprisoned, and exiled to France, where he died in Paray on February 15, 1682, of the pulmonary tuberculosis he had contracted in London. We have from him seventy-nine classical-style sermons, a smaller number of sermon sketches, a selection of retreat notes, and a heavily redacted correspondence, all published beginning in 1684. Claude was beatified by Pius XI (1929) and later canonized by John Paul II (1992).

See also France; Sacred Heart; United Kingdom

Guitton, Georges, *Le Bienheureux Claude La Colombière, son milieu et son temps*. Lyon: Librairie Catholique Emmanuel Vitte, 1943.

La Colombière, Bienheureux Claude, *Écrits spirituels*. 2nd edn. Ed. André Ravier. Paris: Desclée de Brouwer, 1982.

O'Brien, William P., trans. and ed., *Claude La Colombière Sermons*. DeKalb: Northern Illinois University Press, 2014.

William P. O'Brien, SJ

La Storta

The small hamlet of La Storta, located just outside the city of Rome, was the site of a significant vision of St. Ignatius that is directly connected to the subsequent establishment and naming of the Society of Jesus. The event, witnessed by two companions of Ignatius, Diego Laínez and Peter Faber, was later described in numerous accounts of the period, including the *Acta* (autobiography) of Ignatius and the biography written by Pedro de Ribadeneira.

In the autumn of 1537, Ignatius and his companions approached the city of Rome from the north, on the Via Cassia. Throughout the journey from Vicenza, Ignatius had been praying to the Virgin Mary to place him with her son. When they stopped to pray in the dilapidated chapel at La Storta, Ignatius experienced a powerful vision. Ribadeneira (*The Life of Loyola*, 97–98) states:

> Ignatius was praying quite fervently. There, right off, his heart changed and the "eyes of his mind" were so filled with brilliant light that he saw clearly how God the Father commended Ignatius and his companions in a loving way to God the Son as he was carrying the cross, and put them under the protection of his invincible right hand.

The vision concluded with Christ telling Ignatius, "Ego vobis Romae propitius ero" (I will be favorable to you in Rome), which strengthened his resolve to enter Rome and place the group in the hands of the Pope.

The vision of Christ beheld by Ignatius is also connected to the naming of the Order. The first Jesuits had already started referring to themselves as "companions of Jesus" to reflect their belief that they reported to no one but Him. This conception of a "society" took on a more official form when the *Formula of the Institute* was written in 1539; here the Jesuits expressed their desire to be explicitly linked to the name of Jesus and to serve Him. By the time that the Order was confirmed by papal decree a year later, the *Societas Iesu* was firmly established. For Ignatius, the vision of Jesus Christ experienced in the chapel at La Storta, and the promise that Christ would bestow favor upon the companions in Rome, divinely confirmed that this new society was on the correct path.

The Jesuits sent missionaries off to lands unfriendly to Christians from the moment of their establishment, and the emphasis upon the cross in this foundational vision at La Storta links the new Society to the concept of martyrdom as well. Many early Jesuit artistic commissions in Rome focused on images of grisly, tortured, and martyred saints, glorifying the sufferings they underwent for Christ and serving as messages to those who were departing on the missions. Some Jesuit missionaries of the period actively sought this fate as another way of following in the footsteps of Christ. When images of Ignatius and Francis Xavier are paired, the two men are often represented, respectively, by the

Figure 36 Valérien Regnard: *Vision at La Storta*, c. 1622, engraving from *S. Ignatii Loyolæ Soc: Iesv fvndatoris: qvædã miracvla.* Jesuitica Collection, John J. Burns Library, Boston College. Photograph Alison Fleming

"Vision at La Storta," and a scene from Xavier's missions to India or Japan. This is seen on the wooden doors of the Novitiate Church of San Vitale, Rome, where these scenes are coupled with the martyrdoms of Saints Vitale and Valeria.

The "Vision at La Storta" has been artistically represented with great frequency through the years. The episode was first seen, *c.* 1590, in the background of printed images of Ignatius. It was included in all of the illustrated biographies printed in the early seventeenth century to promote and commemorate the beatification and canonization of Ignatius, and it was also incorporated into many painted life cycles in Jesuit churches. Typically, Ignatius is depicted inside the run-down chapel, kneeling in prayer. God the Father and Christ carrying the cross appear above the altar in an illuminated ring of clouds and angels. Laínez and Faber often appear in the chapel's doorway. Occasionally, the episode is set just outside the chapel, with the skyline of Rome in the background. By the late seventeenth century, it is repeatedly represented in apse frescoes or on the high altar of churches, such as Sant'Ignazio in Rome. These images allow the faithful to "place themselves" in the vision of the Jesuit founder and understand the depth of Christ's role in leading the Society.

The chapel at La Storta, noted for its dilapidated condition at the time of Ignatius's vision, was renovated by the Jesuits for the Jubilee of 1700. The chapel later suffered further damage, but it has been rebuilt in modern times.

See also Loyola, Ignatius, SJ, St.; Rome

Fleming, Alison, "St. Ignatius of Loyola's 'Vision at La Storta' and the Foundation of the Society of Jesus." In Maarten Delbeke and Minou Schraven, eds., *Foundation, Dedication, and Consecration in Early Modern Europe*. Leiden: Brill, 2012, pp. 225–49.

Kolvenbach, Peter-Hans, *The Road from La Storta*. St. Louis, MO: The Institute of Jesuit Sources, 2000.

Rahner, Hugh, *The Vision of St. Ignatius in the Chapel of La Storta*. Rome: Centrum Ignatianum Spiritualitatis, 1975.

de Ribadeneira, Pedro, *The Life of Ignatius of Loyola*. St. Louis, MO: The Institute of Jesuit Sources, 2014, pp. 97–99.

Alison Fleming

Labor Schools

The labor school movement was a social justice and adult education initiative inspired by papal social encyclicals and the 1919 US.document "The Bishops' Program of Social Reconstruction." At its peak in the mid-twentieth century, there were as many as 150 labor schools, many operating in tandem with the Association of Catholic Trade Unionists. At least twenty were sponsored by the Society of Jesus throughout the United States, often on the urban campuses of Jesuit high schools and colleges. Unlike most other labor schools, the Jesuit-run endeavors generally preferred the title "Institutes of Industrial Relations" and operated on an ecumenical basis. The last surviving labor school is the Labor Guild of Boston, staffed by Jesuits for a half-century after its founding in 1945.

The Jesuits' "labor school apostolate" supported the rights and dignity of workers by practical means, providing targeted worker education programs, professional training, and leadership development. Labor schools typically ran evening skill-building courses for workers, on topics such as public speaking, union governance, dispute resolution, and the duties of a shop steward.

Although this movement has clearly run its course, its goals remain most admirable and fully relevant. Church agencies seeking to address urgent contemporary social concerns continue to be inspired by this creative effort to support the working masses in the era of industrialization and the Great Depression. The labor-activist priests who ran labor schools sought to overcome the split between secular economic life and the realm of religious values. Jesuits contributed their own distinctive world-affirming spirituality to the noble struggle for worker justice and equitable industrial relations.

See also Corridan, John, SJ; United States of America

Boyle, Edward F., "At Work in the Vineyard: The Jesuit Labor Apostolate." In Joy Heine, ed., *A Worker Justice Reader: Essential Writings on Religion and Labor*. Maryknoll, NY: Orbis Books, 2010, pp. 62–67.

Thomas Massaro, SJ

LaFarge, John, SJ (1880–1963)

By the time John LaFarge became executive editor of *America* magazine in 1942, he had long since distinguished himself as a journeyman among men largely positioned as academics and administrators within high schools, colleges, and universities. Ordained a priest even before entering the Society of Jesus, LaFarge pastored both affluent and poor in rural and urban communities before a career in media took him to the forefront of the struggle for racial justice in the twentieth-century United States. As founder of the Catholic Interracial Council of New York in 1934, LaFarge became the most prominent voice of the Catholic interracial movement at a time when American progressives had only begun to turn their attention to the issue. The nation's struggle against a racist regime in Nazi Germany and the global interests of a Soviet regime eager to exploit racial unrest in the United States brought nationwide discrimination sharply into focus. The emergence of interracialism among mainstream liberals also placed LaFarge's ideas at the center of public discourse on the meaning and consequences of race in postwar America.

This son of a prominent artist and French-American family was born in Newport, Rhode Island, in 1880. LaFarge entered Harvard in 1897 where he studied biblical languages and kept as his confessor Thomas Gasson, the Jesuit rector of Boston College. Gasson encouraged him to pursue theology at the University of Innsbruck. By the time he was ordained to the priesthood in 1905, he was convinced by a retreat director to join the Society of Jesus rather than pursue a career as a diocesan priest. That fall he entered the Jesuit novitiate of St. Andrew-on-Hudson in Poughkeepsie, New York, and later went on to study philosophy at Woodstock College in Maryland in 1908. The physical and mental stresses of his time at Woodstock directed him away from academic life and into parish ministry. His range of encounters as a minister, from indigent and convict communities in New York to poor black farmers in Southern Maryland, defined his commitment to what he considered the Church's failed missions among African Americans.

While in Maryland, LaFarge helped found separate parish schools for black and white students before playing a central role in the 1924 founding of the Cardinal Gibbons Institute, a secondary school for African Americans that closed in 1933. LaFarge's clashes with black laity on the institute's board of directors revealed the tensions inherent within the early Catholic interracial movement. His gradualist approach centered on the educational and cultural uplift of poor blacks within the structures of social and legal segregation. His concerns for black separatism motivated his effort to remove Howard University biologist Thomas Turner, leader of the Federated Colored Catholics, from the organization. The Jesuit nonetheless coordinated a range of social action programs through the Institute of Social Order and the Catholic Interracial Council of New York. He insisted that missionaries move beyond spiritual conversion to address the economic conditions of African Americans.

LaFarge also steered *America* magazine on a more socially engaged tack. Linking it to the social research operation of the Institute for Social Order, he believed that the periodical could disseminate Catholic social philosophy, newly articulated as a "positive and systematic social program," to a broader American public. The emotional and moral sway of communism and socialism among the working masses, he reasoned, demanded a passionate response that acknowledged social realities that they faced and did not simply retreat into anti-Modernist pieties. LaFarge also sought to interpret the meaning of the class-oriented social encyclicals *Rerum novarum* and *Quadragessimo anno* in terms of the race question. His work on race earned him an audience with Pope Pius XI in 1938, with the pontiff seeking a powerful statement against racialist propaganda emanating from Nazi Germany. The ill-fated encyclical failed to materialize after Pius XI's death a year later. While his own passion for ideas confirmed his commitment to traditional forms of Jesuit influence as educators, rather than as social or labor organizers, he demanded active cooperation with non-Catholic influences.

While John LaFarge anticipated some of the most potent social debates of the twentieth century, his age meant that he would play no direct role in the formal struggle for civil rights at mid-century. When he died at age 83 on November 24, 1963, Catholic leaders nonetheless placed him among the "three Johns" (alongside Pope John XXIII and the recently assassinated John F. Kennedy) who contributed so much to Catholicism's social influence in the modern world.

See also America Magazine; Civil Rights Movement (United States); United States of America

LaFarge, John, *The Catholic Viewpoint on Race Relations*. Garden City, NY: Hanover House, 1956.
    The Manner is Ordinary. New York: Harcourt, Brace and Co., 1954.
    The Race Question and the Negro: A Study of the Catholic Doctrine on Interracial Justice. New York: Longmans, Green and Co., 1943.
McDonough, Peter, *Men Astutely Trained: A History of Jesuits in the American Century*. New York, 1992.
McGreevy, John T., *Parish Boundaries: The Catholic Encounter with Race in the Twentieth Century Urban North*. Chicago, IL: University of Chicago Press, 1996.
Southern, David, *John LaFarge and the Limits of Catholic Interracialism, 1911–1963*. Baton Rouge: Louisiana State University Press, 1996.

Justin Poché

Laínez, Diego, SJ (1512–1565)

Born in Spain in 1512 to a wealthy family of New Christians, Diego Laínez (or Laynez) studied philosophy at the University of Alcalá at the same time as Alfonso Salmerón and Ignatius of Loyola. Laínez and Salmerón then traveled to Paris to study theology, where in 1533 they met Ignatius. In 1534 Laínez made the Spiritual Exercises under Ignatius's direction, and he was among the group that professed vows of poverty and chastity at Montmartre that same year. Though he traveled to Venice with the other companions and was ordained a priest there in 1537, he soon left for Rome, where Pope Paul III commissioned Laínez and Peter Faber to teach theology at the University of Rome (La Sapienza). Laínez's expertise in theology led him to be sent to different cities throughout Italy. In 1539 Paul III dispatched him and Faber to Parma and Piacenza, where they preached and gave lectures on the Gospels, and in 1542, Ignatius sent Laínez to Venice at the doge's request. From 1543 to 1544 Laínez traveled around the Veneto, preaching in Brescia, Padua, and Verona, and later he came to Genoa and Naples.

One of Laínez's most important roles was as a theologian at the Council of Trent. Paul III sent him there when the Council opened, and Laínez eventually attended all three phases of the Council – the first two (1545–47, 1551–52) as a papal theologian, and the third (1562–63) as superior general of the Society of Jesus. Laínez's contributions were marked by his championing of papal authority, especially vis-à-vis the episcopacy. In October 1562, for example, Laínez argued that bishops' jurisdiction derived from the papacy, rather than from the office of bishop itself, which led to many protests from bishops at the Council. Perhaps his most famous intervention came in 1546, when he delivered a three-hour speech on justification in opposition to Girolamo Seripando, which the Council fathers praised. Nevertheless, Laínez's support for the papacy did not detract from his desire to see the curia reformed. Besides being involved in the Council's formal work, Laínez was busy preaching and giving the Spiritual Exercises to prelates there as well. Between the Council's phases, Laínez continued his ministry in different towns in Italy, traveling to Venice, Florence, Padua, and elsewhere to preach and hear confessions. As a theologian accompanying Cardinal Ippolito d'Este to France, Laínez forcefully intervened in the Colloquy of Poissy (1561) that aimed at reconciling Catholics and Huguenots, where he bluntly informed Catherine de' Medici that temporal rulers had no authority to manage religious affairs, since that was the prerogative of the papacy. Rather than organizing colloquies such as that at Poissy, Laínez instead recommended the Queen direct religious questions to the general council at Trent.

Laínez was entrusted with increasing responsibility for the Society's governance. In 1552 Ignatius named him provincial of Italy, and immediately following Ignatius's death in 1556, he was named vicar general of the Society until a General Congregation could be convened. In 1558, at age 46, Laínez was elected as Ignatius's successor and became the second superior general in the Society's history. However, Pope Paul IV seized this opportunity to attempt to alter some of the Society's rules, declaring that the superior general should hold office for three years only rather than for life, and insisting that Jesuits should be required to chant the liturgy of the hours in common, as other religious orders did. Laínez agreed to the limiting of the superior general's term, but he only ordered Jesuits in Rome's *casa professa* to chant the liturgical hours. After Paul IV's death in 1559, Laínez secured the favor of his successor, Pius IV, who nullified Paul IV's actions and removed the limit on the superior general's term.

Laínez tried, as far as possible, to maintain continuity in the Society's government following Ignatius's death. The *Constitutions* were formally approved at the 1st General Congregation, and Laínez strove to follow them. His term as general saw the continued, rapid growth of the Society up to nearly 3,000 members at the time of his death in January 1565.

See also Superior General; Trent, Council of

Oberholzer, Paul, ed., *Diego Laínez (1512–1565) and His Generalate*. Rome: Institutum Historicum Societatis Iesu, 2015.
O'Malley, John W., *The First Jesuits*. Cambridge, MA: Harvard University Press, 1993.
Scaduto, Mario, *L'epoca di Giacomo Laínez, 1556–1565: il governo*. Rome: Civiltà cattolica, 1964.
    L'epoca di Giacomo Laínez, 1556–1565: l'azione. Roma: Civiltà cattolica, 1974.
Scaduto, Mario and Mario Colpo, "Diego Laínez (1512–1565)." *Archivum Historicum Societatis Iesu* 59 (1990), 191–225.

Charles Keenan

Lallemant, Louis, SJ (1588–1635)

Louis Lallemant was a French spiritual writer. Born in a significant family of Champagne, he became a Jesuit in 1605. After his novitiate in Lorraine (in Pont-à-Mousson), he was active mostly as a teacher, a spiritual director, and in the training of other Jesuits. In Rouen, the second most important French city at that time, he was for almost ten years master of the novices and director for the third year of probation. Among his trainees were some of the early martyrs of Canada, such as Isaac Jogues and Jean de Brébeuf.

While he did not publish any work during his life, his spiritual teachings seem to have circulated in manuscripts. In 1694 the notes on his instructions taken by Jean Rigoleuc were published in Paris. Rigoleuc underwent tertianship under Lallemant's supervision. Lallemant is a good representative of the mystical turn of the Society, and particularly of French Jesuits, in the first part of the seventeenth century. Among those who influenced Lallemant's work were Isabella Bellinzaga and Achille Gagliardi.

Lallemant was not unimportant in the seventeenth century. He certainly influenced other spiritual figures such as Surin as well as missionaries such as Julien Maunoir. Yet he came to prominence only thanks to the late nineteenth-century and early twentieth-century recasting of early modern spirituality. Bremond, author of the influential *Histoire littéraire du sentiment religieux* turned him into the leader of a school of spirituality.

See also France

Lallemant, Louis, *Doctrine spirituelle*. Ed. Dominique Salin. Paris: Desclée de Brouwer, 2011.

Pottier, Aloys, *Essai de théologie mystique comparée. Le P. Louis Lallemant et les grands spirituels de son temps*. Paris: Téqui, 1927–29.

Jean-Pascal Gay

Lammens, Henri, SJ (1862–1937)

Born in Ghent, Belgium, a Flemish speaker, Lammens first came to Beirut in 1877, where he studied for a year at the Jesuit College and then entered the Order. He would pass the greater part of his life in Beirut and Cairo. He acquired a fluency in Arabic, which allowed him to focus his studies on the history of Islam. He served as editor for the Jesuit publishers in Beirut, al-Machreq and al-Bashir, and then taught in the newly formed Oriental Faculty of St. Joseph University from 1904. His first studies dealt with the Umayyad Dynasty in Syria (the first two Umayyad caliphs, Mu'awiyah I and Yazid I, and their contemporary, the Christian poet al-Akthal). Later he turned to the origins of Islam (*Fātima et les filles de Mahomet*) and especially to the Arabian Peninsula at the origins of Islam. *Le Berceau de l'Islam: l'Arabie occidentale à la veille de l'hégire*, which appeared in 1914, showed the depth of his research into the contemporary physical and social milieu of the peninsula at the rise of Islam. His studies showed clearly the obscurities in the rise of Islam, contrary to earlier claims that "Islam was born in the clear light of history," and it also refuted claims that drought in the Arabian Peninsula explained the spread of Islam. His final study on Syria, *La Syrie: précis historique* (1921), made him a favorite source for twentieth-century Syrian Nationalists with their project for a Greater Syria. His writings did not offer a very favorable view of Islam, and consequently his biography of Muhammad was never published. He contributed some eighty articles to the international *Encyclopedia of Islam* (1913–36) and actively contributed to the formation of an international community for the study of Islam and Arabic.

See also Lebanon; Middle East; Syria

John Donohue, SJ

Lamormaini, William, SJ (1570–1648)

Born in Luxembourg in 1570, William Lamormaini studied at the Jesuit college in Prague and entered the Society of Jesus in 1590. Lamormaini taught philosophy and theology at the University of Graz before serving as its rector from 1613 to 1621. At Graz he met and befriended Archduke Ferdinand. After a short stay in Rome, Lamormaini became rector of the Jesuit college in Vienna. Soon after, in 1624, Lamormaini became confessor to his friend and now emperor, Ferdinand II, a post he held until 1637.

Lamormaini served as confessor during the tumultuous period of the Thirty Years War. He saw the conflict in religious terms, with God aiding Catholics against Protestant states. Lamormaini took a militant position and urged Ferdinand not to grant any concessions to Protestants. He actively sought restitution of Catholic lands that had been seized, looking to found new colleges in many regions of central Europe. He also worked for cooperation among Catholic powers, hoping, in particular, that France and the Empire might work together against the Protestants. Lamormaini vigorously supported the Edict of Restitution (1629), which required the return of all Catholic lands and properties seized by Protestants since 1555. After Ferdinand abandoned a militant path following the Peace of Prague (1635), Lamormaini's influence at court was greatly reduced. Lamormaini composed a lengthy biography of Ferdinand after his death in 1637, entitled *Ferdinandi II Romanorum imperatoris virtutes* (1638). He served as rector of the Jesuit college in Vienna again from 1639 to 1643, and briefly became provincial of Austria from 1643 to 1644. Lamormaini died in 1648.

See also Confession, Confessor; Holy Roman Empire

Bireley, Robert, *Religion and Politics in the Age of the Counterreformation: Emperor Ferdinand II, William Lamormaini, SJ, and the Formation of Imperial Policy*. Chapel Hill: University of North Carolina Press, 1981.

Charles Keenan

Lapide, Cornelius a, SJ (1567–1637)

Cornelius a Lapide, a Belgian Jesuit, studied the humanities, philosophy, and theology before entering the Jesuits at age 25. Ordained three years later (1595), he became a professor of Scripture at Louvain (1596) and taught there for twenty years, until he went to teach Scripture in Rome (1616). He died there in 1637.

Cornelius a Lapide wrote commentaries on all the books of the Canon of Scripture, including the Apocrypha, with the exception only of the Book of Job and the Psalms. His earliest work, a Commentary on Paul's Epistles and a Commentary on the Pentateuch, were followed by Commentaries on the Major and Minor Prophets, the Acts of the Apostles, the Catholic Epistles, the Book of Revelation, the Wisdom of Sirach, and then the Book of Proverbs. His other commentaries were edited after his death. All of his Commentaries were re-edited several times, both separately and collectively. Eleven editions of his commentary on the Epistles of St. Paul, for example, were published during his lifetime. The complete series, with Job and the Psalms added by other hands, was first published in Antwerp, 1681. It would be published at least a dozen more times in various European cities over the course of the following two centuries.

Like most of his predecessors and contemporaries, a Lapide intended to serve not only the historical and scientific study of the Bible, but, even more, the purposes of preaching and pious meditation. That is why his works explain not only the literal but also the allegorical, moral, and anagogical senses of the sacred text and furnish a large number of quotations from the Church Fathers and scriptural commentators of the Middle Ages.

In 1699 an academic dissertation on a Lapide's commentaries was produced that praised him as the most important Catholic writer of his time. Toward the end of the nineteenth century, Thomas Mossman, an Anglican priest, translated a Lapide's commentaries into English and his translations of a Lapide's greatest New Testament works are available for purchase today.

See also Biblical Studies

The Great Commentary of Cornelius a Lapide. Vols. I–VIII. Trans. Thomas W. Mossman. London: Aeterna Press, 2014.

Alice L. Laffey

Lavalette Affair

In the second half of the 1750s, unfortunate developments in the business dealings of Antoine Lavalette (1708–67), a Jesuit in Martinique, resulted in the bankruptcy of his primary creditors, the Lioncys of Marseille. Successful legal action was taken in local courts, but the leaders of the French province, who were responsible for affairs in the overseas missions, registered an appeal with the Parlement of Paris. This proved to be a catastrophic maneuver. Anti-Jesuit elements in the Parlement seized the opportunity to launch a wide-ranging assault on the Society. In May 1761, the Parlement held that the Society was responsible for a debt of more than 1.5 million *livres* owed to the Lioncys and various associates. Other creditors of Lavalette claimed a debt of an additional 4.7 million *livres*. By the end of the year, the French Jesuit superiors had belatedly assumed responsibility for Lavalette's debts and made plans for at least partial financial restitution, but a more momentous process was already underway.

As early as April 1761, the Society's enemies within the Parlement of Paris, with those of Jansenist sympathies leading the charge, had demanded close scrutiny of the Jesuits' Constitutions and enacted legislation that forbade the recruitment of new novices. They subsequently raised the issue of whether the Society of Jesus's Institute enjoyed, or had ever enjoyed, legal existence in France. The Jesuits were positioned as a palpable threat to the well-being of the French body politic. Subsequently, the Society's educational role was eradicated, and unpalatable oaths had to be sworn in order for French Jesuits to embark on alternative clerical careers.

See also Anti-Jesuit Polemic; France; Jansenism; Scandals; Suppression

Thompson, D. Gillian, "The Lavalette Affair and the Jesuit Superiors." *French History* 10 (1996), 206–39.

Thompson, D. Gillian, "The Persecution of French Jesuits by the Parlement of Paris 1761–71." *Studies in Church History* 21 (1984), 289–301.

Jonathan Wright

Least Society

The *General Examen* identifies the Society of Jesus as "this least congregation," a translation of *minima Compañía*, which Ignatius Loyola frequently invoked. Diego Laínez lists three reasons for Ignatius's practice. First, he wished to recognize the inherent human weakness of the Jesuits. Second, by using *minima* he hoped to foster humility in those who would join the Society. Finally, Ignatius recognized the example of earlier orders and wanted to emulate the Franciscan Friars Minor and the Minims of Francesco di Paula.

During their first deliberations in 1539, the companions proposed arguments for and against taking vows as religious. One objection focused on the poor reputation of religious life at the time: "It seems that, on account of our failures and sins, the words 'religious' or 'obedience' have unseemly connotations among the Christian people." Aware of this, Ignatius urged his companions to avoid the honors and ecclesiastical dignities that would distract them from the humility necessary for a reformed religious life. In a letter to King Ferdinand I in 1546, Ignatius argued, "It is the spirit of the Society to go in all humility and simplicity from city to city and place to place ... As the Society of Jesus makes progress in this spirit, God our Lord manifests Himself to it by greater spiritual profit to souls."

Ignatius would also have been aware of the desire for simplicity and humility of two earlier founders. The *Regula Bullata* approved by Pope Honorius III in 1223 identified the first Franciscans as "little brothers" (*fratres minores*). When Francesco di Paula sought approval of his Rule in 1493, he wanted them to be distinguished for their humility as the least (*minimi*) of all. Thus Ignatius followed the example of earlier founders in describing the least Society.

See also Constitutions; *Formula of the Institute*; Humility; Mission; Poverty

The Constitutions of the Society of Jesus. Trans. George Ganss. St. Louis, MO: The Institute of Jesuit Sources, 1970.

Decloux, Simon, *Commentaries on the Letters and Spiritual Diary of St. Ignatius Loyola.* Rome: Centrum Ignatianum Spiritualitats, 1980.

Mark A. Lewis, SJ

Lebanon

Lebanon did not appear on the map as an independent country until 1943. At the time of the early Society, it was spread among two Ottoman provinces, Tripoli and Damascus. The latter included Beirut and Sidon, while the former extended north to Latakiya, Hama, and Homs.

Pope Gregory XIII desired to renew contacts with the Oriental patriarchs once the Council of Trent ended. He commissioned Fr. Jean-Baptiste Eliano to go to Lebanon in 1578. The initial attempt was blocked by the pestilence, but in 1580, Eliano and two other Jesuits began a visit of nearly two years that solidified Roman ties with the Maronites. After that, the Maronite College would be established in Rome and the printing of their liturgical books assured. Three other Jesuits would accompany a papal envoy to visit the Jacobite, Armenian, and Chaldean patriarchs in 1583.

Then in 1625, Pope Urban VIII asked Superior General Vitelleschi to send Jesuits to Aleppo where, under the protection of the Greek Catholic bishop and the French Consulate, the Jesuits established a school and directed three confraternities for men: Greek, Armenian, and Maronite. Once established, the Jesuit residence would be a jumping-off point for Jesuits going east and south.

Missions were opened in Damascus (St. Paul) in 1643, and the following year in Tripoli (St. John), while Fr. François Rigordi came from Damascus to establish the residence of Notre Dame at Sidon. A Maronite bishop from Zghorta-Ehden joined the Jesuits and passed over to them title to a residence and school there that would be attached to Tripoli. From the residences with a chapel and a school, the Jesuits reached out to the Christians in the region, forming confraternities and organizing catechesis.

The central residence, however, would be Antoura, established by coincidences: a French merchant whose contact with Jesuits in the Levant led to his joining the Order, on return to the region in 1657, mistakenly came ashore in the jurisdiction of Abu Nawfal, a Maronite governor happy to find a stray Jesuit. The Residence of St. Joseph at Antoura gave birth to a seminary and school and produced the first catechisms in Arabic printed at nearby Khinshara in 1734 by Fr. Pierre Fromage with the aid of Deacon Abdallah Zalher.

When the Jesuit order was suppressed in 1773, the properties in Lebanon and Syria passed to the Lazarists. The restored Society of Jesus returned to the region under the auspices of the Greek Catholic bishop, Mazlum. He requested them to aid the seminary at Ayn Traz in the Shuf region of Lebanon. Frs. Paul Riccadonna, Benedict Planchet, and Bro. Heinz Henze arrived there in 1831 only to find that the seminary was a project, not a building. Mazlum became patriarch in 1833 and gave the Jesuits their liberty. They had been studying Arabic and investigating possibilities. The Prince Abi al-Lama', in gratitude for the medical care he received from Brother Henze, settled the Jesuits in Bikfaya on the site of a former Maronite hermitage. The Residence dedicated to Our Lady of Deliverance was enlarged, a chapel built and a school opened. Bikfaya would serve as a center for traditional missions to nearby villages and, with time, house several different apostolates: a novitiate, a house for Arabic studies (CREA), and a retreat house.

A residence in the Biqaa valley was established in a suburb of Zahle by Fr. Planchet in 1833. From there, the Jesuits visited the Christian villages of the Biqaa. Later a school was added and a second residence and school in the town of Zahle in 1844. After the Druze massacres of 1860, a retreat house, normal school, and farm were established at nearby Tana'il on land given to the French government in compensation for victims of the massacre. The vineyards of the farm provided grapes for a winery set up nearby at Ksara along with an observatory and seismology station. The Jesuits operated the winery and maintained a residence at Ksara until 1977. In 1979 the observatory ceased operations.

The seminary founded in the village of Ghazir in 1843 added a college in 1855 and would be the nucleus of St. Joseph University when it moved to Beirut in 1875. The university gradually added faculties of medicine, dentistry, pharmacy, law, engineering, and Oriental studies. All but the last were associated with sister institutions in Lyons, France, until 1975 when all were grouped under a Lebanese Charter. The seminary was passed to the Oriental Patriarchs. The Oriental Library and the Jesuit Press (l'Imprimerie catholique), begun in 1852, formed part of the university complex. Of its many publications, perhaps the best known is *al-Munjid*, the Arabic dictionary and encyclopedia that until recently was the Webster's of the Arab world.

The primary and secondary schools, Notre Dame, were moved in 1953 to Jamhour, outside Beirut, and continue in full operation, as does the university, with approximately 11,000 students.

See also Middle East; Syria

Libois, Charles, *La Compagnie de Jésus au Levant: la province du Proche-Orient: notices historiques.* Beirut: Faculté des lettres et des sciences humaines, Université Saint-Joseph/Dar el-Machreq, 2009.

John Donohue, SJ

Ledóchowski, Włodzimir, SJ (1866–1942)

Włodzimir Ledóchowski was the twenty-sixth Jesuit superior general. He was born of Polish nobility in Loosdorf, Austria, on October 7, 1866. The son of Count Antoni Halka Ledóchowski and Countess Josephine (Salis-Zizers) Ledóchowski, he died in Rome, Italy, on December 13, 1942. A page of the Habsburgs, he entered the Jesuit order on September 24, 1889, and was ordained a priest on June 10, 1894. Having served as a Jesuit provincial (1902–06) and an assistant to the superior general (1906–15), he was elected superior general on February 11, 1915, and served until his death. Among his relatives were his sisters, Blessed Maria Teresa Ledóchowski and Saint Ursula Ledóchowski; a brother, Polish Army General Ignacy Kazimierz Ledóchowski; and an uncle, Miesezyslw Cardinal Ledóchowski.

An acute observer of contemporary events, Ledóchowski lived through an era when Poland had been wiped off the map of Europe. Determined to preserve Europe against Germany, he had entertained the view of a united Catholic bloc against the communists in the east and against the Protestants in the west until events had dramatically altered that possibility. He had an accurate view of Adolf Hitler as perfidious, and he was one of the few who foresaw the possible alliance between communism and Nazism because they were much alike in ruthlessly suppressing individual human rights.

Well-informed about world events, Ledóchowski was a strict disciplinarian in the government of the Society of Jesus and was equally zealous in using its resources, especially Vatican Radio operated by the Jesuits, to undermine the Nazis and to help their enemies.

See also Poland; Superior General

Kertzer, David I., *The Pope and Mussolini.* New York: Random House, 2014.
Selected Writings of Father Ledóchowski. Chicago, IL: American Assistancy of the Society of Jesus, 1945.

Vincent A. Lapomarda, SJ

Lessius, Leonard, SJ (1554–1623)

After philosophical studies at the University of Louvain (1567–72), Lessius (Leys) entered the Jesuit novitiate, taught philosophy in Douai, was ordained a priest in 1582, and studied theology in Liège and at the Collegio Romano under Robert Bellarmine and Francisco Suárez, with whom he exchanged many letters. In 1584 he returned to Liège, where he prepared himself for his task as professor of theology for Jesuit students in Louvain. Because of his good judgment, he was appointed "admonitor" of the rector and counselor of the Flemish province until 1615.

As professor he introduced the *Summa theologica* in the Netherlands, which he combined with ideas of his masters and colleagues. His classes were open to the public, which annoyed the theological faculty of the University of Louvain that censured him in 1587 for his theses on grace and free will, but only a year later the pope lifted the censure. The theological ideas of Lessius also caused unrest among his fellow Jesuits, and he was not allowed to publish anymore unless with special permission. The situation of the financial market in Antwerp made him publish *De justitia et iure* (1605), an important work on economic ethics. Because of ill health, he was freed from teaching for the last 23 years of his life. It gave him time to publish many books on apologetics, dogmatics, spirituality, and morals.

On September 30, 2007, the remains of Lessius were transferred to Saint Michael's church in Louvain, where they once belonged.

See also Antwerp; The Netherlands

van Houdt, T., "Jacob Wijns SJ, De vita, et moribus R.P. Leonardi Lessii liber (1640)." In Paul Begheyn, Bernard Deprez, Rob Faesen, and Leo Kenis, eds., *Jesuit Books in the Low Countries 1540–1773*. Leuven: Maurits Sabbebibliotheek/Peeters, 2009, pp. 105–07.

van Houdt, T., and W. Decock, *Leonardus Lessius: traditie en vernieuwing*. Antwerp: Lessius Hogeschool, 2005.

Paul Begheyn, SJ

Letters, Annual

The *litterae annuae*, or annual letters, were an important means of communication throughout the early centuries of the Society. Owing to the rapid and global expansion of the Jesuit order, an orderly system of communication was required. From the start Ignatius laid out the requirements of frequent communication, up and down the levels of hierarchy. The prescribed method for writing the annual letters is contained in the *Institutes*, Vol. 3, *Formula scribendi*, numbers 26–31.

On a yearly basis, each provincial sent a report to Rome, in the form of an official letter. They were put forth from all Jesuit houses or missions and consisted of a summary of all activities undertaken during the year. The annual letters reflected on the state of each province, college, or mission. They were recorded as apologetic and hagiographic accounts, and were often filled with ethnographic information not recorded in other forms. As a result, modern scholars have extensively studied and published annual letters, as they offer insight into various aspects of the missions.

The annual letters were shared, but only among members of the Society. From 1581 until 1654 many annual letters were collected, edited, and printed for distribution. Even those which remained in manuscript form were copied and shared. The holdings of the Archivum Romanum Societatis Iesu (ARSI) include an extensive collection of annual letters. These internal letters exist in a separate category from the letters known as "Relations." Those letters were written expressly for public view and were published until the 1673 decree of Pope Clement X forbidding missionary publications without the approval of the *Propaganda fide*, in the wake of the Chinese Rites Controversy. The ordinary practice of other annual letters continued and was renewed in the restored Society of Jesus post-1814.

See also Archivum Romanum Societatis Iesu (ARSI); Province; *Lettres Édifiantes et Curieuses*

Orschel, Vera, "'Uniting the Dispersed Members': the 'Annual Letters' of the Irish Jesuits." *Studies: An Irish Quarterly Review* 103, 412 (Winter 2014/15), 402–13.

Alison C. Fleming

Letters of Ignatius

During his adult life Ignatius of Loyola wrote close to 7,000 letters. He wrote to family, friends, colleagues, and patrons, offering thanks, spiritual direction, and guidance. He had very specific ideas about letters: what different types of letters should contain, to whom they should circulate, and how frequently they should be sent. Notable letters to early members of the Society, including Peter Faber, Francis Xavier, and Francis Borgia, have detailed instructions for what was required in their letters. Given the rapid pace at which the Society expanded into a worldwide organization, it is no surprise that the letters exchanged between headquarters in Rome and Jesuits across the globe were so essential and needed prescription.

Among the most well known are letters sent to the Society's first missionary, Francis Xavier, including one recalling him to Rome. The slow and inconsistent postal system of the age meant that the letter was written months after Xavier's death. But the letters exchanged between Ignatius and Xavier provide rich details of the far reaches of Asia to which Xavier traveled, and the activities of the missions.

Ignatius wrote a letter regarding obedience to the members of the Society in Portugal in 1553, in the wake of a crisis that had resulted in the replacement of their provincial. The letter was printed and became widely read in Jesuit houses as guidance on this important topic.

The letters of Ignatius that survived to the twentieth century were collected in the twelve volumes of the *Monumenta Ignatiana* series. They have been translated into many languages, with the first substantial collection in English published in 1959; in 2006 a collection of some 400 letters was published in English. The letters of Ignatius continue to provide a rich source for scholars interested in the life of St. Ignatius and in the early years of the Society.

See also Loyola, Ignatius of, SJ, St.; Xavier, Francis, SJ, St.

Ignatius of Loyola, *Letters and Instructions*. Ed. Martin Palmer, John W. Padberg; trans. John L. McCarthy. St. Louis, MO: The Institute of Jesuit Sources, 2006.
Letters of St. Ignatius of Loyola. Selected and trans. William J. Young. Chicago, IL: Loyola University Press, 1959.
Monumenta Ignatiana: Sancti Ignatii de Loyola Societatis Jesu fundatoris epistolae et instructiones. 12 vols. Madrid: G. Lopez de Horno, 1903–11.

Alison C. Fleming

Letters, *Indipetae*

Since the formation of the Society, Jesuits have taken a vow of willingness to travel throughout the world, going to any place where they are needed, in imitation of the Apostles. The first missionaries departed for Asia before the confirmation of the Order was even official, and in the early years of the Society many men desired to participate in the missions. Young Jesuit novices as well as priests made requests, in the form of letters to the superior general, asking to be sent on a mission outside Europe, and often phrased as "to the Indies." The term *indipetae* comes directly from the phrase *Epistolae India petentes*, or the "letters of request to go to the Indies." Jesuits who volunteered for these often-dangerous overseas missions became known as *indipeti*.

As typically it was only the superior general who could grant the official permission for joining a missionary province, the letters were sent to him. The letters are usually passionate, expressing a fervent desire to serve the Society in this capacity. It is estimated that around 24,000 of these letters were written between 1540 and 1773; approximately 14,000 have survived. They are preserved primarily in the Archivum Romanum Societatis Iesu (ARSI). There are also *indipetae* existing for the post-1814 era.

See also Archivum Romanum Societatis Iesu (ARSI); *Lettres Édifiantes et Curieuses*; Superior General

de Andrada Pacheco, Paulo Roberto, and Marina Massimi, "The Experience of 'Consolation' in the *Litterae Indipetae*." *Psicologia em Estudo* 15, 2 (April/June 2010), 343–52.

Clossey, Luke, *Salvation and Globalization in the Early Jesuit Missions*. Cambridge: Cambridge University Press, 2008.

O'Malley, John W., *The First Jesuits*. Cambridge, MA: Harvard University Press, 1993.

Alison C. Fleming

Letters, *Soli*

A letter marked *soli*, a Latin word meaning "for one only," is to be read exclusively by its addressee. According to a long-established practice in the Society of Jesus, any Jesuit may send the provincial or the superior general a *soli* letter, which is to be opened and read by him alone. Such a letter is sent using two envelopes, in which the outer envelope is addressed in the usual way and the inner envelope, duly sealed, is simply marked *soli*.

Under ordinary circumstances, letters sent to the provincial are also read by his *socius*, and the contents may be shared with the province consultors. In like measure, letters sent to the general are ordinarily read by the regional assistant for the region from which the letter was sent, and its contents are shareable among the members of the General Curia. A *soli* letter obviates this process by reserving its material only for the superior in question.

The circumstances for the sending of a *soli* letter are generally extraordinary. They may be used, for instance, in particularly sensitive matters in which confidentiality is imperative or if, in the judgment of an individual Jesuit, the usual course of information has proven non-responsive to a problem. The general expectation is that the content of *soli* letters will be kept confidential, even if exceptions to this practice may be made. Consequently, the *Practica quaedam*, or the Society's *Norms for Correspondence with Father General and Other Concrete Business Matters*, directs Jesuits to send *soli* letters to the general only under very specified circumstances, that is, "concerning matters reserved *exclusively* to Father General, and whose solution does not require consultation with others."

See also Province, Provincial; Superior General

Practica Quaedam: Norms for Correspondence with Father General and Other Concrete Business Matters. Rome: General Curia, 1997.

Henry Shea, SJ

Lettres Édifiantes et Curieuses

Lettres edifiantes et curieuses is the title of a series of letters from missionaries published in French by the Jesuits in Paris between the years 1703 and 1776 (34 vols.). Fr. Le Gobin, former missionary in the Levant, judged that the letters, official and cordial, that missionaries mailed back to superiors and friends merited a broader audience. Each volume opens with a preface addressed to Jesuits; Volume 9 refers to them as "those kept in Europe by *force majeure*." The final title he chose reflected his choice of letters: *edifying* – accounts of the progress of evangelization, the apostolic experience of the missionaries, and the precarious conditions in which they lived; and *curious* – exotic descriptions, geographical and astronomical observations. In short, interesting travelogues support the serious religious discourse of the letters. Alongside the letters there are frequent reports on cities, missions, or recent discoveries.

A second collection of eight volumes (1818–23) followed the first, and a third of 30 volumes appeared between 1827 and 1878.

The letters, written from China, East India, North and South America, and the Middle East, provide a mine of literary and cultural information on a great part of the world in the eighteenth century. They have been studied as travel literature, religious and mission history, and geography. Covering, as they do, an extended time period and geographic area, they are woven into the fabric of the century.

The writers did not look for the exceptional; rather, they talked of the typical, highlighting the characteristics of the area in which they worked. The scientific value of the letters derives from their authors' long years of service among a people whose language they spoke. They had a considerable impact on the intellectual and artistic life of the era.

There have been several editions of the letters, complete and selected, the most recent dating from 1979 and 1987.

See also Archives and Libraries; France

John Donohue, SJ

Liberation Theology, Latin American

Latin American liberation theology is one of the most significant movements in twentieth-century Catholic theology. Its focus on the preferential option for the poor, its criticism of structural sin, and the emphasis it has placed on reimagining the Catholic faith as an instrument for the liberation of the oppressed constitute decisive contributions to Catholic theology. Although Latin American liberation theology is a diverse movement that counts both Catholics and Protestants among its adherents, Jesuits throughout Latin America have played a prominent role in its development and defense – from Juan Luis Segundo (Uruguay), Ignacio Ellacuría (El Salvador), and Jon Sobrino (El Salvador) to Pedro Trigo (Venezuela), Victor Codina (Bolivia), Juan Carlos Scannone (Argentina), and Manuel Diaz Mateos (Peru). Because the influence of the Jesuits on Latin American liberation theology is wide-ranging, the focus here is on three dimensions of this influence: (1) Vatican II and its reception by Jesuits in Latin America; (2) Ignatian spirituality and Latin American liberation theology; (3) Pope Francis and the future of Latin American liberation theology.

The Second Vatican Council (1962–65) reformulated the Church's mission in the world by calling for Catholics to read the signs of the times and respond to the realities of the modern world in the light of the Gospel. Pedro Arrupe, SJ, was elected superior general of the Jesuits on May 22, 1965. As superior general, Arrupe participated in the fourth and final session of the Second Vatican Council (from September 14 to December 8, 1965) which deliberated over *Gaudium et spes*. At the conclusion of the Council, Arrupe argued that the Jesuit order "should be completely pervaded by the spirit of Vatican II." Arrupe interpreted this spirit and the Council's mandate to read the signs of the times in terms of a call for a renewed focus on the liberation of the marginalized from oppression.

This call for renewal was concretized in the context of Latin America in May of 1968 when Arrupe met with the Jesuit provincials of Latin America in Rio de Janeiro, Brazil, for a week of prayer, study, and discernment. At the conclusion of the meeting, the provincials sent a letter to the Jesuits in Latin America that articulated a new vision for their mission in the region. In response to the crisis of widespread poverty – what the authors termed the "social problem in Latin America" – the letter argued that in "all our activities, our goal should be the liberation of humankind from every sort of servitude that oppresses it."

The provincials argued that this reorientation of the "entire apostolate" of Jesuits in Latin America would involve a transformation of their priorities in a number of important ways. First, the provincials called for a specific focus on personal conversion that would entail Jesuits divesting themselves of "any aristocratic attitude" in their public positions, their lifestyle, and the selection of the audiences to whom they minister. The renewal of spirituality was given explicit attention in the letter because the provincials were convinced that without this process of inner conversion the "creation of a new social order" in Latin America would not be possible. Second, the document announced an important shift in relation to the traditional work of the Jesuits in the realm of education. The provincials observed: "we are convinced that the Society of Jesus in Latin America must take a clear stand in defense of social justice, supporting those who lack the basic tools of education, which are so essential for development. Hence we must offer marginal groups the chance for an education." Practically, this meant that that Jesuit "schools and universities accept their role as active agents of national integration and social justice in Latin America." Finally, the provincials acknowledged that this shift in their apostolate would lead to criticism and persecution, but reaffirmed their mission "to preach the gospel to the poor no matter what reactions may be unleashed."

The transformation of the mission of the Jesuits in Latin America was given broader institutional support by the Catholic Church at the meeting of the Second General Conference of the Conference of Latin American Bishops in Medellín, Colombia, from August 26 to September 6, 1968. At this meeting the bishops responded to "a deafening cry" that "pours from the throats of millions of men and women asking their pastors for a liberation that reaches them from nowhere else." It was in response to the "dismal poverty" and "inhuman wretchedness" experienced by millions of Latin Americans that the bishops called for the Catholic Church to place the preferential option for the poor at the center of its activities.

In each province in Latin America Jesuits reflected on their work in response to the call for renewal issued at Vatican II, Rio de Janeiro, and Medellín. Perhaps the most well known of these meetings was the gathering of the Jesuits of Central America from December 24 to December 31, 1969, in San Salvador, El Salvador. The meeting was structured around the Four Weeks of the *Spiritual Exercises*. Miguel Elizondo, Ignacio Ellacuría, and others offered interpretations of the *Exercises* as a means of discerning the proper response of the Jesuits in Central America to a historical situation characterized by social unrest, civil wars, and political violence.

Ellacuría, in particular, called for Jesuits to recognize the reality of social or structural sin and to embody the option for the poor in a way that would actively contest forces of oppression that lead to the suffering of the innocent. In his comments, Ellacuría acknowledged the consequences that would follow from placing the preferential option for the poor at the center of their work in the region. Specifically, he observed that this shift in mission would lead to conflict and advised the Jesuits in Central America to prepare themselves for persecution. Tragically, this warning would prove prescient as Jesuits throughout Latin America – from João Bosco Penido Burnier, SJ, to Rutilio Grande, SJ – were martyred for their radical commitment to the poor. Ellacuría would suffer the fate he described at this meeting of the Central American Jesuits in 1969 almost twenty years later on November 16, 1989, when he was assassinated at the Universidad Centroamericana (UCA) along with five fellow Jesuits, their housekeeper, and her daughter.

In addition to the transformation of the apostolic priorities and educational initiatives in Latin America, Jesuits in the region turned to the *Spiritual Exercises* as an instrument uniquely suited to facilitate the type of discernment that was needed to respond to the transformation of their mission in Latin America. This engagement is evident in Miguel Elizondo's work with the *Exercises* and Manuel Diaz Mateos's analysis of the relationship between Ignatian spirituality and liberation theology (*The God Who Liberates*). Furthermore, this type of engagement is present in the Christological work of Juan Luis Segundo (*The Christ of the Ignatian Exercises*) and Jon Sobrino (*Christology at the Crossroads* and *The True Church and the Poor*).

Ellacuría's work on Ignatian spirituality is broadly representative of the approach taken by Jesuit liberation theologians in their application of the *Spiritual Exercises* to the situation in Latin America. For Ellacuría, the central task of Christian theology and spirituality is to historicize Christianity by incarnating gospel values in new sociopolitical contexts. For Ellacuría, the *Spiritual Exercises* already represent a work of historicization insofar as the program of the *Exercises* is oriented toward the end of producing an encounter with God's concrete will in history. But where Ignatius largely employed the *Exercises* to promote the discernment of God's will for individuals, Ellacuría maintains that in Latin America the *Exercises* should be refocused on the discernment of God's will in the midst of situations of oppression.

In a commencement address at Santa Clara University in 1982, Ellacuría performed a famous historicization of the *Exercises* by reinterpreting the significance of Ignatius's colloquy at the end of the First Week through the lens of Latin American liberation theology. At the end of the First Week, as a means of creating the disposition necessary for the individual exercitant to discern her concrete mission in the world, Ignatius asks the exercitant to stand before Christ crucified and ask: "What have I done for Christ? What am I doing for Christ? And what ought I to do for Christ?" Ellacuría seizes upon this colloquy as a critical tool for spiritual discernment, but reinterprets it by placing it within the social reality of Latin America. Thus, Ellacuría shifts the object of meditation from Christ to the crucified people and suggests that individuals ask these questions as they stand before the crucified people: "What have I done to crucify them? What am I doing to end their crucifixion? What should I do so that this people might rise from the dead?" Ellacuría's sociopolitical reinterpretation of Ignatius's colloquy is only one example of a broader project undertaken by Jesuits in Latin America that not only employed the *Exercises* as a tool of discernment but also utilized Ignatian spirituality as a critical resource for the development of theologies and spiritualities responsive to the suffering of a crucified people in Latin America.

The transformation of institutional priorities in Latin America as well as the critical role the Jesuit theologians played in the development of liberation theologies and spiritualities placed many Latin American Jesuits at the center of debates over liberation theology during the papacies of John Paul II and Benedict XVI. During John Paul II's papacy, the Congregation for the Doctrine of the Faith (CDF), under the leadership of the then Cardinal Joseph Ratzinger, released two critical instructions that attributed "serious ideological deviations" to Latin American liberation theology. This suspicion of the orthodoxy of Latin American liberation theology continued during the papacy of Benedict XVI during which Jon Sobrino's theology was investigated. In 2007 the CDF publicly criticized Sobrino's Christological reflections in *Jesus the Liberator* and *Christ the Liberator* as "erroneous" and "dangerous."

In view of the often tense relationship between Vatican authorities and Latin American liberation theologians, a topic of contemporary interest is how the first Jesuit and Latin American pope will approach liberation theology. As a pope who has deployed concrete gestures as an extraordinarily effective means of communication, Francis has signaled his greater openness to Latin American liberation theology by meeting with Gustavo Gutierrez, OP, at the Vatican, through his beatification – and promotion of the canonization – of Archbishop Oscar Romero (a process which had been stalled under the papacies of John Paul II and Benedict XVI), and through his consultation with Leonardo Boff when preparing his encyclical on the environment. But even more than these gestures, it is evident that Latin American liberation theology has influenced the themes and priorities of Francis's papacy.

In the 1970s, as provincial superior of the Jesuits in Argentina, the then Jorge Mario Bergoglio, SJ, distanced himself from more radical forms of liberation theology that were influencing the Catholic Church in Latin America. While he expressed reservations about specific strands of liberation theology, Bergoglio supported the Argentinian strand of liberation theology known as a "theology of the people" (*teología del pueblo*). This form of liberation theology was developed by Bergoglio's former teacher, Juan Carlos

Scannone, SJ, and differed from other forms of Latin American liberation theology in its explicit concern to distance itself from Marxist analysis and in its emphasis on the significance of popular religiosity. In particular, where some forms of Latin American liberation theology adopted the Marxist criticism of popular religiosity as a source of alienation that engendered submission to the prevailing sociopolitical and economic order, the Argentinian strand focused on the significance of popular piety of the "people of faith" (*pueblo fiel*) as a source of resistance to oppression and as the authentic starting point for theology.

The influence of this Argentinian form of liberation theology on Francis's papacy can be detected in a number of the themes that have been at the center of his speeches and writings as pope. At the outset of his pontificate, Francis called for the renewal of the Catholic Church by returning to its roots as a "church of the poor, for the poor." In the apostolic exhortation *Evangelii gaudium*, Francis elaborated on the significance of this approach to the Church by arguing that "each individual Christian and every community is called to be an instrument of God for the liberation and promotion of the poor." This statement echoes the claim made by Gustavo Gutierrez that the preferential option for the poor is not "optional," but rather an essential component of the Christian life because it is the option that God has taken.

This commitment to the retrieval of the option for the poor as a central, non-negotiable feature of Catholic spirituality has led Francis to criticize those cultural forces that prevent Catholics from reclaiming this option in their lives. For Francis, foremost among these obstacles is the emergence of "new idols" in contemporary culture. In a manner that is redolent of the reflections of Archbishop Oscar Romero, Gustavo Gutierrez, and Jon Sobrino, Francis has argued that the idol that now dominates global culture is money. In *Evangelii gaudium* he observed: "the worship of the ancient golden calf (cf. Exodus 32: 1–35) has returned in a new and ruthless guise in the idolatry of money and the dictatorship of an impersonal economy lacking a truly human purpose."

For Francis, the idolatry of money has given rise to a "culture of prosperity" that promotes a social environment in which the loss of a few points in the stock market is viewed as a tragedy that garners virtually endless amounts of news commentary, but the death of a homeless person from exposure fails to register as an event worthy of attention. But even more than its role in the dissemination of a culture of indifference, Francis contends that this form of idolatry supports an impersonal economy that generates vast amounts of inequality and social exclusion. In *Evangelii gaudium* Francis singled out "trickle down economics" as a particularly pernicious ideology that creates an economic climate in which everything is subsumed under the "laws of competition and the survival of the fittest." Within this context the "powerful feed upon the powerless" and the poor are sacrificed to the "faceless" imperatives of capital accumulation.

This powerful indictment of the global economic order and the inequality it spawns is entirely consistent with the types of criticisms of "neoliberal" capitalism developed by Latin American liberation theologians in the 1970s and 1980s as well as the trenchant criticisms of "neoliberalism" offered by the Jesuit provincials of Latin America in a 1996 document entitled, "A Letter on Neoliberalism in Latin America." And while it is too early to cast any definitive judgment on the matter, the development of these liberationist themes in Francis's papacy appears to signal the end of the dispute between Latin

American liberation theology and the Vatican. Perhaps of even more significance is the fact that Francis appears to be engaged in a retrieval of a non-Marxist form of liberation theology rooted in the conviction that a critical confrontation with the global economic order is necessary to defend the rights of the poor and to ensure a sustainable future for the planet.

It is evident from this brief overview that the history of Latin American liberation theology is linked inextricably to the renewal of the Jesuit order after Vatican II. On the one hand, the direction taken by the Society under the leadership of Arrupe was instrumental in the development of Latin American liberation theology as Jesuits in the region reoriented their apostolate toward the liberation of the poor from oppression. On the other hand, the development of liberation theology in Latin America in the 1960s and 1970s influenced the broader mission of the Jesuit order and led to the codification of liberationist themes in its official documents. Ignacio Ellacuría, for instance, argued that it was the influence of Medellín on Arrupe that led the Society to articulate its mission in terms of the "service of faith and the promotion of justice" at the 32nd General Congregation in 1975.

It remains to be seen what the twenty-first century will hold for Latin American liberation theology, but one could very well imagine a future historian narrating its history by drawing a line from Arrupe's call for the Jesuit order to focus on the liberation of the oppressed to Francis's renewal of liberationist themes during his papacy. What is certain, however, is that no matter how this history is narrated, the Jesuits will be accorded a privileged place in the development and continued relevance of Latin American liberation theology for Catholic theology.

See also Arrupe, Pedro, SJ; Ellacuría, Ignacio, SJ and Companions; Justice; Preferential Option for the Poor; Segundo, Juan Luis, SJ; Service of Faith and Promotion of Justice; Universidad Centroamericana (UCA)

Ashley, J. Matthew, "A Contemplative under the Standard of Christ: Ignacio Ellacuría's Interpretation of Ignatius of Loyola's Spiritual Exercises." *Spiritus: A Journal of Christian Spirituality* 10, 2 (Fall 2010), 192–204.
   "Ignacio Ellacuría and the Spiritual Exercises of Ignatius of Loyola." *Theological Studies* 61, 1 (2000), 16–39.
Ellacuría, Ignacio, "A Latin American Reading of the *Exercises* of Saint Ignatius." *Spiritus: A Journal of Christian Spirituality* 10, 2 (Fall 2010), 205–42.
   "The Task of the Christian University." In Jon Sobrino, Ignacio Ellacuría, and Joseph O'Hare, *Companions of Jesus: The Jesuit Martyrs of El Salvador.* Maryknoll, NY: Orbis Books, 1990, pp. 149–150.
Hennelly, Alfred, *The Documentary History of Latin American Liberation Theology.* Maryknoll, NY: Orbis Books, 1990.
Klaiber, Jeffrey, *Jesuits in Latin America, 1549–2000: 450 Years of Inculturation, Defense of Human Rights, and Prophetic Witness.* St. Louis, MO: The Institute of Jesuit Sources, 2009.
Lasalle-Klein, Robert, *Blood and Ink: Ignacio Ellacuría, Jon Sobrino, and the Jesuit Martyrs of the University of Central America.* Maryknoll, NY: Orbis Books, 2014.
Sobrino, Jon, *Christology at the Crossroads.* Maryknoll, NY: Orbis Books, 1978.
   The True Church and the Poor. Trans. Matthew J. O'Connell. Maryknoll, NY: Orbis Books, 1984.
Valiente, Ernesto, "The Reception of Vatican II in Latin America." *Theological Studies* 73, 4 (2012), 795–823.

Matthew T. Eggemeier

Liberatore, Matteo, SJ (1810–1892)

Matteo Liberatore, as a Jesuit student in Naples of Fr. Luigi Taparelli, SJ, an enthusiast for St. Thomas, was himself influenced to appreciate and espouse Thomism. Taparelli was at that time Jesuit provincial, before which he had been rector of the Gregorian University, where he had managed to interest a young student, Gioacchino Pecci, the future Leo XIII, in St. Thomas. So, while Taparelli by no means succeeded in making everyone with whom he came into contact a disciple of St. Thomas, he did catch some surprisingly big fish. Another was at Modena, prior to his arrival in Naples, when he "captured" for St. Thomas one Giuseppe Pecci, at that time a Jesuit scholastic and brother of the future pope.

Liberatore taught philosophy at the Jesuit college in Naples from 1837 to 1848, after which he became a professor of theology at the Gregorian University in Rome. However, after two years he gave up this professorship to co-found and to write for *La Civiltà Cattolica*, a periodical begun by the Jesuits to support the Church and the papacy and to promote the philosophy and theology of St. Thomas Aquinas. Liberatore had by then become a fervent Thomist and, in a series of articles begun in *La Civiltà Cattolicà* in 1853, presented Thomas's philosophy and theology as a coherent, integrated and, indeed, indispensable system.

Like his Jesuit contemporary, Joseph Kleutgen (although the two worked independently), Liberatore argued that Thomism – conceived in a Suarezian way by him – was superior to any Enlightenment-influenced attempts that drew on post-Cartesian philosophies to meet the philosophical challenges of the day. In *La Civiltà Cattolica* alone, in articles and reviews, Liberatore was responsible for over 900 titles. He also authored works on logic, metaphysics, ethics, and natural law, in addition to a host of articles on anthropological, economic, cultural, and pastoral subjects. He enjoyed the favor of Leo XIII, the "Thomist" pope, in the preparation of whose encyclicals *Aeterni Patris* (1879) and, in particular, *Rerum novarum* (1891) he played a highly influential role.

See also Civiltà Cattolica; Kleutgen, Joseph, SJ; Philosophy; Theology

McCool, Gerald A., *Catholic Theology in the Nineteenth Century: The Quest for a Unitary Method.* New York: The Seabury Press, 1977.

James Corkery, SJ

Lievens, Constant, SJ (1856–1893)

Born to a large, rural Flemish family with ten children, Lievens studied at the minor seminary of Roeselare, together with the Flemish writer Albrecht Rodenbach (1856–80), followed by a year of theology in Bruges. Because he wanted to become a missionary, Lievens joined the Jesuits in 1878 and was sent to India two years later. After only three years of formation, he was ordained in Calcutta (now Kolkata) in 1883. He studied the language and customs of the Munda people whom he joined in 1885. Lievens, popularly known as Libin Saheb, dedicated himself not only to the evangelization of the area but also to education, social work, and human rights, defending the local tribes in the English colonial courts. The Christian population until then numbered only 2,700; two years later 15,000 were baptized, with 40,000 catechumens. Lievens received support from other missionaries and moved to Ranchi in 1888 as director of the mission. In spite of his tuberculosis he continued to work, baptizing many more people, so that the

Christians eventually numbered 73,000. He was sent back to his homeland in order to recuperate. However, he did not survive his illness and died at the age of 37. His ashes were transferred to Saint Mary's Cathedral in Ranchi.

In his hometown Moorslede, a statue was erected in 1929 showing him on horseback, with an identical copy in Torpa, the centre of the Munda region. The minor seminary of Roeselare placed a memorial for Lievens in 1956.

The cause for his beatification started in 1993 in the Diocese of Bruges.

See also India

Houthaeve, Robert, *Brieven van Constant Lievens*. Moorslede: Robert Houthaeve, 1994.

Tete, Peter, *Constant Lievens and the Catholic Church of Chotanagpur*. Ranchi: Archbishop's House, 1993.

Paul Begheyn, SJ

Lith, Frans van, SJ (1863–1926)

Born of humble and pious parents, Frans van Lith entered the Society of Jesus in 1881 and was ordained a priest in 1894. Two years later he was sent to the recently started mission among the Javanese in the Netherlands Indies. He settled in Muntilan where he attempted to insert himself into traditional rural Javanese life. He criticized the traditional Catholic missionary practice and became a representative of what was later called "inculturation." This evoked irritation among his religious superiors, who did not want him to publish his new insights, in which he stated his desire to be Javanese with the Javanese.

In 1904 Van Lith baptized 171 villagers in Sendangsono, now a pilgrimage center. In the same year he opened a simple school in Muntilan for male village teachers. Seven years later two of them asked to be trained as priests and were sent to the Netherlands in 1914. Ten others followed, among them Albert Soegijapranata (1896–1963), later to become Indonesia's first indigenous bishop, who called Van Lith "our emancipator." A short time after Van Lith's initiative, Pope Benedict XV, in his apostolic letter *Maximum Illud* (1919), recommended the training of indigenous priests. From 1920 through 1924 Van Lith returned to his homeland because of his declining health.

This Dutch Jesuit functions as a model of modern Catholicism in Indonesia.

See also Indonesia

van Klinken, Gerry, "Power, symbol and the Catholic mission in Java. The biography of Frans van Lith SJ," *Documentatieblad voor de Geschiedenis van de Nederlandse Zending en Overzeese Kerken* 4 (1997), 43–59.

Rosariyanto, Floribertus Hasto, *Father Franciscus van Lith, SJ (1863–1926): Turning Point of the Catholic Church's Approach in the Pluralistic Indonesian Society*. Rome: Pontifical Gregorian University, 1997.

Paul Begheyn, SJ

Lithuania

Jesuits first arrived in what was then the Polish-Lithuanian Commonwealth in 1569 and, at the invitation of the local nobility, immediately took steps to found a university, which was opened ten years later. This school became an "Academia et Universitas" headed by the famed Polish Jesuit Piotr Skarga, going on to play a major role in the cultural and intellectual life of the Commonwealth until the Suppression. In 1594 the printing house connected with the university produced the oldest-surviving printed book from the Duchy of Lithuania. Another milestone was the Polish–Lithuanian–Latin dictionary *Dictionarium trium linguarum* (1629) by Constantius Szyrwid (1580–1631), who also compiled the first book of grammar of the Lithuanian language (*Lietuvių kalbos raktas*), no copies of which have survived. A Lithuanian province was created in 1608 which included Livonia and Prussia (before its union with Brandenburg). In 1641 the university added a Faculty of Law, and in 1649 a secondary school was founded in Kaunas.

This golden age of the Society in Lithuania saw the publication of *Praxis Oratoria* 1648 by Sigismundus Lauxmin (Žygimantas Liauksminas) (*c.* 1597–1670), a native of Vilnius. Nicolaus Lancicius (Leczyski) (1574–1652), a convert from Calvinism and later provincial of the Lithuanian province, compiled the text of the widely distributed "visual biography" of Ignatius of Loyola.

The Jesuit press in Vilnius produced important scientific works, including those by Boscovic, as well as the first book in Latvian, a Catholic catechism, which appeared in 1585. Albertas Kojalavičius (Kojałowicz) (1609–77) contributed to Lithuanian historiography with *Historiae Lituanae pars prior* (1650–69). Among the distinguished Jesuits associated with Vilnius University was Thomas Zebrowski (1714–58), who designed the observatory that opened in 1753. Among the Lithuanian language publications produced in this period were a catechism, *Pamokslas krikščioniškas* (1670), and a songbook, *Balas sirdies* (1680), both by Franciscus Szrubowski (1620–80). Lithuanian language missions were also undertaken, including one in the Samogitian dialect. However the overall production of Lithuanian language materials was a fraction of that produced in Polish, and the makeup of the Jesuit community in Vilnius retained a significantly Polish character.

Late Baroque Jesuit culture in Vilnius was especially rich. Benedictus Dobszewicz (Dobševičius) (1722–94), professor of the Vilnius Academy, was the author of two extensive works *Placita recentiorum philosophorum explanata* (Vilnius, 1760) and *Praelectiones logicae* (Vilnius 1761), in which he attempted a synthesis of traditional and more modern philosophy. School dramas were produced as late as 1750; modern languages, history, and geography were taught at the university, and a decade before the Suppression a *collegium medicum* appeared. Jesuit brothers left their mark on the province of Lithuania: Stanislas Szymborski (1651–1736) was an outstanding craftsman who designed candelabra for St. John's Church in Vilnius.

Lithuanian Jesuits were also active in China, among them Andrzej Rudomina (Lu an de) (1595–1631). Throughout this period Lithuania, as a field of Jesuit endeavor, cannot be entirely separated from Poland, since the Commonwealth survived until after the Society's suppression. Relations with Jews were often difficult: some Jesuit preachers were involved in the propagation of the Blood Libel, and relations between Jesuits and Jews were often strained in the years before 1773. As in Poland, many Jesuits based in Lithuanian territories continued to teach after the Suppression. Andreas Strzecki (1737–97) published *Ephemerides astronomicae* (1776) while working at the Vilnius observatory.

The restoration of the Society did not see the return of Jesuits to Lithuania, as was the case in many other places in eastern Europe. Not until 1921 and the resurrection of an independent Lithuanian state was the Jesuit presence restored and a secondary school established in Vilnius. The advance of German armies saw the arrest and interment of numerous Jesuits and the closing of their schools, and in 1944 with the advance of the Soviet Army, many Lithuanian Jesuits fled westward, while those who remained were subject to persecution. By the late 1940s Soviet authorities had banned all Catholic religious congregations, and most Jesuits, headed by their provincial, were in prisons and camps. Those who survived were released in the years 1955–56, many of whom returned to serve in Lithuania, while some of these soon went on a mission to diffuse through the territory of the USSR, especially to the thousands of Catholics deported to Siberia and Kazakhstan. Among the Jesuits of the Lithuanian province were Jonas Paukshtis (Yakutia), Fr. Jurgis Smilgyavichyus (Tomsk), Fr. Petras Lygnugaris (Tomsk region, Krasnoyarsk Krai, Irkutsk region, Buryatia), Fr. Antanas Shyashkyavichyus (Altai Territory). Further persecutions ensued with the anti-religious campaigns of 1957 and following years. Meanwhile Jesuits continued their ministry to the Lithuanian diaspora in the New World. After the collapse of Soviet power, Jesuits opened secondary schools in Vilnius and Kaunas, and gained further visibility with the appointments of Jesuits as bishops of Kaunas and Telšiai.

See also Catechims; Eastern Europe; Poland

Grzebień, Ludwik, *Encykolpedia Wiedzy o Jesuitach na Ziemiach Polski i Litwy 1564–1995*. Cracow: WAM, 1996.

Rostowski, Stanislaus, *Lituanicarum Societatis Jesu Historiarum Libri Decem*. Paris: Victor Palmé, 1877.

Paul Shore

Liturgy

From their inception, Jesuits have played a unique role in the liturgy of the Church. In an effort to break from the requirements of the more traditional monastic style of liturgical life (maintained by canons regular and mendicant orders as well) and to maintain the flexibility necessary for their engagement-in-the-world apostolate, Ignatius of Loyola insisted that the clerical members of the Society of Jesus be exempted from the obligation to recite the Divine Office daily *in choro* (*Formula* [8]; *Constitutions* [586]). A structured liturgical life was not completely dispensed with: all Jesuits were expected to go to confession weekly; non-priests would receive communion once a week, while priests "will celebrate Mass more frequently" (*General Examen* [80]-25). Novices received instruction on how to participate in Confession and assist at Mass (*Constitutions* [277]-20); scholastics were given an extra hour for private prayer and meditation, as well as recitation of the Little Office of the Blessed Virgin Mary (*Constitutions* [342]-3); less literate members were to recite the rosary (*Constitutions* [344]-4), and all were to pray before and after each meal (*Constitutions* [251]-5). Prayer in the presence of the Blessed Sacrament was also encouraged. All of these practices could be altered at the discretion of the superior (e.g. *Constitutions* [343]-B). Other liturgical activities, e.g., celebration of Vespers or ceremonies of Holy Week, were to be carried out reverently but simply, and always with "the care of souls" in mind.

Over the next centuries, the influence of Jesuits in the area of liturgy continued, and the Mass and Eucharistic devotions played a key role in the lives of both Jesuits and the communities they served. Their patronage of the Baroque style of church architecture can be seen as a very physical way of drawing the laity closer to liturgical rites, not only the celebration of Mass but also Benediction and the recitation of litanies. In seventeenth-century France, Jesuit theologians, including Denis Pétau, SJ (1583–1652), advocated the practice of frequent communion as spiritual support for the faltering soul, answering attempts by Jansenist writers to insist that reception of communion must be anticipated by strict penitential practices to ensure the purity of the communicant's spiritual state.

The Jesuits also played a role in promoting other private and communal liturgical/devotional activities. Cardinal Robert Bellarmine, SJ (1542–1621), signed the decree establishing the Feast of the Guardian Angels in the Roman Calendar (1607). The growing devotion to the Sacred Heart of Jesus was energized by several generations of Jesuits, starting with Francis Borja and Aloysius Gonzaga, and supported and popularized by later Jesuits, including Claude La Colombière (1641–82), Jean Croiset (1656–1738), and Joseph de Gallifet (1663–1749).

Several Jesuits wrote on liturgy in the early twentieth century; although some remained skeptical of the growing liturgical movement in Europe and North America, they were strong supporters of increased lay participation in the Mass and more frequent communion. The Belgian Jules Lintelo authored two important books on the topic (1908 and 1910); both were translated into English by Francis M. de Zulueta, for use in Great Britain. In Germany, Joseph Kramp (?–1940) and Josef Braun (1857–1947) published on liturgical topics. In the 1930s through the 1950s, an increasing number of Jesuits specialized in liturgy: Joseph Jungmann (1889–1975) in Austria; the Dutch Hermann Schmidt; Clifford Howell (1902–81) in Great Britain; and in the USA, Gerard Ellard (1894–1963) and Edward J. Kilmartin (1923–94), whose work spanned several decades.

In the 1960s, Jesuits were involved in the preparations for and implementation of the Second Vatican Council. Augustin Bea, SJ (later cardinal; 1881–1968), served on both the Commission for Liturgical Reform (1948) and the post-conciliar Consilium. Other Jesuits were also involved with the Consilium: Domenico Grasso (Italy); Louis Ligier (France); Roderick MacKenzie (Canada); Alphonsus Raes, prefect of the Vatican Library; Alois Stenzel (Germany).

Jesuits continue to be locally and globally prominent as liturgical scholars and experts. Examples include the Australian Jesuit and composer Christopher Willcock (b. 1947); the American liturgical theologian John Baldovin (b. 1947); the British Jesuit Edward Yarnold (1926–2002); and on Eastern liturgy, the American Robert Taft (b. 1932). The Jungmann Society, established in 2006, is an international professional association for Jesuit liturgical experts.

See also Baroque Art and Architecture; Bea, Augustin Cardinal, SJ; Communion, Frequent; *Constitutions*; Jungmann, Joseph, SJ

Bugnini, Annibale, *The Reform of the Liturgy, 1948–1975.* Trans. Matthew J. O'Connell. Collegeville, MN: Liturgical Press, 1990 [*La riforma liturgica, 1948–1975,* 1983].

Janssens, John Baptist, "Instruction and Ordinance Concerning the Training of Ours in the Sacred Liturgy." American Assistancy Seminar. *Studies in the Spirituality of Jesuits* 35, 2 (March 2003), 9–37.

Klein, J. Leo, "American Jesuits and the Liturgy." American Assistancy Seminar. *Studies in the Spirituality of Jesuits* 11, 3 (May 1979), 1–30.

Weiss, Joseph, "Jesuits and the Liturgy of the Hours: The Tradition, Its Roots, Classical Exponents, and Criticism in the Perspective of Today." Unpublished Ph.D. dissertation, University of Notre Dame, 1993.

Joanne M. Pierce

Lonergan, Bernard J., SJ (1904–1984)

Bernard Lonergan, philosopher and theologian, was born in Buckingham, Quebec, on December 17, 1904, and died in Pickering, Ontario, on November 26, 1984.

Inspired by both traditional wisdom and modern science, Lonergan engaged in a lifelong pursuit to develop a method that would reconcile the interdisciplinary questions of life. Through the empirical method of self-appropriation, he sought to understand the structure of human consciousness, hoping to reconnect modern thinkers with their ancient and medieval predecessors and by so doing transform contemporary culture and science.

After attending Loyola College in Montreal, Lonergan entered the Jesuit novitiate at Guelph, Ontario, on July 29, 1922, at 17 years of age. Showing exceptional brilliance, he was appointed to teach Latin to his fellow novices and then mathematics to his fellow junior scholastics. From 1926 to 1929 he studied philosophy at Heythrop College, Oxfordshire, and the following year he also received degrees in classics and mathematics from the University of London. After returning to Montreal in 1930, he taught at Loyola College for his regency.

From 1933 to 1937, Lonergan studied theology at the Gregorian University in Rome and worked out his ideas on a new philosophy of history. He was ordained to the priesthood on July 25, 1936 The following year he began a doctorate in theology at the Gregorian University and, with Charles Boyer, SJ, as his director, prepared a study on divine grace and human freedom in Aquinas that revealed considerable independence of thought. Then, in 1940 at Immaculée-Conception, Montreal, he began a 43-year academic career of teaching and writing.

Lonergan published his dissertation in four installments in *Theological Studies* in 1941–42. Next he investigated the cognitional theory of Aquinas and painstakingly elucidated it from 1946 to 1949 in the "Verbum" articles in the same journal.

In 1949, now teaching at Regis College in Toronto, he began his magnum opus, *Insight: A Study of Human Understanding*. Frustrated by the antiquated methods used in theology, he prepared a philosophical prolegomenon to theological method that could also be used for other sciences. By means of a suitable method, he wished to recast the traditional formulations of medieval theologians into literary forms and thought patterns that would incorporate modern discoveries and concepts. Published in 1957, *Insight* was well received by religious and secular scholars, and study clubs were initiated to assimilate and expand its complex thought.

Central to the method of Lonergan was the "appropriation of one's own rational self-consciousness." By intrinsic analysis of the rational life we experience, and proceeding through the steps of experience, understanding, and judgment, we can eventually transform our human situation. This subjective experience is found to be isomorphic with objective understanding and to give a fixed base for understanding the universe. Such a procedure could be used to give meaning to theological formulas and to develop a modern spirituality and mysticism.

Invited in 1953 to teach at the Gregorian University, Lonergan presented questions in a dialectical fashion to students from over eighty countries for over a decade. Using his cognitional theory to shed new light on old theological questions, he published major Latin treatises: *De constitutione Christi ontologica et psychologica*, *De Deo Trino*, and *De Verbo incarnato*. Working always on a very fundamental level, he was less involved than other theologians in the day-to-day controversies in the Church. He was, however, consulted as a *peritus* at the Second Vatican Council. He also later became a member of the first International Theological Commission and served as a consultor to the Secretariat for Non-Believers.

A pipe smoker for thirty years, Lonergan, during a visit to Toronto in 1965, was found to have lung cancer. He remained for medical treatment and never returned to his Roman professorship. After an operation and a lengthy recovery, he resumed work on the theological sequel to *Insight*. It was published in 1972 as *Method in Theology* and reflected the significance of the change from classical to modern culture. For Lonergan theological method was best conceived as a framework for collaborative creativity, demanding conversion of theologians so that they are able to embrace the values about which they seek understanding. Lonergan envisioned the complementary vectors of human creativity and divine healing as central to theological understanding, the former rising up from our perception of values in the world and the latter flowing to effect our surrender to the love of God.

Throughout his career Lonergan gave occasional addresses at various universities on key aspects of his thought. In 1971–72 he was the Stillman Professor of Catholic Studies at Harvard University. Accepting the post of Visiting Distinguished Professor at Boston College in 1975, for eight years he taught seminars, tutored students, and exchanged ideas with faculty. In the late fall of 1983, at 79 years of age and in failing health, he retired to the Jesuit infirmary in Pickering, Ontario. Colleagues, students, and "Lonergan Centers" around the world soon began to incorporate his method of understanding and to disseminate his thought.

See also Canada; Philosophy; Theology

Braman, Brian J., *Meaning and Authenticity: Bernard Lonergan and Charles Taylor on the Drama of Authentic Human Existence.* Toronto: University of Toronto Press, 2008.

Jacques Monet, SJ, written in collaboration with Frederick Crowe, SJ

Lord, Daniel, SJ (1888–1955)

"Silent smut had been bad," Daniel Lord famously wrote. "Vocal smut cried to the censors for vengeance." One of the first modern-day culture warriors, Lord is known as a firebrand who agitated to implement a moral code for motion pictures based on Judeo-Christian values. But Lord was also an apostolic giant of the twentieth century whose work with the sodality movement among young people and as a writer, playwright, and musical composer galvanized an entire generation of American Catholics. He was a communicator and a media mastermind who had a keen ability to reach a wide audience.

Born in 1888 in Chicago, Daniel Aloysius Lord studied at St. Ignatius College and entered the Society of Jesus in 1909. Ordained a priest in 1923, Lord became director of the Sodality of the Blessed Virgin Mary in 1925. He would remain the national director until 1948. The sodality, which had existed as a loose network of student-led devotional groups based at Jesuit high schools and universities, would develop rapidly and dramatically under Lord's leadership, claiming more than 2 million members at its height. He worked to revitalize the sodality's magazine, *The Queen's Work*, with the aim of placing a copy in the hands of every Catholic student in the nation. Lord saw the magazine as a tool for evangelization and catechesis for the Catholic youth of America.

But the magazine was not the sole way in which Lord attempted to reach young people. During his life he employed music and drama (he was an accomplished pianist) and relied on a popular approach that some of his fellow Jesuits and superiors thought beneath the Society. Lord did not write scholarly articles or books, but rather simple poems, cartoons, and songs (some with hokey titles) on topics and themes designed to bring Catholic influence to bear on the dominant culture. These topics included suggestions for a proper devotional life, decorum and modesty, respect for authority, family life, and denunciations against secularism and communism in the wake of World War II. It is estimated that Lord wrote "an average of 20,000 words per month over the course of his 35-year ministry, totaling at least eight million words," published as books, pamphlets, and articles (Endres, "Dan Lord," 21).

In addition to his writings, Lord engaged the young members of his sodality in elaborate theater pieces and dramas, works that would eventually link him to the film industry, where he would be viewed as a meddlesome presence. The theater pieces – he created and staged fifty-eight original musicals – were haphazardly organized yet skillfully accomplished. Often the plots of these productions were centered on moral issues, and the life lessons taught during the plays were intentional. Lord believed Catholicism to be a moral force for good in the world, and his public ministry in its many forms encouraged young people to live out the truths of the faith in the public square, outside of their schools and parishes.

Lord's artistic endeavors and his public insistence on Catholic life and morals collided dramatically in the film industry. After serving as a consultant to the 1927 film "The King of Kings," many began to look to Lord as the authoritative Catholic voice in the industry. Soon, Lord came to see himself in that role, and he took up the charge of censorship, working as a vocal member of the Legion of Decency to develop a production code for motion pictures. Lord sought to imbue the code with a solid theological and moral foundation, and his work, more than any other person, influenced the new guidelines. Lord relished his chance to influence mass recreation for the good. (It is interesting to note here that, although Lord was willing to use various entertainment pursuits to evangelize, he was not willing to allow artistic freedom to impinge upon the moral teachings of the Church.) However, with no effective provisions for enforcement, the Code, as written, faltered. Lord himself pronounced it a failure.

Still, Lord's influence was staggering; a search of *The Queen's Work* will reveal hundreds of pamphlets, books, and plays Lord published through that media enterprise. His ability to communicate effectively with an entire generation of young Catholics through so many different means was unmatched in his era. Lord's was not a scholarly approach, but he employed the most effective means available – from the stage to the screen, from witty cartoons to written word – to pass on the Church's teachings to a new generation.

See also Arts, Performing; Film and Television: Screenwriters, Consultants; Marian Congregations; Theater; United States of America

Endres, Dan, "Dan Lord, Hollywood Priest." *America*. December 12, 2005, pp. 20–21.

Lord, Daniel, *Played by Ear: The Autobiography of Daniel A. Lord, SJ*. Chicago, IL: Loyola University Press, 1956.

Keith Maczkiewicz, SJ

Louis XIV

Louis XIV (who reigned from 1643 until 1715) perpetuated the dynastic tradition of patronage begun by Henry IV. Louis XIV, for instance, kept appointing Jesuit confessors (with such prominent figures as François Annat and François de La Chaize).

The continued support of the monarchy had proved decisive for the expansion of the Order in France. The order had also benefited from the limited competition on the market of higher education in the first half of the century. All the provinces were in place since 1616 and every major French town had a Jesuit college (and sometimes, as for example in Lyon, more). While the bulk of the growth occurred before Louis XIV rose to personal power in 1661, he continued to show support. In 1682 he declared himself the founder of the Parisian Collège de Clermont which changed its name to Louis-Le-Grand. The same year, the French provinces petitioned for the right to found seminaries. They soon were granted a few by the bishops (in Albi and Auch, for instance), or by the King himself (in recently conquered Strasbourg). When the King decided to better the training of navy chaplains, the Society was put in charge of new seminaries in Brest and Toulon. By the end of the reign, there were close to 3,000 Jesuits and 115 Jesuit establishments (of which 91 were colleges) in France. The second half of the century also witnessed a strong Jesuit involvement in the various aspects of French cultural life. In 1701 the Jesuits founded the *Mémoires de Trévoux*, an academic journal that chronicled cultural life.

Before Louis XIV's accession, royal support had already opened extra-European French territories to Jesuit missions (particularly in Canada). Louis XIV not only continued this policy but also used missions to assert the Kingdom's leadership in the Catholic world. The Jesuit missions to the Kingdom of Siam and to Southeast Asia had strong diplomatic overtones.

The presence of the Society remained contentious in France, and the Jesuits had to adapt accordingly. Their decision to petition for the authorization to undertake the responsibility for local seminaries was thus connected to their need for an efficient ecclesiastical strategy. While anti-Jesuit feelings were widespread in some parts of French Society in the early seventeenth century, there is no doubt that starting in the 1630s, the growing division of French Catholicism greatly affected the place of the Society in France. The debate over Jansenism was perceived – somewhat inaccurately – by the public as one pitting an anti-Jesuit party against a pro-Jesuit one. While connections between the Society and local elites remained strong in many places, there is no doubt that the growing phenomenon of religious partisanship could not be escaped. This combined with preexisting political and academic hostility, as well as with new claims coming from a more educated and empowered secular clergy. In such places as the major Archdiocese of Sens, Archbishop de Gondrin, could choose to wage war against the local Jesuits and try to bridle their ministry. These conflicts made the Society increasingly dependent on the King.

This was all the more so, as Louis XIV was intent on asserting his authority over the French Jesuits. His confessors became a key element in the government of the Society in France and were used to relay royal demands to the Roman Curia. He tried to have the geography of the French Assistancy match with the boundaries of his own political rule and asked for the incorporation of colleges and provinces in the territories conquered during the reign. Louis also engaged in a more general competition with the

Habsburg dynasty for patronage over the Order worldwide. During the generalate of Tirso González, these moves came close to altering the structure of the Order. While the General, encouraged by Pope Innocent XI, was perceived by the French court as a political enemy, the King opted for the separation of the French Jesuits from the Jesuit Curia and envisioned an autonomous French Society of Jesus. The possibility would come to be recalled in the eighteenth century.

While French Jesuits reacted in diverse ways to the King's claims, there is no doubt that many regarded them as justified, including for religious reasons. Jesuit historiography has greatly underestimated the influence of Gallicanism and of growing national feelings upon French Jesuits. If some may have proved capable of refusing the new claims of royal authority, most Jesuits acknowledged that the King was master of the public sphere. Many felt much further obliged.

See also Confession, Confessors; France; Jansenism; La Chaize, François de, SJ

Bergin, Joseph, *Church, Society and Religious Change in France*. New Haven, CT/London: Yale University Press, 2009.

Bireley, Robert, *The Jesuits and the Thirty Years War: Kings, Courts and Confessors*. Cambridge: Cambridge University Press, 2003.

Gay, Jean-Pascal, *Jesuit Civil Wars. Theology, Politics and Government under Tirso González (1687–1705)*. Farnham/Burlington, VT: Ashgate, 2012.

Wright, Anthony D., *The Divisions of French Catholicism, 1629–1645: The "Parting of the Ways."* Farnham/Burlington VT: Ashgate, 2011.

Jean-Pascal Gay

Louis XV

France certainly proved instrumental in the process of suppression of the Society of Jesus. After royal approval of the expulsion, it became more difficult for the Society to face its adversaries as the Bourbon dynasty largely dominated Catholic Europe. Expulsion from Spain, from the Kingdom of the Two Sicilies, as well as from the Duchy of Parma is a sign of closer diplomatic connections between Bourbon monarchies after the 1761 Family Compact. French diplomatic pressure played an important part in securing Pope Clement XIV's decision to suppress the Society worldwide. Yet, it would be greatly misleading to limit the history of the Society in France during this long reign to the Suppression, let alone to read this history merely as pointing to it.

While the Society did not grow between 1715 and 1764, it remained strong on the basis of its major seventeenth-century expansion and retained its importance in the making of the French urban elites. The number of French Jesuits remained stable (between 3,000 and 3,500) as did the number of colleges. Jesuit spiritual writers retained great popularity. After a short interruption during the *Régence*, the Jesuits returned as confessors to King Louis XV albeit with less influence than before. The confessors spent less time at court, and the King stopped confessing around 1738.

While the Society remained strong, the enrollment in Jesuit schools dropped drastically because of competition, financial difficulties, the possible aging of Jesuit personnel, as well as hostility to the Society. Despite such efforts as those of Claude Buffier, eighteenth-century French Jesuits also proved unable to adapt their teaching to cultural changes. The syllabus remained rigid and came under strong criticism by the middle of the eighteenth century. In the province of Champagne, while the Jesuits cared for roughly 5,700 students in 1629, they retained only 3,000 in 1761.

This does not mean that the Jesuits could not or did not engage cultural change. They did so all the more as they had managed to consolidate their positions in the Republic of Letters. Many Jesuits welcomed the new expansion of cultural life in France and took part in the flourishing *Académies*. In 1751 the editor of the *Mémoires de Trévoux* saluted the *Encyclopédie* as a noble prospect, though he grew rapidly critical of the professional deontology of its authors. With time the Jesuits became all the more defiant of the religious opinions of the *Philosophes*, as the latter became openly hostile to the Jesuits. Voltaire famously described the Jesuits as the best defenders of Catholicism and therefore advocated actively pursuing their demise.

One of the most unsettling challenges that the Jesuits had to face was the permanence of Jansenism. The crisis reactivated by the papal bull of 1713 (*Unigenitus Dei Filius*) not only revived Jansenist hostility to the Society but also encouraged a rapprochement between supporters of Jansenism and a secular Gallican clergy and accentuated the political turn of Jansenism. The criticism of both royal and Jesuit "despotism" brought the *parlements*, the Jansenists, and the *Philosophes* together.

The multilayered process of suppression took place in the context of the Seven Years War (1756–63). This major setback put the French monarchy in a fragile political position. The legal difficulties of the Jesuits began with their indictment for their responsibility in the financial risk taken by the superior of the Martinique mission, Antoine Lavalette. The Parlement of Paris mounted an attack on the Society predicated upon judicial initiatives as well as on a public campaign of defamation. This forced the King to intervene. In 1762 the Crown tried to find some middle ground and revived the hypothesis of an autonomous French Society. This solution was faced with opposition from Lorenzo Ricci and Pope Clement XIII. Parlement refused to register the edict enacting this middle-way and resumed its assaults on the Society. It started by closing the Jesuit schools in its jurisdiction and then declared the Jesuit order "obnoxious to civic order, violator of the natural law, destroyer of religion and morality." While some of the other regional *parlements* followed suit, others hesitated or even opposed that of Paris. Pressure for a unified Parliamentary front finally triumphed. The King sanctioned and reclaimed the whole process by himself proscribing the Society throughout France in 1764. While most Jesuits disapproved of the national dissolution, not all of them considered it illegitimate. Earlier religious commitment to the authoritarian claims of the monarchy certainly proved essential in encouraging the now former Jesuits into accepting their own situation. The ex-Jesuits certainly cannot be described as a unified group passively or actively expecting the restoration of the Order.

See also Anti-Jesuit Polemic; France; Jansenism; Suppression

McManners, John, *Church and Society in Eighteenth-Century France*. Oxford: Oxford University Press, 1998.

Northeast, Catherine M., *The Parisian Jesuits and the Enlightenment 1700–1762*. Oxford: The Voltaire Foundation, 1991.

Van Kley, Dale, *The Jansenists and the Expulsion of the Jesuits from France 1757–1765*. New Haven, CT/London: Yale University Press, 1975.

Jean-Pascal Gay

Loyola (Place)

Loyola, or Loiola in Basque, was the second surname of St. Ignatius, who was born Iñigo López de Loyola in the Basque country in Spain. The name Loyola specifically made reference to the medieval tower house in which Ignatius was born. At present, the town of Loyola is settled in a small district near the city of Azpeitia in the Gipuzkoa province, and its main point of reference is what is now called the Sanctuary of Loyola, which was raised upon the family home of Ignatius on the banks of the Urola River and integrated into the green, hilly landscape.

In 1681 the original tower house was given to the Jesuits, who built a religious complex around it. In the center there stands a church dominated by a dome and preceded by a wide porch of a Churrigueresque Baroque style. The inside of the church features a silver statue of Ignatius that was donated by the Royal Guipuzcoana Company of Caracas in the mid-eighteenth century.

The Sanctuary of Loyola became dependent on the Spanish government in 1836 after the so-called *Confiscation of Mendizabal*, a series of decrees that resulted in the expropriation of Church properties in Spain. As a result, the Sanctuary has been administered instead by the Gipuzkoa Provincial Council, which still maintains the property today. In 1991, however, the Gipuzkoa Provincial Council restored the tower house itself to the Society of Jesus.

In total, the Baroque architectural complex includes the central nave of the basilica, the tower house, where some childhood memories of Ignatius are preserved and, on the third floor, the room known as the Chapel of the Conversion, where Ignatius

Figure 37 Loyola family coat-of-arms, embedded in stone at Loyola Castle. Photograph Alison Fleming

made his famous convalescence. There is also a Jesuit residence, a public library, and two important archives. The historical archive keeps documents relating to the house and lineage of Loyola as well as documents relating to the history of the early Society, and its more than 40,000 volumes contain works of great significance for Jesuit history. Another archive preserves material related to Nemesio Otaño, the famous twentieth-century Jesuit Basque musicologist and composer. Nearby there is also a Center for Spirituality and a youth hostel where group activities are performed.

See also Azpeitia; Loyola, Ignatius of, SJ, St.; Spain

Achabal, Mª Isabel Astozarain, *El Santuario de Loyola*. San Sebastián: Fundación Cultural, 1988.
Eguillor, José Ramón, *Loyola: Historia y arquitectura*. Guipúzcoa: Diputación Foral de Guipúzcoa, 1991.
Sanctuary of Loyola. www.santuariodeloyola.org/.

Inmaculada Fernández Arrillaga

Loyola, Ignatius of, SJ, St. (1491–1556)

Ignatius of Loyola was born Íñigo Lopez de Loyola in Guipúzcoa (Loyola), in the Basque region of Spain. The seventh and youngest son of thirteen children, most historians place his birth in 1491. He took the name Ignatius during his time in Paris, out of devotion to the martyr of the early Church and also to have a name that was more universally recognizable. His early years followed the pattern of life of a minor Spanish *hidalgo*, i.e., someone who fit into the society of the Spanish court. He would therefore have learned to read and write and even compose verse, the protocols of court, the use of arms, as well as other skills useful to the courtier. He lost his mother in 1506 and his father a year later.

After his mother's death he was sent to live with his uncle, Juan Velásquez de Cuéllar, the chief treasurer of Castile. While he saw himself pursuing a career at court, he received the tonsure (the first Minor Order) in his early teens, probably in order to hold the parish church in Azpeitia, which was in the patronage of the Loyola family. It is from this that the first documented evidence of Ignatius can be found. During Carnival of 1515 he was charged with assault while on a visit back home. He fled to Pamplona claiming clerical jurisdiction because of his tonsure. This was not granted because he neither dressed as a cleric nor behaved as one. However, Ignatius was able to flee back to Arévalo and his duties to Velásquez there. Ignatius remained primarily concerned with advancing his own position at court. Of these early years his autobiography states, "until he was 26 years old he was a man given to the vanities of this world, and principally he delighted in the exercise of arms." This, however, does not make Ignatius a professional soldier. He was a courtier and so at times obliged to resort to weapons when wit and diplomacy failed to serve his mission.

After the death of King Ferdinand II of Aragon, Velásquez lost influence at court; he died in August of 1517. Having experienced the fall from favor of his patron, the young Ignatius went into the service of Don Antonio Manrique de Lara, duke of Nájera, and viceroy of Navarre. After serving the Viceroy on diplomatic missions in Guipúzcoa, Ignatius was wounded at the fortress of Pamplona on May 20, 1521, while helping the Spanish forces defend that town from French troops seeking to return the kingdom of Navarre to Henri d'Albret. After being taken prisoner by the French and receiving the most rudimentary of attention to his wounded leg, Ignatius was returned to his home. His leg was reset at Loyola castle, and he probably suffered from a resulting infection with a high fever and came close to death. The fever broke around the feasts of Saints Peter and Paul (June 29, 1521) and he began to heal. However, his vanity caused him to submit to yet another surgery. The healing bones created a lump under the knee of his right leg, unsightly for a courtier, in his view. He had the protruding bone cut away, and submitted to agonizing traction in order to lengthen his leg. This slow and painful recovery required considerable immobility, and during his convalescence he found himself reading the *Vita Christi* of Ludolph of Saxony, and the *Flos sanctorum*, a selection of lives of the saints gathered by Jacopo de Varazze. It was as a result of his musings on the spiritual adventures which he read that he began to discern the diversity of spirits which attracted or repelled him. This was the beginning of an experience that inspired his imagination in a direction different from his previous desires; he experienced a spiritual conversion and resolved to make a pilgrimage to the Holy Land.

Ignatius left Loyola at the end of February 1522 to begin his pilgrimage. He traveled first to Barcelona, stopping at the monastery of Montserrat to keep a vigil at the shrine of the black Madonna there. In the course of his vigil, he confessed to a French Benedictine, Jean Chanon, and came into contact with elements of the *devotio moderna* through the *Ejercitorio de la vida espiritual* of Garcia Jimenez de Cisneros. Because there was a fear of the plague at Barcelona, Ignatius stopped at the village of Manresa outside the Spanish port city. What was initially intended to be a brief pause became an eleven-month sojourn which allowed him to begin a "little book" that would become the basis for his later *Spiritual Exercises*. The young and inexperienced pilgrim sought to write down those exercises which he had found helpful, as well as some counsels for avoiding some of the mistakes that he had made in his own spiritual journey. The *Spiritual Exercises*, then, are a series of prayer experiences and counsels intended to be given by a guide over a period of four weeks. They combine the use of the imagination in prayer with the purpose of disposing the person making the exercises to a spiritual generosity that might lead to practical resolutions in his or her life.

Ignatius's *Autobiography* recounts many examples from this time in his process of conversion that illustrate an immaturity of experience that could have ended badly. One of the most famous recounts his falling in with a Moor on his journey to Manresa. In the course of their travel together, the Moor disputed with Ignatius the perpetual virginity of Mary. Unable to convince him by argument, he felt the urge to settle the matter with his dagger. Feeling the pull of this interior movement, and another to spare the man's life and continue on his pilgrimage, he decided "to let the mule go with the reins slack," thus allowing the mule to decide the man's fate. The mule took the narrower path onward to Manresa and so the pilgrimage continued without a violent incident.

At the beginning of 1523 he left Manresa for Barcelona. From there he took a ship to Rome where he received the pilgrimage blessing from the recently elected Pope Adrian VI. He embarked on the pilgrim ship from Venice on July 14, 1523, and arrived in Jerusalem on September 3. While he desired to remain there to help souls and seek conversions, he did not receive permission from the Franciscan custodians to do so. Thus he returned first to Italy and then to Spain with the intention of beginning his studies so as to "help souls." In Barcelona he began the study of Latin grammar under Jerónimo Ardévol. While initially distracted by great spiritual consolation in prayer, once he realized that this was a temptation away from his studies he resolved to attend to them with firmer resolve.

Ignatius next made two unsuccessful attempts to study humanities at the universities of Alcalá and Salamanca. While at Alcalá he came under the investigation of the Dominicans of the Spanish Inquisition and spent forty-two days in their custody. Their concern focused on the similarities between the *Spiritual Exercises* and the heresy of the *alumbrados*, as well as the suspicious appearance of both Ignatius and his companions as they went about helping the poor. (They dressed in similarly colored gowns like a religious order.) While the matter was resolved to the satisfaction of the Dominicans, Ignatius sought a less distracting place to complete his studies. He had also learned from his less than successful experience at the Spanish universities that he needed a more disciplined and ordered approach to his studies.

The now middle-aged student (aged 37) arrived at Paris in 1528, though none of the students he had come to know in Spain accompanied him there. To finance his studies, Ignatius traveled to Flanders and as far as London, where he begged alms sufficient for his own needs as well as for several other students with whom he had come into contact. He soon began to gather these other students as "friends in the Lord" who met together for Mass and spiritual conversation. While some had known of him in Spain, others met him for the first time in Paris. In addition to Ignatius's roommate, the Savoyard priest Peter Faber, and his friend Francis Xavier from Navarre, there were Diego Laínez, Alfonso Salmerón, and Nicolás Bobadilla, all Spaniards and former students at Alcalá who joined the group. The Portuguese Simão Rodrigues completed the first seven companions. It was this international group who would come to form the Society of Jesus. In the course of their time at the University of Paris, all of them made the *Spiritual Exercises*. On August 15, 1534, at the chapel of Montmartre outside of Paris, these six companions and Ignatius vowed perpetual poverty and chastity, and resolved to travel to the Holy Land when they had completed their studies.

During his time in Paris, Ignatius saw the practicality of the *modus parisiensis* as an ordered method and curriculum of study. He would remember this "Parisian method" when the first Jesuit schools were founded and adopt the same for them. He also studied theology with the Dominicans at the convent of St. Jacques, where he developed a preference for the scholasticism of St. Thomas Aquinas. This, too, would be enshrined in the Jesuit schools later in the century.

After successfully completing the Arts course at Paris in 1535 (obtaining a master's degree), Ignatius returned home to Spain to settle some personal affairs and regain his health. He reunited with his companions (now nine with the addition of Claude Jay, another Savoyard, and Paschase Broët and Jean Codure, both French) in Venice in 1536. After visiting Rome to receive the blessing of Pope Paul III for their anticipated pilgrimage to the Holy Land, they were ordained by the papal legate in Venice, Vincenzo Nigusanti, in June of 1537.

During their time in Venice, the companions assisted in hospitals for the incurable, preached, taught catechism, and gave the *Spiritual Exercises*. While doing so, they came into contact with other companies of reformers. For his part Ignatius continued his spiritual conversations with friends and benefactors as well as reading theology on his own.

When it became clear that the pilgrim ship would not leave Venice in either 1537 or 1538, Ignatius and his companions (now joined by Diego de Hoces, another Spaniard) returned to Rome to make themselves available to Pope Paul III, a proviso they had made with their vows at Montmartre. On the morning of December 25, 1538, Ignatius, who had delayed celebrating his first Mass in hopes of celebrating it in the Holy Land, finally did so at the basilica of Santa Maria Maggiore at the altar of the Manger. During Lent of 1539 the companions deliberated on their next steps and decided to form themselves into a religious order with direct obedience to the pope regarding being sent on missions. Ignatius was elected to draw up an initial rule, the so-called "Five Chapters" or *Formula of the Institute*. This was approved by Pope Paul III in the bull *Regimini militantis ecclesiae* on September 27, 1540.

Ignatius was elected superior general on April 8, 1541, and the newly approved Jesuit companions professed their solemn vows on April 22 at the basilica of St. Paul outside the walls. As the first Jesuits dispersed for various missions (Francis Xavier had already left for the Indies), Ignatius remained in Rome until his death, tasked with expanding and revising the original rule into *Constitutions* for the Order. In this he was aided significantly by the first secretary of the Society of Jesus, Juan de Polanco.

During this final period of his life, Ignatius saw the Jesuits grow from the initial ten companions to more than 1,000 spread over the continents of Europe, Africa, South America, and Asia. Through a system of letter writing and the naming of superiors, Ignatius was able to act decisively in this global enterprise. As founder and first superior general, Ignatius brought the culture of the late medieval courtier as well as the emerging bureaucracy of the modern age to his task. The Roman Archives of the Society of Jesus conserve, in addition to his *Autobiography*, *Spiritual Exercises*, and *Constitutions*, over 6,000 of Ignatius's letters. His writings reveal someone who could be attentive to the intricate details of houses and missions, yet open to individual initiative and adaptation. Often after writing several pages of detailed instructions on how to proceed in a certain mission, Ignatius would conclude, "but if this does not appear practical to you, do what is more fitting to the actual situation for the greater glory of God."

In evaluating the impact of Ignatius's early, pre-conversion experiences on his later work, some authors have focused on the influence of his courtly training and diplomatic experiences. But most scholars agree that Ignatius lived in a period of transition between the medieval and modern world. Many of his personal characteristics and worldviews derived from the chivalric notions of the late Middle Ages. For example, his "Meditation on the Two Standards" in the *Spiritual Exercises* hark back to his experience attending the court in Valladolid in February of 1518 at the arrival of Carlos I as king of Castile, or even earlier in 1511 to the calling of the crusade in Seville by King Ferdinando II of Aragon. However, elements of the modern age are also visible in his life and work. The *Spiritual Exercises* rely on the developments introduced by the *devotio moderna*; and Jesuit advocacy of frequent confession and communion reflects one aspect of that reform movement. The use of modern means of organization and communication within the Order, the insistence on regular letters reporting on missions sent to a central government rather than more capitular forms of religious government also mark Ignatius and the Society of Jesus as belonging to the Catholic reforms of the early modern period.

Ignatius must also be understood within the tradition of mysticism in the Church. His interior experience of the Trinity at Manresa by the River Cardoner was the first of many key mystical experiences which helped shape his life and mission. In Venice in 1538 he again made the month-long *Spiritual Exercises* at San Pietro in Vivarolo and

Figure 38 Pierre Legros: Portrait of St. Ignatius Loyola, 1700, silver, Chapel of St. Ignatius, Church of Il Gesù, Rome. Photograph Alison Fleming

shortly after had his mystical vision at La Storta outside of Rome. In that vision he saw the Father place him (and his Company) with the Son, and heard the voice of the Lord saying, "I will be propitious to you in Rome." This experience gave him the confidence to continue on to Rome when the way to the Holy Land had closed. In his final years as general, he continued to find an intimacy with God even in the midst of the mundane duties of government. His *Spiritual Journal* (really just a fragment from 1544 to 1545) registers consolations, gifts of tears especially at Mass, and the contemplative insight into the Triune God whom he found not only in quiet prayer but in all of the many tasks and concerns which filled his day.

While Ignatius was knowledgeable of the weakness of papal Rome (where he founded houses for the reform of prostitutes and for the care of their children), he also knew of its potential in bringing about a more universal reform of the Catholic Church. Although his own education came late in life and followed the more traditional forms of scholastic philosophy and theology, he recognized the potential of the new humanist learning as a key instrument for that reform. While in Paris he feared those who studied Greek for their Lutheran tendencies, he nevertheless later adopted the same humanities curriculum for the Jesuit schools. In this he was greatly influenced by early Jesuits such as Diego Laínez and Jerónimo Nadal, who were humanist scholars in their own right.

Ignatius also sought to safeguard the vow of poverty in the fledgling order (aware of the scandal given by some of the mendicant orders at that time), yet he also saw the advantage of having schools made more stable by a substantial endowment. Thus, the *Constitutions* legislate a strict personal poverty on the part of the individual Jesuit, while allowing for the endowment of the colleges. Still, at the end of his life, the Jesuits saw themselves as primarily an order available for missions from the pope, and not as a teaching order. In maintaining this predisposition to papal missions, the Jesuits incorporated Ignatius's initial desire to help others through the spiritual ministries of preaching, hearing confessions, catechism, and the *Spiritual Exercises*.

Ignatius governed the Society of Jesus from Rome for fifteen years, overseeing the foundation of colleges and missions while writing the *Constitutions*. While the latter was still in the final stages of evaluation and approval during the summer of 1556, Ignatius fell ill for the final time with stomach complaints and a high fever. He died on July 31, 1556, and was buried in the small chapel of Santa Maria della Strada. This chapel was later replaced by the Church of the Gesù, and his new tomb there came to symbolize the triumph of the Baroque church. He was beatified in 1609 and canonized by Pope Gregory XV on March 12, 1622. Pope Pius XI named him patron of the *Spiritual Exercises* in 1922.

See also Autobiography; *Constitutions*; Friends in the Lord; Loyola (Place); Manresa; Montmartre; Montserrat; Paris; Rome; *Spiritual Exercises*

de Dalmases, Candido, *Ignatius of Loyola Founder of the Jesuits*. Trans. Jerome Aixalá. St. Louis, MO: The Institute of Jesuit Sources, 1983.

Idígoras, José Ignacio Tellechea, *Ignatius of Loyola the Pilgrim Saint*. Trans. Cornelius Michael Buckley. Chicago, IL: Loyola University Press, 1994.

Martín, Luis Fernandez, *Los años juveniles de Iñigo de Loyola*. Valladolid: Caha de Ahorros Popular de Valladolid, 1981.

Maryks, Robert, ed., *A Companion to Ignatius of Loyola: Life, Writings, Spirituality, Influence*. Leiden: Brill, 2014.

Ravier, André, *Ignatius of Loyola and the Founding of the Society of Jesus*. San Francisco, CA: Ignatius Press, 1987.

Tylenda, Joseph N., *A Pilgrim's Journey: The Autobiography of Ignatius of Loyola*. Wilmington, DE: Michael Glazier, 1985.

Villoslada, Ricardo Garcia, *San Ignacio de Loyola, nueva biografia*. Madrid: B.A.C., 1986.

Mark A. Lewis, SJ

Lubac, Henri de, Cardinal, SJ (1896–1991)

Henri de Lubac was born on February20, 1896, in Cambrai (Nord), France, and died on September 4, 1991, in Paris. He studied law at the Catholic faculty, Lyon, from 1912 to 1913, philosophy on the island of Jersey from 1920 to 1923, and theology in Hastings, England, from1924 to 1926 and at Lyon-Fourvière from 1926 to 1927. De Lubac entered the Society of Jesus in Sussex, England, in 1913. He served in the French Army from 1915 to 1919. He was ordained a priest in 1927 and was professor of fundamental theology at the Institut Catholique de Lyon from 1929 to 1935. He was professor of theology at Fourvière from 1935 to 1950. He was co-founder, with Jean Daniélou, of *Sources Chrétiennes*, in 1940; co-founder, with Henri Bouillard, of the series, *Théologie*, from 1942; and editor of *Recherches de science religieuse* from 1945 to 1950. De Lubac was a member of the Institut de France (Académie des Sciences Morales) from 1953 and a consultor of the preparatory theological commissions for Vatican II from 1960 to 1962. He was a *peritus* at Vatican II (1962–65). Pope John Paul II made him a cardinal in 1983.

Henri de Lubac is the best known of the theologians associated with the theological movement, the *nouvelle théologie*. His first major work, *Catholicisme* (1938), in essence contains the programmatic themes of his theological career. Its subtitle, *A Study of Dogma in Relation to the Corporate Destiny of Mankind*, points to de Lubac's emphasis on the social character of salvation and the solidarity of the human race in its common vocation. This same social emphasis occurs in *Corpus mysticum* (1944), where de Lubac shows that the term *corpus mysticum* originally designated the Eucharist and not the Church, as it has since the shift that occurred after the Eucharistic controversy with Berengar of Tours in the eleventh century. The effect of this change was the divorce of the ecclesial body from the Eucharistic and historical bodies of Christ and a loss of awareness of the social and ecclesial meaning of the Eucharist.

During World War II, de Lubac was actively involved in the French Resistance. He was one of the principal theologians of the clandestine publication *Cahiers du Témoinage chrétien* (1941–44). His memories of the years 1940–44 are recorded in *Résistance chrétienne à l'antisémitisme* (1988). These memories serve as commentary on the nature, limitations, and responsibility inherent in the Church's relation to the temporal order and to the state.

De Lubac's controversial work on the supernatural destiny of the human person, *Surnaturel* (1946), argues that there is only one destiny for an intellectual creature, the supernatural destiny of the beatific vision. This challenged the neo-scholastic interpretation of Thomas Aquinas that upheld the possibility of a purely natural order. This work, in particular, was thought to be implicated among the errors denounced in the encyclical of Pius XII, *Humani generis* (1950), although de Lubac vigorously denied it. His friend, Hans Urs von Balthasar, reported, "his books were banned, removed from the libraries of the Society of Jesus and impounded from the market." De Lubac left Fourvière and moved to Paris in 1950. Although this occurred two months prior to the publication of the encyclical, the two events are often linked together. The theme of nature and grace continued to occupy de Lubac, for in 1965 he published a reworked version of the first three chapters in *Surnaturel* as *Augustianisme et théologie moderne* as well as *Le mystère du surnaturel*. His *Petite catéchèse sur nature et grâce* appeared in 1980.

De Lubac's work on apologetics, revelation, atheism, and the nature of the Church enabled him to be a valuable influence at the Second Vatican Council. Pope John XXIII appointed him a member of the Council's preparatory commission in August 1960. He subsequently served as a *peritus* and was associated with the documents *Dei verbum*, *Lumen gentium*, and *Gaudium et spes*. Of these, he most influenced *Dei verbum* through his work on the spiritual meaning of the Scriptures and the typological relationship between the Old and New Testaments. He completed his four-volume *Exégèse médiévale* (1959, 1961, 1964) during the Council. His journals, *Carnets du Concile*, were published in 2007.

De Lubac became critical of some of the post-conciliar theological and ecclesiastical developments. This conservative turn is not evident in his theological writings, however, which bear witness to a unity in his thought and do not indicate any shifts in his theological positions. The change was due to a shift in the terms of the conversation from the relationship between grace and nature to the relationship between grace and history or between Church and world. This shift is most apparent in de Lubac's criticism of Edward Schillebeeckx in *Petite catéchèse sur Nature et Grâce* (1980) and his 1969 article, "The Church in Crisis."

After the Council, de Lubac was appointed as a member of the International Theological Commission and served as a consultor for the Secretariat for Non-Christians and the Secretariat for Non-Believers. When, on February 2, 1983, Pope John Paul II elevated Henri de Lubac to Cardinal in the Roman Catholic Church, he requested and received a dispensation from the requirement of being ordained a bishop, stating that at his age he could not discharge the duties of a bishop properly and therefore would not do justice to the episcopal office.

See also Ecclesiology; *Nouvelle Théologie*; *Sources Chrétiennes*; Theology

Susan K. Wood

Lumen Vitae Institute (Brussels)

The Lumen Vitae is an international center founded in 1935 by Belgian Jesuit Georges Deleuve with the intention of helping missionaries in foreign lands to develop new catechesis for a new cultural context. The center was primarily dedicated to producing research and textbooks in the field of religious education, a tradition that it continues today. In 1956, however, Father Deleuve organized an international congress with the theme of "Catechism for our time." This congress was a great success, with the participation of 450 people from all over the world, and it led to the establishment of Lumen Vitae as a full-fledged academic institute in Brussels in 1961 that would serve international students from various cultural backgrounds. While the Institute still operates in Brussels, since 1996 it has been officially affiliated with the University of Louvain. It offers second and third cycles of religious, catechetical, and theological formation.

Lumen Vitae has a vibrant community of students coming mostly from Africa, Asia, and Latin America. The presence of students from Latin America has given rise to a deeper understanding of the theology of liberation. The Institute endorsed the paradigm and method of liberation theology to the point of creating tension with the Roman Curia. Salesian priest Father Girardi was accused of being a Marxist, and this led to the closure of the Institute for one academic year (1975–76). The Institute reopened in 1976 and has continued since to remain faithful to its mission, which is the proclamation of the Good News with a special attention to cultural context and the promotion of social justice.

Today the center remains a vibrant and dynamic Jesuit institution that continues to contribute to the evangelization of peoples across the entire world. It continues to communicate the light of life to those who are seeking God through rigorous theological and catechetical study.

See also Catechisms; Justice

Centre International Lumen Vitae. www.lumenvitae.be/.

Luc Bonaventure A. Amoussou, SJ

Macau

Macau long served as the base of operations for the missions in China and Japan; many notable Jesuits spent time here. This territory was established by the Portuguese in 1557 for the purpose of exploration and trade in China. Despite its small size, its prime location on the tip of a peninsula on the southern Chinese coastline facilitated rapid population growth. Most early inhabitants were Portuguese merchants and their families; they were rapidly joined by various religious orders, including the Jesuits. The Christian

Figure 39 Façade of St. Paul's College of Macau, 1602, now in ruins. Photograph © Stephanie Colasanti / The Art Archive at Art Resource, New York

population more than doubled, from 400 to 1,000, in the first twenty-five years of the settlement's existence.

Manuel Teixeira and Francesco Peres established a permanent residence for the Jesuits in Macau in 1565 that would exist until the Suppression. The following year Jesuit bishop Andrea Oviedo (patriarch of Ethiopia) arrived and oversaw the community until the creation of a diocese in 1576. By that time a school had opened, which served 200 students by 1592, and subsequently became St. Paul's University College, issuing degrees by 1597. The college's church burned down in 1601 and was subsequently rebuilt in European style, according to designs by Genoese Jesuit Carlo Spínola. Only the façade and staircase remain as a consequence of another fire in 1835.

Jesuit official visitor Alessandro Valignano arrived in 1577. Ten months spent awaiting favorable weather for sailing to Japan allowed him time to observe and evaluate, and establish the policy of cultural accommodation. Michele Ruggieri arrived in Macau two years later, and Matteo Ricci in 1583. They began studying Chinese language and preparing for their historic mission work there.

Today, the Macau Ricci Institute continues to facilitate the relationship between the Society of Jesus and the people of China.

See also China; Hong Kong; Portugal

Brockey, Liam, *Journey to the East: The Jesuit Mission to China 1579–1724*. Cambridge, MA: Harvard University Press, 2007.

Kaijian, Tang, *Setting off from Macau: Essays on Jesuit History during the Ming and Qing Dynasties*. Leiden: Brill, 2015.

Alison Fleming

MacGregor, Felipe, SJ (1914–2004)

Father Felipe MacGregor was born in Callao, Peru, on September 20, 1914. Educated by the Marist Brothers and later by the Jesuits at the College of San José in Arequipa (Peru), Father MacGregor joined the Society of Jesus and completed his novitiate in Córdoba, Argentina. On December 23, 1944, he was ordained in Buenos Aires, the city where he also finished his philosophy and theology studies. In 1948 he returned to Peru to teach in the Jesuit Colegio de la Inmaculada in Lima. In 1952 he obtained his doctorate from Fordham University and returned to Peru to join the faculty of the Humanities Department of the Pontifical Catholic University of Peru. In 1958 he was named provincial of Peru, and in 1963 he became rector of the Catholic University, a post he held until 1977, when he was designated rector emeritus. Father MacGregor was very active in the organization and advancement of higher education in Latin America. From 1963 he was a member of UNESCO's International Institute for Educational Planning, and he was vice president and president of the Unión de Universidades de América Latina (Association of Latin American Universities) from 1972 to 1976. In 1980 Father MacGregor joined the board of the United Nations University. That same year, he established the Asociación Peruana de Estudios para la Paz (Peruvian Association for Peace Studies), and from 1990 he was the head of the Peruvian Peace Institute. Father Felipe MacGregor died in Lima on October 3, 2004.

See also Peru

Riera, Jorge Capella, and Elsa Tueros Way, "Felipe MacGregor: vida y legado de un maestro." *Educación* (Lima) 14, 27 (2005), 7–22.

Andrés Ignacio Prieto

MacRae, George W., SJ (1928–1985)

George W. MacRae, a member of the New England province of the Society of Jesus, was an internationally renowned New Testament scholar. He received a doctorate from Cambridge University and wrote a dissertation on the relationship between Jewish apocalyptic thought and Gnostic literature. In his academic career he is best known for his work on the translation and interpretation of the Nag Hammadi Library, a collection of Coptic texts discovered in the twentieth century that have significantly impacted biblical studies, and for his collaboration with biblical scholars from diverse religious traditions on the revision of the Revised Standard Version of the Bible.

Father MacRae was born in Lynn, Massachusetts, and entered the Jesuits at age 20 (1948). He did his novitiate at Shadowbrook in Lenox, MA, and was ordained in 1960. During his years of formation, he received a Licentiate in Philosophy in Louvain (1954), a Master of Arts degree in Semitic languages from Johns Hopkins University (1957), and a Licentiate in Sacred Theology from the Weston School of Theology (1960). After his ordination (1961) he completed his doctorate (1966) and returned to Weston to teach (1966–73). In the fall of 1973, he began teaching at Harvard Divinity School, where he taught until his death.

Father MacRae became the first tenured Charles Chauncy Stillman Professor of Roman Catholic Studies at Harvard. Also while at Harvard he served as the rector of the Ecumenical Institute for Theological Research in Tantur, Jerusalem (1979–80). At the time of his death, he had just begun an appointment as acting dean of the Harvard Divinity School.

Father MacRae was both a member and leader of many learned societies; he was known for the diversity of his courses as well as their popularity. Upon his death, Derek Bok, then president of Harvard University, Helmut Koester, his eulogist, and Daniel Harrington, SJ, the homilist at his funeral Mass, all attested that it was Father MacRae's human qualities and virtues – his intelligence, loyalty, wisdom, generosity, and service – that caused him to be both academically successful and genuinely beloved.

See also Biblical Studies; United States of America

Alice L. Laffey

Madagascar

Jesuits played a key role in the evangelization of Madagascar. Their contacts with the people of the Red Island before the nineteenth century were, however, ineffectual. Two Jesuits, vaguely remembered as Luis Mariano (d. *c.* 1630) and Pedro Freire, joined a

Portuguese expedition that was sent from India to Madagascar in 1613. Following the expedition, a Malagasy prince was taken to Goa by force. While there, he received instructions under the Jesuits and was baptized Don André (Andria Ramaka, d. 1651). In 1616 the Jesuits returned to Madagascar accompanied by their convert. For over a decade they attempted to establish a mission on the island, but they were impeded by the Malagasy political class, which was already aligned to the Dutch and was under strong Protestant influence. The Jesuits were expelled from Madagascar in 1621. In a 1667 report of Manuel Barreto, then superior of a Jesuit college at Sena, Mozambique, the Jesuits advised Portugal to conquer Madagascar before the French could do so, probably with the hope of securing Portuguese protection over their missions on the island. The advice bore no results.

Jesuits considered Madagascar again only after the restoration of the order in the nineteenth century. Although the post-restoration missions have been remarkably successful, they are marked by strong Protestant opposition and by a series of expulsions.

In 1844, the general, Jan Roothan (1785–1853), entrusted Madagascar to the Jesuits of Lyon. Six men were immediately assigned to the mission and a local bishop entrusted to them the southern part of the island. As a mark of favorable conditions, a Jesuit, Marc Finaz (1815–80), became prefect-apostolic of the mission from 1851 to 1865. Even then, the Jesuits faced strong opposition from Ranavalona I (c. 1785–1861), a local queen who was generally opposed to European presence and, more specifically, to Catholicism. Some members of her court were inclined to Islam. Moreover, a strong presence of the London Baptist Missionaries in Antananarivo also made it difficult for Catholics to operate in the place. Eventually most Jesuits were forced out of the capital, leaving only a few of them in peripheral parts of Madagascar where they maintained some schools and youth centers.

Ranavalona I was succeeded by Radama II (d. 1863), at which point the Jesuits returned to the center of Madagascar. However, Ranavalona II (1829–83), who ascended the throne in 1863 and was baptized a Protestant in 1869, made Protestantism the state religion and abolished every other form of worship. The Jesuits were once again sent away from Antananarivo. As before, they found refuge among friends on the outskirts of the capital and established thriving missions there. In 1883, for example, there were eighty-three Jesuit stations in Betsiléo alone. Even the Franco-Malagasy War that lasted between 1883 and 1896, which led to yet another expulsion of the Jesuits in 1894, could not smother the zeal for Christianity that was already rooted in the local population. For example, Victoria Rasoamanarivo (1848–94), a woman of great courage and determination, defended the Church against political assault and became the pillar of the Catholic faith in the country after the missionaries had been expelled.

The Menalamba nationalistic movement, which opposed the creation of a French protectorate over the island, was more generally anti-European and, consequently, hostile to missionary Christianity. It was in the context of its resistance that the Jesuit Father (now Saint) Jacques Berthieu (1838–96) was martyred. From 1896, a firmer French colonial hold on Madagascar ushered in a more stable missionary environment. At the beginning of the twentieth century, the Jesuits evangelized mainly in the central and mountainous areas of Madagascar and were responsible for the vicariates apostolic of Fianarantsoa and Antananarivo. They contributed significantly to the training of a strong local clergy. Under their care, St. Michel's College of Antananarivo became a minor seminary in 1910 and a major seminary in 1921. Within their own ranks, the Jesuits had their first Malagasy priests ordained in 1925.

With a strong local membership, the Jesuit vice-province of Madagascar was created in 1958 and was made into a full-fledged province in 1971. Today, the province is made up of 270 Jesuits, most of whom are in training. They continue to invest themselves in youth education, publications, pastoral care, and spirituality ministries. They have also distinguished themselves in the areas of scientific and scholarly research and are visibly present in the Malagasy mass media.

See also France; Martyrs, Ideal and History

Boudou, Adrien, *Les Jésuites à Madagascar au xixe siècle*. 2 vols. Paris: Gabriel Beauchesne et ses Fils, 1940.
Dossou, Davy, and Fulgence Ratsimbazafy, eds., *Revisiter l'histoire et redynamiser la vie spirituelle et missionnaire: Actes du Colloque sur le Bicentenaire de la Restauration de la Compagnie de Jésus, Province de Madagascar*. Antananarivo: Compagnie de Jésus – Province de Madagascar, 2014.
Hübsch, Bruno, ed., *Madagascar et le christianisme*. Antananarivo: Éditions Ambrozontany, 1993.

Festo Mkenda, SJ

Madonna della Strada

In 1541, less than a year after the establishment of the Society of Jesus, Pope Paul III assigned the new order the small church of Santa Maria della Strada (Our Lady of the Wayside), on the Via Papale at Piazza Altieri in Rome. The benefice was facilitated through a member of the Papal Curia, Pietro Codaccio. The church was small, crowded, and in poor condition, but it was centrally located in the city near the Capitoline Hill, an aspect valued by the Order.

The Jesuits acquired land in the neighborhood, and the first members of the Society moved into a house across the street from the chapel almost immediately. The first professed house was built adjacent to the church in 1544; by the death of Ignatius in 1556, there were eighty Jesuits living there. Next, their attention turned to replacing Santa Maria della Strada with a larger structure. Planning discussions began in the early 1550s, but no work was done prior to the death of Ignatius, who was buried in the small church. This original church would later be destroyed completely and replaced by the church of Il Gesù, to which the body of Ignatius was transferred.

One piece of the original church that has been preserved is a fresco fragment depicting the Virgin and Child (fifteenth century), which was located in the chapel dedicated to the Madonna della Strada in the left transept. Although much restored, the fresco recalls icons of the Virgin found in Rome, especially the *Salus Populi Romani* in the Church of Santa Maria Maggiore, which was venerated by the Jesuits and thought to possess miraculous properties. The chapel of the Madonna della Strada is likely the site where St. Bernardino of Siena established the Confraternity of the Holy Name in 1427.

See also Gesù; Rome

Lucas, Thomas, *Landmarking: City, Church and Jesuit Urban Strategy*. Chicago, IL: Loyola Press, 1997, pp. 92–98.

Alison Fleming

Figure 40 *Madonna della Strada*, medieval fresco fragment, Church of Il Gesù, Rome (unknown artist). Photograph Alison Fleming

Magis

The Latin term *magis* (Spanish *más*) serves as shorthand for the dynamism that lies at the heart of Ignatian spirituality. It is characteristic of Ignatius to use the comparative "more" or "greater" in a variety of circumstances. We first encounter it in the First Principle and Foundation in the *Spiritual Exercises*. "Rather, we ought to desire and choose only that which is more conducive to the end for which we are created" (#23). The retreatant is not to be satisfied with whatever may be helpful to the "praise, reverence and service" of God but is to beg for what is *more* helpful. This desire for the "more" introduces an element of tension throughout the Exercises that is not present in all spiritualities.

But it is in the *Constitutions* that the role of the *magis* is most noticeable. In describing the fourth vow of special obedience to the pope, Ignatius writes of the first companions:

> They made the promise or vow in order that His Holiness might distribute them for the greater glory of God, in conformity with their intention to travel throughout the world, and, when they could not find the desired spiritual fruit in one place, to pass on to another and another, ever seeking the greater glory of God our Lord and the greater aid of souls. (*Constitutions*, #605)

He repeats this last formula in discussing the missioning of Jesuits by a superior. "To make the best choice in sending persons to one place or another while having the greater service of God and the more universal good before his eyes as the guiding norm" (*Constitutions*, #622). Having established this overarching criterion, he then discusses the particular criteria of greater need among people, greater fruit to be hoped for, greater indebtedness to some people, the more universal good, and a greater multiplying effect (*Constitutions*, #622). Always the *magis*.

See also Constitutions; *Cura Personalis*; Mission; *Spiritual Exercises*

Rahner, Karl, "Being Open to God Ever Greater: On the Significance of the Aphorism 'Ad Majorem Dei Gloriam.'" In *Theological Investigations*. Vol. VII. London: Darton, Longman & Todd, 1971, pp. 25–46.
Veale, Joseph, "Ignatian Criteria for Choice of Ministries." In *Manifold Gifts: Ignatian Essays on Spirituality*. Oxford: Way Books, 2006, pp. 109–22.

Brian O'Leary, SJ

Malagrida, Gabriel, SJ (1688–1761)

Born in Menaggio, Italy, Malagrida entered the Society of Jesus in 1711, and after a three-decade missionary career in Brazil, which witnessed various conflicts with the local secular authorities, he returned to Lisbon in 1753. In the wake of the devastating Lisbon earthquake of 1755, he published the pamphlet *Juízo da verdadeira causa do Terramoto* (The True Cause of the Earthquake) in which the catastrophe was seen as a divine punishment for Portugal's sins rather than a random natural disaster. The Marquis of Pombal took this as criticism of his polices and embarked upon a campaign against Malagrida. This came to a head following a failed assassination attempt against the king in September 1758. Malagrida, along with fellow Jesuits, was accused of involvement. The charges appear to have been entirely concocted. Malagrida was handed over to the Inquisition and suffered a period of unusually harsh imprisonment. His mental health deteriorated rapidly, and there is still uncertainty about precisely what Malagrida did or did not write and say during this period. Having been condemned for holding heterodox theological opinions and engaging in false prophecy, Malagrida was strangled and burned in Lisbon's Rossio Square on September 20, 1761. The treatment of the aged and disturbed priest provoked a hostile reaction, even from figures such as Voltaire who were not natural allies of the Jesuits.

See also Brazil; Portugal; Suppression

Maxwell, Kenneth, *Pombal: Paradox of the Enlightenment*. New York: Cambridge University Press, 1995.
Vogel, Christine, "Les Lumières face à l'Inquisition portugaise: le procès du jésuite Gabriele Malagrida et l'opinion publique en Europe (1759–1761)." In L. F. Barreto, ed., *Inquisição Portuguesa: tempo, razão e circunstância*. Lisbon: Prefácio, 2007, pp. 375–90.

Jonathan Wright

Malta

Ignatius of Loyola was first approached to open a college in Malta by Bishop Domingo Cubelles (1540–66) in 1553. Conscious of Malta's great potential as a bridge in establishing contact between mainland Europe and the Muslim countries of the Maghreb, Ignatius approved the request. He planned to send Fr. Nicholas Bobadilla to make the preliminary arrangements, but Fr. Bobadilla never reached Malta because a quarrel ensued between the bishop and the Knights of St. John.

The Jesuit college was eventually set up in November 1592. Founded and endowed by Bishop Tomás Gargallo (1578–1614), the college immediately made a great impact among the ruling Knights of Malta and the Maltese alike. Besides teaching, the Jesuit community organized missions, distributed alms, heard confessions, taught Christian doctrine, served as intermediaries between rival families, worked for the conversion of non-Catholics, and established Marian congregations.

Over the years, several grand masters of the Knights of St. John, other dignitaries, and members of the Maltese elite donated generous gifts of land, furniture, and books to the college. The Collegium Melitense, as the college was known, was regarded as having the potential of a university and, by the early seventeenth century, philosophy and theology courses were being taught there.

During the seventeenth and eighteenth centuries, the college served as a link between the Jesuit missionaries from mainland Europe and those in North Africa and parts of the Levant. Maltese Jesuits were considered ideal as missionaries among the Arab-speaking Christians of the Levant mainly because they spoke Maltese, a Semitic language. Gradually, however, the Jesuit superiors became less inclined to send Maltese Jesuits to the missions and began to encourage them to remain in Malta and serve the Maltese community.

Certain Jesuit fathers exerted great influence among the grand masters of Malta, grand crosses of the Order of St. John, and other dignitaries, particularly the apostolic visitor and inquisitor. As a result, several Jesuits functioned as consultants in important Church and State affairs. This caused a strain among the knights, some of whom were anti-Jesuit, and this led to the Jesuits' temporary expulsion in 1639. However, they returned soon after and by 1739 they had opened a house for spiritual exercises. Yet, despite their considerable influence, the Jesuits were expelled in 1768 by the ruling Portuguese Grand Master Pinto de Fonseca who acted in concert with most Catholic sovereigns of Europe.

It took some years after the restoration of the Society in 1814 for the Jesuits to return to Malta. During the mid-nineteenth century, the Jesuit fathers reached Malta from the British province and directly from Sicily. In 1845 the British colonial authorities agreed to allow British Jesuits to open a Jesuit college, but it was closed down again in 1858. Another attempt to open an English-speaking college was made in 1877, but despite its popularity and the sterling pastoral ministries among the British forces, the college was closed down in 1907.

Meanwhile, there were attempts to open a novitiate by the Sicilian Jesuits. The Sicilian Jesuits reached Malta in 1860 and opened a novitiate, under the direction of the province of Sicily, in 1867. Yet it was only in 1897 that they managed to open a permanent residence with the foundation of St. Aloysius College. The direct link with Sicily continued until September, 1940, when the college rector was appointed as the delegate of father general, thus effectively separating the Maltese Jesuits from the Sicilian province. Malta became a vice province in 1947 and a full-fledged province in 1983. A newly built novitiate house eventually came to serve as the center of the new province.

The Maltese Jesuits presently run a House of Retreats in Gozo and have become particularly active in the promotion of social justice, in the dissemination of the social teachings of the Church, in the training and formation of the laity, and of the Maltese society in general. They have also set up a Jesuit Refugee Service to help asylum seekers and refugees. They continue to make a significant contribution to the formation of the Maltese diocesan clergy as well as to the running of the University of Malta Chaplaincy. Several Jesuit fathers have, over the decades, lectured at various departments of the University of Malta such as biology, philosophy, spiritual theology, and Church history.

See also Jesuit Refugee Service; Marian Congregations; Ministries

Borg, Vincent, "Gerolamo Manduca: His Life and Works." *Melita Historica* 7, 3 (1978), 237–57.

Fiorini, Stanley, "The *Collegium Melitense* and the *Universitas Studiorum* to 1798." In Ronald G. Sultana, ed., *Yesterday's Schools. Readings in Maltese Educational History*. Malta: PEG, 2001, pp. 31–58.

Leanza, Antonio, *I Gesuiti in Malta al tempo dei cavalieri gerosolimitani*. Malta: Government Printing Office, 1934.

Scicluna, John, "The History of the Society of Jesus in Malta." www.jrsmalta.org/content.aspx?id=246880#.VG8II00tC1s. Accessed on November 21, 2014.

Carmel Cassar

Manresa

Though Ignatius intended only to pass through the city of Manresa soon after his conversion, he was drawn to remain there for eleven months. During that time, his spiritual experiences would come to define the remainder of his life and directly influence the formation of every man who would later join the Society of Jesus.

Located in the Catalonia region of Spain in the foothills of the Montserrat mountains, the city of Manresa was to be only a brief resting point for the future saint. After his dramatic conversion during his convalescence, Ignatius donned the garb of a pilgrim and began his long journey. He spent time at the Benedictine monastery of Montserrat, where he was led through a series of meditative and contemplative prayers written by Garcias de Cisneros (1455–1510), the abbey's former abbot. These would later become one of the main sources of Ignatius's *Spiritual Exercises*. Following his time there, he went to Manresa simply to record some reflections in the notebook he carried with him. Instead, from March 25, 1522, to mid-February, 1523, Ignatius lived there.

While there, Ignatius's interior life undulated wildly, and he received several significant spiritual insights. In his journals, Ignatius recounts several straight months of tranquility, where a deep sense of peace and joy filled his soul. However, over time he experienced great changes in his soul, feelings of sadness and dryness in prayer. He suffered terribly from scruples during this period and made frequent confessions, seemingly always confessing the same transgressions, racked with self-torturous guilt for weeks at a time. However, Ignatius records that he suddenly became aware that his scruples were falsehoods and lies keeping him from embracing life with God. Thus began his discernment and testing of the various spirits acting upon him. Eventually, Ignatius was freed from the pernicious influence of his scruples, and his tranquility returned. It would not be the last major insight for Ignatius in Manresa.

Ignatius recounts an experience, when sitting on the steps of the Dominican monastery, of seeing the Holy Trinity as three musical keys: each distinct, yet complementary.

Figure 41 *St. Ignatius Writing the Spiritual Exercises*, 17th century, alabaster relief sculpture, Cave of St. Ignatius, Manresa (unknown artist). Photograph Alison Fleming

The insight caused Ignatius to sob almost uncontrollably, so overjoyed and moved by his new interior understanding. He wrote that God was teaching him in Manresa, "much as a schoolteacher teaches a child."

Though Ignatius is often depicted in a cave at Manresa writing down his experiences and composing his *Spiritual Exercises*, the moment of greatest importance in the life of the pilgrim happened on the banks of a river, the Cardoner. In his autobiography, Ignatius describes a spiritual experience he had there in which "the eyes of his understanding were opened" and he was given a new way of seeing all of Creation and how the Creator had imbued everything with Himself. This illumination would come to affect everything in Ignatius's life and give a sort of cohesion to his own blossoming spirituality. Like many spiritual experiences, Ignatius's account of this experience is non-specific, except to say that "everything seemed new to him" afterwards; commentators have offered that Ignatius afterwards came to see as God sees, not through his own biased, limited, human lens.

What should be noted here, however, is that Ignatius's experiences were not isolated; Ignatius writes that there were many moments in which he felt God had invaded his soul, filling him with insights and movements that fleshed out the experience of conversion he first had while convalescing at Loyola. What is clear is that these moments were life-changing and fundamental to who Ignatius would become for the remainder of his life: one wholly aware of the self-communication of a loving and merciful God, the God of grace. It was this interior knowledge that Ignatius eventually shared with others, engaging some in spiritual conversation and leading others through his *Exercises*, all based from his experiences in Manresa and the gifts or graces he received while there.

Many have noted that Manresa was the first real church and true home of St. Ignatius. It was in Manresa that Ignatius was a sort of religious novice, learning the ways in which God had been and continued to be active in his life. Ignatius's growth in discernment of spirits while in Manresa is one that contemporary Jesuits look to as an example. Manresa, therefore, is the spiritual home of each member of the Society of Jesus and all those whose understanding of the world is incarnational, that is, imbued with the sense that God might be found in all things.

See also Loyola, Ignatius of, SJ, St.; *Spiritual Exercises*

Jackson, Charles, "'Something that Happened to Me at Manresa': The Mystical Origin of the Ignatian Charism." *Studies in the Spirituality of Jesuits* 38, 2 (Summer 2006), 1–40.
Segarra, Joan Pijuan, *Manresa and Saint Ignatius of Loyola*. Manresa: Bausili, 1992.
Tylenda, Joseph N., ed. and trans., A *Pilgrim's Journey: The Autobiography of Ignatius of Loyola*. Wilmington, DE: Michael Glazier, 1985.

Keith Maczkiewicz, SJ

Maranhão Mission

Although the Jesuit mission of Maranhão was officially established on June 3, 1639, when Fr. Luís Figueira received legal authorization, its real founder was António Vieira, who, while still in Lisbon in 1652, obtained under royal auspices everything needed to establish the mission.

Vieira's initiatives were the fruit of his political and missionary experiences. Travelling in Indian canoes, he went up the Maranhão and Amazon rivers to open up new fields to evangelization. The Jesuit established farms, cultivating sugar cane and raising cattle. Saint Blaise, on the island of São Luís do Maranhão, had a manual mill to process rice, a flour mill, a sugar cane mill, and a weaver's shop.

In 1655 Vieira went to Lisbon to defend the freedom of Indians. His efforts resulted in the Mission Regulation, which led to the settlers' violent attempt to stem the establishment of reductions similar to the ones in Paraguay, in which the Jesuits would have temporal and spiritual power over native villages.

During the first half of the eighteenth century, the missionary action of the Society of Jesus spread out over the Amazon basin. In 1727 the Maranhão mission was elevated to the status of autonomous vice province. It boasted the College of Saint Alexander in Pará and the College of Our Lady of Light in Maranhão, a novitiate, and studies of philosophy and theology.

The Jesuits in Maranhão devoted themselves to cartography. At Vieira's request, *The Amazons' Great River*, drawn by Fr. Aloisio Conrado Pfeil, was concluded in 1684. In Pará, four years later, Pfeil met Fr. Samuel Fritz, cartographer of the map *El gran Rio Marañon o Amazon*, printed in Quito, in 1707.

The vice province of Maranhão was about to be elevated to a province at the time of the expulsion of the Society in 1760. At the moment of the expulsion, there were about 155 Jesuits in Maranhão.

See also Brazil; Portugal

Benimeli, José Antonio Ferrer, "Pombal y la expulsión de los jesuitas. 1759." In *Expulsión y extinción de los jesuitas (1759–1773)*. Bilbao: Mensajero, 2013.

Leite, Serafim, *História da Companhia de Jesus no Brasil*. Vols. III–IV. Lisbon/Rio de Janeiro: Civilização Brasileira, 1943.

de Madureira, J. M., *A liberdade dos índios: a Companhia de Jesus, sua pedagogia e seus resultados*. 2 vols. Rio de Janeiro: Imprensa Nacional, 1927–29.

Danilo Mondoni, SJ

Marian Congregations

While not the earliest model of Jesuit confraternal activity, the Marian congregations or sodalities represent the hallmark of Jesuit lay associations. Jan Leunis, a Belgian Jesuit from Liège, founded the first Marian sodality for students in the Roman College in 1563. This soon split into four separate groups (named after Marian feasts: the Assumption, the Nativity, the Annunciation, and the Immaculate Conception), and multiple sodalities became common in Jesuit colleges. Similarly, sodalities for adults often clustered around a Jesuit professed house and were organized around social groups, such as for nobles, merchants, artisans, servants, or priests.

Figure 42 Andrea Pozzo, SJ, Engraving of a Forty Hours Devotion, from *Perspectiva pictorum et architectorum Andreae Putei*, 2 vols. (Rome, 1717–23). Rare Books Library, College of the Holy Cross. Photograph Lance Gabriel Lazar

In 1584 Jesuit General Claudio Acquaviva obtained from Pope Gregory XIII the bull *Omnipotentis Dei*, which canonically erected the original sodality, the Prima Primaria, or "first of the firsts," and enabled the affiliation of similar institutions. In 1599, Acquaviva added the Sodality rules to the *Ratio studiorum* and directed rectors to establish sodalities in all Jesuit colleges, soon including other Jesuit residences. By 1748, Pope Benedict XIV had greatly extended the indulgences and privileges of the sodalities and their devotions with the "Golden Bull" *Gloriosae Dominae*. In particular, the Forty Hours Devotion had grown into a grand baroque spectacle promoted by the sodalities. By the Suppression of the Society in 1773, there were roughly 2,500 affiliated Marian congregations, and emperors, popes, kings, and cardinals could be counted among the members.

Having expanded significantly in the nineteenth century, the Marian congregations became the World Federation of Sodalities of Our Lady in 1953 and numbered roughly 80,000 affiliated institutions on six continents. In 1967 they renamed themselves Christian Life Communities but still reflect their Ignatian origins of contemplation in action.

See also Christian Life Communities; Confraternities

Maher, Michael W., "Reforming Rome: The Society of Jesus and Its Congregations." Ph.D. dissertation, University of Minnesota, 1998.
Mullan, Elder, *The Sodality of Our Lady Studied in the Documents*. 3rd edn. New York: P. J. Kennedy and Sons, 1912.

Lance Gabriel Lazar

Marquette, Jacques, SJ (1637–1675)

Jacques Marquette is arguably the best known of all the Jesuits who served in North America during the colonial era. A copy of his detailed diary is the only document that survived the expedition led by his young friend and colleague Louis Jolliet (1645–1700), in 1673, to "discover" the course of the Mississippi. Jolliet's records were lost when his canoe capsized in the Sault St. Louis rapids near Montreal, and as a result, Marquette's became the only documents to ground the French claim to the American Midwest.

He was born in Laon on the Aisne River in northern France on June 10, 1637. The son of pious and prosperous parents, he was a landowners' descendant, and on his father's side, he came from knights famous for heroic deeds in the Catholic cause during the Wars of Religion. His mother, Rose de La Salle, counted several military heroes in her ancestry as well. It was she, he later recounted, who introduced him to the Jesuit *Relations* and their accounts of the heroic tragedy of Huronia and the extraordinary discoveries of the voyageurs.

He entered the Jesuit novitiate in Nancy on October 8, 1654, and very soon volunteered for the missions in Canada. Still, he was kept at home until after the traditional Jesuit formation period of studies and teaching in the humanities and in philosophy. Later his Jesuit peers referred to him as particularly gifted for acquiring foreign languages, and he was fluent in six. He gave special attention to cartography and hydrography. He taught in the Jesuit colleges in Auxerre, Reims, and Pont-à-Mousson; then, in 1665, he began the study of theology and was ordained to the priesthood on March 7, 1666. It was soon afterwards that he received confirmation that he was at last missioned to Canada.

Figure 43 Ronald Knepper: Portrait sculpture of Jacques Marquette, 2005, bronze, Marquette University campus, Milwaukee, WI. Photograph Thomas Worcester, SJ

He left La Rochelle in June 1666 and landed in Quebec on September 20. During the voyage, on July 6, he christened the newborn child of Jean Noland, one of the earliest settlers of Quebec.

After a year in Trois-Rivières learning native languages, Marquette was posted to Chequamegon Bay on Lake Superior, whence he moved in 1668 to found a mission at Sault Ste. Marie and another in 1671 at Michilimackinac.

It was there that on December 8, 1672, he welcomed the Quebec explorer and fur-trader Louis Jolliet, who had been commissioned by Jean Talon, the Intendant of New France, to sail the Mississippi and determine whether the river flowed into the Atlantic Ocean, into the Gulf of Mexico, or again into the Pacific Ocean. Given Marquette's facility with native languages, Jolliet had come to seek his cooperation and help.

They left Michilimackinac on May 17, 1673, traveling southward along the North Shore of Lake Michigan onto the Wisconsin River and finally the Mississippi, which they sailed down in mid-July to point 33° 40' latitude, near the mouth of the Arkansas River. They knew then that the great river flowed into the Gulf of Mexico.

They returned by another route: the Illinois River and the Chicago Portage. By then Marquette was exhausted. He remained at the St. Francis Xavier mission, where he worked on his diaries, dictionaries, maps, and papers before entrusting them to his superior, the noted geographer Claude-Ignace Dablon (1619–97), who annotated them and eventually published a brief *Récit* containing the report of the discovery of the Mississippi. Jolliet went on to Sault Ste. Marie and thence in May 1674 to the tragedy at the Sault St. Louis rapids, where his diary was lost.

In 1674 Marquette mistakenly felt well enough to travel to the Illinois country, where he founded the mission of the Immaculate Conception. There his health truly began to break down. He left for St. Ignace in April 1675 but died on May 18 and was buried by his two companions in the wilderness near the mouth of the river that now bears his name. Two years later, a thirty-canoe flotilla of Native Christians came to transfer his remains to St. Ignace.

Across eastern Canada and the Midwestern United States, Jacques Marquette is commemorated more than any other Jesuit. Cities, towns, and parks are named after him, as are rivers, lakes, and highways. So are public buildings, schools, and church halls. A remarkable museum and a flourishing university both bear his name. And then, representing the state of Wisconsin in the Capitol in Washington, DC, there is the remarkable marble statue of him by the Florentine sculptor Gaetano Trentanove, who is said to have used as his model Jesuit Father Richard Baxter (1821–1904), a thirty-year veteran of the Northern Ontario missions and the first Anglophone Canadian Jesuit.

See also Canada; United States of America

Caffier, Michel, *Le découvreur du Mississippi*. Paris: Presses de la Cité, 2007.
Donnelly, Joseph P., *Jacques Marquette, SJ, 1637–1675*. Chicago, IL: Loyola University Press, 1968.

Jacques Monet, SJ

Martini, Carlo Maria, Cardinal, SJ, (1927–2012)

Carlo Maria Martini, an Italian Jesuit, died as a cardinal of the Roman Catholic Church (1983–2012), but not before serving as archbishop of Milan (1980–2002), one of the largest dioceses in the world, rector of the Gregorian University (1978–79), rector of the Pontifical Biblical Institute (1969–78), and a faculty member for many years at the Pontifical Biblical Institute, where he taught textual criticism. He earned two doctoral degrees, one in fundamental theology from the Gregorian University, where he wrote a dissertation on the resurrection (1958), and the other from the Pontifical Biblical Institute, where he wrote on variations in certain ancient manuscripts of the Gospel of Luke.

All of Carlo Martini's education was with the Jesuits: as a young man at the Istituto Sociale in Turin, as a scholastic at the Jesuit House of Studies at Gallarate where he studied philosophy, and at the faculty of theology in Chieri. He entered the Jesuits at age 17 (1944) and was ordained at 25 (1952).

Carlo Martini possessed a brilliant intellect, as his graduation from both the Gregorian University and the Biblicum *summa cum laude* suggests. He became the only Catholic member of the Institute for New Testament Textual Research. Located at the University of Münster, its central task has been to research the textual history of the New Testament (NT) and to reconstruct the original Greek text on the basis of the entire manuscript tradition, the early translations of the NT, and the citations of the NT in the writings of the Fathers of the Church. Foremost among the results of this research is the ongoing publication of the *Editio Critica Maior*, known more commonly as the *Nestle-Aland Novum Testamentum Graece*. Martini's contribution to this endeavor was so substantial that even in its fourth edition (1993) his name appears as one of the editors.

Cardinal Martini was deeply pastoral. While serving as rector of the Biblicum, he became associated with the Church of Sant'Egidio in Trastevere and was known for "his love for the weak and the poor." His appointment to Milan, though surprising in that few religious become heads of dioceses, was no surprise in so far as it was a logical use of his outstanding administrative skills and his pastoral and spiritual gifts. He was made a cardinal in 1983 and was assigned the title of Cardinal-Priest of Santa Cecilia in Trastevere. The motto he chose for his coat of arms is translated, "For the love of truth, dare to choose adverse situations."

Martini was prolific, especially in the homilies he preached and the lectures he gave, many of which later appeared in published form. To those who could not attend his homilies or lectures, he is well known through his many articles and books. Each of his texts has an historical context. The dates of publication given in the bibliography at the end of this article are deceptive because in most cases they represent the date of the published translation from Italian. Many are meditations on Scripture, directed in their publication to any willing reader. Others, like the book with Umberto Eco, *Belief or Non-Belief?* or *On the Body*, are responses to specific cultural concerns. One volume masterfully brings together Scripture and the *Spiritual Exercises of St. Ignatius*. Many of his monographs have been translated into several languages and some are co-authored. A very small sampling of his writings is included in the bibliography following this article.

Martini possessed the deepest respect for those different from himself and tried to learn from them. He was drawn to ecumenical and interreligious dialogue. While rector of the Pontifical Biblical Institute, he developed relationships of mutual understanding with the Hebrew University and the larger Jewish community in Jerusalem and similarly, as an archbishop, he worked to establish and strengthen ties with the Muslim community in Milan.

Finally, a word should be said about Martini's "liberal leanings." There were those "on the left" who loved him and those "on the right" who did not. From the perspective of Scripture, such categorizing and judging is problematic. Carlo Maria Martini was a man of immense compassion, generous forgiveness, and unbounded love, a man who personally experienced the joy of the Gospel and wanted to share the Good News. He was a Jesuit for whom *Letting God Free Us* was not the title of a book but an affirmation of deep faith. He was a priest, a bishop, a cardinal loyal to the Church. He exemplified the motto he chose for his coat of arms: "For the love of truth, dare to choose adverse situations."

See also Biblical Studies; Cardinals, Jesuits; Pontifical Biblical Institute

Martini, Carlo Maria, *Journeying with the Lord: Reflections for Everyday*. New York: Alba House, 1987.
  Letting God Free Us: Meditations on the Ignatian Spiritual Exercises. New York: New City Press, 1994.
  On the Body: A Contemporary Theology of the Human Person. New York: Crossroad, 2001.
  Once More from Emmaus. Collegeville, MN: Liturgical Press, 1995.
  Our Lady of Holy Saturday: Awaiting the Resurrection with Mary and the Disciples. Liguori, MO: Liguori Publications, 2004.

Pilgrims, Not Strangers: Christian Witness in a Broken World. Boston, MA: Pauline Books and Media, 1993.
Women in the Gospels. New York: Crossroad, 1990.
With Umberto Eco, *Belief or Non-Belief?* New York: Arcade Publishing, 2000.

Alice L. Laffey

Martyrs, Ideal and History

The English word "martyr" comes from the Greek μάρτυς, meaning simply "witness," in the sense of giving witness in a court of law. The martyr bears witness to his or her faith in Christ by the shedding of blood. Martyrdom is therefore the ultimate confession of faith. It produces in the individual a communion with Christ in imitation of Christ's own passion and death. Christ is in a sense the first martyr, a witness to the message of God's love and salvation, and in his death Christ redeemed humanity from its sins. Martyrdom in the Christian tradition arises out of the mission of Christ to his disciples, that they should preach the Gospel to the ends of the earth. The Gospel will meet with opposition and persecution will result.

Christians in the Greco-Roman world were exposed to persecution because Christianity was not an approved religion. Although there were, at times, systematic attempts to destroy the Christian faith in the Roman Empire, such as under Valerian (AD 253–60), Diocletian (AD 284–305) and Galerius (AD 305–11), these were, on the whole, few. Sometimes persecution arose because individuals would blame Christians for natural disasters, seeing in such events a manifestation of the displeasure of the gods because of Christian impiety in not worshiping the state's gods. Such persecutions were aimed at forcing Christians to conform to the religion of the Empire. At other times local factors gave rise to persecution, such as at Lyon in AD 177, a grisly example of hatred for a minority that was regarded by some as an underclass. Here as elsewhere Christians were accused of cannibalism and gross sexual immorality. Nero's persecution in the 60s of the first century was not simply because of his desire to blame Christians for burning Rome but also because he accused them of harboring the hated of the human race. The ideology of martyrdom was strongly emblematic of how Christians saw themselves. The desire to be like Christ in his death so as to be like him in his resurrection was a foundational motif of the early centuries of the faith. At times an obsession with a martyr's death was compulsive, bordering on the fanatical, with some Christians believing that only the martyrs went directly to heaven.

Origen was saved from death in the persecution at Alexandria in AD 202, in which his father died, by the expedient of his mother hiding his clothes. Several of the early Fathers wrote treatises urging Christians not to provoke persecution and not to seek martyrdom for its own sake. With the Edict of Milan in 313, the scope for martyrdom changed and Christians were persecuted only in lands on the fringes of the Empire, such as with the missionary expansion into England. By the time of the foundation of the Jesuit order in 1540, the Church had a long and venerable tradition of venerating martyrs. Prior to the Suppression of the Society, Jesuits were martyred either by orders from government, such as in England and Japan in the sixteenth and seventeenth centuries, or by persecution among the peoples with whom they came into contact, such as the Hurons in the seventeenth century in what is now southern Ontario and upstate

New York. In all, some sixty-seven Jesuits were martyred as a result of the wars of religion that arose in Europe as a result of the Reformation and its aftermath. This number does not include Blessed Ignacio de Azevedo and his thirty-nine companions who were put to death near Santa Cruz de la Palma in 1570 while on their way to strengthen the mission in Brazil. They were intercepted by French Huguenot pirates and killed by either drowning or beheading.

The persecution of Jesuits in virtually every part of the world in which they worked, from Indo-China to South America, was a feature of the Order's history in both its pre- and post-Suppression phases. Of some 350 Jesuits who have been canonized or beatified, or whose cause has been introduced, some 265 were martyred for their faith. In some instances, as in sixteenth- and seventeenth-century England, religious motivation was also inextricably linked with political considerations. Others, such as the Portuguese John de Brito (1647–93), put to death in India by the raja of Marava, were martyred because Christianity threatened to violate local culture by, for example in this instance, forbidding polygamy. In more recent times the term "martyrs" has been used to describe the six Jesuits and their two household servants who were murdered, in November 1989, by a death squad of the military dictatorship during the civil war in El Salvador (1979–92).

See also Canadian/North American Martyrs; Ellacuría, Ignacio, SJ, and Companions; Košice Martyrs; Yad Vashem

Chenu, Bruno, Claude Prud'Homme, France Quéré, and Jean-Claude Thomas., *The Book of Christian Martyrs*. New York: Crossroad, 1990.
Tylenda, Joseph N., *Jesuit Saints and Martyrs*. 2nd edn. Chicago, IL: Loyola Press, 1989.

Oliver P. Rafferty, SJ

Maryland Mission

Jesuits accompanied the first settlers of Maryland, a proprietary colony granted by James I to Cecil Calvert, the second Lord Baltimore, a Catholic. He intended a colony that tolerated all Christians; hence Catholics would be free from British penal laws. At Calvert's request, the English provincial assigned Jesuits to the Maryland mission. They were to be self-supporting as they ministered to their co-religionists and worked to convert Native Americans. Andrew White, John Altham (alias Gravenor), and Brother Thomas Gervase arrived with the first group of 320 settlers in 1634.

Within a few years, they had converted 1,000 Indians and most of the Protestants among the colony's founders, but in 1645 Protestant zealots from Virginia burnt their settlement at St. Mary's City and sent White and Thomas Copley to England in chains. Three other Jesuits disappeared in the bloodshed. Copley returned in 1648 when the Calverts regained control of the colony, but by then the Indians had been driven away. To support their work, the proprietor granted estates to the Jesuits. Eventually they owned 12,000 acres in Maryland in six estates, where, following contemporary developments, they acquired slaves to work the land. St. Thomas Manor, near Port Tobacco, served as Jesuit headquarters, while academies were established briefly at Newtown and

Bohemia Manors. By 1773, there were twenty-three priests in the mission, including several in Pennsylvania.

Under the terms of the Society's suppression, Clement XIV directed local bishops to assume possession of Jesuit properties in their dioceses. Because the English colonies that soon became the United States did not have a bishop, the order was not carried out. Instead, the former Jesuits, under the leadership of John Carroll, formed a corporation, the Select Body of the Clergy, to hold the properties. They obtained a charter from Maryland in 1792 as the Corporation of the Roman Catholic Clergymen. Under Carroll's leadership, this group established the academy that would become Georgetown University. In 1805 five of the surviving ex-Jesuits re-affiliated with the Society, and John Carroll, now bishop, was designated by Franz Gruber, Jesuit general of the partially restored Society in Russia, to select a mission superior. The choice fell to Richard Molyneux, who opened a novitiate and concluded an agreement with Carroll, allowing the Jesuits to regain their former properties. To provide leadership and energy to the elderly American Jesuits and those in the formation programs, eight Europeans were sent to America, including John Anthony Grassi and Anthony Kohlmann. But these newcomers were greeted with suspicion as monarchists by Americans imbued with the republican spirit of the recent revolution and the War of 1812. Moreover, foreigners were not eligible for membership in the corporation that controlled the Jesuit properties.

Shortly after the universal restoration, Father General Brzozowski addressed the difficult issues in the United States by sending Peter Kenney from Ireland as official visitor in 1819 to study the situation, receive accounts of conscience, and offer recommendations regarding this "wretched parish" that included 22 priests, 21 scholastics, and 13 novices. During his stay, Kenney set down rules for the temporal administration of the manors and reported that none of the priests was capable of effective governance, nor of teaching theology or philosophy adequately. He also recommended sending scholastics to Italy to be schooled in theology, leadership, and pedagogy.

After the death of Father Brzozowski, it fell to Father General Luigi Fortis to act on the recommendations. Eight scholastics were sent to Italy, of whom five returned in the late 1820s to animate the work of the mission. To bridge the gap in leadership, Fortis sent to the mission a gifted Pole, Francis Dzierozynski, a veteran of the faculty at Polotzk, whose efforts in America were prodigious. From 1823 to 1830, he served as mission superior (and later as acting provincial for four years); before his death in 1850, he was novice master for a total of fourteen years, also tertian director, and a member of the Georgetown faculty for theology and philosophy.

In 1830 Father General Roothaan sent Peter Kenney back to Maryland as official visitor. During this stay, he tried to arbitrate rising tensions between Jesuits who wanted to reorient the Society's work to the cities and those who favored the traditional pastoral pattern based on manors with a workforce of slaves. Pleased with the contributions being made by the Roman-trained Americans, he supported the idea of raising Maryland to the status of a full province under the leadership of William McSherry, one of the group trained in Europe. Kenney read the formal announcement in June of 1833. There were 38 priests, 20 scholastics, and 32 brothers in the new province.

See also Carroll, John; United States of America

Curran, Robert Emmett, *Shaping American Catholicism*. Washington, DC: The Catholic University of America Press, 2012.

Kuzniewski, Anthony, "Our American Champions." *Studies in the Spirituality of Jesuits* 46, 1 (Spring 2014), 1–43.

Anthony Kuzniewski, SJ

Marzal, Manuel, SJ (1931–2005)

Jesuit priest and anthropologist Manuel Marzal was born in Spain on October 20, 1931. He entered the Society of Jesus in 1949, and two years later was sent to Peru, where he finished his humanities and philosophy studies in the Jesuit novitiate of Miraflores (Lima). He completed his doctorate in Ecuador in 1964 and pursued postgraduate studies in Mexico, obtaining a master's degree in anthropology from the Universidad Iberoamericana in 1968. From that year on, his teaching and research work focused on the anthropology of religions. Back in Peru, he joined the faculty of the Pontifical Catholic University of Peru. His research centered on the study of the religiosity of peasant communities in the Peruvian Andes and the migrants from rural areas to Lima. Among his most notable publications on the subject are *El mundo religioso de Urcos* (The Religious World of Urcos) (Cusco, 1971); *Estudios de religión campesina* (Studies on Peasant Religiosity) (Lima, 1977); *Los caminos religiosos de los inmigrantes de la Gran Lima* (*The Religious Pathways of Immigrants to the Greater Lima*) (Lima, 1988). In the later part of his career, Father Marzal dedicated his efforts to study the processes of change and synthesis in the religiosity of Peru and Latin America; see his *La transformación religiosa peruana* (Peru's Religious Transformation) (Lima, 1983); *El sincretismo iberoamericano* (Iberoamerican Syncretism) (Lima, 1985); and especially *Tierra encantada: Tratado de antropología religiosa de América latina* (Enchanted Land: A Treatise on the Religious Anthropology of Latin America) (Madrid and Lima, 2002). In the last years of his life, Father Marzal successfully devoted his efforts to the creation of the Jesuit University Antonio Ruiz de Montoya, becoming its first president. Father Manuel Marzal died in Lima on July 16, 2005.

See also Peru; Universidad Iberoamericana; Vargas Ugarte, Rubén

Asín, Fernando Armas, "Manuel Marzal (1931–2005)." *Anuario de Historia de la Iglesia* 15 (2006), 426–28.
de Velasco, Francisco Diez, "Manuel Marzal." *Numen* 52, 4 (2005), 496–97.

Andrés Ignacio Prieto

Mayer, Rupert, SJ, Bl. (1876–1945)

Mayer was born in Stuttgart on January 23, 1876. He first encountered Jesuits in 1894, when he did the Spiritual Exercises at their college (Stella Matutina) in Feldkirch, Austria. On May 2, 1899, he was ordained a priest for the Diocese of Rottenburg. On October 1, 1900, Mayer entered the Jesuit novitiate in Tisis near Feldkirch. Before taking his final vows in Tisis on February 2, 1911, he studied philosophy and theology in Valkenburg (1901–04), completed his tertianship (1906), and developed his skills as a preacher by giving parish missions in Germany, Austria, and Switzerland (1908–11). In 1912 Mayer received the pastoral assignment to care for rural migrants to Munich. On August 1, 1914, he volunteered for the German war effort, serving first in a field hospital and then as a military chaplain. In 1915, he was the first Catholic priest to be awarded an Iron Cross, First Class. A serious battle wound suffered at the end of 1916 necessitated the amputation of his left leg from above the knee. Mayer returned to Munich. In 1921 he was stationed at St. Michael's Church. His vigorous engagement in various pastoral ministries and public life won him popular acclaim among Catholics. He became known as the Apostle of Munich. For his vocal opposition to National Socialism, the Nazi authorities forbade Mayer to speak in public (1937) and imprisoned him (1938). After spending a little more than seven months in Sachsenhausen concentration camp, he was transferred in August 1940 to the Benedictine monastery at Ettal, where he lived under house arrest until May 1945. Mayer died of a stroke in Munich on November 1, 1945, and was beatified in 1987.

See also Delp, Alfred, SJ; German-Speaking Lands

Bleistein, Roman, *Rupert Mayer: der verstummte Prophet.* Frankfurt am Main: Knecht, 1993.

Hilmar M. Pabel

McGarry, Cecil, SJ (1929–2009)

Born in Galway, Ireland, in 1929, Cecil McGarry entered the Society of Jesus in 1946, was ordained priest in 1960, and received a doctorate in theology (ecclesiology) at the Gregorian University in 1964. He taught theology at the Jesuit School of Theology in Dublin, became rector of the community there and, in 1968, provincial of Ireland. His theological leadership as rector led to the founding of the Milltown Institute of Theology and Philosophy (1968–2015), a collaborative venture involving several religious orders and congregations. His time as provincial (1968–75) was fruitful but difficult, as it fell to him to update both the works and the communities of the province after Vatican II, not always with the support, in particular, of some of Ireland's senior Jesuits.

In 1975, at the 32nd General Congregation, McGarry was elected one of the four assistants *ad providentiam* to Fr. General Pedro Arrupe, a job he remained in, and that included special responsibility for Formation, until 1983. After Fr. Arrupe's stroke in1981, Fr. Vincent O'Keefe, one of his four assistants, became temporary vicar general. But less than two months later, Pope John Paul II told Arrupe, in a letter delivered by Cardinal Casaroli, his secretary of state, that he was appointing Fr. Paolo Dezza, SJ (at age 79) as his personal delegate to govern the Society. Thus McGarry experienced, at close range, the impact of the Pope's suspension of the Society's normal governing procedures (1981–83).

Cecil McGarry spent the last twenty-five years of his life in academic and spiritual leadership in Africa. He helped set up Hekima College in Nairobi and was its first dean of studies (1984–94). He advised the Kenyan bishops and helped develop the Catholic University of Eastern Africa. From 1995 to 1998 he was rector of Hekima. In 1999 he moved to Mwangaza Retreat Center near Nairobi where he enjoyed a fruitful ministry of spiritual direction. When he died, aged 80, on November 24, 2009, the then provincial of the East African province, Fr. Agbonkhianmeghe Orobator, wrote that, in him, the Irish province "shared with us one of the best Jesuit companions they had."

See also Africa, East; Arrupe, Pedro, SJ; Hekima University College; Ireland

James Corkery, SJ

McKenna, Horace, SJ (1899–1982)

Born in New York City, Horace McKenna first encountered the Society of Jesus while attending Fordham Preparatory School, acquiring an education that he considered "deep, broad and accurate." After vows and regency in the Philippines, he attended Woodstock College, the Jesuit seminary in Maryland, for theology and taught Sunday school to African American children excluded from the Maryland parochial schools. After his ordination in 1929, he became a pastor in southern Maryland for twenty years, driven by what he called a "passionate impatience" with the pace of racial justice. Later in Washington, DC, he worked out of the St. Aloysius Parish basement with the St. Vincent de Paul Society as it witnessed the neighborhood's rapid demographic transformation. White flight and business development created housing shortages affecting the area's poor black population. McKenna co-founded the housing complex Sursum Corda to meet this need. In 1970, he founded SOME (So Others Might Eat) to provide hot meals to neighborhood residents.

McKenna's dedication to parish ministry defined his vocation. He would refer to his confessional as the "peace box," insisting that people would always find peace there. However, when the 1968 encyclical *Humanae vitae* prompted Cardinal O'Boyle, the archbishop of Washington, to direct priests in applying the prohibition of artificial birth control, McKenna argued for pastoral accommodation for married couples. O'Boyle briefly restricted him from hearing confessions as a result.

McKenna's work also drew attention and financial support from the privileged and powerful, even as he joined antiwar marches and protested nuclear proliferation as a self-declared pacifist. Many considered him a future saint, with Mayor Marion Barry of Washington, DC, naming him the "Apostle of the Poor" in 1979. Since McKenna's death from a heart attack in 1982, his memory has continued to inspire ongoing struggles against poverty and gentrification in Washington.

See also United States of America

Monaghan, John S., *Horace: Priest of the Poor*. Washington, DC: Georgetown University Press, 1985.
O'Brien, Kevin, "Horace McKenna, Apostle of the Poor." *America*, September 17, 2007.

Justin Poché

Médaille, Jean-Pierre, SJ (1610–1669)

Born on October 6, 1610, at Carcassonne (Aude), Jean-Pierre entered the Jesuit novitiate in Toulouse (Haute-Garonne, 1626), where he met Jean-François Régis (1597–1640); during tertianship (1642–43) he met future missionary-martyr of New France Noël Chabanel (1613–49). Médaille worked at the college of Saint-Flour (1643–49), during which time he founded (c. 1646) a community of women who desired to live as religious outside of cloister, where they could dedicate themselves to the works of charity in the way that Francis de Sales (1567–1622) originally had envisioned for the Visitandines. This foundation, which Jean-Pierre placed under the patronage of St. Joseph, did not last long; missioned to Aurillac (1650), however, he re-founded the religious community (Sisters of St. Joseph) in the neighboring commune of Le-Puy-en-Velay and received for it canonical recognition under Henri de Maupas, bishop of Le Puy. Jean-Pierre left as writings the *Maximes de perfection* (1657, 1672), which he had composed before, and later adapted for, the religious foundations. We also have the *Lettre Eucharistique* and *Règlements*, which he wrote for Saint-Flour, and the *Constitutions*, written for the Le Puy foundation, the latter of which take the virtues of the Trinity and of the Holy Family as models. He later engaged in missionary work in central France, attached successively to the colleges in Montferrand (1654) and Clermont (1662). Sent to the college of Billom (Puy-de-Dôme) in 1669, he died there on December 30.

See also France

Gondal, Marie-Louise, *Les origines des sœurs de Saint-Joseph au XVIIe siècle: histoire oubliée d'une fondation Saint-Flour-le Puy, 1641–1650–1661*. Paris: Cerf, 2000.

Vacher, Marguerite, *Nuns without Cloister: Sisters of St. Joseph in the Seventeenth and Eighteenth Centuries*. Trans. Patricia Byrne and the United States Federation of the Sisters of St. Joseph. Lanham, MD: University Press of America, 2010.

William P. O'Brien, SJ

"Men and Women for Others"

Anyone who has spent any appreciable time in a Jesuit educational institution will no doubt have run across this phrase, first uttered by Father General Pedro Arrupe while speaking to alumni of Jesuit schools in Valencia, Spain, on July 31, 1973. Arrupe's challenge was both to graduates of Jesuit schools and to the schools themselves and proved to be a harbinger for what would eventually be adopted by the 32nd General Congregation as the Society's mission: the service of faith and promotion of justice. His words, so often truncated and since taken out of context in those same institutions he was calling to account, are worth quoting here:

> Today our prime educational objective must be to form men-and-women-for-others; men and women who will live not for themselves but for God and his Christ – for the God-man who lived and died for all the world; men and women who cannot even conceive of love of God which does not include love for the least of their neighbors; men and women completely convinced that love of God which does not issue in justice for others is a farce.
>
> "Men and Women for Others," in Arrupe and Burke, 173

Kevin Burke writes that Arrupe's original address contained no references to women but that Arrupe later amended the text himself, conscious of the need to include increasing numbers of Jesuit-educated women.

The phrase (or some variant of it) is often used as an official or unofficial motto for Jesuit schools, and it can be counted among Arrupe's most famous remarks. However, the frequency with which it is deployed risks transforming his powerful challenge to upend structural injustice into a domesticated platitude, devoid of its Christocentric focus: Christ as *the* Man-for-others.

See also Arrupe, Pedro, SJ; Education, Secondary and Pre-secondary; Preferential Option for the Poor; Universities, 1773–Present

Arrupe, Pedro, and Kevin Burke, eds., *Pedro Arrupe: Essential Writings*. Maryknoll, NY: Orbis Books, 2004.

Keith Maczkiewicz, SJ

Mental Reservation

Augustine's two treatises on lying (*On Lying, De Mendacio*; *Against Lying, Contra Mendacium*) provided a foundation against which all lying was considered immoral in the Christian tradition. Even though the Scriptures provided sanctioned instances of those lying (the most interesting being the lying midwives who protected the birth of Moses and were rewarded by God, Exodus 1:20), Augustine was exhaustive in anticipating every response one could have to lying. To the Egyptians, he could see that they got their temporal reward since by lying they lost their eternal reward, the same argument he used against lying to protect the life of an innocent person: "Since by lying eternal life is lost, never for any man's temporal life must a lie be told" (*De Mendacio*, 6). Augustine also held that were we to grant this "exception," we would give license to the rule that a lesser evil may be done to prevent another from doing a greater.

Though the Eastern Churches never accepted the absolute prohibition that Augustine proffered, in the West, it was not until Thomas Aquinas that a moment of conflict appeared, when he commented that "it was licit to hide the truth prudently by some sort of dissimulation" (*Summa theologiae* I.II. q. 110. a. 3, ad.4). Similarly, Thomas's fellow Dominican Raymond of Peñafort engaged the question of the innocent man being protected and proposed that one could use "equivocal words" like "non est hic" which can mean "he is not here" or "he does not eat here" (*Summa de Paenitentia* I.x.).

The question of protecting an innocent man's life from a potential murderer shifted to whether a priest could deny something said under the seal of confession. Inasmuch as the Fourth Lateran Council in 1215 imposed severe penalties upon a priest who broke the seal, the confessional seal brought to the surface a question about whether anyone asking a priest a question about the interrogator had any right to this information. Equivocation, like that proposed by Raymond, was often considered: an answer like, "I do not know" and such words as those when used by a priest would mean "I do not know apart from confession," or "I do not know as a human being," or "I have no knowledge of the matter which I can communicate."

This insight, about the right to truth, became a controlling insight later in England, when priests entering Queen Elizabeth I's England were questioned by her troops about whether they were priests. Did they have any right to such information inasmuch as they were servants of a monarch who was not recognized as such? In this light, many casuists argued that for the sake of the souls for whom they were ministering, the priest could equivocate. These two reasons, a grave matter along with the right of the inquirer to know, were central to the casuists' calculus on equivocation, which was later also known as "wide" or "broad mental reservation." Thus, in England, for instance, casuists became stricter on matters of equivocation as Roman Catholics enjoyed greater tolerance. Finally, though Protestants often derided the Roman Catholics in general and the Jesuits, in particular, for the use of equivocation, after the execution of Charles I (January 30, 1649) during the reign of James I, Anglican divines turned to the same approach, contending that equivocation could be permitted for the taking of the "Oath of Engagement."

A further development occurred when Martin Azplicueta, "The Doctor of Navarre" (1492–1586), entertained a case where the equivocation came not from the ambiguity of the words themselves or from the circumstances in which they were uttered (as in a priest protecting the seal of the confessional) but from an added mental reservation exercised by the speaker but heard by no one. This became known as a "strict mental reservation" as distinct from the "broad mental reservation." This newer form could be legitimate, it was argued by Martin, in instances where one, for instance, tells another, "I give you my word," but adds as a strict mental reservation "never!"

On the strict mental reservation there was great division. Francisco Suárez, SJ (1548–1617), and Leonardo Lessius, SJ (1554–1623), recognized the argument as probable and Tomás Sánchez, SJ (1550–1610), appropriated and fortified the argument. Juan Azor, SJ (1535–1603), and Paul Laymann, SJ (1574–1635), repudiated Martin's argument. It was condemned by Pope Innocent XI on March 2, 1679.

See also Casuistry; Confession, Confessor

Jonsen Albert, and Stephen Toulmin, "Perjury: The Case of Equivocation." *The Abuse of Casuistry: A History of Moral Reasoning*. Berkeley: University of California Press, 1988, pp. 195–215.

Slater, Thomas, "On Lying." *A Manual of Moral Theology*. New York: Benziger Brothers, 1906, pp. 464–69.

Sommerville, Johann, "The 'New Art of Lying': Equivocation, Mental Reservation, and Casuistry." In Edmund Leites, ed., *Conscience and Casuistry in Early Modern Europe*. New York: Cambridge University Press, 1988, pp. 159–84.

James F. Keenan, SJ

Mercurian, Everard, SJ (1514–1580)

Born Everard Lardinois in 1514, Mercurian took his surname from the Latin name for his native city, Marcour, in the principality-bishopric of Liège. He studied in Liège with the Brethren of the Common Life and in Louvain. He was ordained in 1546. In 1547 he sought out in Paris Jesuits whom he had met earlier in Louvain. Under them he made the *Spiritual Exercises* and consequently applied for admission. He entered the Society in Paris on September 8, 1548. Ignatius appointed Mercurian minister of the professed house upon his arrival in Rome in March/April, 1552. In May, Ignatius named him founding rector of a new college in Perugia. In 1557 Diego Laínez, vicar general after Ignatius's death, nominated Mercurian his commissary to oversee a new Jesuit province that included northern Germany and Belgium. Mercurian participated in the First General Congregation (1558), at which Laínez, now the new superior general, lauded Mercurian's prudence and administrative skills, and nominated him provincial of Lower Germany, the area where he had been commissary. Lower Germany was divided into two provinces in 1564; Mercurian continued as provincial of the new Belgian province, an office he held until his election as the general's assistant for Germany, that is northern Europe, at the Second General Congregation in 1565. As provincial he opened colleges in Trier (1561), Mainz (1561), Tournai (1562), Dinant (1563), Cambrai (1563) and laid foundations for colleges founded later in Louvain (1565), St. Omers (1567), and Douai (1568). Moreover, he preached the Spiritual Exercises to reformed monastic orders.

In May 1569, Francis Borja, the third superior general, appointed Mercurian official visitor to France, then convulsed by religious strife. But even within the Society, divisions were appearing regarding proper religious discipline and the presence of foreign Jesuits. Through exhortations on the *Spiritual Exercises*, especially the discernment of spirits, and on the Society's *Constitutions*, he advocated mutual charity and religious observance. His authority as visitor expired with the death of Borja.

Pope Gregory XIII, one of the Society's greatest benefactors after whom the Gregorian University was named, intervened in the proceedings of the Third General Congregation (April 1573), to the delight of some and the dismay of many. Many considered Juan de Polanco, Ignatius's secretary and vicar general after Borja's death, the most fit candidate as superior general until the Pope stated his preference for a non-Spaniard. But Gregory persisted and asked at his benediction whether there were no non-Spaniards qualified for the position. With firm backing from the royal family, Portuguese Jesuits warned against the election of a "new Christian," that is someone with Jewish ancestry. Implicit warnings became explicit when Tolomeo Cardinal Galli, secretary of state, ordered the congregation against the election of a Spaniard. After a congregational protest, Gregory eventually granted a free election but clearly stated that a non-Spaniard was his preference. Mercurian was elected on the first ballot. Of the twenty votes that he did not receive, thirteen went to Spaniards! Anti-Spanish bias continued and resulted in the return of many Spaniards to their home provinces after having held many important positions in the central and provincial administrations of the Society. The Society continued its expansion under Mercurian. Numerically, there were circa 1,500 more Jesuits at his death in 1580 than at his election in 1573. Despite some closures, there were twenty-eight more colleges by the time of his death. More important was Mercurian's concern that a distinctive Jesuit infrastructure, harmonious with the principles espoused in the *Spiritual Exercises* and articulated in the *Constitutions*, be created and fostered. He sent official visitors to the Spanish and Portuguese provinces principally because of their strict style of governance. He oversaw the compilation and publication of a summary of the *Constitutions* and of common rules for such important offices as provincial, master of novices, etc., to establish greater uniformity. More controversially, Mercurian prevented teaching and promulgating within the Society types of prayer that fostered a contemplative life that he considered contrary to Ignatian spirituality. Nor would he permit Jesuits to become involved in matters deemed alien to the Society's "way of proceedings," e.g., the Irish Jesuit David Wolfe's close association with a rebellion against English rule. A similar cautious prudence delayed the inauguration of a Jesuit mission to England. His selection of Alessandro Valignano and Matteo Ricci as missionaries to the Far East aptly illustrates his understanding of the Society, its Institute, and its mission. Mercurian died in Rome on August 1, 1580, a victim of an influenza epidemic.

See also Gregory XIII; Superior General

Catto, Michela, *La Compagnia divisa: il dissenso nell'ordine gesuitico tra 500 e 600*. Brescia: Morcelliana, 2009.

McCoog, Thomas, ed., *The Mercurian Project: Forming Jesuit Culture 1573–1580*. Rome: Institutum Historicum Societatis Iesu; St. Louis, MO: The Institute of Jesuit Sources, 2004.

Severin, Tony, *Un grand Belge: Mercurian, 1514–1580 – Curé Ardennais Général des Jésuites*. Liège: H. Dessain, 1946.

Thomas McCoog, SJ

Messina

In the city of Messina, in northeastern Sicily, the early Jesuits established an institution considered one of the most important Jesuit schools for externs. In fact, its success far exceeded similar previous attempts in Goa (1543) and Gandía (1545), and the Messina school strongly influenced Jesuit pedagogy.

In 1547 the Messina Senate with the support of Juan de Vega (r. 1547–57), viceroy of Sicily, invited Jesuits to come to the city and to open a school for lay boys. The city would pay the salaries and the school would be free of charge and open to non-Jesuits. Ignatius responded enthusiastically and sent some of the best talent available in the Society, including Jerónimo Nadal (1507–80).

In its pedagogical approach, the school inaugurated a specific Jesuit style that evolved in the following decades, became the model for hundreds of similar institutions founded by Jesuits during the sixteenth and seventeenth centuries, both for formation of Jesuit scholastics and for externs, and contributed to the development of the *Ratio studiorum*.

The Messina Senate and the Jesuits expected that the school of Messina would become a university, and in 1548 the Jesuits obtained a papal bull authorizing the institution of a *studium generale*. However, both parties wanted full control over the university and they were not able to reach an agreement on the structure, governance, and finances of the planned institution. Jesuits wanted to follow the Paris university model, while the Senate wanted an institution structured like Italian universities. The original project failed, and the city of Messina founded a university in 1597 without Jesuit participation.

See also Education, Secondary and Pre-Secondary; Italy

Grendler, Paul F., *The Jesuits and Italian Universities 1548–1773*. Washington, DC: The Catholic University of America Press, 2016.
Novarese, Daniela, *Istituzioni politiche e studi di diritto fra Cinque e Seicento: Il Messanense Studium Generale tra politica gesuitica e istanze egemoniche cittadine*. Milan: Giuffrè, 1994.

Emanuele Colombo

Mexico, Pre-Suppression (Viceroyalty of New Spain)

During the colonial period, the Viceroyalty of New Spain included California, Florida, the Spanish Caribbean, and, for a period, the Philippines. King Philip II of Spain invited the Society of Jesus to set up colleges and missions in New Spain, and he expressed a desire that they would civilize not only native inhabitants but also the growing population of Spaniards. The Jesuits landed at Vera Cruz in 1572, almost a full fifty years after the Franciscans (1523), who traveled to Mexico at the request of Cortes after the conquest of Tenochtitlán in 1521. By the turn of the seventeenth century, there were approximately 345 Jesuits operating in the Mexican province and, at the date of the expulsion, the members of the Society numbered 678. Late to arrive and subject to an "early" and sudden departure when expelled in 1767, Jesuit establishments – from colleges, haciendas, and mission systems to the very popular lay congregations – were thoroughly integrated into almost every aspect of colonial Mexican society.

Upon arrival, the Jesuits proceeded, as they did in Europe, to establish colleges as centers of education and piety. The first such institution, the college San Pedro y San Pablo (also known as Colegio Máximo), was founded in Mexico City in 1573. A Spanish patron donated urban properties to help the Jesuits establish their presence in Mexico City and, shortly thereafter, in 1576, donated an existing hacienda, Santa Lucia, to

Figure 44 Church of "La Compania de Jesus," 1747–65, Guanajuato, Mexico. Photograph ©
Gianni Dagli Orti / The Art Archive at Art Resource, New York

support directly the newly established Jesuit college. Students were taught Latin and
Greek, and the Jesuits ran a printing press that printed texts of classical authors, such
as Aristotle and Cicero. The construction of the Casa Profesa began in 1592, and the
Jesuit novitiate was firmly established in Tepotzotlán in the early years of the seven-
teenth century, after having moved from Mexico City to Puebla and back to Mexico
City once again.

The Jesuits also established San Gregorio (1586), a college adjoined to the Colegio
Máximo, for the sons of native elites. The Jesuit Church of San Gregorio was established for Indian congregants, but was also attended by Spanish and Creole populations.
The study of local American languages took on a particular urgency for the Mexican
Jesuits. The Spanish Crown had from an early date urged that Americans learn Spanish,
yet the Jesuits, like the Franciscans before them, determined that natives peoples were
best reached through their mother tongue and thus were encouraged to give sermons
and hear confessions in native languages, primarily Nahuatl and Otomí. By the late
eighteenth century, the Jesuits also established a school for elite Indian women, Nuestra
Señora de Guadalupe, in 1751.

Jesuit colleges were established in New Spain's major urban centers, such as Puebla
de Los Angeles (Espíritu Santo, 1578, and San Javier, 1619), but also in major mining

towns (San Luís de Potosí, 1623, and Querétero, 1625). A college and seminary were established in the growing northern city, Guadalajara (1644), the gateway to the northern frontier regions, but also at Parral (1651) in the heart of Jesuit mission territory, which served as an important nodal point between the urban centers and the far-flung mission stations. Late establishments were the Jesuit colleges in Chiapas (1681) and Oaxaca (1700).

From the colleges, the Society established congregations for both students and laypersons. Many took up service to jails and hospitals and other ministries in support of the poor. Ignatian spirituality animated the lives of Catholics largely via lay Congregations dedicated to the Annunciation, St. Francis Xavier, Our Lady of Sorrows, the Sacred Heart of Jesus, and the very popular congregation dedicated to a Good Death.

In undertaking popular missions to both urban centers and outlying rural areas, Jesuit preaching was focused upon animating the desire of the laity to make general confessions and to receive communion. The Jesuits also offered the *Spiritual Exercises* to the laity from the early years of their ministry in New Spain and established retreat houses dedicated to offering the *Exercises* year-round in Puebla (1727) and Mexico City (1751).

The establishment of the Jesuit mission system began in Sinaloa in 1591. The Tarahumara missions were established in the mid-seventeenth century, and the Society moved to expand into California in the late seventeenth century. Gerard Decorme states that the Jesuits in the northern mission-system were responsible for approximately 2 million converts to Catholicism. The frequent uprisings against the missionaries resulted in missionary casualties, and admiration of these Jesuit martyrs fueled further support for evangelical expansion on the Mexican frontiers.

The Jesuits were expelled from the Spanish Americas in 1767 by edict of Charles III. *See also* Baja California; Mexico, Nineteenth Century to Present; Spain

Clossey, Luke, *Salvation and Globalization in the Early Jesuit Missions*. Cambridge: Cambridge University Press, 2008.

Decorme, Gerard, *La obra de los Jesuitas mexicanos durante la epoca colonial, 1572–1767*. Mexico: Antigua Libreria Rebredo de Jose Porrua e Hijos, 1941.

Hausberger, Bernd, *Für Gott und König: die Mission der Jesuiten im kolonialen Mexiko*. Vienna: Verlag für Geschichte und Politik, 2000.

Martinez, John J., *Not Counting the Cost: Jesuit Missionaries in Colonial Mexico: A Story of Struggle, Commitment, and Sacrifice*. Chicago, IL: Jesuit Way, 2001.

Peláez, Agustín Churruca, *Primeras fundaciones jesuitas en Nueva España, 1572–1580*. Mexico City: Editorial Porrúa, 1980.

Melvin, Karen., *Building Colonial Cities of God: Mendicant Orders and Urban Culture in New Spain*. Palo Alto, CA: Stanford University Press, 2012.

Polzer, Charles W., *Rules and Precepts of the Jesuit Missions of Northwestern New Spain*. Tucson: University of Arizona Press, 1976.

J. Michelle Molina

Mexico, Nineteenth Century to Present

The expulsion of the Jesuits from Mexico in 1767 dealt a strong blow to a Society that was at the height of its ministries. In a bold move to placate critics of the Society of Jesus in Europe, King Charles III of Spain expelled them from the country as well as from all Spanish colonies. This expulsion meant that if Jesuits chose to stay in the Society, they would have to leave Mexico to find some kind of refuge in Europe. At the time, the Mexican province, which included Guatemala and Cuba, had 678 members distributed among forty colleges and houses and 114 missions (the majority of the men being Creoles, or Spaniards born in the New World). After their exile, 150 of these Jesuits died before making it to Europe. Soon after, Pope Clement XIV suppressed the entire Society of Jesus in 1773. It was not universally restored until 1814.

Only two years later, in 1816, the Jesuits returned to Mexico after an exile of slightly less than a half-century. One of their first tasks was to gain access once again to their former schools, the first of which was the Colegio de San Ildelfonso, which was soon educating 150 students. A new novitiate, counting six priests among the eight novices, was opened in the same compound. The province soon resumed its other apostolic labors, including the learning of indigenous languages, the instruction of seminarians, the religious instruction of children and adults, preaching in parishes, confessions, visits to hospitals and prisons, and the giving of the *Spiritual Exercises*. The small number of Jesuits at the time was not able to respond to all the requests for schoolmasters that came in from the provinces, though men were sent to Durango and Puebla.

Besides the many apostolic demands, another challenge that the Society met in Mexico from the period 1821–53 was the enactment of laws, both in Spain and in the newly formed country of Mexico, that were antithetical to religious communities. Some such laws even called for their suppression. Father Pedro Canton, the Jesuit provincial at the time, obtained permission from the general in Rome, Luis Fortis, to have the men live outside of communities, supporting themselves by the fruit of their labor. Properties were returned and taken away again, depending on what government was in power. Difficulties for the Mexican Jesuits continued in the years that followed as the country underwent various dramatic changes in government, including a civil war (1858–65).

Starting in 1879, however, the twenty-year leadership of Provincial Father José Alzola would mark a new beginning for the province, which expanded from a mere 40 men to 245. This vibrant period witnessed a return to community life, the promotion of preaching missions in rural areas, and the return in 1900 to the indigenous mission of La Tarahumara in the northern part of the country. A later mission to indigenous peoples was started in 1958 in Bachajón in the state of Chiapas. At various times during this period and the years that followed, Jesuits assumed the responsibility of diocesan seminaries, the most famous of which was El Seminario Interdiocesano de Montezuma, which was actually set up by the US bishops in Las Vegas, New Mexico, and existed in exile there from 1937 to 1972. This seminary, which eventually educated one-fourth of the diocesan clergy of Mexico, produced 1,802 priests and 21 bishops, all of whom returned to work in their native land.

The need for such a national seminary in exile came out of the Church–State conflict that witnessed severe persecution of the Church, a time when many priests and religious women and men went underground or left the country. This was particularly true during the era dubbed the *La Cristiada* or Cristero War (1926–29), in which rural Catholics took up arms against the government in defense of their religious freedom. Among the most famous of the Mexican martyrs of this period is Jesuit Miguel Agustín Pro. During this period, many Mexican Jesuits left the country, and the province established its novitiate and philosophate outside of Mexico in El Paso, Texas, in what become known as Ysleta College. It would not return to Mexico until 1951.

The post-Vatican II period ushered in many changes as it shifted the province's attention from the formal educational realm to works among the poor. Two prestigious schools, one in Mexico City and the other in Chihuahua, Chihuahua, were closed in the early 1970s. The men in formation worked mostly with Christian base communities, cooperatives, popular education projects, the popularization of the *Spiritual Exercises*, and the like. Newer apostolates, such as the founding of a center for human rights, the Centro de Derechos Humanos Miguel Agustín Pro in Mexico City, the Kino Border Initiative in Nogales for the care of immigrants, the expansion of regional campuses for the Universidad Iberoamericana, and the Instituto Superior Intercultural Ayuuk in the state of Oaxaca, which provides university-level education for indigenous persons, are bringing together the Society's centuries-old concern for education, indigenous and vulnerable persons, and human rights. The 2014 catalogue lists 369 Jesuits in the Mexican province, including 75 scholastics.

See also Mexico, Pre-Suppression

de Lara, Pablo López, *Los Jesuitas en México: breve historia de cuatro siglos de la Provincia Mexicana, 1572–1972*. Mexico City: Buena Prensa, 2001.

Eduardo C. Fernández, SJ

Middle East

Ignatius of Loyola's interest in the Middle East is clear from his biography. He visited the Holy Land in 1523 and, although he was evicted by the Franciscans, he had hoped to return. A bull from Julius III (1550–55) granting the Jesuits permission to establish colleges in Constantinople, Jerusalem, and Cyprus remained a dead letter, but the Jesuit Gaspar Barzeus, sent by Francis Xavier from Goa, did establish a mission on Hormuz island in 1549. In 1580 it was turned over to the Augustinians. Not until 1583 was an attempt made to establish a residence at Constantinople, though there had been a few voyages in the region, as well as the ad hoc interventions of the Jesuit Jean-Baptiste Eliano, with the Copts in Egypt (1561, 1582) and the Maronites in Lebanon (1578).

Documents from the period refer to the Jesuit work in the region as Missions to the Greeks (Constantinople and the Aegean Islands), to the Levant (Lebanon, Syria, Palestine, and Egypt), and to Armenia and Persia.

The Jesuit presence in the region required the support of foreign consulates, the French in Ottoman lands, French and Polish in Persia. There was never a question of proseltyzing among Muslims, apparently by papal request.

In 1583 five Jesuits, sent in answer to a request to Pope Gregory XIII by Latin Catholics residing in Constantinople, established the first residence in an abandoned Benedictine convent in Galata. The mission was decimated after a few years by the pestilence. In 1609 the Jesuit presence resumed after Franciscan objections were overruled by the French Consul. Their pastoral work centered on the Greeks, the Armenians, and the Europeans, merchants and prisoners of war in the penal colonies of Constantinople and Crimea. From Constantinople, the Jesuits would slowly reach out to the region between the Black and the Caspian seas and to the south.

Urban VIII, in 1625, asked Father General Vitelleschi to send Jesuits to Syria. The two sent from Lyon arrived in Aleppo the same year, only to be expelled. They managed to make their way to Constantinople, obtain permission from the sultan and the French ambassador and return to Aleppo where the Greek Catholic bishop helped the two priests and two brothers establish their Mission of Notre Dame: catechesis, school, and three confraternities for men (Greek, Armenian, and Maronite). The consulate chapel served as their church. Many Jesuits passed through the city, an important center of the trade route.

From Aleppo, in 1643–44, Fr. Jerome Queyrot founded the Mission of St. Paul in Damascus, Fr. Jean Amieu opened the Mission of St. John at Tripoli, and Fr. François Rigordi opened the Mission of Notre Dame in Sidon.

Fr. Rigordi did not stay in Sidon but continued his journey east. In 1646 he passed briefly through Persia and returned in 1653 to establish a Jesuit residence in Isfahan, which he would later transfer to New Julfa, a suburb populated by Armenians. The mission included a school for Armenian youth.

Jesuit activity would spread north to Armenian centers: Shemakha (Shirvan province), Erivan, and Etchmiadzin. Shemakha was of special interest as a crossroads on the trade route and a passage to Poland and Russia. The Polish Jesuits were instrumental in establishing the mission at Ganja in 1703. Fr. Judasz Krusinksi served the shah as court translator and liaison between the Safavids and the papacy.

In 1722 an Afghan revolt and invasion brought an end to the brilliant Safavid period. Nadir Shah, who inaugurated the Afsharid dynasty in 1736, became indebted to the Jesuit Brother Bazin who, after curing him of an ailment, became his traveling companion. After the assassination of Nadir Shah in 1747, Persia fell prey to divisions, and the Jesuits in Julfa fell victim to the machinations of an Armenian faction. Brother Bazin made his way safely to Bandar Abbas and sailed to Goa. Thus ended the Persian mission. The grave of Fr. Alexandre de Rhodes is still extant in the graveyard of the Episcopal Church in Isfahan.

Some time after the restoration of the Society of Jesus, Leo XIII requested the Jesuits to resume the mission among the Armenians. In 1891–93, Fr. Amédée de Damas saw to the establishment of six Jesuit residences in Adana, Marsivan, Tokat, Marsiva, Sivas, and Amasi. He was headquartered at Constantinople. The outbreak of World War I provoked the closure of the six missions with a total of fifty-seven Jesuits. The Jesuits maintained residence at Constantinople and in 1922 erected a large building, which was finally turned over to the Congregation for the Oriental Churches in 1983. Work with Armenian Catholics was continued in Aleppo at the St. Vartan School and in Beirut at the St. Gregory School.

In 2000 the Jesuits responded to another papal appeal and took over the mission of the Augustinians in Ankara, providing services for resident Catholics and cultivating relations with Turkish Muslims. Fathers Thomas Michel and Christian Troll have participated in faculty exchanges between Turkish religious colleges and the Gregorian University in Rome.

See also Holy Land; Interreligious Dialogue; Lebanon; Syria

Kuri, Sami, *Une histoire du Liban à travers les archives des jésuites, 1816–1845*. Vol. I. Beirut: Dar el-Machreq, 2001.
Libois, Charles, *La Compagnie de Jésus au Levant: la province du Proche-Orient: notices historiques*. Beirut: Faculté des lettres et des sciences humaines, Université Saint-Joseph/Dar el-Machreq, 2009.
Five volumes of: *Lettres édifiantes et curieuses: mémoires du Levant* (Google eBooks).

John Donohue, SJ

Miki, Paul, SJ, St. (1563–1597) and Companions

In 1596 the Spanish galleon *San Felipe* with Franciscans on board sank near Tosa, Japan. Toyotomi Hideyoshi, wary of the Spanish colonialism in Manila, ordered the public execution of six Franciscan missionaries, their seventeen Japanese *dōjuku* and lay leaders, and three Japanese Jesuits. All twenty-six were burnt at the stake in Nagasaki on February 5, 1597.

Paul Miki and two Jesuit brothers were companions of Pedro Morejón, SJ, at the Osaka residence at the time of their arrest on December 9, 1596. Miki was one of the first students in the Jesuit seminary at Azuchi and joined the novitiate in Usuki in 1586. He became one of the most effective preachers in the Kyoto-Osaka area, and preached at his execution. John of Gotō (1578–97) from the Gotō islands studied with the Jesuits in Nagasaki from an early age. In 1590 he became a *dōjuku* at the seminary at Arima, then at Shiki, specializing in visual arts and music. James Kisai (1533–97) lived with his 10-year-old son in Osaka after his wife abandoned the Christian faith and left them. As a *dōjuku* he served as a porter at the Jesuit residence and tea server for their guest house for many years. He was famous for his beautiful calligraphy. On the way to the execution site, at the hospital of Saint Lazarus, Paul Miki renewed his vows and John of Gotō and James Kisai took their vows as Jesuit scholastics.

Paul Miki and the "Nagasaki 26 Martyrs" were beatified in 1627 and canonized on June 8, 1868. In addition, thirty-three Jesuit martyrs from the Christian Century in Japan were beatified in 1867, and four in 2009.

Figure 45 William Lamprecht: *Paul Miki and the Japanese Martyrs*, 1882, mural, St. Francis Xavier Church, NY. Photograph Alison Fleming

See also Japan; Martyrs, Ideal and History

de Medina, Juan G. Ruiz, *El martirologio del Japón (1558–1873)*. Rome: Institutum Historicum Societatis Iesu, 2000.
Website of the Nagasaki Twenty-Six Martyrs Museum. www.26martyrs.com/.

Haruko Nawata Ward

Minister

The minister is the official in a Jesuit community who assists the superior especially regarding the material concerns of the house. He sees to renovations, maintenance, and the purchase of supplies for the community. The minister also sees to the needs of the members of the community (including physical health) and monitors their observance of religious life. He assigns community members to tasks within the house (for its care) and to spiritual ministries undertaken by the community (e.g. Masses for convents, parish supply, etc.). He also serves as prefect of the Church if that is a ministry of the community.

In the absence of the superior from the house, the minister ordinarily takes over his daily duties as well (*locum tenens*), though not making long-term decisions without the superior's approval. While the office of minister is often held by a priest, it can also be held by brothers or scholastics (General Congregation 33, Decree 7, #68). In these cases the provincial also appoints someone from among the priests in the community to act as *locum tenens* in the absence of the superior. If this has not been done, the superior makes the appointment, or, if no one is named, the priest serving longest as house consultor takes his place.

While the minister is appointed by the provincial, it is done in consultation with the local superior, and for larger houses, with the province consultors. There is no term for the minister, and he is usually a house consultor, though not *ex officio*. In larger houses there may also be a house treasurer; when one is not appointed, the minister takes on those responsibilities as well. When there is a treasurer, both minister and superior receive the financial report and approve the budget.

See also Community; Superior, Local

Instruction on the Administration of Goods. Rome: Curia of the Society of Jesus, 2005.
Manual for Juridical Practice of the Society of Jesus. Rome: Curia of the Society of Jesus, 1997.

Mark A. Lewis, SJ

Ministries

From their origins to today, Jesuits have been involved in a great variety of ministries. Unlike some religious orders that are devoted to a particular work, such as teaching, the Jesuits understand themselves as available, individually and collectively, to take up various works according to where the needs are greatest. While such needs may be determined locally, the Society of Jesus also looks to its superior general for guidance and for decisions regarding where and how Jesuit talents will be utilized, and to the pope, the universal pastor, who is thought likely to have the broadest view of where and to what works Jesuits should be missioned. Jesuit obedience concerns above all acceptance of a mission to engage in a certain work, to accept a specific assignment.

The provincial of a Jesuit province is normally the one who missions a Jesuit to an assignment.

Jesuits have worked at all levels of society, including among the poorest of the poor, such as French Jesuit Pierre Ceyrac (1914–2012) in India. Jesuits have worked with and for migrants, the homeless, or refugees; many generations of Jesuits have taught students from middle-class backgrounds; some Jesuits have focused their attention on economic and political and other elites. Such a broad range of people, from the most marginalized to the most powerful, was already engaged by Ignatius and the first generation of Jesuits, as they sought to "help souls" and to do so as companions of Jesus. All age groups have also been a focus, from young children to the elderly and the dying. In the twenty-first century, Jesuit ministry among youth integrates social media and electronic communication. *The Jesuit Post* is a kind of electronic magazine for young adults.

The Society of Jesus has often privileged ministries of the word, including preaching, teaching, hearing confessions, spiritual direction, but also more informal conversation, what some call the conversational word of God. Jesuit priests also exercise their priesthood in sacramental ways, in some cases in parishes, often as chaplains in schools of all kinds, and in hospitals, prisons, and the military. The *Spiritual Exercises* of St. Ignatius, given in preached or directed retreats of various kinds and lengths, have a special place among the diversity of Jesuit ministries, for they inform and inspire and animate all that Jesuits do.

Intellectual life is a major focus of Jesuit work. Some Jesuits devote virtually all their time to scholarly research and publication. Jesuit research may include not only theology or philosophy, fields familiar to every Jesuit ordained a priest, but also all areas of the humanities, as well as of the natural and social sciences, or of law, medicine, business, etc. Some Jesuit scholars combine scholarly pursuits with teaching, and some also with regular commitments to sacramental or other pastoral work. Since its first decades, the Society of Jesus has encouraged its members to publish, and the Society of Jesus has made a very large contribution to the print culture that developed from the era of the Renaissance and Reformation. Jesuit publishing includes both scholarly and more popular journals or periodicals, some of the former and the latter sponsored and published by the Society of Jesus.

In certain cases, Jesuits have been prophetic voices, denouncing injustices, and calling for conversion, from greed and violence and racism, to generosity, to peace, to respect for and fraternal relations among all peoples. Jesuits have at times been arrested and imprisoned for their prophetic ministry: a good example, from the United States, is Daniel Berrigan, best known for his opposition to the Vietnam War. And some have paid with their lives, such as six Jesuits in El Salvador in 1989. Though martyrdom may not be a ministry, certain ministries, lived in integrity and with generosity, may make Jesuits targets for persecution to the point of death.

Jesuits do not belong so much to a particular, local religious community as to a worldwide companionship. Until the most recent decades, Jesuit mobility often meant that European or North American Jesuits were sent as missionaries to parts of Asia, Latin America and the Caribbean, or to Africa. What they did as missionaries varied a good deal, from teaching Christian doctrine, to teaching a wide range of subjects, to engaging in scholarly dialogue with local elites, to caring for those suffering from poverty and disease, to advocating for justice for the oppressed. But as the number of Jesuit vocations has grown in what had once been considered mission territories, and as the number of Jesuit vocations has declined in the "first" world, travel in the opposite direction has become much more frequent.

See also Apostolate; Community; Obedience; Vocation

Berrigan, Daniel, *To Dwell in Peace: An Autobiography.* San Francisco, CA: Harper & Row, 1987.

Ceyrac, Pierre, *Tout ce qui n'est pas donné est perdu!* Paris: Desclée de Brouwer, 2000.

Endean, Philip, "The Spiritual Exercises." In Thomas Worcester, ed., *The Cambridge Companion the Jesuits.* Cambridge: Cambridge University Press, 2008, pp. 52–67.

Wirth, Eileen, *They Made All the Difference: Life-Changing Stories from Jesuit High Schools.* Chicago, IL: Loyola Press, 2007.

Thomas Worcester, SJ

Mission

The Society of Jesus understands itself to have been founded historically for the defense and propagation of the faith and for the rendering of any service to the Church that may be for the glory of God and the common good (*Formula of the Institute*, #1). The insight of Ignatius was that the grace of Christ which enabled and impelled his followers to seek "the salvation and perfection of souls" is the same grace by which they are enabled and impelled to seek their "own salvation and perfection" (*General Examen*, #3). At the very center of this insight is the sense of mission, and the fourth vow of obedience to "the Roman Pontiff, Christ's Vicar on earth" is precisely in function of a radical sense of universal mission, "to be sent wherever there is hope of God's greater glory and the service of men and women" (General Congregation [GC] 32, Decree 2, #13). In the lapidary phrase of GC 32, "A Jesuit, therefore, is essentially a man on a mission: a mission which he receives immediately from the Holy Father and from his own religious superiors, but ultimately from Christ himself, the one sent by the Father" (Decree 2, #14).

Historically, the mission of the Society of Jesus took many forms, with, from early on, a certain privileging of education (the founding of schools all over Europe) and parts of the world which had not yet heard God's word in Christ (evinced by the missionary journeys of Francis Xavier, one of the first companions and a close friend of Ignatius, in the Far East).

In more modern times, under the influence of the Second Vatican Council, the 1971 Synod of Bishops on Justice in the World, and new theological thinking which stressed the links between salvation and human liberation, the mission of the Society of Jesus was significantly rearticulated in Decree 4 of GC 32 (1974–75) in terms of "the service of faith, of which the promotion of justice is an absolute requirement"(#2). It was clearly intended that the justice in question should involve not only the personal but also the institutional: for injustice is "built into economic, social and political structures that dominate the life of nations and the international community" (#6).

There was some initial tension within the Society itself as it strove to understand and internalize this new specificity of mission, not to mention some reservations from Rome, expressed not least by Cardinal Villot, then secretary of state, in his letter on behalf of Pope Paul VI commenting on the decrees of GC 32. However, over time the direction taken by the Society in that period has subsequently been confirmed by three succeeding General Congregations and has become part of the ordinary understanding of the Society's own members. This confirmation has been accompanied by the acknowledgment of some mistakes – in particular an undue stress on the notion of justice understood in an exclusively secular way without acknowledging its roots in the justice of the Kingdom of God and in faith – and a more explicit attention to the elements of culture (not least to the phenomenon of secularization) and interreligious dialogue (GC 34) and to reconciliation (already in the founding documents of the Society) and matters ecological (GC 35).

The mission of the individual Jesuit comes to him from his superior in the context of his vow of obedience, exercised in the context of discernment and dialogue, with the annual account of conscience being of particular significance. The community life of Jesuits, too, is understood within this discerning openness to mission. Occasionally – as occurred at the beginning of GC 31 in 1965 with the request from Paul VI to combat atheism – the Society will receive a particular, immediate mandate from the pope, in the way that Ignatius had originally foreseen. There can also be requests from the bishop of Rome, through the appropriate Jesuit superiors, to individual Jesuits to take up a particular mission or role within the Church.

It should be noted, finally, that for Ignatius the missionary and apostolic dynamic of the Society of Jesus has deep roots in his understanding of the Blessed Trinity and his own experience at La Storta of being placed with the Son of God bearing the cross, so that "he and his companions were drawn into the Son's pattern of life, with its joys and with its sufferings" (GC 35, Decree 2, #6).

See also Constitutions; *Formula of the Institute*; Loyola, Ignatius of, SJ, St.; Service of Faith and Promotion of Justice

Arrupe, Pedro, "The Trinitarian Inspiration of the Ignatian Charism." In *The Trinity in the Ignatian Charism*. Rome: Centrum Ignatianum Spiritualitatis, 1982, pp. 11–69.

The Constitutions of The Society of Jesus and Their Complementary Norms. Ed. John W. Padberg. St. Louis, MO: The Institute of Jesuit Sources, 1996.

O'Leary, Brian, *Sent into the Vineyard: Explorations in the Jesuit Constitutions*. Oxford: The Way, 2012.

Gerard O'Hanlon, SJ

Molina, Luis de, SJ (1535–1600)

Luis de Molina, was a Spanish-born Jesuit who entered the Society at 18 years old. He was the first Jesuit to write commentaries on Thomas Aquinas's *Summa theologica*. Therein Molina sought to counter theologies emerging from the Protestant reformation that insisted upon the depravity of the human will. Against the notion that humans have as much liberty to act as the potter's clay or the swordsman's sword, Molina sought to validate the human capacity to cooperate with God in laboring toward salvation. This philosophical defense became known as *scientia media* (or middle knowledge), wherein Molina argued that God not only knows higher metaphysical truths and what *will* be in historical fact but also possesses a "middle knowledge" of all that *could* be. Neither God's pre-knowledge of the future nor his predestining provision of grace results in a divine imposition, however, that would compromise human freedom. For to know is not to will, and according to Molina, God simply uses God's knowledge of both actual future events and mere possible "futuribles" in order to provide graces precisely tailored to each person so as to be most effective in the particular circumstances of his or her life. These graces are not intrinsically efficacious, however, and the free cooperation of the person is essential to their realization. This was the crux of Molina's efforts to develop a theology that avoided determinism and protected human liberty.

His *Concordia* was published in 1588, but his ideas had been made known and generated controversy through his lectures at Evora in the early 1570s. His writings continued to foment controversy well into the eighteenth century but were most violently opposed at the end of the sixteenth century following the publication of *Concordia*. For almost two decades, the Jesuits and the Dominicans were pitched in fierce theological debate until Molina's ideas were vindicated by Paul V in 1607, seven years after Molina's death.

See also Philosophy; Theology

Flint, Thomas, *Divine Providence: The Molinist Account*. Ithaca, NY: Cornell University Press, 2006.
Kaufmann, Matthias, and Alexander Aichele, eds., *A Companion to Luis de Molina*. Leiden: Brill, 2014.
de Molina, Luis, *On Divine Foreknowledge: Part IV of the Concordia*. Trans. Alfred J. Freddoso. Ithaca, NY: Cornell University Press, 2004.

J. Michelle Molina

Molina González, Juan Ignacio, SJ (1740–1829)

Juan Ignacio Molina was one of the most important Jesuit natural scientists of the eighteenth century. True to the Society's broad pedagogical values, he was also a poet, a philosopher-theologian, and an historian. He was born on June 23, 1740, and began his early schooling at the Jesuit college in the city of Talca (established 1748), but he spent his summers at his family's hacienda, where he entertained himself raising birds. His father had been a collector of natural curiosities such as fossils and minerals from the Andes. All this had a profound influence on his later interest in the natural sciences.

In 1752 he was sent to the city of Concepción to study at the Jesuit seminary and, in 1755, joined the Society of Jesus. He transferred to Santiago and then to Bucalemu for his novitiate. It was in this period that he began to experiment with poetry. In 1761 he continued his studies in philosophy at the College of San Miguel (Santiago). From there, he returned to Talca to teach but by 1766 was once again studying in Santiago – this time, theology. This was abruptly interrupted by the expulsion of the Society on August 26, 1767, when all the Jesuits in Chile were arrested and transported to the nearest port to be sent into exile. The tragedy for Molina was that during the rapid arrest, his detailed fieldwork notes were confiscated.

Molina was never one to let such setbacks suppress his desire to understand more about the world around him (in both theological and scientific terms). Thus, a year after reaching Imola (near Bologna) in 1769, he passed his theology exams and was ordained a priest.

If Molina did not have a firm belief in the mystery of divine providence, it could be understandable were he to think that fate was conspiring against him, because in 1773, only three years after his ordination, Pope Clement XIV ordered the complete suppression of the Society. Molina, now a secular priest, moved to Bologna to work as a tutor.

Bologna, the famous university city, was the ideal location to continue his studies. Once settled there, he became involved in intellectual circles studying the natural sciences.

This should be placed in the context of Cornelius de Paw's publication of *Recherches philosophiques sur les Américains* (Philosophical Research on the Americans) in 1769. De Paw had based his work on that of the French naturalist Georges-Louis Leclerc, the Comte de Buffon (d. 1788). On the basis of profound ignorance of the Americas, these authors deliberately set out to establish a discourse of European superiority by denigrating American people and nature. On reaching Europe, Jesuits born in the Americas quickly became the intellectual champions of their native lands and set about demolishing their opponents through rigorous arguments based on their real-life experience and fieldwork. While it is certain that the work of European writers such as de Paw insulted Creole identities linked to their homeland, which in turn spurred Creole intellectuals to rebut this discourse, Jesuits arguably threw themselves into the debate because these works were also an insult to their intellect and their vast experience of observation and data gathering. They were an assault on truth itself, and so it was the Society's duty to enter the fray. It is precisely in this period that the empirical method for the natural sciences became ever more important.

Molina was in the vanguard of this intellectual struggle to vindicate the Americas. In 1776 he published anonymously his *Compendio della storia geografica, naturale e civile del regno del Chile* (*Compendium of the Geographic, Natural and Civil History of the Kingdom of Chile*) – a remarkable achievement given the loss of his notes a decade earlier. Not long afterwards, the workings of providence (as he would have understood it) caused his long-lost notes to turn up in Bologna. An old class-mate had come by them and traveled to Bologna to return them. This allowed Molina to expand his *Compendio* and to publish the *Saggio sulla storia naturale del Chili* (*Essay on the Natural History of Chile*) (1782 and revised 1810), which moved the famous naturalist and explorer Alexander von Humbolt to pay him a visit. In 1787 Molina published a new work on the civil history of Chile. He donated his estate to the newly independent Chile in order to found the National Institute of Talca (an educational institution) in the year of his death. Juan Ignacio Molina died on September 12, 1829.

See also Chile; Science; Suppression

Charrier, Reynaldo, and Francisco Hervé, "El abate Juan Ignacio Molina: una vida dedicada a la historia natural y civil del reino de Chile." *Revista de la Asociación Geológica Argentina* 68, 3 (2011), 445–63.

Menichetti, Marco, "The Geological Perspective of Italy and Chile by Abbot Juan Ignacio Molina between the 18th and 19th Centuries." *Revista de la Asociación Geológica Argentina* 68, 3 (2011), 464–78.

Prieto, Andrés I., *Missionary Scientists: Jesuit Science in Spanish South America, 1570–1810*. Nashville, TN: Vanderbilt University Press, 2011.

Ronan, Charles E., *Juan Ignacio Molina: The World's Window on Chile*. New York: Peter Lang, 2002.

Andrew Redden

Monita Secreta

This short work, first published under the title *Monita privata Societatis Jesu* in Krakow in 1614, proved to be one of the most influential and enduring anti-Jesuit tracts. Written by Hieronymus Zahorowski, who had recently been dismissed from the Society, it purported to reveal the secret instructions and strategies penned by the Order's superior general and to be deployed by the Jesuits in their alleged campaign to secure financial, cultural, and political influence. It contained tall tales of wily Jesuit confessors manipulating wealthy widows and the ways in which the Society sought to dominate the educational arena. Though a work of fantasy, it went a long way toward establishing perennial themes in anti-Jesuit literature: feigning humility and political obedience while secretly accruing power, and proceeding through slow cultural infiltration rather than overt acts of intrusion. The work was greeted with instant criticism (condemned by the bishop of Krakow in 1615, and by the Holy Office in 1616), and though Jesuits, beginning with Matthaeus Bembus in 1615, produced written rebuttals, the text sustained marked popularity across Europe despite such efforts. There were at least eighteen editions, in various languages, during the seventeenth century; it was still being invoked during the period of the Jesuit suppression in the 1770s, and new editions (often embellished with new accusations) continued to emerge during the nineteenth and twentieth centuries.

See also Anti-Jesuit Polemic; Poland

Pavone, Sabina, "Between History and Myth: The Monita Secreta Societatis Jesu." In John O'Malley, Gauvin A. Bailey, Steven J. Harris, and T. Frank Kennedy, eds., *The Jesuits II: Cultures, Sciences and the Arts, 1540–1773*. Toronto: University of Toronto Press, 2006, pp. 56–65.
The Wily Jesuits and the Monita Secreta: The Forged Secret Instructions of the Jesuits, Myth and Reality. St. Louis, MO: The Institute of Jesuit Sources, 2005.

Jonathan Wright

Montcheuil, Yves de, SJ (1900–1944)

Yves de Montcheuil was a promising French theologian at the Catholic Institute in Paris when in July 1944 he decided to respond to the request of young students engaged in the underground Resistance in southeastern France and to accompany and minister to them. Within a few days, a massive attack of the German army struck the group. Montcheuil was arrested by the Gestapo and executed in Grenoble, only two weeks before the liberation of the city. This tragic end gives testimony to the integrity of a man who was living what he was teaching. Montcheuil was one of the French Jesuit theologians (with Fessard, de Lubac, Daniélou, Bouillard) who contributed to a decisive renewal of theology in the period preceding Vatican II. During his philosophy studies he was particularly interested in Blondel, and the only two books published in his lifetime are editions of selected writings of this philosopher in an attempt to do theology in active dialogue with contemporary philosophy. From 1936 onward he taught courses on the Trinity, the sacraments and more specifically the Eucharist, and the Incarnation and Redemption. Some of his most advanced research on those topics was published by de Lubac after his death (*Problèmes de vie spirituelle*, *L'Église et le monde actuel*, *La conversion du monde*, *Mélanges théologiques*). Alongside his teaching of seminarians, Montcheuil had an influential activity as spiritual adviser of student groups in this troubled period and was insistent in unmasking the evil of the Nazi racist ideology. He also contributed to the clandestine review *Cahiers du témoignage chrétien*. Though remaining rather unknown in comparison with some of his colleagues because of his premature death, Montcheuil was nonetheless one of those great precursors who shaped the theological reflection which would blossom at Vatican II.

See also France; Martyrs, Ideal and History; Theology

Sesboüé, Bernard, *Yves de Montcheuil.* Paris: Cerf, 2006.

                                                                                        Grégoire Catta, SJ

Montmartre

Montmartre is a butte in the north of Paris mined since ancient times for gypsum. Gregory of Tours wrote (575 or 577) of a bishop Dionysius sent from Rome to Paris, where he suffered for Christ and was beheaded (249–251). Hilduin of Saint-Denis indicated (*c.* 835) that a chapel dedicated to this bishop existed on Montmartre, but erroneously identified the bishop with both Dionysius the Areopagite (Acts 17:34) and Pseudo-Dionysius the mystical theologian. In 1133, Louis VI established a foundation of Benedictine nuns, the royal abbey of Montmartre, at the top of the butte and built a chapel on the purported site of the decapitation. The morning of August 15, 1534, Ignatius of Loyola and six companions from the University of Paris requested of the abbey sacristan the key to the chapel, in the crypt of which they pronounced, at a Mass celebrated by Peter Faber, vows of poverty and to make pilgrimage to Jerusalem. Regarding the latter, they determined to decide by majority once in Jerusalem whether to remain there or to return to Europe, where they would put themselves at the service of the Holy Father. Furthermore, they agreed that if for

Figure 46 *Vow at Montmartre*, stained glass window, Casa Professa, Rome (artist unknown). Photograph Alison Fleming

whatever reason they could not depart for Jerusalem, they would offer their services immediately to the pope, which is what eventuated. The martyrium vows thus set the direction for the Society of Jesus that Paul III would later approve (1540). In 1611 Abbess Marie de Beauvilliers renovated the crypt and built a new chapel above it, establishing nearby (1622) a priory to which the nuns would relocate in 1686. The revolutionaries dissolved the Benedictine community and ruined the chapel/priory in 1792. In 1854, however, Jesuit architect Magloire Tournesac claimed to have located the site of the Martyrium, and in 1870 an oratory was built there. This building was replaced by a second chapel (1886–87), of which the crypt, renovated once in 1952 and again in 1988, continues to attract Ignatian pilgrims.

See also Faber, Peter, SJ, St.; Loyola, Ignatius of, SJ, St.; Paris

Crosby, Sumner McKnight, *The Abbey of St. Denis, 475–1122*. Vol. I. New Haven, CT: Yale University Press, 1942.
Martin-Decaen, Bernadette, Chantal de Seyssel, and William Vandevelde, *Le Martyrium de Montmartre*. Paris: Institut des Sœurs Auxiliatrices du Purgatoire, 1998.

William P. O'Brien, SJ

Montserrat

In his autobiography, Ignatius of Loyola describes his journey to Santa Maria de Montserrat, a Benedictine monastery in the saw-toothed mountains near Barcelona, in March of 1522. This visit was made after his recovery from the injury at Pamplona and conversion to a Christian life. His intention was to spend a night in the monastery in

Figure 47 View of Benedictine Abbey of Santa Maria de Montserrat from surrounding mountains. Photograph Alison Fleming

vigil in front of the medieval statue of *La Moreneta*, the Black Virgin, laying down his sword and his worldly clothes, and taking up the life of a pilgrim en route to Jerusalem. Ignatius was familiar with the vigils made by knights of the era, as described in the chivalric romances he had read, and he envisioned a similar action.

Approaching Montserrat he stopped and purchased some rough sackcloth and had it made into a garment that he would wear henceforth. He also bought a staff and drinking gourd, and made his way to the pilgrim's hostel near the monastery. He meditated and fasted, then found a priest and made a full confession on the eve of the feast of the Annunciation. In his new clothing he knelt at the altar, laid down his sword as an ex-voto offering, and spent the night in prayer. At dawn he departed for Manresa.

Ignatius's visit to Montserrat signifies a turning point in his life, the moment when he abandoned the life he had known and made a determined effort to leave it behind, emotionally and physically. The laying down of the sword is central to his effort. The sword remained in Montserrat through the sixteenth century. It was relocated within the church during the beatification process, but later taken to Barcelona where it is preserved.

Tylenda, Joseph N., SJ, trans., *A Pilgrim's Journey: The Autobiography of Ignatius of Loyola*. Rev. edn., San Francisco, CA: Ignatius Press, 2001.

Alison Fleming

Monumenta Historica Societatis Iesu (MHSI)

The series of archival sources of greatest importance for the history of the Society of Jesus began to be published under this title (usually abbreviated as *MHSI*) in 1894 in Madrid; a small group of Spanish Jesuits issued the first volume of the new edition of Saint Ignatius of Loyola's correspondence. Their initiative continued after 1930 in Rome under the supervision of the Jesuit Historical Institute (166 volumes have been published up to 2014). Two main strands of the *MHSI* cover, first, the beginnings of the Society (*Monumenta Ignatiana* [26 vols.] and other documents of the first Jesuits [37 vols.]), and second, the Order's foreign missions (*Monumenta Missionum* [68 vols.]). Other sources have been published as *Monumenta Paedagogica* (8 vols.), and documents concerning some provinces (Austria, Hungary: 6 vols.). To face new circumstances characterized by the decreasing number of Jesuits investigating the Society's past and by the continuing interest of many non-Jesuit historians, a new series of the *Monumenta* started in 2005. Following different editorial rules than in the past, this *Nova Series* contains nine volumes published before 2015. Since 2010 the *Monumenta* series together with the entire editorial work of the Historical Institute have been reorganized within the context of the Jesuit Roman Archives (ARSI) and continue as part of the latter.

See also Archives and Libraries; Archivum Romanum Societatis Iesu (ARSI); Bibliographies

Danieluk, Robert, "*Monumenta Historica Societatis Iesu* – uno sguardo di insieme sulla collana." *Archivum Historicum Societatis Iesu* 81, fasc. 161 (2012), 249–89.
Zubillaga, Félix, and Walter Hanisch, *Guía manual de los documentos históricos de la Compañía de Jesús de los cien primeros volúmenes, que tratan de los orígenes de la Compañía, de san Ignacio, sus*

compañeros y colaboradores, legislación, pedagogía y misiones de Asia y América. Rome: Institutum Historicum S.I., 1971.

Robert Danieluk, SJ

Moon (Craters and Jesuits)

The first recorded observations of the Moon through a telescope were by Thomas Harriott in England in the summer of 1609, but he only produced crude drawings that were not published at that time. Galileo's far superior paintings and writings, based on his observations in December 1609, and his publication of this work in the *Sidereus nuncius* in 1610, were the real beginnings of lunar cartography. A number of lunar maps, each with a different system of nomenclature, were produced in the mid-seventeenth century, but by far the most accurate and influential was the map in Jesuit astronomer Giovanni Battista Riccioli's *New Almagest* (1651), which instituted the system of nomenclature used to this date. Each large dark flat area he termed a *mare* (sea), while craters were given the names of prominent scientists. Among those he so honored were a number of his fellow Jesuits (including himself).

Since the early twentieth century, the nomenclature of planetary surfaces has been determined by the International Astronomical Union. A commission on lunar names in 1935 approved most of Ricciol's nomenclature, including seventeen Jesuit names and another ten Jesuits whose names had been added after Riccioli's time. In 1970, a number of additional planetary surface names were approved, including five more Jesuits. Since 1973, nomenclature issues have been decided by the IAU's Working Group on Planetary System Nomneclature; its present membership inlcudes one Jesuit from the Vatican Observatory.

In total, thirty-three Jesuits have been honored with lunar crater names, often using Latinized versions of their names. These include: Bettinus, Billy, Blancanus, Boscovich, Cabeus, Clavius, Cysatus, De Vico, Fenyi, Furnerius, Grimaldi, Gruemberger, Hagen, Hell, Kircher, Kugler, Malapert, Mayer, McNally, Moretus, Petavius, Riccioli, Riccius, Scheiner, Schomberger, Secchi, Simpelius, Sirsalis, Stein, Tacquet, Tannerus, Zucchius, and Zupus.

See also Astronomy; Vatican Observatory

Whitaker, Ewen A., *Mapping and Naming the Moon: A History of Lunar Cartography and Nomenclature.* Cambridge: Cambridge University Press, 2003.

Guy Consolmagno, SJ

Munzihirwa, Christophe, SJ (1926–1996)

Born in 1926 in Burhale in the Democratic Republic of the Congo (DR Congo), Bishop Munzihirwa was assassinated in Bukavu in the DR Congo on October 29, 1996. He was ordained a diocesan priest on August 17, 1958, but decided to enter the Society of Jesus five years later. He obtained a Licentiate in Social Studies at the Catholic University of Louvain in Belgium in 1969. After further study and pastoral work in Africa, he became rector of the St. Peter Canisius Jesuit Faculty of Philosophy in Kimwenza in 1978. Two years later he was appointed provincial of the Central Africa province. In 1990

Munzihirwa was appointed by Pope John Paul II as an auxiliary bishop of the Diocese of Kasongo, and he became the archbishop of Bukavu in 1994. "Mzee," meaning "The Wise," as he was affectionately called by his peoples, was known as a kind and caring shepherd who ultimately laid down his life for his flock.

During the tension between Rwanda and Congo caused by the presence of Rwandan Hutu refugees in Bukavu, Archibishop Munzihirwa was preaching reconciliation. His call for humanitarian help to secure his diocese from the invasion of Tutsi soldiers from Rwanda received no response from the Congolese authorities in Kinshasa. The international community was also silent to the plea made by the Bishop to help his people and the Rwandan Hutu refugees in his territory. His diocese became a battlefield between armies and rebels. He engaged in tireless efforts to bring peace and security, but those who were seeking revenge perceived him as a hindrance to achieving their own objectives. On the evening of October 29, 1996, his convoy was headed toward the Jesuit Alfagiri College when a Rwandan commando opened fire. Hoping that his two companions might be spared, Munzihirwa surrendered himself. He was quickly interrogated, tortured, and executed. He remains an inspiration for the Jesuits and the Church of Congo, who consider him a martyr and an unforgettable pastor.

See also Congo; Martyrs, Ideal and History

Luc Bonaventure A. Amoussou, SJ

Murmurationes

At a General Congregation convoked to elect a superior general, four days are set aside for the electors to engage in conversations (*murmurationes*) with one another for the purpose of becoming better informed about persons who might be suitable as superior general. Time is set aside for prayer, before the Blessed Sacrament especially. The timetable and the regime for those days is simple, even ascetical. And the electors seek one another out for one-on-one conversations concerning the persons about whom they wish to know more as regards their potential suitability for the office of superior general. The *murmurationes* are not only *about* persons who the elector thinks might be suitable but also *with* such persons, that he may get to know them better and thus be in a position to vote more prudently.

The conversations are frank, but respectful. They center on two questions: what are the qualities of the person under consideration that indicate his suitability for the office of father general and what qualities are lacking in him that it would be desirable for a superior general to possess? The focus is on strengths and weaknesses and not on attempts to discover hidden faults. Anyone coveting the office and observed to have sought it in some way, directly or indirectly, is, if convicted of such behavior, deprived of active and passive voice and excluded from that and all subsequent Congregations.

The purpose of the *murmurationes* is to elicit the kind of information with regard to the suitability of persons for the office of superior general that will be an aid to the electors when they come to cast their vote. The elements of prayer, simplicity, and dedication that mark the *murmurationes* underline that they are part of a discernment process – a way to come to the exercise of a responsible choice, free of disordered attachments and more likely to accord with the divine will rather than simply reflect an elector's own preferences.

See also Congregations; Superior General

The Constitutions of the Society of Jesus and Their Complementary Norms. Ed. John W. Padberg. St. Louis, MO: The Insititute of Jesuit Sources, 1996.

James Corkery, SJ

Murray, John Courtney, SJ (1904–1967)

Murray (born September 12, 1904; died August 16, 1967) was an American Jesuit known for his work on the public role of religion and the relationship between Church and State in the context of democratic pluralism. His defense of the idea that Catholics could endorse – more than just pragmatically – the principle of religious freedom led to his substantive role in the drafting of the Vatican II Declaration on Religious Freedom, *Dignitatis humanae.*

Murray entered the Maryland-New York province of the Jesuits in 1920. He studied in Boston, completed regency at the Ateneo de Manila in the Philippines, and was ordained in 1933. He continued theological studies at the Gregorian University in Rome, earning his doctorate in sacred theology with a dissertation on faith in 1937. Returning to the United States, he was assigned to Woodstock College, the Jesuit house of studies in Maryland, where he taught until his death. In 1941, he became the editor of the prominent Jesuit journal *Theological Studies.*

As his career developed, various consultations and projects (including aspects of postwar reconstruction in Europe) helped Murray gradually build an expertise in the public role of religion. By the early 1950s, he was well known for questioning, as the Church's sole model, the approach employed in a new concordat just being negotiated between Spain and the Vatican, with its ideal in a Catholicism closely intertwined with government. Instead, Murray had begun to advocate for an understanding of the compatibility between Catholicism and Anglo-American pluralist institutions.

The thrust of Murray's argument was that the growth of democratic ideals demonstrated that political debate could be conducive to civil peace and freedom, and that all of these things were moral goods. He saw political ideas and structures as unfolding within specific historical contexts, rather than being founded directly on immutable philosophical and theological principles. Yet, Murray insisted, a democratic society had to operate within a strong moral consensus that, while still foundational to public life, could afford to allow the explicitly political sphere to operate at some distance from the most deeply rooted values. He looked to the American founders' reliance on natural law (enshrined in the Declaration of Independence) to provide this moral framework, but worried that the consensus was eroding in postwar America.

Contemporary critics accused Murray of opening to moral and political relativism. His theories challenged the visions of militant Catholic cultural revival that enjoyed strong popularity during the papacy of Pius XII but also gave little support to the hope that corporatist socioeconomic ideas based on papal encyclicals could help integrate Catholic thought into mainstream American political dialogue. In 1954, the Holy Office pressured Jesuit superiors to force Murray to cease publishing on these topics.

Short of a formal "silencing," Murray was required to submit all such articles to Jesuit authorities in Rome prior to publication, where they were routinely denied. By 1960, however, during the papacy of John XXIII, Murray was able to collect several essays into what became his best-known work, *We Hold These Truths: Catholic Reflections on the American Proposition*.

In 1963 Cardinal Francis Spellman invited Murray to attend the second session of the Vatican Council as *peritus*. In this position, Murray produced two drafts of what eventually became the Declaration on Religious Freedom (originally a chapter of the document on ecumenism). He played a prominent role in long debates about the content and ultimate disposition of the Declaration, until a full Council vote on the text was blocked near the end of the third session in 1964. Illness prevented him from participating in the fourth session (1965), at the end of which a much-amended version of the Declaration was finally promulgated.

Murray's own introduction to the first English translation of the Declaration summarizes some important areas of his own thought. The document affirms three doctrinal tenets: religious freedom is a human right; the functions of government in matters religious are strictly limited; and the freedom of the Church is fundamental to its relationship with the sociopolitical order. Murray points out that the real struggle in the debate about the Declaration was with the notion of development (both in politics and in doctrine), and that religious freedom "in the technical secular sense" was only a "minor issue." However, he anticipates that for the concept of freedom, once evoked, "the ripples will run far," and "the children of God" will "assert it within the Church as well as within the world." These implications were beginning to absorb Murray's intellectual energies at the time of his sudden death.

See also Periti; Theology; United States of America; Vatican II

Hudock, Barry, *Struggle, Condemnation, Vindication: John Courtney Murray's Journey toward Vatican II*. Collegeville, MN: Liturgial Press, 2015.
McDonough, Peter, "Chapter 7: Political Change." In *Men Astutely Trained: A History of the Jesuits in the American Century*. New York: Free Press/Macmillan, 1992, pp. 214–41.
Murray, John Courtney, "Religious Freedom: Introduction and Notes." In Walter M. Abbott, gen. ed., *The Documents of Vatican II*. New York: America Press, 1966, pp. 672–96.
Pelotte, Donald E., *John Courtney Murray: Theologian in Conflict*. New York: Paulist, 1976.

William A. Clark, SJ

Museums

Museums have long occupied a central place in the Society of Jesus. They have showcased the global reach of the Society, supported its efforts to educate the wider public, and provided neutral spaces for scientific and cultural engagement with a broad range of individuals and institutions. They exemplify the syncretism that lies at the heart of the Jesuit mission, but what makes the museum particularly important is its public character – it is here that audiences have, for centuries, encountered a uniquely Jesuit vision of the world and of the Society's own place in it. The museum also demonstrates the outward-looking focus of the Society, its desire to bring together nature and culture for the edification of both its members and the wider populations they serve.

The public character that lies at the heart of the museum was also present in the earliest incarnation of the Society; almost from its inception, its members took an interest in the public demonstration of ideas. In the late sixteenth century, the famed mathematician Christopher Clavius (1538–1612) and his disciple Christoph Grienberger (1561–1636) constructed a small "mathematical museum" in Rome that contained apparatus, machines, and other examples of what early modern thinkers called "mixed" or applied mathematics. This collection acted as the seed for the later, much more spectacular museum housed in the Collegio Romano in the seventeenth century. Curated by Athanasius Kircher (1602–80), this latter museum grew from a small collection housed in Kircher's private apartments to one that easily rivaled anything found in Europe. It contained objects that were common to many museums in this period, such as ancient Roman coins and unusual fossils, but also acted as a spectacular advertisement for the global presence and ingenuity of the Society. Scattered throughout were the preserved remains of animals from around the world, sent by Jesuits living overseas – mentioned in the 1678 catalogue were three rhinoceros horns, brightly colored birds from Mexico, and a crocodile sent all the way from Java – as well as a bewildering array of machines constructed by Kircher himself, powered by hydraulic, pneumatic, or magnetic ingenuity. The strongly philosophical character of the Roman museum meant that, alongside the public displays of mathematical virtuosity used by the Society to tout its intellectual credentials in the seventeenth century, the Kircherian collection was an attempt not merely to impress its visitors with a sumptuous display of Jesuit power but also to instruct them in how the Society studied the world.

The Roman museum existed for decades and welcomed a wide range of illustrious visitors; indeed, so great was its fame that Kircher once claimed that only those who had seen his museum could claim to have truly visited Rome. It disintegrated following Kircher's death in 1680, however, in spite of the efforts to revive it made by Filippo Buonanni (1638–1723) in the early years of the eighteenth century.

Though the museum in the Collegio Romano remains the prime exemplar of a truly Jesuit collection, members of the Society also established museums across the world in the centuries that followed. Not infrequently, these were spaces where the Society could house and display the *naturalia* encountered in far-flung corners of the world; for example, the museum established at the Jesuit college in Manila contained animal specimens used by scientists to further their understanding of local fauna. Not unlike their spectacular progenitor in Rome, these overseas museums had strong ties to the educational character of the Jesuit mission; a paradigmatic example is the colonial museum that was established by a group of French Jesuits in Shanghai in 1868, led by Pierre Heude (1836–1902). Funded and supported by the Collegio Romano, it also had close ties with l'Université l'Aurore, another Jesuit initiative designed to train Franco-Chinese interpreters and to foster closer ties between the Jesuits and the surrounding culture.

Today, museums continue to occupy an important place in modern Jesuit life, though over time their character has become more secular. For example, centers of American Jesuit education such as Boston College, Georgetown University, and Chicago's Loyola University are all home to well-known art museums that display and celebrate a wide range of cultural and artistic perspectives. In other countries, Jesuit history has itself become the subject of entire museums, including Argentina's National Jesuit Museum (Museo Jesuítico Nacional) and Mexico's Jesuit Missions Museum (Museo de las

Misiones Jesuíticas). Here and elsewhere, the accomplishments of the Society remain on display as they were centuries before.

See also Archives and Libraries; Clavius, Christopher, SJ; Encyclopedias; Kircher, Athanasius, SJ

Claypool, Lisa, "Zhang Jian and China's First Museum." *The Journal of Asian Studies* 64, 3 (2005), 567–604.
Findlen, Paula, *Possessing Nature: Museums, Collecting, and Scientific Culture in Early Modern Italy.* Berkeley: University of California Press, 1994.
Sardo, Eugenio Lo, *Athanasius Kircher: il museo del mondo: macchine, esoterismo, arte.* Rome: De Luca, 2001.
Waddell, Mark A., "A Theater of the Unseen: Athanasius Kircher's Museum in Rome." In Allison B. Kavey, ed., *A World Such As This I Dreamed: Cosmogony in the Early Modern Mind.* New York: Palgrave Macmillan, 2010, pp. 67–90.

Mark A. Waddell

Music

The history of the early Jesuit order and music is fairly complicated. The early Jesuits dedicated themselves "to the progress of souls in Christian life and the doctrine and propagation of the faith." They were approved as a religious order in 1540. The approval of this new religious order and spirituality was significant in that the members of the Society of Jesus were released from having to gather together to chant the Divine Office (though Ignatius did not prohibit the members from doing so if it did not conflict with their apostolic duties and ministries).

Unlike the other religious orders, freedom from the compulsory chanting of the Divine Office was mixed with a certain amount of skepticism concerning the ability of music to appeal to the sensuous quality that would be attractive to the emotions of the listener. Many in the Society argued that music should not be given a major position in the tradition of the Order. This view was supported in the formation of Jesuits. Usually the scholastics were not allowed to practice their instruments as it was preventing them from apostolic work. Despite this anti-music bias, a profound musical tradition did emerge: the Society hired the best possible musicians for their colleges, seminaries, and churches. Years later, many musicians who were attracted to the religious life in the Society were able to use and incorporate their talents in their ministries. Francis Borja, the former duke of Gandía and the third father general of the Society, was known to have composed a polyphonic setting of the Mass.

In 1548 the first Jesuit college was founded in Messina, Sicily. By the 1560s the Jesuits established other schools with their own curriculum. Music was seen as a vital and necessary component to the success of the curriculum, along with theology, math, rhetoric, and other areas of study. As music was essential to the Jesuit curriculum, music teachers were hired to teach the students chant and sight-singing, as each school had their own liturgical and para-liturgical services. In addition to these, each school would have theatrical productions as well as collegiate assemblies; each required musical works and musicians to be included in them. As one of the para-liturgical services, the devotion to the Blessed Virgin Mary and other saints by these pious sodalities made it necessary for music to be a natural means of prayer and devotion for these student groups. It is interesting to note that Ignatius said nothing about the necessity of having musical talent or banishing of music from the daily life of the members. This was merely the case of meeting the needs of the people and assisting them in the spiritual life, whether it was in a school or parish.

During the latter half of the sixteenth century, the Society established numerous colleges throughout Europe. Music was given a prominent part of the curriculum. The Jesuits also encouraged the writing of plays, as they were considered a way to bolster the Catholic faith and teach the students the value of good morals and to witness them portrayed on the stage. Thus, the combining of music and the dramatic arts proved to be a valuable educational tool for the Jesuits and their students. In 1556 the first documented drama with music was the *Acolastus*, performed in Lisbon. Up until the time of the Suppression in 1773, hundreds of dramas and comedies were written; music was usually composed for them. Copies of these works were sent from one college to another and translations were made. Unfortunately, the music for these works has not been found and presumably was destroyed following the Suppression.

On August 31, 1552, the Collegio Germanico was established by Pope Julius III through his bull *Dum sollicita*. Ignatius of Loyola and Cardinal Giovanni Morone had petitioned Julius for the foundation of this new seminary. This college was the oldest college seminary in Rome. The Spanish composer Tomás Luis de Victoria came to study music and theology at the college in 1565. In 1571 he was given a position on the faculty at the German College, and in 1573 he replaced Palestrina as the *maestro di cappella*. The Society continued to hire the best musicians for the faculty and chapel positions after the turn of the seventeenth century. Among the list of names of composers who held positions within the Jesuit colleges in Rome are Giovanni Francesco Anerio, Agostino Agazzari (who composed the *Eumelio* during the carnival celebrations of the Roman Seminary in 1606), Giacomo Carissimi, Domenico Massenzio, and Johannes Hieronymous Kapsberger. Kapsberger was hired to compose the music for the opera *Apotheosis sive Consecratio SS Ignatii et Francisci Xaverii*, celebrating their canonization in 1622; the Jesuit librettist was Orazio Grassi.

In 1564 the Seminario Romano was founded to better prepare men for future priestly ministry. Coming out of the reforms of the Council of Trent, the curriculum for the seminary also incorporated musical training of the seminarians. The music faculty was not made up of members of the Jesuit order, since they were neither *maestri di cappella* nor composers in their own right. Therefore, to meet the needs of the seminary and the house chapel and churches that the Order had under its direction, laypersons were hired to teach the lay and clerical students. One of these musicians hired to teach music and direct the choir for Masses and other services was none other than Giovanni Pierluigi da Palestrina.

In 1566 Jerome Nadal, principal assistant to the general of the Jesuits, wrote to the college in Vienna with guidelines on what could or should be sung at the Mass and vespers services. This is the earliest mention of music by any Jesuit in authority. For the Ordinary of the Mass (Kyrie, Gloria, Credo, Sanctus, and Agnus Dei) and for the Magnificat canticle at Vespers, polyphony was allowed. The other vespers psalms were to be sung in *falsobordone* and the remaining prayers and hymns sung to Gregorian chant. Of course, exceptions could always be made with permission either by the rector of the college or the provincial of the province. This probably became the norm throughout the colleges in Europe, as those in authority would refer to the directions given by Nadal in his letter for each new institution. Motets were allowed to be performed at the Masses and during the other liturgical services (Good Friday and the Marian sodalities).

With regard to the missions of the Jesuits, music became the means for catechetical instruction. The missionaries would quickly adopt hymns and other short catechetical works and set them to music and in the language of the people. This was particularly the case with the missions in what is now Canada, Mexico, and in the Paraguayan Reductions. The "Huron Carol" or "Jesous Ahatonhia" is Canada's oldest Christmas carol. The text is attributed to Jean de Brébeuf, SJ, one of the North American Jesuit Martyrs, and was written around 1642. He wrote the lyrics in the native Huron-Wendat language; the melody is based on a sixteenth-century chanson, "Une Jeune Pucelle." What is remarkable about the song is the imagery de Brébeuf used: Jesus is born in a lodge constructed of broken bark, the Magi are foreign chiefs who brought fox and beaver pelts instead of their traditional gifts, and hunters come to adore the child instead of shepherds. These images would have made sense to the people and enabled them to comprehend the Incarnation.

In Mexico and in South America, the music was of a different style from that of the diocesan cathedral music. The music tended to be of a simpler Baroque style than that of the cathedrals in Mexico, South America, and Europe. In the Reductions, the Jesuits established separate small towns for the Guaraní Indians and other native peoples. Almost all of these towns, usually with a population of nearly 2,000 men, women, and children, had their own orchestra. The Jesuits, such as Domenico Zipoli and Martin Schmid, taught the people how to sing in Latin and in their own language, compose music for Masses, processions, civic assemblies, and for the sodalities. Zipoli and Schmid were musicians before they entered the Society, and the Society made full use of their talents. Together with anonymous indigenous composers, Zipoli and Schmid composed the music for a chamber opera, *San Ignacio de Loyola*. It was most likely performed in Santa Ana in honor of the superior, Francisco de Lardin, in mid-1762. It is a tribute to Zipoli, and his music continued to be performed in the churches well after the Suppression of 1773. In fact, much of his music continued to be performed by the indigenous peoples well into the nineteenth century.

The Jesuits frequently corresponded with their European counterparts, asking them to send keyboard instruments (organs, harpsichords), strings (violins, violas, cellos, and double basses), flutes, oboes, and other instruments. Instruction was given to these indigenous people on the construction of new instruments based on the models sent over to the missions. In the larger towns conservatories were built for the making of these instruments. Another musician sent to Paraguay was Antonius Sepp, who as a boy sang in the boys' choir in St. Stephen's Cathedral in Vienna. He oversaw one of the Guaraní conservatories in the making of instruments. Moreover, the Jesuits also asked for copies of the latest-composed music to be sent to these communities. They wanted to be exposed to new genres and styles of music coming over from Europe and then send copies of the music that the Guaraní and other indigenous people had composed.

The cross-cultural mixing of music and musical styles was brought about by the Jesuits and other missionary-focused religious orders. The Jesuits brought European music to South America, India, the Philippines, and to China; they also took with them the musical culture of the people they tried to evangelize. The earliest reference to music for Catholic worship in China was reported by the French Jesuit Henri Bernard. He was in Macau on April 4, 1563, the feast of St. Veronica; the statue of the saint was carried in procession accompanied by dancing and music. Matteo Ricci arrived in Beijing in 1598; in a letter dated February 1, 1605, he wrote that a small chapel had been built, Masses celebrated, sermons preached, and grand rituals held on feast days. A few of these Masses were sung with accompaniment from the clavichord. Other Jesuits who worked in the Chinese missions later in the century were the Belgian Jesuit Ferdinand Verbiest and the German Jesuit Florian Bahr. Emperor Kang Xi appointed Verbiest the master of music in the court. Bahr composed songs and music for the court.

For the court of Emperor Quinlang, there was a choir of eighteen choirboys with violins, cellos, wind instruments, ivory flutes, and a harpsichord during the years 1741–50. In 1751 the French Jesuit Joseph-Marie Amoit arrived in Beijing and remained there until his death in 1793. He composed several musical settings of the canticles from the Scriptures as well as motets to the Virgin (Salve Regina and Ave Maria among many others). In 1710 an anthology was published with the music for the first Mass and canticles in Chinese, entitled *Tianyue zhengyin pu* (Scores Presenting the Correct Sound of Catholic Music). It also included multiple sets of tunes from the north and south of China, along with twenty strophes set to music. Wu Li was the composer of these strophes and known for his delicate landscape paintings. Also known as Yushan, he converted to Roman Catholicism, and in 1682 he entered the novitiate in Macau. He studied Latin, philosophy, and theology and was ordained a priest by the first Chinese bishop, Lou Wencao in 1688.

The Chinese tune *wannian huan* was first mentioned in a geographical work by the French Jesuit Jean-Baptise Du Halde in 1733. Later, in 1768, Rousseau quoted it in his *Dictionnaire de musique*. Through a mistake in the copying of the tune, it was used in Carl Maria von Weber's *Overtura chinesa* of 1806; the music is now lost. Weber used the tune again in his opera *Turandot* in 1809. It has also been used by Paul Hindemith in his *Symphonic Metamorphosis on Themes by Carl Maria von Weber* in 1943.

The largest collection of manuscripts from the missions is located in the episcopal archive in Concepción, Bolivia. There are collections of music or information concerning music of the Jesuits in the libraries in Mexico, Canada (Quebec), Brazil, Colombia, Chile, the Philippines, and China. During the Suppression some of the libraries of the Jesuit colleges survived and were incorporated into the state library. Unfortunately, this was not the case for the music and manuscripts of the college chapels and churches; these scores are lost to history. In the 1990s manuscripts and copies of music from the sixteenth and eighteenth centuries were found in the Church of the Gesú in Rome. It is now held in the Jesuit Archive in Rome.

Before the Suppression of the Society, many members of the Order contributed their talents in the fields of composition, music theory, and musicology. Anthanasius Kircher (1601–80), a critic of Galileo's theories, was a music theorist. William Bathe (1564–1614) was an Irish writer who joined the Jesuits in 1595 at Tournai and was ordained in 1599. He wrote "An Introduction to the True Art of Musicke," in 1584. It is a method of teaching sight-singing to children using the *ut, re, fa, sol*, and *la* to notes on the scale. Conrad Vetter (1546–1622) was a German priest and poet who entered the Order in 1576. Known primarily for his poetry and anti-Lutheran polemics, his verses were combined with melodies by unknown composers. His texts were part of the effort to bring back former Catholics who became Lutheran.

In the eighteenth century, musicians such as Vicente Requeno (1743–1811) entered the Order. He was mainly known as a theorist who wrote on musical temperaments and ratios between intervals. He joined the Society in 1757, and after the expulsion of the Jesuits from Spain in 1769, he moved to Rome. He returned to Zaragoza as the numismatic curator of the Royal Society, but he returned to Italy in 1804 when the Jesuits were reestablished. Juan Andrés (1740–1817) was a Jesuit from Spain as well as a literary historian and music critic. He taught rhetoric and poetry at the University of Gandía until he was exiled with the Spanish Jesuits. He wrote biographies as well as subjects in music: conservatories, singers, opera, and Greek chants.

Even though they were not members of the Jesuit order, the Jesuits evidently thought very highly of the Mozarts. For the Jesuit College in Salzburg, Leopold Mozart, the father of Wolfgang Amadeus, arranged to have his son compose an opera. In 1767, at the age of 11, the young Mozart was commissioned to compose an opera in Latin, *Apollo et Hyacinthus*, as an interlude for the tragedy, *Clementia Croesi*.

After the restoration of the Society, several Jesuits were known for their scholarly work as well as their compositions. The Belgian Jesuit Louis Lambilotte (1796–1855) was a scholar of Gregorian chant and a composer of hymnody. Guido Maria Dreves (1854–1909) was a medieval scholar and co-editor of Analecta Hymnica Medii Aevi (which dealt with Catholic music, hymnody, and religious Latin poetry). Jan Vollaerts (1901–56) was a Dutch musicologist and theorist who authored the book *Rhythmic Proportions in Early Medieval Ecclesiastical Chant*. Jóse López-Calo (b. 1922) is a Spanish musicologist whose research centers on Galician music from the Middle Ages through the Renaissance, and on the music and instruments in the cathedrals of Santiago de Compostela and Palencia.

Joseph Gelineau was a French Jesuit, liturgist, and composer. Given his knowledge of Hebrew, he wrote his own form of psalm responses in French, striving to attain the nuances of both languages. This new approach, with simple melodies for the cantor and the congregation, came to be known as "Gelineau psalmody." An English translation was published in London in 1963 as *The Psalms: A New Translation*. Using his settings as a model, many other settings of the responsorial psalms have emerged over the years. He composed and published several editions of psalms, including *Psaumes* (1953–55, from the Jerusalem Bible) and Masses as the *Festival Mass* (1974).

Clement James McNaspy (1915–95) was a Jesuit author and musicologist. He authored twenty-nine books, including *The Lost Cities of Paraguay*, which provided the story for the movie *The Mission*.

The St. Louis Jesuits are a group of Jesuit composers who modeled their composition in the folk style of church music from the mid-1960s through the mid-1980s. The members of the group, Robert Dufford, SJ, John Foley, SJ, John Kavanaugh, SJ, Timothy Manion, Roc O'Connor, SJ, and Daniel Schutte were Jesuit faculty and scholastics at St. Louis University. Their music continues to be sung today in Catholic and Protestant churches, and they have influenced other American composers of liturgical music. Of these Jesuits, John Foley is best known for his liturgical songs, including "One Bread, One Body," "Come to the Water," and "The Cry of the Poor." His symphonic work, *A Movement for Orchestra*, has been performed by the Louisville Symphony.

Christopher Willcock (b. 1947), an Australian Jesuit, is one of the leading composers of Catholic liturgical music. He studied at the Sydney Conservatorium of Music and

Figure 48 Composer Christopher Willcock at Notre Dame, Paris. Photograph Thomas Worcester, SJ

sacramental and liturgical theology at the Institut Catholique de Paris. His compositions include the *Gospel Bestiary*, commissioned by the Tallis Scholars, as well as the *Missa Messina* and *Psalms for Feasts and Seasons*. Along with these sacred compositions, Willcock is renowned for his choral and instrumental works, including his *Akmatova Requiem* (2001) and the a cappella pieces *Etiquette with Angels* (a poem written by another Australian Jesuit, Andrew Bullen) and a setting of the Latin psalm 50, *Miserere*. He composed the *John Shaw Nielson Triptych* for the Melbourne Symphony Chorus (2004).

Several Jesuits from the Philippines have also contributed liturgical composition from the 1960s to the present. Under the auspices of the Philippine province, the Jesuit Music Ministry began under Eduardo Hontiveros (1923–2008). He was the first Filipino composer of liturgical music in response to the mandates of Vatican II. Some of his songs include "Ama Namin (Our Father)," and "Ang Puso Ko'y Nagpupuri (Magnificat)." Following his lead Nemy Que, Fruto Ramirez, and Danny Isidro, "second generation composers," worked on an album, *Heswita*, celebrating 400 hundred years since the arrival of the Jesuits in the Philippines. In 1994 other Jesuits produced *Himig Heswita*; other contemporary Jesuit composers include Manoling Franciso and Arnel Aquino.

The Society of Jesus enjoys a rich musical tradition, one that began in the sixteenth century and continued after the Suppression and eventual restoration to the present day.

Jesuits from around the world have in the past and still to this day contribute to the treasury of sacred and liturgical music of the Church.

See also Arts, Performing; Charpentier, Marc-Antoine; China; Paraguay Missions ("Reductions"); Saint Louis Jesuits; Zipoli, Domenico, SJ

Bangert, William, *A History of the Society of Jesus*. St. Louis, MO: The Institute of Jesuit Sources, 1986.
Celenza, Anna Harwell, and Anthony DelDonna, eds., *Music as Cultural Mission: Explorations of Jesuit Practices in Italy and North America*. Philadelphia, PA: St. Joseph's University Press, 2014.
McNaspy, Clement J., and Thomas D. Culley, *The Fine Arts in the Old Society: A Preliminary Investigation*. Rome: The Historical Archive of the Society of Jesus, 1972.
O'Malley, John, Gauvin A. Bailey, Steven Harris, and T. Frank Kennedy, eds., *The Jesuits: Cultures, Sciences and the Arts, 1540–1773*. Toronto: University of Toronto Press, 1999.

Charles Jurgensmeier, SJ

Muslims in Indonesia, Jesuit Relations with

With an estimated population of 240 million people, Indonesia is the fourth most-populous nation in the world. It is also the world's third largest democracy. Because it is a strategically located territory and possesses abundant natural resources, Indonesia has been exploited by the chief colonial powers, especially the Netherlands. While other major religions came to Indonesia through Middle Eastern and Asian traders, Christianity entered the island-nation through European missionaries who accompanied European colonial forces. St. Francis Xavier, one of the first Jesuits, was one of them. Joining a Portuguese colonial fleet, he came to the Moluccas (formerly the Spice Islands) in 1546. He and the other missionaries were forced to leave a year later when the Dutch came to rule the islands.

Today Indonesia is a religiously pluralistic nation. There are six religions that are officially acknowledged by the Indonesian government, namely Islam (87.18% of the population according to 2010 census), Protestantism (6.96%), Roman Catholicism (2.91%), Hinduism (1.69%), Buddhism (0.72%), and Confucianism (0.05%). Other forms of religious belief are also acknowledged, but only with smaller number of adherents. Under the official motto of *Bhineka Tunggal Ika* or Unity in Diversity, Indonesia is committed to respect its citizens regardless of their religious belief. The Indonesian Constitution also guarantees the people freedom of religion. Freedom of religion is also guaranteed by Indonesia's five official state principles, namely *Pancasila*. Pancasila acknowledges the central role of religion but without imposing a state religion.

During President Sukarno's administration (1945–65), religious relations in Indonesia were relatively harmonious, but during the period of President Suharto's rule (1966–98) relations were often marked by Muslim–Christian tensions and conflicts. This trend continued even after Suharto's authoritarian government was brought to an end in 1998.

As an overwhelming religious majority in Indonesia, Islam is very influential not only in the nation's religious affairs but also in other matters. Since Indonesia does not uphold the principle of Church–State separation, religions – especially Islam – are very influential in the nation's politics. Most of Indonesian Muslims are traditionally moderate and tolerant, but there have been certain groups that tend to be antagonistic toward non-Muslims, particularly the Christians. Faced with such a situation, the Indonesian province of the Society of Jesus attempts to help open spaces for interfaith dialogues. The dialogues were intended not merely for the interest of the Catholics but also for the country as a whole. Some apostolates were directly and indirectly intended to open dialogues with the Muslims at the intellectual and practical level.

At the intellectual level, for instance, Indonesian Jesuits in collaboration with the Jesuit Conference of Asia-Pacific helped initiate and run the Asia Pacific Theological Encounter Program (APTEP). In the program, participants from countries such as the Philippines, Vietnam, Myanmar, and Thailand spent several days living with students of Islamic boarding schools and involved in daily dialogues with them. In the city of Yogyakarta, the Jesuits open their library at St. Ignatius College theologate to the public, and many Muslim students come and make use of the library's 180,000-strong book collection. Some Jesuits were involved in different groups that promote religious dialogues such as Madia (*Masyarakat Dialog Antar Agama* or the Society for Interreligious Dialogue). Some Jesuits focus their academic works on Islamic studies.

On a more practical level, when the predominantly Muslim province of Aceh, in North Sumatra, was hit by a major earthquake and tsunami in 2004, many Indonesian Jesuits were involved in the disaster relief efforts. This was done particularly through the Jesuit Refugee Service (JRS)-Indonesia. In Central Java, a Jesuit parish priest helped Catholics and Muslims in his parish to work together in building each other's house of worship.

See also Indonesia; Interreligious Dialogue

Prakosa, J. B. Heru, and Greg Soetomo, "A Common House for All Believers." In *Yearbook of the Society of Jesus*. Rome: The General Curia of the Society of Jesus, 2012, pp. 86–88.

Prakosa, J. B. Heru, and Sc. Adrianus Suyadi, "Building Fellowship among Believers in a Plualistic Society." In *Yearbook of the Society of Jesus*. Rome: The General Curia of the Society of Jesus, 2001, pp. 83–84.

Baskara T. Wardaya, SJ

Mveng, Engelbert, SJ (1930–1995)

Engelberg Mveng was born on May 9, 1930, near Yaoundé, Cameroon. He was an historian, anthropologist, theologian, writer, painter, and poet. Mveng entered the Society of Jesus in 1951 at the Djuma novitiate (Democratic Republic of the Congo) and was ordained a priest on September 7, 1963. He defended his doctoral thesis in theology, entitled "Paganisme face au Christianisme dans la correspondance de Saint Augustin," at the University of Lyon in 1964. In 1970 he defended another doctoral thesis in history at Paris-Sorbonne University: "Les sources grecques de l'histoire négro-africaine depuis Homère jusqu'à Strabon." He was strongly convinced that African theology cannot stand alone without an interdisciplinary approach that incorporates history, art, and anthropology. He developed the concept of "anthropological poverty" (*paupérisation anthropologique*) to explain how the African person has been deprived of every value due to historical and colonial happenings.

Mveng believed that highlighting the many great achievements of Africans throughout history could help restore a sense of dignity and creativity among the new African

Figure 49 Englebert Mveng, SJ: Ugandan Martyrs Altar, painting in the chapel at College Libermann, Douala, Cameroon, 20th century. Photograph courtesy of Luc Amoussou, SJ

generation. As a painter, he drew an African Way of the Cross that is deeply rooted in African culture and used colors that are symbolic in traditional African settings. He was commissioned to draw the African Virgin that is in the Church of the Annunciation in Nazareth.

As a theologian, he believed in a contextual theology and advocated a spirituality of liberation for the African context. He promoted a spirituality of life in the spirit of the beatitudes. He actually co-founded a community of religious brothers and sisters called the Beatitudes. As a theologian of inculturation, he advocated an African reading of the Bible and contended that Moses was actually an African.

On April 22, 1995, Mveng was found dead in his apartment in Yaoundé, having been brutally murdered. He was one of several clergy who were murdered in Cameroon at that time. Throughout his lifetime, Mveng published many books and articles, and many more books and articles about his life and work have been published since his assassination.

See also Africa, West; Congo

Luc Bonaventure A. Amoussou, SJ

Nadal, Jerónimo, SJ (1507–1580)

Jerónimo Nadal is a key figure of the foundational years of the history of the Society. Alongside Ignatius, he is the one whose actions had more influence in defining the features of the Society and of Jesuit identity within the Catholic Church.

Born to a prosperous family that lived in the Jewish quarter of Palma de Mallorca, Nadal first studied in Alcalá and then in Paris where he knew Ignatius and his companions but declined to join in their fellowship. In 1536 he stayed in the papal city of Avignon where he was in close but somewhat conflicted relationship with the Jewish community. He then returned to Mallorca a priest and a doctor in theology, and taught Holy Scriptures for a while. Made a chaplain of Emperor Charles V, Nadal was clearly set for a successful ecclesiastical career. After intense spiritual self-examination, and after reading a letter of Xavier from Cochim, Nadal reconsidered joining the Jesuits, which he did after making the *Spiritual Exercises* in Rome. His own difficult discernment played a part in his understanding of the Jesuit charism. Rapidly regarded as a talented Jesuit, he was entrusted with important responsibilities in the early Society and sent on several crucial missions. For instance, he was sent to Portugal to deal with the first major crisis in early Jesuit history that occurred while Simão Rodrigues was provincial and that was caused by diverging visions regarding both the structure and the vocation of the Order. He also played a major part in the government and organization of the Society alongside Laínez and Polanco in the decisive years around the death of Ignatius. In 1557, when Nicolás Bobadilla challenged the authority of the *Constitutions* and of Laínez as Vicar, Nadal sided decisively with Polanco and the future general. He was made one of the assistants of Laínez and worked alongside Polanco on the *Scholia in Constitutiones*. After the reorganization of 1564, Nadal became assistant for Germany and Austria. He remained a central figure during the Second and Third General Congregations of 1565 and 1573, and acted as vicar of the Society during Borja's diplomatic travels in 1571. After 1573 he retired first in Tivoli, then in Tyrol, and later on in Venice where he worked on several texts including some pieces of spiritual literature such as his *Evangelicæ historiæ imagines*.

Nadal played a more than significant part in the transformation of the Society into a teaching order as well as in defining its pedagogy. As early as 1548, he was appointed as the first superior of the group that founded the college of Messina. He also supervised the Collegio Romano for several years. He has been sketched as profoundly influenced by humanism (particularly the philological brand that flourished in Alcalá) and was certainly influential in the making of the Jesuit theological curriculum, with its insistence on Aquinas as a basis for lectures. An able theologian himself, Nadal was appointed as theologian to the Diet of Augsburg in 1555 and again in 1568.

He was instrumental in fostering the Jesuit *esprit de corps* and in strengthening a vision of Jesuit identity defined by Ignatius and the members of the Roman Curia. Nadal enjoyed a close and personal relationship with Ignatius. Both the latter as well as Polanco stressed how much Nadal understood the spirit of the Society. He was therefore chosen in 1553 for the first promulgation of the *Constitutions* in the Spanish and Portuguese provinces where alternative understandings of what the first Society had been about remained strong. Under Ignatius as well as under his first two successors, Nadal traveled a great deal throughout Europe, negotiating the financial foundations of several Jesuit schools, but also discussing with fellow Jesuits the life of Ignatius as well as the *Constitutions*. As John O'Malley wrote, Nadal was perhaps the best known of all the Jesuits in Europe and "practically knew and influenced more members of the Society more immediately than even Ignatius."

Nadal became an ambassador of the Jesuit order not only among members of his own order but in the broader society. He left many documents (letters, commentaries, instructions, etc.) that circulated in the Society both during his lifetime and after. His interpretation of Ignatian spirituality certainly had great influence on several Jesuit spiritual writers. His texts remained a key source for Jesuit self-understanding throughout the early modern era, as well as in the restored Society in the nineteenth and twentieth centuries.

Historians are grateful to his rather bureaucratic spirit. The questionnaires he constructed and administered to individual Jesuits in several places in Europe starting in 1562 provide us with extraordinary and detailed information regarding the first Jesuit generations.

See also Constitutions; Loyola, Ignatius of, SJ, St.; Messina; Mission

Bangert, William W., *Jerome Nadal, SJ (1507–1580): Tracking the First Generation of Jesuits*. Ed. Thomas M. McCoog. Chicago, IL: Loyola Universy Press, 1992.
O'Malley, John W., *The First Jesuits*. Cambridge, MA: Harvard University Press, 1993.
Vercruysse, J., "Nadal et la Contre-Réforme." *Gregorianum* 72 (1991), 289–315.

Jean-Pascal Gay

Nationalism, Nations, Nation-States

From its origins at the University of Paris in the 1530s, the Society of Jesus has been multinational. The first Jesuits were foreign students in Paris, and once the Society was approved by Paul III in 1540, it grew rapidly to include Jesuits in much of Europe and well beyond. Jesuits were and are understood to belong to the entire Society of Jesus, not simply to local communities or provinces, and it has often been the case that Jesuits working in a given country have been missioned there from many others. But such an international vision, in which companions of Jesus are expected to put that companionship ahead of national identities and allegiances, has often been the source of tension and controversy as well.

In the early modern period, Jesuits somehow had to come to terms with the Catholic monarchs and especially the *Padroado* and *Patronato*, in Portugal and Spain and their vast empires, the systems under which the Portuguese state or the Spanish state was both the chief patron of the Church but also a power that directed and dominated the Church in its territories. The Jesuit fourth vow, of obedience to the pope, symbolized and concretized ongoing tension between national churches and the Society of Jesus. The situation in France was one in which the king was called "Most Christian" and chose bishops for dioceses and abbots for monasteries in his kingdom. Gallicanism articulated a French ecclesiology in which the pope played but a minimal role. Jesuits did not fit well, if at all, in such a system.

Many historians use the term "nationalism" to refer specifically to the post-French Revolution understanding of a people as a sovereign nation, and they see the French National Assembly of the 1790s as the means by which France become no longer a kingdom but a nation-state. In this view, nationalism in the last two centuries follows the lead set by France. Such nationalism tended to make the nation itself the object of a kind of religious cult, a cult that glorified universal (male) military service and willingness to die for one's nation on the battlefield (the field of "honor"). Good citizens of such a nation-state were expected to put it above all other considerations or commitments, traditional Christian notions of God or Christ included.

Other historians, however, use the term nationalism more broadly both in chronology and geography and in what is meant by it. For some historians, nationalism is as much ethnic and cultural as it is political, sometimes depending on Christianity or other theistic religions to produce and sustain national cohesion. Xenophobia and national arrogance and racism have often accompanied nationalism in the last two centuries, and if some

Jesuits have themselves adopted such attitudes, perhaps especially in time of war, the Society of Jesus as such has remained committed in principle to an international vision of itself as transcending the narrowness and divisiveness of national flag waving, whatever its origins or motivations. How a Jesuit could be both a "good" citizen of his country and a good Jesuit member of the worldwide Society of Jesus has often been a difficult question. In many times and places, Jesuits have been expelled from a country, and sometimes even killed, because they were perceived as a threat to the cohesion of a nation-state. A prime example is Alfred Delp, a German Jesuit executed by *National* Socialist Germany.

The Society of Jesus continues to live out a tension between its center in Rome, with the Jesuit superior general and his "curia" residing and working but a block from the Vatican, and the vast majority of Jesuits scattered around the world, working in a great variety of ways and places, and attempting to not only take Roman directives seriously but also adapt themselves to local circumstances and the complex realities of the nations where they find themselves. Today, India is the largest democratic state in the world, with a parliament informed by British traditions of governance. It is also home to the largest number of Jesuits in any country, one-quarter of the total. Indian Jesuits, from a great variety of regions and cultures and languages and traditions within India, also play a very major role in the Society of Jesus worldwide, and in living out the vocation common to all Jesuits, of all nations.

See also Cultures; Gallicanism; *Patronato* and *Padroado*

Bell, David, *The Cult of the Nation in France: Inventing Nationalism, 1680–1800*. Cambridge, MA: Harvard University Press, 2001.

Bennette, Rebecca, *Fighting for the Soul of Germany: The Catholic Struggle for Inclusion after Unification*. Cambridge, MA: Harvard University Press, 2012.

Flageat, Marie-Claude, *Les Jésuites des provinces de l'assistance de France et la première guerre mondiale*. Lille: Université de Lille III, 2000.

McKevitt, Gerald, *Brokers of Culture: Italian Jesuits in the American West, 1848–1919*. Stanford, CA: Stanford University Press, 2007.

Murray, John Courtney, *We Hold These Truths: Catholic Reflections on the American Proposition*. New York: Sheed & Ward, 1960.

Thomas Worcester, SJ

Native Americans

The desire to convert Native Americans to Christianity first drew Jesuits to the New World. In North America, the earliest to arrive for this purpose were Spanish, French, and English missionaries. Each nationality employed a mixture of universal Jesuit practices and its own cultural approaches.

All Jesuit missionaries were inspired by the Jesuit *Constitutions*, sought to learn indigenous languages, attempted to convert tribes by first converting their leader, and studied indigenous spiritualities for features compatible with Christian dogma. Parallels were often found to sacramental and incarnational theology, which closely paralleled native imaginings of the divine at work in nature. Later, Italian missionaries found affinities between native and Italian folk religions.

The cultural differences usually involved tactics for meeting Native Americans. In New Spain, the Jesuits opened chapels at the edge of ancient Pueblo settlements from which they sought to turn the villagers Catholic. In New France, Jesuits preferred to accompany fur traders on distant treks into the wilderness, seeking along the whole way a combination of markets and converts.

The Maryland mission was handicapped by English Jesuit eagerness to prove their secular loyalty to the Crown. Thus, the Jesuits avoided settling in native villages when the colonial government ordered them to stay away. The missionaries also bowed to Protestant fears that a Jesuit-French-Native American cabal might emerge to oust English rule. The Maryland Jesuits adapted by embracing an alternative, less controversial ministry to the planter class, its indentured servants, and black slaves that would endure through the Jesuit Suppression and beyond.

Initially, prospects in the independent United States seemed no better. The new federal government envisioned assimilation of Native Americans into a distinctly Protestant civilization. However, the Louisiana Purchase of 1803 doubled the land area of the country with territory more familiar to Spanish and French Jesuits. Refugees from the revolutions of early nineteenth-century Europe provided additional Jesuits for missions in the American West after the Society's restoration in 1814. These fresh immigrants had an advantage over Protestant missionaries of American origin, for the Indians did not regard these Jesuits as Americans and less often associated them with oppression. This may be one reason for the great success that the Belgian Jesuit Peter De Smet had among the peoples of the Mississippi and Missouri River valleys and the trans-Rocky Mountain west. However, the restored Society was much more Eurocentric than the Society had been pre-Suppression, and much of the multicultural approach to ministry was lost for a century and a half.

Eventually the federal government came to rely upon Jesuit help in negotiations with Indians. It also invited them to take limited part in a "Peace Policy" of the 1870s that combined denominational operation of trade and farming schools on reservations with delegation of actual reservation administration to church groups in certain circumstances. The number of reservations thus turned over to Jesuits fell short of the Catholic proportion of the Native American population, but the Church lobbied successfully for its inclusion in a new system of contract schools.

Catholic and Protestant missions shared the general goal of assimilation until the 1930s. President Franklin Roosevelt's "Indian New Deal" then revived tribal government and promoted white respect for Indian cultures. Jesuits responded slowly because of both European cultural bias and American nationalism. After European empires disintegrated following World War II and Vatican II embraced the concept of global Church, the international Society opted for the marginalized at General Congregation 32 in 1975. The United States itself underwent a civil rights revolution. The missions began to celebrate the realization that they had produced a hybrid of Roman Catholic and native spirituality, representing not a failure but an enrichment of the Church and the nation with the greater diversity of Native American adherents and citizens. Jesuits now vigorously oppose "termination" proposals to disband tribes and integrate members into white culture.

Despite this revival of multiculturalism, Native American vocations to the Society have remained neither numerous nor particularly enduring. Jesuits disagree about remedies. Some focus on recruitment and argue that the problem remains an intractable association of the missions with colonialism. Others focus on retention, arguing that the problem is establishing culturally appropriate supports for those who enter. All agree, however, that an increase of stable vocations would greatly enhance Jesuit work among Native Americans in the twenty-first century.

See also Canada; United States of America

Axtell, James, *The Invasion Within: The Contest of Cultures in Colonial North America*. New York: Oxford University Press, 1985.

Curran, Robert Emmett, *American Jesuit Spirituality: The Maryland Tradition, 1634–1900*. Mahwah, NJ: Paulist Press, 1988.

McKevitt, Gerald, *Brokers of Culture: Italian Jesuits in the American West, 1848–1919*. Stanford, CA: Stanford University Press, 2007.

Nash, Gary B., *Red, White, and Black: The Peoples of Early North America*. 4th edn. Upper Saddle River, NJ: Prentice Hall, 2000.

Thomas Murphy, SJ

Nativity School Model

In 1971 the New York Jesuits and lay collaborators opened a school on the lower east side of Manhattan. It was called the Nativity Mission Center School and was designed as a middle school that would provide a quality education in this mostly Hispanic neighborhood considered one of the poorest and most at-risk areas of the city. The founders knew they needed to come up with a different kind of educational model if they really wanted to prepare these underprivileged students to succeed in good academic high schools and later in college so that the cycle of poverty could be broken for them. The challenge was not small. How to provide a quality, middle-school, college-preparatory education affordably for at-risk youth that were so far behind their peers?

They first decided to extend school days, to limit class sizes to around fifteen, and to provide compulsory summer programs and continuous tutoring so that students could reach academic standards similar to their future classmates in high school. Of course, this was not possible without high-quality teachers who could understand and accompany their pupils. From the beginning Nativity schools have used a combination of experienced and volunteer teachers that has proven very effective for this educational model and has kept the schools tuition-free and sustainable despite their small size.

In 1989 another school following the same model opened in Boston under the same name: Nativity Preparatory School. Over the years other schools from different parts of the United States have wanted to provide a similar education in equally challenging contexts. In the late 1990s this ongoing need led to the creation of a network of Nativity schools with the purpose of strengthening the Nativity mission, fund-raising, and sharing best pedagogical practices.

In 2001 it was officially formed as the Nativity Educational Centers Network with an office in Baltimore. The model inspired many other Catholic religious communities working with the poor as well as other Christian, non-Catholic, and lay organizations. In 2006 a new network was established under the name "The NativityMiguel Network of Schools" to reflect the increasing number of schools sponsored by the De La Salle Christian Brothers and with the aim of combining resources and enhancing the support system for the schools. The network grew to sixty-four schools in twenty-seven states with around 5,000 students. In 2012 the network decided to dissolve, though the schools continued on their own.

The network developed nine core mission standards to ensure the effectiveness of the model. These standards were: (1) Explicit faith-based education; (2) At the service of the economically poor and marginalized; (3) A holistic education; (4) Partnered with the family; (5) Extended school day and year; (6) Effective administrative structures to make viable a non-tuition-driven model; and (7) Support for students after graduating so that they can succeed in Secondary and Post-Secondary education; (8) Ongoing assessment requiring schools to be accredited as providing quality education; and (9) Active participation in the network.

The academic success of the model is clearly reflected in some basic statistics from 2009: 89% of its students graduate from high school compared to 61% of their peers; 74% of its students enter private high schools compared to just 6% of their peers; 55% of its students graduate from college compared to 21% of their peers (NativityMiguel Network).

In October 2014, during a conference in Philadelphia, the "NativityMiguel Coalition" was established with the mission of strengthening the NativityMiguel model through three priorities taken from the nine previous standards: (1) Explicit faith-based education at the service of a holistic view of the human being; (2) Effective administrative structures for a non-tuition-driven model; and (3) Support for students after graduation so that students can reach fulfilling personal and professional lives. The coalition has also kept the nine standards under the name of nine core beliefs. It has also retained the motto that made the model famous: Breaking the cycle of poverty through faith-based education.

However, not all previous NativityMiguel schools are participating in this new initiative. Some Jesuit Nativity schools are now participating only in the Jesuit Schools Network of North America (formerly JSEA), and some other Nativity schools have gone their own way.

See also Cristo Rey (Model of Schools); Education, Secondary and Pre-Secondary; Fe y Alegría; United States of America

Fenzel, Mickey, *Improving Urban Middle Schools: Lessons from the Nativity Schools*. Albany: State University of New York Press, 2009.

Nativity Academy at Saint Boniface, The Nativity Model. www.nativitylouisville.org/Nativity AcademyModel.html. Accessed on December 19, 2014.

NativityMiguel Coalition, Our Mission. www.nativitymiguel.org. Accessed on December 19, 2014

NativityMiguel Network of Schools. www.youtube.com/watch?v=IIjJIQC3TL0. Accessed on December 19, 2014.

Seattle Nativity School, What Is a Nativity School. www.seattlenativity.org/about-us/what-nativity-school/. Accessed on December 19, 2014.

José Alberto Mesa, SJ

Nell-Breuning, Oswald von, SJ (1890–1991)

Born in 1890, ordained to the priesthood in 1921, and living until 1991, Fr. von Nell-Breuning was emblematic of recent generations of Jesuits whose academic work spans theology and the social sciences. Although he had a long teaching career as an ethicist in Jesuit institutions in Europe, this distinguished German Jesuit is best remembered for his role in drafting Pius XI's 1931 letter *Quadragesimo anno*, the second of the papal social encyclicals.

Because they involve complex matters of economics and social sciences on which few popes are experts, most social encyclicals are largely ghostwritten. Despite occasional speculation regarding the precise identity of the authors, protocol holds that the names of the writers and the process by which a given encyclical is drafted remain confidential. It is only by exception that the public knows so much about the role of von Nell-Breuning and his collaboration with Pius XI in the months leading up to the May 15, 1931, publication of *Quadragesimo anno*. The ordinary shroud of secrecy was lifted in 1971, when von Nell-Breuning himself published a detailed account of the writing process behind that encyclical on reconstructing the social order and promoting economic justice in *Stimmen der Zeit*, a major theological publication of the German Jesuits.

Von Nell-Breuning's contribution demonstrates acute awareness of the social and economic context of the times. With the unease and disillusionment that followed World War I, European nations were increasingly sharply divided between leftist parties, which were growing in their appeal to the working classes, and right-wing parties, which were gaining ground among the middle and upper classes, most notably in the rise of Nazism in Germany and Fascism in Italy, Spain, and elsewhere. With free-market capitalism and Soviet Communism supplying the polar extremes, many sought a middle ground, often referred to as a "Third Way" between *laissez-faire* capitalist and decidedly socialist approaches to economic relations. Catholic social teaching was emerging as a promising venue to supply a balanced and personalistic alternative to the economic extremes which threatened to dominate the debate and subject the world to disruptive ideological and even armed conflict. The stock market crash of 1929 and the onset of the Great Depression, along with the failure of many banks and financial institutions, raised the stakes considerably, and prompted Pius XI to commission the writing of a social encyclical to provide instruction to Catholics on matters of social justice in challenging times.

Jesuit Superior General Włodzimir Ledóchowski responded to the Pope's request for assistance by turning to von Nell-Breuning, who had received his doctorate in 1928 and, though still an apprentice in academic circles, was well positioned to provide expert advice on economic values and reforms. He brought to the task a thorough knowledge of the works of his many intellectual mentors, including Gustav Gundlach, Heinrich Pesch, and the wider "Konigswinter Group" of Catholic scholars. The text of *Quadragesimo anno* offers a sound diagnosis regarding the roots of economic and social disorder and proposes many helpful suggestions to improve economic relations. Von Nell-Breuning's achievement frequently repeats the moral admonitions of the first social encyclical *Rerum novarum* (particularly on fair wages and protections for worker rights), but also offers creative analysis suited to contemporary challenges. Primary among these novelties is the notion of subsidiarity, a newly articulated moral principle that calls for a careful calibration of public and private economic interventions to be applied at the appropriate level of society. Solutions should be attempted at the local level, but higher-level measures are often necessary and may be readily justified.

On this Jesuit's telling, the most controversial section of *Quadragesimo anno*, namely paragraphs 91–96, turns out to be the sole place where Pius XI inserted text beyond what von Nell-Breuning had drafted. These six brief paragraphs on the topic of corporatist syndicalism are generally interpreted as offering a benevolent nod to Mussolini's preferred style of political authoritarianism, thus prompting the charge that the encyclical represents a "flirtation with fascism" on the part of Church officials trying to curry favor with the Italian dictator and like-minded European leaders.

Nothing in von Nell-Breuning's intellectual profile would suggest as much, although debate continues to swirl about the complex political intentions that may be fairly attributed to Pius XI. *Quadragesimo anno* remains a constructive contribution to "the social question" and even contains some pointed words of praise (para. 143) for one distinctively Jesuit resource for personal as well as social renewal, namely the *Spiritual Exercises* of Saint Ignatius Loyola.

See also Papacy; Pius XI

Hinze, Christine Firer, "Commentary on *Quadragesimo Anno (After Forty Years)*." In Kenneth R. Himes, ed., *Modern Catholic Social Teaching: Commentaries and Interpretations*. Washington, DC: Georgetown University Press, 2005, pp. 151–74.

von Nell-Breuning, Oswald, "The Drafting of *Quadragesimo Anno*." In Charles E. Curran and Richard A. McCormick, eds., *Readings in Moral Theology No. 5: Official Catholic Social Teaching*. New York: Paulist Press, 1986, pp. 60–68.

Thomas Massaro, SJ

Nepal Jesuit Mission

The Jesuit mission in Nepal is a dependent region of the Patna province of Jesuits in India. The formal presence of Jesuits in Nepal is a relatively recent development. Owing to its mountainous terrain and the fact it was a Hindu kingdom, Nepal had been isolated from much foreign influence. Christian missions, therefore, had not been established in Nepal, although missionaries in the seventeenth and eighteenth centuries, including the Jesuit Ippolito Desideri (1684–1733), had passed through Nepal on the way to Tibet.

But as neighboring India achieved independence from British rule (1947) and great plans for its growth and modernization were underway, the royal family of Nepal wanted to address the lack of adequate educational and other opportunities within their borders. Thus the government initiated talks starting in 1949 with the Jesuits of the Patna province in India, to invite them to establish a school in Nepal. Meanwhile in a power struggle within the Nepal government, King Tribuhuvan abdicated and sought asylum in India, resulting in 4-year-old Gyanendra ascending the throne. In January 1951, amid the political instability, Fr. Marshall Moran, SJ, and Fr. Joseph Egan, SJ, the provincial of the Chicago province (which sponsored the Patna province), traveled to Nepal to see the proposed school site and work through the details. Despite this shift in power, the new government remained committed to the invitation to the Jesuits.

In just six months the Jesuits opened their first school in Godavari, 8 miles outside of Kathmandu, at the former summer palace of the prime minister. After renovations and additional construction, the new school opened on July 1, 1951, with sixty boys admitted as the first students. Fr. Marshall Moran was the first principal, and he was joined in this mission by four other Jesuits: Fr. Frank Murphy, Fr. Ed Saxton, Fr. Sanboelle, and Fr. Tom Downing. The school expanded quickly, and in 1954 the Jesuits opened a second school in Jawalakhel as capacity could not keep up with enrollment demand on just one campus. By 1969 the Jesuit schools at Godavari and Jawalhakel, having both undergone major building projects, were distinguished as primary and secondary schools, respectively.

The invitation of the Jesuits to begin work in Nepal was part of a larger opening of Nepal's society to modernization and greater influence from the outside world.

by the charismatic appearance of General Pedro Arrupe. A painful and disastrous polarization followed, visible in many departures from the Society and emigration of Jesuits to quieter countries. Reality constantly thwarted plans for rearrangement and reconsideration. Nevertheless Dutch Jesuits acted as pioneers in theology, education, liturgy, pastoral renewal, and social commitment. Most institutions have been cut back for want of Jesuits. Focus is now most on parish work and Ignatian spirituality. Collaboration with the Flemish, British, and Irish provinces has been developing since the end of the twentieth century.

See also Belgium; Canisius, Peter, SJ, St.

Begheyn, Paul, *A Guide to the History of the Jesuits in the Netherlands, 1540–2000*. 2 vols. Nijmegen: Valkhof Pers, 2002–06.
Jesuit Books in the Dutch Republic and Its Generality Lands 1567–1773. Leiden/Boston: Brill, 2014.
Faesen, Rob, and Leo Kenis, eds., *The Jesuits of the Low Countries: Identity and Impact (1540–1773)*. Leuven: Peeters, 2012.

Paul Begheyn, SJ

Nicaragua

Nicaragua (together with Guatemala, El Salvador, Costa Rica, Panama, and Honduras) belongs to the Central American province of the Society. Four Jesuits arrived in 1579, but then the Jesuits withdrew in 1625. Another group arrived from Ecuador in 1853, but they were allowed to stay for only a few years. Sixty-eight Jesuits forced to leave Guatemala came to Nicaragua in September 1871. Yet while there was a desire to have the Society found a school, the government, wishing to avoid any controversy with Guatemala (where the Society was unwelcome), preferred that they engage in pastoral work; they were received as refugees, not as permanent residents. Nevertheless, given the onslaught of attacks against the Church in the press, and given that Guatemala and El Salvador were pressuring for their expulsion (they had also been unjustly blamed for a local uprising), the Jesuits were once more expelled in 1881. Eventually, Jesuits exiled from Mexico began coming in 1913; they were joined by Jesuits from the Castilla province. Educational ministry predominated. In 1961 they founded the Universidad Centroamericana (UCA), but they were also working among the poor and marginalized.

Nicaragua has had an unsettled history, both because of liberal/conservative tensions within the country that mirrored similar tensions in other parts of Central America, and because the country fell victim to the economic and political interests of the United States, especially under the presidency of Ronald Reagan. Throughout much of the twentieth century, Nicaragua suffered under the dictatorship of the Somoza family, which was finally overthrown by the Sandinista Front for National Liberation in 1979. Throughout the 1970s, the UCA played an important role in terms of social and political critique. In fact, a number of Jesuits worked closely with the revolutionary Sandinista government toward the end of the 1970s and into the 1980s.

The involvement of Jesuits (and Christians in general) with the new government was complicated by the stance of the official Church in the person of Archbishop (and later Cardinal) Miguel Obrando y Bravo. The Archbishop had been a sharp critic of the Somoza regime. Initially sympathetic to the revolution, the Archbishop sensed that the Sandinistas were becoming increasingly ideological and totalitarian, and he found strong support within the Reagan administration, for whom the Sandinistas were simply communists. As a result, the United States began supporting a counter-revolutionary insurgency (the Contras), many of whom had supported Somoza, and the Archbishop supported the Contras.

The history of the Jesuits in Nicaragua in recent times cannot be told without knowledge of what was happening politically and ecclesiastically (the same must be said with respect to most of the other countries in Central and South America). The story of Fernando Cardenal, SJ, is illustrative of the tension that the Society was experiencing. Deeply immersed in the life of his people during the dictatorship, he was a vocal critic of the regime and, like so many other religious and priests who had witnessed the desperate conditions of the Nicaraguan people, supported the revolution. He then served for six years in the new government as minister of education and directed the successful national literacy campaign. Forced to choose between leaving his post and remaining in the Society, he left the Jesuits in 1984; however, after retiring from the government post he was readmitted to the Society twelve years later.

In addition to parish work and the UCA, the Society sponsors two secondary schools in Nicaragua (Colegio Centro América del Sagrado Corazón de Jesús, founded in 1916 by Jesuits from Mexico fleeing persecution, and Instituto Loyola, founded in 1946). Jesuits are engaged in a variety of social and educational projects as well as the Fe y Alegría network. The province publishes the review *Envio*, a monthly analysis of political, cultural, and religious life in Nicaragua and other parts of Central America. The house of studies in Managua is named after Rutilio Grande, SJ, who was murdered in El Salvador.

See also Fe y Alegría; Guatemala; United States of America; Universidad Centroamericana (UCA)

Jerez, César, "Discurso del Rector de la UCA." *Envio* #102, April 1990. Available at www.envio.org. ni/articulo/2492.

Klaiber, Jeffrey L., *The Jesuits in Latin America, 1549–2000: 450 Years of Inculturation, Defense of Human Rights, and Prophetic Witness*. St. Louis, MO: The Institute of Jesuit Sources, 2009.
The Church, Dictatorships, and Democracy in Latin America. Maryknoll, NY: Orbis Books, 1998.

Testamento de Fernando Cardenal. Available at www.manresanet.cat/testamento-fernando-cardenal-s-j/.

Walker Thomas, and Christine Wade, *Nicaragua: Living in the Shadow of the Eagle*. Boulder, CO: Westview Press, 2011.

William Reiser, SJ

Nobili, Roberto de, SJ (1577–1656)

Roberto de Nobili was the first Jesuit to introduce the missionary method of adaptation in India and the first missionary to write books in Tamil. His extensive knowledge and sympathetic view of the sociocultural customs of India, coupled with his conviction that the earliest Christian missionaries and Fathers of the Church guided Christians from different cultures with empathy, gentleness, openness, and tolerance, made him boldly immerse himself in the Indian way as deeply as possible, thus ushering in a new chapter in the history of Christianity in India.

Born in Rome, de Nobili entered the Society of Jesus in 1597 and was ordained in 1603. His provincial sent him to Madurai, India, in 1606 where another Jesuit, Gonçalo Fernandez, SJ, had already been for more than a decade without having successfully converted a single local person to Christianity. De Nobili realized that the negative response to Christianity in Madurai was because the locals called Christianity a *paranghi* (barbarian and foreign) religion, impure and inferior, indulging in practices and relationships abhorrent to the Hindu philosophy and practices, especially of purity and pollution. De Nobili broke through the barriers of misunderstanding and created an atmosphere where Hindus embraced Christianity.

Roberto de Nobili became his own starting point for adaptation; he left the Jesuit residence in Madurai and moved into a house in the Brahmin quarters of Madurai to live like a Hindu ascetic. He changed his food and dress habits, became a vegetarian, and ate only once a day. Instead of the black habit worn by Jesuits, he started wearing the saffron-colored robes of an Indian *sanyasi*. Based on his study of Indian customs, de Nobili made a distinction between religious and cultural customs and allowed the Indian Christians to continue to follow the Indian customs like wearing thread, having a tuft of hair, and using sandal paste. He encouraged them to celebrate *Pongal*, the harvest festival of the Tamils. Although his venture was sanctioned by his provincial, Albert Laerzio, there was strong opposition to his method in both India and Rome. The strategies were considered too conciliatory toward Hinduism and to dilute the importance and radicality of Christianity. These raging controversies sparked three scholarly works in Latin by de Nobili – *The Apology*, *The Narration*, and *Report on Certain Customs of the Indian Nation*. In 1625 Pope Gregory XV decided in favor of de Nobili's adaptation approach, but this issue resurfaced as one of the contested issues known as the Malabar Rites Controversy during the events leading to the Suppression of the Society of Jesus in 1773.

The erudite scholar de Nobili studied Hindu religious texts in Sanskrit and Tamil to such an extent that he has been called the first European Sanskrit scholar, and one of the earliest Christian missionaries to have had an extensive knowledge of Hinduism. He presented Christianity as *Satya Veda* (True Religion). Molded in the missionary spirit, he remained an apologist presenting Christianity as the true religion and deliberately demoting Hinduism as a false religion. Throughout his discussions with Hindus, his sole aim was to convert people to Christianity through arguments and logic. Among his many writings on religious matters, *Tusana Tikkaram* (Refutation of Calumnies) and *Gnana Upatecam* (Catechism) gave a thorough defense and presentation of the Christian beliefs and way of life. De Nobili's new method of approach to Hindus in Madurai and neighboring places proved reasonably successful. The locals came to listen to him and some embraced Christianity.

The conversion movement that began with de Nobili encouraged people of different castes to embrace Christianity. In a surcharged hierarchical caste system prevalent in India, with its discriminations and segregations, he tried to be pragmatic by allowing the converts to worship in the same church but in different places assigned to them. He also created two groups of Jesuit missionaries in the Madurai mission – *Brahminsanyasis* and *Pandarasamis*, the former working with the Brahmins and the people belonging to the dominant castes and the latter with people of other castes. Thus in his appropriation of the *Weltanschauung* of the Brahmininic Hinduism, he accepted also its sociocultural prejudices. He is still criticized for this today, even as he is praised for de-coupling Christianity from European culture and making a home for it in Indian culture.

Though rudimentary, de Nobili inaugurated Indian Christian theology. He called Jesus *satguru* (teacher of truth), a term borrowed from Hindu tradition. His dialogue partners were Brahmins and the Brahminic Hinduism, which all played a vital and restrictive role in his mission paradigm. By contrast, Fr. Joseph Constanzo Beschi, a fellow Jesuit and countryman of de Nobili, came to the Madurai mission a century later and worked as a *pandarasami*, had non-Brahmins as his dialogue partners, and developed an Indian Christian theology by his being immersed in the rich Tamil *bhakti* (devotion) tradition; he also wrote both classical and folk literature.

See also India

de Nobili, Roberto, *Preaching Wisdom to the Wise: Three Treatises*. Trans. and intro. Anand Amaladass and Francis X. Clooney. St. Louis, MO: The Institute of Jesuit Sources, 2000.

Leonard Fernando, SJ

Nóbrega, Manuel da, SJ (1517–1570)

Manuel da Nóbrega was born in Sanfins do Douro, Portugal, on October 18, 1517. Having graduated in canon law from the University of Coimbra in 1541, he was already a priest when he entered the Society of Jesus on November 21, 1544.

He was appointed superior of the first mission of the Society of Jesus in the Americas (1549) and was named provincial of Brazil by Saint Ignatius on July 9, 1553. He helped to found the cities of Salvador, São Paulo, and Rio de Janeiro.

On January 25, 1554, at the Piratininga plateau, Nóbrega founded the house-college of São Paulo, where the Jesuits taught the native people reading, writing, Latin, singing, as well as how to play musical instruments. Nóbrega valued Piratininga as a stopover for many native nations, as well as the safest way to go to preach to the groups living in the wilderness.

In 1558 Nóbrega founded the village of São Paulo at the Bahia de Todos os Santos, choosing it as his habitual residence and establishing it as an experimental station for conversion and for regular learning of the work of planting cotton, spinning, and weaving. Considering it useful and practical to make cloth from the land, Nóbrega promoted the art of weaving in the Indian settlements, and then farming. Following the first two nuclei of foundation – the colleges of Bahia and São Vicente – there was no college, novitiate, or residence of any relevance without one or more cattle farms.

Nóbrega considered African slaves to be essential to maintaining the support of the colleges and thus making possible the education of native children. He traveled through all the captaincies of Brazil, from Pernambuco to São Vicente, promoting catechesis and the education of boys, and fighting for the freedom of the native people.

Portuguese orphan boys played a singular role in the Brazil missions. Nóbrega placed them among native boys – so that the orphans learned Tupi and the natives, Portuguese – and went into the jungle with them. When he went to the villages, he would take with him a small choir: the boys' songs were one of the most effective means of engaging the interest of the native people. For hearing the confession of Indians and mestizos who did not know the confessors' language, he opted for the use of boys as interpreters.

In 1552 Pedro Fernandes Sardinha, bishop of Salvador, forbade this form of confession. He allowed native people and settlers to stay together at the liturgical assembly. Nevertheless, in the face of the Bishop's contrary opinion, in 1554 he had to adopt the custom of dismissing the catechumens at the moment of the offertory.

Nóbrega fought the abuses committed against the native people and strove for Portuguese legislation to support them – he started petitions to free the Indians who had been unjustly captured. He proposed the creation of villages to shelter those native communities who had accepted the Jesuits in exchange for protection from the Portuguese settlers.

He wrote *Letters from Brazil* (1549–70), *Dialogues on the Conversion of the Heathen* (1566–67), and *Civilizing Plan* (1558). These texts deal with the need to catechize the native people, their defense against the white invader, the defense of Christian moral supremacy, and the protection offered by the Portuguese to the natives from the cannibalism believed to be practiced by certain groups.

In *Dialogues on the Conversion of the Heathen* (1566–67) – the first literary work written in Brazil – Nóbrega's fundamental thought is that the non-Christians are capable of conversion given proper education, acculturation, and the help of divine grace. He believed that to achieve this end, external circumstances must be created within a system of paternalistic authority focused on the education of children.

He closed the doors of confession to those who lived publicly out of wedlock or owned unjustly bought slaves. In Nóbrega's view, a man may only renounce his freedom in order to save his life or in other analogous situations, not for a price. Since individual freedom is a natural right, it can be lost solely by causes founded in natural law, not by a mistake or by tyranny. Nóbrega made this argument in 1567 while discussing a recent law that sanctioned "voluntary slavery," when a father sold his child out of great necessity or when an adult sold himself. Nóbrega's *Answer* marks the beginning of philosophy of law in Brazil.

The fathers of the Society of Jesus could baptize adults who were already married according to natural law, excusing them from all positive law. But for those already baptized, canon law authorized their marriage only up to the fourth degree of consanguinity. Nóbrega insisted on a dispensation from these strictures. The brief *Cum gratiarum omnium*, by Pope Pius V (December 15, 1567) allowed the Jesuits of the Portuguese Empire to dispense from all the impediments of positive law.

Nóbrega died on October 18, 1570, at the college of Rio de Janeiro.

See also Brazil; Portugal

Leite, Serafim, *História da Companhia de Jesus no Brasil*. Vols. I–II. Lisbon/Rio de Janeiro: Civilização Brasileira, 1938.

Monumenta Brasiliae. 4 vols. Rome: Monumenta Historica Societatis Iesu, 1956–60.

Novas páginas da história do Brasil. Lisbon: Academia Portuguesa da História, 1962, pp. 3–129.

Danilo Mondoni, SJ

Nouvelle Théologie

Nouvelle théologie is a theological movement attempting to renew theology by a return to biblical and patristic sources. It is associated with the period 1930–60 and the Jesuit faculty at Fourvière, France. Since there was never a specific group of theologians who self-identified as representing a group by this name, a list of those associated with this movement varies from author to author. They certainly include the Jesuits Jean Daniélou, Henri de Lubac, Gaston Fessard, Henri Bouillard, and Pierre Teilhard de Chardin, although the Belgian Dominican M.-D. Chenu is also commonly associated with the thought of this group. The list also includes Hans Urs von Balthasar, who studied theology in Fourvière as a Jesuit.

The first to use the term *la nouvelle théologie* was an Italian, Msgr. Parente, in the February 1942 issue of *L'Osservatore Romano* in reference to two Dominican theologians, M.-D. Chenu and L. Charlier. Réginald Garrigou-Lagrange used it to refer to certain Jesuit theologians in 1946. Those associated with the movement tried to distance themselves from the term, de Lubac calling its existence a "myth," Bouillard saying he had no such aspirations, and Congar calling it "an abusive term." The term strangely contradicts the attempt of these theologians to renew theology by returning to scriptural, patristic, and liturgical sources. The movement was named by its detractors, who feared it to be a return to Modernism.

Jean Daniélou outlined the general orientation of this "new theology" in an article, "Les orientations présentes de la pensée religieuse," in which he noted the gulf that had opened up between theology and the pressing concerns of the day. He lamented a progressive rupture between exegesis and systematic theology, each developing according to its own method, with a resulting aridity within systematic theology. The "new" orientation aimed at a reunification of theology through a return to Scripture, the Fathers, and a liturgical revival. The biblical renewal incorporated an interpretation of the Old Testament that restored its character as prophecy and figure, thereby underscoring its relation to the New Testament. The revival of patristic studies naturally followed the biblical renewal since the work of the Fathers was a commentary on Scripture incorporating just such a figurative interpretation of the Old Testament. The liturgical renewal reaffirmed the sign value of the liturgy and sought to better understand the symbolic elements of liturgical worship to balance a one-sided emphasis on the efficacy of liturgical action.

The *nouvelle théologie* is characterized by the French language of its primary figures, its emphasis on the category of history, its appeal to a positive theology and an inductive method over against a more speculative and deductive theology, and, finally, its critical attitude toward neo-scholasticism in which the conceptual system had priority over the relationship between theology, faith, and life (Mettepenningen, *Nouvelle Théologie*, 9–11). Additional identifying attributes include its emphasis on the "economy" of the saving action of God in history as contrasted with a matrix of doctrines, its return to the dogma of the Mystical Body of Christ as foundational to the social identity of Catholicism, its preference for a kerygmatic theology which announces the Word of God, and its emphasis on the existential dimensions of theology and its impact on a life of faith.

M.-Michel Labourdette, M.-J. Nicolas, and R. Garrigou-Lagrange, all Dominicans and outspoken critics of the *nouvelle théologie*, defended scholasticism against what they perceived to be a theological approach that would jeopardize the immutability of doctrine and would fall into historical relativism. The Jesuits responded in what became a spirited exchange of articles. Joseph Komonchak points to the political ramifications of the debate insofar as Garrigou-Lagrange was a supporter of *Action française* and a defender of Vichy, while many of the Jesuits associated with the *nouvelle théologie* resisted Nazism and the regime in occupied Vichy. When interpreted within its historical context, the *nouvelle théologie* is an argument for the relevance and prophetic voice of Christianity in a cultural milieu threatened by secularism, racism, and anti-Semitism.

Pius XII's encyclical *Humani generis* (1950) put a damper on the *nouvelle théologie* insofar as some thought that it targeted de Lubac's work on the supernatural, a charge that de Lubac vigorously denied. Nevertheless, he was removed from teaching for a time and a number of his books were removed from libraries and bookstores. The movement and its proponents were vindicated when some were appointed as *periti* at the Second Vatican Council.

See also Daniélou, Jean Cardinal, SJ; France; Lubac, Henri de, SJ; Teilhard de Chardin, Pierre, SJ; Theology

Komonchak, Joseph, "Theology and Culture at Mid-Century: The Example of Henri de Lubac." *Theological Studies* 51 (1990), 579–602.

Labourdette, Michel, Marie-Joseph Nicolas, and Raymond-Léopold Bruckberger. *Dialogue théologique: pièces du débat entre "La Revue Thomiste" d'une part et les R.R. P.P. de Lubac, Daniélou, Bouillard, Fessard, von Balthasar, SJ, d'autre part.* Saint-Maximin: Les Arcades, 1947.

Mettepenningen, Jürgen, *Nouvelle Théologie–New Theology: Inheritor of Modernism, Precursor of Vatican II.* New York: T & T Clark, 2010.

Susan K. Wood

Novels

The appearance of Jesuits in novels is frequent and widespread. This is not to say, however, that such appearances were always flattering. In the novels of Czarist Russia and Victorian England, where Jesuits were often looked upon with suspicion, they were often portrayed as scheming, conniving characters with less than holy intentions. In Leo Tolstoy's epic *War and Peace* (1869), the young and beautiful Hélène, desiring to be freed from a previous marriage to wed her lover, is introduced to the aged French Jesuit de Jobert, who charms the moneyed princess with lofty spiritual conversation, causing her eyes to well with tears as "their voices trembled." De Jobert enables Hélène to remarry by bringing her into the Catholic Church, an effort, it is divulged, ultimately designed "to obtain money from her for Jesuit institutions." In Fyodor Dostoevsky's *The Idiot* (1869), Prince Myshkin learns "in horror" that his benefactor Pavlischev was converted to Catholicism by the Jesuits, only to be further informed that the Jesuits "put in a claim under [Pavlischev's] will" when he died.

A more ambiguous portrayal is found in Alexandre Dumas's popular French novels, including *The Three Musketeers* (1844), where a Jesuit and diocesan priest are lampooned for engaging in abstruse, petty arguments in ecclesiastical Latin, and *The Vicomte de Bragelonne* (1850), in which one of the musketeers, Aramis, lays down his sword to become, in a playful twist, the general of the Society of Jesus in his final act.

In the early twentieth century, James Joyce, who was educated at three different Jesuit schools in Ireland, cast his former teachers in a critical light in his first novel, the Modernist *Künstlerroman, A Portrait of the Artist as a Young Man* (1916). Having already appeared in the short stories of *The Dubliners* (1914), Jesuits also turned up in the pages of *Ulysses* (1922) and *Finnegan's Wake* (1939). In spite of Joyce's piquant critique of the religious milieu of his youth, his portrayal of the Jesuits is often conflictive, blending criticism with esteem. In *A Portrait*, when Stephen Daedelus, Joyce's fictional alter ego, is invited by the Jesuit director of the school to consider becoming a Jesuit himself, the youth reflects upon the faces of Jesuits "he had so often seen on wintry mornings," "eyeless and sourfavoured and devout." "His masters," Daedelus notes, "even when they had not attracted him, had seemed to him always intelligent and serious priests."

Various preeminent Catholic authors of the twentieth century wrote novels featuring protagonists based upon heroic Jesuit exemplars. In 1935 Evelyn Waugh released the elegant work of historical fiction *Edmund Campion* (1935), a literary homage to the English Jesuit martyr. In 1939 Graham Greene devoted the prologue of *The Lawless Roads*, a travel account of his journeys in Mexico, to the story of Miguel Pro, a Mexican Jesuit executed by an anticlerical regime in 1927. A year later, Greene's critically acclaimed classic *The Power and the Glory* (1940) featured an unnamed protagonist priest who dies a martyr's death before a Mexican firing squad shouting the same words as Pro: "Viva Cristo Rey!"

Waugh and Greene each enjoyed personal friendships with individual Jesuits, something also true of Flannery O'Connor. In O'Connor's darkly comedic short story "The Enduring Chill," a dying young writer named Asbury is impressed by a Jesuit priest, Ignatius Vogle. Later, Asbury makes a final request to see a priest, "preferably a Jesuit," so that "he could talk to a man of culture before he died."

In 1966 Japanese Catholic author Shusaku Endo published *Silence*, a provocative novel of historical fiction about a persecuted Jesuit missionary in seventeenth-century Japan. The recipient of multiple Japanese literary prizes, *Silence* probes the question of how God relates to suffering through the life and moral dilemmas of Jesuit Father Sebastian Rodrigues. Endo ultimately intimates that God does not merely remain "with folded arms, silent," but came "to share men's pain" in carrying the cross. In 2016 a film version of *Silence*, directed by Martin Scorsese, premiered worldwide.

Multiple other novels with Jesuit protagonists have been made into films, including William Peter Blatty's *The Exorcist* (1971) and Brian Moore's *Black Robe* (1985). Jesuits have also become favored religious characters of science fiction authors, playing leading roles in Arthur C. Clarke's "The Star" (1955) and Mary Doria Russell's *The Sparrow* (1996). They have likewise been featured in recent historical mystery novels, such as the Charles du Luc series of Judith Rock and the Shinobi mysteries of Susan Spann.

Ever since Italian Jesuit Antonio Bresciani (1798–1862) published his serial novels in the pages of *La Civiltà Cattolica*, there have also been Jesuit novelists. The latest of these is the American Jesuit author James Martin, whose debut novel *The Abbey* was released in 2015.

See also Alumni/ae; Film and Television: Themes and Characters; Science Fiction

Bradley, Bruce, "'At School Together in Commee's Time': Some Notes on Joyce's Clongowes Jesuits." *Dublin James Joyce Journal* 3 (2010), 1–18.

Brennan, Michael, "Graham Greene, Evelyn Waugh and Mexico." *Renascence: Essays on Values in Literature* 55 (2002), 7–23.

Cavanaugh, William, "The God of Silence: Shusaku Endo's Reading of the Passion." *Commonweal* 125 (1998), 10–12.

Harrison, Elizabeth, "The Image of the Jesuit in Russian Literary Culture of the Nineteenth Century." *Modern Languages* 1 (2014), 1–17.

Henry Shea, SJ

Novena of Grace

The Novena of Grace is a nine-day devotion honoring Saint Francis Xavier and calling upon his intercession for specific graces. This popular devotion, which has traditionally been celebrated from March 4 through March 12, consists of various prayers and sermons as well as a celebration of the Eucharist and adoration of the Blessed Sacrament anticipating the anniversary of the saint's canonization on the final day. Originating in Naples, the Novena was initially carried out as a private devotion until its public practice began to spread across Europe in the latter half of the seventeenth century.

Traditionally, the Novena was connected with the miraculous recovery of Fr. Marcello Mastrilli, a young Jesuit priest on the brink of death. On December 11, 1633, Mastrilli suffered a hard hit to the head from a heavy hammer that slipped away from a worker's hand from a height of 34 feet. After days of severe pain, Mastrilli prayed for healing through the intercession of St. Francis Xavier and promised to offer his life to the Jesuit mission in the Indies once his health improved. Holding the saint's relic in his hands, an hour later he was completely cured. Remaining true to his promise, Mastrilli went to Japan and was martyred in Nagasaki on October 17, 1637.

After the cure, some of Mastrilli's biographers claim that the saint continued to appear to him, promising similar intercessional healing grace to those who committed themselves to the Novena. The popularity of the Novena has grown not only because of the saint's power of intercession but because of the special indulgences granted by various popes since the eighteenth century to those who made the devotion. This Novena continues in various Jesuit apostolates to this day.

See also Xavier, Francis, SJ, St.

Thompson, Robert, *Handbook of the Novena of Grace Made in Honour of St. Francis Xavier: March 4th to March 12th.* Dublin: Irish Messenger Publications, 1978.

Hưng Trung Phạm, SJ

Novitiate, Novice

A man who believes himself to have a vocation to the Society of Jesus, after having been interviewed and assessed, may be admitted to the novitiate and live as a Jesuit novice for a period of two years, in order to verify his vocation. The novitiate is essentially a time of probation, of radical disconnection and reorientation, to test whether or not God is indeed calling the man to life in the Society and whether he has sufficient interior freedom to be able to choose to follow Christ as a Jesuit.

The verification of the call is carried out by means of the six principal experiments as outlined by St. Ignatius in the *Constitutions*. Of central importance is the experience of the thirty-day *Spiritual Exercises*, in which a novice comes to know through personal experience that a Jesuit is one who is a sinner, yet is loved and called to be a companion of Christ, to help in his salvific mission.

It is vital that novices come to understand the charism of the Society as an apostolic body committed to advancing the Kingdom and saving souls. To that end, novices must complete a close reading of the founding documents (*Formula of the Institute, General Examen*), the so-called *Autobiography of St. Ignatius*, the *Constitutions and Their Complementary Norms*, and the decrees of the last few General Congregations.

If, at the end of the two-year novitiate, a novice has shown "an initial, but tested and authentic, connaturality with our way of proceeding," he may be admitted to first vows (Kolvenbach, *Formation of Jesuits*, 25).

See also Experiment; Formation

The Constitutions of the Society of Jesus and Their Complementary Norms. Ed. John W. Padberg. St. Louis, MO: The Institute of Jesuit Sources, 1996.
Kolvenbach, Peter-Hans, *The Formation of Jesuits*. Rome: General Curia of the Society of Jesus, 2003.

Keith Maczkiewicz, SJ

Obedience

When Ignatius of Loyola and his companions decided in 1539 to vow obedience to one of their number, they effectively determined to found a new religious order of global reach. Thus would they fulfill their desire, aroused by the Gospel through the *Spiritual Exercises* and expressed in their vow at Montmartre in 1534, to be companions of Jesus. The confidence they had in this discernment, recorded as the *Deliberation of the First Fathers*, enabled them to imagine, in the *Formula of the Institute* (1540, revised 1550), a brotherhood structured for apostolic discernment and articulated by relations of obedience. Based roughly on the mendicant orders, their institute's supreme body, the General Congregation, would represent the whole Society in electing their superior general but would otherwise meet as seldom as possible, investing him with authority to govern between meetings. Members would make a special vow of obedience to the pope "with regard to the progress of souls and the propagation of the faith, or wherever he may be pleased to send us" (1540 *Formula*, para. 3).

The *Constitutions of the Society of Jesus*, when they appeared, took an unusual and characteristically dynamic form. Instead of a scholastic treatise beginning with the "end" and then elaborating the means, they followed a developmental logic, starting with the individual Jesuit's admission, formation, and incorporation before addressing the purpose of the Society, which is the missioning and being missioned of Jesuits. Ignatius wrote the *Constitutions* while the shape of the Society was still settling, and he aimed at flexibility and adaptability. In effect, the *Constitutions* institutionalize the "discernment of spirits" of the *Spiritual Exercises* as a mode of apostolic decision-making and execution within a globally extended Society, and obedience, as Ignatius understood it, was key.

Jesuit obedience is sometimes depicted as "military" and Ignatius as a "soldier," appealing to a misunderstanding of the term "superior general." Militaristic language does appear in the *Exercises*, the *Formula*, and the *Constitutions*. But though he participated in battle, Ignatius was never a soldier in our modern sense; furthermore, his images for obedience owe more to chivalric notions through which, in the *Exercises*, he explained what it was to choose in personal freedom to follow Christ.

The only section of the *Constitutions* devoted specifically to obedience occurs as part of the treatment of the personal life of Jesuits in Part VI. Ignatius desired that Jesuits distinguish themselves in it "not only in the matters of obligation but also in the others" and devote "very special care to the virtue of obedience shown first to the sovereign pontiff and then to the superiors of the Society" (#547). He used a rhetoric of "blind obedience," giving edifying examples such as the willingness to "leave unfinished any letter" of the alphabet in order to obey with alacrity, and images such as the "lifeless body" (*perinde ac cadaver*) and the "old man's staff" (#547). In 1553 Ignatius had cause to write to the Jesuits in Portugal and this "Letter on Obedience" was cited by both friends and enemies of the Society in defense of the idea of "blind obedience." The *Constitutions* themselves, however, provide a richer account than these traditional tropes, by appealing directly to each Jesuit's experience of the *Exercises* and his resulting strong desire to obey "God our Creator and Lord." Jesuits would therefore wish to obey "not as men troubled by fear" but "in a spirit of love," ready to receive the command "just as if it were coming from Christ our Savior" (#547), showing great "reverence" and "warm love" to their superiors who make possible the following of this vocation (#551). In the requirement to manifest their consciences to their superiors, keeping hidden "nothing exterior or interior" so that those superiors would be "the better able to direct them in everything along the path of salvation and perfection" (#551), they would recognize the key mechanism of spiritual discernment, as well as Ignatius's own experience of general confession. Ignatius deployed the traditional distinction between three degrees of obedience developmentally: Jesuits will desire to progress from the least perfect (merely *executing* the command), to the more perfect (executing and *willing* it), and ultimately to the most perfect (executing, willing, and successfully aligning one's *judgment* to the superior's) (#550). This ideal is actually the opposite of blind obedience: at its most perfect, the Society would be a single body agreeing freely, willingly, and with full understanding, if from differing points of view, on the means to their common end.

Beyond the personal asceticism of Jesuits, obedience is structurally fundamental to Parts VII (missioning and being missioned), VIII (means to retain union among Jesuits), and IX (governing the global Society of Jesus). Regarding missions, Ignatius begins with the "special" or "fourth vow" of obedience to the pope, intended to help the Society "avoid erring in the path of the Lord" (#605). This, however, referred not to the loyalty owed to the pope by every Catholic, in which Jesuits desired in any case to be exemplary. Rather, it was an application to their original desire to be sent "to any regions whatsoever" of the Ignatian principle that "the more universal the good, the more divine" (#622). For, as they saw it, the pope possessed the more universal view and would be in the best position to determine where they could be most fruitfully sent. It was, therefore, a mode of apostolic discernment; and its "entire purport … was and is with regard to missions" (#529). Actually, the *Constitutions* envision such papal missions as limited and rather restless journeyings: "the original design of our Institute" was, as they put it, "to travel through various regions, staying for longer or shorter times in accordance with the fruit that is seen" (#626). Those sent should ask the pope for precise instructions, in writing, regarding means and purpose; they should represent to him any problems or advice, including the abandonment of the mission, "while finally leaving the entire matter to the decision of His Holiness" (#607). Obedience by no means precluded judgment or creativity: on the contrary, no opportunity for some initiative giving hope of fruitful "service to God our Lord" should – "without prejudice to the principal mission and intention of the sovereign pontiff" – be neglected (#616).

The same principles applied to obedience to a Jesuit superior: obedience "is not violated if someone represents the motions [a technical term in Ignatian spirituality] and thoughts that occur to him contrary to an order received, meanwhile submitting his entire judgment and will to the judgment and will of his superior who is in the place of Christ" (#627). The *Constitutions* recognize that this demands from both superiors and subjects great psychological and spiritual maturity (the "mortification" of vices) (#657) and provide certain helps, especially the provision of "consultors" for each superior whose advice he is obliged to hear but not necessarily to follow (#810) or the "collateral associate" (no longer used) who, neither under obedience to the superior nor interfering in his legitimate authority, accompanies him in the exercise of his office (#659).

The hierarchy of obedience within the Society is notably short, from the more "universal" to the less: "It is thus from the general as head that all authority of the provincial should flow, from the provincials that of the local superiors, and from the local superiors that of the individual members" (#666). Presupposed in this is the principle of subsidiarity: the legitimate authority of superiors at each level should only exceptionally and for good reasons be short-circuited either by appeals from below or interventions from above (#662). At the apex, the superior general is elected for life (#719) and has "complete authority" to summon General Congregations, appoint provincials and assign missions (##736–65). But his authority is itself subject to a still more universal perspective, namely, that of the whole Society either represented in a General Congregation or through the assistants elected by the Congregation for that purpose and empowered to convoke a Congregation if necessary. "This arrangement is made so that all may have full power for good and that, if they do poorly, they may be fully in subjection" (#820).

Thus obedience, a structure for apostolic discernment, is also a means to the necessary apostolic unity of the Society, insofar as all within it seek, as in the *Exercises*, the will of God above all else. For then the love of God will almost of itself circulate throughout, among, and between members, both subjects and superiors, in the form of charity and all the virtues (#671). The primary means of preserving and increasing the Society, that is to say, must be spiritual: "the means which unite the human instrument with God and so dispose it that it may be wielded well by his divine hand are more effective than those which equip it in relation to human beings" (#813). Not that the latter are unnecessary: superiors should employ "all possible love, modesty and charity in our Lord, so that subjects may be disposed to have greater love than fear for their superiors, though at times both are useful" (#667). Superiors should leave some matters to their subjects, accompanying them and sympathizing with them, and visiting their communities regularly (#670). Such love will be sustained by frequent communication, especially letters, for which the *Constitutions* made precise recommendations (##673–76).

The *Constitutions*, then, presuppose considerable spiritual maturity and provide great flexibility in the hands of a creative leader like Ignatius, who in 1540 famously dispatched Francis Xavier to India with enormous latitude and with spectacular results. When the Society began receiving requests to start or run colleges and universities, Ignatius did not take long to respond positively and vigorously, radically broadening thereby the "original vision." Adaptability, raised to a missionary principle, was key to the success of missions to India, Japan and China, and the New World. It was also, however, near the center of controversies such as the "Chinese Rites" and "Malabar Rites" that precipitated determined opposition to the Society. Together with the "Jesuit position" in arguments with Dominicans and Jansenists about free will, they enabled its enemies to associate the Society with disobedience and disloyalty, and contributed to the complex processes leading to its suppression in 1773.

The Society's reconstitution of itself after the restoration in 1814, though highly successful in terms of numbers and institutions, was shaped by a reactionary international and ecclesiastical climate and the limited array of documentary resources rescued from the dissolution of Jesuit houses. What was restored was a Jesuit past represented in a collection mostly of normative documents: the *Spiritual Exercises*, the *Constitutions*, and the *Ratio studiorum*, certain letters of Ignatius, some specific ordinances of superiors general, and rules regulating daily life. From these emerged an obedience conceived primarily as an ascetical matter achieved through the "Observation of Rules," the title of a treatise in *The Practice of Perfection and Christian Virtues*, a seventeenth-century exhortatory text prominent in post-restoration Jesuit formation until the mid-twentieth century. Meanwhile, however, a wider range of sources was gradually reassembled and, when the Second Vatican Council (1962–65) called for the renewal of the original charisms of religious institutes, the Jesuits had a head start.

The story of the Society of Jesus after the Second Vatican Council is of its response to the arrival of postmodernity, in which issues of authority and obedience, including obedience to Church and pope, were central. The Jesuits successfully retrieved from their tradition an understanding of obedience as a mode of both union and apostolic discernment, and reaffirmed it at subsequent General Congregations. Nevertheless, and perhaps in consequence, their obedience to Church and pope was again questioned.

The Society's response to the Second Vatican Council came in its General Congregation 31 (1965–66) which elected Pedro Arrupe as superior general and produced a new and influential vision of its identity and mission. Its decree on obedience, "conscious of the social change in our day which gives rise to a new awareness of the brotherhood of men and a keener sense of liberty and personal responsibility, along with an excessively critical attitude and an overly naturalistic view of the world," did not retreat from the vision of the *Constitutions* but did strike some distinctive notes (Decree 17, #1). It acknowledged for the first time, and even offered a remedy for, the problems of conscience that could arise, arguing that Jesuit obedience did not take away but rather presupposed the obligation of personal responsibility, and that even obedience of judgment could be achieved without abusing the intellect or going against reason or the evidence of truth (##10–12).

In the turbulent reactions of the 1960s and 1970s, particularly to Paul VI's encyclical *Humanae vitae* and to liberation theology, it was the obedience and loyalty of the Society under Pedro Arrupe in doctrinal matters that were questioned. General Congregation 32 (1974–75) admitted Jesuit mistakes but comprehensively confirmed Arrupe's leadership, even refocusing the Society's constitutive mission as the "struggle for faith and that struggle for justice which it includes" (Decree 2, #2). It also made more explicit the communitarian dimension of Jesuit apostolic discernment as involving the participation of both subjects and superiors (Decree 11, #18). It acknowledged a tension in practice between, on the one hand, the "reverence and fidelity" owed by Jesuit teachers to the magisterium and to the pope and, on the other, the Jesuits' "proper responsibility" to the Church (Decree 3, ##1, 2). As the Congregation proceeded, the Society had its own direct and painful experience of obedience when, following a mandate from the previous Congregation, it addressed the numerous petitions (*postulata*) from Jesuits regarding the distinction of grades in the Society. Pope Paul VI's intimation that he did not favor any change in this matter was not understood by the Congregation as a prohibition of what it regarded as its duty in obedience: namely, to represent its discerned view to its superior, the pope, while affirming his right to make the final determination. To Paul, this seemed to be disobedience, if not defiance.

Pope John Paul II, elected in 1978, also seemed at first to mistrust the Society and Pedro Arrupe. When Arrupe suffered an incapacitating stroke in 1981, John Paul suspended the prescribed procedure for electing a successor and appointed his own vicar, a Jesuit, Fr. Paulo Dezza, arousing fears of a second suppression. Normal governance of the Society was restored, however, in just over a year. Concerns about the loyalty of Jesuit theologians resurfaced under Pope Benedict XVI, who in 2008 felt it necessary to remind General Congregation (GC) 35 of the Society's "vow of immediate obedience to the Successor of Peter *perinde ac cadaver*," and to hope that the Congregation would "reaffirm, in the spirit of St. Ignatius, its own total adhesion to Catholic doctrine" (GC 35, Letter to Fr. Kolvenbach, January 10, 2008). In a later audience, however, Benedict expressed a more reassuring confidence; and in its decree on obedience, the Congregation responded with a robust description of the fourth vow as that which gives the Society structural incorporation into the life of the Church and guarantees the universality of its mission (Decree 4, #31).

The Jesuits have also made structural changes to the institutions of the Society which affect their practice of obedience. The role of local superiors, situated between the provincial who gives the mission and the subject who receives it, was perhaps never easy to delineate in practice. Now local superiors have to adapt to the assumption of General Congregation 32 that communities, not only individuals, receive missions, and to its requirement that each Jesuit discern, together with his superior but under the latter's final decision, how to fulfill his mission (Decree 11, #18). The increasingly important distinction between local superiors and "directors of works" who have "true religious authority in directing the efforts" of Jesuits (#29) was further complicated when General Congregation 34 acknowledged that that director may be a layperson (Decree 13, #13).

The creation of new structures for "interprovincial and supraprovincial cooperation" was recommended by General Congregation 31 in the form of standing conferences of the major superiors of roughly continental regions (Decree 48), and their status and operation were addressed at General Congregations 34 and 35. They may need to be revisited. While these conferences "do not constitute a new level of government between the General and the Provincials" and have no faculty to own and administer funds in their own right, they are "oriented for mission" rather than merely for coordination, are expected to do apostolic planning at the interprovincial level, and may have works and houses directly dependent on them (GC 35, Decree 5). Some conference statutes empower their presidents to mission Jesuits to interprovincial works; most, however, can only request men from their provincials (GC 35, Decree 5).

Especially in mission territories, many Jesuits have been ordained bishops; more recently, a Jesuit has been elected pope. Ignatius himself resisted the pressure sometimes placed on Jesuits to accept bishoprics; the *Constitutions* require each professed Jesuit to promise not to ambition for any prelacy and, if they were ordained bishop, always to be willing to listen to the views of the superior general (#817). A Jesuit bishop, and *a fortiori* a Jesuit pope, cannot receive a mission from a Jesuit superior and does not cease to be a bishop on retirement, even if he chooses to live in a Jesuit community.

New challenges for the traditional practice of obedience are posed by increasingly corporate styles of governance in Jesuit institutions. Jesuits now work through boards of trustees, governors, and management that are more closely regulated by civil law, and demand new sensitivities and modes of planning, participation, and accountability. On the other hand, secular management consultants claim to have found helpful models of leadership in traditional Jesuit practices of obedience, such as the combination of "indifference" (the ability to both give and take orders), quick and effective decision-making, subsidiarity, creativity, and adaptability.

See also Chastity; Community; *Constitutions*; Mission; Papacy; Poverty; Province, Provincial; Superior General

Padberg, John W., ed., *Jesuit Life and Mission Today: The Decrees and Accompanying Documents of the 31st–35th General Congregations of the Society of Jesus.* St. Louis, MO: The Institute of Jesuit Sources, 2009.

Stephen Buckland, SJ

Ogilvie, John, SJ, St. (1579–1615)

Born in 1579 into a well-to-do Calvinist family in Banffshire, Scotland, Ogilvie was educated at Regensburg and at the Jesuit College at Olmutz. A convert to Catholicism, he joined the Jesuits in Brno, southern Moravia, in 1599. On completion of his studies, he was sent to France and was ordained in Paris in 1611. Assigned to the Jesuit College in Rouen, he asked to be sent back to his native Scotland. Masquerading as a horse trader under the name of Captain Watson, he landed at Leith in the fall of 1613 accompanied by another Jesuit, Fr. Moffet. Having ministered initially in the area between Aberdeen and Banff, after Christmas 1613 he went to Edinburgh.

Early the following year, Ogilvie made a mysterious visit to London; some think it was to try to negotiate a *modus vivendi* for Scottish Catholics with the government. He went to Paris, possibly to report on his activities, but received a cool reception from his superiors and was summarily sent back to Scotland. Again in Edinburgh, he soon transferred his apostolic labors to Glasgow, hoping to make converts or reconcile lapsed Catholics to the Church. Betrayed by Adam Boyd, who had expressed an interest in Catholicism, he was brought before the Protestant archbishop of Glasgow, John Spottiswode. The encounter was not a happy one. Ogilvie was taken to Edinburgh where he was tortured, but did not reveal any of the names of his Catholic associates. Returned to Glasgow for trial, he wrote from prison a number of letters to his Jesuit brethren, including father general, discussing the circumstances of his capture, and the inducements his jailers offered him to abandon the faith. Executed at Glasgow Cross on February 28, 1615, he flung his rosary from the scaffold, and it struck Jean de Eckersdorft, who subsequently became a Catholic. Ogilvie was canonized by Pope Paul VI in October 1976.

See also Martyrs, Ideal and History; United Kingdom

Carrell, Christopher, and Mark Dilworth, eds., *St. John Ogilvie SJ, 1579–1615.* Glasgow: Third Eye Centre, 1979.
Collins, Thomas, *Martyr in Scotland: The Life and Times of John Ogilvie.* London: Burns and Oates, 1955.

Oliver P. Rafferty, SJ

O'Keefe, Vincent T., SJ (1917–2012)

Father Vincent O'Keefe, SJ, stands out as a major figure for implementing the Jesuit response to the Second Vatican Council. At General Congregation 31 in Rome in 1965 he was elected to serve as one of four general assistants to the newly elected Jesuit superior general, the Rev. Pedro Arrupe, SJ.

The years following the Second Vatican Council brought vast changes in an extremely short period of time. What had seemed changeless, such as the Tridentine Latin Mass, was suddenly changing. The Jesuits were in the middle of this whirlwind of change.

"Vinnie" and "Don Pedro" Arrupe became fast friends. And seven years later, in the midst of several critiques of the direction the Jesuits were taking, General Congregation 32 (1974–75) strongly affirmed the leadership of Father Arrupe, and it laid out a new articulation of its mission: a fundamental commitment to faith and justice. Jesuits throughout the world, but especially in Latin America, worked on behalf of the disadvantaged and oppressed and challenged the elite establishment, often facing reprisals from military governments.

Jesuit theologians, such as Jon Sobrino and Richard McCormick, offered critical, theological assessments of the practices of the Church.

Some of the leading cardinals in the Vatican were not at all pleased. Some Catholics accustomed to an unchanging Church felt threatened by these "revolutionary" steps taken by the Society of Jesus. Father O'Keefe was at the vortex of all these currents. Through it all he provided balance, kept his genial composure, and offered his wise counsel in the deliberations with Father Arrupe and the leadership council.

The gathering storm came to a head in 1981. On returning from a trip to Asia, Father Arrupe suffered a massive stroke at Fiumicino Airport in Rome. With his friend "Don Pedro" incapacitated, Father O'Keefe, in his role as vicar general informed the Vatican of the Jesuits' desire to hold a General Congregation to elect a successor to Father Arrupe. But Pope John Paul II reacted by initiating a form of papal receivership. He abruptly suspended the ordinary governance of the Society of Jesus. He had Father O'Keefe removed as vicar general, and in his stead, appointed Rev. Paolo Dezza, SJ, as his personal delegate to govern the Society of Jesus until such time as a General Congregation seemed timely. The Pope also appointed Giuseppe Pittau, the Jesuit provincial of Japan, as Father Dezza's assistant in governance since Dezza was in his eighties, and, although of sound mind, he was nearly blind.

This unprecedented decision by the Pope sent shock waves through the Society, but contrary to Vatican expectations, not a single Jesuit left the Society because of this extraordinary intervention. Father O'Keefe received the decision with great equanimity, but years later, these events also provided endless, humorous, sometimes poignant stories for Father O'Keefe to share with young Jesuits in formation. Father Dezza moved rather quickly and astutely to have the Pope agree to allowing him to convoke a General Congregation (GC). In September 1983, GC 33 elected Rev. Peter-Hans Kolvenbach as the successor to Father Arrupe.

After GC 33, Father O'Keefe returned to the United States where he continued to lead in other capacities, including as rector of the Jesuit community at Fordham University; as key staff person at the National Jesuit Conference for planning Assembly 89 at Georgetown University, the first-ever gathering of Jesuits and their colleagues from the twenty-eight Jesuit colleges and universities; and as superior of the Jesuit community at America House in Manhattan. Eventually he retired to Fordham University (2007) and then (2009–2012) the province infirmary at Murray-Weigel until his death.

During his years in Rome, Father O'Keefe was a lively commentator for ABC News for such events as the death of Pope Paul VI in 1978 and the two papal conclaves that followed. His friends affirmed that he was fluent in Latin, Italian, French, Spanish, and German, but always spoke with a strong Jersey accent.

He grew up in Jersey City, NJ, the youngest of eight children. He entered the Jesuits in 1937 at Wernersville, PA. He did philosophy studies at Woodstock College (1941–44) and taught for three years at Regis High School in New York City.

His studies led him to Europe and then back again to the United States: theology at Louvain, Belgium; tertianship in Germany; a doctorate at the Gregorian University in Rome. He taught theology at Woodstock College (1954–60) and then was in administration at Fordham, prior to succeeding Rev. Laurence J. McGinley, SJ, as president in 1963.

He was quick-witted and humorous, and a wonderful raconteur who was a welcomed presence in every Jesuit gathering.

See also Arrupe, Pedro SJ; Dezza, Paolo, SJ; John Paul II, United States of America; Vatican II

Archives of the New York province, which includes the "Obituary of Fr. Vincent T. O'Keefe, SJ," by Peter Schineller, SJ.

Patrick J. Howell, SJ

Oliva, Gian (Giovanni) Paolo, SJ (1600–1681)

Eleventh superior general of the Society of Jesus and celebrity preacher of Baroque Rome, Oliva was born on October 4, 1600, in Genoa, Italy, of an eminent patrician family. With an excellent education and a devoutly spiritual temperament already to his credit, he entered the Society in December 1616 in Rome. Likewise in Rome were his ordination to the priesthood (1628) and pronouncement of final vows (1633). Upon ordination he taught humanities at the Collegio Romano for several years and began what was to be a long, illustrious career as preacher, both in Rome and other Italian cities. In 1651 he was appointed preacher to the Papal Court by Pope Innocent X, a position of great prestige and responsibility which he held under the three successive popes (Alexander VII, Clement IX, and Clement X) as well, until his retirement in 1675.

Oliva's first experience with governance dates to 1641 with his appointment as superior of the community at Sant'Andrea al Quirinale, which included the novitiate of the Roman province. In 1651 he assumed the rectorship of the Collegio Germanico, serving in that office until 1654 (with a brief return in 1657 as interim rector) and achieving great success in reviving the fortunes of that institution. By 1661 the health of 80-year-old Father General Goswin Nickel had declined to such a degree that he could no longer effectively govern; hence, in June 1661 the 11th General Congregation elected Oliva as perpetual vicar general of the Society, possessing all necessary powers for governance and the right of succession. Succession took place in July 1664, Oliva serving as superior general until his own death in November 1681.

Even though Oliva strenuously opposed his own election and received only forty-nine of the eighty possible votes, rarely has the Society of Jesus had a man so eminently qualified on so many fronts – spiritual, intellectual, administrative, diplomatic, and cultural – serving as its superior general. Perhaps the greatest tribute to his abilities as the leader of this by now large, complex, international organization came from King Louis XIV of France, who publicly expressed his deep esteem for Oliva's "singular virtue ... stupendous political skill [and] extraordinary authority among princes" (ARSI, Vitae, 158, fol. 246, letter from French Jesuit Jean Adam), an opinion confirmed by the highly laudatory obituary published upon Oliva's death by the all-but-official periodical of the French court, the *Journal des Savants* (February 1682 issue).

In the late seventeenth century, the Society of Jesus was perhaps at the historical apex of its power and influence within the Catholic world (and beyond), but these were still perilous times for the Order often caught in the dangerous crossfires between the ambitions and wars of the European courts (especially France and Spain) in this "Age of Absolutism" and the clashes of authority between the papacy and the same secular powers (e.g., the clash between the Holy See and Gallicanism). Even within the Catholic world, Jesuits faced severe opposition and intrigue from other religious orders and other sectors within the Church (most notably the Jansenists) on matters of doctrinal interpretation (especially probabilism in the realm of moral theology) and, on the foreign mission front, of territoriality and methodology. Moreover, as always in the history of the Society, continual need for conflict resolution and disciplining by Father General Oliva rose from within the ranks of the Jesuits themselves, not all of whom were living up to the ideals of founder Ignatius of Loyola, especially with respect to worldly honors and ambitions (e.g., the cases of Austrian Father Eberhard Nithard and Portuguese Father Manuel Fernandes). Oliva was not able to always achieve the outcomes he desired, but for twenty years he succeeded in keeping the ship of the Society ably afloat and coursing forward amid ever-shifting, challenging waters.

One of the great celebrities of Baroque Europe, Oliva would, nonetheless, probably be all but forgotten today outside the Jesuit world were it not for his achievements as promoter of the fine arts, most specifically, his decisive role in promoting the dramatic Baroque decoration of the Jesuit churches of Rome, especially the mother church of the Gesù, whose spectacular *trompe l'oeil* ceiling was executed under commission from Oliva by the young artist Gaulli, protegé of eminent Roman artist Bernini. Oliva is also known to history as one of the few personal friends of (and, in effect, spiritual director to) Bernini, who supplied frontispieces to two volumes of Oliva's collected sermons. Several hundred sermons by Oliva were published in the last decades of his life, many posthumously published in Latin translation. Also published, just after his death, was a collection of his many letters to heads of state and other prominent personages of Europe, as well as a biblical commentary and preacher's aide, *In selecta Scripturae loca ethicae commentationes*.

See also Bernini, Gianlorenzo; Gesù, Rome; Superior General

Fois, Mario, "Il generale Gian Paolo Oliva tra obbedienza al Papa e difesa all'ordine." *Quaderni franzoniani* 5, 2 (1992), 29–40.

"Oliva, Jean Paul." In Augustin de Backer, Aloys de Backer, and Carlos Sommervogel, eds., *Bibliothèque de la Compagnie de Jésus*. Vol. V. Louvain: Éditions de la Bibliothèque SJ, Collège philosophique et théologique, 1960, pp. 1884–92.

Patrignani, Giuseppe, "Del R. P. Giampaolo Oliva, XI. Generale della Compagnia di Gesù." In *Menologio di pie memorie d'alcuni religiosi della Compagnia di Gesù*. Vol. IV. Madrid: Pezzana, 1730, pp. 189–91.

Franco Mormando

Ong, Walter J., SJ (1912–2003)

As a young Jesuit in 1968–69, I had the good fortune of living with Fr. Ong who manifested a voracious intellectual curiosity in conversations throughout that year. While recognizing that he was a polymath as well as a man of immense charm, friendliness, and modesty, I had no idea that he was so distinguished an intellectual, probably one of the three most accomplished twentieth-century American Jesuit thinkers along with Bernard Lonergan and John Courtney Murray. Ong successfully embodied within himself the key dimensions in the dynamic tension of Jesuit life. On the one hand, there is an existentialist concern with personal self-scrutiny, decisiveness, and self-appropriation that the *Spiritual Exercises* of St. Ignatius directs. On the other hand, there is a worldly reaching out to vast fields of human accomplishment, particularly, for Ong, how cultures come to organize knowledge, and that sweep is guided by the Ignatian prayer of "finding God in all things." As Ong said: "Inner-directedness is not antisocial. By inner-directedness I mean an attention to oneself in all one's dimensions. The drive comes from within but moves out" ("Interview with Walter Ong," in *An Ong Reader* [hereafter *OR*] 88). His solitary engagement as an author produced an extensive series of books and articles in diverse fields, and this wide range fashioned his identity as a personalist philosopher of culture.

His teaching career centered on his beloved St. Louis University where he taught for over thirty years and where he and the communications theorist Marshall McLuhan dialogued with one another in the 1930s and 1940s. Ong also lived in a distinguished international academic universe where he held visiting professorships at New York University, the University of Chicago, and Washington University among others. He was elected president of the large and influential Modern Language Association, and he lectured throughout the Americas and Europe but also in Africa, Asia, and the Middle East. He attributed his particular intellectual passion, noetics or the structures of our knowing, to two sources: his early training in a Thomistic philosophy that, in his case at least, opened to other non-philosophical domains, and a recommendation from McLuhan to look at the work of the Harvard intellectual historian Perry Miller who had written about the influence of the French philosopher Peter Ramus (1515–72) on colonial New England. These two sources led him to his own investigation of Ramus as a figure of transition from medieval culture to our modern worldview. At the heart of this transition for Ong was the development from an oral culture to a print culture in which knowledge would be mapped. "Ramus bridges antiquity and modern technology because he intensified and accentuated the visualist element in verbal cognition. What made this possible for him was the printing press" (*OR*, 82)

His interpretation of Ramus provided the foundation for Ong's ongoing investigations of the technologies through which we know and within which we fashion the meaning of our lives. These studies established the central place in his thought for the genius of interpersonal communication. In direct contrast to rhetoric with its maintenance of a defined position, Ong envisioned a dialogic culture of intellectual openness: "The dialogic approach means you don't know where you are coming out. You stand to be modified by the other man; he stands to be modified by you" (*OR*, 91) In addition to the premodern primary orality, Ong also held for a secondary orality "induced by radio and television." In contrast to many other cultural theorists, Ong formulated positive ways of dealing with technology and the secondary orality for a humanity that is "overwhelmed with awareness":

> [Oral] communication, which is built into existential actuality more directly than written, has within it a momentum that works for the removal of masks. Lovers try to strip off all masks. And in all communication, in so far as it is related to actual experience, there must be a movement of love. Those who have loved over many years may reach a point where almost all masks are gone. But never all … When the last mask comes off, sainthood is achieved, and the vision of God. But this can only be with death.
>
> ("The Writer's Audience Is Always a Fiction," *OR*, 425–26)

See also Rhetoric(s); Saint Louis University; United States of America

Farrell, Thomas J., *Walter Ong's Contributions to Cultural Studies*. Cresskill, NJ: Hampton Press, 2000.

Ong, Walter, *An Ong Reader: Challenges for Further Inquiry*. Ed. Thomas J. Farrell and Paul A. Soukup. Cresskill, NJ: Hamton Press, 2002.

    Orality and Literacy: The Technologizing of the Word. London: Methuen, 1982.

    Ramus, Method and the Decay of Dialogue. Cambridge, MA: Harvard University Press, 1958.

James Bernauer, SJ

Orate Pro Societate

While the Latin term *orate pro Societate* (pray for the Society) constitutes an essential part of the mission of all Jesuits, it is usually applied to the final assignment of the sick or elderly. The mission to pray for the Society is described eloquently in Part X of *The Constitutions of the Society of Jesus*. Since the Society of Jesus cannot be maintained by human means, "the first and appropriate means will be the prayers and Masses which ought to be offered for this holy intention." In current practice this includes the obligation to offer one Mass a month for the needs of both the Church and the Society. The Complementary Norms of the *Constitutions* (#244) further clarifies the mission: "Major superiors should give to our elderly and infirm members a special mission to pray for the Church and Society and to unite their personal sufferings and limitations to [it]."

The mission of the Jesuit, then, includes prayer, and the formation of a habit of personal and sacramental prayer. While the *Constitutions* do not set rules concerning how or when to pray, the Jesuit must find a balance between sufficient prayer and the needs of active ministry. This tension between contemplation and action remains constant in the life of the active Jesuit, and is monitored by superiors, spiritual directors, and confessors. But arriving at the maturity of later years when the active apostolate diminishes, the Jesuit is called to embrace the contemplative, offering the end of his life "for the Lord's blessing on the work of the Church and his fellow Jesuits."

See also Community; Mission

The Constitutions of the Society of Jesus and Their Complementary Norms. Ed. John W. Padberg. St. Louis, MO: The Institute of Jesuit Sources, 1996.
Padberg, John W., ed., *Jesuit Life and Mission Today: The Decrees and Accompanying Documents of the 31st–35th General Congregations of the Society of Jesus*. St. Louis, MO: The Institute of Jesuit Sources, 2009.

Mark A. Lewis, SJ

Paccanarists

The Society of the Faith of Jesus (or Fathers of the Faith) was founded by Niccolò Paccanari (1774–1811) in 1797. It drew immediate and controversial comparisons with the Society of Jesus, which was formally suppressed at this time. Though there were clear points of similarity (the group's name, codes of dress, a focus on popular missions, etc.), Paccanari had established a distinctive group and some of his emphases (the role of visions and ecstatic experiences, for example) had little in common with the Ignatian legacy. Plans to establish a female branch of the order were also an innovation. In 1799 there was a union with the Society of the Sacred Heart of Jesus (founded in 1794), and this marked the beginning of a period of expansion. Houses and schools were established in Germany, France, Holland, and England, and a motherhouse was established at Rome in 1801. By 1803 there were some 130 members of the order. Their missions and spiritual retreats acquired considerable popularity.

The Paccanarists also received criticism, however, from some ex-Jesuits, notably Luigi Mozzi de'Capitani who charged Paccanari with, as it were, hijacking the Jesuit legacy. More seriously, from 1801 Paccanari came under close scrutiny from the Holy Office for his "pretence of holiness" and his alleged sexual misconduct, and in 1806 he was sentenced to ten years' imprisonment. Over the coming years the congregation was abandoned by most of its members and became defunct.

It is notable that a number of former members and associates (for instance Luis Rozaven and Anton Kohlmann) played a significant role in the restored Society of Jesus.
See also Suppression

Castelli, Eva Fontana, "The Society of Jesus under Another Name: The Paccanarists in the Restored Society of Jesus." In Robert Maryks and Jonathan Wright, eds., *Jesuit Survival and Restoration: A Global History, 1773–1900*. Leiden: Brill, 2014, pp. 197–211.

Jonathan Wright

Pacific Worlds

Starting with Magellan's act of naming the planet's largest body of water, Europeans left their cultural and political mark on the Pacific Ocean, its wide-ranging coasts, and innumerable islands. Jesuits took an active role in this process. The establishment of the Manila galleon trade was particularly consequential because alongside forging powerful economic links between Asia, the Americas, and Europe, it opened up a major channel for the flow of Jesuit missionaries and materials.

New Spain, the galleon trade's anchor in the Americas, became the training center for European Jesuits on their way to Pacific missions and Asia. The lure of China loomed large for those who boarded the galleon and those stationed in New Spain. Chinese commodities reaching New Spain also proved highly attractive to Jesuits. They took such a liking to Chinese porcelain that a particular genre with Christian motifs became known as "Jesuit ware." However, the most crucial commodity that arrived with the galleon was information about Asia. New Spain quickly developed into the major hub for collecting, editing, printing, and distributing this information to audiences in the Americas and Europe.

Across the Pacific in Manila, the galleon's point-of-origin, Jesuits produced, printed, and packaged much information about Asia. China loomed larger still in the Philippines with its strong commercial ties to China and its sizable Chinese population. Spanish sources often referred to both China and the Philippines as "La Gran China," and China exerted such a pull on some Jesuits in the Philippines that General Claudio Acquaviva felt the need to issue a travel ban to forestall defections. Jesuits in the Philippines compiled pioneering studies of the indigenous peoples and the archipelago's fauna and flora. Brother Georg Kamel was the first to classify the archipelago's plants, animals, and minerals, and his plant descriptions were published by the famous English Naturalist John Ray in his *Historia plantarum* in 1703. Father Murillo Velarde put together the first major cartographic work for the Philippines that also featured depictions of various ethnic groups, cities, and islands, and key maritime routes such as the one to New Spain. Engraved in the Jesuit College press, Velarde's *Mapa hydrográfica* (1734) served as the benchmark for admiralty proceedings until the end of the eighteenth century.

Jesuits further made a mark on the islands where the galleon had its sole but central stopover in Guam. Magellan christened the archipelago Ladrones, and Spain claimed the islands in 1565. A colonial government was not established there until 1668 and then only because Father Diego de Sanvitores persuaded the Crown to fund and support the archipelago's evangelization with a boat and a garrison. Sanvitores subsequently changed the islands' name to Marianas in recognition of the mission's patronage by the Regent-Queen Mariana. Father Alonso López produced the first detailed map of Guam and the Mariana Islands. His cartographic work appeared in Father Charles Le Gobien's "Histoire des Isles Marianes" in 1700. Le Gobien's work did much to disseminate Jesuit information about the Marianas mission, the archipelago, and its Chamorro inhabitants to a broader European public. On the islands themselves, Jesuits became deeply embroiled in violent conflict between Spanish colonial authorities and a Chamorro resistance. They supported the late seventeenth-century relocation of the inhabitants of the northern islands to Guam, a reduction that hastened a dramatic demographic decline of the Chamorro population to levels near extinction. A high proportion of missionaries fell victim to bloodshed, and the Marianas gained a reputation as a place where martyrs were still being made, attracting many applicants from Europe.

The islands to the southwest of the Marianas that later became known as the Carolines also caught the attention of Jesuits in Manila and Guam. While the Society did not succeed in establishing a permanent mission in the Carolines, Jesuits produced vital ethnographic and geographic knowledge about this island world. Father Paul Klein questioned a group of Carolinian castaways in the Philippines in 1696 and summarized his findings about the archipelago and its inhabitants in a long letter that circulated widely. Klein is also credited with the first European map of the archipelago, which was drawn up from pebbles that the castaways laid out in the sand. The map reflects the distinct spatial perspective of Carolinian navigators and is a precious record of their mental maps, which were otherwise passed down only orally. In 1720 Father Antonio Cantova encountered another group of castaways on the Mariana Islands. After spending eight months with the castaways, Cantova produced an ethnographic account and a new, more detailed map that adhered more closely to European conventions and served as a cartographic point of reference for later scientific expeditions in Micronesia.

See also Asia; China; Philippines; Spain

Clossey, Luke, "Merchants, Migrants, Missionaries, and Globalization in the Early Modern Pacific." *Journal of Global History* 1 (2006), 41–58.

de la Costa, Horacio, *The Jesuits in the Philippines, 1581–1768*. Cambridge, MA: Harvard University Press, 1961.

Hezel, Francis X., "From Conversion to Conquest: The Early Spanish Mission in the Marianas." *Journal of Pacific History* 17, 3 (1982), 115–37.

Reyes, Raquel A. G., "Botany and Zoology in the Late Seventeenth-Century Philippines: The Work of Georg Josef Camel SJ (1661–1706)." *Archives of Natural History* 36, 2 (2009), 262–76.

Strasser, Ulrike, "Die Kartierung der Paläosinseln: Geographische Imagination und Wissenstransfer zwischen europäischen Jesuiten und mikronesischen Insulanern um 1700." *Geschichte und Gesellschaft* 36 (2010), 197–230.

Ulrike Strasser

Pamplona

Pamplona, known as Irunea in the Basque language, is surrounded by a mountainous belt with an altitude of around 1,000 meters and contains a population of over 300,000 inhabitants.

In 1521 Ignatius was part of the garrison that defended the city of Pamplona from invading French troops. In this confrontation, on May 20, Pentecost Monday, he was seriously wounded when a cannonball shattered his right leg. To heal his wounds, Ignatius was moved to his family home in Loyola. During his convalescence he had an important spiritual transformation that led him to conversion.

In 1580 the Society of Jesus founded a college in Pamplona through the sponsorship of local nobleman Juan Piñeiro and the assistance of St. Teresa of Avila in spite of an unfavorable political context and opposition from several sections of society. The Jesuits in Pamplona promoted Latin, rhetoric, literature, and, at the request of the city council, historical studies. Of especial significance in this regard was the later publication of the *Annals of the Kingdom of Navarre (1684–1715)*, an historical work compiled by Fathers Moret and Alesón that marked the awakening of an historical consciousness of Navarre.

Today, the Jesuits of Pamplona belong to the Territorial Apostolic Platform (PAT) of Loyola as part of the Local Apostolic Commissions (CAL), joining the communities and Jesuit works of Pamplona, Tudela, and Javier. They are placed in a large architectonic complex that includes the Colegio San Ignacio, which was founded in 1946 and provides education from kindergarten through high school, the Church of the Immaculate Conception, and the Loyola Cultural Center. Also in Pamplona are the regional headquarters of ALBOAN, a Jesuit NGO that works for cooperative development.

Militiam sequutus Ignatius, ictu muralis globi crure perfracto à defensione arcis Pampelonæ semianimis excutitur vt sęcu-lari militia relicta, ad diuinam se tranfferat.
2.

Figure 50 Jean-Baptiste Barbé: *Battle at Pamplona*, 1609, engraving from *Vita beati P. Ignatii Loiolae Societatis Iesu fundatoris*. Jesuitica Collection, John J. Burns Library, Boston College. Photograph Alison Fleming

See also Loyola, Ignatius of, SJ, St.; Spain

Colectivo Cultural, "Íñigo Arista." *Conozcamos Pamplona y sus ciudades hermanas.* Pamplona: Excelentísimo Ayuntamiento de Pamplona, 1991.

Inmaculada Fernández Arrillaga

Papacy

The Jesuits are inconceivable without the papacy. From its inception, the Society of Jesus has existed "to serve the Lord alone and the Roman Pontiff, his Vicar on earth" (*Formula of the Institute*, #1, 1540). After the earliest Jesuit companions, in their deliberations of summer 1539, discerned that they would stay together and communicated their intentions in an initial five-point draft to Pope Paul III, he approved their project orally in September 1539 and formally in the bull *Regimini militantis Ecclesiae* one year later. The service to be rendered by the members of the Society that was to be designated with the name of Jesus was one that would be carried out under the Vicar of Christ on earth, the Pope. Ten years later, in a second papal document entitled *Exposcit debitum* and issued by Pope Julius III, the words quoted above from the 1540 text were expanded to include mention also of the Church. The new text said: "to serve the Lord alone and his bride the Church under the Roman Pontiff, the Vicar of Christ on earth." There were further approbations of the Society subsequently by various popes, but it was definitively established initially in 1540 and availability to serve the papacy has been a hallmark of it ever since.

Jesuits, the Papacy, and the Counter-Reformation

The *Formula of the Institute* of 1540 spoke of the purpose of the Society as being "to strive especially for the progress of souls in Christian life and doctrine and for the propagation of the faith by the ministry of the word" as well as by spiritual, charitable, and catechetical means. Thus it is hardly surprising that, just five years after the Society was confirmed, and when the Council of Trent (1545–63) opened, Jesuits were sent there by Paul III as his (papal) theologians. The chief purposes of the Council were to deal with the theological challenges arising from the Reformation and with reform of the Church. Two of the first Jesuit companions, Spaniards Diego Laínez (1512–65) and Alfonso Salmerón (1515–85), were present at all three sessions of the Council and made important contributions to the discussions and debates leading to a number of its decrees. Laínez attended the final session (1562–63) as superior general of the Jesuits, but otherwise he and Salmerón attended as theologians to the Pope, who never attended the Council – in the first session to Paul III, in the second to Julius III, and in the third to Pius IV. When the last of these died in 1565, many cardinals wanted Laínez to be his successor, but he succeeded in eluding them and also the papacy! So, very early in the life of the Society, a Jesuit pope became a serious possibility; and this occurred subsequently also (in Robert Bellarmine's case, for example, in 1605, and in Carlo Maria Martini's, in 2005). It became a reality on March 13, 2013, when Jorge Mario Bergoglio, SJ, was elected pope and took the name of Francis.

The foundation of the Society at a time when the Reformation was spreading rapidly led to Jesuits becoming best known, in northern Europe especially, for being at the forefront of the Counter-Reformation, as they served and defended the doctrinal interests of the papacy, even if their becoming so-called "storm-troopers of the Counter-Reformation" had not initially been an explicit intention of Ignatius. In addition to Laínez and Salmerón, two other Jesuits more or less of this era also stand out: the Dutchman, Peter Canisius (1521–97), and the Italian, Robert Bellarmine (1542–1621). Canisius stated Catholic doctrine with great clarity at different academic levels and produced three catechisms, two while he was also provincial of Germany (1556–59). Bellarmine was a first-rate theologian, highly skilled in handling the theological controversies of the post-Reformation era. In 1576, he was given the (then recently founded) chair of Controversies at the Roman College of the Jesuits and from his lectures there produced his famous, three-volume work, *Disputationes de Controversiis Christianae Fidei adversus hujus temporis haereticos*, which was said to have so ably systematized the controversies of the time that in Protestant Germany and England special university chairs were to be founded in order to refute it.

Despite its excellence and usefulness for the Church, Bellarmine's *De controversiis* did not prevent him from running foul of Pope Sixtus V (1585–90), who wanted to place the work's first volume on the Index because it contained a theory assigning only *indirect* power over temporal matters to the Pope. Fortunately, a crisis was averted by the death of Sixtus. But Bellarmine again fell out of papal favor some years later. Having been appointed by Pope Clement VIII (1592–1605) as his theologian in 1597, they disagreed five years later and Bellarmine became an embarrassment and had to be sent away from Rome; he was made archbishop of Capua. Later again he regained papal favor – with Paul V (1605–21), who kept him in Rome after the conclave (which Bellarmine attended as a cardinal) that elected him, assigning various, highly significant theological roles to him. Bellarmine's life at the end of the sixteenth and beginning of the seventeenth century shows that to serve the papacy was not always to enjoy smooth relations with it. Notwithstanding this, however, it must be acknowledged that, institutionally, the Society enjoyed much papal trust in the latter part of the sixteenth century. In 1564 Pius IV (1559–65) entrusted to its care the first seminary of the Diocese of Rome, and Gregory XIII (1572–85), an enthusiastic supporter of the Society's 1551-founded Collegio Romano, built a magnificent building for it that still stands in the center of Rome today (although no longer in Jesuit hands).

Jesuit Missions and the Papacy: India, China, and Paraguay

Relations between the papacy and Jesuit missionaries and their methods reveal a character ranging from papal approval to papal condemnations. From the Society's missionary beginnings with the arrival of Francis Xavier in Goa in May 1542, other Jesuits soon followed – to India, Japan, China, and elsewhere. It took time for the Jesuit missionaries to develop methods of evangelization that were effective. In their initial efforts they were often unsuccessful, not least because of their failure to immerse themselves in the languages, cultures, and traditions of those to whom they were sent. If Xavier was perhaps naïve at first, he quickly learned; and certainly by 1549, following his arrival in Japan, the importance of learning the local language and understanding the customs of the people was not lost on him. Jesuits who followed him developed more effective strategies. Gradually, mainly through the methods of "accommodation" or "adaptation" – today we would say "inculturation" – of men like Alessandro Valignano (1539–1606) in Japan and China, Matteo Ricci (1552–1610) in China, and Roberto de Nobili (1577–1656) in India, the Jesuits' missionary activity became more successful. It was de Nobili who first introduced the method of adaptation to India, immersing himself in Hindu modes of thinking and living, studying Sanskrit, developing a deep knowledge of Hinduism, and distinguishing between what were religious and what were simply cultural customs. He also allowed Indian Christians to keep many of their own customs and celebrations. In China, Matteo Ricci acted similarly, with even greater success. He arrived in China in 1582 and died there in 1610. He developed a profound respect for the Chinese people and made friends with them, dressing also in their clothing (eventually in the garb of their literati or scholars) and immersing himself in their language and culture. His first book in Chinese was a treatise on friendship and it gained the admiration of Chinese scholars. Ricci was the first foreigner to be given, by the emperor, a plot of Chinese land as his burial place.

Successful though they were, the methods of de Nobili and Ricci proved controversial. De Nobili's approach won the approval of his provincial in India and, in 1623, Pope Gregory XV ruled in favor of his adaptation approach. But not all of his fellow missionaries (among them Jesuits) agreed with his methods; neither did the archbishop of Goa.

If he enjoyed a certain approval during his lifetime, over a century later, in 1744, Pope Benedict XIV condemned some of his innovations. A controversy was also sparked by the missionary methods of Ricci in China. This so-called Chinese Rites Controversy of the seventeenth and eighteenthth centuries centered around what, for many, was the questionable compatibility of certain Chinese and Confucian ritual practices with the Catholic faith. The Jesuit historian, Norman Tanner, reports how, in China, while Jesuit missionaries Valignano, Ricci, and others showed great openness to the language and religious customs of the Chinese, their persistent and successful methods of inculturation caused divisions and Rome eventually ruled against them in the decree *Ex quo singulari* of Pope Benedict XIV in 1742. The practices of the Jesuits in China had already been condemned by Pope Clement XI in 1715, but this had neither ended the controversy nor cleared up suspicions against the Jesuits, which continued, contributing to their eventual suppression later in the century.

Turning briefly to Latin America, in Paraguay during the seventeenth and eighteenth centuries, the Jesuits evangelized the indigenous peoples – in a manner that respected both their culture and their freedom. They established settlements, so-called "Reductions," among, mainly, the Guaraní people, with whom they lived and worked and to whom they taught Christian doctrine, as well as many other things. The Reductions were successful, religiously and also agriculturally and commercially. The Spanish colonists did not live within the territory of the Reductions and were suspicious of and hostile toward them. The Spanish Crown supported and protected the Reductions, for the most part, and the Spanish governors in Paraguay, as well as the local bishops, were also generally favorable. In time, however, jealousy and suspicion, particularly on the part of the disaffected Spanish colonists, led to the Jesuits being expelled from several of their colonies. What was relayed to Europe, in addition to other oppositions already brewing there against the Jesuits, turned the tide against the Society further, and in 1767 a weak and yielding Charles III of Spain signed an edict decreeing the Jesuits' expulsion from the Spanish possessions in Latin America. This dealt a blow to the Reductions from which they could never recover. And it marked, further, the reversed fortunes of the Order in Europe that were already mentioned in relation to the rites controversies. The Jesuits were being opposed on every front: theologically, by Jansenists and Gallicans, and also, in some cases, by members of other religious congregations and orders; and politically, not least through virulent opposition to them on the part of Ministers Choiseul (France), Pombal (Portugal) and Aranda (Spain). Enlightenment intellectuals often hated them too, since they were the ablest opponents of their theories. And the Catholic monarchs – in Spain, Portugal, and France – were bitterly against them also because of their loyalty to the papacy, the weakening of which the monarchs were attempting to bring about. In the end, the monarchs succeeded in exerting such pressure on Pope Clement XIV that he yielded to it and suppressed the Society of Jesus, issuing a bull to that effect, entitled *Dominus ac Redemptor*, on July 21, 1773.

Suppression (1773) and Restoration (1814)

If it seems odd that the suppression and restoration of the Society of Jesus are treated under a single heading, this is because, for the topic "The Papacy and the Jesuits," there is not much to write for the period of Suppression itself! The Suppression removed the

Society from actual existence and was, without doubt, the lowest point in the history of its relations with the papacy. While it is true that Clement XIV's action was not effective everywhere, particularly in Russia, where Catherine the Great ignored the papal bull, it was also true that, for forty-one years the Society of Jesus did not officially exist and many of its members during that time became diocesan priests; many more died; and some returned to secular occupations. From 1800 on, when the Benedictine, Pius VII, became pope, there was a papacy favorable to the Society of Jesus once again and, in due course, following his release from imprisonment by Napoleon, Pius VII did in fact restore the Society of Jesus on August 7, 1814, with the bull *Sollicitudo omnium ecclesiarum*.

The Nineteenth Century

The Society's relationship to the papacy was somewhat different after the restoration from how it had been before it. It is hard to characterize it in a single phrase, but the relationship after the restoration was, overall, more on the side of being very closely allied with the papal agenda, politically and theologically, rather than sometimes being in tension with it, such as had occurred from the mission territories, or with regard to theological questions, during the seventeenth and eighteenth centuries. The century of the restoration, the nineteenth century, was also, to an extent, a century of restoration itself in that the Church's desire was to restore pre-revolutionary circumstances, which included the monarchy – although it was ironic that Jesuits should support this because it was the Catholic kings who had pressured for the Society's dissolution. Nonetheless it was so. As historian John O'Malley puts it: "'Restored' in an era of restoration, the Jesuits, and other orders as well, embraced a conservative, sometimes full-blown reactionary approach to politics and church life not characteristic of them earlier" (*History of the Popes*, 237).

Being closely allied with the papacy in the nineteenth century meant, for the Society, a significant involvement in the pope's political and intellectual agenda, these two being inextricably interwoven. The contributions of Jesuits such as Matteo Liberatore, SJ (1810–92), and Joseph Kleutgen, SJ (1811–83), to the development of a philosophical-theological system based on Thomas Aquinas's thought during the reigns of Pius IX (1846–78) and Leo XIII (1878–1903) meant that the papacy was equipped with an intellectual synthesis of faith and reason that served its interests doubly: first, by providing a foundation for the kind of independent relations between Church and State that it desired; and second, by charting a credible course between those extremes of rationalism and fideism to which Enlightenment thought forms had inevitably given rise. The first served the papacy well – although not, ultimately, successfully – in its struggle to retain the Papal States in the face of ongoing attacks from the forces for Italian unification. And the second enabled Catholicism to become a force once again in the academic world of philosophy and theology. In 1850, the Jesuit, quasi-official papal journal, *La Civiltà Cattolica*, was founded – as a mouthpiece for papal (Pius IX's) ideas and concerns – and it still operates along fairly similar lines. For a period of time, everything written in it was overseen by the Vatican Secretariat of State and even today, through the close collaboration between Pope Francis and *La Civiltà's* current editor, Fr. Antonio Spadaro, SJ, it continues to further, or at least to exhibit compatibility with, the current papal worldview.

The Twentieth Century

Changes came in the twentieth century – for the Church itself and for the Society of Jesus. Many of the changes were theological in nature, but born of events that called for changed theological thinking. Protestants and Catholics fighting and dying side by side during the two world wars and chaplains from different Christian confessions laboring together for the troops fostered levels of ecumenical understanding hitherto unimagined, but important for ecumenical relations later in the century. Many Jesuits, such as the German Augustin Bea, were prominent in the ecumenical movement. In Scripture studies, too, Jesuits made their mark. The Society, asked by Pope Pius X (1903–14) to take charge of the Pontifical Biblical Institute (PBI) that he founded in 1909 to counter historical trends in the study of the Scriptures, did assume this responsibility but, in quite a short time, came round to accepting, and promoting, the very methods the PBI was initially founded to counteract. Pope Pius XI (1922–39) entrusted the management of Vatican Radio to the Society when he set it up in 1931 and the Jesuits continued to lead this work until recently (2016), Pope Francis changed this. From all these activities, it is evident that the Society, by and large, enjoyed papal confidence during the first half of the twentieth century.

In theology, however, twentieth-century Jesuits' relations with the papacy were decidedly mixed. Sebastian Tromp, the Dutch Jesuit at the Gregorian University in Rome, had an important role in the preparatory work for the Second Vatican Council (1962–65); he also wrote Pius XII's encyclical on the Church, *Mystici corporis* (1943). Augustin Bea, SJ, together with the Dominican, Jacques Marie Vosté, wrote Pius XII's encyclical on the study of the Scriptures, *Divino afflante Spiritu*. (Jesuits ghostwriting encyclicals had already become a practice in the nineteenth century with Kleutgen's work on *Aeterni Patris* and Liberatore's on *Rerum novarum*). However, the 1950 encyclical of Pius XII, *Humani generis* (alleged by some to have been influenced by Sebastian Tromp), was very negative toward certain trends emerging in pre-Conciliar theology and, while the name of Henri de Lubac, SJ, was not actually mentioned in it, the position he espoused on the relationship between nature and grace was targeted. Fr. de Lubac spent almost ten years, beginning in 1950, barred from teaching theology. His older French confrère, Pierre Teilhard de Chardin, SJ, had suffered this fate – and a ban on publishing his work – for a much longer period. The German Jesuit Karl Rahner was informed by the Prefect of the Holy Office, Cardinal Ottaviani, that a special censor had been appointed to read his work. US Jesuit John Courtney Murray was told to stop publishing on religious freedom and Church–State relations following pressure from the Vatican's Holy Office in 1954. These Jesuits (except for Teilhard de Chardin, who died in 1955) became, during and after the Second Vatican Council, as respected as they had previously been suspected.

After the Council's first session, John XXIII died and his successor, Paul VI (1963–1978), was generally appreciative of Jesuit theologians, during the Council and after it. He gave the Society a special mission to combat atheism. But there were tensions too – on the issue of "grades," when the Society wished to explore the possibility of eliminating the traditional grade of "spiritual coadjutor"; on the very strong emphasis on justice in the Society's rearticulation of its mission in 1975, when the Pope feared it might be losing sight of its essentially spiritual purpose; and on adherence to the papal magisterium, perhaps especially in the wake of Paul's encyclical *Humanae vitae* issued in 1968. Paul VI was cautious in style and always seeking consensus; Jesuits of his era were sometimes impatient with the slowness of pace that seemed to result from this. Looking back, it may be that they did not always appreciate the extent to which Paul VI was in fact a friend of the Society, but perhaps Pope John Paul II's dramatic suspension of the normal government of the Society in 1981 enabled them to recognize this more fully in subsequent years.

The action, just mentioned, of Pope John Paul II (1978–2005) is treated in this encyclopedia in a separate article under that pope's name. Here it need only be said that the Pope, in leaving the Society without normally elected leadership for two years (1981–83) and naming two Jesuits of his own choosing to take the helm, sent shock waves through the Society. When the astute, competent, and diplomatic rector of the Oriental Institute, Father Peter-Hans Kolvenbach, took over as superior general in 1983, his election marking a return to normal government, relations with the papacy improved and remained on a more even keel for the rest of Pope John Paul II's life. However, some tensions remained, especially in relation to Jesuit theologians, particularly those writing in the areas of liberation theology and interreligious dialogue. These two areas were of great concern both to Pope John Paul II and to his successor, Benedict XVI, and Jesuits Roger Haight, Jacques Dupuis, and Jon Sobrino were investigated, and censured, during their papacies. Tensions over theology led the Society, in a document of the 35th General Congregation ("With Renewed Vigor and Zeal") in 2008, to acknowledge imperfections in its intellectual apostolate and to recommit itself to a service at once creative and faithful. Benedict XVI addressed the members of the same Congregation encouragingly on February 21, 2008. After his papacy a unique circumstance arose that still (2016) obtains: a Jesuit was elected pope! If the Suppression of the Society marked the lowest point of Jesuit relations with the papacy, the present situation witnesses to unusually harmonious relations, with Francis as the first Jesuit pope. However, what the future will bring for the Society's relationship with the papacy, not least as a consequence of a Jesuit now actually being pope, remains to be seen.

See also Clement XIV; John Paul II; Julius III; Paul III; Paul VI; Pius VII; Pius XI; Pius XII; Suppression; Vatican I; Vatican II

Corkery, James, and Thomas Worcester, eds., *The Papacy since 1500: From Italian Prince to Universal Pastor*. Cambridge: Cambridge University Press, 2010.
O'Malley, John W., *A History of the Popes: From Peter to the Present*. Plymouth, MA: Rowman and Littlefield Publishers, 2010.
Tanner, Norman, *New Short History of the Catholic Church*. London/New York: Burns and Oates, 2011.

James Corkery, SJ

Paraguay Missions ("Reductions")

Although the province of Paraguay was created by General Claudio Acquaviva in 1604, the Jesuit presence in those territories goes back to 1585, when Fathers Alonso Barzana and Francisco Angulo arrived at Tucuman (today's Argentina) from Peru. In 1587 Fathers Manoel Ortega, Juan Saloni, and Thomas Fields arrived at Buenos Aires, coming from Brazil. Owing to administrative difficulties and facing political opposition from the Spanish settlers, the Jesuits abandoned Paraguay in 1593. Only Fields remained in Asunción, keeping operative the residence the Jesuits had opened in the city and which eventually would become the center of their operations there. In 1607 General Acquaviva appointed Diego de Torres Bollo as provincial of Paraguay. The territories of the new province included the modern Brazilian states of Parana and the western portion of Sao Paulo, modern Paraguay, Uruguay, Chile, Argentina, and the eastern portion of Bolivia.

Under Torres Bollo's leadership, missionaries such as Roque González and Antonio Ruiz de Montoya began establishing permanent missions among the Guaraní groups that populated the area. By 1630 the Jesuits had ten mission towns in Parana (also known as the Guaira Reductions). However, the settling of the Guaraní groups in the Jesuit missions made them easy targets for the Portuguese slave raiders, who began attacking the Reductions and selling off the captured neophytes in Sao Paulo. The situation became so dire that Antonio Ruiz de Montoya, superior of the Guaira Reductions, decided to move all ten towns further south to protect them from the Portuguese. The Jesuits led approximately 12,000 Guaraní to today's Paraguay and the Argentine province of Misiones. In 1639 Ruiz de Montoya, acting as a proxy of the Paraguayan Jesuits in Madrid, secured a royal authorization allowing the Jesuits to provide firearms to the reduction of Guaraní. In 1641 a group of Guaraní forces, led by the Jesuit lay brother Domingo de Torres, defeated a large Portuguese expedition in Mbororé, after which the Portuguese incursions became more and more scarce until they finally stopped at the beginning of the eighteenth century.

For about a century after Mbororé, the Jesuit missions (thirty in total) flourished, reaching a population peak of 150,000 by the mid-eighteenth century. The missions (also known as "reductions") were modeled after the famous doctrine of Juli, in the shores of the Titicaca Lake (present-day Bolivia), where Jesuit missionaries in South America received their training. Typically manned by at least a Jesuit priest and a lay brother, the missions were built as towns around a central plaza dominated by a church, next to which was the house of the priests, sometimes referred to as a "college." Although authority in the reductions ultimately rested in the Jesuits' hands, each mission was governed by a town council (*cabildo*), which appointed a *corregidor*, charged with policing and with the punishment of offenders. The *cabildo*, and all other municipal offices, were filled by native leaders, or *caciques*. Life in the reductions was marked both by the seasonal rhythms and the Catholic ritual calendar. The semi-nomadic Guaraní that settled in the reductions changed their lifestyle and economy toward agriculture. Over time, the cultivation and harvesting of *yerba maté* would become a major source of income for the Jesuit reduction system, along with cattle ranching. By 1750 the reductions boasted more than 200,000 *maté* trees and hundreds of thousands of cattle heads. Attendance at catechism was mandatory, as well as at Mass on Sundays. The Jesuits encouraged frequent confession, as well as membership of sodalities under the advocacy of the Virgin Mary and other saints. Children were taught basic literacy and music; some were trained as artisans and painters. These Guaraní artists worked recreating European styles, developing along the way a recognizable style, patterned originally on Italian classicism and, later, on Roman and Bavarian Baroque. Young women, widows, and those whose husbands were away lived and worked in the *cotiguazu*, the House of the Widows, devoting

Figure 51 Detail of Jesuit reduction at Trinidad, Paraguay, 2013. Photograph Eric Studt, SJ

their time to spinning cotton or wool thread, and to devotional activities. By 1700 there was a functioning printing press servicing the reductions. Under the direction of Father Pablo Restivo, in 1724 the Guaraní Nicolás Yapeyú published an annotated catechism (*Explicación del catecismo en lengua guaraní*), and a collection of sermons (*Sermones y ejemplos en lengua guaraní*) in 1727, both written in the Guaraní language.

In 1750 Spain and Portugal signed the Treaty of Madrid that redefined their boundaries in South America. As a result, seven Jesuit reductions east of the Uruguay River found themselves suddenly situated in Portuguese dominions. The Jesuits tried all means at their disposal to get the Spanish court to nullify the treaty, while at the same time trying to prevent an uprising of the nearly 30,000 Guaraní affected by it. The rebellion broke out in 1753, and in 1754 the Guaraní forces defeated a joint Spanish-Portuguese force sent to subdue them. By 1756, however, the Guaraní had been defeated by the Iberian armies; estimates put the number of Guaraní casualties close to 10,000. By the next year, two-thirds of the remaining inhabitants of the seven Uruguayan reductions had been relocated to other missions. In 1761 the Treaty of Pardo nullified the Treaty of Madrid, but it was already too late. In 1767 the Jesuits were expelled from all Spanish American dominions by a royal decree signed by Charles III.

See also Argentina; Bolivia; Brazil; Chile; González, Roque, SJ, St.; Portugal; Ruiz de Montoya, Antonio, SJ; Uruguay

Caraman, Philip, *The Lost Paradise: An Account of the Jesuits in Paraguay, 1607–1768*. London: Sidgwick & Jackson, 1975.

Ganson, Barbara, *The Guarani under Spanish Rule in the Rio de la Plata*. Stanford, CA: Stanford University Press, 2003.

Andrés Ignacio Prieto

Paris

It would be hard to overstate the importance of Paris in Jesuit history. The origins of the Society of Jesus are found in a group of foreign students at the University of Paris, 1528–35. After some years of false starts in Spain in obtaining the education he wanted for the sake of being able to minister to others, Ignatius succeeded in obtaining a Master of Arts degree in Paris. At the same time, Ignatius gave his *Spiritual Exercises* to fellow students, especially to some who shared his origins on the Iberian Peninsula. On August 15, 1534, Ignatius and six of these men formed the nucleus of what would become the Society of Jesus: they made a vow to go to Jerusalem, or, if this were not possible, to go to Rome and offer to go wherever the pope sent them.

After formal approval by Pope Paul III in 1540, the Society of Jesus grew rapidly in Europe and beyond. But Paris was one of the places where there was enduring opposition: from those that saw the papist Jesuits as a threat to Gallican traditions; from older religious orders opposed to Jesuit innovations in religious life (such as Jesuit omission of the Divine Office in choir); from university professors seeking to avoid competition; from xenophobic Frenchmen who dismissed Jesuits as but Spaniards (the chief rivals of the French in the 1500s). Establishment of the Jesuits in Paris was an uphill battle, one that would succeed when and if the French monarchy supported Jesuit presence and ministries.

The seventeenth century was an era of generally good relationships between the king and the Jesuits, despite accusations that Jesuits were disloyal and regicidal. In Paris, the Jesuits built a new church, dedicated to Saint Louis, holy ancestor of King Henri IV (r. 1589–1610). Meanwhile, Jesuits served as royal confessors. As such they not only heard the king's confession, but advised the king on the morality or immorality of proposed actions, such as declarations of war. But by the 1640s, Jansenists were gaining many adherents in Paris, especially in the Parisian law court (Parlement), in certain religious communities, especially the convent just outside Paris at Port-Royal, and among a literate laity. Jansenists, adopting a dour vision of life in which sin abounded, grace was scarce, and damnation awaited most people, took the relatively optimistic Jesuits to be their arch-enemies, and they pursued a bitter polemic against them all the way to the dissolution of the Society in France, in the 1760s, and indeed beyond.

Following the 1814 restoration of the Society by Pope Pius VII, Jesuits in Paris were soon faced, as earlier, with the need for support, or at least tolerance, by the state. The changing political arrangements in nineteenth-century France (various forms of empire, monarchy, republic) meant hot/cold relations with the state and its heads. While the Second Empire (1852–70) was relatively supportive of Jesuits, the Paris Commune of 1871 was extraordinarily hostile to the Church, Jesuits included. Five French Jesuits were martyred during the Commune. The Third Republic that followed promoted a version of *la laïcité* that had no room for schools run by religious orders, especially not the ultramontanist Jesuits. The 1880 expulsion of Jesuits from France was followed by a 1901 law on associations that meant expulsion for nearly all French religious orders.

The return of large numbers of Jesuits to Paris was prepared by hundreds of French Jesuits (and other religious) who had returned from exile in order to enlist and fight for their *patrie* in 1914–18. This led to greater tolerance of the Church by the postwar French state. In the 1930s, the Jesuits built a very large new residence on the rue de Grenelle, in the seventh *arrondissement*. Here and in other houses, Parisian Jesuits endured the Nazi occupation of 1940–44. A few Jesuits risked their lives by denouncing Nazi actions, by aiding the Resistance, and/or by helping Jews and others to avoid arrest. An example is Michel Riquet (1898–1993), who, among other things, helped Allied soldiers escape from occupied Paris. Riquet survived two Nazi concentration camps, and upon his return to Paris, he became a well-known preacher at Notre-Dame cathedral and an advocate of good relations between Christians and Jews.

In recent decades, the number of French Jesuits has fallen a great deal. Many Jesuit houses in France have closed. But Paris has become more than ever the focal point for Jesuits in France, with the merger of four provinces into one, with its headquarters in Paris, and with the creation of the Centre Sèvres as the sole Jesuit faculty of philosophy and theology for France.

See also Centre Sèvres; Charpentier, Marc-Antoine; France; Jansenism; Montmartre

Lécrivain, Philippe, *Paris in the Time of Ignatius of Loyola*. Trans. Ralph Renner. St. Louis, MO: The Institute of Jesuit Sources, 2011.

Ranum, Patricia, ed. and trans. *Beginning to be a Jesuit: Instructions for the Paris Novitiate circa 1685*. St. Louis, MO: The Institute of Jesuit Sources, 2011.

Riquet, Michel, *Le rebelle discipliné: entretiens avec Alain-Gilles Minella*. Paris: Mame, 1993.

Saint-Paul – Saint Louis: Les Jésuites à Paris. Paris: Musée Carnavalet, 1985.

Thomas Worcester, SJ

Parishes

Ignatius did not think that the Society should have parishes because he desired the Society to be marked by spiritual freedom for mission and by freedom from benefices and regular income. But the reasons he advanced for the sixteenth century no longer hold true. Handsome revenues no longer obtain, and the new Code of Canon Law (1983) mandates term limits for pastors, so a lengthy tenure of a pastor is increasingly unlikely.

A tension exists, however, for Jesuit parishes. The parish is the ordinary ministry of the Church. It is subject to the direct authority of the local bishop. The ordinary authority for a Jesuit is his provincial, and he is expected to fulfill the mission of the Society. So, in addition to being attuned to the regional, pastoral needs of the Church, the challenge for Jesuit pastors is to "make their apostolic contribution to the local church, while at the same time being faithful to their charism and keeping their freedom for mission" (General Congregation 34, Decree 6, #175).

At the same time the Jesuit parish can be an excellent base from which to move out and reach people on the margins who are alienated from the Church or from religion and to be an apostolic center where the charisms of the Society for the faith that does justice, engages cultures, and welcomes interfaith dialogue can flourish. Through the centuries the Jesuit parish, or more often the church attached to a Jesuit college or university, has been noted for its outstanding preaching and for lively devotions, such as the devotion to the Sacred Heart and the Novena of Grace. The faithful often gravitate to Jesuit confessors to receive the Sacrament of Reconciliation.

Often the modern parish is the Ignatian equivalent of "the public squares and markets, hospitals, and prisons, ships in dock, fortresses, playing fields, hospices and hostels"

Figure 52 Exterior view of Church of Saint Louis, Paris, constructed by Étienne Martellange, SJ, 17th century. Photograph Thomas Worcester, SJ

where the early Jesuits engaged people through preaching, spiritual conversations, and eventually the sacraments.

Up until General Congregation 34 (1975), however, parishes were officially considered an exception for Jesuit ministry or acknowledged as a temporary mission. This reluctance seems rather amazing considering that in 1975 nearly 3,200 Jesuits were serving in more than 2,000 parishes throughout the world.

Central to the life of a parish is the gathering (the *ek-klesia*) to celebrate the community's joys, struggles, and hopes in Word and Sacrament. Liturgies need care so that they are well-planned, creative, and inculturated. Such a parish "becomes an evangelizing community committed to 'justice and reconciliation' and makes its popular devotions relevant to contemporary needs" (Byrne, "Jesuits and Parish Ministry," 26).

Jesuit parishes, whether serving the highly educated or the poor, offer a forum for the gift of Jesuit spirituality – experienced through the *Spiritual Exercises* and the practice of personal and communal discernment. The *Spiritual Exercises* in everyday life have flourished in diverse places, such as St. Joseph's in Seattle, Holy Trinity in Washington, DC, and Holy Name in Camden, NJ.

During the time of communism in eastern Europe, often the only public ministry available to Jesuits was in a state-recognized parish. In Slovenia, for instance, parishes were the only source of regular income and support. Likewise Jesuit parishes among the Dalits, the lowest caste in India, have played a critical role in recognizing the dignity of all peoples and have been a major source for evangelization.

Parish ministers can make an explicit appeal to faith-based language and symbols that immensely aid the process of communal discernment. Some Jesuit parish councils, led by their pastors, have adopted a regular method of communal discernment for key decisions relating to leadership, budget, and mission. Discernment helps parishioners to realize that the Lord's will is not always manifest by majority vote. At times alone, prophetic voice can articulate the deeper values of the Gospel out of which a decision may flow.

Since the Second Vatican Council, Jesuits are much more attuned to the dynamics, rhythm, and beauty of the liturgy of the Church which desires that "all the faithful should be led to that fully conscious and active participation" demanded by the very nature of the liturgy.

The deeper embrace of the baptismal call for every Christian leads naturally to the recognition of the multitude of gifts present within the parish and calls for an awakening of lay leadership, not only as in earlier Catholic Action groups overseen by the hierarchy, but within the celebration of the liturgy itself and within the leadership structures of the Church. Consequently, Jesuit parishes have often been at the forefront of encouraging and establishing lay ecclesial ministry.

See also Apostolate; Liturgy; Ministries; Preaching

Byrne, Peter D., "Jesuits and Parish Ministry." *Studies in the Spirituality of Jesuits* 29, 3 (May 1997), 1–31.

General Congregation 34, Decree 19, "Parish Ministry." In John L. McCarthy, ed., *Documents of the Thirty-Fourth General Congregation of the Society of Jesus*. St. Louis, MO: The Institute of Jesuit Sources, 1995.

Patrick J. Howell, SJ

Pascal, Blaise

Pascal (1623–1662) was one of the most brilliant minds and pens of his age and author of one of the most lasting attacks in literature on the Society of Jesus. A precocious mathematical genius, Blaise wrote a treatise on sound at the age of 12 and studied mathematics among some of the greatest mathematical and scientific minds of the age, including René Descartes. At the age of 16 Pascal wrote a treatise on the geometry of cones which contained what came to be known as Pascal's Theorem. His physical and nervous health caused him lifelong difficulties, but he managed to overcome them, working on Pascal's Triangle, the theory of probabilities, and the inventions of a calculator, the hydraulic press, the syringe, and improvements to the barometer. He is also credited with being the inventor of public transport according to a fixed itinerary.

In 1646 Pascal came across the works of Jean Duvergier de Hauranne, the abbé de Saint-Cyran (1581–1643), spiritual director of the monastery of Port-Royal. He counted this as his first conversion, one that he eventually shared with the rest of his family. By 1648 he and his sister Jacqueline were in close contact with the Port-Royal circle, including Antoine Singlin, who had followed Saint-Cyran as spiritual director to the nuns. A period of intense mathematical and scientific activity followed as well as a time of engagement in what he later described as "worldly pursuits" in the aftermath of Jacqueline's entry into the novitiate at Port-Royal. From 1654 he began to feel a disgust for the world, and to retire increasingly into religious and mathematical solitude, corresponding with Fermat on the theory of probabilities and the calculus of probabilities. On the night of November 23 of that year, he had a powerful and lasting mystical experience, known as the Night of Fire, which replaced his previous doubts, anxieties, and hesitations with overwhelming peace and tears of joy. His brief jottings on that experience have survived, in a style reminiscent of his later *Pensées*, which also give an insight into his later main theological arguments. They extol the God of biblical revelation, as opposed to the God of the learned philosophers, and he prays never again to be separated from Jesus Christ, to whom he desires to submit himself entirely. He saw this experience as his second conversion.

Pascal made a retreat at the monastery of Port-Royal des Champs and became attached to the community there although he would remain independent of it. When Antoine Arnauld was condemned by the Sorbonne in 1655 for refuting the existence of five alleged heretical propositions in Jansen's *Augustinus*, Pascal began to write his *Lettres provinciales* (*The Provincial Letters*), published under a pseudonym between 1656 and 1657. They constituted a devastating attack on the casuistry of the Jesuits and on the Jesuits themselves as purveyors of cheapened sacramental grace to the morally lax. The letters shocked the enemies of Port-Royal and delighted its adherents. Considered then and now a masterpiece of the French language, they were to prove immensely popular and had a major influence on the subsequent work of Voltaire and Rousseau, as well as setting the tone of French anti-Jesuit propaganda to the present day. The *Letters* were condemned and burned by order of Louis XIV and placed on the Index by the pope in 1657. In the same year Pascal began his major religious work, *The Truth of the Christian Faith*. He and Jacqueline led the radical opposition to the Formulary condemning Jansenism. In the aftermath of the closure of Port-Royal and Jacqueline's death in 1661, he experienced his definitive conversion and abandoned religious polemics, dying in 1662 with his greatest work, the *Pensées*, unfinished.

Pascal's famous wager suggests that it is in our interest to believe in God, even without definitive evidence that such a God exists, since we stand to receive an eternal reward if God does exist, and to lose nothing if he does not, while we stand to be eternally punished for unbelief in a God who does exist and to lose nothing for believing in the same God if he does not. Pascal's *Pensées* are a work of cryptic genius which has kept editors busy attempting to work out their meaning and proper order for centuries. He makes clear his fideist position, seeing religious belief as dependent on revelation rather than on reason, and opposes the skepticism of Montaigne and the stoicism of Epictetus with a finely balanced portrayal of the human condition as halfway between grandeur and nothingness. The two major themes of his *Pensées*, which in their challenge and poetic beauty are as fresh today as when first published, are the wretchedness of humanity without God and the greatness of humanity with God. His is an extraordinarily broad vision of the human soul.

See also Anti-Jesuit Polemic; Arnauld, Antoine; Casuistry; France; Jansenism

Ferreyrolles, Gérard, *Blaise Pascal: "Les Provinciales."* Paris: Presses Universitaires de France, 1984.
Hunter, Graeme, *Pascal the Philosopher: An Introduction.* Toronto: University of Toronto Press, 2013.

Mesnard, Jean, *Pascal: l'homme et l'oeuvre*. Bruges: Desclée de Brouwer, 1965.
Sellier, Philippe, *Blaise Pascal: Pensées*. Paris: Bordas, 1991.

Gemma Simmonds, CJ

Patronato and *Padroado*

The *patronato* and *padroado* were agreements between the popes and the Spanish and Portuguese kings that provided for precise duties and rights to the Crowns in the ecclesiastical affairs in the territory of the Iberian Kingdoms. The Crowns were empowered to nominate bishops, collect tithes, and approve the construction of religious edifices. In return, they took responsibility for various needs of the Church. The *patronato* and *padroado* evolved and assumed various forms, and during the early modern and modern periods they exercised great influence on the extra-European missions.

In 1508, with the bull *Universalis Ecclesiae* of Julius II (r. 1503–13), the *Real Patronato de Indias* was created. A number of popes subsequently confirmed the *Patronato* and granted it to the kings of Spain to facilitate their support of evangelization in the New World. Franciscans, Augustinians, Dominicans, and later Jesuits who went to the mission lands under the control of the Spanish Empire had to be approved by the *Consejo de Indias* in Madrid; Spanish and Italian missionaries were usually welcomed.

The Portuguese *Padroado* dates back to the first half of the fifteenth century and was confirmed in 1515 by Leo X (r. 1513–21). It was called, at different stages, *Padroado Real*, *Padroado Ultramarino Português*, and, after 1911, *Padroado Português do Oriente*; it provided a series of benefices to the Portuguese Crown to assist in the control of ecclesiastical life in the Portuguese *ultramar*.

For more than a century, the Catholic missionary enterprise outside Europe was under the control of the *patronato* and *padroado*. In the second half of the sixteenth century, after the Council of Trent (1545–63), the Church of Rome felt the need to limit the power of the Iberian Crowns and to develop central control over the missions. For more than fifty years there were attempts to create a Roman congregation for the missions that succeeded only in 1622 with the founding of *Propaganda fide* by Pope Gregory XV (r. 1621–23). Many Jesuits were involved in this effort, including Francis Borja (1510–72) and one of the pioneers of the project, Antonio Possevino (1533–1611). Possevino faced the opposition of General Claudio Acquaviva (1543–1615) who desired to preserve the privileges of the Jesuit missions without harming the interests of the Spanish Crown.

Propaganda fide did not have a great impact on the missions in Spanish America because of the strong opposition of the Habsburg kings, and the missions during the seventeenth and eighteenth centuries continued to be under the *patronato*. During the seventeenth century, the Spanish Crown wanted to strictly control the entrance of foreign (non-Spanish) Jesuits, in particular those from France, the Dutch Republic, and also, after 1640, from Portugal. Later, during the second half of the seventeenth century, Philip IV (r. 1621–65) allowed more foreign missionaries into Spanish America, as long as they were subjects of the *Austrias*. At the beginning of the eighteenth century, under the Bourbon dynasty, the Crown became more open to foreign missionaries, but the hostility toward the Society started to grow, leading to the expulsion of Jesuits from the territories of the Spanish Empire in 1767 with a decree by Charles III (r. 1759–88). The long tradition of the *patronato* in Spanish America was dismantled during the 1830s by Gregory XVI (r. 1831–46).

In Brazil the *padroado* lasted, with minor disputes, until the independence from Portugal. In Asia, *Propaganda fide* enjoyed greater influence and controlled the missions through the action of vicars apostolic. The vicarial intervention in India, China, and Japan, often in conflict with the tradition of the *padroado*, caused recurrent tensions with the Portuguese Crown, but also with the Jesuits, who were often accused of disobeying the vicars. The presence of several dioceses with double jurisdiction – the *padroado* and *Propaganda fide* –was resolved between the Holy See and Portugal over the course of a century through several bilateral concordats (1850s–1950s). The dismantling of the *padroado* in India and in the Far East was a slow process supported by many non-Portuguese bishops (many of whom were Jesuits), and was accomplished only in the second half of the twentieth century.

See also China; India; Japan; Portugal; Spain

Alden, Dauril, *The Making of an Enterprise: The Society of Jesus in Portugal, Its Empire, and Beyond 1540–1750*. Stanford, CA: Stanford University Press, 1996.

Donnelly, John Patrick, "Antonio Possevino's Plan for World Evangelization." In J. Cummins, ed., *Christianity and Missions, 1450–1800*. Aldershot/Brookfield, VT: Ashgate, 1997, pp. 37–56.

Hermann, Christian, *L'Eglise d'Espagne sous le Patronage (1476–1834): essai d'ecclésiologie politique*. Madrid: Casa de Velazquez, 1988.

Pizzorusso, Giovanni, *La Compagnia di Gesù, gli ordini regolari e il processo di affermazione della giurisdizione pontificia sulle missioni tra fine XVI e inizio XVII secolo: tracce di una ricerca*. In P. Borggio, F. Cantù, P.-A. Fabre, and A. Romano, eds., *I gesuiti ai tempi di Claudio Acquaviva: strategie politiche, religiose e culturali tra Cinque e Seicento*. Brescia: Morcelliana, 2007, pp. 55–85.

Emanuele Colombo

Paul III

Alessandro Farnese was born in 1468 to a family known for its military expertise, having counted a number of *condottieri*, or mercenary leaders, among its members. Given a humanistic education, he studied in Florence, Rome, and Pisa before Pope Alexander VI (r. 1492–1503) created him a cardinal. Later named bishop of Parma, Farnese underwent something of a religious conversion in the 1510s, breaking off relations with his mistress and becoming ordained as a priest in 1519. The oldest member of the Sacred College of Cardinals at the time, Farnese was later elected as Pope Paul III in 1534.

Despite some actions typical of a Renaissance pope – elevating his grandsons to the cardinalate, commissioning art by Michelangelo, beginning construction on his family's Palazzo Farnese – it was under Paul III that reform began in earnest, epitomized by the opening of the Council of Trent in 1545 after manifold delays. Paul III lived through the first phase of the Council's sessions, which met between 1545 and 1547. The Pope's attempts at reform extended beyond the Council as well. He elevated other reform-minded men to the cardinalate, including Gasparo Contarini, Reginald Pole, and Marcello Cervini, and in anticipation of the upcoming council, he charged a committee of nine men, led by Contarini, to draw up a plan for reforming the Church. Their result was the famous *Consilium de emendanda ecclesia* (1537), which was never put into effect. Paul III also organized the Roman Inquisition in 1542.

Equally significant, Paul III approved the Society of Jesus as a new religious order. Paul III first encountered Ignatius of Loyola in 1537, when Ignatius and other companions approached the Pope with their plan to travel to the Holy Land. Paul III gave them both his blessing and funds for the journey. After the companions found no available passage in Venice, Ignatius, Peter Faber, and Diego Laínez returned to Rome in 1538, where the Pope missioned Faber and Laínez to begin teaching theology at the University of Rome (La Sapienza). After the companions had drafted the "Five Chapters" in 1539, Ignatius gave them to Cardinal Contarini to pass along to the Pope, which he did in September 1539. Some members of the curia raised concerns over the chapters' details, including the Jesuits' decision not to chant the liturgical hours in common every day as other religious orders did. Contarini defended the text, and the following year, Paul III officially recognized the Society of Jesus with his bull *Regimini militantis ecclesiae*, promulgated September 27, 1540. The bull capped the Society's membership at sixty, a restriction that was later removed. In numerous artistic depictions of the scene of Pope Paul III's approval of the Society of Jesus, depictions commissioned by the new order, Paul III is represented on the papal throne, blessing the kneeling Ignatius, who holds the bull.

Figure 53 Angelo De Rossi: *Pope Paul III Approves the Society of Jesus in 1540*, 1695–99, marble relief sculpture from the Chapel of St. Ignatius, Church of Il Gesù, Rome. Photograph Alison Fleming

Paul III called upon the first Jesuits throughout his papacy. When the *Spiritual Exercises* were first printed in 1548, they included a statement of Paul III's approval. The Pope continued to use the first Jesuits at his discretion, sending Faber and Laínez to Parma and Piacenza in 1539, and Nicolás Bobadilla to Calabria in 1540. Paul III also asked for Jesuits to be sent to India, the mission that Francis Xavier eventually undertook in 1540. Later, Paul III also gave Jesuits permission to preach anywhere in the world, if their superiors approved. By these actions we can see Paul III's direct role in the shaping of the early Society's itinerant nature. At the same time, the Pope sought to include the Jesuits in the Council of Trent, appointing Laínez and Alfonso Salmerón as papal theologians to the Council. Paul III died in 1549, yet even beyond his death, the connection to the Jesuits that he established lingered. His grandson, Cardinal Alessandro Farnese (1520–89), spent a vast sum sponsoring the building of the church of Il Gesù. He commissioned artists, was actively involved in the construction, and was buried in front of the high altar of the church. Later, Alessandro's great-nephew, Cardinal Odoardo Farnese (1573–1626), commissioned the professed house next door. A painting still hanging in the sacristy of Il Gesù depicts the two Farnese cardinals in the church, marking the Farnese family's long support of the Society of Jesus.

See also Contarini, Gasparo; Loyola, Ignatius of, SJ, St.; Papacy

Benzoni, Gino, "Paolo III." In Massimo Bray, ed., *Enciclopedia dei papi*. Vol. III. Rome: Istituto della Enciclopedia Italiana, 2000, pp. 91–111.

Capasso, Carlo, *Paolo III (1534–1549)*. Messina: Casa Editrice G. Principato, 1924.

O'Malley, John W., *The First Jesuits*. Cambridge, MA: Harvard University Press, 1993.

Robertson, Clare, *'Il Gran Cardinale': Alessandro Farnese, Patron of the Arts*. New Haven, CT/ London: Yale University Press, 1992.

Charles Keenan

Paul VI

Giovanni Battista Montini, born in Lombardy in 1897, was archbishop of Milan from 1953, made a cardinal in 1958, and elected Pope Paul VI in 1963 in succession to John XXIII. Paul continued with the Second Vatican Council, convoked by his predecessor, and saw it through to its conclusion in 1965. His papacy was marked by the fall-out from the Council, and not least by the publication in 1968 of his last encyclical, *Humanae vitae*, on the regulation of birth.

Montini knew the Jesuits well, having been educated by them as a boy and then later, as a seminarian, at the Gregorian University in Rome. In his address to the Jesuit delegates at the opening of the 32nd General Congregation (GC 32) in 1974 he repeated the notes of "joy and trepidation" that he had already sounded in May and November of 1965 at the opening and closing of GC 31. The joy is due "to the witness of Christian apostolate and of fidelity which you give us and in which we rejoice." Later on, in the same address, he notes that "wherever, in the Church, even in the most difficult and extreme fields, in the crossroads of ideologies, in the front line of social conflict, there has been and there is confrontation between the deepest desires of men and women and the perennial message of the Gospel, here also there have been, and there are, Jesuits." It was against this background that he mandated the Jesuits at GC 31 to confront atheism "with forces united."

The causes of his trepidation in relation to the Society of Jesus were several, some of which were articulated before, during, and after GC 32 in 1974–75. First, there was the matter of "grades," in particular the move, already flagged in GC 31, Decree 5, to suppress the grade of spiritual coadjutor. While the Society saw this in terms of the mandate of *Perfectae caritatis* in Vatican II to return to "the original spirit of the institutes, and the adaptation of the institutes to the changed conditions of the times" (#2), the Pope saw this effort at egalitarian renewal as a threat to the "essentials" of the Jesuit vocation and identity and, in his own words, was impelled "to interpose our authority with the superiors of your society" in order to prohibit any implementation in GC 32 (see Decree 8) of the direction proposed in GC 31.

Then, as was expressed in the appendix to the letter of Cardinal Villot, then secretary of state, written on behalf of Paul, to the Jesuits and commenting on the decrees of GC 32, there were reservations about the decisive shift in the Jesuit understanding of mission, articulated in particular in Decree 4 of GC 32, with its linking of salvation with human liberation. The fear seemed to be that this link would be extolled in such a way that the Society could forget that it was founded "for a particularly spiritual and supernatural end." And finally, in terms of substantive issues, there was expressed an appreciation that the Society had, at GC 32 (Decree 3), affirmed its traditional fidelity to the "Magisterium and the Holy Father," but a warning that the encouragement to intellectual freedom should not be construed in a way that weakened that fidelity.

It should be remembered that the immediate aftermath of Vatican II – the period with which we are concerned – was a turbulent one for the Church. The "anthropological turn" that had occurred in theology, to be followed by a political dimension, would take time to be assimilated by the Church in a balanced way and was bound to lead to tensions. These were exacerbated by the fall-out from the publication of *Humanae vitae*, with its implications not just for sexual teaching but also for ecclesiology and the status of authority in the Church. For the more cautiously inclined Paul VI, the Society of Jesus must sometimes have become a thorn in his side, with its more prophetically driven dynamism towards reform and renewal – as indeed the Society itself acknowledged (see GC 32, Decree 1, #4 and Decree 3).

However, it is clear that for Paul his concern about the Society was precisely in the context of his appreciation of its great contribution and its significance for the whole Church – "Your Society is, we say, the test of the vitality of the Church throughout the centuries; it is perhaps one of the most meaningful crucibles in which are encountered the difficulties, the temptations, the efforts, the perpetuity and the successes of the whole Church" (opening address to GC 32). There are, then, reasonable grounds to speculate that, for Paul, the balance between joy and trepidation came down positively.

See also Papacy; Vatican II

Papal Addresses to GC 31 and GC 32. In John W. Padberg, ed., *Jesuit Life and Mission Today: The Decrees and Accompanying Documents of the 31st–35th General Congregations of the Society of Jesus*. St. Louis, MO: The Institute of Jesuit Sources, 2009.

Gerard O'Hanlon, SJ

Peace and Reconciliation

The Society of Jesus has been engaged in promoting peace and reconciliation since its foundation. In the *Spiritual Exercises*, the founder of the Jesuits, Ignatius of Loyola, proposes a contemplation on the Trinity looking down on the universe and seeing contrary situations where some people are happy and others are sad; some suffering and others celebrating; some in conflict and others in peace. As a mission of the Jesuits, peace and reconciliation come under the broader category of faith and justice. Over the last four decades, the Jesuits have made a deliberate commitment to faith and justice, actively working against unjust structures by instituting social justice centers all over the world. These social centers form the hub of the ministry of peace and reconciliation in the Society.

The 32nd General Congregation set the tone for a more authentic approach to living the gospel values in the promotion of faith and justice. This came at the time when there was excessive militarization of conflicts in many parts of the world, particularly in Latin America and Africa. The 34th and 35th General Congregations confirmed that the work of faith and justice is not a specialized apostolate but, rather, an integral part of every Jesuit apostolate. As a consequence, the expanded vision of peace and reconciliation takes into account the analysis of the structures that create and sustain conflict and violence, such as systematic marginalization of the majority of the population, migration and refugee movements, environmental and ecological degradation, and new inequalities engendered by marketization and the privatization of economies.

In Africa the work of peace and reconciliation has focused largely on addressing the social-economic injustices at the root of conflict and violence. For example, CEPAS, a research and social justice center in the Democratic Republic of the Congo (DRC), has for more than forty years been involved in conducting research and conscientizing the population through its writings and seminars on situations of injustice in the country as well as the need for equitable distribution of natural resources. Similarly, CEFOD, a research and social justice center in Chad, has focused on social research and advocacy for economic justice. The two centers have advocated for the right to own and manage mineral resources as a common good for the benefit of all citizens. At the Jesuit Hakimani Centre (JHC) in Nairobi, Kenya, the main focus has been peace and reconciliation. Following the post-election violence in 2008, the JHC put into place a team of leaders from different sectors known as "ambassadors for peace" who traversed the country, mobilizing the population to end the violence and live harmoniously. The center continues to conduct research and advocate for peace and reconciliation. The social apostolate coordinating office of the Jesuits of Africa and Madagascar conducts advocacy and popular education on ecology, peace building, and economic justice.

In India the Jesuits have worked with marginalized communities and consistently advocated against human rights violations and economic injustices. The India Social Institute has been at the forefront of conducting research and social action that empower marginalized groups, especially the Dalits, tribals, women, children, and minority communities, who are victims of multiple forms of violence.

The Jesuit Refugee Service (JRS) International Office in Rome has an international reconciliation team that has been developing context-sensitive reconciliation tools that can be applied to different parts of the world. Comillas Pontifical University in Madrid, Spain, conducts interdisciplinary research on reconciliation. In Mexico, IBERO University in Mexico City conducts research and teaching on trauma healing.

Other Jesuit universities in Africa, the United States, and Europe have been actively engaged in peace and reconciliation research as well as advocacy that is critical for conflict resolution. Hekima University College Institute of Peace Studies and International Relations (HIPSIR) in Nairobi offers a Master of Arts degree in Peace Studies and International Relations as well as specialized practitioners' training in conflict analysis, diplomacy, peace building, and reconciliation for people from different parts of Africa and elsewhere. Marquette University in Milwaukee, Wisconsin, USA, runs a center for peacemaking. Deusto University, Bilbao, Spain, conducts research and teaching on transitional justice.

In Latin America, a strategic focus of JRS Colombia is to develop methodological tools for reconciliation that would facilitate working with communities of refugees and displaced people. This also includes a pedagogy of forgiveness and reconciliation with youth. The pilot project has focused on working with communities of victims in the areas of forgiveness and reconciliation. Another project in Latin America is the collaborative educational program named Schools of Forgiveness and Reconciliation (ESPERE) in Mexico, Peru, Dominican Republic, Cuba, and Ecuador. Peace Education for youth is being conducted in Fe y Alegría schools in Venezuela, Bolivia, Dominican Republic, and Colombia. At CINEP, the social justice center in Colombia, the "Program for Peace" (*Programa por la Paz*) and publication of "reconciliation learning experiences" are among the activities geared toward peace and reconciliation.

See also Africa, East; Africa, West; Hekima University College; Jesuit Refugee Service; Justice; Kenya; Service of Faith and Promotion of Justice

Arlen Amanda Chinchilla et al., "La paz completa?" *Cien días*. Center for Research and Popular Education/Peace Program (CINEP/PP) (December 2015), 1–23.
Nicolás, Adolfo, "*Hospitality on the Frontiers: 34 Years of Service to Refugees.*" Colloquium. Rome: Jesuit Refugee Service International Office, November 2014.
Padberg, John W., ed., *Jesuit Life and Mission Today: The Decrees and Accompanying Documents of the 31st–35th General Congregations of the Society of Jesus.* St. Louis, MO: The Institute of Jesuit Sources, 2009.
"Seeking Peace in a Violent World: New Challenges." *Promotio Iustitiae* 89 (2005), 15–24.

Agbonkhianmeghe Orobator, SJ

Periti

(Lat., singular, *peritus*: "expert" or "consultant"). Throughout the history of general Church councils, theologians have played various roles, ranging from witnesses, expert advisers, and even full voting members. According to Nelson Minnich, the status of theologians at general councils varied according to the nature of "the troubles" the Church was experiencing at the time and shifting ecclesiologies that emphasized either conciliar or papal authority.

The general councils held between 1409 and 1511 had allowed theologians deliberative votes during their proceedings. In 1511, however, this practice was halted and the role of the theologian became a purely consultative one of assisting bishops who lacked the theological training needed to make doctrinal judgments. In some cases they were simply listed as "witnesses" in the council *acta*, along with the ambassadors, knights, and curial officials who were present.

Among the theological consultants, or *periti*, invited to the Council of Trent (1545–63) were three Jesuits: Diego Laínez, Alfonso Salmerón, and Claude Jay. Laínez attended the first two sessions as a theological adviser and the third session as a voting member, since by then he had succeeded Ignatius of Loyola as the second superior general of the Society of Jesus. Salmerón attended all three sessions as a papal theologian, and Jay served as procurator for the bishop of Augsburg. The German Jesuit Peter Canisius also made a brief appearance at the end of the first session.

At Trent the *periti* examined the doctrinal issues in the Reformers' writings in order to ferret out heretical statements. They formulated these as "articles" on which they gave their opinions in serial fashion, defending or opposing the Protestant positions. The bishops responded, offering their opinions also in serial fashion. After a number of sessions with the help of the *periti*, a group of bishops would draft a decree, discuss, and (if necessary) amend it. Finally, it would be brought to a formal vote in a session open to the public. Despite their inability to vote, theologians clearly "played an indispensable role at Trent and were fully integrated into the Council's functioning" (O'Malley, *Trent*, 84–85).

Of the ninety-six *periti* who prepared materials for the First Vatican Council (1869–70), eight were Jesuits. Three, all Germans from the "Roman school," stand out for their significant contributions: John Baptist Franzelin and Klemens Schrader as the principal drafters of the proposed Constitutions on the Catholic Faith (*Dei Filius*) and on the Church (*De Ecclesia*), and Joseph Kleutgen, who together with Franzelin, took an active part in drafting the Council's definition of papal infallibility.

Of the 480 officially appointed *periti* at the Second Vatican Council (1962–65), forty-eight were Jesuits. Five other Jesuits, including ecumenists Maurice Bévenot and Gustave Weigel, served as translators and also participated in the commissions. As at Trent, since not all bishops were theologians, Pope John XXIII officially invited theologians to assist the bishops in their deliberations. These *periti* often gave informal lectures and circulated articles to the bishops from their national and linguistic groups in order to update them on the latest theology. They helped to draft conciliar schemas and attended the general sessions, but they neither addressed the Council fathers nor voted. Nevertheless, they had many informal opportunities for contact with the bishops.

The influence of *periti* at Vatican II cannot be overestimated. For example, in the case of the document on revelation, *Dei Verbum*, two *periti*, Joseph Ratzinger and Karl Rahner, SJ, drafted an alternative text which they deemed more adequate than the text *De fontibus revelationis* proposed by "the Roman school." They gave their text to Cardinal Frings of Cologne, who delivered it to other episcopal conferences. Thus, the Vatican II *periti* were sometimes humorously referred to as "the cooks of the council." "Their work nevertheless remained outside the Council Hall," notes Karl Heinz Neufeld, [thus] "it was essentially a hidden service." Jesuit *periti* at Vatican II who made the most significant contributions included Charles Boyer, Jean Daniélou, and Henri de Lubac (France); Aloysius Grillmeier, Josef Jungmann, Otto Semmelroth, and Karl Rahner (Germany); Peter Smulders and Sebastian Tromp (Netherlands); and John Courtney Murray (United States).

See also Kleutgen, Joseph, SJ; Laínez, Diego, SJ; Murray, John Courtney, SJ; Rahner, Karl, SJ; Trent, Council of; Vatican I; Vatican II

Acta Synodalia Concilii Oecumenici Vaticani II, Indices, 935–49.

Bangert, William, *Claude Jay and Alfonso Salmerón: Two Early Jesuits*. Chicago, IL: Loyola University Press, 1985.

Dulles, Avery, "Jesuits and Theology." *Theological Studies* 52 (1991), 524–38.

Minnich, Nelson, "The Voice of Theologians in General Councils from Pisa to Trent." *Theological Studies* 59 (1998), 420–41.

Neufeld, Karl Heinz, "In Service of the Council: Bishops and Theologians at the Second Vatican Council." In René Latourelle, ed., *Vatican II: Assessment and Perspectives: Twenty-Five After (1962–1987)*. Vol. I. New York: Paulist Press, 1988, pp. 74–105.

O'Malley, John W., *Trent: What Happened at the Council*. Cambridge, MA: Harvard University Press, 2013.

Tanner, Norman, *Decrees of the Ecumenical Councils*. Vol. II: *Trent to Vatican II*. London: Sheed and Ward, 1990.

Veliath, Dominic, "The Theologian and the Church." In Jacob Kavunkal, Errol D'Lima, and Evelyn Monteiro, eds., *Vatican II: A Gift and a Task*. Bombay: Saint Paul Society, 2006, pp. 100–15.

Mary Ann Hinsdale, IHM

Persons (Parsons), Robert, SJ (1546–1610)

Robert Persons resigned his Oxford position in 1574 for religious reasons; in 1575 he entered the Jesuit novitiate in Rome where he remained after his ordination in 1578. (Pope Pius V excommunicated and deposed Elizabeth and encouraged subjects to rise up against her.) Unlike his contemporary Edmund Campion, Persons agitated for a Jesuit mission to England. With William Allen (president of the English College, Douai) as his advocate and in anticipation of religious liberties after the projected marriage of Queen Elizabeth and François, duke of Anjou, Persons secured Acquaviva's permission. Accompanied by a reluctant Campion, Persons left Rome in April 1580. Instead of toleration, they found renewed persecution within England as marital negotiations collapsed and a Papal-Spanish military expedition landed in Ireland. Campion was captured in July, 1581. *Post hoc* (and according to Persons's opponents *propter hoc*) Persons escaped to the continent to confer with Allen and to write.

Persons published about thirty treatises in Latin and English on theological, religious, and political issues, including the persistent problem of Catholic attendance at Protestant services. His extant correspondence, currently being edited, will comprise four volumes. The English prose style is considered among the best of the period. His nimble pen could quickly turn poisonous in his attacks. These works are now read only by scholars, with the exception of the very influential Ignatian spiritual work *The First Book of Christian Resolution* (generally referred to as *The Christian Directory*). Purified of its popish, superstitious doctrines by a godly Protestant Edward Bunny – to the anger and dismay of Persons – *The Christian Directory* became a best-seller in Elizabethan England.

On the continent Persons and Allen played integral roles as various coalitions of Spain, the Papacy, Scotland, and the French Catholic League (headed by the Guises) conspired and planned an invasion of England to liberate the captive Mary, Queen of Scots (a Guise) and install her as the rightful queen of England. After her execution in 1587 and her son King James's subsequent reconciliation with Queen Elizabeth, Allen and Persons abandoned the Stuarts to support the Spanish princess as Elizabeth's successor. In 1588, after the defeat of the Spanish Armada, Acquaviva sent Persons to Spain for two reasons: to keep English affairs on Philip II's agenda; and to use his influence at court against Acquaviva's Spanish Jesuit opponents, the *memorialistas*. Persons secured endowments from the King and various nobles and bishops for the foundation of English seminaries at Valladolid and Seville, and a college for English boys at St. Omers, then in the Spanish Netherlands. A decree from the 5th General Congregation

(1593–94) prohibiting Jesuit involvement in political matters alarmed Persons who protested that, at least in England, political and religious matters were so intertwined that he would need a dispensation. Acquaviva clarified the issue: Persons's activities were not political because they were undertaken to advance the Kingdom of God and not a particular state or dynasty.

The cracks within the English Catholic community, skillfully but superficially covered by Allen, broke open after his death in 1594. In the subsequent controversies, clerical and lay opponents of Jesuit activity, occasionally with support from the Elizabethan government, blamed the Society and Persons in particular for the religious persecution which resulted from their participation in treasonous plots and interference in the question of the succession, an area declared off-limits by the government for anyone. They agitated for the Society's withdrawal from the mission, a goal which they nearly achieved. As the disturbances spread to the English College, Rome, Persons was summoned from Spain to become rector in 1597. In the following year two novel structures were introduced: an archpriest to govern the secular clergy in England; and a prefect (Persons) to coordinate the activities of English Jesuits in the continental seminaries and on the mission. Neither resolved the problem: other Jesuits protested institutions within their geographical provinces over which they had limited if any control; secular clergy wanted guarantees that Jesuits were not involved in their ecclesiastical structure. Using his Roman contacts, Persons successfully defeated Appellant efforts to exclude the Society, but he failed to preserve the integrity of the mission.

The peaceful accession of King James I in 1603 left Persons in the embarrassed position of having backed a loser. First through the mediation of courtiers and then directly with the King, Persons attempted to establish contact. James was not interested and apparently influenced Pope Clement VIII's suggestion that Persons prolong his sojourn in Naples until further notice: he remained there until Clement's death in 1605. Some scholars seek to involve Persons in or hold him responsible for the Gunpowder Plot, but there is no evidence. Despite his problems with James, Persons consistently counseled Catholics to patience and against violence. The introduction of an oath of allegiance after the plot occasioned the last major controversy in which Persons was involved. Persons served as prefect and rector until his death in 1610.

See also Campion, Edmund, SJ; Gunpowder Plot; United Kingdom

Edwards, Francis, *Robert Persons: The Biography of an Elizabethan Jesuit, 1546–1610*. St. Louis, MO: The Institute of Jesuit Sources, 1995.

Houliston, Victor, *Catholic Resistance in Elizabethan England: Robert Persons's Jesuit Polemic, 1580–1610*. Aldershot: Ashgate; Rome: Institutum Historicum Societatis Iesu, 2007.

McCoog, Thomas M., *The Society of Jesus in Ireland, Scotland, and England 1541–1588: "Our Way of Proceeding?"* Leiden: Brill, 1996.

The Society of Jesus in Ireland, Scotland, and England, 1589–1597. Building the Faith of Saint Peter upon the King of Spain's Monarchy. Farnham: Ashgate; Rome: Institutum Historicum Societatis Iesu, 2012.

Thomas McCoog, SJ

Peru

In 1568 a group of Jesuit priests and lay brothers led by Jerónimo Ruiz del Portillo arrived at Peru, thus beginning the Jesuit presence in Spanish America. Although the Society of Jesus had established itself in Portuguese Brazil as early as 1549, previous attempts to found a mission in the Spanish-controlled areas of the continent had failed. Twice while superior of Spain had Francis Borja attempted to send missionaries to America (in 1555 and again in 1559), only to see the expeditions fail at the last minute. Yet, in 1566, a letter from King Philip II revived the plans, and on November 4, 1567, eight Jesuits set sail from San Lúcar de Barrameda to found a college in Lima.

The College of San Pablo opened its doors shortly after the arrival of the Jesuits. Besides teaching the usual courses on philosophy and humanities, the Jesuits devoted their time to preaching and tending to the spiritual needs of the Spanish, native, and African communities in the city. They immediately made their presence felt in the Peruvian society, and, by the end of that first year, the Jesuits had accepted several new recruits, increasing their ranks to thirty individuals. Among the novices were some of mestizo origins (sons of Spanish fathers and native mothers), such as Blas Valera and Bartolomé de Santiago. Mestizos were accepted into the Society because their mastery of native languages was considered essential for the task of evangelizing the native population of Peru. This fact trumped all racially based misgivings some Spanish Jesuits had manifested. The issue of mestizo priesthood remained a controversial one, however, and in 1582, the 3rd Provincial Congregation of Peru unanimously barred mestizos from entering the Order.

Some months after the arrival of the Jesuits, Francisco de Toledo entered Lima to take possession of the office of viceroy. Although Toledo had always had friendly relations with the Society of Jesus (he was a personal friend of Father General Borj and brought with him several Jesuits to Peru, including Bartolomé Hernández, his personal confessor), his mandate to reform the civil and ecclesiastical government of Peru soon put him at odds with the Peruvian Jesuits. Toledo's ecclesiastical reforms focused on two main goals: to strengthen the Royal Patronage (the right of the Spanish Crown to make ecclesiastical appointments in the Americas), and to create new parishes around the towns in which he was resettling the scattered native population of Peru. Based on a rigorist interpretation of the Royal Patronage, Toledo tapped into the religious orders to get the personnel needed to fill these new positions. The Jesuits, who were forbidden by their *Constitutions* to become parish priests, resisted Toledo's pressures. Ultimately, they would only take care of two native parishes for any meaningful period of time: Santiago del Cercado, in the outskirts of Lima, and Juli, in present-day Bolivia, on the shores of Lake Titicaca. In time, Juli would become a training ground for Jesuit missionaries. In 1594, the 5th General Congregation of the Society made knowledge of native languages mandatory for all Jesuits working in the Americas. In order to maximize their exposure to native languages and the pastoral methods of the Order, Juli was designated as a residence for all young Jesuits undergoing their third probation in Peru. Two Jesuits, Diego González de Holguín and Ludovico Bertonio, produced the most important grammars and dictionaries of Quechua and Aymara, respectively, the two main native languages spoken in Peru.

Even if the Jesuits did not have a significant impact as parish priests, they deeply influenced the pastoral methods employed in the Indian parishes. Two figures in particular stand out: José de Acosta (1540–1600) and Pablo Joseph de Arriaga (1564–1622). Acosta was among the brightest Jesuits of his generation. His *Historia natural y moral de las Indias* (1590) was one of the most widely read accounts of the nature and peoples of the New World ever written, being translated into most European languages and praised by

Enlightened philosophers such as William Robertson and Alexander von Humboldt. But Acosta's influence on the American Church was due not to his masterpiece of natural history, but rather to his technical interventions as a theologian during his fifteen years in Peru, namely, his missiological treatise, *De procuranda Indorum salute* (composed in 1576; published in 1589), and his participation in the 3rd Council of Lima, convened in 1582 by Archbishop Toribio de Mogrovejo. The Council reformed Church practices, implementing in South America the dispositions of the Council of Trent. Among the measures adopted by the Lima Council were a number of suggestions from Acosta's *De procuranda*, such as the use of native languages for evangelization, the publication of a corpus of pastoral texts of mandatory use in the native parishes, and a renewed emphasis on the importance of administering the sacrament of penance to the natives. Acosta's hand was behind the main outcomes of the Third Lima Council. He edited the acts of the meetings as well as the trilingual (Quechua, Aymara, and Spanish) confession handbook, the brief and long catechisms, and the sermon collection published under the auspices of the Council. These texts – the first books printed in South America – would remain in use until the eighteenth century.

If Acosta prepared an educational program for the indoctrination of Andean catechumens, Arriaga became the leader and ideologue of a harsher approach to native spirituality. From 1609 onwards, in the Archdiocese of Lima (and, sporadically, in other bishoprics), teams of inspectors (known as *extirpadores*) visited native communities with the declared objective of eradicating indigenous ritual practices and strengthening Christianity. These campaigns to extirpate idolatry, initiated by Archbishop Bartolomé Lobo Guerrero, were soon controlled by the Society of Jesus with the political backing of Viceroy Francisco de Borja, prince of Esquilache. Even though Arriaga did not hold any official position, he quickly became the acknowledged leader of the extirpation campaigns, especially from 1619 onwards. In 1621 he published his handbook for extirpators, *Manual de extirpación de las idolatrías*, where he detailed not only a good deal of native ritual practices but, more importantly, the standard procedure for the inspections, beginning with the preparations for the arrival of the extirpating team to a village, the proper way of conducting interrogations and gathering information regarding cultic objects, to the sermons to be preached and the different punishment of the idolaters.

Acosta's *De procuranda* (along with the pastoral corpus published by the Third Lima Council) and Arriaga's *Manual de extirpación* are the two poles around which much of the missionary and evangelizing activity of the Peruvian Jesuits revolved. Although complementary – Acosta mentioned the need to punish contumacious idolaters, while Arriaga recommended sermons taken from Acosta's writings – these texts embodied different ways of understanding native evangelization. But aside from their differences, both represented an official position regarding the evangelization of the native peoples in a colonial setting, a position that oscillated between persuasion and repression. Whereas the influence of the Jesuit-inspired pastoral corpus published by the Third Lima Council would have a more lasting impact, campaigns to extirpate idolatries would be established periodically during the seventeenth century, almost all of them including a strong Jesuit element.

The original Jesuit province of Peru spanned from Panama to Chile, covering an area that more or less coincided with that of the Viceroyalty of Peru. The immense distances in the continent meant that, as soon as the Jesuits began expanding their activities outside of the central Andean region (roughly, the central area of today's Peru), governance and logistic problems arose. As a result, new administrative divisions were carved out from the Peruvian province to facilitate work in the new missions and colleges scattered throughout South America. The province of Paraguay was founded in 1604, encompassing modern Paraguay, Uruguay, Argentina, and Chile. In 1605 Quito became a semi-autonomous vice province depending on Peru, covering the territories of today's Colombia, Ecuador, and Venezuela.

Alongside the expansion came the foundation of colleges and residences. Although modern scholars tend to focus on the missionary endeavors of the Jesuits in South America, in their contemporaries' eyes the Jesuits were first and foremost educational agents. The Jesuits, in fact, opened up schools in every important city in the continent. Just a few decades after their arrival in Peru, they had opened up colleges in Cuzco, Potosi, Chuquisaca (modern-day Sucre), Quito, Buenos Aires, Asunción, Córdoba, and Santiago. The center of this network of colleges was San Pablo, in Lima. Although during the 1570s General Mercurian had hoped to raise San Pablo to the level of the most prestigious Jesuit universities in Europe, in 1578 Viceroy Toledo, seeking to protect the interests of the newly founded Royal University of San Marcos (also situated in Lima), forbade all lay students from attending private colleges. This forced the Jesuits to close San Pablo's doors. By virtue of a royal decree dated 1580, the Jesuits were allowed to resume the teaching of Latin, humanities, philosophy, and theology to all students at San Pablo. The decree, however, forbade the Jesuits from conferring degrees. In practice, this transformed the College of San Pablo into the entryway to the University of San Marcos, a situation that was made official by a royal decree of 1621, which required every student looking for admission at the university to present a certificate signed by the Jesuits at San Pablo.

In spite of these restrictions, San Pablo quickly became one of the most important intellectual centers of the Peruvian Viceroyalty. Its faculty collaborated closely with the university's faculty; several Jesuits (among them José de Acosta, Esteban de Ávila, Juan Pérez Menacho) held the Chair of Theology at San Marcos. The Jesuit College's library housed one of the finest collections in the South America, holding over 25,000 books by 1767. Perhaps more importantly, San Pablo played a crucial role in the development of other Jesuit colleges in the continent. Since the creation of the office of procurator for the West Indies in 1575, books were regularly sent to Spanish America in order to supply the colleges. The books sent by the procurator arrived in San Pablo and from there were distributed to the different Jesuit colleges and residences in South America.

Even though the Jesuits at San Pablo could not confer higher education degrees on their pupils, in areas that were too far away from Lima to make it practical for students to attend San Marcos, the Society was allowed to establish universities. In the province of Peru proper, the Jesuits operated two universities: the University of Saint Ignatius Loyola, in Cuzco (est. 1621) and the College of Santiago, in Chuquisaca, elevated to the rank of university in 1622. Attached to these institutions of higher learning were boarding schools (known as *colegios convictorios*), in which students from other cities could take the humanities courses in preparation for their university studies. The oldest of these boarding schools was the College of Saint Martin, in Lima, founded in 1587. The College of Saint Bernard, in Cuzco, opened its doors in 1619, and the College of Saint John the Baptist in Chuquisaca began its classes in October 1623.

Aside from secondary and higher education, the Jesuits maintained grammar schools wherever they had a residence. The Jesuits taught literacy, arithmetic, the Christian doctrine, and, in some cases, basic Latin to local children free of charge. The Society of Jesus also opened two colleges for the education of the native nobility, one of them in Santiago del Cercado, just outside Lima, and the other in Cuzco. Even though formally referred to as "colleges," these institutions were more akin to the grammar schools operated by the Jesuits, with the difference that the students boarded in the colleges, in order to expose them to a more exacting religious instruction. The College of El Cercado was inaugurated in 1618, and remained open even after the expulsion in 1767. The College of Cuzco was opened on November 1, 1622.

After the separation of Paraguay, Chile, and Quito from the Jesuit province of Peru, the Peruvian Jesuits did not engage in new missions among unconverted native groups until the second half the seventeenth century. In 1668 Father José Bermudo and Brother Juan de Soto entered the Moxos region, in the Bolivian Amazonia, where they founded the Reduction of Trinidad. The reductions at Moxos were modeled after the more famous Paraguayan missions. By 1749 there were twenty-one reductions, manned by forty-six missionaries, who tended to a population of some 20,000 individuals.

The Jesuit ministries in Peru came to an end in 1767, when the Spanish Crown decided to expel the Society of Jesus from its dominions. The Royal Edict was read first in Chuquisaca on August 17, and in Lima on September 9. The Jesuits from today's Bolivia and Southern Peru were gathered in the port of Arica, where they embarked in a ship bringing about 200 Jesuits from Lima. From there, the ship proceeded to the port of Valparaiso in order to pick up another 200 priests from the Chilean province. After a long and taxing voyage, the exiled Jesuits from Peru finally were relocated in the city of Ferrara, Italy.

As it also happened in other areas of South America, the Jesuits did not come back to Peru immediately after the restoration of the Order in 1814. The return of the Jesuits to the now independent Republic of Peru was engineered by Manuel Teodoro del Valle, bishop of Hanuco. In 1869, on the occasion of his stay in Rome for the First Vatican Council, Bishop Valle formally requested from General Pieter Beckx the return of the Society to Peru. On September 15, 1871, four Jesuits from France disembarked in Callao, Lima's seaport, thus resuming Jesuit activity in what had been their first and most important province in Spanish America. For the next century, the Peruvian Jesuits would be part, administratively, of the Jesuit province of Toledo (Spain). In 1968 General Pedro Arrupe elevated Peru again to the level of independent province. Today, the Peruvian province boasts more than 170 priests, most of them born and raised in Peru. Aside from their social and pastoral ministries, the Peruvian Jesuits again play an important role in education. The Order maintains nine elementary and secondary schools in the country, and one institution of higher learning, the Universidad Antonio Ruiz de Montoya. They are also co-founders of the Universidad del Pacífico. The Order is in charge of the Seminary San Luis Gonzaga in Jaen, in the Cajamarca region, in northern Peru, where they train future diocesan priests.

See also Acosta, José de, SJ; Education, Secondary and Pre-Secondary; Paraguay Missions ("Reductions"); Spain; Suppression; Universities, 1540–1773; Vargas Ugarte, Rubén, SJ

Albó, Xavier, "Jesuitas y culturas indígenas en el Perú, 1568–1606." *América indígena* 26, 3(1966), 249–308, and 26, 4 (1966), 395–445.

Griffiths, Nicholas, *The Cross and the Serpent: Religious Repression and Resurgence in Colonial Peru.* Norman/London: University of Oklahoma Press, 1996.

Martin, Luis, *The Intellectual Conquest of Peru: The Jesuit College of San Pablo, 1568–1767.* New York: Fordham University Press, 1968.

Vargas Ugarte, Rubén, *Historia de la Iglesia en el Peru.* 5 vols. Lima: Imprenta Santa María, 1953–62.

Andrés Ignacio Prieto

Pharmacy/Pharmacology

Thanks to their involvement in overseas missions, Jesuits enjoyed a leading role in the discovery and spread of herbals and other pharmacological remedies in the early modern period. Partly because of the cost of obtaining European medicine overseas, Jesuits turned to local flora in seeking out remedies. However, because the Society's *Constitutions* forbade professed priests from studying or engaging in medical work, most of the pharmacological work was undertaken by the Society's temporal coadjutors, who were trained as apothecaries and stationed in pharmacies attached to Jesuit colleges in the New World and in Europe.

Most famous among the medical agents Jesuits identified and transported to Europe was cinchona, an antifebrile containing quinine that became an effective remedy for malaria. Jesuits initially noticed Indians' use of the agent near Quito in the early seventeenth century, and after some testing it was shipped back to Rome, arriving by the 1640s at the latest. From there it was sent to other Jesuit colleges throughout Europe. The Society's role in cinchona's spread was well known, for the substance was commonly called "Jesuit's bark," and, in powdered form, "Jesuit's powder." The Jesuits also identified and transported guaiacum, sarsaparilla, aguaribay, and ipecacuanha root, among many other items (Anagnostou, "Jesuits in Spanish America," 4). They also provided descriptions of thousands of species of plants. The Jesuits' temporal coadjutors generally published little, but some treatises did appear, including Pedro Montenegro's *Materia médica misionera* (eighteenth century) and Johann Steinhöfer's *Florilegio medicinal de todas las enfermedades* (1712). In addition, many natural histories of the Americas written by Jesuits also described local flora and its uses, including José de Acosta's *Historia natural y moral de las Indias* (1590).

Though herbals and other remedies were initially intended for use by members of Jesuit colleges, in time the Society's apothecaries began to serve cities and the countryside surrounding the colleges as well. In many cases, Jesuit missionaries relied on native populations for information about local flora and herbals, observing the use of medicinal agents in indigenous societies. At the same time, Jesuits were wary of embracing what they saw as pagan use of such materials, especially in non-Christian rituals. Missionaries instead sought to control access to medicinal agents and medical knowledge, recognizing the advantages for their mission if they held such expertise. Thus, many Jesuit missionaries attempted to portray themselves as healers in the hope of facilitating conversions to the Catholic faith.

Meanwhile, the Jesuits' communication networks meant that herbals and other pharmacological products could easily be transported back to Europe and distributed there. As the center of Catholic networks for information and administration, Rome became a key locus in the spread of Jesuits' pharmacological products and medical knowledge.

A pharmacy was built at the Roman College in the early seventeenth century, with a Jesuit designated as head pharmacist. Interest in the new medical remedies was not restricted to the temporal coadjutors who studied and practiced medicine. From his seat in Rome, where he studied all manner of objects brought back from the Society's missions, the Jesuit polymath Athanasius Kircher also became interested in new pharmaceuticals, even composing a treatise on the plague, its causes, and possible remedies in 1658 (*Scrutinium physico-medicum contagiosae luis, quae dicitur pestis*). Although many Jesuits, like the majority of their contemporaries, believed illness and plague had a moral cause – that individual or collective sin lay at the root of illness – Jesuits did embrace the use of so-called temporal remedies. As noted, Jesuit temporal coadjutors served in pharmacies, and Jesuit novices served in hospitals, tending to the sick and administering medicine under a physician's watch.

The influx of medicinal products from the Americas brought the Society's European members several benefits. First and foremost, the medical agents could be used to treat the Society's own members who had fallen ill. At the same time, Jesuit pharmacies could sell these new agents for profit, and Jesuit priests could also offer new herbal remedies to powerful patrons. The Jesuits could thus act as healers both in the overseas missions and at European courts.

The Jesuit missionaries enjoyed nearly unrestricted access to medicinal herbs and other pharmacological agents in the Americas until the eighteenth century, when the Society's members were expelled from Portuguese territories in 1759 and Spanish ones in 1767.

See also Acosta, José de, SJ; Ecuador; Kircher, Athanasius, SJ; Plague; Science

Anagnostou, Sabine, "Jesuits in Spanish America and Their Contributions to the Exploration of the American *Materia Medica*." *Pharmacy in History* 47, 1 (2005), 3–17.

Harris, Steven J., "Jesuit Scientific Activity in the Overseas Missions, 1540–1773." *Isis* 96, 1 (2005), 71–79.

Jarcho, Saul, *Quinine's Predecessor: Francesco Torti and the Early History of Cinchona*. Baltimore, MD: Johns Hopkins University Press, 1993.

Parsons, Christopher, "The Natural History of Colonial Science: Joseph-François Lafitau's Discovery of Ginseng and Its Afterlives." *The William and Mary Quarterly* (3rd Series) 73, 1 (2016), 37–72.

Prieto, Andrés I., *Missionary Scientists: Jesuit Science in Spanish South America, 1570–1810*. Nashville, TN: Vanderbilt University Press, 2011.

Charles Keenan

The Philippines

In the span of almost four centuries, the Jesuit mission in the Philippine archipelago has undertaken diverse ministries in response to changes in the world as well as within the Church. From 1581 onwards, save during the Society's suppression, it faced difficult challenges during Spanish and American colonial periods and after Philippine independence in 1946.

In nearly four centuries of Spanish colonization (1521–1898), all missionaries including the Jesuits, mostly Spaniards with other Europeans, worked within the *Patronato Real de las Indias* between the papacy and Spanish monarchy. The archipelago became a strategic post for religious and colonial missions within the Asia Pacific region, and

Jesuits went on such missions; for instance, to the Moluccas in the late sixteenth century, and Marianas in the seventeenth.

Religious orders were assigned to different islands. Jesuits served in provinces near Manila but shifted from the late sixteenth century to indigenous and Moslem settlements in many islands of Visayas and Mindanao. These missions were frequently plagued by tropical diseases and natural calamities such as earthquakes and storms, and also disrupted by armed conflicts and pirate raids for the slave trade. Though some Jesuits helped build fortifications and even took on military roles, their overall approach of working with local leaders and incorporating music and other native elements proved more effective. From the restored Society's return in 1859, Jesuit missionary efforts extended across Mindanao, covering the Magindanao, Zamboanga, and Caraga regions, among others. During the American colonial period (1898–1946), many missions were turned over to diocesan clergy and other religious orders.

Education was crucial to mission. Ensuring instruction before and after baptism, Jesuits began to establish different schools for both native and Spanish students. They offered basic education in Cavite, Panay, and elsewhere, but by the early seventeenth century, Colegio de San Jose (present-day San Jose Seminary), and Colegio de San Ignacio (short-lived university) were founded. After the Society's restoration and upon the request of Spanish colonial authorities, Jesuits established Escuela Municipal de Manila, the alma mater of some leaders of the late nineteenth-century nationalist and revolutionary movements and the precursor of Ateneo de Manila University. During the twentieth century, four more institutions for tertiary education would open, and three for basic education of Chinese Filipinos initiated by Jesuits exiled during the 1949 Chinese Revolution.

These schools also functioned as social ministry centers. Besides promoting works of mercy, they began programs with marginalized sectors of the population. From the 1930s onward, Jesuits Joseph Mulry and Walter Hogan together with their students formed labor organizations that rejected communist ideology but also provoked condemnation from the local hierarchy. Their efforts led to the establishment of the Institute of Social Order in 1947. Under the Marcos dictatorship (1972–86), Jesuit institutions, inspired by recent General Congregations, worked with others in Church and civil society for constitutional democracy.

Jesuit contributions to cultural and scientific development have also been significant. Early missions introduced methods of agriculture and built churches with native elements. Many did not survive; the beautiful 1890 San Ignacio was bombed during World War II, and the 1734 Loboc, Bohol, church was damaged by the 2013 earthquake. Jesuits also produced much writing and engaged in research in diverse fields. With the Church's decision to evangelize in the native languages, many translated European works and wrote original manuscripts in various languages. Juan de Noceda and Pedro de San Lucar redacted the classic *Vocabulario dela lengua tagala* (1754); Juan Alcina recorded local plant and animal species as well as native customs in Samar; Georg Josef Kamel studied native plants, one of which was named after him. From the 1860s as well, Manila Observatory under the Jesuit Federico Faura was a highly regarded center for meteorological and seismic studies, and its work later was supported by the American colonial government. It has focused now on environmental research and risk reduction management.

The Jesuit mission in the Philippines has accompanied the Church and nation through changing times. It began under Spanish Jesuit jurisdiction, then was turned over in 1927 to the Maryland-New York province (when Irish-American Jesuits were politically unacceptable for mission to India), became an independent province in 1958, and was led by the first Filipino provincial Horacio de la Costa in 1965. Today it numbers around 250 members and has established new institutions to address emerging concerns – notably, Loyola School of Theology, centers of Ignatian spirituality, and psychospiritual formation, as well as social research and advocacy institutes such as the Institute for Church and Social Issues and Environmental Science for Social Change. The Jesuit pastoral ministry has focused on indigenous communities and prison and hospital chaplaincies. Filipino Jesuits have been sent to interprovincial missions in Timor Leste and Cambodia.

See also Asia; Ateneo de Manila University; East Asian Pastoral Institute (EAPI); Korea and Cambodia; Pacific Worlds; Spain; Timor Leste; United States of America

de la Costa, Horacio, *The Jesuits in the Philippines 1581–1768*. Cambridge, MA: Harvard University Press, 1961.

Fabros, Wilfredo, *The Church and Its Social Involvement in the Philippines, 1930–1972*. Quezon City: Ateneo de Manila University Press, 1988.

Moreno, Antonio F., *Church, State, and Civil Society in Postauthoritarian Philippines: Narratives of Engaged Citizenship*. Quezon City: Ateneo de Manila University Press, 2006.

Schumacher, John N., ed., *Readings in Philippine Church History*. Quezon City: Loyola School of Theology, 1979.

Jose Mario C. Francisco, SJ

Philosophy

The philosophical activity of Jesuits has been burdened by the same conflict as have its spirituality and its style of religious life. On the one hand, there is a spirit of adventure and openness to the present that has enabled some Jesuits to appreciate the modern age and, indeed, to make a contribution to its growth in knowledge. On the other hand, there has frequently been an abject submissiveness to authority that sabotaged any independent thinking. Not surprisingly for a sixteenth-century document, the Jesuit *Constitutions* indicated that the "doctrine of Aristotle" was to be followed and a special esteem accorded his successor, St. Thomas Aquinas. Typically for his cast of mind, though, Ignatius was not intimidated by the possibility of a more pluralistic philosophical scene. This flexibility was reflected in 1593 at the 5th General Congregation which acknowledged that departures from a narrow Thomistic path would be taken: "And it is not fitting that Ours be more tightly bound to St. Thomas than are the Thomists themselves." The most influential of Jesuit Thomists was Francisco Suárez (1548–1617) whose innovative interpretations came to split Jesuit philosophers into different polemical camps. Probably the most prominent creative philosopher of the early Society was Balthasar Gracian (1601–58) whose internationally regarded work *The Art of Worldly Wisdom* embodied Jesuit practicality as the most desirable direction for philosophy: "What is knowledge good for if it has no practical application? To know how to live is true knowledge."

All too often under the direction of the nineteenth-century papacy, Jesuit philosophy became an apologetics for a Church which felt threatened by the age and its scientific advances. Debates gave way to uniformity and ideological correctness. Jesuits armed themselves with a polemical defensiveness that fed Vatican paranoia and repression.

As the distinguished Jesuit historian Frederick Copleston asserted, philosophy was taught in the Catholic world "in a dogmatic manner analogous to that which Marxism-Leninism is taught in Communist-dominated education" (A *History of Philosophy*, Vol. IX, 251). Personally, I recall the advice that my own very well educated Jesuit teacher of modern philosophy gave our class in 1968 in the one lecture in the course he devoted to Marx: "Gentlemen, my advice to you is that, should you ever meet a Marxist, go for his jugular." Fortunately, in that tumultuous year there were competing Jesuit voices that encouraged intellectual encounter with Marxism, scholars such as Henri de Lubac and Quentin Lauer. Still in 1974, as a modern expression of their very vow of obedience, Jesuits were summoned by Pope Paul VI to a new sort of crusade, a resistance to the many forms of atheism.

There have been more critical currents among some Jesuits who were in dialogue either with Maurice Blondel or with Kantian thought. The latter led to the influential work of Joseph Maréchal. Others went back behind Aquinas to ancient thinkers as a way of escaping an inclination among Thomists to confuse substantial philosophical issues with textual exegesis of Aquinas. Broader Jesuit openings to the contemporary age were led by such powerful thinkers as de Lubac, Karl Rahner, John Courtney Murray, and Bernard Lonergan. It was Lonergan who perhaps best showed the transformation in Christian thinking that is necessitated by the modern revolution in notions of science and history. He called for an appreciation of the radical novelty of these revolutions and accused Catholic thinkers of failing to appreciate that a philosophical thinking is required that is adequate to historical and scientific reflection. While Lonergan celebrated the contemporary release from the earlier philosophical regimentation, he also worried that too many Jesuits in the post-Vatican II Church would regard philosophy itself as dispensable. Current Jesuit approaches to philosophy still operate between lively engagement with contemporary thinkers and lack of confidence in the love of wisdom itself.

See also Copleston, Frederick, SJ; Formation; Lonergan, Bernard, SJ; Suárez, Francisco, SJ

Caruana, Louis, "The Jesuits and the Quiet Side of the Scientific Revolution." In Thomas Worcester, ed., *The Cambridge Companion to the Jesuits*. Cambridge: Cambridge University Press, 2008, pp. 243–60.

Clooney, Francis, ed., *Jesuit Postmodern: Scholarship, Vocation and Identity in the 21st Century*. Lanham, MD: Lexington Books, 2006.

Copleston, Frederick, *A History of Philosophy*. 9 vols. New York: Image Books, 1993–94.

Lonergan, Bernard, "Questionnaire on Philosophy." *Method: Journal of Lonergan Studies* 2, 2 (October 1984), 1–35.

Rafferty, Oliver P., "The Thomistic Revival and Relations between the Jesuits and the Papacy, 1878–1914." *Theological Studies* 75, 4 (December 2014), 746–73.

Schloesser, Stephen. "Recent Works in Jesuit Philosophy." *Journal of Jesuit Studies* 1 (2014), 105–26.

James Bernauer, SJ

Photography

Photography is a way to catch moments in time and to document faces, spaces, and events. Two significant Jesuit photographers – the Irishman Frank Browne (1880–1960)

Figure 54 Don Doll, SJ: Alice New Holy and her granddaughter, photograph from his book *Vision Quest: Men, Women and Sacred Sites of the Sioux Nation* (Random House, 1994). Photograph © Don Doll, SJ

and American Don Doll (b. 1937) – have used this medium to capture people and places in order to preserve them and reveal them to the world. Their images document the worldwide presence of the Society and its interaction with others, sharing ideas, encounters, and images. Browne took photographs of the Titanic on her maiden voyage and the trenches of World War I, along with thousands of images taken on travels through twenty-eight countries. Doll began taking photographs while living on the Rosebud Sioux reservation in South Dakota in the early 1960s. His photographs have contributed to a better understanding of Native Americans and document the important interactions between the Jesuits and other groups.

Photographs of Jesuits have also been taken by professional lay photographers. In the 1950s, American photographer Margaret Bourke-White spent six months visiting Jesuits throughout the United States and recording images of the people and activities she encountered. These images first appeared in a *Life* magazine photo-essay (October 11, 1954), introducing the Society in the United States to a wide audience. She subsequently collaborated with Jesuit John LaFarge on a book, *A Report on the American Jesuits*, in which dozens of her photographs accompany an exploration of who and what the Society was in 1956. Her photographs captured a wide range of Jesuits, young and old, living and working all over the United States, engaged in a variety of activities. The images helped put real and individual faces on the story of the Society.

Photographs taken both of and by Jesuits have been collected in archives worldwide. They continue to play a significant role in Jesuit life, as records and documents of the past, and as works of art in their own right. Today, most Jesuit houses display photographs of the pope and the superior general, and occasionally of the local bishop.

See also Arts, Visual; Browne, Francis, SJ

Doll, Don, *A Call to Vision: A Jesuit's Perspective on the World*. Omaha: Magis Productions, 2012.
LaFarge, John, and Margaret Bourke-White, *A Report on the American Jesuits*. New York: Farrar, Straus and Cudahy, 1956.
McCoog, Thomas, *A Guide to Jesuit Archives*. St. Louis, MO: The Institute of Jesuit Sources, 2001.

Alison Fleming

Pignatelli, Joseph, SJ, St. (1737–1811)

Pignatelli was born, of noble descent, in Saragossa, Spain. He lost both his parents at a young age. He entered the Society's novitiate at Tarragona in 1753, professed his vows in 1755, and was ordained in 1762. His early ministries focused on the education of youths and the visitation of prisoners. In 1767 King Charles III of Spain banished the Society from his realms, and Pignatelli emerged as a leading figure in the ensuing Italian exile. Because of his noble status, Pignatelli was offered exemption from the expulsion edict, but he flatly refused. He settled first on Corsica, then briefly in Ferrara, and spent two decades in Bologna, from which city he worked hard to sustain Jesuit (and, post-1773, ex-Jesuit) solidarity.

Pignatelli showed interest in joining the fragment of the Society in the Russian Empire, but he was destined to play the leading role in reigniting a formal Jesuit presence in Italy. In 1793 Ferdinand II of Parma had welcomed a small group of Jesuits to his duchy, and Pignatelli, after renewing his vows in 1797, joined them. He had previously conducted missions in the Parmesan countryside and was on friendly terms with the duke. He played a major role in attracting Spanish ex-Jesuits to the duchy and was appointed master of novices at Colorno in 1799. This was the only Jesuit novitiate in western Europe at the time, and its establishment marked a significant moment on the road to Jesuit restoration. It would train, under Pignatelli's leadership, many leading figures in the Jesuits' future, including Angelo Mai and Giovanni Grassi. Success in Parma also encouraged official papal recognition of the Russian Society in 1801. Pignatelli was named provincial of all Italy in 1803 (appointed by Father General Gabriel Gruber in 1803), and he played a leading role in securing formal papal recognition of the Society in Naples and Sicily through the 1804 papal brief *Per alias*. There was considerable growth in the new province, with as many as 124 members by 1806 and the reopening of institutions including the Noblemen's College, the Casa Professa, and the Naples novitiate. In February 1806, however, further intrusions by Napoleonic troops obliged Pignatelli and his confrères to move to Rome. This in spite of the fact that they had offered oaths of allegiance to the invaders. Pignatelli moved to the Roman College, and Jesuits from Naples and elsewhere took up teaching positions in a number of cities, including Orvieto, Tivoli, and Palestrina.

Pignatelli is rightly credited with making a major contribution to the survival of the Ignatian ideal during the Suppression era although this role was not always straightforward. Significant tensions emerged within the Italian Jesuit communities over the route towards restoration (in terms of both speed and extent) and concerning the identity of any restored order. Some, notably Gaetano Angiolini (1748–1816), wanted a restored Society to retain its *Constitutions* but to develop a revised administrative structure. This was just one aspect of a simmering conflict between the exiled community and their hosts, and between the new and the old guard. There was also tension between different Iberian communities, with the Castilian Manuel Luengo charging Pignatelli with favoring his Aragonese countrymen. In any event, however, Pignatelli's contribution during the Suppression period was momentous, and there was sadness in the fact that Pignatelli did not live to see the global restoration of the Order in 1814. His chief goal, throughout his long exile, was to ensure that any restored Society of Jesus was, in every available sense, the direct continuation of the Order founded by Ignatius of Loyola in the sixteenth century. He took care to renew interest in the *Spiritual Exercises*, the order's original rules, and the *Ratio studiorum*. He would presumably have looked askance at the notion of his being regarded as one of the Jesuits' "second founders." For Pignatelli, beatified in 1933 and canonized by Pius XII in 1954, such a second foundation was not necessary: the original foundation remained fully operative.

See also Italy; Saints; Suppression

Arrilaga, Inmaculada Fernandez, and Niccolò Guasti, "The Exiled Spanish Jesuits and the Restoration of the Society of Jesus." In Robert Maryks and Jonathan Wright, eds., *Jesuit Survival and Restoration: A Global History, 1773–1900*. Leiden: Brill, 2014, pp. 178–96.

Ferrer Benimeli, José Antonio, *José Pignatelli, SJ (1737–1811): la cara humana de un santo*. Bilbao: Mensajero, 2011.

Iappelli, Filippo, "Francesco de Gregorio e Giuseppe Pignatelli: due uomini fra 'vecchia' e 'nuova' Compagnia." *Societas* 4–5 (1987), 107–18.

Jonathan Wright

Pilgrimage (in the Life of Ignatius and the Early Jesuits)

Pilgrimages figured prominently among the early Jesuits. It was a means of instilling the Ignatian principles of personal interior development and, as such, very effective in spiritual formation. As a result, the early Jesuits came to conceive of themselves primarily as "pilgrims," or as "apostles" who, like St. Paul, traveled from one place to another to spread the teachings of the Gospel. They essentially saw themselves as itinerant preachers, like Jesus and his disciples, and were mainly concerned with inculcating holiness in the hearts of their listeners, converting them to the "true path." This ideal remained central to the Jesuit creed.

Rome (the holy city of Christianity), Jerusalem, and the Holy Land ranked highly as pilgrim destinations. This was due, in part, to the fact that in the early phase of his vocation – from the 1520s to the 1530s – Ignatius of Loyola was convinced that his true vocation was to travel to the Holy Land and spend the rest of his life in devotion and penance in Jerusalem. In a sense, Ignatius was following an ideal common among many

Figure 55 Michael A. Onu, SJ, a Jesuit from Nigeria, on a pilgrimage to the memorial Church of St. Francis Xavier at Malindi, Kenya. Photograph courtesy of Festo Mkenda, SJ

devout Catholics of his times. Going to Jerusalem and the Holy Land meant experiencing the life of Christ, the Virgin, and the Apostles as well as reliving the many Old Testament events which took place in that special holy region.

Ignatius did go to Jerusalem, but he had to return to Spain soon after for reasons beyond his control. In 1534, when Loyola and his six companions took their vows at Montmartre, they resolved to travel to Jerusalem. However, the raging conflict between Christians and Muslims in the Mediterranean disrupted their plans. Ignatius and his companions never managed to go to Jerusalem.

They turned their attention instead to Protestantism which was then gaining ground and spreading fast, especially throughout the central and northern parts of Europe. The early Jesuits devoted their efforts to promulgating the teachings of the Catholic faith and inculcating among the masses frequent confession, devotions to the Eucharistic, the Sacred Heart of Jesus, the Forty Hours Devotion, and other practices such as those to the Sacred Heart of Mary and the saints.

Among the Jesuits themselves, periodic pilgrimages to sanctuaries, in the vicinity, or further away, were seen as a way to help strengthen and maintain unity among the Jesuit brothers. Jesuits who wished to go on a pilgrimage were often made to go poorly clothed. They were to travel on foot, without money, and under all weather conditions.

They had to beg for alms. Pilgrimages were often directed to Marian sanctuaries which heightened their devotion to the Virgin. But although they revered the Virgin, as she was much more than other saints, their main focus was obviously on Jesus, as their name implies.

The significance of pilgrimage among the early Jesuits is best appreciated within the context of the wide range of activities which they conducted in line with the principles of the Council of Trent. The Council sought to revive the cult of the saints, especially the Marian cult, which had suffered in popularity after the spread of Protestantism. This is why the Jesuits set up Marian congregations and encouraged them to go on pilgrimages to sanctuaries dedicated to the Virgin. The congregations, under the direction of the Jesuit community, were advised to seek the protection of the Virgin. Devotional statues, distributed along the route to the place of pilgrimage, coupled with indulgences for those who prayed fervently for their salvation, helped to keep the devotees in a state of grace. The frequent pilgrimages to sanctuaries dedicated to the Virgin helped to make these places highly regarded among the masses.

These Jesuit-run congregations were, therefore, very much in line with the ideology of the Council of Trent. And so, through their efforts in organizing pilgrimages, mainly directed to Marian sanctuaries, the Jesuits had thus come to play a vital role in Catholic piety until the early decades of the twentieth century.

See also Loyola, Ignatius of, SJ, St.; Marian Congregations; Middle East; Rome

Donnelly, John Patrick, ed., *Jesuit Writings of the Early Modern Period, 1540–1640*. Indianapolis, IN: Hackett Publishing, 2006.

Idígoras Tellechea, José Ignacio, *Ignatius of Loyola: The Pilgrim Saint*. Ed. and trans. Cornelius Michael Buckley. Chicago, IL: Loyola University Press, 1994.

Meissner, William, *Ignatius of Loyola: The Psychology of a Saint*. New Haven, CT: Yale University Press, 1992.

Carmel Cassar

Pius VII

Pius VII, Barnaba Chiaramonti, who brought about the universal restoration of the Society of Jesus, was born on August 14, 1742, at Cesena in Italy. After entering the Benedictines in 1756, he studied at Padua and Rome, and then taught philosophy and Church history in Parma and Rome. In 1783 Pope Pius VI appointed him bishop of Tivoli, and in 1758, cardinal and bishop of Imola.

After the French Revolution broke out in 1789, it became for more than the next quarter century part of the context of the life and accomplishments of Pius VII. His firmness with principles, his flexibility in their implementation, and, above all, his concern for the spiritual needs of those committed to his care stood him in good stead when the French invaded the Papal States in 1796.

After Pius VI died in 1799, a prisoner of revolutionary France, the papal conclave began on December 8, 1799, in Venice because French troops were occupying Rome. The meeting deadlocked for thirteen weeks, between the so-called *politicanti* and *zelanti* cardinals. The former recognized that the Church had to deal with a world changed in many ways by the revolution. The latter longed to restore a pre-revolutionary world and Church. The deadlock finally was broken on March 14, 1800, by the election of

Figure 56 Sir Thomas Lawrence: *Portrait of Pope Pius VII*, 1819, oil on canvas. © Royal Collection Trust/Her Majesty Queen Elizabeth II 2014

Cardinal Chiaramonti, who took the papal name Pius VII. But the division continued to exist in the papal curia and in the Church itself beyond his pontificate.

Pius VII's first public act with respect to the Society of Jesus took place on March 7, 1801, when the papal letter *Catholicae fidei* formally and publicly gave recognition to the continuing corporate existence of the Society in the Russian Empire. After Pope Clement XIV had suppressed the Jesuits in 1773, a remnant of the Society continued an anomalous existence and apostolic activities in Russia because its ruler, Catherine the Great, had forbidden any promulgation of the papal document of suppression. Now the superior general in Russia could also accept into membership in the Society even men who lived and worked outside of Russia. And in 1804, another papal letter, *Per alias*, extended this corporate restoration to the Two Sicilies.

Meanwhile, and for years to come, the rise of Napoleon made the Pope's reign increasingly difficult. Very quickly after the papal election, Napoleon had proposed a concordat with France. Pius accepted the offer despite strong opposition by the *zelanti* cardinals and despite the domineering attitude of Napoleon. The result was the Concordat of 1801, with terms fundamentally favorable for the Church. Of course, Napoleon unilaterally altered the agreement by adding to it his Gallicanist Organic

Articles. And it was clear that Napoleon would by no means tolerate the legal existence of Jesuits in France.

The Pope was even willing to go to Paris in 1804 for the imperial coronation of Napoleon. But as the Emperor extended French rule and the Napoleonic system throughout Europe, it became clear that the Holy See was to become an appanage of France, and the Pope, the sacristan of an imperially ruled Church. Pius resisted all these moves. The French invaded Rome on February 18, 1808, annexed the Papal States to France, and in 1809 carried off the Pope as prisoner to Savona near Genoa, and then in 1812 to Fontainebleau in France.

Finally, Pius VII was freed and returned to Rome on May 24, 1814. He had already determined to restore universally the Society of Jesus, intending to do so on July 31, the feast of St. Ignatius. Disagreements within the papal curia about how to take account of Clement XIV's past suppression of the Jesuits and about the future juridical status of the Society delayed the preparation of the papal bull. On August 7, 1814, the octave of the feast of St. Ignatius, Pius, after celebrating Mass at the Church of the Gesù, published at the Jesuit Curia *Sollicitudo omnium ecclesiarum*, which fully and universally restored the Society of Jesus.

The Papal States that Pius returned to in 1814 were troubled internally and needed reorganization. Such was true also of the Society of Jesus. One example of such trouble that engaged the Pope's attention was its first post-restoration General Congregation in 1820. Serious differences occurred on several questions, especially on the validity of the profession of vows of the delegates who had made such professions in the Society in Russia. The Pope had to intervene by confirming their validity.

Pius VII has rightly been called the pope of the new post-revolutionary age. The Society of Jesus, thanks to him, was present to help confront that new age through the rest of the nineteenth century and well into the twentieth.

See also France; Papacy; Suppression

Dansette, Adrien, *Religious History of Modern France*. Trans. John Dingle. 2 vols. New York: Herder and Herder, 1961.

Hales, G. G. Y., *Revolution and Papacy, 1769–1846*. New York: Hanover House, 1960.

Leflon, J., *La crise révolutionnaire, 1789–1846. (Histoire de l'Église depuis les origines jusqu'à nos jours, tome 20)*. Ed. A. Fliche and V. Martin. Paris: Bloud & Gay, 1949.

O'Dwyer, Margaret M., *The Papacy in the Age of Napoleon and the Restoration*. Lanham, MD: University Press of America, 1985.

John W. Padberg, SJ

Pius XI

Pius XI (Ambrogio Damiano Achille Ratti b. 1857) (r. 1922–39) was the pope perhaps most influenced by the Society of Jesus in the era after its suppression. The son of an Italian silk manufacturer, Achille Ratti was privately tutored as a boy and entered the major seminary in Milan. Ordained in 1879, he came under the influence of the Jesuits late in his education, attaining three doctorates – canon law, theology, and philosophy – at the Gregorian University in 1882. From 1888 to 1911, Ratti served on the staff of the Ambrosian Library in Milan.

During these years, Ratti was greatly influenced by the Jesuit social thinker Luigi Taparelli d'Azeglio (1793–1862), whose writings Ratti began to translate into German.

Tapparelli is widely recognized as the first writer to use the term "social justice" (*giustizia sociale*). Although his understanding of social justice was preservationist of the prevailing social order, it introduced Ratti to new concepts about the relationship of individuals to society. Taparelli promoted the core concept of society as consisting of relational "units," with larger units being responsible for intervening on behalf of smaller, independent units. Ratti embraced this understanding and refined it during his pontificate.

Jesuit influences were even more pronounced, however, in Ratti's 1931 encyclical on labor and society, *Quadragesimo anno*. Two German Jesuits, in particular, had deep influence on the construction of the encyclical. Its intellectual foundations had been laid by Jesuit economist Heinrich Pesch and his theory of "solidarism." At its core, solidarism sought to balance economic forces, labor, and individualistic tendencies with the larger social role of "human fulfillment." Even though Pesch was five years deceased, his ideas on issues such as a living wage continued to resonate. The actual drafting of the encyclical fell to a student of Pesch, Oswald von Nell-Breuning, the primary ghostwriter of the text. Its publication thrust the papacy to the forefront of global discussions on economic distributionism, subsidiarity, workers' rights, and the living wage. Four paragraphs about Italian Fascism, a phenomenon that would perplex and infuriate Ratti until the end of his pontificate, were written exclusively by the Pope (paragraphs 91–95).

Ratti tussled with conservative movements in the Church throughout his pontificate. Bernardi points out that many French Jesuits, including Cardinal Louis Billot, had extolled Charles Maurras's *Action française*. Reported Jesuit attempts to stay a condemnation of *Action française* were fruitless, and in 1927 the Holy See promulgated its decree of condemnation.

When Mussolini declared his Fascist state in 1922, however, the Holy See opened up communications with the *Duce* through the Jesuit Church historian, Pietro Tacchi Venturi. Venturi once described himself in a letter to Mussolini as "a good Jesuit and a good fascist." Over time, he became an unofficial liaison between the Pope and Mussolini. Many historians see him as a behind-the-scenes architect of the 1929 Lateran Accords, which reconciled the Holy See with the Italian state.

Ratti fulminated against the Italian racial laws of 1938, which severely impacted Jews' civil rights. That same year he famously stated that it was "inadmissible" for Catholics to hold anti-Semitic views because, "spiritually, we are all Semites." Yet, inasmuch as Ratti publicly supported Italy's Jewish population, he complicated matters by permitting the Jesuit-run journal *La Civiltà Cattolica* to publish a series of highly anti-Semitic articles during the 1930s.

It is possible that Ratti attempted to correct this oversight when he privately commissioned an American Jesuit, John LaFarge, to prepare an encyclical entitled *Humani generis unitas* (On the Unity of the Human Race). Extant preliminary drafts of the encyclical show a clear condemnation of anti-Semitism and a call for human solidarity. Once LaFarge revealed his papal commission to Jesuit General Ledóchowski, the General arranged for two other Jesuits to assist LaFarge, Gustave Desbuquois and Gustav Gundlach. The encyclical was created secretly at a time when Ratti was experiencing the onset of his terminal illness. Many historians see the self-insertion of Ledóchowski into the process as the main reason that the draft never reached the desk of Ratti's successor.

In his spiritual life, Ratti remained close to the Society of Jesus. Jesuit priest Celestino Alisiano befriended Ratti when he was at the Ambrosian Library and became his confessor from that time through the larger part of his pontificate. Ratti made an annual retreat based on the *Spiritual Exercises* that was preached in the Sistine Chapel. Among the Jesuit saints canonized by Pope Pius XI were Robert Bellarmine, the North American Martyrs, Peter Canisius, and Andrew Bobola. Canisius and Bellarmine were also declared doctors of the Church.

See also Anti-Semitism; Jews and Jesuits; LaFarge, John, SJ; Nell-Breuning, Oswald von, SJ; Papacy; Vatican Radio

Bernardi, Peter, "French Jesuits and Action Française." In James Bernauer and Robert Maryks, eds., *The Tragic Couple: Encounters between Jews and Jesuits*. Leiden/Boston: Brill, 2014, pp. 183–202.

Maryks, Robert, "The Jesuit Pietro Tacchi Venturi and Mussolini's Racial Laws." In Charles Gallagher, David Kertzer, and Alberto Melloni, eds., *Pius XI and America: Proceedings of the Brown University Conference*. Berlin: Lit, 2012, pp. 303–28.

Passelecq, Georges, and Bernard Suchecky, *L'Encyclique Cacheé de Pie XI*. Paris: La Découverte, 1995. Trans. Steven Rendall as *The Hidden Encyclical of Pius XI*. New York: Harcourt Brace, 1997.

Charles Gallagher, SJ

Pius XII

Eugenio Maria Giuseppe Giovanni Pacelli, the future Pope Pius XII (r. 1939–58) was ordained a priest on April 2, 1899. From 1894 to 1895, Pacelli studied philosophy at the Gregorian University. In 1901 he entered the Academy of Ecclesiastical Nobles, the Holy See's training school for ecclesiastical diplomats. Pacelli rose through the ranks of the Secretariat of State of the Holy See to become secretary of state on February 7, 1930. In this meteoric rise, Jesuits played little part. Pacelli's diplomatic patron was Pietro Gasparri, the able secretary of state of Pius XI. Gasparri shaped much of the young diplomat's thinking in legal and political affairs. Pacelli helped Gasparri codify the 1917 Code of Canon Law. Without citation, John Cornwell argues that Pacelli was influenced in canon law theory by Franz Xaver Wernz, SJ. This claim is hard to verify since Gasparri and all those who collaborated in compiling the 1917 Code were in one way or another influenced by Wernz's formidable *Jus decretalium* (Rome, 1898).

The main Jesuit issue which straddled the transition between Pius XI and Pius XII was the disposition of the LaFarge, Gundlach, and Desbuquois draft encyclical *Humani generis unitas*. Many historians conclude that Pope Pius XI would have issued the encyclical if he had not received it only twenty days before his death, when he was critically ill. Obviously, its publication would have infuriated both Hitler and Mussolini. Pope Pius XII decided to shelve the encyclical and pursue a less confrontational and more diplomatic course.

In many ways, the affair of the "lost encyclical" signaled how Pacelli would differ from his predecessor in his employment of the Society of Jesus to meet papal goals. Over the course of his pontificate, Pius XII would certainly employ various Jesuits to advise him and write policy. But whereas Ratti was often deferential on matters of Jesuit expertise, many times allowing solely Jesuit-generated ideas to hold sway in his encyclicals, Pacelli viewed Jesuit advice more critically. Pius XII saw the Society less as generators of points of theological doctrine and more as a resource. In many cases, Pacelli viewed himself as a co-expert, and always relegated final decisions on content and structure to himself.

Jesuit behind-the-scenes influence also waned under Pius XII because of Pacelli's interest in jurisprudence and concordat diplomacy as primary ways of achieving world peace. Few Jesuits occupied ranks within the Secretariat of State of the Holy See. Moreover, as a diplomat, Pacelli spurned what today would be called "track two diplomacy," or interactions of statecraft exercised by groups or individuals outside of formal negotiation processes and institutions. In 1944, when the Jesuit-educated Cardinal Secretary of State Luigi Maglione died, Pius consolidated the position of secretary of state into his papacy and acted in this role until his own death in 1958.

Robert Lieber, SJ, whom historian Susan Zuccotti has called "Pius XII's closest adviser throughout his papacy," served as the Pope's private personal secretary from 1939 to 1958. While there is some evidence showing that Lieber had contact with representatives of various German anti-Hitler and French underground resistance movements, in the end it was Pius XII who made resistance decisions alone. Gauging Lieber's role in influencing the Pope's political decisions is precarious, since the Jesuit secretary destroyed all of his personal papers shortly prior to his death. Overall, the posture of the Society of Jesus during the pontificate of Pius XII fits into three phases: (1) an early alignment with his goals after his election; (2) lock-step support for his policies during the war, and (3) vigorous defense of his policies after the war and after his death. From the 1960s to the 1990s, many Jesuit historians staunchly defended Pius XII's legacy in the wake of the global critique of his actions in connection with the Holocaust.

Theologically, Pius XII relied on the writings of the Belgian Jesuit Émile Mersch, SJ, to align his thoughts on the concept of the mystical body of Christ. After Mersch's death in 1940, the main ecclesiologist moving the discussion forward was another Jesuit ecclesiologist, the Dutchman Sebastian Tromp. Reputedly, Tromp was the primary drafter of Pius XII's important 1943 encyclical *Mystici corporis*. Although not contemporaneous, theologians Edward Kilmartin and Robert Daly have noted the profound impact that the Eucharistic theology of the Jesuit St. Robert Bellarmine had on Pius XII. In his 1947 encyclical on the liturgy, *Mediator Dei*, Pius adopted Bellarmine's thoughts on priestly consecration of the Eucharist verbatim.

Pope Pius XII canonized only two Jesuit saints – St. John de Britto in 1947 and St. Joseph Pignatelli in 1954.

See also Jews and Jesuits; Papacy; Pius XI

Lapomarda, Vincent A., *The Jesuits and the Third Reich*. Lewiston, NY: Edwin Mellen Press, 1989.
Ventresca, Robert A., *Soldier of Christ: The Life of Pope Pius XII*. Cambridge, MA: The Belknap Press of Harvard University Press, 2013.

Charles Gallagher, SJ

Plague

Until the late 1800s, when a bacterium was identified as the cause of bubonic plague, with its characteristic blackened swellings, the term "plague" was used to refer to almost any disease perceived as contagious, epidemic, and frequently fatal. The term was also used as a metaphor for heresy and other threats to society.

Though the biggest outbreak of a plague in Europe occurred *c.* 1350, smaller, more localized outbreaks continued to take place for centuries beyond that era, and in various parts of the world. Jesuits responded to such outbreaks in several ways: with homilies and treatises and sacramental ministry designed to console the sick and to turn their attention to preparation of their souls for a good death; by caring for the bodies of the sick in hospitals and other institutions; with composition of narrative, descriptive accounts of what happened in time of plague; with provision of herbal and other remedies thought to be helpful against such diseases. The best-known Jesuit to have worked among those suffering from plague was Aloysius Gonzaga (1568–91); from one of the most prominent families in Italy, he overcame parental opposition to his Jesuit vocation, and as a young Jesuit in Rome worked among plague victims and died of plague himself or at least of some disease contracted while engaged in such work. A canonized saint, Aloysius Gonzaga has more recently been named patron for those suffering from HIV/AIDS.

See also Gonzaga, Aloysius, SJ; HIV/AIDS

Martin, A. Lynn, *Plague? Jesuit Accounts of Epidemic Disease in the 16th Century.* Kirksville, MO: Sixteenth Century Journal Publishers, 1996.
Worcester, Thomas, "Plague as Spiritual Medicine and Medicine as Spiritual Metaphor: Three Treatises by Etienne Binet, SJ (1569–1639)." In Franco Mormando and Thomas Worcester, eds., *Piety and Plague: From Byzantium to the Baroque.* Kirksville, MO: Truman State University Press, 2007, pp. 224–36.

Thomas Worcester, SJ

Poetry

Aside from Gerard Manley Hopkins, Robert Southwell, and perhaps Daniel Berrigan in our own time, there are few Jesuits whose poems are anthologized and widely known in the English-speaking world today. On the other hand, Hopkins's poems are among the most read and admired of all poets, and have been translated into German, French, Italian, Russian, and Japanese. Moreover, his work has had and continues to have a profound impact on poets as diverse as Hart Crane, W. H. Auden, Robert Lowell, John Berryman, and Elizabeth Bishop, to name a few.

What places Hopkins's poems distinctively in the Jesuit tradition is their foundational connection with the Ignatian *Spiritual Exercises*, especially in employing Ignatius's compositions of place, which are usually but not exclusively biblical in their focus, infolded with prayer and the imagination. Beyond this, there is the deep sense of spiritual meditation, contemplation, and the profound understanding that all of creation is suffused with the reality of the Incarnation, with the resultant understanding of God's shining in and with and through his creation.

Of necessity there are many overlays, resonances, and counterpointings in the various ways in which biblical imagery and language, together with the intentionality of the poet in the act of composing, and the understanding that the act of poesis is inextricably linked with prayer itself. It should also be understood that many poets have borrowed or co-opted the Scriptures for their own aesthetic and philosophical ends, often to the point of running counter to the spirit of the Scriptures themselves (*vide* Blake, Dickinson, Swinburne, Hardy, Yeats, Pound, William Carlos Williams, and Hecht, to name a few).

But what sets poetry in the Ignatian tradition apart from what these poets do centers around the conviction that a sacramental and incarnational reality rather than the ego-centered design of the poet is what is necessarily at the heart of the poem – what Hopkins called its inscape – and that this focus can result in a creation stemming from the poet's wording or fleshing out of the ineffable Word. This will be so, in fact, even when the poem performs not only a rounding back to its beginning as with a circle in imitation of the great *De Processu*, but when the poet uses a figure eight, seeming to move away from the spiritual only to return to it again in the end in a way that instresses its deeper meaning upon the reader.

It is also of great advantage to employ the *Spiritual Exercises* in reading poems as one might read a biblical text, in order to come to a deeper understanding of what a poem has to offer us. The manner of reading a text thus begins with a turning in on oneself in some quiet place to allow oneself to become aware of the deeper, God-centered reality one may be privileged to discover there. Once in that space, it is useful to read through the poem silently several times, until its radiance begins to shine through. One might then read the poem aloud to oneself, speaking it as the voice of the poem dramatically leads one, aware of the words – phrases, alliterations, consonances, rhymes, refrains, parallelisms, etc. – as if one were reading a musical score. Further, one should note – as in reading a biblical text – which image or phrase or word in the poem seems to call out to you, and then pondering how these words speak to your own life. Following the spirit of the *Exercises*, one might read the poem again, this time addressing that deeper, God-saturated reality that surrounds one, and waiting to see if there is an epiphany, as if God has something to say to you through the poem.

On retreats, for instance, spiritual directors might suggest a poem for the retreatant to read and ponder over for as much as a day. Examples might be a poem by Denise Levertov, such as her "Annunciation," or a sonnet by Hopkins, such as "God's Grandeur" or "As kingfishers catch fire," or a section from one of Dante's cantos, or a poem by John Donne, George Herbert, Robert Herrick, Mary Karr, Marilyn Nelson, Franz Wright, Luci Shaw, Scott Cairns, or any number of other poets. Another exercise might be to meditate on a religious painting by Giotto, Cimabue, Caravaggio on up through such artists as Rouault, Dalí, Chagall, and Matisse's stained glass windows at the Chapel of the Rosaire in Vence, which so deeply influenced the poet Wallace Stevens, giving him a way of understanding God's rainbow radiance in his own time. Then, after an ekphrastic and spiritual meditation on the painting or sculpture, one might consider translating that experience into a poem as well. These are just a few of the profound gifts which the *Spiritual Exercises* can offer the poet and the reader of poetry, the fruit of this exercise being a poetic, prayer-like response, where our words speak as they can to the ineffable Word.

See also Hopkins, Gerard Manley, SJ; Wu, Li, SJ; Southwell, Robert, SJ; *Spiritual Exercises*

Berrigan, Daniel, *Essential Writings*. (Modern Spiritual Masters Series). Selected with an Introduction by John Dear. Maryknoll, NY: Orbis Books, 2009.

Sweeney, Anne R., *Robert Southwell: Snow in Arcadia: Redrawing the English Lyric Landscape, 1586–1595*. Manchester: Manchester University Press, 2006.

Paul Mariani

Polanco, Juan Alfonso de, SJ (1517–1576)

From a wealthy merchant family in Burgos, Spain, Juan Alfonso de Polanco studied humanities and philosophy at the University of Paris (1535–38). He worked as a notary (*scriptor apostolicus*) in the papal curia in Rome before joining the Society in 1541.

After studying theology at the University of Padua, he was ordained a priest in 1546; in 1547 he was appointed secretary of the Society and became Ignatius's closest collaborator. He worked with Ignatius on the *Constitutions* and was responsible for the Latin translation from the Spanish autograph.

Polanco continued to serve as secretary of the Society under Generals Diego Laínez (1512–65) and Francis Borja (1510–72), and held various appointments within the Society. He also participated in the fourth session of the Council of Trent (1563).

At the death of Borja, Polanco, who had been nominated vicar general, was considered the favorite candidate for superior of the Society. However, the preference of Gregory XIII (r. 1572–85) for a non-Spanish general and the strong Italo-Portuguese campaign against Polanco based on his alleged Jewish ancestry contributed to the election of the Walloon Jesuit Everard Mercurian (1514–80).

In the following years, at the request of the new general, Polanco compiled the *Chronicon Societatis Iesu*, a year-by-year systematic history of the activities of the Society from 1537 to the death of the founder. Polanco also authored other works on the history of the Society, instructions for Jesuit confessors, and several spiritual books. Sent to Sicily as official visitor (1575), he returned sick to Rome where he died in 1576.

See also Loyola, Ignatius of, SJ, St.; *Constitutions*

Coupeau, José Carlos, "Juan de Polanco's role as Secretary of Ignatius of Loyola: 'his memory and hands'." In Thomas McCoog, ed., *"Ite inflammate omnia": Selected Historical Papers from Conferences Held at Loyola and Rome in 2006*. Rome: IHSI, 2010, pp. 109–27.

Donnelly, John Patrick, ed., *Year by Year with the Early Jesuits, 1537–1556: Selections from the Chronicon of Juan de Polanco, SJ*. St. Louis, MO: The Institute of Jesuit Sources, 2004.

Emanuele Colombo

Poland

The Jesuits arrived in Poland in 1564, five years before the creation of the Poland-Lithuania Commonwealth, which throughout its existence until the partitions of the late eighteenth century (which coincided with the papal suppression of the Society in 1773), included parts of present-day Poland, Lithuania, Latvia, Belarus, Hungary, and Ukraine. Independent Poland was created after World War I (1918) but occupied by Nazi Germany and the Soviet Union during World War II (1939–45), after which it remained under the Communist regime until 1989.

1564–1773. Called by Cardinal Stanisław Hozjusz, the Jesuits founded a significant number of influential schools for the formation of the youth in liberal arts as well as

seminaries for the formation of the clergy, including a college in Vilnius which soon
became a renowned university and a home for a printing press and astronomical observatory. Printing, missionary activity, and public discussions with Protestants became
means of producing conversions of not a few politically influential noblemen who had
abandoned the Catholic Church. The number of Jesuits grew rapidly: by the end of the
sixteenth century there were 800. Some of them influenced Polish literary culture significantly: Piotr Skarga published the popular *Lives of the Saints* (1579); Jakub Wujek provided the first translation of the Bible into Polish (1599); Grzegorz Knapski (Knapius)
composed a standard Polish–Latin–Greek dictionary (1621); Francziszek Bohomolec
issued his work on the purity of the Polish language, *Rozmowa o języku polskim* (1752);
and Adam Naruszewicz wrote a major history of the Polish nation, *Historia narodu pol-
skiego* (1780–86). Polish Jesuits became especially prominent in the 1700s. They published a number of important periodicals: *Monitor* (edited by Franciszek Bohomolec);
Zabawy przyjemne i pożyteczne (Jan Albertrandi and Adam Naruszewicz); *Kalendarz
polityczny* (Francziszek Paprocki). The Suppression of the Society coincided with the
establishment of the Enlightenment-inspired Commission for National Education
and the Society of Textbooks. As a result, hundreds of experienced Jesuit teachers participated in its programs, including Grzegorz Piramowicz, the author of a guide for
teachers, *Obowia̧zki nauczyciela* (1787). No less important (and controversial) was the
Jesuits' role as royal preachers and military chaplains. Polish Jesuits were also known for
their dedication to the cause of the Uniate Catholics. Perhaps the most famous Polish
missionary of this period was Michał Boym, who designed several maps of China and
authored a work on Chinese flora (1656).

1820–1918. As a result of the expulsion of the Jesuits from Russia (1820), a group of
Jesuits returned to Galicia (southeast Poland), which was then under the Austrian occupation, and engaged mainly in pastoral and missionary work. Almost immediately, however, they also opened a couple of schools for external and internal students. After the
temporal suppression caused by the revolutionary events of 1848, the Jesuits expanded
their presence in the region. They founded a publishing house in Krakow, which produced a number of periodicals, including *Posłaniec Serca Jezusowego* and *Przegla̧d
Powszechny*. A few Jesuits were able to work in the Prussia-occupied territory but the
anti-Jesuit law of Bismarck (1872) put an end to it until the fall of the Second Reich.

1918–1945. With the fall of the Russian, Austrian, and German empires by the end
of World War I, the Jesuits were able to recuperate some of their earlier residences,
schools, and churches, and therefore expand their activities beyond Galicia in a newly
established Polish province by Polish Superior General Włodzimierz Ledóchowski,
which in a few years was divided in two because of the rapid growth of the Society in
independent Poland. With a new center in Warsaw, one of the major enterprises in
this period was publishing. The Jesuits continued producing several periodicals and
established a series of books dedicated to spiritual life, Biblioteka Życia Wewnętrznego.
Other ministries included a few schools, so-called popular missions in parishes, and
Marian congregations for intellectuals. During the war, about one-fourth of the Jesuits
were murdered, died in camps, or disappeared. Not a few, like Józef Warszawski, Tomasz
Roztworowski, and Czesław Białek, served as chaplains in the underground military
organizations.

1945 onwards. Because of major border changes as a result of the new postwar political order, the Society lost a number of important institutions in the east, including those

in Vilnius, Lvov, Pińsk, and Tarnów, but established new ones in the territories lost by Germany in the west. Because the new Communist regime prohibited the religious from running schools, the Jesuits concentrated their activities on pastoral and catechetical ministries in parishes, including the so-called Sacred Heart missions. They continued publishing, with intervals depending on the political atmosphere in Church–State affairs, but were limited just to two periodicals, *Przegla̧d* and *Posłaniec*. After the fall of Communism, the Society found new possibilities of apostolate in running programs for radio and TV.

See also German-Speaking Lands; Russia; Skraga, Piotr, SJ; Suppression

Grzebień, Ludwik, ed., *Encyklopedia wiedzy o jezuitach na ziemiach Polski i Litwy 1564–1995*. Krakow: WAM, 1996.
Załęski, Stanisław, *Jezuici w Polsce*. 11 vols. Lvov-Krakow: Anczyc, 1900–06.

Robert A. Maryks

Pombal, Marquis

The most influential Portuguese minister during the reign of Joseph I and the chief architect of the assault on the Jesuits in Portugal and its overseas territories during the 1750s, Sebastião José de Carvalho e Melo (1699–1782) did not become marquis of Pombal until 1770, but in the literature he is usually referred to by this title at all stages of his career: a convention followed here. Following an unremarkable military career, Pombal made headway in the realm of diplomacy, notably as an envoy extraordinary at the English court between 1738 and 1745. After a spell in Vienna, he returned to Lisbon in 1749 and on the accession of Joseph I was unexpectedly appointed as minister of foreign affairs and secretary of state. It has been suggested that this appointment owed something to the intervention of local Jesuits. Given subsequent events, this would be ironic, though there is no firm evidence to support the theory.

It can be stated, however, that prior to the 1750s Pombal exhibited little conspicuous animosity toward the Society and had various Jesuit correspondents. By the middle of that decade, however, Pombal's attitudes had shifted. He appears to have regarded the Society of Jesus as an obstacle to both his own accretion of power and the centralizing ambitions of the royal government. Pombal seized upon a number of events in order to diminish Jesuit influence at court and to cast the Society as a dangerous threat to the Portuguese body politic. These included the devastating Lisbon earthquake of 1755 (in the wake of which Jesuits, including Gabriel Malagrida, wrote critically about Portugal's cultural trajectory); a popular revolt at Oporto in 1757 and rebellions and disturbances in Portugal's South American territories (for both of which, on scant evidence, Jesuits were blamed); and, most importantly of all, a failed assassination attempt against the king in September 1758. By this date Pombal had already taken strides in attacking the Society (securing, for instance, the removal of Jesuit confessors from court).

In April 1758 Pope Benedict XIV had succumbed to pressure from Pombal and issued the brief *In specula supremae dignitatis*. This mentioned a need for reform within the Society of Jesus, and Pombal's ally, Cardinal Francisco de Saldanha da Gama, was appointed as official visitor of the Portuguese Assistancy. It was the attempt against the king's life, however, that allowed Pombal to deal a devastating blow. Despite a lack of genuine evidence against them, ten Jesuits were imprisoned in January 1759, including the provincial João Henriques and Gabriel Malagrida. Later in the month, a royal letter accused the Jesuits of lending moral support to the attempted attack on the king. Subsequently, Portugal's Jesuits were confined to their houses, and their possessions were confiscated. In July 1759 it was ordered that all Jesuit schools and colleges in Portugal and its overseas possessions were to be closed and, on September 3, 1759, a royal decree formally expelled the Jesuits from the Kingdom of Portugal and its dominions.

It is crucial to stress the specific, local factors behind Pombal's animus, but his fostering of anti-Jesuit sentiment, especially the promotion of acerbic books and pamphlets, had a significant impact beyond Portugal. These included the *Relação abreviada* (Short Account of the Republic Which the Jesuits Have Established in Spanish and Portuguese Dominions of the New World) published anonymously in December 1757, though almost certainly from Pombal's own pen, and the highly influential four-volume *Dedução cronológica e analítica* by José Seabra da Silva, published in 1767–68 at Pombal's behest. Compared to their French and Spanish counterparts, the agents and ambassadors of Portugal played a minor role in pressuring the papacy towards the global suppression of the Jesuits: formal relations between Portugal and Rome had been severed in 1760 and only began to be restored during the reign of Clement XIV.

Pombal was nonetheless delighted when news of the papal brief of suppression arrived: he ordered that Lisbon's lights should burn all night in celebration. Pombal's influence came to an end with the death of Joseph I and, in 1777, he was dismissed from his offices. He emerged unscathed from post-ministerial investigations into his conduct and died of natural causes in 1782.

See also Anti-Jesuit Polemic; Portugal; Suppression

Brazão, Eduardo, "Pombal e os jesuítas." In Luis Reis Torgal and Isabel Vargues, eds., *O Marquês de Pombal e o seu Tempo*. Coimbra: University of Coimbra, 1982–83, pp. 329–65.

Diaz, Belmonte, "La expulsión de los jesuitas de Portugal en la 'era pombalina.'" *Arbor: Ciencia, Pensamiento, y Cultura* 190 (2014), 1–13.

Maxwell, Kenneth, *Pombal: Paradox of the Enlightenment*. New York: Cambridge University Press, 1995.
    "The Spark: Pombal, the Amazon, and the Jesuits." *Portuguese Studies* 17 (2001), 168–83.

Jonathan Wright

Pontifical Biblical Institute (PIB/PBI)

The Pontifical Biblical Institute was founded in Rome by Pope Pius X in 1909 and entrusted to the Jesuits. The Biblicum (or PIB), as the Institute is familiarly called, emerged as a response to many factors of the previous century, including Modernism and the publication of Charles Darwin's *On the Origin of Species* (1859). To attempt to counteract the privileging of reason over faith and the challenge to Creation (Genesis 1–3) that evolutionary biology posed, Leo XIII issued an encyclical *Providentissimus Deus*, "On the Study of Holy Scripture" (1893), in which he reviewed the history of Bible study from the time of the Church Fathers to the present, spoke against the errors of the Rationalists and "higher critics," and outlined principles of Scripture study and guidelines for how Scripture was to be taught in seminaries. He also addressed the issues of apparent contradictions between the Bible and physical science, or between one part of Scripture and another, and how such apparent contradictions could be resolved.

Nine years after the encyclical, in 1902, Pope Leo XIII instituted the Pontifical Biblical Commission, composed at its founding of three cardinals and twelve consultors whose duties included the following: (1) to protect and defend the integrity of the Catholic faith in biblical matters; (2) to further the progress of biblical understanding and exposition, taking into account all recent discoveries; (3) to decide controversies on grave questions that might arise among Catholic scholars; and (4) to publish studies on Scripture as occasion might demand. In 1904 Pope Pius X issued an apostolic letter *Scripturae sanctae*, giving the Biblical Commission the power to grant pontifical academic degrees in biblical studies, including to graduates of the École Biblique et Archéologique Française de Jérusalem, a school for biblical studies that had been founded by the Dominicans in 1890. It was not until almost twenty years after the Biblicum's founding that it could award its own degrees, independent of the Commission; only in 1928, when Pius XI created the Consortium of the Gregorian University, did the Biblicum and the Oriental Institute finally gain complete autonomy from the Biblical Commission.

Still, as late as 1934 an atmosphere of anti-Modernism prevailed. In 1910 Pius X had established an Oath against Modernism and required that all teachers of Scripture take the oath. The practice continued officially until it was abolished by Pope Paul VI in 1967 (although unofficially it persisted much longer). It was in such an atmosphere that the Pontifical Biblical Institute was born and spent its early years.

Not too long after the founding of the Biblicum, plans began to take shape for the school to establish an arm in Jerusalem. What was envisioned was not a separate school but a place in the Holy Land where students of the Roman school could do research or further study. Such a site was opened in 1927. To this day, it has not become a school separate from the Institute in Rome but, more recently, it has worked in collaboration with the Hebrew University (since 1975), the École Biblique (since 1984), and the Studium Biblicum Franciscanum (since 2000) to provide Biblicum students with additional academic opportunities.

An encyclopedia entry of this length cannot detail the development of the school's curriculum, from a more traditional interpretation of Scripture with heavy emphasis on philology, to greater appreciation of archaeology and the world of the Ancient Near East, to a respectful embrace of historical criticism. No precise dates can account for the evolution of thinking in an institution; it is difficult enough to render such an account in the mind of an individual. Nevertheless, such an evolution did take place, partly nurtured by the publication in 1943 of the encyclical *Divino afflante Spiritu*, which granted freedom and promoted modern exegesis of the Old Testament, and then, by the advent of the Second Vatican Council, particularly its Dogmatic Constitution on "Divine Revelation."

In addition to the scholarship published by individual faculties of the Biblicum, the school as an institution contributes to the fields of biblical and Ancient Near Eastern studies through major publications. These include *Biblica* and *Orientalia*; the *Elenchus Biblica*, published annually, which annotates all the work on biblical subjects produced each year, and four monograph series, the *Analecta Biblica*, *Subsidia Biblica*, *Biblica et Orientalia*, and *Studia Pohl*.

The professors of the biblical faculty of the PIB are engaged in teaching Old and New Testament exegesis, biblical Hebrew and Greek, allied subjects (e.g., textual criticism,

Patristic exegesis), and ancient Judaism. In the Faculty of Studies of the Ancient East, a small number of dedicated professors cover the field of ancient Semitic languages as well as Hittite, Egyptian, and Coptic. In its areas of expertise, the PIB's library stands out as one of the best in the world.

See also Biblical Studies; Rome

Gilbert, Maurice, *The Pontifical Biblical Institute: A Century of History (1909–2009)*. Rome: Pontifical Biblical Institute, 2009.

Alice L. Laffey

Pontifical Oriental Institute (POI)

The Pontifical Oriental Institute (POI, or Pontificio Istituto Orientale/Pontificium Institutum Orientalium Studiorum) in Rome is a center of superior studies dedicated to the Eastern Christian Churches, both the Byzantine ones (Bulgarian, Georgian, Greek, Melkite, Romanian, Russian, Ruthenian, Serbian, Ukrainian) and the others (Antiochene, Assyro-Chaldean, Armenian, Coptic, Ethiopic, Malabar, Malankar, Maronite). It offers courses in theology (including spirituality), liturgy, history, and canon law, as well as in the respective languages of these Churches. It is often called idiomatically "the Orientale."

Pope Benedict XV founded it with the *motu proprio, Orientis catholici*, on October 15, 1917, a few months after the founding of the Vatican's Congregation for the Oriental Churches. Antoine Delpuch, the vice-procurator of the White Fathers (the Missionaries of Africa), was the first director of the POI (1918) with the title of President-Delegate or Propresident, but the final responsibility remained in the hands of Niccolò Cardinal Marini, the Secretary of the Congregation for the Oriental Churches.

In the summer of 1919, Delpuch was sent on a papal mission to Georgia, which had been separated from the Russian Empire but was not yet a Soviet republic. He was succeeded on October 3, 1919, by Idelfonso Schuster, OSB, abbot of St. Paul Outside the Walls in Rome and a professor of liturgy at the POI since its founding. In 1920, during his presidency, the power to grant academic degrees, including the doctorate, was granted to the POI. Owing to the small number of students, Schuster suggested to Pope Pius XI the combination of the POI with the Pontifical Biblical Institute, which was already under the direction of the Society of Jesus. In 1922 the Pope decreed the combination of the two institutes and put both under the direction of the Society. The superior general named Michel d'Herbigny as head of the POI. A Jesuit community was established to replace the previous professors.

The combination of the two institutes ended in 1926–27 when the POI opened a new campus on Piazza Santa Maria Maggiore. Together with d'Herbigny at the dedication on November 14, 1926, was the apostolic visitor to Bulgaria, Angelo Roncalli (later Pope St. John XXIII). In his encyclical *Rerum orientalium* (1928), Pope Pius XI assigned a major role to the POI in the study and the appreciation of the Eastern Christian Churches. On September 30, 1928, Pius XI formed an academic union of the three institutions of superior studies directed by the Society (the Pontifical Gregorian University, the Pontifical Biblical Institute, and the POI), while insisting that each retain its own autonomy. On August 15, 1929, the Pope created the Pontifical Russian College

(Russicum), closely connected to the POI, which was also placed under the direction of the Society. In accordance with the apostolic constitution *Deus scientiarum Dominus*, the POI reformed its statutes and programs in August 1934.

For a number of years the POI's Faculty of Eastern Ecclesiastical Studies had four sections: theology, liturgy, history, and canon law. In 1963 the Sacred Congregation for Universities and Seminaries transformed the POI's section on canon law into a special section of the Gregorian University's Faculty of Canon Law dedicated to the Eastern Churches, an intermediary step in the creation of the POI's own Faculty of Canon Law in 1971, the only such faculty in the world.

Approximately 200 professors, more than half Jesuits, have taught at the POI. Many have been major leaders in their fields. Among the Jesuits is Guillaume de Jerphanion, a specialist on Byzantine archaeology, who studied the earliest churches in Cappadocia. Irenée Hausherr and Tomáš Špidlík are recognized authorities on spirituality; Bohumil Spáčil, Mauricio Gordillo, and Stanisław Tyśkiewicz on theology; Georg Hoffman, Albert Amman, and Joseph Gill on Church history; Juan Mateos, Miguel Arranz, and Robert Taft on liturgy; and Emil Herman and Ivan Žužek on canon law.

Since its beginning the POI has had approximately 5,000 students, including both those who completed degrees and those who did special programs of studies. In the early years (1919–31) the POI had between eight and thirty-three students. The number grew first in the 1960s and later in the 1990s.

Among its alumni are many bishops and archbishops of the Eastern Catholic, Orthodox, Oriental Orthodox, and Assyrian Churches. Since 1991, an alumnus of the POI has been the head of the Orthodox Church, Ecumenical Patriarch Bartholomew of Constantinople. Many graduates of the POI teach in Catholic and Orthodox universities and seminaries around the world.

Its most important periodical publications are the semi-annual *Orientalia Christiana Periodica*, the monograph series *Orientalia Christiana Analecta*, and the canon law series *Kanonika*.

See also Eastern Catholic Churches; Rome; Špidlík, Tomáš, SJ

Poggi, Vincenzo, *Per la storia del Pontificio Istituto Orientale: saggi sull'istituzione, i suoi uomini e l'Oriente cristiano*. (Orientalia Christiana Analecta 263). Rome: Pontifical Oriental Institute, 2000.

Steven Hawkes-Teeples, SJ

Popish Plot (1678)

The Popish Plot was the most violent anti-Catholic moral panic in seventeenth-century England. Titus Oates's tales of conspiracies and regicide fanned fears of godly Protestants as they pondered the implications of the probable succession of King Charles II's Catholic brother James, duke of York. A protracted Exclusion Crisis tried to bypass his candidacy or impede his accession. Oates, a former Protestant reprobate who studied briefly at the English Jesuit College in St. Omer and did occasional jobs for the province, and Israel Tonge, an aggressively anti-Catholic minister, disclosed a vast conspiracy in which Jesuits would assassinate the King. Charles II dismissed the stories as lies. Other officials, intent on using the plot in their campaign against James, ordered an investigation. The murder of Sir Edmund Berry Godfrey as he opened his examination of the plot made the outlandish claims more credible. Catholic lords, Jesuits, priests, and other religious were arrested. Between 1678 and 1679 Jesuit presence within England declined by nearly forty as many fled to continental safety. The major Jesuit community at Combe near Hereford, a flourishing spiritual center/college since the early 1620s, was invaded and destroyed with most of its library ending up at Hereford Cathedral. Other pursuivants were more interested in discovering the legendary Jesuit wealth. Indeed some of the Society's lay agents did disclose Jesuit assets often to save their own lives. Nine Jesuits were executed; twelve others died in prison; the deaths of at least three others can be attributed to the plot. The most notable non-Jesuits executed were William Howard, Viscount Stafford, and Oliver Plunkett, archbishop of Armagh. As the plot waned, Oates himself was denounced and imprisoned. English Jesuit recovery – initially slow – accelerated with the accession of the Catholic James in 1685, but the province suffered a more severe setback with the so-called "Glorious Revolution" of 1688.

See also Anti-Jesuit Polemic; United Kingdom

Kenyon, John, *The Popish Plot.* London: Heinemann, 1972.
Miller, John, *Popery and Politics in England 1660–1688.* Cambridge: Cambridge University Press, 1973.

Thomas McCoog, SJ

Portugal

The first Jesuits to reach Portugal, invited by King John III, were Simão Rodrigues and Francis Xavier in 1540. The latter set sail for India, initiating the Jesuit missions overseas, while Rodrigues coordinated the first steps of the Society of Jesus in Portugal, where the House of S. Antão in Lisbon and the College of Jesus in Coimbra were founded in 1542. After some initial mistrust regarding their spirituality, the court, aristocracy, and bishops helped the Jesuits to set down roots in the kingdom, spreading the practice of the *Spiritual Exercises*. The creation of the Portuguese province (1546) under the charismatic Rodrigues was followed by the opening of a college in Évora (1551), which was later elevated to the status of a university (1559). In 1553 the House of S. Roque was opened in Lisbon and the first internal missions were begun, while other contingents were sent to territories of Portuguese royal patronage (by 1700 more than 2,000 Jesuits had left for Asia and Africa, and around 500 for Brazil). There was a serious crisis in 1551–53, when Rodrigues was accused by Rome of being too autonomous in his running of the province and of favoring extreme forms of penitential asceticism. His removal led to a hemorrhage of fathers and brothers from the province of Portugal and to the success of the rigorist current guided by Luís Gonçalves da Câmara, which remained dominant until 1574. Thanks to their accord with Cardinal Prince Henry, inquisitor general and regent from 1562 to 1568, the Jesuits' influence increased. Counselors of King Sebastian and confessors of the royal family, they worked for better religious education and frequent access to confession and communion, opened colleges and schools, collaborated with the diocesan clergy, and participated in the Inquisition, even becoming part of its General Council (1571–92). They also opposed the admission of *conversos* of Jewish origin to the Society, having a crucial influence in the general prohibition of 1593.

Despite some difficulties in the early years of the dynastic union between Portugal and Spain under the Habsburg Crown (1580–1640), due to suspicions of Jesuit political opposition, their number continued to grow (620 in 1603, 640 in 1649, 716 in 1700, and 818 in 1754). The Society established itself as a characteristic presence in the Portuguese Counter-Reformation and Baroque era. This was thanks to the intellectual contribution of the fathers of Coimbra and Évora, the celebrated edition of Aristotle's works with a commentary by the fathers of Coimbra (1591–1606), and Jesuit involvement in education and the sacramental life of the faithful. Favorable to the restoration of an autochthonous dynasty, the Jesuits lent their support to the prophetic interpretations that accompanied the Braganzas' rise to the throne in 1640. In the difficult years that followed independence from Spain, the province temporarily split in two (1653–65) and the Jesuits often clashed with the Inquisition, particularly during the trial against António Vieira (1663–67), a famous Jesuit preacher, missionary in Brazil, and diplomat in the courts of Europe.

They became a target of criticism in the Enlightenment, when Jesuit teaching was singled out as a principal cause of the ills of the kingdom. But what caused the real downturn in their fortunes was the conflict with the minister of King Joseph I, Sebastião José de Carvalho e Melo (marquis of Pombal from 1770), a typical representative of enlightened despotism. The missions in Maranhão (Brazil) had caused problems, but these were exacerbated by the Jesuits' supernatural interpretation of the Lisbon earthquake (1755). Accused of collaborating in an attack on the King (1758), they were expelled a year later from the territories of the Portuguese Crown, and in 1761 Gabriele Malagrida, perhaps the most famous exponent of the supernatural interpretation of the earthquake, was condemned to death by the Inquisition. These events inaugurated the period of the Suppression of the Society of Jesus.

An aggressive anti-Jesuit myth marked Portuguese culture in the decades that followed, but this did not prevent the Society, once it was reestablished (1814), from being readmitted to Portugal (1829). There were ups and downs in its fortunes as a result of political clashes and repeated waves of liberal anticlericalism. Expelled in 1834, the Jesuits returned, their presence officially reestablished in 1858, and they distinguished themselves in education as well as the training of missionaries. Banned once again in 1910 after the Republic was proclaimed, they trickled back from the 1920s on, opening various residences, until, under the Salazar dictatorship, they once again enjoyed full official approval. Since then they have enlivened religious life in the community, also doing cultural work and university teaching. In 2013 the province counted 237 members, of whom 160 were resident in Portugal.

See also Brazil; Coimbra; Gonçalves da Câmara, Luís, SJ; India; Macau; *Patronato* and *Padroado*; Pombal, Marquis of; Rodrigues, Simão, SJ; Vieira, António, SJ.

A Companhia de Jesus na Península Ibérica nos sécs. XVI e XVII: espiritualidade e cultura. 2 vols. Porto: Universidade do Porto, 2004.

Alden, Dauril, *The Making of an Enterprise: The Society of Jesus in Portugal, Its Empire, and Beyond, 1540–1750*. Stanford, CA: Stanford University Press, 1996.

Rodrigues, Francisco, *História da Companhia de Jesus na Assistência de Portugal*. 4 vols. Porto: Apostolado da Imprensa, 1931–50.

Giuseppe Marcocci

Possevino, Antonio, SJ (1533–1611)

Born in Mantua in 1533, Antonio Possevino was educated as a humanist and served as a tutor to two young Gonzaga princes. He entered the Society of Jesus in 1559, and after only two months in the novitiate, Diego Laínez sent him to Piedmont, where for two years he sought to combat the Waldensians and to found a college there. He was ordained a priest in 1561. Then, for ten years (1562–72), he was in France, preaching, writing, and serving as rector of colleges in Avignon and Lyon. When Everard Mercurian was elected as superior general of the Society in 1573, he selected Possevino as his secretary, a post Possevino held until 1577. Among his other duties as secretary, Possevino prepared the Society's annual letters and handled correspondence with Pope Gregory XIII (r. 1572–85), a firm supporter of the Jesuits. Possevino disliked this desk work and requested to be sent on missions to eastern Europe, but Mercurian denied these requests. Stuck in Rome, Possevino preached to the Jewish community at the Congregation of the Holy Trinity, hoping to effect conversions there.

The second phase of Possevino's life began in 1577, when Gregory XIII selected him to go to Sweden and negotiate the conversion of King John III (r. 1568–92) to Roman Catholicism. Possevino arrived in late 1577, and John III converted on the condition that the Pope grant certain concessions to him and his subjects, including liturgy in the vernacular, communion in both kinds, and married clergy. Possevino duly returned to Rome in early 1578, but Gregory and other curial officials were unwilling to grant these concessions. Possevino returned to Sweden carrying this news and found John displeased. The King abandoned his conversion, and soon after the Society was expelled from the kingdom. The mission thus ended unsuccessfully in 1580, though a number of Scandinavians were recruited to join the priesthood.

Possevino was then sent as a diplomat to the Polish-Lithuanian Commonwealth and Muscovy. Gregory XIII charged him with negotiating a peace settlement between the two powers, which was realized in the Treaty of Jam Zapolski (1582). Possevino also worked to reunite the Orthodox Churches with the Roman Church, although nothing was accomplished on this front. Possevino remained in Poland until 1587, preaching and founding seminaries in Olomouc, Braniewo, Vilnius, Riga, Tartu, and elsewhere. He also took up his pen, and his *Moscovia* (1586) remains an important document for its descriptions of his mission and the court of Ivan IV. Possevino also described the religious atmosphere of Russia and gave his opinions on how best to spread the Catholic faith there.

Possevino was recalled by Superior General Claudio Acquaviva in 1587, and he taught theology in Padua until 1591, where St. Francis de Sales was among his students. Possevino briefly reprised his role as a diplomat in 1593 during the negotiations for Henry IV of France's conversion to Catholicism when Clement VIII ordered Possevino to meet with the Duke of Nevers on this matter.

The most significant result of Possevino's later years was his *Bibliotheca selecta*, published in 1593. The *Bibliotheca selecta* was intended as a guide to "good" Catholic books that Possevino had selected for the reader, ones that were in line with Catholic doctrine and teaching. In this way, the *Bibliotheca selecta* was meant to complement the *Index librorum prohibitorum*; if the latter were books that should not be read, the former was a list of books that would take their place. The text was meant to be used in teaching those who would become civil or ecclesiastical leaders. The *Bibliotheca selecta* was actually composed of two parts, the *De cultura ingeniorum*, in which Possevino laid out his system of classifying knowledge – where theology was the only true science – and the *Apparatus sacer*, which was a list of approved authors and their works. The two sections were sometimes published independently of one another.

Possevino remained in Padua during the Venetian Interdict crisis (1606–07), writing numerous polemical works against Paolo Sarpi and the Venetian republic under pseudonyms. When the Jesuits were expelled from Venetian territories in 1606, Possevino relocated to Ferrara, where he died in 1611.

See also Eastern Europe; Gregory XIII; Italy; Jews and Jesuits; Mercurian, Everard, SJ; Scandinavia

Castaldini, Alberto, ed., *Antonio Possevino: i gesuiti e la loro eredità culturale in Transilvania*. Roma: Institutum Historicum Societatis Iesu, 2009.

Colombo, Emanuele, "The Watershed of Conversion: Antonio Possevino, New Christians, and Jews." In James William Bernauer and Robert A. Maryks, eds., *"The Tragic Couple": Encounters between Jews and Jesuits*. Leiden: Brill, 2014, pp. 25–42.

Donnelly, John Patrick, "Antonio Possevino's Plan for World Evangelization." *The Catholic Historical Review* 74, 2 (1988), 179–98.

Karttunen, Liisi, *Antonio Possevino: un diplomate pontifical au XVIᵉ siècle*. Lausanne: Imprimerie Pache-Varidel & Bron, 1908.

Charles Keenan

Postulate

A *postulate* is a request that is made by Provincial Congregations either to an upcoming General Congregation or to the superior general. Postulates are received before or even during a Provincial Congregation, where they are debated, frequently reformulated, sometimes screened out, and other times approved – for sending either to the superior general or to the forthcoming General Congregation.

The *Formula for a Provincial Congregation*, which was recently revised following a directive from General Congregation 35 in 2008 that such revision be undertaken, stipulates that postulates to the superior general should be "such that they offer him useful knowledge about those matters that should be corrected or encouraged in the province, touch on personal reflection or the help of souls, or propose to him suitable means to achieve this same goal" (see *Formula for a Provincial Congregation*, 78 #1, 2).

It is evident that the word "postulate," as it is used in its technical sense in the Society of Jesus, lies somewhat outside the everyday use of English as it is spoken today. Generally in the context of Congregations, it is used in Latin and in the plural – *postulata* – and, in more colloquial English, it means something like "items for potential discussion," or "subjects that Provinces wish to have discussed at a General Congregation." Basically, postulates are requests for consideration of a matter that many Jesuits have come to see as important. For example, in 2008, General Congregation 35 received quite a number of *postulata* concerned with ecology and with the significance for the Society of Jesus of proper stewardship of the earth.

See also Congregations; Superior General

Letter of Father General Adolfo Nicolás SJ to All Major Superiors: "Convocation of the 70th Congregation of Procurators," March 12, 2011. www.sjweb.info.

James Corkery, SJ

Postulator General (Causes of Saints)

Broadly speaking, a postulator is a person, ordained or lay, who has the responsibility of guiding a proposed cause for beatification or canonization through the formal processes that have been established by the Church. Owing to the demands of the various stages of the judicial process, the postulator must be an expert in canonical, theological, and historical matters. The Society of Jesus, like most major religious orders, appoints one of its own members as postulator general, who oversees the beatification or canonization process of Jesuits or individuals who have been commended to the Society. In the normal course, the postulator presents to the bishop of the diocese where the candidate died supporting documents, including a biography highlighting the candidate's heroic virtues or martyrdom, as well as his or her writings. If the cause proceeds to the stage of a wider diocesan inquiry, the investigation focuses on evidence of heroic virtues or martyrdom, as well as signs or miracles, typically medical healings, attributed to the candidate's intercession. If such evidence is found, the case is forwarded to the Congregation for the Causes of Saints in Rome. "New Laws for the Causes of Saints" were promulgated in 1983. To date, fifty-four Jesuits have been formally named as saints by the Church.

See also Curia, Jesuit; Saints

Woodward, Kenneth L., *Making Saints: How the Catholic Church Determines Who Becomes a Saint, Who Doesn't, and Why*. New York: Simon & Schuster, 1996.

Robert E. Scully, SJ

Poverty

Poverty, a primary characteristic of Ignatian spirituality and a Jesuit way of life, is an effort to imitate Jesus, who became poor for our sake. The spiritual foundation of Ignatian poverty is found in the teaching and life of Jesus and the early apostles, who lived completely in abandonment to divine providence. They had no material possessions, relied on supporters, and shared everything in common (Luke 8:3, Acts 2:44–45).

Ignatius's attitude toward evangelical poverty began with his initial conversion at Loyola in 1521. During his long months of convalescence, Ignatius meditated on the lives of Christ and of the saints, fostering a desire to live like them (*Autobiography*, ##6–9). After recovering, he decided to take on the life of a pilgrim, dressing in sackcloth and begging for daily necessities (*Autobiography*, ##17–19). From his time at Manresa to his days in Paris, a total reliance on divine providence and the goodwill of others enabled Ignatius to become closer to Christ the King (*Autobiography*, ##35–36), whom he asked to accept him under His banner (*SpEx* ##98, 147).

The first companions were inspired by Ignatius's personal example; together they vowed to live like Christ "for the good of souls" (*Autobiography*, #85). When circumstances prevented them from going to the Holy Land, they made themselves available for the service of the Church. In Rome, they learned to practice a new form of poverty: providing *gratuitous* ministry to those who needed their service (*Constitutions*, #565). Like the "third type of person" in the *Spiritual Exercises*, they were opened to God's will in the disposition of their possessions (*SpEx* ##155, 157). Content to live close to the poor, they accepted no fixed revenue, either for individuals or for their established communities.

As their apostolic scope grew, the early Jesuits began to corporately modify their attitude toward material poverty. They discerned through Ignatian indifference that the vow of poverty should be subordinated to the primary goal of fulfilling the apostolic mission set before them, and as they began to institutionalize their educational enterprises, they modified its norms. It was decided that, for the sake of the greater service to the Lord that these enterprises made possible, the newly formed Society could own land, possess buildings, and have endowments as long as they were necessary to maintain their colleges. Nevertheless, no fixed revenue was permitted for their "houses of the professed" (*Constitutions*, ##554–57). Individual Jesuits could live off the income from these educational institutions but should be ready to beg "when obedience or necessity requires it" (*Constitutions*, #569).

After the restoration, Jesuit poverty was understood more in the context of obedience. Individual Jesuits had to ask for permission for everything they spent or kept (GC 20, Decree 7) and be dependent on the Society entirely for their material needs (GC 22, Decrees 25–26). Poverty became a religious attitude of living frugally within what the Society provided. The restored Society continued to rely on the support from its institutions, which were becoming more financially complex in keeping with modern developments.

Contemporary Jesuit understandings of poverty follow the directions of recent General Congregations. Jesuits should live their vow of poverty with integrity (GC 30, Decree 22), as "disciples of a poor Christ [who] do not exceed what men of moderate means can allow themselves" (GC 30, Decree 46, #4). Their life of poverty must be marked by "sincerity," "devotion to work," and "charity" (GC 31, Decree 18, ##6–9). Not only is it a form of individual self-abnegation and a communal sharing of resources (GC 32, Decree 12, ##8, 24–31), but it also includes a social concern for justice and preferential option for the poor, conforming to an apostolic value of self-giving toward a "generous and ready service of all the abandoned" (GC 32, Decree 12, #4). Most recently, the personal and communal poverty of Jesuits were understood as a means to bear real and prophetic witness to their service of and solidarity with the poor (GC 34, Decree 9, ##5–6).

The pontificate of Pope Francis, whose own example has reflected the practice of Jesuit poverty, is deeply grounded in these congregations. As a Jesuit formed in the spirit of social justice developed by the Latin American Bishops' Conferences at Medellin, Puebla, and Aparecida, Jorge Mario Bergoglio understood Jesuit poverty as a self-emptying movement toward the peripheries of society. Thus, the Pope's washing the feet of women prisoners and refusal to live in traditional papal luxury are concrete examples of Jesuit poverty in action.

While the understanding of poverty has evolved throughout the history of the Society, one feature remains constant. Jesuit poverty is linked to humility and self-denying as a way to imitate Christ (*SpEx* #167). However, it is evangelical and centered upon the mission rather than a privatized, ascetical lifestyle. Thus, it functions as an effective value that permeates all apostolic activities. In short, Jesuit poverty is contextual: all are called to a real and brotherly poverty yet always interpreted and practiced in appropriate discernment for the sake of the mission and its apostolic witness.

See also Chastity; Community; Gratuity of Ministries; Humility; Obedience; Preferential Option for the Poor

Aguilla, Mario I., *Pope Francis: His Life and Thought.* Cambridge: Lutterworth Press, 2014.
Ivens, Michael, "Poverty in the Constitutions and Other Ignatian Sources." *The Way Supplement* 61 (1988), 76–88.
Knight, David, "Saint Ignatius' Ideal of Poverty." *Studies in the Spirituality of Jesuits* 4, 1 (1972), 1–37.
Tetlow, Joseph A., "The Transformation of Jesuit Poverty." *Studies in the Spirituality of Jesuits* 18, 5 (1986), 1–37.

Anh Q. Tran, SJ

Pozzo, Andrea, SJ (1642–1709)

Andrea Pozzo was a Jesuit brother, and perhaps the most accomplished artist of the Society. He mastered the art of *trompe l'oeil* painting in seventeenth-century Italy and used this skill to decorate numerous Jesuit churches. He also wrote a treatise that outlined his technique, which was widely read and translated toward the end of his life. Almost all of the art he created was produced for the Jesuits.

Pozzo was born in Trent on November 30, 1642, and educated by the Jesuits in that city. He studied with a local painter for three years and began a career as an artist. He entered the Society of Jesus in Milan at the age of 23 and spent his years as a novice in Piedmont. He lived in the professed house at San Fedele in Milan 1667–69, and his first works for the Jesuits date to this period: panel paintings of Saints Ignatius and Francis Xavier, for the Church of Santa Maria di Brera. His design for an *apparato* for the celebration of St. Francis Borgia's canonization in 1671 brought his work to the attention of many and led to subsequent projects for the Jesuits throughout northern Italy: in Genoa (1673), Mondovì (1675–78), Turin (1678), and Como (1680–81). These early successes, particularly the decoration of the church dedicated to St. Francis Xavier in Mondovì, brought him to the attention of General Giovanni Paolo Oliva in Rome.

His first project in Rome was the painting of a corridor in the professed house (1682–86), depicting scenes from the life of St. Ignatius, who had lived there. This space was a challenge for the artist, because of its size, but Pozzo succeeded in creating a visually engaging space celebrating the miracles performed by the Society's founder, within an illusionistic framework. In this period Pozzo also began to design stage sets and *apparati* for Forty Hours Devotion. Over the years Pozzo would create numerous *apparati* of this type for liturgical celebrations in the Church of Il Gesù.

In 1687 he began work at the new Church of Sant'Ignazio, frescoing the tribune and ceiling. The fictive dome Pozzo painted in this space is often considered his greatest achievement; it is in fact one of five such illusionistic domes that he created in his career. Various factors, including the low light level of the church and its high ceiling, contribute to the strong illusionistic effect. The *trompe l'oeil* ceiling frescoes in the nave, showcasing the Jesuit missions, date to 1691–94. All of his work at Sant'Ignazio was completed by 1698; he then turned his attention to the Church of Il Gesù, executing altars dedicated to St. Ignatius and St. Luigi Gonzaga.

Figure 57 Andrea Pozzo, SJ: Corridor frescoes in Casa Professa, Rome, 1582–86. Photograph Alison Fleming

Pozzo's illusionistic style of painting is believed to have been influenced by contemporary scientific developments, especially those connected to astronomy and optics. In particular, the optical experiments conducted by his fellow Jesuit Athanasius Kircher at the Collegio Romano were known by Pozzo and would have offered the artist additional knowledge of the field.

In addition to his numerous paintings and architectural designs, Pozzo was also a theoretician. He followed in the footsteps of artists and treatise writers Leon Battista Alberti and Sebastiano Serlio, and furthered theories of painting in perspective. The first volume of Pozzo's *Perspectiva Pictorum et Architectorum* (*Perspective in Architecture and Painting*) was published in 1693, and the second volume followed in 1700. It is essentially a series of engravings with commentary on the principal ideas of perspectival painting, and may be regarded as an instructional manual for artists. Many of the prints illustrate Pozzo's own works, including the fictive dome of Sant'Ignazio, and they illuminate the connections between real and painted architecture. An English translation of the treatise appeared in 1707, and the book was quite rapidly translated into numerous other languages, including Chinese, emphasizing both the global footprint of the Order and the popularity of Pozzo's art. His appointment at the court of Vienna shortly after publication of the treatise cemented his international reputation and further spread his ideas.

Pozzo's final projects took him away from Rome. He departed from the city in 1702, stopping in Montepulciano to paint a salone for the Contucci family en route to Vienna, where he painted for both the Jesuits (a final fictive dome in the Jesuit church) and the Holy Roman Emperor (in the Liechtenstein Palace). Pozzo died in that city on August 31, 1709, and is buried in the Jesuit church.

See also Arts, Visual; Baroque Art and Architecture; Brothers; Gesù, Rome; Sant'Ignazio, Rome

Burda-Stengel, Felix, *Andrea Pozzo and Video Art*. Philadelphia, PA: St. Joseph's University Press, 2013.
De Feo, Vittorio, and Valentino Martinelli, eds., *Andrea Pozzo*. Milan: Electa, 1996.
Pozzo, Andrea, *Perspective in Architecture and Painting: An Unabridged Reprint of the English-and-Latin Edition of the 1693 "Perspectiva Pictorum et Architectorum."* New York: Dover, 1989.

Alison Fleming

Pray, György, SJ (1723–1801)

Born at Érsekújvár, György Pray entered the Society of Jesus in 1745 and enjoyed a successful pre-Suppression academic career, culminating at Buda, where he taught from 1760. Pray is in many ways emblematic of ex-Jesuits' ability to weather the storms of the post-Suppression period. He moved from Buda to the court of Maria Theresa where he was imperial historiographer for a spell and, in 1777, returned to Buda when the University of Nagy-Szombat transferred to that city. He served as a highly capable head of the university library, to which he gave important manuscript collections. During the remainder of his career, Pray took up clerical positions at Grosswardein and Tormowa, and even served as a representative in the Hungarian diet, but he is best remembered for his historical scholarship.

Pray had already published groundbreaking works on Hungarian history before the Suppression, including the impressively wide-ranging *Annales veteres Hunnorum, Avarum et Hungarorum, ab anno ante natum Christum CCX. ad annum Christi CMXCVII. deducti ac maximam partem ex orientis, occidentisque rerum scriptoribus congesti* (1761) and the more specialized *Dissertatio historico-critica de sacra dextera divi S. Stephani primi Hungariae regis* (1771), but his mightiest achievements were to come later in his career, notably the multi-volume history of the kings of Hungary, *Historia regum Hungariæ, cvm notitiis praeviis ad cognoscendum veterem regni statum pertinentibus*, which appeared in the year of his death in Pest.

See also Eastern Europe; Suppression

Shore, Paul, "Ex-Jesuits in the East Habsburg Lands, Silesia and Poland." In Jonathan Wright and Jeffrey Burson, eds., *The Jesuit Suppression in Global Context: Causes, Events, and Consequences*. Cambridge: Cambridge University Press, 2015, pp. 216–28.
Shore, Paul, *Narratives of Adversity: Jesuits in the Eastern Peripheries of the Habsburg Realms (1640–1773)*. Budapest: Central European University Press, 2012.

Jonathan Wright

Preaching

Preaching has been a foundational component of Jesuit life and ministry since the founding of the Society of Jesus. In the 1550 *Formula of the Institute of the Society of Jesus*, approved and confirmed by Pope Julius III, the Society was founded chiefly for the defense and propagation of the faith and the good of souls first and foremost through "public preaching, lectures, and any other ministration whatsoever of the word of God." Such ministries of the Word, and formal preaching in particular, constituted an essential component of any work that the Society undertook. The apostolic work of preaching, therefore, was understood in the early Society in the broadest sense and as part of what John O'Malley calls a "triad of word-sacrament-works," which together open up the revelatory word of God proclaimed in the life and ministry of Jesus, Incarnate Word of God, and handed on to the Church in the canonical scriptures. Jerónimo Nadal wrote to the early Society that giving the *Spiritual Exercises*, so central to Jesuit mission and spirituality, was a ministry in which "the word of God is declared." Even after the first decade of the Society's history, when the intellectual apostolate had acquired greater prominence, O'Malley notes, the preaching event itself continued to have focal priority in Jesuit apostolic ministry. A robust *ordo* of preaching was introduced that included Sundays outside of Advent and Lent, an expansion upon the earlier norm.

Preaching the word of God, therefore, became the wellspring and summit of all Jesuit ministries, and it fed a hunger among those to whom the first Jesuits were sent for a deepening union with Christ and a restored relationship with the Church. This focus reflected the mandate of the Society's *Constitutions*, which specified that if circumstances and needs were equal, preference should be given to preaching and to communicating the word of God through lectures and other public encounters because these yield the "more universal good and extend to the aid of greater numbers of our neighbors" (*Constitutions*, #623). This multidimensional understanding of proclamation as including "lectures and other public encounters" has characterized the Society of Jesus throughout its history. Such preaching, at the discretion of the superior, could take place beyond the Society's own churches to include "other churches, squares, or places of the region," provided that the greater glory of God remained the constant goal in the choice of such ministries (*Constitutions*, ##645–47). In all its modes, Jesuit preaching shares the Church's own mission of proclamation, which is charismatic and kerygmatic, i.e., it is a response to a Spirit-filled summons born of faith, and it is a proclaimed word, a dynamic event "fulfilled in our hearing" (Luke 4:21). Both the summons and the eventful proclamation bear the initiative of God, who first speaks the Word of grace and stirs hearts to hear and proclaim it.

By identifying themselves early on with this mission, the first Jesuits built upon the mendicant tradition of the followers of Francis and Dominic in responding to the malaise of faith and practice in their own time, fueled particularly by the atmosphere of the Counter-Reformation in which the Society was born. Suspicion about lapses in matters of faith often prevailed and provided a context in which the urgency of preaching took hold. Though often polemical and motivated by a call to moral conversion, the spiritual dimension of union with Christ in the midst of everyday living, as well as the faith needed to sustain it, motivated Jesuits to draw more and more people into the embrace of the Church. Spiritual conversion and a deepening of one's faith were a fruit of hearing the Word, but always within the safe haven of the Church, understood as a keeper and sure foundation for one's access to salvation. This response to the unique signs of the times and the needs of the age called Jesuits to pay particular attention to their Ignatian charism in order to be persuasive and effective heralds of the Good News. The preaching ministry relied upon the eloquence and faith of the individual preacher, but it also shared an ecclesial and Jesuit identity, received first from Christ, the redemptive Word made flesh, and handed on in the apostolic tradition, guided in every age by an impelling Spirit that was seen as "ever ancient and ever new." The preached Word, then and now, is a communal Word, not one's own.

Such a mission demanded intellectual and practical training in rhetoric, Scripture, and theology, but the end and purpose was always to stir the souls of all their hearers and to reconcile hearts that have been alienated from the love of God revealed in Christ. Such preaching, as twentieth-century Jesuit liturgical historian Josef Jungmann described it, announces in every time and season "that the kingdom of God has entered the world, thus disclosing salvation to [humankind]." The time is now and at hand, and Jesuit preaching reflected that immediacy and urgency.

Preaching as Spiritual Conversation and Moment of Divine Encounter

The dynamic character of such a Word-event was particularly suited to the Society's "way of proceeding," for it took its inspiration from the *Spiritual Exercises* themselves, where the Triune God looks down upon the world and sees the joys and struggles of human lives. Out of love and compassion, the Trinity desires to enter into communication with this world and invites all people to respond to the call of Christ the King, first by "not being deaf to his call" but hearers of the Word, and then by choosing to follow him ("ready and diligent") as the Body of Christ in the world (*SpEx* ##91, 102). For Jesuits, this proclamation and response relationship with Christ was fundamental to being a Companion of Jesus and to their religious identity as "servants of his mission," as later documents would call it (GC 34, Decree 1, #7). Laboring with Christ who is laboring in the world, they carry that word into the lives and struggles of the cultural and religious contexts in which they dwell among the people, "to bring the Gospel into their lives and labors" (GC 34, Decree 1, #7). Without that immersion into real lives and cultural contexts, the biblical word and witness remain static and lifeless, rather than what the Letter to the Hebrews called a Word that is "living and active, sharper than any two-edged sword, piercing until it divides soul from spirit, joints from marrow" (Hebrews 4:12). From a Jesuit perspective, that summons engenders a spiritual freedom that looks only to "what is most conducive for us to the end for which we are created," as the First Principle and Foundation of the *Exercises* situated the end and purpose of all human longing. Such liberation allows one to desire and choose the "greater glory of God." Human longing meets a saving Word in that incarnational encounter.

Seen from this perspective of human engagement with the mystery of God at every level of life, and animated by the greater good, Jesuit preaching reaches beyond the formal moments of liturgical preaching within defined liturgical rites to include a way of being in the world that is always seeking to facilitate a new hearing of an ancient promise of God revealed in Christ and refreshed in every age through the power of the Holy Spirit. This primary initiative of a loving God invigorates each proclamatory event as a fresh word and a renewed call to fidelity to God, speaking within every aspect of human life. Such preaching took place in Jesuit churches and centers of apostolic ministry as the Society moved from its beginnings in Rome to spread rapidly throughout the world. It was this character of charismatic and kerygmatic preaching that both endeared the

Society to the people served and brought Jesuits into religious and political conflict with Church authorities and political structures, from the time of Ignatius to the present. It highlights the vulnerability and importance of preaching, for it is nothing less than "God's self-disclosure in word," as Karl Rahner describes this divine communication, a "word of grace, reconciliation, and eternal life." Jesuits understood this through the lens of their own spiritual heritage of "finding God in all things." Its interactive dynamic highlights the unique roles of both the preacher and the hearer of the Word as essential to the communication of the very mystery of God himself. In line with the Roman Catholic tradition of sacramentality, the locus of revelation is the world, real persons and lives, speaking and listening and acting, bodying forth the matter and form of the presence of Christ.

The Renewed Preaching Ministry after Vatican II

Proclaiming and preaching the Word was later articulated by the Second Vatican Council as a mode of Christ's presence in the liturgy, a presence that leads to true communion "through him, with him, and in him, in the unity of the Holy Spirit," to the Father's praise and glory. These ancient words correspond with the First Principle and Foundation of the *Spiritual Exercises*, where the "praise, reverence, and service of God" is identified as the end and purpose of human life. The liturgical renewal inspired by the Second Vatican Council included a renewal and deepening of the ministry of preaching. The four constitutions of the Council, *Sacrosanctum concilium*, *Dei Verbum*, *Lumen gentium*, and *Gaudium et spes*, reflected the work of a number of prominent Jesuit theologians and paved the way for liturgical reform. Jesuit Cardinal Augustin Bea was seminal in the renewal of biblical studies and the emphasis on the revelatory character of the Word of God. Jesuits Josef Jungmann, Otto Semmelroth, Henri de Lubac, and Karl Rahner, preeminent theologians and spiritual scholars of the time, each used their scholarly expertise to shed light on the pastoral mission of announcing the Word of God. Of particular importance was the German Semmelroth, whose writing on a theology of proclamation did much to reintegrate the relationship between the Liturgy of the Word and the Liturgy of the Eucharist in the reformed rites following the Council. In a time of sparse Roman Catholic literature on the theology of preaching, he articulated a way of uniting ambo and altar as one redemptive dialogue in which the incarnate Christ is both Word and Answer (*Wort und Antwort*) and in which all are invited to share. Karl Rahner would mine this insight to speak of liturgy and the Christian life as "one whole word of God." He provided a specifically theological interpretation of the revised lectionary's summons to a richer and more abundant fare at the Table of God's Word and Sacrament, which together form "one single act of worship." Renewed theological reflection on preaching, which began before the Council and continued after its conclusion, highlighted a seminal feature of the liturgical reform of Vatican II and the reintegration of preaching into the life of the Church. Preaching was no longer considered, at best, as a talk about God gleaned from a static text, but a revelatory moment in which Christ can speak in the preaching event itself. The liturgy is a particularly privileged moment of this charismatic and kerygmatic encounter, and Jesuit churches and ministries have often been noted and sought out in contemporary times because of the attention paid to the importance of preaching as a vehicle of grace.

Contemporary Jesuit Spirituality and the Preaching Ministry

With the tradition of scholarship and spiritual ministry that has shaped contemporary Jesuit ministries around the world, a rich dialogue has begun about what characterizes Jesuit preaching that embraces both the theological *ressourcement* of the Council and the renewed identity of the Society in recent General Congregations and documents. Fathers General Arrupe and Kolvenbach contributed to this reengagement of the Word in the midst of what *Gaudium et spes* called "the joy and hope, the grief and anguish of the people of our time," which all companions of Jesus share and take to heart. The evangelical character of Arrupe's clarion call to a faith that does justice asks that preachers "labor with Christ who is laboring in the world" (GC 34, Decree 1, ##4–5) and find that echo in the lives of those whom they are called to serve and shape into communities of faith. Kolvenbach invited the Society to plumb the poetic and symbolic richness of the Word beneath the words. His reflections suggest that the vision of La Storta, where Ignatius asked to be "placed with Christ," is an image of Jesuit preaching that is truly a labor in companionship, a tilling of the soil beneath the surface of text and context and their meeting in the preaching moment. The choice to be "placed with Christ" is to share the vulnerability of One who chose to enter into human suffering and struggle, as well as human solidarity and joy, to announce that it is here that Christ is speaking "when the holy scriptures are read in the Church" (Vatican II, *Sacrosanctum concilium*, #7).

Preaching is an ecclesial mission that Jesuits share with the global Church. The Benedictine tradition of *lectio continua* within the rhythm of the communal office and the daily work (*Ora et labora*) provides a contemplative perspective on this ministry. Members of the Order of Preachers understand contemplation as the primary foundation for sharing the fruits of that contemplation in their lives of service (*Contemplata aliis tradere*). The Franciscan tradition offers preaching in images and themes common to the people, as a model of humility and poverty with the itinerant Christ, "using words if necessary." Jesuit preaching, as part of this matrix of preaching charisms, emanates from a Society "placed as companions with a laboring Word." Jesuits are sent on mission to preach out of the center of the Church, the *totus Christus* (Head and members), to the margins of peoples and cultures, recognizing themselves first as sinners who are called to be in companionship with Christ and inseparable from the Church, united with him as the sacramental Body of Christ in the world. Christ's heart is at the center and interprets all texts, and it is the Spirit's hallowing that shapes the Word that is preached. This requires receptivity and willingness to be taken, blessed, broken, and shared with Christ for the life of the world, which is the field in which the tilling of the soil takes place and is the locus of the harvest proclamation. The spiritual discernment cultivated in the *Exercises* provides a freedom to explore both the darkness and the shadows, the hollow and dry areas of human living, as well as the unexpected grace and deep joy that comes when the "Contemplation to Attain the Love of God," the culminating prayer of the *Exercises* (#230), finds poetic expression in the famous *Suscipe*, which is the prayer of total surrender in response to the grace given to love God in all things. Such preaching wrestles with the texts and eschews easy answers or platitudes. It always seeks to find a thread of grace weaving itself through saint and sinner alike, the powerfully placed and the voiceless. This understanding of preaching, as the history attests, bears great risk and promises much. Its mission of attempting "to feel and to taste" (*sentir y gustar*) the presence and activity of God in all the persons and circumstances of the world places Jesuits at the center of a tension pulling them both to God and to the world at the same time, being firmly rooted in God at all times, while simultaneously being plunged into the heart of the world (GC 35, Decree 2). Jesuit history, spirituality, and contemporary experience have traced "the footprints of Christ everywhere," as that recent Congregation attested.

In the end, the story of Jesuit preaching is most articulated, yet hidden, in the daily ministries and Sunday gatherings in which countless Jesuit preachers of the word have labored week after week. There Jesuits have gathered in faith the words and images to preach a fresh word and a consoling grace amid every human emotion that shapes the lives of the communities in which they are placed. Walter Burghardt in North America, Rupert Mayer in Europe, Paul Lungu in Africa, and Rutilio Grande in Central America are all members of a "great cloud" of faithful Jesuit preachers throughout the Society's history who have struggled to name in their own time and place the grace of Christ, who "plays in ten thousand places, / Lovely in limbs and lovely in eyes not his / To the Father through the features of men's faces," as the Jesuit poet Gerard Manley Hopkins proclaimed in "As Kingfishers Catch Fire." The labor of Jesuit preaching, embodied in such men, is a privileged expression of the Society's self-offering to the Church. Its art, creativity, and dynamism suggest that new voices and different modes of communication may surely be welcomed into what Ignatius articulated from the beginning as an apostolic mandate of the highest priority and a "pathway to God." This priority has been reaffirmed in recent *Complementary Norms* in all its complex reality as integral to the evangelizing mission of the Society within the Church today, "which aims at the realization of the Kingdom of God in the whole of human society, not only in the life to come, but in this life" as well (*Complementary Norms*, 245, #1).

See also Biblical Studies; Liturgy; Ministries; Mission; Rhetoric(s); *Spiritual Exercises*

Janowiak, Paul A., "Lex Orandi, Lex Praedicandi: Placed in Companionship with a Labouring Word." *Review of Ignatian Spirituality* 30, 3 (2004), #107.

Jungmann, Joseph, *Announcing the Word of God.* Trans. Ronald Walls. New York: Herder and Herder, 1967.

Kolvenbach, Peter-Hans, *The Road from La Storta: Peter-Hans Kolvenbach, SJ, on Ignatian Spirituality.* Ed. Carl Starkloff. St. Louis, MO: The Institute of Jesuit Sources, 2000.

O'Malley, John W., *The First Jesuits.* Cambridge, MA: Harvard University Press, 1993.

Rahner, Karl, *The Church and the Sacraments.* Trans. W. J. O'Hara. New York: Herder and Herder, 1963. "The Word and the Eucharist." *Theological Investigations.* Vol. IV. New York: Crossroad, 1960, pp. 213–88.

Semmelroth, Otto, *The Preaching Word: On the Theology of Proclamation.* Trans. John Jay Hughes. New York: Herder and Herder, 1965.

Vatican Council II. Ed. Austin Flannery. Northport, NY: Costello Publishing Co., 1996.

Paul A. Janowiak, SJ

Preferential Option for the Poor

This recent phrase encapsulates the Christian attitude toward the poor: a commitment to action, advocacy, and solidarity with the most disadvantaged, inspired by Jesus's proclamation: "The Spirit of the Lord is upon me, because he anointed me to preach the gospel to the poor" (Luke 4:18ff.).

In 2000, Jesuit Superior General Peter-Hans Kolvenbach claimed that a preferential option for the poor, in various forms, "has marked the whole history of the Society" ("On the Social Apostolate," #2). Its articulation, however, developed following Leo XIII's

Rerum novarum (1891), which included the line: "God Himself seems to incline rather to those who suffer misfortune" (#24). Subsequent papal encyclicals called for action on behalf of the poor including, beyond temporary relief, detailed social analysis and reform. In 1971, Paul VI referred to a "preferential respect due to the poor" (*Octogesima adveniens*, #23). In 1979, the Latin American bishops reaffirmed their mission of justice and entitled a chapter of their document "A Preferential Option for the Poor." The expression appears frequently in Church documents thereafter.

Under Superior General Pedro Arrupe (1965–81) – often credited with first use of the phrase – focus on justice in the service of faith became central to Jesuit identity. In a well-known address (1981), he presented "a preferential care for the poor, the weak and the oppressed" as an essential corrective to overly juridical approaches to justice ("Rooted and Grounded In Love," #61). In 1983, the 33rd General Congregation brought together nearly a century of Jesuit discussion in the statement, "We wish to make our own the Church's preferential option for the poor," noting that the preference comes from "a desire to heal the whole human family" and "excludes no one but neither does it excuse anyone from its demands" (Decree 1, #48). The particular implications of the "preferential option" in the contemporary world have been further elaborated by the most recent General Congregations.

See also Arrupe, Pedro, SJ; Justice; Liberation Theology; Mission; "Men and Women for Others"; Poverty; Service of Faith and Promotion of Justice

Sobrino, Jon, *No Salvation Outside the Poor: Prophetic Utopian Essays*. Maryknoll, NY: Orbis, 2008.

William A. Clark, SJ

Presupposition

The term "presupposition" refers to a directive that Ignatius of Loyola gives near the beginning of the *Spiritual Exercises*. There he counsels the "one who is giving the *Spiritual Exercises* and the one who receives them" that it should be "presupposed" that each will always be "more ready to save the proposition of the neighbor than to condemn it." If one cannot "save the proposition," Ignatius advises, he should ask the other how he understands it, seeking out "every suitable means" by which it may be saved and, only if necessary, "corrected with love." Many commentators have suggested that Ignatius wrote this as a result of his experience of being unfairly accused of heresy by the Spanish Inquisition earlier in life.

In the years following the Second Vatican Council, twentieth-century Jesuit General Pedro Arrupe placed special emphasis upon the importance of the presupposition as a basis for dialogue and inculturation. It encourages a "broad understanding," explained Arrupe, that objectively considers first "the positive values" of another's statement and avoids "one-sided exaggerations or purely emotional reactions." In keeping with Arrupe's observation, Carl Starkloff has argued that the "tremendous potential" of the presupposition "for creating a dynamic of trust and collaboration between persons" makes it an apt principle for any type of conversation.

See also Direction, Spiritual; *Spiritual Exercises*

Arrupe, Pedro, "On Inculturation." In Jerome Aixala, ed., *Other Apostolates Today: Selected Letters and Addresses*. Vol. III. St. Louis, MO: The Institute of Jesuit Sources, 1981.

A *Planet to Heal: Reflections and Forecasts*. Rome: International Center for Jesuit Education, 1977.

Ivens, Michael, *Understanding the Spiritual Exercises*. Leominster: Gracewing, 1998.

Starkloff, Carl, "As Different as Night and Day: Ignatius's Presupposition and Our Way of Conversing across Cultures." *Studies in the Spirituality of Jesuits* 28, 4 (September 1996), 1–21.

Henry Shea, SJ

Priesthood

Not all Jesuits are priests – some are brothers or "temporal coadjutors" – but as Paul VI reminded General Congregation (GC) 32 in 1975, ministerial priesthood is an essential character of the Society of Jesus. When, in 1540, the first ten companions decided to stay together and to form a religious order under the leadership of Ignatius, all of them were already priests. The *Constitutions* stipulate that those who are called to priesthood need to be ordained before they take their final vows. Nonetheless, from the personal history of Ignatius and the first companions and from the way the Society developed since then, it appears that it is not so much a particular understanding of priesthood which shapes the Jesuit identity than it is the Jesuit identity which shapes the way Jesuits are priests. Ordained priesthood in the Society of Jesus is instrumental in order to fulfill its mission within the Church and in the world which Ignatius saw broadly as "helping souls" and which has been formulated more recently as "the service of faith, of which the promotion of justice is an absolute requirement" (cf. GC 32, Decree 4).

In the documentary sources of the Society (*Constitutions*, Ignatius's *Autobiography* and *Letters*), there is no in-depth reflection about priesthood. Ignatius and the early companions took it for granted. In the medieval understanding they inherited, holy orders conferred the powers to celebrate the Eucharist and to hear confessions, two sacraments central to their ministries. Therefore ordination was necessary for their mission. Ignatius and four companions were ordained in Venice in 1537 *ad titulum paupertis et sufficientis litteraturae*, "under the title of poverty and sufficient knowledge," which means that their ordination was not attached to a particular place or office providing an income as was usually the case, but also that it was recognized that they had studied at length. This reflects well three main orientations for Jesuit ministries as they appear in the *Formula of the Institute* approved by Pope Paul III in 1540 and as Ignatius and the first companions already practiced them before ordination. First, there were the ministries of the Word which includes preaching and various forms of teaching in order to spread the Gospel. Second, there were the ministries of the *Spiritual Exercises* and all that can foster among people an intimate and personal union with God, such as spiritual conversations or personal advice. Third, there were the ministries of charity in solidarity with the poor, starting with the education of children and unlettered persons. The solid and long education of the first Jesuits was necessary for the first two. Their commitment to poverty was the basis for the last. Another characteristic of their being priests was their readiness to be sent wherever there would be greater need for the Church, even to the most remote places of the world. Hence, they were not to be immediately at the service a local bishop but rather they put themselves at the disposition of the Roman Pontiff.

Those characteristics continue to shape the Jesuit priesthood today even as a more general understanding of priesthood has evolved since Vatican II with the recovery of the centrality of the Word of God and of the notion of a common priesthood of the faithful. According to more recent documents of the Society, which show a greater reflection about the meaning of Jesuit priesthood than the early sources did, no ministry or particular profane activity is a priori outside the scope of Jesuit priests. Their mission is directed, "inseparably, towards justice for the poor and the reconciliation of the world to God through the preaching of the Gospel" (cf. GC 34, Decree 6); they strive to reach out to those cultural and geographical places which are at the frontiers of the Church. To do so they develop the resources of their own spirituality rooted in the *Spiritual Exercises*, collaborating with others in and outside the Church and engaging in open dialogue with sciences, religions, and cultures. Though sometimes in a position of direct service of the institutional Church, their priesthood is more prophetic in the sense of speaking out the Good News in any way it could be heard, than it is cultic or kingly in the sense of being focused on the pastoral administration of a Christian community. It is an apostolic priesthood in the missionary style of Saint Paul. As "companions of Jesus," Jesuits find in him and his way of ministering to people the model of their priesthood.

See also Confession, Confessors; Formation; Liturgy; Ministries; Preaching

Buckley, Michael J., "Jesuit Priesthood: Its Meaning and Commitments." *Studies in the Spirituality of Jesuits* 8, 5 (December 1976), 135–62.

Harmless, William, "Jesuits as Priests: Crisis and Charism." *Studies in the Spirituality of Jesuits* 19, 3 (May 1987), 1–49.

"The Jesuit Priest: Ministerial Priesthood and Jesuit Identity." General Congregation 34, Decree 6. In John W. Padberg, ed., *Jesuit Life and Mission Today: The Decrees and Accompanying Documents of the 31st–35th General Congregations of the Society of Jesus.* St. Louis, MO: The Institute of Jesuit Sources, 2009, pp. 559–69.

Grégoire Catta, SJ

Principle and Foundation

The text of the Principle and Foundation occupies a unique place in the *Spiritual Exercises*. It is written differently than the meditations and reads like a brief theological statement. Most scholars believe that Ignatius did not assemble the text in its current form until his studies in Paris, further refining it during his initial years in Rome. The early directories of the *Exercises*, however, do propose using the Principle and Foundation as a meditation at the outset of the First Week, noting that it serves as a propaedeutic to the overarching dynamisms of the retreat.

The text begins with the lapidary observation that the human person "is created to praise, reverence and serve God our Lord and by means of this to save his soul." As a result, Ignatius counsels, each person ought to make themselves "indifferent to all created things," desiring "only what is more conducive to the end for which we are created" (*SpEx* #23). The Principle and Foundation is thus the primary source for the practice of "Ignatian indifference." Hugo Rahner, moreover, suggests that the desire "only for what is more conducive" represents the beginning of a thread within the *Exercises* that continues through the meditations of the Second Week into the Election, where the language of the Principle and Foundation is repeated almost verbatim. In this way the Principle and Foundation lays the groundwork for those later meditations in which one is invited to identify with Christ, even Christ poor and crucified.

See also Indifference; *Spiritual Exercises*

Ivens, Michael, *Understanding the Spiritual Exercises*. Leominster: Gracewing, 1998.

Rahner, Hugo, "The Christology of the Spiritual Exercises." In *Ignatius the Theologian*. Trans. Michael Barry. San Francisco: Ignatius, 1990, pp. 53–135.

Royón, Elías, "*Principio y fundamento*." In *Diccionario de espiritualidad Ignaciana (G–Z)*. Vol. II, ed. José García de Castro. Bilbao: Ediciones Mensajero, 2007, pp. 1490–98.

Henry Shea, SJ

Pro Juárez, Miguel Agustín, SJ, Bl. (1891–1927)

The son of a mining engineer and mine owner, Miguel Pro was born on January 13, 1891, in the town of Guadalupe in the Mexican state of Zacatecas to Miguel and Josefa Juárez, their third child. His mother, known for her charity toward mining families, started a small hospital. Having been sent to study at the Jesuit college in Saltillo, with two of his sisters already in the convent, Miguel joined the Jesuits in 1911 at El Llano, Michoacán, at the age of 20. Because of the tumultuous Church–State conflict that followed, especially with the Mexican government's anticlerical policies, he was sent out of the country during his juniorate and spent some time at Los Gatos, California (1913–14), after which he did philosophy in Granada, Spain (1915–18), regency at the Jesuit college in Granada, Nicaragua (1918–22), and then finally theology in Sarriá de Barcelona (1922–23) as well as Enghien, Belgium (1924–26), because of his interest in working with the labor movement. Ordained on August 31, 1925, without having done tertianship because of his precarious health, he was sent back to Mexico at the height of the Church–State conflict. He worked clandestinely in Mexico City for a short time, from July 1926 to November 1927, until he was accused of being part of a plot to assassinate presidential candidate Alvaro Obregón, an accusation never proven since he and his companions were never granted a trial, despite pleas from foreign governments. Miguel Pro was executed before a firing squad with one of his brothers, Humberto, on the morning of November 23, 1927, the international press having been invited to witness the spectacle. A last-minute intervention by the consul of Argentina saved the life of his younger brother, Roberto. Miguel Pro's final cry as he extended his arms forming a cross, "Viva Cristo Rey!" (Long live Christ the King!), was heard the world over. Photographs of his execution soon became holy cards, and crowds filled the streets for his funeral. His following continues to this day.

Despite the brevity of his final apostolate in Mexico City, about sixteen months in total, he worked tirelessly in many underground settings. The atmosphere between Church and State was extremely tense during this time. When Plutarco Elías Calles became president in 1924, he continued the Revolution's process of land distribution and inaugurated an ambitious program of public works and fiscal reform. While his predecessor, Alvaro Obregón, had generally ignored the anticlerical articles of the Constitution, Calles was determined to enforce them. He forbade religious processions and closed Church schools, convents, and monasteries. He required, furthermore, that Mexican priests register with the civil authorities. In response to these repressive anticlerical laws, the Mexican hierarchy retaliated by suspending religious services throughout Mexico. This suspension took place on July 31, 1926, the same month Pro returned to Mexico from Europe. The Church–State conflict took a dramatic turn when Mexican *campesi-nos*, persons from rural areas in several of the central states, under the partial leadership of the *Liga* (La Liga Nacional Defensora de la Libertad Religiosa), which was more centered in the cities, especially Mexico City, took up arms and engaged in guerilla-type warfare with the government troops. These rural, armed groups became known as the *Cristeros*, because of their cry, "Viva Cristo Rey!" The *Cristeros* were not able to defeat the federal army nor was the army able to suppress them.

It was within this tense, conflictive environment of the mid-1920s that Pro took up his apostolic labors, which included work with students and office workers, not to mention domestic workers, taxi-cab drivers, unmarried mothers, and reformed prostitutes. Besides giving retreats to many of these groups, he celebrated the sacraments for them clandestinely. He came to the aid of many victims connected with the Cristero Rebellion, especially widows and orphans. While he did not promote violence, like many of the Mexican Jesuits, he felt that these persons had a right to take up arms in defense of their religious liberties. Stories abound of the many ingenious ways he eluded police, often engaging in humor and donning a million disguises right under their noses, and photographs document these disguises. In 1988, the Mexican province established the Centro de Derechos Humanos Miguel Agustín Pro Juárez near the site of his execution, the same year in which he was beatified by Pope John Paul II.

See also Blesseds; Martyrs, Ideal and History; Mexico, Nineteenth Century to Present

Dragón, Antonio, *Vida Íntima del Padre Pro*. Trans. from French by Rafael Martínez del Campo. México: Buena Prensa, 1990.
Fanchón, Royer, *Padre Pro*. New York: P. J. Kennedy & Sons, 1954.
Muller, Gerald F., *With Life and Laughter: The Life of Father Pro*. Boston, MA: Pauline Books and Media, 1996.

Eduardo C. Fernández, SJ

Probabilism

Probabilism is a hermeneutical school of interpreting the moral law and was first articulated by the Spanish Dominican Bartolomé de Medina (1527–80), in his *Expositio in Summa Theologiae partem, I-II* (1577): "if an opinion is probable it is licit to follow it, even if the opposite is more probable." Contemporary English reads "probable" as "arguable" and therefore a probable opinion was a cogent interpretation of the law held by a competent moralist. That probable opinion could be held even if another opinion had stronger arguments for a stricter interpretation of the law.

Inasmuch as confessors looked to moral theologians to determine what belonged to sin and what did not, probabilism gave to the confessor the pastoral freedom in conscience to accept the stated opinion of any moralist who was recognized as an authoritative moralist. Effectively, a confessor could be as lenient or as strict as any recognized moralist.

Though penitents too tried to find moralists whose positions conformed to their own, once a penitent entered a confessional, though he might argue with the confessor that the moralists the confessor was following were too stringent, the confessor had no obligation at all to follow another opinion. The tribunal of the confessor was his and not the penitent's.

Almost all Jesuit moralists were probabilists. As they emerged, most Dominicans developed a more conservative position, "probabiliorism." Probabiliorists held that if a confessor had two opinions, he was obliged to follow the stricter one unless a weightier (more probable) argument was given for the more lenient interpretation. Probabliorists effectively restricted the freedom that probabilists extended both to fellow manualists and to confessors.

To mediate the two positions, the Redemptorist casuist, Alphonsus Liguori (1696–1787), originally a probabilist, later proposed "equiprobabilism," which contended that to follow a more lenient opinion its arguments had to be as weighty as the more strict interpretation of the law.

Two other concepts describe the opposite ends of the probable spectrum: laxism and absolute tutiorism. Laxism is not a hermeneutical position per se, but rather a judgment that dismisses an opinion as effectively not respecting the force of a law. The Holy Office frequently condemned opinions that it deemed were lax in 1665, 1666, and 1679. On the other hand, absolute tutiorism is a hermeneutical position that holds that only the strictest interpretation of the law could be considered safe. In 1690 Pope Alexander VIII (1610–91) condemned absolute tutiorism.

Conceptually these differences were clearly understandable, but in practice the differences were problematic. A confessor normally had access to only one or two works of moralists. Though he could see that on some matters one moralist was more lenient than another, how was the confessor to determine whose position was stronger? The confessor was only competent to read what was available; he could not judge another as more probable. Furthermore, was the confessor obliged to simply look for the more stringent interpretation, and if so, at what point was he obliged to stop? Would he not effectively have to become an absolute tutiorist, that is, one who held that only the most stringent position is the safe one?

Still, Jesuit probabilists were attacked by Blaise Pascal (1623–62) who, in his *Provincial Letters* (1656–57), cited and ridiculed the opinions of Antonio Escobar (1589–1669) in particular. Pascal claimed that the whole Jesuit probabilist position in general was nothing more than moral laxism.

Prior to Pascal's attacks, however, the Society of Jesus tried to restrict any signs of laxism. In 1612 Superior General Claudio Acquaviva condemned the position that excused from mortal sin any slight pleasure in deliberately sought venereal desires. Herein is the teaching that there is no parvity (lightness) of matter with regard to the sixth commandment. Not only did Acquaviva bind Jesuits to obey the teaching under pain of excommunication, he imposed on them the obligation to reveal the names of those Jesuits who violated even the spirit of the decree. By 1650 the Society imposed a strict structure of review and censorship within its ranks.

Finally, a Spanish Jesuit, Tirso González de Santalla (1624–1705), tried to publish an argument in favor of probabiliorism but was prohibited in 1674 by Giovanni Paolo Oliva (1600–81), the superior general, who feared that the work would suggest that the Jesuits were becoming probabiliorists. In 1687, Tirso González was elected general, by the intervention of Pope Innocent XI (1611–89). Though his work was not published until 1691, he spent his generalate refuting the probabilists.

Nonetheless, almost all Jesuit moralists upheld probabilism through the manualist period, well into the twentieth century.

See also Casuistry; Confession, Confessor; Ethics; González de Santalla, Tirso, SJ; Pascal, Blaise

Fleming, Julia, *Defending Probabilism: The Moral Theology of Juan Caramuel*. Washington, DC: Georgetown University Press, 2006.
Mahoney, John, *The Making of Moral Theology*. New York: Oxford University Press, 1987.
Maryks, Robert Aleksander, *Saint Cicero and the Jesuits*. Burlington, VT: Ashgate, 2008.

James F. Keenan, SJ

Probation

According to the Complementary Norms of the *Constitutions* of the Society of Jesus, "The novitiate is a time at once of formation and of probation, during which the grace of vocation should be cultivated and during which it should already manifest its fruitfulness" (44, #1). Unlike most Catholic religious orders, which have a one-year novitiate, the Jesuit novitiate lasts for two years, a term that was finalized in 1550 after a decade of some flux. During the novitiate there is a first probation, generally lasting from twelve to fifteen days, to test a candidate's initial suitability for religious life, followed by a longer second probation, upon completion of which a novice takes simple vows as a temporal coadjutor (brother) or a scholastic (preparing for the priesthood). In the period of probation, a novice undergoes six "experiences" or "experiments," which serve the double purpose of testing and training the individual for life in the Society according to its Institutes. The six experiments normally include, first and foremost, the *Spiritual Exercises*, in addition to some type of pilgrimage, service of the sick in hospitals, teaching Christian doctrine (catechism), preaching, and hearing confessions (if one is already ordained, as many of the first Jesuits were). After first vows, studies, and other ministries, and, normatively, within several years after ordination, a Jesuit completes a third year of probation or tertianship. Variously known as a school of the heart, of the will, or of virtues, this involves further spiritual and ministerial experiences, including those of the novitiate – and centrally, once again, the *Spiritual Exercises*. Upon completion of tertianship, and with the approval of superiors, a Jesuit priest takes final vows as either a spiritual coadjutor or a fully professed member of the Society.

See also Experiment; Formation; Novitiate, Novice; Tertianship, Tertians

de Aldama, Antonio M., *An Introductory Commentary on the Constitutions*. Trans. Aloysius J. Owen. St. Louis, MO: The Institute of Jesuit Sources, 1989.
The Constitutions of the Society of Jesus and Their Complementary Norms. Ed. John W. Padberg. St. Louis, MO: The Institute of Jesuit Sources, 1996.

Robert E. Scully, SJ

Professed, Professed House

The Jesuit *Constitutions* describe four "categories," often referred to as "grades," of Jesuits: novices, approved scholastics, formed coadjutors, and the professed or "principal members" (192, 194). After the two years of novitiate, all Jesuits make "simple" vows of poverty, chastity, and obedience and "promise to enter" the Society. At the time of final vows following tertianship, they officially enter the Society as non-ordained brothers ("temporal coadjutors"), "spiritual coadjutors," or "professed members." Coadjutors repeat the same "simple" vows, but this time "into the hands of" the general of the Society or his delegate, while for the professed the three vows, as well as a promise "of special obedience to the sovereign pontiff in regard to the missions," are regarded as "solemn." The current *Code of Canon Law* (1983) does not use the terms "simple" and "solemn" in regard to vows of religious life, but according to the law of the Society, the distinction is that a provincial superior can dismiss a Jesuit in simple vows, while only the general can dismiss those professed of solemn vows (*Constitutions*, 93). The solemnly professed also make five simple vows: never to change the prescriptions of the *Constitutions* on poverty, except to make them stricter; never to seek promotion to a prelacy or dignity within the Society; never to seek promotion outside the Society, or consent to it, unless ordered by a Jesuit superior to do so; and to report anyone else seeking promotion or prelacy to a superior (*Constitutions*, 207). Certain privileges and offices are reserved to these "principal members," selected at the discretion of the general with special regard to their academic prowess and skill at preaching, and from the earliest days the division of the priests of the Society into two classes has led to hurts and hard feelings. From the time of the restoration of the Society until the 1970s, the decision about whether a man would take vows as a spiritual coadjutor or as a professed member was normally based on his performance on the philosophy examination given midway in the course of formation. It is unlikely that St. Ignatius intended the grades to be a permanent feature of Jesuit life (O'Malley, *First Jesuits*, 346), and in the years since Vatican II there have been attempts to do away with them. General Congregation 32 was inclined to admit all Jesuits to the four solemn vows, but Pope Paul VI was unwilling to permit this change to the *Formula of the Institute* (*Jesuit Life*, 272). Nevertheless, in the 1970s, many Jesuits who had been spiritual coadjutors were subsequently solemnly professed, and in many Jesuit provinces solemn profession for all priests became common practice. At the time of General Congregation 34, Pope John Paul II reaffirmed the papal refusal to grant permission to amend the *Constitutions* in favor of one grade for all (*Jesuit Life*, 696), and the beginning of the twenty-first century saw the custom of separating Jesuit priests into the two grades returning to favor with the leadership of the Society itself, although decisions were often based on considerations other than a Jesuit's academic performance.

The Jesuit *Constitutions* envisioned two kinds of communities: "professed houses" and "colleges" (228, 230). Professed houses were to be residences for "the professed Society," Jesuits solemnly professed of four vows, and these houses were to have no fixed revenue and to survive on alms and remuneration for labor. The colleges, which were allowed to have income from rents and endowments, were to be residences for spiritual coadjutors, brothers, and men in formation. The intention was that most Jesuits would live in professed houses, but within twenty years of the foundation of the Society the situation was radically reversed, so that most Jesuits lived in houses associated with colleges, and professed houses without income were the rare exception (O'Malley, *First Jesuits*, 350–51). This situation did not change until the late twentieth century, when General Congregation 32 mandated that a juridical distinction be made between apostolic institutes, including schools and colleges, and the communities that serve them. Since then, the "colleges" and other apostolic institutes may possess endowments, but the communities associated with them "are assimilated to 'professed house,' and may have no stable revenues from capital" (*Jesuit Life*, 357). Seminaries, houses of formation, and infirmaries for the aged or sick have their own regime of poverty and may be endowed (*Jesuit Life*, 359).

See also Community; Formation; Grades; Poverty

The Constitutions of the Society of Jesus and Their Complementary Norms: A Complete English Translation of the Official Latin Texts. Ed. John W. Padberg. St. Louis, MO: The Institute of Jesuit Sources, 1996.
O'Malley, John W., *The First Jesuits*. Cambridge, MA: Harvard University Press, 1993.
Padberg, John W., ed., *Jesuit Life and Mission Today: The Decrees and Accompanying Documents of the 31st–35th General Congregations of the Society of Jesus*. St. Louis, MO: The Institute of Jesuit Sources, 2009.

Martin Chase, SJ

Propagation of the Faith, Congregation of

The Congregation of the Propagation of the Faith (*Propaganda fide*) is one of the congregations that comprise papal administration. It is also one of the most powerful and influential, responsible for managing Catholic missionary territories and institutions across the globe. Despite its importance, the history of this Congregation remains surprisingly understudied, especially for the first centuries of its existence. The origins of this institution lay in a sixteenth-century Church embattled from within by the forces of internal reform and from without by the growing power of many European states. It responded in particular to a concern in papal circles about the weakness of papal authority vis-à-vis its missionary traditions at a time when the global boundaries of the Church were expanding at an unprecedented rate, and Protestantism was spreading rapidly throughout the Christian body of Europe. Prior to the sixteenth century, missions were largely the purview of missionary orders such as the Franciscan and Dominican. Many in fact had received faculties that granted them extensive jurisdiction. Further hindering papal influence over Catholic missions by the sixteenth century was the authority of European monarchs. Agreements brokered between the papacy and the Portuguese (1453) and Spanish monarchies (1493), for example, granted the monarchs spiritual jurisdiction in the Atlantic. By the 1520s, these states were establishing missions in their colonies that lay under the jurisdiction of state authorities and over which the papacy had little influence.

It was during the pontificate of Pius V (1566–72) that the first serious efforts were made to establish a central administration for Catholic missions based in Rome. Pius V was a Dominican and thus a member of one of the great missionary orders. This pontiff was also a proponent of the reform initiatives promulgated at the Council of Trent (1545–63), reforms which embraced a centralized papacy as a foundation of a stronger, revitalized Church. As early as 1568, Pius V in consultation with the Jesuit General Francis Borgia and Alvaro Castro, the Portuguese ambassador, formed a commission dedicated to the conversion of "infidels." This body did not survive long, though experimentations with similar commissions continued over the next decades, laying the groundwork for the formal establishment of the Congregation of the Propagation of the Faith in 1622.

The bull *Inscrutabili*, published on June 6, spoke to the importance of this new congregation for strengthening the global authority of the papacy. Comprising thirteen Cardinals, the Congregation of the Propagation of the Faith was given jurisdiction over all missionary territories in matters pertaining to the propagation of the faith, including the establishment and management of missions, the mediation of disputes, and the performance of the liturgical rites. These extensive privileges ensured that the authority of the body faced serious resistance in many quarters from the start. Portugal and Spain almost immediately excluded the Congregation from operating in their dominions. The established religious orders were also less than pleased to find the operations of their missions under close papal scrutiny.

In reality, it would take considerable time and perseverance on the part of the Congregation to assert itself in the older, established missionary zones for the reasons stated above. It was in part to obviate the authority of the established missions and royal influence that the Congregation introduced a new hierarchy of missionary officials (apostolic vicars and prefects) as early as the 1650s. By the end of the seventeenth century, the Congregation was successfully pressuring the regular orders of missionaries to recognize the superior authority of the vicars. However, relations with the regular orders were not always contentious. The Jesuits in particular were frequent beneficiaries of the Congregation's authority. The support of the Congregation enabled the Jesuits, for example, to establish missions in the Ottoman regions of the eastern Mediterranean after 1622.

Within a few decades of its foundation, the Congregation had established itself as a powerful organ of the Catholic Church with global reach. It oversaw a school in Rome to train missionaries in the "oriental" languages known as the Pontifical College of the *Propaganda fide* (1627), and a printing press to produce Catholic texts in multiple languages. The Congregation also established colleges in many missions. Following Vatican II, Pope Paul VI reorganized the Congregation to meet its directives, outlined in the bull *Ad gentes*. The name of the Congregation was changed to the "Evangelization of the Peoples," and its mandate included greater engagement with local bishops and communities in the operation of foreign missions. Today the Congregation for the Evangelization of the Peoples continues to manage missions across the globe including Albania, the Antilles, New Zealand, Palestine, and Turkey. The Pontifical Urbaniana University (formerly the Pontifical College) in Rome remains under its direction and is dedicated to preparing students from mission countries for taking holy orders.

See also Gregory XV; Papacy

Codignola, Luca, "Roman Catholic Conservativism in a New North Atlantic World, 1760–1829." *William and Mary Quarterly* 64 (2007), 717–56.

Guilday, Peter, "The Sacred Congregation of the Propaganda Fide (1622–1922)." *The Catholic Historical Review* 6 (1921), 478–94.

Song, R. H., *The Sacred Congregation for the Propagation of the Faith*. Washington, DC: Catholic University of America Press, 1961.

Megan C. Armstrong

Province, Provincial

Jesuit communities and apostolic works are organized by provinces, which belong to one of nine assistancies around the world. The Jesuit superior general appoints a provincial for a six-year term to head up each province. The provincial, in turn, appoints several assistants to help in the apostolic direction (*cura apostolica*) of the province and the spiritual care (*cura personalis*) of each Jesuit.

The Society of Jesus, as of January 1, 2016, was divided into seventy-seven provinces with four independent regions and six dependent regions (for example, South Africa, a region dependent on the British province).

For greater apostolic effectiveness and also because of fewer Jesuits, provinces throughout the world are being amalgamated. For instance, all of Italy is now one province, instead of five as it was formerly. The United States is rapidly moving from a peak of eleven provinces in the 1960s to four provinces by 2021.

Although candidates to the Jesuits enter a specific province, they, in fact, join the worldwide Order and can be missioned by their superior to any part of the world.

As candidates surged into the new Society of Jesus (1541), Ignatius quickly saw the need for organizational structures more sophisticated than he and the early companions had first envisioned. In 1547 he appointed Antonio Araoz as the first provincial of Spain. Shortly after, Diego Laínez became the first provincial of Italy. By 1558 when Laínez was elected the second superior general, the Society had over 1,000 members in twelve different provinces, including three outside of Europe: Brazil, Ethiopia, and India.

At the moment India has the greatest number of provinces: nineteen in all. As communication shrinks distances, more provinces will combine to facilitate good governance.

See also Community; Curia, Jesuit; Region; *Socius*

The Jesuit Curia in Rome. www.sjweb.info.
O'Malley, John W., *The First Jesuits*. Cambridge, MA: Harvard University Press, 1993.

Patrick J. Howell, SJ

Pseudonyms

There has been a long practice in the Jesuit order of the adoption of pseudonyms: "false names." In general this occurred for one of two reasons. In countries such as England in the sixteenth and seventeenth centuries, members of the Society were subject to systematic persecution; hence, the need to adopt an "alias" as a means of evading detection by the authorities. In the Reformation and post-Reformation period, Jesuit authors also used pseudonyms because of the controversial nature of theological disputes in which they became involved. Sometimes pseudonyms were used for books written on matters that seemed inappropriate for Jesuits. It is estimated that in the last two decades of the seventeenth century alone nine Jesuits wrote works on the subject of the architecture of military fortifications, all published under pseudonyms. By 1643 Philippe Alegambe, building on Pedro Ribadeneira's *Illustrium scriptorum religionis Societatis Jesu catalogus* (1602), had carried out an important investigation into the practice, not only listing anonymous and pseudonymous Jesuit works but also discussing the propriety of identity concealment in theological controversies. He concluded that such a practice was permissible for "legitimate reasons."

Alegambe's work has been augmented over the centuries, most importantly by that of Nathaniel Sotwell (1676), Carlos Sommervogel (1890–1932), and José De Uriarte (1904–16). Volume 11 of Sommervogel's bibliographical work reproduces a list of 11,000 titles of Jesuit anonymous and pseudonymous works since 1540, and of the latter only 1,600 have been unambiguously attributed. The practice of using pseudonyms on the English mission endured from the time of Edmund Campion ("Mr. Edmonds") until well into the nineteenth century. When William Scott died in 1894, it was said of him that he belonged to the last set of those who, upon entering the Society in England, had the letter "A" written against his name in the province register to indicate that it was his authentic name, and not a pseudonym.

See also Bibliographies; Campion, Edmund, SJ; Sommervogel, Carlos, SJ; United Kingdom

Basset, Bernard, *The English Jesuits From Campion to Martindale*. New York: Herder and Herder, 1967.
Taylor Archer, and Fredric J. Mosher, *The Bibliographical History of Anonyma and Pseudonyma*. Chicago, IL: University of Chicago Press, 1951.

Oliver P. Rafferty, SJ

Puerto Rico

Two Jesuits on their long route to Japan stopped in the island of Puerto Rico in the late sixteenth century, the future martyrs Charles Spinola and Jerome de Angelis. Waiting for a ship to take them to New Spain and from there to Southeast Asia, they preached to scattered settlers on the island and sent to Rome a short and graphic account of their experiences. There are occasional subsequent mentions of Jesuits stopping at Aguada, on the northwest coast, on their way to New Spain. In their letters to the generals, some of which have been published, they briefly described their impressions of the population. But no Jesuit community was established in Puerto Rico until the nineteenth century.

Negotiations between the Spanish government and the Jesuit Curia in the mid-nineteenth century allowed the Jesuits to establish a novitiate in Loyola. In exchange the Order promised to establish schools in the three principal remaining Spanish colonies. Thus were born the Ateneo de Manila and the Colegio de Belén in Cuba. In Puerto Rico, the Jesuits assumed the direction of the diocesan seminary, which accepted students not destined for priesthood. Besides participating in temporary missions in the outlying towns, they ministered to the inmates of the state penitentiary, established a sodality, and occupied the old Dominican church of Santo Tomás de Aquino, which they renamed San José. The province of Castile sent to the Colegio many young scholastics.

The diocesan seminary and the Jesuit school separated in the late 1870s. The Colegio de San Ignacio moved to a government-built facility in Santurce, a ward of San Juan. In 1886, the Jesuit province of Toledo (of which Puerto Rico was dependant) decided to withdraw its remaining men from San Juan and send them to Lima. Two young Puerto Rican Jesuits remained in Spain.

Between 1886 and 1946, Jesuits from Castile, and eventually the León province, sporadically came to the island to preach or to direct the Spiritual Exercises. After the American invasion of 1898, Bishop James Blenk unsuccessfully offered the Jesuits a parish on the island.

It was descendants of the old Colegio de San Ignacio's alumni who lobbied for the foundation of a Jesuit school and a renewed Jesuit presence on the island. In 1945 Father Antonio Quevedo and a lay brother arrived in San Juan. The bishops of the two dioceses entrusted the Society with the minor seminary, which was relocated to a farm in the outskirts of Aibonito. The new Colegio de San Ignacio opened its doors in 1952. The Colegio moved to its present location in Urbanización Santa María in September of 1955. Jesuits from the Antilles province, with the assistance of scholastics and priests from New Orleans, California, and Mexico, staffed the Colegio in its first seven years of existence. At the same time, the bishop of San Juan entrusted the Society with a new parish adjoining the Colegio and the managing of the Catholic Center at the University of Puerto Rico in Río Piedras.

In 1959 Puerto Rico was incorporated into the Jesuit province of New York, where it remained until 1987. All the Jesuit scholastics who had entered in the previous ten years were transferred to New York. Several of the Antilles men remained in Puerto Rico for the rest of their lives, and others came to Puerto Rico when the political situations in Cuba and the Dominican Republic resulted in their expulsion. During this period, the Colegio de San Ignacio became one of the most prestigious educational institutions on the island and received many awards and recognitions. In 1980 a Jesuit novitiate was founded in Caimito. This led to a surge of vocations to the Society in the 1980s. Expectations of growth were high when Father Kolvenbach created the Independent Region of Puerto Rico in 1987. The Region became part of the Northern Latin American Assistancy and, eventually, of the Conference of Latin American Provincials.

In recent years, the Region formulated its Apostolic Plan, in which emphasis was given to the intellectual apostolate, work with youth, and the *Spiritual Exercises*. Crossing all the fields is the dimension of working with the poor. In November, 2014, the Region became part of the Central South province of the United States.

See also Caribbean; Spain; United States of America

Archivum Romanum Societatis Jesu. Provinciae Hispaniae Historiae et Litterae Annuae.
    Provinciae Castellanae Litterae Annuae.
    Provinciae Toletanae Litterae Annuae.
Frías, Lesmes, *Historia de la Compañía de Jesús en su asistencia moderna de España*. 2 vols. Vol. II
    (1835–1868). Madrid: Administración de Razón y fe, 1944.
Picó, Fernando, "Alberto Boysen, Sacerdote Jesuita." In *Contra la Corriente: Seis Microbiografías de los
    Tiempos de España*. San Juan: Ediciones Huracán, 1995, pp. 75–97.
de Portillo, Enrique, *La Provincia de Toledo de la Compañía de Jesús 1880–1914*. Madrid: Est.
    Tipográfico Sucesores de Rivadeneyra, 1916.
de Santa Anna, Antonio López, *Los Jesuitas en Puerto Rico, 1858–1886*. Santander: Bedia, 1958.

Fernando Picó, SJ

Québec

Québec (Kébec) is the spelling and pronunciation of the name given by the early French explorers to the site on the St. Lawrence River at the foot of Cape Diamond. In 1534 the discoverer Jacques Cartier understood it to mean "narrowing of the waters." In founding it as a permanent settlement on July 4, 1608, Samuel de Champlain saw it as becoming the capital of the French Empire in North America. In 1627 he officially became King Louis XIII's representative, and Québec, in law as well as in fact, became the Royal Capital. Henceforth, it was from Québec that the government and development of New France, and of the Jesuits within it, would be planned and carried out.

At the Treaty of Vervins in 1598, Henri IV wrested from the Spanish the right to spread French influence and institutions throughout eastern North America. It was one small step further for the King to send missionaries. And, his confessor being the Jesuit Pierre Coton (1564–1626), an even smaller one to choose Jesuits.

Pierre Biard (1567–1622) and Ennemond Massé (1574–1646) were the first to come, landing at Port-Royal in Acadia (now Nova Scotia) on May 22, 1611; they were the first of some 330 who crossed to Canada until the death of the last one, Jean-Joseph Casot (1728–1800).

All were Frenchmen except one, Giuseppe Bressani (1612–72), who was Roman. Their ministry among the native peoples brought the Gospel from Québec to the heart of the continent: Gabriel Druillettes (1610–81) preached along the Atlantic Coast; Charles Albanel (1616–96) went to Hudson Bay; Claude Allouez (1622–89), Jean-Pierre Aulneau (1705–36), and Godefroy Coquart (1706–65) scoured 3,000 miles around the Great Lakes as far as Winnipeg; most famously, Jacques Marquette (1637–75) became known for the voyage that discovered the Mississippi.

It was from Jesuit headquarters in Québec that these missionary explorations were decided upon, funded, and equipped, the Jesuit superior working out the modalities with the governor, the fur-trading companies, and the benefactors. Of the twenty-two Jesuit superiors whose terms coincided with the *Ancien Régime* (1611–1800), the terms and accomplishments that most stand out are those of Paul Le Jeune (1632–39) and Jérôme Lalemant (1645–50, 1659–65). The first was the founder in 1635 of what became the first parish in Canada, as well, in the same year, as the Collège des Jésuites, the first institution of higher studies in North America. He wrote, in 1632, the first of the famous Jesuit *Relations* and brought to Québec in 1639 both the hospital Sisters of St. Joseph and the Ursuline community led by St. Marie de l'Incarnation. Later, in 1658, he was responsible for the appointment of St. François de Laval to the primatial see of Québec. When the nuns came, it was the first time in history that religious women had left their cloister to travel to a foreign mission.

Later, Jérôme Lalemant introduced the *Ratio studiorum* to the Collège and set up the administration of the "Jesuit estates," those considerable properties donated to the Jesuits by the kings of France and other major benefactors in order to support the missions.

Thanks to an understanding between Governor Carleton and Bishop Briand of Québec in 1773, the Society was never suppressed in Canada. Unable to recruit, however, it disappeared by attrition in 1800, a date that marked the end of Jesuit government from Québec. When Jesuits returned in 1842, their headquarters would be in Montreal.

See also Canada; Canadian/North American Martyrs

Monet, Jacques,"*Les archives des Jésuites: lieu de mémoire et d'inspiration.*" *Relations* 758 (August 2012), 18–19.

True, Micah, *Masters and Students: Jesuit Mission Ethnography in Seventeenth-Century New France.* Montreal/Kingston: McGill-Queen's University Press, 2015.

Jacques Monet, SJ

Rahner, Hugo, SJ (1900–1968)

German Church historian, theologian, and rector of the University of Innsbruck and the Collegium Canisianum, among whose chief contributions was his presentation of the "living, everyday holiness of Ignatius," as opposed to the inflated hagiography of the "soldier-saint." Rahner's historical work on Ignatius, rendered even more impressive when placed alongside his many patristic studies, has become so widely accepted that, according to Philip Endean, its originality has been obscured. Rahner's legacy endures also in the works of his younger brother, Karl (1904–84), another Jesuit and theologian. The Rahner brothers offered many spiritual conferences together, including the *Spiritual Exercises*, which they co-directed many times. Their publications interlace with mutual citation. Though Hugo became the less famous of the Rahner brothers, his gifts to the Society and the Church remain in generations of European Jesuits influenced by his spiritual direction, and, for a wider public, a greater understanding of the person, theology, and spirituality of Ignatius.

Rahner was born in Pfullendorf, Baden, Germany, on May 3, 1900, to a traditional Catholic family, the third of seven children to Karl (1868–1934) and Luise (1875–1976). After a quiet upbringing, mostly in Freiburg im Breisgau, he served six months in World War I, and upon his discharge he joined the Jesuits (January 11, 1919). He studied philosophy at Valkenburg, the Netherlands (1920–23), worked at the Jesuits' Stella Matutina *Gymnasium* at Feldkirch, Austria (1923–26), and studied theology at the University of Innsbruck (1926–31), culminating in a doctoral thesis on Christian piety in the Church's first three centuries (1931). He was ordained to the priesthood at Pullach, Bavaria (July 26, 1929). Following his time at Innsbruck, he earned a D.Phil. at the University of Bonn in Church History (1931–34), leading to his appointment as a lecturer and then Professor of Church History, History of Dogma, and Patristics at Innsbruck (1935, 1937), where he served as vice-rector of the Jesuit community. When the Nazi takeover of the university forced the Jesuits to relocate, Rahner moved to Sion, Switzerland, and taught in the Pontifical Faculty of Theology (1938–45). The war's end brought the reestablishment of the Catholic theological faculty at Innsbruck, and Rahner's return. Over the next decade he would serve twice as dean of the faculty (1945–49, 1952–53) and once as rector of the university (1949–50). He was also rector of the Collegium Canisianum, the Society's international theological college at Innsbruck, from 1950–56. He represented the Austrian province to General Congregation 30 (1957). Throughout his time in teaching and administration, Rahner actively pursued research in patristics, Mariology, ecclesiology, and Ignatius. He fell ill with Parkinson's disease in 1963, which he battled for half a decade before his death in Munich (December 21, 1968). He was buried at the Jesuit cemetery in Pullach.

From early in his time in the Society, Rahner positioned himself to advance historical study of Ignatius and the early Jesuits. Already in 1922 he produced a catalogue of relevant primary sources. He worked further on this catalogue with his brother Karl, and they translated into German an address by Jerónimo Nadal (1507–80) on prayer (1935). From the 1920s through the end of his career, in earnest from 1935, Rahner devoted himself to close and careful study of numerous recently available Ignatian and early Jesuit sources, such as the *Monumenta Ignatiana* (four series, 1903–55), the critical edition *Fontes Narrativi de Sancto Ignatio* (3 vols., 1943–60), and sets of letters from Ignatius, Francis Xavier, Nadal, Francis Borja, and others (1890s forward). Rahner edited and published two volumes of Ignatius's letters. The collection of Ignatius's letters to women (1956) was perhaps more significant, especially for its remembrance of women's roles in the Society's early history. On the theological side, the slim volume, *The Spirituality of St. Ignatius Loyola, An Account of Its Historical Development*

(1947), and the larger *Ignatius Loyola as Man and Theologian* (1964), made major inroads toward establishing Ignatius as a first-order mystical theologian. Andreas Batlogg reports that, even with Rahner's major achievements in Ignatian scholarship, his *magnum opus*, a biography of Ignatius, was left unfinished. Parkinson's disease cut short Rahner's career, but his Ignatian scholarship still bears great fruit, whenever we consider Ignatius as an historical person who experienced the nearness of God's mysterious presence.

See also German-Speaking Lands; Loyola, Ignatius, SJ, St; Rahner, Karl, SJ

Batlogg, Andreas R., "Hugo Rahner als Mensch und Theologe." *Stimmen der Zeit* 218 (2000), 517–30.
Endean, Philip, *Karl Rahner and Ignatian Spirituality*. Oxford: Oxford University Press, 2001, pp. 68–98.
Rahner, Hugo, *Ignatius the Theologian*. Trans. M. Barry. Freiburg: Herder and Herder, 1968.
    Saint Ignatius: Letters to Women. Trans. K. Pond and S. Weetman. Freiburg: Herder and Herder, 1960.

                                                                            Peter Joseph Fritz

Rahner, Karl, SJ (1904–1984)

While the famous twentieth-century German theologian Karl Rahner is most often treated as simply a *Catholic* theologian, to understand him rightly one must take seriously and centrally his life as a Jesuit.

Rahner was born in Freiburg im Breisgau on March 5, 1904, to a traditional Catholic family, the fourth of seven children to parents Karl (1868–1934) and Luise (1875–1976) Rahner. He attended primary and secondary school in Freiburg, an unremarkable student not taking great interest in his studies. Three weeks after finishing secondary school, he entered the Jesuit novitiate at Feldkirch, Austria (April 20, 1922). His parents and a high school English teacher thought he was too gruff and unsocial to join in a religious community, but he did it, partially because his brother Hugo (1900–68) had three years earlier (1919). Later in life, Rahner claimed that his entrance into the Society was at first a vague decision, but it grew on him over time.

On April 27, 1924, Rahner pronounced his first vows in the Jesuits and proceeded to philosophical studies at Feldkirch (1924–25) and Pullach (1925–27). He spent two years teaching Latin at the novitiate in Feldkirch, where Alfred Delp, who would later perish at the hands of the Nazis, was one of his students (1927–29). Theological studies followed at Valkenburg in Holland (1929–33), spurring Rahner's interest in medieval theologians like Bonaventure and the Church Fathers: their mysticism, view of the Church, and theologies of penance. Rahner was ordained a priest on July 26, 1932, by Cardinal Michael Faulhaber in St. Michael's Church, Munich. After a tertianship year in the Lavanttal valley of southern Austria (1933–34), Rahner was sent to Freiburg to pursue a doctorate in philosophy (1934–36). His provincial intended for Rahner to serve the Society as a professor of philosophy. This would prove a fecund time in Rahner's life. He studied under Martin Heidegger and continued serious study of the theological tradition, but difficulties with his dissertation director Martin Honecker impeded completion of the doctorate. In the summer of 1936, Rahner returned to Innsbruck and before the year was out finished a doctorate in theology with a dissertation on the Church's birth from the side of Christ (cf. John 19:34).

His teaching career commenced the following year with a course on grace, but in 1938 it was interrupted when the Nazis abolished the Innsbruck Theological Faculty. Rahner made final vows on August 15, 1939, at the Austrian Jesuit novitiate at St. Andrea in Carinthia. Afterward he was offered refuge in Vienna, where he worked in the diocesan pastoral office (1939–44). This time of pastoral work made a lasting impression on Rahner. Later in life, whenever he returned to Vienna, he would stay in Caritas House, a residence for former convicts. During the final year of World War II, Rahner lived in the small village of Mariakirchen in Bavaria, providing pastoral care for people there, including refugees (1944–45). He remained in Bavaria in the war's aftermath to lecture and preach at Berchmans College in Pullach, where the Jesuits were trying to reestablish philosophical studies (1945–48). Soon he was recalled to the reopened Innsbruck theological faculty where for over a decade he lectured on creation, grace, and the sacraments (1948–64). Jesuits housed at the Canisianum made up a critical mass of his students. Rahner's publication career was, by this point, proceeding apace, with many authored and edited volumes. His scholarship was delayed somewhat when his Jesuit superiors notified him that he must submit his writings for prior approval by Rome before publication (1962). This order was lifted the next year.

Rahner's participation as Franz Cardinal König's *peritus* (official theological expert) at the Second Vatican Council (1962–65) cemented his status as an internationally renowned theologian. His influence is apparent in the Council's teachings on the mystery of the Church, the Eucharist, revelation, Mariology, the permanent diaconate, atheism, ecumenism, missiology, and ecclesial engagement with the modern world. He moved during the Council to Munich where, with the approval of his Jesuit superiors, he assumed the Chair of Christianity and Philosophy of Religion formerly held by Romano Guardini (1964). Three years later Rahner was appointed Professor of Dogmatic Theology at Münster, where he taught before retiring in 1971. He split the next thirteen years between two Jesuit communities in Munich, the Jesuit writers' house (1971–73) and Berchmans College (1973–81), and the Jesuit College in Innsbruck (1981–84). Rahner died on March 30, 1984, in Innsbruck, three weeks after his 80th birthday, which was widely celebrated by his students, colleagues, and others familiar with his astoundingly rich contributions to Catholic theology and life. He was buried in the Jesuit Church of the Trinity at Innsbruck.

Interpretation of Rahner's theological works is fiercely contested. Arno Zahlauer offers helpful guidelines for interpreting Rahner as a specifically Jesuit theologian. Zahlauer presents a four-stage schema for arranging commentaries on Rahner and Ignatius. Avery Dulles's 1965 treatment of Rahner as an interpreter of Ignatius epitomizes stage one. Dulles aimed to correct the limited perception that Rahner was merely a speculative theologian. Second, commentators like Klaus Fischer came to see Rahner as a theologian whose thinking was significantly marked by Ignatius's spirituality. Third, scholars like Philip Endean went further to suggest that Rahner's views on Ignatius might serve as tools for developing scholarship on Ignatian spirituality. Fourth, Karl H. Neufeld brought things full circle by referring the whole of Rahner's corpus back to his *Ordensexistenz*, his life as a Jesuit.

Surely Rahner's theology bears an ineluctable relation to his being a Jesuit. As Harvey Egan amply illustrates, Rahner adapts his major ideas from Ignatius. His complex view of freedom bears an Ignatian stamp. Many recurring themes in his work, especially prior to the Council, like Mary and the Sacred Heart of Jesus, appear because of Jesuits' special devotion to them. Rahner wrote frequently on religious life (obedience, poverty, chastity) and the priesthood, usually with the express intent of aiding the practice of his Jesuit brothers. Even his philosophical work has an Ignatian cast, at least according to prominent Rahnerians like Neufeld, Herbert Vorgrimler, William Dych, and Leo O'Donovan.

In 1922, the year that Rahner entered the Jesuits, his brother Hugo produced a catalogue of primary sources relevant to historical study of the Society. Karl worked further on this catalogue with Hugo during the 1920s, and by 1935 they had translated into German an address by Jerónimo Nadal on prayer. From the 1920s through the end of his career, in earnest from 1935, Hugo devoted himself to close and careful study of numerous recently available Ignatian and early Jesuit sources, such as the *Monumenta Ignatiana* (four series, 1903–55), the critical edition *Fontes Narrativi de Sancto Ignatio* (3 vols., 1943–60), and sets of letters from Ignatius, Francis Xavier, Nadal, Francis Borja, and others (1890s forward). Though Karl would not remain as closely tied as he once was to Hugo's historical work on Ignatius and the first Jesuits, his brother kept him abreast of his findings, and Karl cites Hugo with relative frequency. If Rahner creatively interprets the spirituality of the founder of his order, he does so from a well-informed position.

The year after producing the Nadal translation, Rahner finished his philosophical dissertation (revised and published as *Geist in Welt*, 1939). He also published "The Ignatian Mysticism of Joy in the World" (1936), a brief essay whose title he did not choose, but which he uses constructively. Rahner sees Ignatian spirituality as bearing a twofold relationship to the world: flight from it and active life in it. Ignatian acceptance of the world hinges upon flight from it. As Rahner understands him, Ignatius insists upon God's sovereignty over the world. Christian devotion to God entails death to the world. But since this sovereign God elects to relate to the world freely and out of love, so must the Christian. Ignatian flight from the world prepares Christians for deep, active engagement with the world.

This view of Ignatian spirituality coheres well with *Geist in Welt*, which interprets Thomas Aquinas's metaphysics of knowledge. Aquinas, as Rahner depicts him, becomes an exponent of the dual spirituality of Ignatius. For the Rahnerian Aquinas, knowledge comes through a twofold movement of abstraction from the world and return to it. An encounter with absolute being, which exceeds the world, makes possible rich apprehension of worldly beings. The concluding page of *Geist in Welt* is decisive and suggests the project's roots in Ignatian spirituality, which centers on the life of Christ. Aquinas's metaphysics of knowledge surpasses ordinary western metaphysics when it calls people back to the world as the arena for God's self-revelation in Christ. Rahner enunciates what Roman Siebenrock calls the double movement of the *Spiritual Exercises*: God's movement toward a human person (or the world), and the human person's movement toward God.

This double movement is refined in writings of the 1950s. "Ignatian Spirituality and Devotion to the Sacred Heart of Jesus," originally delivered as three meditation-preparations at the Canisianum (June 1955), discusses three characteristics of Ignatian spirituality, associated dangers, and how Sacred Heart devotions inoculate practitioners against these dangers. Ignatian indifference risks a cold death to the world. Ignatian "existentialism" – care for individual vocation – risks solitariness. Ignatian service to the Church risks partisan fanaticism. Devotions focused on Christ's heart, pierced out of love for sinners, correct potential excesses of Ignatian spirituality. Indifference blossoms from devotion to Christ's burning heart as the center of all things. Existentialism blossoms from devotion to Christ's divine-human heart as the concreteness of God's infinite love. Service to the Church blossoms from Christ's pierced heart as the source of reconciliation for sinners. Ignatian spirituality might be seen primarily as movement toward God beyond the world. But the pierced heart of Jesus entails that any movement beyond must entail a loving return to the world. We die in order to live. Vocational uniqueness fosters interpersonal discovery and service. Being Church means loving all people.

"The Ignatian Logic of Existential Decision" (1956) intensifies Rahner's thinking on the "existential" moment of Ignatian spirituality. This piece confirms Andreas Batlogg's view that Rahner discovers in Ignatius not just a spiritual teacher, but a theologian. It centers on the problem of election. The genius of the *Exercises* lies in its singular focus on "vital decision." Ignatius sets forth rules to guide people in discerning God's specific will for them. Individuals will not deduce this from a general rule set by reason or Church doctrine. Instead, through experience, they will find a unique instantiation of God's will, given for them. In Ignatius's *Exercises*, then, Rahner finds a challenge to the deductive moral theology into which he was educated, and to new currents like situation ethics. Ignatius's time may well be yet to come.

He continues this thought in a 1972 essay he wrote for a *Festschrift* honoring the Spanish Jesuit Joaquín Salaverri: "Reflections on a New Task for Fundamental Theology." Since Ignatius's complex view of decision has not yet been appropriated by theology, it presents a new possible path. Fundamental theology is the branch of theology dedicated to the relationship between "grounds of credibility of Christian revelation" and "the actual decision to believe." Most modern fundamental theology prior to the Second Vatican Council (including Salaverri's) insisted that a decision to believe be made on firm rational grounds. Ignatius's logic of existential decision offers fundamental theology a way for discussing decision as total commitment made without rational analysis of a specified object. The affective states involved in decision-making in the *Exercises* tend not to present perspicuous rational content. Rahner concludes by lamenting that Jesuit theology has not effectively used the Ignatian heritage to make sense of Christian faith. He calls for Jesuits to recast theology using insights from Ignatius.

A 1959 essay on the Ignatian motto *Ad majorem Dei gloriam* is worth noting, as are transcripts of conferences on the *Exercises* that Rahner gave in the 1950s and 1960s that were published as two books (*The Spiritual Exercises* and *The Priesthood*). More remarkable for Rahner's work as a Jesuit is the work he called his "last will and testament": "Ignatius of Loyola Speaks to a Jesuit Today" (1977). Rahner states in the foreword that he wrote this piece by default: the Herder Press wanted a biographical piece on Ignatius; their first two preferred authors, Hugo Rahner and Burkhardt Schneider, were both deceased. Rahner, a self-proclaimed non-expert on Ignatius, does not attempt to capture Ignatius's biography. He "translates" Ignatius for the late twentieth century.

Rahner has Ignatius contest contemporary Jesuit theology and practice. He scolds the Jesuits for betraying his legacy by using theology to enforce docility among the laity. He enjoins them instead to foster joy and hope, to trust in the measurelessness of God's love. He designates giving the *Exercises* as the primary task of Jesuits, from which other tasks distract them. Through the *Exercises* the Jesuits will foster Christians' inner lives. They will assist Christians in recognizing that Christian life "coactualizes" God's descent to the world in Jesus Christ.

Rahner's Ignatius emphasizes the *descent* of Christ: Jesus's poverty and humility. Using language reminiscent of Rahner's famous student, the political theologian Johann Baptist Metz, Rahner's Ignatius insists that poverty and humility signify a "critical sting" in the contemporary world, where the "dangerous memory of Jesus" threatens business as usual in society and the Church. He encourages his fellow Jesuits to ask how their Society may be a "community of radical discipleship" and then lists proper names of people who enacted such discipleship. He begins with a non-Jesuit, Helder Câmara, as a model bishop who integrates radical discipleship with ecclesial institution. Then he names Jesuits from earlier in the Society's history: Peter Claver, Francis Regis, and Friedrich von Spee. Each followed closely the poor and humble Jesus. He finishes the list with Alfred Delp. Today's Jesuits must seek what it would look like for a Christian to be a follower of the poor and humble Jesus tomorrow.

Continued reflection on the history of the Jesuits will be crucial. Rahner's Ignatius castigates the Jesuits for their history of being "underlings" to worldly authorities. He interrogates them regarding why they allowed themselves to be overtaken by colonial powers in Latin America. He demands that the Jesuits remember their earliest days – begging, founding orphanages, opening a food pantry, and establishing a Martha-house for penitent prostitutes in Rome. He poses an incisive question at a Society that risks laxity and luxury: "has the Order forgotten this side of my life?" By contrast, Rahner's Ignatius applauds General Congregation 32's reframing of the Jesuits' mission as a "struggle for faith and justice."

It becomes clear in Rahner's "translation" of Ignatius that Rahner felt deep resonances with the new tone Superior General Pedro Arrupe set for the Society. He underscores Jesus's poverty and humility, and pleads that Jesuits center their work on pursuing justice. Themes of Rahner's earlier writings on Ignatius – mission to the world grounded in a transcendent encounter with God, active service out of love for Jesus's Sacred Heart, vital decision for God's love – become even more concrete.

The social-political tenor of the "Ignatius Speaks" piece is developed and applied in the 1982 lecture, "The Situation of the Society of Jesus since Its Difficulties with the Vatican." The lecture concerns Pope John Paul II's appointment of Father Paolo Dezza, SJ, as a papal delegate to the Jesuits, charged with ensuring that they follow the wishes of the Pope with respect to theology and ministry. Rahner considers two main themes from documents authored by Dezza: obedience to the Magisterium and problems related to work for justice. He objects to the latent ecclesiastical totalitarianism in Dezza's writings, which is patent in Dezza's overzealous demands for Jesuit theologians to unquestioningly obey Church (read: Vatican) officials. To do so, Rahner maintains, would mean the death of theology – not because Jesuits stand above the Magisterium, but because obedience is far more complex than Dezza allows. Similarly, as would become a hallmark of the Congregation of the Doctrine of the Faith and its associates in the 1980s, Dezza misunderstands his fellow Jesuits' work for the advancement of justice as "horizontalism" and an overstepping of limitations to priestly life. Rahner sternly rebuffs both perceptions. Love of God and love of neighbor are not collapsed into one another, but neither should they be separated. Clearly Jesuit priestly life is limited (Jesuits are neither Mother Teresa, nor Carthusians), but the Society's sphere of action should not be too closely circumscribed. These thoughts show that right up to the end of his life Rahner remained intensively engaged with the life of the Society that he joined six decades before. The Jesuits' love of God and their apostolate in the world remained ever in his thoughts, and governed his living.

Alfons Klein, SJ, was Rahner's provincial at the time of his death and gave his funeral Mass homily. Most people know Rahner as a famous theologian, but Klein demands a properly sharp frame of reference: Rahner must be seen as a true Jesuit. Klein states, "Just as Nathaniel was a true Israelite so Rahner was a true Jesuit – with a daily workload, with all the advantages, with all the hardships and with all the suffering which is associated with that."

See also Dezza, Paolo, Cardinal, SJ; Loyola, Ignatius, SJ, St.; Rahner, Hugo, SJ; *Spiritual Exercises*; Theology

Batlogg, Andreas R., Melvin E. Michalski, and Barbara G. Turner, eds., *Encounters with Karl Rahner: Remembrances of Rahner by Those Who Knew Him.* Milwaukee, WI: Marquette University Press, 2009.

Egan, Harvey D., *Karl Rahner: Mystic of Everyday Life.* New York: Crossroad, 1998.

Endean, Philip, *Karl Rahner and Ignatian Spirituality.* Oxford: Oxford University Press, 2001, pp. 68–98.

Rahner, Karl, "The Ignatian Mysticism of Joy in the World." In *The Theology of the Spiritual Life.* Trans. Karl H and Boniface Kruger. New York: Crossroad, 1982, pp. 277–93.

"Ignatian Spirituality and Devotion to Sacred Heart of Jesus." In *Christian in the Market Place.* Trans. C. Hastings. New York: Sheed and Ward, 1966.

Ignatius of Loyola Speaks. Trans. Annemarie S. Kidder. South Bend, IN: St. Augustine's Press, 2013.

Peter Joseph Fritz

Ratio studiorum

The *Ratio studiorum* (full title: *Ratio atque Institutio Studiorum Societatis Iesu*) was the Jesuit "plan of study" that defined the Society's educational program, formally codified in 1599. From the 1540s, Ignatius had identified education as a key ministry for the Society, and after opening their first school in Messina in 1548, the Jesuits were running nearly 800 schools and colleges around the world at the time of their suppression in 1773. As the number of Jesuit-run educational institutions grew, questions arose over how to organize their curriculum. The prefect of studies at the Roman College composed a list of orders and regulations between 1563 and 1564 that was given to the superior general, Francis Borja. This document, the *Ratio studiorum Borgiana,* was then sent to various provinces in 1569 with Borja's instructions that it be adapted to local circumstances.

It soon became apparent that more standardization was needed, given the amount of disagreement on how to teach certain topics, especially theological issues. In 1583 Claudio Acquaviva set up a commission of six Jesuits charged with composing an order of study. The following year they submitted two documents, the *Delectus opinionum* (a list of propositions drawn from Aquinas's *Summa theologica*) and the *Praxis et ordo studiorum,* which outlined the material that was to be taught in Jesuit schools. Both documents were revised by the Roman College and issued to the entire Society in 1586, with Acquaviva's instructions that provinces review them and send their comments back to Rome. This 1586 *Ratio* was revised in 1591. Then, the Society's 5th General

Congregation (1593–94) decided that a definitive order of study was needed, and so from 1595 to 1598 three Jesuits sharply reduced the number of rules contained in the 1591 *Ratio*. The list of speculative prescriptions for teaching drawn from Aquinas – what had been the *Delectus opinionum* – was removed from the *Ratio* altogether. The definitive *Ratio studiorum* was then printed in Naples in 1599.

According to the 1599 *Ratio*, students progressed from "lower faculties" to "higher ones." Students began with Latin classes, focusing sequentially on grammar, humanities, and rhetoric. Ideally some Greek would also be taught. Then came three years of philosophy, based on Aristotle's works. This, too, was taught in a sequence that included logic, natural philosophy, and metaphysics. The final stage was four years of theology, chiefly based on Aquinas and the Sacred Scriptures. Though the *Ratio* aimed at standardization, it is clear that local colleges made adjustments to the curriculum, sometimes teaching mathematics or vernacular languages. Absent from the curriculum were law and medicine, seen as pre-professional fields addressed by other universities. Also absent was politics, since history was only taught as a field of rhetoric.

In practice the Jesuits drew from the "Parisian method" of teaching, then in vogue at the University of Paris. (However, it is likely that Ignatius and several other companions first encountered this method of instruction at the University of Alcalá prior to their arrival in Paris.) Students were divided into classes and graduated from one class to another upon demonstrating the necessary proficiency. Professors lectured frequently, but students were expected to be active participants in the classroom via compositions and recitations, beyond merely reading classical authors. Jesuits favored competition in the classroom, often dividing students into two or more groups to compete against one another. Jesuit schools were also famous for their use of theater, with students putting on classical plays as well as reading them. The aim of this style of education was the intellectual and moral formation of young men. The Society's schools were open to all young men – the Society's own as well as externs – and they especially encouraged poorer students to enroll in their schools.

The 1599 *Ratio* remained in effect with only slight alterations until the Society's suppression in 1773. Superior General Jan Roothaan attempted to revise the *Ratio* after the Society's restoration in 1814, sending a revised version to the provinces in 1832, but it was rejected as antiquated, impossible to put into effect given the changing world around the Society. Nevertheless, the spirit of the *Ratio* continued to influence Jesuit education, albeit informally, into the 1960s. Many Jesuit schools continued to teach classical languages and maintained a focus on the humanities similar to what had been prescribed by the 1599 *Ratio*.

See also Acquaviva, Claudio, SJ; Education, Secondary and Pre-Secondary; Universities, 1540–1773; Universities, 1773–Present

Brizzi, Gian Paolo, ed., *La "Ratio studiorum": modelli culturali e pratiche eduative dei Gesuiti in Italia tra Cinque e Seicento*. Rome: Bulzoni, 1981.

Duminuco, Vincent, ed., *The Jesuit Ratio Studiorum: 400th Anniversary Perspectives*. New York: Fordham University Press, 2000.

Hinz, Manfred, Roberto Righi, and Danilo Zardin, eds., *I gesuiti e la "Ratio studiorum"*. Rome: Bulzoni, 2004.

Pavur, Claude Nicholas, ed., *The Ratio Studiorum: The Official Plan for Jesuit Education*. St. Louis, MO: The Institute of Jesuit Sources, 2005.

Charles Keenan

Reformers, Catholic

Whether Ignatius of Loyola can be classified a Catholic reformer is a question that has generated significant historical debate in recent years. For this reason we need to understand the meaning of reform in the early modern Catholic tradition, and the place of the Society of Jesus within it. This is by no means an easy task, however, given that neither contemporaries nor historians agree on a specific definition. Efforts aimed at purifying Church administration of worldliness and corruption, restoring Christian dogma to its original, and thus authentic, biblical interpretation as well as more popular impulses directed at personal renewal have all been considered manifestations of Catholic reform. In a persuasive article published in 1981, John O'Malley argued that Ignatius had never intended to alter or restore the structure of the Church and for this reason is better understood as a reformer "by osmosis." Others have pointed to Ignatius's extensive networks of relations with well-known reformers across Europe, the innovative nature of the *Spiritual Exercises*, and the new Jesuit model of ministry as evidence of a reformist agenda.

Assuming a broader definition, this entry considers Catholic reformers to be those men and women who worked within the structure of the Catholic Church to effect religious change during the early modern period. To be sure, reformers existed in the Catholic tradition much earlier. Early modern scholars, however, differentiate between "Catholic" and "Protestant" Reformers. Whereas Luther and his followers ultimately rejected the Catholic Church as too corrupted to be saved after 1517, Catholic reformers initiated their visions of reform as active members of its body.

This decision to stay, however, should not be considered as a sign of consensus among Catholic reformers on the state of the Church, let alone on a shared vision of a restored Christian body. Some of the more widely held concerns about the clergy pivoted around the issues of education, pastoral care, and such insidious clerical practices as nepotism and the buying and selling of spiritual offices (venality). A desire to create a better-trained and moral clergy underlay the reforming measures of many Church leaders by the early sixteenth century. Deep divisions among reformers also existed over conceptions of the path to perfection, spawning the Observant reform movements visible in many of the medieval orders by the fifteenth century as well as the simultaneous appearance of many new orders in the European marketplace, including the Jesuits, Oratorians, and Ursulines.

Ignatius of Loyola had ties with many well-known reformers, especially in Spain, Italy, and France, where he spent much of his life developing his new model of ministry. A consideration of some of these individuals along with broader strands of reform in the Church will help us better understand Ignatius as a product of his time as well as assess the uniqueness of his vision of the ideal religious life. Of the broader impulses, two of the most influential first emerged during the late medieval period, namely, conciliarism and Christian humanism.

The Christian Humanists. The influence of Christian humanism upon the spirituality of the first Jesuits is well known and treated at greater length elsewhere in this encyclopedia. These men, mostly clerics and learned laymen, were concerned with signs of ecclesiastical worldliness, abuse, and excessive piety. Their focus was on recapturing and disseminating the simpler piety found in early Christian writings, texts they considered closer to the true nature of Christian spirituality. We know from the early Jesuit writings that Ignatius read and was influenced by Desiderius Erasmus (1466–1536) and his devotional writings. Other famous humanists that Ignatius may well have read but certainly knew about included Thomas More (1478–1535), the English author of *Utopia*, and the Spanish scholar Juan Luis Vives (1493–1540). Ignatius would have encountered their work while still in Spain. Erasmus's work, in particular, was published in many languages before fear of Protestantism tainted his work as suspect. Humanists could be found at the University of Alcalá as well as at the Collège de France at the University of Paris, two institutions important to Ignatius's theological and spiritual formation. The University of Paris was a renowned center of scholastic theology and biblical scholarship, while the Collège de France in particular was an active center of Christian humanism. It held two widely recognized royal lectures in Greek and Hebrew that became central to humanist scholarship in France.

By the 1530s, the biblical scholarship of these reformers became tainted by Protestantism, and many, including Erasmus, found their works on the Index of Forbidden Books. Even so, these reformers left as a legacy a new approach to biblical scholarship and a powerful new language for communicating religious change. They were also celebrated as authors of popular devotional treatises and education. Indeed, their focus upon moral reform, rhetoric, and education as critical paths to spiritual perfection informed Ignatius's model of ministry.

Conciliarism and the Conciliarists. Conciliarism was another influential reforming impulse that shaped the world in which Ignatius and his followers defined their new ministry. It was arguably one of the most important legacies of the great schism of the Church in the fourteenth century, though it drew its inspiration from earlier, biblical models of Christian governance. Conciliarism was motivated by growing disillusionment with papal direction of the Church and signs of worldliness in its myriad institutions. Led by high-ranking clerics – bishops, cardinals, as well as the superiors of many religious orders – conciliarists thought that reform could be facilitated by submitting papal authority to the will of a General Church Council. It reached its greatest vigor in the fifteenth century, most visibly at the Council of Constance (1414–18), which ended the papal schism. Though the sixteenth century would see the papacy work hard to reclaim its authority, the influence of the conciliarists upon the early modern Church is impossible to ignore. Many of the more reform-minded cardinals and popes of the sixteenth century were influenced by conciliarist ideas, such as the need for improved pastoral care through the creation of a better-educated and trained priesthood, and the abolition of the most egregious worldly practices amongst the episcopacy, such as absenteeism and simony. The Cardinals Gasparo Contarini (1483–1542), Gian Pietro Carafa (1476–1559), and Charles Borromeo (1538–84) reflect the penetration of conciliarist ideas into the very core of papal governance by the middle of the sixteenth century. Perhaps the most significant legacy of conciliarism was the organization of the Council of Trent (1545–63). While the Council did in the end reaffirm papal supremacy, it also implemented wide-ranging reforms in the body of the Church, including the introduction of seminaries to train priests, greater attention to clerical discipline, and diocesan reform. Arguably the most influential exponent of diocesan reform was Cardinal Charles Borromeo, the archbishop of Milan. Borromeo was instrumental in the organization of the final session of Trent, which finished in 1563. To implement reform in his diocese, Borromeo insisted upon the regular episcopal visitation of parishes and held provincial councils. He also called upon the Jesuits, along with members of other new orders, to organize a seminary in Milan that became a model of clerical training in other dioceses.

As John O'Malley has argued, the kinds of concerns that motivated the conciliarists and their successors by the sixteenth century were not those that necessarily drove the spiritual agenda of Ignatius of Loyola. The founder of the Jesuits even discussed recalling his three delegates from the Council of Trent in 1547 in favor of putting them to tasks he considered more worthy, notably those of mission. It is worth noting, however, that Ignatius knew many of the men who operated at the heart of ecclesiastical reform in Rome. He had ties in particular with two new religious organizations that included many well-known reformers among their membership: the Oratory of Divine Love and the Theatine order. The Oratory of Divine Love began as a confraternity, founded by the layman Ettore Vernazza in the city of Genoa. Typical of late medieval confraternities, it was devoted to charity and personal sanctification. Between 1514 and 1517, it established a branch in Rome, one that quickly attracted prominent ecclesiastics, including Carafa, Contarini, and Gaetano da Thiene (d. 1547).

Thiene is most closely associated with the Theatines, a religious order that emerged out of the Oratory in 1524. Along with the Oratory, the Theatine order is considered one of the great catalysts in the spread of Catholic reform in Italy after this time. Thiene was a curial official when he first joined the Oratory. The order he created from it, the Theatines, was an order of clerks regular. While Thiene is generally considered its founder, an achievement which earned him canonization later on as Saint Cajetan, Cardinal Carafa was also involved from its inception. Carafa came from an illustrious Neapolitan family with deep roots in the Roman Curia. The name of the new order in fact came from the city of Theata, the seat of the bishopric of Chieti that belonged to Carafa's uncle Cardinal Oliviero. Carafa was known during his lifetime as a fierce and tireless reformer, presiding over the introduction of the Roman Inquisition and the Index of Forbidden Books. These legacies have largely cemented his historical reputation as an uncompromising enemy of doctrinal heterodoxy. As Pope Paul IV (1555–59), Carafa also promoted the work of the Theatines as part of broader-ranging initiatives aimed at ecclesiastical reform and pastoral care. But as early as the 1530s the order had become an influential agent of reform, espousing a new clerical ideal that emphasized public modesty in dress and comportment as well as clerical discipline. It was also one of the new orders more focused upon pastoral work, though the model of life was monastic in form: members had a rule, took vows, and lived in common.

Ignatius of Loyola met Carafa during his time in Rome, though scholars suggest that that relationship was less than cordial. Ignatius resisted pressure, for example, to incorporate his own fledgling order into the Theatines. For these and other reasons, Ignatius did not welcome news of Carafa's accession to the papal throne in 1555. And yet, his correspondence shows that Ignatius had a great deal of respect for the order itself and its founder Thiene, whom he seemed to have known quite well. Indeed, they had much in common. The Theatines, like the Jesuits, valued clerical education and embraced a pedagogy that mixed humanist and scholastic elements.

Religious Orders. As the history of these two congregations suggests, the paths of reform were varied during the early modern period, especially with regard to new models of the religious life. Two other distinct and influential religious congregations that emerged in Italy during this period included the Oratorians, established by Philip Neri (d. 1595) in 1575, and the Barnabites. The Oratorians – not to be confused with the

Oratory of Divine Love – mixed clerics and laymen in a new model of communal life. The Barnabites began earlier in 1530, in Milan, and were formally recognized in 1579. Cardinal Borromeo was named its protector. Similar to the Theatines, the Barnabites were dedicated to pastoral care and became known for their attention to preaching, catechism, education, and the care of prisoners. The Barnabites were also known for their fourth vow never to take high office. Fairly quickly, the order expanded outside the boundaries of Milan as another one of the myriad new missionary orders emerging at this time. Their work was so highly regarded by the celebrated reformer Francis de Sales (1567–1622) that he invited them to set up colleges in his diocese in Annecy. Henry IV of France (1594–1610) invited them to organize missions in Bearn, a stronghold of Calvinism, after he assumed control of the throne. Their most vigorous areas of activity throughout the early modern period were in Italy, Savoy, Austria, Bohemia, and France.

As the above discussion suggests, Italy was a hotbed of reform by the sixteenth century, and many of its impulses resonated in other parts of Europe. This had a great deal to do with its association with the seat of Catholic authority – the papacy – as well as its location in the middle of Europe. The fact remains that Europe teemed with reforming impulses throughout the early modern period, and many of them took the form of new religious orders and congregations. Indeed, the diverse and innovative nature of many of these traditions is striking. For John O'Malley and Robert Bireley, among others, this was above all a great era of mission and pastoral outreach. Some of the most influential religious orders to emerge at this time were the initiatives of women. Two in particular deserve attention here because of their broad influence in Europe and importance in the history of the Jesuit tradition: the discalced Carmelites and the Ursulines. The discalced Carmelites had their roots in Observant reform, in this case that of the medieval Carmelite tradition. It was also Spanish in origin, the inspiration of the female Carmelite Teresa of Avila (1515–82). A product of a noble home, Teresa developed a reputation as a mystic from a young age. Her renown and reputation for austerity earned her a wide following among members of the Spanish elite. By the 1560s, she was the mother superior of her convent in Avila and began implementing a more rigorous model of Carmelite spirituality. This new model inspired the formation of reformed male houses as well. The discalced – or shoeless – Carmelites became one of the most influential religious orders of the early modern period. Both female and male branches flourished in many regions, notably in France where they received the patronage of the noblewoman Barbe Acarie and the Savoyard reformer Francis de Sales. The male order proved to be one of the more active of the new missionary traditions to emerge in this period, alongside the Jesuits and the Capuchins, the latter a reformed branch of the Franciscan tradition.

The Jesuits also played an important role in the history of Teresan reform. They were advisers and confessors to the future saint. Indeed, in her autobiography Teresa gave her Jesuit confessors credit for validating her spiritual experiences when previous confessors would not. It is worth noting, as well, that Ignatius and his fellow Jesuit Francis Xavier were canonized on the same day as Teresa of Avila, March 12, 1622, along with the Roman reformer Philip Neri, and Isidore the Farmer (d. 1130). Besides the rapidity of the process in the case of the four early modern reformers – a matter of a few decades for each one – the group canonization underscores their association in the eyes of contemporaries.

Another newly formed female order that was perhaps even more important historically to the Society of Jesus, however, was the Ursuline. The order was not French but
Italian in origin, formed by Angela Merici (1474–1540) in Brescia in 1535. In contrast
to Teresan reform, Merici oriented her new model of female religious toward the care of
the poor; it was less focused upon the contemplative life, in other words, and more on
outreach. The education of poor girls became a defining concern of the order from early
on, a role that gave them important common ground with the Jesuits. Indeed, the significance of the Ursulines for the Jesuit mission in New France is difficult to overstate. The
letters of the nun and future saint, Marie de l'Incarnation (1599–1672), are especially
revealing in this regard, depicting a close working relationship with the Jesuits as well
as an active role for these female religious in the education and spiritual formation of
indigenous girls. The nuns first arrived in New France in 1639 for this purpose and were
trained in the indigenous languages to help with their work.

Studied alongside these men and women, one can understand why Ignatius of Loyola
has often been labeled a Catholic reformer. He created a new religious tradition that by
any standard was innovative, especially in terms of organization, education, and pastoral
care. At the same time, Ignatius had very little interest in the kind of structural changes
under discussion at the Council of Trent. What was important to him, according to John
O'Malley and Philip Endean, among others, was the pursuit of personal sanctification,
a state best achieved, to his mind, through following his *Spiritual Exercises* – one of the
most influential contributions of early modern Catholicism.

See also Erasmus; Humanism, Renaissance; Loyola, Ignatius, SJ, St.; *Spiritual
Exercises*; Trent, Council of

Bilinkoff, Jodi, *The Avila of Saint Teresa: Religious Reform in a Sixteenth-Century City.* Ithaca, NY:
  Cornell University Press, 1989.
Bireley, Robert, *The Refashioning of Catholicism 1450–1700.* Cambridge: Cambridge University
  Press, 1999.
Diefendorf, Barbara, *From Penitence to Charity: Pious Women and the Catholic Reformation in France.*
  Oxford: Oxford University Press, 2002.
Endean, Philip, "The Spiritual Exercises." In Thomas Worcester, ed., *The Cambridge Companion to
  the Jesuits.* Cambridge: Cambridge University Press, 2008, pp. 52–67.
Gleason, Elizabeth, *Gasparo Contarini: Venice, Rome and Reform.* Berkeley: University of California
  Press, 1993.
Greer, Allan, "Colonial Saints: Gender, Race and Hagiography in New France." *The William and
  Mary Quarterly* 57 (2000), 323–48.
Oakley, Francis, *The Conciliarist Tradition: Constitutionalism in the Catholic Church, 1300–1870.*
  Oxford: Oxford University Press, 2003.
Olin, John C., *The Catholic Reformation from Cardinal Ximenes to the Council of Trent, 1495–1563.*
  New York: Fordham University Press, 1990.
O'Malley, John W., "Was Loyola a Reformer? How to Look at Early Modern Catholicism." *The
  Catholic Historical Review* 77 (1991), 177–93.
Quinn, Peter A., "Ignatius Loyola and Gian Pietro Carafa: Catholic Reformers at Odds." *The Catholic
  Historical Review* 67 (1981), 386–400.

Megan C. Armstrong

Regency, Regent

In a word, Jesuit formation is long, with multiple stages and various periods of testing.
The stage known as regency plays a "special role in the overall formation of a Jesuit,"

where growth in self-knowledge and discipline meets the demands of full-time ministry and apostolic community life (Kolvenbach, *Formation of Jesuits*, 79).

Normally a two or three-year period following philosophy studies, regency is, for the Jesuit (known as a regent), the first time he lives and works full-time in an apostolic work and community of the Society. Though the man will have had previous experiments as a novice and apostolic experiences during philosophy, regency provides a Jesuit with an opportunity for a distinct, serious commitment to apostolic work. Traditionally high school or university teaching, the work of a regent varies according to the man's gifts, the needs of the Society, and the man's formational needs. The work undertaken is understood to be a mission given by a superior (or his delegate) who has received the man's account of conscience and therefore knows the man well.

The demands of full-time work that a regent undertakes are to be understood as the regular and principal rhythm of his future life as a Jesuit. With that in mind, a regent will undergo frequent testing of his abilities and limitations (and come to know the limitations of others), deal with a constant challenge to balance work with a commitment to prayer, and have the real-time opportunity to work collaboratively with other Jesuits and laypeople, developing qualities of generosity and service fit for an apostle and future priest, if he is a scholastic.

See also Course of Studies; Formation; Scholastic

Kolvenbach, Peter-Hans, *The Formation of Jesuits*. Rome: General Curia of the Society of Jesus, 2003.
The Constitutions of the Society of Jesus and Their Complementary Norms. Ed. John W. Padberg. St. Louis, MO: The Institute of Jesuit Sources, 1996.

Keith Maczkiewicz, SJ

Region

As a truly international organization, the Society of Jesus is organized into various subdivisions. Specifically, as stated in the Complementary Norms of the Jesuit *Constitutions*, "The Society is divided into provinces and regions (which can also be called missions)" (387, #1). Further, there are two types of regions within the Society: "Regions (missions) are either dependent on some province or immediately subject to the superior general; in the latter case, they are called independent" (387, #2). In other words, a dependent region is one that is connected to a particular province and is subject to its governance, whereas an independent region is directly under the governance of the superior general. The Norms make clear the general's ultimate authority regarding both provinces and regions: "By universal law and our own law, the general can establish, unite, divide, or suppress provinces and regions (missions), once he has given the matter careful consideration and has discussed it with the general counselors" (388, #1). According to the 33rd General Congregation, "communal apostolic discernment [is] central to 'our way of proceeding,' a practice rooted in the Exercises and Constitutions. This way of proceeding calls for a review of all our ministries, both traditional and new" (Decree 1, Part II, #42). This process of discernment should be undertaken "in the local community, province, or region, [leading] to apostolic decisions made by superiors, after normal consultation and with accountability to Father General" (Decree 1, Part II, #43). Therefore, discernment should be normative at the local level as well as at the provincial and regional levels.

See also Constitutions; Province

The Constitutions of the Society of Jesus and Their Complementary Norms. Ed John W. Padberg. St. Louis, MO: The Institute of Jesuit Sources, 1996.

Padberg, John W., ed., Jesuit Life and Mission Today: The Decrees and Accompanying Documents of the 31st–35th General Congregations of the Society of Jesus. St. Louis, MO: The Institute of Jesuit Sources, 2009.

Robert E. Scully, SJ

Regis High School (New York)

Founded in 1914 by virtue of an originally anonymous bequest from a Manhattan family, this highly selective secondary school sponsored by the Society of Jesus has operated continuously on a tuition-free basis – the only all-scholarship Jesuit high school in the United States. Noteworthy is how this arrangement fulfills the original intention of the first Jesuits for "gratuity of ministries," a principle that has been attenuated by the contingencies of high educational costs. As a result of the remarkable generosity of the founders and the New York province of the Society of Jesus in contributing the services of hundreds of Jesuits over the school's history, Regis has opened the door to secondary and higher education for thousands of sons of immigrants who otherwise would not have been able to attend any Catholic or private school.

In recent decades, the now mixed (lay and Jesuit) Regis board of trustees has debated strategies for achieving the twin priorities of maintaining high academic standards and ready access to a Regis education for less-advantaged youth. REACH (Recruiting Excellence in Academics for Catholic High Schools) was established in 2002 as an enrichment program to groom academically talented but indigent Catholic middle-school boys who might succeed in the Regis admissions exam, or in another selective academic environment.

With fewer Jesuits available for assignment, the school's faculty increasingly consists of highly dedicated Catholic laity. The all-male student body of Regis continues to number about 550. Although Regis teams enjoy only occasional success in athletic competition, the school has won national renown in competitions in speech and debate, chess and Latin sight translation.

See also Education, Secondary and Pre-Secondary; United States of America

Andreassi, Anthony D., Teach Me to Be Generous: The First Century of Regis High School in New York City. New York: Empire State Editions of Fordham University Press, 2014.

Thomas Massaro, SJ

Régis, Jean-François, SJ, St. (1597–1640)

Born January 31, 1597, in the village of Fontcouverte (Aude), Jean-François entered the Jesuit novitiate in Toulouse (Haute-Garonne) on December 8, 1616, later teaching in the colleges of Billom, Le Puy, and Auch. As he began his theology studies in Toulouse (October 1628), a plague epidemic prompted the theologians to move to the country. Wanting to help the plague victims, Jean-François asked for and received ordination (May 1630) before completing his studies, which meant that he would forgo full profession in the Society. He devoted his final ten years to catechism and instruction among the Calvinists, sex workers, and rural poor, gaining a reputation for tireless zeal. It appears, however, that this same zeal led to complaints from Louis de Suze, bishop of Viviers, which resulted in Jean-François receiving a reprimand from his superiors, who nonetheless sent him to the college of Aubenas from which he gave missions to the surrounding areas. In 1636 his superiors sent him back to the college of Le Puy, where the simplicity and creativity of his catechesis had great success, in particular among children. Finally, his intense work and devotional exercises during the Christmas season in La Louvesc (Ardèche) contributed to his contracting pneumonia, from which he died on December 31, 1640. Many pilgrims visited his tomb at La Louvesc, and he was beatified in 1716 and canonized in 1737. Étienne Terme founded (1821) at Aps the Sisters of Saint Regis, from which would develop, under the leadership of Thérèse Couderc (1805–85) at La Louvesc, the Sisters of Our Lady of the Cenacle.

See also Catechism; France; Plague

Cros, Léonard-Joseph-Marie, *Saint Jean-François Régis de la Compagnie de Jésus*. Toulouse: Librairie A. Loubens, 1894.
Guitton, Georges, *Après les guerres de religion: Saint Jean François Régis (1597–1640)*. París: Éditions Spes, 1937.

William P. O'Brien, SJ

Revues/Journals

A long tradition of publishing runs throughout the history of the Society of Jesus. Ever since Ignatius purchased a printing press for the Society in 1556, publishing has been viewed as a vital medium through which the Society can fulfill its mission. It is no surprise, therefore, that the first Jesuit printing presses were occupied primarily with publishing materials to accompany ministerial efforts in education, catechesis, and spirituality. By the 1570s, these presses also began to publish notable quantities of serious academic texts, beginning with works of theology. After the Society was restored in the nineteenth century, an array of new publications were soon founded, some of which are still in print. Today Jesuits are involved in the publication of scores of journals and periodicals in a host of different contexts and cultures across the globe. The following is an historical overview of the many scholarly publications of the Society, as well as those aimed at a broader audience.

In 1850 *La Civiltà Cattolica* was founded by the Italian Jesuits as a locus of reflection upon intellectual and cultural questions in light of Catholic faith, and it remains today the oldest Italian periodical in print. The French journal *Études* (1856) was founded six years later as a revue of philosophy and theology, though its scope gradually expanded to include broader cultural questions. In 1865 the German Jesuits founded what eventually became the preeminent journal of theology and culture, *Stimmen der Zeit*. After illegally publishing *Mit brennender Sorge*, Pius XI's 1937 encyclical denouncing developments in Nazi Germany, the journal was suppressed by the Third Reich. It was not to reappear until 1946, a year after one of its editors, German Jesuit Alfred Delp, had been executed. In the 1950s, *Stimmen der Zeit* began to publish myriad articles, most notably from Karl Rahner, that laid theological groundwork for the new phase of openness and *aggiornamento* associated with the Second Vatican Council. Jesuit journals with a similar focus upon theology and culture include *Razón y fe* (Spain, 1901); *Brotéria* (Portugal, 1902); *Studies* (Ireland, 1912); *Streven* (Belgium, 1931), and *Choisir* (Switzerland, 1959).

In 1921 Jesuits teaching at the Institut d'Études Théologiques in Brussels were given editorial responsibility for the already existing *Nouvelle Revue Théologique*, founded in 1847. In the decades that followed, numerous eminent theologians associated with the *nouvelle théologie* published their work in its pages, including Balthasar, Congar, and Daniélou. Other notable European Jesuit academic journals of theology include the *Gregorianum*, founded in 1920 by the Pontificia Università Gregoriana in Rome, and *Estudios Eclesiásticos*, published by the Universidad Pontificia Comillas since 1922.

Among the many Jesuit publications written for a more popular audience, national journals worthy of note include *Posłaniec Serca Jezusowego*, first published in 1872 and now the oldest Catholic monthly in Poland; *Mensaje* (1951), founded in Chile by Chilean Jesuit Alberto Hurtado, who was canonized in 2005; *Signum*, the only Catholic journal in Sweden (1975); *Australian Catholics* (1993), Australia's largest Catholic magazine; and most recently, *Thinking Faith*, the online journal of the British Jesuits established in 2008. In recent years Jesuit-sponsored regional media have also emerged, such as *Jivan*, a publication of the Jesuit Conference of South Asia based in Gujarat, India; *Mirada Global*, an online magazine featuring contributions from across Latin America; and *Europeinfos*, a collaborative monthly publication sponsored by the Bishops' Conferences of the European Union and the Jesuit European Office.

In the United States, the national weekly magazine *America*, established in 1909 to reflect upon faith and culture for a popular audience, was followed by the academic journal of theology, *Theological Studies*, founded in 1940. Other American Jesuit academic journals include *New Testament Abstracts* (1956), now published out of Boston College, and the *International Philosophical Quarterly* (1961), founded by Jesuits in the philosophy department of Fordham University.

In Asia, Jesuits have published three important academic journals of history and cultural studies: the *Monumenta Nipponica* at Sophia University in Japan since 1938, *Philippine Studies* at the Ateneo de Manila since 1953, and *Indica* at St. Xavier's College in Mumbai since 1964. In 1975 *The Clergy Monthly* in India was transformed into the *Vidyajyoti Journal of Theological Reflection*, a monthly publication of the Vidyajyoti College of Theology in India.

Among the many Jesuit journals of spirituality still published today, one finds the following: *Sacred Heart Messenger* (Ireland, 1888); *Madonna* (Australia, 1897); *Manresa* (Spain, 1925); *Geist und Leben* (Germany, 1926); *Christus* (France, 1954); *The Way* (United Kingdom, 1961); *Studies in the Spirituality of Jesuits* (United States, 1969); *Ignis* (India, 1972); *Telema: lève-toi et marche!* (Congo, 1975); *Cahiers de Spiritualité Ignatienne* (Canada, 1976); *Revista Diakonia* (El Salvador, 1977); *Cuadernos de Espiritualidad* (Chile, 1980); *Itaici* (Brazil, 1989); and *Ignaziana* (Rome, 2006).

In keeping with a renewed commitment of the Society to social justice, a series of journals were also established in the twentieth century to focus on social issues, including *Relations* (Canada, 1941); *La Revista de Fomento Social* (Spain, 1946); *Aggiornamenti Sociali* (Italy, 1950); *Congo-Afrique* (Congo, 1961); *Envío* (Nicaragua,

1981); *Eureka Street* (Australia, 1991); *Promotio Iustitiae* (Rome, 1992); and *Migraciones* (Comillas, 1996).

 See also America Magazine; *Civiltà Cattolica*; *Études*

Henry Shea, SJ

Rhetoric(s) and *Eloquentia Perfecta*

The Society of Jesus was founded during the era of the great European Renaissance, when rich adaptations of classical knowledge, increasingly disseminated through published texts, shaped the development of Christian humanism. One of the distinguishing marks of this era was the revitalization of classical rhetoric, the art of persuasion. It is no wonder, therefore, that a newly founded religious order, with its first members educated into this world of eloquence and letters, would engage the power of rhetoric to instruct (*docere*), persuade (*movere*), and inspire (*delectare*).

 The term "Jesuit rhetoric" is a capacious one with several facets of meaning. Indeed, it might be easier to refer to *Jesuit rhetorics*. From the beginning, the Society of Jesus held the discursive arts close to its heart, identifying its work as ministries of the word of God and works of mercy. In one sense, then, the term refers to the ways in which the Jesuits valued the power of speech to move listeners toward the good and trained their own members to become effective preachers and orators. During this period of Church reform and strident, even violent, confessionalism, effective and persuasive communication became all the more exigent. The scope of the term Jesuit rhetorics also extends to the many treatises Jesuits wrote about preaching (sacred rhetorics), collections of sermons and orations, and their correspondence in larger debates about sermonic genres and styles. Similarly, studies of Jesuit rhetoric include the works of great Jesuit preachers of the pre-Suppression Society (e.g., Canisius, Caussin, Bourdaloue, Jouvancy, Coton, Segneri, Vieira, Binet) or those trained by the Jesuits (e.g., Bossuet, de Sales).

 Ignatius Loyola himself developed a set of intimate rhetorical-discursive "exercises," now called the *Spiritual Exercises*. Based on inner dialogue, conversation with a spiritual director, prayer, and meditation, these exercises became a central part of Jesuit spirituality and have been shared with countless people across the centuries, often in forms tailored to the circumstances of those receiving them. More broadly, John O'Malley explains: "Beginning with the *Exercises* themselves, the Jesuits were constantly advised to adapt what they said and did to times, circumstances, and places. The rhetorical dimension of Jesuit ministry in this sense transcended the preaching and lecturing in which they were engaged ... it was a basic principle in all their ministries, even if they did not explicitly identify it as such" (*First Jesuits*, 255).

 Since the Jesuits were contemplatives-in-action, they lived and enacted their mission in the larger world rather than cloistering themselves in monasteries. Thus, they engaged in rhetorics of encounter: missionary work that required great facility in languages and the willingness to undertake substantial cultural accommodation. The Jesuits also employed civic rhetorics: exercising public roles in Church councils and debates, reconciling hostilities between noble families or principalities, and negotiating treaties. Over time the rhetorical power of the Jesuits came in for significant criticism from both Protestant and competing Catholic quarters. Their mastery of rhetoric in multiple domains was perceived by some as wily manipulation, and Jesuits were sometimes stereotyped as intriguers who would stop at nothing to win arguments.

By far their greatest public endeavor, however, was the creation of a worldwide system of schooling, the humanistic Jesuit college and university system that became their central ministry. As with most Renaissance education, a large portion of the curriculum was devoted to teaching classical and, to a lesser extent, vernacular languages, grammar, and the humanities (the close reading and composing of historical and literary texts), all of which culminated in the capstone course in rhetoric. The Jesuits favored Cicero and Quintilian, along with many other classical and patristic authors. The aim of this program of study was *eloquentia perfecta*, the formation of erudition, wisdom, virtue, and eloquence as an integrated whole. The Jesuit conception of rhetoric encompassed all the literary, communicative, and symbolic arts: they viewed art, architecture, theater, music, and even ballet as forms of rhetoric in action, and they engaged students in visual and performative events (public oratory, festivals, plays) as part of the larger educational culture.

Over time this rich, embedded rhetorical training was abandoned by most other school traditions. In the nineteenth and early twentieth centuries, Jesuit colleges and universities reformed and updated their curricula as well, making room for modern disciplines. But inadvertently, the integrative transdisciplinary fabric of rhetoric as meaning-making and symbolic action was nearly lost. In the twenty-first century, many scholars and teachers at Jesuit institutions in the United States and elsewhere are working to restore the place of rhetoric and *eloquentia perfecta* as a hallmark of Jesuit education worldwide.

See also Arts, Performing; Education, Secondary and Pre-Secondary; Preaching; *Ratio Studiorum*; *Spiritual Exercises*; Universities

Abbot, Don Paul, "Reading, Writing, and Rhetoric in the Renaissance." In James Murphy, ed., *A Short History of Writing Instruction from Ancient Greece to Contemporary America*. 3rd edn. New York: Routledge, 2012, pp. 148–71.

Fumaroli, Marc, "The Fertility and Shortcomings of Renaissance Rhetoric: The Jesuit Case." In John O'Malley, Gauvin A. Bailey, Steven J. Harris, and T. Frank Kennedy, eds., *The Jesuits II: Culture, Sciences and the Arts, 1540–1773*. Toronto: University of Toronto Press, 1999, pp. 90–106.

Gannett, Cinthia, and John Brereton, eds., *Traditions of Eloquence: The Jesuits and Modern Rhetorical Studies*. New York: Fordham University Press, 2016.

O'Malley, John W., *The First Jesuits*. Cambridge, MA: Harvard University Press, 1993.

Owen, Diana, "*Eloquentia Perfecta* and the New Media Landscape." *Conversations on Jesuit Higher Education* 43 (2013), 14–17.

Cinthia Gannett

Rhodes, Alexandre de, SJ (1593–1660)

Alexandre de Rhodes was born in 1593 to a Catholic family of Jewish descent in Avignon. His grandparents, having fled from persecution in Spain at the end of the fifteenth century, had changed their family name from Rueda to de Rhodes. On April 14, 1612, de Rhodes was admitted to the Jesuit novitiate of Sant'Andrea al Quirinale in Rome. He chose to join the Jesuits because he believed that "in this Holy Order, it is easier to go to those beautiful lands, where so many souls perished because of the lack of preachers." De Rhodes's desire for the missions continued to deepen during his subsequent studies at the Roman College, and he repeatedly petitioned the Jesuit superior general to be sent to the Indies. On Easter Sunday of 1618, de Rhodes received General Vitelleschi's approval to work in the Jesuit mission in Japan.

In October of 1618, de Rhodes left Rome for Avignon to bid farewell to his family. After Avignon, he journeyed via Lisbon and arrived in Goa a year later. Owing to the ongoing persecution of Christians in Japan, however, de Rhodes was asked to wait in Goa upon his arrival in India. After two and a half years of active waiting, he left Goa and arrived in Macau on May 29, 1623. During his stay in Macau, de Rhodes actively engaged in ministry and proved to be an observant learner who maintained a deep respect for the native cultures. He strongly believed that Christian conversion entailed an ongoing process that grounded itself in a change of heart in the light of the Gospel rather than external appearances or habits.

In 1623 de Rhodes was among a group of Jesuits sent to work with the Japanese Christian community in Cochinchina. He was sent to minister in an area near the Gianh River where Tonkin and Cochinchina – the two Vietnamese-speaking kingdoms – bordered one another. After four months of studying Vietnamese, he was able to preach and to hear confession. He returned to Macau in July of 1626. Eight months later, because of his advanced language skills, de Rhodes was sent to establish a Jesuit mission in Tonkin. For the next three years, he championed the Jesuit method of accommodation, incorporating *thày gia'ng* (native catechetical teachers) into the Jesuits' work of evangelization. He composed the *Cathechismus* in Vietnamese, which served as a manual for teachers to use both in instructing others and for their own ongoing training and formation. De Rhodes's *Cathechismus*, which was printed in Rome in 1651, remains the first publication in *chu˜ quÓc ngu˜* (Vietnam's modern script).

Because Christian teaching on monogamy caused conflict with royal interests, de Rhodes was ordered to leave Tonkin indefinitely. In May of 1630, he returned to Macau and taught Christian morality for the next ten years. In 1640 he returned to the Jesuit mission in Cochinchina and served as its superior. For the next six and a half years, with frequent expulsion and imprisonment, de Rhodes strove to demonstrate that Christianity was very much alive within Vietnamese cultures and in the same way that Vietnamese cultures were at home with Christianity. With his words and deeds, de Rhodes, who was once a stranger in Vietnam, had now won over and found a home in the heart of Vietnamese Christians.

After being ordered to leave under penalty of death, de Rhodes left Vietnam for good on July 3, 1645. Of this experience, he recalled: "I left Cochinchina in body but certainly not in my heart, as it was with Tonkin." Remaining true to his words, de Rhodes continued to labor unceasingly for the Jesuit mission in Vietnam. He was instrumental in inspiring interest among the founding members of the Foreign Missionaries of Paris (MEP) in continuing the work of evangelization throughout Southeast Asia.

De Rhodes's direct involvement with the Jesuit mission in Vietnam, which came under the authority of Rome, ended abruptly due to its opposition with the Portuguese. To avoid further conflict, de Rhodes was sent to the Jesuit mission in Persia. In November of 1654, he left Marseille and arrived in Isfahan a year later. For the next five years, he once again learned a new language and labored quietly in his newly assigned mission. On November 5, 1660, Alexandre de Rhodes died a peaceful death in Isfahan, a year after Tonkin and Cochinchina had been established as the two new vicariates in Southeast Asia.

Among de Rhodes's own writings are his *Histoire du royaume de Tunquin* (Lyon, 1651), *Dictionarium annamiticum lusitanum et latinum* (Rome, 1651), and *Divers voyages et missions* (París, 1653).

See also Asia; Catechisms; Japan; Macau; Middle East; Vietnam

Pham, Hung T., "Composing a Sacred Space: A Lesson from the Cathechismus of Alexandre de Rhodes." *Studies in the Spirituality of Jesuits* 46, 2 (2014), 1–34.
Phan, Peter, *Mission and Catechesis: Alexandre de Rhodes and Inculturation in Seventeenth Century Vietnam.* Maryknoll, NY: Orbis Books, 1998.

Hưng Trung Phạm, SJ

Ribadeneira, Pedro de, SJ (1526–1611)

Pedro de Ribadeneira (or Ribadeneyra) was one of the first Jesuits, closely connected to Ignatius of Loyola, and was the founder's first biographer. A Spaniard, he was born in Toledo in 1526. His mother, widowed young, desired to give him a good education and hoped that he would become a priest. Thus, she consented to send him to Italy as a page to Cardinal Alessandro Farnese, who visited Toledo in 1539. Although he lived in the luxury of Farnese's household, after meeting Ignatius he was increasingly drawn to him. He embraced Ignatius's life of poverty, and his ideas concerning helping souls, and leaned on him for fatherly guidance. Ribadeneira was received into the Society on September 18, 1540, just days before the Order was officially confirmed. He was 14 years old.

Ribadeneira worked as secretary to Ignatius before pursuing university studies in Paris and Louvain. He suffered a crisis of conscience and considered leaving the Society in 1543, but fell ill, and recovered with a renewed sense of commitment, taking vows in 1545. After additional studies in theology at Padua, he taught in Palermo and at the German College in Rome. In December 1553 he was ordained a priest, and he celebrated his first Mass on Christmas in the chapel of the Crib in Santa Maria Maggiore, as Ignatius had done fifteen years before. After the death of Ignatius, Ribadeneira held many administrative positions within the Society, including provincial of Tuscany and Sicily. He also preached extensively and served in a diplomatic capacity, attempting to promote the Society in England. In 1574 he returned to his native Toledo in poor health. He lived in Spain (primarily Madrid) until his death in 1611, devoting his time to writing.

Around 1566, Ribadeneira was asked to write a biography of Ignatius by the General of the Society, Francis Borgia. He was ideally suited for this endeavor, having been a close companion of the founder and present for many of the key events of his life (and of the Society). He understood the personality of Ignatius, revealed by the many anecdotes related in the biography. He also had access to a great many documents, as Borgia had requested that all provinces send pertinent material to Rome for Ribadeneira to consult. He also had access to the *Acta* (autobiography) that Ignatius had dictated to Luís Gonçalves da Câmara and Ignatius's *Spiritual Diary.* The biography was written between 1567 and 1569, undergoing a "peer-review" before being published in Naples in 1572. The fact that it was written in Latin indicates that the intended audience was the members of the Society, who shared this as their common language, worldwide.

A second version, which corrected and added information, was published in Spanish in 1583, for a wider audience. A new Latin edition was published in 1586. In 1610, an illustrated version of Ribadeneira's biography of Ignatius was produced by the Galle workshop in Antwerp. Detailed engravings with specific references to Ribadeneira's text brought the work to an even larger audience. Within decades, other biographies of Ignatius had been written, but Ribadeneira's remained the best known and the source of most of what is known about Ignatius today. His *Life of Ignatius* has been translated into many languages; the first English translation of the complete version became available in 2014.

Ribadeneira presents Ignatius as the defender of the modern Church, and a vigorous combatant against heresy. The biography is, in fact, more than an account of the life of Ignatius, because it also examines the establishment of the Order, its focus on education, and its worldwide expansion. In this manner, the life of the man and the life of the Society become intertwined. The first edition stated that Ignatius had not performed any miracles, save the foundation of the Society. That stance was amended in later editions, as the push for the beatification and canonization of Ignatius would require accounts of miracles he performed.

In addition to his biography of Ignatius, Ribadeneira also wrote accounts of the second and third generals of the Order (Diego Laínez and Francis Borgia), an autobiography, and a collection of the lives of the saints known as the *Flos sanctorum*. He is regarded as a writer who transformed the genre of hagiography, writing accounts that were modern and straightforward. He also wrote works of history, spirituality, and philosophy. The *Historia eclesiástica del scisma del reino de Inglaterra* (1588–94) resulted from his 1558 travels to England, and another work, the *Tratado de la religión* (1595) has become known as a refutation of Niccolò Machiavelli's *The Prince*.

See also Antwerp; Autobiography of St. Ignatius; Loyola, Ignatius, SJ, St.

Bilinkoff, Jodi, "The Many 'Lives' of Pedro de Ribadeneyra." *Renaissance Quarterly* 51 (1999), 180–96.

O'Reilly, Terence, "Ignatius of Loyola and the Counter-Reformation: The Hagiographic Tradition." *The Heythrop Journal* 31 (1990), 439–70.

de Ribadeneira, Pedro, *The Life of Ignatius of Loyola*. Trans. Claude Pavur. St. Louis, MO: The Institute of Jesuit Sources, 2014.

Alison Fleming

Ribas, Andrés Pérez de, SJ (1575–1655)

Andrés Pérez de Ribas was born in 1575 in Córdoba, Spain, where he became a priest (1601) and joined the Society of Jesus (1602) in the same year that he departed for New Spain. He completed his novitiate in Puebla de Los Angeles (1604) and shortly thereafter was sent to Sinaloa (northern Mexico) as a missionary. He returned to Mexico City to take his final vows in 1612 and was again sent to the missions in northern Mexico. Recalled to Mexico City in 1619 because of illness, he recuperated while serving as rector at Tepotzotlán, the Jesuit novitiate. Thereafter, he remained in the central valley of Mexico where, among other roles, he served as rector at the Casa Profesa, and, ultimately, as Jesuit provincial of the province of New Spain. He returned to Spain and Rome in 1643–45 to represent the province in the 8th General Congregation of the

Society of Jesus. In 1645 he published *Historia de los triumphos de nuestra santa fe*, and in 1653 he completed his *Corónica y historia religiosa*, though its publication was suppressed. He died at the Colegio Máximo in Mexico City in 1655.

He is best known for his *Historia de los triumphos de nuestra santa fe*, in which he gave an eyewitness account of events in New Spain as a story of the unveiling of God's plan, highlighting the role of Jesuits as apostles of Christ. Pérez de Ribas, whose "edifying cases" narrated the requisite characteristics of the Jesuit who would take up the strenuous labor of evangelization on the frontier, directed the book to his fellow missionaries. Yet modern scholars have also utilized the text to learn about the indigenous cultures of northern Mexico, the nature of the Spanish conquest, and Jesuit evangelization methods in this frontier region.

See also Mexico; Spain

J. Michelle Molina

Ricci, Lorenzo, SJ (1703–1775)

Lorenzo Ricci was born in Florence to an eminent Tuscan family, members of which had long held important positions in Church and State. He received his education from the Jesuits at Prato and joined the Society at the age of 15, entering the S. Andrea novitiate in Rome. Ricci held significant teaching positions in Siena and at the Roman College, offering instruction in philosophy, theology, and rhetoric and, at the Roman College, he also played a leading role in spiritual direction. Even Ricci's critics would concede that he was a man of deep and heartfelt piety. He was made secretary of the Society in 1755 before his election as superior general in 1758. His generalate was dominated by the national assaults on the Society in Catholic Europe from the late 1750s and the global suppression of the Order in 1773. Ricci has often been criticised for his failure to stem these attacks but, in fairness, he had very little room for maneuver. There was nothing he could do concerning the Portuguese expulsion of 1759, and he was powerless to prevent the Spanish expulsion of 1767, an event that King Charles III of Spain was determined to carry through. Indeed, Charles and many of his leading ministers believed (with no justification) that Ricci had played a role in igniting the series of riots in 1766 that had convulsed dozens of Spanish cities and sent Charles scurrying from Madrid. During these years, it seems likely that Ricci took papal advice that maintaining a patient and peaceable approach was the most astute tactic

In the case of France, there was, potentially, an opportunity to contain the situation. In the midst of the the Parlement of Paris's prolonged attack on the French branch of the Society during the first half of the 1760s, the Jesuit leadership in Paris seriously entertained the idea of making the French Jesuit province quasi-independent and subject to a French vicar general. Ricci rejected this idea, announcing that "Aut sint ut sunt aut non sint" ("They shall be as they are or they shall not be"). This was not, however, stubbornness on Ricci's part. First, such a development would have represented a revolution in the inner workings of the Jesuit order. Second, Ricci's position was entirely shared by the reigning pope, Clement XIII, and, third, it is highly unlikely that such a move would have satisfied the Jesuits' French enemies. There is room for more legitimate criticism when assessing Ricci's response to the arrival of Spanish Jesuit exiles in Italy during the late 1760s. There was certainly grumbling within Iberian ranks that the Father General, beyond the limited measure of logistical support he provided, might have done more to ease the exiles' transition. Again, however, there were mitigating circumstances, notably the fear that providing too much help would have done significant damage to the financial situation of the Italian assistancy.

Nuance is also required when adjudicating Ricci's reaction to the gathering storm following Clement XIV's election in 1769, which culminated in the 1773 global suppression. Clement came under extraordinary pressure from the Bourbon powers to carry through the Suppression, and during the first years of the 1770s Ricci's access to leading figures in the papal curia was greatly curtailed. In any event, Ricci suffered dreadfully in the wake of the brief of suppression. He received news of *Dominus ac Redemptor* on August 16, 1773, was moved to the English college the next day, and then dragooned to the Castel Sant'Angelo. Despite repeated appeals for release and concerted attempts to defend the Society's past, he would endure two years of harsh incarceration: prevented from hearing Mass or receiving visitors, and denied access to news from beyond his prison cell. He died on November 24, 1775, and at his 1776 memorial service, held in Prussia where the brief of suppression had not been promulgated, an orator declared Ricci "a man whose dignity has made him a father to us, and whose charity has made him a brother." A satisfactory modern account of Ricci remains to be written, which is curious given his role in such a pivotal series of events in Jesuit history, but a likely conclusion is that he was an unexceptional figure confronting an exceptional situation. His friend and early biographer Giulio Cordara concluded that he would have been an excellent general in easier times.

See also Anti-Jesuit Polemic; Charles III; Clement XIV; Italy; Suppression

Coralli, Filippo, ed., "La vita del P. Lorenzo Ricci, generale della Compagna di Gesù. Biografia inedita del P. Tommaso Termanini SJ." *Archivum Historiae Pontificiae* 44 (2006), 35–139.

Thompson, D. Gillian, "General Ricci and the Suppression of the Jesuit Order in France, 1760–64." *The Journal of Ecclesiastical History* 37, 3 (1986), 426–41

Jonathan Wright

Ricci, Matteo, SJ (1552–1611)

Matteo Ricci was born in Macerata, Italy, on October 6, 1552. After studies of law, Ricci entered the Society of Jesus in Rome in 1571 and left seven years later for India (Goa), where he completed his theological studies and was ordained. In 1582, Alessandro Valignano (1539–1606), the Jesuit visitor in Asia, called Ricci to Macau to study Chinese. In 1583 Ricci and Michele Ruggieri (1543–1607) received permission from Chinese officials to settle in Zhaoqing (near Canton). They first dressed as Buddhist monks, but after about ten years of experience Ricci changed this accommodation into one with the Confucian elite. Meanwhile, the world map displayed in the Jesuit residence drew the attention of the Chinese literati and Ricci, with the help of Chinese scholars, made several Chinese versions of it, placing China in the center of the map. Ricci was responsible for the move northwards, first to the center of the country, next to the capital Beijing in 1598.

After a temporary return to the center, he definitively settled in Beijing in 1601, and on that occasion he offered two clocks to the emperor. He became acquainted with several leading literati and statesmen, who were often amazed by his prodigious memory of Chinese texts. One of his earlier works was devoted to the art of memory (*Xiguo jifa*). Among the scholars were Li Zhizao (1571–1630) and Xu Guangqi (1562–1633), who helped him with the translation of European astronomical and mathematical works, among others Euclid's *Elements*, edited by his former teacher at the Roman College, Christopher Clavius (1538–1612). Besides the mathematical texts, Ricci wrote humanistic treatises, such as a treatise on "Friendship" (*Jiaoyou lun*, 1595), based upon Andreas Eborensis's *Sententiae et exempla* (1569), and *Ershiwu yan* (Twenty-Five Sayings, 1605), which is basically a translation of a Latin version of Epictetus's *Encheiridion*. By selecting passages by Stoic authors that were compatible with Christianity, Ricci entered into dialogue with Confucianism and stressed the compatibility between the two ethical systems. His catechism based on natural theology was entitled the "Solid Meaning of the Lord of Heaven" (*Tianzhu shiyi*, 1603). The most original aspect of this work, with far-reaching consequences, is that Ricci cites the Chinese classics, demonstrating that in ancient times Chinese had a natural knowledge of God. He identifies the terms *tian* (heaven) and *shangdi* (high lord) in these texts with the Christian God (*Tianzhu*: Lord of Heaven). Regarding the later commentaries on the Chinese classics, Ricci was of the opinion that they were too much influenced by Buddhism and often departed from what he considered the original meaning of the text. After an initial purist and exclusivist attitude, Ricci very gradually adopted a more open view regarding certain Chinese ritual practices, such as ancestral worship and funeral rites. This became fully manifested only at his own funeral because of the initiatives of both Christian and non-Christian Chinese. Nicolas Trigault (1577–1628) who arrived in China the year that Ricci died, and returned to Europe a few years later, published *De Christiana expeditione apud Sinas suscepta ab Societate Iesu* through which Ricci's work became well known in Europe. Ricci died in Beijing on May 11, 1610. His tombstone and grave (without his remains) is still preserved in Beijing in a burial place that was originally granted by the emperor in 1611.

See also Asia; China; Cultures; Interreligious Dialogue

Bernard-Maître, Henri, *Le père Matthieu Ricci et la société chinoise de son temps 1552–1610*. 2 vols. Tientsin: Hautes études, 1937.

Bettray, Johannes, *Die Akkommodationsmethode des P. Matteo Ricci SJ in China*. Rome: Pontifical Gregorian University, 1955.

Gallagher, Louis J., trans., *China in the Sixteenth Century: The Journals of Matthew Ricci, 1583–1610*. New York: Random House, 1953.

Malatesta, Edward, and Gao Zhiyu, eds., *Departed, Yet Present: Zhalan, The Oldest Christian Cemetry in Beijing*. Macau: Instituto Cultural, 1995.

Ricci, Matteo, *Fonti Ricciane*. 3 vols. Ed. Pasquale M. d'Elia. Rome: La Libreria dello Stato, 1942–49.

  Le sens réel de «Seigneur du ciel». Trans. Thierry Meynard. Paris: Les Belles Lettres, 2013.

  The True Meaning of the Lord of Heaven (T'ien-chu Shih-i). Trans. Douglas Lancashire and Peter Hu Kuo-chen, ed. Edward J. Malatesta. St. Louis, MO: The Institute of Jesuit Sources; Taipei: Ricci Institute, 1985.

Spence, Jonathan D., *The Memory Palace of Matteo Ricci*. London/Boston: Faber and Faber, 1990.

Standaert, Nicolas, "Matteo Ricci and the Chinese: Spaces of Encounter between the Self and the Other." *Euntes docete* 63, 1 (2010), 101–21.

Trigault, Nicolas, and Matteo Ricci, *De Christiana expeditione apud Sinas, suscepta ab Societate Iesu. Ex P. Matthaei Ricij eiusdem Societatis commentarijs, Libri V. Ad S. D. N. Paulum V. In quibus*

Sinensis Regni mores, leges atq instituta et novae illius Ecclesiae difficillima primordia accurate et summa fide describuntur. Auctore P. Nicolao Trigaultio Belga ex eadem Societate. Augsburg: Christoph Mang, 1615.

Nicolas Standaert, SJ

Rodrigues, Simão, SJ (1510–1579)

Of aristocratic origins, Simão Rodrigues (b. Vouzela, 1510, d. Lisbon, July 15, 1579) studied in Paris, where he met Ignatius of Loyola and became a part of the nucleus of the future first Jesuits. He was, with Francis Xavier, the first Jesuit to enter Portugal (1540). Unlike Xavier, who moved on to India, Rodrigues remained to coordinate the first steps of the Society, becoming provincial (1546). He ruled independently, receiving reminders from Rome of the need for obedience. His alignment with the main trends in the kingdom was clear in his denunciations of the humanist Damião de Góis and the (failed) attempt to forbid the admission of *conversos* to the Society. In 1554 he also wrote a letter from Venice to King John III calling for measures against the Portuguese *conversos* who had fled to Ancona. He had left Portugal the year before, after a serious crisis marked by the accusation of tolerance on his part, if not actual encouragement, of extreme forms of penitential spirituality. Ignatius removed him from his post in 1551, but Rodrigues hung on for two more years. His expulsion led to the departure of many of his followers from the Society. The new dominant current was led by Luís Gonçalves da Câmara. After twenty years in Italy and Spain, Rodrigues was finally rehabilitated. In 1573 the balance of power changed after Everard Mercurian was elected general of the Jesuits, and he returned to Portugal as a visitor, supporting the nomination of an adversary of da Câmara as provincial, Manuel Rodrigues. He spent the last years of his life in Lisbon, in the House of S. Roque, where he also wrote an historical account of the origin and progress of the Jesuits.

See also Gonçalves da Câmara, Luís, SJ; Portugal

de Carvalho, José Vaz, "Simão Rodrigues, 1510–1579." *Archivum Historicum Societatis Iesu* 59 (1990), 295–314.
Pacheco, José Carlos Monteiro, *Simão Rodrigues: Iniciador da Companhia de Jesus em Portugal.* Braga: Editorial A.O.; São Paulo: Edições Loyola, 1987.

Giuseppe Marcocci

Rodriguez, Alphonsus, SJ, St. (1532–1617)

St. Alphonsus Rodriguez, born in 1532, was the son of a cloth merchant in Segovia, Spain. At the age of 12, Alphonsus was sent to the Jesuit school in Alcalá, but within a year he had to withdraw because of the death of his father.

In 1558 he married Maria Francisco Suárez, with whom he eventually had three children. Alphonsus's life, however, was not a happy one, and within ten years he experienced the death of his wife and three children and the failure of the family business.

In 1568 Alphonsus went back to school, this time at the Jesuit school in Valencia. His goal was to finish his studies and then to enter the Society of Jesus and become a priest. Citing his age and delicate health, however, the Spanish Jesuits would not allow him to enter. Alphonsus then reapplied for admission as a Jesuit brother. Despite misgivings about his health, the provincial relented, allegedly saying that if Alphonsus wasn't qualified to become a brother or a priest, then he could at least enter and become a saint.

Thus, on January 31, 1571, Alphonsus entered the Society of Jesus as a brother novice. Six months later, he was sent to work at the new Jesuit college in Majorca. Alphonsus professed his vows in 1573, and in 1579 he received the job for which he is now famous: door-keeper of the Jesuit college. As door-keeper Alphonsus's job was to receive students and visitors, give advice and encouragement, and deliver messages to and from the other Jesuits of the college. His humility and prayerfulness impressed all who came to know him, including a young student named Peter Claver, who would also go on to become a Jesuit saint.

Alphonsus Rodriguez died on October 31, 1617. In 1888, he was canonized by Pope Leo XIII, together with Peter Claver, and became the first Jesuit brother to be declared a saint.

See also Brothers; Claver, Peter, SJ, St.; Saints; Spain

Tylenda, Joseph N., *Jesuit Saints and Martyrs.* 2nd edn. Chicago, IL: Loyola Press, 1998.

Jonathan Stott SJ

Roma (Gypsies)

The Society's contacts with Roma appear to have begun in Naples and the Low Countries. Pietro Antonio Spinelli and Aloysisus la Nuza taught catechism to Roma in the former city during the mid-sixteenth century while Bernardus Oliverius (1523–56) was one of the first Jesuits to attempt missionary work among them north of the Alps. Although there is no evidence that Diego Laínez had any direct contact with Roma, he lumped them together with "Hebrews and Infidels" in his *Disputationes Tridentinae* as vagabonds and practitioners of magic.

While for a long time Roma had relatively little direct contact with the Society's schools, even before the Habsburg reconquest of the Danube Basin and Transylvania, Jesuits working in these regions had continual contact with Roma, many of whom were Muslim, while Jesuits in western Europe tried to come to grips with Romany history, linguistics, and culture, but often with less direct contact with this population. Some Jesuits such as Johannes Bisselius simply linked "Zingari" with immorality and blasphemy, while Matthias Faber emphasized Romany involvement in prognostications and Nicholas Baldellus (1573–1655) referred specifically to their practice of palm reading. Historian Ladislaus Turoczi wrote with sympathy and outrage at the persecution of Roma in Hungary during the mid-sixteenth century, and the skills of Roma as metal workers were known to other eighteenth-century Hungarian Jesuits.

Jesuit missionaries encountered dialects and social customs of Romany but had little real understanding of these, sometimes drawing excessively optimistic conclusions about conversion efforts, which were perhaps influenced by excessive reliance on interpreters. Sebastianus Beretarius perceived similarities between Roma and the indigenous peoples of Brazil. Franciscus Partinger produced a collection of emblems, one of which appears to show a Roma musician with his performing bear, while Gaspar Schott and Matthias Faber noted Roma involvement in fortune-telling, and Franciscus Fasching praised Roma musical and metalworking skills. A few Jesuit historians strove to place the Roma in a historical context: Stephanus Menochius traced the history of Roma people from their arrival in western Europe in 1417, and Rudolf Bzensky (1631–1715) mentioned the arrival of the Roma in Transylvania in his manuscript *Origines propagationis variae fidei in Transylvania* (1710). Johannse Rhò perpetuated the legend of Roma origins in Egypt, and epigramist Giovanni Battista Bargiocchi wrote of a Roma who gave his life for a friend. The Jesuit philologist Lorenzo Hervás y Panduro (1735–1809) theorized that the Roma of western Europe had lost their original tongue and instead spoke a sort of "robbers' jargon." At least one Roma child – a girl – was enrolled in a pre-Suppression school founded by Jesuits in Transylvania. Roma figured in at least one post-Suppression drama, *La Zingara* by former Jesuit Enrique García Álvarez, which premiered in Venice in 1781. Some Jesuits shared the more general anti-Roma prejudice. Francisco Rávago, confessor to King Fernando VI of Spain, supported the cruel "Gran Redada de Gitanos" in 1749.

In modern times a few scholars have linked Jesuits, Jews, and Roma among the "outsiders" of Europe who were viewed as lacking a home, an honest mode of presentation, or geographic loyalty – references that John Adams had made in a famous passage about Jesuits in 1816.

The restored Society, focusing as it did in eastern Europe on highly academic secondary schools, and with reduced resources to undertake major missionary campaigns, at first made little systematic effort to engage Roma in this region, but since 1989 contacts with this population have increased. Today Jesuits operate a primary school for Roma near Satu Mare, Romania, and Roma students are taught in a Jesuit school in Budapest. There are also summer camps for Roma children in Slovakia, and Jesuits work with Roma in Poland where a Jesuit has been appointed national Catholic minister to the Roma community. Summer camps for Roma are run by the Society in Kyrgyzstan. Pope Francis, a Jesuit, has called attention to the plight of Roma, noting that they are among the most vulnerable of Europe's peoples.

See also Cultures; Eastern Europe; Preferential Option for the Poor

Nemeshegyi, Péter, *Jezsuiták Sárospatakon*. www.asziv.hu/archivum/2013/november/vilagegyhaz/jezsuitak-sarospatakon.

Shore, Paul, *Jesuits and the Politics of Religious Pluralism in Eighteenth-Century Transylvania*. Aldershot: Ashgate, 2007.

Narratives of Adversity. Budapest: CEU Press, 2012.

Turoczi, Laudislaus, *Ungaria suis cum regibus compendio data*. Trnava: Typis Academicis Soc. IESU per Fridericum Gall, 1739.

Paul Shore

Roman College (Gregorian University)

The Collegio Romano emerged from Ignatius of Loyola's vision of an international university at the service of the Holy See. The College opened its doors in a rented house on the via Capitolina on February 23, 1551, with a basic program in the humanities (four years) and in philosophy and theology (seven years). In 1551, after flooding and other problems, the College moved to Palazzo Salvati, and in 1556 it received the right to grant degrees – and the accompanying university status – from Pope Paul IV (1476–1559). In 1564 the pope also gave the Society charge of the Roman seminary, thereby establishing the College as the principal institution of clergy formation.

Figure 58 Exterior view of the Gregorian University, Rome. Photograph Thomas Worcester, SJ

The College gained even greater prestige through the support of Pope Gregory XIII (r. 1572–1585), who both endowed the institution and gave funds for a permanent building. The architect Bartolomeo Ammanati (1511–92) designed the new structure for the location across from the Palazzo Doria Pamphilii. The foundation stone was laid on January 11, 1581, and the doors opened in 1584. New disciplines, such as astronomy and moral philosophy, also entered the College's curriculum.

During its early years the College boasted an impressive and internationally renowned faculty. In the fields of philosophy and theology, such luminaries as Francisco Suárez (1548–1617), Gabriel Vásquez (1549–1604), and the future cardinal, Robert Bellarmine (1542–1621) shone with their scholarship and influence upon future Church leaders. The burgeoning sciences also found significant practitioners in its halls: the brilliant mathematician and creator of the Gregorian calendar, Christopher Clavius (1538–1612), the astronomer Christopher Grienberger (1561–1636), and the charismatic polymath Athanasius Kircher (1601–80) added to the College's growing luster. It is estimated that by the mid-seventeenth century over 2,000 international students were attending lectures at the College, demonstrating the renown and success of Ignatius's dream.

The Suppression of the Society, however, radically affected the College's future. The machinations of various European powers, accompanied by rivalries within the Church, led to the elimination of the Jesuits for a 41-year period. In 1772, Pope Clement XIV (r. 1769–74) removed the Roman seminary from the Society's direction and in 1773 officially suppressed the Order in the papal brief *Dominus et Redemptor*. The Roman College entered diocesan hands under the direction of three cardinals: Marcantonio Colonna (1724–93), Andrea Corsini (1735–95), and Francesco Saverio de Zelada (1717–1801). Courses resumed in 1774 under the new authorities and, despite numerous financial problems during this period, the College maintained a regular academic program and even acquired a new observatory in 1787.

Though Pius VII (r. 1800–23) restored the Society in 1814 with the bull *Sollicitudo omnium ecclesiarum*, the Jesuits would not resume direction of the College until the publication of Leo XII's (r. 1823–29) brief, *Cum multa in urbe*, in 1824. During the tumultuous years of the nineteenth century, the College reasserted itself as one of the premier intellectual institutions in Europe through such scholars as Luigi Taperelli (1793–1862), founder of the journal *Civiltà Cattolica*, and the theologian Giovanni Perrone (1794–1876). The institution suffered, however, under the vicissitudes of Italian politics until its formal takeover by the New Kingdom of Italy in 1870. In 1873 the College reopened in the building of the old German College in the Palazzo Boromeo and, by the authority of Pope Pius IX (r. 1846–78), acquired its modern title, the Pontifical Gregorian University.

The Gregorian survived these lean years, growing from a mere 415 students in 1880 to over a thousand students by the end of the century. In 1876 Pius IX established a new faculty of Canon Law, and between 1919 and 1922, Benedict XV (r. 1914–22) would expand the University's offerings with such subjects as paleography, modern philosophy, and the history of religions. In 1920 the publication of the journal *Gregorianum* began, and in 1928 Pius XI (r. 1922–1939) officially placed three major academic institutions under the Society's direction: the Pontifical Gregorian University, the Pontifical Biblical Institute, and the Pontifical Oriental Institute. The University moved to its current location in the Piazza della Pilotta in 1930.

The Gregorian University remains one of the most significant centers of scholarship and religious formation in the Roman Catholic Church. Seventeen popes have been Gregorian alumni; numerous bishops continue to emerge from its lecture halls; and seventy-two saints and blessed received formation from its Jesuit faculty. Today nearly 4,000 religious and lay students from 150 countries attend its classes and lectures.

See also Gregory XIII; Papacy; Pontifical Biblical Institute; Pontifical Oriental Institute; Rome; Universities

Caraman, Philip, *University of the Nations: The Story of the Gregorian University of Rome from 1551 to Vatican II*. New York: Paulist Press, 1981.

Cerchiai, Claudia, ed., *Il Collegio Romano dalle origini al Ministero per i Beni e le Attività Culturali*. Rome: Instituto poligrafico e Zecca dello Stato, 2003.

Gilbert, Maurice, *The Pontifical Biblical Institute: A Century of History (1909–2009)*. Rome: Editrice Pontificio Istituto Biblico, 2009.

John Gavin, SJ

Rome

No other religious order has had the same kind of presence in Rome as the Society of Jesus, and Rome has been affected by Jesuits more than any other city.

The centrality of Rome to the Jesuits appeared well before Ignatius's arrival in the eternal city. When he gathered with his companions in Montmartre, on August 15, 1534, the first destination of the group was Jerusalem, a city that had dominated his dreams for years. However, the "friends in the Lord" stated that if it were not possible to go there, they would go to Rome and put themselves at the service of the pope. Later, in 1538, while Ignatius was traveling to Rome with Diego Laínez (1512–65) and Peter Faber (1506–46), he experienced in prayer one of his best-known illuminations, related in different versions by the Jesuit literature. In the village of La Storta, on the outskirts of Rome, he saw Jesus carrying his cross with God the Father at his side. In the vision, God the Father placed Ignatius with Christ and told him, "I will be propitious to you in Rome."

Elected superior general of the Society of Jesus in 1541, Ignatius spent the rest of his life in Rome dedicating himself to the ministries of the Society, drafting the *Formula*, a canonical description of the Jesuits' life, working on the *Constitutions* (published in 1558 after his death), and writing letters. The standard edition of his correspondence includes more than 5,300 letters to Jesuits. From that time up to the present, the superior general of the Society has resided in Rome (with a few temporary exceptions), described by the *Constitutions* as the best place to communicate with the rest of the world.

The importance of Rome for the Society was due not only to the presence of the superior general and his assistants (whose innovative role was later imitated by other religious orders) but also to the key role of the secretary, a role that was more important than in other religious orders. In 1547 Juan Alfonso de Polanco (1517–76), who had previously worked in the papal administration, became the secretary and began building an extremely efficient system of centralized communication. Polanco established the tradition of sending circular letters to Jesuits spread around the world, in which he described in detail the many accomplishments of the Society. Aimed at spiritual edification, Polanco's letters – that evolved into different forms over the years – communicated to the Jesuits what was known within the Society as "our way of proceeding." Ignatius and Polanco developed the administrative system of the Society, which found in Rome its center and in the letters its privileged instrument: Rome became the sorting, selecting, and sending center of the official documents of the Society. It was not a completely new approach, but the extent of the system and the way in which the letters were used was definitely an innovation.

Rome was not only the headquarters of the Society of Jesus but also the place where most Jesuits were trained and lived. When Ignatius died in 1556, Jesuits numbered about 1,000, organized into twelve provinces; almost 200 of them lived in Rome. Additionally, the Society created in Rome pioneering institutions that were imitated in the rest of the world.

The first Jesuits undertook what the *Formula* called "works of charity" in the hospitals, in prisons, and with the prostitutes. In Rome – at that time one of the European capitals of prostitution – Ignatius founded the Casa Santa Marta (1543). It was a house that provided temporary shelter and assistance to women who wanted a better future. The house had the capacity to host sixty women, who were either unmarried prostitutes or women who had turned to prostitution after becoming estranged from their husbands. For the former, dowries were collected, and the women could choose either marriage or a monastic vocation. The married women were encouraged to reconcile with their husbands or, if that was unsuccessful, to live in the same manner as nuns, even though still married. Life in Casa Santa Marta was like that of a convent, and the women promised to stay until they were settled into a morally upright life. Several noble families in Rome supported this ministry, but Casa Santa Marta was unable to maintain its mission for a long time, and by 1573 it had become a monastery reserved for virgins.

Education, not included in the first projects of Jesuits, became very early on a fundamental ministry. The first Jesuit educational institution in Rome was the Roman College. Founded in 1551 at the request of Ignatius after the founding of the College of Messina (1548), it became the premier scholarly enterprise of the Society of Jesus. It soon received the right to confer university degrees in theology and philosophy, was strongly supported by Roman elites, and attracted an international community of faculty and students. A printing press established in the College printed the first version of the *Ratio studiorum*, the curriculum and teaching method of the Society, in 1591 (the final version was completed in 1599). The Roman College became the model for several similar foundations in Rome and throughout the world. It was also the headquarters of the Sodality of Our Lady (1563), a Marian congregation of lay students that spread throughout Europe and attracted thousands of members. In Rome, the Jesuits also established a number of colleges for the education of clergy from other parts of Europe. The German College, the Hungarian College, the Greek College, the Roman Seminary, and the English College were crucial in the training of clergy who had to live out their vocations in the context of the period's many religious conflicts.

Rome was also the center of Jesuit architectural and artistic culture, and many of the Jesuit buildings in Rome became prototypes for the entire Society. The monumental Church of the Gesù, one of the most important churches built in the sixteenth century, had a unique status for Jesuits, since it was the church that Ignatius had desired to build adjacent to the Jesuit headquarters. It was situated near the center of the city and very close to the Palazzo Venezia, a papal residence until 1564. The church was thus centrally located, both for members of the Society and for those who came to avail themselves of the Order's various ministries. To the extent the Jesuits had a particular style of architecture, it was modeled on the style of the Church of the Gesù. Together with other Jesuit buildings in Rome, such as the Roman College, the Church of Sant'Ignazio, and the novitiate and Church of Sant'Andrea al Quirinale, the Church of the Gesù represented a sort of architectural canon that was imitated all over the world, from China to South America.

Rome witnessed both the triumphs and the most dramatic events in Jesuit history. The Roman port of Civitavecchia harbored the Jesuits expelled from the Kingdoms of Portugal and Spain from 1759 to 1768. Welcomed in the Papal States, after the Suppression (1773), the expelled Jesuits traveled to many Italian cities. The apex of the drama was reached in 1775, when Lorenzo Ricci (1703–75), the eighteenth superior general of the Society, died in Castel Sant'Angelo, the ancient fortress that in the early modern period was used as a papal shelter, archive, and prison. Ricci had been detained there since the Suppression of the Jesuits.

Only in 1820, six years after the restoration of the Order, did General Luigi Fortis (1748–1829) go back to Rome, which again became the location of the General Curia of the Society. After that, there were only short periods in which the Curia was moved outside Rome or the generals had to abandon the city. General Jan Philipp Roothaan (1785–1853) was obliged to flee to Marseille in 1848–50 during the Italian wars. Later, in 1870, the Curia was moved to Florence and Fiesole because of the difficult political situation in Rome, under the generalates of Pieter Beckx (1759–1887) and Anton Anderledy (1819–92). Luis Martín (1846–1906), elected during General Congregation 24 gathered in Loyola, Spain (1892), succeeded in transferring the headquarters of the Society back to Rome in 1895. Since then, the Curia has remained in Rome, but General Włodimir Ledóchowski (1866–1942), who was an Austrian subject, had to flee to Switzerland in the years 1915–18 during World War I.

After the restoration and up to the present, Rome has been the center of the Society's life. In Rome, the Jesuits have assumed the leadership of important research and teaching institutions of theology, sacred history, and Scripture. The Roman College, renamed the Pontificia Università Gregoriana in 1873 after its great patron Gregory

XIII (r. 1572–85), is still considered one of the most prominent Jesuit universities. In 1909, Pius X (r. 1903–14) entrusted to the Society of Jesus the newly founded Pontifical Biblical Institute, a university-level institution of the Holy See for the study of the Sacred Scripture, and in 1928 Pius XI (r. 1922–39) brought into association the Gregorian University, the Pontifical Biblical Institute, and the Pontifical Oriental Institute. The last of these was founded in 1917 by Pope Benedict XV (r. 1914–22) to be a center dedicated to advanced studies in Eastern Christianity. The three institutions have the same Vice-Grand Chancellor (the superior general of the Society of Jesus), but each has its own statutes.

Rome has also seen the flourishing of Jesuit scientific studies. In the seventeenth and eighteen centuries, the Roman College hosted a series of prominent scholars, including the Jesuit mathematician and astronomer Christopher Clavius (1538–1612), who calculated the new Gregorian Calendar (1582); Athanasius Kircher (1602–80), who established in the College a museum with an impressive collection of archaeological and scientific artifacts; and Roger Joseph Boscovich (1711–87), who published important works on contemporary scientific developments and on astronomical observations and mathematics. After the restoration of the Order, Jesuits began to found observatories in their universities and colleges. The first one, established at the Roman College in 1824, became a model for about seventy Jesuit observatories throughout the world that flourished in the late nineteenth and early twentieth centuries. One of the most important directors of the observatory at the Roman College was Angelo Secchi (1818–78), considered the Italian founder of meteorology, who obtained excellent results with his observations of the stars and in solar physics. In 1906, Pope Pius X entrusted the Vatican Observatory, founded in 1890 by Pope Leo XIII (r. 1878–1903), to the Jesuits. The role of its first director, Johann Georg Hagen, SJ (1847–1931), was central to the development of Jesuit contributions to science. In 1935 the Vatican Observatory was moved to Castel Gandolfo, the papal summer residence near Rome, where it is still directed and staffed by Jesuits.

In Rome, Jesuits have been in charge of important projects of media communication. The still-active biweekly journal *La Civiltà Cattolica*, founded in 1850, is one of the oldest Italian journals, and its goal is to promote Catholic culture, thought, and civilization in the modern world. The first issue was published in Naples, but the editorial offices were then moved to Rome, where the journal came to be regarded as the unofficial voice of the Holy See. In 1931, with the collaboration of the Italian engineer Guglielmo Marconi (1874–1937), Vatican Radio, the official broadcasting service of the Vatican, was created. Since 1938 it has been maintained by the Society of Jesus. This radio service played a crucial role during World War II, when it was used to send messages of peace from Pope Pius XII (r. 1939–58) and as a source of information for the Allies. Today its programs are offered in forty-seven languages.

Since the foundation of the Society, Rome has also been the center of the conservation of the Order's history. The Archivum Romanum Societatis Iesu (ARSI) is the archive of the central government of the Society of Jesus. It was begun at the time of the Society's founding and received crucial input from Polanco, who carefully organized it. The archive is today divided into two main sections: the Old Society (1540–1773) and the New Society (1774–present). Owing to the exceptional number of documents archived and its meticulous organization, it is one of the most visited archives maintained by any religious order, daily hosting researchers from all over the world. The

Roman Archive is housed in the Institutum Historicum Societatis Iesu, an institute founded in Madrid at the end of the nineteenth century and transferred to Rome in 1930 by General Ledóchowski. The main historiographical products of the Institute are local histories of the Society, the *Monumenta Historica Societatis Iesu* – a massive series of modern editions of primary sources – and monographs on the history and spirituality of the Society. In 1932 the Institute began publishing a quarterly journal on the history of the Society, *Archivum Historicum Societatis Iesu*.

According to some historians, Pedro Arrupe (1907–91), the twenty-eighth superior general of the Society (1965–83), opened a new chapter in the history of the Society. After Vatican II, in which Jesuit bishops and *periti* (expert theologians) had great influence, the Society began to emphasize the importance of social justice in Jesuit ministries. During Arrupe's generalate, Jesuits created many innovative institutions to serve the poor and the abandoned; one of them is the Jesuit Refugee Service, created in 1980. Facing the flood of refugees from the Vietnam War and other conflicts throughout the world, Arrupe suggested using the Jesuit network in order to accompany, serve, and advocate on their behalf. Its headquarters is in Rome, in the Curia of the Society of Jesus, and since 2000 it has been officially registered with the Vatican State as a foundation.

It is not possible to discuss Jesuits in Rome without mentioning their relationship with the popes. Two facts make this relationship particularly important. First, the superior general of the Society of Jesus is elected for life and has extraordinary power within the Order. For this reason he has often been depicted as an alternative pope, a fact that in the nineteenth century won him the nickname of "black pope." Second, most Jesuits take the Fourth Vow *circa missiones*, a vow of obedience to the pope, in which they declare their availability for mission anywhere in the world. These facts have contributed to making the connection between the Jesuits and the popes stronger and at the same time more delicate than those of other religious orders. Throughout its long history, the Society's relationship with individual popes has varied considerably, ranging from strong papal support to outright hostility.

To illustrate these variable relationships, some examples can be considered. Paul III (r. 1534–49), who officially approved the Society in 1540, bestowed extensive pastoral privileges on it that were confirmed and sometimes extended by his successor. These privileges inevitably caused resentment among bishops and the older orders, but they engendered in the Jesuits a deep sense of gratitude and loyalty to the Pope. Later, Paul IV (r. 1555–59) adopted a more hostile policy toward the Society: he did not accept the fact that the general was elected for life and obliged the Jesuits to chant or recite the Hours in common – a practice that was not included in their original rule and that was abandoned after the death of Paul IV.

In the second half of the eighteenth century, in the delicate period that led to the Suppression of the Society, two popes adopted very different attitudes. The pontificate of Clement XIII (r. 1758–69) was dominated by the Jesuit affair: he had to face Jesuit expulsion from Portugal, France, and Spain, pressure from the Bourbon kings, and the campaigns of Italian anti-Jesuit circles. The Pope and his secretary of state, Cardinal Ludovico Maria Torregiani (1697–1777) provided a bulwark of support against the Suppression of the Order. Upon the death of Clement XIII on February 2, 1769, the Holy Roman Emperor, Joseph II (r. 1765–90), and his brother Leopold, grand duke of Tuscany (r. 1765–90), arrived in Rome. The College of Cardinals was already under immense pressure from the Bourbon powers to elect a pope who would suppress the

Society of Jesus, and the Emperor's unprecedented participation in the conclave provided him with an opportunity to apply even more pressure. Clement XIV (r. 1769–74), the newly elected pope, and a Conventual Friar Minor, was not in sympathy with the Society and, after resisting for a few years, signed the brief of suppression on July 21, 1773.

An episode exhibiting significant tension between a pope and the Society occurred at the end of the twentieth century, during the pontificate of John Paul II (r. 1978–2005) and under the generalate of Pedro Arrupe. In 1980, Arrupe had decided to call a General Congregation and to present his resignation for reasons of age. In early 1981 he met twice with Pope John Paul II, who was concerned by some aspects of Jesuit life. The assassination attempt on John Paul's life that May, and a stroke suffered by Arrupe, interrupted their dialogue. Suffering from the consequences of the stroke, Arrupe appointed his vicar, Vincent O'Keefe (1920–2012), one of his closest collaborators, to take over his duties; however, John Paul II appointed as a delegate the Jesuit Paolo Dezza (1901–99), who was very critical of Arrupe's leadership. Arrupe resigned and was subsequently replaced during General Congregation 33 (1983). It was the first time a superior general had resigned, and it left an indelible mark. In fact, Arrupe's successor, Peter-Hans Kolvenbach (b. 1928), resigned as superior general when he turned 80, in 2008, and Superior General Adolfo Nicolás (b. 1936), resigned in 2016, at the age of 80.

The relationship between the Society of Jesus and the bishop of Rome took a new turn on March 13, 2013, when for the first time a Jesuit was elected pope. The Argentinian Jesuit Jorge Mario Bergoglio (b. 1936), who has taken the name Francis, has mentioned many times the deep influence of Ignatian spirituality on his actions as the bishop of Rome. The consequences of this event for the Society of Jesus in Rome and in the world are part of a future history.

See also Constitutions; Curia, Jesuit; Gesù, Rome; Loyola, Ignatius, SJ, St.; Italy; Obedience; Papacy; Roman College; Sant'Ignazio, Rome; Superior General

Catto, Michela, and Claudio Ferlan, eds., *I gesuiti e i papi*. Bologna: Il Mulino, 2016.
Friedrich, Markus, "Governance in the Society of Jesus 1540–1773," *Studies in the Spirituality of Jesuits* 40, 1 (2009), 1–42.
Guidetti, Armando, *Le missioni popolari: i grandi gesuiti italiani. Disegno storico-biografico delle missioni popolari dei gesuiti d'Italia dalle origini al Concilio Vaticano II*. Milan: Rusconi, 1988.
Lazar, Lance G., "The First Jesuit Confraternities and Marginalized Groups in Sixteenth-Century Rome." In Nicholas Terpstra, ed., *The Politics of Ritual Kingship: Confraternities and Social Order in Early Modern Italy*. Cambridge: Cambridge University Press, 2000, pp. 132–49.
Martina, Giacomo, *Storia della Compagnia di Gesù in Italia (1814–1983)*. Brescia: Morcelliana, 2003.
Murphy, Paul V., "Jesuit Rome and Italy." In Thomas Worcester, ed., *The Cambridge Companion to the Jesuits*. Cambridge: Cambridge University Press, 2008, pp. 71–87.
Scaduto, Mario, *Storia della Compagnia di Gesù in Italia*. Rome: La Civiltà Cattolica, 1930–64.
Udías, Augustín, *Jesuit Contribution to Science: A History*. Dordrecht: Springer, 2015.

Emanuele Colombo

Roothaan, Jan Philip, SJ (1785–1853)

Jan Roothaan was the twenty-first general of the Society of Jesus, serving between 1829 and 1853. He was born in Amsterdam and was the youngest of three brothers. The former Jesuit Adam Beckers played a leading role in his education, a fact that is significant because Roothaan is accurately portrayed as representing one of the crucial bridges between the pre-Suppression and post-restoration Society.

In 1804 Roothaan traveled to the Russian Empire, at that time an outpost of Jesuit survival. He entered the novitiate at Dunaburg, professed his vows in 1806, and was ordained in 1812. He pursued his education, notably at Polotsk, and took on a number of teaching positions in the Russian Empire down to 1820, in which year the Jesuits were expelled by Alexander I. Roothaan subsequently taught in Switzerland and at Turin (where he was rector of the local college) before being appointed vice provincial of Italy in 1829. This role was short-lived as he was elected superior general (on the fourth ballot) at the Order's 21st General Congregation later the same year.

The cornerstone of Roothaan's generalate was to revive central aspects of the Jesuits' enterprise, and to sustain links with the past in a much-changed religious and cultural landscape. From early in his generalate, there was a need to confront urgent internal problems: the end of the Maryland province's slave plantations is a notable example. Nonetheless, Roothaan was deeply committed to the cause of continuity. He oversaw a new edition of the *Spiritual Exercises* and (in 1832) a revision of the *Ratio studiorum*, and he laid great emphasis on the two central planks of earlier Jesuit activity: education and mission. During his tenure major Jesuit educational initiatives were launched, notably in the United States: these included Fordham in New York City, Holy Cross in Worcester, St. Joseph's in Philadelphia, and St. Louis University. He fostered the expansion of missionary work around the globe, notably in the United States, Canada, India, Australia, and China. Roothaan's missiological goals tied in with his broader quest for linkages between past and present. Missionaries in the American West, for example, were encouraged to read reports about the earlier missions in Paraguay; Roothaan believed that the continuation of the earlier "intellectual/scientific" evangelism in China was appropriate; in the revived Madurai mission field, he found natural allies in figures such as Joseph Bertrand, who were determined to sustain the spirit and goals of previous Indian missionary ventures.

Transnational correspondence had always been a hallmark of the Jesuit enterprise, and Roothaan recognized its continuing potential to foster Jesuit solidarity. His long letters on, among much else, tribulation, study, the Sacred Heart of Jesus, and devotion to Mary were circulated throughout the Jesuit fraternity around the globe. Roothaan's generalate also witnessed a series of banishments (from Spain in 1835, from Switzerland in 1847, for instance, and from a number of South American countries). At one stage he lamented that "there is no place in the world wherein we are not the target for the poisoned shafts of our enemies." Roothaan would experience this at first hand and, with his fellow Jesuits, was forced to flee Rome in disguise during the revolutionary turmoil of 1848. He returned in May 1849, and within a year all of the Society's Italian colleges and houses were back in operation. His death in 1853 followed several painful months stemming from heart disease.

Under Jan Roothaan the Society witnessed considerable numerical expansion. While never avoiding the manifold challenges presented by the nineteenth century, Roothaan saw sense in avoiding unnecessary controversy: his objections to the founding of *La Civiltà Cattolica* in 1850 are perhaps a symptom of this tendency. His fears proved to be prophetic, and the journal's editorial line provoked, by turns, praise and condemnation from those of both liberal and conservative tastes. Roothaan was by no means enamored of the cultural, intellectual, and social trends of the nineteenth century, and frequently said so: he found the American promotion of unfettered individual liberty deeply troubling, for instance. Roothaan sometimes struggled with the challenges facing a Jesuit superior general during the first half of the nineteenth century, but his crucial generalate can be credited with reestablishing the Society of Jesus as a dynamic, well-organized presence across the globe. He would also be remembered for his simple lifestyle.

See also Civiltà Cattolica; Rome; Superior General; Suppression

de Jonge Ludovicus, and Petrus Pirri, eds., *Opera Spiritualia: Ioannis Phil. Roothaan Societatis Jesu praepositi generalis XXI*. Rome: Typis Pontificiae Universitatis Gregorianae, 1936.

Lighthart, Cornelius J., *The Return of the Jesuits: The Life of Jan Philip Roothaan*. London: Shand Publications, 1978.

McKevitt, Gerald, *Brokers of Culture: Italian Jesuits in the American West 1848–1919*. Stanford, CA: Stanford University Press, 2007.

Sijkerman, Jan, "Roothaan and the First Novitiate in India of the Restored Jesuit Order." *Indian Church History Review* 9, 1 (1976), 23–54.

Jonathan Wright

Rougemont, François de, SJ (1624–1676)

François de Rougemont was born in Maastricht (now the Netherlands) on August 2, 1624. He entered the Society of Jesus at Mechelen in 1641. After the visit of Martino Martini (1614–61) to Leuven, he applied for the China mission. After his arrival in Macau in 1658, de Rougemont was assigned to the Jiangnan mission in the middle region of the country, which was the most flourishing mission with *c.* 50,000 Christians. They were organized in "congregations," which gathered together for prayer and instruction, even in the absence of a priest. De Rougemont was strongly involved in pastoral and missionary activities among these communities, which proved their operational significance during exile of the missionaries to Canton in 1665–71.

During his stay in Canton, de Rougemont participated in the "Canton Conference" (1668) held among representatives of the Jesuits, Dominicans, and Franciscans, dealing with missionary methods and questions about Chinese rites. In this context he wrote an essay on the need for an indigenous clergy. He also contributed to the first Latin translation of some of the major Confucian classics, published as *Confucius Sinarum philosophus* (Paris, 1687).

After the exile de Rougemont returned to Changshu from where he administered many Christian communities with the help of catechists. One of them was Li Wu (1632–1718), a famous painter who later became a Jesuit priest. A unique document left behind by de Rougemont is his *Account Book*, which covers the years 1674–76 and records, among others, his expenses during ten pastoral tours. This book constitutes a rare source of information on daily missionary life. At the same time, it abounds in information on the local Chinese economy. He died in Changshu on November 9, 1676.

See also China

Golvers, Noël, *François de Rougemont, SJ, Missionary in Ch'ang-shu (Chiang-nan): A Study of the Account Book (1674–1676) and the Elogium*. Leuven: Leuven University Press, 1999.

Nicolas Standaert, SJ

Rousselot, Pierre, SJ (1878–1915)

Pierre Rousselot was born on December 29, 1878, in Nantes, France, and died on April 25, 1915, in Eparges, France. He received licentiates in classical and modern languages from the Sorbonne in 1899, studied philosophy at the French Jesuit House of Studies, Jersey, England, from 1900 to 1903 and theology at the French Jesuit House of Studies, Hastings, England, from 1905 to 1909. He earned a Ph.D. at the Sorbonne in 1908. Rousselot entered the Jesuits in Canterbury in 1895 and was ordained a priest in 1908. He was a professor of dogmatic theology at the Institute Catholique, Paris, from 1909 to 1914. In that year he was mobilized and was killed in action in 1915.

Rousselot pursued a philosophy of knowledge, love, participation, and connaturality in the work of St. Thomas for his two Sorbonne theses: *L'intellectualisme de saint Thomas* (1908) and *Pour l'histoire du problème de l'amour au Moyen Âge* (1908). The first of the transcendental Thomists, Rousselot demonstrated that the "intellectualism" of St. Thomas was completely different from static rationalism and discursive reason. He showed that for Thomas, the highest form of knowledge was the preconceptual insight of the *intellectus*, an immediate grasp of the singular under the influence of love, the kind of knowledge exercised by God and the angels and also by humans in the Beatific Vision. Likewise, intelligence for Thomas is the synthesis of cognition and affection. His interpretation of Thomas significantly influenced Joseph Maréchal and Bernard Lonergan.

Rousselot applied this philosophy to the theology of faith in his essay, "Les yeux de la foi" (1910). The eye of faith is an act of insight by which a person, under the influence of love and connaturality, grasps a truth of faith.

Father Włodzimir Ledóchowski, the superior general of the Jesuits, issued a letter July 15, 1920, forbidding Rousselot's opinions to be taught or defended by Jesuits. Father General Jean-Baptiste Janssens later upheld the prohibitions on the basis of passages in Pius XII's encyclical *Humani generis* (1950) on the rational character of the credibility of the Christian faith. Since Vatican II, these prohibitions are no longer considered to be binding.

See also France; Philosophy; Theology

Susan K. Wood

Royackers, Martin, SJ (1959–2001)

Martin Royackers, SJ, Canadian missionary to Jamaica, pastor from 1994, was found murdered at the side door to St. Theresa's Church in Annotto Bay, Jamaica, on June 21, 2001. At the time of his murder, St. Mary's Cooperative, a farming cooperative partly sponsored by the Jesuits, acquired 60 acres of government land for poor farmers. It is believed that his murder may have been a reprisal directed toward the Jesuits for their support of the land acquisition initiated on behalf of the farmers. Royackers, a farmer since childhood, was a strong advocate for both the practical and the spiritual empowerment of the people. In an article on the evangelical importance of lay catechists, he said: "there are many churches with no priest who depend on lay leaders to be their pastors … Catechists are lay people who are at the frontlines of making the Gospel and the Church a part of people's ordinary lives." The people empowered Royackers to be a voice of critique of North Atlantic culture, and by extension ecclesial culture. Royackers argues, 1996: "We have lights and can no longer see stars. We listen to radios and can no longer hear one another. Technology is weaving a cocoon around us, and what will emerge?" Royackers anticipated the teachings of John Paul II's *Ecclesia in America* (*EA*; January 22, 1999) and Pope Francis's apostolic exhortation *Evangelii Gaudium* (*EG*; November 24, 2013) regarding how the in-breaking of the reign of God is inextricably linked to the good of all in the concrete "social order" of the world today (*EA*, #27 in *EG*, #182).

See also Jamaica; Martyrs, Ideal and History

Palmisano, Joseph, "Martin Royackers, SJ (1959–2001) and the Church in Annotto Bay, Jamaica: *Ecclesia in America*'s 'Reciprocal Solidarity' as an *Aggiornamento* Moment for Contemporary Missiology." *One in Christ* 45, 1 (July 2011), 111–41.
Royackers, Martin, "Lay Catechists Are in the Front Lines of the Church." *Canadian Messenger of the Sacred Heart* (July 2001), 10.

Joseph Palmisano, SJ

Rubens, Peter Paul

A leading Netherlandish painter of the seventeenth century, Peter Paul Rubens became the artist of choice for many religious reform orders, including the Society of Jesus. For the Jesuits, Rubens painted vivid and dramatic religious scenes in bright colors and bold perspectives, thus creating a new type of communicative and rhetorical image that captured the eyes and hearts of the congregation. Rubens's close affiliation with the Jesuit order started during his stay in Italy (1600–09). His patron Duke Vincenzo Gonzaga commissioned him to paint three paintings for the family's chapel in the Jesuit church in Mantua. In this early Jesuit commission (1605), Rubens juxtaposed two apparitions of the Trinity, the *Baptism of Christ* and the *Transfiguration* with a painting depicting members of the Gonzaga family adoring the Trinity. In 1604 Marcello Pallavicini, a Jesuit priest and member of a noble Genoese family, contracted Rubens to paint an altarpiece for the high altar of the newly built Genoese church of the Jesuits, St. Ambrogio. The altarpiece (1605) depicted the Circumcision, the ritual of the naming of Jesus, which was of particular importance to the Jesuits. Rubens engages the viewer through his use of primary colors and his emphasis on the melancholic attitude of the Virgin, who has turned her head away from the dramatic ritual.

Rubens's association with the Jesuits continued after his return to his native Antwerp. In 1609 he became a member of the Jesuit sodality of married men in Antwerp, and in that same year he supplied the organization with a painting of the *Annunciation*. In the second decade of the seventeenth century, he became involved with the decoration of the major Jesuit churches in Brussels, Neuburg an der Donau, and Antwerp. In Brussels, he painted two pendants of Ignatius of Loyola, the founder of the Order, and Francis Xavier, the Order's famous missionary to the East (1616), which were displayed on the pillars flanking the high altar. Almost immediately thereafter, he painted for the Jesuit church in Neuburg the Michelangelo-inspired *Great Last Judgment*, which was to be installed on the high altar, and the *Adoration of the Shepherds* and the *Descent of the Holy Spirit* intended for the two side altars.

Figure 59 Peter Paul Rubens: *The Miracles of Saint Ignatius Loyola*, 1617–18, oil on canvas. Kunsthistorisches Museum, Vienna. Photograph © Erich Lessing / Art Resource, New York

Rubens made his greatest contribution to the Jesuit church in Antwerp (now St. Carolus Borromeus). For this structure (1615–21), Rubens provided two monumental altarpieces of Ignatius and Francis Xavier, which were painted in advance of the Jesuits' canonization in 1622. For two of the side chapels, he supplied altarpieces of the *Assumption of the Virgin* and the *Flight into Egypt*. Rubens also designed an aedicula frame for the high altar, executed by Hans van Mildert, as well as a series of thirty-nine ceiling paintings, painted between 1620 and 1621, that were installed in the vaults of the side aisles and upper galleries (destroyed in 1718). Finally, he made two drawings for reliefs on the façade.

Rubens's large decorative program for the Antwerp church engaged the surrounding church environment and the spectator in new and dynamic ways. The altarpiece of Ignatius was illuminated by light from an oculus in the semi-dome above. The surrounding polychrome marble altar frame, which featured a white marble statue of the Virgin and Child rising through a broken pediment, further augmented the altarpiece's effect. Rubens's ceiling paintings, which combined scenes from the Old and New Testament with portrayals of the Church Fathers and early Christian female saints, transported the spectator to a heavenly realm through feats of foreshortening and daring illusionism.

Taken together, the church's highly ornamented exterior and interior acted as a type of epideictic rhetoric that was aimed at involving and persuading the spectator.

During the second decade of the seventeenth century, Rubens also participated in smaller projects for the Flemish members of the Society. In 1613 he designed illustrations and a frontispiece for François Aguilonius's book on optics, the *Opticorum libri sex*, and in the following years he provided title pages for books written by various Jesuit authors, including Carolus Scribani, Baltasar Cordier, Leonardus Lessius, Heribert Rosweyde, and Cornelis à Lapide. In 1617 he also drew a portrait of the famous missionary Nicolas Trigault, who had returned to Europe from China in 1614 to raise funds for the Chinese mission. Rubens's last major commission for the Flemish Jesuit province was an altarpiece of the *Martyrdom of Saint Livinus* intended for the Jesuit church in Ghent and executed in 1633.

See also Antwerp; Art Patronage; Baroque Art and Architecture

Göttler, Christine, "'Actio' in Peter Paul Rubens' Hochaltarbildern für die Jesuitenkirche in Antwerpen." In Joseph Imorde, Fritz Neumeyer, and Tristan Weddigen, eds., *Barocke Inszenierung*. Emsdetten, Zürich: Edition Imorde, 1999, pp. 10–31.
Knaap, Anna C., "Seeing in Sequence: Rubens's Ceiling Cycle for the Jesuit Church in Antwerp." *Netherlands Yearbook for History of Art / Nederlands Kunsthistorisch Jaarboek* 55 (2004), 154–95.
Martin, John Rupert, *The Ceiling Paintings for the Jesuit Church in Antwerp, Corpus Rubenianum Ludwig Burchard*. Pt. 1. London/New York: Phaidon, 1968.
Vlieghe, Hans, *Saints: Corpus Rubenianum Ludwig Burchard*. London/New York: Phaidon, 1972.

Anna C. Knaap

Rubio, José María, SJ, St. (1864–1929)

St. José María Rubio Peralta was born in the small town of Dalías (Almería) on July 22, 1864. He was a farmer's son and the oldest of thirteen children. At age 11, he began secondary school in Almería, where he entered the seminary a year later, in 1876. He studied the humanities and a year of philosophy before moving to the major seminary in Granada in 1879, where he studied philosophy, theology, and canon law. In 1886, he traveled to Madrid with the sponsor of his studies, Joaquín Torres Asensio, where he was ordained a diocesan priest in 1887. He felt called at this time to the Society of Jesus, but because of his responsibilities in caring for Asensio, an elderly priest, he could not yet fulfill this desire. He provided pastoral ministry instead as a parish priest in surrounding villages and slums. At the same time he was teaching Latin, metaphysics, and pastoral theology at the seminary in Madrid. In 1897 he finished a doctorate in canon law in Toledo.

In 1904 he made a pilgrimage to Rome and another pilgrimage to the Holy Land the year after. These seriously increased his interest in joining the Society of Jesus, which he did by entering the novitiate in 1906 in Granada. He made his tertianship at Manresa, and from there, he was sent to Madrid two years later. Once in the capital, he became popular as a preacher and confessor, growing rapidly in this popularity because of his support for social associations and schools in the slums and poor areas of the city.

After his death in Madrid on May 2, 1929, Archbishop Garay de Eijo described him as "Apostle of Madrid" in a pastoral letter in which he was praised for his exemplary behavior. Father Rubio was beatified by John Paul II in 1985 and canonized in Madrid by the same pontiff on May 4, 2003. His remains lie in the parish of Saint Francis Borja in Madrid. The well-known message of José María Rubio, "To do what God wants and to want what God does," perfectly sums up his manner of thinking and way of being.

See also Saints; Spain

Lamet, Pedro Miguel, *Como lámpara encendida: José María Rubio (1867–1929)*. Barcelona: Belacqva, 2003.

Inmaculada Fernández Arrillaga

Ruiz de Montoya, Antonio, SJ (1585–1652)

Founder and superior of the Paraguayan Reductions, Antonio Ruiz de Montoya was born in Lima, Peru, on June 13, 1585. Having lost both his father and his mother by 1593, he was entrusted to the Jesuit Royal College of San Martin in Lima. After completing the Spiritual Exercises at the Jesuit College of San Pablo, Ruiz de Montoya joined the Society of Jesus in 1606 and was sent to finish his studies in Santiago del Estero, present-day Argentina. In 1612 he was ordained and was sent to work among the Guaraní natives in the Paraguayan missions.

The missions were by then located in the area known as Guaira, which occupied roughly the territories of the present-day Brazilian state of Parana and the western portion of the state of São Paulo. Ruiz de Montoya founded thirteen missions or "reductions" – thus known because the natives were "reduced" or settled in Spanish-style towns. In order to convince the semi-nomadic Guaraní of settling in the new towns, Ruiz de Montoya and his Jesuit confrères taught them European agricultural techniques, gave them metal tools, and acted as physicians during the relatively frequent outbreaks of typhus and smallpox brought about by the Europeans. Ruiz de Montoya also organized the religious life of the reductions, establishing the frequency with which native neophytes had to confess and take communion, and founding in each reduction a sodality under the advocacy of the Virgin Mary.

The settlement of the Guaraní in fixed towns, however, made them an easy prey for the *bandeirantes*, slave-raiding parties from the Portuguese enclave of São Paulo. Ruiz de Montoya, who in 1620 had been elected superior of the Guaira Reductions, decided to organize a massive retreat in order to protect the natives from the attacks of the *bandeirantes*. In 1630, under Ruiz de Montoya's leadership, the Jesuits and approximately 12,000 Guaraní initiated a difficult journey to the south, toward today's Paraguay and the Argentine province of Misiones. In 1636 Ruiz de Montoya was elected superior of all the Paraguayan missions and procurator or proxy of Paraguay in Madrid. In that capacity, he traveled the following year to Spain in order to lobby for the manumission of the Guaraní sold in São Paulo (Portugal and its colonies were under Spanish control from 1580 to 1640).

In Madrid, Ruiz de Montoya published the first descriptions of the Guaraní language, on which he had been working since 1620: *Arte y vocabulario de la lengua guaraní* (Grammar and Vocabulary of the Guaraní Language, 1640) and the *Tesoro de la lengua guaraní* (Thesaurus of the Guarani Language, 1640). He also published a translation of the catechism into Guaraní (*Catecismo de la lengua guaraní*, 1639). While in Madrid, Ruiz de Montoya also published the first history of the Paraguayan Reductions, *La conquista espiritual del Paraguay, Uruguay y Tape* (*The Spiritual Conquest of Paraguay, Uruguay, and Tape*, 1639). In it, Ruiz de Montoya detailed the Jesuit efforts to evangelize the Guaraní in the reductions, emphasizing the opposition from native shamans and, particularly, the harm done to the missionary efforts by the *bandeirantes*. Ruiz de Montoya concluded the *Spiritual Conquest* with a reminder to the King of Spain of the dangers that might come by allowing the Portuguese to come too close to Peru. This warning was designed to help Ruiz de Montoya's main goal while in Madrid: to gain permission to arm the Guaraní reduction with firearms and thus be able to repel the attacks from São Paulo.

In 1640 King Philip IV, following a recommendation from the Council of Indies, signed a decree authorizing the Jesuits to form a Guaraní militia in order to defend the boundaries of the Spanish Empire against the Portuguese. In 1641 a group of Guaraní forces, led by the Jesuit lay brother Domingo de Torres, defeated a large Portuguese expedition in Mbororé, after which the *bandeirante* incursions became more and more scarce until they finally stopped at the beginning of the eighteenth century. Antonio Ruiz de Montoya returned to Lima to oversee at the Viceregal court the implementation of the royal decrees he had just obtained.

He died in Lima in 1652, leaving behind two unpublished works: a mystical work titled, *Sílex del divino amor* (Silex of the Divine Love), written in 1650 and published in 1991, and a defense of the use of Guaraní for evangelizing purposes, *Apología de la lengua guaraní* (Apology of the Guaraní Language), completed in 1651 and published in 1996.

See also González, Roque, SJ, St.; Paraguay Missions ("Reductions"); Peru

Lacouture, Jean, *Jesuits: A Multibiography*. Washington, DC: Counterpoint, 1995.
Rouillón, José Luis, *Antonio Ruiz de Montoya: Biografía*. Lima: Fondo Editorial Universidad Antonio Ruiz de Montoya, 2001.

                                                                                          Andrés Ignacio Prieto

Russia

The Society of Jesus has been present in Russia intermittently from the sixteenth century to the present. One of the periods of the most extensive work in Russia was precisely when the Society was suppressed in the rest of the world (1773–1814).

The first notable involvement of the Society in Russia was the mission of Antonio Possevino in 1581–82. Ivan IV ("Ivan the Terrible") sent a legate to Pope Gregory XIII seeking a mediator to negotiate a treaty with Poland and to unite the Christian powers against the Ottoman Empire – a successful mission politically, less so in terms of Church union.

The next mission of Jesuits to Russia involved the presence of a young Russian, who claimed to be Dmitrij, the son of Ivan IV. It is now clear that the young man was not who he claimed to be and is now known as False Dmitrij (Лжедмитрий in Russian). He arrived in Moscow in June 1605 with a Polish delegation, including two Jesuits. He was crowned czar and served until his assassination in May 1606.

From 1684 onwards there was a mission of Jesuits to serve the needs of the Catholics in Moscow. The Jesuits were expelled in 1689, but others came to Russia in 1698. Czar Peter the Great allowed the Jesuits to build a church and establish a school in the early 1700s. A small group also worked in St. Petersburg from 1713 to 1719, when all Jesuits were expelled from Russia.

In the 1772 Partition of Poland, 201 members of the Mazovian Jesuit province came under Russian rule. Czarina Catherine II, also known as Catherine the Great, refused to promulgate the papal brief of suppression, *Dominus ac Redemptor* (1773). From 1776 to 1780, the life of the Jesuits in White Russia improved with the acceptance of some Mazovian Jesuits there. Twenty-one priests were ordained, and a novitiate was opened in 1780. In 1782 the Jesuits in White Russia elected Stanisław Czerniewicz as vicar general. In 1801 Lithuanian Jesuit Franciszek Kareu was serving as vicar general when Pope Pius VII promulgated a decree recognizing the existence of the Society in Russia. The decree also directed that Kareu be given the title of superior general of the Society, even though his jurisdiction was still limited to Russia. The worldwide restoration of the Society in 1814 would give Tadeusz Brzozowski, then superior general in Russia, universal jurisdiction over the Society throughout the world.

During the reigns of Czarina Catherine II (1762–96) and of Czar Paul I (1796–1801), Jesuits in Russia had a very supportive government that favored their educational work and their contacts with western Europe.

From 1800 onward, the White Russian Jesuits undertook missions throughout Russia, even in Siberia. The college at Polotsk became a university in 1812. There were colleges in St. Petersburg, Daugavpils, Vitebsk, Mogilev, Mstsislaw, Orsha, and Romanov. The schools specialized particularly in sciences and foreign languages. In 1802 the White Russian Jesuits had 247 members, and by 1805, there were 333 members, of whom many were students of ex-Jesuits from France, Germany, Belgium, and the Netherlands.

The situation took a dramatic turn for the worse with the ascent of Czar Alexander I in 1801. He adopted a much more nationalistic line and was increasingly hostile to the Society. In 1820 the 348 Jesuits in Russia were expelled. From this expulsion until the Edict of Toleration in 1905, a few Jesuits entered the country in order to support Catholics in Russia. Their number and their activities increased until the Russian Revolution in 1917. After the revolution, a number of Jesuits continued to work especially among Polish Catholics in the western areas of the USSR.

From 1922 to 1924, a number of Jesuits came to Russia with a papal mission sent in response to an appeal for food, medicine, and clothing in the aftermath of the Civil War. Directed by American Jesuit Edmund Walsh, from an office in Moscow, the work lasted two years and nourished 35,000 people directly and furnished food and goods distributed by others to another 158,000.

Under the harsh Soviet repression, French Jesuit Michel d'Herbigny was sent to Russia in 1926 to establish a clandestine Catholic Church structure. Along the way he was ordained a bishop in secret by Eugenio Pacelli in Berlin (later Pope Pius XII) for the sake of ordaining future bishops within Russia.

For most of the rest of the twentieth century, single Jesuits worked clandestinely in Russia. Among the best known of these was the American Walter Ciszek (1904–84), who was active in Russia from 1940 to 1963, spending most of that time in Soviet prisons.

Shortly after the fall of Communism (1989), a "Russian Independent Region" of the Society was created. It has had a growing number of members (twenty-eight in 1992, forty-two in 1996, including Joseph Werth, Bishop of Novosibirsk). In Moscow Jesuits run the St. Thomas Institute of higher education, which teaches theology in a university system. The Iñigo Cultural and Spiritual Center in Novosibirsk organizes various courses and programs. In Moscow and Novosibirsk Jesuits do pastoral work in Catholic parishes. They also offer the *Spiritual Exercises* in retreat houses and elsewhere. The region has houses in Moscow, Novosibirsk, and Tomsk, as well as in Belarus, Kazakhstan, Kirghizstan, and Ukraine.

See also Catherine II ("the Great") of Russia; Ciszek, Walter, SJ; Suppression

Steven Hawkes-Teeples, SJ

Sacred Heart

The term "Sacred Heart" refers to both (1) the person of Jesus Christ, presented or considered under the form of his physical heart, and (2) devotion, both general and specific, to (1). From this perspective, Christ's heart, located at the center of his physical and spiritual life, represents the sum of his entire being, above all his universal, redemptive love for humanity.

Scriptural antecedents for the Sacred Heart thus include the entire covenant tradition, beginning with the friendship that God develops with Abraham and continuing through the Deuteronomic History in expressions of God's faithful love for wayward Israel. Christians see this tradition fulfilled in Jesus of Nazareth as the eternal word made flesh, from whose pierced side flow the sacramental blood and living waters of the Holy Spirit that bring believers into participation with the paschal mystery (John 7:37–39; 19:33–37). Likewise, on the human level, the Beloved Disciple reclines on the bosom (*kolpos*) of Jesus (John 13:23), who describes himself as rest-giving and "meek and humble of heart" (Matthew 11:28–29).

Devotion to the Sacred Heart developed through the patristic and medieval periods into the modern era, when the Society of Jesus took responsibility for its promotion at the direction of visitation nun Margaret Mary Alacoque (1647–90). Beginning in December 1673, Margaret Mary had been receiving visions of the Sacred Heart of Jesus at her convent in Paray-le-Monial, located in east-central France. In the first vision, which occurred on the feast of John the Evangelist (December 27, 1673), Margaret Mary experienced herself reposing on the breast of Jesus, who commissioned her to spread devotion to his heart. She reports that he granted her a sense of her own unworthiness and the grace of experiencing in her side an enduring, mystical pain that he would renew on the first Friday of each month. On one such occasion (June 1674), when his five wounds appeared as five suns, he revealed to her his pain at his unrequited love for humankind and asked her to make reparation, through mystical suffering, for their offenses.

In February 1675, French Jesuit Claude La Colombière (1641–82) arrived on assignment to Paray-le-Monial. Having met with Margaret Mary at the convent in early March, he effectively declared to her superior that he considered her visions authentic. Three months later, on or about June 16, during the octave of Corpus Christi, Margaret Mary had another revelation during which Jesus instructed that the Church establish a feast in honor of his heart for the Friday after the Solemnity of Corpus Christi and promised the grace of final repentance to all who received communion on nine consecutive First Fridays. Although his extant sermons make no mention of the Sacred Heart, presumably because the Church had not yet approved of the devotion for universal use, Claude's spiritual journal contains an Act of Consecration to the Sacred Heart, a primitive form of which he may have pronounced as early as 1675.

Claude later would serve (1679–81) as spiritual father of the Jesuit students in Lyon, where contact with Jean Croiset (1656–1738) and Joseph de Gallifet (1663–1749) inspired them to promote the devotion in France and Rome. After Claude's death, Margaret Mary wrote a letter to her superior, Marie-Françoise de Saumaise, in which she related a vision of July 2, 1688, wherein the Virgin Mary entrusted promulgation of the devotion to the Jesuit fathers. The Jesuits would work to this end through the foundation, beginning in 1690, of confraternities of the Sacred Heart, and through their publications, notably Croiset's *La dévotion au Sacré Cœur* (1691) and Gallifet's *De cultu Sacrosancti Cordis Dei* (1726) and *De l'excellence de la dévotion au Sacré Cœur* (1733). Their efforts would culminate, through much resistance from a variety of opponents, in the declaration whereby Pius IX extended the feast of the Sacred Heart to the universal Church (August 23, 1856). This sociopolitical dimension of the devotion appears especially in the efforts of Jesuit Henri Ramière (1821–84), whose foundations of both the Apostleship of Prayer (approved by Pius IX in 1854) and the *Messager du Cœur de Jésus* (1861) had an enormous and lasting effect on popular Catholicism through the twentieth century. Decree 46 of the 23rd General Congregation of the Society of Jesus (1883) reaffirmed the Society's commitment to the *munus suavissimum* ("most pleasant duty") of promoting the devotion, which the governance of the Society has reiterated even amid the transformation of popular devotions since Vatican II.

See also Apostleship of Prayer; Confraternities; La Colombière, Claude, SJ, St.

Bea, Augustin, Hugo Rahner, Henri Rondet, and Friedrich Schwendimann, eds., *Cor Jesu: Commentationes in litteras encyclicas Pii XII "Haurietis aquas."* Rome: Herder, 1959.
Darricau, Raymond, and Bernard Peyrous, eds., *Sainte Marguerite-Marie et le message de Paray-le-Monial*. Paris: Desclée de Brouwer, 1993.
Hamon, Auguste, *Histoire de la dévotion au Sacré Cœur*. 5 vols. Paris: Gabriel Beauchesne, 1923–39.

William P. O'Brien, SJ

Saint Louis Jesuits

The Saint Louis Jesuits are a group of Jesuit composers who modeled their composition in the folk style of Church music from the mid-1960s through the mid-1980s. The members of the group, Robert Dufford, SJ, John Foley, SJ, John Kavanaugh, SJ, Timothy Manion, SJ, Roc O'Connor, SJ, and Daniel Schutte, SJ, were Jesuit faculty and scholastics at St. Louis University, though some later left the Jesuits. They incorporated acoustic guitars in their music, creating melodies and rhythms to accompany scriptural and other religious texts sung in English, as one of the many musical responses to the reforms put forth by the Second Vatican Council.

Their earliest music was composed in 1964, and many of these songs were on the first album, *Neither Silver nor Gold*. The popularity of these songs, which have simple and singable melodies, made them quite useful for the Masses and liturgies on the campus. Because of the wide appeal of their music, copied by many before it was officially published, the group came to be identified as "The Saint Louis Jesuits."

Their second recording, *Earthen Vessels*, sold over 1 million albums, further establishing the songs within the repertoire of contemporary liturgical music. During the 1970s and 1980s their music was published by North American Liturgy Resources and is currently published by Oregon Catholic Press. Other recordings followed including, *A Dwelling Place* (1976), *Gentle Night* (1977), and *Lord of Light* (1980). They have had a profound and lasting influence on contemporary Church music. Their music has been printed in contemporary Episcopal, Lutheran, and Presbyterian hymnals. Their work has been translated into several languages, including Spanish and Vietnamese. During the 1980s the group formally disbanded as Schutte and Manion left the Society and continued to write and record as solo artists. They came back together and recorded a new album *Morning Light* (2005).

See also Music; Saint Louis University; United States of America

Gale, Michael, ed., *The St. Louis Jesuits: Thirty Years*. Portland: Oregon Catholic Press, 2006. Reviewed by Jeffrey Tucker, in *Sacred Music* 133, 3 (2006), 27–36.
McDermott, James, "Sing a New Song: Part 2. The St. Louis Jesuits: Earthen Vessels." *America*, May 30, 2005.

Charles Jurgensmeier, SJ

Saint Louis University

In 1818 Louis William DuBourg, the first bishop resident in Saint Louis, founded Saint Louis Academy. In 1823 he brought to Saint Louis as missionaries a group of ten Belgian Jesuits and gave them rural property near Saint Louis to establish a school for Native Americans. While the rural project did not succeed, the college in the city increasingly taxed the resources of the diocesan clergy faculty. At DuBourg's urging, the Jesuits assumed responsibility for the college. In 1829 it opened with Jesuit personnel in a new building at a city location donated for that purpose. The college quickly attracted both day and boarding students, 150 within the first several weeks.

The success under its first Jesuit president, Fr. Peter Verhaegen, a man of great vision and ability, was such that in 1832 he petitioned and was granted by the Missouri legislature a civil charter of incorporation as a university. This was the first such institution in all of the two-thirds of the United States west of the Mississippi River and also the first Jesuit educational institution in the United States specifically chartered as a university.

Verhaegen immediately began to organize educational programs beyond the undergraduate level. The year 1832 marked the beginning of the graduate school. A School of Divinity opened in 1834. In 1836 a medical faculty took form, and classes began in the School of Medicine in 1842. In 1843 a law school was established, but at the time it lasted only a few years. The University continued to flourish until the violently anti-Catholic Know-Nothing movement of the 1850s threatened the University as a whole, and in particular, the School of Medicine. The two institutions separated in 1855 as a way of assuring the continued existence of both of them. Then, with the coming of the Civil War, the University lost a large number of students who had originally come from states in the south of the country.

The late nineteenth and early twentieth centuries saw a significant expansion and development of the University and its academic programs. In 1888 the University moved to midtown Saint Louis, erected new quarters and built an imposing church that has functioned ever since as an archdiocesan parish, a university church, and a familiar landmark in the city. In 1889 the School of Philosophy and Letters was founded; the

School of Divinity, which had been closed since the time of the Civil War, reopened. In 1903 the University acquired a formerly proprietary medical college, which became the Saint Louis University School of Medicine. Some five years later the Law School again reopened, and in 1910 the School of Commerce and Finance was founded. In 1928 the School of Nursing was established, and a few years later, in 1933, the School of Social Work.

With the end of the World War II and the implementation of the "G.I. Bill," which made available to all veterans of that war the financial resources for a college education, the University enrollment vastly increased, now with a national outreach because of an increasingly large number of boarding students. Locally, it played a major role in the urban redevelopment of a central part of the city of Saint Louis. It turned its attention, too, to intellectual outreaches. Significant among them was that in 1950, with the permission of the Holy See, the University undertook a multi-year project to microfilm and make available to scholars many of the manuscript resources of the Vatican Library in Rome.

In 1967 the University, while continuing to maintain its Jesuit character and the sponsorship of the University by the Society of Jesus as a Jesuit work, entrusted its governance to a predominantly lay board of trustees, the first major Catholic educational institution in the world to do so. In subsequent years, almost all United States Catholic colleges and universities made a similar move.

As of the year 2015, the University enrolled more than 13,000 students, in excess of 8,500 undergraduates and 4,700 post baccalaureate students in nearly 100 undergraduate and 80 graduate programs. Almost 1,000 of these are international students. The faculty numbers more than 3,000. They are supported academically in their teaching and research by library holdings of more than 2 million volumes and access to some 45,000 electronic resources, and supported financially by a 1-billion-dollar endowment. They teach in the eleven colleges and schools of the University and on the Madrid campus in Spain: the College of Arts and Sciences; the College for Public Health and Social Justice; the Edward and Margaret Doisy College of Health Sciences; the John Cook School of Business; Parks College of Engineering, Aviation and Technology; the School for Professional Studies; the School of Law; the School of Medicine; the School of Nursing; the College of Education and Public Service; and the College of Philosophy and Letters.

See also AJCU (USA); Saint Louis Jesuits; United States of America; Universities, 1773–Present

John W. Padberg, SJ

St. Omers (Saint-Omer), English College

Informed by friends within England that the Elizabethan government planned new, more severe restrictions on the education of Catholics, Robert Persons secured an annual pension from King Philip II of Spain for a college at St. Omers (then in the Spanish Netherlands) in 1593. The college's foundation proved problematic in that it was an "ecclesiastical peculiar," an institution located within a geographical province but not totally under the jurisdiction of the provincial. For decades the Jesuit general tried to balance the authorities of the local provincial, of the rector, and of the superior (and later prefect and provincial) of the English mission, generally to the dissatisfaction of one party. Twice destroyed by fire (1684 and 1725), the college usually numbered about 25 Jesuits and 130 students, not a large student population by Jesuit standards but larger than any other English Catholic college. Many Jesuit vocations were produced within its halls.

The St. Omers Press published numerous spiritual and devotional works, often reflecting the Ignatian/Jesuit tradition, for use within England. In 1635 Muzio Vitelleschi entrusted the initial publication of the Society's complete Institute (16 octavo volumes) to the press. The college enjoyed a high reputation. Its dramatic tradition has been extensively studied by scholars; more recently the Academy has discovered its musical heritage.

Attempts to exempt the college from the Society's expulsion from France in 1762 (Saint-Omers passed to the French Crown in 1677) failed, possibly because of machinations of English secular clergy. The college migrated to Bruges, and with the universal Suppression of the Society in 1773, it moved to Liège where it merged with the former English Jesuit theologate to become the English Academy. The Academy fled to Stonyhurst in 1794 to escape the armies of the French Revolution.

See also Persons, Robert, SJ; Stonyhurt; United Kingdom

Chadwick, Hubert, *St Omers to Stonyhurst: A History of Two Centuries*. London: Burns and Oates, 1962.
Whitehead, Maurice, *English Jesuit Education: Expulsion, Suppression, Survival and Restoration, 1762–1803*. Farnham: Ashgate, 2013.

Thomas McCoog, SJ

Saints

The saints of the Society of Jesus number fifty-four, including both priests and brothers, and they come from all the continents of the world. The majority of them were also martyrs.

Beginning with Africa, Jacques Berthieu (1838–96) was a Jesuit who served as a missionary priest and martyr in Ambiatibe, Madagascar.

In North America, there were Jesuit martyrs in Canada: John de Brébeuf (1593–1649), Anthony Daniel (1601–48), Charles Garnier (1606–49), Gabriel Lalemant (1610–49), and Noël Chabanel (1613–1649), all priests. In what is now the United States, Isaac Jogues (1607–46), a priest, and René Goupil (1608–42), and John de La Lande (c. 1627–46), both brothers, were also martyrs. In South America, four countries produced saints: in Brazil, José de Anchieta (1534–97) was known as "The Apostle of Brazil"; in Chile, Alberto Hurtado Cruchaga (1901–52) was a leader in the social apostolate; in Colombia, Peter Claver (1580–1654) provided pastoral care to black slaves, baptizing over 300,000; in Paraguay, Juan del Castillo (1596–1628), Roch Gonzáles de Santa Cruz (1576–1628), and Alphonsus Rodriguez (1598–1628), all priests, gave their lives defending the native peoples in the River Plate.

In Asia, there were a host of Jesuit martyrs and saints. In China, Léon-Ignatius Mangin (1857–1900), and his three Jesuit companions, Modeste Andlauer (1847–1900), Paul Denn (1847–1900), and Rémy Isoré (1852–1900), stand out as French priests and martyrs who shed their blood for their faith during the Boxer Rebellion. In India, there was the preeminent Francis Xavier (1506–52), a priest and a co-founder of the Jesuits, and later John de Brito (1647–93), a priest and a martyr. In Japan, Paul Miki (1564–97) and John Soan de Goto (1578–97), both scholastics, and Vincent Kaun (1579–1626), a Korean noble, and James Kisai (1533–97), both brothers, were among the Jesuit martyrs who labored on behalf of the Gospel in Nagasaki. In Korea itself, there were the martyrs Paul Chong Hasang (c. 1794–1839), and Andrew Kim Taegon (1821–46), who were priests associated with the Jesuits. And in Vietnam, there was Andrew Dung-Lac (1795–1839), a diocesan priest; he and his 116 companions were not Jesuits but products of the Jesuit mission.

In Europe, Jesuit saints were also many. In Belgium, John Berchmans (1599–1621) became a model for young Jesuit scholastics. In Czechoslovakia, Stephan Pongrácz (1582–1619) and Melchior Grodziecki (1584–1619) were martyred priests at Košice during the religious wars. In England, there were Edmund Arrowsmith (1585–1628), Edmund Campion (1540–81), Robert Southwell (1561–95), and companions like Alexander Briant (1556–81) and Thomas Garnet (1575–1608). Henry Morse (1595–1645) and Henry Walpole (1558–95), both priests, and Nicholas Owen (c. 1550–1606), a brother, all suffered martyrdom. In France, there were John Francis Regis (1597–1640) and Claude de la Colombière (1641–82), Jesuit priests who were also preachers and confessors. In Germany, Peter Canisius (1521–97), a priest, was indefatigable in his apostolic labors. In Italy, there was of course Ignatius Loyola (1491–1556), priest and founder of the Society of Jesus. Apart from Aloysius Gonzaga (1568–91), a scholastic, the other Italian Jesuit saints were priests: Robert Bellarmine (1542–1621), who also became a bishop and cardinal, Bernardino Realino (1530–1616), Francis de Geronimo (1642–1716), and Joseph Pignatelli (1737–1811). In Poland, there was Stanislaus Kostka (1550–68), a young, devout novice, followed by Andrew Bobola (1591–1657), a courageous priest and martyr. In Savoy, Peter Faber (1506–46), co-founder of the Jesuits, was the first Jesuit priest canonized by the first Jesuit pope. In Scotland, John Ogilvie (1579–1615), a priest, was martyred for his unwillingness to deny the spiritual primacy of the papacy. In Spain, the canonized include Francis Borja (1510–72), also a priest, Alphonsus Rodriguez (1533–1617), a brother, and Joseph Mary Rubio (1864–1929), a priest known as "The Apostle of Madrid." And in Wales, David Lewis (1616–79) and Philip Evans (1645–1679), priests, were also martyrs.

See also Blesseds; Martyrs, Ideal and History

del Rio, Jorge Delpiano, and Victor Gana Edwards, *Testigos de Santidad en la Compañia de Jesus.* Santiago, Chile: Manuel Salas, 2008.
Rochford, Tom, ed. *The Complete List of Jesuit Saints and Blesseds.* Rome: The Jesuit Curia, 2016.
Tylenda, Joseph N., *Jesuit Saints and Martyrs.* 2nd edn. Chicago, IL: Loyola University Press, 1998.

Vincent A. Lapomarda, SJ

Salmerón, Alfonso, SJ (1515–1585)

Alfonso Salmerón was born in Toledo, Spain, on September 8, 1515. His parents, Maria and Alfonso, provided him with a superb education in Toledo and the University of Alcalá. During his studies in the latter, he befriended the older Diego Laínez, who encouraged Salmerón to join him for further studies in Paris. The two Spaniards arrived in 1533 and soon entered the small band of companions surrounding the charismatic figure of Ignatius of Loyola. Salmerón became one of the founders of the Society of

Jesus, taking part in its early formation and contributing to its juridical establishment. His later missions would include an arduous journey to Ireland as a papal representative (1542), as well as preaching and teaching in Austria, Germany, Poland, the Netherlands, and Italy. He died in Naples on February 13, 1585, one of the last witnesses of the burgeoning Society's humble beginnings.

Salmerón stands out from among his early companions in three ways. First, his stature as a theologian made him a highly sought adviser during the tumultuous debates of the Reformation period. In particular, he participated in all three sessions of the Council of Trent (1545–63) as an adviser and preacher. Second, he contributed to the governance of the Society through his work on the composition of the *Constitutions*, his leadership as a provincial and vicar general, and his participation in General Congregations 1–4. Finally, his greatest legacy remains his sixteen-volume commentary on the New Testament.

See also Laínez, Diego, SJ; Loyola, Ignatius, SJ, St.; Spain

Bangert, William, *Claude Jay and Alfonso Salmerón*. Chicago, IL: Loyola University Press, 1985.
Willis, John D., "A Case Study in Early Jesuit Scholarship: Alfonso Salmerón, SJ, and the Study of Sacred Scripture". In Christopher Chapple, ed., *The Jesuit Tradition in Education and Missions: A 450-Year Perspective*. Scranton, PA: Scranton University Press, 1993, pp. 52–80.

John Gavin, SJ

Sanata Dharma University

Sanata Dharma University (known as Universitas Sanata Dharma in Indonesia) is a Catholic and Jesuit university, located in the town of Yogyakarta, Indonesia. In 1955 the University began as Sanata Dharma Higher Education Institute for Teacher Training. It was founded as a result of collaboration between the Congregation for the Propagation of the Faith in Rome and the superior of the Jesuit mission in Indonesia. Father Nicolaus Driyarkara, SJ, a native Indonesian Jesuit, was the institute's first president.

In 1958 the institute was extended into Sanata Dharma Faculty of Teacher Training and Education. In 1965 it was upgraded into a teacher training and education institute called Sanata Dharma Institute of Teacher Training and Education (known nationally as "IKIP Sanata Dharma"). Finally, in 1993 it was developed into a full university, called Sanata Dharma University. The term *sanata dharma*, which originates from Sanskrit, means "true dedication" or "real service." Traditionally, the University has been led by Jesuit presidents, but from 1988 to 1993 the president was a layperson, and this is also the case in 2014–18.

Today Sanata Dharma University is a thriving higher learning educational institution with nearly 11,000 students, 42,000 alumni, 700 faculty and staff, and five campuses located in different parts of the town. Its fields of study stretch from technology to theology. Despite its Catholic identity, students of the University have different religious backgrounds, although the majority of them are Catholic. Most of the students come from Java, but almost every province of Indonesia is represented in the student body.

The University is an active member of Indonesia's Association of Catholic Higher Education (APTIK) and Association of Christian Universities and Colleges in Asia (ACUCA), Association of Southeast & East Asian Catholic Colleges & Universities

(ASEACCU) and Association of Jesuit Colleges & Universities-Asia Pacific (AJCU-AP). It was officially named as one of Indonesia's fifty most promising universities. It maintains close collaboration with Jesuit colleges and universities worldwide.

See also Indonesia; Universities, 1773–Present

Iskarna, Tatang, ed., *The Sanata Dharma University Prospectus*. Yogyakarta, Indonesia: Public Relations of Sanata Dharma University, 2004.

Baskara T. Wardaya, SJ

Santa Clara University

"I think we ought not to show ourselves indifferent" to a place "that will not fail to offer considerable advantages." With those words the Jesuit missionary Michele Accolti lobbied superiors in Rome to launch an educational ministry in Gold Rush California. Although Superior General Jan Roothaan had chided American Jesuits for expanding too rapidly, Accolti's proposal was accepted. In 1851 an all-male boarding college was opened at the former Franciscan mission of Santa Clara. Today's Santa Clara University is California's oldest institution of higher learning.

The school typified the Society's early educational ministry in the United States. Santa Clara, like many Jesuit colleges, benefited from unrest in Europe that drove clergy from their homelands after 1848. Jesuits banished from northern Italy during the Risorgimento adopted the American West Coast as a mission field in 1854, thus guaranteeing a flow of teachers to California's pioneer college. Planted in a populated urban frontier with few educational facilities, Santa Clara College drew an ethnically diverse student body. The cultural ambivalence of the Italian Jesuits was an asset because it enabled them to work effectively among Hispanic, European, and Anglo cultures and to build bridges between them. By 1868 students of Hispanic origin constituted 25 percent of the school's enrollment of 216 students. The College actively recruited Spanish-speaking pupils by publishing a Spanish-language edition of its bulletin.

The College embraced both Italian and American educational traditions. Transplanted school masters championed training in Latin and Greek in the New World just as they had in the Old. Attempts to impose a classical education met with mixed results on the frontier, however. "Oh what a waste of time are Latin and Greek," a Jesuit lamented in 1866, "for so many students that I now see working for a living – as grocer, butcher, and who knows what else!" Commercial and scientific training were more popular. Mirroring student interest and the Italians' own training, the California school offered more instruction in the sciences than did many Jesuit institutions in the east. To make its curriculum relevant to western needs, Santa Clara taught assaying and chemical analysis. The apex of all study was rhetoric. Masterful eloquence meant not merely easy, elegant communication, but the ability to harmonize virtue and learning. The school promoted spiritual values and moral training through a network of devotional symbols suffusing every aspect of campus life. Religious holidays abounded while Marian sodalities promoted piety and good example. Discipline was strict, co-founder Accolti boasted, but "of course not so stringent as that enforced at West Point."

As Italian supervision of operations in California declined at century's end, an ascendant American-born faculty adopted more mainstream curriculum and policies. With the waning popularity of Lain and Greek, other subjects filled the vacuum, especially theology and philosophy. Once a capstone in the senior year, philosophy was now distributed over four undergraduate years as the distinguishing feature of a Santa Clara education. Theology, formerly imparted by devotional practice and catechetical instruction, advanced to a more prominent academic place. In 1912 the inauguration of graduate and professional divisions prompted the college to assume a new title as Santa Clara University. Once confined to a small Catholic milieu, the institution sought greater public recognition through fund-raising and intercollegiate athletics. No force was as powerful in reshaping the educational landscape as accrediting associations that upgraded curricula and faculty.

World War II accelerated still greater conformity with other US colleges and universities. Enrollments, which first broke the 1,000 mark in 1947, swelled to 5,000 twenty years later in response to California's postwar growth. Curricular expansion meant that women entered Santa Clara's classrooms, first as wartime students in professional programs, and then as undergraduates in 1961. As the institution grew in size and complexity, it relied more than ever on a non-clerical professorate. In response to the Second Vatican Council and upheavals in American society in the 1960s, secularization advanced ever more swiftly. Required courses in philosophy and theology were reduced to accommodate trends in American higher education and make way for more electives. Mirroring a shift in contemporary Catholic higher education, Santa Clara became more secular in governance as well as in curricula. In 1968 a board of trustees on which laypersons constituted the majority assumed ownership and control. Vigorous fund-raising led by board chair Benjamin H. Swig and Jesuit president Patrick A. Donohoe paved the way for major capital improvements. As scholarly achievement and professionalism took precedence over Catholic distinctiveness, critics began to ask, "Is Santa Clara still Catholic?" In 1995 the University moved toward a new self-definition by educating for faith and justice in accord with recent reorientations of the Society of Jesus. Enrolling about 5,250 undergraduates and 3,269 graduate students in 2014, the institution continued to profess a dedication to Catholic education in the Jesuit tradition.

See also AJCU (USA); United States of America; Universities, 1773–Present; University of San Francisco (USF)

McKevitt, Gerald, *The University of Santa Clara: A History, 1851–1977.* Stanford, CA: Stanford University Press, 1979.

Gerald McKevitt, SJ

Sant'Ignazio, Rome

The Jesuits' second major church in Rome, dedicated to the Order's founder was built between 1626 and 1650, initially under the patronage of the papal nephew, Cardinal Ludovico Ludovisi (1595–1632), following the canonization of Ignatius in 1622. It formed part of the Collegio Romano, replacing the small Church of Santa Maria Annunziata. The relationship between the patron and the Jesuits was evidently fraught. The principal architect, imposed by the Order, seems to have been the Jesuit architect and mathematician, Orazio Grassi (1583–1654), although Carlo Maderno (1556–1629) had some input, and Domenichino, supported by Ludovisi, and Borromini also produced designs. The final plan was closely based on that for the Church of Il Gesù, Rome, with three interconnecting side-chapels on either side of a wide nave.

Figure 60 View of interior with frescoes by Andrea Pozzo, Church of Sant'Ignazio, Rome, 17th century. Photograph Alison Fleming

Following the death of Ludovisi in 1632, the Jesuits struggled to raise funds for the decoration of the new church and initially had one of their members, the indifferent painter Pierre de Lattre, decorate some of the altars and the sacristy. Despite the Order's relative poverty, the interior was richly decorated with polychrome marble and stucco. The sculptor Alessandro Algardi (1598–1654) provided figures of *Religion* and *Magnificence* for the entrance wall in 1650, as well as a frieze of putti around the nave's cornice.

The most important decoration in the church was carried out by another Jesuit artist, Andrea Pozzo (1642–1709), who worked there between 1685 and 1698. He painted the high altar chapel with scenes from the life of St. Ignatius: *Ignatius's Vision at La Storta*, flanked by *Ignatius sending Francis Xavier to the Indies*, and *Ignatius welcoming Francisco Borgia into the Company of Jesus*. In the apse above he frescoed *Saint Ignatius in Glory*. Pozzo was a specialist in perspective, and his skills were put to good use in the frescoed decoration of the nave vault. In a remarkable demonstration of illusionistic *quadratura*, he painted St. Ignatius welcomed into Heaven with other saints, including Aloysius Gonzaga and Stanislaus Kostka. The vault also represents an allegory of the Jesuits' missions with groups of figures standing for the continents, which freely tumble over the fictive architecture. The ceiling takes as its starting point G. B. Gaulli's nave decorations in the Gesù but is even more elaborate.

The Jesuits could not afford to build a dome for the church, and Pozzo's illusionistic skills were required once more. On a huge canvas he painted what appears to be an entirely convincing view into a real dome, when seen from the correct viewing point. He was also responsible for the pendentives of the "dome," frescoed with Old Testament subjects: David, Samson, Judith, and Jael.

The right transept contains the lavish funeral monument to St. Aloysius Gonzaga, who had studied at the Collegio Romano. This monument was commissioned by Prince Scipione Lancellotti. Designed by Pozzo, it has a marble relief showing the saint in glory, by Pierre Legros (1666–1719), a follower of Bernini, which is flanked by monumental pairs of green marble solomonic columns, and allegorical figures of *Mortification* and *Purity*, as well as two standing angels by Bernardino Ludovisi (1713–49). Legros was simultaneously working on the tomb of Ignatius in the left transept of the Gesù. Opposite the Gonzaga monument, an equally sumptuous altar was dedicated to the Annunciation and St. John Berchmans. It contains a corresponding structure designed by Pozzo, a marble altarpiece by Filippo Valle (1698–1770), and figures by Pietro Bracci (1700–73).

A key figure behind the lavish nature of the decorations at the Gesù and Sant'Andrea al Quirinale, as well as at Sant'Ignazio was the general of the Order between 1664 and 1681, Gian Paolo Oliva, as Francis Haskell demonstrated. By the early eighteenth century, Oliva's ideas had been put into practice on a grand scale at Sant'Ignazio.

See also Baroque Art and Architecture; Gesù, Rome; Grassi, Orazio, SJ; Oliva, Gian Paolo, SJ; Pozzo, Andrea, SJ; Roman College

Bösel, Richard, *Jesuitenarchitektur in Italien, 1540–1773*. Vol. I. Vienna: Verlag der Österreichischen Akademie der Wissenschaften, 1985, pp. 191–200.

Bösel Richard, and Lydia Salviucci Insolera, eds., *Mirabili Disinganni: Andrea Pozzo (Trento 1642–Vienna 1709). Pittore e architetto gesuita*. Rome: Artemide, 2010, pp. 119–35.

Carlucci, Zaccaria, *La chiesa di S. Ignazio di Loyola in Roma*. Rome: Chiesa di Sa. Ignazio, 1995.

Haskell, Francis, "The Role of Patrons: Baroque Style Changes." In Irma Jaffé and Rudolph Wittkower, eds., *Baroque Art: The Jesuit Contribution*. New York: Fordham University Press, 1972, pp. 51–62.

Levy, Evonne, "'A Noble Medley and Concert of Materials and Artifice': Jesuit Church Interiors in Rome, 1567–1700." In Thomas M. Lucas, ed., *Saint, Site and Sacred Strategy: Ignatius, Rome and Jesuit Urbanism*. Vatican: Biblioteca Apostolica Vaticana, 1990, pp. 51–56.

Clare Robertson

Scandals

The *Universal Catechism of the Catholic Church* (CCC) defines a scandal as "an attitude or behavior which leads another to do evil" and which "takes on a particular gravity by reason of the authority of those who cause it or the weakness of those who are scandalized" (CCC, ##2284–85). Based upon Jesus's warning in the Gospel of Matthew (18:6): "whoever causes one of these little ones who believe in me to sin, it would be better for them to have a great millstone fastened round their neck and so to be drowned in the depths of the sea," the *Catechism* further observes that "Scandal is grave when given by those who by nature or office are obliged to teach and educate others."

During its almost 500-year history, the Society of Jesus, as individual members and in their exercise of administrative policy, has not been exempt from giving scandal. Although what constitutes "scandal" often lies in the eye of the beholder, and may even shift meaning from one historical period or cultural location to another, generally scandalous behavior or practices involve an abuse of trust – most often seen in financial mismanagement, sexual impropriety, or political despotism.

In 1731 Catherine Cadière, a young French woman accused her Jesuit spiritual director, Jean-Baptiste Girard, of using witchcraft to seduce her and procure an abortion for her subsequent pregnancy. Appearing before the Parlement of Aix-en-Provence, Girard countered that Catherine was a disturbed young woman, prone to hysterics, who used her own menstrual blood in order to fake reception of the wounds of Christ. The trial ended in a deadlock with twelve members voting for Girard to be burnt alive and twelve voting for Catherine to be hanged. In the end, Catherine was sent home to her mother and Jean-Baptiste handed over to ecclesiastical authorities. He died two years later.

The scandal continued to be a national obsession, however, with vitriolic pamphlets, erotic illustrations, bawdy songs and doggerel that contributed to the sordid myth of the "wanton Jesuit." The story of Father Girard would spread across Europe contributing to anti-Jesuit polemic that already had been stirred up in 1613 by the *Monita secreta* which detailed the "secret rubrics" by which Jesuits could talk newly widowed wealthy women into donating their inheritance to the Society among other secret practices. What at first blush appeared as a local sex scandal would end up becoming a microcosm for the larger political and ecclesiastical threat that the Jesuits represented to their foes, like the Jansenists, who were already seething from the imposition of the papal bull *Unigenitus*.

Another example of Jesuit scandal is "the tragic and disgraceful affair" of 1838 concerning the selling of 272 slaves owned by the Maryland Jesuits by the former president of Georgetown, Thomas Mulledy. The Jesuit superior general had approved the sale of the slaves two years earlier, provided that (1) their religious needs be met; (2) that families not be separated; and (3) that the money from the sale be invested to support the education of Jesuits. Mulledy, however, now as provincial superior, sold all the slaves to Louisiana planters for $115,000. He subsequently loaned $25,000 of the profits to Georgetown and, accompanied by local sheriffs, "swept unannounced through the province's four plantations," and had the slaves "dragged off by force" to be shipped to the Deep South (Curran, *Bicentennial History*). Catholics and Protestants alike were scandalized and Jesuits themselves complained about the sale. In the end, Mulledy resigned as provincial and was sent to France. His exile was short-lived, however, when in 1843 he was appointed president of the College of the Holy Cross. In the second decade of the twenty-first century, student and faculty protests set off in the wake of the US "Black Lives Matter" movement were successful in bringing Georgetown administrators to rename university buildings named after Mulledy and William McSherry (who had sold some of the Jesuits' slaves before Mulledy) (*The Washington Post*, November 15, 2015).

In 1862 the famous Jesuit Neo-Thomist, Joseph Kleutgen, SJ, was condemned by the Holy Office of the Inquisition for promoting "false mystics" and for violating "the seal of the confessional." Kleutgen, along with Giuseppe Leziroli, SJ, served as extraordinary confessor to the Franciscan convent of Sant'Ambrogio. Both Jesuits were accused and convicted of violating the cloister and of engaging in sexual relationships with one of the nuns, Maria Luisa Ridolfi. Kleutgen, the close confidant of Pope Pius IX and later reputed author of Vatican I's "Decree on Papal Infallibility," as well as a major drafter of its two constitutions, was sentenced to five years of imprisonment for "formal heresy" (Wolf, *The Nuns*, 351). However, this penalty was later reduced to just two years, one of which was spent in a Jesuit retreat in the lovely Alban Hills outside of Rome.

This extremely sordid affair, which also involved the attempted poisoning of the widowed German princess Katharina von Hohenzollern, came to light only when the Archives of the Holy Office were opened by John Paul II in 1998 and Münster Church historian Hubert Wolff stumbled upon it in his research. In what was perhaps a harbinger of the way the Jesuit sex abuse scandals of the early twenty-first century would be handled by ecclesiastical superiors, one of Kleutgen's biographers refers to his temporary banishment as "an unfortunate incident," one which clearly did not diminish his reputation, as evidenced by his subsequent appointment to curial office and as *peritus* to the First Vatican Council (Finkenzeller, "Joseph Kleutgen," 323).

See also France; Georgetown University; Kleutgen, Joseph SJ; Sexual Abuse by Jesuits

Choudhury, Mita, *The Wanton Jesuit and the Wayward Saint: A Tale of Sex, Religion, and Politics in Eighteenth-Century France*. University Park, PA: Pennsylvania State University Press, 2015.

Curran, Robert Emmet, *The Bicentennial History of Georgetown University: From Academy to University, 1789–1889*. Vol. I. Washington, DC: Georgetown University Press, 1993.

Finkenzeller, Josef, "Joseph Kleutgen (1811–1833)." In Heinrich Fries and George Schwaiger, eds., *Katholische Theologen Deutschlands im 19. Jahrhundert*. Munich: Kosel Verlag, 1975, pp. 318–34.

Murphy, Thomas, *Jesuit Slaveholding in Maryland, 1717–1838*. New York: Routledge, 2001.

Wolf, Hubert, *The Nuns of Sant'Ambrogio: The True Story of a Convent in Scandal*. Trans. Ruth Martin. New York: Alfred A. Knopf, 2015.

Mary Ann Hinsdale, IHM

Scandinavia

The Protestant Reformation was a gradual process in Scandinavia, but in 1536 both Denmark-Norway and Sweden made the break with Rome official and unilateral. Jesuits seem to have begun to work clandestinely in the North shortly thereafter. In the 1560s two Norwegians studying in Copenhagen, Rikard Pedersson and Laurentius Nicolai Norvegus, entered the Society at Louvain. In 1568, when the Catholic-sympathetic John III and his Polish queen ascended to the throne of Sweden, Norvegus was sent there posing as a Lutheran clergyman. The King took a liking to him and made him founding rector of the Collegium Regium Stockholmense, the new (Lutheran) theological faculty at the University of Stockholm. At the university he was able to make a number of converts and send them to Rome for further study. This enterprise came to an abrupt end in 1579, when Antonio Possevino, SJ, the papal emissary, ordered Norvegus and his Jesuit confrères to reveal themselves in hopes of precipitating the King's conversion. Instead, they were banished. Possevino's next project was the founding of papal seminaries, staffed by Jesuits, at Prague, Graz, Braunsberg, Olomouc, Vilna, and Dorpat, as well as the Collegium Germanicum in Rome for the education of expatriate Scandinavian Catholics.

In the seventeenth century, Jesuits were increasingly permitted to work in Scandinavia, especially in Denmark, as chaplains to diplomats and mercenary soldiers from Catholic countries, though they were forbidden to associate with local citizens. Two Danes, Theodor Atsche (1652–92) and Johannes Ring (1674–1753) are known to have entered the Society during this period. In 1686 King Christian V granted the Jesuit military chaplains permission to establish a church in Fredericia, the first post-Reformation Catholic church in Denmark. Jesuits maintained the mission in Fredericia until the Suppression of the Society, when it was entrusted to secular priests from Germany. After the restoration, Jesuits continued to be active as diplomatic and military chaplains in Copenhagen and Fredericia. When the Danish Constitution of 1849 granted freedom of religion, the German Jesuits began to investigate possibilities for missionary work there. In 1873 they opened the Sankt Andreaskolleg at Ordrup, a suburb of Copenhagen. This was a boarding school for German boys, made necessary by the closing of Catholic schools in Germany as a part of Bismarck's *Kulturkampf*. Sankt Andreaskolleg closed in 1920, but its chapel became a parish church and was manned by Jesuits until 1953. In the 1880s the German Jesuits opened parishes and grammar schools for Danish students in Copenhagen and Århus, and in 1950 a Danish gymnasium, the only Catholic secondary school in Scandinavia, was founded in Copenhagen. Niels Steensens Gymnasium was from the beginning coeducational, the first Jesuit school to admit girls. A number of alumni of the schools entered the Society, including Hans L. Martensen, Bishop of Copenhagen (1965–95). In the decades following World War II, the German Jesuits in Denmark were joined by Jesuits from Holland, England, Mexico, Italy, and the United States. The beginning of the twenty-first century saw Jesuit apostolates in Denmark much diminished: they are now limited to Niels Steensens Gymnasium and the parish and grammar school in Århus. The German Jesuits have withdrawn and Denmark is now a mission of the Polish provinces of the Society.

German Jesuits returned to Sweden in 1879 to take charge of the Church of St. Eugenia, founded in 1837 and the only Catholic church in Stockholm. They subsequently took on pastoral work in Göteborg, Gävle, and Norrköpping. In 1936 a Jesuit house was established in the university town of Uppsala. This community became a flourishing intellectual center and the home of the journal *Signum*. In 2001 the Newmaninstitutet was founded there as the sole Catholic institution of higher education in Scandinavia and the first since the Reformation. Granting baccalaureate degrees in philosophy and theology, the college also serves as the seminary for the Roman Catholic Diocese of Stockholm. Sweden continues to be a mission of the German province of the Society.

In Norway, the Constitution of 1814 denied Jesuits entry to the country, and the "Jesuit paragraph" was not amended until 1956, after a heated parliamentary debate provoked by an invitation extended to Heinrich Roos, SJ, of the University of Copenhagen, to lecture at the University of Oslo. It was this same "Jesuit paragraph" that prevented Norway from signing the United Nations Declaration of Human Rights ("News, Notes, & Texts," p. 19). In 1960 Hungarian Jesuits came to Norway and remained until the 1980s to minister to refugees from the Hungarian Revolution.

See also Christina of Sweden; German-Speaking Lands; Poland; Possevino, Antonio, SJ

Garstein, Oskar, *Rome and the Counter-Reformation in Scandinavia*. 3 vols. Vols. I–II. Oslo: Universitetsforlaget, 1963, 1980; Vol. III. Leiden: Brill, 1992.

Holzapfel, Helmut, *Unter nordischen fahnen*. Paderborn: Bonifatiusverein, 1954.

"News, Notes, & Texts." *The Tablet*. December 10, 1955, p. 19.

Schatz, Klaus, *Geschichte der deutschen Jesuiten (1814–1983)*. 4 vols. Münster: Aschendorff Verlag, 2013.

Martin Chase, SJ

Schall von Bell, Johann Adam, SJ (1592–1666)

Schall was born in Cologne, Germany, on May 1, 1592. After his early studies, he went to Rome to study for the priesthood at the German College and entered the Society of Jesus in 1611. He was among the Jesuits who set sail for China with Nicolas Trigault (1577–1628) in 1618, when the latter returned to China. In 1629, after a failure of official astronomers to accurately predict an eclipse, a proposal by the Chinese Christian Xu Guangqi (1562–1633) to put the Jesuits to work on the calendar reform was accepted, and Xu was given charge of establishing a new Calendar Office for that purpose. Johann Schall von Bell, Johann Terrenz Schreck (1576–1630), and Giacomo Rho (1592–1638), with the help of some Chinese specialists, began compiling an astronomical compendium. The result of this work, *Chongzhen lishu* (Calendar Compendium of the Chongzhen Era, 1631–35), comprised 137 volumes of books and astronomical atlases. It included Schall's *Yuanjing shuo* (Explanation of the Telescope, 1626), which contained the first account of the Tychonic world system in Chinese. With the hope of converting the Ming emperor, Schall also compiled several religious texts, such as an illustrated life of Christ (*Jincheng shuxiang*, 1640) and *Zhuzhi qunzheng* (All signs proving the rule of the Lord, 1636) which was based on Leonard Lessius's (1554–1623) *De providentia Numinis et animi immortalitate libri duo adversus Atheos et Politicos* (Antwerp, 1613).

After the suicide of the last Ming emperor and the fall of Beijing in 1644, Schall remained in Beijing and put his astronomical skills in the service of the new Manchu rulers. They entrusted him with the calendar of the new dynasty and appointed him Administrator of the Calendar in the Astronomical Bureau. This position in the Chinese bureaucracy did not go unchallenged, since Schall was accused by fellow Jesuits in the China mission of usurping too much power and of backing superstitious practices. In this dispute, Rome sided with Schall, since he had secured the Jesuits' position in Beijing. With additional honorary titles, his position at court made him the protector of the Christian missions throughout China. In 1650 he received imperial permission to build a new mission compound in the capital, later called the Nantang (South Church).

Yet Schall's advantageous position was to change. In 1657 one of the astronomers of the Muslim section of the Astronomical Bureau, Wu Mingxuan, accused him of having made wrong predictions; this accusation was judged to be unfounded and led to the closure of the Muslim section. Two years later, Yang Guangxian (1597–1669) presented to the Board of Rites documents attacking Schall in the name of Confucian orthodoxy. With a new accusation, namely that Schall had deliberately chosen an inauspicious date and site for the burial of a prince, thus causing the death of the emperor's favorite consort, Yang succeeded in bringing the case to court in 1664. In 1665 Schall and several Chinese Christian astronomers were sentenced to lingering deaths. However, an earthquake occurred on the following day and was interpreted as a sign against this sentence. The Jesuits were therefore pardoned, but five Chinese astronomers were executed. Having suffered partial paralysis in 1664, Schall died on August 15, 1666. In 1669 he was rehabilitated and received imperial sponsorship for his funeral.

See also Astronomy; China

Bornet, Paul, and Henri Bernard, *Lettres et mémoires d'Adam Schall SJ: relation historique. Texte latin avec traduction française.* Tianjin: Hautes Études, 1942.

Malek, Roman, ed., *Western Learning and Christianity in China: The Contribution and Impact of Johann Adam Schall von Bell, SJ (1592–1666)*. 2 vols. Nettetal: Steyler Verlag, 1998.

Väth, Alfons, *Johann Adam Schall von Bell SJ: Missionar in China, kaiserlicher Astronom und Ratgeber am Hofe von Peking, 1592–1666: Ein Lebens- und Zeitbild*. Nettetal: Steyler Verlag, 1991.

Nicolas Standaert, SJ

Scheiner, Christoph, SJ (1573–1650)

Christoph Scheiner was a German Jesuit, astronomer, and instrument builder. A contemporary of Galileo, Scheiner made the first systematic observations of the sun and is credited with making a number of fundamental discoveries in solar astronomy.

Even as a young Jesuit, Scheiner showed an aptitude for building scientific instruments. In 1603, even before he had completed his studies for the priesthood, Scheiner invented his first important instrument: the pantograph. Commonly used by artists and draftsmen before computers became widespread, a pantograph is an apparatus for tracing out reproductions of an original drawing or diagram. Depending on how the pantograph is used, these reproductions can be scaled up or down, enlarging or reducing the original drawing.

Another important early work of Scheiner was his 1619 *Oculus hoc est: fundamentum opticum*, which was the first modern scientific explanation for the operation of the human eye. While Johannes Kepler had previously published a correct optical theory, he did not provide any experimental proofs. Scheiner proved Kepler's theory by taking the eyeballs of slaughtered bulls and shaving away the tissue at the back of the eye until he could see the light being focused on to the back of the eyeball, which proved that vision took place at the back of the eye and not inside the lens (as Aristotle had taught). Along with providing the experimental proof of Kepler's theory, Scheiner also made a number of additional discoveries on the physiology of the eye, including the roles of the retina and the optic nerve in vision.

Again building on an idea first proposed by Kepler, Scheiner was also the first to construct an improved telescope for astronomical observations. By changing the shape of one of the lenses in Galileo's original telescope design, Scheiner's modified telescopes produced a much larger field of view, making observations easier to perform.

What Scheiner is best known for today, though, is his work on solar astronomy and his dispute with Galileo over credit for the discovery of sunspots. Both Galileo and Scheiner independently observed sunspots beginning sometime in 1611. Scheiner, under the pseudonym "Apelles latens post tabulam," published his discovery in 1612 and proposed that sunspots were produced by hidden moons orbiting the sun. Galileo responded with his own set of letters in 1613 and argued that the sunspots had to be on the surface of the sun, a view which Scheiner would later concede to be the correct explanation.

As Galileo's disputes with the Church and the Jesuits of the Roman College grew more heated, though, Galileo started claiming that he, and not Scheiner, was in fact the first to discover sunspots (although modern historians agree that Thomas Harriot was their actual discoverer). In *The Assayer* (1623) and then in his *Dialogue Concerning the Two Chief World Systems* (1630), Galileo even went so far as to accuse Scheiner of plagiarism, although it was Galileo himself who had copied Scheiner rather than the other way around. That Scheiner was a firm geocentrist who tried to find empirical flaws in Galileo's heliocentrism did not improve the tone of the exchange.

Unlike Galileo, who stopped observing the sun in 1613, Scheiner continued to make observations of the sun over the course of fifteen years. Scheiner then published his observations in his book *Rosa ursina sive sol*, which was published in four volumes between 1626 and 1630. The first volume deals with his dispute with Galileo and gives a reasonably accurate account of who had made which discoveries concerning sunspots and when. The second volume has a discussion of telescopes and other instruments for observing the sun, including several of Scheiner's own designs. The most important of these was something Scheiner called the "heliotropii telioscopici." Two things made this a historically important instrument. First, it combined a telescope and a *camera oscura* to create a device, now called a helioscope, which allows the sun to be viewed safely at any time of the day. Second, Scheiner's heliotropii used a mounting system, invented by a fellow Jesuit Christoph Grienberger but first realized by Scheiner, which allowed his helioscope to track the sun all day long without rotating the image it produced. This mount was the direct ancestor of the equatorial mount still used on modern astronomical telescopes. The third volume is a summary of Scheiner's observations, while the fourth volume discusses his discoveries. In addition to his work on sunspots, Scheiner is also credited with being the first to observe solar flares, the rotation of the sun, solar differential rotation, and the inclination of the solar axis.

Christopher Scheiner died in 1650 at the Jesuit college in Neisse, Silesia (modern Nysa, Poland).

See also Astronomy; Galileo; Science

MacDonnell, Joseph, *"Jesuit Geometers."* St. Louis, MO: The Institute of Jesuit Sources; Rome: Vatican Observatory, 1989.
Mitchel, Walter M., "The History of the Discovery of the Solar Spots." Repr. from *Popular Astronomy* 24 (1916).
Southall, J., "Early Pioneers in Physiological Optics." *Journal of the Optical Society of America* 6 (1922), 827–42.

Jonathan Stott, SJ

Schmid, Martin, SJ (1694–1772)

Martin Schmid was born in Baar, Switzerland, in 1694, the son of Martin and Maria Katharina Hurter Schmid. He studied at the Jesuit gymnasium in Lucerne from 1710 to 1716. In 1717 he entered the Jesuit novitiate in Landberg am Lech (Bavaria); he studied theology in Hall in Tirol (Tyrol) and Ingolstadt (Bavaria). In 1726 he was ordained a priest and received permission to travel to South America as a missionary. Owing to the Spanish-English War, he was unable to travel until 1728, making use of this time to study Spanish.

After landing in Buenos Aires, he and the other missionaries traveled several months to Potosí, eventually arriving at the Jesuit mission of the Chiquitos in 1730. He worked at the mission of San Javier for ten years, preaching, celebrating the various liturgies and sacraments, as well as teaching the indigenous peoples the catechism. He also taught music and established a music school and trained the people to recreate the European musical instruments for their use in their own orchestra. Among other things, he helped them learn carpentry, building, brick-making, and other skills. During this time he was active as a composer. From 1745 through 1755 he oversaw the construction of churches in San Rafael and Concepción (now Bolivia) in what would be later called a colonial Baroque style. While at San Rafael he incorporated Zipoli's and unknown indigenous composers' music in fashioning a chamber opera celebrating the lives of Saints Ignatius of Loyola and Francis Xavier. The libretto is in Spanish, with the conclusion in the Chiquitano language summarizing the moral of the play.

After nearly forty years of work in the Reductions, he and the other Jesuit missionaries were deported back to Spain. He returned to his province in 1770 and died in Lucerne in 1772.

See also Bolivia; Music; Paraguay Missions ("Reductions")

Kühne, Eckart, *The Mission Churches of Chiquitos in the Lowlands of Bolivia: Construction and Restoration of Church by Martin Schmid (1694–1772)*. Zurich: Swiss Federal Institute of Technology, 2008.

Charles Jurgensmeier, SJ

Scholastic

Though the word "scholastic" comes from the Latin *scholasticus* and the Greek *scholastikos*, meaning simply a student or one devoted to study, the term "scholastic" in the Society of Jesus is most commonly used juridically and is associated with the Society's formulation of grades or levels as outlined in the *Constitutions*, written by Ignatius.

In the Society, the term scholastic includes those Jesuits in formation who have not yet completed future studies in anticipation of ordination to the priesthood and those ordained Jesuit priests who have yet to pronounce final vows. This scholastic "track" is separate from that of Jesuits who enter the Society with the intention to live as vowed brothers, not as ordained priests. Thus, the juridical progression for priests in the Society of Jesus is from novice-scholastic to approved scholastic (a vowed Jesuit who progresses through philosophy studies, regency, and theology studies to ordination as a priest). Canonically, a Jesuit ceases to be scholastic upon pronouncing his final vows, wherein his grade changes to spiritual coadjutor (if he pronounces three vows) or solemnly professed father (if he pronounces four vows).

By utilizing the term scholastic, it should be noted that therein lies a reference, however obliquely, to scholasticism, the system of study of philosophy and theology taught in medieval universities across Europe. Like all formation in the Society, the future study that Jesuit scholastics undertake is to be seen as having a priestly character to it, preparing the Jesuit to serve God and God's people with apostolic zeal and great love.

See also Course of Studies; Formation; Grades

Brown, Donald, *The Origins of the Grades in the Society of Jesus 1540 to 1550*. Rome: Pontifical Gregorian University, 1971.
The Constitutions of the Society of Jesus and Their Complementary Norms. Ed. John W. Padberg. St. Louis, MO: The Institute of Jesuit Sources, 1996.

Keith Maczkiewicz, SJ

Schoonenberg, Piet, SJ (1911–1999)

Piet Schoonenberg, Dutch Jesuit, was a professor of theology at Maastricht in the Netherlands (1948–53), a teacher at the Higher Catechetical Institute in Nijmegen (1953–64), and professor of systematic theology at the Catholic University of Nijmegen (1964–76). His was a major theological voice in the production of *A New Catechism* (1967), widely referred to as "The Dutch Catechism" (another major voice was that of Edward Schillebeeckx, OP). Fr. Schoonenberg made distinct contributions to the development of Christology "from below," that is, a theological study of the person of Jesus that begins with his humanity (*The Christ: A Study of the God–Man Relationship in the Whole of Creation and in Jesus Christ*, 1971), and to the development of an understanding of original sin that takes into account both modern biblical scholarship and the contemporary evolutionary perspective on human origins (*Man and Sin: A Theological View*, 1965). His Christology represented an effort to think beyond the thought-world bequeathed to the later Church in the creed of the Council of Chalcedon (AD 451) and to introduce, he said, "a less static, a more dynamic concept of God." His understanding of original sin moved away from the suggestion that original sin is transmitted through the process of being born (almost as if inherited from Adam physically) and toward a more sociological view (the human being as born into and thus shaped by social and cultural surroundings, where "original sin" more properly resides). Social birth thus becomes more theologically significant than biological birth. Such a shift of anthropological perspective requires adjustments in how we understand Church and sacraments, and how, historically and in day-to-day life, redemption takes place.

The Dutch Catechism was strongly criticized (though never condemned) by the Congregation for the Doctrine of the Faith because it departed from traditional Church teaching on a number of points, although it was not the only post-Vatican II catechism to come under close scrutiny. An international commission of cardinals reviewed the book and asked for revisions, which came in the form of a supplement to subsequent editions of the catechism – though not in a change of the original text. (See Murray, "The Dutch Catechism Dispute".) All this took place before liberation theology, with its attention to the human, historical Jesus, washed over Christological reflection like a tidal wave.

See also Catechisms; Theology

Murray, Robert, "The Dutch Catechism Dispute." *The Tablet*. November 15, 1969.
Schoonenberg, Piet, *The Christ: A Study of the God–Man Relationship in the Whole of Creation and in Jesus Christ*. Trans. Della Couling. New York: Herder and Herder, 1971.
Schoonenberg, Piet, *Man and Sin: A Theological View*. Trans. Joseph Donceel. Notre Dame, IN: University of Notre Dame Press, 1965.

William Reiser, SJ

Science

Although much has been written about the life and activities of the Society of Jesus, until recently very little has been published on its contribution to modern science. This is quite surprising since a considerable mass of data exists to show that the Jesuits were a major player in the field of modern science, particularly in its infancy. Not only did several of its members make important contributions to different branches of science, but its educational institutions also produced many outstanding scientists and thinkers.

Some Historical Data

The involvement of Jesuits in modern science was active and productive, both individually and institutionally. It is true that none of them rose to the stature of a Descartes, Kepler, or Newton – perhaps a few of them could have, had the circumstances and conditions been different – but they made substantial contributions to the origin and development of science. When Poggendorff published his *Biographisch-Literarische Handwörterbuch zur Geschichte der exakten Wissenschaften*, a biographical history of all scientists up until 1858, he listed 8,847 scientists, about 10 percent of whom are priests and religious, and among whom almost half are Jesuits. Sommervogel's twelve-volume work *Bibliothèque de la Compagnie de Jésus* gives the names and works of 631 Jesuit geometers from the first two centuries of Jesuit history. William Ashworth considers the Society of Jesus as the scientific order without rival in seventeenth-century Catholicism. According to well-known historian of science George Sarton, one cannot talk about mathematics in the sixteenth and seventeenth centuries without seeing a Jesuit at every turn. John Heilbron believes that the Jesuit order was the single most important contributor to experimental physics in the seventeenth century. Coming to India and Asia, well-known historian of science M. Razaullah Ansari points out that the Jesuits were the first Europeans to introduce modern western astronomy into South and Southeast Asia.

The merit and significance of the Jesuit contribution to science can also be assessed from the honors accorded to it by the scientific community over the centuries. To list a few, there are more than thirty lunar craters named after Jesuits. Similarly four asteroids have been named after Jesuits, two of whom – George Coyne, former director of the Vatican Observatory, and Guy Consolmagno, current director of the Observatory – are alive and currently active in the field. In India alone more than forty-four species of plants and an insect have been named after Jesuit scientists.

Jesuit Contributions to the Different Branches of Science

Mathematics. The field of mathematics is one of the areas in which the Jesuits were most conspicuous. Not only did they continue some of the groundbreaking work done by others, but they made their own original contributions as well. Christopher Clavius (1537–1612), often recognized as the "Father of Jesuit Science," was called "the Euclid of the sixteenth century." Gregory Saint Vincent (1584–1667) pioneered the field of infinitesimal analysis. Guldin's Theorem in mathematics is named after the Jesuit Paul Guldin (1577–1643). Girolamo Saccheri's (1667–1733) work on non-Euclidean (hyperbolic) geometry was considered the most significant discovery of his century. Vincenzo Riccati (1707–75) was credited as the inventor of hyperbolic functions.

Astronomy. The Collegio Romano, the flagship of Jesuit science, was one of the first colleges to have an observatory using a telescope. In fact, the scientists there were the first to independently verify the telescopic discoveries of Galileo and to congratulate and honor him for his original work. Clavius was also highly recognized in astronomy, and hence he became the natural choice to head the team appointed for the Gregorian calendar reform. His highly popular *In Sphaeram Ioannis de Sacro Bosco commentarius* was for a long time considered the authoritative book on the astronomy of the day. Christopher Grienberger (1561–1636), Clavius's successor, was celebrated for the invention of the still used equatorial mount, an ingenious arrangement in which the telescope and the earth rotate about parallel axes. Christopher Scheiner (1575–1650) was another outstanding astronomer who discovered the sunspots, an issue that embroiled him in a bitter dispute with Galileo. He also discovered *faculae*, bright cloud-like objects seen chiefly near the edge of the sun. Orazio Grassi (1583–1654) was a much appreciated Italian Jesuit mathematician, astronomer, and architect, although Galileo attacked and ridiculed him in a bitter controversy on the comets.

The Vatican Observatory, entrusted to the Jesuits by the Holy See in 1934, continues this great astronomical tradition. The Vatican Observatory Research Group in Tucson, Arizona, operates its state-of-the-art 1.8 meter Alice Lennon Telescope and Thomas Bannan Astrophysics Facility on Mount Graham and has become one of the leading observatories in the world.

When early Jesuits arrived in China and India, they also made remarkable contributions to astronomy there. Owing to their outstanding work in China, the astronomer-trio – Matteo Ricci (1552–1610), Johann Adam Schall von Bell (1591–1666), and Ferdinand Verbiest (1623–88) – were accorded the rare honor of national heroes. In India the Jesuits were the first to make use of the telescope, giving a much-needed boost to astronomical observations both qualitatively and quantitatively. J. Richaud (1633–93), sent by the French king as "mathematician of France," made the first credited scientific discovery in India in 1689 when he discovered the binary nature of Alpha-Centauri and Alpha-Cruis. Claude Boudier (1686–1757) was considered the most important French contributor to science in India. He was one of the principal astronomers who helped Maharaja Sawai Jai Singh II of Jaipur, the Indian astronomer-king, in his ambitious astronomical project.

Spectroscopy. Angelo Secchi (1818–78) is rightly regarded as the "Father of Spectroscopy." His study of the sunspots and other phenomena were a great help to our understanding of the astronomical world. Stephen Perry (1833–89) was a physicist, astronomer, and schoolmaster, who made considerable contributions to astrophysics. Among other things, his detailed study confirmed the existence of an eleven-year solar cycle of sunspot activity.

Creative Scientific Theories. In the field of creative scientific ideas and original techniques, the Jesuits also left their mark. For instance, Francesco Grimaldi (1618–63) has been recognized for formulating the geometrical basis for the wave theory of light, anticipating Robert Hooke and Christian Huygens. Ignace-Gaston Pardies also worked on the properties of light, particularly on the theory of colors. Roger Boscovich (1711–87) is honored for presenting in the eighteenth century the first coherent description of an atomic theory when he introduced a new concept of matter as made up of countless "point-centers" of force instead of being a continuous assortment of different solid atoms.

Seismology. The Jesuit contribution to seismology is unparalleled, so much so it is called the "Jesuit science." Jesuits did pioneering work in this field in various parts of the world. This tradition continues, albeit on a small scale, mostly in the United States and specifically in the Boston College Educational Seismology Project.

Geophysics and Geographical Explorations. Jesuits in various parts of the world took a special interest in geographical explorations – observing carefully the different conditions of nature, exploring the rivers and their bases, charting their courses, preparing accurate maps of the regions, studying their flora and fauna, etc. José de Acosta (1540–1600) was the first to describe the natural conditions in the Americas. He carefully observed, recorded, and analyzed earthquakes, volcanoes, tides, currents, etc. Cristóbal de Acuña (1598–1670) made the first map of the Amazon River in 1641, while Samuel Fritz made the first scientific map of the Amazon from source to mouth. The Paraguay River was also mapped by the Jesuits in the seventeenth century. José Gumilla prepared the first accurate map of Orinoco and its tributaries in 1741. The great rivers of North America also fascinated the Jesuit explorers. Jacques Marquette mapped the Mississippi River in the mid-seventeenth century and Peter De Smet mapped much of northwest America, including the Rocky Mountains. Pedro Páez in 1613 located the source of the Blue Nile.

In the East the Jesuits also made an invaluable contribution to geographical exploration and cartography. In 1584 Ricci published the first maps of China ever available to the West. Anthony Monserrate (1536–1600) was the first to complete a map of India around 1590. Jean-Venant Bouchet (1655–1732) and Joseph Tieffenthaler (1710–85) also made very valuable contributions in this field.

Aeronautics. Francesco Lana-Terzi (1631–87) did pioneering work in this field and has been called "the Father of Aviation." He was the first to study and publish a scientific treatise on a heavier-than-air-flying machine.

Physics and Chemistry. Several Jesuits have been active in physics and chemistry. Charles Racine (1897–1976) was well-versed in relativity, celestial mechanics, etc., and Lourdu Yeddanapalli (1904–70) did important work in the field of chemical kinetics and high polymers.

Technology and Instrumentation. In the field of technology and instrumentation, the Jesuits also left their mark, particularly in making clocks and telescopes. Scheiner is given credit for the invention of the refracting telescope and the pantograph; Clavius for anticipating the Vernier Scale; Verbiest for making astronomical instruments and cannons; Athanasius Kircher (1602–80) for the magic lantern, an early form of optical projector of still pictures, and Jan Ciermans for anticipating Blaise Pascal's calculating machine.

Botany. Given the Ignatian spirituality of having a positive attitude toward the physical universe, a keen Jesuit interest in the life sciences is a natural expectation. Immediately following the discovery of the New World, the Jesuits extended their activities to these new areas. José de Acosta's *Historia natural y moral de las Indias*, published in 1590, had a lasting impact on Jesuit naturalists of the Americas. He advocated the need to go beyond the traditional Aristotelian categories by pointing out their inadequacy to explain some of the things observed in the New World. Cristóbal de Acuña's study of the fauna of the Amazon region has been quite valuable. Bernabé Cobo's (1580–1657) book *Historia del Nuevo Mundo*, published in 1653, describes 108 different species of plants original to South and Central America, along with 87 others that are also found in Europe. In Argentina and Paraguay, Sánchez Labrador's (1717–98) publications *Paraguay natural* and *El Paraguay Católico* describe the region of Río de la Plata and the plants, animals, and customs of its inhabitants. In this context the works of Thomas Falkner (1702–84) in Argentina and José Jolís (1728–90) in Paraguay are also significant. Ramón Termeyer's (1737–1814) treatise on the environment in Argentina, *Opuscoli scientifici d'entomologia, di fisica e d'agricoltura*, published from 1807 to 1809 in five volumes, proved an original and valuable study. Also remarkable is the contribution of

Chilean Juan Molina (1740–1829), who in his 1820 book, *Analogia de los tres reinos de la naturaleza*, gave a foretaste of evolution by proposing continuity between the worlds of non-living minerals, living plants, and conscious animals.

In the East, João de Loureiro (1717–91) worked in South Vietnam, Cambodia, Sumatra, and Malaysia. In his 1790 publication on the flora of Cochinchina, *Flora Cochinchinensis*, he classifies 2,000 species of plants in the Linnaean system. George Kamel (1661–1706), who worked in the Philippines, was the first to describe the camellia, which is named after him. His works were published in *Philosophical Transactions* of the Royal Society.

In India the Jesuits have a long-standing tradition of engaging seriously in the study of the flora of the region. Toward the end of the nineteenth century, the Sacred Heart College of Shembaganur, Tamil Nadu, became a rich nursery of many future scientists, particularly in the field of plant taxonomy. Louis Anglade (1873–1953), Alfred Rapinat (1892–1959), Mathew Koyapillil (1930–2004), and Visuvasam Manickam (1944–2012) were the most notable among them. In the western part of India, similar work was done by Ethelbert Blatter (1877–1934), Hermenegild Santapau (1903–70), and Cecil Saldanha (1926–2002). All of them made valuable contributions in the study and identification of many new species of plants. They were noted for making internationally recognized collections of botanical specimens, setting up world-class herbariums like Rapinat Herbarium in Tiruchirappalli and Blatter Herbarium in Mumbai, and running innovative research centers.

Medicine. In the medical field too, particularly in practical medicine, the Jesuits made a name for themselves. José de Acosta is considered one of the pioneers of modern aeronautical medicine. Barnabé de Cobo and Bartolomé Tafur were the first to introduce quinine to Europe. Kircher's microscopic and bacteriological discoveries in 1646 were a great step in understanding the cause of certain diseases.

Some Other Contributions

Scientific Writing. The Jesuits were also voluminous writers in the area of science. According to Dhruv Raina, between the years 1600 and 1773, Jesuit scientists authored more than 4,000 published works in differing fields like natural philosophy, medicine, astronomy, and mathematics. Some estimates show that after 1700 they penned about 1,000 book manuscripts and 600 journal articles.

Educators. Imparting outstanding scientific education has been one of the trademarks of the Jesuits all through their history. They have also encouraged critical and progressive thinking. Their institutions have produced many outstanding scientists and geniuses. Among them are Abdul Kalam, world-renowned scientist and former president of India; Sabeer Bhatia, founder of Hotmail; Georges Buffon, French naturalist; François d'Aguilon, Belgian mathematician and physicist; Jean Delambre, French mathematician and astronomer; Jérôme Lalande, French astronomer; Georges Lemaitre, Belgian priest and cosmologist; Voltaire, French thinker and author. Eugene Lafont (1837–1908) in Kolkata and D. Honore (1862–1934) in Tiruchirapalli were also outstanding in this regard. Lafont's collaboration with Mahendralal Sircar (1833–1904) in founding the Indian Association for the Cultivation of Science (IACS), the Indian counterpart of the British Royal Society for the advancement of science, was so noteworthy that he is often considered the co-founder of IACS.

Disseminators of Scientific Ideas. The Jesuits participated not only in the creation and development of scientific ideas but also in their dissemination to other countries and peoples. For instance, they were the first to confirm Galileo's telescopic discoveries. Galileo published them in his *Starry Messenger* in 1610. Within five years the Jesuit missionaries in Beijing gave an account of these historic discoveries.

Distinctive Features of Jesuit Science

Although there were a number of creative and original scientists in the ranks of the Jesuits, by and large Jesuit science showed limited creativity. The Jesuits only rarely broke new ground. They mostly worked on the theories and ideas of others – modifying them, bringing out their significant implications, putting them to important practical uses, etc. In astronomy, for instance, they mostly limited themselves to positional astronomy – accurate observation of the position of the different stars and other heavenly bodies, determining the longitudes and latitudes of different places and cities, etc. In the life sciences, taxonomy and related areas were their principal focus.

For most Jesuit scientists, engaging in science was part of their apostolate and as such pastoral concern came uppermost in their priorities. Hence, they often focused on the practical aspects of science, particularly how it could benefit the people among whom they lived and worked. This emphasis also prevented them from moving deeply into the theoretical realm to come up with more creative new theories.

The Jesuits gave very little publicity to the great work they were doing in the field of science. They kept very meticulous records of their work and shared it with their superiors and companions, but never bothered much about its publicization. Perhaps a paradigm case of this attitude of self-abnegation is Christoph Grienberger, the successor of Clavius. Although some of his contemporaries considered him "the Archimedes of our time," as one who could creatively blend the most ingenious practices and machines with very acute theories, it is reported that he spared no pains to ensure that his name appeared neither in the texts written by him nor in the instruments designed by him. The same attitude in varying degrees can be found in many others as well. This is perhaps the main reason why Jesuit science has long remained little known.

Conclusion: The Source and Motivation of Jesuit Science

Although there were many religious orders like the Dominicans with an outstanding track record of intellectual and academic pursuit, only the Society of Jesus took to science in a big way. In fact, the study of natural science was part of the curriculum for their training, particularly in the Old Society before its suppression in 1773. Furthermore, in the case of many individual Jesuits, engagement with science was a lifetime commitment. What made the difference for the Jesuits? Joseph Needham, the well-known Cambridge biologist-turned-sinologist, in his monumental series *Science and Civilization in China*, gives purely religious reasons to explain this point. In his view the Jesuits engaged in science because it gave them access to the forbidden territory of China, and acceptability and credibility among the rulers and intelligentsia; it also served as a means to show the superiority of the Christian religion over eastern religions. Although, to some extent, this may have been true in the specific case of China, this cannot be taken as a general strategy. After all, Jesuit science was far more active in Europe where missionary activity was never a concern. Furthermore, it is clear that even in missionary territories where science was helpful for Christianization, their engagement with science continued undiminished even after its successful completion.

Rather, Jesuit science, far from being an avocation, was firmly rooted in the Jesuit charism and Jesuit spirituality. Given certain elements of the Jesuit charism and certain fundamental features of modern science, one could expect the Society of Jesus to be naturally inclined to pursue science. The fundamental mission of the Jesuits is the attainment of "the greater glory of God and the salvation of souls," which involves the service of humanity. Jesuit scientists have been looking upon science as a service that broadens our understanding of nature and thereby brings glory to the Creator of this marvelous universe. At the same time, being mostly practical and pastoral in their approach, the Jesuits' engagement with science has been focused upon the service of humanity as a primary objective. A positive attitude to the material universe is also fundamental for modern science. The Jesuits shared this attitude because they were disposed to see "God in all things," including the whole created universe, as described in the *Contemplatio ad amorem* of the *Spiritual Exercises*, the fountain-head of Jesuit spirituality. Thus, a Jesuit scientist sees no undesirable tension between his religiosity and modern science. In fact, the life and work of Jesuit scientists is perhaps the best demonstration that a constructive and fruitful interaction between genuine science and true religion is not only possible but also needs to be cultivated in our world today

See also Astronomy; China; Clavius, Christopher, SJ; Galileo; Moon; Pharmacy/Pharmacology; Vatican Observatory

Bishop, George, *Jesuit Pioneers of Modern Science and Mathematics*. Anand, India: Gujarat Sahitya Prakash, 2005.
Kozhamthadam, Job, "Christian Contribution to Science in India." In A. V. Afonso, ed., *Indian Christianity*. New Delhi: Centre for Studies in Civilizations, 2009, pp. 451–77.
MacDonnell, Joseph, *Jesuit Geometers*. St. Louis, MO: The Institute of Jesuit Sources, 1989.
Udías, Agustín, *Jesuit Contribution to Science: A History*. New York: Springer, 2015.

Job Kozhamthadam, SJ

Science Fiction

Jesuits figure so prominently among other members of the clergy as characters in the science fiction of the twentieth and twenty-first centuries for several possible reasons: their reputation for high intelligence; the professional diversity of their membership; their rigorous theological training and intense spiritual formation; their past history as missionaries in foreign lands; and their "open-mindedness" coupled with their dedication to the Catholic Church and its ministry. Science fiction writers use Jesuit characters to examine the interaction between theology and science, and to probe the limits of faith.

A few of the most prominent examples include some science fiction classics. In "The Star" (1955), Arthur C. Clarke's Jesuit astrophysicist struggles to reconcile his faith in the goodness of God with the shattering results of an astronomical catastrophe. James Blish, in his novella *A Case of Conscience* (1959), follows a Jesuit who comes to a shocking conclusion about an apparently "sinless" race of aliens. A Jesuit geophysicist sees the hand of God in an unexpected chemical analysis on Saturn's moon, Titan, in Hilbert Schenck's "The Theology of Water" (1982). The protagonist in Damien Broderick's "The Magi" (1982) is a Jewish physicist who becomes a Jesuit priest, only to be expelled from Earth along with the last 500 Jesuits; his faith is shaken during two missions on the starship *Loyola*. The troubled Jesuit in Dan Simmons' *Hyperion* (1989) has been "exiled" to an anthropological study on a backwater planet; what he finds is an alien mockery of bodily resurrection. In Mary Doria Russell's *The Sparrow* (1996), the Jesuits sponsor a "first contact" spaceflight; the Jesuit linguist assigned experiences intense suffering because of later cross-cultural misunderstandings. There are many other examples in contemporary literature.

See also Film and Television: Characters and Themes; Novels

"Mainstream Science Fiction and Fantasy with Jesuit Characters and References." www.adherents. com/lit/sf_jesuit.html. Accessed on September 17, 2015.
Russell, Mary Doria, *The Sparrow*. Ballantine, 1997.

Joanne M. Pierce

Scribani, Carlo, SJ (1561–1629)

Scribani, only child of an Italian nobleman and sister of the Antwerp bishop Levinus Torrentius (van der Beke), joined the Jesuits in Trier in 1582, taught rhetoric at the colleges of Molsheim, Trier, and Liège, and was ordained in 1590 by his uncle. Most of his life he would stay in Antwerp as prefect of studies and college rector, and from 1613 as first provincial of the independent Flemish province. He commissioned the building of the superb Ignatius Church (now Carolus Borromeus) in Antwerp. Scribani was a member of a network of influential politicians and artists, like Justus Lipsius and Erycius Puteanus, Peter Paul Rubens and Anthony van Dyck, duke Maximilian of Bavaria and archdukes Albrecht and Isabella.

Scribani was a prolific writer, whose early publications were directed against the Protestants, like the anonymous pamphlets *Veridicus Belgicus* and *Apocalypsis Batavica* on the Dutch revolt, both from 1625. In two works he highly praised the city of Antwerp: *Antverpia* and *Origines Antverpiensium*. Between 1613 and 1620 he published several books on spiritual topics, as does his very last publication *Christus Patiens* in 1629. He also wrote some important political books, among them the anti-Machiavellian treatise *Politico-Christianus* from 1624, dedicated to King Philip IV of Spain. In all his writings Scribani stressed his attachment to the Catholic faith, his faithfulness to the legal Spanish authority, and his love for the Netherlands. His writing style is rather baroque.

His portrait by Anthony van Dyck is now in the Kunsthistorisches Museum in Vienna. *See also* Antwerp

Brouwers, Lodewijk, and Jean-François Gilmont, *Carolus Scribani*. Brussels: Archief- en Bibliotheekwezen in België, 1977.
Vanwelden, Sarah, "Carolus Scribani's Veridicus Belgicus and Apocalypsis Batavica: The Dissemination of Two Controversial Pamphlets on the Dutch Revolt." *De Gulden Passer* 91 (2013), 21–36.

Paul Begheyn, SJ

Sebastian, King of Portugal

Grandson of John III, Sebastian of Aviz (b. Lisbon, January 20, 1554; d. Ksar el-Kebir, August 4, 1578) was the son of Prince John, who died before his birth, and Princess Joanna of Austria. He came to the throne in June 1557. As the only heir to the throne, great hopes had been focused on him since birth. Until he came of age, the regency was assumed by Queen Catherine of Austria, his grandmother, and by the Cardinal Prince Henry, his uncle, the inquisitor general. Henry smoothed the way for the nomination of the Jesuit Luís Gonçalves da Câmara, leader of what was then the most powerful current in the Society of Jesus, as preceptor of the young king (1560) and, later, his confessor. Sebastian received a fervent religious education, growing up in a climate marked by an alliance between the Jesuits and the Crown that was unparalleled in Europe at the time. Its fruits included the opening of the University of Évora (1559), which was entrusted to the Society, the foundation of new colleges, and the encouraging of new missions overseas. Even before Sebastian assumed the government himself (1568), the secular theologian Martim Gonçalves da Câmara, Luís's brother, had begun his rise at court, later becoming the King's main political counselor. The image of a young sovereign in the hands of the two brothers dominated the first years of his direct reign. But the relationship soured, partly because of their opposition to Sebastian's expansionist designs: as early as 1574 he personally led the first armed expedition to Morocco. The King freed himself of both of them and, increasingly isolated, threw himself into a new Moroccan adventure, which ended with the battle in which he himself lost his life, opening a serious dynastic crisis.

See also Gonçalves da Câmara, Luís, SJ; Portugal

Cruz, Maria Augusta Lima, *D. Sebastião*. Lisbon: Círculo de Leitores, 2006.
Cruz, Maria do Rosário de Sampaio Themudo Barata de Azevedo, *As regências na menoridade de D. Sebastião: elementos para uma história estrutural.* 2 vols. Lisbon: INCM, 1992.

Giuseppe Marcocci

Seghers, Daniel, SJ (1590–1661)

Daniel Seghers was a Jesuit brother in seventeenth-century Antwerp and a painter of extraordinarily detailed flower pictures. His works are unusual for the period in that they are almost all collaborations with other artists, in which he executed elaborate bouquets or garlands of flowers around religious images created by other artists.

Seghers was born in Antwerp in 1590. After the death of his father, his mother moved the family back to her native Utrecht, where they converted to Calvinism, and Seghers started training as a painter. The family returned to Antwerp in 1610. There he was apprenticed to Jan Brueghel the Elder, with whom he lived and worked for four years. His specialization as a flower painter is directly attributable to this training; Brueghel was a master painter of still lifes and flower garlands. In collaboration with Hendrick van Balen, Brueghel first executed a "flower garland painting" (a small painting of the Virgin and Child, on a silver panel, set into a floral wreath), commissioned by Federico Borromeo in 1607. Later garland paintings by Brueghel were likely produced during the years that Seghers was a member of his workshop, and Seghers may have assisted with the painting of the flowers. The earliest recorded work by Seghers independently is a representation of a vase of flowers, owned by Brueghel, and dated to *c.* 1611–14.

Figure 61 Daniel Seghers, SJ: *Madonna and Child with Garlands, c.* 1645, oil on canvas. Gift of the Chicago-Detroit Province of the Society of Jesus. Photograph © Jesuit School of Theology of Santa Clara University, Berkeley, CA, and reproduced by permission

Seghers converted back to Catholicism and entered the Society as a lay brother at the novitiate in Mechelen in 1614. Most of what is known about his early life comes from the autobiographical statement he gave at his entrance. He took his first vows two years later and his final vows in 1625, while living in Brussels. During his novitiate he began to execute the type of works for which he is best known. A painting of floral garlands surrounding the figure of St. Francis Xavier (attributed to his younger brother Gerard Seghers) dates to about 1617. Seghers spent two years in Italy after pronouncing his final vows, and then he returned to Antwerp, where he lived until his death. In each place he sought out exotic flowers and plants to draw; his notebooks, filled with these recordings, served as his guide throughout his artistic career.

Between 1618 and 1621 Seghers lived at the professed house in Antwerp. It has been suggested that he contributed to the decoration of the Church of St. Ignatius, consecrated in 1621. Records of the paintings removed from that church at the time of the Society's suppression attributed over twenty to Seghers; two of them can be connected to his works now in Vienna.

As many as nine other artists collaborated with Seghers over the course of his career. All of these painters produced the central images of the works, generally depicting Christ, the Virgin Mary, or saints (including Jesuit saints Ignatius of Loyola and Francis Xavier). Most frequently he worked with Cornelis Schut and Erasmus Quellinus II; other collaborators include Simon de Vos, Abraham van Diepenbeeck, Gerard Seghers, Peter Paul Rubens, Thomas Willeboirts Bosschaert, Hendrick van Balen, and Antoine Goubau. It has also been said that he added garlands to two paintings by Domenichino during the period spent in Rome. In a few works there is a symbolic connection between the flowers and the scenes they surround, such as in the thorny plants that frame a scene of the Mocking of Christ (c. 1643), suggesting a specifically planned collaboration. The religious scenes are sometimes executed in full color, but especially after the 1640s and in his collaborations with Quellinus, they were rendered in grisaille cartouches, as if they were sculptures.

Owing to the status of Seghers as a Jesuit brother, he did not sell his works, but presented them as gifts. He often selected the recipient because of their status or reputation as collectors: paintings were gifted to Christina of Sweden, Philip IV of Spain, Marie de' Medici, Charles I of England, and Archduke Leopold of Austria. Other times they were given as souvenirs to visitors to his studio. On occasion they were commissioned, despite the fact that he did not receive payment for them. Instead, he was given gifts, sometimes of extraordinary value, such as solid gold brushes. His reputation as a Jesuit appealed to his patrons; in turn, his works engendered goodwill and publicity for the Society.

A notable feature of Seghers's oeuvre is that throughout his life he kept a list of all the paintings he produced: *Cataloge van de Bloem-stukken, die ik selfs met mijn hand heb geschildert en voor wie* (Catalog of flower-still lifes, which I have painted and for whom). The original has been lost, but it exists in an eighteenth-century copy.

See also Antwerp; Arts, Visual; Brothers

Burke-Gaffney, M. W., *Daniel Seghers, 1590–1661: A Tercentenary Commemoration*. New York: Vantage Press, 1961.

Merriam, Susan, *Seventeenth-Century Flemish Garland Paintings: Still Life, Vision, and the Devotional Image*. Farnham: Ashgate, 2012.

Alison Fleming

Segundo, Juan Luis, SJ (1925–1996)

Juan Luis Segundo was born in Montevideo, Uruguay, on March 31, 1925. He entered the Society of Jesus in 1941 and pursued studies in philosophy in San Miguel, Argentina. Segundo was ordained a priest in 1955 and gained a licentiate in sacred theology from Louvain, Belgium, in 1956. He obtained a doctorate in literature at the Sorbonne in Paris in 1963. In 1965 he founded the Peter Faber Pastoral Center in Montevideo. This center offered programs that educated the laity about the relationship between religion and society. At this time, he also founded *Perspectivas de diálogo*, a journal that examined important philosophical and theological issues from a Latin American perspective. Segundo never held a permanent academic position but nevertheless taught theology at various institutions in both North America (Harvard, the University of Chicago, and Regis College in Toronto) and Latin America. He died on January 17, 1996.

Often cited as one of the earliest Latin American liberation theologians, Segundo published *Función de la Iglesia en la realidad rioplatense* in 1962 and *Concepción cristiana del hombre* in 1964. In these works Segundo developed a liberationist interpretation of the Christian tradition that predates the emergence of European political theology and thereby falsifies the often-made claim that Latin American liberation theology is little more than an application of European political theology to the Latin American situation.

Segundo's most important contribution to Latin American liberation theology was in the area of theological method. Segundo argued that it is critical that Christians engage in the process of reinterpreting the significance of the Bible and the Christian tradition in conversation with changing individual circumstances and current sociopolitical conditions. For Segundo, this entails the use of a hermeneutic circle as the broad methodological basis for liberation theology. According to Segundo, the hermeneutical circle involves a four-step dialectical process: (1) a commitment to liberating the poor from oppressive situations; (2) ideological suspicion toward the dominant social order that produces innocent suffering and those ideologies that legitimate it; (3) exegetical suspicion toward those religious ideologies that purport to disseminate timeless truths and which, in the end, provide support to the dominant social order; (4) finally, the development of a "new hermeneutic" that leads to a more critical and nuanced interpretation of the current social order and that generates new theologies and spiritualities rooted in commitment to the liberation of the oppressed.

Beyond his work in theological method, Segundo produced an ambitious five-volume Christology that included an analysis of the Christology of the *Spiritual Exercises* of Ignatius of Loyola (*The Christ of the Ignatian Exercises*). Segundo also wrote a book-length response to the Congregation for the Doctrine of the Faith's criticism of liberation theology entitled *Theology and the Church: A Response to Cardinal Ratzinger and a Warning to the Whole Church*. In this work, he contested what he viewed as the reductionistic analysis of the relationship between Latin American liberation theology and Marxism. Finally, Segundo examined the significance of Ignatian spirituality from a liberationist perspective in "Ignatius Loyola: Trial or Project?" In this essay, Segundo argued that the *Spiritual Exercises* represent an example of a spirituality of trial that focuses on the avoidance of sin as a means of escaping eternal damnation. Segundo criticizes the spirituality because it leads to the devaluation of this world. He argues, however, that as superior general of the Society of Jesus Ignatius developed an alternative form of spirituality that focuses on one's life before God as a project. This spirituality views the world as the site at which humans are invited to collaborate with God in the creation of a more just world. In conclusion, Segundo argues that because the spirituality of the life-project supports the fundamental commitments of Latin American liberation theology, Jesuits would be well served to broaden the scope of their analysis of Ignatian spirituality beyond the *Spiritual Exercises*.

See also Liberation Theology; Uruguay

Goizueta, Roberto, "Juan Luis Segundo." In Donald W. Musser and Joseph L. Price, eds., *A New Handbook of Christian Theologians*. Nashville, TN: Abingdon Press, 1996, pp. 419–26.

Haight, Roger, "Juan Luis Segundo." In Kwok Pui-lan, Don H. Campier, and Joerg Rieger, eds., *Empire and the Christian Tradition: New Readings of Classical Theologians*. Minneapolis: Fortress Press, 2007, pp. 439–53.

Hennelly, Alfred T., "The Challenge of Juan Luis Segundo." *Theological Studies* 38, 1 (1977), 125–35.

Segundo, Juan Luis, *The Christ of the Ignatian Exercises*. Maryknoll, NY: Orbis Books, 1987.

Concepción cristiana del hombre. Montevideo: Mimeográfica "Luz," 1964.

Función de la Iglesia en la realidad rioplatense. Montevideo: Barreiro y Ramos, 1962.

The Liberation of Theology. Maryknoll, NY: Orbis Books, 1976.
Signs of the Times: Theological Reflections. Maryknoll, NY: Orbis Books, 1993.
Theology and the Church: A Response to Cardinal Ratzinger and a Warning to the Whole Church.
Minneapolis, MN: Winston Press, 1985.

Matthew T. Eggemeier

Seminary of Painters in Japan

The Seminary of Painters in Japan, founded by the Jesuits in 1583, was the largest missionary art school in Asia. It reveals a fascinating legacy of Catholic art in Asia and Jesuit missionary history. In the older scholarship, this seminary was somehow inaccurately referred to as "Academy of St. Luke," never confirmed by any source, as Rome's Accademia di San Luca was founded just five years previously.

The founding of this seminary was closely associated with the official Jesuit visitor Alessandro Valignano, who had on his first visit proposed an attitude toward and a method for adapting to Japanese culture for European missionaries coming in contact with the local people. Under this policy, the Seminary of Painters was officially formed soon after Valignano left in 1582. The Japan mission expanded considerably and the need for devotional images greatly exceeded the supply from Europe after the 1580s.

The first artist commissioned to teach at the seminary was Giovanni Niccolò or Cola (1563–1626), a native of Naples, who arrived in Japan in 1581. The seminary constantly moved; it was located for a long time in Nagasaki before moving to Macau in 1614, when all missionaries were exiled from Japan. Textual sources highly praise the broad scope of the educational activities of the seminary and the achievements of local Japanese students in supplying devotional images throughout Japan and even to China and the Philippines. The peak came around the 1590s: there was a record number of ninety-three students in the seminary in 1596.

Many surviving Christian images and Namban screens or objects show the blending of European skills and Japanese indigenous elements. However, because of the limited number of sources documenting the high number of visual materials, the scholarship can only ambiguously attribute them to the seminary.

See also Arts, Visual; Asia; Japan; Valignano, Alessandro, SJ

Bailey, Gauvin A., *Art on the Jesuit Missions in Asia and Latin America 1542–1773.* Toronto: University of Toronto Press, 1999, pp. 52–81.

Hui-Hung Chen

Separate Incorporation

The Second Vatican Council (1962–65) opened up new horizons for a more dynamic Church with lay leadership at its core. This emphasis on lay leadership coincided in the late 1960s with major social and ecclesial upheavals, which precipitated the need for Jesuit high schools, colleges, and universities to search for new ways of governing themselves, since the older ways were simply not up to the task.

Until the mid-sixties, Jesuit institutions had often commingled their operation and resources with those of the religious community. But this model was no longer effective. The institutions responded by: (1) staking out a claim to a necessary autonomy; (2) encouraging separate incorporation of the religious community from the college or university; (3) developing independent boards of trustees composed of both religious and lay members. These steps could have been (and often were) interpreted as lessening an interest in Catholic and Jesuit identity, but actually each step was taken with an explicit commitment to preserve that identity.

Already in 1965, Fr. John McGrath, canon lawyer at the Catholic University of America, had argued that if an institution had been civilly incorporated, it was no longer a "juridic person" in canon law. Thus, the institution was not "ecclesiastical property" and the religious community no longer owned it. McGrath argued for other ways of keeping educational institutions "Catholic," that is, through charter and bylaw provisions.

In 1967 Saint Louis University became the first major Catholic institution to vest legal ownership and control in a board composed of both laymen and clergy. Fr. Paul Reinert, SJ, the university president, had consulted widely in the United States and in Rome before receiving approval from Father General Pedro Arrupe, SJ.

Soon after approving the St. Louis governance change, Fr. Arrupe commissioned the American provincials to draw up a statement on ownership, separate incorporation, and freedom. The statement sought to "establish that our colleges and universities and high schools, if they were civilly incorporated, are not ecclesiastical property, or if they were, were alienated upon becoming civilly incorporated."

By November 1967, Fr. Arrupe was beginning to worry about the "identity of an institution as Jesuit, if the responsible superiors of the Society could exercise no authority in it." But American Jesuit presidents pointed out that the Society had often had its name associated with apostolic causes without owning or controlling them. The crucial element was not structure but rather the extent of the commitment of the Society to a corporate apostolic activity.

In 1968 Fr. Arrupe, apparently having resolved his doubts, gave his general approval for separate incorporation of communities from institutions. Within a few years, most Jesuit schools moved in the direction of separate incorporation, but none asked permission from the Vatican to alienate property.

In 1973 Fr. (later Cardinal) Adam Maida published his view opposing the McGrath thesis, arguing that civil incorporation does not destroy the canon law status of Catholic institutions or their nature as ecclesiastical goods. But by the time the Maida critique of the McGrath thesis appeared, twenty of the twenty-eight Jesuit colleges and universities had already undergone separate incorporation.

In April 1975, Cardinal Garrone, prefect of the Sacred Congregation on Catholic Education, wrote to Father Arrupe, asking him to inform "appropriate Jesuit authorities in the U.S." that the McGrath thesis has "never been considered valid by our congregations, and has never been accepted." He asked Father Arrupe to ask "all those responsible to prepare to rescind any possibly invalid actions on this basis that have been made in the past." By then it was too late to change.

In 1976 the National Catholic Educational Association (NCEA) produced a document, "Relations of American Catholic Colleges and Universities with the Church," seeking to combine affiliation with the Church and institutional autonomy. The document asserts that a juridical relationship between the Church and university is neither desirable nor possible in the American context. It sought "both healthy distance and needed closeness."

Despite the insistence on institutional autonomy, relationships between American Catholic colleges and universities and American bishops remained healthy. A committee of bishops and presidents was established in 1974 to deal with the possible tension between the rights of ecclesiastical teaching authority and the rights related to academic freedom.

The third step taken to adjust governance was the development of boards of trustees independent of the sponsoring congregation, which included both religious and lay members.

Jesuit high schools, colleges, and universities under the new dispensation not only have made major strides in increased strength, quality, professionalism, and respect among peers, but have arguably become more intentionally Jesuit and Catholic because of the many and varied steps taken to foster that identity.

See also Collaboration; Poverty; United States of America; Universities, 1773–Present

An abridgement of an article by Charles Currie, "Seeking a Responsive Governance for a New Age." *Conversations* 46 (January 2014).

Patrick J. Howell, SJ

Service of Faith and the Promotion of Justice

The expression "service of faith and promotion of justice" comes from Decree Four of the 32nd General Congregation of the Society (1974–75): "The mission of the Society of Jesus today is the service of faith, of which the promotion of justice is an absolute requirement." The decree continues, "In one form or another, this has always been the mission of the Society," citing the Society's foundational document, the *Formula of the Institute*.

From one point of view, the linking of faith and justice simply makes concrete in today's world Jesus's words: "Not everyone who says to me 'Lord, Lord,' will enter the kingdom of heaven, but only the one who does the will of my Father in heaven" (Matthew 7:21). The will of God is that justice should be done in the world. Thus hearing the word of God is not sufficient; one must also put that word into practice (Luke 11:28). To paraphrase James 2:17, faith without justice is dead. From another point of view, pairing faith with justice (perhaps more so than with love, mercy, or solidarity) represents the Society's appropriation of the insight of liberation theology, since this coupling foregrounds so sharply the Gospel's understanding of the reign of God. The reign of God is about being set free from every form of oppression – political, economic, social, cultural, ethnic, racial – the demonic in every form; the reign of God means freedom. "Service of faith and the promotion of justice" was building on *Justice in the World*, the document issued by the 1971 Synod of Bishops. Faith and justice, as a way of defining the Society's mission today, is also very much connected to "the preferential option for the poor" and "solidarity." "Option for the poor," a phrase often associated with liberation theology, has entered into the Church's mainstream; it was used by Pedro Arrupe, by the bishops of Latin America, and by John Paul II. So, too, the term "solidarity."

Decree 4 called Jesuits to "a thoroughgoing reassessment of our traditional apostolic methods, attitudes and institutions" (#9) with an eye to the transformation of social structures (#40). "[S]olidarity with men and women who live a life of hardship and who are victims of oppression ... should be a characteristic of all of us (#48) ... It will therefore be necessary for a larger number of us to share more closely the lot of families who are of modest means, who make up the majority of every country, and who often are poor and oppressed (#49) ... To promote justice, to proclaim the faith and to lead others to a personal encounter with Christ are the three inseparable elements that make up the whole of our apostolate (#51)." Decree 4 was insisting that all the ministries of the Society worldwide – educational institutions, retreat houses, research centers, mass media, spiritual direction, parishes – should be rethought in terms of the role they play in the transformation of social structures and the protection of basic human rights.

The service of faith and the promotion of justice are not only a way of defining the Society's mission, however. This coupling also supposes a particular experience of God, a distinctive way of knowing the divine mystery, which comes from the heart of the Gospel. In it, the mystical and prophetic dimensions of Christian religious experience come together. Ultimately, the commitment to justice is grounded in the experience of loving and being loved by God, a love which becomes simultaneously a love of neighbor. In the next three General Congregations (GC 33, GC 34, and GC 35), the Society would expand the scope of Decree 4 by including dialogue with other religious traditions, the environment, and the challenges of globalization as central to its mission and as further areas for the promotion of justice.

The relation between faith and justice has been developed in many numbers of *Promotio Iustitiae*, published by the Social Justice and Ecology Secretariat of the Society in Rome.

See also Calvez, Jean-Yves, SJ; Justice; Mission; Preferential Option for the Poor

Calvez, Jean-Yves, *Faith and Justice: The Social Dimension of Evangelization*. St. Louis, MO: The Institute of Jesuit Sources, 1991.

Cook, Michael L., "Jesus' Parables and the Faith that Does Justice." *Studies in the Spirituality of Jesuits* 24, 5 (1992), 1–35.

Ivern, Francisco, "The Future of Faith and Justice: A Critical Review of Decree 4." *Studies in the Spirituality of Jesuits. Studies in the Spirituality of Jesuits* 14, 5 (1982), 1–30.

Kolvenbach, Peter-Hans, "The Service of Faith and the Promotion of Justice in Jesuit Higher Education." In George W. Traub, ed., *A Jesuit Education Reader*. Chicago, IL: Loyola University Press, 2008, pp. 144–62.

Kolvenbach, Peter-Hans, and Pedro Arrupe, "Faith, Justice, and American Jesuit Higher Education." *Studies in the Spirituality of Jesuits* 33, 1 (2001), 1–29.

Franco, Fernando Fernández, "Fe-Justicia." In *Diccionario de espiritualidad Ignaciana*. Vol. I, ed. José García de Castro. Bilbao: Ediciones Mensajero/Editorial Sal Terrae, 2007, pp. 877–85.

William Reiser, SJ

Sexual Abuse by Jesuits

In 2002 in Boston, Massachusetts, the clerical sex abuse scandal broke as a result of journalistic investigative reporting by *The Boston Globe*. In actuality, the "scandal" had been simmering for many years. What shocked most readers was not only the crimes committed by the abusing priests, but the deliberate cover-up of these offenses on the part of knowledgeable bishops and religious superiors. Their failure to protect vulnerable children and young adults would lead to much institutional soul-searching on the part of the Roman Catholic Church, especially its hierarchy and religious orders. Sadly, individual Jesuits and their superiors have not been immune from these accusations.

As early as 1985 Jason Berry, an investigative reporter writing in the *National Catholic Reporter*, publicized the case of a Louisiana diocesan priest who pled guilty to eleven counts of molestation of boys (Berry, *Lead Us Not*). What ensued was an avalanche of cases of clerical sexual abuse ranging over the entire United States and, eventually, throughout the world. The response of bishops and religious superiors was to "contain scandal" by imposing silence, sending the accused men for therapeutic treatment, or – and perhaps most insidious – removing them from the scene, but sending them to other assignments only with the admonition to "practice prudence" and not have any contact with children or adolescents.

Among the most notorious cases of sex abuse by US Jesuits were those members of the Oregon province who ministered in Alaska. In 2011 the province agreed to pay 250 million dollars to some 700 victims, most of them Native American and Alaska natives. These cases of abuse were perpetrated by some fifty-seven Jesuit priests and brothers, most of whom are now deceased. This same province had previously settled 200 cases and had filed for bankruptcy in 2009 ("Briefly Noted").

According to the watchdog group, BishopAccountability.org, which was established in 2003, 127 US Jesuits have been accused of abusing minors and at least two have been convicted and are serving prison sentences. Outside the United States, reports of Jesuits involved in sexual abuse soon began surfacing in England, Ireland, and Germany, and continue to make headlines.

Perhaps the most egregious offender among American Jesuits is the case of Donald McGuire, "a globe-trotting, spiritual retreat leader who counted Mother Teresa among his fans" (Rezendes, "For the Jesuits"). McGuire abused twenty-eight young men between the 1960s and 2004. In 2009 he was sentenced to twenty-five years in a federal prison. According to a positive act of the appropriate ecclesiastical authorities, which included the approval of the Jesuits' superior general, McGuire was dismissed from the Society and removed (laicized) from the priesthood.

Unfortunately, as a result of further allegations and litigation against McGuire, it came to light that four different provincial superiors had long known about his abuse but had taken no action until 1991. At that time McGuire was evaluated and sent for six months of treatment in a facility in Pennsylvania that deals with sexual disorders. When McGuire stopped cooperating with his treatment after only a few months, his provincial considered seeking his removal from the Jesuits. However, fearing McGuire's ability to wreak havoc within the Order, he allowed McGuire to continue his ministry, merely barring him from traveling with anyone under the age of 21. Four years later, additional complaints about McGuire's behavior with boys surfaced; still there was no confrontation by any Jesuit provincial authority. The most recent lawsuits against McGuire surfaced correspondence between him and his Jesuit superiors that has led to the resignation of at least one of these provincials from boards and positions of authority within Jesuit institutions (Rezendes, "For the Jesuits").

After the United States Conference of Catholic Bishops (USCCB) issued its *Charter for the Protection of Children and Young People* in 2002, the Society of Jesus in the United States engaged Praesidium, Inc., to aid them in developing "standards for accreditation" which would educate their members to the tragic consequences of sexual abuse and call both leaders and members to greater accountability and transparency in handling allegations of sexual abuse, as well as instructing them on follow-up and outreach to victims and on how members charged with sexual abuse should be supervised. Known as "Instruments of Hope and Healing: Safeguarding Children and Young People," these standards were adopted by the US Conference of Major Superiors of Men (CMSM) in 2012. All US Jesuits are now required every three years to receive three hours of professional education in the areas of sexual abuse prevention, response, and supervision guidelines.

In Europe the Society of Jesus has become involved in an initiative located at the Pontifical Gregorian University in Rome that focuses on the prevention of sexual abuse of children and vulnerable persons. Known as the Centre for the Protection of Minors, it is part of the academic structure of the university and is headed by Fr. Hans Zollner, SJ, assisted by Professor Karlijn Demasure as its executive director.

See also Scandals; United States of America

Applewhite, Monica, and Paul Macke, "The Response of Religious Institutes of Men to the Crisis of Sexual Abuse in the Roman Catholic Church in the United States." In Thomas G. Plante and Kathleen L. McChesney, eds., *Sexual Abuse in the Catholic Church: A Decade of Crisis 2001–2012*. Santa Barbara, CA: Praeger, 2011, pp. 225–28.

Berry, Jason, *Lead Us Not into Temptation: Catholic Priests and the Sexual Abuse of Children*. Urbana: University of Illinois Press, 2000.

"Briefly Noted." *The Christian Century*. April 11, 2011.

"The Jesuits and Donald McGuire SJ." www.bishopaccountability.org/docs/jesuits/McGuire_Donald/Punitive_Damages_Motion/#klein. Accessed on February 28, 2016.

Rezendes, Michael, "For the Jesuits, a Long Road to Accountability." *The Boston Globe*, April 15, 2012. www.bostonglobe.com/metro/2012/04/14/for-jesuits-long-road-accountability/FG0IkXq2vO9EsyjSW3RRTJ/story.html. Accessed on February 28, 2016.

Mary Ann Hinsdale, IHM

Sicard, Claude, SJ (1677–1726)

Born in Aubagne, France, Sicard entered the Jesuits in Avignon in 1692. He was professor at Lyons before being sent as a missionary to Syria. In Aleppo he first concentrated on the study of Arabic before being sent to Egypt in 1707. He would spend the rest of his life there working with the Copts and discovering the forgotten monuments of Egypt, publishing the first results in 1717. It is said that he shortened his nights in order to meet the request of the regent of France (Duke of Orleans) and his own superior general to record Egypt's ancient monuments. He documented twenty of the major pyramids, twenty-four complete temples, and over fifty decorated tombs. He also produced the first modern map of Egypt. He was one of the early visitors to the Coptic desert monasteries as well as to the Valley of the Kings in Upper Egypt. He traveled the shores of the Red Sea, calculating the crossing of the Hebrews in the Exodus; he described Mount Sinai, the cataracts, the Etephantine monuments and Philae. He sketched the plans of the buildings and cities he discovered.

In 1718 he founded, in Akhmim, the first Coptic Catholic community. He refused to separate the Catholics from the Orthodox in the administration of the sacraments and fought long with the Roman authorities in defense of his view.

In 1726, he left aside scientific pursuits entirely to aid the people stricken by the pestilence in Cairo. He contracted the sickness himself and died in April at the age of

49 years. Sicard's works were reproduced in the *Lettres édifiantes et curieuses*, Volume V. A critical edition of his writings was published by the Institut français d'Archéologie orientale: *Oeuvres* (3 vols., Cairo, 1982).

    See also Eygpt; *Lettres Édifiantes et Curieuses*; Syria

John Donohue, SJ

Sitjar, Tomas, SJ, Bl. (1866–1936), and His Companions

Tomas Sitjar Fortiá was born on March 21, 1866, in Gerona (Catalonia) and was admitted to the Society of Jesus in the novitiate of Veruela (Zaragoza) on July 21, 1880. After studying philosophy at Tortosa (Catalonia), he taught philosophy for eight years at the Diocesan Seminary of Montevideo (Uruguay). He returned to Tortosa for health reasons to study theology and was ordained to the priesthood in 1900. From 1902 to 1921 he taught philosophy to Jesuit scholastics in that city and later on at Sarriá.

In 1923 he was appointed superior of the residence of Tarragona, a position he kept until 1929 when he became rector of the Novitiate College of Gandía (Valencia). He was working there until 1932 when the Society of Jesus was suppressed throughout Spain and most of the Spanish Jesuits went away into exile. Others decided to stay, as Father Sitjar did, sharing an apartment with another Jesuit called Brother Pedro Gelabert Amer, who was born in Manacor (Balearic Islands) on March 29, 1887.

In 1936, the first year of the Spanish Civil War, a violent phenomenon of persecution against members of the Catholic Church became widespread throughout the Iberian Peninsula, with special radicalism in Catalonia and Valencia. There were also occasional episodes against Catholics and other confessions in the *Nacional* area, dominated by Franco's troops, although these episodes were few and far between. In Valencia, the persecutions resulted in the destruction of an architectural, artistic, and documentary religious heritage and culminated in the execution of many people, including secular clergy as well as religious orders and subordinate organizations of the Catholic Church. The fact that Franco and his followers called these victims "martyrs," extending that term to those who died defending the Franco dictatorship, still generates controversy and rejection.

In this context of violence and war, Father Sitjar was arrested, compelled to leave his house by force on July 25, 1936, and sent to a provisional prison. There he met his partner, Brother Pedro Gelabert and two other Jesuits, Father Constantine Carbonell Sempere and Ramón Grimaltos Monllor. Brother Gelabert entered the Society when he was 20 years old and in 1936 was serving in Gandía. He had previously worked in the Majorcan Montesion College, the Jesuit college in Alicante and at the Veruela Juniorate, where he stood out for his expertise in electricity. Father Carbonell was born on April 12, 1866, in the industrial city of Alcoy (Alicante) and he joined the Society at age 20. His last assignment was also the residence of Gandía and he was, like Father Sitjar, 70 years old at the time of his arrest. For his part, Brother Grimaltos, born on March 3, 1861, in the little Valencian village of Puebla Larga, had entered the Society of Jesus in 1890 and lived at the residence of Gandía doing housework before the Society was suppressed.

Father Tomas Sitjar's judgment took place on August 18, and he was executed in Palma de Gandía two days later. The other three aforementioned Jesuits were also shot in the Valencian town of Valldigna de Tabernes on August 23, 1936.

But these four Jesuits were not the only ones who suffered persecution and death during this period of war, since twelve more members of the Society suffered the same destiny in the Valencian area. Among them was Brother Joseph Tarrats Comaposada, born in Manresa on August 29, 1878. He had joined the Society at age 17 and worked as a tailor in the scholasticate at Tortosa and later as an infirmarian at the professed house in Valencia. Upon the dissolution of the Society, he remained in Spain to care for sick Jesuits, and he was working at the Asilo de Valencia (Nursing Home) in 1936 when he was arrested and executed on September 28.

Father Paul Bori Puig, born in Vilet de Malda (Tarragona) on November 12, 1864, was also at this nursing home. He was ordained a priest in 1888 and entered the Society of Jesus three years later. He had served in the houses of Barcelona, Veruela, and Gandía. He was executed in Benimaclet (Valencia) on the day after Joseph Tarrats's execution.

The ailing Juan Bautista Ferreres Boluda, a well-known professor of moral theology and canon law, was also arrested and imprisoned. His imprisonment is believed to have hastened his death, which happened on December 29 in Valencia, the city of his birth (on November 28, 1861).

Another group of Jesuits was shot in the town of Paterna. Fr. Darío Hernández Morato, born October 25, 1880, in Valencia, was killed on September 29, 1936; he was executed along with Jesuit Brother Vicente Sales Genovés, also Valencian, born October 15, 1881. On October 15, Narciso Baste y Baste was killed, born December 16, 1866, in San Andrés de Palomar (Barcelona). Baste y Baste had served as the director of the Board of Youth Workers in Valencia. On November 29, Alfredo Simon Colomina (born in Valencia on March 8, 1877) also fell.

Father Sitjar and all the aforementioned Jesuits were part of the group of 233 religious beatified by John Paul II together, on March 11, 2001, calling them "Martyrs of the Spanish Civil War." This designation generated a mixed popular reaction of applause and rejection.

See also Blesseds; Martyrs, Ideal and History; Saints; Spain

Segura, Ramón Correcher, *Beatos Tomás Sitjar Fortiá, Constantino Carbonell Sempere, Pedro Gelabert Amer, Ramón Grimaltos Montllor de la Compañía de Jesús, mártires.* (Mártires de Cristo, vol. 87). Valencia: Archdiocese of Valencia, 2001.

Inmaculada Fernández Arrillaga

Skarga, Piotr, SJ (1536–1612)

Piotr Skarga (Pawe̜ski, Powe̜ski) was born in 1536 in Grójec (central Poland) and died in Krakow in 1612. After his studies at Krakow University in the early 1550s, he was appointed head of the parish school at the St. John church in Warsaw, cathedral canon in Lvov, and chancellor of the chapter house. In 1568 he traveled to Rome where he entered the novitiate of the Society the next year and completed his studies in theology. Upon his return to Poland in 1571, Skarga was appointed preacher and professor in Pułtusk and Vilnius, and subsequently the first rector of the Vilnius Academy (1579–84). Between 1584 and 1588, Skarga was the superior of the St. Barbara residence in Krakow, where he founded a number of charitable organizations. The turning point of Skarga's career was his appointment in 1588 as royal preacher to King Sigismund III, a crucial office of political influence that he held almost until his death. But Skarga exerted an even greater impact through his publications. Along with some minor polemical works, including his treatise *On the Unity of the Church of God*, Skarga published a history of the Church and *The Lives of Saints* (Vilnius, 1579), arguably one of the most widely read books of the time. No less important are collections of his sermons: *Sermons for Sundays and Holidays* (Krakow, 1595), *Sermons on the Seven Sacraments* (Krakow, 1600), and *Sermons Preached to the Diet* (1597). These sermons are considered to be among the finest works of Polish literature before the Commonwealth's partitions of the late eighteenth century. Shadowed by myths, Skarga became a symbol of both staunch anti-Protestantism and patriotism.

See also Poland; Preaching

Obirek, Stanisław, *Wizja Kościoła i państwa w kazaniach ks. Piotra Skargi SJ*. Krakow: WAM, 1994.
Tazbir, Janusz, *Piotr Skarga, szermierz kontrreformacji*. Warsaw: Wiedza Powszechna, 1983.

Robert A. Maryks

Slavery

In 1537 Pope Paul III condemned the international slave trade. Three years later, Paul approved the founding of the Jesuits. The Society of Jesus was thus born into a Church at the outset of a tortuous analysis of modern slavery. Jesuits paralleled the wider Church in more consistently critiquing the slave trade than slavery itself.

Jesuits felt that this trade impeded the evangelization of indigenous peoples. The reductions they established in South America were designed to shield potential victims from the trade. Like other religious orders, however, Jesuits sometimes succumbed to the temptation to rationalize the importation of African labor as a less objectionable alternative to indigenous slavery. Hoping to sustain their practice of offering ministries *gratis*, many Jesuits also entertained the hope that plantations might provide the necessary financial foundation.

Meanwhile, some Jesuits followed the example of Peter Claver in seeking to mitigate the slave trade by tending to the spiritual and corporal needs of its victims. Jesuit protests against Spanish and Portuguese practice of the trade eventually became a major cause of the Suppression. The Society's solicitude for American indigenous peoples paralleled their determination to protect Asians from the excesses of European colonialism.

Slavery itself, however, had explicit scriptural warrant, the endorsement of most Greco-Roman philosophers, and the sanction of both Church Fathers and scholastic theologians. When Christian abolitionism appeared in the western world during the latter part of the eighteenth century, its roots in both the Reformation churches and the Enlightenment prompted many Jesuits to regard it as heretical. Jesuits were slow to realize that modern economics had created a form of slavery beyond the competence of traditional thinking. A lack of historical consciousness also impeded reflection.

English-speaking Jesuits became involved in slavery through the Maryland mission. As Native American presence there diminished, Jesuits concentrated on ministry to lay planter elites and their slaves. It is probable that gifts from benefactors among these elites began the Society's practice of possessing its own slaves. Jesuits practiced catechesis evenhandedly, seeing both planters and slaves as fully entitled to Catholic formation.

Protestants assaulted Maryland Catholics with the charge that they forfeited the civil liberties of property-holding Englishmen by clinging to their faith. The Society fought this claim by articulating its corporate right to all forms of property ownership, including slaveholding. Thus, there emerged a fateful decision to accommodate slavery as an assertion of religious liberty. In the wake of the Suppression and the achievement of American independence, former Jesuits formed a clergy corporation under Maryland law so that they could continue this accommodation.

After the founding of Georgetown in 1789, the plan that the estates would support the new academy financially was never fulfilled. In 1820 and 1830, the Roman Jesuit Curia appointed the Irish Jesuit Peter Kenny as official visitor to the mission. He first decreed strict restrictions on direct Jesuit oversight of slaves, but during the second visitation recommended that the slaves be sold. As Catholic immigration increased, many abolitionists embraced nativism as well. Jesuit officials had decided it would not secure Catholic liberty to provoke controversy with such a coalition. Furthermore, the estates were still financially unsound and the demographics of immigration suggested the desirability of shifting ministry to cities. In 1838 most of the Maryland slaves were sold to a planter in Louisiana.

American Jesuits sought to maintain internal unity during the Civil War by no longer discussing slavery within their communities. After emancipation in 1865, they agreed with the American hierarchy that it had been poorly prepared for and executed too abruptly.

By 1890 international slavery seemed moribund and Pope Leo XIII had issued a clearer condemnation of the practice than any predecessor had. Jesuits retained, however, a slaveholding legacy of condescension toward descendants of African slaves. Not until the 1960s did a combination of developments – post-colonialism, the international human and civil rights revolutions, the promotion of indigenous clergy throughout the Church, and the Vatican II spirit of critical engagement with the world – finally prompt the Society to question this attitude. With involuntary human trafficking reviving in the world in the early twenty-first century, a Society transformed by Pedro Arrupe's attentiveness to political and social refugees sought to accelerate its reckoning with its earlier practice of slaveholding for the sake of making its opposition to contemporary forms of bondage more effective.

See also Claver, Peter, SJ, St.; Haciendas (and Jesuit Estates); Maryland Mission; Scandals; Vieira, Antonio, SJ

Davis, David Brion, *The Problem of Slavery in Western Culture.* New York: Oxford, 1966.
Murphy, Thomas, *Jesuit Slaveholding in Maryland, 1717–1838.* New York: Routledge, 2001.
Ross, Andrew C., *A Vision Betrayed: The Jesuits in Japan and China, 1542–1742.* Maryknoll, NY: Orbis Books, 1994.
Zanca, Kenneth J., ed., *American Catholics and Slavery, 1789–1866: An Anthology of Primary Documents.* Lanham, MD: University Press of America, 1994.

Thomas Murphy, SJ

Smulders, Pieter, SJ (1911–2000)

Smulders, from a family of three boys and three girls, and a Jesuit since 1930, was appointed by Augustin Bea in 1937 to study dogmatic theology in Rome, where he published his dissertation on the Trinitarian doctrine of Hilary of Poitiers (1944), later followed by the edition of his *De Trinitate* (1979). A collection of studies on Hilary, entitled *Hilariana*, was never finished. He taught dogmatic theology in Maastricht and Amsterdam, where he was rector between 1974 and 1977, and published books and articles on the sacraments, the creed, and Christological dogma. In all his research he tried to discover continuity between the thoughts of the Church Fathers, the scholastic teachers of the Middle Ages, and contemporary theological reflection. In 1962 he published an "attempt at theological appreciation" of Pierre Teilhard de Chardin, translated into several languages.

Just before the Second Vatican Council, he was asked to become *peritus* (expert) of the Indonesian bishops' conference. He contributed greatly to the first and fourth chapter of *Dei Verbum*, the dogmatic constitution on divine revelation, to the text of the permanent diaconate, and to the chapter on the task of the Church in the world in *Gaudium et spes*. He confessed more than once that "ecclesiastical authorities were afraid of the blowing of the Spirit". Later he became a member of the theological commission of the Pastoral Council of the Dutch Church Province (1966–70).

His papers are kept in the archives of the Dutch Jesuits, and in the Catholic Documentation Centre, both at Nijmegen.

See also The Netherlands; *Periti*; Vatican II

Fides Sacramenti, Sacramentum Fidei: Studies in Honour of Pieter Smulders. Assen: Van Gorcum, 1981. Wicks, Jared, "Pieter Smulders and Dei Verbum" (5 parts). *Gregorianum* 82–86 (2001–05).

Paul Begheyn, SJ

Soares-Prabhu, George, SJ (1929–1995)

George Soares-Prabhu was a Jesuit from the western Indian state of Maharashtra. Although he started his undergraduate education in the sciences, later on, as a Jesuit, he became a renowned biblical theologian. During his education in India, Italy, and France, Soares-Prabhu trained in the historical-critical method. His doctoral dissertation on Matthew 1–2 was published as *The Formula Quotations in the Infancy Narrative of Matthew: An Enquiry into the Tradition History of Matthew*, by the Pontifical Biblical Institute in 1976. He went on to pioneer an Indian hermeneutic for biblical exegesis, a method that approaches the Scriptures contextually from within the Indian social, cultural, and religious milieu, in which, for example, the majority of Indian Christians are Dalits, outcastes from the prevailing caste hierarchy, and seen as a source of ritual pollution. Soares-Prabhu drew upon liberation theology, which he adapted from its original Latin American roots and applied to the Indian context, where the roots of structural injustice are more religious and social than economic and political. At the time of his sudden death in a road accident in 1995, much of his work was yet unpublished. A series of editors have compiled his writings on biblical spirituality and contextual liberationist exegesis, including *The Dharma of Jesus* (1997), *Biblical Themes for a Contextual Theology Today* (1999), *A Biblical Theology for India* (1999), *Theology of Liberation: An Indian Biblical Perspective* (2001), and *Biblical Spirituality of Liberative Action* (2003). George Soares-Prabhu, SJ, has received growing international recognition as a biblical theologian.

See also Biblical Studies; Dalits and Dalit Theology; India; Liberation Theology

D'Sa, Francis X., ed., *The Dharma of Jesus: Interdisciplinary Essays in Memory of George Soares-Prabhu, SJ*. Pune: Institute for the Study of Religion; Anand, India: Gujarat Sahitya Prakash, 1997.

D'Sa, Francis X., and Isaac Padinjarekuttu, eds., *Biblical Themes for A Contextual Theology Today: Collected Writings of George M. Soares-Prabhu, SJ*. 2 vols. Pune: Jnana-Deepa Vidyapeeth, 1999.

Brent Howitt Otto, SJ

Socius

Socius (from the Latin word for companion) is a term ordinarily used to refer to the assistant to the provincial. The role commonly involves a combination of functions like administrator, executive assistant, confidant, and sounding-board. In the *Manual for Juridical Practice of the Society of Jesus* (#287, par. 1) it is stated that "to him in due measure should be accommodated what is said about the Secretary of the Society in the *Constitutions* Part IX c. 6, n. 8, E (800, 801)." In this part of the *Constitutions*, the secretary is referred to as one who ordinarily accompanies the general and who "should be his memory for everything which he must write and discuss, and finally for all the affairs of his office." He also manages all of the correspondence and reports coming across the general's desk. The *Socius* is, by office, a province consultor and is ordinarily the admonitor of the provincial (*Manual*, #287, pars. 2 and 3; #272, par. 2). In addition, if the provincial dies without designating a vice provincial, then until the general makes provision his place will be taken by the *socius*, if he is professed of four vows (*Manual*, #286, par. 2, 1).

A good *socius*, in particular one who can combine gifts of administration with personal wisdom, discretion, and sensitivity, who has the humility required to be the "number two" man, and who enjoys the trust of the members of the province, can be of enormous help to a provincial and to the sound governance of the province.

It should be noted, finally, that the term *socius* is also used to designate the assistant to the master of novices, should one be required (*Manual*, #66, par. 2).

See also Province

Manual for Juridical Practice of the Society of Jesus. Rome, 1997; English edition 1999.

Gerard O'Hanlon, SJ

Sogang University

The Korean Church hierarchy requested Vatican help to establish "a Catholic college for the spiritual and intellectual formation of Korean youth" in Korea. In 1948, Pope Pius XII (1939–58) encouraged them to establish an educational institution. The Pope entrusted this project to the Society of Jesus. Fr. Jean-Baptiste Janssens, SJ (1889–1964), Jesuit superior general, entrusted the project to the Japanese vice province of the Society. However, the Korean War (1950–53) interrupted all efforts to bring the Jesuits to Korea. When the war ended, this project was resumed. Fr. Pedro Arrupe, SJ (1907–91), vice provincial of the Japanese vice province, made a special visit to study the feasibility of establishing a Jesuit college in Korea. Subsequently, Fr. Thedore Geppert, SJ (1905–2002), a German missionary and former rector of Sophia (Jesuit) University in Tokyo, was sent to Korea in 1954 in order to begin preliminary preparation for a Catholic college. In his decree of establishment of the Korea mission in 1955, Fr. Janssens transferred the project of the establishment of Sogang College to the Wisconsin Jesuit province. In the same year, two Wisconsin Jesuits, Fr. Kenneth Killoren, SJ, and Br. Arthur Dethlefs, SJ, arrived in Korea to work with Fr. Geppert.

Eventually, under the motto of *Obedire Veritati*, Sogang College was officially opened in Seoul on April 18, 1960, based on the Catholic faith and on Jesuit educational ideals, with six departments and 158 students. Sogang quickly became famous for its innovative manner of educational organization, such as having an international standard curriculum, a sabbatical year for professors, and an emphasis on English language teaching. In addition, the international Jesuit network contributed to quality in the education provided. From its founding many Jesuit scholars from abroad visited Sogang to teach on either a short-term or a long-term basis. Sogang soon became one of the leading schools in Korea.

In 1970 Sogang opened a new chapter in its history. It established several new departments, such as science and engineering. A small Catholic liberal arts college thus began its growth into a large university. Fr. John P. Daly, SJ, became the first president of Sogang University. In 1985 Korea, until then a dependent region of the Wisconsin Jesuit province, became an independent region of the Society of Jesus and a Korean Jesuit became president of Sogang for the first time. Twenty years later, in 2005, a lay Catholic became the president of Sogang University.

One very important characteristic of Sogang from its beginning and up to the present has been cooperation with lay Catholics and even with non-Catholics. Since Korea is religiously very diverse, and Catholics are a small minority (10 percent of Korea's whole population was Catholic in 2014), Jesuits in Korea had to work with openness. As a result, from the start Sogang has been a place where people of various beliefs worked together, even before the Church began to put a stress on cooperation with laity and on interreligious dialogue.

As the world becomes more globalized, Sogang also turns its eyes abroad. It has established a sister-relationship with 268 universities abroad: 60 in Asia; 100 in Europe; 84 in North America; 12 in South America; 9 in Oceania; and 3 in Africa. Especially significant since 2010 has been the annual Sogang-Sophia Festival of Exchange (SOFEX), in which members of Sogang and Sophia universities have academic and cultural exchanges, along with friendly sports events.

Sogang University has continued to grow. In recent years, it has operated twenty-seven departments in nine schools (School of Humanities and International Cultures, School of Social Sciences, School of Integrated Knowledge, School of Natural Sciences, School of Engineering, School of Economics, Sogang Business School, School of Communication, and Interdisciplinary Programs). Twelve graduate schools and thirty-five institutes for research in various areas are attached to Sogang. The number of students is about 16,000, and there are about 800 professors, including fourteen Jesuits and temporary lecturers, teaching in Sogang. It has about 60,000 alumni.

However, Sogang's successful growth has another side. Growth presents many challenges to the University in the course of fulfilling its mission, especially in a very highly competitive and rapidly changing Korean society. Key questions are the following. How can Sogang keep its Catholic and Jesuit identity? How can it foster the practice of *cura personalis*? How can Sogang promote a faith that does justice to its members? How can it form men and women for and with others? How can Sogang keep its academic excellence? Since its foundation, Sogang University has enjoyed great success within a relatively short time in Korea. It now faces a new critical phase with crucial challenges. The future of Sogang will be measured by how it responds to these.

See also Interreligious Dialogue; Korea-Cambodia; Sophia University; Universities, 1773–Present

Yongsu Paschal Kim, SJ

Sommervogel, Carlos, SJ (1834–1902)

Born on January 8, 1834, in Strasbourg (Bas-Rhin), Carlos Sommervogel entered the Society on February 2, 1853, in Issenheim (Haut-Rhin). After studies at Saint-Acheul (Amiens), he worked as prefect of discipline at Paris-Vaugirard, where he collected books while studying philosophy in private. In 1865 he returned to Amiens, where he studied theology privately while continuing as prefect of discipline (1865–67). He then worked on the staff of the journal *Études* (1867–79) and was decorated for chaplaincy (1870–71) during the Franco-Prussian War. Having made a list of errors that he had discovered in Augustin and Aloys de Backer's *Bibliothèque des écrivains de la Compagnie de Jésus*, Sommervogel helped them bring their work to completion (3 vols., 1869–76). After serving briefly as *socius* to the provincial (1880–83), he continued his collaboration with the de Backers until the death of Aloys in 1883. Missioned to succeed the de Backers, he moved to Louvain (1885) where he began work on a third edition of the *Bibliothèque* (9 vols., 1890–1900). Sommervogel returned to Paris in 1895, where he served for three years as superior of *Études* while contributing bibliographical notes to the journal (1895–1901). He died on May 4, 1902, while working on the index (vol. 10) of the *Bibliothèque*, which Pierre Bliard would complete. Bliard also realized Sommervogel's plan to revise, as a second part of the *Bibliothèque* (vol. 11), Auguste Carayon's 1864 *Bibliographie historique de la Compagnie de Jésus*. Ernest-M. Rivière produced a supplement (vol. 12) to the *Bibliothèque*.

See also Bibliographies; *Études*; France; Pseudonyms

Danieluk, Robert, *La bibliothèque de Carlos Sommervogel: le sommet de l'œuvre bibliographique de la Compagnie de Jésus (1890–1932)*. Rome: Institutum Historicum Societatis Iesu, 2006.
Sommervogel, Carlos, *Bibliothèque de la Compagnie de Jésus*. 12 vols., 2nd edn. Brussels: Oscar Schepens; Paris: Alphonse Picard, 1890–1932.

William P. O'Brien, SJ

Sophia University

The story of the first Catholic university in Japan begins with the arrival of Francis Xavier in Kagoshima in August 1549. In a missive to Rome, he wrote of his intention "first to go to Miyako [Kyoto], where the king resides; and then to visit the various colleges where people engage in learning." This was a reference to the various Buddhist schools that reminded him of the colleges of the University of Paris, where he had studied. A generation later, Alessandro Valignano (1539–1606) established a college of higher studies for European and Japanese Jesuits studying for the priesthood at Funai (Ōita) under the patronage of Ōtomo Sōrin (1530–87). Unlike any other college before it, its curriculum attempted to integrate the humanist traditions of late Renaissance Europe with the classical texts of Japan and China.

Following an extended period of persecution (1614–1873), religious tolerance was enshrined in law by the Meiji government in 1873. Several decades later, in 1903, the German Orientalist, Joseph Dahlmann, SJ, visited Japan and met with Pope Pius X in 1905. After papal envoy Bishop William Henry O'Connell met with Emperor Meiji and Prime Minister Katsura Tarō and gained their support for the project, the Pope asked the Society of Jesus to establish a new Catholic university in Tokyo. As a result, Dahlmann returned to Japan in 1908 accompanied by James Rockliff of Great Britain and Henri Boucher, a Frenchman who had been rector of the Jesuits at Zikawei in Shanghai. Two years later, they were joined by another German Jesuit, Hermann Hoffmann, who would become the first president of the university.

The school's legal corporation was established in 1911, and in 1912 the Jesuits purchased prime land in the historic Kioi-chō area of Tokyo, formerly part of the holdings of the Owari clan during the Edo period. In April 1913, the Ministry of Education approved its status as a private "college" (*senmon gakkō*). It began with fifteen students and three departments, Philosophy, German Literature, and Commerce, organized into a two-year preparatory and a three-year main course program.

The meeting of eastern and western learning, which Valignano had strived for centuries earlier, was reflected in the choice of name for the new Jesuit university. Officially named Universitas Sedis sapientiae (or University of the "Seat of Wisdom," after a title of the Virgin Mary), students began to use the Greek word "Sophia" in the 1920s in conjunction with the Japanese "Jōchi," a classical Buddhist word for "wisdom" or "higher knowledge."

On September 1, 1923, the Great Kanto Earthquake leveled most of Tokyo. But Sophia rebuilt and in 1928 was formally granted full university (*daigaku*) status. On May 5, 1932, a group of sixty students was taken by their Sophia military officer to Yasukuni Shrine to pay their respects, but a group of Catholics refused to bow and declared that forcing such acts upon them violated their freedom of conscience and religion. A crisis ensued that cast a long shadow over the University throughout the years of militarist government until the end of World War II. Many Sophia students were conscripted and died during the war.

Despite these setbacks, a study-abroad program was launched in 1935 and marked the beginning of Sophia's history as a university actively engaged in student exchanges throughout the world – which has developed into present agreements with 245 universities in forty-nine countries (August, 2015). A number of important academic projects marked the first decades. In 1938 the German Jesuit Johannes Kraus launched *Monumenta Nipponica*, one of the most prestigious western-language journals of Japanese studies in the world today; and in 1939 Johannes Laures, another German Jesuit, founded the Japanese Christian Research Institute (later Kirishitan bunko). The following year marked the publication of the first volume of the Japanese *Catholic Encyclopedia*.

Postwar years saw the reconstruction of buildings destroyed by the Tokyo air raids, purchase of new land adjacent to the existing campus in Yotsuya, and the arrival of many young Jesuits from all over the world to help educate the next generation of Japanese

Figure 62 Students on the campus of Sophia University Yotsuya campus on "Yukata (kimono) Day" 2015. Photograph Antoni Ucerler, SJ

youth, on whose shoulders would fall the heavy responsibility of rebuilding their country. In 1957–58 the first women were admitted as students.

The Shakujii campus for the Faculty of Theology opened in 1947; and the "International Division" (presently the Faculty of Liberal Arts) was launched in 1949. The Faculty of Science and Technology, founded in 1962, was followed by the School of Social Welfare in 1963. In 1973 a two-year Junior College for Women was started on a new campus in Hadano (Kanagawa Prefecture); and in 2011 Sophia took over the Nursing program from Seibo Gakuen. In 2013 Sophia celebrated its centennial anniversary. The University enrolled 12,475 undergraduates and 1,340 graduate students in the academic year 2015. Thus, Xavier's dream to found a university in the "Capital" of Japan had become a reality.

See also Japan; Sogang University; Universities, 1773–Present; Xavier, Francis, SJ, St.

M. Antoni J. Ucerler, SJ

Sources Chrétiennes

Sources Chrétiennes, published by Éditions du Cerf in Paris, is a bilingual collection of the most important texts from the first 1,400 years of the Church. Founded in Lyon in 1942 by Jean Daniélou, SJ, Henri de Lubac, SJ, and Claude Mondésert, SJ, the collection today numbers approximately 530 volumes and is edited by the Institut des Sources

Chrétiennes whose current director is Bernard Meunier. This institute is now affiliated with the Centre National de la Recherche Scientifique (CNRS).

The first volume of the series was a translation by Jean Daniélou of Gregory of Nyssa's *Contemplation sur la vie de Moïse*, a subtle reminder of the Semitic origins of Christianity at a time of French occupation by an anti-Semitic regime.

The series consists principally of Greek and Latin early texts, although it also includes some eastern (Syriac, Armenian, and Coptic) texts along with some medieval works by authors such as Bernard of Clairvaux and Simeon the New Theologian. Greek authors include Basil of Caesarea, Gregory of Nazianzus, John Chrysostom, Cyril of Alexandria, and Theodoret of Cyr (sometimes rendered as Cyrrhus), among others. Representative Latin authors include Tertullian, Cyprian, Hilary of Poitiers, Ambrose, and Gregory the Great. The texts include apologetics, biblical commentary, sermons, treatises, letters, liturgies, poems and hymns, dialogues, ascetic writings, Church canons, and history.

The original text is on the left-hand page with a new French translation on the right. Some eastern texts (in Armenian, Syriac) are available only in translation. The critical apparatus, including introductions, notes, and indexes, helps scholars and the educated layperson to access Christian biblical, liturgical, and patristic sources.

Sources Chrétiennes also oversees the *Biblindex* project, an Index of Biblical Quotations and Allusions in Early Christian Literature. A parallel collection of the works of Philo of Alexandria has developed. A similar German bilingual collection, *Fontes Christani*, is currently published by Brepols of Turnhout, Belgium.

See also Archives and Libraries; Bibliographies; Daniélou, Jean, Cardinal, SJ; France; Lubac, Henri de, Cardinal, SJ

Susan K. Wood

South Asia Jesuit Colleges and Universities

Jesuit efforts in Indian tertiary education have been growing rapidly over the past century. The Jesuit presence in tertiary institutions today comprises colleges (50), technical institutes (22), management/business schools (15), specialized engineering colleges (4), and one autonomous Jesuit university. This growth in part has been a response to India's rapidly growing economy over the past twenty years, particularly in the information technology sector, which has created a high demand for training in business management, engineering, and other technical fields. The mission of Jesuit tertiary education also underwent a shift of focus after the Second Vatican Council (1962–65) and the 32nd General Congregation (GC 32) of the Jesuits (1974–75). GC 32 called for a greater emphasis on justice and serving the poor and marginalized. In the Indian context this drew attention to the needs of *adivasis* (tribal groups) and Dalits (untouchables), by broadening their educational scope. Some institutions also shifted to teaching in the vernacular language to expand access.

Seeing a need to organize and support Jesuit educational efforts across India, the major superiors of India founded the Jesuit Educational Association of India (JEA) in 1961. JEA was a separately incorporated body, which subsequently was folded into the Jesuit Conference of India (JCI) when JCI was legally incorporated as a body to help coordinate the works of the various Jesuit provinces. JEA, and subsequently the Education Section of the JCI, had a purview that entailed all educational efforts at every level. The scope of its mission was eventually too broad, so the Jesuit Higher Education Association of South Asia (JHEASA) has now been created to deal only with tertiary-level institutions.

See also Asia; India; Universities, 1773–Present

"Higher Education – JHEASA." Jesuit Higher Education Secretriat. Accessed December 28, 2014.

Parkhe, Camil, *Contribution of Christian Missionaries in India.* Anand, India: Gujarat Sahitya Prakash, 2007.

Brent Howitt Otto, SJ

Southwell, Robert, SJ (1561–1595)

Southwell's initial application for the Jesuits was deferred; he eventually entered the novitiate in Rome in 1578. After ordination, he served as prefect of studies at the English College, Rome. Jesuit General Claudio Acquaviva refused Robert Persons's request that Southwell be sent to the dangerous English mission because the General believed him to be too young and his work at the College too important. Acquaviva finally agreed, and Southwell departed with Henry Garnet in 1586. Southwell was based in London where he received incoming clergy, known to him because of his work at the English College, and distributed them in Catholic households. Circa 1590 he moved to a London house of Anne Dacre Howard, countess of Arundel, whose husband Philip was then imprisoned in the Tower of London. Southwell developed a series of consolatory letters to the imprisoned earl into *An Epistle of Comfort*, important for the introduction of Ignatian spirituality into the English devotional tradition. Thus was the only prose work published during his lifetime. A *Humble Supplication to Her Majestie* appeared posthumously, published by English secular clergy intending to use its lavish praise of Queen Elizabeth against the perceived pro-Spanish myopia of other English Jesuits. Various domestic presses published his poems anonymously. Their quality has secured him a place in the English literary canon; attempts to establish kinship between him and William Shakespeare on the basis of a posthumous dedication to a "W.S." have been less successful, and remain contentious.

Richard Topcliffe, a most notorious and cruel anti-Catholic pursuivant, tracked Southwell with information provided by Anne Bellamy. Topcliffe apprehended Southwell at the Bellamy home in Uxenden, Harrow, in June 1592. Imprisoned and tortured, he was found guilty of being a priest and executed on February 21, 1595. During the trial, Southwell was blamed for the introduction of the subversive doctrine and practice of Jesuit equivocation into English discourse.

See also Poetry; Martyrs, Ideal and History; Mental Reservation; United Kingdom

Devlin, Christopher, *The Life of Robert Southwell, Poet and Martyr.* London: Longmans, Green & Co., 1956.

Southwell, Robert, *Collected Poems.* Ed. Anne Sweeney and Peter Davidson. Manchester: Manchester University Press, 2007.

Thomas McCoog, SJ

Spain

The first Jesuits to arrive in Spain were Antonio de Araoz and Peter Faber, who, despite diplomatic obstacles, obtained key contacts for the establishment of the

Society of Jesus. In 1542 these Jesuits met in Barcelona with Francis Borja, then viceroy of Catalonia. Several years later, Borja himself would become a Jesuit and the superior general of the same Society. In 1545 Araoz and Faber accompanied and assisted Princess Maria Manuela de Aviz at the royal court of Valladolid, Spain. The young princess, fiancée of the future Philip II of Spain, died shortly after their arrival in Valladolid.

Other powerful individuals also further helped to establish the Society in Spain. Among them was Juana de Austria, regent of Spain (1554–59) and daughter of Emperor Charles V. St. Ignatius accepted her request to become a member of the Society, and she was secretly known as Mateo Sánchez or Brother Montoya. Juana facilitated the expansion of the Society over the wide territories of Philip II.

In 1544 Father Jerome Domenech founded the College of Valencia, the first Jesuit college in Spain. A year later, Ignatius approved a new college in Gandia, built with funds donated by Borja. By 1546 Borja was widowed and asked to join the Society of Jesus. Though he would not officially enter until 1551, Borja remained throughout a prominent supporter and successful representative of the Jesuits in Spain and Portugal.

Araoz created the Jesuit province for Spain, on September 1, 1547. In 1552, Spain's province was split into two: Castile and Aragon. In 1554 Andalucía and the Canary Islands became a third province. A fourth province, Toledo, was created in 1562. All four provinces constituted the Spanish Assistancy. An agreement in 1659, however, ceded the Perpignan colleges to the French Assistancy.

In less than forty years, the Society of Jesus created five new provinces in Hispanic territories. In 1568 the Jesuits arrived in the Viceroyalty of Peru and organized its first Spanish province in the Americas there in September 1572. The province of Mexico would be established in that same year, and the Society would open seven colleges there by 1600. In 1588 the first Jesuits were missioned permanently to Paraguay, and by 1604 a new Jesuit province of Paraguay was established. In 1605 an independent province of the Philippines was founded with its center in Manila, where the Jesuits already ran two colleges. An array of Jesuit colleges and missions in present-day Colombia and Ecuador would become an independent province in 1607.

This gradual but determined progress caused problems, and the sixteenth-century Spanish Assistancy was attacked by early detractors. The most impassioned was Juan Martinez Guijarro, the archbishop of Toledo (also called "Silicio" or sackcloth), and the Dominican Melchior Cano. Both accused the Jesuits of teaching *alumbrista*, theological errors. In this controversy, Juana de Austria, governor queen of Spain, protected the Jesuits. Throughout the next century, royal protection of the Society's efforts continued. However, Jesuit political influence became so strong that serious penalties were levied on some of its members, including Juan de Mariana. The Society was opposed by rigorous Jansenists and challenged by the lax morals of the late Baroque period. They enjoyed the backing of Philip IV, however, who supported the Jesuit Imperial College in Madrid. This period also saw the popularity of *misiones populares* in Spain that used dramatic effects to energize Spain's Catholic believers.

The Jesuit historian Isidoro Pinedo divides the last years of the pre-Suppression Society into three stages. In the first period, during the late seventeenth century until the end of the War of Succession in 1700, the Society grew in membership but showed no signs of change or pastoral initiatives. A second stage, one of splendor, spanned the middle years of Philip V's reign with his wife Elizabeth Farnese, and included the reign of Ferdinand VI. The third period, one of decline, began with the political fall of the Marquis de la Ensenada and culminated in 1767. In that year King Charles III decreed the expulsion of all Jesuits from his expansive domains.

Different political forces caused the expulsion of the Jesuits. First, the Marquis de la Ensenada, a very efficient minister who had administered almost all government operations except for the *Estado*, was impeached and banished. Then the Jesuit Father Rávago gave up his privileges as the King's confessor. No Jesuit would replace him. Third, the new king, the reform-minded Charles III, a champion of monarchical power, alarmed the Jesuits. Complaints against the Jesuits in Spain proliferated. In the universities, *Suaristas* competed with Thomists and *colegiales* (nobility) with *manteistas* (reformers). The Jesuits monopolized secondary schools, intensifying tensions with a new religious teaching order, the *escolapios*. In addition, the Jesuits challenged the Carmelites' advocacy for sainthood of a bishop with whom they had disagreements in Mexico, the Venerable John of Palafox and Mendoza. Finally, Jesuit Father Francisco de Isla published a novel, *Fray Gerundio de Campazas*, with a scathing caricature of the friars. As its popularity grew, the enmity of other clergy increased. Criticism of the Jesuits by the rigorously devout Jansenists was now joined by critics of a very different kind, namely the *philosophes* and supporters of the Enlightenment, who shared a more secularist perspective.

In 1759 Portugal expelled its Jesuits, and in 1762, the Society was banned from France. It was expected that the Spanish Crown would follow suit. And so it happened. In 1767, for reasons never explained, King Charles III expelled all Jesuits from his dominions. The procedure was finely orchestrated: in the early morning of April 2, the army surrounded every Jesuit college in the provinces of Andalucía, Aragon, Castile, and Toledo. The Jesuits were assembled in dining halls and were read the King's decree of expulsion, the *Pragmatica Ley*. A few days later they were taken to different ports to sail for the Roman harbor of Civitavecchia.

The exiled Jesuits were shocked when they saw the cannons of Pope Clement XIII pointed at their ships. The Pope refused the Jesuits entry into his territories. Without a destination, over 2,000 men remained on the ships. Diplomatic efforts allowed them to disembark on the island of Corsica, then fighting a civil war. There the Jesuits lived in harsh conditions for more than a year.

The 1767 *Pragmatica* also ordered the expulsion of Jesuits living overseas. Their transport was more difficult. Jesuits in the Philippines would not reach Cádiz for almost two years after the King's notification. Jesuits in Peru, Mexico, Paraguay, Santa Fe, Quito, and Chile waited in Atlantic ports until assigned ships took them to exile. Their distressing journey from Hispanic America stopped first in Havana and then off the coast of Cádiz. In El Puerto de Santa Maria, 4,000 Jesuits disembarked and were hosted by all the convents in the area.

Meanwhile in Corsica, the already dismal conditions for the Jesuits worsened when France purchased the island. In such troubled times, the Pope allowed the Jesuits to discreetly move into the Papal States, which meant staying near Genoa rather than in the Roman port. The Jesuits had to walk across the Apennines without a clear destination to reach the pontifical legacies intended for them in Emilia Romagna. During nearly fifty years of exile, their situation was somewhat relieved by the meager pensions that the Spanish king granted them for their *temporalidades* (payments for the sales and rents of their properties). The exile became more difficult by the summer of 1773 when Pope Clement XIV signed *Dominus ac Redemptor*, suppressing the entire Society of Jesus.

It is surprising that the Jesuits remained together, despite the exile's hardships, the Suppression of their Order, and the pressures of the Spanish court. However, the Jesuits maintained their identity, keeping the names of their former communities. Membership in the Society remained almost the same throughout the period when it was declared extinct. Not many Jesuits embraced secularization, despite the repeated attempts of royal commissioners. Also significant was the high number of novices who voluntarily followed the exiled Jesuits, although they were free to leave the Society.

In 1814 Pius VII restored the Society and efforts were made to return the Jesuits to their homeland. King Ferdinand VII favored their return to Spain, but liberals opposed it. They feared a strengthened partnership between Church and State that might overthrow the constitution initiated in 1812 by the *Cortes de Cádiz*. However, in May 1815, the Jesuits were able to return to sites assigned by the government. In August of that year, they were allowed to embark for America, and on May 3, 1816, Ferdinand VII fully restored the Society of Jesus in Spain.

At this time, the Order was affected by the political upheavals that shook their country. The liberal triennium of 1820–23 suppressed the Society for illegalities in the 1815 royal restoration. The Society was reinstated in 1823. Ten years after Ferdinand VII died, anticlerical protests shattered the Imperial College in Madrid and killed fourteen Jesuits. Suppressed again in 1835, the Jesuits voluntarily went back into exile. In 1852 Queen Isabel II allowed the Society to establish houses and colleges on the condition that they would promote overseas missions. However, the 1868 September revolution resulted in a third suppression of the Jesuits in Spain, though they were allowed to return a few years later.

The reign of Alfonso XIII (1886–1931) assisted in the restoration of the Society, but it ended abruptly on April 14, 1931, when the Second Spanish Republic was proclaimed. Article 26 of the new constitution prohibited religious orders from obeying any mandate other than State authority. On January 24, 1932, the official newspaper *Gaceta de Madrid* announced the dissolution of the Society of Jesus and the expropriation of its properties. The Jesuits had to choose between exile or risking an underground existence. The host countries offering asylum were Portugal, Holland, Belgium, and Italy. This time Italian Jesuits welcomed their brothers, unlike in the eighteenth century, when the Spanish deportees were not even allowed to consult their libraries.

On May 3, 1938, during the Spanish Civil War (1936–39), the army revolted against the government and promulgated the Jesuits' return to the *Sector Nacional*. The following year, after Francisco Franco's victory, his regime returned the Society's assets and proclaimed it an exemplar of traditional values. On the whole, the Jesuits greatly benefited during Franco's dictatorship. In 1941 it restored almost all their schools and by 1953 the number of Jesuits had grown by 16 percent. However, two small groups remained dissatisfied with Franco's dictatorship: the Catalan Jesuit circle and those who sympathized with Basque nationalism.

The Society accepted new challenges both in teaching and in intellectual work. It strengthened *escuelas profesionales* such as the SAFA network (schools in Andalucía), highlighted the Writers House in Madrid, and, in the late 1960s, improved the faculties of philosophy and theology. Jesuits spread their ideas through academic magazines (*Archivo Teológico Granadino*, *Miscelánea*) and the more widespread *Razón y Fe*, *Manresa*, *Estudios Eclesiásticos*, and *Pensamiento*, which began publication in 1945.

In addition, the Society was commissioned to train the clergy and to direct minor and major seminaries. Its *misiones populares* spread across the countryside. Factory workers participated in the *Spiritual Exercises* of St. Ignatius and the *Congregaciones Marianas* prospered. Both the increasing number of Spanish Jesuits in the early fifties and their missionary tradition increased their presence in the USA, Latin America, and Asia. The vitality of the Spanish Jesuit provinces also brought many changes. Father Llanos's work, which promoted contacts between universities and workers, both resistant to Franco's dictatorship, had a significant social impact. The majority in Spanish Jesuit provinces welcomed Vatican II and Father Arrupe's generalship with enthusiasm.

In the 1980s a vocational crisis occurred, forcing the merging of the provinces. Efforts had begun as early as 1970 to coordinate the existing provinces in Spain. On November 14, 2008, Father General Adolfo Nicolás approved the integration of five provinces – Andalucía, Aragon, Castile, Loyola, and Tarraconense – into one Spanish province. It was successfully established in 2014.

As organized today, the Society of Jesus in Spain works by *Sectores* (areas) to coordinate different fields of apostolate (education, social, etc.). At the same time, Plataformas Apostolicas Locales (PAL) oversees the efforts of Jesuits and laypeople working together in Spain. The two exceptions are Loyola and Cataluña. Together they form the Plataformas Apostolicas Territoriales (PLT), preserving the cultural characteristics of their respective populations and recognizing the different national sensibilities of people in Spain today.

See also Anti-Jesuit Polemic; Borja (Borgia), Francis, SJ, St.; Charles III; Juana of Austria; Laínez, Diego, SJ; Loyola, Ignatius SJ, St.; Mexico; Paraguay Missions ("Reductions"); *Patronato* and *Padroado*; Peru; Philippines; Suppression; Xavier, Francis, SJ, St.

Benimelli, José Antonio Ferrer, *Expulsión y extinción de los jesuitas (1759–1773)*. Bilbao: Mensajero, 2014.
Callahan, William James, *Church, Politics and Society in Spain, 1750–1875*. (Harvard Historical Monographs, 73). Cambridge, MA: Harvard University Press, 1984.
González, Manuel Revuelta, *El restablecimiento de la Compañía de Jesús*. Bilbao: Mensajero, 2014.
Jesuitas España. www.jesuitas.es/.
O'Malley, John W., *The First Jesuits*. Cambridge, MA: Harvard University Press, 1995.
Roehner, Bertrand M., "Jesuits and the State: A Comparative Study of Their Expulsions (1590–1990)." *Religion* 27 (1997), 165–82.

Inmaculada Fernández Arrillaga

Spee von Langenfeld, Friedrich, SJ (1591–1635)

The years *c.* 1550–1650 were, in parts of Europe, years of prosecution (and persecution) of persons said to be witches. The accused had few, if any, rights and could be tortured to obtain an admission of guilt and the names of accomplices; a guilty verdict often meant a death sentence. Rare were the voices to speak out in defense of the victims, often poor women. One such voice in Germany was the Jesuit Friedrich Spee von Langenfeld. A philosophy teacher, catechist, and poet, Spee took up the defense of accused "witches" after being assigned to administer the sacrament of penance to some of them. Against what was the prevailing opinion, Spee argued that torture, far from eliciting the truth, elicited whatever words, lies included, that the tortured believed could stop the torture. For Spee, the witch trials were a travesty of justice that enriched lawyers and encouraged any persons seeking revenge to accuse their enemies of witchcraft. Many Jesuits disagreed with Spee, most notably Martin Delrio (1551–1608), who urged judges to punish witches, though he did argue for provision of legal counsel for the accused and for some restrictions on use of torture. Spee had the protection of Goswin Nickel (1584–1664), who became the provincial of Spee's Jesuit province, and later the Jesuit superior general (1652–64). Spee's major work against witch trials, the *Cautio criminalis*, was first published in 1631. He died in 1635, apparently from plague contracted while providing pastoral care for soldiers wounded in the Thirty Years War.

See also German-Speaking Lands; Plague

Machielsen, Jan, *Martin Delrio: Scholarship and Demonology in the Counter-Reformation.* Oxford: Oxford University Press, 2015.

Modras, Ronald, "A Jesuit in the Crucible: Friedrich Spee and the Witchcraft Hysteria in Seventeenth-Century Germany." *Studies in the Spirituality of Jesuits* 35, 4 (September 2003), 1–46.

Spee von Langenfeld, Friedrich, *Cautio criminalis, or, A Book on Witch Trials.* Trans. Marcus Hellyer. Charlottesville: University of Virginia Press, 2003.

Thomas Worcester, SJ

Špidlík, Tomáš Cardinal, SJ (1919–2010)

Tomáš Špidlík was born on December 17, 1919, in Boskovice, Moravia (Czechoslovakia, now the Czech Republic). He studied Slavic and Latin philology at the University of Brno and in 1940 entered the Jesuit novitiate in Benešov. He did philosophy studies in Velhrad (1942–45), though these were often interrupted by forced labor for the occupying Germans, Romanians, or Russians. After regency in Velhrad and theology studies in Maastricht, he was ordained a priest in 1949. Since he could not return to his homeland because of the Communist takeover, he did his tertianship in Florence and then went to Rome to give radio broadcasts for Vatican Radio. From 1951 to 1955, he was a student at the Pontifical Oriental Institute (POI) and successfully defended his doctoral dissertation on Joseph of Volokolamsk in 1955. He remained as professor at POI from 1955 to 1992.

Špidlík spent much of his life in Italy, dedicating himself to the translation of the riches of Eastern Christianity to the West, with a particular emphasis upon the Slavic tradition. He published over 140 books and articles, including *The Spirituality of Eastern Christianity: A Systematic Manual* (1978) and *Ignatius of Loyola and Eastern Spirituality* (1995), and gave conferences throughout Europe. He was also a beloved spiritual father for Czech students at the Pontifical College Nepomuceno (1951–89). Among his numerous prizes and honors, he was named a cardinal by Pope John Paul II in 2003. He died on April 16, 2010. Pope Benedict XVI called him "a distinguished Jesuit and zealous servant of the Gospel."

See also Cardinals, Jesuit; Eastern Catholic Churches

Čemus, Richard, "Con l'Europa nel cuore: ricordando il Cardinale Tomáš Špidlík, SJ, nel primo anniversario della morte." *Orientalia Christiana Periodica* 77 (2011), 5–24.

Špidlík, Tomáš, *The Spirituality of the Christian East*. Trans. Anthony P. Gytheil. Collegeville, MN: Liturgical Press, 1986.

John Gavin, SJ

Spirits, Good and Evil

In two appendices at the end of the *Spiritual Exercises* (*SpEx*), Ignatius provides "rules" for "the discernment of spirits," or the practice of distinguishing between interior "movements in the soul." Such movements are generally sifted into two categories, identified either as coming from the "good" or "evil" spirit. These terms, however, are not necessarily limited to any particular being. For Ignatius, the term "good spirit" could refer alternately to the direct activity of God or the mediation of this activity through a spiritual creature. In the second appendix, Ignatius says that "it belongs only to the Creator to give consolation to the soul without previous cause," whereas an affective movement of consolation preceded by an intermediary cause can derive either from *"el buen ángel"* (the good angel) or from the *"el mal ángel"* (the evil angel) (*SpEx* ##330–31). In the first appendix, however, Ignatius identifies God as the ultimate source of all genuine consolation (*SpEx* #322). God, then, is the fundamental "good spirit." In a similar way, Ignatius routinely speaks of "the enemy of our human nature," identified as "Satan" in the meditation on the Two Standards (*SpEx* ##136–42), as the predominant "evil spirit."

In Ignatian spirituality, good and evil spirits have characteristic ways of acting. For those striving to advance "in the service of God," it is of the good spirit, Ignatius writes, to give "encouragement, strength, consolations, tears, inspirations, and peace." By contrast, the evil spirit attempts to impede progress by "disquieting with false reasons" and producing anxiety and sadness (*SpEx* #315). Whereas the evil spirit acts in ways that are "violent" and "aggravating," as "a drop of water falls upon stone," the good spirit is characteristically "delicate and gentle," as "a drop of water upon a sponge," engendering "true joy and spiritual gladness" (*SpEx* ##329, 335).

See also Consolation; Desolation; Discernment; *Spiritual Exercises*

Gallagher, Timothy V., *The Discernment of Spirits: An Ignatian Guide for Everyday Living*. New York: Crossroad, 2005.

Toner, Jules J., *A Commentary on Saint Ignatius' Rules for the Discernment of Spirits*. St. Louis, MO: The Institute of Jesuit Sources, 1982.

Henry Shea, SJ

Spiritual Exercises

Ignatius Loyola's most important writing, *Spiritual Exercises*, is a collection of resources for people seeking to develop their lives as Christians. It presents various techniques of prayer, supplemented by maxims of practical wisdom and approaches to decision-making. Though much of this material is presented within a program for a month's silent retreat, the text itself explicitly encourages adapted uses of the material in other contexts (##18–19). Ignatius explains his title at the outset (#1) in terms of an analogy: just as physical exercise fosters a general state of health, so "spiritual exercises" foster a life in authentic relationship with God, free of "inordinate affections," and conformed to the ultimate purpose of God's creation.

A key statement at the outset of *Spiritual Exercises* at once indicates the reality haunting the book and renounces any strategy to specify or describe it. It is *immediate* – immediately, directly, without mediation – that the Creator should operate "with the creature and the creature with its Creator and Lord" (#15) – just as the *Constitutions* seek merely to open the way for something that only divine grace can bring about (IV.8.8 [414]). Ignatius does not presume to specify or predict the reality around which nevertheless his whole program is ordered. The central significances of his text do not lie on its surface. Moreover, what Ignatius sees as the effect of divine action will vary, depending on God's freedom and the personal responses of exercitants. Thus, despite the obvious centrality of *Spiritual Exercises* to Jesuit life in all periods, caution is required in making connections between the text and elements of Jesuit practice. Though reference to *Spiritual Exercises* is a constant throughout Jesuit history, the text's effects vary according to the diversity of religious cultures. Veneration for the Ignatian heritage itself has never been separated from – to echo the subtitle of a standard current English translation – "a contemporary reading."

The Content of *Spiritual Exercises*

After the *Anima Christi* by way of frontispiece, Ignatius offers twenty "annotations" – an almost random collection of more or less rich comments "to give some understanding of the spiritual exercises which follow." Perhaps intentionally, the dryness and lack of structure deters casual or linear reading. An expanded version of the title and purpose follows (#21), and then a further annotation, or "presupposition," before the main program of the month-long retreat begins.

The program falls into four sections called, perhaps misleadingly, "weeks" (#4). The First Week is about sin. It opens with the Principle and Foundation, a statement about the dependence of humanity on God and the ethical corollaries. Without comment, Ignatius then provides various resources for the examination of conscience and confession, before presenting a program of five exercises that the exercitant should normally do each day of the First Week. The first, sometimes called "the history of sin" or "the triple sin," begins with meditation on the fall of the Angels, on Adam and Eve in the garden, and about a hypothetical mortal sinner now damned. Then, abruptly, it confronts us with the figure of Christ crucified. We are invited to enter into imaginative conversation (colloquy) with him, asking what we have done for him, what we are doing for him, and what we ought to be doing for him (#53). The second exercise focuses on the exercitant's personal history and characteristic patterns of sinfulness, culminating in wonder and gratitude "that He has given me life up to now" (##60–61). The third and fourth exercises are "repetitions" in a special technical sense that involves concentration on points "in which I have felt greater consolation or desolation, or greater spiritual feeling" (#62). At this point Ignatius introduces the "triple colloquy" (#63) of prayer to Mary, Jesus, and the Father, not only for a deeper abhorrence of sin but also for gifts of insight into the dynamics of sinfulness. The final exercise is a contemplation on Hell, not in the threatening spirit of the preacher in James Joyce's *A Portrait of the Artist as a Young Man*, but, rather, in a spirit of gratitude for having been delivered from disaster. The First Week material ends with some "additional directions" for the exercitant, focusing on particular practices that will foster the process at this stage. Modifications to these directions are indicated in each of the subsequent weeks.

The Second Week begins with an exercise comparing the call of Christ with that of "a human king." This introduces a program of imaginative contemplation on the life of Christ, interspersed with more specifically Ignatian material. Again, a regular structure of five exercises is proposed for each day: typically, two contemplations of events of Christ's life, followed by two repetitions, and finally "the prayer of the senses," seemingly a more intuitive exercise invoking "the five senses of the imagination" (#121). The aim is growth in knowledge, love, and service of Christ. After prayer around Christ's incarnation, birth, and youth, Ignatius lays down for the fourth day exercises more specifically oriented to the choice of a way of life. His concern is that generous people learn to recognize "the deceits of the bad chief" (#140) and temptations "under the appearance of good" (#10). He offers "a meditation on two standards," contrasting diabolic temptations to pursue riches, honor, and pride with a more Christ-like path of poverty, humiliations, and injuries (##136–47). On the same day, and with the same end in view, Ignatius also invites us to consider strategies for managing a sum of money acquired – like all goods in the real world – through morally ambiguous means. Ignatius focuses not on what is done with the money, but on the self's disordered *attachments* that complicate such a decision. Drawing on a trope of medieval moral theology (*tres binarios* – conventionally "three classes"), he invites us to consider three scenarios: indefinite procrastination; subtle interior bargaining and rationalization; pure surrender of the attachment. These two exercises, like that on the earthly king at the outset and on the three kinds of humility that will follow, end with a complex petition, often oversimplified in the secondary literature. Each invokes what seems a reasonable response of complete availability for God's work, "the highest spiritual poverty," but then goes further: provided there is no dishonor caused to God thereby, or sin committed, one expresses a preferential choice for union with Christ in actual poverty and suffering insults (#168).

To the extent that these dispositions are in place, the exercitant can undertake a discernment of a way of life in the subsequent days of the Second Week, breaking with the standard rhythm of contemplations as seems appropriate. Ignatius describes three "times" when a choice is well made: the first when the subject is subjectively incapable of doubting its rightness; the second, through reflection on his or her subjective reactions to it; the third, through a dispassionate evaluation of arguments for and against the alternatives in question.

Ignatius then outlines the Third Week, containing several days of prayer on the passion and death of Christ, seeking a grace of "shatteredness (*quebranto*) with Christ shattered" (#203). At this point he offers guidelines for well-ordered eating. The Fourth Week begins with prayer on Christ's resurrection appearances. Here too the purpose, though elliptically expressed, evokes the possibility of an imaginative sharing in Christ's own experience (#221). There follows a "Contemplation to Attain Love," and an outline of three methods of prayer.

By way of appendix, there follows a long series of presentations of gospel incidents structured round points for the exercitant to contemplate. Finally, there are five sets of guidelines or rules. The first two are about discernment of spirits, the latter being reserved for those facing more subtle temptation. There follow rules for almsgiving, rules for the handling of scruples, and finally rules "for the true sense that in the Church militant we must have" (#352).

The Exercises and the Jesuits

The writing of *Spiritual Exercises* and his leading role in the founding of the Society of Jesus are Ignatius Loyola's two most important achievements. But the relationships between the two are paradoxical.

On the one hand, the text of *Spiritual Exercises* makes no direct reference to the foundation of a religious community. The three iterations of the *Formula of the Institute* name the giving of spiritual exercises as only one activity among others, and not the first, in which Jesuits engage. *Spiritual Exercises* clearly envisages a choice between different ways in which a person can find authentic union with God, and from the beginning, many have made the full Spiritual Exercises without being, or subsequently becoming, Jesuits. Vatican II's proclamation of a universal call to holiness has given new impetus to movements more or less attached to the Jesuits claiming a spirituality based on the Exercises; ecumenical initiatives have made the Exercises popular even beyond Roman Catholicism. The shifts in religious sensibility that these changes reflect may also be leading contemporary Jesuits to articulate their distinctive spiritual identity in new ways: less in terms of the *Spiritual Exercises* that they share widely, and more in terms of vowed consecration, celibacy, mission, and the *Constitutions*.

On the other hand, the connections between *Spiritual Exercises* and the Jesuits are multiple and evident. From Ignatius's first companions onwards, the Jesuits' processes of recruitment, initiation, and formation have centered on programs of spiritual exercises based on Ignatius's text. *Spiritual Exercises* has served throughout Jesuit history as the analogue to a monastic Rule, the principal source of corporate myth and spirituality. Conventional narratives of Jesuit spirituality present the consolidation of the Society's spiritual identity and the stabilization of the interpretation of *Spiritual Exercises* as one and the same process.

The Impact of Jesuit Routines

Jesuit consolidation occasioned some important shifts in the interpretation and practice of elements in *Spiritual Exercises*, a text seemingly presupposing an individually guided process, lasting a month, and undertaken once in a lifetime. The need for regular programs of Jesuit spiritual renewal, based on *Spiritual Exercises*, became evident already in Ignatius's lifetime. During the generalate of Acquaviva, practices were codified: a full thirty-day retreat for all novices and all tertians, and an annual retreat for all lasting eight or ten days. Such retreats were generally given collectively, and the delivery of talks became the director's main task. Particularly in such contexts, the intimate, intuitive features of Ignatius's original text were marginalized. Such versions of his process fit well within interpretations of Catholicism in modernity as a form of social disciplining.

Jesuits also looked to *Spiritual Exercises* to resource their daily prayer. The rule of an hour's daily prayer established by Borja drew on Ignatius's gospel contemplations, but the different life-setting changed their character. Elements of freedom, however, were never fully absent. Ignatius's own *Spiritual Diary* and that of Pierre Favre reveal intense engagements with God, drawing creatively and explicitly on motifs from *Spiritual Exercises*, but in ways far beyond what the text envisages. In particular, they apply the teachings of *Spiritual Exercises* regarding discernment of a state of life to face questions arising in daily life, whether major or trivial, sometimes with great subtlety. The oldest substantial commentary on *Spiritual Exercises*, that of Achille Gagliardi, shows that examination of conscience in daily practice could take on a contemplative richness overshooting the penitential practice envisaged in *Spiritual Exercises*.

Twentieth-Century Renewal

In this context, the contemporary retrieval of the individually guided retreat, provoked by historical researches published in the mid-twentieth century and by the movements of intellectual *ressourcement* and institutional *aggiornamento* within Roman Catholicism, represented a revolution, particularly in the English-speaking world. The mystical element in *Spiritual Exercises* had been handled cautiously, in ways perhaps conditioned by inquisitorial nervousness in Ignatius's lifetime. Though the possibility of such union with God was never denied outright, the stress fell on the need for disciplined preparation and the dangers of illusion. In the Vatican II period, the possibility of direct encounter between creator and creature emerged, or re-emerged, as the central reality of *Spiritual Exercises*, and in the hands of some interpreters the Contemplation to Attain Love took on a newly central significance. The associations with Jesuit discipline suddenly appeared as at best accidental, at worse misguided.

The renegotiations of Jesuit identity this movement provoked remain a work in progress. It is attractive, but it may also be anachronistic, to draw links between what have only recently become mainstream interpretations of *Spiritual Exercises* and initiatives for which pre-Suppression Jesuits are noted in the educational, scientific, and artistic fields, and in accommodation to cultures outside Europe.

The Text and Its History

Tradition has linked *Spiritual Exercises* to Ignatius's initial conversion experience in Loyola, and to his sojourn in Manresa, although the standard accounts, themselves from the 1540s and 1550s, recount powerful experiences linked with only some of the many elements in the text. *Spiritual Exercises* in its present form involves an unrecorded process of codification, quite remarkable in what it demonstrates of Ignatius's ability to abstract from his own personal experiences to facilitate the growth of others. Its originality is a matter more of its form and genre than of its content, which echoes many commonplaces of medieval piety. Attempts to show literary dependence to an extent that would determine overall interpretation have failed to convince.

The earliest written version of *Spiritual Exercises* dates from the mid-1530s, recording a retreat given to John Helyar, and in Paris by either Ignatius himself or Favre. Written in Latin, it differs in significant respects from the standard text. The written texts of *Spiritual Exercises* standardly used today depend chiefly on a Spanish manuscript dating from 1544, conventionally entitled the "Autograph" because some corrections are in Ignatius's own hand. A manuscript of a Latin translation dates from 1541. Stylistic analysis of this latter document suggests that a core of the text is relatively crude, possibly deriving from Ignatius himself, and dating from shortly after his arrival in Paris in 1528.

Further passages were added during the 1530s in more sophisticated Latin, probably firstly by Favre and then by Salmerón. These differences may indicate developments in lost Spanish versions. The states of the text before 1528 remain a matter of yet more tenuous conjecture.

The version officially published in 1548 was a polished, and rather free, Latin translation by André des Freux. This remained the standard text until Roothaan retranslated the original Spanish into Latin in 1835. Tacitly, the Spanish "Autograph" has gradually replaced Roothaan's text as normative, though some experts prefer to work from the Vulgate. Critical parallel text editions were published in the *Monumenta Historica Societatis Iesu*; the first, in 1919, was replaced as the series' centenary volume in 1969. The plurality of texts coincides nicely with the contemporary sense that Ignatius's words are in any case secondary to the exercitant's lived experience.

Interpreting the Text

In 1599 *Spiritual Exercises* was supplemented with an *Official Directory* setting out what had by then become consensus positions of interpretation and practice. One central question runs through the disputes during the preparation of that document, and through many subsequent discussions of particular passages of *Spiritual Exercises*. How seriously is the interpreter to take Ignatius's systematic relativizing of his own text? Reverence for tradition and a concern for good order lead some to insist on a strict, ascetical observance of Ignatius's directives. Others are more impressed both by the need to apply the text to the dispositions of the one receiving the Exercises (#18), and by a sense of the text's purpose as opening the self to the sovereign freedom of God working mystically, overruling human prescriptions. Both approaches can find justification in Ignatius's writings; both have had cogent and influential advocates; each nevertheless generates a quite different account of Ignatian and Jesuit spirituality. Successful attempts to articulate the significance of *Spiritual Exercises* among and beyond the Jesuits need somehow to negotiate this duality.

See also Contemplation; Contemplation to Attain Love; *Constitutions*; Direction, Spiritual; Discernment; Finding God in All Things; Imagination; Loyola, Ignatius, SJ, St.; Manresa

Begheyn, Paul, and Kenneth Bogart. A *Bibliography on St. Ignatius's Spiritual Exercises*. St. Louis, MO: The Seminar on Jesuit Spirituality, 1991.

Delmage, Lewis, *The Spiritual Exercises of Saint Ignatius Loyola: An American Translation from the Final Version of the Exercises, the Latin Vulgate, into Contemporary English*. Boston, MA.: St. Paul Editions, 1978.

Fleming, David L., *Draw Me into Your Friendship: A Literal Translation and a Contemporary Reading of the Spiritual Exercises*. St. Louis, MO: The Institute of Jesuit Sources, 1996.

García-Mateo, Rogelio, "The 'Accommodated Texts' and the Interpretation of the *Spiritual Exercises*." *The Way* 44, 1 (January 2005), 101–16.

Ivens, Michael, *Understanding the Spiritual Exercises*. Leominster: Gracewing, 1998.

Palmer, Martin E., *On Giving the Spiritual Exercises: The Early Jesuit Manuscript Directories and the Official Directory of 1599*. St. Louis, MO: The Institute of Jesuit Sources, 1996.

Roothaan, Jan Philipp, "On the Spiritual Exercises." In *Renovation Reading*. Woodstock, MD: Woodstock College, 1931, pp. 68–82.

Philip Endean, SJ

Stonyhurst College

Stonyhurst traces its origins to the college founded at St. Omer by the Jesuit Robert Persons in 1593. The institution quickly emerged as a major center for the education of English Catholics. With the attacks on the Society of Jesus during the second half of the eighteenth century, the College was forced to move to Bruges in 1762 and then to Liège in 1773. Two decades later, in 1794, with the intrusion of French Revolutionary troops, the College transferred across the English Channel. Thomas Weld, a former pupil at St. Omer, gifted Stonyhurst Hall in Lancashire and 30 acres of accompanying land. Stonyhurst College has been on this site in the Ribble Valley ever since and has been described by Maurice Whitehead in his history of English Jesuit education as "one of the most extraordinary phenomena in British educational history" (*English Jesuit Education*, 179). Stonyhurst firmly established itself as a school of choice within the higher social reaches of the English Catholic community, but from the mid-nineteenth century it also took on great importance as a center, even a refuge, for continental Catholic clerics during a turbulent period of revolution. Italian Jesuits were particularly drawn to the College, including the celebrated astronomer Angelo Secchi and the philosopher and mathematician Giuseppe Bayma who came to Stonyhurst in 1858 and served as a professor for ten years. In recent times the physical Jesuit presence at the College has diminished and the first lay headmaster was appointed in 1986. Today Stonyhurst is home to a little under 500 pupils of both sexes, aged between 13 and 18, roughly three-quarters of whom are boarders. Alumni include the novelist Arthur Conan Doyle, the leading peace activist Bruce Kent, and the actor Charles Laughton.

See also Education, Secondary and Pre-Secondary; Persons, Robert, SJ; St. Omers (Saint-Omer); United Kingdom

Muir, T. E., *Stonyhurst College, 1593–1993*. London: James and James, 1992.

Whitehead, Maurice, *English Jesuit Education: Expulsion, Suppression, Survival and Restoration, 1762–1803*. Farnham: Ashgate, 2013.

Jonathan Wright

Suárez, Francisco, SJ (1548–1617)

Francisco Suárez, whom Pope Paul V called the *doctor eximius et pius*, was born in Granada, Spain, to Antonia Vázquez de Utiel and Gaspar Suárez de Toledo on January 5, 1548. He was the second of eight children.

He began his studies at the University of Granada and transferred to the University of Salamanca in 1561 to study law. The Jesuits turned down his application twice because of his lackluster academic performance. Yet familial connections finally elicited a positive response from the provincial, and he entered the novitiate in Medina del Campo in June, 1564.

After taking vows in 1566, he began his studies at the University of Salamanca. He arrived to enjoy the fruits of the golden age of Iberian philosophy, planted by such luminaries as Domingo de Soto (1494–1560), Francisco de Vitoria (1483–1546), and Melchior Cano (1509–60). Furthermore, Pius V, having declared Thomas Aquinas a Doctor of the Church in 1567, inspired a "new scholasticism" in Europe that led to a critical study of primary sources. Francisco plunged into the rich intellectual currents of Salamanca and flourished.

He was ordained in 1572. From 1571 to 1576 he taught and gave spiritual direction in a variety of posts, including Segovia, Valladolid, and Avila. While teaching in Valladolid (1576–80), he received criticism for his "pedagogical novelties" in teaching the philosophy of Thomas Aquinas: instead of strictly repeating the text and established opinions, Suárez sought to examine each problem anew and to relate the conclusions to contemporary issues and controversies. Despite such attacks, he was called to Rome in 1580 to teach at the Roman College. It was during this period that he composed some of his first writings, including the *De Incarnatione*.

Suffering from poor health, he left Rome in 1585 to teach in Alcalá. In 1592 he returned to Salamanca to teach metaphysics. This series of lectures would result in his most well-known composition, the *Disputationes metaphysicae*. In this celebrated work of fifty-four disputations, Suárez systematically examined the opinions of some 250 authors in the investigation of "being insofar as it is real being." Though highly respectful of his sources, he did not hesitate to disagree even with Thomas regarding such teachings as the distinction between essence and existence, which he considered to be only a mental distinction in finite beings, and the principle of individuation, which he believed was found in the *entitas* of a thing and not in designated matter. Though his intellectual daring would win him many admirers, it also inspired controversies with such figures as the Jesuit Gabriel Vázquez (1549–1604), who even accused Suárez of adopting a lax and privileged lifestyle.

In 1596 Phillip II (1527–98) chose Suárez over his controversial brother Jesuit Luis Molina (1535–1600) for a chair at the University of Coimbra. This post demanded that he finally obtain a doctorate, which he defended at the University of Evora on June 4, 1597. He then assumed the position that he would retain until his death. During these years he composed such influential works as *De sanctissimo Trinitatis mysterio* (1606), *De gratia* (1619) – a work that emerged from his involvement in the *De auxiliis* Controversy – *De angelis* (1620), and *De fide, spe et charitate* (1622). His most important work of this period, however, was *De legibus* (1612), which established him as a major authority on law and political theory. He advanced a voluntarist theory of law – the obligations of both natural and positive law are derived from the will of a sovereign (God or the ruler) – though he avoided the arbitrary nature of such a view by grounding principles in their fittingness and goodness for human nature. His ideas contributed to discussions on natural law, positive law, custom, the role of the state, and canon law. Many of his works would be published only after his death on September 25, 1617.

Francisco Suárez was both the product of Jesuit formation and a major influence upon that formation's development. On the one hand, his respect for previous authorities – especially Thomas Aquinas – and his willingness to critique them reflected the principles of the Jesuit *Ratio studiorum*. On the other hand, his style and synthetic vision shaped the intellectual and spiritual lives of Jesuits even into the twentieth century. The Society supported Suárez's ideas through its institutions, helping to make his works an important bridge between medieval scholasticism and early modernity.

See also Philosophy; Spain; Theology

Forlivesi, Marco, "Francisco Suárez and the *rationes studiorum* of the Society of Jesus." In Marco Sgarbi, ed., *Francisco Suárez and his Legacy*. Milan: Vita e Pensiero, 2010, pp. 77–90.

Hill, Benjamin, and Henrik Lagerlund, eds., *The Philosophy of Francisco Suárez*. Oxford: Oxford University Press, 2012.

Schwarz, Daniel, ed., *Interpreting Suarez*. Cambridge: Cambridge University Press, 2012.

John Gavin, SJ

Superior, Local

In addition to a superior general and to provincial superiors, the Society of Jesus also has local superiors. A local superior is in charge of a community of Jesuits, such as one devoted mainly to a particular work, as in an educational institution. But Jesuit communities often also include men doing a variety of works or who are retired from active ministry; the superior is to have care for all of the individual Jesuits in his community, their spiritual, physical, and intellectual well-being, as well as care for the community as such and for its corporate effectiveness and witness to Christ. In the financial and material dimensions of community life, the superior is assisted by a Jesuit appointed by the provincial and who holds the title "minister."

Normally, local superiors serve for six years and are appointed by the provincial superior after broad consultation. In larger communities the superior holds the title "rector," and rectors are appointed by the superior general, also normally for six years. Only rarely, and for very specific reasons, is the term of local superiors or rectors extended beyond six years; sometimes it is shorter, depending on how well he does as superior, or on whether or not other needs of the Society lead to his being missioned elsewhere before the end of six years. A local superior or rector is aided in his work by four consultors, Jesuits from within the community named by the provincial; meeting at regular intervals, the consultors' main task is to assist the superior in making decisions. One of the consultors, or another member of the community, has the role of admonitor, and the admonitor meets privately with the superior to offer criticism of how well he is fulfilling his mission.

See also Community; Minister

The Constitutions of the Society of Jesus and their Complementary Norms. Ed. John W. Padberg. St. Louis, MO: The Institute of Jesuit Sources, 1996.

Thomas Worcester, SJ

Superior General

The head of the Society of Jesus is known as the superior general. He is elected for life by a General Congregation, but he may resign from office. While the supreme legislative authority for Jesuits is the General Congregation, the superior general's authority is very extensive and includes the appointment of provincials and rectors as well as making major decisions in accord with the *Constitutions* and *Complementary Norms* of the Society of Jesus. The *Constitutions* provide detailed descriptions of what an ideal superior general should be and do. In addition to Ignatius of Loyola, one other Jesuit superior general has thus far been canonized as a saint: Francis Borja. In recent decades the superior general has often traveled to various parts of the world in order to better know and support a variety of Jesuit works and ministries. A list of the thirty superiors general follows in chronological order, with the dates of their generalate in parentheses.

The most significant superiors general, from Ignatius of Loyola to Pedro Arrupe, have their own entries in this encyclopedia, indicated here by the inscription of their names in uppercase letters. Editorial norms precluded those still living from having their own entry in this compilation; as a result, Peter-Hans Kolvenbach and Adolfo Nicolás Pachón have instead been treated below under superiors general 29 and 30.

1. IGNATIUS OF LOYOLA (1541–56): Spain.
2. DIEGO LAÍNEZ (1558–65): Spain.
3. FRANCIS BORJA (1565–72): Spain.
4. EVERARD MERCURIAN (1573–80): Belgium.
5. CLAUDIO ACQUAVIVA (1581–1615): Italy.
6. MUZIO VITELLESCHI (1615–45): Italy.
7. Vincenzo Carafa (1646–49): Italy.
8. Francesco Piccolomini (1649–51): Italy.
9. Luigi Gottifredi (1652): Italy.
10. Goswin Nickel (1652–64): Germany.
11. GIOVANNI PAOLO OLIVA (1664–81): Italy.
12. Charles de Noyelle (1682–86): Belgium.
13. TIRSO GONZALEZ DE SANTALLA (1687–1705): Spain.
14. Michelangelo Tamburini (1706–30): Italy.
15. Frantisek Retz (1730–50): Bohemia.
16. Ignazio Visconti (1751–55): Italy.
17. Luigi Centurione (1755–57): Italy.
18. LORENZO RICCI (1758–73): Italy.
19. TADEUZ BRZOZOWSKI (1814–20): Russia.
20. Luigi Fortis (1820–29): Italy.
21. JAN ROOTHAAN (1829–53): Netherlands.
22. Pieter Jan Beckx (1853–87): Belgium.
23. Anton Maria Anderledy (1887–92): Switzerland.
24. Luis Martín Garcia (1892–1906): Spain.
25. Franz Xavier Wernz (1906–14): Germany.
26. WŁODZIMIR LEDÓCHOWSKI (1915–42): Austria.
27. Jean-Baptiste Janssens (1946–64): Belgium.
28. PEDRO ARRUPE (1965–83): Spain.
29. Peter-Hans Kolvenbach (1983–2008): Born in Druten in Holland on November 30, 1928, the son of a Dutch father and an Italian mother, Kolvenbach entered the Jesuit novitiate on September 7, 1948, and was ordained a priest of the Armenian rite on June 29, 1961. Having studied general and Oriental linguistics at the Sorbonne and the University of the Hague, he taught linguistics at St. Joseph's University in Lebanon (1968–81) and served as vice provincial of the Jesuits in the Near East (1974–81) as well as rector of the Oriental Institute in Rome (1981–83). Elected general at the 33rd General Congregation in 1983, he renewed the relationship between the Vatican and the Society of Jesus as he promoted the apostolates of education and the *Spiritual Exercises*, continued the Society's promotion of faith that does justice, and coped with a decline in Jesuit vocations and the reality of sexual abuse scandals in the Church. He called a 34th General Congregation

(1995) that dealt with a wide range of questions, including collaboration of Jesuits with others, especially women. By the end of Kolvenbach's tenure, John Paul II had beatified and canonized more Jesuits and elevated more of them to the College of Cardinals than any other pope in history. Fr. Kolvenbach submitted his resignation at the 35th General Congregation in 2008.

30.   Adolfo Nicolás Pachón (since 2008): Born in 1936 in Villamuriel de Cerrato, Spain, he entered the Jesuit order in 1953 and was ordained a priest on March 17, 1967. Educated at Alcalá, Tokyo, and Rome, he became a professor in theology at Sophia University in Tokyo in 1971. He would later become director of the East Asian Pastoral Institute (1978–84) in the Philippines, rector of the Jesuit theologate in Tokyo (1991–93), and provincial of the Jesuit province of Japan (1993–99), followed by four years helping the poor among Tokyo's immigrants. Returning to the Philippines in 2004, he became president of the Jesuit Conference for Eastern Asia and Oceania before his election as superior general in 2008. As general, he focused on updating the structure of the Jesuit Curia in Rome, emphasizing availability for mission among Jesuits, providing support to Pope Francis, the first Jesuit pope, and preparing for the 36th General Congregation, at which he submitted his resignation, in 2016.

See also Black Pope; *Constitutions*; Curia, Jesuit

Dillon, Meaghan, "New Jesuit Superior General Elected." *The Fordham Observer*, February 14, 2008.

Kolvenbach, Peter-Hans, *Men of God, Men for Others*. Trans. Alan Neame. New York: Alba House, 1990.

McCarthy, Michael, Thomas Massaro, Thomas Worcester, and Michael A. Zampelli, "Four Stories of the Kolvenbach Generation." *Studies in the Spirituality of Jesuits* 42 (Spring 2010), 1–41.

Padberg, John W., Martin D. O'Keefe, and John L. McCarthy, *For Matters of Greater Moment*. St. Louis, MO: The Institute of Jesuit Sources, 1994.

van Westerhout, Arnoldo, *Ritratti de' prepositi generali della Compagnia di Gesù*. Rome: Monaldini, 1748.

Zeyen, Thomas E., *Jesuit Generals*. Scranton, PA: University of Scranton Press, 2004.

Vincent A. Lapomarda, SJ

Suppression

The papal brief *Dominus ac Redemptor* (July 21, 1773) ordered the global suppression of the Society of Jesus. It followed a series of national attacks on the Jesuits in many of Catholic Europe's leading nations: key moments in this process included the expulsion of Jesuits from Portugal and its overseas territories in 1759, Spain and its empire in 1767, and the assault on the French branch of the Society between 1762 and 1764. Recent historical debate has focused on the degree to which these regional variants of anti-Jesuitism were linked and whether they created an inexorable process that culminated in global suppression. Separate political events clearly triggered the local attacks on the Society: in Portugal the Marquis of Pombal's animus against the Jesuits, and trumped-up charges of Jesuit involvement with an assassination attempt against the king; in France, the dubious business dealings of the Jesuit Antoine Lavalette, which opened up an opportunity for the Society's Jansenist and Gallican enemies within the Parlement of Paris to strike; in Spain, the regalist agenda of Charles III and unwarranted charges of Jesuit involvement with the devastating riots of 1766. A run of unusually bad historical luck therefore goes some way toward explaining the immediate causes of the national attacks upon the Society, but some scholars have sought to identify the role of an international network of anti-Jesuits (notably Jansenists in France, the Italian States, and the Austrian Netherlands, and those of regalist sympathies across the continent) in seizing their moment and fostering a coherent campaign against the Society of Jesus which led to global suppression.

It is also noteworthy that, from the late 1750s onwards, there was widespread circulation and translation of anti-Jesuit tracts that originated in different countries. The scope and potency of such an anti-Jesuit "conspiracy" remains a matter of debate, but it is clear that by the late 1760s the individual Bourbon powers who had attacked the Society now aimed at global suppression. This is perhaps best construed as the result of a primarily political, rather than philosophical, logic. There was a need to justify earlier actions. The conclave that resulted in the election of Clement XIV in 1769 was dominated by the "Jesuit issue" and the agents of the Bourbon powers interfered unabashedly in proceedings: it was made abundantly clear that any candidate with conspicuous pro-Jesuit sympathies stood little chance of securing election. There was a tangible sense in some Jesuit circles that Clement's election made global suppression more likely and, over the coming years, great pressure was applied to the Pope to bring this to pass. The process took longer than expected, and Clement appears to have been reluctant but, in 1773, the axe finally fell.

The consequences of Clement's action were momentous. Hundreds of schools were closed or were handed over to the secular clergy, other religious orders, or the state; mission fields around the globe were abandoned, libraries were dispersed, and thousands of men became ex-Jesuits. This did not mark the end of the Jesuit enterprise, however. In some places (Prussia, for a short while, and the Russian Empire throughout the Suppression era) the Jesuit corporate existence survived. In other places, Jesuit life was rekindled ahead of the formal restoration of the Society in 1814: Parma, Naples, and the United States, for instance. This leads to a key interpretative question concerning the Suppression: did it mark a watershed moment in Jesuit history that separates an "old" and a "new" Society of Jesus? The event was patently traumatic but, throughout the Suppression era there were pockets of meaningful Jesuit survival and, within formally ex-Jesuit circles, determined attempts to sustain the Ignatian legacy: France and the exiled Spanish ex-Jesuits in Italy provide key examples of this process. The restored Society clearly regarded itself as the continuation of a project begun in 1530s Paris. At the same time it was fully aware that the events of 1773 had turned the Jesuit world upside down and that adjustment would be required.

See also Clement XIV; *Dominus ac Redemptor*; France; Portugal; Russia; Spain

Van Kley, Dale K., "Jansenism and the International Expulsion of the Jesuits." In S. Brown and T. Tackett, eds., *Reawakening Revolution, 1660–1815*. Cambridge: Cambridge University Press 2006, pp. 302–28.

Vogel, Christine, *Der Untergang der Gesellschaft Jesu als Europäisches Medienereignis (1758–1773)*. Mainz: Verlag Philipp von Zabern, 2006.

Worcester, Thomas, "A Restored Society or a New Society of Jesus?" In Robert Maryks and Jonathan Wright, eds., *Jesuit Survival and Restoration: A Global History 1773–1900*. Leiden: Brill, 2014, pp. 13–33.

Wright, Jonathan, "The Suppression and Restoration." In Thomas Worcester, ed., *The Cambridge Companion to the Jesuits*. Cambridge: Cambridge University Press, 2008, pp. 263–77.

Jonathan Wright

Surin, Jean-Joseph, SJ (1600–1665)

Born February 9, 1600, in Bordeaux (Gironde), Jean-Joseph Surin made, by his acquaintance with the Spanish mystics and through his own religious experience and writings, a major contribution to seventeenth-century French spirituality. Having completed his tertianship (1629) under the direction of Louis Lallemant (1578–1635), Surin worked as both minister and home missioner before his provincial sent him (December 1634) to serve as exorcist to the Ursulines of Loudun, where he provided great help to their prioress, Jeanne des Anges (1602–65). His already fragile health severely compromised by this mission, Surin was sent (1639 or 1640) to the infirmary in Bordeaux where he remained invalid for twenty years. Suffering from acute mental illness, he attempted suicide in 1645. Having made progress, he began to dictate and later himself to write his major works, slowly returning to pastoral and sacramental ministry. This union of the experiential and the speculative apparent in Surin as in the mystical authors he admired lent a credibility to his theological writings, of which his *Catéchisme spirtuel* (1657, rev. 1659, 1661) and posthumously published *Dialogues spirituels* (1704–09) had considerable influence. For Surin, as for Lallemant and the author of *L'Abandon à la providence divine*, familiarity and union with God require purity of heart. Yet Bossuet defended Surin's orthodoxy against charges of quietism, as did Surin himself in his *Questiones importantes à la vie spirituelle* (1664). After a brief illness, Surin died in Bordeaux in 1665, leaving in addition to the works mentioned a significant correspondence.

See also Asceticism and Mysticism; France

de Certeau, Michel, *The Possession at Loudun*. Trans. Michael B. Smith. Chicago, IL: University of Chicago Press, 2000.

Goujon, Patrick, *Prendre part à l'intransmissible: la communication spirituelle à travers la correspondance de Jean-Joseph Surin*. Grenoble: Jérôme Millon, 2008.

Surin, Jean-Joseph, *Guide Spirituel*. Ed. Michel de Certeau. Paris: Desclée de Brouwer, 1963.

William P. O'Brien, SJ

Suscipe

The word *Suscipe* comes from the opening of a prayer of Ignatius Loyola in the meditation entitled "Contemplation to Attain Love," placed at the end of the *Spiritual Exercises*. In Latin the prayer begins, "Suscipe, Domine, universam meam libertatem," which is rendered in English, "Take, Lord, receive all my liberty." Because the Latin verb *suscipere* can mean "to receive" as well as "to take up," the English translation usually includes both verbs in order to convey the full meaning of the original expression.

In the "Contemplation," Ignatius provides the words of the *Suscipe* as an offering to be made after someone has "pondered with great affection how much God our Lord has done for me" and how much God "desires to give me." It is, therefore, a prayer of gratitude that flows from the experience of the love of God. In response to the superabundance of divine love, which gives inexhaustibly of itself, Ignatius encourages the retreatant to make this prayer of total self-gift in return: "Take, Lord, and receive all my liberty, my memory, my understanding, and my entire will, all that I have and possess. You have given all to me; to you, Lord, I return it. All is yours; dispose of it according to your will. Give me only your love and your grace; these are enough for me."

Karl Rahner notes that the "Contemplation to Attain Love," though placed at the end of Ignatius's text, technically lies "outside of the body of the Exercises." But this is fitting, he observes, for its dynamic contains in itself the whole of the retreat and is "present in all the meditations."

See also Contemplation to Attain Love; Grace; *Spiritual Exercises*

de Guibert, Joseph, *The Jesuits: Their Spiritual Doctrine and Practice – A Historical Study*. Trans. William Young. St. Louis, MO: The Institute of Jesuit Sources, 1986, pp. 109–39.
Rahner, Karl, *Spiritual Exercises*. Trans. Kenneth Baker. New York: Herder and Herder, 1965, pp. 270–77.

Henry Shea, SJ

Syria

The Jesuits are present in three cities of Syria: Damascus, Aleppo, and Homs. The residence at Damascus was established in 1872 with two priests and a brother. They reached out to the Hauran and Jabal Druze. In addition to the ministries of confraternities, visits to schools, catechesis, and confessions, the Jesuits compiled a library for the use of university students and, following the Armenian disaster (1915), schools for Armenian refugees were established in Damascus as well as in Aleppo. Given the demographic changes in Damascus, the Jesuits left their residence at Bab al-Touma in 1965 and installed the university library and residence in apartments at Azbakiye.

The Aleppo residence dates from 1873 when three Jesuits came to Aleppo from Ghazir. Later, in 1882, they constructed an ample residence, classrooms, and a church in a quarter overlooking the city. The years of World War I devastated the city and dispersed the Jesuits. Under the Mandate a school was opened, only to be closed four years later when the Armenian school of St. Vartan commenced. The latter school is still in operation, as is the residence.

A residence and school in Homs date from 1882. They passed under the jurisdiction of the Greek Catholic patriarch in 1961.

In 1931, a tribal dispute among the Alawites set off a movement of conversions to Christianity and led to the founding of the mission among the Alawites, with a center at Tartous and schools and clinics at four other locations. It lasted until 1945.

Since the closure of private schools in 1967, work has been confined to a social center at Nouzha and to another socio-religious and agricultural center outside the city.

See also Lebanon; Middle East

Kuri, Sami, *Une histoire du Liban à travers les archives des jésuites, 1816–1845*. Vol. I. Beirut: Dar el-Machreq, 2001.
Libois, Charles, *La Compagnie de Jésus au Levant: la province du Proche-Orient: notices historiques*. Beirut: Faculté des lettres et des sciences humaines, Université Saint-Joseph/Dar el-Machreq, 2009.

John Donohue, SJ

Tacchi Venturi, Pietro, SJ (1861–1956)

Pietro Tacchi Venturi was born to Antonio Tacchi Venturi and Orsola Ceselli in San Severino (Marche) on August 12, 1861. After some time in Rome, he continued his education in San Severino and in Macerata, the birthplace of Matteo Ricci. Tacchi Venturi would later publish Ricci's works on China. Subsequently, he moved back to Rome, where he attended the Roman Seminary (1876–78). In 1878 Tacchi Venturi departed for the novitiate in France. Owing to the anti-Jesuit measures of the government, he and his confrères had to be transferred to Naples to complete his novice formation. Subsequently, he studied rhetoric first in Naples and then in Castel Gandolfo. In 1882 Tacchi Venturi was sent to Rome and then to Naples in order to complete his high school exams, which he had missed before joining the Society. Having passed the exams, Tacchi Venturi returned to Rome to continue for two years (1883–85) his training in philosophy at the Pontifical Gregorian University. Consecutively, he was sent for the so-called regency at the boarding school in Mondragone. Toward the end of this experience, marked by an illness, Tacchi Venturi was transferred to Rome with a task of pursuing studies in literature. He therefore enrolled at the Royal University of Rome, where in 1891 he earned his MA degree. Afterwards, he enrolled at the Gregorian University, where he studied theology until 1895. One year later, Tacchi Venturi received from the superior general his first major mission: to write a history of the Jesuits in Italy. He would continue to work on this project intermittently until his nineties. The first part of the first volume of *La storia della Compagnia di Gesù in Italia* was published in 1910. The second part of the second volume was published in 1951, shortly before he died in 1956.

With the beginning of World War I, Tacchi Venturi's activity as a writer was interrupted, for Superior General Franz Xavier Wernz appointed him secretary general of the Society (1914). This office, which he held until 1921, became particularly crucial when the new superior general Włodzimierz Ledóchowski, who was not allowed to stay in Rome, left much of the Order's daily government affairs in the hands of Tacchi Venturi.

His role as the Vatican's "fiduciary" in dealings with the Palazzo Venezia began in 1922, when Pope Pius XI requested that he negotiate with the newly appointed minister of external affairs, Benito Mussolini, the purchase of the Chigi Library for the Vatican. As he later put it, the donation of the Chigi Library "was the beginning of my acquaintance and conversation that I had with the Duce from December 1922 until the first months of 1943." Tacchi Venturi's role in the reconciliation between the Vatican and the Italian state is abundantly documented, yet unstudied. His archive in Rome contains an ample file of correspondence with the governmental officials, and the notes Tacchi Venturi made of his numerous audiences with Mussolini himself, which reveal his zealous and constant engagement in Church–State affairs leading to the Lateran Pacts and its subsequent preservation. In his vision of Italian society as traditionally Catholic, he sought not only the reconciliation of the Church–State animosity that had resulted from the role the liberal and anticlerical Risorgimento had played in the limitation of the papal temporal power but also the conciliation of Fascist ideology with Catholicism, which for him would guarantee society's moral order. It is not surprising, therefore, to see Tacchi Venturi eagerly collaborate with the Fascist government in about 4,000 affairs related to keeping Catholic culture and morality dominant, if not exclusive, in Italian society. The Duce recognized Tacchi Venturi's merits by awarding him in 1931 the highest civil decoration, the Knight Grand Cross of the Order of SS. Maurice and Lazarus. One of the most controversial negotiations in which Tacchi Venturi participated was the Vatican's assurance of not criticizing Mussolini for the introduction of the racial laws (1938) in exchange for the governmental noninterference in the affairs of the ecclesiastical organization Azione Cattolica Italiana. Nevertheless, Tacchi Venturi spent most of his time in 1938–43 helping Jews and former Jews in overcoming the racial legislation.

Besides his political engagement, Tacchi Venturi was an editor of the *Storia delle religioni*; an author of many articles in Treccani's monumental *Enciclopedia Italiana*, and a writer for *La Civiltà Cattolica*, in whose pages he published more than a hundred articles.

See also Civiltà Cattolica; Italy; Jews and Jesuits; Pius XI

Pierre Blet, Angelo Martini, Burkhart Schneider, and Robert A. Graham, *Actes et documents du Saint Siège relatifs à la Seconde Guerre mondiale*. Città del Vaticano: [Libreria editrice vaticana], 1965.

Kertzer, David I., *The Pope and Mussolini: The Secret History of Pius XI and the Rise of Fascism in Europe*. New York: Random House 2014.

Maryks, Robert A., *"Pouring Jewish Water into Fascist Wine": Untold Stories of (Catholic) Jews from the Archive of Mussolini's Jesuit Pietro Tacchi Venturi*. Leiden: Brill, 2012.

Scaduto, Mario, "P. Pietro Tacchi Venturi." *Archivum Historicum Societatis Iesu* 25 (1956), 229–30.

Robert A. Maryks

Taiwan

Taiwan belongs to the Chinese province (headquarters in Macau) of the Conference of Asia Pacific (headquarters in the Philippines) in the Society of Jesus. The first Jesuit to visit Taiwan was Father Edward Murphy (Chinese name Mu Yucai 牧育才) in 1951. He taught at National Taiwan University when Ying Qianli 英千里 (Ignatius, 1901–69), the Catholic director of the Department of Foreign Language and Literature, hired several Catholic priests as faculty. In 1950, numerous Jesuits fled China and moved to Macau, Hong Kong, and Taiwan because the new Communist government expelled foreign missionaries and ministers. In March of 1954, the first church built by the Jesuits in Taiwan was dedicated to the Holy Mother and consecrated in Zhudong 竹東, County of Hsinchu (新竹縣) in North Taiwan. Father Alonso, who was previously stationed in Anqing 安慶, province of Anhui 安徽 in China, decided to build the first Jesuit church in Taiwan to signify their arrival rather than being transient after the expulsion from China. Hsinchu had been assigned to the Jesuits by the pope to develop their initial evangelization in Taiwan in 1952, and thus a central place formed to receive financial aid from overseas. Because of support from the Philippines mission and the papacy, the number of Jesuits in Taiwan peaked in 1968 and was the highest among the missions in the Jesuit province of East Asia (renamed the Chinese province in 1970).

Dedication to education and culture is among the most substantial legacies of the Jesuits in Taiwan. The Tien Education Center in Taipei was founded in 1963 and has become an active secular institute that upholds Jesuit evangelization and Catholic activities. The name "Tien" refers to the first cardinal from Asia, Thomas Tien Ken-Sin, SVD (Chinese name 田耕莘, 1890–1967), who was a former archbishop in Beijing, China. Furthermore, to provide a more accessible venue to the public, the Cardinal Tien Cultural Foundation was established in 1990, enhancing Jesuit social engagement. In 2000 the Ignatian Spirituality Center, which belonged to the Tien Education Center, was founded. It promotes Ignatius's spirituality according to the founder's pedagogy. In addition, the Taipei Ricci Institute was founded by the French Jesuits Yves Raguin

(1912–98) and Jean Almire Robert Lefeuvre (1922–2010) in 1966. The institute was named after one of the most famous Jesuits in China, Matteo Ricci, and continues Jesuit sinological research and promotes religious and cultural comparative studies between China and the West. Currently, the institute has individual offices in Macau, Paris, and San Francisco. The institute's most acclaimed publication is *Le Grand Ricci*, the largest Chinese–French dictionary in the world, comprising seven volumes and published in 2001 after nearly fifty years. Since the 1990s, the institute has also focused on Taiwan studies, such as indigenous languages and cultures, and further included the fields of the Pacific Ocean and the Austronesian languages and peoples.

In contemporary Taiwan, two Jesuit fathers have made a particularly positive impact on Asian society. Cardinal Paul Shan Kuo-His 單國璽 (1923–2012), the first cardinal elected from Taiwan, was probably the most well-known and respected Jesuit in Taiwan in recent decades. He used his high status to effect social changes, and his lectures on peace and faith were widely acclaimed after he retired from the cardinalate in 2006 because of cancer. Unlike Cardinal Paul, who was Chinese, Father Barry Martinson (b. 1945, Chinese name Ding Songqing 丁松青) was an American from California who arrived in Taiwan in 1969. He began learning Chinese at the Jesuit college in Hsinchu. In addition to this college (since 1957), the Jesuits had their Shanghai college reopened in Catholic Fujen University in Taipei in 1968, entitled Fujen Faculty of Theology of St. Robert Bellarmine. Martinson's first mission to Koto island (politically belonging to Taiwan), near the coast of southeast Taiwan, began in 1971. After living among native Tao people, he developed a love for the islands and peoples of Taiwan. In 1976, he was assigned to a mountain village, Qingquan 清泉 in Hsinchu, and began his second residential mission to the aboriginal people. To date Father Martinson remains in Qingquan, and because of his artistic creation, the Catholic church in the village has become famous for its mural paintings, stained glass, and mosaics that depict native Atayal people's devotion and incorporate indigenous elements. A Jesuit priest as well as an anthropologist, Martinson has helped the Atayal people reestablish their identity with their indigenous culture.

Before the previously mentioned fathers, the Swiss Jesuit Franz Burkhardt (1902–2002, Chinese name Pu Mindao 蒲敏道) was the longest-living Jesuit who devoted himself to charity in Taiwan since 1959. A former official visitor for China and provincial of East Asia, he was abundantly awarded by the Taiwanese president and the pope.

See also Asia; China; Philippines

Zhirong, Fang, 房志榮, "1949 nian yihou de yesuhui zai zhongguo" 1949年以後的耶穌會在中國 [The Jesuits in China after 1949]. *Shenxue lunji* 神學論集 [*Anthology of Theology*] 153 (Fall 2007), 331–52.

Hui-Hung Chen

Tarahumara

In the seventeenth century Jesuit missionaries moved into the frontier regions of northern Mexico to convert and minister to the Tarahumara, a group of non-sedentary and semi-sedentary peoples who inhabited the Sierra Madre Occidental. At the point of contact with the Spanish, the Tarahumara numbered approximately 100,000 persons.

The Jesuits attracted the original mission inhabitants through gifts of cloth, tools, axes, seeds, and cattle. The Tarahumara mission system placed Jesuits and Indians alongside the Spanish settlers who had moved north in search of silver. The missions, with their labor pool and their livestock, were integrated into the local mining and ranching economies, but the missions were also subsidized by the Crown, supported by income from the Society's haciendas in central Mexico, and received lay donations. Some missions had financial success with the marketing of their cattle and crops, such as the central mission at Huejotitlán. Jesuit mission churches were richly decorated, their reliquaries imported from Italy, sculptures from Spain and Mexico City, paintings from Italy and Mexico City. Tarahumara mission libraries and individual cells were well-stocked with books and prints, and mission kitchens and churches boasted Chinese vases and dishes.

Given the labor demands of the mining economy, the Jesuit missionaries walked something of a middle line between advocating for better terms for Indian subjects, but also justifying their presence to the Crown and local miners by their ability to corral a pool of indigenous labor in a single location. By the eighteenth century, mission remuneration in the form of gifting and feasting had given way to a wage-labor system, augmented by rations of meat and corn. Missions were no longer entirely Indian by the eighteenth century, as both Spanish and *castas* occupied Indian villages. Culturally assimilated, an eighteenth-century Jesuit visitor complained that the inhabitants of lower Tarahumara were "not very Indian" (Deeds, *Defiance and Deference*, 142).

The Tarahumara mission system saw its fair share of strife, especially during the 1652 Toboso-led insurrection. Quelled by Spanish troops, the continuing periodic raids, coupled with episodes of disease that decimated populations, made the late seventeenth century an unstable period in the missions' history. Eventually, the Jesuits secularized a portion of their missions (1753) in favor of developing the California missions.

See also Mexico

Bargellini, Clara, "At the Center on the Frontier: The Jesuit Tarahumara Missions of New Spain." In Thomas Kaufmann and Elizabeth Pilliod, eds., *Time and Place: The Geohistory of Art.* Farnham: Ashgate, 2005, pp. 5–19.

Deeds, Susan, *Defiance and Deference in Mexico's Colonial North: Indians under Spanish Rule in Nueva Vizcaya.* Austin: University of Texas Press, 2003.

J. Michelle Molina

Teilhard de Chardin, Pierre, SJ (1881–1955)

During the first half of the twentieth century, at a time when the Catholic Church was still ambivalent about the theory of evolution and its impact on doctrine, Jesuit Pierre Teilhard de Chardin set about articulating how this theory actually enhances the doctrine of the Incarnation. Despite his efforts, very few people attended Teilhard's funeral Mass at St. Ignatius Church in New York City or joined the funeral procession to the Jesuit novitiate in Poughkeepsie, NY. Indeed, most of his religious writings had not yet been published and few beyond his professional and personal circles knew of his work until the appearance of his magnum opus, *The Phenomenon of Man*, several months after he died. Yet, as volumes containing his religious essays appeared gradually over the ensuing years, his inspiring mystical interpretation of evolution captivated many. In less than a decade, his name became commonplace; his vision influenced the proceedings of the Second Vatican Council, particularly the document *Gaudium et spes*; and many were reading his work, which the Holy Office had, by then, officially declared dangerous.

Today, as scholars plumb the richness and variety of his work, the magnitude of his contribution has become apparent. Eleven volumes of his published scientific papers, technical notes, and geological maps deal mainly with the geology and paleontology of China, although his early work and occasional work at excavation sites that he visited later in life are also included. Of particular note are his contributions to the Peking Man project. His religious essays comprise another thirteen volumes, not to mention twelve volumes of collected letters. In his short work on spirituality, *The Divine Milieu*, Teilhard provides a cosmic context for divine action and emphasizes the value of the human as co-creator in the evolutionary process. Grounded in the *Spiritual Exercises*, he raises Ignatius's exhortation to find God in all things to cosmic dimensions, encouraging the mystic to find God at work in the evolutionary dynamics of the universe.

Pierre Teilhard de Chardin grew up in central France where his father stimulated interest in natural history and his mother inspired devotion to the Sacred Heart. In his autobiographical essay "The Heart of Matter," Teilhard relates how the seeds of his synthesis began to germinate very early in life. One day as a young boy of 5 or 6, as he was having a haircut by a fireplace, he held a lock of his hair close to the fire and watched part of himself burn to ash. This traumatic experience sparked his lifelong research project – the search for an absolute, an imperishable consistency, an answer to the question, "what holds everything together?" To console himself at the time, he began secretly to "worship" iron and then rock – anything hard and durable. This intense interest led naturally to his choice of geology as a field of graduate study.

Teilhard's formal education began at Notre Dame de Mongré, a Jesuit boarding school in Villefranche-sur-Saône, where he excelled in all subjects though he always preferred science. Spurred on by a desire to be and do what is perfect, he entered the Jesuit novitiate of the Lyon province at Aix-en-Provence in 1899. His formation was typical: a thirty-day retreat, two years of orientation to Jesuit spiritual life, first vows in 1901, followed by four years of college education. Because of laws restricting the activities of religious orders in France, in 1902 he and his Jesuit companions were transferred to a temporary juniorate on the Isle of Jersey in the English Channel to complete their course work. In 1905 Teilhard received a three-year assignment to Holy Family, a Jesuit junior college in Cairo, Egypt, where he taught physics and chemistry, curated a small museum, and often spent weekends collecting marine fossils with colleagues.

During his early years as a Jesuit, he struggled to reconcile his passion for God with his equally deep passion for rock. It was not until he immersed himself in theological studies in Hastings, England, and encountered the theory of evolution that the seeds of his gestating synthesis began to sprout. With the aid of the scriptural text, "All things hold together in Him" (Colossians 1:17), a spark ignited and his world caught fire. He resolved to devote his life to achieving "communion with God through Earth" and to showing others the way. He was ordained in the chapel of the Jesuit theological seminary in Hastings on August 24, 1911, and after a tertianship experienced in the trenches of World War I, he pronounced his solemn vows on May 26, 1918.

During his stay in Hastings, he befriended Charles Dawson, a paleontologist who turned out to be the architect of a massive deception. Dawson claimed to have discovered a skull and jawbones of an early hominid known as Piltdown Man. Once more sophisticated analytic techniques were developed, the fossil was shown to be a Neolithic human skull fitted with a modern orangutan jaw holding teeth that were artificially filed and dyed a fossil-like color. Though an amateur at the time, Teilhard was always suspicious of the find. Unfortunately, his involvement with Dawson encouraged Teilhard's later opponents to implicate him. However, evidence shows that Teilhard knew nothing of the hoax until it was revealed in 1953.

In 1912, under the supervision of the renowned paleontologist Marcellin Boule, a specialist in an extinct species of pre-humans called Neanderthals, Teilhard began graduate studies at the Museum of Natural History in Paris. Boule, who was impressed with Teilhard's independence of mind and his gifts for minute analysis and wide synthesis, encouraged him to pursue his interest in mammals of the lower Eocene, a geological epoch marked by the emergence of placental mammals and primates. Teilhard also traveled to the northwest region of Spain to participate in excavations at several caverns known for their prehistoric cave paintings.

However, at the outbreak of World War I, Teilhard's studies were interrupted when he volunteered to serve on the front line, not as a chaplain, but as a stretcher-bearer, one of the most humble positions in the military. His service was exemplary. He was loved by the men in his regiment, promoted to the rank of corporal, cited several times for bravery, and awarded the Croix de Guerre, the Médaille Militaire, and the Chevalier of the Légion d'Honneur.

The war was a true trial by fire, one that had a profound effect on Teilhard's personality and spiritual vision. Living and working closely with soldiers from all parts of the French Empire, experiencing the deplorable conditions of the trenches, comforting the dying, carrying the wounded from the battlefield, feeling the solidarity that is only possible at times of great crisis drew him out of himself and helped him to fashion a vision in which humanity would one day become one. During the lulls between battles, he began to explore his new ideas in a series of essays now published in *Writings in Time of War*. The first of these, "Cosmic Life," was to be his intellectual testament in case he was killed in battle. When he was not writing essays, he continued as always to hunt for fossils, some of which were useful to his graduate research project.

After the war, Teilhard returned to Paris, completed his graduate work, and defended his thesis with distinction on March 22, 1922. He was quickly recognized as a brilliant scholar: appointed chair of the geology department at the Institut Catholique in Paris; awarded the Prix Viquesnel by the Société Géologique de France in 1922 and the Prix Roux by the Académie des Sciences in 1923; and elected to the Société de Biogéographie in 1925. During this period he was making valuable contacts with world-class experts in his field.

In 1923 Teilhard spent a year in China with Jesuit Father Émile Licent, who had established a small museum in Tientsin. Licent had invited Teilhard to help classify some of his fossils. Together they explored the regions surrounding Beijing, gathering fossils and stone implements. During their first expedition to the Ordos desert, as Teilhard found himself without the bread and wine needed to celebrate the Eucharist, he completed an intensely moving and cosmic refashioning of the Eucharistic Prayer, "The Mass on the World," a prayer that he had been developing since his time in the trenches.

On his return to Paris, Teilhard took up his position at the Institut Catholique, reconnected with other scholars, and continued to study the fossils of mammals from the Tertiary and Quaternary periods, particularly rodents. Because his ideas were fresh and alive and came from his life experience, he quickly gained popularity as a lecturer with students and young seminarians. However, Church officials in Rome, who were making massive efforts to halt the Modernist trend in Catholic thinking, were concerned with Teilhard's interpretation of original sin. When, in 1926, a document written by Teilhard for private study entitled "Note on Some Possible Historical Representations of Original Sin" mysteriously landed on the desk of the Jesuit General Włodimir Ledóchowski, Teilhard came under yet further scrutiny. Because of increased pressure from the Vatican, Ledóchowski asked Teilhard to sign an agreement never to speak or write about religious matters, to confine himself to purely scientific publications, and to leave Paris. Though deeply distressed, he submitted reluctantly to this request. By the end of April, he was on his way to China, his connection with the Institut Catholique permanently severed. In exile, he was allowed only brief visits to Paris and was sometimes refused permission to travel to scientific conferences. However, he did continue to write and to sharpen his synthetic vision of science and faith. He sent completed essays to his cousin or to a friend who distributed them to his circle of followers.

In China, Teilhard's life as a scientist flourished. He collaborated with both local and foreign researchers working in Beijing, and always took particular care to mentor and encourage the young Chinese scientists with whom he worked. At Chóu-Kóu-Tien, 30 miles southwest of Peking, Teilhard and his companions discovered the well-preserved skull of a pre-human species they called *Sinanthropus* or Peking Man. Having lived some 500,000 years ago, Peking Man used stone tools and possibly fire. One of Teilhard's main contributions as chief geologist was his discovery of an enormous filled-in cavern where the fossils were eventually found. At his lab at the Beijing Union Medical College, he continued for many years to classify and provide a thorough inventory of the fossils.

Teilhard's geological interests focused primarily on Earth's underlying geological structure rather than restricting his work to the collection of specimens. In 1931 he was invited to join the Croisière Jaune or Yellow Crossing, a nine-month automobile expedition into the interior of China, as its official geologist. This allowed him to integrate his knowledge of the geology of regions around Beijing with the overall geology of China. Expeditions to other parts of Asia, to Africa, Europe, and the Americas offered him a still more global picture. Always interested in an interdisciplinary approach to scientific problems, in 1940, he and his friend Pierre Leroy established the Beijing Institute of Geobiology. During his China years, he was sometimes able to attend international conferences, and in 1939 Villanova University awarded him the Mendel Medal for his work on human paleontology.

By 1929 Teilhard had completed his first major work, *The Divine Milieu*, in which he sets out a cosmic spirituality, one that promotes the value of work and highlights the immanent presence of the divine in all of creation. As his religious thought developed, he dreamed of writing a comprehensive treatise that would integrate all aspects of evolution. His work with fossils and geological formations convinced him that Earth was indeed much older than many were imagining and that it had undergone considerable change throughout its lifetime.

Over the years, his attention turned from the emergence of the human to the future of humanity. He had contemplated the mass of humanity from the battlefield and had realized the boundless potential of this dynamic living organism that covers Earth's surface and in which "thought" had recently emerged in natural history. He called this layer of human consciousness the "noosphere" and began to emphasize the human phenomenon with its special role in the forward movement of evolution. He was anxious that others see what he was seeing: the immensity of space, the eons of time, the incredibly large number of species, the rise of novelty, the organic nature of the cosmos, the interdependence of all things, the potential for life and thought present from the beginning, the growth of consciousness in tandem with the ongoing complexification of matter, the human not as an epiphenomenon but as truly embedded within the evolutionary process, and most especially, the divine milieu, in which the cosmos is bathed.

From 1938 to 1940, Teilhard worked every day on *The Phenomenon of Man*, the treatise in which he integrated his vision into a coherent whole. Following the complexification of matter through several critical points – the emergence of matter, the emergence of life, and the emergence of thought – he speculated about the next critical point in the evolution, when humanity would learn to harness the power of love and live in communion.

Perhaps Teilhard's most creative contribution was his discovery of what he calls the law of complexity-consciousness and its corollary, creative union. Studies of mole rat fossils, showing a correlation between brain size and consciousness, indicated to him that matter and spirit are not two separate entities but two aspects of one and the same cosmic reality. He noted that new levels of complexity emerge from the union of agents at the next lower level. Each ascending level shows an increase in consciousness. His succinct statement of the law, "Union Differentiates," indicates that complexity and consciousness evolve hand in hand. Teilhard envisaged a final cosmic synthesis, one in which cosmogenesis coincides with Christogenesis, arriving finally at what he called the Omega Point. At this point of convergence, the universe and humanity will have been gathered into the fullness of the body of Christ.

Teilhard's final years in China were difficult. By 1939 the Sino-Japanese War was ravishing the country; his activities were curtailed; fieldwork was impossible; and most laboratories were transferred to the south of China. Alone and often depressed, Teilhard remained at his laboratory in Beijing caring for the Peking Man fossils. Eventually, the fossils were packed in strong boxes to be sent to the United States by way of its military for safekeeping. In the process, however, the fossils disappeared. Perhaps they were confiscated by the Japanese or lost during the bombing of Pearl Harbor.

Teilhard was also anxious to see his manuscript of *The Phenomenon of Man* published. He waited several years to find someone who could deliver it to the censors in Rome. The censors were not pleased and suggested that he revise the work and resubmit it. Several attempts at revision were to no avail. On his return to Paris in 1946, he continued to pursue the possibility of publication. In June 1947, he suffered a serious heart attack which was probably partly due to the stress of the last few years.

In recognition of outstanding service to the intellectual and scientific influence of France, in 1947, the French Foreign Affairs Ministry promoted Teilhard to the rank of officer of the Legion of Honor citing his international standing in the fields of geology and paleontology. He was offered the chair of prehistory at Collège de France,

Figure 63 Gravestone of Pierre Teilhard de Chardin, SJ, Hyde Park, New York. Photograph Thomas Worcester, SJ

but his superiors in Rome would not permit his returning to Paris. Instead he settled for a position as research associate at the Wenner-Gren Foundation in New York City, a foundation dedicated to anthropological research. There he worked until his death from a heart attack on Easter Day, April 10, 1955. Fortunately, he had bequeathed his manuscripts to his secretary Jeanne Mortier who immediately began preparing them for publication.

In 1962 the Vatican issued a warning that Teilhard's works contained dangerous ideas and were not to be housed in seminary libraries or sold in Catholic bookstores. Although the warning was never officially lifted, both Popes John Paul II and Benedict XVI have praised Teilhard's work and studies continue to plumb the richness of his vision – a vision that resulted from Teilhard's focusing on a question that mattered to him, one that needed a scientific as well as a religious answer. Ignited in childhood beside a fireplace, this question burned within him throughout his life until it blazed out in an explosion of dazzling flashes and culminated in a unique vision of Christ radiating from the heart of the cosmos as its divine milieu, of Christ up ahead in the future as its Omega Point, drawing all things to himself. It was a daring synthesis of evolution and Incarnation couched in poetic language for which he paid a great price. Remaining faithful to the voice of God burning in his heart while at the same time obeying his religious superiors required unmatched discernment, courage, and fortitude.

Yet even today, not all embrace his vision. Many scientists are skeptical and many Christians continue to read Scripture literally. But for those who have embraced the vision, traditional dogma has acquired a new vigor, and its implications – the unity of all things, the interdependence of humanity with the rest of creation, each person's role as co-creator with the Cosmic Christ – continue to challenge life in an unfinished universe.

See also Aseticism and Mysticism; China; France; Science

Cuénot, Claude, *Teilhard de Chardin: A Biographical Study.* Trans. V. Colimore. London: Burns & Oates, 1965.
Duffy, Kathleen, *Teilhard's Mysticism: Seeing the Inner Face of Evolution.* Maryknoll, NY: Orbis Books, 2014.
King, Thomas, *Teilhard de Chardin.* Wilmington, DE: Michael Glazier, 1988.
King, Ursula, *Spirit of Fire: The Life and Vision of Teilhard de Chardin.* Maryknoll, NY: Orbis Books, 1996.
Lukas, Mary, and Ellen Lukas, *Teilhard.* Garden City, NY: Doubleday, 1977.
Mortier, Jeanne, and Marie-Louise Auboux, *Teilhard de Chardin: Album.* New York: Harper & Row, 1966.
Teilhard de Chardin, Pierre, *The Heart of Matter.* Trans. René Hague. New York: Harcourt Brace Jovanovich, 1978.

Kathleen Duffy, SSJ

Tertianship, Tertians

The term Tertianship stands for the Latin *tertia probatio* or third probation. A Jesuit's first probation consists of a brief period before entering the novitiate. The two years of novitiate are his second probation. The third probation, usually lasting eight to ten months, takes place after priestly ordination and before a person's final vows. Jesuit brothers make their tertianship about ten years after their first vows. Those engaged in making the tertianship are called tertians.

In 1537, having received Holy Orders, Ignatius and his companions went to live in small groups in some of the towns of northern Italy. There they led a mixed life, alternating withdrawal and apostolic engagement. When he came to write the *Constitutions*, Ignatius drew on this experience as a prototype for the final period of a Jesuit's probation. He also envisaged it as a second novitiate but adapted to men who were familiar with the ways of the Spirit and Jesuit life. He wrote (*Constitutions*, #516):

> it will be helpful for those who had been sent to studies, upon finishing the work and effort of intellectual formation, to apply themselves during the period of final probation to the school of the heart (*schola affectus*), exercising themselves in spiritual and corporal pursuits ...

The tertian makes the full Spiritual Exercises, which underpin all that follows. He then undertakes other experiments such as service in hospitals, pilgrimage, etc. as described in the *General Examen* in relation to novices (*Constitutions*, ##64–70). Study of the *Constitutions* and other Jesuit documents is another core component of tertianship. The makeup of contemporary tertianships tends to be international and so offers an experience of the universality of the Society. The renewal of the tertianship, called for by General Congregations 31 and 32, has borne fruit and restored the *schola affectus* to its rightful place in Jesuit formation.

See also Course of Studies; Formation

Ruhan, Anthony, "The Origins of the Jesuit Tertianship." In Raymond Schroth, ed., *Jesuit Spirit in a Time of Change.* Westminster, MD: Newman, 1967, pp. 99–117.

Brian O'Leary, SJ

Theater

Historians of performance and culture have long recognized Jesuit theater as a potent dramatic form within the larger genus of early modern scholastic drama. Even as the professional theater was emerging in Europe, Catholics and Protestants were producing amateur academic and confessional dramas to form moral consciences and impart good religion. Along with the Franciscans and Piarists, the Jesuits employed theater in the service of education and evangelization. More particularly, Jesuit theatrical production aimed at cultivating the verbal and physical eloquence necessary for engaging public life as well as forming hearts in the human and Christian virtues required for becoming a moral person. In relationship to other species of Catholic school drama, Jesuit theater proved distinctive in the extraordinary number of plays produced, the geographical reach of the dramas, and the extensive investment of resources in theatrical presentation.

Jesuit theater was born in schools that aimed to impart a deeply humanistic education to young laymen preparing to take their places on the early modern public stage. As early as 1551, three years after the establishment of the Society's first college in Messina, Sicily, the Jesuits began staging full-scale theatrical productions. In addition to the dialogues and orations that were already a standard part of the curriculum, every Jesuit school throughout Europe and the mission territories staged tragedies, comedies, biblical dramas, saint plays, and/or history plays. Theatrical productions, many of which incorporated music and/or dance, took place twice per year, often at Carnival and then again at the annual distribution of prizes. Patronal feasts, the visitation of ecclesiastical or political dignitaries, and special civic celebrations provided additional occasions for performance. These theatrical events allowed students to demonstrate their educational progress to a broad audience while publicizing the good reputation of the school. Involving citizens in these productions and/or staging the plays in important public spaces served to nourish the relationship between the Jesuit college and the locality.

As Jesuit dramas were aimed at performance rather than publication, their authors, usually professors of poetry or rhetoric, frequently remained anonymous; however, some Jesuit playwrights (e.g., Stefano Tuccio, Jakob Bidermann) achieved notoriety when other schools in the extensive Jesuit network staged their plays, a phenomenon facilitated by the ubiquity of Latin. Because the plays were instruments for cultivating *eloquentia perfecta Latina*, they were composed entirely in Latin, though vernacular elements were incorporated with increasing frequency, particularly for the sake of invited audiences.

Jesuit theater, like Jesuit education itself, was an integrative experience that touched the participants' minds, hearts, and spirits by appealing to the senses. As such, these didactic school dramas paid particular attention to *mise-en-scène*. Because the colleges could marshal a variety of resources in service of the dramatic project, especially the technical and artisanal skills of Jesuit brothers like Andrea Pozzo, the Jesuits made significant strides in scenography, stagecraft, and lighting. Most professional theaters of the period could not hope to compete with the Jesuit colleges in staging splendor. Jesuit theater became well known for scenes of transformation in which stage settings changed miraculously before the audience's eyes, anticipating the more interior transformations that might be wrought in the observers.

Despite the vigor with which the Jesuits "trod the boards" prior to the Suppression, the investment in theatrical performance was by no means uncontested. Various editions of the *Ratio studiorum* reveal an internal schizophrenia about the theater's place in the educational project; though theater was clearly valuable, its natural exuberance and sensuality needed to be contained by legislative norms (honored more in the breach than in the observance). To critics of the Society like the Jansenists, Jesuit theatricals pointed to a more thoroughgoing laxity characterizing the Order's approach to the Christian life. Still, despite the anxieties, Jesuit theater disseminated a vibrant approach to education that encouraged effective communication, embodied human and Christian virtues, and fostered ongoing dialogue with religious and civic cultures.

Discussions of Jesuit theater often terminate with the Suppression, yet the restored Society continued to employ theatrical performance, particularly in the Americas, not only to educate and evangelize but also to publicize the Society's emerging institutions. Dialogues, orations, and full-scale theatrical productions were presented in nearly every Jesuit school, particularly at public exhibitions and Commencement Exercises, to exercise students' ability at public speaking, assist with language acquisition, and develop a cultured Catholic presence within an American, democratic context. Vestiges of this tradition can be found today in Jesuit high school theater programs and in theater companies advancing the Society's work of serving faith and promoting justice (e.g., Teatro la fragua, National Theatre Workshop for the Handicapped, etc.).

See also Arts, Performing; Education, Secondary and Pre-Secondary; *Ratio Studiorum*; Universities

Bloemendal, Jan, and Howard B. Norland, *Neo-Latin Drama and Theatre in Early Modern Europe*. Leiden: Brill, 2013.

Griffin, Nigel, *Jesuit School Drama: A Checklist of Critical Literature, Supplement No. 1*. London: Grant and Cutler, 1986.

Knapp, Eva, *The Sopron Collection of Jesuit Stage Designs*. Budapest: Enciklopédia Publishing House, 1999.

Shore, Paul, "Counter-Reformation Drama." In Alexandra Bamji, Geert H. Janssen, and Mary Laven, eds., *The Ashgate Research Companion to the Counter-Reformation*. Burlington, VT: Ashgate, 2013, pp. 355–72.

Michael A. Zampelli, SJ

Theology

Theology has been a central occupation of Jesuits since the founding of the Society of Jesus. There is, however, no clearly identifiable "Jesuit theology." The US Jesuit theologian Avery Dulles (1918–2008) said recently: "If one were to look for a common bond among Jesuit theologians, it would be found not so much in theology itself as in spirituality" (Dulles, "Jesuits and Theology," 525). Drawing on the personal, practical, and ecclesial mysticism of St. Ignatius, the founder of the Society of Jesus, Jesuits exercise their mission of theological reflection animated by the spirit of Ignatius and the vision of the world that he had; but they do not receive from this vision a specific theological content or method. It is true that in the history of Jesuit intellectual formation, certain tendencies prevailed, such as a preference for the scholasticism of the Spanish Jesuit Francisco Suárez (1548–1617) over the more strict Thomism of the Dominicans, a preference that lasted into the nineteenth century and that caused not a little Jesuit–Dominican tension. Yet

Jesuits have generally been free to think and write creatively as professional theologians without having to follow some Jesuit "party line." What Jesuits have had in common, always, is their formation according to the *Spiritual Exercises* of St. Ignatius, which, drawing on the saint's mystical experiences, shape every Jesuit's spirituality and understanding of God. Thus the God (and world) of the *Exercises* influence Jesuits to practice theology in a spirit that approaches the world as Ignatius did, that is, with a loving but also critical attitude, ready to find God at work in the depths of all things while seeking, practically, to discern the import of this active divine presence for the situations in which they live.

Doing theology is thus an *apostolate* for Jesuits, not a purely academic exercise. Their ministry of theology is carried out as a service to the Church and to the world in social, cultural, and ecclesial circumstances in which a theological response is required. The fact that the Society of Jesus exists "to serve the Lord alone and his vicar on earth" (*Formula of the Institute*, #1, 1540) and to engage in the ministry of "defense and propagation of the faith" (*Formula of the Institute*, #1, 1550) has caused Jesuits, from the beginning, to engage in theology on behalf of (and even at the behest of) the pope. Also influential were the overseas missions of the Society, which started with Francis Xavier's arrival in India in 1542. And historical factors of various kinds have also played a central role in why and how Jesuits do theology, devoting attention to specific areas within it, as we shall see.

The Society's Purpose and Papal Missions

Scarcely had the Society begun when Jesuits were engaged in theology on behalf of the pope. Diego Laínez and Alfonso Salmerón, two of the earliest companions, were papal theologians for most of the three sessions of the Council of Trent (1545–63), with Laínez attending the last session as superior general of the Society. Pierre Favre, Claude Jay, and Peter Canisius (third session) went to the Council as theologians also. Laínez, more than the others, proved to be an important voice during the background theological discussions that led up to what eventually became the Council's Decree on *Justification*; and for some of its other texts, he was also significant. Laínez had to provide nuanced arguments for the balancing of the grace (*sola gratia*) championed by the reformers with the Council's wish to insist also on a role for human freedom in the process of justification. Jesuits have contributed from that time to the present to the area of grace and freedom. In what would be called *theological anthropology* in our time, Jesuits exhibited a positive estimate of the gifts of created human nature – consistent with their early humanist heritage (Dulles, "Jesuits and Theology," 526).

Jesuit thinking on grace and freedom sometimes caused controversy. For example, in the late sixteenth and early seventeenth centuries a dispute arose – and continued for an extended time – between, mainly, Jesuits and Dominicans, in relation to the respective roles of divine grace and human freedom in the performance of good acts that could be meritorious for salvation. The central Jesuit in the controversy was Luis de Molina (1535–1600); the main Dominican was Domingo Bañez (1528–1604). Known as the *De auxiliis* Controversy – because focused, precisely, on the "helps" afforded by grace and freedom respectively in the doing of good acts – it was marked by protraction even beyond the main protagonists' death and by debate at times in the presence of popes, until finally, in 1607, a papal decree put an end to it, permitting each side to continue defending its doctrine, without censoring or condemning that of the other. A decree of the Apostolic See was promised in order to settle the matter; it has yet to arrive!

Spanish Jesuits like Francisco Suárez (1548–1617) and Juan Martínez de Ripalda (1594–1648) followed – albeit with modifications – in the Molina line that embodied a positive estimate of human freedom. This approach to human freedom, as well as Ripalda's argument that any naturally good, free human act elevated by the grace of God could contribute toward the salvation of non-believers, led to Jesuits being opposed by conservative Protestants, and by Jansenists in the seventeenth century, who viewed human nature as completely corrupt and grace as present only within the visible Church. The renowned Jansenist Blaise Pascal (1623–62) considered Jesuits to be erroneous anthropologically and lax morally, attributing to them the moral system, "probabilism," even though – while most Jesuit moralists espoused it – it actually owed its origin to the Dominican Bartolomé de Medina (1527–80). Probabilism held that, in interpreting moral laws, it was permissible to follow a probable opinion even if there existed another opinion with stronger arguments supporting a stricter interpretation of the law. So Jesuits were once again placing value on human freedom here – in the balancing of liberty and law – and, as with the positions taken by Molina and Ripalda, so too now, in moral theology, they incurred strong opposition. Nonetheless this emphasis has continued into (and beyond) twentieth-century Jesuit theological reflection on freedom and grace and is evident, in different ways, in the work of Henri de Lubac, Karl Rahner, Bernard Lonergan, Edward Yarnold (UK), Roger Haight (USA), and Jean-Marc Laporte (Canada). Karl Rahner's theory of *anonymous Christianity* was influenced – as he himself admitted – by the work of Ripalda over three centuries before him.

Moving from grace and freedom to ecclesiology (and to controversial theology), the figure of Robert Bellarmine, SJ (1542–1615), looms large. He occupied a number of important theological positions in the Church. He held key positions in the Society of Jesus also, such as the Chair of "Controversies" in the Roman College, where he wrote his multi-volume work *Disputationes de controversiis Christianae Fidei adversus hujus temporis haereticos*. This was such an able summary of the theological controversies of the sixteenth century that it gave rise to vigorous attempts to refute it, above all in Germany and England. The known Ultramontanism of Bellarmine and his support for papal infallibility long before it became a dogma of the Church, as well as the *institutional* model of the Church which he articulated, demonstrated how he was, with other Jesuits of the Counter-Reformation era, very loyal to the papacy and to what St. Ignatius called the "hierarchical church," while also limiting papal power in temporal matters, much to the annoyance of Pope Sixtus V (1585–90). Ecclesiology has been a theological interest of Jesuits from the time of Bellarmine until now, with names such as Henri de Lubac, Karl Rahner, Medard Kehl, Avery Dulles, Francis Sullivan, and Michael Fahey being particularly prominent; some are still writing today.

Bellarmine and Peter Canisius, as early members of a Society founded "especially for the defense and propagation of the faith," became involved in what today we call fundamental theology. They wrote influential catechisms; in all, Peter Canisius wrote three. It was not only in the sixteenth and early seventeenth centuries that Jesuits engaged in theology in a way that defended and promoted the faith. This has been a continuous pursuit, referred to as "apologetics" in earlier times. Jesuits devised effective responses to several Enlightenment *philosophes* during the eighteenth century, at times with such success that these responses, together with other factors (political and religious, for example), contributed to the hatred that led to the Suppression of the Society of Jesus in 1773.

In the nineteenth century, following the restoration of the Society in 1814, many Jesuits became involved in apologetic theology, a number within the scholastic revival of that time. There were Jesuits also, in the late nineteenthth/early twentieth century, who, in rejecting the rationalistic, non-experiential neo-scholastic line, argued so strongly in a contrary (experiential) direction as to run foul of the ecclesiastical authorities and – in the case of Irishman George Tyrrell (1861–1909) – to end up outside the Society, accused of being a "Modernist" during the papacy of Pius X (1903–14). Others fared better, circumventing neo-scholastic rationalism to open other paths that prepared the way for a more creative contribution to a revitalised Thomism that eventually became the "transcendental Thomism" that flourished in the mid-twentieth century. With its origins in the thought of such Jesuits as the Frenchman Pierre Rousselot (1878–1915) and the Belgian Joseph Maréchal 1878–1944), it came to fruition in the work of the twentieth-century Jesuit theological "giants," Karl Rahner (1904–84) and Bernard Lonergan (1904–88). After them, work in fundamental theology remained a Jesuit preoccupation, as the writings of René Latourelle, Gerald O'Collins, Ignacio Ellacuría and Jon Sobrino, Karl-Heinz Neufeld, Franz Jozef van Beeck, and Avery Dulles demonstrate. The *Dictionary of Fundamental Theology* edited by René Latourelle, SJ, of the Pontifical Gregorian University in Rome and by Rino Fisichella, now head of the Pontifical Council for the New Evangelization, is an abiding contribution to fundamental theology containing entries from several Jesuits.

The Influence of the Society's Overseas Missions

The early Jesuit overseas missions to India, Japan, China, and Latin America proved a challenging context for Jesuit theologians, raising questions about what today would be called inculturation of the Gospel and also about the possibility of access to salvation for those who had never heard of Christ. Regarding the latter, reference has been made already to the work of the Spanish Jesuit, Juan Martinez de Ripalda, SJ. On adapting Christianity to new cultures, Avery Dulles, SJ has written that Jesuit missionaries in Asia and in the Americas quickly saw the need for adaptation of Christianity to the local cultures and developed styles of theology that enabled it to be transmitted in ways accommodated, particularly, to the cultures of India and China. Rome later issued condemnations of some of these methods, to the disagreement of many, Dulles said, adding that adaptation is being practiced afresh today in our multicultural world, and "inculturation" is what it is called (Dulles "Jesuits and Theology," 528). The condemnations to which Dulles refers are those of the Chinese Rites in 1742 and of the Malabar Rites in 1744 by Pope Benedict XIV, these "rites" being associated respectively with the practices of Matteo Ricci (1552–1610) in China and Roberto de Nobili (1577–1656) in India in the seventeenth century. Despite these setbacks, Jesuits have habitually espoused a generous attitude toward the cultural practices of indigenous peoples, and openness to cultures and optimism about human nature and about the presence of God in ways known only to God continue to mark Jesuit theology today. This is evident in the positive approach to cultures (and religions) of which the 34th General

Congregation (1995) speaks (in Decree 2: #17, also #20; and in Decrees 4 and 5). The same is evident in the 35th General Congregation (2008) in its third decree (##3 and 4). Since 1995, dialogue with cultures and interreligious dialogue have been seen as "integral dimensions" of the mission of the contemporary Society of Jesus. Intercultural and interreligious dialogue have explicitly marked the life of the Society for fifty years: from Father General Pedro Arrupe (1965–83), writing to the whole Society about inculturation after the 32nd General Congregation (1974–75), to the intercultural and interreligious work of such Jesuits as Peter Schineller (USA), Jacques Dupuis (Belgium and India), Michael Amaladoss (India), Michael Barnes (UK), Aloysius Pieris (Sri Lanka), Christian Troll (Germany), Felix Wilfrid (India), and Daniel Madigan and Francis Clooney (Georgetown and Harvard universities, USA, respectively).

Various Historical Factors (18th to 19th Centuries)

Gallicanism and Ultramontanism. Added to the opposition of Jansenists and conservative Protestants to Jesuits' positive views on human nature and on the salvation of nonbelievers was an opposition also between ultramontane Jesuit papalists and Gallicans, many but not all of whom were French and were inclined, in their movements, to fragment the Church along national lines. In response to this, "Jesuits promoted the universal authority of the Holy See and missionary outreach to all nations" (Dulles, "Jesuits and Theology," 529). In the late seventeenth century (1682), the Declaration of the Gallican Clergy, or Gallican Articles, was signed following pressure from Louis XIV of France. Rome, not surprisingly, reacted negatively to this, although never pronouncing it heretical, and Jesuit writers, in the ultramontane tradition of Robert Bellarmine (who was already being read extensively long before this) moved in on the papalist side. "The devotion of Jesuit theologians to the Holy See provoked bitter antagonism on the part of Gallicans in France, and like-minded groups in other countries, who wanted greater autonomy for national Churches. This antagonism, indeed, was a major factor leading to the suppression of the Society of Jesus in 1773" (Dulles, "Jesuits and Theology," 528).

Nineteenth-Century Ecclesiastical Centralization. The nineteenth century saw the restoration of the Society (in 1814) and Jesuits staying in close relationship to the papacy. Jesuits aided the papacy of Pius IX (1846–78) in its centralizing and of Leo XIII (1878–1903) in its enshrining of neo-Thomism as Catholicism's preferred intellectual synthesis and system of training for Catholic seminarians. Giovanni Perrone (1794–1876), who entered the Society of Jesus just after its restoration, already had a doctorate in theology and worked all his life, except for one four-year period as a superior outside of Rome, in the Roman College, once it had been returned to the Society by Leo XII in 1824. He was instrumental in the drafting of the 1854 statement on the immaculate conception of Mary and the statement on papal infallibility at Vatican Council I (1869–70). Perrone had distinguished Jesuit pupils, such as the Germans Johann Baptist Franzelin (1816–86) and Clemens Schrader (1820–75), who "were the principal authors, respectively, of the proposed constitutions on Catholic faith and on the Church" (Dulles, "Jesuits and Theology," 530) in the First Vatican Council.

Neo-scholasticism/Neo-Thomism. While Perrone, Franzelin, and Schrader were decided contributors to the neo-scholastic "refrain" in papal and Roman College theology, their specifically *Thomist* character was not as pronounced as that of Jesuits Luigi Tapparelli (1793–1862), Matteo Liberatore (1810–92) and Josef Kleutgen (1811–83). Tapparelli, from his time of teaching as a young man in Naples – and having had as one of his students, Giuseppe Pecci, SJ, the brother of the future Pope Leo XIII – was an enthusiast for Thomism and caught big fish for it such as Pecci, and Liberatore. The latter wrote countless articles commending Thomism in the 1850-founded "quasi-papal" Jesuit periodical, *La Civiltà Cattolica* (Tapparelli was one of the founders, along with Carlo Maria Curci SJ). Josef Kleutgen, also a convinced Thomist, argued in his multivolume works *Philosophie der Vorzeit* and *Theologie der Vorzeit* that Thomism was the only synthesis of philosophy and theology that could stand up in the face of challenges from various modern philosophies. These Jesuits contributed a huge amount to the Thomist renewal promoted in particular in the late nineteenth century by Pope Leo XIII, and Kleutgen is said to have drafted the encyclical *Aeterni Patris* (1879), in which Leo called for a revival of St. Thomas's thought. Jesuits also supported Leo XIII in his social writings. This pope's encyclical on capital and labor, *Rerum novarum* (1891), inaugurated the tradition of what today is referred to as Catholic Social Teaching and Matteo Liberatore contributed very significantly to it. In Germany in the twentieth century, Jesuits continued to advise popes writing in this tradition, Pius XI (1922–39) and Pius XII (1939–58) in particular. The well-known names are Heinrich Pesch (1854–1926), Oswald von Nell-Breuning (1890–1991), and Gustav Gundlach (1892–1963).

A Glance at the Multifaceted 20th and 21st Centuries

Leo XIII's successor was Pius X, who entrusted the Pontifical Biblical Institute to the Society in 1909, mainly to counter developing historical trends in the study of the Scriptures, although within a short period the Institute became a skilled user of these. Key Jesuits in the Institute's activities before (and after) the Second Vatican Council were Stanislas Lyonnet and Maximilian Zerwick (both of whom were suspended from teaching for a short period in the early 1960s) and Ignace de la Potterie. Historical studies became very important in Scripture and theology in the early part of the twentieth century and, by midcentury, several Jesuits were involved in the theological research that provided the necessary background reflection for the Second Vatican Council (1962–65) and that made that Council so fruitful. The main French Jesuits were Henri de Lubac (1896–1991), Jean Daniélou (1905–74) and Teilhard de Chardin (1881–1955). A host of German Jesuits made their mark already prior to – and in preparation of – the Council also. Famous above all the others was Karl Rahner (1904–84). Augustin Bea (1881–1968) and Aloys Grillmeier (1910–98) were major influences in ecumenism and Christology respectively. In the twentieth century, in sacramental and liturgical theology, Josef Jungmann (1889–1975) and Otto Semmelroth (1912–79) were the key thinkers. At the Gregorian University in Rome, where a host of international Jesuits taught theology in the mid-to-late twentieth century, the Dutchman Sebastian Tromp (1889–1975) and the German moral theologian Joseph Fuchs (1912–2005) stand out as influential, on the conservative and progressive sides respectively. Also at the Gregorian were the Spaniard Juan Alfaro (1914–93), as well as the "duo," Italian Maurizio Flick and Hungarian Zoltan Alszeghy, who published many influential articles in dogmatic, fundamental, and moral theology together. The most famous North American was the Canadian, Bernard Lonergan (1904–84), known, above all, for his writing on method in theology.

US Jesuits Avery Dulles, Michael Fahey, and Thomas P. Rausch have been prominent in ecumenism in the latter half of the twentieth century. Other fields of importance are ecclesiology (Dulles again, also Francis Sullivan), the theology of Karl Rahner (Leo O'Donovan, Harvey Egan, William Dych), the theology of Bernard Lonergan (Fred Lawrence and those who meet annually at Boston College, especially Robert Doran of Marquette University), Christology (Brian McDermott and Roger Haight), historical theology (Brian Daley), and liturgical theology (Robert Taft, John Baldovin, Bruce Morrill). Prominent in theological ethics have been Jesuits Richard McCormick, who taught at the University of Notre Dame and wrote the Moral Theology Notes for many years in *Theological Studies*, and James Keenan and David Hollenbach of Boston College, together with their many well-known colleagues such as Lisa Sowle Cahill. Theological scholarship in Jesuit institutions throughout the United States is enriched by the presence of non-Jesuit colleagues. US Jesuits in the twentieth to twenty-first centuries have also included prominent biblical scholars: George MacRae, the first Jesuit to teach at Harvard; Daniel Harrington, editor for over forty years of *New Testament Abstracts* and also of the *Sacra Pagina* commentaries; and Joseph Fitzmyer, author of many books on New Testament and other topics and collaborator on key biblical commentaries of the twentieth century.

Latin American liberation theology, which flourished in the 1970s and 1980s and clashed significantly with both civil and ecclesiastical authorities, was supported and engaged in not only by particular Jesuits like Juan Luis Segundo (1925–96), Ignacio Ellacuría (1930–89, when he was assassinated), and Jon Sobrino (b. 1938), but also, to a large extent, by the Society of Jesus itself, at its 32nd General Congregation (1974–75) when it made the promotion of justice integral to its service of faith. In Asia and Africa, increasingly, Jesuit theologians have been active. For example, at Hekima College, Kenya, Agbonkhianmeghe Orobator enjoys widespread recognition for his writings in theological ethics; and in Asia, at the East Asian Pastoral Institute in Manila, creative theological work has been going on for decades and continues to flourish. It is to these two continents, rich in Jesuit vocations, that we shall have to look in the future as theology remains, undoubtedly, a key element in the Jesuit story.

See also Ecclesiology; Ecumenism; Ethics; Fundamental Theology; Grace; Interreligious Dialogue; Liberation Theology; Liturgy; Ultramontanism

Costigan, Richard F., *The Consensus of the Church and Papal Infallibility*: A Study in the Background of Vatican I. Washington, DC: The Catholic University of America Press, 2005.
Daniélou, Jean, "The Ignatian Vision of the Universe and of Man." *Cross Currents* 4, 4 (Fall 1954), 357–66.
Dulles, Avery, "Jesuits and Theology: Yesterday and Today." *Theological Studies* 52 (1991), 524–38.
"Saint Ignatius and the Jesuit Theological Tradition." *Studies in the Spirituality of Jesuits* IV, 2 (March 1982), 1–21.
Rahner, Hugo, *Ignatius the Theologian*. London: Chapman; New York: Herder and Herder, 1968.

James Corkery, SJ

Timor Leste

The presence of the Society of Jesus in Timor Leste – formerly East Timor, comprising the eastern half of the Timor Island – began in 1897. In that year two Jesuits,

Fr. Sebastião Maria Aparício da Silva and Fr. Manuel Fernandes Ferreira, arrived in the territory to join the Soibada Mission, when the territory was still a Portuguese colony. In the mission they built a church and a rectory. They also ran a school for boys, called Colégio Nuno Alvares. In 1910, however, they were expelled from the territory following the issuance in Lisbon of the mandate for the Expulsion of all Religious Orders in all the Portuguese Colonies.

Upon their return to the territory several decades later, the Jesuits restarted their service to the people of Timor Leste by running a pre-seminary and a minor seminary. Their presence and service remained strong when the territory was occupied by Indonesia beginning in 1975. During this period the Timor Leste mission of the Society of Jesus was entrusted to the Indonesian province of the Jesuits. Along with the remaining Portuguese Jesuits, Indonesian Jesuits provided various ministries including services at Timor Timur University, Colégio de São José, and an agricultural center.

In the wake of Timor Leste's vote for independence in 1999, two Indonesian Jesuits, namely Fr. Tarcisius Dewanto, SJ, and Fr. Albrecht Karim Arbie, SJ, were killed while helping the people. Following independence, Jesuits from several countries joined forces to serve the new nation's people. They provided various ministries, including parish works, education, and youth ministries. The Jesuits also established a high school called the Colégio de Santo Inácio de Loiola, dedicated on January 25, 2014, by Jesuit Superior General, Father Adolfo Nicolás, SJ. To prepare senior secondary school teachers of Timor Leste, the Jesuits established another educational institution called Instituto São João de Brito.

See also Indonesia; Portugal

Goh, Karen, "A Window to a Brighter Future." In Guiseppe Bellucci, ed., *Yearbook of the Society of Jesus, 2014*. Rome: The General Curia of the Society of Jesus, 2013, pp. 125–27.

Baskara T. Wardaya, SJ

Transcribe

This is the formal process by which a Jesuit officially changes membership from one province to another. According to the Complementary Norms of the *Constitutions* of the Society of Jesus, "Each person belongs to that province to which he was admitted; it is the prerogative of the general alone to transcribe someone definitely into another province" (389, #1). As the Norms suggest, it does not happen often that a Jesuit transcribes into another province. A typical situation in which this might occur would be if someone spent or was likely to spend almost all of his Jesuit life and ministry living and working outside of his home province, such as teaching and getting tenure at a university in another province. In such a case, he could ask to be transcribed to that province. At that point, the provincials of both his home province and his prospective province would have to agree. If they are in agreement, the provincial requesting the transcription must send a letter to Rome with an explanation of the reasons for the change, along with the other provincial's letter of approval. Then, as the Norms indicate, father general is the one who gives final approbation. If he does so, he then informs both provincials of the transcription.

See also Province; Applied

The Constitutions of the Society of Jesus and Their Complementary Norms. Ed. John W. Padberg. St. Louis, MO: The Institute of Jesuit Sources, 1996.

Robert E. Scully, SJ

Trent, Council of

Responding to the successes of the Protestant Reformation, the bishops and delegates of the nineteenth ecumenical council met in three sessions over eighteen years, from 1545 to 1563, and thereby established a blueprint for early modern Catholicism. From the outset, there were contrasting positions regarding the scope and focus of the Council, most notably regarding whether it should address dogma and doctrine, as advocated by the popes, or discipline and the reform of morals, as advocated by Emperor Charles V. In a characteristic compromise, the delegates opted to discuss theological and reform issues concurrently. This slowed the pace and assured a more limited scope, but the canons and decrees of Trent established norms lasting into the nineteenth century and beyond.

The first phase (December 13, 1545, to March 11, 1547; sessions 1–8) established the dual parameters of doctrine and discipline, while addressing Scripture, original sin, and justification – issues that touched the heart of Protestant criticisms of Catholic dogma. Session 7 addressed the sacraments in general, while the eighth session transferred the Council to Bologna due to an epidemic, effectively ending the first phase.

The second phase (May 1, 1551, to April 28, 1552; sessions 11–16, as sessions 9–10 related to postponements from Bologna) was reconvened in Trent by Pope Julius III. Many German bishops attended, and even some Protestant delegates arrived, but they did not formally participate in the Council due to disagreements about preconditions for their involvement. Session thirteen dealt with the Eucharist, affirming transubstantiation and repudiating the Lutheran, Calvinist, and Zwinglian interpretations, while session fourteen addressed the sacraments of Penance and Extreme Unction. Renewed hostilities and Protestant military victories in nearby Tyrol prompted the early conclusion of this phase.

Pope Pius IV convoked the third and final phase (January 18, 1562, to December 4, 1563; sessions 17–25). With some 200 bishops and other delegates, this was the most geographically diverse and best-attended phase. Sessions 21 through 25 addressed Communion, the Mass, holy orders, diocesan reform, marriage, and a concluding session concerning purgatory, saints, relics, and other subjects. On January 26, 1564, soon after the close of the Council, Pius IV issued a bull approving and commencing implementation of the Council's canons and decrees.

Four Jesuits were present at Trent. Diego Laínez was the most noteworthy theologian among the original companions of Ignatius, and he and Alfonso Salmerón were among the very few theologians who attended all three sessions of Trent over eighteen years, and as papal theologians, they were given some precedence. Claude Jay attended the first session as the procurator of the Prince-Bishop Otto Truchsess von Waldburg, and Peter Canisius arrived late in the first session, also at the behest of Waldburg. Laínez and

Salmerón contributed briefs on sacramental teaching, confession, the Eucharist, holy orders, and marriage. They also weighed in significantly during the first session on the central issue of justification by successfully opposing the theory of justification advanced by the influential Augustinian Cardinal Girolamo Seripando. In his capacity as general and successor to Ignatius during the third session, Laínez distinguished himself on the controversial matter of the residency of bishops and helped the papal legate, Cardinal Giovanni Morone, to achieve the eventual compromise.

Besides such direct personal engagement, the Jesuits broadly influenced the interpretation and application of the Council's decrees. One of the most consequential decrees (Session 23, Chapter 18) mandated that every diocese provide seminaries to support poor boys for the priesthood. This had enormous impact on the training and education of the clergy worldwide, and a familiar model came from the German College in Rome, founded in 1552 by the Jesuits to educate German boys for the priesthood to compete successfully against Lutheran ministers. Similarly, the willingness of the Jesuits to dispute central matters of the faith, like justification, led to their entanglement in many polemical controversies not only with Calvinists and Lutherans but also with other Catholics. The *De auxiliis* Controversy between the Spanish Dominicans and the Jesuits over the issue of human agency and salvation erupted in the 1580s and was concluded only by a papal order to end debate by Paul V in 1607. Calvinist factions soon fought over similar issues in the Arminian controversy, as did the Jesuits and the Jansenists later in the seventeenth century.

The Jesuits also left a strong mark on the historiography of the Council through publications opposing the many Protestant condemnations of the Council. The two-volume *History of the Council of Trent*, published in 1656–57 by Jesuit Cardinal Pietro Sforza Pallavicino, served as the definitive Catholic response and interpretation through the nineteenth century.

See also Faber, Peter, SJ, St.; Julius III; Laínez, Diego, SJ; *Periti*; Salmerón, Alfonso, SJ

Bangert, William V., *Claude Jay and Alfonso Salmerón: Two Early Jesuits*. Chicago, IL: Loyola University Press, 1985.

Jedin, Hubert, *Geschichte des Konzils von Trient*. 4 vols. in 5. Freiburg im Breisgau: Herder Verlag, 1949–1975. First two volumes translated into English: *A History of the Council of Trent*. Trans. Ernest Graf, 2 vols. St. Louis: Thomas Nelson and Sons, 1957–61.

O'Malley, John W., *Trent: What Happened at the Council*. Cambridge, MA: Harvard University Press, 2013.

Lance Gabriel Lazar

Trigault, Nicolas, SJ (1577–1628)

Nicolas Trigault was born in Douai (now France) on March 3, 1577, and entered the Gallo-Belgian province in 1594. In 1607 he left Lisbon for Goa, India, and reached Macau by 1610. His first stay in China was relatively short, because he was soon appointed procurator to explain the needs of the mission in Rome, where he arrived at the end of 1614. Through the mediation of, among others, Robert Bellarmine (1542–1621), he received papal permission for a Chinese translation of the Bible and the approval for Chinese priests to celebrate Mass in Chinese. In order to get support for the China mission, Trigault traveled extensively in Europe (Peter-Paul Rubens made a drawing of him

Figure 64 Peter Paul Rubens: *Portrait of the Jesuit Nicolas Trigault in Chinese Costume*, 1617, black, red, and white chalk, blue pastel, and pen and brown ink on light brown laid paper. The Metropolitan Museum of Art. Photograph © Art Resource, NY

in Antwerp). He played a key role in the spread of knowledge about China in Europe, publishing among others *De Christiana expeditione apud Sinas* (1615), a Latin translation of a history of Christianity in China written in Italian by Matteo Ricci.

Accompanied by new missionaries and carrying a large Renaissance library, he returned to Macau in 1619. He established a mission in Shaanxi Province, where he was the first European to see the Nestorian monument of 781. In these years, Trigault produced a syllabary or phonetic dictionary entitled *Xiru ermu zi* (Aid to the Eyes and Ears of Western Literati, 1626). He died in Hangzhou on November 14, 1628.

See also Antwerp; China

Dehaisnes, Chrétien, *Vie du Père Nicolas Trigault*. Tournai: Casterman, 1864.

Lamalle, Edmond, "La propagande du P. N. Trigault en faveur des missions de Chine (1616)." *Archivum Historicum Societatis Iesu* 9 (1940), 49–120.

Logan. Anne-Marie, and Liam M. Brockey, "Nicolas Trigault, SJ: A Portrait by Peter Paul Rubens." *Metropolitan Museum Journal* 38 (2003), 157–67.

Standaert, Nicolas, *An Illustrated Life of Christ Presented to the Chinese Emperor: The History of Jincheng Shuxiang (1640)*. Nettetal: Steyler Verlag, 2007.

Nicolas Standaert, SJ

Tyrrell, George

Born into a Church of Ireland family in Dublin, as a teenager Tyrrell (1861–1909) found his way to the fashionable Jesuit church at Farm Street, London, where he was baptized in May 1879. Almost immediately he declared that he wanted to enter the Society, but the provincial decided that he should wait for a year. During that time he taught in Jesuit schools, first in Cyprus and then in Malta. He joined the novitiate at Roehampton, London, in September 1880 and was ordained in 1891. After tertianship, and a brief period of pastoral work, he was sent to teach philosophy at St. Mary's Hall, Stonyhurst, in 1894. Almost immediately he came into conflict with some of the other Jesuits on the staff, whom he accused of not adhering strictly to the teaching of Pope Leo XIII on the promotion of Thomist thought as outlined in the encyclical *Aeterni Patris* (1879). He made representations on the matter to both Fr. General Luis Martín and Cardinal Camillo Mazzella, SJ. Mazzella informed Tyrrell that his approach was in perfect conformity with the mind of the Pope. Armed with this assurance, Tyrrell became disruptive of the discipline of the philosophate, and although a gifted teacher who made a deep impression on the more talented scholastics, he was removed from his post.

He was now assigned to the house of writers at Farm Street and, after a hesitant beginning, his work for *The Month* made Tyrrell well known in Catholic England. The years 1896–1900 were a period of great creativity for him as a theological writer. However, he began to develop an approach to religion that was quite different from the position he championed at St. Mary's Hall. In particular he became concerned that conventional theological and spiritual doctrine, as taught and practiced at that stage of the nineteenth century, was not meeting the intellectual and spiritual needs of "modern" man. Not only did he embrace the higher criticism of the German school in matters of theology, biblical studies, and archaeology, he increasingly became disillusioned with Catholic theological views and with ecclesiastical censorship of his work.

Tyrrell also became friendly with a number of leading Modernists such as Henri Bremond, Maude Petre, and especially the Baron Frederick von Hügel, who for a time exercised great influence over him. Tyrrell was fascinated with the idea that Catholicism was a sort of elemental religion. He asserted that there was a substantial unity in the human mind that underlay all surface diversity and gave a substantial unity to all who believed in God. From this principle there flowed his conviction that Christianity had to be a religion of the many and not a philosophical system for an intellectual elite. For Tyrrell, faith was based on the experiential, and this experience had to take priority over theological formulation. Although increasingly convinced that the Catholic Church's leadership acted like a dead hand upon belief, he was nevertheless convinced that, dead or alive, Catholicism's claims to be the authentic tradition of Christianity were incontestable.

As time passed, Tyrrell's public presentations of Catholic doctrines were increasingly controversial. In December 1899 he published an article in the *Weekly Register* on the unlikely subject of hell, characterizing much of the Catholic attitude to the matter as "A perverted devotion." The piece was delated to Rome, and Fr. Martín now placed severe restrictions on Tyrrell. At his own request he was moved to Richmond, Yorkshire, and he began to publish anonymously and pseudonymously, and he also started to suffer from the early onset of Bright's disease. His disaffection with the Church and the Society was such that in February 1904 he wrote to the Jesuit general saying that the Society was doing everything it could to make intelligent faith impossible. He was dismissed from the Order following the publication of an excerpt from his *Letter to a University Professor* which appeared in *Corriere della Sera* in December 1905. But it was his letters to *The Times* of London on September 30 and October 1, 1907, denouncing Pius X's encyclical *Pascendi domini gregis* that brought about his excommunication from the Church.

Tyrrell continued to write and publish until his death in July 1909. Before his death at Storrington in West Sussex, he was attended by no fewer than four priests who, at different times, heard his confession and administered to him the last rites. However, Maude Petre published a letter in the press saying that Tyrrell stood by all he had ever written. In any event the local bishop, Peter Amigo of Southwark, had already decided that unless Tyrell publicly repudiated his writings he would not have a Catholic burial. He is buried in the Anglican cemetery in Storrington, symbolically halfway between the Catholic and Anglican parish churches. His gravestone states that he was a Catholic priest and that he died "Fortified by the Rites of the Church."

See also Dismissal; Ex-Jesuits; United Kingdom

Petre, M. D., *Autobiography and Life of George Tyrrell*. 2 vols. London: Edward Arnold, 1912.
Rafferty, Oliver P., ed., *George Tyrrell and Catholic Modernism*. Dublin: Four Courts Press, 2010.

Oliver P. Rafferty, SJ

Ultramontanism

Concerned, as it is, with the exercise of authority, Ultramontanism emphasizes the position and role of the papacy in the Church almost to the exclusion of any other consideration. St. Robert Bellarmine, SJ (1542–1621), is often regarded as the father of the movement. In Bellarmine's view Christ has given the perfect order of hierarchy to the Church. General councils may be needed from time to time for practical reasons but, strictly, are not absolutely necessary; the pope has jurisdiction over the entire Church. Given the Jesuit special vow of obedience to the pope, it seemed natural that when the neo-ultramontane movement got underway in the second decade of the nineteenth century, soon after the restoration of the Society, the Jesuits would play a prominent part in the revival of Ultramontanism.

The idea of separation of Church and State following the Enlightenment and the expansion of the Church in missionary countries paradoxically played into the hands of the ultramontanes. Since many states were no longer involved in the appointment of bishops, the papacy began to reserve that authority exclusively to itself. Joseph de Maistre's *Du Pape* (1819) became a foundational text for the movement. The infallible declaration of the Immaculate Conception of the Blessed Virgin Mary in 1854 was an expression of Ultramontanism also. The foundation, four years earlier, of the Jesuit-sponsored but Vatican-controlled *La Civiltà Cattolica* was also significant in that *Civiltà* became the most important mouthpiece for ultramontane ideas in the decades before Vatican I (1869–70). The loss of the Papal States in the Italian Risorgimento was also a factor; the assertion of supreme papal spiritual power seemed to flow organically from the forfeiture of the pope's temporal authority. In addition to the promulgation of the Immaculate Conception, ultramontanes had set themselves three other goals: the declaration of papal infallibility, achieved at Vatican I, at which two Jesuits, Johannes Franzelin and Josef Kleutgen, played a prominent role; the canonization of Bellarmine

(1930); and the extension of the Roman rite of the Mass to the universal Church, a feat paradoxically accomplished only as a result of the "liberal" reforms of Vatican II (1962–65).

See also Bellarmine, Robert, SJ, St.; *Civiltà Cattolica*; Papacy; Theology; Vatican I

Costigan, Richard F., *The Consensus of the Church and Papal Infallibility: A Study in the Background of Vatican I*. Washington, DC: Catholic University of America Press, 2005.

Oliver P. Rafferty, SJ

Union of Minds and Hearts

A fleshed-out English translation of the Latin *unio animorum*, "union of minds and hearts," has become a refrain for Jesuits on a par with "friends in the Lord." A major treatment of the topic was given in Decree 11 of General Congregation 32:

> Moreover, that very union of minds and hearts which participation in Christ's mission requires will at the same time be a powerful aid to that mission, since it will be a visible sign of the love of the Father for all men (*sic*). In the following orientations, therefore, we treat of our *union with God in Christ*, from which flows our *brotherly communion with one another*, a communion strengthened and made apostolically efficacious by the *bond of obedience*.

This triple division of the topic and its theological formulations are based on Ignatius's teaching in Part VIII of the *Constitutions*. Union of minds and hearts is not simply a human construct but a gift given *de arriba* (from above). "The chief bond to cement the union of the members among themselves and with their head is the love of God our Lord." When Jesuits are in close relationship with God, "they will very easily be united among themselves, through that same love which will descend from the Divine Goodness and spread to all other persons, and particularly to the body of the Society" (*Constitutions*, #671).

It is understood that the primary community to which a Jesuit belongs is the universal body of the Society. Union of minds and hearts, therefore, is not simply a mark of local community. Furthermore, the context of this teaching is always that Jesuits exist "for mission." Hence, their union (with God and with one another) is itself a *sine qua non* for mission and may even be said *to be mission*.

See also Community; Friends in the Lord

Osuna, Javier, *Amigos en el Señor: unidos para la dispersión*. Bilbao: Mensajero, 1997.
Osuna, Javier, *Friends in the Lord*. Part I of *Amigos en el Señor*. Trans. Nicholas King. London: Way Books, 1974.

Brian O'Leary, SJ

United Kingdom

In the late 1570s, the Order's father general, Everard Mercurian, proposed a Jesuit mission to the hostile environment of Elizabeth I's Protestant England. Edmund Campion, Robert Persons, and Ralph Emerson were the first to embark in 1580. Campion would be captured and then executed in December 1581. This marked the beginning of a long roster of English Jesuit martyrs during the reigns of Elizabeth I and James I, including

Ralph Ashley, Alexander Briant, John Cornelius, Thomas Garnet, Nicholas Owen, Francis Page, Robert Southwell, and Hugh Walpole.

The English government enacted a series of measures that made life unusually dangerous for Jesuit missionaries or those who lent them assistance. Priests were obliged to travel in disguise, and complex debates raged about how captured Jesuits ought to behave under interrogation: was it legitimate, for instance, to employ evasive methods when faced with incriminating questions? Figures such as Persons did little to soften the regime's attitude by supporting plans to invade England and depose the Queen. Another notable factor was rivalry between Jesuits and members of the secular clergy. The Society, through its stewardship of the English College in Rome (from 1579), quickly emerged as the dominant force in the English mission, but a fierce internecine war of words developed concerning the best way to sustain Catholicism in the British Isles. At the turn of the seventeenth century, the rhetoric of the Jesuits' Catholic rivals in England sometimes came close to matching the splenetic outbursts of the Society's Protestant enemies. There was unhelpful animosity on both sides.

Elsewhere there was progress: the founding of English seminaries at Valladolid (1589), Seville (1592), and an English College at St. Omer (1593). There was also a need to establish a suitable administrative structure, and in 1598 England became a prefecture. By 1619 it had acquired the status of a vice province and full provincial status was granted in 1623. The tides of persecution had not diminished (notably around the time of the Gunpowder Plot of 1605), but the seventeenth century witnessed notable expansion. English Jesuits played a major role in the founding of the Maryland colony, and by 1640, there were as many as 350 members of the English province.

The later Stuart era was less stable. Jesuits faced accusations of treachery during the English Civil War, at the time of the so-called Popish Plot (1678), and following the deposition of James II in 1688. Through the following century, the English province was at its weakest, with predictable charges of disloyalty being leveled during the Jacobite rebellions. Misfortune also resulted from the series of national attacks on the Society during the 1750s and 1760s. In 1762 the English college at St. Omer was obliged to move to Bruges (owing to events in France) and, following the global suppression in 1773, English Jesuits faced potentially difficult circumstances. In fact, there was a concerted attempt to sustain solidarity within Jesuit ranks. The residents of the Bruges college moved to Liège and, in 1794, arrived at Stonyhurst in Lancashire. Throughout the nineteenth century, Stonyhurst would serve as a safe harbor for many Jesuits who were forced to flee from the recurrent series of banishments endured by the Society.

At the beginning of that century, there was also a passion to create links with the thriving Jesuit community in the Russian Empire, and in 1803, thirty-five former Jesuits renewed their vows at Stonyhurst with Marmaduke Stone serving as the first provincial of a restored English province. Following the global restoration in 1814, there was a period of significant expansion. Jesuit colleges opened in, among other places, Liverpool (1842), Glasgow (1857), Preston (1865), Wimbledon (1893), and Stamford Hill (1894). Campion Hall was founded at Oxford in 1896. There were similar signs of revival across the British Empire. During the twentieth century, education would continue to be the primary mission of the English Jesuits, and in 1953, the province contained 905 members. During the nineteenth and twentieth centuries, the province produced notable contributors to a host of disciplines: the poet Gerard Manley Hopkins, historians such as Henry Foley and Philip Caraman, and spiritual writers including Bernard Basset. The English province was renamed the British province in 1985, and British Jesuits retain an important role in a host of social ministries and educational establishments, including eleven schools. The Farm Street parish in London's Mayfair remains the heart of the British province.

See also Campion, Edmund, SJ; Gunpowder Plot; Heythrop College; Martyrs, Ideal and History; Persons, Robert, SJ; Popish Plot; Stonyhurst College

McCoog, Thomas M., *"And Touching Our Society": Fashioning Jesuit Identity in Early Modern England*. Toronto: Pontifical Institute of Medieval Studies, 2013.

Pullan, Malcolm, *The Lives and Times of the Forty Martyrs of England and Wales, 1535–1660*. London: Athena Press, 2008.

Whitehead, Maurice, *English Jesuit Education: Expulsion, Suppression, Survival and Restoration, 1762–1803*. Farnham: Ashgate, 2013.

Jonathan Wright

United States of America

The foundation of the Society of Jesus during the early stages of European penetration of the Americas assured that Jesuits would seek to evangelize there, especially in the Spanish, French, and English colonies that would eventually become the contiguous United States. The initial goals were to convert native peoples and restrain their exploitation. The fortunes of these endeavors varied, but even in colonies where they did not prosper, Jesuits also answered many demands for ministry among European settlers and their indentured servants and slaves. These situations endured until the Suppression in 1773. A major consequence was that most of the early Jesuit presence in North America was in wilderness and rural settings. Even the Spanish possessions were among the least urbanized parts of that empire.

The first Jesuits who would call themselves United States citizens were those based in Maryland and neighboring Pennsylvania. The proximity of the Suppression to the American Revolution launched these missionaries on a twin adaption to a changed Church and a new nation. These priests were virtually the only ordained clergy within the original boundaries of the United States at the proclamation of independence.

These men were in a similar situation to that of the very first Jesuits during the "prologue" phase of the Society's development, the first of four "foundations" which John O'Malley has identified as essential to Jesuit history. The dissolution of their canonical religious status returned them to the informal community initially practiced by Ignatius and the early companions. Desiring more than the remaining tie of a common ordained priesthood, they also sought to continue to share spirituality, zeal for common life, and a common approach to ministry to souls. Their geographical isolation, as well as their paucity of communication with the wider Church due to the Revolutionary War, allowed them to preserve much of their practice of the First Foundation of the Society, the *Formula of the Institute* as decreed in 1540 and revised in 1550. Adding to this good fortune was the emergence of separation of Church and State in the New American republic, whose secular authorities now abandoned any desire to intervene in religious matters.

Suppressed Jesuits found in John Carroll a figure much like Ignatius, combining charismatic spiritual leadership and superior organizational skills. By the mid-1780s, Carroll had led them in organizing a clerical association that enjoyed recognition as a corporation in Maryland law, a development that would help them remain distinct even after an American episcopacy was established under Carroll. In 1789 they recollected the Second Foundation of the Society by imitating the first companions in making a major commitment to educational work through the founding of Georgetown Academy. It soon became clear that Georgetown would be part of the new national capital. This was an exciting prospect to Carroll and others who believed that the reunion of Christianity was more likely to take place in a free republic than anywhere else. The Maryland mission had long struggled to support itself through plantation income, but resolved now to try to support Georgetown through the same means.

The hope of reviving the Society worldwide remained. In 1805 the Marylanders were allowed to join the never-suppressed White Russian province, a prelude to the universal restoration of 1814. This event, identified as the Third Foundation of the Society, complicated American Jesuit life for the next 150 years. They had to function in a liberal country as members of an international Society revived as part of a European conservative reaction to the French Revolution. American members sought to reconcile this dichotomy by emphasizing the different character of their own revolution. Jesuits who emigrated from Europe to work in the United States were urged to embrace the republican ways of the young nation. However, the ultramontane character of the increasingly centralized nineteenth-century Church meant that much of the structure and outlook of the Society in the United States remained fundamentally European.

Meanwhile the republic spread west rapidly. The Louisiana Purchase of 1803, the Oregon Treaty of 1846, and the Mexican War of 1846–48 stretched the nation from the Atlantic to the Pacific Oceans. One consequence was a revival of Native American ministries in the west under the leadership of Jesuits like Peter De Smet. These ministries remain in operation today but have gradually shifted their model from a pursuit of assimilation of native peoples to a Euro-American way of life to an appreciation for native culture as worthy in its own right and itself compatible with evangelization. Native American ministry also encouraged the early westward spread of other apostolates, drawing Jesuits into the Mississippi Valley and the Upper Midwest.

As the nineteenth century unfolded, a number of Jesuits discerned the need for the Society's greater presence in urban America. Industrialization and immigration were swelling the cities, in which many Catholic newcomers settled. By the 1830s, the Jesuits increasingly took steps to follow them. The newly autonomous Maryland province pursued the sale of its slaves in part through a desire to end its focus on rural plantations. Eventually, the shift to cities also meant that the clientele of Jesuit schools would change from rural country gentlemen to the offspring of a Catholic laboring class. Jesuit apostolates soon spread from Maryland to places like Massachusetts, Pennsylvania, and New Jersey.

Conditions remained difficult for European Jesuits, and many came to the United States as refugees from anticlerical governments and political movements. French exiles, for example, established major apostolates in New York City, Alabama, and Louisiana. Their German counterparts spread the Society along the shores of Lake Erie. Italians established the Society's presence in California and other far western states. These new arrivals steadily increased the Society's size in the United States but also deepened the gulf between its American situation and its still largely European orientation. Episcopal advocates of a more Americanized Church kept a wary distance from Jesuits well into the twentieth century. Frustration over this situation prompted a few individual Jesuits to wonder if the Church might ever be reconciled with American ideals of religious liberty, but no formula for this would be found until the middle of the twentieth century.

The Civil War of 1861–65 created further complications. The Union was preserved, but the egalitarian North replaced the hierarchical South as the nation's dominant political, economic, and cultural region. The North's new hegemony was also a major triumph for a nativist-abolitionist coalition not noted for its affinity with Catholicism. Within five years of the conclusion of the war, Vatican I's declaration of papal infallibility deepened the chasm. To all appearances the Church had moved in a sharply more authoritarian direction than ever before just as the United States seemed to be becoming ever more democratic. The interval between Vatican I and Vatican II would see Jesuits tugged in these two opposing directions. Their long-standing answer was to declare, relatively consistently, that one could be a loyal American and a loyal Catholic at the same time, often simply ignoring any evidence to the contrary.

During these decades Jesuits lost little opportunity to demonstrate that their ministries contributed to the common good of the United States. They stressed that their parishes among immigrant communities helped to maintain a sense of order among the newcomers, providing them with essential social services too. It could be said that the basic welfare provided in a Jesuit parish matched or exceeded the work of urban political machines on the same issue. Jesuit schools emphasized their teaching of the virtues of loyal citizenship. Jesuits also sought to assist the United States in times of war, serving in high numbers as military chaplains and often with great heroism. The cultivation of patriotism also led Jesuits to emphasize their opposition to communism during the Cold War; they seized upon the common enmity of their country and Church to Marxism as a major opportunity to establish the compatibility of the American and Catholic systems. One example of this resolve was the emergence of a school of foreign service at Georgetown.

Some wondered, however, whether this loyalty was maintained at the price of an uncritical attitude toward both American culture and outmoded Church structures. As the twentieth century approached, the wider American educational community asked serious questions about the usefulness of the *Ratio studiorum*, the foundation of the curriculum of all Jesuit schools since the late sixteenth century. Its humanistic program failed to anticipate the modern hard and social sciences; could a modern educated American function professionally without exposure to these new fields? The Jesuit schools were slow to respond, but eventually the fact that alumni were failing to win admission to graduate studies due to this issue forced an adaptation. Gradually Jesuits pursued a compromise that kept the essence of the humanities while making room for the new disciplines. Breaking the taboo that the *Ratio* could not be reformed was an essential first step toward some radical changes in Jesuit education during the second half of the twentieth century. Colleges and universities began to take research seriously, and to require from prospective Jesuit faculty the same professional credentials as any other academics. The need to find suitable research projects prompted Jesuit academics to increase their queries about problems and injustices in American life. Meanwhile, the schools served the socioeconomic function of creating a wider Catholic middle class, especially after World War II, when the federal government's generous provision of educational assistance to veterans made higher education affordable to more young Catholics than ever before. Furthermore, the increasing admission of women to Jesuit schools in the United States, both secondary and higher, helped pave the way for the worldwide Society to address the issue of women in the Church and the modern world during the 34th General Congregation of 1995.

As the Third Foundation of the Society continued, its American branch was noted for surface uniformity. The myth of a "long black line" continued to win admiration from many Catholics and alarm from some outside observers. Beneath the surface, however, there were prophetic currents. Individual Jesuits raised serious questions about race relations and the rights of labor, advocates of the latter position drawing inspiration from the social teachings that developed in the universal Church beginning with the reign of Pope Leo XIII. A new journal of public cultural and social analysis, *America*, began in 1909. It provided comment on the American way of life from a Catholic perspective. Also, John Courtney Murray, arguably the most important American Jesuit since John Carroll, took up the issue of finding a formula that would finally overcome the Roman Curia's intense opposition to American thinking on religious liberty. His eventual formula was that the old teaching was not wrong, just archaic, and that the American position could be taken up without contradiction of the previous teaching. Murray's position was vindicated by Vatican II's Decree on Religious Liberty, *Dignitatis humanae*, in 1965. Coming at the very end of the Third Foundation of the Society, this document essentially ended the contradiction that American Jesuits had lived with since the restoration between a liberal republic and an authoritarian Church. It was a key psychological turning point because it liberated American Jesuits from worries that they would be perceived as unpatriotic when criticizing their own culture.

The year 1965 also began the Fourth Foundation of the Society itself with the election of a new general, Pedro Arrupe, during the 31st General Congregation. Arrupe assumed office just as Vatican II asked all religious orders to renew their founding charisms. The combination of the Decree on Religious Liberty, the Council's call for renewal, and the charismatic personality of Arrupe unleashed currents of upheaval within the American Society. A survivor of the American atomic bombing of Hiroshima, Japan, at the conclusion of World War II, Arrupe encouraged American Jesuits in fresh thinking about war and peace, as well as social justice. Arrupe's honesty about his experiences at Hiroshima also encouraged American Jesuits to question the benevolence of their government in unprecedented ways.

Within just a few years of the conclusion of Vatican II and the election of Arrupe, American Jesuits took leading roles in questioning their own nation's foreign policy, particularly its involvement in, and in some cases instigation of, wars in Vietnam, Central America, Iraq, and Afghanistan. In 1989 the assassination in El Salvador of six Jesuits and two of their employees by American-trained counter-revolutionary soldiers dramatized the extent to which Jesuits were now both opponents and in some cases victims of oppressive action by the American government. American Jesuits also embraced the global Society's option for the poor as articulated at General Congregation 32 in 1975, voicing increasing questions about the fairness of the American economy and the global capitalism it engendered. While Jesuit schools continued to produce alumni who both operated and profited from this American system, the same schools also sought increasingly to foster a spirit of global service among their students and alumni. A major consequence of General Congregation 32 was that Jesuit apostolates within the United States often twinned themselves with equivalent apostolates in the developing world and with communities of the poor in their own localities.

Another way of entering the spirit of renewal was to reform the manner in which American Jesuits both experienced and presented the *Spiritual Exercises* of St. Ignatius. During the Third Foundation, perhaps under the influence of the large numbers of Jesuit novices and tertians generally characteristic of that era, the predominant trend had become to offer the *Exercises* in a preached rather than a directed manner. Jesuits became accustomed to making the retreat a series of quasi-classroom lectures. Vatican II's challenge to retrieve original charisms, however, led to the rediscovery that Ignatius himself had imagined retreats as encounters within the context of one-to-one spiritual direction and personal prayer. The United States became a major base of a new directed retreat movement. This had at least two effects upon the American Society. Crucially, it revived the sense that what all Jesuits had in common was essentially the shared experience of the *Exercises* at least twice in each Jesuit's lifetime. Also, it encouraged the training of laypeople and other Jesuits in spiritual direction, creating a vital set of partners in Ignatian ministry.

A further feature of the Fourth Foundation of the Society has been a tension between established and prophetic models of ministry. The Third Foundation had seen the establishment of many Jesuit institutions in the United States, among them schools, parishes, and retreat houses. Increasingly, some Jesuits saw the demands of these institutes as barriers to choosing fresh opportunities for ministries. They also worried that these institutes were barriers to working among the poor and obstacles to challenging American culture. However, the emergence of new creative models of middle and secondary education, including the Nativity and Cristo Rey models of schools for the poor, offered chances for traditional ministries to operate with renewed focus. A major question for the future is whether such models will penetrate higher education. Meanwhile, the American Jesuits have sought strenuously to hold both old and new models of ministry together in a continued union of hearts and minds.

The Fourth Foundation saw the demographics of both the international and the American Society change dramatically. Jesuits from Europe and North America steadily declined, while Jesuits from Africa and Asia grew prodigiously. American Jesuits, used to explaining themselves to Europeans, now must adjust to explaining themselves to parts of the world that most Americans have traditionally understood less well than Europe. However, the United States has also opened itself more to immigration from the areas where the Society is growing. A consequence has been an increase in American Jesuit vocations from among men of these origins. Such new Jesuits are likely to be main actors in future dialogue between American Jesuits and the international Society.

American Jesuits have struggled to understand the cause of their own relative decline in numbers without consensus. It is at least clear that this decline has occurred in tandem with a major institutional decline of the entire American Church. It is also helpful to compare the increased departures from religious life with a growing social acceptance of divorce. In recent years, with no signs of the downward trend of the American Jesuits reversing, many Jesuits have emphasized the increasing importance of shared ministry with like-minded religious, especially the laity. This may be the best way of maintaining the Jesuit heritage in the United States. In 2013, however, renewed hope for the future came with the election of Pope Francis, not only the first Jesuit pontiff, but also the first from the western hemisphere.

Some say that jazz is the characteristic American music because it features minimum structure and maximum improvisation. If this combination indeed summarizes the American character, then the Jesuit way of proceeding is compatible with the American way of life. Jesuits in the United States have long been able to adapt their principles to fresh situations, adapting to republican government, urban and immigrant ministry, changes in the higher education apostolate, and the renewal of Vatican II among other challenges. Without ever losing continuity with Ignatius and his minimal structure for an adaptable religious order, they have been able, however slowly, to seize opportunities and adapt to an evolving world.

See also AJCU; *America* Magazine; Carroll, John; Civil Rights Movement; Dulles, Avery, SJ, Cardinal; Education, Secondary and Pre-Secondary; Maryland Mission; Murray, John Courtney, SJ; Universities, 1773–Present

Ellis, John Tracy, *Documents of American Catholic History*. 3 vols., 4th edn. Wilmington, DE: Michael Glazier, 1986.
Hennesey, James, *American Catholics: A History of the Roman Catholic Community in the United States*. New York: Oxford, 1981.
Mahoney, Kathleen M., *Catholic Higher Education in Protestant America: The Jesuits and Harvard in the Age of the University*. Baltimore, MD: Johns Hopkins University Press, 2003.
McDonough, Peter, *Men Astutely Trained: A History of the Jesuits in the American Century*. New York: Free Press, 1992.
O'Malley, John W., *The Jesuits: A History from Ignatius to the Present*. Lantham, MD: Rowman and Littlefield, 2014.
Schroth, Raymond J., *The American Jesuits: A History*. New York: New York University Press, 2007.

Thomas Murphy, SJ

Universidad Alberto Hurtado (UAH, Santiago de Chile)

The Universidad Alberto Hurtado (UAH) (Santiago de Chile) was founded on October 20, 1997. The context was one of major growth in the non-state education sector. In part this process was begun by the extreme neo-liberalism of the Pinochet dictatorship. Nevertheless, the growth in non-state education continued during the 1990s under the democratic *Concertación* government of Eduardo Frei. The Society of Jesus saw this as an opportunity to found a university with the aim of propagating its own Jesuit values of Catholic humanism. Indeed, in his inaugural speech, Rector Fernando Montes, SJ, talked about the foundation as a new mission, a way of contributing to the holistic and ethical formation of students who would go on to participate in the rebuilding of Chilean society in the spirit of Christian respect, pluralism (although not relativism), and justice. The namesake and patron of the university, St. Alberto Hurtado, embodied this holistic mission that sought the unity of studies with action, science with theology and the humanities, and Christian spirituality with social engagement.

The UAH differed from other higher education institutions in that its foundation as an undergraduate institution came about through the collaboration of two already existing and successful graduate institutions, the Instituto Latinoamericano de Doctrina y Estudios Sociales (the Latin American Institute of Doctrine and Social Studies – ILADES), and the Centro de Investigación y Desarrollo de la Educación (Center for Investigation and Educational Development – CIDE). These two graduate centers came together with the Jesuit Centro de Investigación Sociocultural (the Center for Sociocultural Investigation) and the Chilean Society of Jesus in order to build the undergraduate programs that altogether became the university. Ten years on, the university had 4,277 students across twenty-two different programs and at undergraduate and postgraduate levels.

See also Chile; Universities, 1773–Present

Fernando Montes, Fernando, *Discursos del Rector*. www.uahurtado.cl/universidad/discursos-del-rector/. Accessed November 24, 2014.
Swope, John, "New Charter." *Company* (Spring 1998), 12–14.

Andrew Redden

Universidad Centroamericana (UCA)

While UCA also refers to the Jesuit university in Nicaragua, the UCA "José Simeón Cañas" in El Salvador is better known because of the assassination of six Jesuit educators in 1989. That event led Jesuit universities worldwide to think long and hard about higher education's role in the promotion of faith and justice, and a Catholic university's responsibility in the matter of transforming social structures. They reflected on the mission of Jesuit schools, given the scandalous inequalities and oppressive economic arrangements that prevent human flourishing; and they began by examining what the UCA Jesuits were doing that brought about such prophetic witness to the service of faith and promotion of justice.

The UCA "José Simeón Cañas" was founded in 1965. Ten years later, the school's leadership, particularly in the person of Ignacio Ellacuría, undertook a review of the school's first decade. They did so in light of El Salvador's changing political reality and major Church statements, especially Paul VI's 1967 encyclical *Populorum progressio*, the final document of the 1968 meeting of the Latin American Bishops Conference in Medellín, Colombia, and, for Jesuits, Decree 4 of the Society's 32nd General Congregation in 1974–75. They understood that the University could help in shaping El Salvador's future. "Developmentalism," so promoted by wealthy countries in the 1960s for the betterment of Central and South America, had proved to create increasing dependency. The University, the Jesuits argued, had a critical role to play in uncovering structures of oppression through rigorous research and analysis, and by bringing students into close contact with the social conditions that needed to be addressed. Today the UCA remains firmly committed to fostering social change through research, teaching, and envisioning an ever more just society.

See also Ellacuría, Ignacio, SJ, and Companions; Liberation Theology; Nicaragua

Sobrino, Jon, "The University's Christian Inspiration." In *Companions of Jesus: The Jesuit Martyrs of El Salvador*. Maryknoll, NY: Orbis Books, 1990, pp. 152–73.
Whitfield, Teresa, *Paying the Price: Ignacio Ellacuría and the Murdered Jesuits of El Salvador*. Philadelphia, PA: Temple University Press, 1994.

William Reiser, SJ

Universidad Iberoamericana

Universidad Iberoamericana started as a school of philosophy in Mexico City in 1943 and was affiliated at the time with the national university, the Universidad Nacional Autónoma de México. Ten years later, it became a full-scale university and was renamed the Universidad Iberoamericana. The university has existed in several physical sites throughout its seventy-plus-year history. In 1982 it began construction on its latest campus in Sante Fe, outside of Mexico City, and it now has campuses throughout the country, mainly in Torreon, Tijuana, and Puebla. Its umbrella also includes a joint venture in higher education for indigenous peoples with the Instituto Superior Intercultural Ayuuk in the state of Oaxaca. The Sante Fe campus alone sustains an enrollment close to 12,000 students. Like its sister school also run by the Jesuits of the Mexican province, the Instituto Technológico y de Estudios Superiores de Occidente (ITESO), located in Guadalajara, Jalisco, whose enrollment is similar, its mission is to contribute to the attainment of a more just, free, inclusive, productive, and peaceful society by means of the development and diffusion of professional knowledge and research. According to its 2012–20 strategic plan, the Universidad Iberoamericana is committed to high-quality research that is not only competent at an international level but also oriented toward the greater service of all and inspired by authentic human, social, and transcendental values. It sponsors thirty-four undergraduate and thirty-five graduate programs, and its curriculum engages two major vehicles for learning: critical academic reflection, that is the cultivation of skills whereby students occupy themselves with exploring the meaning and value of human life, and social service, an opportunity for engaged, holistic learning in various social contexts that not only helps to improve the lives of those being served but also engenders future ongoing solidarity and commitment.

See also Mexico, Nineteenth Century to Present; Universities, 1773–Present

Universidad Iberoamericana. www.uia.mx/.

Eduardo C. Fernández, SJ

Universities, 1540–1773

From the founding of the Society of Jesus until its suppression, the Jesuits created the largest, most comprehensive system of colleges and universities the world has ever known. Earning the accolade of "the schoolmasters of Europe," Jesuits educated young men from all social classes throughout Europe and across the globe for over 250 years. At first, the Jesuits had not identified formal schooling as one of their ministries, focusing instead on preaching, catechism, spirituality, mission work, and other works of charity. Rather, they became the first *teaching* order in the Catholic Church almost by accident.

One reason for this transition is that the first Jesuits were themselves highly educated. Critically, Ignatius of Loyola and his six companions had come together while in graduate studies at the renowned University of Paris, and the early Jesuits drew much from its structures and pedagogy, the *modus Parisiensis*. Here and elsewhere humanism had engendered changed forms of learning, such as the *collège*, which became a hallmark of Jesuit education, both countering and complementing the scholasticism of medieval universities. The older university system, built on a rigorous examination of Aristotelian philosophy and logic, had functioned as preparation for the learned professions: law, medicine, and theology. Students entered in their early teens and finished the full course of study well into their twenties or later.

By contrast, humanistic education, which the Jesuits would adapt and disseminate globally, offered a shorter (five–seven year) program of study based on the *studia humanitatis*. Intended to teach wisdom, eloquence, and moral formation, these studies began with classical languages, grammar, and humanities, culminating in rhetoric. There was a coherent and sequenced developmental approach to the curriculum, which contrasted with the *modus Italicus*, a model in which students took courses at any level and in any order. Combining portions of current secondary school and the first years of higher education, the *collège* accepted students from 10 years of age on. Complete in itself and a full preparation for most occupations, the *collège* also acted as a foundation for advanced university study.

Born well into the Renaissance, as newly rediscovered Greek and Latin classics were repurposed in the service of Christian humanism, the Jesuits understood that discursive power was paramount in an age of social turmoil and religious reform movements. Thus, the Society first entered the ministry of teaching to improve the formation of its own members and to meet the broader exigence for a more informed and effective clergy. From the beginning, Jesuits were asked to teach theology in Rome. By 1542, some were sent to the Royal College in Coimbra, Portugal, while others were sent to teach humane letters in Goa, India. The first formal Jesuit *collège* started in Messina (1548) when the town elders offered to endow a Jesuit school if their own sons could be educated along with those desiring to take orders. Other cities soon clamored for the Jesuits to open schools, sometimes resulting in four or five new schools a year. Ignatius and his company quickly realized that this ministry of schooling could be an enduring means of "helping souls." In 1551 the esteemed Collegio Romano (now the Pontifical Gregorian University) was founded. It would become a great university and a model for Jesuit pedagogy.

Notably, the early schools were free, except for boarding students. Most Jesuits taught in the colleges during their formation, supplying countless hours of instruction across levels and subjects. As a result, Jesuit colleges and universities were generally able to offer a rigorous and effective education at little or no cost.

In order to create consistency and coherence across this global enterprise, Jesuits worldwide constructed a complete plan of studies – sometimes called the *magna carta* of Jesuit education – the *Ratio studiorum* (1599). A detailed educational plan, it combined elements from both the humanistic and university systems. While most Jesuit schools did not develop the full university curriculum, and few students finished the final course of studies beyond rhetoric, the Society did develop several excellent universities, primarily for philosophical and theological study, which built upon the humanistic foundation of the *collège* and integrated it into a distinctive synthesis.

Jesuit colleges and universities also became important centers for sponsoring spirituality, scholarship, and arts. They promoted piety and devotion in the larger communities through their confraternities, Masses, retreats, pageants, and processions. They created intellectual resources: well-endowed libraries, museums, observatories, and laboratories. Many Jesuits contributed to scholarship, producing thousands of treatises, textual analyses, and commentaries, and textbooks in all fields, including emerging areas of scientific inquiry and applied mathematics. Interestingly, their mission work, which took them into places unknown to Europe, enabled them to undertake geographic, ethnographic, linguistic, and scientific studies of a high order. The schools also acted as regional centers for arts and culture, as the Jesuits saw in the arts a means of teaching through all the senses to join intellect and affect. They sponsored theater, music, and dance in sacred and civic events for the whole municipality.

Of course, like all educational systems, the Jesuit educational system was imperfect. It grew too quickly, and episodically suffered from lack of resources and underprepared teachers. The downside of free tuition was that the Jesuits had to rely on municipalities, bishops, or other powerful donors for support, rendering their schools vulnerable to the changing allegiances of elites. Reliance on elites also meant some accommodation to their interests in educating their children, which marked the Jesuits as bearing allegiance to the *ancien régime*. Even so, by the universal Suppression (1773), the Jesuit educational network comprised well over 800 institutions of higher learning around the globe.

See also Coimbra; Humanism, Renaissance; Paris; Roman College; *Ratio Studiorum*; Universities, 1773–Present

Ganss, George, *Saint Ignatius' Ideal of the Jesuit University*. Milwaukee, WI: Marquette University Press, 1954.

Giard, Luce, "The Jesuit College: A Center for Knowledge, Art, and Faith 1548–1773." *Studies in the Spirituality of Jesuits* 40 (2008), 1–31.

Grendler, Paul, *Schooling in Renaissance Italy: Literacy and Learning, 1300–1600*. Baltimore, MD: Johns Hopkins University Press, 1989.

Duminuco, Vincent, ed., *The Jesuit Ratio Studiorum: 400th Anniversary Perspectives*. New York: Fordham University Press, 2000.

O'Malley, John, "Jesuit Schools and the Humanities Yesterday and Today." *Studies in the Spirituality of Jesuits* 47 (2015), 1–34.

Scaglione, Aldo, *The Liberal Arts and the Jesuit College System*. Amsterdam: John Benjamins, 1986.

Cinthia Gannett

Universities, 1773–Present

With the universal Suppression of the Society of Jesus in 1773 by Pope Clement XIV, the Jesuit educational mission was largely dismantled. Almost overnight most of the 845 colleges, universities, and seminaries were closed, the Jesuit faculty forced into exile, their facilities confiscated, destroyed, or sold. Over 200,000 students around the world were displaced. In France alone, twenty-two universities closed, and 40,000 students were forced to find other education or forgo higher education completely. Only a few colleges survived in what is now Russia and Poland, thanks to the refusal of Frederick the Great and Catherine the Great to implement the order of suppression.

The Suppression was lifted by Pope Pius VII on August 7, 1814, primarily to restore the Jesuits' educational work. Only a handful of colleges had survived: including one in White Russia, four in the Kingdom of the Sicilies, one in the United States (Georgetown), and a few in France. With only 600 Jesuits, the Society set about restoring its schools with few teachers, fewer facilities, and little financial support. Even more important, perhaps, the Jesuits had to rebuild their educational network in new, post-revolutionary political circumstances, which included frequent expulsions and state-enforced secularization of education in many countries. But by 1896, there were 209

Jesuit colleges and universities worldwide, serving over 50,000 students. Given the trauma of the Suppression, the restored Society, working slowly to rebuild its global educational project, tended to be conservative, sometimes even insular, in its approach.

The Jesuit educational system would never be fully refashioned in Europe, given the secularization of European education across the nineteenth century. But Jesuit higher education would remake itself, accommodating its curricula and methods to new contexts, creating new kinds of institutional structures, and identifying new sites for development in India, Latin America, and the United States.

Efforts started immediately to update the curriculum established by the *Ratio studiorum* of 1599, and a new, provisional *Ratio* had developed by 1832. While respecting the spirit of the older *Ratio* and retaining much of its classical content and focus on moral formation, the *Ratio* of 1832 provided for greater training in vernacular languages, mathematics, history, and the physical sciences. The new *Ratio* was never formally adopted, however. Discussion continued until 1906, when it was decided that each province could create its own educational plan while retaining key pedagogical principles from the earlier versions of the *Ratio*. The *Ratio* of 1832 may not have fully engaged the new intellectual milieu, but more importantly, it was simply impossible to create a set curriculum that would fit the changed, and changing, circumstances across the globe.

One major growth area was the United States, where Jesuits expelled from European provinces established colleges and universities to support the waves of Catholic immigrants marginalized from access to higher education. Starting with Georgetown (1789), its first American university, the Jesuits developed twenty-eight colleges and universities in the United States, which now serve over 200,000 students and have over 2 million living alumni. American Jesuit higher education has flourished, with most of the twenty-eight colleges and universities ranking in the upper segment of each institution's classification category in the *US News and World Report 2015 College Rankings*. Thirty-one other Jesuit universities are dispersed across the continents, with 14 in Latin America, 9 in East Asia, 7 in Europe, and one in the Middle East, serving nearly 400,000 students in total.

The twentieth century saw an increase in the size, number, and types of schools. Globally, there are now 89 Jesuit-affiliated colleges (undergraduate) or universities, and 100 Jesuit seminaries or residences for Jesuit students. The Society of Jesus has also adapted to new educational structures. There are 24 University Colleges that are part of a government university, as in the British system. In other countries, such as Spain, France, Belgium, and India, the Jesuits are affiliated with 36 specialized state-controlled professional schools in areas such as engineering, business, music, and education, where special residence halls offer tutoring, advising, and Christian development for students.

In the second half of the twentieth century, the Jesuit educational apostolate worked to construct a diverse, but consistent and integrated, worldwide educational network by creating international associations, holding regular conferences, sharing comprehensive reports, and publishing journals such as *Conversations*.

In the twenty-first century, Jesuit education is remaking itself again, by: (1) addressing the changing face of Jesuit education – fewer Jesuits and many more lay faculty and administrators, (2) constructing a global network of schools which are both locally appropriate and yet still *Jesuit* in some enduring way, (3) offering education to increased numbers of students from diverse socioeconomic backgrounds to promote social justice, and (4) working across cultural, political, and linguistic borders to promote transformative learning in a global age.

See also AJCU; South Asia Jesuit Colleges and Universities; Universidad Alberto Hurtado

Bonachea, Rolando E., ed., *Jesuit Higher Education: Essays on an American Tradition of Excellence.* Pittsburgh, PA: Duquesne University Press, 1989.

Buckley, Michael, *The Catholic University as Promise and Project: Reflections in a Jesuit Idiom.* Washington, DC: Georgetown University Press, 2007.

Codina, Gabriel, "A Century of Jesuit Education, 1900–2000." In *Jesuits: Yearbook of the Society of Jesus. 2000.* Trans. John Dullea. Rome: Jesuit Curia, 1999.

Duminuco, Vincent, ed., *The Jesuit Ratio Studiorum: 400th Anniversary Perspectives.* New York: Fordham University Press, 2000.

Leahy, William, *Adapting to America: Catholics, Jesuits, and Higher Education in the Twentieth Century.* Washington, DC: Georgetown University Press, 1991.

Padberg, John W., *Colleges in Controversy: The Jesuit Schools in France from Revival to Suppression, 1815–1880.* Cambridge, MA: Harvard University Press, 1969.

Traub, George, *The Jesuit Education Reader.* Chicago, IL: Loyola Press, 2008.

Tripole, Martin, ed., *Promise Renewed: Jesuit Higher Education for a New Millennium.* Chicago, IL: Loyola Press, 1999.

Cinthia Gannett

University of San Francisco (USF)

To recount the story of the University of San Francisco is to recount the story of an educational enterprise that took place at a number of significant historical crossroads. Among the principal protagonists were the Italian Jesuits of the Turin province. Exiled from their homeland in the aftermath of the Risorgimento, they reached the shores of the Pacific just as the Gold Rush was taking hold of the American West and arrived in San Francisco in 1849. The Jesuits concluded that one of the best ways to engage the needs of the new immigrants, coming both from abroad and from other parts of the United States, would be to offer them a quality education.

As a result, the Italian Jesuit Michele Accolti received permission in 1851 to establish a school. On account of the chaos Accolti and his fellow Jesuits, Antonio Maraschi and Giovanni Nobili, experienced after their arrival in San Francisco, they opted instead for Santa Clara, the site of the former Franciscan mission, originally founded in 1777, where they established their first college in California. Despite these initial misgivings, the Jesuits returned to San Francisco, where in the fall of 1855 Maraschi established St. Ignatius Academy, the first school of higher learning in a city that Accolti described as "the leading commercial place of California and soon … of the entire world." At first an informal one-room schoolhouse, it was renamed St. Ignatius College in 1859, after Maraschi obtained a charter from the State of California. It granted its first undergraduate degree in 1863 and its first graduate degree in 1867.

The school rapidly expanded and by the 1870s it had developed one of the most advanced science programs in the whole country. The faculty included the world-renowned Jesuit mathematicians Giuseppe Bayma and Luigi Varsi, as well as the physicist Giuseppe Neri, who was the first person to show electric light to the inhabitants of San Francisco and illuminate all of Market Street. By 1900 it also boasted one of the most extensive college libraries in the western United States.

Figure 65 Towers and dome on campus of the University of San Francisco. Photograph Thomas Worcester, SJ

A prolonged debate took place over the curriculum among those advocating for the original emphasis on the classical tradition of Latin and Greek studies and others who argued for a more pragmatic course of learning. Eventually, the pragmatists prevailed and acknowledged the importance of a greater variety of fields of study, including journalism, business, and law, among others.

Originally built on what would later become Market Street, the college moved locations in 1880 and 1906. In 1927 it relocated to its present location on the corner of Fulton and Parker Streets. In 1930 St. Ignatius College changed its name and became the University of San Francisco (USF). Originally an all-male school, with women attending evening programs since 1927, it became fully coeducational in 1964 and in 1978 merged with Lone Mountain College, originally San Francisco College for Women, founded by the Religious of the Sacred Heart. From its inception, the history of the University has been inextricably linked to that of St. Ignatius Church, which since 1855 has played an important role in the life of both the city and USF.

Throughout its history, the University had to overcome many challenges, including major financial crises in the late 1880s and in 1912. The latter followed the devastating earthquake of April 18, 1906, which reduced its buildings to a heap of rubble and ashes. It also lost many of its students, who valiantly gave up their lives in the two world wars.

In 2015 the USF had an enrolment of over 11,000 students, with approximately 7,000 undergraduates and 4,000 graduate students, who pursue their studies in the College of Arts and Sciences (1925) or in one of four schools, the School of Law (1912), the School of Management (1925), the School of Education (1947), and the School of Nursing and Health Professions (1954). It also offers classes at branch campuses in Sacramento, San Jose, Santa Rosa, and Pleasanton – with two locations outside the main 55-acre campus in downtown San Francisco and at the Presidio.

The University has always been a pioneer of diversity. In 1951, the *Dons*, arguably the best college football team in the country that year, refused to take part in the Orange Bowl in protest over the discrimination of African American players. Beginning with the early Irish, Italian, Chinese, and Filipino immigrants of the late nineteenth and early twentieth centuries, it continues to reflect a rich ethnic and racial mix among students, staff, and faculty. In 2014, 20 percent of the student body were international students from over eighty countries.

USF strives to continue its tradition of Jesuit education with a global perspective while maintaining its mission of service to the citizens of San Francisco, who so generously supported and defined the University throughout its 160-year history.

See also Santa Clara University; United States of America; Universities, 1773–Present

M. Antoni J. Ucerler, SJ

Urbanism

Although St. Ignatius was born in a rural valley in the Basque region, he evolved into a resolutely urban being. By the time he reached Rome in 1537, he had visited or lived in most of the important Catholic cities of Europe, with the exception of the Kingdom of Naples and Southern Germany. His youthful travels with the peripatetic Spanish court, visits to Jerusalem, Antwerp, and London, studies in Barcelona, Alcalá, Salamanca, Paris, and pastoral work in Venice and the cities of northern Italy acquainted him with the dynamics and possibilities of urban ministry at the beginning of the early modern era.

In Rome, Ignatius and his companions targeted the urban core, and six weeks after the approval of the Society (1540) obtained title to a small Church of Santa Maria della Strada and its adjoining properties. Strategically located on a busy corner between the papal summer palace of San Marco, the Campidoglio or city hall, the Jewish ghetto, a redevelopment zone and the red-light district, this first downtown emplacement became the paradigm for all that followed. The earliest works included street-corner preaching, direct ministries to the poor and excluded (i.e., prostitutes, daughters of prostitutes, orphans, Jewish catechumens) as well as lecturing at the papal university. Although neighborhood opposition frustrated Ignatius's attempts to build a large church on the della Strada site, Francis Borja succeeded in raising the Chiesa del Gesù there beginning in 1568. The Casa Professa adjoining the church was added in the early seventeenth century. Major Roman constructions included the four-square-block Roman College/Chiesa di Sant'Ignazio complex, the large Germanicum-Hungaricum college near Piazza Navona, smaller residential colleges for English, Maronite, and Greek Catholic seminarians and Bernini's jewel box chapel for the novitiate on the Quirinale.

The early Jesuits deliberately chose downtown locations for their colleges, college chapels, professed houses, and outreach ministries in order to maximize their impact on the cities they sought to serve. The Jesuit *Constitutions* directly addressed the issue of siting in paragraph 622e: "Preference should be shown to aid which is given to great nations such as the Indies, or to important cities, or to universities, which are generally attended by persons who by being aided themselves can become laborers for the help of others."

Inverting the centrifugal impulse of monasticism and early mendicant establishments that usually were built outside city gates, the Jesuits strategically targeted downtown sites. Ignatius's extensive correspondence (more than 6,800 extant letters) is peppered with some 2,300 references to property transactions, siting, and strategy issues for Jesuit urban

ROMA.

Figure 66 Map of Rome with Jesuit buildings marked, from *Vita beati patris Ignatii Loyolae religionis Societatis Iesu fundatoris ad viuum expressa ex ea quam ...*, 1610, engraving. Jesuitica Collection, John J. Burns Library, Boston College. Photograph Alison Fleming

ministries (churches, colleges, and social services centers), and staffing and financing such works. Some 600 references instruct Jesuits how to negotiate for a "convenient" urban property "not too far from the conversation of the city." The rationale spelled out typically included greater utility to the city and its rulers; richer educational opportunities for a broad spectrum of students; and greater pastoral, preaching, and sacramental availability for the Jesuits and those they served.

The explosive demand for Jesuit colleges strained both the Society's human and economic resources and its relationships with local bishops, canons, and other religious orders. Medieval rules had legislated a fixed distance between mendicant churches, parishes, and cathedral, but the Jesuits regularly received papal dispensations from the law. Papal bulls (Pius IV's *Etsi ex debito*, 1561, and Gregory XIII's *Salvatoris Domini*, 1576) eventually gave the Society extraordinary privileges to build anywhere it chose, although such freedom was regularly contested by irate Ordinaries from Cuzco in the seventeenth century to San Francisco in the nineteenth and Seattle in the twentieth century.

Peter Canisius took advantage of these papal exemptions when he negotiated the purchase or donation of huge college properties in the hearts of Munich, Prague, and Vienna. In seventeenth-century Mexico City, no less than three colleges and a large professed house were built within a five-block radius of the Cathedral. In Paris, the seventeenth-century Jesuit Church of St. Paul and St. Louis at the professed house in the Marais and the College Louis-le-Grand in the Latin quarter became important cultural landmarks. The Jesuit College of St. Paul in Macau abutted the hilltop fortress just above the town square, and Matteo Ricci obtained downtown property in Beijing for the first of three distinct Jesuit churches in the south (the "Nantang," 1605), east (the "Dontang" 1665), and north (the "Beitang," 1703) quadrants of the city. The Kangxi emperor granted property and permission for construction of a magnificent Baroque North Church (the original "Beitang" adjacent to the Forbidden City) to French Jesuits to reward them for curing him of malaria with "Jesuit bark" or quinine.

While the Suppression of the Society spelled the end of a great real estate empire, the urban mission remains very much a part of Jesuit DNA as Jesuit works continue to be founded in cities around the world.

See also Constitutions; Loyola, Ignatius, SJ, St.; Mission; Paris; Rome; Universities, 1540–1773

Lucas, Thomas, *Landmarking: City, Church and Jesuit Urban Strategy*. Chicago, IL: Loyola Press, 1997.

Thomas Lucas, SJ

Uruguay

The beginnings of the Society's mission work in Uruguay, in the seventeenth century, were complicated by confrontations between Spain and Portugal; even the Guaraní from the reductions were drawn into the conflict. A residence and school in Montevideo were founded in 1746, which lasted until the Jesuits were expelled from Latin America in 1767. The Society returned to the region in 1841 and embarked upon a number of educational, spiritual, and pastoral works. But the nineteenth century found the Jesuits facing strong opposition from the Masons, who accused them of undermining familial and civic life. Jesuits were expelled in 1859 but then returned in 1872 as part of the Chilean-Paraguayan mission, taking up once more the Society's traditional ministries and evangelizing, as well as assuming direction of a college seminary in 1880. Again, the Masons were soon their enemies, together with those free thinkers who connected the Jesuits with clericalism and the Church's resistance to development and modernity, and with Ultramontanism. In 1880 there began the gradual de-Christianizing of the Republic, and unlike other Latin American countries, Uruguay became strongly secular and remained so. In 1861 the government decreed the secularization of cemeteries, crucifixes were removed from hospitals (1906), divorce was legalized (1907), religious instruction removed from public schools (1909), and separation of Church from State was completed in the Constitution of 1919.

A repressive civilian-military dictatorship ruled the country from 1973 to 1984, coinciding with the Dirty War in Argentina. This prompted the creation of the Service of Justice and Peace Commission for Uruguay (SERPAJ), spearheaded by Luis Pérez Aguirre, a Jesuit from Montevideo; in 1989 the Commission published *Uruguay: Nunca Más*, a record of the atrocities. The liberation theologian Juan Luis Segundo, also from Montevideo, co-founded the Peter Faber Center for Theological and Social Studies (1965), which was closed by the dictatorship; he was forced to leave the country. Over the years, Jesuits in Uruguay have been involved in both seminary and secondary education, and in maintaining parishes. The Catholic University of Montevideo, opened in

1882 and then reopened in 1985, is under the direction of the Society. Uruguay became part of the Argentine-Chilean province in 1918, and then part of the Argentina province in 1937. In 1950 it became an independent region, a vice province in 1961, and its own province in 1983. Uruguay rejoined Argentina in 2010 to form the Argentine-Uruguayan province.

See also Argentina; Paraguay Missions ("Reductions"); Segundo, Luis, SJ

Klaiber, Jeffrey, The Jesuits in Latin America, 1549–2000. St. Louis, MO: The Institute of Jesuit Sources, 2009.
Monreal, Susana, "Antijesuitismo en Montevideo a comienzos del siglo XX: los folletos de la Asociación de Propaganda Liberal (1900–1905)." Estudos Ibero-Americanos 39, 2 (2013), 285–303.
Jesuitas Provincia Argentino-Uruguaya (Uruguay province website). www.jesuitasaru.org.
Universidad Católica del Uruguay. www.ucu.edu.uy.

William Reiser, SJ

Valdivia, Luis de, SJ (1561–1642)

Born in Granada (Spain) in 1561, Valdivia entered the Society of Jesus on April 2, 1581. Soon after being ordained, Valdivia was sent to Peru, where he began learning native languages. In 1593 he was part of the first group of Jesuits sent to establish a mission in Chile. There he occupied the rectorate of the College of San Miguel in Santiago and was charged with preaching to the native population of the city. In 1602 Valdivia returned to Lima. He made a second trip to Chile in 1605 and returned to Peru in 1606. From there, Valdivia traveled to Spain to lobby the Crown to halt all military actions against the Mapuche in southern Chile, to establish a frontier between Spanish and Mapuche territories, and to send missionaries into Mapuche lands to preach the Gospel and obtain the voluntary submission of the Mapuche to the Spanish Crown. In 1612 Valdivia went back to Chile, endowed with ample powers to implement what has come down in Chilean historiography as the defensive war strategy. He devoted his time to pacify the Mapuche and to establish missions among them. In 1619 he returned to Peru and then to Spain. In 1621 he took residence in the Jesuit college in Valladolid. Once in Spain, Valdivia published his Nueve sermones en lengua de Chile, a translation into the Mapuche language of the first nine sermons written by José de Acosta and published in 1584 by the Third Lima Council. Previously, Valdivia had also published translations into Mapuche and the Allentaiac and Millcayac languages of the catechism and the confession manuals sanctioned by the Third Lima Council. Valdivia died in Valladolid, on November 5, 1642.

See also Chile; Peru; Spain, Valladolid

Andrés Ignacio Prieto

Valera, Blas, SJ (1544–1597)

Blas Valera was born in Chachapoyas, Peru, in 1544, as the son of Luis Valera, a Spanish conquistador, and a native woman named Francisca Pérez. A native speaker of both Quechua and Spanish, Valera joined the Society of Jesus in 1568, the same year of the Order's arrival in Peru. Between 1570 and 1583, Valera worked as a missionary among the native peoples of Huarochiri, Lima, Cusco, Juli, and Potosí. In April 1583, however, Valera was taken prisoner on charges that are still a matter of debate among scholars. After three years in prison and eight years of house arrest, Valera was finally exiled to Spain. He arrived in Cádiz in 1596, where he was badly injured during the English raid of the city that same year. Valera died from his wounds in April 1597.

Although none of his writings survive in complete form, Valera has been a looming presence in Andean studies, shrouded in mystery. As a scholar of ancient Peru, Valera influenced writers such as Giovanni Anello Oliva (1574–1642) and Garcilaso de la Vega, El Inca (1539–1616). Valera's major work (and the only one firmly established as his own), titled *Historia Occidentalis*, survives only in passages quoted by Garcilaso. Another manuscript, titled *De las costumbres antiguas de los naturales del Pirú* (*c.* 1594), has been attributed to Valera by some scholars, although debate regarding its authorship continues. Recently, a group of documents have been found in a private collection in Naples, allegedly dating from the seventeenth century. Among these documents are some signed by Valera. These documents claim that Valera did not die in Cádiz in 1597 but instead secretly returned to Peru, where he wrote the *Primer nueva corónica y buen gobierno*, a manuscript generally accepted as having been written by the native intellectual Felipe Guamán Poma de Ayala. The Naples documents also claim that Valera taught a phonetic system for recording information using the traditional Andean *khipus*, or knot-based recording system. Although some scholars defend the authenticity of the Naples documents, the general consensus is that they are either colonial or modern forgeries.

See also Peru

Andrés Ignacio Prieto

Valignano, Alessandro, SJ (1539–1606)

Francis Xavier is credited with having founded the Jesuit missions in South, Southeast, and East Asia as a result of the work of evangelization that he carried out from India to Japan for a period of ten years between 1542 and 1552. A generation later, Alessandro Valignano was responsible for creating the structures and policies that would influence the progress of those missions for almost two centuries thereafter.

An Italian, born in 1539 in Chieti, in the Abruzzi region in the Kingdom of Naples ruled by Spain, he belonged to an influential noble family. He was given a late Renaissance education, which included the study of "letters" as well as chivalry. In 1557 he was awarded a doctorate *in utroque iure*, i.e., in both civil and canon law, from the University of Padua. After a wild youth, including time spent in prison in Venice, he experienced a conversion and joined the Society of Jesus in 1566.

After his studies at the Roman College, a year at the novitiate at Sant'Andrea in Rome, and several months in Chieti, he became rector of the Jesuit college in Macerata. Ordained a priest in 1571, two years later he was appointed official "visitor" of the Jesuit superior general, Everard Mercurian. His new position gave him authority over all Jesuit missions of the East Indies, i.e., from Mozambique to Japan. These territories were all part of the *Padroado Real* of Portugal – in accordance with the Treaty of Tordesillas of 1494 between Portugal and Spain. Thus, his authority did not extend to the Philippines, which remained under Spanish rule.

Valignano spent considerable time in India, between 1574 and 1577, 1583 and 1588, and 1595 and 1597. He then visited Malacca in 1577 and Macau, the Portuguese trade entrepôt in China, where he stayed in 1578, 1588–90, 1592–94, and 1603–06. He also carried out three visitations of Japan, from 1579 to 1582, 1590 to 1592, and 1598 to 1603.

While in India, Valignano visited the missions from Goa to Kochi and promoted the formation of a native Indian clergy. His most controversial actions involved the St. Thomas Christians of Kerala and his attempts, on behalf of the archbishop of Goa, to pressure the local bishop and clergy of the Syro-Malabar rite to adapt and submit themselves to the customs and ecclesiastical jurisdiction of the Latin Church.

It was in Japan that Valignano's policies would have the longest and most significant impact. When he arrived in 1579, he found Japan in the midst of civil war. Many of the Christian warlords complained about the Jesuits' lack of knowledge and respect for Japanese culture. In response, he composed a treatise in which he ordered all Jesuits to follow customs similar to those adopted by the monks at Nanzenji temple in Kyoto. He then set up seminaries at Arima, Azuchi, and Funai, and admitted Japanese novices to the Society of Jesus at Usuki in 1580. He also founded a college of higher studies at Funai under the patronage of Ōtomo Sōrin (1530–87), daimyō of Bungo. The college would train students in both European *studia humanitatis* as well as Japanese classical "scholarship" (*gakumon*).

To further this aim, he acquired a Gutenberg handpress and movable type from Lisbon, and encouraged the printing of books in Japanese translation of catechisms and dictionaries, as well as works of early modern devotion, including those by Thomas à Kempis (*c.* 1380–1471) and Luis de Granada (1504–88). On his orders, in 1593 the Spanish Jesuit, Pedro Gómez, completed a tripartite compendium of astronomy, philosophy, and theology, which was then translated for the first time into Japanese.

To protect the precarious position of Christians in the domains of Ōmura Sumitada (1533–87), Valignano accepted ownership of the small town of Nagasaki, which soon became the major port of trade between Japan and Portugal. To finance the mission, Valignano negotiated Jesuit involvement in the silk trade.

In 1582 he chose four young boys of noble lineage and sent them to see Christian Europe and act as ambassadors of the Christian community in Japan. The "Tenshō Embassy" (1582–90) was warmly received and accorded diplomatic honors by two popes, the king of Spain, and numerous nobles throughout Italy, Spain, and Portugal.

Equally significant were his efforts on behalf of the Chinese mission. He called the Italian Jesuits Michele Ruggieri and Matteo Ricci to Macau and ordered them to make every effort to master the Chinese language and classics. In 1594 Valignano founded a university college in Macau to educate Jesuits to work in the Chinese mission. By the time he died in 1606, Ricci had been accepted at the Chinese court as a western scholar worthy of respect and known for his many published works in classical Chinese. Thus, Valignano's policies of "cultural accommodation" were to bear fruit for generations thereafter. A prolific writer, he produced dozens of reports and hundreds of letters.

See also Asia; China; Cultures; India; Japan; Visitation

M. Antoni J. Ucerler, SJ

Valladolid

This city in northern Spain became the site of the first of several English seminaries established in the realm of the "Most Catholic Kings" in the late sixteenth and early seventeenth centuries. Despite the founding of English colleges at Douai (1568) and Rome (1579), the need for a continual supply of priests for the English-Welsh mission led the Jesuit Robert Persons, in conjunction with the crucial support of King Philip II, to establish several additional seminaries in Spain. The first and arguably the most significant of these was founded at Valladolid in 1589. In addition to being the traditional court capital, Valladolid was the third largest city in the kingdom, was an important center of communications, and was home to both a university and a Jesuit college. In terms of its important connections to both Spain and the Society of Jesus, the rectors of the seminary were Spanish Jesuits, at least during its first few decades. The first English rector was the Jesuit William Weston, who had survived many years of ministry and imprisonment on the English mission. As clear signs of royal approbation, Philip II visited the seminary in 1592, as did Philip III in 1600. Yet the vital link to the English Catholic mission was clear from the outset, as the seminary was named St. Alban's, after the first English Christian martyr. The first thirty years of the institution have been called its "golden age." In all, more than twenty of its graduates were martyred on the English mission, five of whom were later canonized. This "school of martyrs" was buttressed by additional seminaries in Seville (1592) and Madrid (1611), known collectively as "islands of England" in the heart of Spain.

See also Spain; United Kingdom

Murphy, Martin, *St. Gregory's College, Seville, 1592–1767*. London: Catholic Record Society, 1992.
Williams, Michael E., *St. Alban's College, Valladolid: Four Centuries of English Catholic Presence in Spain*. New York: St. Martin's Press, 1986.

Robert E.Scully, SJ

Vargas Ugarte, Rubén, SJ (1886–1975)

One of the most prominent historians of Peru, Rubén Vargas Ugarte was also the third rector of the Pontifical Catholic University of Peru from 1947 to 1953, and head of the Peruvian National Library from 1955 to 1962. Vargas Ugarte was born in Lima on October 22, 1886, and entered the Society of Jesus in 1904 in Pifo, Ecuador, where he completed his novitiate. He studied philosophy in Spain, at the Jesuit College of Granada, and was ordained in 1921 in Barcelona, where he also completed his theology studies. It was during his time in Spain that Vargas Ugarte began researching the history of the Viceroyalty of Peru, making use of the extensive records housed at the Archivo General de Indias in Seville. He also consulted the documentation regarding the early history of the Society of Jesus in Peru in the Vatican archives. In 1924 Vargas Ugarte returned to Peru, and in 1931 he joined the faculty of the Pontifical Catholic University, occupying the chairs of Peruvian History and of History of the Americas. Vargas Ugarte's most important and enduring contributions came from his work as a historian of the Society of Jesus and as a Church historian more generally. His *Historia de la Compañía de Jesús en el Perú* (History of the Society of Jesus in Peru, 4 vols.,

1963–67), *Historia de la Iglesia del Perú* (History of the Peruvian Church, 5 vols., 1953–62), and his edition of the proceedings of the councils of the Archdiocese of Lima, *Los concilios limenses, 1551–1772* (The Lima Councils, 1551–1772, 3 vols., 1951–54) are all indispensable sources for the study of the Viceroyalty of Peru. Vargas Ugarte was awarded the Peruvian National Prize for History in 1953. He passed away in Lima on February 14, 1975.

See also Furlong Cardiff, Guillermo, SJ; Marzal, Manuel, SJ; Peru

Nieto Vélez, Armando, "P. Rubén Vargas Ugarte, SJ, 1886–1975." *Archivum Historicum Societatis Iesu* 44 (1975), 424–39.

Andrés Ignacio Prieto

Vatican I

The First Vatican Council (1869–1870) produced just two documents, *Dei Filius* and *Pastor Aeternus.* The former dealt with the subjects of revelation, faith and the relations between faith and reason, and the latter with papal primacy, including the controversial topic of the infallibility of the pope.

Both documents bear strong marks of Jesuit influence, *Dei Filius* particularly. From its beginnings in the Preparatory Commission preceding the Council, the purpose of what eventually became *Dei Filius* was not to provide a comprehensive treatment of the subjects of faith, revelation, reason, and related matters, but rather to clarify "Catholic faith" in contradistinction to the chief errors that were seen to abound in its regard in the nineteenth century. The document steers a path between the extremes of rationalism and fideism and its fourth chapter, on the relationship between faith and reason, is unmistakably Thomist in character, due in large measure to the involvement in its preparation of the prominent Jesuit neo-Thomist, Joseph Kleutgen. He acted as theologian to a commission of three bishops who, prior to the Council, had been asked to revise a preparatory schema on the relations of faith and reason that another Jesuit, Johann Baptist Franzelin, had composed, but that was thought to be too long and unwieldy. Kleutgen also exerted influence on *Pastor Aeternus*, although its statement on papal infallibility does not owe its formulation to him.

Not all nineteenth-century Jesuits in Rome were champions of neo-scholasticism, Thomist style, but those who were had the most impact on Vatican I – and not exclusively on *Dei Filius*. Matteo Liberatore SJ, chief among them, worked and wrote extensively for the Jesuit-run, quasi-official organ of the papacy, *La Civiltà Cattolica*, which championed papal infallibility in the run-up to the Council. He belonged to the infallibilist circles that flourished at that time, and his key role in *La Civiltà Cattolica* ensured the journal's support for infallibility also.

See also Kleutgen, Joseph, SJ; Liberatore, Matteo, SJ; *Periti*; Ultramontanism

Dulles, Avery, *The Assurance of Things Hoped For: A Theology of Christian Faith*. Oxford/New York: Oxford University Press, 1994.
Kerr, Fergus, *After Aquinas: Versions of Thomism*. Malden, MA/Oxford: Blackwell Publishing, 2002.

James Corkery, SJ

Vatican II, Jesuits and

Any evaluation of what Jesuits contributed to the Second Vatican Council (1962–65) must also take into account what they had already done toward preparing the Council's work and what they would do toward implementing its teaching.

Augustin Bea (1881–1968) enjoyed more official clout at the Council than any other Jesuit. In 1959 Pope John XXIII had made him a cardinal and in 1960 the first president of the Secretariat for Promoting Christian Unity, a post which he held until his death and through which he promoted relations with other Christians and with the Jewish people. As co-drafter of Pius XII's 1943 encyclical on biblical studies, Bea helped prepare Vatican II's teaching on the Sacred Scriptures. His appreciation for the word of God made him reject the 1962 official schema on "the Sources of Revelation" that endorsed Scripture and tradition as parallel sources of revelation. The draft was withdrawn and sent for revision to a "mixed commission" drawn from Bea's own Secretariat for Promoting Christian Unity and the Theological Commission. In 1965 the bishops approved the Dogmatic Constitution on Divine Revelation (*Dei Verbum*), a text which enjoys theological priority in the sixteen documents of Vatican II. Bea was also a decisive force in securing the Council's repudiation of anti-Semitism in its Declaration on the Relation of the Church to Non-Christian Religions, *Nostra aetate*. He welcomed observers from other Christian churches who attended the Council and let their views be heard in revising texts, notably *Dei Verbum*, the Dogmatic Constitution on the Church (*Lumen gentium*), and the Decree on Ecumenism (*Unitatis redintegratio*).

Together with Henri de Lubac (1896–1991), Jean Daniélou (1905–74) had led a patristic revival that renewed theology by engaging with the full tradition of the Church Fathers. Together they founded *Sources Chrétiennes* (1942–). As a *peritus* at the Council, Daniélou was active in communicating ideas and rallying the support of bishops. He contributed to the making of *Dei Verbum* through a November 1962 draft "On Revelation and the Word of God."

Another French Jesuit, Joseph Gélineau (1920–2008), helped open the way for liturgical reform through his musical compositions, historical scholarship, and pastoral skills. He was responsible for reintroducing into the Roman Missal the responsorial psalm that had disappeared for more than one thousand years. He also contributed to the revision of the Eucharistic Prayers, and reintroduced the acclamations after the words of institution.

Aloys Grillmeier (1910–98) came to the Council as a consultant for Bishop Wilhelm Kempf of Limburg. In 1963 he became an official *peritus*, served on the Theological Commission (1963–65), and had a hand in drafting *Lumen gentium*, *Dei verbum*, and the Pastoral Constitution on the Church in the Modern World (*Gaudium et spes*). In the aftermath of the Council, Grillmeier put his knowledge of the ancient Christological controversies at the service of dialogues with the Oriental Orthodox Churches, which had rejected the Council of Chalcedon (AD 451). The dialogues bore fruit in official, joint confessions of faith in Christ (1973 with the Copts, 1994 with the Assyrian Church of the East, and 1996 with the Armenians).

Through his two-volume *Missarum Solemnia* (German original, 1949; translation, *The Mass of the Roman Rite*, 1950) and other writings, the Austrian Josef Jungmann (1889–1975) had prepared the way for liturgical reform. After joining the Preparatory

Commission on the Liturgy, he became a Council *peritus* and then a consultant for implementing what the Constitution on the Sacred Liturgy (*Sacrosanctum concilium*) had mandated.

Before the Council, de Lubac developed a theology that creatively retrieved historical sources, not least the exegesis of the Fathers and their successors. After being forbidden to teach by the Roman authorities (1950–58), he was appointed in 1960 a consultant for the Preparatory Theological Commission and then in 1962 an official *peritus*. De Lubac had challenged a neo-scholastic separation of grace and nature, insisting that there is only one order of human existence, called by supernatural grace to the destiny of glory. In general, Vatican II followed de Lubac by avoiding language that would separate grace and nature. Specifically, he contributed to the making of *Lumen gentium*, *Dei Verbum*, and *Gaudium et spes*. Through dialogue with Orthodox theologians, he developed the theme that "the Eucharist makes the Church," a principle embodied to a degree in *Sacrosanctum concilium*. He had published on Pierre Teilhard de Chardin (1881–1955) and helped communicate some of Teilhard's evolutionary optimism to *Gaudium et spes*. Like Daniélou, de Lubac later proved less than fully enthusiastic in implementing the Council's teaching.

John Courtney Murray (1904–67) came to the Council as Cardinal Francis Spellman's consultant, was appointed a *peritus* in 1963, and helped draft the third and fourth versions of the Declaration on Religious Liberty, *Dignitatis humanae*.

Before John XXIII announced the Council, Karl Rahner (1904–84) had already updated numerous themes of fundamental and systematic theology: e.g., grace as God's self-communication; revelation being mediated through words and deeds in the history of salvation; the graced situation before God of those of "other" faiths or of no faith at all; the Church as sinful and needing reformation; and the historical development of the sacrament of penance. Right through his theological career, Rahner was deeply concerned to let faith address the needs and questions of the modern world. After being a consultant for the Preparatory Commission on the Sacraments, he became a *peritus* and quickly made his presence felt. He produced a critical *Disquisitio brevis* on the question of Scripture and tradition. Together with Joseph Ratzinger, he drafted a replacement for the schema on "the Sources of Revelation" and had 2,000 copies distributed to the bishops in November 1962 just before they began discussing that schema. Various themes from Rahner's *Disquisitio* and the draft he wrote with Ratzinger made their way into the final text of *Dei Verbum*. Directly or indirectly, Rahner contributed to other Council documents, and in the post-Vatican II period he never stopped communicating the Council's teaching and significance.

Others from among the forty-six Jesuit *periti* should be recalled. Otto Semmelroth helped prepare *Lumen gentium*, *Dei Verbum*, and *Gaudium et spes*. Five articles by Jared Wicks published in *Gregorianum* (2001–05) have spelled out the major role played by Pieter Smulders in developing *Dei Verbum*. Domenico Grasso contributed to the Decree on the Church's Missionary Activity (*Ad gentes*), while Johannes Hirschmann and Roberto Tucci were involved in fashioning *Gaudium et spes* and Paolo Dezza in preparing *Optatam totius*, the Decree on the Training of Priests.

Without becoming official *periti*, Gustave Martelet and Henri Rondet proved effective consultants for bishops from Africa. Finally, a few Jesuit *periti* worked against the aims of the Council: Wilhelm Bertrams, Charles Boyer, Édouard Dhanis, Franz

X. Hürth, Joaquin Salaverri, and Sebastian Tromp. As secretary of the Preparatory Theological Commission and then of the Council's Doctrinal Commission, Tromp hindered the updating of Church teaching. But, from the first session of 1962, his influence waned.

A complete account would examine how the (few) Jesuit bishops (e.g., Archbishop Thomas Roberts) performed at Vatican II, and how the Jesuit institutions in Rome collaborated in the work of the Council. Jesuit journalists (e.g., Giovanni Caprile, Mario von Galli, and Daniel O'Hanlon) kept the wider Catholic public informed about the progress and implementation of Vatican II. Walter Abbott quickly produced an English translation of the Council's documents that sold more than a million copies. Other Jesuits, such as Jacques Dupuis, René Latourelle, John O'Malley, Jared Wicks, and those who collaborated in writing major commentaries for Cerf, Herder and Herder, and Paulist Press have done much to interpret and implement the work of Vatican II. Lastly, from the 31st General Congregation of the Jesuits (1965), the Council has had its impact on Jesuit governance, life, and ministry (including theological ministry). In that sense "Jesuits and Vatican II" remains an unfinished story.

See also Arrupe, Pedro, SJ; Bea, Augustin, Cardinal, SJ; Murray, John Courtney, SJ; Paul VI; *Periti*; Rahner, Karl, SJ

Gerald O'Collins, SJ

Vatican Observatory

The Specola Vaticana (Vatican Observatory) is the official astronomical observatory of the Holy See, acting as a national observatory for the Vatican City State.

Its origins reach back to the sixteenth-century reform of the calendar by Pope Gregory XIII (r. 1572–85). Following the instructions of the Council of Trent, he promulgated a method for keeping calendar dates in line with the seasons and determining (by a formula, rather than observation) the date of Easter and other movable feasts. Among the astronomers working on this reform was the Jesuit mathematician at the Roman College, Christopher Clavius (1537–1612), who explained and defended the new calendar. Following his work, astronomy was a prominent part of the work at the Roman College for the next two 200 years.

After the Suppression of the Jesuits, a Pontifical Observatory at the Roman College was formally established in 1774. Though at first it was neither well equipped nor well financed, Pope Pius VII (r. 1800–23) provided significant support after observing a near-total solar eclipse there in 1804. With the restoration of the Jesuits in the early nineteenth century, astronomical research returned to the Roman College. Its most notable astronomer was Angelo Secchi (1818–78), the first to classify stars by their spectra. In parallel with the observatory at the Roman College, the popes also had a separate astronomical observatory on the Capitoline Hill, expanded in 1848 by Pope Pius IX (r. 1846–78), which collected data on stellar positions, the orbits of solar system objects, and the solar chromosphere. The unification of Italy in 1870 led to the confiscation of these observatories by the anticlerical Italian government; however, because of his reputation, Secchi was allowed to continue his work until his death in 1878.

In 1891 Pope Leo XIII established the Specola Vaticana as an astronomical research center at the Vatican. Telescopes were built on the walls surrounding the gardens behind St. Peter's, and instruments were installed in the Tower of the Winds atop the Vatican Library. Pope Leo's reasons were straightforward: "This plan is simply that everyone might see clearly that the Church and her Pastors are not opposed to true and solid science, whether human or divine, but that they embrace it, encourage it, and promote it with the fullest possible dedication." Having such a national observatory also served as a sign of the Vatican's independence from Italy.

The first project of the new Vatican Observatory was to take part in the *Carte du Ciel* program, a major international activity organized by the Paris Observatory to map the positions of the stars using large telescopic cameras. This work was begun by Giuseppe Lais (1845–1921) and the first Jesuit director, Johann Hagen (1847–1930).

In the 1930s, under the new director Johan Stein (1871–1951), the Observatory moved to the Pope's summer home in the hills of Castel Gandolfo to escape Rome's light pollution. Two new telescopes were constructed on the roof of the Papal Summer Palace in 1934 and Pope Pius XI dedicated the new facility in 1935. At the time of the move, the staffing of the Observatory was entrusted to the Jesuits.

Among the features of the new site was a space designed for a large meteorite collection, from which a catalogue of meteorite physical properties has been established, and a laboratory to study the spectra of pure metals needed for interpreting the composition of stars from their spectra. In addition, the Vatican Observatory has developed an active program in studying the history and philosophy of science and the relationship between astronomy, philosophy, and religion.

When city lights eventually reached Castel Gandolfo itself, observing was transferred to the deserts of southern Arizona. There, in 1993, the Vatican Observatory opened its Vatican Advanced Technology Telescope, pioneering revolutionary design techniques now in use at many of the world's largest telescopes. In 2009 the Vatican provided the observatory with newly remodeled headquarters and expanded laboratory facilities in the papal summer gardens at Castel Gandolfo; these new facilities were personally dedicated by Pope Benedict XVI.

Research today continues in Arizona and Castel Gandolfo, in fields ranging from the Big Bang to the structure of galaxies, from mapping stars in our Milky Way to understanding meteors and meteorites in our own solar system. Vatican astronomers, an international community drawn from Europe, Africa, Asia, and the Americas, have collaborated with astronomers from every major observatory. Several Vatican astronomers have been elected to leadership positions in a number of international astronomical organizations, including the presidency of divisions of the International Astronomical Union and the American Astronomical Society.

In summary, the Vatican supports the Observatory and asks the Jesuits to staff it with astronomers in order to show the world in a visible way that it does not fear science but rather embraces it. This follows the long tradition of seeing knowledge of the created world as a path to the Creator.

See also Astronomy; Moon; Papacy; Science

Maffeo, Sabino, *The Vatican Observatory: In the Service of Nine Popes*. South Bend, IN: University of Notre Dame Press, 2002.

Udías, Augustín, *Jesuit Contribution to Science: A History*. London: Springer, 2015.

Guy Consolmagno, SJ

Vatican Radio

The emergence and growth of Vatican Radio (*Radio Vaticana*) was the product of both papal acceptance of modern technologies in the use of evangelization, and the ability of the Society of Jesus to provide a transnational platform for the application of the new technologies. During the 1930s, Pope Pius XI adopted a number of technologies – radio, cinema, and aviation – to push the Gospel message toward some of the remotest areas of the globe. In the course of this new arrangement, Pius XI looked to the Society of Jesus to administrate its new radio broadcasting station. Many historians have seen the use of the Jesuits, with their fourth vow of allegiance to the papacy and direct-reporting of the Jesuit father general to the pope, as an astute mechanism of papal control. However, the pan-European and global proposals connected to the new radio station played into the strengths of the Jesuits as a missionary order which could supply ready commentary according to both language groups and geography. Moreover, the adoption of technology on a global scale fit with the Jesuits' own spiritual and evangelical concept of *tantum quantum*: "that man should make use of all creation so far as (*tantum quantum*) they do help him towards his end, and should withdraw from them so far as they are a hindrance to him in regard to that end."

Jesuits had been interested in radio telegraphy since the 1890s. According to historian Gerald McKevitt, Father Richard Bell, SJ, began studying the experiments of Guglielmo Marconi since his days as a theologian in Rome during the 1890s. Bell modeled his radio laboratory at Santa Clara University on Marconi's, and by 1903 was transmitting wirelessly from Los Gatos to San Francisco. In the meantime, it was Marconi who was looking for the opportunity to transmit via radio waves worldwide. Radio historian Suzanne Lommers has shown that in 1929 Marconi was notified that the League of Nations was hoping to construct a global radio network. But the League's compromise plan of joint public-private ownership with Radio-Swiss S.A. meant bureaucratic hurdles would stymie the outlay of the plan until 1932. Spurning the League, Marconi may have been persuaded to take the call of the Vatican to establish a similar global radio station simply because of the free hand he would be given in creating the network. Vatican Radio was inaugurated by Pope Pius XI on February 12, 1931. A plaque dedicating its operation implored that the voice of the Supreme Shepherd might "be heard through the ether to the end of the globe for the salvation of souls."

The political history of Vatican Radio might be divided into three phases: protest in the era of the dictators, anti-communism during the Cold War, and modernization. Historian John Pollard has noticed that from the onset of war in 1939 through the American deployments in 1942, Vatican Radio exercised an often radically critical tone against the fascist government of Nazi Germany and even of Italy. Priests from occupied countries were allowed to broadcast on conditions in France and Poland, while anonymous speakers protested various fascist moves. Vatican Radio broadcasts vexed the Nazis so much, Pollard claims, that civilians caught listening to Vatican Radio in Nazi-occupied eastern Europe "were severely punished and even executed."

During the postwar period, the Vatican of Pope Pius XII girded itself for a transnational confrontation with global communism. Accordingly, Vatican Radio ramped up its broadcast power and battled for the airwaves. In 1957 a new 1,000-acre transmitting station was inaugurated by Pius XII at Santa Maria di Galeria, about 11 miles north of Rome. This new station, staffed by twenty Jesuits, boasted 24 shortwave antennas and one medium-wave antenna. Its four transmitters were expected "to pierce the Communist bloc's barrage of jamming against Western broadcasts" and "reach the Church of Silence," those jailed and persecuted Catholics behind the Iron Curtain.

As the Cold War dissipated, and the Vatican's own Ostpolitik changed, so did the thrust of broadcasting on Vatican Radio. The ten-minute news spots introduced in 1957 became longer, multilingual, and professionalized. Classical music interspersed with scriptural readings was introduced. In 1970 Jesuit General Pedro Arrupe used Vatican Radio to speak out against legalized abortion, calling it an "explosion [of death] which was much more dangerous" than any potential nuclear war. During the 1980s and 1990s, as some Jesuit theologians seemed to be out of step with the papacy of Pope John Paul II, there were rumblings that Vatican Radio would be handed over to the lay prelature Opus Dei. These rumors were dispelled by 2000, as Jesuit technical leadership held sway and Jesuit fidelity to the papacy was reaffirmed. On June 27, 2015, a *Motu proprio* by Pope Francis created the Secretariat of Communications which folded Vatican Radio into a new Dicastery. On February 22, 2016, Rev. Federico Lombardi, SJ, general director of Vatican Radio since 2005, stepped down and was not to be replaced because of the new consolidation.

See also Papacy; Pius XI; Pius XII

Matelski, Marilyn J., *Vatican Radio: Propagation by the Airwaves*. Westport, CT: Praeger Publishers, 1995.
Pollard, John F., "Electronic Pastors: Radio, Cinema, and Television from Pius XI to John XXIII." In James Corkery and Thomas Worcester, eds., *The Papacy since 1500: From Italian Prince to Universal Pastor*. Cambridge: Cambridge University Press, 2010, pp. 182–203.

Charles Gallagher, SJ

Venezuela

Originally, Venezuela was part of the Jesuit province of the New Kingdom of Granada. In 1607 the Jesuits Bernabé Rojas and Vicente Imperial led a mission to Caracas. On May 14, 1628, Father Ventura de la Peña founded the college of Mérida. In 1728 the Jesuits started a residence where the youth were instructed. They struggled to open the college of Caracas, and it was not until December 20, 1752, that they obtained a royal license to launch the project. The college functioned until 1767.

In addition to teaching in schools, the Jesuits engaged in missionary work in the Orinoco. This work can be characterized in several stages. First, in 1621, there was an attempt to penetrate the indigenous territories of the Orinoco across the Andes. This effort concluded in 1628 when the archbishop of Santafé ordered the Jesuits to abandon their missions. The most important missionaries were José Dadey and Miguel Jerónimo Tolosa.

Following these initial efforts, there were several attempts to open new missionary fields in 1646. There were other expeditions between 1653 and 1664 led by the French missionaries Pierre Pelleprat and Denis Mesland. Three villages were founded between 1668 and 1681, but lacking sufficient personnel, the Jesuits decided to leave the mission in 1681. This missionary action was extended to the Tunebos, Achaguas, Giraras, Guahivos, and Chiricoas indigenous groups.

The period between 1669 and 1716 was characterized by an entry into the Orinoco region and the foundation of Our Lady of the Saliva Reduction in 1669 by Antonio Monteverde. In this period the missionaries encountered violent resistance from the Carib people, who killed a significant number of religious. Given the situation the Jesuits debated whether to stay or leave the Orinoco, but as the civil authorities insisted that they stay, the Jesuits were forced to devise a new strategy for evangelization.

Several indigenous reductions were founded between 1716 and 1730. The most important missionary of this period was José Gumilla, who became superior of the mission in 1723. The missions in the region of the Orinoco were consolidated between 1730 and 1741. This period is characterized by two events: the settlement with Canary families and the incursions of the indigenous Caribs in the reductions to hunt other indigenous populations, who were then sold as slaves to the Dutch. From 1741 until 1767, the missions grew until their dissolution at the hands of King Carlos III of Spain.

The exiled Jesuits coming from the Orinoco missions arrived at Cádiz on April 30 and a week later moved to Urbino, Italy. Among the exiles to Italy was Father Philippo Salvatore Gilii, who in 1771 published his *Sagio di storia americana*, an important work on the nature, peoples, and languages of South America.

The Jesuits returned to Venezuela only in 1916. The tensions between the Venezuelan government and the Church in the nineteenth century affected all religious congregations, which had been dissolved by the February 25, 1837, and May 5, 1874, laws. President José Tadeo Monagas issued a decree on August 31, 1848, forbidding the entry of foreign priests, especially members of the Society of Jesus. However, from 1889, civil society and the press in Venezuela began calling for the return of the religious orders, including the Jesuits.

In 1916, at the request of the apostolic delegate, Carlo Pietropaoli, and with the support of the secretary of state of the Vatican, the first steps were taken to entrust the Diocesan Seminary of Caracas to the Society of Jesus. Superior General Włodimir Ledóchowski entrusted this project to the province of Castilla, which then administered Venezuela along with Panama. On September 8, 1929, the superior of the so-called "Mission of Venezuela and Panama" was appointed. On December 12, 1936, Panama joined the newly created vice province of Central America. On March 25, 1958, Venezuela became an independent vice province and on January 1, 1971, it became an independent province with a total of 288 members and nineteen works.

The work of the Jesuits in this period focused on the educational apostolate, opening the high schools of Saint Ignacio in Caracas, Saint José in Merida, Gonzaga in Maracaibo, Jesús Obrero in Caracas, Saint Francis Xavier in Barquisimeto, and the Gumilla Institute of Puerto Ordaz opening between 1916 and the present day. The Catholic University Andrés Bello opened in 1953. In 1962 a branch office in San Cristobal was founded, which later became the Catholic University of Táchira. Since the 1960s the Jesuits have been popular with Fe y Alegría education, a work begun in 1955 by José María Vélaz, SJ, with a group of university students.

See also Fe y Alegría; Spain; Suppression

Fajardo, José del Rey, *La biografía de un Exilio, 1767–1916. Los Jesuitas en Venezuela: siglo y medio de ausencia*. Caracas: Universidad Católica Andrés Bello, 2014.

Los Jesuitas en Venezuela: Fuentes. Caracas-Bogotá: Universidad Católica Andrés Bello-Pontificia Universidad Javeriana, 2006.

Los Jesuitas en Venezuela: Los hombres. Caracas-Bogotá: Universidad Católica Andrés Bello-Pontificia Universidad Javeriana, 2006.
Los Jesuitas en Venezuela: Topo-Historia. 2 vols. San Cristóbal: Fondo Editorial Simón Rodríguez de la Lotería del Táchira, 2011.

Jorge Salcedo, SJ

Verbiest, Ferdinand, SJ (1623–1688)

Verbiest was born in Pittem, Belgium, on October 9, 1623, and joined the Society of Jesus in 1641. He studied philosophy in Leuven, and theology in Rome and Seville; he was also a mathematical autodidact, starting his teaching in Coimbra. In 1658 he arrived in Macau and two years later was called to Beijing to assist Johann Adam Schall von Bell in astronomical calculations. He soon became involved in the conflict about the calendar in which Schall was accused of having made wrong calculations. This led to his imprisonment, followed by a house arrest. Freed in 1669, he sought and obtained the rehabilitation of Schall. Verbiest himself was appointed administrator of the calendar in the Astronomical Bureau. He corrected the calendar calculations and became an instructor of the Kangxi emperor (r. 1662–1722), teaching him mathematics and astronomy. In 1671 he obtained the permission for missionaries to return to their missions after their exile in Canton.

Verbiest undertook many projects, including hydraulic constructions, the compilation of a world map and star charts, the building of new instruments for the Beijing Observatory, and even the creation of an automobile. He became most respected for the casting of several series of cannon. In his *Astronomia Europaea* (1687), he reflected on his years at the court: how European astronomy succeeded in resuming its former position, and how fourteen distinct mathematical and mechanical sciences helped the revival of the Jesuit mission. He died in Beijing on January 28, 1688.

See also Astronomy; Cartography in China; China; Schall von Bell, Johann Adam, SJ; Science

Golvers, Noël, *The "Astronomia Europæa" of Ferdinand Verbiest, SJ (Dillingen, 1687)*. Nettetal: Steyler Verlag, 1993.
Ferdinand Verbiest, SJ (1623–1688) and the Chinese Heaven: The Composition of the Astronomical Corpus, Its Diffusion and Reception in the European Republic of Letters. Leuven: Leuven University Press, 2003.
Witek, John W., ed., *Ferdinand Verbiest (1623–1688): Jesuit Missionary, Scientist, Engineer and Diplomat*. Nettetal: Steyler Verlag, 1994.

Nicolas Standaert, SJ

Vidyajyoti

Vidyajyoti is committed to seeking God, the light that shines in human knowledge, to reflect on it, to let it shine in new human insight and expression, and expel the darkness which envelops the world. *Vidyajyoti*, the name adopted by the Society of Jesus in South Asia for its College of Theology in Delhi in 1972, is a combination of two Sanskrit words: *vidyā* (knowledge) and *jyoti* (light); when combined it would mean "pour forth the Light of Knowledge."

Vidyajyoti has a history that dates back 140 years to 1879, when it began as a seminary for Jesuit missionaries in Asansol, West Bengal. In 1889 it was transferred to the hills of Kurseong, Darjeeling district, West Bengal, where it was named St. Mary's Seminary. In 1932 the Holy See accredited it as a Faculty with the authority to confer the degrees of Bachelor of Theology, Master of Theology, and Doctor of Theology. It was transferred to Delhi in 1972 and was re-christened the Vidyajyoti Institute of Religious Studies, Faculty of Theology. In 1993 it changed its name to Vidyajyoti College of Theology. The transfer from the hills to the capital city of India, Delhi, was envisaged as placing it in an apt milieu for studying theology in the midst of contemporary Indian realities. Vidyajyoti became an Open Faculty in December 1973 with the authority to confer degrees on any qualified student, and its statutes were approved by the Congregation for Catholic Education in 1989.

Vidyajyoti is committed to developing an Indian/Asian theology. An Indian Academy was created in the Seminary in 1905 for research on Indian religions and cultures in order to respond effectively and creatively in pluri-religious and multicultural India. Continuing in that tradition, Vidyajyoti College of Theology engages in contextual theology that partly draws its content from the particular context. This is possible only when there is a dialogue between the contextual realities and the faith experience.

Active apostolic involvements (fieldwork) on a regular basis throughout the academic year and subsequent reflection on these are integral parts of theological formation in Vidyajyoti. Under the guidance of staff members, students do fieldwork and reflect on their involvement in the life struggles of the people. The objectives of the fieldwork are: (1) to give poverty a face – an essential reference for all the students' theological reflections; (2) to provide formation in personal holistic attitudes and skills; and (3) to initiate a theological reflection geared toward transformative and life-affirming praxis.

In addition to regular fieldwork, the staff and students participate in diverse local educational, cultural, and social programs that enlighten and challenge people on a wide range of issues. Moreover, the Vidyajyoti Institute of Islamic Studies (VIDIS) promotes dialogue with Muslims and scholarly research and writing on Islam.

The College has been publishing the *Vidyajyoti Journal of Theological Reflection* (earlier called *The Clergy Monthly*) for over seventy-five years. This monthly journal is a platform for theological reflection on India/South Asia. It aims at promoting dialogue between Christianity and the plurality of cultures in Asia; the different religious traditions of Asia; and between theology, social movements, and human sciences.

The students have two monthly publications – *Ave* in English and *Vachan Sudha* in Hindi – both containing reflections on the readings of the day for the liturgical cycle. In the pages of *Tatvaviveka*, an annual student magazine, Christian sources of theology – Scripture and Tradition – are applied to the theological resources and the contextual realities of Asia, especially those that have affected the students.

With the aim of promoting theological reflection within the framework of regional realities representing extensive cultural and linguistic differences in India, Vidyajyoti has created the Regional Theology Centers (RTC) as extension centers. Currently, they operate in Chennai, Patna, Ranchi, and Varanasi. Students in these RTCs take up to two years of theology in their region and then join the other students in Delhi for their third-year bachelor course in theology. Through this venture, the Faculty seeks a better understanding and respect for the multicultural reality of India and promotes the integration and unity of the country.

The Distance Education Programme in Theology (DEPTh) is a new initiative of Vidyajyoti College, introduced in 2013. It focuses particularly on the theological education of the lay faithful – in India and elsewhere. It is designed as a diploma course and is offered in both correspondence and online formats. Students receive a diploma after completing 60 credits in Theology and Scripture in a minimum period of two years.

Vidyajyoti has a library of about 140,000 volumes and 300 journals in a variety of languages. It has a collection of rare books from the sixteenth and eighteenth centuries on India and ancient Christian culture.

Vidyajyoti motto: *tam eva bhāntam aabubhāti sarvam*

("everything shines only after that shining light")

         – *Katha Upanishad* II.2.15

See also Asia; India; Interreligious Dialogue; Theology; Universities, 1773–Present

Vidyajyoti College of Theology. www.vidyajyoti.in.

                                   Leonard Fernando, SJ

Vieira, António, SJ (1608–1697)

Born on February 6, 1608, in Lisbon. In 1616 his family moved to Salvador, Bahia. He studied at the Jesuit College in Salvador and joined the Society of Jesus on May 5, 1623. He taught humanities and rhetoric at Bahia and Olinda colleges. He studied philosophy and theology in Salvador and was ordained presbyter on December 10, 1634.

At the time of the Restoration of Portugal in 1640, he was a member of the embassy of submission to Dom John IV. Besides appointing him royal preacher in 1644, from 1646 to 1650 the King kept him busy in several embassies in France, England, Holland, and Rome.

Because of his support of the Jesuits who were beyond the Tagus, in 1649 he was dismissed by the General, but the King interceded on his behalf. He refused the episcopal miter in a difficult moment of his religious life.

From 1652 to 1661 he was superior and official visitor of the Maranhão and Pará missions, in Brazil. Between 1658 and 1660 he wrote the Village Rules, consisting of three parts: what belongs to religious observance by priests, to spiritual healing of souls, and to the temporal administration of Indians. The internal statute of the Portuguese missions of the Society of Jesus in Maranhão, Pará, and Amazonas was in force for one whole century.

The alluring method of Manuel da Nóbrega's catechesis – song teaching and use of musical instruments – was spread by Vieira in Maranhão and Pará.

From the pulpit he preached against Indian enslavement. When summoned to go to the wilderness and catch slaves, he answered that the land economic difficulties were not caused solely by the lack of slaves.

Noticing the African slaves' devotion to Our Lady of the Rosary, he was convinced that their enslavement was divinely ordered so they could achieve freedom in the afterlife.

He adopted the view that the advancement of Christianity justified African slavery. In spite of his rhetorical attempt to convince slaves that their life was worth living, he was the seventeenth-century thinker who denounced most clearly the abuses and cruelty of African slavery.

Following a settlers' revolt, he was exiled to Porto in 1662 and denounced to the Inquisition because of his writings, especially *Hopes of Portugal, the Fifth Empire of the World*, where he spoke of Dom John IV's resurrection. The book had been sent to the queen at the suggestion of his confessor, the Jesuit André Fernandes. After his only appearance in front of the tribunal, on October 1, 1665, Vieira ended up in the Coimbra jail for forty-four days. On December 23, 1667, he was forbidden to preach and to be elected to office. With the new regent Peter, he was readmitted at the palace, and his penalties were gradually abrogated.

Vieira appealed to Rome. Fearing that the Portuguese Inquisition would fall out with the Society, the General did not authorize resources; with the resurgence of the question of the Jewish converts to Christianity, this was definitely renounced in 1671. In Rome he dazzled the pontifical court with sermons and discourses, and he persisted in denouncing the style of the Portuguese Inquisition.

He obtained from Pope Clement X the brief *Religionis zelus* (April 17, 1675), exempting him from the Portuguese Inquisition and submitting him to the Roman Inquisition. At the regent's request, on August 23, 1675, he went back to Lisbon – if he stayed in Rome he would be a hindrance to the Portuguese Inquisition. He undertook the publication of the first volume of *Sermons*. In 1676 he was appointed a consultant for the Portuguese province.

Vieira went back to Bahia in January 1681 and prepared the rest of his works for publication (*Sermons* and *Key for the Prophets*). He went to Quinta do Tanque together with Fr. José Soares, his secretary and confidant. In 1687 he was appointed official visitor of Brazil and Maranhão. From 1688 to 1691 he exchanged Quinta for a college. He resigned and withdrew again to the Quinta.

In 1697 he went back to the college in Bahia, where he died on July 18, 1697. Diplomat, social reformer, apostle, and protector of Indians, administrator, preacher, and literate who knew how to use spoken and written words, he withstood harsh battles on behalf of Portugal, of the natives' freedom, and of the Jewish converts to Christianity.

Vieira was one of the greatest figures of seventeenth-century Luso-Brazilian thought. He preached with the same ease, understanding, loftiness, and formal beauty to the African slaves in a sugar plantations, to Indians in the missions on the banks of the Amazon River, in moments of national crisis – awakening consciences against the Dutch invasion of Pernambuco and the Castilian one of Alentejo – and he felt at ease in pulpits of Bahia and Maranhão, of the Lisbon royal chapels, and of the pontifical court of Rome.

See also Brazil; Maranhão Mission; Portugal; Slavery

Abraão, Maria, *Lembra-te do futuro: a teologia de Antônio Vieira à luz da História do futuro*. São Paulo: Edições Loyola, 2012.

Leite, Serafim, *História da Companhia de Jesus no Brasil*. Vols. III–IV. Lisbon/Rio de Janeiro: Civilização Brasileira, 1943.

Margutti, Paulo, "Padre Antônio Vieira." In *História da Filosofia do Brasil: O período colonial (1500–1822)*. São Paulo: Edições Loyola, 2013, pp. 244–67.

Danilo Mondoni, SJ

Vietnam

Viet Nam, officially the Socialist Republic of Vietnam, occupies the easternmost part of the Indochinese Peninsula in Southeast Asia. "Viet" refers to a group of peoples that for centuries inhabited parts of Indochina, and the title Vietnam, which means the "Viet of the South," was first officially adopted by the emperor Gia Long in 1802. The country exceeds 127,000 square miles and, as of 2014, is home to over 90 million people. Perspectives on Vietnam's history are as diverse and complex as the history itself. All Vietnamese, however, share a 4,000-year-old history and a common cultural heritage that makes them, according to ancient Vietnamese folklore, "children of Dragon and descendants of Fairy." In addition, Vietnamese Catholics have proudly claimed 117 martyrs from their motherland.

The presence of Christianity in Vietnam was first recorded in the Vietnamese Imperial Historical Records in 1533, which retell the story of a Westerner named Inêkhu who secretly preached the doctrine of Christianity in a village of the Sơn Nam Province (Nam Định today). Later, Portuguese Dominicans and Spanish Franciscans were among the first Christian missionaries and entered Vietnam as early as 1550 and 1583, respectively. The royal courts, however, forbade these early missionaries to preach to Vietnamese natives. Instead, these missionaries worked exclusively with Japanese or Portuguese Christians in Faifo (Hội An today). After laboring for some years, most of them left.

In 1615, at the request of Fernandes de Costa, the captain of a Portuguese merchant ship, Fr. Valletim Carvalho, then provincial of the Japanese province, sent Frs. Francesco Buzomi, Diogo Carvalho, and Br. Antonio Dias to minister to the Japanese Christian community in Cochinchina, one of two Vietnamese-speaking kingdoms in seventeenth-century Indochina. Subsequently, more Jesuit priests and brothers as well as Japanese catechists (*dōjukus*) were sent to extend their ministry to the native Vietnamese. Twelve years later, Jesuits were invited to start their mission in Tonkin, the other Vietnamese-speaking kingdom at this time. Among those who arrived in Tonkin in 1627 were Jesuit Frs. Pedro Marques and Alexandre de Rhodes as well as a few Japanese catechists.

The main challenge that confronted Jesuits in Vietnam was how to relate Christianity to the *Đạo Thờ Trời* (The Way of Heaven), Vietnam's indigenous religion and, more specifically, its beliefs regarding heaven and filial piety. In addition, the Jesuit efforts at evangelization were carried out in dialogue with Taoism, Confucianism, and Buddhism, each of which had contributed to the philosophical and religious character of Vietnamese culture. Even after the Vietnamese had been baptized, certain Christian concepts and beliefs remained difficult for them to comprehend. Thus, the cultivation of a personal and intimate relationship with God remained essential to Jesuit instruction on the Christian faith. The Jesuits had to negotiate with both the Portuguese authorities to acquire sufficient funding for their mission *and* the Vietnamese royal courts in order to gain permission to evangelize freely among the people.

Despite all these difficulties, the labor of the Jesuit missionaries combined with the rich religious sensibility of the Vietnamese produced an overwhelming success. By 1663, 350,000 Christians were reported in Cochinchina and Tonkin combined. The Society welcomed its first Vietnamese brother in 1669 and its first Vietnamese priest in 1694. Various catechisms and prayers were composed in *chữ Nôm* (Vietnam's demotic script) and *chữ quốc ngữ* (Vietnam's modern script). Generally, the success of the Jesuit mission in Vietnam during this period was attributed to four elements: the Jesuits' effective training of dedicated native Vietnamese catechists; the Jesuits' personal relationships with those they met; the Jesuits' celebration of elaborate funeral rites and anniversaries of the dead; and as a result, an observable change in the behavior of those in positions of authority and power, particularly Christians. By the time of the Suppression of the Society in 1773, approximately 160 Jesuits had served in Vietnam, 13 of whom were native-born Vietnamese.

In 1957, at the invitation of the government in then South Vietnam, the Jesuits returned to Indochina and engaged primarily in issues of education and the formation of young adults. In 1975, after the Communist government from the North took over the South, foreign Jesuits were expelled from the country. Vietnamese Jesuits were sent to labor camps or reeducation centers. Most Jesuit properties were confiscated. A few activities continued, but most were sent underground. In 2007 Jesuit Superior General Peter-Hans Kolvenbach made Vietnam, which had previously operated as an independent region, a new province of the Society. One of the fastest-growing provinces in the Society, at the beginning of 2015 the Vietnam province consisted of 212 Jesuits, including one bishop, 55 priests, 96 scholastics, 18 brothers, and 42 novices. Today Jesuits in Vietnam are engaged in a variety of ministries, including the giving of the Spiritual Exercises, evangelization, seminary formation, and pastoral work focused upon the poor, university students, and internal migrants.

See also Asia; Interreligious Dialogue; Rhodes, Alexandre de, SJ

Chính, Đỗ Quang, *Dòng Tên trong xã hội Đại Việt, 1615–1773* [The Society of Jesus in Vietnam 1615–1773]. T. P. Hồ Chí Minh: Nhà Xuất Bản Tôn Giáo, 2008.
Ngọc, Hữu, *Wandering through Vietnamese Culture*. Hà Nội: Thế Giới Publishers, 2012.
Pham, Hung, "Composing a Sacred Space: A Lesson from the Cathechismus of Alexandre de Rhodes." *Studies in the Spirituality of Jesuits* 46, 2 (2014), 1–34.
Taylor, Keith W., *A History of the Vietnamese*. Cambridge: Cambridge University Press, 2013.

Hưng Trung Phạm, SJ

Villa

Though a word often associated with grandiose or ostentatious living, Jesuits have long used the term "villa" to refer to a place of respite or repose separate from the full-time, common house shared by an apostolic community. Ignatius, himself a sickly man throughout much of his life, understood the value of "pure air" for one's health (the last line of the *Constitutions* of the Society makes a reference to its benefits) and so made provision in the rules of the Society for Jesuit communities to maintain a villa or farm to take time away for convalescence and restoration so as to remain zealous and active apostles.

In seeking rest and relaxation, early Jesuits were in plentiful company. To escape the sweltering summer heat of Rome, Pope Paul III, inspired by the ancient tradition of *villeggiatura all'antica*, sought to develop Frascati, in the Tusculan hills. Frascati's accessibility and splendid views of Rome made it the ideal place for Church dignitaries to establish a country seat for the Roman papal court. Those who journeyed to Frascati came not only to escape the heat but also to restore their health, enjoying time hunting and eating alfresco. Jesuits stationed at the Roman College eventually established a presence in Frascati, purchasing a modest structure with small-scale gardens and fountains and, just like their counterparts in the episcopacy, they retreated to their villa during the hot summer months.

See also Community; Paul III; Roman College

Ehrlich, Tracy, *Landscape and Identity in Early Modern Rome: Villa Culture at Frascati in the Borghese Era*. Cambridge: Cambridge University Press. 2002.
Franck, Carl Ludwig, *The Villas of Frascati, 1550–1750*. New York: Transatlantic Arts, 1966.

Keith Maczkiewicz, SJ

Vineyards, Literal and Metaphorical

Established in 1851, the last remaining Jesuit-owned and active winery in the world is situated at Sevenhill, South Australia. Originally, it produced for sale only altar wine, but in recent times it has added fine-quality red and white wines to be sold commercially. Nowadays its altar wine is distributed to churches and religious houses in Australia, Asia, and Oceania – modern "missionary" work.

When Ignatius and his companions came to Rome in 1539, they lived in a house surrounded by vineyards above the Spanish Steps. In the old Society, Jesuit vineyards producing altar wine were common, especially in Europe and the Americas. Some notable examples are the Jesuitengarten, Trier, and the Jesuit estates in Tucumán, Argentina. Other Jesuit wineries were in Arizona, Mexico, and Romania.

In the restored Society, there were wineries at Chateau Ksara in Lebanon (1857) and at Los Gatos in California (1888). The former winery was closed in 1972; the latter was sold for commercial use in 1986.

In the iconography for their churches, from the beginning, Jesuits used the image of the vineyard. A striking example is a painting by Hieronymous Wierix (in the St. Francis Xavier Church, Amsterdam) that depicts the crucifixion on a grapevine that emerges from a chalice and carries the words, "I am the true vine, and you the branches" (see John 15). Israel was the choice vineyard planted by God (Isaiah, 5:1–7), but that failed. Jesus had become the true Israel, the vine in which his followers "abide" and bear fruit.

After using the military and pilgrim image, the laborer in the Lord's vineyard took over in Ignatius's writing. In the *Constitutions* he outlined the personal qualities needed by such a laborer and the norms for choosing a particular field in the Lord's vineyards.

See also Australia; Images

Schineller, J. Peter, "The Pilgrim Journey of Ignatius, from Soldier to Labourer in the Lord's Vineyard and Its Implications for Apostolic Lay Spirituality." *Studies in the Spirituality of Jesuits* 31, 4 (September 1999), 1–41.

David Strong, SJ

Viscardo y Guzmán, Juan Pablo, SJ (1748–1798)

Born in Arequipa, Peru, this Creole and his younger brother entered the Society of Jesus only to find their vocational plans terminated by the expulsion of the Jesuits from

Spanish territories. Spending most of the second half of his life in Europe, Juan Pablo Viscardo y Guzmán is still cited frequently as having played a notable role in encouraging movements seeking independence from the Spanish Crown. In London for most of the 1790s, he entrusted his papers before his death to Rufus King, United States ambassador (minister) to Great Britain. King worked with Francisco de Miranda to facilitate publication of Viscardo's "Letter to the Spanish Americans," in Spanish, French, and English versions, published in various places.

Though some historians may pass lightly over Viscardo's Jesuit identity, focusing instead on the last decade of his life, a recent essay by Karen Stolley suggests that he was throughout his life much affected by the Suppression of the religious order he had chosen to join, and that his hostility to the Spanish monarchy and its empire is properly understood in the light of his lifelong sense of exile as a "suppressed" Jesuit. Stolley also shows how Viscardo appealed to an understanding of God's providence in order to lambast Spanish exploitation of New World inhabitants as a kind of blasphemy against the divine will.

See also Peru; Spain; Suppression

Klaiber, Jeffrey, *The Jesuits in Latin America, 1549–2000*. St. Louis, MO: The Institute of Jesuit Sources, 2009.

Simmons, Merle, *Los escritos de Juan Pablo Viscardo y Guzmán: precursor de la Independencia Hispanoamericana*. Caracas: Universidad Católica Andrés Bello, 1983.

Stolley, Karen, "Writing Back to Empire: Juan Pablo Viscardo y Guzmán's 'Letter to the Spanish Americans.'" In *Liberty! Egalité! ¡Independencia!: Print Culture, Enlightenment, and Revolution in the Americas, 1776–1838*. Worcester, MA: American Antiquarian Society, 2007, pp. 117–32.

Viscardo y Guzmán, Juan Pablo, *Obra completa*. Lima: Ediciones del Congreso del Perú, 1988.

Thomas Worcester, SJ

Visitation

The classic "visitation" was the review of a province by a "visitor," appointed by the general with all the powers of a provincial. Usually some grave issue was at stake, such as financial mismanagement or some continuing spiritual malaise because of poor governance that had overtaken the province. In the United States Fr. Zacheus Maher, SJ, the US assistant to the general, made a visitation in 1938 to the whole American assistancy and composed a rather famous "Memoriale," addressing all the various problems facing American Jesuits and pulling them back into the norms and standards of the Society at that time.

Today, however, a visitation simply involves the visit of the regional provincial to the Jesuit houses and apostolates. During this annual visit, the provincial meets with each man individually to receive his manifestation of conscience, which has the purpose of allowing the Jesuit to be transparent and open to God in all humility. And it serves the primary apostolic purpose of enabling the provincial to "mission" the man, congruent with the man's abilities, to the most urgent needs of the Church and the Society. This frank manifestation is at the heart of Jesuit obedience and calls for great discretion on the part of the provincial. During the visitation, the provincial also meets with the leadership of the Jesuit community (rector and consultors) and with the leadership of the apostolate: the president of the university and the chair of the board; or the pastor and the pastoral staff; or the high school president, the principal, and the board. With increasing lay leadership, these conversations are vital for sustaining the Jesuit mission.

See also Province; Valignano, Alessandro, SJ

Maher, Zacheus, "Memoriale on Visiting the American Assistancy," 1938, in several province archives. "Office of Visitor." *Woodstock Letters* 75 (1946), 371–72.

Patrick J. Howell SJ

Vitelleschi, Muzio, SJ (1563–1645)

Born into a noble Roman family, Muzio Vitelleschi studied at the Roman College, where he later taught philosophy and theology. He was appointed rector of the Roman College (1588–91), of the English College (1592–94 and 1597–98), and of the College of Naples (1594–97). He was named provincial of the Neapolitan (1602) and the Roman province (1606), as well as assistant for the Italian provinces (1608).

In 1615 Vitelleschi was elected the sixth superior general, in spite of having powerful internal opponents who accused him of political maneuvering and unsuccessfully took their case to the French and Spanish ambassadors and to Pope Paul V (r. 1605–21).

His generalate, after the stormy period of Acquaviva (1581–1615), was directed at stabilizing the Society and carrying out existing programs. During his thirty-year leadership, the Society experienced growth in the number of its members, houses, and colleges, both in Europe and in mission lands. Those years were marked also by triumphal celebrations: the canonization of Ignatius of Loyola and Francis Xavier (1622) and the centenary of the papal approval of the Society (1640), the latter marked by the publication of the *Imago primi saeculi Societatis Iesu*.

Vitelleschi strongly supported extra-European missions in Paraguay, where the system of the reductions (*reducciones*) was developed, and in the Philippines, China, and New France. Additionally, he began the Jesuit mission in Maryland.

Vitelleschi's generalate was marked by the Thirty Years War (1618–48), a time of intense princely rivalries when many Jesuits were involved in the life of European courts as influential confessors. During those critical years, Vitelleschi worked to eliminate divisions arising from nationalism and to keep the Society united using prudence and political cleverness.

See also Imago Primi Saeculi; Nationalism; Superior General

Bireley, Robert, *The Jesuits and the Thirty Years War*. Cambridge: Cambridge University Press, 2003.
O'Malley, John W., ed., *Art, Controversy and the Jesuits: The Imago Primi Saeculi*. Philadelphia, PA: St. Joseph University Press, 2015.

Emanuele Colombo

Vocation

"Vocation" denotes a "calling" to live a life and/or engage a work whose meaningfulness transcends categories of "job" or "career." The Jesuit purchase on "vocation" is inflected by the experiences of St. Ignatius of Loyola. "Jesuit vocation" emphasizes an evolving relationship with the Father who, in the power of the Spirit, communicates with people through their deepest desires and calls them to serve him in the company of his Son who carries the cross. In considering a Jesuit vocation, one explores deeply personal longings alongside the wide-ranging needs pressing upon the Church and world. In the discernment process a person inevitably becomes aware of his own sinfulness; however, rather than being a stumbling block to pursuing God's call, this awareness serves to remind him of his dependence upon God's love and grace and that these, in the end, "will be enough." Though personal and particular, a Jesuit vocation is necessarily communitarian: one is called to be a companion of Jesus in a diverse company of others who are likewise called to serve the Church and the world. Pope Francis, in a 2013 interview with *Civiltà Cattolica*, responded to the question, "Who is Jorge Mario Bergoglio?" by stating, "I am a sinner." This striking response by the first Jesuit pope echoes the contemporary understanding of Jesuit vocation enunciated in 1975 by the 32nd General Congregation: "What is it to be a Jesuit? It is to know that one is a sinner, yet called to be a companion of Jesus as Ignatius was … [and] to engage, under the standard of the Cross, in the crucial struggle of our time: the struggle for faith and that struggle for justice which it includes."

See also Discernment; Election; Ministries; Mission

Padberg, John W., ed., *Jesuit Life and Mission Today: The Decrees and Accompanying Documents of the 31st–35th General Congregations of the Society of Jesus.* St. Louis, MO: The Institute of Jesuit Sources, 2009, pp. 291–97.

Michael A. Zampelli, SJ

Voltaire, François-Marie Arouet de

Voltaire's literary career was marked by a series of controversies. As early as 1734 his "Philosophical Letters" were being condemned across France, and during the 1750s, his most productive period, he routinely came into conflict with Church and State authorities. The later part of Voltaire's life was noteworthy for his musings on toleration and his bitter attacks on what he regarded as religious fanaticism: this began with his response to the killing of Jean Calas, a Protestant accused of murdering his Catholic son, by the Parlement of Toulouse in 1762. There is little surprise that much of Voltaire's life was spent in exile, most notably at Ferney on the Franco-Swiss border from 1759 until a few weeks before his death, when he returned to Paris, the city of his birth.

Voltaire (1694–1778) clearly possessed conflicted opinions regarding organized religion: these included his attitude toward the Society of Jesus. His approach to the Jesuits can be glimpsed in his entry on the Society in his *Dictionnaire philosophique*. He begins harshly, claiming that Europe had become "weary" and disgusted by the Order, but quickly admits that it still contains "individuals of extraordinary merit."

Voltaire explains that "six thousand volumes" have been written about the Jesuits' supposed "lax morality," but opines that this morality was no more lax than that of other orders. He mentions their "doctrines relating to the safety of the person of kings" but emphasizes that this should not be equated with the "horn handled knife" of the would-be regicide. Voltaire is hardly kind to the Jesuits, but he is a little less harsh than some of his *philosophe* contemporaries. This pattern was reflected in his attitude to the Society throughout his life. He said some uncomplimentary things about his education at the

Jesuits' Louis-le-Grand college but fully realized that, at bottom, he owed his teachers there a significant debt. In his dictionary entry, Voltaire puts the contemporary attack on the Jesuits down to the Society's "pride." He offers a long list of Jesuits, past and present, whose behavior he deplores and homes in on perennial themes in anti-Jesuit literature, notably dominance in the royal confessional and an attempted stranglehold on education: he writes of the "contempt" in which they supposedly held "every university where they had not been educated, every book which they had not written." He cannot help but concede, however, that "there have been among them, certainly, men of knowledge, eloquence, and genius." He ends with a piece of not particularly friendly advice: "O monks, monks! be modest, as I have already advised you; be moderate, if you wish to avoid the calamities impending over you."

Any gaps between Voltaire's private feelings about the Society and his public utterances remain a matter of debate. It can be stated, however, that aspects of the Jesuit enterprise clearly influenced his own thought: these ranged from the musings of the philosopher Claude Buffier, to the outpourings of the *Journal de Trévoux*, to the reports sent back to Europe by Jesuit missionaries in China. Voltaire was also entirely capable of sustaining friendly personal relations with individual Jesuits and engaged others in meaningful debate: with d'Olivet regarding Locke's theories on human understanding, for instance.

Often, Voltaire's criticism of the Society took the form of mockery rather than bilious attack: in *Candide*, for example, he paints a portrait of unseemly luxury in the Jesuits' Paraguayan Reductions, where the fathers eat sumptuous breakfasts from gold dishes, while the Guaraní have to make do with maize served in wooden bowls. Elsewhere, he expressed admiration for some of the Jesuits' overseas adventures. In sum, Voltaire was certainly not "pro-Jesuit" and he voiced no overt opposition to the attack on the Society in 1760s France. Indeed, in that dictionary article, he stressed that the French branch of the Society was not suffering simply because of the dubious Caribbean business dealings of Antoine Lavalette: rather, a long catalogue of intrusions and misdemeanors were, in Voltaire's opinion, to blame. Then again, Voltaire clearly felt that some Jesuits had their virtues or at least warranted a place in his intellectual life: he would correspond with Roger Boscovich and, so the story goes, play chess with other members of the Society. It is also worth noting that Voltaire found some of the excesses of the assault on the Jesuits unpalatable, as witnessed by his response to the execution of the aged and mentally unstable Gabriel Malagrida in Pombal's Portugal.

See also Alumni/ae; Enlightenment; Suppression

Fumaroli, Marc, "Voltaire jésuite." *Commentaire* 69 (1995), 107–14.
Pearson, Roger, *Voltaire Almighty: A Life in Pursuit of Freedom*. London: Bloomsbury, 2005.
Pomeau, René, *La religion de Voltaire*. Paris: Nizet, 1969.
Todd, Christopher, *Voltaire: Dictionnaire Philosophique*. London: Grant and Cutler, 1980.

Jonathan Wright

Ward, Mary

Mary Ward (1585–1645) was born in Yorkshire, England, of Catholic recusant parents who were part of an extended network served by the Jesuits. Hers was the first sustained attempt to found a congregation of religious women on the Jesuit model. While the

Figure 67 *Mary Ward and her family consulting with Father Richard Holtby, SJ, about her vocation*, oil on canvas (artist unknown). Photograph Gemma Simmonds, CJ

order of "English Ladies" flourished and spread in its early years, opposition from within the Society of Jesus and from Rome resulted in the suppression of the congregation by Pope Urban VIII in 1631 with the bull *Pastoralis Romani Pontificis*. Despite this, the congregation survived beyond her death, though it struggled for centuries to overcome canonical opposition to her original plan and to her being recognized as the founder. She received final vindication from Rome in 1909 and in 2009, 400 years after the founding of her congregation, was declared venerable by Pope Benedict XVI.

Two unfortunate episodes involving influential women, Isabel Roser and Juana of Austria, sister to Philip II of Spain, made Ignatius determined to avoid having a female branch of the Jesuit order. He successfully appealed to free the Jesuits in perpetuity from responsibility for any women living together in community and wishing to place themselves under obedience to his Society. Many groups of women sought to imitate Ignatius's emergent Society, but the Council of Trent confirmed the imposition of strict enclosure on all nuns begun by the constitution *Periculoso* of Boniface VIII (1294–1309) and confirmed by Pius V's constitution *Circa pastoralis* (1566). Full approbation was not given to women attempting to live an apostolic life under simple vows until nearly three centuries later.

In the absence of established Catholic clergy or hierarchy in England, many Catholic women assumed positions of religious leadership, working in apostolic collaboration with Jesuits while not being professed religious. Mary determined to become a nun but encountered strong opposition from her family who had a dynastic marriage in mind. Three of her uncles died implicated in the Gunpowder Plot along with Jesuits Oswald Tesimond, Edward Oldcorne, Henry Garnet, superior of the English mission, and John

Gerard, who escaped to become a staunch supporter of Mary Ward and her English Ladies. Most of Mary's companions had relatives implicated in the Gunpowder Plot and were connected to the Jesuit networks in the Catholic underground of the time.

Mary's reluctant parents took her to London to consult Fr. Richard Holtby, a Jesuit living in hiding there. A picture from the *Painted Life*, held in Augsburg, Germany, shows him spilling the chalice at Mass. This convinced him not to oppose Mary's vocation, and with his blessing she made her way to St. Omer in Flanders, entering the order of Poor Clares there but subsequently leaving. Jesuit Roger Lee became her spiritual director and was so involved in her subsequent story that she and her companions were dubbed "Rogerites." Returning to London, she began doing apostolic work and with a group of like-minded companions set sail again for St. Omer in 1609. In 1611 Mary received an intellectual understanding that she and her companions were to "... 'Take the same of the Society.'" While remaining autonomous, they attempted to take the Jesuit Constitutions and live a religious life as closely resembling that of the Jesuits as was possible for women, using the name Society of Jesus. This brought them into direct conflict with the Council of Trent and the Jesuits. Communities under Mary's authority multiplied across Europe, their apostolic aims spreading from the education of girls to any appropriate apostolic work. Jesuit Superior General Muzio Vitelleschi, while kind and personally supportive of Mary herself, was immovably opposed to these "Jesuitesses."

In 1631 Mary's Institute was suppressed and she herself imprisoned on a charge of heresy. Her surviving sisters gathered in Rome, Munich, and England, where Mary died during the English Civil War in 1645. Those remaining became a network of apostolic women under Jesuit inspiration, eventually known as the Institute of the Blessed Virgin Mary. In 1749 Benedict XIV's apostolic constitution *Quamvis justo* conceded a measure of papal approval for a permitted "new" institute, while denying that Mary Ward was its founder. In 1823 Frances Teresa Ball founded a second branch of the order, known as Loreto Sisters, in her native Ireland, which spread to North America, India, Australia, and beyond. Final confirmation of Mary Ward's order and her rehabilitation by the Church came in 1909. In 1979 and 1983 respectively, the oldest two branches of the IBVM adopted edited forms of the Jesuit *Constitutions*. The first branch adopted the fullest possible text, including the Jesuit fourth vow of universal mission, in 2004 along with a change of name to the Congregation of Jesus.

See also Women, as Co-Workers with Jesuits

Littlehales, Margaret Mary, *Mary Ward: Pilgrim and Mystic*. London: Burns & Oates, 1988.

Orchard, Gillian Emmanuel, ed., *Till God Will: Mary Ward through Her Writings*. London: Darton, Longman and Todd, 1985.

Simmonds, Gemma, "Women Jesuits?" In Thomas Worcester, ed., *The Cambridge Companion to the Jesuits*. Cambridge: Cambridge University Press, 2008, pp. 120–35.

Wright, Mary, *Mary Ward's Institute: The Struggle for Identity*. Sydney: Crossing Press, 1997.

Gemma Simmonds, CJ

Way of Proceeding

The final and, in many ways, integrative decree (Decree 26) of the 34th General Congregation of the Society (GC 34, 1995) was entitled "Characteristics of Our Way of Proceeding." The decree opens with an explanation of this important phrase in the life of Jesuits: "Certain attitudes, values, and patterns of behavior join together to become what has been called the Jesuit way of proceeding. The characteristics of our way of proceeding were born in the life of St. Ignatius and shared by his first companions" (#659). Thus, various defining and distinctive features of the life and ministry of Ignatius and the first Jesuits came to characterize the early Society. This *esprit de corps* was grounded perhaps most of all in an experiential knowledge and promotion of the *Spiritual Exercises*. It was also based on what, for the sixteenth century, was the Jesuits' unique ministry of the *colegios*, a growing network of schools for lay students, which collectively had a far-reaching intellectual, spiritual, and cultural impact. Besides these central ministries, key documents of the early Society, especially the *Constitutions*, helped to define and promote its way of proceeding. These characteristics have, of course, developed over the life of the Society, but they echo the sentiments of the first companions. GC 34 aptly summarizes these motivating factors in a Jesuit's life as follows: having a "deep personal love for Jesus Christ," being a "contemplative in action," seeing the Society as "an apostolic body in the Church," being "in solidarity with those most in need," promoting a "partnership with others," being "called to learned ministry," recognizing that Jesuits are "men sent, always available for new missions," and, at the very heart of Jesuit life, "ever searching for the *Magis*" (##659–64).

See also Community; Loyola, Ignatius, SJ, St.; Mission; *Spiritual Exercises*

"Characteristics of Our Way of Proceeding." General Congregation 34, Decree 26. In John W. Padberg, ed., *Jesuit Life and Mission Today: The Decrees of the 31st–35th General Congregations of the Society of Jesus*. St. Louis, MO: The Institute of Jesuit Sources, 2009.
O'Malley, John W., *The First Jesuits*. Cambridge, MA: Harvard University Press, 1993.

Robert E. Scully, SJ

Weigel, Gustave, SJ (1906–1964)

Born in Buffalo, New York, on January 15, 1906, Gustave Weigel was the son of Alsatian immigrants. He entered the Jesuit novitiate at St. Andrew-on-Hudson after his graduation from Canisius High School at the age of 16, having skipped several grades. After his philosophy studies at Woodstock College in Maryland, Weigel spent only one year of what was normally a three-year period of Jesuit "regency" teaching at Loyola College in Baltimore. To Weigel's chagrin, the rector of Woodstock was impressed with the young Jesuit's philosophical gifts and planned to send him for doctoral studies. Weigel returned to Woodstock in 1930 to spend four years doing theological studies in a program he found narrow and outdated.

Ordained to the priesthood in 1933, Weigel began doctoral studies in dogmatic theology the following year at the Gregorian University in Rome. The analytical section of his dissertation, a discussion of the semi-Pelagian views of the fifth-century bishop Faustus of Riez, received some criticism from his examiners; nevertheless, the historical section was published as *Faustus of Riez: An Historical Introduction* (1938).

Although slated to return to Woodstock as a member of the faculty, the critique of his dissertation caused him to be assigned instead to the Catholic University in Santiago, Chile. Thus began a sojourn of eleven happy years as professor and dean of the faculty, during which, in his own words, he "came to know Chileans intimately and loved them intensely." In 1948, while away on a visit to the United States, "the Gringo," as he was affectionately known by Chilean students and friends, was suddenly recalled to Woodstock. The removal seems to have been instigated by his Chilean Jesuit superiors, who were not happy with Weigel's American frankness and pragmatism. They regarded such traits as an implicit criticism of the Spanish Jesuit manner of being and working in Chile. Weigel's "lasting contributions" were later recognized by the Chilean government, which awarded him the *Orden al Merito*, a special honor accorded to foreigners, giving him great solace.

Returning to Woodstock inaugurated a new epoch in Weigel's life: a theological career in ecumenism. Throughout the 1950s Weigel wrote on Protestant theology and the Eastern Churches. His embrace of ecumenism stemmed from a challenge given him by the German Reformation scholar Joseph Lortz, who said it was a "disgrace and a sin" that Christians were not working for unity in the United States. Weigel's response to the challenge was to emphasize friendly conversation and hospitable understanding: "Unless we understand each other," he wrote, "we cannot possibly achieve real unity." He mistrusted overly irenic approaches, insisting that doctrinal unity must precede actual union. But his grasp of tradition earned him the respect of Protestant theologians, who could always be assured that he was giving the Catholic position. Christian unity, he claimed, "was God's work" and would be accomplished by God's grace alone.

Pope John XXIII's surprise announcement in 1959 of an ecumenical council unleashed a series of massive preparations, which included the establishment of a secretariat to address a main purpose of the council: the problem of Christian unity. Weigel was appointed one of five North American consultors to the Secretariat for the Promotion of Christian Unity. Although originally pessimistic about what John XXIII could accomplish, the Pope's opening address gave Weigel new enthusiasm for the council and the issues he had come to champion: a new definition of episcopal power, more involvement of the laity, clarification of Church–State relations, and the possibility of married deacons and priests.

Possibly owing to other consultors' perceptions of his understanding of ecumenism as being outdated, Weigel's contributions to the Secretariat for Promoting Christian Unity (SPCU) meetings were minimal. He was assigned to work with English-speaking ecumenical observers, for whom he instantaneously translated Latin speeches, offering interpretations which his hearers found immensely valuable and often amusing. A further contribution was his service to the US bishops' press panel, where his blunt, logical, and witty rejoinders to journalists were legendary. After the council's first session, Weigel traveled throughout the United States discussing the progress of the council, preferring the terms "open-door" and "closed-door" rather than "liberal" and "conservative" to describe bishops' viewpoints.

Weigel's hopes for the council were tempered during the second session. Although he was pleased with the schema on ecumenism and its encouragement of "dialogue," he lamented the lack of any admission of responsibility by the Catholic Church for its role in rupturing Christian unity. He strongly supported "collegiality" and applauded the understanding of the Church as the People of God, which stressed the equality of all believers. But he regretted that the chapters on Jewish relations and religious liberty did not come to a vote. Having determined not to return for the third session, he died of acute coronary thrombosis in New York City on January 3, 1964.

See also Chile; Ecumenism; Theology; United States of America; Vatican II

Collins, Patrick, *Gustave Weigel: A Pioneer of Reform*. Collegeville, MN: The Liturgical Press, 1992.
Murray, John Courtney, ed., *One of a Kind: Essays in Tribute to Gustave Weigel*. Wilkes Barre, PA: Dimension Books, 1967.
Weigel, Gustave, *A Catholic Primer on the Ecumenical Movement*. Westminster, MD: Newman, 1959.

Mary Ann Hinsdale, IHM

Welt-Bott

The premier Catholic missionary periodical in German-speaking lands, the *Welt-Bott* (*World-Messenger*) was modeled after the French *Lettres édifiantes et curieuses*. The first volumes featured translations of French Jesuit letters, but the *Welt-Bott* soon went beyond Le Gobien's model and materials to become the first serialized publication of German Jesuits' reports from all over the world in German. It comprises 812 texts, arranged in forty parts and published in five volumes between 1726 and 1761, amounting to over 4,500 densely printed folio pages. It also contains images, maps, and explanatory materials, such as a table that converts the Chinese calendar into a Christian framework. The majority of letters stem from East and South Asia and the Americas, with many others from Pacific islands and the Near East. There are also letters from Turkey, Africa, Russia, and Sweden.

Like the *Lettres édifiantes* and the contemporary Protestant *Halle'sche Berichte*, the *Welt-Bott* pursued a dual aim of combining the edifying with the educational to appeal to a confessional audience as well as a broader interested public. The journal's twin goal is reflected in the visual language of the frontispiece, which amalgamates Christian evangelization with classical learning. It depicts a flying Hermes who carries a staff with the Jesuit monogram and a pile of missionary letters while also delivering the world in the shape of a globe. Alongside stories of conversion and martyrdom, all aspects of natural history received coverage in the *Welt-Bott*, situating the journal in the context of physico-theological and early Enlightenment thinking.

The *Welt-Bott* was launched by the Bavarian-born Jesuit Joseph Stöcklein, who had served as an imperial military chaplain and unsuccessfully applied to "the Indies" during the last decade of his life in Graz. In response to a call for contributions by German Jesuits, Stöcklein received a flood of submissions that would not abate for many years. Volume 1 appeared in 1726 in Augsburg, a nodal point in Germany's national and transnational trade network and a traditional center of the printing industry. Stöcklein cleverly partnered with the Augsburg printer Veith, which had a subsidiary and bookstore in Stöcklein's Graz and possessed a large distribution network across Catholic and Protestant areas.

A heavy-handed editor and skilled designer, Stöcklein transformed a heterogeneous multitude of handwritten letters into an appealing and recognizable print product. He divided the texts geographically by region, made summaries in different fonts, and provided an index for further orientation. He also edited each letter for repetitions, orthography, and word choice, eliminating dialect in favor of a standardized German. Linguistic uniformity made it possible to market the journal successfully on the Catholic imperial book market of the South as well as on the Saxon book market dominated by Protestant print. Stöcklein set the pattern for subsequent editors and the *Welt-Bott*'s long-term success. It appeared in fairs and bookstores from Vienna and Linz to Regensburg, Frankfurt, and Leipzig. The journal's popularity in turn contributed to Augsburg's meteoric rise as Germany's hub for missionary literature and overseas accounts.

Stöcklein also assembled Volume 2 and had it printed by the Veiths in 1730, but he died in 1733 while working on Volume 3. His confrère Karl Meyer completed the volume using Stöcklein's materials, and Volume 3 was again printed in the Veith shop in Augsburg in 1736. Owing to the outbreak of the War of the Austrian Succession in 1740, editorial and printing efforts had to be moved to Vienna, and production temporarily ground to a halt. The imperial print shop of Leopold Johann Kaliwoda, adjacent to the Viennese Jesuit College, put out the final two volumes in 1755 and 1761. Peter Probst, Franz Keller, and (in 1761) Franz Xaver Zacher did the editorial work. The last volumes show a decline in quality, including fewer letters from fewer regions and fewer supplementary materials.

The *Welt-Bott* garnered a wide trans-confessional readership. The periodical earned entries in renowned encyclopedias of the time, a testimony to its popularity. Catholic religious orders owned copies and enjoyed reading them aloud during meals. But the journal's volumes also found their way into the library holdings of Protestant princes and Protestant theological seminars like the *Evangelische Stift* in Tübingen. Excerpts and maps from the *Welt-Bott*, albeit often without proper attribution, were reprinted in scientific and scholarly publications long after the periodical had gone out of print.

See also German-Speaking Lands; *Lettres Édifiantes et Curieuses*

Borja, Galaxis, *Jesuitische Berichterstattung über die Neue Welt. Zur Veröffentlichungs-, Verbreitungs- und Rezeptionsgeschichte jesuitischer Americana auf dem deutschen Buchmarkt*. Göttingen: Vandenhoeck & Ruprecht, 2011.

Borja, Galaxis, and Ulrike Strasser, "The German Circumnavigation of the World: Missionary Writing and Colonial Identity Formation in Joseph Stöcklein's *Neuer Welt-Bott*." In Markus Friedrich and Alex Schunka, eds., *Reporting Christian Missions*. Wiesbaden: Harrassowitz Verlag, 2017, pp. 73–92.

Dürr, Renate, "Der 'Neue Welt-Bott' als Markt der Informationen? Wissenstransfer als Moment jesuitischer Identitätsbildung." *Zeitschrift für historische Forschung* 34, 3 (2007), 441–66.

Hausberger, Bernd, "El padre Joseph Stöcklein o el arte de inscribir el mundo a la fe." In Karl Kohut and María Cristina Torales Pacheco, eds., *Desde los confines de los imperios ibéricos*. Madrid: Iberoamericana, 2007, pp. 631–62.

Ulrike Strasser

Wierix Brothers

The three Wierix brothers, Jan (*c.* 1549–*c.* 1618), Hieronymus (1553–1619), and Anton II (*c.* 1555/59–1604), were among the most prolific and talented of the numerous engravers active in Antwerp in the second half of the sixteenth and early seventeenth centuries. They were the sons of Anton I Wierix (*c.* 1522–*c.* 1572), an obscure painter and engraver, and Cornelia Embrecht. Jan and Hieronymus probably trained with a goldsmith, and Anton II presumably studied with his brother Jan. At an early age the two oldest sons already engraved prints by Albrecht Dürer and others. In 1620 Christine, one of the daughters of Hieronymus, married the engraver Jan Baptist Barbé (1578–1649). The brothers often worked together, and they engraved in styles virtually indistinguishable from one another. Most of their work is based on compositions by other artists, whether a painting, drawing, or print.

Figure 68 Anton Wierix: *The Healing of the Paralytic*, engraving in Jerome Nadal's *Evangelicae historiae imagines* (Antwerp, 1593). Photograph Paul Begheyn, SJ

Despite their superb works of art, all three brothers were also famous for their disorderly conduct, and in a letter of 1587 the Antwerp publisher Christophe Plantin (1520–89) complained that whoever wanted to employ the Wierix brothers had to go and look for them in the taverns, pay their debts and fines, and recover their tools, which they had pawned. Listed as Lutherans in 1585, the Wierix brothers returned to Catholicism soon afterwards, because many of their engraved works were commissioned by Jesuits and other Catholic patrons.

The Wierix brothers worked for a number of publishers like Plantin, but also published their own prints. An example of the latter is the collection of seventy-five copperplates by the Wierix brothers and their relative Barbé, discovered in 2000 in the Jesuit De Krijtberg church in Amsterdam.

The most important book illustrated by the Wierix brothers (and others) is *Evangelicae historiae imagines* by Spanish Jesuit Jerónimo Nadal (1507–80), published by the Plantinian press in Antwerp in 1593, followed two years later by a textbook *Adnotationes et meditationes in evangelia*. This book had a long prehistory. Shortly before his death, Ignatius of Loyola (1491–1556) had assigned Nadal to edit an illustrated edition of his meditation method for Jesuits, especially for those still in formation. But only twenty years later, in October 1575, the project seemed finished. The young Dutch Jesuit Jan Zonhoven (1543–80) had been able to translate Nadal's theology into dramatic prose and to render the language of the Gospel into powerful images. But the size of the original illustrations of Livio Agresti did not fit into the layout Plantin had in mind. The whole project threatened to come to an end with the deaths of Nadal, Zonhoven, and Plantin. Nevertheless, in 1593 Martin Nutius, successor to Plantin, was able to publish the folio book with 153 engravings, in an edition of 3,000 copies, and the texts a year later, in 2,500 copies. The drafts were the work of Jesuit Giovanni Battista Fiammeri, Bernardino Passeri, and Maerten de Vos. The engravings were made by the Wierix brothers, Adriaen Collaert, and Karel van Mallery. The book was dedicated to Pope Clement VIII.

In the work of Nadal the life of Jesus is presented according to the set-up of the Second, Third, and Fourth week of the *Spiritual Exercises*. They are ordered according to the liturgical calendar of the sixteenth century, beginning with Advent.

Re-editions in Latin were published in the sixteenth and seventeenth centuries. Three different French translations and one Spanish translation appeared in the nineteenth century; an Italian translation was published in 1599, and reprinted in 1839. An English edition was published in the United States (2003–07).

In Europe Nadal's book was used as a model for local artists like Spaniard Francesc Ribalta and could be found in many Jesuit libraries. Recently, a complete woodcut copy of the engravings, by Christoffel van Sichem, published in Amsterdam in 1629, has been discovered.

Jesuits who were sent as missionaries to America and Asia carried the book in their luggage, so that the engravings could inspire local artists in Peru and elsewhere. The *Akbarnama*, the official chronicle of the reign of Akbar, the third Mughal emperor, contains three illustrations copied from Nadal's book.

The work had great impact in China. Already in 1599 the Jesuits there asked for a copy. The illustrated Chinese version of the *Rules for Praying the Rosary*, translated by Portuguese Jesuit João da Rocha and printed about 1619, includes fifteen woodcuts inspired by Nadal's work. This is also the case with fifty-six illustrations in the life of Christ, published for the first time by Jesuit Giulio Aleni in 1637. At least ten engravings from Nadal's work appear in a Chinese translation of a *Life of Christ* by German Jesuit Adam Schall von Bell.

See also Antwerp; Art Patronage; China; Images; Nadal, Jéronimo, SJ

Begheyn, Paul, "The Collection of Copperplates by Members of the Wierix Family in the Jesuit Church 'De Krijtberg' in Amsterdam." *Quaerendo* 31 (2001), 192–204.

Rheinbay, Paul, *Biblische Bilder für den inneren Weg. Das Betrachtungsbuch des Ignatius-Gefährten Hieronymus Nadal (1507–1580)*. Egelsbach: Hänsel-Hohenhausen, 1995.

Paul Begheyn, SJ

Women, as Co-Workers with Jesuits

The relationship between the first members of the Society of Jesus and women is revealed through the words of Ignatius of Loyola. Among the large number of letters he wrote are many to women, from royal ladies to the mothers of fellow Jesuits. His closest female correspondents include his benefactress and mother-figure Ines Pascual, in whose house

Ignatius had boarded during his student days in Barcelona, and Isabel Roser, who sought to become a female Jesuit, after years of epistolary dialogue in spiritual matters with Ignatius. The fact that Roser's foray into the Society did not end well – amid claims of financial impropriety, eventually disproved, Ignatius petitioned the pope to permanently release the Society from the spiritual direction of women living in community – has led many to conclude that the Society possessed an animosity toward women in general. However, the episode encompassed a series of incompatible elements that should not adversely color the larger picture. The Jesuits in Rome had, in fact, enjoyed strong relations with female patrons of artistic and architectural projects, including Marchesa Vittoria della Tolfa, Giovanna d'Aragona Colonna, and Isabella Feltria della Rovere Sanseverino. By 1543 they had also established the Casa Santa Marta, with the aim of rehabilitating prostitutes, devoting significant amounts of time and resources to these women. And one woman, the Infanta Juana of Austria (sister of Philip II of Spain) did secretly become a Jesuit scholastic in 1554. The preserved correspondence of Ignatius and other early modern documents connected to the Society demonstrate their ongoing concern for women and meaningful spiritual relationships with them, despite the absence of "official" female Jesuits after the late sixteenth century.

As attitudes toward women in general society have evolved, so has the approach of the Society. Decree 14 of the 34th General Congregation of the Society (1995) specifically addressed "Jesuits and the Situation of Women in Church and Civil Society." The last section of the decree encourages Jesuits to listen to the experiences of women, find appropriate places for them in Jesuit ministries and institutions, and promotes respectful cooperation with female colleagues. It also notes that the Society should strive for the "genuine involvement of women in consultation and decision-making in our Jesuit ministries." In the two decades since, there has been a notable increase in the presence of laywomen in Jesuit institutions, holding positions as teachers, professors, chaplains, and spiritual directors, and working collegially with members of the Society. There have also been clear indications that these words have been taken seriously and that women have established an important and influential presence in many Jesuit institutions.

Most Jesuit colleges and universities in the United States began as single-sex institutions, with Marquette University as the first to admit women, in 1909. Over the past century additional strides toward the inclusion of women have occurred, from women joining the faculty, to the establishment of women's studies programs, and most recently, women taking on significant leadership roles – including deans, provosts, and now even presidents – at these institutions. While a nun, Sister Maureen Fay, OP, served as president of the University of Detroit Mercy (1990–2004), the first laywoman to serve in this capacity was Linda LeMura, at LeMoyne College (2014–). JoAnn Rooney was announced as the new president of Loyola University Chicago in 2016. As over one-third of Jesuit colleges and universities in the United States now have lay presidents, it is likely that more women will lead them in the future. They are indicative of the many women who closely work with Jesuits at their institutions, who have become accepted as not just colleagues, but collaborators. They bring different perspectives and reflect diverse backgrounds that complement those of the members of the Society, as these respective groups work together to educate and instruct students at Jesuit institutions.

Outside of the academic world Jesuits work closely with women as well. A leading periodical, *America*, includes women among its editors, and women hold numerous positions at other organizations including the Jesuit Volunteer Corps, the Ignatian

Solidarity Network, and the Jesuit Refugee Service. As the world has changed since 1540, so has the Society.

See also Barat, Sophie, St.; Catechists, Women and the Jesuits in Japan; Juana of Austria; "Men and Women for Others"; Ward, Mary

Boryczka, Jocelyn M., and Elizabeth Petrino, eds., *Jesuit and Feminist Education: Intersections in Teaching and Learning for the Twenty-First Century.* New York: Fordham University Press, 2012.
Cahill, Lisa Sowle, "Women and Men Working Together in Jesuit Institutions of Higher Learning." *Conversations on Jesuit Higher Education* 4 (Fall 1993). http://epublications.marquette.edu/cgi/viewcontent.cgi?article=1583&context=conversations.
Hufton, Olwen, "Altruism and Reciprocity: The Early Jesuits and Their Female Patrons." *Renaissance Studies* 15 (2001), 328–53.
Rahner, Hugh, *St. Ignatius Loyola: Letters to Women*, revised edn. New York: Crossroad Publishing, 2007.
Simmonds, Gemma, "Women Jesuits?" In Thomas Worcester, ed., *The Cambridge Companion to the Jesuits.* Cambridge: Cambridge University Press, 2008, pp. 120–35.
Ross, Susan A., "The Jesuits and Women: Reflections on the 34th General Congregation's Statement on Women in Church and Civil Society." *Conversations on Jesuit Higher Education* 16 (Fall 1999). http://epublications.marquette.edu/cgi/viewcontent.cgi?article=1451&context=conversations.

Alison C. Fleming

Wu, Li, SJ (*c.* 1632–1718)

Li Wu 吳歷 is a Chinese Jesuit painter and poet of the seventeenth century. He was born in Changshu 常熟 of Suzhou 蘇州, and also known as his *zi* 字, Yushan 漁山, and *hou* 號, Mojing daoren 墨井道人. It is said that he was baptized in childhood and named Simon-Xavier a Cunha, but it is now thought more likely that his contact with Catholicism did not start until around 1676 because he was attracted to Buddhism in his early years. His earliest documented contact with the West is that he met the Jesuit Francois de Rougemont (1624–76) in 1676. One of Wu's best friends in the 1670s was among the pro-Catholic literati. Even so, it has never been confirmed whether his decision to accept Catholicism was solely influenced by the two Jesuits he met. Wu later met another Jesuit, Philippe Couplet (1624–92), who was sent to Suzhou for evangelization after 1664. One opinion holds that he could have entered the Society of Jesus around 1680, when he decided to accompany Couplet on a trip to Europe. Both of them arrived in Macau in this year. However, for some unknown reason, Wu did not continue the journey and stayed in Macau to study at the Jesuit college of St. Paul, being officially admitted to the Society of Jesus there. The earliest instance of a Jesuit record containing his name is a document from 1683 stating his entry. Around 1682, at the age of 50, he returned to Suzhou and the Jiangnan 江南 coastal area as a Chinese Jesuit, and subsequently began his catechesis near Shanghai 上海 and Jiading 嘉定.

Wu was ordained a priest by the first Chinese bishop, Luo Wenzao 羅文藻 (1615 or 1616–1691; baptized as Gregorio), in 1688. This ordination was also the first one for three Chinese. By the age of 66, Wu had not only missionized Jiangnan but also become a highly regarded painter and poet. Inexplicably, among later generations, his work as a painter and poet overshadowed his work as a Jesuit priest and his contribution to Jiangnan missions. Moreover, his achievements in painting obscured his pursuit of poetry. He is praised in Chinese history as one of the six orthodox masters of painting during the early Qing Dynasty, and all of his paintings that have survived to the present show the literati taste and Confucian morality. Details of his early learning of painting remains unknown, except for the information that he studied painting under another orthodox master, Wang Shihmin 王時敏 (1592–1680).

He studied poetry under Qian Qianyi 錢謙益 (1582–1664) and was a disciple of the leading Confucian scholar Chen Hu 陳瑚 (1613–75) in his youth. As scholars attempt to probe the conversion mentality of several Chinese literati, Wu's conversion to Catholicism has also been studied, and some possible reasons for his conversion have been inferred with his rejection of Neo-Confucian cosmology and his dissatisfaction with Buddhism. Although his spirituality toward Catholic Heaven is to a certain degree a myth, like most cases of Chinese literati conversion, his poems reflect his admiration for Catholicism and are thought to be the first Chinese Christian poetry in the exquisite classical Chinese style. Regarding his paintings, the influence of western spatial perspective and the light–shadow effect continue to be debated; his paintings merely show classical Chinese formats and style. Furthermore, Wu himself claimed that he stopped painting, especially after his ordination. Thus, his poetry was more closely associated with his Catholic life and evangelical experience. He composed thirty poems in seven-character quatrains on Macau, including the seashore landscape and religious life in this Portuguese foothold. This anthology, entitled *Sanba Ji* 三巴集 (Anthology of St. Paul), is a vivid and valuable record of his observations during his sojourn. Moreover, he has been close to the circle of poets responsible for the revival of Song Dynasty poetry, which emphasized realism (evident in Wu's poems on Macau) and spiritual enlightenment. Wu would have transformed and interpreted the spirituality according to those of Catholicism. In his poems he often referred to himself as a shepherd or fisherman, both terms having Christian significance. Wu died and was buried in Shanghai in 1718.

See also Arts, Visual; China; Poetry

Chaves, Jonathan, *Singing of the Source: Nature and God in the Poetry of the Chinese Painter Wu Li*. Honolulu: University of Hawaii Press, 1993.
Hao, Fang, 方豪, *Zhongguo tianzhujiao shi rewuzhuan qingdai pian* 中國天主教史人物傳清代篇 [Bibliography of People in Chinese Catholic History: Qing]. Taipei: Mingwen shuju 明文書局, 1985, pp. 203–20.

Hui-Hung Chen

Xavier, Francis, SJ, St. (1506–1552)

Francis Xavier was the first Jesuit to arrive in India in 1542. For the next 200 years, over 2,100 Jesuits followed him to the East until the expulsion of the Jesuits from Portuguese domains in 1759. The numerous institutions and persons bearing the name of Francis Xavier, his 137 extant letters, the writings about him, and the vast number of pilgrims who throng to the Basilica of Bom Jesus, Goa, and the Church of the Gesù, Rome, to venerate St. Francis Xavier reflect his popularity among Catholics and people of different religious traditions.

Francis Xavier was born on April 7, 1506, in the Castle of Xavier in Navarre, northern Spain, as the fifth and last child of Dr. Juan de Jassu, president of the Royal Council of Navarre, and Maria de Azpilcueta, daughter of the royal Chamberlain.

In September 1525 he enrolled at the University of Paris in the College of Sainte-Barbe, where he met two students who greatly influenced his life – Peter Faber (1526) and Ignatius of Loyola (1529). In 1530 Xavier obtained a master's degree in philosophy. He worked as instructor in philosophy in the college of Beauvais from 1530 to 1534, when he began his theology studies.

Ignatius of Loyola, who had come to Paris to study in 1528, tried to bring about change in Francis Xavier but met with limited success. Ignatius himself confessed later that Francis was "the toughest dough he had ever handled." By mid-1533 Xavier decided to follow Ignatius and a year later made the thirty days *Spiritual Exercises* under the direction of Ignatius himself. The *Spiritual Exercises* transformed the ambitious and worldly Xavier into an ascetic unattached to physical comfort, power, or privilege. The effect of Ignatius and his spirituality on the life of Xavier was so deep that Fr. Peter-Hans Kolvenbach, the superior general of the Society of Jesus, addressed Xavier as "Our brother Francis Xavier in whom Ignatian spirituality was well incarnated" ("Francis Xavier and the Asian Jesuits," 716).

By 1540 Ignatius Loyola was ready to send Jesuits to India at the request of King John III of Portugal (1502–57) and Pope Paul III (1468–1556). Nicolas Bobadilla was the Jesuit originally chosen for the mission to India, but he fell ill and could not travel. Ignatius asked Xavier instead, who was the acting secretary of the Society of Jesus at that time, to leave for Lisbon with Dom Pedro Mascarenhas, the Portuguese ambassador to the Holy See. Since the Society of Jesus had not yet received official approbation from Paul III, Xavier signed three documents on March 15, 1540, before leaving Rome, in which he promised to obey the future Constitutions and Rules of the Society; pronounced his vows to take effect when the Society was approved; and cast his vote for the superior general's election. Xavier traveled to Lisbon via Bologna and continued by ship to India.

The arrival of Francis Xavier and his Jesuit companions in India is closely linked to the conversion movement in the Pearl Fishery Coast in Tamil Nadu, India, in the sixteenth century. The Pearl Fishery Coast, the *pescaria* of the Portuguese, extends from Kanyakumari to Rameshwaram and from there to Mannar off the coast of Sri Lanka. King John III of Portugal asked Pope Paul III specifically for members of the fledgling Society of Jesus to give religious instruction to the men and women in the Fishery Coast who were baptized between 1535 and 1537 but had not yet received any religious instruction. Since the King had also been informed of the possibility of a further conversion movement to Christianity, he hoped that the new missionaries would found new Christian communities in India.

On April 7, 1541, Xavier left Lisbon via Mozambique with Martin Affonso de Souza, the newly appointed Portuguese governor of India, never to return to Europe. He landed in Goa on May 6, 1542, but the monsoon season made it impossible for him to travel onwards to the Fishery Coast where he had originally been sent on mission. During the four months in Goa, Xavier preached to the Portuguese and local Christians, applying a method which he had used in the streets of Bologna and Lisbon. A ringing bell drew the attention of the people who were gathered on the main square of Goa, and he asked them to send their children and slaves for catechism. The faithful were catechized on the outskirts of the city with a simplified Portuguese language and many songs, a method that proved so successful that the Bishop subsequently recommended that other priests adopt it as well.

The governor of Goa asked Xavier for Jesuits for the College of St. Paul (also known as the College of the Holy Faith), a seminary founded in Goa in 1541 by the secular clergy and supported by the laypeople. The main purpose of this college was to educate Indian and East Asian Catholic boys for the priesthood. Xavier was open to the proposal and appointed Jesuits to teach and carry out spiritual ministries. By 1548 the Jesuits were asked to take over the administration of the college, and three years later King John III donated the college to the Society of Jesus in perpetuity. The College of St. Paul became the first Jesuit educational institution – "school" – in the world.

Toward the end of September 1542, Xavier left for the Fishery Coast accompanied by three seminarians from Tuticorin (in the Fishery Coast), who were studying in the College of St. Paul for the priesthood – deacons Gaspar and Manuel and a minor seminarian. They acted as his interpreters and collaborators in the mission, initially as seminarians and later on as priests.

Francis Xavier landed on the Fishery Coast at Manappad in October 1542. He traveled along the coastal area on foot in order to better acquaint himself with the local inhabitants. The travel was laborious but Xavier's ministry remained undaunted by the inclement weather and different food habits. He baptized the children of Catholic families born after 1537, had the catechism book translated into Tamil, and memorized a sermon in Tamil that he repeated in every village. In time, the local Tamil Christians learned the prayers Francis taught them through repetition and were able to actively participate during worship and prayer services.

He stood by the people in their moments of agony and triumph. When the Badaga soldiers of the king of Vijayanagar attacked the Christians near Kanyakumari, Xavier remained with the people for a month, arranged for food and drink for them, and even chastised the soldiers for their errant behavior. This exemplary and courageous act of Xavier won the hearts of people and greatly influenced others along the Travancore Coast to embrace Catholicism. Xavier baptized them when their king granted permission to embrace the Catholic faith and then made further arrangements for their religious instruction.

Francis Xavier appointed catechists in every coastal village to strengthen the faith and help improve the quality of life. He paid them for their work from the money given to him by the King. He was a pioneer who entrusted the new Christians with great responsibilities and saw to it that the work he began continued to bear fruit. He guided the Jesuit companions sent to labor with him through letters and personal interactions.

After a number of years of preaching and working with the people in Goa, the Fishery Coast, and Travancore Coast, Xavier decided to preach the Christian faith and establish new Christian communities in Indonesia, Japan, and China. He met Yajiro, a Japanese Samurai from Kagoshima in 1547 at the Portuguese fort of Malacca, who convinced Xavier to come and preach the Christian faith in Japan. In December 1547 Yajiro and two other Japanese attended the College of St. Paul to receive instruction in Christian faith. They were baptized on May 20, 1548. Then Xavier chose two Jesuit companions – Cosme de Torres (1510–70) and Juan Fernández (1526–67) – to accompany him and the three Japanese Catholics on their journey to Japan. On August 15, 1549, they reached Kagoshima, in the feudal kingdom of Satsuma. At that time Japan was divided into sixty-six kingdoms and was in the midst of a chaotic civil war, but within two years Xavier was able to establish Christian missions in the kingdoms of Satsuma, Hirado, and Yamaguchi. He also interacted with Ōtomo Yoshishige (1530–87), the Daimya of Bungu, who converted to Christianity in 1578 and played a vital role in the activities of the Jesuits in Japan.

Ignatius elevated India to the third province of the Society (after Spain and Portugal) and appointed Francis Xavier as the first provincial in a letter of October 10, 1549, which reached Xavier only in November 1551.

From Japan, Xavier continued en route to China and reached the island of Sancien, off the shore of China, where he fell ill. In his last letter written from Sancien, Xavier expressed his hope of going to China in spite of the many hurdles ahead. Francis Xavier died on December 3, 1552, at the age of 46 without ever reaching the shores of China. His last words were taken from Psalm 31:2 in Latin: "In te Domine, speravi, non confundar in aeternum" ("In you, O Lord, have I hoped, let me never be confounded"). In the Lord he trusted all through his life and to the service of His people he gave his whole being. He was a pilgrim on the move, a pioneer ready to brave any hazard in life.

One constant factor that remained with Francis Xavier from the time of his conversion was his unassailable trust in God. The mission that was entrusted to him was the decisive factor that defined his life. Availability and adaptability made this missionary.

After undergoing the *Spiritual Exercises* and committing himself to God's ways, Xavier led a simple and austere life. Frugality and poverty were values he cherished and lived by, and he refused to accept any favor or privilege shown to him for his own benefit. The Count of Castanheira was asked by the King of Portugal to provide supplies for Xavier's journey. The Count asked Xavier to take a servant along with him so as not to diminish his credibility and authority, but Xavier thought otherwise. His response to the Count: "Sir, it is credit and authority acquired by the means you suggest which have reduced the Church of God and their prelates to their present plight. The right way to acquire them is by washing one's own clothes and boiling one's own pot, without being beholden to anybody" (on this letter, see Schurhammer, *Francis Xavier*, I, 707–08). During his travel from Lisbon to Goa, when the vessel Santiago in which he was traveling became almost a floating hospital with people groaning in agonies and unable to take care of their basic needs, Xavier ministered to the sick with affection despite his own seasickness.

Upon reaching Goa he continued to give expression to this spirit of humility and lowliness all through his life. In spite of the title and authority of papal nuncio and with King John as his patron, Xavier did not seek the privileges connected with the office and stayed in a humble cottage next to the main building of the city hospital in Goa. He continued the mendicant lifestyle, an itinerant preacher who begged food for the sick and the prisoners whom he served.

Francis Xavier did not adhere blindly to the frugal life or rejection of respectability. Success of the mission remained at the forefront of his strategy. This is illustrated by how, when Miyako in Japan demanded another missionary approach, Xavier did not hesitate to march in great pomp and circumstance to meet the prince and offer him the gifts his friend Pedro de Silva had provided for the purpose. This adaptability to the demands of situations opened the doors of Japan to Christianity.

Xavier was a man fondly attached to his Jesuit companions, and he kept their signatures close to his heart. He wrote to his companions: "In these regions, my dearest brothers, my recreations consist in frequently calling you to mind and the time when, through the great mercy of God our Lord, I knew and conversed with you" (Letter 20). He had a deep affection for Ignatius of Loyola whom he called fondly "the father of my soul" and spoke of as his "only father in the love of Christ." The deep love that

Xavier had for Ignatius of Loyola is manifested in his letter dated January 29, 1552: "And among the many other very saintly words and consolations which I read in your letter were these last, which said 'Entirely yours, without my being able to forget you at any time, Ignatius'; and just as I then read them with tears, so I am now writing these with tears, as I recall times past and the great love which you ever had, and still have, for me" (Letter 97).

Xavier was a person of deep prayer. One of the places where he retreated often in the midst of his busy apostolic life is a grotto hewn from the rock near the seashore in Manappad, Tamil Nadu, popularly known today as the Xavier grotto. Thomas Fernandes, one of the eyewitnesses, testified that Xavier spent a great part of the night and of the day in prayer and that he had frequently seen him raised a little above the floor, his face and eyes glowing with light, especially during the celebration of Mass. Xavier was also blessed with tears of consolation and ecstasy. While he celebrated his first mass in Vicenza on September 30, 1537, he received a profusion of tears of consolation. This gift of tears remained constant with him.

Xavier went through a discernment process before venturing into new missions. In his discernment method, he relied on the inner movements of his soul – consolation and desolation – to decipher God's will. Xavier's methodology is documented in his letter to Diogo and Micer Paolo, his fellow Jesuits in Goa: "I deemed it my duty to engage myself in asking God our lord to grant me to feel within my soul his most holy will … and with great interior consolation I have felt, and have come to know, that it is his will that I go to those regions of Malacca" (Letter 51).

A saint remains a human person, ever marked by weaknesses, and St. Francis Xavier is no exception.

His mother tongue was Basque, though Xavier spoke Spanish, French, Portuguese, Italian, and Latin. He relied heavily on interpreters for his missionary work except for this time in Goa, where he could still communicate in Portuguese. He often expressed his frustration at this handicap and once wrote that he was alone among the people without an interpreter, they not understanding him and he understanding them even less. It was up to his successors in the Indian mission and elsewhere, to people like Antonio Criminali and Henri Henriques, to master the language of the local people. Xavier insisted on their learning the language of the people so as to be effective in their work among them.

Xavier did not find Indians suitable as new recruits for the Society of Jesus. He wrote to Ignatius a letter from Cochin dated January 12, 1549: "From the experience which I have had here, I clearly see, my dearest Father, that our society can in no way be perpetuated by native Indians, and that they will remain Christians only as long as we who are already here, or others whom you will have sent from Europe, will live and remain here" (Letter 70). Ignatius did not share this view and suggested other approaches to promote local vocations in his letter to Xavier dated October 11, 1549. The number of Indian Jesuits today working in India and in other parts of the world is a sure proof that Xavier was wrong in his views about Indians becoming Jesuits.

Xavier was a man of his times. Like many of his contemporaries, he too had a false theology of religions. He struggled with the conviction that baptism was necessary in order to gain eternal salvation and that those not baptized would suffer eternal damnation. He wrote that few, from India, would attain paradise other than those who died in the state

Figure 69 Nicholas Poussin: *Saint Francis Xavier Resuscitates a Woman*, 1641, oil on canvas. Louvre, Paris. Photograph © RMN-Grand Palais / Art Resource, New York

of innocence, that is, aged 14 or younger. As Kolvenbach observed: "For his total dedication, Xavier remains a model, but not for the motivation behind it" ("Francis Xavier and the Asian Jesuits," 719).

Xavier was frequently on mission journeys to the different parts of Asia. Throughout these travels he opened new lands and people to the Good News of Jesus Christ. Given communication limitations between himself and the people in these distant lands, the mission administration proved to be difficult. His continuous absences from the mission stations created information gaps that affected decisions on important issues. Francis had the habit of often using the phrase "in virtue of holy obedience" in his letters of instruction to his Jesuit companions, a phrase which Ignatius used only sparingly in comparison. Opinions on Xavier as a superior are divided. Some approved of his forthright dealings and strong measures, while others found him too exacting and harsh.

St. Francis Xavier is intricately intertwined with Christianity in Asia. When his sacred remains were brought to Goa in 1554, people thronged in great numbers to receive him whom they already revered as a saint. Veneration of Francis Xavier remains unabated, having achieved much in a short time. His intense missionary life grounded in his intimacy with God, was a life in which people and mission to them took precedence over his own comforts and well-being. His battle cry of a life "not for gain nor in vain" remains a challenge today not only to Jesuits but also to all.

See also Asia; China; India; Japan; Loyola, Ignatius, SJ, St.; Saints; Spain

Costelloe, M. Joseph, trans. and intro., *The Letters and Instructions of Francis Xavier*. St. Louis, MO: The Institute of Jesuit Sources, 1992.

Kolvenbach, Peter-Hans, "Francis Xavier and the Asian Jesuits." *Vidyajyoti Journal of Theological Reflection* 66 (2002), 716–24.

Schurhammer, Georg, *Francis Xavier, His life, His Times*. 4 vols. Rome: The Jesuit Historical Institute, 1973–82.

Leonard Fernando, SJ

Yad Vashem

Yad Vashem, the Holocaust Martyrs' and Heroes' Remembrance Authority in Jerusalem, is Israel's agency that honors Gentiles who risked their lives to save Jews during the Holocaust. They number about 25,000, among them fourteen Jesuit priests: five from Belgium, five from France, and one each from Greece, Hungary, Italy, and Poland.

The Belgians are Jean-Baptiste De Coster (1896–1968), Emile Gessler (1891–1958), Jean-Baptiste Janssens (1889–1964), Alphonse Lambrette (1884–1970), and Henri van Oostayen (1906–45). Except for van Oostayen, who died a martyr at Bergen-Belsen for helping Jews in the Resistance, the other four Jesuits, under the leadership of Janssens, protected Jewish children at the Jesuit colleges in Brussels: St. John Berchmans (De Coster and Gessler) and St. Michael's (Lambrette).

The French are Roger Braun (1910–81), Pierre Chaillet (1900–72), Jean Fleury (1905–82), Emile Planckaert (1906–2006), and Henry Revol (1904–92). Braun, founder of *Reconntre*, helped Jews escape the Gestapo as a chaplain in prison camps. Chaillet published *Témoignage chrétien*, which inspired the Resistance. Fleury, at St. Joseph's College in Poitiers, saved more than a thousand Jews. Planckaert obtained identification papers for Jews. Finally, Revol enabled about eighty Jews to escape into Switzerland.

The other Europeans are Ioannis Marangas (1901–89) from Greece, Jacob Raille (1894–1949) from Hungary, Raffaele de Chantuz Cubbe (1904–83) from Italy, and Adam Sztark (1907–42), a martyr from Poland. Marangas hid one Jew in the Jesuit residence in Athens. Raille assisted many Jews in Budapest. Cubbe disguised Jewish youngsters as Jesuit novices at the College of Nobles in Mondragone in Italy. Sztark saved many children in the area of Słonim, Poland.

At least another hundred Jesuits risked their lives for Jews. Their names are found in the studies listed below.

See also Jews and Jesuits; Martyrs, Ideal and History

Lapomarda, Vincent A., *The Jesuits and the Third Reich*. 2nd edn. Lewiston, NY: Mellen, 2005.
100 Heroic Jesuits of the Second World War. Worcester, MA: np, 2015.

Vincent A. Lapomarda, SJ

Zambia-Malawi

In the second half of the nineteenth century, the Catholic Church began recovering from the turmoil of the French Revolution and its consequences, to launch its missionary efforts and to catch up with the various Protestant missions especially in Africa. The Zambesi mission was begun in 1879 under the leadership of Henry Depelchin, and after four months they covered the 1,100 miles from Grahamstown (South Africa) to King Lobengula's kraal in Bulawayo. The three further outreaches to the Nguni in East Zimbabwe, to the Tonga across the Zambezi River, and to the Lozi of the western province of Zambia, all failed. It was a mission too far, and they were devastated by malaria. Some years later (1895), the White Fathers successfully planted the Church in the north of Zambia and did splendid work among the Bemba.

The second Jesuit attempt was with Rhodes Pioneer Column in 1890 and was successful. Fifteen years later two Frenchmen (Joseph Moreau and Jules Torrend) crossed into Zambia and set up Chikuni (1905) near Monze and Kasisi near present-day Lusaka. Both began primary evangelization separately, but Moreau transformed Tongaland by introducing the plough while Torrend developed his unique linguistic skills in writing grammars and dictionaries.

In 1910 the republican government in Portugal expelled all Jesuits from the home country and its colonies. About forty Jesuits in Mozambique had to abandon their fledgling missions and were reassigned elsewhere. However, a small group, mostly Poles, crossed the Luangwa River and set up a mission at Katondwe (1912) and later at Chingombe (1914). Soon the Polish province took responsibility and, despite a difficult beginning, eventually linked up with the railway line and in time incorporated both Kasisi and later Chikuni into the Luangwa mission. From this missionary effort the Church of Lusaka was founded.

In 1927 Msgr. Bruno Wolnik was appointed apostolic delegate of Broken Hill (Kabwe), and one of his first accomplishments in 1931 was to hand over the Copperbelt province to the Conventual Franciscans and the Western province to the Capuchin Franciscans. With Bishop Hinsley's mission from the Vatican in 1928, the Catholic evangelization in Africa became more focused on education as the point of insertion into the new Africa.

After World War II, other Jesuits were invited from eastern Europe. They were later joined by Americans of the Oregon province and some Canadians. The pastoral challenge of the variety of languages helped them later to cope with the rising national centers of Lusaka (the capital in 1935) and Kabwe.

In 1950 Adam Kozlowiecki took over, and soon Lusaka became an archdiocese. Irish Jesuits began coming in large numbers in the 1950s and evangelized the populace of the Southern province from Chikuni mission, and in 1962 the Diocese of Monze was created under James Corboy. They developed Canisius Secondary School and later, at the request of the bishops, opened the government-supported Charles Lwanga Teacher Training College. The Jesuits managed over 200 primary schools before handing them over to the government in the late sixties. Later their educational interest led them to become involved in the new university in Lusaka, where they still have a presence today.

Within a few years of independence in 1964, the archbishop of Lusaka handed over the diocese to a young dynamic diocesan priest, Emmanuel Milingo, who continued the rapid expansion of the young Church with its local liturgical music. By the nineties the archdiocese claimed to have registered its millionth Catholic. Today the country is about 25 percent Catholic.

In 1969 Fr. Arrupe, superior general, made a province of the two missions of Lusaka and Chikuni. In 1975 the Jesuits began working on the Copperbelt in chaplaincies and later a parish. Soon afterward they set up a community in Malawi. They helped run the national theological seminary of St. Peter's in Zomba for ten years until there were sufficient local priests to carry on the work. Today they run a parish and recently opened a secondary school at Kasungu in Lilongwe Archdiocese.

In the mid-eighties the Jesuit regional novitiate in Lusaka began to receive a number of local candidates and today most of the hundred Jesuits in the province are local Jesuits running the province and developing their own identity: in education, with three secondary schools, a college of education, and an agricultural college; in social work, with institutions such as the Jesuit Centre for Theological Reflection in Lusaka; and in media work, with the Chikuni Radio station and Loyola Productions, as well as eight parishes.

The younger generation is open to the regional restructuring of the Jesuits in southern Africa which now comprises Zimbabwe, Mozambique, and South Africa, with Zambia/Malawi to join in the near future.

See also Zimbabwe

Hinfelaar, Hugo, *History of the Catholic Church in Zambia*. Lusaka: Bookworld Publishers, 2004.
Murphy, Edward, ed., *A History of the Jesuits in Zambia*. Nairobi: Paulines, 2003.

Edward P. Murphy, SJ

Zeal for Souls

The phrase "zeal for souls" (*zelus animarum* in Latin, *celo por las almas* in Spanish), which can be traced to a sermon by Gregory the Great, is often associated with Ignatius of Loyola and has become ingrained in the Society's vocabulary. Like similar phrases in the Jesuit lexicon (such as "helping souls"), "zeal for souls" points to the active and pastoral nature of the Society of Jesus, describing diverse Jesuit ministries, including education, spiritual direction, and missionary work. To be clear, the "souls" in question are those of the living, referring to the entire person. The phrase reflects the Society's goal, as stated in the *Formula of the Institute*, "to strive ... for the progress of souls in Christian life and doctrine."

Ignatius frequently used this phrase in his own writings, and early accounts of his life (by Luís Gonçalves da Câmara and Pedro de Ribadeneira, for example) are peppered with references to Ignatius's zeal. In addition, the *Constitutions* and *Complementary Norms* underline that this is fundamental to the Society. Candidates for the Society as well as those admitted should possess a "zeal for the salvation of souls" (*Constitutions*, #156) – meaning not just their own, but those of their neighbors as well – and "charity and zeal for souls" is upheld as what characterizes the activity of the Society as a whole (#163). Later, the phrase would be used to describe the lives of many famous Jesuits, and especially the Society's missions around the world.

See also Loyola, Ignatius, SJ, St.; Mission

O'Malley, John W., *The First Jesuits*. Cambridge, MA: Harvard University Press, 1993.

Charles Keenan

Zimbabwe

In 1560, four years after Ignatius of Loyola's death, Gonçalo da Silveira, a Portuguese Jesuit from India, traveled from Mozambique up the Zambezi River to the Mutapa kingdom, a successor to the southern Shona kingdom of Zimbabwe (*dzimba dzemabwe*, "houses of stone"), dying there in 1561. Three hundred years later, Fr. Alfred Weld, English assistant to Father General Beckx, planned the "Zambesi Mission" covering present-day Zimbabwe, south and west Zambia, and parts of Malawi, Mozambique, and Congo. In 1875 Jesuits took over St. Aidan's College in Grahamstown, South Africa, invited by Bishop Ricards, vicar apostolic of the Eastern Cape; and in 1879 the international Jesuit team, led by Fr. Henry Depelchin, trekked the 1,100 miles northward to the mission. Within ten years, however, debilitated by malaria, inexperience, and the magnitude of their task, they withdrew to regroup in South Africa.

Another opportunity came in 1890, though this time not without entanglement in entrepreneurial colonialism. Jesuits and Dominican sisters accompanied as chaplains, teachers, and nurses the settlers of Cecil Rhodes's British South Africa Company which held a royal charter to territories north of the Limpopo – excluding what was to become the Mozambique region, which was assigned in 1893 to the Portuguese province. In 1894 the Salisbury mission was entrusted to the English (later British) province, and a network of missions, hospitals, and schools quickly grew, mostly to serve rural Africans: Chishawasha (1892), Bulawayo (1894), St. George's College (1895), Gokomere (1896), Mutare (1899), with others following. Chikuni and Kasisi (1905) and Katondwe (1912) were founded north of the Zambezi, but in 1912 these were separated off as the Luangwa mission under the Polish province, the beginning of today's Zambia-Malawi province.

Figure 70 Children at a Jesuit school in Zimbabwe. Photograph courtesy of Stephen Buckland, SJ

In 1923 the British Crown adopted "Southern Rhodesia" as a self-governing colony. The settlers had created "native reserves," taxed villagers to produce labor, and suppressed early African resistance which reemerged in classic African nationalist form in the 1960s. The white minority refused to accept majority rule and unilaterally declared independence from Britain in 1965 under an apartheid-style constitution, provoking the nationalists to an armed guerilla struggle in which perhaps 20,000 civilians died, including seven Jesuits. Before and during that war, some Jesuits established personal relationships, important for the future, with Robert Mugabe whose party won elections under a majority-rule constitution when the war ended in 1979. Mugabe, educated on a Jesuit mission by Marist brothers, with numerous degrees and more than ten years in prison, never hid his Catholicism and Jesuit connections, and invited Church collaboration in dramatic expansions of national education and health services even as he professed Marxist-Leninism and excoriated bishops. Pragmatism and patronage tempered ideology over time, however, and in 2015, after more than one disputed election, Mugabe was still president aged 91.

The first prefects apostolic of the Salisbury mission were English Jesuits; in 1931 Aston Chichester became vicar apostolic, first bishop and then, in 1955, archbishop of Salisbury, his successor being another English Jesuit. Jesuits ran the major seminary from 1935 until 1979. Plans for a separate German Jesuit missionary territory were delayed by World War II, but in 1957 the Sinoia mission (later Chinhoyi Diocese) in the north was given to the East German province, which established new missions in Guruve (1958), Centenary (1962), Karoi, Chitsungo, and Banket (1963), and elsewhere; its first two bishops were German Jesuits. There was impressive growth in both Sinoia and Salisbury missions during the 1960s, including early social initiatives in the spirit of the Second Vatican Council: St. Peter's Kubatana community school (1963), Silveira House, and the School of Social Work (both 1964). Such significant Jesuit contributions to national infrastructure were funded from largely Catholic overseas sources, notably through appeals by missionaries on home leave and through Jesuit Mission offices in Germany and Britain.

In 1979 the Sinoia mission was united with the Salisbury mission north of the Limpopo as the independent "Vice-Province (later Province) of Zimbabwe," leaving South Africa a separate region dependent on the British province. The first Zimbabwean provincial, Fr. Fidelis Mukonori, was appointed in 2001. In 2015 province membership remains around 120, but now with 50% in formation, 33% 70 years old or over, and 65% of Zimbabwean origin. Jesuits are responsible for seventeen schools, some diocesan and all largely lay-run; ten parishes and rural missions; and works for streetchildren, orphans, HIV/AIDS prevention, and youth. In 1994 the province became host to Arrupe College, an interprovincial formation house for English-speaking Africa with around a hundred Jesuit students and staff.

General Congregation 35, in 2008, called Jesuits to reevaluate province boundaries. On December 6, 2014, in an historic retrieval, father general united the Mozambique region with the Zimbabwe province as the "Province of Zimbabwe-Mozambique," upon which would depend, from December 31, 2015, the South African region.

See also Arrupe College; HIV/AIDS; Zambia-Malawi

Creary, Nicholas, *Domesticating a Religious Import: The Jesuits and the Inculturation of the Catholic Church in Zimbabwe, 1879–1980*. New York: Fordham University Press, 2011.

Dachs A. J., and W. F. Rea, *The Catholic Church and Zimbabwe 1879–1979*. Gwelo: Mambo Press, 1979.

Stephen Buckland, SJ

Zipoli, Domenico, SJ (1688–1726)

Born in Prato, Italy, in 1688, Domenico Zipoli was an Italian organist and composer. He was the sixth child born to Sabatino Zipoli and Eugenia Varrochi. The family were peasants, living outside the walls of the city on the property of the Naidini family. He took organ lessons from two Florentine organist-directors: Ottavio Termini and Giovanni Francesco Beccatelli. On September 12, 1707, he wrote to Cosimo III, grand duke of Tuscany, for six scudi monthly so that he could study at Florence. His teacher was Giovanni Maria Casini, the cathedral organist. Supported by another grant from the Duke, he moved to Naples in 1709 in order to study with Alessandro Scarlatti. He left the same year following disagreements with the composer and traveled to Bologna to study with the organist Lavinio Felice Vannucci. In the same year he went to Rome to study with Bernardo Pasquini. He became a member of the Order of Santa Cecilia; the order commissioned from him a vespers service and Mass for the feast of San Carlo, and he eventually worked as the organist at the Chiesa San Carlo di Catinari. He remained in Rome following Pasquini's death in 1710; while there he composed two oratorios. The music is lost but the librettos survive, *San Antonio di Padova* (1712) and *Santa Caterina Vergine e martire* (1714). In 1715 he was appointed organist of the Jesuit Church of the Gesù in Rome and came into contact with the Society of Jesus. The next year he published the keyboard collection on which his fame rests, *Sonate d'intavolatura per organo e cimbalo*. It was published on January 1, 1716, with a dedication to Maria Teresa Strozzi, principessa di Forano (who was the subject of his cantata *Delle offese a vendicarmi*). These works for the organ or harpsichord were to be performed at various times during the Mass. The collection of pieces is quite polished and makes it difficult to consider these pieces their author's first work.

The collection is divided into two parts, the first intended for the organ. This first part contains music for the Mass: *Toccata, Versi, Canzone, Offertorio-Elevatione, Post Communio e Pastorale*. The second part has pieces for harpsichord: *Preludij, Allemande, Correnti, Sarabande, Gighe, Gavotte e Partite*. The second half is a traditional suite for the harpsichord and not intended for liturgical purposes. The *Toccata* alternates chordal sections with moments of virtuosic passagework. The *Versi* are four small verses that have an improvisatory character to them, responding to the *cantus firmus*. In some cases Zipoli asked for particular effects of timbre, using the *Co' flauti* for the *Post Communio* and the *Co' flauti* and *Piva* for the *Pastorale*.

He entered the novitiate on July 1, 1716. He seems to have expressed a strong desire for the missions for he was soon sent to Seville in order to book passage to the Paraguayan Reductions. On April 5, 1717, he and fifty-three other Jesuits sailed from Cádiz and reached Buenos Aires in July. After a couple of weeks the group set out for Córdoba. By 1724 he had completed his philosophical and theological studies with distinction at the Jesuit Colegio Máximo in Córdoba. During these years he worked as the music director for the various Jesuit churches, his duties including playing the organ at the various religious services, composing settings of Masses, hymns, vesper psalms, canticles, and oratorios as well as additional vocal and instrumental music for processions and special feast days of the liturgical year. He was ready to be ordained a priest in 1725, but no bishop could be found to ordain him. He died from an infectious disease (possibly tuberculosis) on January 2, 1726.

He is remembered for his instrumental and vocal works. His music was extremely popular throughout the Reductions and many copies were made nearly fifty years after his death. In 1782 a copy of his three-part concerted Mass was made in Potosí and delivered in Sucre. He was held in high esteem by the Yapeyú and Guaraní Indians, so much so that they continued to perform his music in the parish church even following the expulsion of the Society in 1773. In Europe his fame rested on his organ and harpsichord music, and in South America his fame was due to the significant contributions to the mission style of sacred music. Lastly, three sections of the chamber opera compiled by Martin Schmid, SJ, *San Ignacio de Loyola*, have been attributed to Zipoli (based on the surviving manuscripts found in the churches). Schmid and other anonymous indigenous composers wrote music for the opera.

See also Argentina; Bolivia; Gesù, Rome; Music; Paraguay Missions ("Reductions"); Schmid, Martin, SJ

Kennedy, Thomas F., "Colonial Music from the Episcopal Archive at Concepción, Bolivia." *Latin American Music Review* 9 (1988), 1–17.

Nawrot, Piotr, *Musica de visperas en las reducciones de Chiquitos-Bolivia (1691–1767): Obras de Domenico Zipoli y maestros jesuitas e indígenas anónimos.* Concepción: Archivo Musical Chiquitos, 1994.

Charles Jurgensmeier, SJ

Index

Acosta, José de, SJ
  early life and writing of, 11–12
  in Peru, 604–05
Acquaviva, Claudio, SJ, 12–13, 233
Acta Sanctorum, 110–11
Action Populaire, 14–15, 435
ad gradum exam, 16
Adnotationes et meditationes in Evangelia, 58
Africa, Central
  Congo, 190–91
  Jesuits in, 108–09, 533–34
  theology, 788
Africa, East
  Hekima University College, 359
  Jesuit history in, 16–18
Africa, Northwest, 18–19
Africa, South
  Zambia-Malawi, 853–54
  Zimbabwe, 855–56
Africa, West
  Jesuit history in, 20–21, 358
  and Mveng, 545–46
African American Civil Rights movement. *See* Civil
    Rights movement
African Institute of Economic and Social
    Development (INADES), 20
African Jesuit AIDS Network, 362–63
AIDS. *See* HIV/AIDS
AJCU (Association of Jesuit Colleges and
    Universities), 22
Akbar, Mughal emperor, 14
Albania, 257
Alcalá de Henares, 22–23
alcoholism, 302
Alegambe, Philippe, 656
alumbrados, 23
alumni
  Descartes, 225–26
  Georgetown University, 327
  Jesuit university, 24–25
  Roman College, 688
  Voltaire, 834–35
AMDG (*Ad majorem Dei gloriam*), 25–26
America (periodical)

and Leonard Feeney, 296
as major journal, 676
temperateness of, 26–27
and Thurston Davis, 220–21
American Indians. *See* Native Americans
Anchieta, José de, SJ, St., 27–28, 118
Anima Christi, 29
anti-Jesuit polemic
  the Lavalette affair, 457
  locations
    in German-speaking lands, 330
    in Portugal, 627–28
    in Spain, 751–55
  Monita secreta, 528–29
  people involved
    and *alumbrados*, 23
    Arnauld, 47
    Charles III, 156
    jesuitical Jesuits, 423
    Pascal, 592–93
    Ricci, 682–83
  Popish Plot, 631–32
  written discourses in, 30–34
anti-Semitism, 35–36, 310, 620
Antwerp
  architecture in, 56
  Imago primi saeculi, 385
  Jesuit history in, 36–37
  Scribani, Carlo, SJ in, 729
AOP. *See* Apostleship of Prayer
apologetic theology, 784–85
Apostle of Blacks. *See* Claver,
    Peter, SJ, St.
Apostleship of Prayer (AOP), 37–38
apostolate
  and Apostleship of Prayer, 38–39
  Jesuit, 333
  and ministries, 523–25
  and parishes, 590–92
  and Sacred Heart, 704
  and science, 727
  social, 434–35
applied (process), 39, 221
Aquinas, Thomas, 238

Index

Index

Index

Index